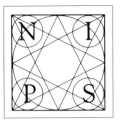

ADVANCES IN

NEURAL INFORMATION PROCESSING SYSTEMS 2

Other Titles of Interest from
Morgan Kaufmann Publishers

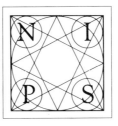

ADVANCES IN

NEURAL INFORMATION PROCESSING SYSTEMS 2

EDITED BY

DAVID S. TOURETZKY

CARNEGIE MELLON UNIVERSITY

MORGAN KAUFMANN PUBLISHERS
2929 CAMPUS DRIVE
SUITE 260
SAN MATEO, CALIFORNIA 94403

Editor   *Bruce M. Spatz*
Production Manager   *Shirley Jowell*
Cover Designer   *Jo Jackson*
Compositor   *Technically Speaking Publications*

ISSN 1049-5258
ISBN 1-55860-100-7
MORGAN KAUFMANN PUBLISHERS, INC.
Editorial Office:
   2929 Campus Drive
   San Mateo, California
Order from:
   P.O. Box 50490
   Palo Alto, CA 94303-9953
©1990 by Morgan Kaufmann Publishers, Inc.
All rights reserved.
Printed in the United States.

CONTENTS

PART 1: NEUROSCIENCE

PART II: SPEECH AND SIGNAL PROCESSING

PART III: VISION

PART IV: OPTIMIZATION AND CONTROL

PART V: OTHER APPLICATIONS

PART VI: NEW LEARNING ALGORITHMS

PART VII: EMPIRICAL ANALYSES

PART VIII: THEORETICAL ANALYSES

PART IX: HARDWARE IMPLEMENTATION

PART X: HISTORY OF NEURAL NETWORKS

Preface

This volume contains the collected papers of the 1989 IEEE Conference on Neural Information Processing Systems–Natural and Synthetic, held November 27-30, 1989, in Denver, Colorado.

Neural networks are often described as an enthusiastically interdisciplinary field. A reliable sign that one has embarked on a course of truly interdisciplinary research is the discovery that one can't understand what most of one's colleagues are talking about. Previous NIPS conferences brought together physicists, biologists, computer scientists, and engineers to discuss their respective research programs, but each spoke mostly in his or her "native" language. It was difficult to pursue multi-disciplinary conversations to any great depth.

In Denver this past November, the situation appeared to have changed. People were talking to each other more easily than in the past. It seems we've all been busy learning about each other's specialties, aided periodically by direct exposure at conferences such as this. A related feature of this year's conference was an increase in reports of interdisciplinary collaborations. I hope I'm not being too optimistic when I say that the news from NIPS-89 is that our field is maturing.

The papers in this volume are organized into ten parts. Part I, Neuroscience, includes some stunning demonstrations of the interaction of computational modeling techniques with classical neuroscience. One example is the paper by Lockery *et al.* on distributed representations in the leech. Some major application areas are covered in Part II, Speech and Signal Processing, Part III, Vision, and Part IV, Optimization and Control. Part V, Other Applications, spans a wide range of topics, from natural language processing to character recognition. An impressive handwritten digit recognizer developed at Bell Labs was demonstrated live, in real time, at the conference. It is described in the paper by LeCun *et al.*

Part VI offers a collection of new learning algorithms. Several papers describe network-growing algorithms, in which new units or connections are added dynamically to produce a network just large enough to solve a particular supervised learning problem. There are papers on unsupervised learning as well. Part VII presents empirical analyses of various networks' behavior, while Part VIII is devoted to theoretical analyses. Part IX, Hardware Implementation, is concerned both with analog VLSI implementation of neural circuitry and with the simulation of networks on digital parallel processors.

At the conference banquet, Jack Cowan of the University of Chicago gave a delightful after-dinner speech on the early days of neural networks. As someone who knew many of the pioneering figures personally and made important contributions of his own to the field, he is in a unique position to tell young scientists what things were like in the "pre-Perceptrons" period from 1943 to 1968. Professor Cowan kindly agreed to put his historical and personal observations from that evening into print, and they are included here as Part X.

I would like to congratulate my colleagues on the NIPS-89 organizing and program committees for their success in putting together such a first rate conference, especially General Chairman Scott Kirkpatrick and Program Chair Rich Lippmann. Shirley Jowell at Morgan Kaufmann was primarily responsible for the smooth and rapid production of this volume; it is always a pleasure to work with her. Thanks also to Chris McConnell, a graduate student here at Carnegie Mellon, for preparing the subject index.

One never knows what exciting developments will surface at next year's neural net conferences. Many of us are already looking forward with anticipation to our return to Denver in November. We hope to see you there.

February, 1990

David S. Touretzky
Carnegie Mellon

NIPS-89 Organizing Committee

General Chair	Scott Kirkpatrick, IBM
Program Chair	Richard Lippmann, MIT Lincoln Lab
Treasurer	Kristina Johnson, UC Boulder
Publicity Chair	Steve Hanson, Siemens Research
Local Arrangements	Kathy Hibbard, UC Boulder
Workshop Program	Alex Waibel, Carnegie Mellon
Workshop Local Arrangements	Howard Wachtel, UC Boulder
IEEE Liaison	Edward Posner, Caltech
APS Liaison	Larry Jackel, AT&T Bell Labs
Neurosciences Liaison	James Bower, Caltech
Publications Chair	David Touretzky, Carnegie Mellon

NIPS-89 Program Committee

CHAIR
Richard Lippmann, MIT Lincoln Lab

COCHAIRS
Eric Baum, NEC Resarch Institute
James Bower, Caltech
John Moody, Yale
Jay Sage, MIT Lincoln Lab

MEMBERS
David Ackley, Bellcore
Paul Adams, SUNY Stonybrook
Joshua Alspector, Bellcore
Dana Anderson, U.C. Boulder
Joseph Atick, Princeton
Brian Aull, MIT Lincoln Lab
Pierre Baldi, JPL
Dana Ballard, Uiversity of Rochester
Andy Barto, U. Mass.
Herve Bourlard, Philips Research Labs
Avis Cohen, Cornell
Jack Cowan, University of Chicago
John Denker, AT&T Bell Labs
David van Essen, Caltech
Scott Fraser, U.C. Irvine
Walter Freeman, U.C. Berkeley
Lee Giles, AFOSR
Stephen Hanson, Siemens Research
Geoffrey Hinton, Toronto
Larry Jackel, AT&T Bell Labs
Steven Judd, Caltech

(continued)

Ido Kanter, Princeton
James Keeler, MCC
Scott Kirkpatrick, IBM
Paul Kolodzy, MIT Lincoln Lab
Alan Lapedes, Los Alamos National Laboratory
Yann LeCun, AT&T Bell Labs
Heung Leung, MIT
Ralph Linsker, IBM
James Mann , MIT Lincoln Lab
Eve Marder, Brandeis
John Miller, U.C. Berkeley
Aaron Owens, E.I. DuPont
Andrew Penz, Texas Instruments
Tommaso Poggio, MIT
Daniel Sabbah, IBM
Idan Segev, Hebrew U.
Terry Sejnowski, The Salk Institute
Allen Selverston, U.C. San Diego
Sara Solla, AT&T Bell Labs
Richard Sutton, GTE Labs
Gerry Tesauro, IBM
Anil Thakoor, JPL
Richard Thompson, USC
David Touretzky, Carnegie Mellon
Santosh Venkatesh, University of Pennsylvania
Deborah Walters, SUNY Buffalo

PART 1:
NEUROSCIENCE

Acoustic-Imaging Computations by Echolocating Bats: Unification of Diversely-Represented Stimulus Features into Whole Images.

James A. Simmons
Department of Psychology
and Section of Neurobiology,
Division of Biology and Medicine
Brown University, Providence, RI 02912.

ABSTRACT

The echolocating bat, *Eptesicus fuscus*, perceives the distance to sonar targets from the delay of echoes and the shape of targets from the spectrum of echoes. However, shape is perceived in terms of the target's range profile. The time separation of echo components from parts of the target located at different distances is reconstructed from the echo spectrum and added to the estimate of absolute delay already derived from the arrival-time of echoes. The bat thus perceives the distance *to* targets and depth *within* targets along the same psychological range dimension, which is computed. The image corresponds to the crosscorrelation function of echoes. Fusion of physiologically distinct time- and frequency-domain representations into a final, common time-domain image illustrates the binding of within-modality features into a unified, whole image. To support the structure of images along the dimension of range, bats can perceive echo delay with a hyperacuity of 10 nanoseconds.

THE SONAR OF BATS

Bats are flying mammals, whose lives are largely nocturnal. They have evolved the capacity to orient in darkness using a biological sonar called *echolocation*, which they use to avoid obstacles to flight and to detect, identify, and track flying insects for interception (Griffin, 1958). Echolocating bats emit brief, mostly ultrasonic sonar sounds and perceive objects from echoes that return to their ears. The bat's auditory system acts as the sonar receiver, processing echoes to reconstruct images of the objects themselves. Many bats emit frequency-modulated (FM) signals; the big brown bat, *Eptesicus fuscus*, transmits sounds with durations of several milliseconds containing frequencies from about 20 to 100 kHz arranged in two or three harmonic sweeps (Fig. 1). The images that *Eptesicus* ultimately perceives retain crucial features of the original sonar wave-

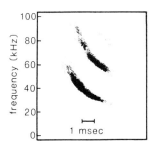

Figure 1: Spectrogram of a sonar sound emitted by the big brown bat, *Eptesicus fuscus* (Simmons, 1989).

forms, thus revealing how echoes are processed to reconstruct a display of the object itself. Several important general aspects of perception are embodied in specific echo-processing operations in the bat's sonar. By recognizing constraints imposed when echoes are encoded in terms of neural activity in the bat's auditory system, recent experiments have identified a novel use of time- and frequency-domain techniques as the basis for acoustic imaging in FM echolocation. The intrinsically reciprocal properties of time- and frequency-domain representations are exploited in the neural algorithms which the bat uses to unify disparate features into whole images.

IMAGES OF SINGLE-GLINT TARGETS

A simple sonar target consists of a single reflecting point, or *glint*, located at a discrete range and reflecting a single replica of the incident sonar signal. A complex target consists of several glints at slightly different ranges. It thus reflects compound echoes composed of individual replicas of the incident sound arriving at slightly different delays. To determine the distance to a target, or target range, echolocating bats estimate the delay of echoes (Simmons, 1989). The bat's image of a single-glint target is constructed around its estimate of echo delay, and the shape of the image can be measured behaviorally. The performance of bats trained to discriminate between echoes that jitter in delay and echoes that are stationary in delay yields a graph of the image itself (Altes, 1989), together with an indication of the accuracy of the delay estimate that underlies it (Simmons, 1979; Simmons, Ferragamo, Moss, Stevenson, & Altes, in press). Fig. 2 shows

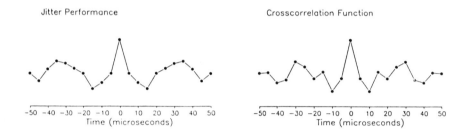

Figure 2: Graphs showing the bat's image of a single-glint target from jitter discrimination experiments (left) for comparison with the crosscorrelation function of echoes (right). The zero point on each time axis corresponds to the objective arrival-time of the echoes (about 3 msec in this experiment; Simmons, Ferragamo, et al., in press).

the image of a single-glint target perceived by *Eptesicus*, expressed in terms of echo delay (58 μsec/cm of range). From the bat's jitter discrimination performance, the target is perceived at its true range. Also, the image has a fine structure consisting of a central peak corresponding to the location of the target and two prominent side-peaks as ghost images located about 35 μsec or 0.6 cm nearer and farther than the main peak. This image fine structure reflects the composition of the waveform of the echoes themselves; it approximates the crosscorrelation function of echoes (Fig. 2).

The discovery that the bat perceives an image corresponding to the cross-correlation function of echoes provides a view of the hidden machinery of the bat's sonar receiver. The bat's estimate of echo delay evidently is based upon a capacity of the auditory system to represent virtually all of the information available in echo waveforms that is relevant to determining delay, including the phase of echoes relative to emissions (Simmons, Ferragamo, et al, in press). The bat's initial auditory representation of these FM signals resembles spectrograms that consist of neural impulses marking the time-of-occurrence of successive frequencies in the FM sweeps of the sounds (Fig. 3). Each nerve im-

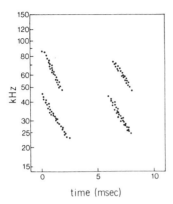

time (msec)

Figure 3: Neural spectrograms representing a sonar emission (left) and an echo from a target located about 1 m away (right). The individual dots are neural impulses conveying the instantaneous frequency of the FM sweeps (see Fig. 1). The 6-msec time separation of the two spectrograms indicates target range in the bat's sonar receiver (Simmons & Kick, 1984).

pulse travels in a "channel" that is tuned to a particular excitatory frequency (Bodenhamer & Pollak, 1981) as a consequence of the frequency analyzing properties of the cochlea. The cochlear filters are followed by rectification and low-pass filtering, so in a conventional sense the phase of the filtered signals is destroyed in the course of forming the spectrograms. However, Fig. 2 shows that the bat is able to reconstruct the crosscorrelation function of echoes from its spectrogram-like auditory representation. The individual neural "points" in the spectrogram signify instantaneous frequency, and the recovery of the fine structure in the image may exploit properties of instantaneous frequency when the images are assembled by integrating numerous separate delay measurements across different frequencies. The fact that the crosscorrelation function emerges from these neural computations is provocative from theoretical and technological viewpoints--the bat appears to employ novel real-time algorithms that can transform echoes into spectrograms and then into the sonar ambiguity function itself.

The range-axis image of a single-glint target has a fine structure surrounding a central peak that constitutes the bat's estimate of echo delay (Fig. 2). The width of this peak corresponds to the limiting accuracy of the bat's delay estimate, allowing for the ambiguity represented by the side-peaks located about 35 μsec away. In Fig. 2, the data-points are spaced 5 μsec apart along the time axis (approximately the Nyquist sampling interval for the bat's signals), and the true width of the central peak is poorly shown. Fig. 4 shows the performance of three *Eptesicus* in an experiment to measure this width with smaller delay steps. The

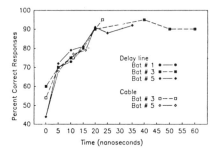

Figure 4: A graph of the performance of *Eptesicus* discriminating echo-delay jitters that change in small steps. The bats' limiting acuity is about 10 nsec for 75% correct responses (Simmons, Ferragamo, et al., in press).

bats can detect a shift of as little as 10 nsec as a hyperacuity (Altes, 1989) for echo delay in the jitter task. In estimating echo delay, the bat must integrate spectrogram delay estimates across separate frequencies in the FM sweeps of emissions and echoes (see Fig. 3), and it arrives at a very accurate composite estimate indeed. Timing accuracy in the nanosecond range is a previously unsuspected capability of the nervous system, and it is likely that more complex algorithms than just integration of information across frequencies lie behind this fine acuity (see below on amplitude-latency trading and perceived delay).

IMAGES OF TWO-GLINT TARGETS

Complex targets such as airborne insects reflect echoes composed of several replicas of the incident sound separated by short intervals of time (Simmons & Chen, 1989). For insect-sized targets, with dimensions of a few centimeters, this time separation of echo components is unlikely to exceed 100 to 150 μsec. Because the bat's signals are several milliseconds long, the echoes from complex targets thus will contain echo components that largely overlap. The auditory system of *Eptesicus* has an integration-time of about 350 μsec for reception of sonar echoes (Simmons, Freedman, *et al.*, 1989). Two echo components that arrive together within this integration-time will merge together into a single compound echo having an arrival-time as a whole that indicates the delay of the first echo component, and having a series of notches in its spectrum that indicates the time separation of the first and second components. In the bat's auditory representation, echo delay corresponds to the time separation of the emission and echo spectrograms (see Fig. 3), while the notches in the compound echo spectrum appear as "holes" in the spectrogram--that is, as frequencies that fail to appear in echoes. The location and spacing of these notches or holes in *frequency* is related to the separation of the two echo components in *time*. The crucial point is that the constraint imposed by the 350-μsec integration-time for echo reception disperses the information required to reconstruct the detailed range structure of the complex target into both the time and the frequency dimensions of the neural spectrograms.

Eptesicus extracts an estimate of the overall delay of the waveform of compound echoes from two-glint targets. This time estimate leads to a range-axis image of the closer of the two glints in the target (the target's leading edge). This part of the image exhibits the same properties as the image of a single-glint target--it is encoded by the time-of-occurrence of neural discharges in the spectrograms and it resembles the crosscorrelation function for the first echo component (Simmons, Moss, & Ferragamo, 1990; Simmons, Ferragamo, et al., in press; see Simmons, 1989). The bat also perceives a range-axis image of the farther of the two glints (the target's trailing edge). This image is located at a perceived distance that corresponds to the bat's estimate of the time separation of the two echo components that make up the compound echo. Fig. 5 shows the performance of *Eptesicus* in a jitter discrimination experiment in which one of the

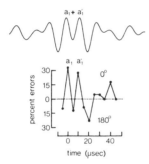

Figure 5: A graph comparing the crosscorrelation function of echoes from a two-glint target with a delay separation of 10 μsec (top) with the bat's jitter discrimination performance using this compound echo as a stimulus (bottom). The two glints are indicated as a_1 and a_1' (Simmons, 1989).

jittering stimulus echoes contained two replicas of the bat's emitted sound separated by 10 μsec. The bat perceives two distinct reflecting points along the range axis. Both glints appear as events along the range axis in a time-domain image even though the existence of the second glint could only be inferred from the frequency domain because the delay separation of 10 μsec is much shorter than the receiver's integration time. The image of the second glint resembles the crosscorrelation function of the later of the two echo components. The bat adds it to the crosscorrelation function for the earlier component when the whole image is formed.

ACOUSTIC-IMAGE PROCESSING BY FM BATS

Somehow *Eptesicus* recovers sufficient information from the timing of neural discharges across the frequencies in the FM sweeps of emissions and echoes to reconstruct the crosscorrelation function of echoes from the first glint in the complex target and to estimate delay with nanosecond accuracy. This fundamentally time-domain image is derived from the processing of information initially also represented in the time domain, as demonstrated by the occurrence of changes in apparent delay as echo amplitude increases or decreases: The location of the perceived crosscorrelation function for the first glint can be shifted by predictable amounts along the time axis according to the separately-measured amplitude-latency trading relation for *Eptesicus* (about -17 μsec/dB; Simmons, Moss, & Ferragamo, 1990; Simmons, Ferragamo, et al., in press), indicating that neural response latency--that is, neural discharge timing--conveys the crucial information about delay in the bat's auditory system.

The second glint in the complex target manifests itself as a crosscorrelation-like image component, too. However, the bat must transform spectral information into the time domain to arrive at such a time- or range-axis representation for the second glint. This transformed time-domain image is added to the time-domain image for the first glint in such a way that the absolute range of the second glint is referred to that of the first glint. Shifts in the apparent range of the first glint caused by neural discharges undergoing amplitude-latency trading will carry the image of the second glint along with it to a new range value (Simmons, Moss, & Ferragamo, 1990). Evidently, the psychological dimension of absolute range supports the image of the target as a whole. This helps to explain the bat's extraordinary 10-nsec accuracy for perceiving delay. For the psychological range or delay axis to accept fine-grain range information about the separation of glints in complex targets, its intrinsic accuracy must be adequate to receive the information that is transformed from the frequency domain. The bat achieves fusion of image components by transforming one component into the numerical format for the other and then adding them together. The experimental dissociation of the images of the first and second glints from different effects of latency shifts demonstrates the independence of their initial physiological representations. Furthermore, the expected latency shift does not occur for frequencies whose amplitudes are low because they coincide with spectral notches; the bat's fine nanosecond acuity thus seems to involve removal of discharges at "untrustworthy" frequencies prior to integration of discharge timing across frequencies. The delay-tuning of neurons is usually thought to represent the conversion of a temporal code (timing of neural discharges) into a "place" code (the location of activity on the neural map). The bat's unusual acuity of 10 nsec suggests that this conversion of a temporal to a "place" code is only partial.

Not only does the site of activity on the neural map convey information about delay, but the timing of discharges in map neurons may also play a critical role in the map-reading operation. The bat's fine acuity may emerge in the behavioral data because initial neural encoding of the stimulus conditions in the jitter task involves the same parameter of neural responses--timing--that later is intimately associated with map-reading in the brain. Echolocation may thus fortuitously be a good system in which to explore this basic perceptual process.

Acknowledgments

Research supported by grants from ONR, NIH, NIMH, DRF, and SDF.

References

R. A. Altes (1989) Ubiquity of hyperacuity, *J. Acoust. Soc. Am.* 85: 943-952.

R. D. Bodenhamer & G. D. Pollak (1981) Time and frequency domain processing in the inferior colliculus of echolocating bats, *Hearing Res.* 5: 317-355.

D. R. Griffin (1958) *Listening in the Dark*, Yale Univ. Press.

J. A. Simmons (1979) Perception of echo phase information in bat sonar, *Science*, 207: 1336-1338.

J. A. Simmons (1989) A view of the world through the bat's ear: the formation of acoustic images in echolocation, *Cognition* 33: 155-199.

J. A. Simmons & L. Chen (1989) The acoustic basis for target discrimination by FM echolocating bats, *J. Acoust. Soc. Am.* 86: 1333-1350.

J. A. Simmons, M. Ferragamo, C. F. Moss, S. B. Stevenson, & R. A. Altes (in press) Discrimination of jittered sonar echoes by the echolocating bat, *Eptesicus fuscus*: the shape of target images in echolocation, *J. Comp. Physiol. A*.

J. A. Simmons, E. G. Freedman, S. B. Stevenson, L. Chen, & T. J. Wohlgenant (1989) Clutter interference and the integration time of echoes in the echolocating bat, *Eptesicus fuscus*, J. Acoust. Soc. Am. 86: 1318-1332.

J. A. Simmons & S. A. Kick (1984) Physiological mechanisms for spatial filtering and image enhancement in the sonar of bats, *Ann. Rev. Physiol.* 46: 599-614.

J. A. Simmons, C. F. Moss, & M. Ferragamo (1990) Convergence of temporal and spectral information into acoustic images perceived by the echolocating bat, *Eptesicus fuscus*, *J. Comp. Physiol. A* 166:

The Computation of Sound Source Elevation in the Barn Owl

Clay D. Spence
John C. Pearson
David Sarnoff Research Center
CN5300
Princeton, NJ 08543-5300

ABSTRACT

The midbrain of the barn owl contains a map-like representation of sound source direction which is used to precisely orient the head toward targets of interest. Elevation is computed from the interaural difference in sound level. We present models and computer simulations of two stages of level difference processing which qualitatively agree with known anatomy and physiology, and make several striking predictions.

1   INTRODUCTION

The auditory system of the barn owl constructs a map of sound direction in the external nucleus of the inferior colliculus (ICx) after several stages of processing the output of the cochlea. This representation of space enables the owl to orient its head to sounds with an accuracy greater than any other tested land animal [Knudsen, et al, 1979]. Elevation and azimuth are processed in separate streams before being merged in the ICx [Konishi, 1986]. Much of this processing is done with neuronal maps, regions of tissue in which the position of active neurons varies continuously with some parameters, e.g., the retina is a map of spatial direction. In this paper we present models and simulations of two of the stages of elevation processing that make several testable predictions. The relatively elaborate structure of this system emphasizes one difference between the sum-and-sigmoid model neuron and real neurons, namely the difficulty of doing subtraction with real neurons. We first briefly review the available data on the elevation system.

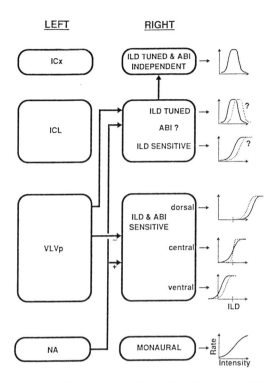

Figure 1: Overview of the Barn Owl's Elevation System. ABI: average binaural intensity. ILD: Interaural level difference. Graphs show cell responses as a function of ILD (or monaural intensity for NA).

2   KNOWN PROPERTIES OF THE ELEVATION SYSTEM

The owl computes the elevation to a sound source from the inter-aural sound pressure level difference (ILD).[1] Elevation is related to ILD because the owl's ears are asymmetric, so that the right ear is most sensitive to sounds from above, and the left ear is most sensitive to sounds from below [Moiseff, 1989].

After the cochlea, the first nucleus in the ILD system is nucleus angularis (NA) (Fig. 1). NA neurons are monaural, responding only to ipsilateral stimuli.[2] Their outputs are a simple spike rate code for the sound pressure level on that side of the head, with firing rates that increase monotonically with sound pressure level over a rather broad range, typically 30 dB [Sullivan and Konishi, 1984].

---

[1] Azimuth is computed from the interaural time or phase delay.

[2] Neurons in all of the nuclei we will discuss except ICx have fairly narrow frequency tuning curves.

Each NA projects to the contralateral nucleus ventralis lemnisci lateralis pars posterior (VLVp). VLVp neurons are excited by contralateral stimuli, but inhibited by ipsilateral stimuli. The source of the ipsilateral inhibition is the contralateral VLVp [Takahashi, 1988]. VLVp neurons are said to be sensitive to ILD, that is their ILD response curves are sigmoidal, in contrast to ICx neurons which are said to be tuned to ILD, that is their ILD response curves are bell-shaped. Frequency is mapped along the anterior-posterior direction, with slabs of similarly tuned cells perpendicular to this axis. Within such a slab, cell responses to ILD vary systematically along the dorsal-ventral axis, and show no variation along the medio-lateral axis. The strength of ipsilateral inhibition[3] varies roughly sigmoidally along the dorsal-ventral axis, being nearly 100% dorsally and nearly 0% ventrally. The ILD threshold, or ILD at which the cell's response is half its maximum value, varies from about 20 dB dorsally to −20 dB ventrally. The response of these neurons is not independent of the average binaural intensity (ABI), so they cannot code elevation unambiguously. As the ABI is increased, the ILD response curves of dorsal cells shift to higher ILD, those of ventral cells shift to lower ILD, and those of central cells keep the same thresholds, but their slopes increase (Fig. 1) [Manley, et al, 1988].

Each VLVp projects contralaterally to the lateral shell of the central nucleus of the inferior colliculus (ICL) [T. T. Takahashi and M. Konishi, unpublished]. The ICL appears to be the nucleus in which azimuth and elevation information is merged before forming the space map in the ICx [Spence, et al, 1989]. At least two kinds of ICL neurons have been observed, some with ILD-sensitive responses as in the VLVp and some with ILD-tuned responses as in the ICx [Fujita and Konishi, 1989]. Manley, Köppl and Konishi have suggested that inputs from both VLVps could interact to form the tuned responses [Manley, et al, 1988]. The second model we will present suggests a simple method for forming tuned responses in the ICL with input from only one VLVp.

3   A MODEL OF THE VLVp

We have developed simulations of matched iso-frequency slabs from each VLVp in order to investigate the consequences of different patterns of connections between them. We attempted to account for the observed gradient of inhibition by using a gradient in the number of inhibitory cells. A dorsal-ventral gradient in the number density of different cell types has been observed in staining experiments [C. E. Carr, et al, 1989], with GABAergic cells[4] more numerous at the dorsal end and a non-GABAergic type more numerous at the ventral end.

To model this, our simulation has a "unit" representing a group of neurons at each of forty positions along the VLVp. Each unit has a voltage v which obeys the equation

$$C\frac{dv}{dt} = -g_L(v - v_L) - g_E(v - v_E) - g_I(v - v_I).$$

---

[3] measured functionally, not actual synaptic strength. See [Manley, et al, 1988] for details.

[4] GABAergic cells are usually thought to be inhibitory.

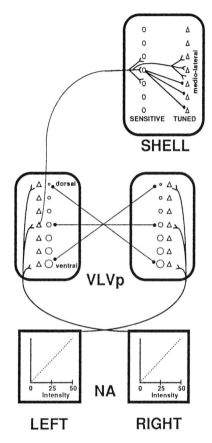

Figure 2: Models of Level Difference Computation in the VLVps and Generation of Tuned Responses in the ICL. Sizes of Circles represent the number density of inhibitory neurons, while triangles represent excitatory neurons.

This describes the charging and discharging of the capacitance C through the various conductances g, driven by the voltages v_N, all of these being properties of the cell membrane. The subscript L refers to passive leakage variables, E refers to excitatory variables, and I refers to inhibitory variables. These model units have firing rates which are sigmoidal functions of v. The output on a given time step is a number of spikes, which is chosen randomly with a Poisson distribution whose mean is the unit's current firing rate times the length of the time step. g_E and g_I obey the equation

$$\frac{d^2 g}{dt^2} = -\gamma \frac{dg}{dt} - \omega^2 g,$$

the equation for a damped harmonic oscillator. The effect of one unit's spike on another unit is to "kick" its conductance g, that is it simply increments the conductance's time derivative by some amount depending on the strength of the connection.

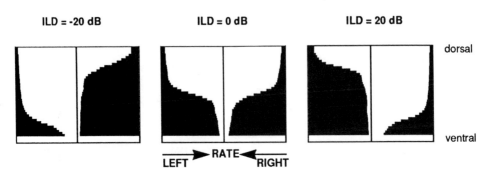

Figure 3: Output of Simulation of VLVps at Several ILDs. Position is represented on the vertical axis. Firing rate is represented by the horizontal length of the black bars.

Inhibitory neurons increment dg_I/dt, while excitatory neurons increment dg_E/dt. γ and ω are chosen so that the oscillator is at least critically damped, and g remains non-negative. This model gives a fairly realistic post-synaptic potential, and the effects of multiple spikes naturally add. The gradient of cell types is modeled by having a different maximum firing rate at each level in the VLVp.

The VLVp model is shown in figure 2. Here, central neurons of each VLVp project to central neurons of the other VLVp, while more dorsal neurons project to more ventral neurons, and conversely. This forms a sort of "criss-cross" pattern of projections. In our simulation these projections are somewhat broad, each unit projecting with equal strength to all units in a small patch. In order for the dorsal neurons to be more strongly inhibited, there must be more inhibitory neurons at the ventral end of each VLVp, so in our simulation the maximum firing rate is higher there and decreases linearly toward the dorsal end. A presumed second neuron type is used for ouput, but we assumed its inputs and dynamics were the same as the inhibitory neurons and so we didn't model them. The input to the VLVps from the two NAs was modeled as a constant input proportional to the sound pressure level in the corresponding ear. We did not use Poisson distributed firing in this case because the spike trains of NA neurons are very regular [Sullivan and Konishi, 1984]. NA input was the same to each unit in the VLVp.

Figure 3 shows spatial activity patterns of the two simulated VLVps for three different ILDs, all at the same ABI. The criss-cross inhibitory connections effectively cause these bars of activity to compete with each other so that their lengths are always approximately complementary. Figure 4 presents results of both models discussed in this paper for various ABIs and ILDs. The output of VLVp units qualitatively matches the experimentally determined responses, in particular the ILD response curves show similar shifts with ABI. for the different dorsal-ventral positions in the VLVp (see Fig. 3 in [Manley, et al, 1988]). Since the observed non-GABAergic neurons are more numerous at the ventral end of the VLVp and

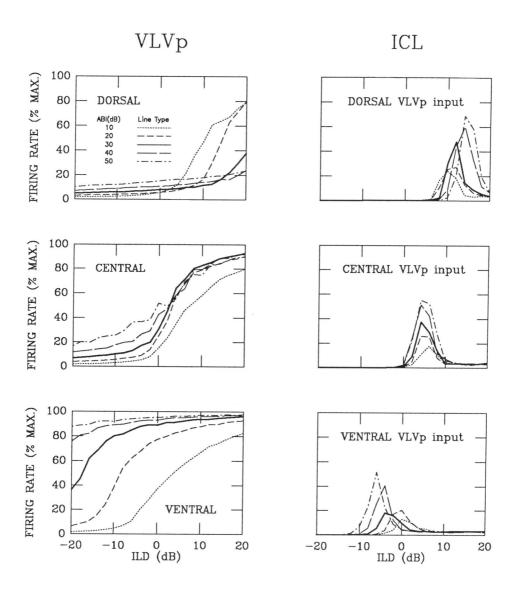

Figure 4: ILD Response Curves of the VLVp and ICL models. Curves show percent of maximum firing rate versus ILD for several ABIs.

our model's inhibitory neurons are also more numerous there, this model predicts that at least some of the non-GABAergic cells in the VLVp are the neurons which provide the mutual inhibition between the VLVps.

4   A MODEL OF ILD-TUNED NEURONS IN THE ICL

In this section we present a model to explain how ICL neurons can be tuned to ILD if they only receive input from the ILD-sensitive neurons in one VLVp. The model essentially takes the derivative of the spatial activity pattern in the VLVp, converting the sigmoidal activity pattern into a pattern with a localized region of activity corresponding to the end of the bar.

The model is shown in figure 2. The VLVp projects topographically to ICL neurons, exciting two different types. This would excite bars of activity in the ICL, except one type of ICL neuron inhibits the other type. Each inhibitory neuron projects to tuned neurons which represent a smaller ILD, to one side in the map. The inhibitory neurons acquire the bar shaped activity pattern from the VLVp, and are ILD-sensitive as a result. Of the neurons of the second type, only those which receive input from the end of the bar are not also inhibited and prevented from firing.

Our simulation used the model neurons described above, with input to the ICL taken from our model of the VLVp. Each unit in the VLVp projected to a patch of units in the ICL with connection strengths proportional to a gaussian function of distance from the center of the patch. (Equal strengths for the connections from a given neuron worked poorly.) The results are shown in figure 4. The model shows sharp tuning, although the maximum firing rates are rather small. The ILD response curves show the same kind of ABI dependence as those of the VLVp model. There is no published data to confirm or refute this, but we know that neurons in the space map in the ICx do not show ABI dependence. There is a direct input from the contralateral NA to the ICL which may be involved in removing ABI dependence, but we have not considered that possibility in this work.

5   CONCLUSION

We have presented two models of parts of the owl's elevation or interaural level difference (ILD) system. One predicts a "criss-cross" geometry for the connections between the owl's two VLVps. In this geometry cells at the dorsal end of either VLVp inhibit cells at the ventral end of the other, and are inhibited by them. Cells closer to the center of one VLVp interact with cells closer to the center of the other, so that the central cells of each VLVp interact with each other (Fig. 2). This model also predicts that the non-GABAergic cells in the VLVp are the cells which project to the other VLVp. The other model explains how the ICL, with input from one VLVp, can contain neurons tuned to ILD. It does this essentially by computing the spatial derivative of the activity pattern in the VLVp. This model predicts that the ILD-sensitive neurons in the ICL inhibit the ILD-tuned neurons in the ICL. Simulations with semi-realistic model neurons show that these models are plausible, that is they can qualitatively reproduce the published data on the responses of neurons in the VLVp and the ICL to different intensities of sound in the two ears.

Although these are models, they are good examples of the simplicity of information processing in neuronal maps. One interesting feature of this system is the elaborate mechanism used to do subtraction. With the usual model of a neuron, which calculates a sigmoidal function of a weighted sum of its inputs, subtraction would be very easy. This demonstrates the inadequacy of such simple model neurons to provide insight into some real neural functions.

Acknowledgements

This work was supported by AFOSR contract F49620-89-C-0131.

References

C. E. Carr, I. Fujita, and M. Konishi. (1989) Distribution of GABAergic neurons and terminals in the auditory system of the barn owl. *The Journal of Comparative Neurology* **286**: 190–207.

I. Fujita and M. Konishi. (1989) Transition from single to multiple frequency channels in the processing of binaural disparity cues in the owl's midbrain. *Society for Neuroscience Abstracts* **15**: 114.

E. I. Knudsen, G. G. Blasdel, and M. Konishi. (1979) Sound localization by the barn owl measured with the search coil technique. *Journal of Comparative Physiology* **133**:1–11.

M. Konishi. (1986) Centrally synthesized maps of sensory space. *Trends in Neurosciences* April, 163–168.

G. A. Manley, C. Köppl, and M. Konishi. (1988) A neural map of interaural intensity differences in the brain stem of the barn owl. *The Journal of Neuroscience* **8**(8): 2665–2676.

A. Moiseff. (1989) Binaural disparity cues available to the barn owl for sound localization. *Journal of Comparative Physiology* **164**: 629–636.

C. D. Spence, J. C. Pearson, J. J. Gelfand, R. M. Peterson, and W. E. Sullivan. (1989) Neuronal maps for sensory-motor control in the barn owl. In D. S. Touretzky (ed.), *Advances in Neural Information Processing Systems 1*, 748–760. San Mateo, CA: Morgan Kaufmann.

W. E. Sullivan and M. Konishi. (1984) Segregation of stimulus phase and intensity coding in the cochlear nucleus of the barn owl. *The Journal of Neuroscience* **4**(7): 1787–1799.

T. T. Takahashi. (1988) Commissural projections mediate inhibition in a lateral lemniscal nucleus of the barn owl. *Society for Neuroscience Abstracts* **14**: 323.

MECHANISMS FOR NEUROMODULATION OF BIOLOGICAL NEURAL NETWORKS

Ronald M. Harris-Warrick
Section of Neurobiology and Behavior
Cornell University
Ithaca, NY 14853

ABSTRACT

The pyloric Central Pattern Generator of the crustacean stomatogastric ganglion is a well-defined biological neural network. This 14-neuron network is modulated by many inputs. These inputs reconfigure the network to produce multiple output patterns by three simple mechanisms: 1) determining which cells are active; 2) modulating the synaptic efficacy; 3) changing the intrinsic response properties of individual neurons. The importance of modifiable intrinsic response properties of neurons for network function and modulation is discussed.

1   INTRODUCTION

Many neural network models aim to understand how a particular process is accomplished by a unique network in the nervous system. Most studies have aimed at circuits for learning or sensory processing; unfortunately, almost no biological data are available on the actual anatomical structure of neural networks serving these tasks, so the accuracy of the theoretical models is unknown. Much more is known concerning the structure and function of motor circuits generating simple rhythmic movements, especially in simpler invertebrate nervous systems (Getting, 1988). Called Central Pattern Generators (CPGs), these are rather small circuits of relatively well-defined composition. The output of the network is easily measured by monitoring the motor patterns causing movement. Research on cellular interactions in CPGs has shown that simple models of fixed circuitry for fixed outputs are oversimplified. Instead, these neural networks have evolved with maximal flexibility in mind, such that modulatory inputs to the circuit can reconfigure it "on the fly" to generate an almost infinite variety of motor patterns. These modulatory inputs, using slow transmitters such as monoamines and peptides, can change every component of the network, thus constructing multiple functional circuits from a single network (Harris-Warrick, 1988). In this paper, I will describe a model biological system to demonstrate the types of flexibility that are built into real neural networks.

2   THE CRUSTACEAN STOMATOGASTRIC GANGLION

The pyloric CPG in the stomatogastric ganglion (STG) of lobsters and crabs is the best-understood neural circuit (Selverston and Moulins, 1987). The STG is a tiny ganglion of 30 neurons that controls rhythmic movements of the foregut. The pyloric CPG controls the peristaltic pumping and filtering movements of the pylorus, or posterior part of the foregut. This network contains 14 neurons, each of which is unambiguously assignable to one of 6 cell types (Figure 1A). Since each neuron can be identified from preparation to preparation, detailed studies of the properties of each cell are possible. Thanks to the careful work of Selverston and Marder and their colleagues, the anatomical synaptic circuitry is completely known (Fig.1A), and consists of chemical synaptic inhibition and electrotonic coupling; there is no chemical excitation in the circuit (Miller,1987).

Despite the complete knowledge of the synaptic connections within this network, the major question of "how it works" is still an important topic of neurobiological research. Early modelling efforts (summarized in Hartline, 1987) showed that, while the pattern of mutual synaptic inhibition provided important insights into the phase relations of the neurons active in the three-phase motor pattern, pure connectionist models with simple threshold elements for neurons were insufficient to explain the motor pattern generated by the network. It has been necessary to understand the intrinsic response properties of each neuron in the circuit, which differ markedly from one another in their responses to identical stimuli. Most importantly, as will be described below, all 14 neurons are conditional oscillators, capable (under the appropriate conditions) of generating rhythmic bursts of action potentials in the absence of synaptic input (Bal et al, 1988). This and other intrinsic properties of the neurons, coupled with the pattern of mutual synaptic inhibition within the circuitry, has generated relatively good models of the pyloric motor pattern under a specified set of conditions (Hartline, 1987).

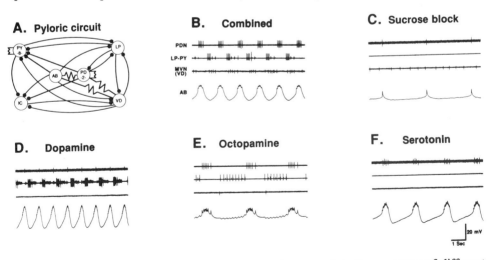

Figure 1: Multiple motor patterns from the pyloric network in the presence of different neurotransmitters. **A.** Synaptic wiring diagram of the pyloric CPG. **B.-F.** Motor patterns observed under different conditions (see text). PDN,LP-PY,MVN traces: extracellular recordings of action potentials from indicated neurons. AB: intracellular recording from the AB interneuron. From Harris-Warrick and Flamm (1987a).

3 MULTIPLE MOTOR PATTERNS PRODUCED BY AN ANATOMICALLY FIXED NEURAL NETWORK

When the STG is dissected with intact inputs from other ganglia, the pyloric CPG generates a stereotyped motor pattern (Miller,1987). However, *in vivo*, the network generates a widely varying motor pattern, depending on the feeding state of the animal (Rezer and Moulins, 1983). The motor pattern varies in the cycle frequency and regularity, which cells are active, the intensity of cell firing, and phase relations.

This variability can be mimicked *in vitro*, where experimental control over the system is better. Two major experimental approaches have been used. First, transmitters and modulators that are present in the input nerve to the STG can be bath-applied, producing unique variants on the basic motor theme. Second, identified modulatory neurons can be selectively stimulated, activating and altering the ongoing motor pattern.

As an example, the effects of the monoamines dopamine (DA), serotonin (5HT) and octopamine (OCT) on the pyloric motor pattern are shown in Figure 1. When modulatory inputs from other ganglia are present, the pyloric rhythm cycles strongly, with all neurons active (Combined). Removal of these inputs usually causes the rhythm to cease, and cells are either silent or fire tonically (Sucrose Block). Bath application of some of the transmitters present in the input nerve can restore rhythmic cycling. However, the motor pattern induced is different and unique for each transmitter tested: clearly the patterns induced by DA, 5HT and OCT differ markedly in frequency, intensity, active cells and phasing (Flamm and Harris-Warrick, 1986a). The conclusion is that an anatomically fixed network can generate a variety of outputs in the presence of different modulatory inputs: the anatomy of the network does not determine its output.

4 MECHANISMS FOR ALTERATION OF NEURAL NETWORK OUTPUT BY NEUROMODULATORS

We have studied the cellular mechanisms used by monoamines to modify the pyloric rhythm. To do this, we isolate a single neuron or single synaptic interaction by selective killing of other neurons or pharmacological blockade of synapses (Flamm and Harris-Warrick, 1986b). The amine is then added and its direct effects on the neuron or synapse determined. Nearly every neuron in the network responded directly to all three amines we tested. However, even in this simple 14-neuron circuit, different neurons responded differently to a single amine. For example, DA induced rhythmic oscillations and bursting in one cell type, hyperpolarized and silenced two others, and depolarized the remaining cells to fire tonically (Fig.2). Thus, one cannot use the knowledge of the effects of a transmitter on one neuron to infer its actions on other neurons in the same circuit.Our studies of the actions of DA, 5HT and OCT on the pyloric network have demonstrated three simple mechanisms for altering the output from a network.

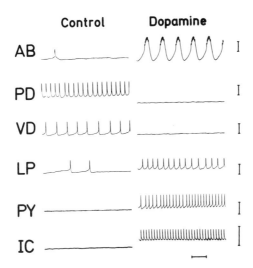

Figure 2: Actions of dopamine on isolated neurons from the pyloric network. **Control**: Activity of each neuron when totally isolated from all synaptic input. **Dopamine**: Activity of isolated cell during bath application of 10^{-4}M dopamine.

4.1 ALTERATION OF THE NEURONS THAT ARE ACTIVE PARTICIPANTS IN THE FUNCTIONAL CIRCUIT

By simply exciting a silent cell or inhibiting an active cell, a neuromodulator can determine which of the cells in a network will actively participate in the generation of the motor pattern. Some cells thus are physiologically inactive, even though they are anatomically present.

However, in some cases, unaffected cells can make a significant contribution to the motor pattern. Hooper and Marder (1986) have shown that the peptide proctolin activates the pyloric rhythm and induces rhythmic oscillations in one neuron. Proctolin has no effect on three other neurons that are electrically coupled to the oscillating neuron; these cells impose an electrical drag on the oscillator neuron, causing it to cycle more slowly than it does when isolated from these cells. Thus, the unaffected cells cause the whole motor pattern to cycle more slowly.

4.2 ALTERATION OF THE SYNAPTIC EFFICACY OF CONNECTIONS WITHIN THE NETWORK

The flexibility of synaptic interactions is well-known and is used in virtually all models of plasticity in neural networks. By changing the amount of transmitter released from the pre-synaptic terminal or the post-synaptic responsiveness (either by altering the membrane resistance or the number of receptors), the strength of a synapse can be altered over an order of magnitude. Obviously, this will have important effects on the phase relations of neurons firing in the network.

In the STG, the situation is complicated by the fact that graded synapses are the primary form of chemical communication: the cells release transmitter as a continuous function of membrane potential, and do not require action potentials to trigger release (Graubard,

1978). Some neurons even release transmitter at rest and must be hyperpolarized to block release. We have shown that graded synaptic transmission is also strongly modulated by monoamines, which can completely eliminate some synapses while strengthening others (Fig.3; Johnson and Harris-Warrick, 1990). Amines can change the apparent threshold for transmitter release or the functional strength of the synapse. Modulation of graded transmission thus allows delicate adjustments of the phasing between cells in the motorpattern, which is often determined by synaptic interactions. Graded synaptic transmission occurs in many species, so this could turn out to be a general form of plasticity.

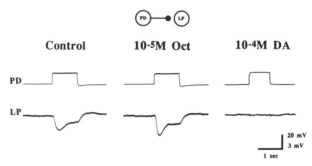

Figure 3: Modulation of graded synaptic transmission from the PD neuron to the LP neuron by octopamine and dopamine. Experiment done in the presence of tetrodotoxin to abolish action potentials. Other synaptic inputs to these cells have been eliminated.

In one case, modulation of graded transmission results in a sign reversal of the synaptic interaction between two cells (Johnson and Harris-Warrick, 1990). In the pyloric CPG, the PD neurons weakly inhibit the IC neuron by a graded chemical mechanism, but in addition the two cells are weakly electrically coupled. This mixed synapse is weak and variable. Dopamine weakens the chemical inhibition: the electrical coupling dominates and the IC cell depolarizes upon PD depolarization. Octopamine strengthens the chemical inhibition, and the IC cell hyperpolarizes upon PD depolarization. Combined chemical and electrical synaptic interactions have been detected in many other preparations, and thus can underly flexibility in the strength and sign of synaptic interactions.

4.3   ALTERATION OF THE INTRINSIC RESPONSE PROPERTIES OF THE NETWORK NEURONS

The physiological response properties of neurons within a network are not fixed, but can be extensively altered by neuromodulators. As a consequence, the response to an identical synaptic input can vary radically in the presence of different neuromodulators.

4.3.1   Induction of bistable firing properties

Many neurons in both vertebrates and invertebrates are capable of firing in "plateau potentials", where a brief excitatory stimulus triggers a prolonged depolarized plateau, with tonic spiking for many seconds, which can be prematurely truncated by a brief hyperpolarizing input (Hartline et al, 1988). Thus, the neuron shows bistable properties: brief synaptic inputs can step it between two relatively stable resting potentials which differ markedly in spike frequency. This property is plastic, and can be induced or suppressed by neuromodulatory inputs. For example, Fig. 4 shows the DG neuron in the STG. Under control conditions, a brief depolarizing current injection causes a small depolarization that is subthreshold for spike initiation. However, after stimulating a serotonergic/cholinergic modulatory neuron (called GPR), the same brief current injection induces a prolonged burst of spikes on a depolarized plateau potential (Katz and Harris-Warrick, 1989). Similar results have been obtained in turtle and cat spinal motor neurons after application of monoamines such as serotonin or its biochemical precursor (Hounsgaard et al,1988; Hounsgaard and Kiehn,1989). Stimulation of a modulatory neuron can also disable the plateau potentials that are normally present in a neuron (Nagy et al, 1988).

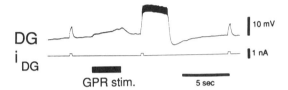

Figure 4: Induction of plateau potential capability in DG neuron by stimulation of a serotonergic/cholinergic sensory neuron, GPR.

4.3.2 Induction of endogenous rhythmic bursting

A more extreme form of modulation can occur where the modulatory stimulus induces endogenous rhythmic oscillations in membrane potential underlying rhythmic bursts of action potentials. For example, in Figure 4, the pyloric AB neuron shows no intrinsic oscillatory capabilities when it is isolated from all synaptic input. Bath application of monoamines such as DA, 5HT and OCT induce rhythmic bursting in this isolated cell (Flamm and Harris-Warrick, 1986b). Brief stimulation of the serotonergic/cholinergic GPR neuron can also induce or enhance rhythmic bursting that outlasts the stimulus by

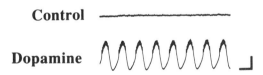

Figure 5: Induction of rhythmic bursting in a synaptically isolated AB neuron by bath application of dopamine (10^{-4}M).

several minutes. The quantitative details of the bursting (cycle frequency, oscillation amplitude, spike frequency, etc.) are different with each amine, due to different ionic mechanisms for burst generation (Harris-Warrick and Flamm, 1987b). Since the AB neuron is the major pacemaker in the pyloric CPG, these differences underly the marked differences in pyloric rhythm frequency seen with the amines in Fig.1. Induction of rhythmic bursting by neuromodulators has been observed in vertebrates (for example, Dekin et al,1985), and this is likely to be a general mechanism.

4.3.3   Modulation of post-inhibitory rebound

Most neurons show post-inhibitory rebound, a period of increased excitability following strong inhibition. This is probably due in part to the activation of prolonged inward currents during hyperpolarization (Angstadt and Calabrese, 1989). This property can be modified by biochemical second messengers used by neuromodulators. For example, elevation of cAMP by forskolin enhances post-inhibitory rebound in the pyloric LP neuron (Figure 5; Flamm et al, 1987). As a consequence of this modulation, the cell's response to a simple inhibitory input is radically changed to a biphasic response, with an initial inhibition followed by delayed excitation.

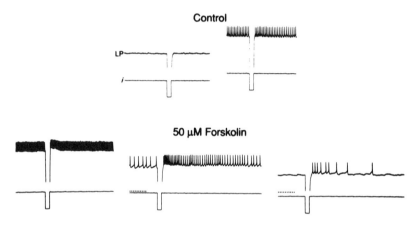

Figure 6: Induction of post-inhibitory rebound by forskolin, which elevates cAMP levels, in the LP neuron. **Control:** Hyperpolarizing current injection does not induce post-inhibitory rebound, measured at two different resting potentials. **Forskolin:** Elevation of cAMP depolarizes LP and induces tonic spiking (left). At all membrane potentials, a hyperpolarizing pulse is followed by an enhanced burst of action potentials.

5 ENDOGENOUS RELEASE OF NEUROMODULATORS FROM IDENTIFIED NEURONS

Most of the results I have described were obtained with bath application of amines or peptides, a method that can be criticized as being non-physiological. To test this, a number of neurons containing identified neuromodulators have been found, and the action of the naturally released and bath-applied modulator directly compared. An immediate complication arose from these studies: the majority of the known modulatory neurons contain more than one transmitter. All possible combinations have been observed, including a slow transmitter with a fast transmitter, two or more slow transmitters, and multiple fast transmitters. To fully understand the complex changes in network function induced by activity in these neurons, it is necessary to study the actions of all the co-transmitters on all the neurons in the network. This has been recently accomplished in the STG. Here, serotonin is released by a set of sensory cells responding to muscle stretch (Katz et al, 1989). These cells also contain and release acetylcholine (Katz et al,1989). In studying the actions of the two transmitters, remarkable flexibility was uncovered (Katz and Harris-Warrick, 1989,1990). First, not all target neurons responded to both released transmitters: some responded only to 5HT, while one cell responded only to ACh. Second, the responses to released 5HT were all modulatory, but varied markedly in different cells, mimicking the bath application studies described earlier. Finally, the two transmitters acted over entirely different time scales. ACh induced rapid EPSPs lasting tens to hundreds of msec via nicotinic receptors, while 5HT induced slow prolonged responses lasting many seconds to minutes (for example, Fig.4).

It is now clear that neural networks are targets for multiple neuronal inputs using many different transmitters and modulators. For example, the STG contains only 30 neurons, but is innervated by over 100 axons from other ganglia. Twelve neurotransmitters have thus far been identified in these axons (Marder and Nusbaum,1989), and these are probably a minority of the total that are present. In recordings from the input nerve to the ganglion, many axons are spontaneously active. Thus, the pyloric network is continuously bathed with a varying mixture of transmitters and modulators, allowing for very subtle changes in the firing pattern. *In vivo*, we expect that each modulator plays a small role in the overall mixture that determines the final motor pattern.

6 CONCLUSION

The work described here shows conclusively that an anatomically fixed neural network can be modulated to produce a large variety of output patterns. The anatomical connections in the network are necessary but not sufficient to understand the output of the network. Indeed, it is best to think of these networks as libraries of potential components, which are then selected and activated by the modulatory inputs. In addition to altering which neurons are active and altering the synaptic strength in the circuits, I have emphasized the important role of modulation of the intrinsic response properties of the network neurons in determining the final pattern of output. Indeed, if this aspect of modulation is ignored, predictions of the actions of modulators on the final motor pattern are grossly in error.

Many modellers claim that this emphasis on the intrinsic computational properties of single neurons is unique to the invertebrates, which have few cells to work with. In the vertebrates, they argue, the enormous increase in numbers of cells changes the computational rules such that each cell is a simple threshold element, and complex transformations only take place with changes in synaptic efficacy in the circuits. There are absolutely no data to support this hypothesis of "simple cells" in vertebrates. In fact, a great deal of careful work has shown that vertebrate neurons are dynamic elements that show all the complex intrinsic response properties of invertebrate neurons (Llinás,1988). These properties can be changed by neuromodulators, just as in the crustacean STG, such that vertebrate cells can have radically different physiological "personalities" in the presence of different modulators. Network models which ignore the complex computational properties of single neurons thus do not reflect the richness and variability of biological neural networks of both invertebrates and vertebrates alike.

Acknowledgments: Supported by NIH Grant NS17323 and Hatch Act NYC-191410.

7 BIBLIOGRAPHY

Angstadt, J.D., Calabrese, R.L. (1989) A hyperpolarization-activated inward current in heart interneurons of the medicinal leech. *J. Neurosci.* 9: 2846-2857.

Bal, T., Nagy, F., Moulins, M. (1988) The pyloric central pattern generator in Crustacea: a set of conditional neuronal oscillators. *J. Comp. Physiol.* A 163: 715-727.

Dekin, M.S., Richerson, G.B., Getting, P.A. (1985) Thyrotropin-releasing hormone induces rhythmic bursting in neurons of the nucleus tractus solitarius. *Science* 229:67-69.

Flamm, R.E., Harris-Warrick, R.M. (1986a) Aminergic modulation in lobster stomatogastric ganglion. I. The effects on motor pattern and activity of neurons within the pyloric circuit. *J. Neurophysiol.* 55: 847-865.

Flamm, R.E., Harris-Warrick, R.M. (1986b) Aminergic modulation in lobster stomatogastric ganglion. II. Target neurons of dopamine, octopamine, and serotonin within the pyloric circuit. *J. Neurophysiol.* 55: 866-881.

Flamm, R.E., Fickbohm, D., Harris-Warrick, R.M. (1987) cAMP elevation modulates physiological activity of pyloric neurons in the lobster stomatogastric ganglion. *J. Neurophysiol.* 58: 1370-1386.

Getting, P.A. (1988). Comparative analysis of invertebrate central pattern generators. in: Cohen, A.H., Rossignol, S., Grillner, S. (eds.), Neural Control of Rhythmic Movements in Vertebrates, John Wiley and Sons, New York, pp. 101-127.

Graubard, K. (1978) Synaptic transmission without action potentials: input-output properties of a non-spiking presynaptic neuron. *J. Neurophysiol.* 41: 1014-1025.

Harris-Warrick, R. M. (1988) Chemical modulation of central pattern generators. in: Cohen, A.H., Rossignol, S., Grillner, S.(eds.) Neural Control of Rhythmic Movements in Vertebrates, John Wiley & Sons, New York. pp 285-331.

Harris-Warrick, R.M., Flamm, R.E. (1987a) Chemical modulation of a small central pattern generator circuit. *Trends in Neurosci.* 9: 432-437.

Harris-Warrick, R.M., Flamm, R. E. (1987b) Multiple mechanisms of bursting in a conditional bursting neuron. *J. Neurosci.* 7: 2113-2128.

Hartline, D.K. (1987) Modeling stomatogastric ganglion. in: Selverston, A.I., Moulins, M. (eds.), The Crustacean Stomatogastric System. Springer-Verlag, Berlin, pp. 181-197.

Hartline, D.K., Russell, D.K., Raper, J.A., Graubard, K. (1988) Special cellular and synaptic mechanisms in motor pattern generation. *Comp. Biochem. Physiol.* 91C:115-131.

Hooper, S.L., Marder, E (1987) Modulation of the lobster pyloric rhythm by the peptide proctolin. *J. Neurosci.* 7:2097-2112.

Hounsgaard, J., Kiehn, O. (1989) Serotonin-induced bistability of turtle motoneurones caused by a nifedipine-sensitive calcium plateau potential. *J. Physiol.* 414:265-282.

Hounsgaard, J., Hultborn, H., Jespersen, B., Kiehn, O. (1988) Bistability of alpha-motoneurones in the decerebrate cat and in the acute spinal cat after intravenous 5-hydroxytryptophan. *J. Physiol.* 405:345-367.

Jan, L.Y., Jan, Y.N. (1982) Peptidergic transmission in sympathetic ganglia of the frog. *J. Physiol.* 327: 219-246.

Johnson, B. R., Harris-Warrick, R.M. (1990) Aminergic modulation of graded synaptic transmission in the lobster stomatogastric ganglion. *J. Neurosci.*, in press.

Katz, P.S., Eigg, M.H., Harris-Warrick, R.M. (1989) Serotonergic/cholinergic muscle receptor cells in the crab stomatogastric nervous system. I. Identification and characterization of the gastropyloric receptor cells. *J. Neurophysiol.* 62: 558-570.

Katz, P.S., Harris-Warrick, R.M. (1989) Serotonergic/cholinergic muscle receptor cells in the crab stomatogastric nervous system. II. Rapid nicotinic and prolonged modulatory effects on neurons in the stomatogastric ganglion. *J. Neurophysiol.* 62: 571-581.

Katz, P.S., Harris-Warrick, R. M. (1990) Neuromodulation of the crab pyloric central pattern generator by serotonergic/cholinergic proprioceptive afferents. *J. Neurosci.*, in press.

Llinás, R.R. (1988) The intrinsic electrophysiological properties of mammalian neurons: insights into central nervous function. *Science* 242: 1654-1664.

Marder, E., Nusbaum, M.P. (1989) Peptidergic modulation of the motor pattern generators in the stomatogastric ganglion. in: Carew, T.J., Kelley, D.B. (eds.), <u>Perspectives in Neural Systems and Behavior</u>, Alan R. Liss, Inc., New York. pp 73-91.

Miller, J.P. (1987) Pyloric mechanisms. <u>in</u>: Selverston, A.I., Moulins, M. (eds.) <u>The Crustacean Stomatogastric System</u> , Springer-Verlag, Berlin, pp. 109-136.

Nagy, F., Dickinson, P.S., Moulins, M. (1988) Control by an identified modulatory neuron of the sequential expression of plateau properties of, and synaptic inputs to, a neuron in a central pattern generator. *J. Neurosci.* 8:2875-2886.

Rezer, E., Moulins, M. (1983) Expression of the crustacean pyloric pattern generator in the intact animal. *J. Comp. Physiol.* 153:17-28.

Selverston, A.I., Moulins, M. (eds.) (1987) <u>The Crustacean Stomatogastric System</u> Springer-Verlag, Berlin, 338 pp.

Neural Network Analysis of Distributed Representations of Dynamical Sensory-Motor Transformations in the Leech

Shawn R. Lockery, Yan Fang, and Terrence J. Sejnowski
Computational Neurobiology Laboratory
Salk Institute for Biological Studies
Box 85800, San Diego, CA 92138

ABSTRACT

Interneurons in leech ganglia receive multiple sensory inputs and make synaptic contacts with many motor neurons. These "hidden" units coordinate several different behaviors. We used physiological and anatomical constraints to construct a model of the local bending reflex. Dynamical networks were trained on experimentally derived input-output patterns using recurrent back-propagation. Units in the model were modified to include electrical synapses and multiple synaptic time constants. The properties of the hidden units that emerged in the simulations matched those in the leech. The model and data support distributed rather than localist representations in the local bending reflex. These results also explain counterintuitive aspects of the local bending circuitry.

INTRODUCTION

Neural network modeling techniques have recently been used to predict and analyze the connectivity of biological neural circuits (Zipser and Andersen, 1988; Lehky and Sejnowski, 1988; Anastasio and Robinson, 1989). Neurons are represented as simplified processing units and arranged into model networks that are then trained to reproduce the input-output function of the reflex or brain region of interest. After training, the receptive and projective field of hidden units in the network often bear striking similarities to actual neurons and can suggest functional roles of neurons with inputs and outputs that are hard to grasp intuitively. We applied this approach to the local bending reflex of the leech, a three-layered, feed-forward network comprising a small number of identifiable neurons whose connectivity and input-output function have been determined physiologically. We found that model local bending networks trained using recurrent back-propagation (Pineda, 1987; Pearlmutter, 1989) to reproduce a physiologically determined input-output function contained hidden units whose connectivity and temporal response properties closely resembled those of identified neurons in the biological network. The similarity between model and actual neurons suggested that local bending is produced by distributed representations of sensory and motor information.

THE LOCAL BENDING REFLEX

In response to a mechanical stimulus, the leech withdraws from the site of contact (Fig. 1a). This is accomplished by contraction of longitudinal muscles beneath the stimulus and relaxation of longitudinal muscles on the opposite side of the body, resulting in a U-shaped local bend (Kristan, 1982). The form of the response is independent of the site of stimulation: dorsal, ventral, and lateral stimuli produce an appropriately oriented

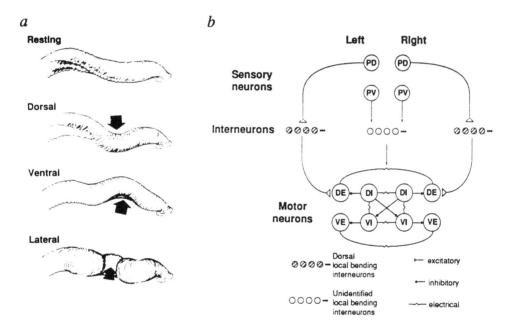

Figure 1: *a*. Local bending behavior. Partial view of a leech in the resting position and in response to dorsal, ventral, and lateral stimuli. *b*. Local bending circuit. The main input to the reflex is provided by the dorsal and ventral P cells (PD and PV). Control of local bending is largely provided by motor neurons whose field of innervation is restricted to single left-right, dorsal-ventral quadrants of the body; dorsal and ventral quadrants are innervated by both excitatory (DE and VE) and inhibitory (DI and VI) motor neurons. Motor neurons are connected by electrical and chemical synapses. Sensory input to motor neurons is mediated by a layer of interneurons. Interneurons that were excited by PD and which in turn excite DE have been identified (hatched) ; other types of interneurons remain to be identified (open).

withdrawal. Major input to the local bending reflex is provided by four pressure sensitive mechanoreceptors called P cells, each with a receptive field confined to a single quadrant of the body wall (Fig. 1b). Output to the muscles is provided by eight types of longitudinal muscle motor neurons, one to four excitatory and inhibitory motor neurons for each body wall quadrant (Stuart, 1970; Ort et al., 1974). Motor neurons are connected by chemical and electrical synapses that introduce the possibility of feedback among the motor neurons.

Dorsal, ventral, and lateral stimuli each produce a pattern of P cell activation that results in a unique pattern of activation and inhibition of the motor neurons (Lockery and Kristan, 1990a). Connections between sensory and motor neurons are mediated by a layer of interneurons (Kristan, 1982). Nine types of local bending interneurons have been identified (Lockery and Kristan, 1990b). These comprise the subset of the local bending interneurons which contribute to dorsal local bending because they are excited by the dorsal P cell and in turn excite the dorsal excitatory motor neuron. There appear to be no functional connections between interneurons. Other interneurons remain to be identified, such as those which *inhibit* the dorsal excitatory motor neurons.

Interneuron input connections were determined by recording the amplitude of the postsynaptic potential in an interneuron while each of the P cells was stimulated with a standard train of impulses (Lockery and Kristan, 1990b). Output connections were determined by recording the amplitude of the postsynaptic potential in each motor neuron when an interneuron was stimulated with a standard current pulse. Interneuron input and output connections are shown in Figure 2, where white squares are excitatory connections, black squares are inhibitory connections, and the size of each square indicates connection strength. Most interneurons received substantial input from three or four P cells, indicating that the local bending network forms a distributed representation of sensory input.

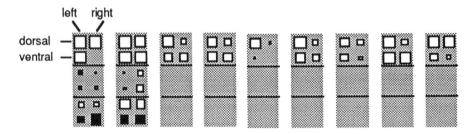

Figure 2: Input and output connections of the nine types of dorsal local bending interneurons. Within each gray box, the upper panel shows input connections from sensory neurons, the middle panel shows output connections to inhibitory motor neurons, and the lower panel shows output connections to excitatory motor neurons. Side-length of each box is proportional to the amplitude of the connection determined from intracellular recordings of interneurons or motor neurons. White boxes indicate excitatory connections and black boxes indicated inhibitory connections. Blank spaces denote conections whose strength has not been determined for technical reasons.

NEURAL NETWORK MODEL

Because sensory input is represented in a distributed fashion, most interneurons are active in all forms of local bending. Thus, in addition to contributing to *dorsal* local bending, most interneurons are also active during *ventral* and *lateral* bending when some or all of their output effects are inappropriate to the observed behavioral response. This suggests that the inappropriate effects of the dorsal bending interneurons must be offset by other as yet unidentified interneurons and raises the possibility that local bending is the result of simultaneous activation of a population of interneurons with multiple sensory inputs and both appropriate and inappropriate effects on many motor neurons. It was not obvious, however, that such a population was sufficient, given the well-known nonlinearities of neural elements and constraints imposed by the input-output function and connections known to exist in the network. The possibility remained that interneurons specific for each form of the behavior were required to produce each output pattern. To address this issue, we used recurrent back-propagation (Pearlmutter, 1989) to train a dynamical network of model neurons (Fig 3a). The network had four input units representing the

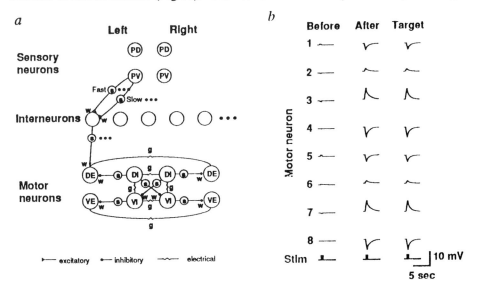

Figure 3: *a*. The local bending network model. Four sensory neurons were connected to eight motor neurons via a layer of 10 interneurons. Neurons were represented as single electrical compartments whose voltage varied as a function of time (see text). Known electrical and chemical connections among motor neurons were assigned fixed connection strengths (g's and w's) determined from intracellular recordings. Interneuron input and output connections were adjusted by recurrent back-propagation. Chemical synaptic delays were implemented by inserting s-units between chemically connected pairs of neurons. S-units with different time constants were inserted between sensory and interneurons to account for fast and slow components of synaptic potentials recorded in interneurons. *b*. Output of the model network in response to simultaneous activation of both PDs (stim). The response of each motor neuron (rows) is shown before and after training. The desired response contained in the training set is shown on the right for comparison (target).

four P cells, and eight output units representing the eight motor neuron types. Between input and output units was a single layer of 10 hidden units representing the interneurons. Neurons were represented as single electrical compartments with an input resistance and time constant. The membrane potential (V_i) of each neuron was given by

$$T_i \, dV_i/dt = -V_i + R_i(I_e + I_c)$$

where T_i and R_i are the time constant and input resistance of the neuron and I_e and I_c are the sum of the electrical and chemical synaptic currents from presynaptic neurons. Current due to electrical synapses was given by

$$I_e = \Sigma_j \, g_{ij} \, (V_j \text{-} V_i)$$

where g_{ij} is the coupling conductance between neuron i and j. To implement the delay associated with chemical synapses, synapse units (s-units) were inserted between between pairs of neurons connected by chemical synapses. The activation of each s-unit was given by

$$T_{ij} \, dS_{ij}/dt = -S_{ij} + f(V_j)$$

where T_{ij} is the synaptic time constant and $f(V_j)$ was a physiologically determined sigmoidal function ($0 \le f \le 1$) relating pre- and postsynaptic membrane potential at an identified monosynaptic connection in the leech (Granzow et al., 1985). Current due to chemical synapses was given by

$$I_c = \Sigma_j \, w_{ij} \, S_{ij}$$

where w_{ij} is the strength of the chemical synapse between units i and j. Thus, synaptic current is a graded function of presynaptic voltage, a common feature of neurons in the leech (Friesen, 1985; Granzow et al., 1985; Thompson and Stent, 1976) and other invertebrates (Katz and Miledi, 1967; Burrows and Siegler, 1978; Nagayama and Hisada, 1987).

Chemical and electrical synaptic strengths between motor neurons were determined by recording from pairs of motor neurons and were not adjusted by the training algorithm. Interneuron input and output connections were given small initial values that were randomly assigned and subsequently adjusted during training. During training, input connections were constrained to be positive to reflect the fact that only excitatory interneuron input connections were seen (Fig. 2), but no constraints were placed on the number of input or output connections. Synaptic time constants were assigned fixed values. These were adjusted by hand to fit the time course of motor neuron synaptic potentials (Lockery and Kristan, 1990a), or determined from pairwise motor neuron recordings (Granzow et al., 1985).

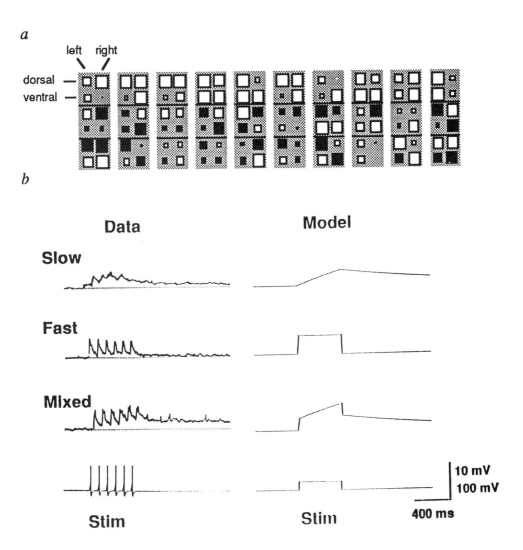

Figure 4: *a.* Input and output connections of model local bending interneurons. Model interneurons, like the actual interneurons, received substantial inputs from three or four sensory neurons and had significant effects on most of the motor neurons. Symbols as in figure 2. *b.* Actual (data) and simulated (model) synaptic potentials recorded from three types of interneuron. Actual synaptic potentials were recorded in response to a train of P cell impulses. Simulated synaptic potentials were recorded in response to a pulse of current in the P cell which simulates a step change in P cell firing frequency.

RESULTS

Model networks were trained to produce the amplitude and time course of synaptic potentials recorded in all eight motor neurons in response to trains of P cell impulses

(Lockery and Kristan, 1990a). The training set included the response of all eight motor neurons when each P cell was stimulated alone and when P cells were stimulated in pairs. After 6,000 - 10,000 training epochs, the output of the model closely matched the desired output for all patterns in the training set (Fig. 3b). To compare interneurons in the model network to actual interneurons, simulated physiological experiments were performed. Interneuron input connections were determined by recording the amplitude of the postsynaptic potential in a model interneuron while each of the P cells was stimulated with a standard current pulse. Output connections were determined by recording the amplitude of the postsynaptic potential in each motor neuron when an interneuron was stimulated with a standard current pulse. Model interneurons, like those in the real network, received three or four substantial connections from P cells and had significant effects on most of the motor neurons (Fig. 4a). Most model interneurons were active during each form of the behavior and the output connections of the interneurons were only partially consistent with each form of the local bending response. Thus, the appropriate motor neuron responses were produced by the summation of many appropriate and inappropriate interneuron effects. This result explains the appropriate and inappropriate effects of interneurons in the leech.

There was also agreement between the time course of the response of model and actual interneurons to P cell stimulation (Fig. 4b). In the actual network, interneuron synaptic potentials in response to trains of P cell impulses had a fast and slow component. Some interneurons showed only the fast component, some only the slow, and some showed both components (mixed). Although no constraints were placed on the temporal response properties of interneurons, the same three types of interneuron were found in the model network. The three different types of interneuron temporal response were due to different relative connection strengths of fast and slow s-units impinging on a given interneuron (Fig. 3a).

CONCLUSION

Our results show that the network modeling approach can be adapted to models with more realistic neurons and synaptic connections, including electrical connections, which occur in both invertebrates and vertebrates. The qualitative similarity between model and actual interneurons demonstrates that a population of interneurons resembling the identified dorsal local bending interneurons could mediate local bending in a distributed processing system without additional interneurons specific for different forms of local bending. Interneurons in the model also displayed the diversity in temporal responses seen in interneurons in the leech. Clearly, the training algorithm did not produce exact matches between model and actual interneurons, but this was not surprising since the identified local bending interneurons represent only a subset of the interneurons in the reflex. More exact matches could be obtained by using two pools of model interneurons, one to represent identified neurons, the other to represent unidentified neurons. Model neurons in the latter pool would constitute testable physiological predictions of the connectivity of unidentified local bending interneurons.

Acknowledgements

Supported by the Bank of America-Giannini Foundation, the Drown Foundation, and the Mathers Foundation.

References

Anastasio, T. and Robinson, D. A. (1989) Distributed parallel processing in the vestibulo-oculomotor system. Neural Comp. 1:230-241.

Burrows, M., and M.V.S. Siegler (1978) Graded synaptic transmission between local interneurones and motor neurones in the metathoracic ganglion of the locust. J. Physiol. 285:231-255.

Friesen, W.O. (1985) Neuronal control of leech swimming movements: interactions between cell 60 and previously described oscillator neurons. J. Comp. Physiol. 156:231-242.

Granzow, B., W.O. Friesen, and W.B. Kristan Jr. (1985) Physiological and morphological analysis of synaptic transmission between leech motor neurons. J.Neurosci. 5:2035-2050.

Katz, B., and Miledi, R. (1967) Synaptic transmission in the absence of nerve impulses. J. Physiol. 192:407-436.

Kristan Jr., W.B. (1982) Sensory and motor neurons responsible for the local bending response in leeches. J. Exp. Biol. 96:161-180.

Kristan, W.B. Jr., S.J. McGirr, and G.V. Simpson (1982) Behavioral and mechanosensory neurone responses to skin stimulation in leeches. J. Exp. Biol. 96:143-160.

Lehky, S.R., and T.J. Sejnowski (1988) Network model of shape-from-shading: neural function arises from both receptive and projective fields. Nature 333:452-454.

Lockery, S.R., and W.B. Kristan Jr. (1990) Distributed processing of sensory information in the leech. I. Input-output relations of the local bending reflex. J. Neurosci. (in press).

Lockery, S.R., and W.B. Kristan Jr. (1990) Distributed processing of sensory information in the leech. II. Identification of interneurons contributing to the local bending reflex. J. Neurosci. (in press).

Nagayama, T., and M. Hisada (1987) Opposing parallel connections through crayfish local nonspiking interneurons. J. Comp. Neurol. 257:347-358.

Nicholls, J.G., and D. Purves (1970) Monosynaptic chemical and electrical connexions between sensory and motor cells in the central nervous system of the leech. J. Physiol. 209:647-667.

Nicholls, J.G., and B.G. Wallace (1978) Quantal analysis of transmitter release an in inhibitory synapse in the CNS. J. Physiol. 281:157-170.

Ort, C.A., W.B. Kristan Jr., and G.S. Stent (1974) Neuronal control of swimming in the medicinal leech. II. Identification and connections of motor neurones. J. Comp. Physiol. 94:121-154.

Stuart, A.E. (1970) Physiological and morphological properties of motoneurones in the central nervous system of the leech. J. Physiol. 209:627-646.

Thompson, W.J., and G.S. Stent (1976) Neuronal control of heartbeat in the medicinal leech. J. Comp. Physiol. 111:309-333.

Zipser, D., and R.A. Andersen (1988) A back-propagation programmed network that simulates response properties of a subset of posterior parietal neurons Nature 331:679-684.

Reading a Neural Code

William Bialek, Fred Rieke, R. R. de Ruyter van Steveninck[1] **and**
David Warland
Department of Physics, and
Department of Molecular and Cell Biology
University of California at Berkeley
Berkeley, California 94720

ABSTRACT

Traditional methods of studying neural coding characterize the encoding of known stimuli in average neural responses. Organisms face nearly the opposite task — decoding short segments of a spike train to extract information about an unknown, time-varying stimulus. Here we present strategies for characterizing the neural code from the point of view of the organism, culminating in algorithms for real-time stimulus reconstruction based on a single sample of the spike train. These methods are applied to the design and analysis of experiments on an identified movement-sensitive neuron in the fly visual system. As far as we know this is the first instance in which a direct "reading" of the neural code has been accomplished.

1   Introduction

Sensory systems receive information at extremely high rates, and much of this information must be processed in real time. To understand real-time signal processing in biological systems we must understand the representation of this information in neural spike trains. We ask several questions in particular:

- Does a single neuron signal only the occurrence of particular stimulus "features," or can the spike train represent a continuous time-varying input?

[1] Rijksuniversiteit Groningen, Postbus 30.001, 9700 RB Groningen The Netherlands

- How much information is carried by the spike train of a single neuron?
- Is the reliability of the encoded signal limited by noise at the sensory input or by noise and inefficiencies in the subsequent layers of neural processing?
- Is the neural code robust to errors in spike timing, or do realistic levels of synaptic noise place significant limits on information transmission?
- Do simple analog computations on the encoded signals correspond to simple manipulations of the spike trains?

Although neural coding has been studied for more than fifty years, clear experimental answers to these questions have been elusive (Perkel & Bullock, 1968; de Ruyter van Steveninck & Bialek, 1988). Here we present a new approach to the characterization of the neural code which provides explicit and sometimes surprising answers to these questions when applied to an identified movement-sensitive neuron in the fly visual system.

We approach the study of spiking neurons from the point of view of the organism, which, based only on the spike train, must estimate properties of an unknown time-varying stimulus. Specifically we try to solve the problem of *decoding* the spike train to recover the stimulus in real time. As far as we know our work is the first instance in which it has been possible to "read" the neural code in this literal sense. Once we can read the code, we can address the questions posed above. In this paper we focus on the code reading algorithm, briefly summarizing the results which follow.

2   Theoretical background

The traditional approach to the study of neural coding characterizes the *encoding* process: For an arbitrary stimulus waveform $s(\tau)$, what can we predict about the spike train? This process is completely specified by the conditional probability distribution $P[\{t_i\}|s(\tau)]$ of the spike arrival times $\{t_i\}$ conditional on the stimulus $s(\tau)$. In practice one cannot characterize this distribution in its entirety; most experiments result in only the lowest moment — the firing rate as function of time given the stimulus.

The classic experiments of Adrian and others established that, for static stimuli, the resulting constant firing rate provides a measure of stimulus strength. This concept is easily extended to any stimulus waveform which is characterized by constant parameters, such as a single frequency or fixed amplitude sine wave. Much of the effort in studying the encoding of sensory signals in the nervous system thus reduces to probing the relation between these stimulus parameters and the resulting firing rate. Generalizations to time-varying firing rates, especially in response to periodic signals, have also been explored.

The firing rate is a continuous function of time which measures the probability per unit time that the cell will generate a spike. The rate is thus by definition an average quantity; it is not a property of a single spike train. The rate can be estimated, in principle, by averaging over a large ensemble of redundant cells, or by averaging responses of a single cell over repeated presentations of the same stimulus. This latter approach dominates the experimental study of spiking neurons. Measurements of firing rate rely on some form of redundancy — either the spatial redundancy of identical cells or the temporal redundancy of repeated stimuli. It is simply not clear that such redundancy exists in real sensory systems under natural stimulus conditions. In the absence of redundancy a characterization of neural responses in terms of firing rate is of little relevance to the signal processing problems faced by the organism. To say that "information is coded in firing rates" is of no use unless one can explain how the organism could estimate these firing rates by observing the spike trains of its own neurons.

We believe that none of the existing approaches[2] to neural coding addresses the basic problem of real-time signal processing with neural spike trains: The organism must extract information about continuously varying stimulus waveforms using only the discrete sequences of spikes. Real-time signal processing with neural spike trains thus involves some sort of interpolation between the spikes that allows the organism to estimate a continuous function of time.

The most basic problem of real-time signal processing is to *decode* the spike train and recover an estimate of the stimulus waveform itself. Clearly if we can accomplish this task then we can begin to understand how spike trains can be manipulated to perform more complex computations; we can also address the quantitative issues outlined in the Introduction. Because of the need to interpolate between spikes, such decoding is not a simple matter of inverting the conventional stimulus-response (rate) relations. In fact it is not obvious *a priori* that true decoding is even possible.

One approach to the decoding problem is to construct models of the encoding process, and proceed analytically to develop algorithms for decoding within the context of the model (Bialek & Zee, 1990). Using the results of this approach we can predict that linear filtering will, under some conditions, be an effective decoding algorithm, and we can determine the form of the filter itself. In this paper we have a more limited goal, namely to see if the *class* of decoding algorithms identified by Bialek and Zee is applicable to a real neuron. To this end we will treat the structure of the decoding filter as unknown, and find the "best" filter under given experimental conditions.

We imagine building a set of (generally non-linear) filters $\{F_n\}$ which operate on the spike train to produce an estimate of the stimulus. If the spikes arrive at times $\{t_i\}$, we write our estimate of the signal as a generalized convolution,

$$s_{est}(t) = \sum_i F_1(t - t_i) + \sum_{i,j} F_2(t - t_i, t - t_j) + \cdots. \tag{1}$$

---

[2]Higher moments of the conditional probability $P[\{t_i\}|s(\tau)]$, such as the inter-spike interval distribution (Perkel & Bullock, 1968) are also average properties, not properties of single spike trains, and hence may not be relevant to real-time signal processing. White-noise methods (Marmarelis & Marmarelis, 1978) result in models which predict the time-varying firing rate in response to arbitrary input waveforms and thus suffer the same limitations as other rate-based approaches.

How good are the reconstructions? We separate systematic and random errors by introducing a frequency dependent gain $g(\omega)$ such that $\langle|\tilde{s}(\omega)|\rangle = g(\omega)\langle|\tilde{s}_{est}(\omega)|\rangle$. The resulting gain is approximately unity through a reasonable bandwidth. Further, the distribution of deviations between the stimulus and reconstruction is approximately Gaussian. The absence of systematic errors suggests that non-linearities in the reconstruction filter are unlikely to help. Indeed, the contribution from the second order term in Eq. (1) to the reconstructions is negligible.

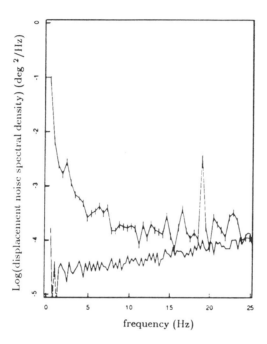

Figure 2: Spectral density of displacement noise from our reconstruction (upper curve). By multiplying the displacement noise level by a bandwidth, we obtain the square of the angular resolution of H1 for a step displacement. For a reasonable bandwidth the resolution is much less than the photoreceptor spacing, 1.35° — *"hyperacuity."* Also shown is the limit to the resolution of small displacements set by noise in the photoreceptor array (lower curve).

We identify the noise at frequency ω as the difference between the stimulus and the normalized reconstruction, $\tilde{n}(\omega) = \tilde{s}(\omega) - g(\omega)\tilde{s}_{est}(\omega)$. We then compute the spectral density (noise power per unit bandwidth) of the displacement noise (Fig 2). The noise level achieved in H1 is astonishing; with a one second integration time an observer of the spike train in H1 could judge the amplitude of a low frequency dither to 0.01° — more than one hundred times less than the photoreceptor spacing! If the fly's neural circuitry is noiseless, the fundamental limits to displacement resolution

stimulus,

$$F_1(\tau) = \int \frac{d\omega}{2\pi} e^{-i\omega\tau} \frac{\left\langle \tilde{s}(\omega) \sum_j e^{-i\omega t_j} \right\rangle}{\left\langle \sum_{i,j} e^{i\omega(t_i - t_j)} \right\rangle}. \tag{2}$$

The averages $\langle \cdots \rangle$ are with respect to an ensemble of stimuli $s(\tau)$.

2. Minimize χ^2 with respect to purely causal functions. This may be done analytically, or numerically by expanding $F_1(\tau)$ in a complete set of functions which vanish at negative times, then minimizing χ^2 by varying the coefficients of the expansion. In this method we must explicitly introduce a delay time which measures the lag between the true stimulus and our reconstruction.

We use the filter generated from the first method (which is the best possible linear filter) to check the filter generated by the second method. Fig. 1 illustrates reconstructions using these two methods. The filters themselves are also shown in the figure; we see that both methods give essentially the same answer.

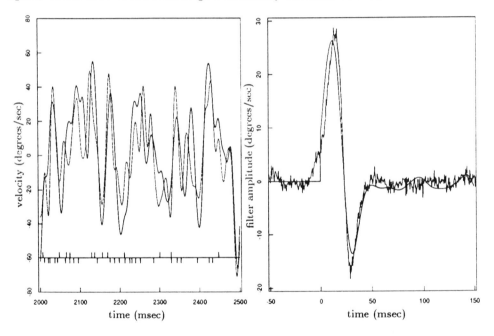

Figure 1: First order reconstruction $s_{est}(\tau)$ using method 1 (solid line). The stimulus is shown here as a dotted line for comparison. The reconstruction shown is for a segment of the spike train which was not used in the filter calculations. The spike train is shown at the bottom of the figure, where the negative spikes are from the "other eye" (cf. footnote 3). Both stimulus and reconstruction are smoothed with a 5 msec half-width Gaussian filter. The filters calculating using both methods are shown on the right.

We define the optimal filter to be that which minimizes $\chi^2 = \int dt |s(t) - s_{\text{est}}(t)|^2$, where $s(t)$ is the true stimulus, and the integration is over the duration of the experiment.

To insure that the filters we calculate allow real-time decoding, we require that the filters be causal, for example $F_1(\tau < 0) = 0$. But the occurrence of a spike at t' conveys information about the stimulus at a time $t < t'$, so we must delay our estimate of the stimulus by some time $\tau_{delay} > t' - t$. In general we gain more information by increasing the delay, so we face a tradeoff: Longer waiting times allow us to gain more information but introduce longer reaction times to important stimuli. This tradeoff is exactly the tradeoff faced by the organism in reacting to external stimuli based on noisy and incomplete information.

3   Movement detection in the blowfly visual system

We apply our methods in experiments on a single wide field, movement-sensitive neuron (H1) in the visual system of the blowfly *Calliphora erythrocephela*. Flies and other insects exhibit visually guided flight; during chasing behavior course corrections can occur on time scales as short as 30 msec (Land & Collett, 1974). H1 appears to be an obligatory link in this control loop, encoding wide field horizontal movements (Hausen, 1984). Given that the maximum firing rate in H1 is 100-200 Hz, behavioral decisions must be based on the information carried by just a few spikes from this neuron. Further, the horizontal motion detection system consists of only a handful of neurons, so the fly has no opportunity to compute average responses (or firing rates).

In the experiments described here, the fly is looking at a rigidly moving random pattern (de Ruyter van Steveninck, 1986). The pattern is presented on an oscilloscope, and moved horizontally every 500 μsec in discrete steps chosen from an ensemble which approximates Gaussian white noise. This time scale is short enough that we can consider the resulting stimulus waveform $s(t)$ to be the instantaneous angular velocity. We record the spike arrival times $\{t_i\}$ extracellularly from the H1 neuron.[3]

4   First order reconstructions

To reconstruct the stimulus waveform requires that we find the filter F_1 which minimizes χ^2. We do this in two different ways:

1. Disregard the constraint that the filter be causal. In this case we can write an explicit formula for the optimal filter in terms of the spike trains and the

---

[3] There is one further caveat to the experiment. The firing rate in H1 is increased for back-to-front motion and is decreased for front-to-back motion; the dynamic range is much greater in the excitatory direction. The fly, however, achieves high sensitivity in both directions by combining information from both eyes. Because front-to-back motion in one eye corresponds to back-to-front motion in the other eye, we can simulate the two eye case while recording from only one H1 cell by using an antisymmetric stimulus waveform. We combine the information coded in the spike trains corresponding to the two "polarities" of the stimulus to obtain the information available from both H1 neurons.

are set by noise in the photoreceptor array. We have calculated these limits in the case where the displacements are small, which is true in our experiments at high frequencies. In comparing these limits with the results in H1 it is crucial that the photoreceptor signal and noise characteristics (de Ruyter van Steveninck, 1986) are measured under the same conditions as the H1 experiments analyzed here. It is clear from Fig. 2 that H1 approaches the theoretical limit to its performance. We emphasize that the noise spectrum in Fig. 2 is not a hypothetical measure of neural performance. Rather it is the real noise level achieved in our reconstructions. As far as we know this is the first instance in which the equivalent spectral noise level of a spiking neuron has been measured.

To explore the tradeoff between the quality and delay of the reconstruction we measure the cross-correlation of the smoothed stimulus with the reconstructions calculated using method 2 above for delays of 10-70 msec. For a delay of 10 msec the reconstruction carries essentially no information; this is expected since a delay of 10 msec is close to the intrinsic delay for phototransduction. As the delay is increased the reconstructions improve, and this improvement saturates for delays greater than 40 msec, close to the behavioral reaction time of 30 msec — the structure of the code is well matched to the behavioral decision task facing the organism.

5   Conclusions

Learning how to read the neural code has allowed us to quantify the information carried in the spike train independent of assumptions regarding the structure of the code. In addition, our analysis gives some hopefully more general insights into neural coding and computation:

1. The continuously varying movement signal encoded in the firing of H1 can be reconstructed by an astonishingly simple linear filter. If neurons summed their inputs and marked the crossing of thresholds (as in many popular models), such reconstructions would be impossible; the threshold crossings are massively ambiguous indicators of the signal waveform. We have carried out similar studies on a standard model neuron (the FitzHugh-Nagumo model), and find results similar to those in the H1 experiments. From the model neuron studies it appears that the linear representation of signals in spike trains is a general property of neurons, at least in a limited regime of their dynamics. In the near future we hope to investigate this statement in other sensory systems.

2. The reconstruction is dominated by a "window" of ∼ 40 msec during which at most a few spikes are fired. Because so few spikes are important, it does not make sense to talk about the "firing rate" — estimating the rate *vs.* time from observations of the spike train is at least as hard as estimating the stimulus itself!

3. The quality of the reconstructions can be improved by accepting longer delays, but this improvement saturates at ∼ 30 − 40 msec, in good agreement with behavioral decision times.

4. Having decoded the neural signal we obtain a meaningful estimate of the noise level in the system and the information content of the code. H1 accomplishes a real-time version of hyperacuity, corresponding to a noise level near the limits imposed by the quality of the sensory input. It appears that this system is close to achieving *optimal* real-time signal processing.

5. From measurements of the fault tolerance of the code we can place requirements on the noise levels in neural circuits using the information coded in H1. One of the standard objections to discussions of "spike timing" as a mechanism of coding is that there are no biologically plausible mechanisms which can make precise measurements of spike arrival times. We have tested the required timing precision by introducing timing errors into the spike train and characterizing the resulting reconstructions. Remarkably the code is "fault tolerant," the reconstructions degrading only slightly when we add timing errors of several msec.

Finally, we wish to emphasize our own surprise that it is so simple to recover time dependent signals from neural spike trains. The filters we have constructed are not very complicated, and they are linear. These results suggest that the representation of time-dependent sensory data in the nervous system is much simpler than we might have expected. We suggest that, correspondingly, simpler models of sensory signal processing may be appropriate.

6   Acknowledgments

We thank W. J. Bruno, M. Crair, L. Kruglyak, J. P. Miller, W. G. Owen, A. Zee, and G. Zweig for many helpful discussions. This work was supported by the National Science Foundation through a Presidential Young Investigator Award to WB, supplemented by funds from Cray Research and Sun Microsystems, and through a Graduate Fellowship to FR. DW was supported in part by the Systems and Integrative Biology Training Program of the National Institutes of Health. Initial work was supported by the Netherlands Organization for Pure Scientific Research (ZWO).

7   References

W. Bialek and A. Zee. *J. Stat. Phys.*, in press, 1990.

K. Hausen. In M. Ali, editor, *Photoreception and Vision in Invertebrates*. Plenum Press, New York and London, 1984.

M. Land and T. Collett. *J. Comp. Physiol.*, 89:331, 1974.

P. Marmarelis and V. Marmarelis. *Analysis of Physiological Systems. The White Noise Approach*. Plenum Press, New York, 1978.

D. Perkel and T. Bullock. *Neurosciences. Res. Prog. Bull.*, 6:221, 1968.

R. R. de Ruyter van Steveninck and W. Bialek. *Proc. R. Soc. Lond. B*, 234:379, 1988.

R. R. de Ruyter van Steveninck. *Real-time Performance of a Movement-sensitive Neuron in the Blowfly Visual System*. Rijksuniversiteit Groningen, Groningen, Netherlands, 1986.

Neural Implementation of Motivated Behavior: Feeding in an Artificial Insect

Randall D. Beer[1,2] and **Hillel J. Chiel**[2]

Departments of [1]Computer Engineering and Science, and [2]Biology
and the Center for Automation and Intelligent Systems Research
Case Western Reserve University
Cleveland, OH 44106

ABSTRACT

Most complex behaviors appear to be governed by internal motivational states or drives that modify an animal's responses to its environment. It is therefore of considerable interest to understand the neural basis of these motivational states. Drawing upon work on the neural basis of feeding in the marine mollusc *Aplysia*, we have developed a heterogeneous artificial neural network for controlling the feeding behavior of a simulated insect. We demonstrate that feeding in this artificial insect shares many characteristics with the motivated behavior of natural animals.

1   INTRODUCTION

While an animal's external environment certainly plays an extremely important role in shaping its actions, the behavior of even simpler animals is by no means solely reactive. The response of an animal to food, for example, cannot be explained only in terms of the physical stimuli involved. On two different occasions, the very same animal may behave in completely different ways when presented with seemingly identical pieces of food (e.g. hungrily consuming it in one case and ignoring or even avoiding it in another). To account for these differences, behavioral scientists hypothesize internal motivational states or drives which modulate an animal's response to its environment. These internal factors play a particularly important role in complex behavior, but are present to some degree in nearly all animal behavior. Behaviors which exhibit an extensive dependence on motivational variables are termed *motivated behaviors*.

While a rigorous definition is difficult to state, behaviors spoken of as motivated generally exhibit some subset of the following six characteristics (Kupfermann, 1974): (1) grouping and sequencing of component behaviors in time, (2) goal-directedness: the sequence of component behaviors generated can often be understood only by reference to some internal goal, (3) spontaneity: the behavior can occur in the absence of any recognizable eliciting stimuli, (4) changes in responsiveness: the effect of a motivational state varies depending upon an animal's level of arousal, (5) persistence: the behavior can greatly outlast any initiating stimulus, and (6) associative learning.

Motivational states are pervasive in mammalian behavior. However, they have also proven to be essential for explaining the behavior of simpler animals as well. Unfortunately, the explanatory utility of these internal factors is limited by the fact that they are hypothetical constructs, inferred by the theorist to intervene between stimulus and action in order to account for otherwise inexplicable responses. What might be the neural basis of these motivational states?

In order to explore this question, we have drawn upon work on the neural basis of feeding in the marine mollusc *Aplysia* to implement feeding in a simulated insect. Feeding is a prototypical motivated behavior in which attainment of the goal object (food) is clearly crucial to an animal's survival. In this case, the relevant motivational state is hunger. When an animal is hungry, it will exhibit a sequence of *appetitive behaviors* which serve to identify and properly orient the animal to food. Once food is available, *consummatory behaviors* are generated to ingest it. On the other hand, a satiated animal may ignore or even avoid sensory stimuli which suggest the presence of food (Kupfermann, 1974).

This effort is part of a larger project aimed at designing artificial nervous systems for the flexible control of complete autonomous agents (Beer, 1989). In addition to feeding, this artificial insect is currently capable of locomotion (Beer, Chiel, and Sterling, 1989; Chiel and Beer, 1989), wandering, and edge-following, and possesses a simple behavioral hierarchy as well. A central theme of this work has been the utilization of biologically-inspired architectures in our neural network designs. To support this capability, we make use of model neurons which capture some of the intrinsic properties of nerve cells.

The simulated insect and the environment in which it exists is designed as follows. The insect has six legs, and is capable of statically stable locomotion and turning. Its head contains a mouth which can open and close, and its mouth and two antennae possess tactile and chemical sensors. The insect possesses an internal energy supply which is depleted at a fixed rate. The simulated environment also contains unmovable obstacles and circular food patches. The food patches emit an odor whose intensity is proportional to the size of the patch. As this odor diffuses through the environment, its intensity falls off as the inverse square of the distance from the center of the patch. Whenever the insect's mouth closes over a patch of food, a fixed amount of energy is transferred from the patch to the insect.

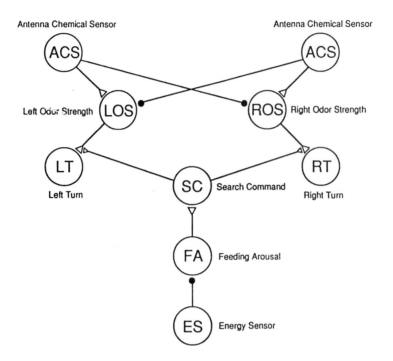

Figure 1: Appetitive Controller

2   APPETITIVE COMPONENT

The appetitive component of feeding is responsible for getting a hungry insect to a food patch. To accomplish this task, it utilizes the locomotion, wandering, and edge-following capabilities of the insect. The interactions between the neural circuitry underlying these behaviors and the feeding controller presented in this paper are described elsewhere (Beer, 1989). Assuming that the insect is already close enough to a food patch that the chemical sensors in its antennae can detect an odor signal, there are two separate issues which must be addressed by this phase of the behavior. First, the insect must use the information from the chemical sensors in its antennae to turn itself toward the food patch as it walks. Second, this orientation should only occur when the insect is actually in need of energy. Correspondingly, the appetitive neural controller (Figure 1) consists of two distinct components.

The orientation component is comprised of the upper six neurons in Figure 1. The odor signals detected by the chemical sensors in each antenna (ACS) are compared (by LOS and ROS), and the difference between them is used to generate a turn toward the stronger side by exciting the corresponding turn interneuron (LT or RT) by an amount proportional to the size of the difference. These turn interneurons connect to the motor neurons controlling the lateral extension of each front leg.

The second component is responsible for controlling whether or not the insect actually orients to a nearby patch of food. This decision depends upon its internal energy level, and is controlled by the bottom three neurons in Figure 1. Though the odor gradient is continuously being sensed, the connections to the turn interneurons are normally disabled, preventing access of this information to the motor apparatus which turns the insect. As the insect's energy level falls, however, so does the activity of its energy sensor (ES). This decreasing activity gradually releases the spontaneously active feeding arousal neuron (FA) from inhibition. When activity in FA becomes sufficient to fire the search command neuron (SC), the connections between the odor strength neurons and the turn neurons are enabled by gating connections from SC, and the insect begins to orient to food.

3   CONSUMMATORY COMPONENT

Once the appetitive controller has successfully oriented the insect to food, the consummatory component of the behavior is triggered. This phase consists of rhythmic biting movements which persist until sufficient food has been ingested. Like the appetitive phase, consummatory behavior should only be released when the insect is in need of energy. In addition, an animal's interest in feeding (its *feeding arousal*), may be a function of more than just its energy requirements. Other factors, such as the exposure of an animal to the taste, odor, or tactile sensations of food, can significantly increase its feeding arousal. This relationship between feeding and arousal, in which the very act of feeding further enhances an animal's interest in feeding, leads to a form of behavioral hysteresis. Once food is encountered, an animal may feed well beyond the internal energy requirements which initiated the behavior. In many animals, this hysteresis is thought to play a role in the patterning of feeding behavior into discrete meals rather than continuous grazing (Susswein, Weiss, and Kupfermann, 1978). At some point, of course, the ingested food must be capable of overriding the arousing effects of consummatory behavior, or the animal would never cease to feed.

The neural controller for the consummatory phase of feeding is shown in Figure 2. When chemical (MCS) and tactile (MTS) sensors in the mouth signal that food is present (FP), and the insect is sufficiently aroused to feeding (FA), the consummatory command neuron (CC) fires. The conjunction of tactile and chemical signals is required in order to prevent attempts to ingest nonfood patches and, due to the diffusion of odors, to prevent biting from beginning before the food patch is actually reached. Once CC fires, it triggers the bite pacemaker neuron (BP) to generate rhythmic bursts which cause a motor neuron (MO) to open and close the mouth. Because the threshold of the consummatory command neuron (CC) is somewhat lower than that of the search command neuron (SC), an insect which is not sufficiently aroused to orient to food may nevertheless consume food that is directly presented to its mouth.

The motor neuron controlling the mouth also makes an excitatory connection onto the feeding arousal neuron (FA), which in turn makes an excitatory modulatory synapse onto the connection between the consummatory command neuron (CC)

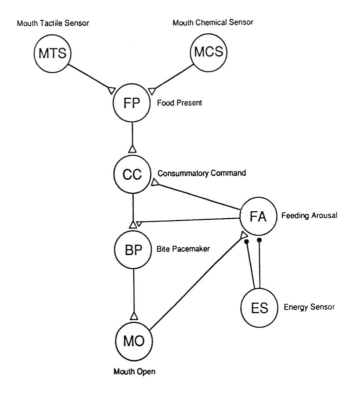

Figure 2: Consummatory Controller

and the bite pacemaker (BP). The net effect of these excitatory connections is a positive feedback loop: biting movements excite FA, which causes BP to cause more frequent biting movements, which further excites FA until its activity saturates. This neural positive feedback loop is inspired by work on the neural basis of feeding arousal maintenance in *Aplysia* (Weiss, Chiel, Koch, and Kupfermann, 1986).

As the insect consumes food, its energy level begins to rise. This leads to increased activity in ES which both directly inhibits FA, and also decreases the gain of the positive feedback loop via an inhibitory modulatory synapse onto the connection between MO and FA. At some point, these inhibitory effects will overcome the positive feedback and activity in FA will drop low enough to terminate the feeding behavior. This neural mechanism is based upon a similar one hypothesized to underlie satiation in *Aplysia* (Weiss, Chiel, and Kupfermann, 1986).

4   RESULTS

With the neural controllers described above, we have found that feeding behavior in the artificial insect exhibits four of the six characteristics of motivated behavior which were described by Kupfermann (1974):

Grouping and sequencing of behavior in time. When the artificial insect is "hungry", it generates appetitive and consummatory behaviors with the proper sequence, timing, and intensity in order to obtain food.

Goal-Directedness. Regardless of its environmental situation, a hungry insect will generate movements which serve to obtain food. Therefore, the behavior of a hungry insect can only be understood by reference to an internal goal. Due to the internal effects of the energy sensor (ES) and feeding arousal (FA) neurons on the controllers, the insect's external stimuli are insufficient to account for its behavior.

Changes in responsiveness due to a change in internal state. While a hungry insect will attempt to orient to and consume any nearby food, a satiated one will ignore it. In addition, once a hungry insect has consumed sufficient food, it will simply walk over the food patch which initially attracted it. We will examine the arousal and satiation of feeding in this artificial insect in more detail below.

Persistence. If a hungry insect is removed from food before it has fed to satiation, its feeding arousal will persist, and it will continue to exhibit feeding movements.

One technique that has been applied to the study of feeding arousal in natural animals is the examination of the time interval between successive bites as an animal feeds under various conditions. In *Aplysia*, for example, the interbite interval progressively decreases as an animal begins to feed (showing a build-up of arousal), and increases as the animal satiates. In addition, the rate of rise and fall of arousal depends upon the initial degree of satiation (Susswein, Weiss, and Kupfermann, 1978).

In order to examine the role of feeding arousal in the artificial insect, we performed a similar set of experiments. Food was directly presented to insects with differing degrees of initial satiation, and the time interval between successive bites was recorded for the entire resulting consummatory response. Above an energy level of approximately 80% of capacity, insects could not be induced to bite. Below this level, however, insects began to consume the food. As these insects fed, the interbite interval decreased as their feeding arousal built up until some minimum interval was achieved (Figure 3). The rate of build-up of arousal was slowest for those insects with the highest initial degree of satiation. In fact, an insect whose energy level was already 75% of capacity never achieved full arousal. As the feeding insects neared satiation, their interbite interval increased as arousal waned. It is interesting to note that, regardless of the initial degree of satiation, all insects in which biting was triggered fed until their energy stores were approximately 99% full. The appropriate number of bites to achieve this were generated in all cases.

What is the neural basis of these arousal and satiation phenomena? Clearly, the answer lies in the interactions between the internal energy sensor and the positive feedback loop mediated by the feeding arousal neuron, but the precise nature of the interaction is not at all clear from the qualitative descriptions of the neural controllers given earlier. In order to more carefully examine this interaction, we produced a phase plot of the activity in these two neurons under the experimental

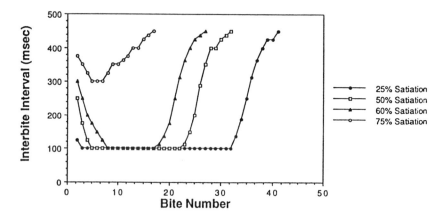

Figure 3: Build-Up of Arousal and Satiation

conditions described above (Figure 4).

An insect with a full complement of energy begins at the lower right-hand corner of the diagram, with maximum activity in ES and no activity in FA. As the insect's energy begins to fall, it moves to the left on the ES axis until the inhibition from ES is insufficient to hold FA below threshold. At this point, activity in FA begins to increase. Since the positive feedback loop is not yet active because no biting has occurred, a linear decrease in energy results in a linear increase in FA activity. If no food is consumed, the insect continues to move along this line toward the upper left of the diagram until its energy is exhausted.

However, if biting is triggered by the presence of food at the mouth, the relationship between FA and ES changes drastically. As the insect begins consuming food, activity in FA initially increases as arousal builds up, and then later decreases as the insect satiates. Each "bump" corresponds to the arousing effects on FA of one bite via the positive feedback loop and to the small increase of energy from the food consumed in that bite. Trajectories are shown for energy levels of 25%, 50%, 60%, 65%, and 75% of capacity. The shape of these trajectories depend upon the activity level of FA and the gain of the positive feedback loop in which it is embedded, both of which in turn depend upon the negative feedback from the energy sensor. We must therefore conclude that, even in this simple artificial insect, there is no single neural correlate to "hunger". Instead, this motivational state is the result of the complex dynamics of interaction between the feeding arousal neuron and the internal energy sensor.

References

Beer, R. D. (1989). *Intelligence as Adaptive Behavior: An Experiment in Computational Neuroethology.* Ph.D. Dissertation, Dept. of Computer Engineering and Science, Case Western Reserve University. Also available as Technical Report TR

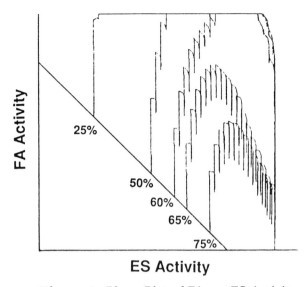

Figure 4: Phase Plot of FA vs. ES Activity

89-118, Center for Automation and Intelligent Systems Research.

Beer, R. D., Chiel, H. J. and Sterling, L. S. (1989). Heterogeneous Neural Networks for Adaptive Behavior in Dynamic Environments. In D.S. Touretzky (Ed.), *Advances in Neural Information Processing Systems 1* (pp. 577-585). San Mateo, CA: Morgan Kaufmann Publishers.

Chiel, H. J. and Beer, R. D. (1989). A lesion study of a heterogeneous neural network for hexapod locomotion. *Proceedings of the International Joint Conference on Neural Networks* (IJCNN 89), pp. 407-414.

Kupfermann, I. J. (1974). Feeding behavior in *Aplysia*: A simple system for the study of motivation. *Behavioral Biology* 10:1-26.

Susswein, A. J., Weiss, K. R. and Kupfermann, I. (1978). The effects of food arousal on the latency of biting in *Aplysia*. *J. Comp. Physiol.* 123:31-41.

Weiss, K. R., Chiel, H. J., Koch, U. and Kupfermann, I. (1986). Activity of an identified histaminergic neuron, and its possible role in arousal of feeding behavior in semi-intact *Aplysia*. *J. Neuroscience* 6(8):2403-2415.

Weiss, K. R., Chiel, H. J. and Kupfermann, I. (1986). Sensory function and gating of histaminergic neuron C2 in *Aplysia*. *J. Neuroscience* 6(8):2416-2426.

Neural Network Simulation
of
Somatosensory Representational Plasticity

Kamil A. Grajski
Ford Aerospace
San Jose, CA 95161-9041
kamil@wdl1.fac.ford.com

Michael M. Merzenich
Coleman Laboratories
UC San Francisco
San Francisco, CA 94143

ABSTRACT

The brain represents the skin surface as a topographic map in the somatosensory cortex. This map has been shown experimentally to be modifiable in a use-dependent fashion throughout life. We present a neural network simulation of the competitive dynamics underlying this cortical plasticity by detailed analysis of receptive field properties of model neurons during simulations of skin co-activation, cortical lesion, digit amputation and nerve section.

1 INTRODUCTION

Plasticity of adult somatosensory cortical maps has been demonstrated experimentally in a variety of maps and species (Kass, et al., 1983; Wall, 1988). This report focuses on modelling primary somatosensory cortical plasticity in the adult monkey.

We model the long-term consequences of four specific experiments, taken in pairs. With the first pair, behaviorally controlled stimulation of restricted skin surfaces (Jenkins, et al., 1990) and induced cortical lesions (Jenkins and Merzenich, 1987), we demonstrate that Hebbian-type dynamics is sufficient to account for the inverse relationship between cortical magnification (area of cortical map representing a unit area of skin) and receptive field size (skin surface which when stimulated excites a cortical unit) (Sur, et al., 1980; Grajski and Merzenich, 1990). These results are obtained with several variations of the basic model. We conclude that relying solely on cortical magnification and receptive field size will not disambiguate the contributions of each of the myriad circuits known to occur in the brain. With the second pair, digit amputation (Merzenich, et al., 1984) and peripheral nerve cut (without regeneration) (Merzenich, et al., 1983), we explore the role of local excitatory connections in the model cortex (Grajski, *submitted*).

Previous models have focused on the self-organization of topographic maps in general (Willshaw and von der Malsburg, 1976; Takeuchi and Amari, 1979; Kohonen, 1982; among others). Ritter and Schulten (1986) specifically addressed somatosensory plasticity using a variant of Kohonen's self-organizing mapping. Recently, Pearson, et al., (1987), using the framework of the Group Selection Hypothesis, have also modelled aspects of normal and reorganized somatosensory plasticity.

Elements of the present study have been published elsewhere (Grajski and Merzenich, 1990).

2 THE MODEL

2.1 ARCHITECTURE

The network consists of three heirarchically organized two-dimensional layers shown in Figure 1A.

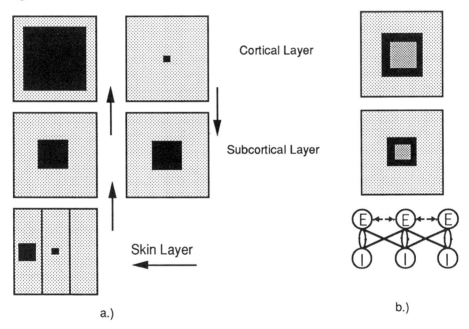

Figure 1: Network architecture.

The divergence of projections from a single skin site to subcortex (SC) and its subsequent projection to cortex (C) is shown at left: Skin (S) to SC, 5 x 5; SC to C, 7 x 7. S is "partitioned" into three 15 x 5 "digits" Left, Center and Right. The standard S stimulus used in all simulations is shown lying on digit Left. The projection from C to SC E and I cells is shown at right. Each node in the SC and C layers contains an excitatory (E) and inhibitory cell (I) as shown in Figure 1B. In C, each E cell forms excitatory connections with a 5 x 5 patch of I cells; each I cell forms inhibitory connections with a 7 x 7 path of E cells. In SC, these connections are 3 x 3 and 5 x 5, respectively. In addition, in C only, E cells form excitatory connections with a 5 by 5 patch of E cells. The spatial relationship of E and I cell projections for the central node is shown at left (C E to E shown in light gray, C I to E shown in black).

2.2   DYNAMICS

The model neuron is the same for all E and I cells: an RC-time constant membrane which is depolarized and (additively) hyperpolarized by linearly weighted connections:

$$\dot{u}_i^{C,E} = -\tau_m u_i^{C,E} + \sum_j v_j^{SC,E} w_{ij}^{C,E:SC,E} + \sum_j v_j^{C,E} w_{ij}^{C,E:C,E} - \sum_j v_j^{C,I} w_{ij}^{C,E:C,I}$$

$$\dot{u}_i^{C,I} = -\tau_m u_i^{C,I} + \sum_j v_j^{C,E} w_{ij}^{C,I:C,E}$$

$$\dot{u}_i^{SC,E} = -\tau_m u_i^{SC,E} + \sum_j \delta_j^S w_{ij}^{SC,E:S} + \sum_j v_j^{C,E} w_{ij}^{SC,E:C,E} - \sum_j v_j^{SC,E} w_{ij}^{SC,E:SC,I}$$

$$\dot{u}_i^{SC,I} = -\tau_m u_i^{SC,I} + \sum_j v_j^{SC,E} w_{ij}^{SC,I:SC,E} + \sum_j v_j^{C,E} w_{ij}^{SC,I:C,E} - \sum_j v_j^{SC,E} w_{ij}^{SC,E:SC,I}$$

$u_i^{X,Y}$ - membrane potential for unit i of type Y on layer X; $v_i^{X,Y}$ - firing rate for unit i of type Y on layer X; δ_j^S - skin units are OFF (=0) or ON (=1); τ_m - membrane time constant (with respect to unit time); $w_{ij}^{post(x,y):pre(X,Y)}$ - connection to unit i of post-synaptic type y on postsynaptic layer x from units of presynaptic type Y on presynaptic layer X. Each summation term is normalized by the number of incoming connections (corrected for planar boundary conditions) contributing to the term. Each unit converts membrane potential to a continuous-valued output value v_i via a sigmoidal function representing an average firing rate ($\beta = 4.0$):

$$v_i = g(u_i) = \begin{cases} \frac{1}{2}(1+\tanh(\beta(u_i-\frac{1}{2}))) & u_i \geq 0.02, \\ 0 & u_i < 0.02 \end{cases}$$

2.3   SYNAPTIC PLASTICITY

Synaptic strength is modified in three ways: a.) activity-dependent change; b.) passive decay; and c.) normalization. Activity-dependent and passive decay terms are as follows:

$$\Delta w_{ij} = -\tau_{syn} w_{ij} + \alpha v_i v_j$$

w_{ij} - connection from cell j to cell i; $\tau_{syn}=0.01\tau_m=0.005$ - time constant for passive synaptic decay; $\alpha=0.05$, the maximum activity-dependent step change; v_j, v_i - pre- and post-synaptic output values, respectively. Further modification occurs by a multiplicative normalization performed over the incoming connections for each cell. The normalization is such that the summed total strength of incoming connections is R:

$$\frac{1}{N_i} \, \Sigma_j w_{ij} \; = \; R$$

N_i - number of incoming connections for cell i; w_{ij} - connection from cell j to cell i; R = 2.0 - the total resource available to cell i for redistribution over its incoming connections.

2.4 MEASURING CORTICAL MAGNIFICATION, RECEPTIVE FIELD AREA

Cortical magnification is measured by "mapping" the network, e.g., noting which 3x3 skin patch most strongly drives each cortical E cell. The number of cortical nodes driven maximally by the same skin site is the cortical magnification for that skin site. Receptive field size for a C (SC) layer E cell is estimated by stimulating all possible 3x3 skin patches (169) and noting the peak response. Receptive field size is defined as the number of 3x3 skin patches which drive the unit at ≥50% of its peak response.

3 SIMULATIONS

3.1 FORMATION OF THE TOPOGRAPHIC MAP ENTAILS REFINEMENT OF SYNAPTIC PATTERNING

The location of individual connections is fixed by topographic projection; initial strengths are drawn from a Gaussian distribution ($\mu = 2.0$, $\sigma^2 = 0.2$). Standard-sized skin patches are stimulated in random sequence with no double-digit stimulation. (Mapping includes tests for double-digit receptive fields.) For each patch, the network is allowed to reach steady-state while the plasticity rule is ON. Synaptic strengths are then renormalized. Refinement continues until two conditions are met: a.) fewer than 5% of all E cells change their receptive field location; and b.) receptive field areas (using the 50% criterion) change by no more than ±1 unit area for 95% of E cells. (See Figures 2 and 3 in Merzenich and Grajski, 1990; Grajski, *submitted*).

3.2 RESTRICTED SKIN STIMULATION GIVES INCREASED MAGNIFICATION, DECREASED RECEPTIVE FIELD SIZE

Jenkins, et al., (1990) describe a behavioral experiment which leads to cortical somatotopic reorganization. Monkeys are trained to maintain contact with a rotating disk situated such that only the tips of one or two of their longest digits are stimulated. Monkeys are required to maintain this contact for a specified period of time in order to receive food reward. Comparison of pre- and post-stimulation maps (or the latter with maps obtained after varying periods without disk stimulation) reveal up to nearly 3-fold differences in cortical magnification and reduction in receptive field size for stimulated skin.

We simulate the above experiment by extending the refinement process described above, but with the probability of stimulating a restricted skin region increased 5:1. (See Grajski and Merzenich (1990), Figure 4.) Figure 2 illustrates the change in size (left) and synaptic patterning (right) for a single representative cortical receptive field.

Figure 2: Representative co-activation induced receptive field changes.

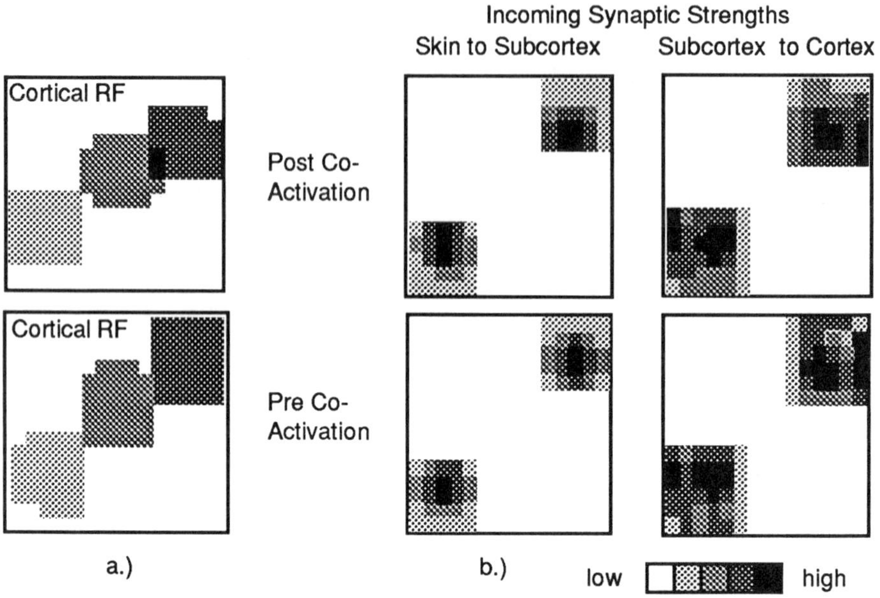

Incoming Synaptic Strengths
Skin to Subcortex   Subcortex to Cortex

Cortical RF

Post Co-
Activation

Cortical RF

Pre Co-
Activation

a.)   b.)   low □▨▨▨■ high

3.3   AN INDUCED, FOCAL CORTICAL LESIONS GIVES DECREASED MAGNIFICATION, INCREASED RECEPTIVE FIELD SIZE

The inverse magnification rule predicts that a decrease in cortical magnification is accompanied by an increase in receptive field areas. Jenkins, et al., (1987) confirmed this hypothesis by inducing focal cortical lesions in the representation of restricted hand surfaces, e.g. a single digit. Changes included: a.) a re-emergence of a representation of the skin formerly represented in the now lesioned zone in the intact surrounding cortex; b.) the new representation is at the expense of cortical magnification of skin originally represented in those regions; so that c.) large regions of the map contain neurons with abnormally large receptive fields.

We simulate this experiment by eliminating the incoming and outgoing connections of the cortical layer region representing the middle digit. The refinement process described above is continued under these new conditions until topographic map and receptive field size measures converge. The re-emergence of representation and changes in distributions of receptive field areas are shown in Grajski and Merzenich, (1990) Figure 5. Figure 3 below illustrates the change in size and location of a representative (sub) cortical receptive field.

3.4   SEVERAL MODEL VARIANTS REPRODUCE THE INVERSE MAGNIFICATION RULE

Repeating the above simulations using networks with no descending projections or using networks with no descending and no cortical mutual exciatation, yields largely normal topography and co-activation results. Restricting plasticity to excitatory pathways alone also yields qualitatively similar results. (Studies with a two-layer network yield qualitatively similar results.) Thus, the refinement and co-activation experiments alone are insufficient to discriminate fundamental differences between network variants.

Figure 3: Representative cortical lesion induced receptive field changes.

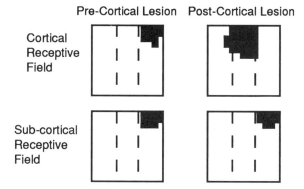

3.5 MUTUALLY EXCITATORY LOCAL CORTICAL CONNECTIONS MAY BE CRITICAL FOR SIMULATING EFFECTS OF DIGIT AMPUTATION AND NERVE SECTION

The role of lateral excitation in the cortical layer is made clearer through simulations of nerve section and digit amputation experiments (Merzenich, et al., 1983; Merzenich, et al., 1984; see also Wall, 1988). The feature of interest here is the cortical distance over which reorganization is observed. Following cessation of peripheral input from digit 3, for example, the surrounding representations (digits 2 and 4) expand into the now silenced zone. Not only expansion is observed. Neurons in the surrounding representations up to several 100's of microns distant from the silenced zone shift their receptive fields. The shift is such that the receptive field covers skin sites closer to the silenced skin.

The deafferentation experiment is simulated by eliminating the connection between the skin layer CENTER digit (central 1/3) and SC layers and then proceeding with refinement with the usual convergence checks. Simulations are run for three network architectures. The "full" model is that described above. Two other models strip the descending and both descending and lateral excitatory connections, respectively.

Figure 4 shows features of reorganization: the conversion of initially silenced zones, or refinement of initially large, low amplitude fields to normal-like fields (a-c). Importantly, the receptive field farthest away from the initially silenced representation (d) undergoes a shift towards the deafferented skin. The shift is comprised of a translation in the receptive field peak location as well as an increase (below the 50% amplitude threshold, but increases range 25 - 200%) in the regions surrounding the peak and facing the silenced cortical zone (shown in light shading). Only the "full" model evolves expanded *and* shifted representations. These results are preliminary in that no parameter adjustments are made in the other networks to coax a result. It may simply be a matter of not enough excitation in the other cases. Nevertheless, these results show that local cortical excitation can contribute critical activity for reorganization.

Figure 4: Summary of immediate and long-term post-amputation effects.

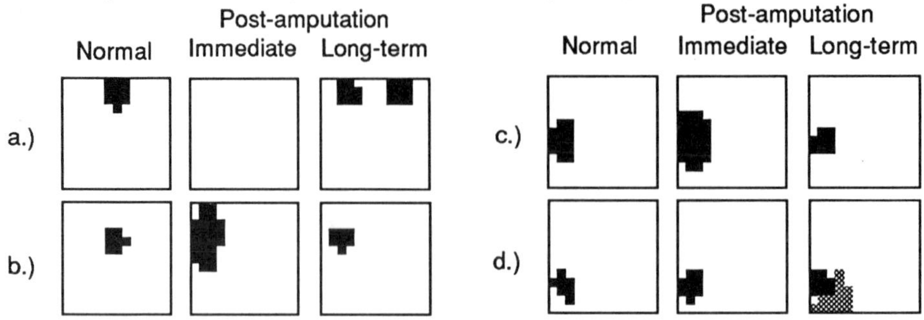

4 CONCLUSION

We have shown that a.) Hebbian-type dynamics is sufficient to account for the quantitative inverse relationship between cortical magnification and receptive field size; and b.) cortical magnification and receptive field size alone are insufficient to distinguish between model variants.

Are these results just "so much biological detail?" No. The inverse magnification-receptive field rule applies nearly universally in (sub)cortical topographic maps; it reflects a fundamental principle of brain organization. For instance, experiments revealing the operation of mechanisms possibly similar to those modelled above have been observed in the visual system. Wurtz, et al., (1990) have observed that following chemically induced focal lesions in visual area MT, surviving neurons' visual receptive field area increased. For a review of use-dependent receptive field plasticity in the auditory system see Weinberger, et al., (1990).

Research in computational neuroscience has long drawn on principles of topographic organization. Recent advances include those by Linsker (1989), providing a theoretical (optimization) framework for map formation and those studies linking concepts related to localized receptive fields with adaptive nets (Moody and Darken, 1989; see Barron, this volume). The experimental and modelling issues discussed here offer an opportunity to sustain and further enhance the synergy inherent in this area of computational neuroscience.

4.0.1   Acknowldegements

This research supported by NIH grants (to MMM) NS10414 and GM07449, Hearing Research Inc., the Coleman Fund and the San Diego Supercomputer Center. KAG gratefully acknowledges helpful discussions with Terry Allard, Bill Jenkins, John Pearson, Gregg Recanzone and especially Ken Miller.

4.0.2   References

Grajski, K. A. and M. M. Merzenich. (1990). Hebb-type dynamics is sufficient to account for the inverse magnification rule in cortical somatotopy. *In Press. Neural Computation.* Vol. 2. No. 1.

Jenkins, W. M. and M. M. Merzenich. (1987). Reorganization of neocortical representations after brain injury. In: **Progress in Brain Research.** Vol. 71. Seil, F. J., et al., Eds. Elsevier. pgs. 249-266.

Jenkins, W. M., et al., (1990). Functional reorganization of primary somatosensory cortex in adult owl monkeys after behaviorally controlled tactile stimulation. *J. Neurophys. In Press.*

Kaas, J. H., M. M. Merzenich and H. P. Killackey. (1983). The reorganization of somatosensory cortex following peripheral nerve damage in adult and developing mammals. *Ann. Rev. Neursci.* 6:325-356.

Kohonen, T. (1982). Self-organized formation of topologically correct feature maps. *Biol. Cyb.* 43:59-69.

Linsker, R. (1989). How to generate ordered maps by maximizing the mutual information between input and output signals. *IBM Research Report No. RC 14624*

Merzenich, M. M., J. H. Kaas, J. T. Wall, R. J. Nelson, M. Sur and D. J. Felleman. (1983). Topographic reorganization of somatosensory cortical areas 3b and 1 in adult monkeys following restricted deafferentation. *Neuroscience.* 8:1:33-55.

Merzenich, M. M., R. J. Nelson, M. P. Stryker, M. Cynader, J. M Zook and A. Schoppman. (1984). Somatosensory cortical map changes following digit amputation in adult monkeys. *J. Comp. Neurol.* 244:591-605.

Moody, J. and C. J. Darken. (1989). Fast learning in networks of locally-tuned processing units. *Neural Computation* 1:281-294.

Pearson, J. C., L. H. Finkel and G. M. Edelman. (1987). Plasticity in the organization of adult cerebral cortical maps. *J. Neurosci.* 7:4209-4223.

Ritter, H. and K. Schulten. (1986). On the stationary state of Kohonen's self-organizing sensory mapping. *Biol. Cyb.* 54:99-106.

Sur, M., M. M. Merzenich and J. H. Kaas. (1980). Magnification, receptive-field area and "hypercolumn" size in areas 3b and 1 of somatosensory cortex in owl monkeys. *J. Neurophys.* 44:295-311.

Takeuchi, A. and S. Amari. (1979). Formation of topographic maps and columnar microstructures in nerve fields. *Biol. Cyb.* 35:63-72.

Wall, J. T. (1988). Variable organization in cortical maps of the skin as an indication of the lifelong adaptive capacities of circuits in the mammalian brain. *Trends in Neurosci.* 11:12:549-557.

Weinberger, N. M., et al., (1990). Retuning auditory cortex by learning: A preliminary model of receptive field plasticity. *Concepts in Neuroscience. In Press.*

Willshaw, D. J. and C. von der Malsburg. (1976). How patterned neural connections can be set up by self-organization. *Proc. R. Soc. Lond.* B. 194:431-445.

Wurtz, R., et al. (1990). Motion to movement: Cerebral cortical visual processing for pursuit eye movements. In: **Signal and sense: Local and global order in perceptual maps.** Gall, E. W., Ed. Wiley: New York. *In Press.*

Computational Efficiency: A Common Organizing Principle for Parallel Computer Maps and Brain Maps?

Mark E. Nelson   James M. Bower
Computation and Neural Systems Program
Division of Biology, 216-76
California Institute of Technology
Pasadena, CA 91125

ABSTRACT

It is well-known that neural responses in particular brain regions are spatially organized, but no general principles have been developed that relate the structure of a brain map to the nature of the associated computation. On parallel computers, maps of a sort quite similar to brain maps arise when a computation is distributed across multiple processors. In this paper we will discuss the relationship between maps and computations on these computers and suggest how similar considerations might also apply to maps in the brain.

1   INTRODUCTION

A great deal of effort in experimental and theoretical neuroscience is devoted to recording and interpreting spatial patterns of neural activity. A variety of map patterns have been observed in different brain regions and, presumably, these patterns reflect something about the nature of the neural computations being carried out in these regions. To date, however, there have been no general principles for interpreting the structure of a brain map in terms of properties of the associated computation. In the field of parallel computing, analogous maps arise when a computation is distributed across multiple processors and, in this case, the relationship between maps and computations is better understood. In this paper, we will attempt to relate some of the mapping principles from the field of parallel computing to the organization of brain maps.

2   MAPS ON PARALLEL COMPUTERS

The basic idea of parallel computing is to distribute the computational workload for a single task across a large number of processors (Dongarra, 1987; Fox and Messina, 1987). In principle, a parallel computer has the potential to deliver computing power equivalent to the total computing power of the processors from which it is constructed; a 100 processor machine can potentially deliver 100 times the computing power of a single processor. In practice, however, the performance that can be achieved is always less efficient than this ideal. A perfectly efficient implementation with N processors would give a factor N speed up in computation time; the ratio of the actual speedup σ to the ideal speedup N can serve as a measure of the efficiency ϵ of a parallel implementation.

$$\epsilon = \frac{\sigma}{N} \tag{1}$$

For a given computation, one of the factors that most influences the overall performance is the way in which the computation is mapped onto the available processors. The efficiency of any particular mapping can be analyzed in terms of two principal factors: load-balance and communication overhead. Load-balance is a measure of how uniformly the computational work load is distributed among the available processors. Communication overhead, on the other hand, is related to the cost in time of communicating information between processors.

On parallel computers, the load imbalance λ is defined in terms of the average calculation time per processor T_{avg} and the maximum calculation time required by the busiest processor T_{max}:

$$\lambda = \frac{T_{max} - T_{avg}}{T_{avg}} \tag{2}$$

The communication overhead η is defined in terms of the maximum calculation time T_{max} and the maximum communication time T_{comm}:

$$\eta = \frac{T_{comm}}{T_{max} + T_{comm}} \tag{3}$$

Assuming that the calculation and communication phases of a computation do not overlap in time, as is the case for many parallel computers, the relationship between efficiency ϵ, load-imbalance λ, and communication overhead η is given by (Fox et al.,1988):

$$\epsilon = \frac{1-\eta}{1+\lambda} \tag{4}$$

When both load-imbalance λ and communication overhead η are small, the inefficiency is approximately the sum of the contributions from load-imbalance and communication overhead:

$$\epsilon \approx 1 - (\eta + \lambda) \tag{5}$$

When attempting to achieve maximum performance from a parallel computer, a programmer tries to find a mapping that minimizes the combined contributions of load-imbalance and communication overhead. In some cases this is accomplished by applying simple heuristics (Fox et al., 1988), while in others it requires the explicit use of optimization techniques like simulated annealing (Kirkpatrick et al., 1983) or even artificial neural network approaches (Fox and Furmanski, 1988). In any case, the optimal tradeoff between load imbalance and communication overhead depends on certain properties of the computation itself. Thus different types of computations give rise to different kinds of optimal maps on parallel computers.

2.1   AN EXAMPLE

In order to illustrate how different mappings can give rise to different computational efficiencies, we will consider the simulation of a single neuron using a multicompartment modeling approach (Segev et al., 1989). In such a simulation, the model neuron is divided into a large number of compartments, each of which is assumed to be isopotential. Each compartment is represented by an equivalent electric circuit that embodies information about the local membrane properties. In order to update the voltage of an individual compartment, it is necessary to know the local properties as well as the membrane voltages of the neighboring compartments. Such a model gives rise to a system of differential equations of the following form:

$$C_m \frac{dV_i}{dt} = \sum_k g_k(V_i - E_k) + g_{i-1,i}(V_{i-1} - V_i) + g_{i+1,i}(V_{i+1} - V_i) \tag{6}$$

where C_m is the membrane capacitance, V_i is the membrane voltage of compartment i, g_k and E_k are the local conductances and their reversal potentials, and $g_{i\pm1,i}$ are coupling conductances to neighboring compartments.

When carrying out such a simulation on a parallel computer, where there are more compartments than processors, each processor is assigned responsibility for updating a subset of the compartments (Nelson et al., 1989). If the compartments represent equivalent computational loads, then the load-imbalance will be proportional to the difference between the maximum and the average number of compartments per processor. If the computer processors are fully interconnected by communication channels, then the communication overhead will be proportional to the number of interprocessor messages providing the voltages of neighboring compartments. If

A   B   C

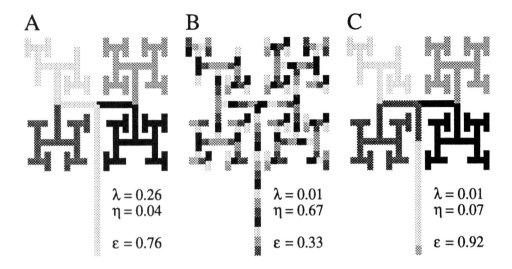

$\lambda = 0.26$
$\eta = 0.04$

$\varepsilon = 0.76$

$\lambda = 0.01$
$\eta = 0.67$

$\varepsilon = 0.33$

$\lambda = 0.01$
$\eta = 0.07$

$\varepsilon = 0.92$

Figure 1: Tradeoffs between load-imbalance λ and communication overhead η, giving rise to different efficiencies ϵ for different mappings of a multicompartment neuron model. (A) a minimum-cut mapping that minimizes communication overhead but suffers from a significant load-imbalance, (B) a scattered mapping that minimizes load-imbalance but has a large communication overhead, and (C) a near-optimal mapping that simultaneously minimizes both load-imbalance and communication overhead.

neighboring compartments are mapped to the same processor, then this information is available without any interprocessor communication and thus no communication overhead is incurred.

Fig. 1 shows three different ways of mapping a 155 compartment neuron model onto a group of 4 processors. In each case the load-imbalance and communication overhead are calculated using the assumptions listed above and the computational efficiency is computed using eq. 4. The map in Fig. 1A minimizes the communication overhead of the mapping by making a minimum number of cuts in the dendritic tree, but is rather inefficient because a significant load-imbalance remains even after optimizing the location of each cut. The map is Fig. 1B, on the other hand, minimizes the load-imbalance, by using a scattered mapping technique (Fox et al., 1988), but is inefficient because of a large communication overhead. The map in Fig. 1C strikes a balance between load-imbalance and communication overhead that results in a high computational efficiency. Thus this particular mapping makes the best use of the available computing resources for this particular computational task.

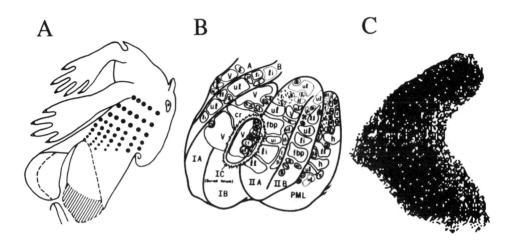

Figure 2: Three classes of map topologies found in the brain (of the rat). (A) continuous map of tactile inputs in somatosensory cortex (B) patchy map of tactile inputs to cerebellar cortex and (C) scattered mapping of olfactory inputs to olfactory cortex as represented by the unstructured pattern of 2DG uptake in a single section of this cortex.

3   MAPS IN THE BRAIN

Since some parallel computer maps are clearly more efficient than others for particular problems, it seems natural to ask whether a similar relationship might hold for brain maps and neural computations. Namely, for a given computational task, does one particular brain map topology make more efficient use of the available neural computing resources than another? If so, does this impose a significant constraint on the evolution and development of brain map topologies?

It turns out that there are striking similarities between the kinds of maps that arise on parallel computers and the types of maps that have been observed in the brain. In both cases, the map patterns can be broadly grouped into three categories: continuous maps, patchy maps, and scattered (non-topographic) maps. Fig. 2 shows examples of brain maps that fall into these categories. Fig. 2A shows an example of a smooth and continuous map representing the pattern of afferent tactile projections to the primary somatosensory cortex of a rat (Welker, 1971). The patchy map in Fig. 2B represents the spatial pattern of tactile projections to the granule cell layer of the rat cerebellar hemispheres (Shambes et al., 1978; Bower and Woolston, 1983). Finally, Fig. 2C represents an extreme case in which a brain region shows no apparent topographic organization. This figure shows the pattern of metabolic activity in one section of the olfactory (piriform) cortex, as assayed by 2-deoxyglucose (2DG) uptake, in response to the presentation of a particular odor (Sharp et al., 1977). As suggested by the uniform label in the cortex, no discernible odor-specific patterns are found in this region of cortex.

On parallel computers, maps in these different categories arise as optimal solutions to different classes of computations. Continuous maps are optimal for computations that are local in the problem space, patchy maps are optimal for computations that involve a mixture of local and non-local interactions, and scattered maps are optimal or near-optimal for computations characterized by a high degree of interaction throughout the problem space, especially if the patterns of interaction are dynamic or cannot be easily predicted. Interestingly, it turns out that the intrinsic neural circuitry associated with different kinds of brain maps also reflects these same patterns of interaction. Brain regions with continuous maps, like somatosensory cortex, tend to have predominantly local circuitry; regions with patchy maps, like cerebellar cortex, tend to have a mixture of local and non-local circuitry; and regions with scattered maps, like olfactory cortex, tend to be characterized by wide-spread connectivity.

The apparent correspondence between brain maps and computer maps raises the general question of whether or not there are correlates of load-imbalance and communication overhead in the nervous system. In general, these factors are much more difficult to identify and quantify in the brain than on parallel computers. Parallel computer systems are, after all, human-engineered while the nervous system has evolved under a set of selection criteria and constraints that we know very little about. Furthermore, fundamental differences in the organization of digital computers and brains make it difficult to translate ideas from parallel computing directly into neural equivalents (c.f. Nelson et al., 1989). For example, it is far from clear what should be taken as the neural equivalent of a single processor. Depending on the level of analysis, it might be a localized region of a dendrite, an entire neuron, or an assembly of many neurons. Thus, one must consider multiple levels of processing in the nervous system when trying to draw analogies with parallel computers.

First we will consider the issue of load-balancing in the brain. The map in Fig. 2A, while smooth and continuous, is obviously quite distorted. In particular, the regions representing the lips and whiskers are disproportionately large in comparison to the rest of the body. It turns out that similar map distortions arise on parallel computers as a result of load-balancing. If different regions of the problem space require more computation than other regions, load-balance is achieved by distorting the map until each processor ends up with an equal share of the workload (Fox et al., 1988). In brain maps, such distortions are most often explained by variations in the density of peripheral receptors. However, it has recently been shown in the monkey, that prolonged increased use of a particular finger is accompanied by an expansion of the corresponding region of the map in the somatosensory cortex (Merzenich, 1987). Presumably this is not a consequence of a change in peripheral receptor density, but instead reflects a use-dependent remapping of some tactile computation onto available cortical circuitry.

Although such map reorganization phenomena are suggestive of load-balancing effects, we cannot push the analogy too far because we do not know what actually corresponds to "computational load" in the brain. One possibility is that it is associated with the metabolic load that arises in response to neural activity (Yarowsky and Ingvar, 1981). Since metabolic activity necessitates the delivery of an adequate supply of oxygen and glucose via a network of small capillaries, the efficient use of the capillary system might favor mappings that tend to avoid metabolic "hot spots" which would overload the delivery capabilities of the system.

When discussing communication overhead in the brain, we also run into the problem of not knowing exactly what corresponds to "communication cost". On parallel computers, communication overhead is usually associated with the time-cost of exchanging information between processors. In the nervous system, the importance of such time-costs is probably quite dependent on the behavioral context of the computation. There is evidence, for example, that some brain regions actually make use of transmission delays to process information (Carr and Konishi, 1988). However, there is another aspect of communication overhead that may be more generally applicable having to do with the space-costs of physically connecting processors together. In the design of modern parallel computers and in the design of individual computer processor chips, space-costs associated with interconnections pose a very serious constraint for the design engineer. In the nervous system, the extremely large numbers of potential connections combined with rather strict limitations on cranial capacity are likely to make space-costs a very important factor.

4   CONCLUSIONS

The view that computational efficiency is an important constraint on the organization of brain maps provides a potentially useful new perspective for interpretting the structure of those maps. Although the available evidence is largely circumstantial, it seems likely that the topology of a brain map affects the efficiency with which neural resources are utilized. Furthermore, it seems reasonable to assume that network efficiency would impose a constraint on the evolution and development of map topologies that would tend to favor maps that are near-optimal for the computational tasks being performed. The very substantial task before us, in the case of the nervous system, is to carry out further experiments to better understand the detailed relationships between brain maps, neural architectures and associated computations (Bower, 1990).

Acknowledgements

We would like to acknowledge Wojtek Furmanski and Geoffrey Fox of the Caltech Concurrent Computation Program (CCCP) for their parallel computing support. We would also like to thank Geoffrey for his comments on an earlier version of this manuscript. This effort was supported by the NSF (ECS-8700064), the Lockheed Corporation, and the Department of Energy (DE-FG03-85ER25009).

References

Bower, J.M. (1990) Reverse engineering the nervous system: An anatomical, physiological, and computer based approach. In: *An Introduction to Neural and Electronic*

Networks. (S. Zornetzer, J. Davis, and C. Lau, eds), pp. 3-24, Academic Press.

Bower, J.M. and D.C. Woolston (1983) Congruence of Spatial Organization of Tactile Projections to Granule Cell and Purkinje Cell Layers of Cerebellar Hemispheres of the Albino Rat: Vertical Organization of Cerebellar Cortex. *J. Neurophysiol.* **49**, 745-756.

Carr, C.E. and M. Konishi (1988) Axonal delay lines for time measurement in the owl's brain stem. *Proc Natl Acad Sci USA* **85**, 8311-8315.

Dongarra, J.J. (1987) *Experimental Parallel Computing Architectures*, (Dongarra, J.J., ed.) North-Holland.

Fox, G. C., M. Johnson, G. Lyzenga, S. Otto, J. Salmon, D. Walker (1988) *Solving Problems on Concurrent Processors*, Prentice Hall.

Fox, G.C. and W. Furmanski (1988) Load Balancing loosely synchronous problems with a neural network. In: *Proceedings of the Third Conference on Hypercube Concurrent Computers and Applications*, (Fox, G.C., ed.), pp.241-278, ACM.

Fox, G.C. and P. Messina (1987) Advanced Computer Architectures. *Scientific American*, October, 66-74.

Kirkpatrick, S., C.D. Gelatt and M.P. Vecchi (1983) Optimization by Simulated Annealing. *Science*, **220**, 671-680.

Merzenich, M.M. (1987) Dynamic neocortical processes and the origins of higher brain functions. In: *The Neural and Molecular Bases of Learning*, (Changeux, J.-P. and Konishi, M., eds.), pp. 337-358, John Wiley & Sons.

Nelson, M.E., W. Furmanski and J.M. Bower (1989) Modeling Neurons and Networks on Parallel Computers. In: *Methods in Neuronal Modeling: From Synapses to Networks*, (Koch, C. and I. Segev, eds.), pp. 397-438, MIT Press.

Segev, I., J.W. Fleshman and R.E. Burke (1989) Compartmental Models of Complex Neurons. In: *Methods in Neuronal Modeling: From Synapses to Networks*, (Koch, C. and I. Segev, eds.), pp. 63-96, MIT Press.

Shambes, G.M., J.M. Gibson and W. Welker (1978) Fractured Somatotopy in Granule Cell Tactile Areas of Rat Cerebellar Hemispheres Revealed by Micromapping. *Brain Behav. Evol.* **15**, 94-140.

Sharp, F.R., J.S. Kauer and G.M. Shepherd (1977) Laminar Analysis of 2-Deoxyglucose Uptake in Olfactory Bulb and Olfactory Cortex of Rabbit and Rat. *J. Neurophysiol.* **40**, 800-813.

Welker, C. (1971) Microelectrode delineation of fine grain somatotopic organization of SMI cerebral neocortex in albino rat. *Brain Res.* **26**, 259-275.

Yarowsky, P.J. and D.H. Ingvar (1981) Neuronal activity and energy metabolism. *Federation Proc.* **40**, 2353-2263.

Associative Memory in a Simple Model of Oscillating Cortex

Bill Baird
Dept Molecular and Cell Biology,
U.C.Berkeley, Berkeley, Ca. 94720

ABSTRACT

A generic model of oscillating cortex, which assumes "minimal" coupling justified by known anatomy, is shown to function as an associative memory, using previously developed theory. The network has explicit excitatory neurons with local inhibitory interneuron feedback that forms a set of nonlinear oscillators coupled only by long range excitatory connections. Using a local Hebb-like learning rule for primary and higher order synapses at the ends of the long range connections, the system learns to store the kinds of oscillation amplitude patterns observed in olfactory and visual cortex. This rule is derived from a more general "projection algorithm" for recurrent analog networks, that analytically guarantees content addressable memory storage of continuous periodic sequences — capacity: $N/2$ Fourier components for an N node network — no "spurious" attractors.

1 Introduction

This is a sketch of recent results stemming from work which is discussed completely in [1, 2, 3]. Patterns of 40 to 80 hz oscillation have been observed in the large scale activity of olfactory cortex [4] and visual neocortex [5], and shown to predict the olfactory and visual pattern recognition responses of a trained animal. It thus appears that cortical computation in general may occur by dynamical interaction of resonant modes, as has been thought to be the case in the olfactory system. Given the sensitivity of neurons to the location and arrival times of dendritic input, the sucessive volleys of pulses that are generated by the collective oscillation of a neural net may be ideal for the formation and reliable longe range transmission of the collective activity of one cortical area to another. The oscillation can serve a macroscopic clocking function and entrain the relevant microscopic activity of disparate cortical regions into well defined phase coherent macroscopic collective states which overide uncorrelated microscopic activity. If this view is correct, then oscillatory network modules form the actual cortical substrate of the diverse sensory, motor, and cognitive operations now studied in static networks, and it must ultimately be shown how those functions can be accomplished with these dynamic networks.

In particular, we are interested here in modeling category learning and object recognition, *after* feature preprocessing. Equivalence classes of ratios of feature outputs in feature space must be established as prototype "objects" or categories that are invariant over endless sensory instances. Without categories, the world never repeats. This is the kind of function generally hypothesized for prepyriform cortex in the olfactory system[6], or inferotemporal cortex in the visual system. It is a different oscillatory network function from the feature "binding", or clustering role that is hypothesized for "phase labels" in primary visual cortex [5], or from the "decision states" hypothesized for the olfactory bulb by Li and Hopfield. In these preprocessing systems, there is no modification of connections, and no learning of particular perceptual objects. For category learning, full adaptive cross coupling is required so that all possible input feature vectors may be potential attractors. This is the kind of anatomical structure that characterizes prepyriform and inferotemporal cortex. The columns there are less structured, and the associational fiber system is more prominent than in primary cortex. Man shares this same high level "association" cortex structure with cats and rats. Phylogenetically, it is the preprocessing structures of primary cortex that have grown and evolved to give us our expanded capabilities. While the bulk of our pattern recognition power may be contributed by the clever feature preprocessing that has developed, the object classification system seems the most likely locus of the learning changes that underlie our daily conceptual evolution. That is the phenomenon of ultimate interest in this work.

2   Minimal Model of Oscillating Cortex

Analog state variables, recurrence, oscillation, and bifurcation are hypothesized to be essential features of cortical networks which we explore in this approach. Explicit modeling of known excitatory and inhibitory neurons, and use of only known long range connections is also a basic requirement to have a biologically feasible network architecture. We analyse a "minimal" model that is intended to assume the least coupling that is justified by known anatomy, and use simulations and analytic results proved in [1, 2] to argue that an oscillatory associative memory function can be realized in such a system. The network is meant only as a cartoon of the real biology, which is designed to reveal the general mathematical principles and mechanisms by which the actual system might function. Such principles can then be observed or applied in other contexts as well.

Long range excitatory to excitatory connections are well known as "associational" connections in olfactory cortex[6], and cortico-cortico connections in neocortex. Since our units are neural populations, we know that some density of full cross-coupling exists in the system[6], and our weights are the average synaptic strengths of these connections. There is little problem at the population level with coupling symmetry in these average connection strenghts emerging from the operation of an outer product learning rule on initially random connections. When the network units are neuron pools, analog state variables arise naturally as continuous local pulse densities and cell voltage averages. Smooth sigmoidal population input-output functions, whose slope increases with arousal of the animal, have been measured in the olfactory system[4]. Local inhibitory "interneurons" are a ubiquitous feature of the anatomy of cortex throughout the brain[5]. It is unlikely that they make long range connections (> 1 mm) by themselves. These connections, and even the debated interconnections between them, are therefore left out of a minimal model. The resulting network is actually a fair caricature of the well studied circuitry of olfactory (prepyriform) cortex. This is thought to be one of the clearest cases of a real biological network with associative memory function [6]. Although neocortex is far more complicated, it may roughly be viewed as two olfactory cortices stacked on top of each other. We expect that analysis of this system will lend insight into mechanisms of associative memory there as well. In [3] we show that this model is capable of storing complicated multifrequency spatio-temporal trajectories, and argue that it may serve as a model of memory for sequences of actions in motor cortex.

For an N dimensional system, the "minimal" coupling structure is described mathematically by the matrix

$$T = \begin{bmatrix} W & -hI \\ gI & 0 \end{bmatrix},$$

where W is the $N/2 \times N/2$ matrix of excitatory interconnections, and gI and hI are $N/2 \times N/2$ identity matrices multiplied by the positive scalars g, and h. These give the strength of coupling around local inhibitory feedback loops. A state vector is composed of local average cell voltages for $N/2$ excitatory neuron populations $\vec{x}$ and $N/2$ inhibitory neuron populations $\vec{y}$ (hereafter notated as $x, y \in \mathbf{R}^{N/2}$). Standard network equations with this coupling might be, in component form,

$$\dot{x}_i = -\tau x_i - h\sigma(y_i) + \sum_{j=1}^{N/2} W_{ij}\sigma(x_j) + b_i \qquad (1)$$

$$\dot{y}_i = -\tau y_i + g\sigma(x_i), \qquad (2)$$

where $\sigma(x) = tanh(x)$ or some other sigmoidal function symmetric about 0. Intuitively, since the inhibitory units y_i receive no direct input and give no direct output, they act as hidden units that create oscillation for the amplitude patterns stored in the excitatory cross-connections W. This may be viewed as a simple generalization of the analog "Hopfield" network architecture to store periodic instead of static attractors.

If we expand this network to third order in a Taylors series about the origin, we get a network that looks something like,

$$\dot{x}_i = -\tau x_i - h y_i + \sum_{j=1}^{N/2} W_{ij} x_j - \sum_{jkl=1}^{N/2} W_{ijkl} x_j x_k x_l + b_i, \qquad (3)$$

$$\dot{y}_i = -\tau y_i + g x_i, \qquad (4)$$

where $\sigma'(0) = 1$, and $\frac{1}{3!}\sigma'''(0)(< 0)$ is absorbed into W_{ijkl}. A sigmoid symmetric about zero has odd symmetry, and the even order terms of the expansion vanish, leaving the cubic terms as the only nonlinearity. The actual expansion of the excitatory sigmoids in (1,2) (in this coordinate system) will only give cubic terms of the form $\sum_{j=1}^{N/2} W_{ij} x_j^3$. The competitive (negative) cubic terms of (3) therefore constitute a more general and directly programmable nonlinearity that is independent of the linear terms. They serve to create multiple periodic attractors by causing the oscillatory modes of the linear term to compete, much as the sigmoidal nonlinearity does for static modes in a Hopfield network. Intuitively, these terms may be thought of as sculpting the maxima of a "saturation" landscape into which the stored linear modes with positive eigenvalues expand, and positioning them to lie in the directions specified by the eigenvectors of these modes to make them stable. A precise definition of this landscape is given by a strict Liapunov function in a special polar coordinate system[1, 3]. Since we have had no success storing *multiple* oscillatory attractors in the sigmoid net (1,2) by any learning rule, we are driven to take this very effective higher order net seriously as a biological model. From a physiological point of view, (3,4) may be considered a model of a biological network which is operating in the linear region of the known *axonal* sigmoid nonlinearities[4], and contains instead sigma-pi units or higher order *synaptic* nonlinearities.

2.1   Biological justification of the higher order synapses

Using the long range excitatory connections available, the higher order synaptic weights W_{ijkl} can conceivably be realized locally in the axo-dendritic interconnection plexus known as "neuropil". This a feltwork of tiny fibers so dense that it's exact circuitry is impossible to investigate with present experimental techniques. Single axons are known to bifurcate into multiple branches that contribute separate synapses to the dendrites of target cells. It is also well known that neighboring synapses on a dendrite can interact in a nonlinear fashion that has been modeled as higher order synaptic terms by some researchers. It has been suggested that the neuropil may be dense enough to allow the crossing of every possible combination of *jkl* axons in the vicinity of some dendritic branch of at least one neuron in neuron pool *i* (B. Mel). Trophic factors stimulated by the coactivation of the axons and the dendrite could cause these axons to form of a "cluster" of nearby synapses on the dendrite to realize a *jkl* product synapse. The required higher order terms could thus be created by a Hebb-like process. The use of competitive cubic cross terms may therefore be viewed physiologically as the use of this complicated nonlinear *synaptic/dendritic* processing, as the decision making nonlinearity in the system, as opposed to the usual sigmoidal *axonal* nonlinearity. There are more weights in the cubic synaptic terms, and the network nonlinearity can be programmed in detail.

3   Analysis

The real eigenvectors of W give the magnitudes of the complex eigenvectors of T.

Theorem 3.1 *If α is a real eigenvalue of the $N/2 \times N/2$ matrix W, with corresponding eigenvector x, then the $N \times N$ matrix*

$$T = \begin{bmatrix} W & -hI \\ gI & 0 \end{bmatrix}$$

has a pair of complex conjugate eigenvalues $\lambda_{1,2} = 1/2(\alpha \pm \sqrt{\alpha^2 - 4hg}) = 1/2(\alpha \pm i\omega)$, for $\alpha^2 < 4hg$, where $\omega = \sqrt{4hg - \alpha^2}$. The corresponding complex conjugate pair of eigenvectors are

$$\begin{bmatrix} x \\ \frac{\alpha+\omega}{2h}x \end{bmatrix} \pm i \begin{bmatrix} x \\ \frac{\alpha-\omega}{2h}x \end{bmatrix}.$$

The proof of this theorem is given in [2]. To more clearly see the amplitude and phase patterns, we can convert to a magnitude and phase representation, $z = |z|e^{i\theta}$, where $|z_i| = \sqrt{\Re_{z_i}^2 + \Im_{z_i}^2}$, and $\theta_i = \arctan(\Im_{z_i})/(\Re_{z_i})$. We get, $|z_{x_i}| = \sqrt{x_i^2 + x_i^2} = \sqrt{2}|x_i|$, and

$$|z_{y_i}| = \sqrt{\frac{2(\alpha^2 + \omega^2)}{4h^2}x_i^2} = \sqrt{\frac{4hg}{2h^2}}|x_i| = \sqrt{\frac{2g}{h}}|x_i|.$$

Now $\theta_x = \arctan 1 = \pi/4, \theta_y = \arctan \frac{\alpha-\omega}{\alpha+\omega}$. Dividing out the common $\sqrt{2}$ factor in the magnitudes, we get eigenvectors that clearly display the amplitude patterns of interest.

$$\begin{bmatrix} |x|e^{i\theta_x} \\ \sqrt{\frac{g}{h}}|x|e^{i\theta_y} \end{bmatrix}, \quad or \quad \begin{bmatrix} |x|\cos\theta_x \\ \sqrt{\frac{g}{h}}|x|\cos\theta_y \end{bmatrix} \pm i \begin{bmatrix} |x|\sin\theta_x \\ \sqrt{\frac{g}{h}}|x|\sin\theta_y \end{bmatrix}$$

Because of the restricted coupling, the oscillations possible in this network are standing waves, since the phase θ_x, θ_y is constant for each kind of neuron x and y, and differs only between them. This is basically what is observed in the olfactory bulb (primary olfactory cortex) and prepyriform cortex. The phase of inhibitory components θ_y in the bulb lags the phase of the excitatory components θ_x by approximately 90 degrees. It is easy to choose α and ω in this model to get phase lags of nearly 90 degrees.

3.1   Learning by the projection algorithm

From the theory detailed in [1], we can program any linearly independent set of eigenvalues and eigenvectors into W by the "projection" operation $W = BDB^{-1}$, where B has the desired eigenvectors as columns, and D is a diagonal matrix of the desired eigenvalues. Because the complex eigenvectors of T follow from these learned for W, we can form a projection matrix P with those eigenvectors of T as columns. Forming also a matrix J of the complex eigenvalues of T in blocks along the diagonal, we can project directly to get T. If general cubic terms $T_{ijkl}\,x_j x_k x_l$, also given by a specific projection operation, are added to network equations with linear terms $T_{ij}\,x_j$, the complex modes (eigenvectors) of the linearization are analytically guaranteed by the projection theorem[1] to characterize the periodic attractors of the network vector field. Chosen "normal form" coeficients Amn [1] are projected to get the higher order synaptic weights T_{ijkl} for these general cubic terms. Together, these operations constitute the "normal form projection algorithm":

$$T = PJP^{-1} \ , \quad T_{ijkl} = \sum_{m,n=1}^{N} P_{im} A_{mn} P_{mj}^{-1} P_{nk}^{-1} P_{nl}^{-1}.$$

Either member of the pair of complex eigenvectors shown above will suffice as the eigenvector that is entered in the P matrix for the projection operation. For real and imaginary component columns in P,

$$P = \begin{bmatrix} |x^s|\cos\theta_x^s & |x^s|\sin\theta_x^s & \cdots \\ \sqrt{\frac{g}{h}}|x^s|\cos\theta_y^s & \sqrt{\frac{g}{h}}|x^s|\sin\theta_y^s & \cdots \end{bmatrix} \Rightarrow X^s(t) = \begin{bmatrix} |x^s|e^{i\theta_x^s + i\omega^s t} \\ \sqrt{\frac{g}{h}}|x^s|e^{i\theta_y^s + i\omega^s t} \end{bmatrix},$$

where $X^s(t)$ is an expression for the periodic attractor established for pattern s when this P matrix is used in the projection algorithm.

The general cubic terms $T_{ijkl}\,x_j x_k x_l$, however, require use of unlikely long range inhibitory connections. Simulations of two and four oscillator networks thus far (N=4 and N=8), reveal that use of the higher order terms for only the anatomically justified long range excitatory connections W_{ijkl}, as in the cubic net (3,4), is effective in storing randomly chosen sets of desired patterns. The behavior of this network is very close to the theoretical ideal guaranteed above for a network with general higher order terms. There is no alteration of stored oscillatory patterns when the reduced coupling is used.

We have at least general analytic justification for this. "Normal form" theory[1, 3] guarantees that many other choices of weights will do the same job as the those found by the projection operation, but does not in general say how to find them. Latest work shows that a perturbation theory calculation of the normal form coefficients for general high dimensional cubic nets is tractable and in principle permits the removal of all but N^2 of the N^4 higher order weights normally produced by the projection algorithm. We have already incorporated this in an improved learning rule (non-Hebbian thus far) which requires even fewer of the excitatory higher order weights $((N)^2$ instead of the $(N/2)^4$ used in (3)), and are exploring the size of the "neighborhood" of state space about the origin in which the rule is effective. This should lead as well to a rigorous proof of the performance of these networks.

3.2   Learning by local Hebb rules

We show further in [2, 1] that for orthonormal static patterns x^s, the projection operation for the W matrix reduces to an outer product, or "Hebb" rule, and the projection for the higher order weights becomes a *multiple* outer product rule:

$$W_{ij} = \sum_{s=1}^{N/2} \alpha^s x_i^s x_j^s \ , \quad W_{ijkl} = c \, \delta_{ij}\delta_{kl} - d \sum_{s=1}^{N/2} x_i^s x_j^s x_k^s x_l^s \ . \tag{5}$$

The first rule is guaranteed to establish desired patterns x^s as eigenvectors of the matrix W with corresponding eigenvalues α^s. The second rule, with $c > d$, gives higher order weights for the cubic terms in (3) that ensure the patterns defined by these eigenvectors will appear as attractors in the network vectorfield. The outer product is a *local* synapse rule for synapse ij, that allows additive and incremental learning. The system can be truly self-organizing because the net can modify itself based on its own activity. The rank of the coupling matrix W and T grows as more memories are learned by the Hebb rule, and the unused capacity appears as a degenerate subspace with all zero eigenvalues. The flow is thus directed toward regions of the state space where patterns are stored.

In the minimal net, real eigenvectors learned for W are converted by the network structure to standing wave oscillations (constant phase) with the absolute value of those eigenvectors as amplitudes. From the mathematical perspective, there are $(N/2)!$ eigenvectors with different permutations of the signs of the same components, which lead to the same positive amplitude vector. This means that nonorthogonal amplitude patterns may be stored by the Hebb rule on the excitatory connections, since there may be many ways to find a perfectly orthonormal set of eigenvectors for W that stores a given set of nonorthogonal amplitude vectors. Given the complexity of dendritic processing discussed previously, it is not impossible that there is some distribution of the signs of the final effect of synapses from excitatory neurons that would allow a biological system to make use of this mathematical degree of freedom.

For different input objects, feature preprocessing in primary and secondary sensory cortex may be expected to orthogonalize outputs to the object recognition systems modeled here. When the rules above are used for nonorthogonal patterns, the eigenvectors of W and T are no longer given directly by the Hebb rule, and we expect that the kind of performance found in Hopfield networks for nonorthogonal memories will obtain, with reduced capacity and automatic clustering of similar exemplars. Investigation of this unsupervised induction of categories from training examples will be the subject of future work[3].

3.3 Architectural Variations — Olfactory Bulb Model

Another biologically interesting architecture which can store these kinds of patterns is one with associational excitatory to inhibitory cross-coupling. This may be a more plausible model of the olfactory bulb (primary olfactory cortex) than the one above. Experimental work of Freeman suggests an associative memory function for this cortex as well[4]. The evidence for long range excitatory to excitatory coupling in the olfactory bulb is much weaker than that for the prepyriform cortex. Long range excitatory tracts connecting even the two halves of the bulb are known, but anatomical data thus far show these axons entering only the inhibitory granuel cell layers.

$$T = \begin{bmatrix} gI & -hI \\ W & 0 \end{bmatrix} \quad , \quad \lambda_{1,2} = 1/2(g \pm \sqrt{g^2 - 4\alpha g}) = 1/2(g \pm i\omega),$$

for $g^2 < 4\alpha g$, where $\omega = \sqrt{4\alpha g - g^2}$. The eigenvectors are,

$$\begin{bmatrix} x \\ \frac{g+\omega}{2h}x \end{bmatrix} \pm i \begin{bmatrix} x \\ \frac{g-\omega}{2h}x \end{bmatrix}, \quad \Rightarrow \quad P = \begin{bmatrix} |x^s|\cos\theta_x^s & |x^s|\sin\theta_x^s & \cdots \\ \sqrt{\frac{\alpha}{h}}|x^s|\cos\theta_y^s & \sqrt{\frac{\alpha}{h}}|x^s|\sin\theta_y^s & \cdots \end{bmatrix},$$

in polar form, where $\theta_x^s = \pi/4$, and $\theta_y^s = \arctan\frac{g-\omega}{g+\omega}$.

If we add inhibitory population self-feedback $-f$ to either model, this additional term appears subtracted from α or g in the real part of the complex eigenvalues, and added to them in all other expressions[2]. Further extensions of this line of analysis will consider lateral inhibitory fan out of the inhibitory - excitatory feedback connections. The $-hI$ block of the coupling matrix T becomes a banded matrix. Similarly, the gI and $-fI$ may be banded, or both full excitatory to excitatory W and full excitatory to inhibitory V coupling blocks may be considered. We conjecture that the phase restrictions of the minimal model will be relaxed with these further degrees of freedom available, so that traveling waves may exist.

3.3.1   Acknowledgements

Supported by AFOSR-87-0317. It is a pleasure to acknowledge the support of Walter Freeman and invaluable assistance of Morris Hirsch.

References

[1] B Baird. A bifurcation theory approach to vector field programming for periodic attractors. In *Proc. Int. Joint Conf. on Neural Networks, Wash. D.C.*, page I381, June 18 1989.

[2] B. Baird. Bifurcation and learning in network models of oscillating cortex. In S. Forest, editor, *Proc. Conf. on Emergent Computation, Los Alamos, May 1989*, 1990. to appear-Physica D.

[3] B. Baird. *Bifurcation Theory Approach to the Analysis and Synthesis of Neural Networks for Engineering and Biological Modelling*. Research Notes in Neural Computing. Springer, 1990.

[4] W.J. Freeman. *Mass Action in the Nervous System*. Academic Press, New York, 1975.

[5] C. M. Grey and W. Singer. Stimulus dependent neuronal oscillations in the cat visual cortex area 17. *Neuroscience [Suppl]*, 22:1301P, 1987.

[6] Lewis B. Haberly and James M. Bower. Olfactory cortex: model circuit for study of associative memory? *Trends in Neuroscience*, 12(7):258, 1989.

Collective Oscillations in the Visual Cortex

Daniel Kammen & Christof Koch
Computation and Neural Systems
Caltech 216-76
Pasadena, CA 91125

Philip J. Holmes
Dept. of Theor. & Applied Mechanics
Cornell University
Ithaca, NY 14853

ABSTRACT

The firing patterns of populations of cells in the cat visual cortex can exhibit oscillatory responses in the range of $35 - 85\ Hz$. Furthermore, groups of neurons many mm's apart can be highly synchronized as long as the cells have similar orientation tuning. We investigate two basic network architectures that incorporate either nearest-neighbor or global feedback interactions and conclude that non-local feedback plays a fundamental role in the initial synchronization and dynamic stability of the oscillations.

1   INTRODUCTION

$40 - 60\ Hz$ oscillations have long been reported in the rat and rabbit olfactory bulb and cortex on the basis of single- and multi-unit recordings as well as EEG activity (Freeman, 1972; Wilson & Bower 1990). Recently, two groups (Eckhorn *et al.*, 1988 and Gray *et al.*, 1989) have reported highly synchronized, stimulus specific oscillations in the $35 - 85\ Hz$ range in areas 17, 18 and PMLS of anesthetized as well as awake cats. Neurons with similar orientation tuning up to $7\ mm$ apart show phase-locked oscillations, with a phase shift of less than $3\ msec$. We address here the computational architecture necessary to subserve this process by investigating to what extent two neuronal architectures, nearest-neighbor coupling and feedback from a central "comparator", can synchronize neuronal oscillations in a robust and rapid manner.

It was argued in earlier work on central pattern generators (Cohen *et al.*, 1982), that in studying coupling effects among large populations of oscillating neurons, one can ignore the details of individual oscillators and represent each one by a single periodic variable: its *phase*. Our approach assumes a population of neuronal oscillators, firing repetitively in response to synaptic input. Each cell (or group of tightly electrically coupled cells) has an associated variable representing the membrane potential. In particular, when $\theta_i = \pi$, an action potential is generated and the phase is reset to its initial value (in our case to $-\pi$). The number of times per unit time θ_i passes through π, i.e. $d\theta_i/dt$, is then proportional to the firing frequency of the neuron. For a network of $n + 1$ such oscillators, our basic model is

$$\frac{d\theta_i}{dt} = \omega_i + f_i(\theta_0, \theta_1, ..., \theta_n), \tag{1}$$

where ω_i represents the synaptic input to neuron i and f, a function of the phases, represents the coupling within the network. Each oscillator i in isolation (i.e. with $f_i = 0$), exhibits asymptotically stable periodic oscillations; that is, if the input is changed the oscillator will rapidly adjust to a new firing rate. In our model ω_i is assumed to derive from neurons in the lateral geniculate nucleus (LGN) and is purely excitatory.

2   FREQUENCY AND PHASE LOCKING

Any realistic model of the observed, highly synchronized, oscillations must account for the fact that the individual neurons oscillate at different frequencies in isolation. This is due to variations in the synaptic input, ω_i, as well as in the intrinsic properties of the cells. We will contrast the abilities of two markedly different network architectures to synchronize these oscillations. The "chain" model (Fig. 1 top) consists of a one-dimensional array of oscillators connected to their nearest neighbors, while in the alternative "comparator" model (Fig. 1 middle), an array of neurons project to a single unit, where the phases are averaged (i.e. $(1/n)\sum_{i=0}^{n} \theta_i(t)$). This average is then feed back to every neuron in the network. In the continuum limit (on the unit interval) with all $f_i = f$ being identical, the two models are

$$(Chain \ \ Model) \quad \frac{\partial \theta(x,t)}{\partial t} \ = \ \omega(x) + \frac{1}{n}\frac{\partial f}{\partial x}(\phi) \tag{2}$$

$$(Comparator \ \ Model) \quad \frac{\partial \theta(x,t)}{\partial t} \ = \ \omega(x) + f\left(\theta(x,t) - \int_0^1 \theta(s,t)ds\right), \tag{3}$$

where $0 \le x \le 1$ and ϕ is the phase gradient, $\phi = \frac{1}{n}\frac{\partial\theta}{\partial x}$. In the chain model, we require that f be an odd function (for simplicity of analysis only) while our analysis of the comparator model holds for any continuous function f. We use two spatially separated "spots" of width δ and amplitude α as visual input (Fig. 1 bottom). This pattern was chosen as a simple version of the double-bar stimulus that (Gray *et al.* 1989) found to evoke coherent oscillatory activity in widely separated populations of visual cortical cells.

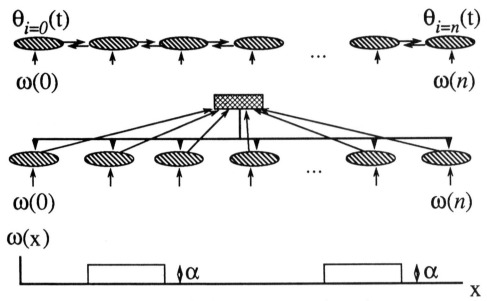

Figure 1: The linear chain (top) and comparator (middle) architectures. The spatial pattern of inputs is indicated by $\omega_i(x)$. See equs. 2 & 3 for a mathematical description of the models. The "two spot" input is shown at bottom and represents two parts of a perceptually extended figure.

We determine under what circumstances the chain model will develop frequency-locked solutions, such that every oscillator fires at the same frequency (but not necessarily at the same time), i.e. $\partial^2\theta/\partial x \partial t \equiv 0$. We prove (Kammen, *et al.* 1990) that frequency-locked solutions exist as long as $|n(\overline{\omega}x - \int_0^x \omega(s)ds)|$ does not exceed the maximal value of f, $f_{\max}$ (with $\overline{\omega} = \int_0^1 \omega(s)ds$ the mean excitation level). Thus, if the excitation is too irregular or the chain too long ($n \gg 1$), we will not find frequency-locked solutions. Phase coherence between the excited regions is *not* generally maintained and is, in fact, strongly a function of the initial conditions. Another feature of the chain model is that the onset of frequency locking is slow and takes time of order $\sqrt{n}$.

The location of the stimulus has no effect on phase relationships in the comparator model due to the global nature of the feedback. The comparator model exhibits two distinct regimes of behavior depending on the amplitude of the input, α. In the case of the two spot input (Fig. 1 bottom), if α is small, all neurons will frequency-lock regardless of location, that is units responding to both the "figure" and the background ("ground") will oscillate at the same frequency. They will, however, fire at different times, with $\theta_{fig} \neq \theta_{gnd}$. If α is above a critical threshold, the units responding to the "figure" will decouple in frequency as well as phase from the background while still maintaining internal phase coherency. Phase gradients *never* exist within the excited groups, no matter what the input amplitude.

We numerically simulated the chain and comparator models with the two spot input for the coupling function $f(\eta) = sin(\eta)$. Additive Gaussian noise was included in the input, ω_i. Our analytical results were confirmed; frequency and phase gradients were always present in the chain model (Fig. 2A) even though the coupling strength was ten times greater than that of the comparator model. In the comparator network small excitation levels led to frequency-locking along the entire array and to phase-coupled activity within the illuminated areas (Fig. 2B), while large excitation levels led to phase and frequency decoupling between the "figure" and the "background" (Fig. 2C). The excited regions in the comparator settle very rapidly – within 2 to 3 cycles – into phase-locked activity with small phase-delays. The chain model, on the other hand, exhibits strong sensitivity to initial conditions as well as a very slow approach to coherence that is still not complete even after 50 cycles (See Fig. 2).

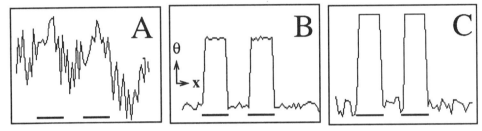

Figure 2: The phase portrait of the chain (A), weak (B) and strongly (C) excited comparator networks after 50 cycles. The input, indicated by the horizontal lines, is the two spot pattern. Note that the central, unstimulated, region in the chain model has been "dragged along" by the flanking excited regions.

3   STABILITY ANALYSIS

Perhaps the most intriguing aspect of the oscillations concerns the role that they may play in cortical information processing and the labeling of cells responding to a single perceptual object. To be useful in object coding, the oscillations must exhibit some degree of noise tolerance both in the input signal and in the stability of the population to variation in the firing times of individual cells.

The degree to which input noise to individual neurons disrupts the synchronization of the population is determined by the ratio $\frac{input\ noise}{coupling\ strength} = \frac{\omega_i(t)}{f(\cdot)}$. For small perturbations, $\omega(t) = \omega_0 + \epsilon(t)$, the action of the feedback, from the nearest neighbors in the chain and from the entire network in the comparator, will compensate for the noise and the neuron will maintain coherence with the excited population. As ϵ is increased first phase and then frequency coherence will be lost.

In Fig. 3 we compare the dynamical stability of the chain and comparator models. In each case the phase, θ, of a unit receiving perturbated input is plotted as the deviation from the average phase, θ_0, of all the excited units receiving input ω_0. The chain in highly sensitive to noise: even 10% stochastic noise significantly perturbs the phase of the neuron. In the comparator model (Fig. 3B) noise must reach the

40% level to have a similar effect on the phase. As the noise increases above $0.30\omega_0$ even *frequency* coherence is lost in the chain model (broken error bars). Frequency coherence is maintained in the comparator for $\epsilon = 0.60\omega_0$.

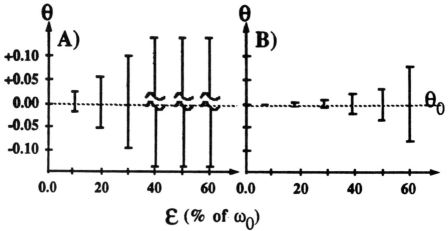

Figure 3: The result of a perturbation on the phase, θ, for the chain (A) and comparator (B) models. The terminus of the error bars gives the resulting deviation from the unperturbed value. Broken bars indicate both phase and frequency decoupling.

The stability of the solutions of the comparator model to variability in the activity of individual neurons can easily be demonstrated. For simplicity consider the case of a single input of amplitude ω_1 superposed on a background of amplitude ω_0. The solutions in each region are:

$$\frac{d\theta_0}{dt} = \omega_0 + f\left(\frac{\theta_0 - \theta_1}{2}\right) \tag{4}$$

$$\frac{d\theta_1}{dt} = \omega_1 + f\left(\frac{\theta_1 - \theta_0}{2}\right). \tag{5}$$

We define the difference in the solutions to be $\phi(t) = \theta_1(t) - \theta_0(t)$ and $\Delta\omega = \omega_1 - \omega_0$. We then have an equation for the rate the solutions converge or diverge:

$$\frac{d\phi}{dt} = \Delta\omega + f\left(\frac{\phi}{2}\right) - f\left(-\frac{\phi}{2}\right). \tag{6}$$

If the solutions are stable (of constant velocity) then $d\theta_1/dt = d\theta_0/dt$ and $\theta_1 = \theta_0 + c$ with c a constant. We then have the stable solution $\phi^* = c$ $d\phi^*/dt = \Delta\omega + f(\frac{c}{2}) - f(-\frac{c}{2}) = 0$. Stability of the solutions can be seen by perturbing θ_1 to $\theta_1 = \theta_0 + c + \epsilon$ with $|\epsilon| < 1$. The perturbed solution, $\phi = \phi^* + \epsilon$, has the derivative $d\phi/dt = d\epsilon/dt$. Developing $f(\phi)$ into a Taylor series around ϕ^* and neglecting terms on the order of ϵ^2 and higher, we arrive at

$$\frac{d\epsilon}{dt} = \frac{\epsilon}{2}\left[f'\left(\frac{c}{2}\right) + f'\left(\frac{-c}{2}\right)\right]. \tag{7}$$

If $f(\phi)$ is odd then $f'(\phi)$ is even, and eq. (7) reduces to

$$\frac{d\epsilon}{dt} = \epsilon f'(\frac{c}{2}).$$ (8)

Thus, if $f'(c/2) < 0$ the perturbations will decay to zero and the system will maintain phase locking within the excited regions.

4   THE FREQUENCY MODEL

The model discussed so far assumes that the feedback is only a function of the phases. In particular, this implies that the comparator computes the average phase across the population. Consider, however, a model where the feedback is proportional to the average firing frequency of a group of neurons. Let us therefore replace phase in the feedback function with firing frequency,

$$\frac{\partial\theta(x,t)}{\partial t} = \omega(x) + f\left(\frac{\partial\theta(x,t)}{\partial t} - \frac{\overline{\partial\theta(x,t)}}{\partial t}\right)$$ (9)

with $\frac{\overline{\partial\theta}}{\partial t} = \frac{\partial}{\partial t}\int_0^1 \theta(s,t)ds = \frac{\partial\overline{\theta}}{\partial t}$. This is a very special differential equation as can be seen by setting $v(x,t) = \partial\theta(x,t)/\partial t$. This yields an algebraic equation for v with no explicit time dependency:

$$v(x) = w(x) + f(v(x) - \overline{v}(x))$$ (10)

and, after an integration, we have,

$$\theta(x,t) = \int_0^t v(x)dt = v(x)t + \theta_0(x).$$ (11)

Thus, the phase relationships depend on the initial conditions, $\theta_0(x)$, and no phase locking occurs. While frequency locking only occurs for $w(x) = 0$ the feedback can lead to tight frequency coupling among the excited neurons.

Reformulating the chain model in terms of firing-frequencies, we have

$$\frac{\partial\theta(x,t)}{\partial t} = \frac{1}{n}\left(\frac{\partial\omega(x)}{\partial x} + \frac{1}{n}\frac{\partial^2}{\partial x^2}f\left(\frac{\partial\theta(x,t)}{\partial t}\right)\right)$$ (12)

under the assumption that $f(-x) = -f(x)$. With $\gamma(x,t) = \frac{\partial\phi(x,t)}{\partial t}$, we again arrive at a stationary algebraic equation

$$\gamma(x) = \frac{1}{n}\left(\frac{\partial w}{\partial x} + \frac{1}{n}\frac{\partial^2}{\partial x^2}f(\gamma(x))\right),$$ (13)

and

$$\phi(x,t) = \int_0^t \gamma(x)dt = \gamma(x)t + \phi_0(x)$$ (14)

In other words, the system will develop a time-dependent phase gradient. Frequency locked solutions of the sort $\frac{\partial\theta}{\partial t} = 0$ everywhere only occur if $w(x) = 0$ everywhere. Thus, the chain architecture leads to very static behavior, with little ability to either phase- or frequency-lock.

5   DISCUSSION

We have investigated the ability of two networks of relaxation oscillators with different connectivity patterns to synchronize their oscillations. Our investigation has been prompted by recent experimental results pertaining to the existence of frequency- and phase-locked oscillations in the mammalian visual cortex (Gray *et al.*, 1989; Eckhorn *et al.*, 1988). While these $35 - 85\ Hz$ oscillations are induced by the visual stimulus, usually a flashing or moving bar, they are not locked to the frequency of the stimulus. Most surprising is the finding that cells tuned to the same orientation, but separated by up to 7 *mm*, not only exhibit coherent oscillatory activity, but do so with a phase-shift of less than 3 *msec* (Gray *et al.*, 1989).[1]

We have assumed the existence of a population of cortical oscillators, such as those reported in cortical slice preparations (Llinás, 1988; Chagnac-Amitai and Connors, 1989). The issue is then how such a population of oscillators can rapidly begin to fire in near total synchrony. Two neuronal architectures suggest themselves.

As a mechanism for establishing coherent oscillatory activity the comparator model is far superior to a nearest-neighbor model. The comparator rapidly (within $1 - 3$ cycles) achieves phase coherence, while the chain model exhibits a far slower onset of synchronization and is highly sensitive to the initial conditions. Once initiated, the oscillations in the two models exhibit markedly different stability characteristics. The diffusive nature of communication in the chain results in little ability to regulate the firing of individual units and consequently only highly homogeneous inputs will result in collective oscillations. The long-range connections present in the comparator, however, result in stable collective oscillations even in the presence of significant noise levels. Noise uniformly distributed about the mean firing level will have little effect due to the averaging performed by the comparator unit.

A more realistic model of the interconnection architecture of the cortex will certainly have to take both local as well as global neuronal pathways into account and the ever-present delays in cellular and network signal propagation (Kammen, *et al.*, 1990). Long range (up to 6 *mm*) lateral excitatory connections have been reported (Gilbert and Wiesel, 1983). However, their low conduction velocities ($\approx 1\ mm/msec$) would lead to significant phase-shifts in contrast to the data. While the cortical circuitry contains both local as well as global connection, our results imply that a cortical architecture with one or more "comparator" neurons driven by the averaged activity of the hypercolumnar cell populations is an attractive mechanism for synchronizing the observed oscillations.

We have also developed a model where the firing frequency, and not the phase is involved in the dynamics. Coding based on phase information requires that the cells track the time interval between incident spikes whereas the firing frequency is available as the raw spike rate. This computation can be readily implemented

---

[1] Note that this result is obtained by averaging over many trials. The phase-shift for individual trial may possibly be larger, but could be randomly distributed from trial to trial around the origin.

neurobiologically and is entirely consistent with the known biophysics of cortical cells.

Von der Malsburg (1985) has argued that the temporal synchronization of groups of neurons labels perceptually distinct objects, subserving figure-ground segregation. Both firing frequency and inter-cell phase (timing) relationships of ensembles of neurons are potential channels to encode the signatures of various objects in the visual field. Perceptually distinct objects could be coded by groups of synchronized neurons, all locked to the same frequency with the groups only distinguished by their phase relationships. We do not believe, however, that phase is a robust enough variable to code this information across the cortex, A more robust scheme is one in which groups of synchronized neurons are locked at different firing frequencies.

Acknowledgement

D.K. is a recipient of a Weizman Postdoctoral Fellowship. P.H. acknowledges support from the Sherman Fairchild Foundation and C.K. from the Air Force Office of Scientific Research, a NSF Presidential Young Investigator Award and from the James S. McDonnell Foundation. We would like to thank Francis Crick for useful comments and discussions.

References

Chagnac-Amitai, Y. & Connors, B. W. (1989) *J. Neurophys.*, **62**, 1149.

Cohen, A. H., Holmes, P. J. & Rand R. H. (1982) *J. Math. Biol.* **3**, 345.

Eckhorn, R., Bauer, R., Jordan, W., Brosch, M., Kruse, W., Munk, M. & Reitboeck, H. J. (1988) *Biol. Cybern.*, **60**, 121.

Freeman, W.J. (1972) *J. Neurophysiol.* **35**, 762.

Gilbert, C. D. & T.N. Wiesel (1983) *J. Neurosci.* **3**, 1116.

Gray, C. M., König, P., Engel, A. K. & Singer, W. (1989) *Nature* **338**, 334.

Kammen, D. M., Koch, C. and Holmes, P. J. (1990) *Proc. Natl. Acad. Sci. USA*, submitted.

Kopell N. & Ermentrout, G. B. (1986) *Comm. Pure Appl. Math.* **39**, 623.

Llinás, R. R. (1988) *Science* **242**, 1654.

von der Malsburg, C. (1985) *Ber. Bunsenges Phys. Chem.*, **89**, 703.

Wilson, M. A. & Bower, J. (1990) *J. Neurophysiol.*, in press.

Computer Simulation of Oscillatory Behavior in Cerebral Cortical Networks

Matthew A. Wilson and James M. Bower[1]
Computation and Neural Systems Program
Division of Biology, 216-76
California Institute of Technology
Pasadena, CA 91125

ABSTRACT

It has been known for many years that specific regions of the working cerebral cortex display periodic variations in correlated cellular activity. While the olfactory system has been the focus of much of this work, similar behavior has recently been observed in primary visual cortex. We have developed models of both the olfactory and visual cortex which replicate the observed oscillatory properties of these networks. Using these models we have examined the dependence of oscillatory behavior on single cell properties and network architectures. We discuss the idea that the oscillatory events recorded from cerebral cortex may be intrinsic to the architecture of cerebral cortex as a whole, and that these rhythmic patterns may be important in coordinating neuronal activity during sensory processing.

1   INTRODUCTION

An obvious characteristic of the general behavior of cerebral cortex, as evident in EEG recordings, is its tendency to oscillate. Cortical oscillations have been observed both in the electric fields generated by populations of cells (Bressler and Freeman

---

[1] Please address correspondence to James M. Bower at above address.

1980) as well as in the activity of single cells (Llinas 1988). Our previous efforts to study this behavior involve the construction of realistic, large scale computer simulations of one particular cortical area, the piriform (olfactory) cortex (Wilson and Bower 1989). While the oscillatory behavior of this region has been known for some time (Adrian 1942; Bressler and Freeman 1980), more recent findings of oscillations within visual cortex (Eckhorn et al.,1988; Gray et al. 1989) have generated increased interest in the role of oscillations in cerebral cortex in general. It is particularly intriguing that although these cortical areas receive very different kinds of sensory information, the periodic activity seen in both structures share a common principle frequency component in the range of 30-60 Hz. At the same time, however, the phase relationships of activity across each cortex differ. Piriform cortex displays systematic phase shifts in field potential responses to afferent activation (Freeman 1978; Haberly 1973), while correlations of neuronal activity in visual cortex indicate no such systematic phase shifts (Gray et al. 1989).

In order to compare this oscillatory behavior in these two cortical systems, we have developed a model of visual cortex by modifying the original piriform cortex model to reflect visual cortical network features.

2   MODEL STRUCTURE

2.1   COMMON MODEL FEATURES

Each simulation has at its base the three basic cell types found throughout cerebral cortex (Figure 1). The principle excitatory neuron, the pyramidal cell, is modeled here as five coupled membrane compartments. In addition there are two inhibitory neurons one principally mediating a slow K+ inhibition and one mediating a fast Cl-inhibition. Both are modeled as a single compartment. Connections between modeled cells are made by axons with finite conduction velocities, but no explicit axonal membrane properties other than delay are included. Synaptic activity is produced by simulating the action-potential triggered release of presynaptic transmitter and the resulting flow of transmembrane current through membrane channels. Each of these channels is described with parameters governing the time course and amplitude of synaptically activated conductance changes. The compartmental models of the cells integrate the transmembrane and axial currents to produce transmembrane voltages. Excursions of the cell body membrane voltage above a specified threshold trigger action potentials. Details of the modeling procedures are described in Wilson and Bower (1989).

Each model is intended to represent a 10 mm x 6 mm cortical region. The many millions of actual neurons in these areas are represented by 375 cells of the three types for a total of 1125 cells. The input to each cortex is provided by 100 independent fibers.

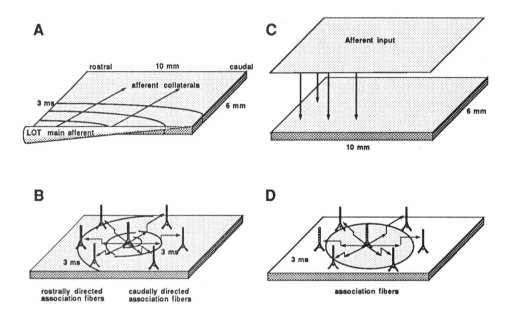

Figure 1: In the piriform cortex, input (A) and association fiber (B) projections make distributed lateral contacts with cells over the extent of the cortex. In the visual cortex model, input projections make local contact with cells over a 1 mm radius in a point-to-point fashion (C) and association fibers connect to cells within a limited radius (D).

While both the piriform and visual cortex models reflect these basic features of cerebral cortical architecture, both also contain major structural simplifications. The model referred to as "visual cortex", is particularly simplified. Our objective was to reproduce cortical oscillations characteristic of visual cortex by modifying those basic architectural features that differ between these two brain regions.

2.2   MODEL DIFFERENCES

The principle differences between the model of piriform and visual cortex involve changes in the topography of input projections, and in the extent of intrinsic connections within each model. In piriform cortex, afferent input from the olfactory bulb arrives via a tract of axons (LOT) projecting across the surface of the cortex (Fig. 1A) with no topographic relationship between the site of origin of individual LOT axons in the olfactory bulb and their region of termination in the cortex (Haberly 1985). In contrast, projections from the lateral geniculate nucleus to visual cortex are highly topographic, reflecting the retinotopic organization of many structures in the visual system (Van Essen 1979). In piriform cortex, excitatory intrinsic association connections are sparse, distributed, and non-topographic, extending across the entire cortex (Fig. 1C) (Haberly 1985). In the visual cortex, this association fiber system is much more limited in extent (Gilbert 1983).

3   RESULTS

Space limitations do not allow a complete discussion of previous results modeling piriform cortex. Readers are referred to Wilson and Bower (1989) for additional details. Here, we will describe data obtained from the modified piriform cortex model which replicate results from visual cortex.

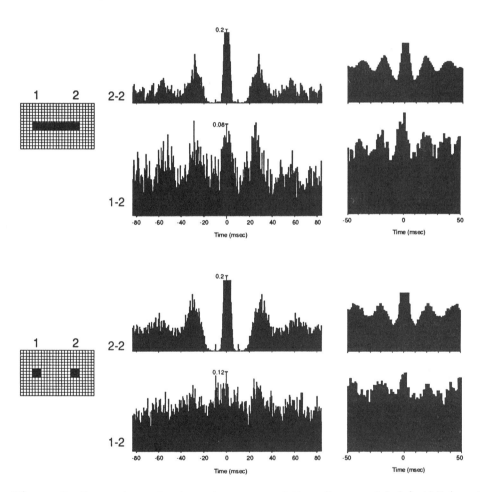

Figure 2: Comparison of auto and cross correlations from modeled (middle) and actual (right) (modified from Gray et al. 1989) visual cortex. The left column shows a diagram of the model with the stimulus region shaded. The numbers indicate the location of the recording sites referred to in the auto (2-2) and cross (1-2) correlations. The correlations generated by presentation of a continuous and broken bar stimulus are shown in the upper and lower panels respectively.

Figure 2 shows a comparison of auto and cross correlations of neuronal spike activity taken from both simulated and actual (Gray et al. 1989) experimental data. In each case the two recording sites in visual cortex are separated by approximately 6 mm. Total cross correlations in the modeled data were computed by averaging correlations from 50 individual 500 msec trials. Within each trial simulated activity was generated by providing input representing bars of light at different locations in the visual field. In these cases the model produced oscillatory auto and cross correlations with peak energy in the 30-60 Hz range. As in the experimental data, this effect is most clearly seen when the stimulus is a continuous bar of light activating cells between the two recorded sites (fig. 2). A broken bar which does not stimulate the intermediate region produces a weaker response (fig. 2), again consistent with experimental evidence.

The oscillatory form of the the cross correlation function suggests coherent firing of neurons at the two recorded locations. In order to determine the degree of synchrony between modeled neurons, the difference in phase between the firing of cells in these locations was estimated by measuring the offset of the dominant peak in the cross correlation function. These values were consistent with measurements obtained both through chi-square fitting of a modified sinc function and measurement of the phase of the peak frequency component in the correlation function power spectra. These measurements indicate phase shifts near zero ($<$ 3 msec).

3.1 STIMULUS EFFECTS

As shown in figure 2, correlations are induced by the presence of a stimulus. However, in both experimental and simulated results these correlations cannot be accounted for through a simple stimulus locking effect. Shuffling the trials with respect to each other prior to calculating cross correlation functions showed oscillations which were greatly diminished or completely absent. At the same time, simulations run in the absence of bar stimuli produced low baseline activity with no oscillations. These results demonstrate that while the stimulus is necessary to induce oscillatory behavior, the coherence between distant points is not due to the stimulus alone.

3.2 FREQUENCY

The visual cortex model generates oscillatory neural activity at a frequency in the range of 30-60 Hz, consistent with actual data. As found in the model piriform cortex, the frequency of these oscillations is primarily determined by the time course of the fast feedback inhibitory input. Allowing inhibitory cells to inhibit other inhibitory cells within a local region improved frequency locking and produced auto and cross correlations with more pronounced oscillatory characteristics.

3.3 COHERENCE

In order to demonstrate the essential role of the association fiber system in establishing coherent activity, simulations were performed in which all long-range ($>$ 1 mm) association fibers were eliminated. Under these conditions the auto correlations at each recording site continued to show strong oscillatory behavior, but oscillations in the cross correlation function were completely eliminated. Increasing the range of association fibers from 1 to 2 mm restored coherent oscillatory behavior. This demonstrates that long-range association fibers are critical in establishing coherence while local circuitry is sufficient for sustaining oscillations.

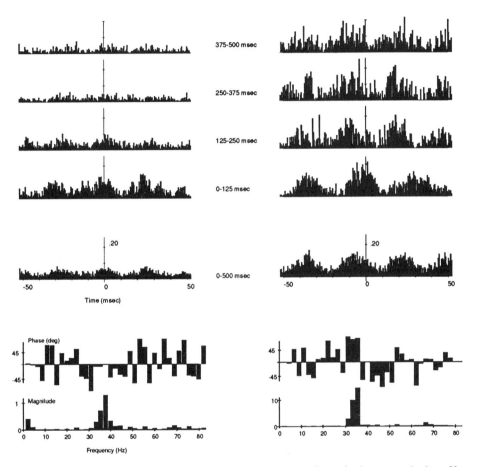

Figure 3: Time course of cross correlation functions for relative association fiber coupling strengths of 200 (left) and 300 (right). Upper traces display correlations taken at successive 125 intervals over the 500 msec period. The bottom-most correlation function covers the entire 500 msec interval. The lower panels display the power spectra of the overall correlation function.

3.3.1 Association Fiber Delay

To examine the dependence of zero-phase coherence between distant sites on association fibers characteristics, the propagation velocity for spikes travelling between pyramidal cells was reduced from a mean of 0.86 m/s to 0.43 m/s. Under these conditions the phase shift in the cross correlation function for a continuous bar stimulus remained less than 3 msec. This result indicates that the zero-phase coherence is not a direct function of association fiber delays.

3.3.2 Coupling Strength

As shown in figure 3, increasing the degree of association fiber coupling by increasing synaptic weights produced a transition from zero-phase coherence to a coherence with an 8 msec phase shift. Intermediate shifts were not observed. Figure 3 also illustrates the time course of coherence and phase relationships. There is a tendency for the initial stimulus onset period (0-125 msec) to show zero-phase preference. Later periods (> 125 msec) reflect the association coupling induced phase shift. For weak coupling which produces zero-phase behavior, the correlation structure decays over the 500 msec stimulus period. Increased coupling strength provides more sustained coherence, as does the addition of mutual inhibition.

4 DISCUSSION

Analysis of the behavior of the models shows that several components are particularly important in establishing the different phase and frequency relationships. A key factor in establishing zero-phase coherence appears to be the stimulation of a cellular population which can activate, via association fibers, adjacent regions in a symmetric fashion. In the case of the continuous bar, this intermediate region lies in the center of the bar. This is consistent with experimental results which indicate reduced coherence with bar stimuli which do not excite this region. The model also indicates that frequency can be effectively modulated by inhibitory feedback. The fact that inhibitory events with similar temporal properties are found throughout the cerebral cortex suggests that oscillations in the 30-60 Hz range will be found in a number of different cortical areas.

Interpreting phase coherence from correlation functions produced from the average of many simulation trials pointed out the need to distinguish average phase effects from instantaneous phase effects. Instantaneous phase implies that the statistics of the correlation function taken at any point of any trial are consistent with the statistics of the combined data. Average phase allows for systematic within-trial and between trial variability and is, therefore, a weaker assertion of actual coherence. This distinction is particularly important for theories which rely on phase encoding of stimulus information. Analysis of our model results indicates that the observed phase relationships are an average rather than an instantaneous effect.

Based on previous observations of the behavior of the piriform cortex model, we have proposed that high frequency oscillations may reflect the gating of intrinsic network integration intervals. This modulatory role would serve to assure that cells do not fire before they have received the necessary input to initiate another round of cortical activity. While this is clearly only one possible functional role for oscillations in piriform cortex, the model is being used to extend this idea to processing in the visual cortex as well.

Acknowledgements

This research was supported by the NSF (EET-8700064), the ONR (Contract N00014-88-K-0513), and the Lockheed Corporation.

References

Adrian, E.D. 1942. Olfactory reactions in the brain of the hedgehog. J. Physiol. (Lond.) 100, 459-472.

Bressler, S.L. and W.J. Freeman. 1980. Frequency analysis of olfactory system EEG in cat, rabbit and rat. Electroenceph. clin. Neurophysiol. 50, 19-24.

Eckhorn, R., R. Bauer, Jordan, M. Brosch, W. Kruse, M. Munk, and H.J. Reitboeck. 1988. Coherent oscillations: A mechanism of feature linking in the visual cortex? Biol. Cybern. 60, 121-130.

Freeman, W.J. 1978. Spatial properties of an EEG event in the olfactory bulb and cortex. Electroenceph. clin. Neurophysiol. 44,586-605.

Gilbert, C.D. 1983. Microcircuitry of the visual cortex. Ann. Rev. Neurosci. 6,217-247.

Gray, C.M., P. Konig, A.K. Engel, W. Singer. 1989. Oscillatory responses in cat visual cortex exhibit inter-columnar synchronization which reflects global stimulus properties. Nature 338, 334-337.

Haberly, L.B. 1985. Neuronal circuitry in olfactory cortex: anatomy and functional implications. Chem. Senses 10, 219-238.

Haberly, L.B. 1973. Summed potentials evoked in opossum prepyriform cortex. J. Neurophysiol. 36, 775-788.

Kammen, D.M., P.J. Holmes, and C. Koch. 1989. Cortical architecture and oscillations in neuronal networks: Feedback versus local coupling. In: Models of Brain Function R.M.J. Cotterill, Ed. (Cambridge Univ. Press.)

Llinas, R. 1988. The intrinsic electrophysiological properties of mammalian neurons: Insights into central nervous system function. Science 242:1654-1664.

Wilson, M.A. and J.M Bower. 1989. The simulation of large scale neuronal networks. In Methods in Neuronal Modeling: From Synapses to Networks C. Koch and I. Segev, Eds. (MIT Press, Cambridge, MA.) pp. 291-334.

Van Essen, D.C. 1979. Visual areas of the mammalian cerebral cortex. Ann. Rev. Neurosci. 2, 227-263.

Development and Regeneration of Eye-Brain Maps: A Computational Model

J.D. Cowan and **A.E. Friedman**
Department of Mathematics, Committee on
Neurobiology, and Brain Research Institute,
The University of Chicago, 5734 S. Univ. Ave.,
Chicago, Illinois 60637

ABSTRACT

We outline a computational model of the development and regeneration of specific eye-brain circuits. The model comprises a self-organizing map-forming network which uses local Hebb rules, constrained by molecular markers. Various simulations of the development of eye-brain maps in fish and frogs are described.

1 INTRODUCTION

The brain is a biological computer of immense complexity comprising highly specialized neurons and neural circuits. Such neurons are interconnected with high *specificity* in many regions of the brain, if not in all. There are also many observations which indicate that there is also considerable circuit *plasticity*. Both specificity and plasticity are found in the development and regeneration of eye-brain connections in vertebrates. Sperry (1944) first demonstrated specificity in the regeneration of eye-brain connections in frogs following optic nerve section and eye rotation; and Gaze and Sharma (1970) and Yoon (1972) found evidence for plasticity in the expanded and compressed *maps* which regenerate following eye and brain lesions in goldfish. There are now many experiments which indicate that the formation of connections involves both specificity and plasticity.

1.1 EYE-BRAIN MAPS AND MODELS

Fig. 1 shows the retinal map found in the optic lobe or *tectum* of fish and frog. The map is topological, i.e.; neighborhood relationships in the retina are preserved in the optic tectum. How does such a map develop? Initially there is considerable disorder in the

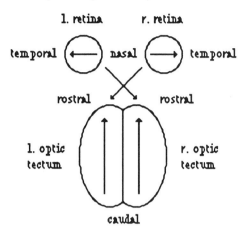

Figure 1: The normal retino-tectal map in fish and frog. Temporal retina projects to (contralateral) rostral tectum; nasal retina to (contralateral) caudal tectum.

pathway: retinal ganglion cells make contacts with many widely dispersed tectal neurons. However the mature pathway shows a high degree of topological order. How is such an organized map achieved? One answer was provided by Prestige & Willshaw (1975): retinal axons and tectal neurons are *polarized* by contact adhesion molecules distributed such that axons from one end of the retina are stickier than those from the other end, and neurons at one end of the tectum are (correspondingly) stickier than those at the other end. Of course this means that isolated retinal axons will all tend to stick to one end of the tectum. However if such axons *compete* with each other for tectal terminal sites (and if tectal sites compete for retinal axon terminals), less sticky axons will be displaced, and eventually a topological map will form. The Prestige-Willshaw theory explains many observations indicating neural specificity. It does not provide for plasticity: the ability of retino-tectal systems to adapt to changed target conditions, and vice-versa. Willshaw and von der Malsburg (1976, 1977) provided a theory for the plasticity of map reorganization, by postulating the synaptic growth in development is Hebbian. Such a mechanism provides self-organizing properties in retino-tectal map formation and reorganization. Whitelaw & Cowan (1981) combined both sticky molecules and Hebbian synaptic growth to provide a theory which explains both the specificity and plasticity of map formation and reorganization in a reasonable fashion.

There are many experiments, however, which indicate that such theories are too simple. Schmidt & Easter (1978) and Meyer (1982) have shown that retinal axons interact with each other in a way which influences map formation. It is our view that there are (probably) at least two different types of sticky molecules in the system: those described above which mediate retino-tectal interactions, and an additional class which mediates axo-axonal interactions in a different way. In what follows we describe a model which incorporates such interactions. Some aspects of our model are similar to those introduced by Willshaw & von der Malsburg (1979) and Fraser (1980). Our model can simulate almost all experiments in the literature, and provides a way to titrate the relative strenghts of intrinsic *polarity* markers mediating retino-tectal interactions, (postulated) *positional* markers mediating axo-axonal interactions, and stimulus-driven Hebbian synaptic changes.

2 MODELS OF MAP FORMATION AND REGENERATION

2.1. THE WHITELAW-COWAN MODEL

Let s_{ij} be the strength or weight of the synapse made by the ith retinal axon with the jth tectal cell. Then the following differential equation expresses the changes in s_{ij}:

$$\dot{s}_{ij} = c_{ij} (r_i - \alpha) t_j - \tfrac{1}{2} (N_r^{-1} \textstyle\sum_i + N_t^{-1} \sum_j)(c_{ij} (r_i - \alpha) t_j) \qquad (1)$$

where N_r is the number of retinal ganglion cells and N_t the number of tectal neurons, c_{ij} is the "stickiness" of the ijth contact, r_i denotes retinal activity and $t_j = \Sigma_i s_{ij} r_i$ is the corresponding tectal activity, and α is a constant measuring the rate of receptor destabilization (see Whitelaw & Cowan (1981) for details). In addition both retinal and tectal elements have fixed lateral inhibitory contacts. The dynamics described by eqn.1 is such that both $\Sigma_i s_{ij}$ and $\Sigma_j s_{ij}$ tend to constant values T and R respectively, where T is the total amount of tectal receptor material available per neuron, and R is the total amount of axonal material available per retinal ganglion cell: thus if sij increases anywhere in the net, other synapses made by the ith axon will decrease, as will other synapses on the jth tectal neuron. In the current terminology, this process is referred to as "winner-take-all".

For purposes of illustration consider the problem of connecting a line of N_r retinal ganglion cells to a line of N_t tectal cells. The resulting maps can then be represented by two-dimensional matrices, in which the area of the square at the ijth intersection represents the weight of the synapse between the ith retinal axon and the jth tectal cell. The normal retino-tectal map is represented by large squares along the matrix diagonal., (see Whitelaw & Cowan (1981) for terminology and further details). It is fairly obvious that the only solutions to eqn. (1) lie along the matrix diagonal, or the anti-diagonal, as shown in fig. 2. These solutions correspond, respectively, to normal and inverted topological maps. It follows that if the affinity c_{ij} of the ith retinal ganglion cell for the jth tectal neuron is constant, a map will form consisting of normal and inverted local patches. To obtain a globally normal map it is necessary to *bias* the system. One way to do this is to suppose that $c_{ij} = \xi a_i a_j$, where a_i and a_j are respectively, the concentrations

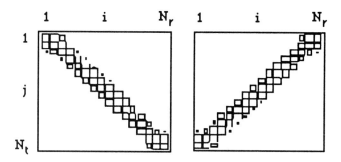

Figure 2: Diagonal and anti-diagonal solutions to eqn.1. Such solutions correspond, respectively, to normal and inverted maps.

of sticky molecules on the tips of retinal axons and on the surfaces of tectal neurons, and ξ is a constant. A good candidate for such a molecule is the recently discovered toponymic or TOP molecule found in chick retina and tectum (Trisler & Collins, 1987). If a_i and a_j are distributed in the *graded* fashion shown in fig. 3, then the system is biased in favor of the normally oriented map.

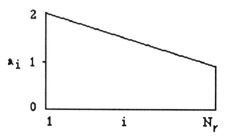

Figure 3: Postulated distribution of sticky molecules in the retina. A similar distribution is supposed to exist in the tectum.

2.2 INADEQUACIES

The Whitelaw-Cowan model simulates the normal development of monocular retinotectal maps, starting from either diffuse or scrambled initial maps, or from no map. In addition it simulates the compressed, expanded, translocated, mismatched and rotated maps which have been described in a variety of surgical contexts. However it fails in the following respects: a. Although tetrodotoxin (TTX) blocks the refinement of retinotopic maps in salamanders, a coarse map can still develop in the absence of retinal activity Harris (1980). The model will not simulate this effect. b. Although the model simulates the formation of double maps in "classical" compound eyes {made from a half-left and a half right eye} (Gaze, Jacobson, & Szekely, 1963), it fails to account for the reprogramming observed in "new" compound eyes {made by cutting a slit down the middle of a tadpole eye} (Hunt & Jacobson, 1974), and fails to simulate the forming of a

normal retinotopic map to a compound tectum {made from two posterior halves}
(Sharma, 1975).

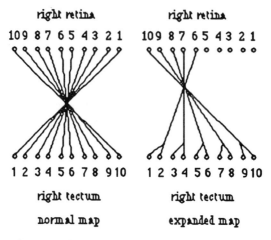

Figure 4: The normal and expanded maps which form after the prior
expansion of axons from a contralateral half-eye. The two maps are
actually superposed, but for ease of exposition are shown separately.

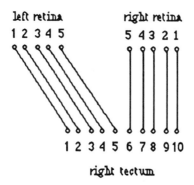

Figure 5: Results of Meyer's experiment. Fibers from the right half-
retina fail to contact their normal targets and instead make contact with
available targets, but with reversed polarity.

c. More significantly, it fails to account for the apparent retinal *induction* reported by
Schmidt, Cicerone & Easter (1978) in which following the expansion of retinal axons
from a goldfish half-eye over an entire (contralateral) tectum, and subsequent sectioning
of the axons, diverted retinal axons from the other (intact) eye are found to expand over
the tectum, as if they were also from a half-eye. This has been interpreted to imply that
the tectum has no intrinsic markers, and that all its markers come from the retina (Chung
& Cooke, 1978). However Schmidt et.al. also found that the diverted axons also map
normally. Fig. 4 shows the result. d. There is also an important mismatch experiment

carried out by Meyer (1979) which the model cannot simulate. In this experiment the left half of an eye and its attached retinal axons are surgically removed, leaving an intact normal half-eye map. At the same time the right half the other eye and its attached axons are removed, and the axons from the remaining half eye are allowed to innervate the tectum with the left-half eye map. The result is shown in fig. 5.   e. Finally, there are now a variety of chemical assays of the nature of the affinities which retinal axons have for each other, and for tectal target sites. Thus Bonhoffer and Huff (1980) found that growing retinal axons stick preferentially to rostral tectum. This is consistent with the model. However, using a different assay Halfter, Claviez & Schwarz (1981) also found that tectal fragments tend to stick preferentially to that part of the retina which corresponds to caudal tectum, i.e.; to *nasal* retina. This appears to contradict the model, and the first assay.

3 A NEW MODEL FOR MAP FORMATION

The Whitelaw-Cowan model can be modified and extended to replicate much of the data described above. The first modification is to replace eqn.1 by a more nonlinear equation. The reason for this is that the above equation has no threshold below which contacts cannot get established. In practice Whitelaw and I modified the equations to incorporate a small threshold effect. Another way is to make synaptic growth and decay exponential rather than linear. An equation expressing this can be easily formulated, which also incorporates *axo-axonal interactions*, presumed to be produced by neural contact adhesion molecules (nCAM) of the sort discovered by Edelman (1983) which seem to mediate the axo-axonal adhesion observed in tissue cultures by Boenhoffer & Huff (1985). The resulting equations take the form:

$$\dot{s}_{ij} = \lambda_j + c_{ij} [\mu_{ij} + (r_i - \alpha)t_j] s_{ij}$$
$$- \tfrac{1}{2} s_{ij} (T^{-1}\textstyle\sum_i + R^{-1}\textstyle\sum_j)\{\lambda_j + c_{ij} [\mu_{ij} + (r_i - \alpha)t_j] s_{ij}\} \qquad (2)$$

where λ_j represents a general nonspecific growth of retinotectal contacts, presumed to be controlled and modulated by nerve growth factor (Campenot, 1982). The main difference between eqns. 1 and 2 however, lies in the coefficients c_{ij}. In eqn. 1, $c_{ij} = \xi a_i a_j$. In eqn. 2, c_{ij} expresses several different effects: (a). Instead of just one molecular species on the tips of retinal axons and on corresponding tectal cell surfaces, as in eqn.1, two molecular species or two states of one species can be postulated to exist on these sites. In such a case the term $\xi a_i a_j$ is replaced by $\sum \xi_{ab} a_i b_j$ where a and b are the different species, and the sum is over all possible combinations aa, ab etc. A number of possibilities exist in the choice of ξ_{ab}. One possibility that is consistent with most of the biochemical assays described earlier is $\xi_{aa} = \xi_{bb} < \xi_{ab} = \xi_{ba}$ in which each species prefers the other, the so-called heterophilic case. (b) The mismatch experiment cited earlier (Meyer, 1979) indicates that existing axon projections tend to exclude other axons, especially inappropriate ones, from innervating occupied areas. One way to incorporate such geometric effects is to suppose that each axon which establishes contact with a tectal neuron *occludes* tectal markers there by a factor proportional to its synaptic weight s_{ij}. Thus we subtract from the coefficient c_{ij} a fraction proportional to $T^{-1}\sum'_k s_{kj}$ where $\sum_k$ means $\sum_{k \neq i}$. (c) The mismatch experiment also indicates that map formation depends in part on a tendency for axons to stick to their retinal neighbors, in addition to their tendency to stick to tectal cell surfaces. We therefore append to c_{ij} the term $\sum'_k \bar{s}_{kj} f_{ik}$ where $\bar{s}_{kj}$ is a local average of s_{kj} and its nearest tectal neighbors, and where f_{ik} measures the mutual stickiness of the ith and kth retinal axons: non-zero only for nearest *retinal* neighbors. {Again we suppose this stickiness is produced by the interaction of two molecular species etc.; specifically the neuronal CAMs discovered by Edelman, but we do not go into the details}. (d) With the introduction of occlusion effects and axo-axonal interactions, it becomes apparent that *debris* in the form of degenerating axon fragments adhering to tectal cells, following optic nerve sectioning, can also influence map formation. Incoming nerve axons can stick to debris, and debris can occlude markers. There are in fact four possibilities: debris can occlude tectal markers, markers on other debris, or on incoming axons; and incoming axons can occlude markers on debris. All these possibilities can be included in the dependence of c_{ij} on s_{ij}, s_{kj} etc.

The model which results from all these modifications and extensions is much more complex in its mathematical structure than any of the previous models. However computer simulation studies show it to be capable of correctly reproducing the observed details of almost all the experiments cited above. Fig. 6, for example shows a simulation of the retinal "induction" experiments of Schmidt *et.al.*

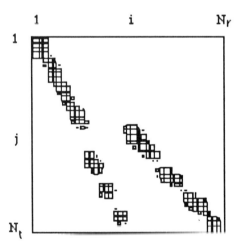

Figure 6: Simulation of the Schmidt *et.al.* retinal induction experiment. A nearly normal map is intercalated into an expanded map.

This simulation generated both a patchy expanded and a patchy nearly normal map. These effects occur because some incoming retinal axons stick to debris left over from the previous expanded map, and other axons stick to non-occluded tectal markers. The axo-axonal positional markers control the formation of the expanded map, whereas the retino-tectal polarity markers control the formation of the nearly normal map.

4 CONCLUSIONS

The model we have outlined combines Hebbian plasticity with intrinsic, genetic eye-brain and axo-axonic markers, to generate correctly oriented retinotopic maps. It permits the simulation of a large number of experiments, and provides a consistent explanation of almost all of them. In particular it shows how the apparent induction of central markers by peripheral effects, as seen in the Schmidt-Cicerone-Easter experiment (Schmidt *et.al.* 1978), can be produced by the effects of debris; and the polarity reversal seen in Meyer's experiment (Meyer 1979), can be produced by axo-axonal interactions.

Acknowledgements

We thank the System Development Foundation, Palo Alto, California, and The University of Chicago Brain Research Foundation for partial support of this work.

References

Boenhoffer, F. & Huf, J. (1980), Nature, **288**, 162-164.; (1985), Nature, **315**, 409-411.
Campenot, R.B. (1982), Develop. Biol., **93**, 1.
Chung, S.-H. & Cooke, J.E. (1978), Proc. Roy. Soc. Lond. B *201*, 335-373.
Edelman, G.M., (1983), Science, **219**, 450-454.
Fraser, S. (1980), Develop. Biol., **79**, 453-464.
Gaze, R.M. & Sharma, S.C. (1970), Exp. Brain Res., 10, 171-181.
Gaze, R.M., Jacobson, M. & Szekely, T. (1963), J. Physiol. (Lond.), **165**, 484-499.
Halfter, W., Claviez, M. & Schwarz, U. (1981), Nature, **292**, 67- 70.
Harris, W.A. (1980), J. Comp. Neurol., **194**, 303-323.
Hubel, D.H. & Wiesel, T.N. (1974), J. Comp. Neurol. **158**, 295-306.
Hunt, R.K. & Jacobson. M. (1974), Devel. Biol. **40**, 1-15.
Malsburg, Ch.v.d. & Willshaw, D.J. (1977), PNAS, **74**, 5176-5178.
Meyer, R.L. (1979), Science, **205**, 819-821; (1982), Curr. Top. Develop. Biol., **17**, 101-145.
Prestige, M. & Willshaw, D.J. (1975), Proc. Roy. Soc. **B**, 190, 77-98.
Schmidt, J.T. & Easter, S.S. (1978), Exp. Brain Res., **31**, 155-162.
Schmidt, J.T., Cicerone, C.M. & Easter, S.S. (1978), J. Comp. Neurol., **177**, 257-288.
Sharma, S.C. (1975), Brain Res., **93**, 497-501.
Sperry, R.W. (1944), J. Neurophysiol., **7**, 57-69.
Trisler, D. & Collins, F. (1987), Science, **237**, 1208-1210.
Whitelaw, V.A. & Cowan, J.D. (1981), J. Neurosci., **1**, *12*, 1369-1387.
Willshaw, D.J. & Malsburg, Ch.v.d. (1976), Proc. Roy. Soc. **B**, 194, 431-445; (1979), Phil. Trans. Roy. Soc. (Lond.), **B**, *287*, 203-254.
Yoon, M. (1972), Amer. Zool., **12**, 106.

The Effect of Catecholamines on Performance: From Unit to System Behavior

David Servan-Schreiber, Harry Printz and Jonathan D. Cohen
School of Computer Science and Department of Psychology
Carnegie Mellon University
Pittsburgh, PA 15213

ABSTRACT

At the level of individual neurons, catecholamine release increases the responsivity of cells to excitatory and inhibitory inputs. We present a model of catecholamine effects in a network of neural-like elements. We argue that changes in the responsivity of individual elements do not affect their ability to detect a signal and ignore noise. However, the same changes in cell responsivity in a *network* of such elements do improve the signal detection performance of the network as a whole. We show how this result can be used in a computer simulation of behavior to account for the effect of *CNS* stimulants on the signal detection performance of human subjects.

1   Introduction

The catecholamines—norepinephrine and dopamine—are neuroactive substances that are presumed to modulate information processing in the brain, rather than to convey discrete sensory or motor signals. Release of norepinephrine and dopamine occurs over wide areas of the central nervous system, and their post-synaptic effects are long lasting. These effects consist primarily of an enhancement of the response of target cells to other afferent inputs, inhibitory as well as excitatory (see [4] for a review).

Increases or decreases in catecholaminergic tone have many behavioral consequences including effects on motivated behaviors, attention, learning and memory, and motor behavior. At the information processing level, catecholamines appear to affect the ability to detect a signal when it is imbedded in noise (see review in [3]).

In terms of signal detection theory, this is described as a change in the *performance* of the system. However, there is no adequate account of how these changes at the system level relate to the effect of catecholamines on individual cells. Several investigators [5,12,2] have suggested that catecholamine-mediated increases in a cell's responsivity can be interpreted as a change in the cell's signal-to-noise ratio. By analogy, they proposed that this change at the unit level may account for changes in signal detection performance at the behavioral level.

In the first part of this paper we analyze the relation between unit responsivity, signal-to-noise ratio and signal detection performance in a network of neural elements. We start by showing that the changes in unit responsivity induced by catecholamines do *not* result in changes in signal detection performance of a single unit. We then explain how, in spite of this fact, the aggregate effect of such changes in a *chain* of units can lead to improvements in the signal detection performance of the entire network.

In the second part, we show how changes in gain – which lead to an increase in the signal detection performance of the network – can account for a behavioral phenomenon. We describe a computer simulation of a network performing a signal detection task that has been applied extensively to behavioral research: the continuous performance test. In this simulation, increasing the responsivity of individual units leads to improvements in performance that closely approximate the improvement observed in human subjects under conditions of increased catecholaminergic tone.

2   Effect of Gain on a Single Element

We assume that the response of a typical neuron can be described by a strictly increasing function $f_G(x)$ from real-valued inputs to the interval $(0, 1)$. This function relates the strength of a neuron's net afferent input x to its probability of firing, or *activation*. We do not require that f_G is either continuous or differentiable.

For instance, the family of logistics, given by

$$f_G(x) = \frac{1}{1 + e^{-(Gx+B)}}$$

has been proposed as a model of neural activation functions [7,1]. These functions are all strictly increasing, for each value of the *gain* $G > 0$, and all values of the *bias B*.

The potentiating effect of catecholamines on responsivity can be modelled as a change in the shape of its activation function. In the case of the logistic, this is achieved by increasing the value of G, as illustrated in Figure 1. However, our analysis applies to *any* suitable family of functions, $\{f_G\}$. We require only that each member function f_G is strictly increasing, and that as $G \to \infty$, the family $\{f_G\}$ converges monotonically to

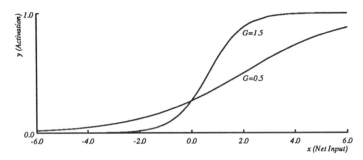

Figure 1: Logistic Activation Function, Used to Model the Response Function of Neurons. Positive net inputs correspond to excitatory stimuli, negative net inputs correspond to inhibitory stimuli. For the graphs drawn here, we set the bias B to -1. The asymmetry arising from a negative bias is often found in the response function of actual neurons [6].

the unit step function u_0 almost everywhere.[1] Here, u_0 is defined as

$$u_0(x) = \begin{cases} 0 & \text{for} \quad x \leq 0 \\ 1 & \text{for} \quad x > 0 \end{cases}$$

This means that as G increases, the value $f_G(x)$ gets steadily closer to 1 if $x > 0$, and steadily closer to 0 if $x \leq 0$.

2.1   Gain Does Not Affect Signal Detection Performance

Consider the signal detection performance of a network in which the response of a single unit is compared with a threshold to determine the presence or absence of a signal. We assume that in the presence of the signal, this unit receives a positive (excitatory) net afferent input x_S, and in the absence of the signal it receives a null or negative (inhibitory) input x_A. When zero-mean noise is added to this quantity, in the presence as well as the absence of the signal, the unit's net input in each case is distributed around x_S or x_A respectively. Therefore its response is distributed around $f_G(x_S)$ or $f_G(x_A)$ respectively (see Figure 2).

In other words, the input in the case where the signal is present is a random variable X_S, with probability density function (pdf) ρ_{X_S} and mean x_S, and in the absence of the signal it is the random variable X_A, with pdf ρ_{X_A} and mean x_A. These then determine the random variables $Y_{GS} = f_G(X_S)$ and $Y_{GA} = f_G(X_A)$, with pdfs $\rho_{Y_{GS}}$ and $\rho_{Y_{GA}}$, which represent the *response* in the presence or absence of the signal for a given value of the gain. Figure 2 shows examples of $\rho_{Y_{GS}}$ and $\rho_{Y_{GA}}$ for two different values of G, in the case where f_G is the biased logistic.

If the input pdfs ρ_{X_S} and ρ_{X_A} overlap, the output pdfs $\rho_{Y_{GS}}$ and $\rho_{Y_{GA}}$ will also overlap. Thus for any given threshold θ on the y-axis used to categorize the output as "signal present" or "signal absent," there will be some misses and some false alarms. The best

---

[1] A sequence of functions $\{g_n\}$ converges almost everywhere to the function g if the set of points where it diverges, or converges to the wrong value, is of measure zero.

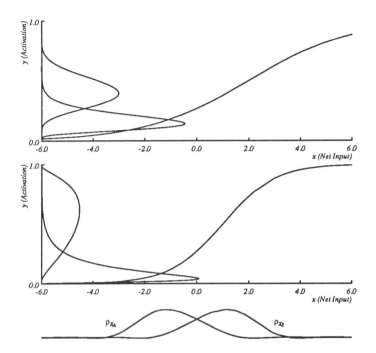

Figure 2: Input and Output Probability Density Functions. The curves at the bottom are the pdfs of the net input in the signal absent (left) and signal present (right) cases. The curves along the y-axis are the response pdfs for each case; they are functions of the activation y, and represent the distribution of outputs. The top graph shows the logistic and response pdfs for $G = 0.5$, $B = -1$; the bottom graph shows them for $G = 1.0$, $B = -1$.

the system can do is to select a threshold that optimizes performance. More precisely, the expected payoff or *performance* of the unit is given by

$$E(\theta) = \lambda + \alpha \cdot \Pr(Y_{GS} \geq \theta) - \beta \cdot \Pr(Y_{GA} \geq \theta)$$

where λ, α, and β are constants that together reflect the prior probability of the signal, and the payoffs associated with correct detections or *hits*, correct *ignores*, *false alarms* and *misses*. Note that $\Pr(Y_{GS} \geq \theta)$ and $\Pr(Y_{GA} \geq \theta)$ are the probabilities of a hit and a false alarm, respectively.

By solving the equation $dE/d\theta = 0$ we can determine the value $\theta^\star$ that maximizes E. We call $\theta^\star$ the *optimal threshold*. Our first result is that for *any* activation function f that satisfies our assumptions, and *any* fixed input pdfs ρ_{X_S} and ρ_{X_A} the unit's performance at optimal threshold is the same. We call this the Constant Optimal Performance Theorem, which is stated and proved in [10]. In particular, for the logistic, increasing the gain G does *not* induce better performance. It may change the value of the threshold that yields optimal performance, but it does not change the actual performance at optimum. This is because a strictly increasing activation function produces a point-to-point mapping between the distributions of input and output values. Since the amount of overlap between the two input pdfs ρ_{X_S} and ρ_{X_A} does not change as the gain varies, the amount of overlap in the response pdfs does not change either, even though the shape of the response pdfs does change when gain increases (see Figure 2). [2]

3   Effect of Gain on a Chain of Elements

Although increasing the gain does not affect the signal detection performance of a single element, it does improve the performance of a *chain* of such elements. By a chain, we mean an arrangement in which the output of the first unit provides the input to another unit (see Figure 3). Let us call this second element the response unit. We monitor the output of this second unit to determine the presence or absence of a signal.

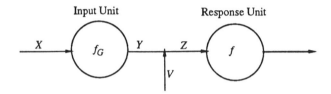

Figure 3: A Chain of Units. The output of the unit receiving the signal is combined with noise to provide input to a second unit, called the *response unit*. The activation of the response unit is compared to a threshold to determine the presence or absence of the signal.

As in the previous discussion, noise is added to the net input to *each* unit in the chain in the presence as well as in the absence of a signal. We represent noise as a random variable V, with pdf ρ_V that we assume to be independent of gain. As in the single-unit case, the input to the first unit is a random variable X_S, with pdf ρ_{X_S} in the presence of the signal and a random variable X_A, with pdf ρ_{X_A} in the absence of the signal. The output of the first unit is described by the random variables Y_{GS} and Y_{GA} with pdfs $\rho_{Y_{GS}}$ and $\rho_{Y_{GA}}$. Now, because noise is added to the net input of the response unit as well, the input of the response unit is the random variable $Z_{GS} = Y_{GS} + V$ or $Z_{GA} = Y_{GA} + V$, again depending on whether the signal is present or absent. We write $\rho_{Z_{GS}}$ and $\rho_{Z_{GA}}$ for the pdfs of these random variables. $\rho_{Z_{GS}}$ is the convolution of $\rho_{Y_{GS}}$ and ρ_V, and $\rho_{Z_{GA}}$ is the convolution of $\rho_{Y_{GA}}$ and ρ_V. The effect of convolving the output pdfs of the input unit with the noise distribution is to increase the overlap between the resulting distributions ($\rho_{Z_{GS}}$ and $\rho_{Z_{GA}}$), and therefore decrease the discriminability of the input to the response unit.

How are these distributions affected by an increase in gain on the input unit? By the Constant Optimal Performance Theorem, we already know that the overlap between $\rho_{Y_{GS}}$ and $\rho_{Y_{GA}}$ remains constant as gain increases. Furthermore, as stated above, we have assumed that the noise distribution is independent of gain. It would therefore seem that a change in gain should not affect the overlap between $\rho_{Z_{GS}}$ and $\rho_{Z_{GA}}$. However, it is

---

[2]We present the intuitions underlying our results in terms of the overlap between the pdfs. However, the proofs themselves are analytical.

possible to show that, under very general conditions, the overlap between $\rho_{Z_{GS}}$ and $\rho_{Z_{GA}}$ *decreases* when the gain of the input unit increases, thereby improving performance of the two-layered system. We call this the chain effect; the Chain Performance Theorem [10] gives sufficient conditions for its appearance. [3]

Paradoxically, the chain effect arises because the noise added to the net input of the response unit is not affected by variations in the gain. As we mentioned before, increasing the gain separates the means of the output pdfs of the input unit, $\mu(Y_{GS})$ and $\mu(Y_{GA})$ (eventhough this does not affect the performance of the first unit). Suppose all the probability mass were concentrated at these means. Then $\rho_{Z_{GS}}$ would be a copy of ρ_V centered at $\mu(Y_{GS})$, and $\rho_{Z_{GA}}$ would be a copy of ρ_V centered at $\mu(Y_{GS})$. Thus in this case, increasing the gain *does* correspond to rigidly translating $\rho_{Z_{GS}}$ and $\rho_{Z_{GA}}$ apart, thereby reducing their overlap and improving performance.

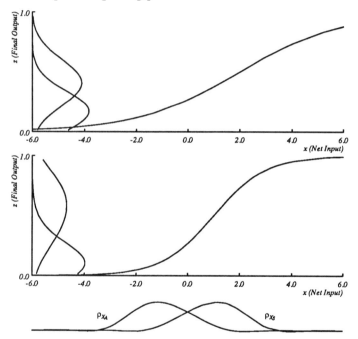

Figure 4: Dependence of Chain Output Pdfs Upon Gain. These graphs use the same conventions and input pdfs as Figure 2. They depict the output pdfs, in the presence of additive Gaussian noise, for $G = 0.5$ (top) and $G = 1.0$ (bottom).

A similar effect arises in more general circumstances, when $\rho_{Y_{GS}}$ and $\rho_{Y_{GA}}$ are not concentrated at their means. Figure 4 provides an example, illustrating $\rho_{Z_{GS}}$ and $\rho_{Z_{GA}}$ for three different values of the gain. The first unit outputs are the same as in Figure 2, but

---

[3]In this discussion, we have assumed that the same noise was added to the net input into each unit of a chain. However, the improvement in performance of a chain of units with increasing gain does not depend on this particular assumption.

these have been convolved with the pdf ρ_V of a Gaussian random variable to obtain the curves shown. Careful inspection of the figure will reveal that the overlap between $\rho_{Z_{GS}}$ and $\rho_{Z_{GA}}$ decreases as the gain rises.

4   Simulation of the Continuous Performance Test

The above analysis has shown that increasing the gain of the response function of individual units in a very simple network can improve signal detection performance. We now present computer simulation results showing that this phenomenon may account for improvements of performance with catecholamine agonists in a common behavioral test of signal detection.

The continous performance test (CPT) has been used extensively to study attention and vigilance in behavioral and clinical research. Performance on this task has been shown to be sensitive to drugs or pathological conditions affecting catecholamine systems [11,8,9]. In this task, individual letters are displayed tachystoscopically in a sequence on a computer monitor. In one common version of the task, a target event is to be reported when two consecutive letters are identical. During baseline performance, subjects typically fail to report 10 to 20% of targets ("misses") and inappropriately report a target during 0.5 to 1% of the remaining events ("false alarms"). Following the administration of agents that directly release catecholamines from synaptic terminals and block re-uptake from the synaptic cleft (i.e., CNS stimulants such as amphetamines or methylphenidate) the number of misses decreases, while the number of false alarms remains approximately the same. Using standard signal detection theory measures, investigators have claimed that this pattern of results reflects an improvement in the discrimination between signal and non-signal events (d'), while the response criterion (β) does not vary significantly [11,8,9].

We used the backpropagation learning algorithm to train a recurrent three layer network to perform the CPT (see Figure 5). In this model, several simplifyng assumptions made in the preceding section are removed: in contrast to the simple two-unit assembly, the network contains three layers of units (input layer, intermediate – or hidden – layer, and output layer) with some recurrent connections; connection weights between these layers are developed entirely by the training procedure; as a result, the activation patterns on the intermediate layer that are evoked by the presence or absence of a signal are also determined solely by the training procedure; finally, the representation of the signal is distributed over an ensemble of units rather than determined by a single unit.

Following training, Gaussian noise with zero mean was added to the net input of each unit in the intermediate and output layers as each letter was presented. The overall standard deviation of the noise distribution and the threshold of the response unit were adjusted to produce a performance equivalent to that of subjects under baseline conditions (13.0% misses and 0.75% false alarms). We then increased the gain of all the intermediate and output units from 1.0 to 1.1 to simulate the effect of catecholamine release in the network. This manipulation resulted in rates of 6.6% misses and 0.78% false alarms. The correspondence between the network's behavior and empirical data is illustrated in Figure 5.

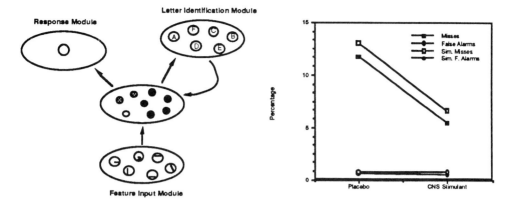

Figure 5: Simulation of the Continuous Performance Task. **Left panel:** The recurrent three-layer network (12 input units, 30 intermediate units, 10 output units and 1 response unit). Each unit projects to all units in the subsequent layer. In addition, each output unit also projects to each unit in the intermediate layer. The gain parameter G is the same for all intermediate and output units. In the simulation of the placebo condition, $G = 1$; in the simulation of the drug condition, $G = 1.1$. The bias $B = -1$ in both conditions. **Right panel:** Performance of human subjects [9], and of the simulation, on the CPT. With methylphenidate misses dropped from 11.7% to 5.5%, false alarms decreased from 0.6% to 0.5% (non-significant).

The enhancement of signal detection performance in the simulation is a robust effect. It appears when gain is increased in the intermediate layer only, in the output layer only, or in both layers. Because of the recurrent connections between the output layer and the intermediate layer, a chain effect occurs between these two layers when the gain is increased over any one of them, or both of them. The impact of the chain effect is to reduce the distortion, due to internal noise, of the distributed representation on the layer receiving inputs from the layer where gain is increased. Note also that the improvement takes place even though there is no noise added to the input of the response unit. The response unit in this network acts only as an indicator of the strength of the signal in the intermediate layer. Finally, as the Constant Optimal Performance Theorem predicts, increasing the gain only on the response unit does not affect the performance of the network.

5   Conclusion

Fluctuations in catecholaminergic tone accompany psychological states such as arousal, motivation and stress. Furthermore, dysfunctions of catecholamine systems are implicated in several of the major psychiatric disorders. However, in the absence of models relating changes in cell function to changes in system performance, the relation of catecholamines to behavior has remained obscure. The findings reported in this paper suggest that the behavioral impact of catecholamines depend on their effects on an ensemble of units operating in the presence of noise, and not just on changes in individual unit responses.

Furthermore, they indicate how neuromodulatory effects can be incorporated in parallel distributed processing models of behavior.

References

[1] Y. Burnod and H. Korn. Consequences of stochastic release of neurotransmitters for network computation in the central nervous system. *Proceedings of the National Academy of Science*, 86:352–356, 1988.

[2] L. A. Chiodo and T. W. Berger. Interactions between dopamine and amino acid-induced excitation and inhibition in the striatum. *Brain Research*, 375:198–203, 1986.

[3] C. R. Clark, G. M. Geffen, and L. B. Geffen. Catecholamines and attention ii: pharmacological studies in normal humans. *Neuroscience and Behavioral Reviews*, 11:353–364, 1987.

[4] S. L. Foote. Extrathalamic modulation of cortical function. *Ann. Rev. Neurosci.*, 10:67–95, 1987.

[5] S. L. Foote, R. Freedman, and A. P. Olivier. Effects of putative neurotransmitters on neuronal activity in monkey auditory cortex. *Brain Research*, 86:229–242, 1975.

[6] W. J. Freeman. Nonlinear gain mediating cortical stimulus-response relations. *Biological Cybernetics*, 33:243–247, 1979.

[7] G. E Hinton and Sejnowski T. J. Analyzing cooperative computation. *Proceedings of the Cognitive Science Society*, 1983.

[8] R. Klorman, L. O. Bauer, H. W. Coons, J. L. Lewis, L. J. Peloquin, R. A. Perlmutter, R. M. Ryan, L. F. Salzman, and J. Strauss. Enhancing effects of methylphenidate on normal young adults cognitive processes. *Psychopharmacology Bulletin*, 20:3–9, 1984.

[9] L. J. Peloquin and R. Klorman. Effects of methylphenidate on normal children's mood, event-related potentials, and performance in memory scanning and vigilance. *Journal of Abnormal Psychology*, 95:88–98, 1986.

[10] H. Printz and D. Servan-Schreiber. *Foundations of a Computational Theory of Catecholamine Effects*. Technical Report CMU-CS-90-105, Carnegie Mellon, School of Computer Science, 1990.

[11] J. Rapoport, M. S. Buchsbaum, H. Weingartner, T. P. Zahn, C. Ludlow, J. Bartko, E. J. Mikkelsen, D. H. Langer, and Bunney W. E. Dextroamphetamine: cognitive and behavioral effects in normal and hyperactive boys and normal adult males. *Archives of General Psychiatry*, 37:933–943, 1980.

[12] M. Segal. Mechanisms of action of noradrenaline in the brain. *Physiological Psychology*, 13:172–178, 1985.

Non-Boltzmann Dynamics in Networks of Spiking Neurons

Michael C. Crair and William Bialek
Department of Physics, and
Department of Molecular and Cell Biology
University of California at Berkeley
Berkeley, CA 94720

ABSTRACT

We study networks of spiking neurons in which spikes are fired as
a Poisson process. The state of a cell is determined by the instantaneous firing rate, and in the limit of high firing rates our model
reduces to that studied by Hopfield. We find that the inclusion
of spiking results in several new features, such as a noise-induced
asymmetry between "on" and "off" states of the cells and probability currents which destroy the usual description of network dynamics in terms of energy surfaces. Taking account of spikes also allows us to calibrate network parameters such as "synaptic weights"
against experiments on real synapses. Realistic forms of the post
synaptic response alters the network dynamics, which suggests a
novel dynamical learning mechanism.

1   INTRODUCTION

In 1943 McCulloch and Pitts introduced the concept of two-state (binary) neurons
as elementary building blocks for neural computation. They showed that essentially
any finite calculation can be done using these simple devices. Two-state neurons are
of questionable biological relevance, yet much of the subsequent work on modeling of
neural networks has been based on McCulloch-Pitts type neurons because the two-
state simplification makes analytic theories more tractable. Hopfield (1982, 1984)

showed that an asynchronous model of symmetrically connected two-state neurons was equivalent to Monte-Carlo dynamics on an 'energy' surface at zero temperature. The idea that the computational abilities of a neural network can be understood from the structure of an effective energy surface has been the central theme in much recent work.

In an effort to understand the effects of noise, Amit, Gutfreund and Sompolinsky (Amit et al., 1985a; 1985b) assumed that Hopfield's 'energy' could be elevated to an energy in the statistical mechanics sense, and solved the Hopfield model at finite temperature. The problem is that the noise introduced in equilibrium statistical mechanics is of a very special form, and it is not clear that the stochastic properties of real neurons are captured by postulating a Boltzmann distribution on the energy surface.

Here we try to do a slightly more realistic calculation, describing interactions among neurons through action potentials which are fired according to probabilistic rules. We view such calculations as intermediate between the purely phenomenological treatment of neural noise by Amit et al. and a fully microscopic description of neural dynamics in terms of ion channels and their associated noise. We find that even our limited attempt at biological realism results in some interesting deviations from previous ideas on network dynamics.

2 THE MODEL

We consider a model where neurons have a continuous firing rate, but the generation of action potentials is a Poisson process. This means that the "state" of each cell i is described by the instantaneous rate $r_i(t)$, and the probability that this cell will fire in a time interval $[t, t + dt]$ is given by $r_i(t)dt$. Evidence for the near-Poisson character of neuronal firing can be found in the mammalian auditory nerve (Siebert, 1965; 1968), and retinal ganglion cells (Teich et al., 1978, Teich and Saleh, 1981). To stay as close as possible to existing models, we assume that the rate $r(t)$ of a neuron is a sigmoid function, $g(x) = 1/(1 + e^{-x})$, of the total input x to the neuron.

The input is assumed to be a weighted sum of the spikes received from all other neurons, so that

$$ r_i(t) = r_m g \left[\sum_\mu \sum_j J_{ij} f(t - t_j^\mu) - \Theta_i \right]. \qquad (1) $$

J_{ij} is the matrix of connection strengths between neurons, r_m is the maximum spike rate of the neuron, and Θ_i is the neuronal threshold. $f(t)$ is a time weighting function, corresponding schematically to the time course of post-synaptic currents injected by a pre-synaptic spike; a good first order approximation for this function is $f(t) \sim e^{-t/\tau}$, but we also consider functions with more than one time constant. (Aidley, 1980, Fetz and Gustafsson, 1983).

We can think of the spike train from the ith neuron, $\sum_\mu \delta(t - t_i^\mu)$, as an approximation to the true firing rate $r_i(t)$; of course this approximation improves as the spikes come closer together at high firing rates. If we write

$$\sum_{\mu} \delta(t - t_i^{\mu}) = r_i(t) + \eta_i(t) \tag{2}$$

we have defined the noise η_i in the spike train. The equations of motion for the rates then become

$$r_i(t) = r_m g \left[\sum_{j} J_{ij} f \circ r_j(t) - \Theta_i + N_i(t) \right], \tag{3}$$

where $N_i(t) = \sum_{j} J_{ij} \eta_j(t)$ and $f \circ r_j(t)$ is the convolution of $f(t)$ with the spike rate $r_j(t)$. The statistics of the fluctuations in the spike rate $\eta_j(t)$ are $\langle \eta_j(t) \rangle = 0$, $\langle \eta_i(t) \eta_j(t') \rangle = \delta_{ij}(t - t') r_j(t)$.

3 DYNAMICS

If the post-synaptic response $f(t)$ is exactly exponential, we can invert Eq. (3) to obtain a first order equation for the normalized spike rate $y_i(t) \equiv r_i(t)/r_m$. More precise descriptions of the post-synaptic response will yield higher order time derivatives with coefficients that depend on the relative time constants in $f(t)$. We will comment later on the relevance of these higher order terms, but consider first the lowest order description. By inverting Eq. (3) we obtain a stochastic differential equation analogous to the Langevin equation describing Brownian motion:

$$\frac{dg^{-1}(y_i)}{dt} = -\frac{dE}{dy_i} + N_i(t), \tag{4a}$$

where the deterministic forces are given by

$$\frac{dE}{dy_i} = \frac{g^{-1}(y_i)}{\tau} - r_m \sum_{j} J_{ij}(y_j - 1/2). \tag{4b}$$

Note that Eq. (4) is nearly equivalent to the "charging equation" Hopfield (1984) assumed in his discussion of continuous neurons, except we have explicitly included the noise from the spikes. This system is precisely equivalent to the Hopfield two-state model in the limit of large spike rate ($r_m \tau \Rightarrow \infty, J_{ij} = $ constant), and no noise. In a thermodynamic system near equilibrium, the noise "force" $N_i(t)$ is related to the friction coefficient via the fluctuation dissipation theorem. In this system however, there is no analogous relationship.

A standard transformation, analogous to deriving Einstein's diffusion equation from the Langevin equation (Stratonovich, 1963, 1967), yields a probabilistic description for the evolution of the neural system, a form of Fokker-Planck equation for the time evolution of $P(\{y_i\})$, the probability that the network is in a state described by the normalized rates $\{y_i\}$; we write the Fokker-Planck equation below for a simple case.

A useful interpretation to consider is that the system, starting in a non-equilibrium state, diffuses or evolves in phase space, to a final stationary state.

We can make our description of the post-synaptic response $f(t)$ more accurate by including two (or more) exponential time constants, corresponding roughly to the rise and fall time of the post synaptic potential. This inclusion necessitates the addition of a second order term in the Langevin equation (Eq. 4). This is analogous to including an inertial term in a diffusive description, so that the system is no longer purely dissipative. This additional complication has some interesting consequences. Adjusting the relative length of the rise to fall time of the post synaptic potential effects the rate of relaxation to local equilibrium of the system. In order to perform most efficaciously as an associative memory, a neural system will "choose" critical damping time constants, so that relaxation is fastest. Thus, by adjusting the time course of the post synaptic potential, the system can "learn" of a local stationary state, without adjusting the synaptic strengths. This novel learning mechanism could be a form of fine tuning of already established memories, or could be a unique form of dynamical short-term memory.

4   QUALITATIVE RESULTS

In order to understand the dynamics of our Fokker-Planck equation, we begin by considering the case of two neurons interacting with each other. There are two limiting behaviors. If the neurons are weakly coupled ($J < J_c$, $J_c = 4/r_m \tau$), then the only stable state of the system is with both neurons firing at a mean firing rate, $\frac{1}{2} r_m$. If the neurons are strongly (and positively) coupled ($J > J_c$), then isolated basins of attraction, or stationary states are formed, one stationary state corresponding to both neurons being active, the other state has both neurons relatively (but not absolutely) quiescent. In the strong coupling limit, one can reduce the problem to motion along the a collective coordinate connecting the two stable states. The resulting one dimensional Fokker-Planck equation is

$$\frac{\partial}{\partial t} P(y, t) = \frac{\partial}{\partial y} \left[U'(y) P(y, t) + \frac{\partial}{\partial y} T(y) P(y, t) \right],$$

(5)

where $U(y)$ is an effective potential energy,

$$U'(y) = y(1 - y)[\frac{g^{-1}(y)}{\tau} - \frac{1}{2} r_m J(y - \frac{1}{2}) + \frac{1}{4} J^2 r_m y(3 - 5y)],$$

(6)

and $T(y)$ is a spatially varying effective temperature, $T(y) = \frac{1}{6} J^2 r_m y^3 (1 - y)^2$. One can solve to find the size of the stable regions, and the stationary probability distribution,

$$P^s(y) = \frac{B}{T(y)} \exp \left[- \int_{\frac{1}{2}}^{y} \frac{U'(y)}{T(y)} dy \right].$$

(7)

We have done numerical simulations which confirm the qualitative predictions of the one dimensional Fokker-Planck equation. This analysis shows that the non-uniform and asymmetric temperature distribution alters the relative stability of the stable states, in the favor of the 'off' state. This effect does have some biological pertinence, as it is well known that on average neurons are more likely to be quiescent then active. In our model the asymmetry is a direct consequence of the Poisson nature of the neuronal firing.

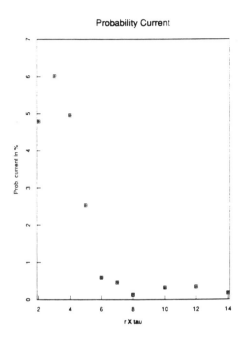

Figure 1: Probability current in the stationary state for two neurons that are strongly interacting. Computed as a ratio of the number of excess excursions in one direction to the total number of excursions, in percent. In thermodynamic equillibrium, detailed balance would force the current to be zero. Shown as a function of the number of spikes in an e-folding time of the post-synaptic response.

There are further surprises to be found in the simple two neuron model. Since the interaction between the neurons is not time reversal invariant, detailed balance is not maintained in the system. Thus, even the stationary probability distribution has non-zero probability current, so that the system tends to cycle probabilistically through state space. The presence of the current further alters the relative probability of the two stable states, as confirmed by numerical simulations, and renders the application of equilibrium statistical mechanics inappropriate.

Simulations also confirm (Fig. 1) that the probability current falls off with increasing maximum spike rate ($r_m \tau$), because the effective noise is suppressed when the spike rate is high. However, at biologically reasonable spike rates ($r_m \sim 150\,\mathrm{s}^{-1}$), the probability current is significant. These currents destroy any sense of a global energy function or thermodynamic temperature.

One advantage of treating spikes explicitly is that we can relate the abstract synaptic strength J to observable parameters. In Fig. 2 we compare J with the experimentally accessible spike number to spike number transfer across the synapse, for a two neuron system. Note that critical coupling (see above) corresponds to a rather large value of $\sim 4/5^{th}$ of a spike emitted per spike received.

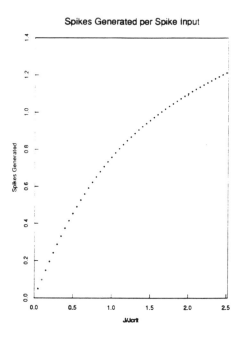

Spikes Generated per Spike Input

Figure 2: Single neuron spike response to the receipt of a spike from a coupled neuron. Since response is probabilistic, fractional spikes are relevant. Computed as a function of $J/J_{critical}$, where $J_{critical}$ is the minimum synaptic strength necessary for isolated basins of attraction.

Many of the simple ideas we have introduced for the two neuron system carry over to the multi-neuron case. If the matrix of connection strengths obeys the "Hebb" rule (often used to model associative memory),

$$J_{ij} = \frac{1}{N}J \sum_{\mu} \xi_i^{\mu} \xi_j^{\mu}, \qquad (8)$$

then a stability analysis yields the same critical value for the connection strength J (note that we have scaled by N, and the sum on μ runs from 1 to p, the number of memories to be stored). Calculation of the spike-out/spike-in ratio for the multi-neuron system at critical coupling shows that it scales like $(\alpha/N)^{\frac{1}{2}}$, where $p = \alpha N$.

Since most neural systems naturally have a small spike-out/spike-in ratio, this (together with Fig. 2) suggests that small networks will have to be strongly driven in order to achieve isolated basins of attraction for "memories;" this is in agreement with the one available experiment (Kleinfeld et al., 1990). In contrast, large networks achieve criticality with more natural spike to spike ratios. For instance, if a network of $10^4 - 10^5$ connected neurons is to have multiple stable "memory" states as in the original Hopfield model, we predict that a neuron needs to receive 100-500 contiguous action potentials to stimulate the emission of its own spike. This prediction agrees with experiments done on the hippocampus (McNaughton et al., 1981), where about 400 convergent inputs are needed to discharge a granule cell.

5   CONCLUSIONS

To conclude, we will just summarize our major points:

- Spike noise generated by the Poisson firing of neurons breaks the symmetry between on/off states, in favor of the "off" state.

- State dependent spike noise also destroys any sense of a global energy function, let alone a thermodynamic 'temperature'. This makes us suspicious of attempts to apply standard techniques of statistical mechanics.

- By explicitly modeling the interaction of neurons via spikes, we have direct access to experiments which can guide, and be guided by our theory. Specifically, our theory predicts that for a given connection strength between neurons, larger networks of neurons will function as memories at naturally small spike-input to spike-output ratios.

- More realistic forms of post synaptic response to the receipt of action potentials alters the network dynamics. By adjusting the relative rise and fall time of the post-synaptic potential, the network speeds the relaxation to the local stable state. This implies that more efficacious memories, or "learning", can result without altering the strength of the synaptic weights.

Finally, we comment on the dynamics of networks in the $N \rightarrow \infty$ limit. We might imagine that some of the complexities we find in the two-neuron case would go away, in particular the probability currents. We have been able to prove that this does not happen in any rigorous sense for realistic forms of spike noise, although in practice the currents may become small. The function of the network as a memory (for example) would then depend on a clean separation of time scales between relaxation into a single basin of attraction and noise-driven transitions to neighboring basins. Arranging for this separation of time scales requires some constraints on synaptic connectivity and firing rates which might be testable in experiments on real circuits.

References

D. J. Aidley (1980), *Physiology of Excitable Cells, 2nd Edition*, Cambridge University Press, Cambridge.

D. J. Amit, H. Gutfreund and H. Sompolinsky (1985a), *Phys. Rev. A*, **2**, 1007-1018.

D. J. Amit, H. Gutfreund and H. Sompolinsky (1985b), *Phys. Rev. Lett.*, **55**, 1530-1533.

E. E. Fetz and B. Gustafsson (1983), *J. Physiol.*, **341**, 387.

J. J. Hopfield (1982), *Proc. Nat. Acad. Sci. USA*, **79**, 2554-2558.

J. J. Hopfield (1984), *Proc. Nat. Acad. Sci. USA*, **81**, 3088-3092.

D. Kleinfeld, F. Raccuia-Behling, and H. J. Chiel (1990), *Biophysical Journal*, in press.

W. S. McCulloch and W. Pitts (1943), *Bull. of Math. Biophys.*, **5**, 115-133.

B. L. McNaughton, C. A. Barnes and P. Anderson (1981), *J. Neurophysiol.* **46**, 952-966.

W. M. Siebert (1965), *Kybernetik*, **2**, 206.

W. M. Siebert (1968) in *Recognizing Patterns*, p104, P.A. Kohlers and M. Eden, Eds., MIT Press, Cambridge.

R. L. Stratonovich (1963,1967), *Topics in the Theory of Random Noise*, Vol. I and II, Gordon & Breach, New York.

M. C. Teich, L. Martin and B.I. Cantor (1978), *J. Opt. Soc. Am.*, **68**, 386.

M. C. Teich and B.E.A. Saleh (1981), *J. Opt. Soc. Am.*, **71**, 771.

A computer modeling approach to understanding the inferior olive and its relationship to the cerebellar cortex in rats

Maurice Lee and James M. Bower
Computation and Neural Systems Program
California Institute of Technology
Pasadena, CA 91125

ABSTRACT

This paper presents the results of a simulation of the spatial relationship between the inferior olivary nucleus and folium crus IIA of the lateral hemisphere of the rat cerebellum. The principal objective of this modeling effort was to resolve an apparent conflict between a proposed zonal organization of olivary projections to cerebellar cortex suggested by anatomical tract-tracing experiments (Brodal & Kawamura 1980; Campbell & Armstrong 1983) and a more patchy organization apparent with physiological mapping (Robertson 1987). The results suggest that several unique features of the olivocerebellar circuit may contribute to the appearance of zonal organization using anatomical techniques, but that the detailed patterns of patchy tactile projections seen with physiological techniques are a more accurate representation of the afferent organization of this region of cortex.

1 INTRODUCTION

Determining the detailed anatomical structure of the nervous system has been a major focus of neurobiology ever since anatomical techniques for looking at the fine structure of individual neurons were developed more than 100 years ago (Ramón y Cajal 1911). In more recent times, new techniques that allow labeling of the distant targets of groups of neurons have extended this investigation to include studies of the topographic relationships between different brain regions. In general, these so-called "tract-tracing" techniques have greatly extended our knowledge of the interrelationships between neural structures, often guiding and reinforcing the results of physiological investigations (DeYoe & Van Essen 1988). However, in some cases, anatomical and physiological techniques have been interpreted as producing conflicting results. One case, considered here, involves the pattern of neuronal projections from the *inferior olivary nucleus* to the *cerebellar cortex.* In this paper we describe the results of a computer modeling effort, based on the structure of the olivocerebellar projection, intended to resolve this conflict.

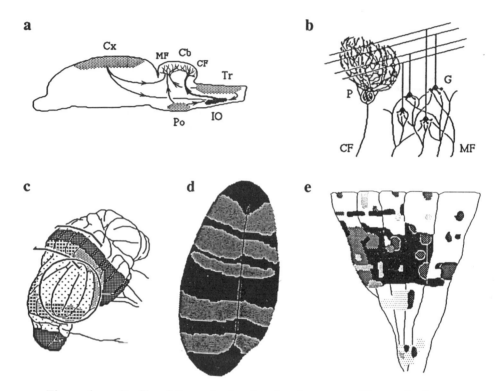

Figure 1. a: Profile of the rat brain, showing three areas (Cx, cerebral cortex; Po, pons; Tr, spinal trigeminal nucleus) that project to the cerebellum (Cb) via both climbing fiber (CF) pathways through the inferior olive (IO) and mossy fiber (MF) pathways. **b:** Magnified, highly simplified view of the cerebellar cortex, showing a Purkinje cell (P) being supplied with climbing fiber input, directly, and mossy fiber input, through the granule cells (G). **c:** Zonal organization of the olivocerebellar projection. *Different shading patterns* represent input from different areas of the inferior olive. Adapted from Campbell & Armstrong 1983. *Circled area* (crus IIA/crus IIB) is enlarged in Figure 1d; *bracketed area* (anterior lobe) is enlarged in Figure 1e. **d:** Detail of zonal organization. Dark areas represent bands of Purkinje cells that stain positive for monoclonal antibody Zebrin I. According to Gravel *et al.* 1987, these bands have boundaries similar to those resulting from partial tracer injections in the inferior olive. Adapted from Gundappa-Sulur *et al.* 1989. **e:** Patchy organization of the olivocerebellar projection (partial map). *Different shading patterns* represent input through the olive from different body surfaces. The horizontal and vertical scales are different. Adapted from Logan & Robertson 1986.

2 THE OLIVOCEREBELLAR SYSTEM

Purkinje cells, the principal neurons of the cerebellar cortex, are influenced by two major excitatory afferent projections to the cerebellum, the *mossy fiber system* and the *climbing fiber system* (Palay & Chan-Palay 1973). As shown in Figures 1a and 1b, mossy fibers arise from many different nuclei and influence Purkinje cells through granule cells within the cortex. Within the cortex the mossy fiber-granule cell-Purkinje cell circuit is characterized by enormous divergence (a single mossy fiber may influence several thousand Purkinje cells) and convergence (a single Purkinje cell may be influenced by several hundred thousand mossy fibers). In contrast, as also shown in Figures 1a and 1b, climbing fibers arise from a single source, the inferior olive, and exhibit severely limited divergence (10-15 Purkinje cells) and convergence (1 Purkinje cell).

Because the inferior olive is the sole source of the climbing fiber projection to the entire cerebellar cortex, and each Purkinje cell receives only one climbing fiber, the spatial organization of the olivocerebellar circuit has been the subject of a large research effort (Brodal & Kawamura 1980). Much of this effort has involved anatomical tract-tracing techniques in which injections of neuronally absorbed substances are traced from the inferior olive to the cerebellum or vice versa. Based on this work it has been proposed that the entire cerebellum is organized as a series of strips or zones, oriented in a parasagittal plane (Figures 1c, 1d: Campbell & Armstrong 1983; Gravel *et al.* 1987). This principle of organization has served as the basis for several functional speculations on the role of the cerebellum in coordinating movements (Ito 1984; Oscarsson 1980). Unfortunately, as suggested in the introduction, these anatomical results are somewhat at odds with the pattern of organization revealed by detailed electrophysiological mapping studies of olivary projections (Robertson 1987). Physiological results, summarized in Figure 1e, suggest that rather than being strictly zone-like, the olivocerebellar projection is organized more as a mosaic of parasagittally elongated patches.

3 THE MODEL

Our specific interests are with the tactilely responsive regions of the lateral hemispheres of the rat cerebellum (Bower *et al.* 1981; Welker 1987), and the modeling effort described here is a first step in using structural models to explore the functional organization of this region. As with previous modeling efforts in the olfactory system (Bower 1990), the current model is based on features of the anatomy and physiology of the real system. In the following section we will briefly describe these features.

3.1 ANATOMICAL ORGANIZATION

Structure of the inferior olive. The inferior olive has a complex, highly folded conformation (Gwyn *et al.* 1977). The portion of the olive simulated in the model consists of a folded slab of 2520 olivary neurons with a volume of approximately 0.05 mm^3 (Figure 2a).

Afferent projections to the olive. While inputs of various kinds and origins converge on this nucleus, we have limited those simulated here to tactile afferents from those perioral regions known to influence the lateral cerebellar hemispheres (Shambes *et al.* 1978). These have been mapped to the olive following the somatotopically organized pattern suggested by several previous experiments (Gellman *et al.* 1983).

Structure of the cerebellum. The cerebellum is represented in the model by a flat sheet of 2520 Purkinje cells with an area of approximately 2 mm² (Figure 2a). Within this region, each Purkinje cell receives input from one, and only one, olivary neuron. Details of Purkinje cells at the cellular level have not been included in the current model.

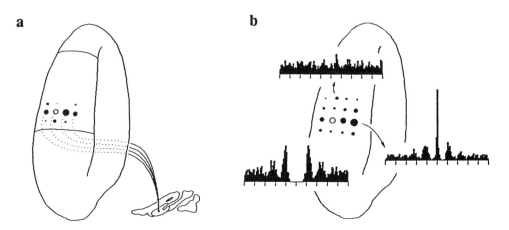

Figure 2. a: Basic structure of the model. Folia crus IIA and crus IIB of the cerebellum and a cross section of the inferior olive are shown, roughly to scale. The regions simulated in the model are outlined. *Clusters* of neighboring olivary neurons project to parasagittal *strips* of Purkinje cells as indicated. This figure also shows simulated correlation results similar to those in Figure 1b. **b:** Spatial structure of correlations among records of climbing fiber activity in crus IIA. Sizes of filled circles represent cross-correlation coefficients with respect to the "master" site (open circle). Sample cross-correlograms are shown for two sites as indicated. The autocorrelogram for the "master" site is also shown. Adapted from Sasaki *et al.* 1989.

3.2 PHYSIOLOGICAL ORGANIZATION

Spatially correlated patterns of activity. When the activities of multiple climbing fibers are recorded from within cerebellar cortex, there is a strong tendency for climbing fibers supplying Purkinje cells oriented parasagittally with respect to each other to be correlated in their firing activity (Sasaki *et al.* 1989: Figure 2b). It has been suggested that these correlations reflect the fact that direct electrotonic couplings exist between olivary neurons (Llinás & Yarom 1981a, b; Benardo & Foster 1986). These physiological results are simulated in two ways in the current model. First, neighboring olivary neurons are electrotonically coupled, thus firing in a correlated manner. Second, small clusters of olivary neurons have been made to project to parasagittally oriented strips of Purkinje cells. Under these constraints, the model replicates the parasagittal pattern of climbing fiber activity found in certain regions of cerebellar cortex (compare Figures 2a and 2b).

Topography of cerebellar afferents. As discussed above, this model is intended to explore spatial and functional relationships between the inferior olive and the lateral hemispheres of the rat cerebellum. Unfortunately, a physiological map of the climbing fiber projections to this cerebellar region does not yet exist for the rat. However, a detailed map of mossy fiber tactile projections to this region is available (Welker 1987). As in the climbing fiber map in the anterior lobe (Robertson 1987; Figure 1e) and mossy fiber maps in various areas in the cat (Kassel *et al.* 1984), representations of different parts of the body surface are grouped into patches with adjacent patches receiving input from nonadjacent peripheral regions. On the assumption that the mossy fiber and climbing fiber maps coincide, we have based the modeled topography of the olivary projection to the cerebellum on the well-described mossy fiber map (Figure 3a). In the model, the smoothly varying topography of the olive is transformed to the patchy organization of the cerebellar cortex through the projection pathways taken to the cerebellum by different climbing fibers.

a   b

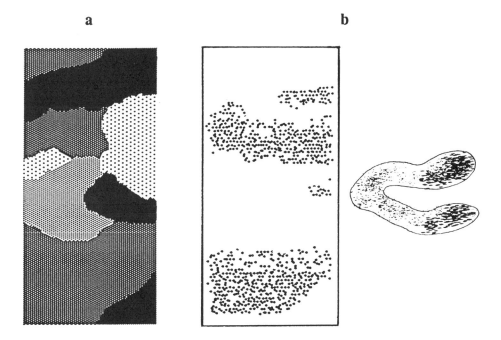

Figure 3. a: Organization of receptive field map in simulated region of crus IIA. *Different shading patterns* represent input from different perioral surfaces. **b:** Simulated tract-tracing experiment. *Left*, tracer visualization (dark areas) in the cerebellum. *Right*, tracer uptake (dark areas) in the inferior olive.

4 RESULTS: SIMULATION OF ZONAL ORGANIZATION

Having constructed the model to include each of the physiological features described above, we proceeded to replicate anatomical tract-tracing experiments. This was done by simulating the chemical labeling of neurons within restricted areas of inferior olive and following their connections to the cerebellum. As in the biological experiments, in many cases simulated injections included several folds of the olivary nucleus (Figure 3b). The results (Figure 3b) demonstrate patterns of labeling remarkably similar to those seen with real olivary injections in the rat (compare Figures 1d and 3b).

5 CONCLUSIONS AND FURTHER WORK

These simulation results have demonstrated that a broadly parasagittal organization can be generated in a model system which is actually based on a fine-grained patchy pattern of afferent projections. Further, the simulations allow us to propose that the appearance of parasagittal zonation may result from several unusual features of the olivary nucleus. First, the folding characteristic of the inferior olive likely places neurons with different receptive fields within a common area of tracer uptake in any given anatomical experiment, resulting in co-labeling of functionally different regions. Second, the tendency for local clusters of olivary neurons to project to parasagittal strips of Purkinje cells could serve to extend tracer injection in the parasagittal direction, enhancing the impression of parasagittal zones. This is further reinforced by the tendency of the patches themselves to be somewhat elongated in the parasagittal plane. Finally, the restricted resolution of the anatomical techniques could very well contribute to the overall impression of parasagittal zonation by obscuring small, unlabeled regions more apparent using physiological procedures. Modeling efforts currently under way will extend these results to more than one cerebellar folium in an attempt to account for the appearence of transfolial zones in some preparations.

In addition to these interpretations of previous data, this model also provides both directions for further physiological experiments and predictions concerning the results. First, the model assumes that mossy fiber and climbing fiber projections representing the same regions of the rat's body surface overlap in the cerebellum. We take the similarity in modeled and real tract-tracing results (Figures 1d and 3b) as suggesting strongly that this is, in fact, the case; however, physiological experiments are currently underway to test this hypothesis. Second, the model predicts that the parasagittal pattern of climbing fiber correlations found in a particular cerebellar region will be dependent on the pattern of tactile patches found in that region. Those regions containing large patches (*e.g.* the center of crus IIA) should clearly show parasagittal strips of correlated climbing fiber activity. However, in cortical regions containing smaller, more diverse sets of patches (*e.g.* more medial regions of crus IIA), this correlation structure should not be as clear. Experiments are also under way to test this prediction of the model.

Acknowledgements

This model has been constructed using GENESIS, the Caltech neural simulation system. Simulation code for the model presented here can be accessed by registered GENESIS users. Information on the simulator or this model can be obtained from genesis@caltech.bitnet. This work was supported by NIH grant BNS 22205.

References

Benardo, L. S., and R. E. Foster 1986. Oscillatory behavior in inferior olive neurons: Mechanism, modulation, cell aggregates. *Brain Res. Bull.* 17:773-784.

Bower, J. M. 1990. Reverse engineering the nervous system: An anatomical, physiological, and computer based approach. In *An introduction to neural and electronic networks*, ed. S. Zornetzer, J. Davis, and C. Lau, pp. 3-24. Academic Press.

Bower, J. M., and J. Kassel 1989. Variability in tactile projection patterns to crus IIA of the Norway rat. *J. Neurosci.* (submitted for publication).

Bower, J. M., D. H. Beermann, J. M. Gibson, G. M. Shambes, and W. Welker 1981. Principles of organization of a cerebro-cerebellar circuit. Micromapping the projections from cerebral (SI) to cerebellar (granule cell layer) tactile areas of rats. *Brain Behav. Evol.* 18:1-18.

Brodal, A., and K. Kawamura 1980. Olivocerebellar projection: A review. *Adv. Anat. Embryol. Cell Biol.* 64:1-140.

Campbell, N. C., and D. M. Armstrong 1983. Topographical localization in the olivocerebellar projection in the rat: An autoradiographic study. *Brain Res.* 275:235-249.

DeYoe, E. A., and D. C. Van Essen 1988. Concurrent processing streams in monkey visual cortex. *Trends Neurosci.* 11:219-226.

Gellman, R., J. C. Houk, and A. R. Gibson 1983. Somatosensory properties of the inferior olive of the cat. *J. Comp. Neurol.* 215:228-243.

Gravel, C., L. M. Eisenman, R. Sasseville, and R. Hawkes 1987. Parasagittal organization of the rat cerebellar cortex: Direct correlation between antigenic Purkinje cell bands revealed by mabQ113 and the organization of the olivocerebellar projection. *J. Comp. Neurol.* 265:294-310.

Gundappa-Sulur, G., H. Shojaeian, M. Paulin, L. Posakony, R. Hawkes, and J. M. Bower 1989. Variability in and comparisons of: 1) tactile projections to the granule cell layers of cerebellar cortex; and 2) the spatial distribution of Zebrin I-labeled Purkinje cells. *Soc. Neurosci. Abstr.* 15:612.

Gwyn, D. G., G. P. Nicholson, and B. A. Flumerfelt 1977. The inferior olivary nucleus of the rat: A light and electron microscopic study. *J. Comp. Neurol.* 174:489-520.

Ito, M. 1984. *The cerebellum and neural control.* Raven Press.

Kassel, J., G. M. Shambes, and W. Welker 1984. Fractured cutaneous projections to the granule cell layer of the posterior cerebellar hemispheres of the domestic cat. *J. Comp. Neurol.* 225:458-468.

Llinás, R., and Y. Yarom 1981a. Electrophysiology of mammalian inferior olivary neurones in vitro. Different types of voltage-dependent ionic conductances. *J.*

Physiol. (Lond.) 315:549-567.

Llinás, R., and Y. Yarom 1981b. Properties and distribution of ionic conductances generating electroresponsiveness of mammalian inferior olivary neurones in vitro. *J. Physiol. (Lond.)* 315:568-584.

Logan, K., and L. T. Robertson 1986. Somatosensory representation of the cerebellar climbing fiber system in the rat. *Brain Res.* 372:290-300.

Oscarsson, O. 1980. Functional organization of olivary projection to the cerebellar anterior lobe. In *The inferior olivary nucleus: Anatomy and physiology*, ed. J. Courville, C. de Montigny, and Y. Lammare, pp. 279-289. Raven Press.

Palay, S. L., and V. Chan-Palay 1973. *Cerebellar cortex: Cytology and organization.* Springer-Verlag.

Ramón y Cajal, S. 1911. *Histologie du système nerveux de l'homme et des vertèbres.* Maloine.

Robertson, L. T. 1987. Organization of climbing fiber representation in the anterior lobe. In *New concepts in cerebellar neurobiology*, ed. J. S. King, pp. 281-320. Alan R. Liss.

Sasaki, K., J. M. Bower, and R. Llinás 1989. Multiple Purkinje cell recording in rodent cerebellar cortex. *Eur. J. Neurosci.* (submitted for publication).

Shambes, G. M., J. M. Gibson, and W. Welker 1978. Fractured somatotopy in granule cell tactile areas of rat cerebellar hemispheres revealed by micromapping. *Brain Behav. Evol.* 15:94-140.

Welker, W. 1987. Spatial organization of somatosensory projections to granule cell cerebellar cortex: Functional and connectional implications of fractured somatotopy (summary of Wisconsin studies). In *New concepts in cerebellar neurobiology*, ed. J. S. King, pp. 239-280. Alan R. Liss.

Can Simple Cells Learn Curves? A Hebbian Model in a Structured Environment

William R. Softky
Divisions of Biology and Physics
103-33 Caltech
Pasadena, CA 91125
bill@aurel.caltech.edu

Daniel M. Kammen
Divisions of Biology and Engineering
216-76 Caltech
Pasadena, CA 91125
kammen@aurel.cns.caltech.edu

ABSTRACT

In the mammalian visual cortex, orientation-selective 'simple cells' which detect straight lines may be adapted to detect curved lines instead. We test a biologically plausible, Hebbian, single-neuron model, which learns oriented receptive fields upon exposure to unstructured (noise) input and maintains orientation selectivity upon exposure to edges or bars of all orientations and positions. This model can also learn arc-shaped receptive fields upon exposure to an environment of only circular rings. Thus, new experiments which try to induce an abnormal (curved) receptive field may provide insight into the plasticity of simple cells. The model suggests that exposing cells to only a single spatial frequency may induce more striking spatial frequency and orientation dependent effects than heretofore observed.

1   Introduction

Although most mathematical theories of cortical function assume plasticity of individual cells, there is a strong debate in the biological community between "instructional" (plastic) and "selectional" (hard-wired) models of orientation-selective cells (which we will call "simple cells") in striate visual cortex. Thus, a theory of simple cell learning which can make experimental predictions is desirable.

1.1 Overview of Plasticity Experiments

The most illuminating experiments addressing the plasticity of visual cortex are collectively called "stripe-rearing." Such experiments artificially restrict the visual environment of animals (usually kittens) to a few straight, dark, parallel lines (e.g. 3 vertical stripes.) In the many cases studied, examination of the visual cortex reveals that animals which viewed such limited visual environments posses more simple cells tuned to the exposed orientation than tuned to other orientations. (For comparison, the simple cells of animals with normal visual experience are equally distributed among all orientations.) But the observed changes in cell populations can be equally well explained by "instructional" and "selectional" hypotheses (Stryker *et al.*1978).

Although many variations on stripe-rearing have been tried (different orientations for each eye, one eye closed, etc.), only environments spanning a very restricted subset (straight lines) of the natural environment have been studied (Hirsch *et al.* 1983, Blakemore *et al.* 1978, and see references therein). Conclusions regarding plasticity have been based on changes in populations of simple cells, rather than on changes in individual cells. Statistical arguments based on changes in large groups of cells are questionable, since the well-documented lateral interactions between cortical neurons may constrain population ratios, e.g. limit the fraction of neurons responding to a single orientation.

1.2 New Experimental Approach

We propose several experiments to alter the receptive field (RF) of a single cell (see also Fregnac *et al.* 1988). How might that be done? The RF of a simple cell has only one characteristic spatial frequency (Jones & Palmer 1987 and ref's therein). To try altering the shape of that RF, it is necessary to present a pattern which is different from a simple bar or edge, but is still sufficiently similar in spatial frequency to activate the same population of retinal cells that detect the bar. An arc-shaped RF satisfies this condition; to generate an arc-shaped RF, an environment of circular rings (rather than bent bars) is necesary, since complete circles lack sharp end-effects which could overexcite spatial opponent cells and thus disturb learning.

This paper proposes a very simple Hebbian model of a neuron, and examines the resulting plasticity upon exposure to edge, bar, and arc-shaped stimuli.

2 Mathematical Model

The model applies a simple Hebbian learning rule to an array of about 400 synapses. There are several important features of this model. One is that the stimulus is a visual environment of structured input (bars, edges, or circles) rather than only stochastic (noise) input, as was used in the previous Hebb-learning models of Linsker (1986) and Kammen & Yuille (1988). (For a review of Hebbian learning and neural development see Kammen and Yuille 1990). Second, the input is Laplace filtered to simulate the retinal processing stage; and third, all connections are rectified to be excitatory, like direct afferent input to simple cells.

2.1 Overview

We model the neuron as an array of non-negative synapses, distributed within a circular region. To let the neuron "see" a single pattern in the visual environment (see Figure 1, end of text), the array is overlaid on a much larger positive array (the filtered image), which represents the environment. Each synapse value is multiplied by its corresponding input pixel, and the sum of these products forms the neuron's "output." If the output is above a threshold value, each synapse is changed slightly to make it more like its corresponding pixel (the synapse is increased for a positive pixel, and decreased for a zero pixel.) If the output is low, nothing is changed. This process implements the correlation-based ("Hebbian") learning rule for synapse modification. To ensure maturation, we presented roughly one million training images to each neuron. Because there are many filtered images, only one is chosen at random for each iteration, and the neuron is overlapped at some random spatial offset.

2.2 Input Filtering Process

The visual environment is a collection of N black-on-white pictures of a single shape (such as straight lines), at fixed contrast. The environment seen by the neuron is a set of N filtered images, whose non-negative elements are produced from the pictures by a rectified, Laplace-like, center-surround process similar to that of the mammalian retina (Van Essen & Anderson 1988). To determine the RF of a mature array of synapses, the combined efficacy of all synapses is calculated for each pixel, and displayed as a grey scale (white = excitatory, black = inhibitory). See Figure 2, at end of text, for several examples of mature RF's.

2.3 Plasticity Under Visual Stimulation

The neuron's input synapses cover a circle much smaller than the filtered image. A single exposure to the environment overlaps the synapse array at a random position on the input image (chosen randomly from the training set). This overlap pairs each synapse with an input from a filter whose center has like polarity (on or off), so that each synapse represents a definite polarity of retinal cell.

A typical run involves perhaps 10^6 exposures. There is no time variable, so that motion and temporal correlations between images are entirely absent. During each exposure a Hebb rule (section 2.4) changes synaptic weights based on current cell output and input values. When the neuron is exposed to filtered stochastic input ("noise-rearing"), synapses are intitialized randomly. When the neuron is exposed to structured environments, synapses are initialized with the orderly synapse arrays which *result* from noise-rearing. (As in animals, synapses may evolve in response to filtered random input before they are exposed to the external environment.)

2.4   A Choice of Hebb Rules for Learning Plasticity

Hebb postulated (1949) that neurons modify their synapses according to the following rule: the synapse will increase in efficacy if the post-synaptic and presynaptic excitations are coincident. There are many different formulae which satisfy Hebb's criterion; this model explores some simple representative ones. During each exposure to input, the synapses are adjusted according to the following type of hard-limited Hebb rule:

$$out \; = \; \sum_i syn_i \times in_i \tag{1}$$

And if $(out - thresh) > 0$:

$$\Delta syn_i \; = \; (out - thresh)^n \times in_i \times growth \tag{2}$$
$$\text{if } in_i > 0 \text{ and } syn_i < 10$$
$$= \; -(out - thresh)^n \times decay \tag{3}$$
$$\text{if } in_i = 0 \text{ and } syn_i > 0.5$$
$$= \; 0 \quad \text{otherwise} \tag{4}$$

The constants *growth* and *decay* are positive, and the exponent n is at least one. Both types of threshold depend on the neuron's recent output history: either the average of the previous 200 outputs, or one half the maximum previous output (decaying by .9995 each exposure until a new $\frac{max}{2}$ exceeds it). This Hebb Rule assumes that the cell can detect the current input value *before* its modification by a synapse.

2.5   Choice of Parameters

The constants *growth* and *decay* are not sensitive parameters. We found that only three parameter regimes exist: all synapses saturate at maximum, all saturate at minimum, or some at maximum and some at minimum. Only the latter regime is of interest, because only it contains structured RF's.

Most simulations used $n = 1, 2, 3$ with both thresholds. The threshold based on maximum output enhances learning selectivity, while the averaged output version can be derived from a principle of "excess information" (See Appendix). Because simple cell RF's have approximately Gaussian envelopes (Jones & Palmer 1987), some simulations were done with Gaussian envelopes modulating the maximum synapse values. That modification made no difference in the results observed.

3   Results and Discussion

The production of oriented RFs during exposure to unstructured input confirms previous results by Linsker (1986) and Yuille *et al.* (1989), but with some important differences. Like those models, the neurons simulated here learn oriented stripe-patterns as a kind of lowest-energy configuration under exposure to spatially correlated inputs. But unlike those models, we do not use: inhibitory connections or synapses; a synaptic-density gradient; a global conservation of synapse strength; or adjustable free parameters which can yield differently-shaped RFs. (In Linsker 1986 the ratio of "on" to "off" synapses is an adjustable parameter ; here, on and off pixels are represented equally.) Also, unlike previous models, mature RF's could have more than 3 lobes, depending on the ratio of filter size to RF size (Figure 2).

Under exposure to images of bars at all orientations, the neuron developed a mature RF matching a single one of them. Under exposure to stripes of nearly a single orientation, development of a mature RF depended on the stripes' spatial frequency.

In all cases, input patterns were learned much more quickly and strongly when their spatial frequency corresponded to the frequency of the Laplace filters. For input frequencies near the filter frequency, the resulting RF had a spatial frequency intermediate between the two. Otherwise, no learning occured unless the input frequency was a harmonic of the filter frequency, in which case the filter frequency was learned. Thus, this model predicts that enhanced learning might take place in kittens exposed to stripes of a single frequency, if that frequency is typical of simple-cell RF frequencies.

Under exposure to arcs or circles (with diameter $\approx 3 \times$ annular width), the model consistently developed RF's which matched a portion of the circle. These results suggest that animals which see only circles of a certain scale during the critical period may develop curved RFs (Barrow 1987) which differ qualitatively from those observed by such experiments as Jones & Palmer's (1987), who report seeing *no* curved contours in their point-by-point mappings of the RFs of normally-reared kittens. As with the stripes, the circles' annular width determines the spatial frequency of the retinal and simple cells which will respond best.

Such predictions must be treated with caution, because this paper does *not* simulate any version of the competing "selectional" model. It is possible that some of the effects predicted here for the "instructional" Hebbian model could also be observed by a "selectional" system.

To experimentally observe such effects in laboratory animals, many other known biological influences (eye acuity, interneuron effects, etc.) must be accounted for. We consider such problems elsewhere (Softky & Kammen *in preparation*), because they are of secondary importance to the striking and robust results of the model.

In summary, we have a single-cell model which contains essential biological features (such as all-excitatory input and synapses, and no global renormalizations). This model developes mature, oriented receptive fields under exposure to stochastic input for a wide variety of Hebb rules and for all non-trivial parameter regimes studied, with no apparent limitations on the number of lobes learned. Under exposure to structured input characteristic of normal environments, the model maintains oriented RF's; under exposure to input of "resonant" spatial frequency, the model develops RF's which reflect any novel orientation, spatial frequency, or curvature of the stimuli. This general, rule-independent response to the spatial frequency of a stimulus – and the specific mechanism for generating abnormally curved RF's – may be useful in deciding experimentally whether simple cortical cells are indeed modifiable by Hebbian mechanisms.

This model does not attempt to explain curve-detection in a normal visual system. We already know that normal simple cells are not tuned for curves, and there are credible theories of normal curve-detection (Dobbins *et al.* 1987.) Rather, this model proposes using stimuli tuned to the natural spatial frequency of simple cells to induce a RF property which is distinctly abnormal, in order to better understand the rules by which normal visual properties emerge.

4   Appendix – Choice of Thresholds for the Hebb Rule

The choice of the average output as a threshold for a Hebb rule can be interpreted as follows. Consider a developing neuron whose output is the sum of N inputs, each of which has independent probability distribution of mean α and standard deviation σ. We can calculate the information content in that sum, whose value has probability distribution (from the central limit theorem) of

$$P(out) \quad \propto \quad \exp\left(\frac{-(out - \langle out \rangle)^2}{2\sigma^2}\right). \tag{5}$$

The Shannon information (Shannon & Weaver 1962) carried by the sequence is

$$H(event) \quad = \quad -\ln P(event). \tag{6}$$

The excess information above the information carried by the average is thus

$$H_{excess} \quad = \quad H(out) - H(< out >) \tag{7}$$

$$\propto \quad \frac{(out - \langle out \rangle)^2}{2\sigma^2} \tag{8}$$

Thus, a Hebb rule using $n = 2$ and $thresh = \langle out \rangle$ is equivalent to learning based on the excess information carried in the output of an immature neuron.

The alternate threshold ($\frac{1}{2}max$) enhances selective learning for the following reason. If we consider the whole ensemble of patterns and shifts, the output characteristic which best distinguishes a matched synapse pattern from a random one is not its average output (the two averages are comparable for the all-excitatory case), but its maximum output. Thus, if a neuron can only 'remember' one characteristic number to serve as a threshold, then a number which changes during evolution (e.g. the maximum output) will refine selectivity more than one which is relatively constant. In addition, storing a maximum rather than an average removes the need to compute a running average, allowing unhindered evolution even after long periods of no input.

Acknowledgements

D.K. is a Weizmann Postdoctoral Fellow and acknowledges support from the Weizmann Foundation, the James S. McDonnell Foundation and a NSF Presidential Young Investigator Award to Christof Koch.

References

Barrow, H. (1987) "Learning Receptive Fields." *First I.E.E.E. Conference on Neural Networks*, **IV**, 115-121.

Blakemore C., Movshon J.A., & Van Sluyters R.C. (1978) "Modification of the Kitten's Visual Cortex by Exposure to Spatially Periodic Patterns." *Exp. Brain Res.*, **31**, 561-572.

Dobbins A., Zucker S. & Cynader M. (1987) "Endstopped Neurons in the Visual Cortex as a Substrate for Calculating Curvature." *Nature*, **329**, 438-441.

Fregnac Y., Shultz D., Thorpe S. & Bienenstock E. (1988) "A cellular analog of visual cortical plasticity." *Nature*, **333**, 367-370.

Hebb, D.O. (1949) "The Organization of Behavior: A Neuropsychological Theory." Wiley & Sons, New York.

Hirsch H., Leventhal A., McCall M. & Tieman D. (1983) "Effects of Exposure to Lines of One or Two Orientations on Different Cell Types in Striate Cortex of Cat." *J. Physiol.*, **337**, 241-255.

Jones J. & Palmer L. (1987) "The Two-Dimensional Spatial Structure of Simple Receptive Field in Cat Striate Cortex." *J. Neurophys.*, **58**, 1187-1232.

Kammen D.M. & Yuille A. (1988) "Spontaneous Symmetry-Breaking Energy Functions and the Emergence of Orientation Selective Cortical Cells." *Biol. Cybern.*, **59**, 23-31.

Kammen D.M. & Yuille A. (1990) "Self-Organizing Networks of Neural Units: Hebbian Learning in Development and Biological Computing." In:*Advances in Control Networks and Large Scale Distributed Processing Models,* Ablex Publishing, New Jersey.

Linsker R. (1986) "From basic network principles to neural architecture: Emergence of orientation-selective cells." *Proc. Natl. Acad. Sci. USA*, **83**, 8390-8394.

Shannon C. & Weaver W (1962) *The Mathematical Theory of Communication,* Univ. of Illinois Press, Urbana.

Stryker M., Sherk H., Leventhal A. & Hirsch H. (1978) "Physiological Consequences for the Cat's Visual Cortex of Effectively Restricting Early Visual Experience with Oriented Contours." *J. Neurophys.*, **41**, 896-909.

Van Essen D. & Anderson C. (1988) "Information Processing Strategies and Pathways in the Primate Retina and Visual Cortex." In: *Intro. to Neural and Electronic Networks*, Academic Press, Florida.

Yuille A., Kammen D.M. & Cohen D. (1989) "Quadrature and the Development of Orientation Selective Cortical Cells by Hebb Rules." *Biol. Cybern.*, **61**, 183-194.

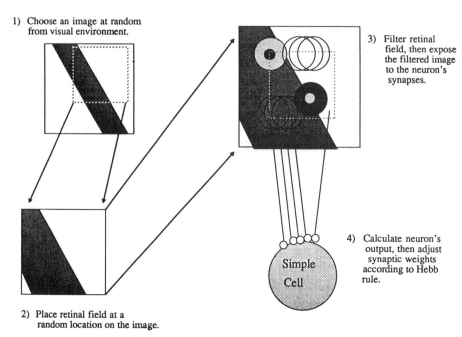

1) Choose an image at random from visual environment.

2) Place retinal field at a random location on the image.

3) Filter retinal field, then expose the filtered image to the neuron's synapses.

4) Calculate neuron's output, then adjust synaptic weights according to Hebb rule.

Simple Cell

Figure 1: Synapses Change Slightly During Each of a Million Iterations

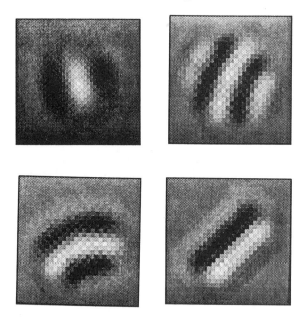

Figure 2: Learned Receptive Fields. Top row: Random pixel input, large (l) and small (r) filter sizes. Bottom row: Structured input, circular rings (l) and edges at different orientations (r).

Note on Development of Modularity in Simple Cortical Models

Alex Chernjavsky[1]
Neuroscience Graduate Program
Section of Molecular Neurobiology
Howard Hughes Medical Institute
Yale University

John Moody[2]
Yale Computer Science
PO Box 2158 Yale Station
New Haven, CT 06520
Email: moody@cs.yale.edu

ABSTRACT

The existence of modularity in the organization of nervous systems (e.g. cortical columns and olfactory glomeruli) is well known. We show that localized activity patterns in a layer of cells, *collective excitations*, can induce the formation of modular structures in the anatomical connections via a Hebbian learning mechanism. The networks are spatially homogeneous before learning, but the spontaneous emergence of localized collective excitations and subsequently modularity in the connection patterns breaks translational symmetry. This spontaneous symmetry breaking phenomenon is similar to those which drive pattern formation in reaction-diffusion systems. We have identified requirements on the patterns of lateral connections and on the gains of internal units which are essential for the development of modularity. These essential requirements will most likely remain operative when more complicated (and biologically realistic) models are considered.

[1] Present Address: Molecular and Cellular Physiology, Beckman Center, Stanford University, Stanford, CA 94305.

[2] Please address correspondence to John Moody.

1   Modularity in Nervous Systems

Modular organization exists throughout the nervous system on many different spatial scales. On the very small scale, synapses appear to be clustered on dendrites. On the very large scale, the brain as a whole is composed of many anatomically and functionally distinct regions. At intermediate scales, the scales of networks and maps, the brain exhibits columnar structures.

The purpose of this work is to suggest possible mechanisms for the development of modular structures at the intermediate scales of networks and maps. The best known modular structure at this scale is the column. Many modality- specific variations of columnar organization are known, for example orientation selective columns, ocular dominance columns, color sensitive blobs, somatosensory barrels, and olfactory glomeruli. In addition to these anatomically well-established structures, other more speculative modular anatomical structures may exist. These include the frontal eye fields of association cortex whose modular structure is inferred only from electrophysiology and the hypothetical existence of minicolumns and possibly neuronal groups.

Although a complete biophysical picture of the development of modular structures is still unavailable, it is well established that electrical activity is crucial for the development of certain modular structures such as complex synaptic zones and ocular dominance columns (see Kalil 1989 and references therein). It is also generally conjectured that a Hebb-like mechanism is operative in this development. These observations form a basis for our operating hypothesis described below.

2   Operating Hypothesis and Modeling Approach

Our hypothesis in this work is that localized activity patterns in a layer of cells induce the development of modular anatomical structure within the layer. We further hypothesize that the emergence of localized activity patterns in a layer is due to the properties of the intrinsic network dynamics and does not necessarily depend upon the system receiving localized patterns of afferent activity.

Our work therefore has two parts. First, we show that localized patterns of activity on a preferred spatial scale, *collective excitations*, spontaneously emerge in homogeneous networks with appropriate lateral connectivity and cellular response properties when driven with arbitrary stimulus (see Moody 1990). Secondly, we show that these collective excitations induce the formation of modular structures in the connectivity patterns when coupled to a Hebbian learning mechanism.

The emergence of collective excitations at a preferred spatial scale in a homogeneous network breaks translational symmetry and is an example of spontaneous symmetry breaking. The Hebbian learning freezes the modular structure into the anatomy. The time scale of collective excitations is short, while the Hebbian learning process occurs over a longer time scale. The spontaneous symmetry breaking mechanism is similar to that which drives pattern formation in reaction-diffusion systems (Turing 1952, Meinhardt 1982). Reaction-diffusion models have been applied to pattern for-

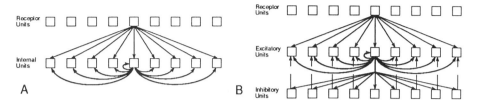

Figure 1: Network Models. A: Additive Model. B: Shunting Inhibition Model. Artwork after Pearson et al. (1987).

mation in both biological and physical systems. One of the best known applications is to the development of zebra stripes and leopard spots. Also, a network model with dynamics exhibiting spontaneous symmetry breaking has been proposed by Cowan (1982) to explain geometrical visual hallucination patterns.

Previous work by Pearson et al. (1987) demonstrated empirically that modularity emerged in simulations of an idealized but rather complex model of somatosensory cortex. The Pearson work was purely empirical and did not attempt to analyze theoretically why the modules developed. It provided an impetus, however, for our developing the theoretical results which we present here and in Moody (1990).

Our work is thus intended to provide a possible theoretical foundation for the development of modularity. We have limited our attention to simple models which we can analyze mathematically in order to identify the essential requirements for the formation of modules. To convince ourselves that both collective excitations and the consequent development of modules are somewhat universal, we have considered several different network models. All models exhibit collective excitations. We believe that more biologically realistic (and therefore more complicated) models will very likely exhibit similar behaviors.

This paper is a substantially abbreviated version of Chernjavsky and Moody (1990).

3   Network Dynamics: Collective Excitations

The analysis of network dynamics presented in this section is adapted from Moody (1990). Due to space limitations, we present here a detailed analysis of only the simplest model which exhibits collective excitations.

All network models which we consider possess a single layer of receptor cells which provide input to a single internal layer of laterally-connected cells. Two general classes of models are considered (see figure 1): additive models and shunting inhibition models. The additive models contain a single population of internal cells which make both lateral excitatory and inhibitory connections. Both connection types are additive. The shunting inhibition models have two populations of cells in the internal layer: excitatory cells which make additive synaptic axonal contact with other cells and inhibitory cells which shunt the activities of excitatory cells.

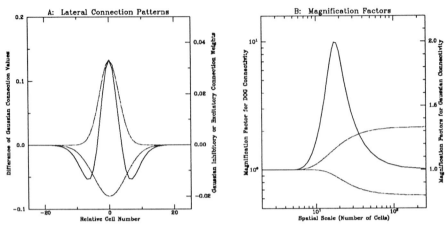

Figure 2: A: Excitatory, Inhibitory, and Difference of Gaussian Lateral Connection Patterns. B: Magnification Functions for the Linear Additive Model.

The additive models are further subdivided into models with linear internal units and models with nonlinear (particularly sigmoidal) internal units. The shunting inhibition models have linear excitatory units and sigmoidal inhibitory units. We have considered two variants of the shunting models, those with and without lateral excitatory connections.

For simplicity and tractability, we have limited the use of nonlinear response functions to at most one cell population in all models. More elaborate network models could make greater use of nonlinearity, a greater variety of cell types (eg. disinhibitory cells), and use more ornate connectivity patterns. However, such additional structure can only add richness to the network behavior and is not likely to remove the collective excitation phenomenon.

3.1   Dynamics for the Linear Additive Model

To elucidate the fundamental requirements for the spontaneous emergence of collective excitations, we now focus on the minimal model which exhibits the phenomenon, the linear additive model. This model is exactly solvable.

As we will see, collective excitations will emerge provided that the appropriate lateral connectivity patterns are present and that the gains of the internal units are sufficiently high. These basic requirements will carry over to the nonlinear additive and shunting models.

The network relaxation equations for the linear additive model are:

$$\tau_d \frac{d}{dt} V_i = -V_i + \sum_j W_{ij}^{aff} R_j + \sum_j W_{ij}^{lat} E_j \tag{1}$$

where R_j and E_j are the activities (firing rates) of the jth receptor and internal cells respectively, V_i is the somatic potential of the ith internal cell, W_{ij}^{aff} and W_{ij}^{lat} are the afferent and lateral connections respectively, and τ_d is the dynamical relaxation time. The somatic potentials and firing rates of the internal units are linearly related by $E_i = (V_i - \theta)/\epsilon$ where θ is an offset or threshold and ϵ^{-1} is the gain.

The steady state solutions of the network equations can be solved exactly by reformulating the problem in the continuum limit $(i \mapsto x)$:

$$\tau_d \frac{d}{dt} V(x) = -V(x) + A(x) + \int dy \, W^{lat}(x-y)E(y) \tag{2}$$

$$A(x) \equiv \int dy \, W^{aff}(x-y)R(y) \tag{3}$$

The functions $R(y)$ and $E(y)$ are activation densities in the receptor and internal layers respectively. $A(x)$ is the integrated input activation density to the internal layer. The functions $W^{aff}(x-y)$ and $W^{lat}(x-y)$ are interpreted as connection densities. Note that the network is spatially homogeneous since the connection densities depend only on the relative separation of post-synaptic and pre-synaptic cells $(x-y)$. Examples of lateral connectivity patterns $W^{lat}(x-y)$ are shown in figure 2A. These include local gaussian excitation, intermediate range gaussian inhibition, and a scaled difference of gaussians (DOG).

The exact stationary solution $\frac{d}{dt} V(x) = 0$ of the continuum dynamics of equation 2 can be computed by fourier transforming the equations to the spatial frequency domain. The solution thereby obtained (for $\theta = 0$) is $E(k) = M(k)A(k)$, where the variable k is the spatial frequency and $M(k)$ is the network *magnification function*:

$$M(k) \equiv \frac{1}{\epsilon - W^{lat}(k)}. \tag{4}$$

Positive magnification factors correspond to stable modes. When the magnification function is large and positive, the network magnifies afferent activity structure on specific spatial scales. This occurs when the inverse gain ϵ is sufficiently small and/or the fourier transform of the pattern of lateral connectivity $W^{lat}(k)$ has a peak at a non-zero frequency.

Figure 2B shows magnification functions (plotted as a function of spatial scale $2\pi/k$) corresponding to the lateral connectivity patterns shown in figure 2A for a network with $\epsilon = 1$. Note that the gaussian excitatory and gaussian inhibitory connection patterns (which have total integrated weight ± 0.25) magnify structure at large spatial scales by factors of 1.33 and 0.80 respectively. The scale DOG connectivity pattern (which has total weight 0) gives rise to no large scale or small scale magnification, but rather magnifies structure on an intermediate spatial scale of 17 cells.

We illustrate the response of linear networks with unit gain $\epsilon = 1$ and different lateral connectivity patterns in figure 3. The networks correspond to connectivities

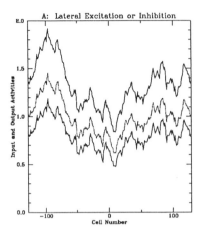
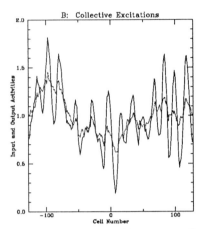

Figure 3: Response of a Linear Network to Random Input. A: Response of neutral (dashed), lateral excitatory (upper solid), and lateral inhibitory (lower solid) networks. B: Collective excitations (solid) as response to random input (dashed) in network with DOG lateral connectivity.

and magnification functions shown in figure 2. Part A, shows the response $E(x)$ of neutral, gaussian excitatory, and gaussian inhibitory networks to net afferent input $A(x)$ generated from a random $1/f^2$ noise distribution. The neutral network (no lateral connections) yields the identity response to random input; the networks with the excitatory and inhibitory lateral connection patterns exhibit boosted and reduced response respectively. Part B shows the emergence of collective excitations (solid) for the scaled DOG lateral connectivity. The resulting collective excitations have a typical period of about 17 cells, corresponding to the peak in the magnification function shown in figure 2. Note that the positions of peaks and troughs of the collective excitations correspond approximately to local extrema in the random input (dashed).

It is interesting to note that although the individual components of the networks are all linear, the overall response of the interacting system is nonlinear. It is this collective nonlinearity of the system which enables the emergence of collective excitations. Thus, although the connectivity giving rise to the response in figure 3B is a scaled sum of the connectivities of the excitatory and inhibitory networks of figure 3A, the responses themselves do not add.

3.2 Dynamics for Nonlinear Models

The nonlinear models, including the sigmoidal additive model and the shunting models, exhibit the collective excitation phenomenon as well. These models can not be solved exactly, however. See Moody (1990) for a detailed description.

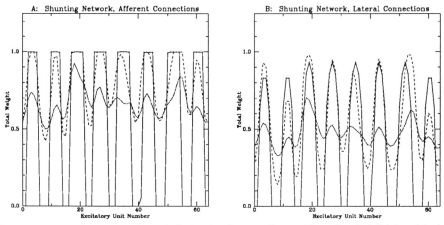

Figure 4: Development of Modularity in the Nonlinear Shunting Inhibition Model. Curves represent the average incoming connection value (either afferent connections or lateral connections) for each excitatory internal unit. A: Time development of Afferent Modularity. B: Time development of Lateral Modularity. A and B: 400 iterations (dotted line), 650 iterations (dashed line), 4100 iterations (solid line).

4 Hebbian Learning: Development of Modularity

The presence of collective excitations in the network dynamics enables the development of modular structures in both the afferent and lateral connection patterns via Hebbian learning. Due to space limitations, we present simulation results only for the nonlinear shunting model. We focus on this model since it has both afferent and lateral plastic connections and thus develops both afferent and lateral modular connectivities. The other models do not have plastic lateral connections and develop only afferent connectivity modules. A more detailed account of all simulations is given in Chernjavsky and Moody (1990).

In our networks, the plastic excitatory connection values are restricted to the range $W \in [0, 1]$. The homogeneous initial conditions for all connection values are $W = 0.5$. We have considered several variants of Hebbian learning. For the simulations we report here, however, we use only the simple Hebb rule with decay:

$$\tau_{Hebb}\frac{d}{dt}W_{ij} = M_i N_j - \beta \qquad (5)$$

where M_i and N_j are the post- and pre-synaptic activities respectively and β is the decay constant chosen to be approximately equal to the expected value $\bar{M}\bar{N}$ averaged over the whole network. This choice of β makes the Hebb similar to the covariance type rule of Sejnowski (1977). τ_{Hebb} is the timescale for learning.

The simulation results illustrated in figure 4 are of one dimensional networks with 64 units per layer. In these simulations, the units and connections illustrated are intended to represent a continuum. The connection densities for afferent and lateral excitatory connections were chosen to be gaussian with a maximum fan-out of 9 lattice units. The inhibitory connection density had a maximum fan-in of 19 lattice units and had a symmetric bimodal shape. The sigmas of the excitatory and inhibitory fan-ins were respectively 1.4 and 2.1 (short-range excitation and longer range inhibition). The linear excitatory units had $\epsilon = 1$ and $\theta = 0$, while the sigmoidal inhibitory units had $\epsilon = 0.125$ and $\theta = 0.5$.

The input activations were uniform random values in the range $[0, 1]$. The input activations were spatially and temporally uncorrelated. Each input pattern was presented for only one dynamical relaxation time of the network (10 timesteps).

The following adaptation rate parameters were used: dynamical relaxation rate $\tau_d^{-1} = 0.1$, learning rate $\tau_{Hebb}^{-1} = 0.01$, weight decay constant $\beta = 0.125$.

Acknowledgements

The authors wish to thank George Carman, Martha Constantine-Paton, Kamil Grajski, Daniel Kammen, John Pearson, and Gordon Shepherd for helpful comments. A.C. thanks Stephen J Smith for the freedom to pursue projects outside the laboratory. J.M. was supported by ONR Grant N00014-89-J-1228 and AFOSR Grant 89-0478. A.C. was supported by the Howard Hughes Medical Institute and by the Yale Neuroscience Program.

References

Alex Chernjavsky and John Moody. (1990) Spontaneous development of modularity in simple cortical models. Submitted to *Neural Computation.*

Jack D. Cowan. (1982) Spontaneous symmetry breaking in large scale nervous activity. *Intl. J. Quantum Chemistry*, 22:1059.

Ronald E. Kalil. (1989) Synapse formation in the developing brain. *Scientific American* December.

H. Meinhardt. (1982) *Models of Biological Pattern Formation.* Academic Press, New York.

John Moody. (1990) Dynamics of lateral interaction networks. Technical report, Yale University. (In Preparation.)

Vernon B. Mountcastle. (1957) Modality and topographic properties of single neurons of cat's somatic sensory cortex. *Journal of Neurophysiology*, 20:408.

John C. Pearson, Leif H. Finkel, and Gerald M. Edelman. (1987) Plasticity in the organization of adult cerebral cortical maps: A computer simulation based on neuronal group selection. *Journal of Neuroscience*, 7:4209.

Terry Sejnowski. (1977) Strong covariance with nonlinearly interacting neurons. *J. Math. Biol.* 4:303.

Alan Turing. (1952) The chemical basis of morphogenesis. *Phil. Trans. R. Soc.*, B237:37.

Effects of Firing Synchrony on Signal Propagation in Layered Networks

G. T. Kenyon,[1] E. E. Fetz,[2] R. D. Puff[1]

[1]Department of Physics FM-15, [2]Department of Physiology and Biophysics SJ-40
University of Washington, Seattle, Wa. 98195

ABSTRACT

Spiking neurons which integrate to threshold and fire were used to study the transmission of frequency modulated (FM) signals through layered networks. Firing correlations between cells in the input layer were found to modulate the transmission of FM signals under certain dynamical conditions. A tonic level of activity was maintained by providing each cell with a source of Poisson-distributed synaptic input. When the average membrane depolarization produced by the synaptic input was sufficiently below threshold, the firing correlations between cells in the input layer could greatly amplify the signal present in subsequent layers. When the depolarization was sufficiently close to threshold, however, the firing synchrony between cells in the initial layers could no longer effect the propagation of FM signals. In this latter case, integrate-and-fire neurons could be effectively modeled by simpler analog elements governed by a linear input-output relation.

1 Introduction

Physiologists have long recognized that neurons may code information in their instantaneous firing rates. Analog neuron models have been proposed which assume that a single function (usually identified with the firing rate) is sufficient to characterize the output state of a cell. We investigate whether biological neurons may use firing correlations as an additional method of coding information. Specifically, we use computer simulations of integrate-and-fire neurons to examine how various levels of synchronous firing activity affect the transmission of frequency-modulated

(FM) signals through layered networks. Our principal observation is that for certain dynamical modes of activity, a sufficient level of firing synchrony can considerably amplify the conduction of FM signals. This work is partly motivated by recent experimental results obtained from primary visual cortex [1, 2] which report the existence of synchronized stimulus-evoked oscillations (*SEO's*) between populations of cells whose receptive fields share some attribute.

2   Description of Simulation

For these simulations we used integrate-and-fire neurons as a reasonable compromise between biological accuracy and mathematical convenience. The subthreshold membrane potential of each cell is governed by an over-damped second-order differential equation with source terms to account for synaptic input:

$$\left(\tau_r \frac{\partial^2}{\partial t^2} + \frac{\partial}{\partial t} + \frac{1}{\tau_d}\right)\phi_k = \sum_{j=1}^{N}\sum_{t'_j} T_{kj}\delta(t - t'_j) + \sum_{p_k} T_P\delta(t - p_k) \tag{1}$$

where ϕ_k is the membrane potential of cell k, N is the number of cells, T_{kj} is the synaptic weight from cell j to cell k, t'_j are the firing times for the jth cell, T_P is the synaptic weight of the Poisson-distributed input source, p_k are the firing times of Poisson-distributed input, and τ_r and τ_d are the rise and decay times of the *EPSP*. The Poisson-distributed input represents the synaptic drive from a large presynaptic population of neurons.

Equation 1 is augmented by a threshold firing condition

$$\text{if} \quad \left\{ \begin{array}{l} \phi_k(t) = \theta(t - t'_k) \\ \dot{\phi}_k(t) > 0 \\ t - t'_k > \tau_a \end{array} \right. \quad \text{then} \quad \left\{ \begin{array}{l} \phi_k(t + 0^+) = \phi_r \\ \dot{\phi}_k(t + 0^+) = \dot{\phi}_r \end{array} \right. \tag{2}$$

where $\theta(t - t'_k)$ is the threshold of the kth cell, and τ_a is the absolute refractory period. If the conditions (2) do not hold then ϕ_k continues to be governed by equation 1.

The threshold is ∞ during the absolute refractory period and decays exponentially during the relative refractory period:

$$\theta(t - t'_k) = \left\{ \begin{array}{ll} \infty, & \text{if } t - t'_k < \tau_a; \\ \theta_p e^{-(t - t'_k)/\tau_r} + \theta_0, & \text{otherwise,} \end{array} \right. \tag{3}$$

where, θ_0 is the resting threshold value, θ_p is the maximum increase of θ during the relative refractory period, and τ_p is the time constant characterizing the relative refractory period.

2.1   Simulation Parameters

τ_r and τ_d are set to 0.2 msec and 1 msec, respectively. T_P and T_{kj} are always $(1/100)\theta_0$. This strength was chosen as typical of synapses in the CNS. To sustain

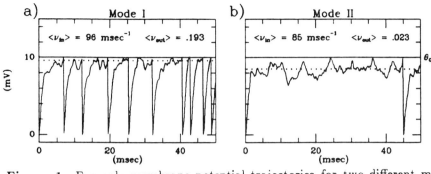

Figure 1: Example membrane potential trajectories for two different modes of activity. *EPSP's* arrive at mean frequency, ν_{in}, that is higher for mode I (a) than for mode II (b). Dotted line below threshold indicates asymptotic membrane potential.

activity, during each interval τ_d, a cell must receive $\approx (\theta_0/T_P) = 100$ Poisson-distributed inputs. Resting potential is set to 0.0 mV and θ_0 to 10 mV. ϕ_τ and $\dot{\phi}_\tau$ are set to 0.0 mV and -1.0 mV/msec, which simulates a small hyperpolarization after firing. τ_a and τ_p were each set to 1 msec, and θ_p to 1.0 mV.

3   Response Properties of Single Cells

Figure 1 illustrates membrane potential trajectories for two modes of activity. In mode I (fig. 1a), synaptic input drives the membrane potential to an asymptotic value (dotted line) within one standard deviation of θ_0. In mode II (fig. 1b), the asymptotic membrane potential is more than one standard deviation below θ_0.

Figure 2 illustrates the change in average firing rate produced by an *EPSP*, as measured by a cross-correlation histogram (*CCH*) between the Poisson source and the target cell. In mode I (fig. 2a), the *CCH* is characterized by a primary peak followed by a period of reduced activity. The derivative of the *EPSP*, when measured in units of θ_0, approximates the peak magnitude of the *CCH*. In mode II (fig. 2b), the *CCH* peak is not followed by a period of reduced activity. The *EPSP* itself, measured in units of θ_0 and divided by τ_d, predicts the peak magnitude of the *CCH*. The transform between the *EPSP* and the resulting change in firing rate has been discussed by several authors [3, 4]. Figures 2c and 2d show the cumulative area (*CUSUM*) between the *CCH* and the baseline firing rate. The *CUSUM* asymptotes to a finite value, Δ, which can be interpreted as the average number of additional firings produced by the *EPSP*.

Δ increases with *EPSP* amplitude in a manner which depends on the mode of activity (fig. 2e). In mode II, the response is amplified for large inputs (concave up). In mode I, the response curve is concave down. The amplified response to large inputs during mode II activity is understandable in terms of the threshold crossing mechanism. Populations of such cells should respond preferentially to synchronous synaptic input [5].

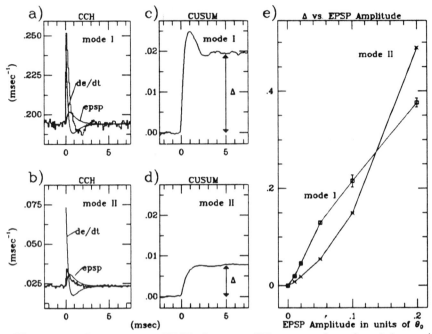

Figure 2: Response to *EPSP* for two different modes of activity. a) and b) Cross-correlogram with Poisson input source. Mode I and mode II respectively. c) and d) *CUSUM* computed from a) and b). e) Δ vs. *EPSP* amplitude for both modes of activity.

4   Analog Neuron Models

The histograms shown in Figures 2a,b may be used to compute the impulse response kernel, U, for a cell in either of the two modes of activity, simply by subtracting the baseline firing rate and normalizing to a unit impulse strength. If the cell behaves as a linear system in response to a small impulse, U may be used to compute the response of the cell to any time-varying input. In terms of U, the change in firing rate, δF, produced by an external source of Poisson-distributed impulses arriving with an instantaneous frequency $F_e(t)$ is given by

$$\delta F(t) = \int_{-\infty}^{t} U(t - t')F_e(t')T_e dt' \tag{4}$$

where, T_e is the amplitude of the incoming *EPSP's*. For the layered network used in our simulations, equation 4 may be generalized to yield an iterative relation giving the signal in one layer in terms of the signal in the previous layer.

$$\delta F_{i+1} = N \int_{-\infty}^{t} U(t - t')\delta F_i(t')T_{i+1,i} dt' \tag{5}$$

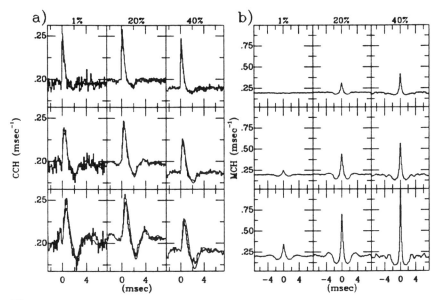

Figure 3: Signal propagation in mode I network. a) Response in first three layers due to a single impulse delivered simultaneously to all cells in the first layer. Ratio of common to independent input given by percentages at top of figure. First row corresponds to input layer. Firing synchrony does not effect signal propagation through mode I cells. Prediction of analog neuron model (solid line) gives a good description of signal propagation at all synchrony levels tested. b) Synchrony between cells in the same layer measured by *MCH*. Firing synchrony within a layer increases with layer depth for all initial values of the synchrony in the first layer.

where, δF_i is the change in instantaneous firing rate for cells in the ith layer, $T_{i+1,i}$ is the synaptic weight between layer i and $i + 1$, and N is the number of cells per layer. Equation 5 follows from an equivalent analog neuron model with a linear input-output relation. This convolution method has been proposed previously [6].

5   Effects of Firing Synchrony on Signal Propagation

A layered network was designed such that the cells in the first layer receive impulses from both common and independent sources. The ratio of the two inputs was adjusted to control the degree of firing synchrony between cells in the initial layer. Each cell in a given layer projects to all the cells in the succeeding layer with equal strength, $\frac{1}{100}\theta_0$. All simulations use 50 cells per layer.

Figure 3a shows the response of cells in the mode I state to a single impulse of strength $\frac{1}{100}\theta_0$ delivered simultaneously to all the cells in the first layer. In this and all subsequent figures, successive layers are shown from top to bottom and synchrony (defined as the fraction of common input for cells in the first layer) increases from

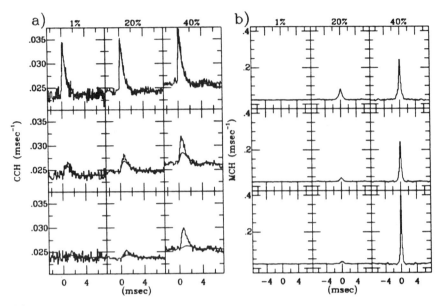

Figure 4: Signal propagation in mode II network. Same organization as fig. 3. a) At initial levels of synchrony above $\approx 30\%$, signal propagation is amplified significantly. The propagation of relatively asynchronous signals is still adequately described by the analog neuron model. b) Firing synchrony within a layer increases with layer depth for initial synchrony levels above $\approx 30\%$. Below this level synchrony within a layer decreases with layer depth.

left to right. Figure 3a shows that signals propagate through layers of interneurons with little dependence on firing synchrony. The solid line is the prediction from an equivalent analog neuron model with a linear input-output relation (eq. 5). At all levels of input synchrony, signal propagation is reasonably well approximated by the simplified model.

Firing synchrony between cells in the same layer may be measured using a mass correlogram (MCH). The MCH is defined as the auto-correlation of the population spike record, which combines the individual spike records of all cells in a given layer. Figure 3b shows that for all initial levels of synchrony produced in the input layer, the intra-layer firing synchrony increased rapidly with layer depth.

The simulations were repeated using an identical network, but with the tonic level of input reduced sufficiently to fix the cells in the mode II state (fig. 4). In contrast with the mode I case, the effect of firing synchrony is substantial. When firing is asynchronous only a weak impulse response is present in the third layer (fig. 4a, bottom left), as predicted by the analog neuron model (eq. 5). For levels of input synchrony above $\approx 30\%$, however, the response in the third layer is substantially more prominent. A similar effect occurs for synchrony within a layer. At input

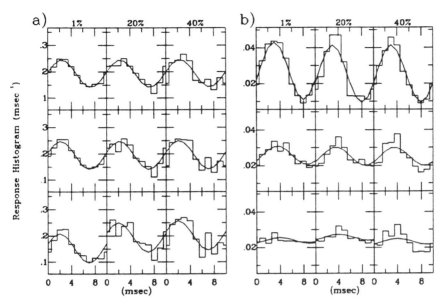

Figure 5: Propagation of sinusoidal signals. Similar organization to figs. 3,4. Top row shows modulation of input sources. a) Mode I activity. Signal propagation is not significantly influenced by the level of firing synchrony. Analog neuron model (solid line) gives reasonable prediction of signal tranmission. b) Mode II activity. At initial levels of firing synchrony above $\approx 30\%$, signal propagation is amplified. The propagation of asynchronous signals is still well described by the analog neuron model. Period of applied oscillation = 10 msec.

synchrony levels below $\approx 30\%$, firing synchrony between cells in the same layer (fig. 4b) falls off in successive layers. Above this level, however, synchrony grows rapidly from layer to layer.

To confirm that our results are not limited to the propagation of signals generated by a single impulse, oscillatory signals were produced by sinusoidally modulating the firing rates of both the common and independent input sources to the first layer (fig. 5). In the mode I state (fig. 5a), we again find that firing synchrony does not significantly alter the degree of signal penetration. The solid line shows that signal transmission is adequately described by the simplified model (eqs. 4,5). In the mode II case, however, firing synchrony is seen to have an amplifying effect on sinusoidal signals as well (fig. 5b). Although the propagation of asynchronous signals is well described by the analog neuron model, at higher levels of synchrony propagation is enhanced.

6   Discussion

It is widely accepted that biological neurons code information in their spike density or firing rate. The degree to which the firing correlations between neurons can code additional information by modulating the transmission of FM signals, depends strongly on dynamical factors. We have shown that for cells whose average membrane potential is sufficiently below the threshold for firing, spike correlations can significantly enhance the transmission of FM signals. We have also shown that the propagation of asynchronous signals is well described by analog neuron models with linear transforms. These results may be useful for understanding the role played by synchronized SEO's in primary visual cortex [1, 2]. Such signals may be propagated more effectively to subsequent processing areas as a consequence of their relative synchronization.

These observations may also pertain to the neural mechanisms underlying the increased levels of synchronous discharge of cerebral cortex cells observed in slow wave sleep [7]. Another relevant phenomenon is the spread of synchronous discharge from an epileptic focus; the extent to which synchronous activity is propagated through surrounding areas may be modulated by changing their level of activation through voluntary effort or changing levels of arousal. These physiological phenomena may involve mechanisms similar to those exhibited by our network model.

Acknowledgements

This work is supported by an NIH pre-doctoral training grant in molecular biophysics (grant # T32-GM 08268) and by the Office of Naval Research (contract # N 00018-89-J-1240).

References

[1] C. M. Gray, P. König, A. K. Engel, W. Singer, *Nature* **338**:334–337 (1989)

[2] R. Eckhorn, R. Bauer, W. Jordan, M. Brosch, W. Kruse, H. J. Reitboeck, *Bio. Cyber.* **60**:121–130 (1988)

[3] E. E. Fetz, B. Gustafsson, *J. Physiol.* **341**:387–410 (1983)

[4] P. A. Kirkwood, *J. Neurosci. Meth.* **1**:107–132 (1979)

[5] M. Abeles, *Local Cortical Circuits: Studies of Brain Function.* Springer, New York, Vol. **6** (1982)

[6] E. E. Fetz, *Neural Information Processing Systems* American Institute of Physics. (1988)

[7] H. Noda, W.R.Adey, *J. Neurophysiol.* **23**:672-684 (1970)

A Systematic Study of the Input/Output Properties of a 2 Compartment Model Neuron With Active Membranes

Paul Rhodes
University of California, San Diego

ABSTRACT

The input/output properties of a 2 compartment model neuron are systematically explored. Taken from the work of MacGregor (MacGregor, 1987), the model neuron compartments contain several active conductances, including a potassium conductance in the dendritic compartment driven by the accumulation of intradendritic calcium. Dynamics of the conductances and potentials are governed by a set of coupled first order differential equations which are integrated numerically. There are a set of 17 internal parameters to this model, specificying conductance rate constants, time constants, thresholds, etc.

To study parameter sensitivity, a set of trials were run in which the input driving the neuron is kept fixed while each internal parameter is varied with all others left fixed.

To study the input/output relation, the input to the dendrite (a square wave) was varied (in frequency and magnitude) while all internal parameters of the system were left fixed, and the resulting output firing rate and bursting rate was counted.

The input/output relation of the model neuron studied turns out to be much more sensitive to modulation of certain dendritic potassium current parameters than to plasticity of synapse efficacy per se (the amount of current influx due to synapse activation). This would in turn suggest, as has been recently observed experimentally, that the potassium current may be as or more important a focus of neural plasticity than synaptic efficacy.

INTRODUCTION

In order to model biologically realistic neural systems, we will ultimately be seeking to construct networks with thousands of neurons and millions of interconnections. It is therefor desireable to employ basic units with sufficient computational simplicity to make meaningful simulations tractable, yet with sufficient fidelity to biological neurons that we may retain a hope of gleaning by these simulations something about the activity going on during biological information processing.

The types of neuron models employed in the computational neuroscience literature range from binary threshold units to sigmoid transfer functions to 1500 compartment neurons with Hodgkin-Huxley kinetics for a whole set of active conductances and spines with rich internal structure. In principle, a model neuron's functional participation in the operation of a network may be fully characterized by a complete description of its transfer function, or input-output relation. This relation would necessarily be parameterized by a host of internal variables (which would include conductance rate constants and parameters defining the neuron's morphology) as well as a very rich space characterizing possible variations in input (including location of input in dentritic tree). In learning to judge which structural elements of highly realistic models must be preserved and which may be simplified, one approach will be to test the degree to which the input-output relation of the simplified neuron (given a physiologically relevant parameter range and input space) is sufficiently close to the input-output properties of the highly realistic model.

To define 'sufficiently close', we will ultimately refer to the operation of the network as a whole as follows: the transfer function of a simplified neuron model will be considered 'sufficiently close' to a more realistic neuron model if a chosen information processing task carried out by the overall network is performed by a network built up of the simplified neurons in a manner close to that observed in a network of the more realistic neurons.

We propose to begin by exploring the input/output properties of a greatly simplified 2 compartment model neuron with active conductances. Even in this very simple structure there are many (17) internal parameters for things like time constants and activation rates of currents. We wish to understand the parameter sensitivity of this model system and characterize its input-output relation.

1.0 DESCRIPTION OF THE MODEL NEURON

THE MODEL NEURON CONSISTS OF A SOMA WITH A VOLTAGE-GATED POTASSIUM CONDUCTANCE AND A SINGLE COMPARTMENT DENDRITE WITH A VOLTAGE-GATED CALCIUM CONDUCTANCE AND A [CA]-GATED POTASSIUM CONDUCTANCE

We will choose for this study a simple model neuron described by MacGregor (1987). It possesses a single compartment dendrite. This is viewed as a crude approximation to the lumped reduction of a dendritic tree. In this approximation, we are neglecting spatial and temporal summing of individual synaptic EPSP's distributed over a dendritic tree, as well as the spatial and temporal dispersion (smearing) due to transmission to the soma. The individual inputs we will be using are large enough to drive the soma to firing, and so would represent the summation of many relatively simultaneous individual EPSP's, perhaps as from the set of contacts upon a neuron's dendritic tree made by the arborization of one different axon. The dendritic membrane possesses a potassium conductance gated by intradendritic calcium concentration and a voltage gated calcium conductance. The soma contains its own voltage-gated potassium channels and membrane time constants. Electrical connection between soma and dendrite is expressed by an input impedance in each direction. The soma fires an action potential, simply expressed by raising its voltage to 50 mv for one msec after its internal voltage has been driven to firing threshold.   Calcium accumulation in the dendrite is modelled assuming accumulation proportional to calcium conductance. Calcium conductance itself increases in proportion to the difference between the dendrite's voltage and a threshold, and calcium is removed from the dendrite by means of an exponential decay. This system is modelled by a set of coupled first order differential equations as follows:

1.1   THE SET OF EQUATIONS GOVERNING THE DYNAMIC VARIABLES OF THIS MODEL

The soma's voltage ES is governed by:

$$dES/dt=\{-ES+SOMAINPUT+GDS*(ED-ES)+GKS*(EK-ES)\}/TS$$

where SOMAINPUT is obtained by dividing the input current by the total resting conductance of the dendrite (therefor it has units of voltage). GDS is proportional to input resistance from dendrite to soma, and multiplies the difference between the dendrite's voltage ED and the soma's voltage ES; GKS is the soma's aggregate potassium conductance (modelled below); EK is the voltage of the potassium battery (assumed constant at -10mv); and TS is the soma's time constant. All potentials are relative to resting potential, and all conductances are dimensionless.

The dendrite's voltage ED is govened by:

$$dED/dt=\{-ED+DENDINPUT+GSD*(ES-ED)+GCA*(ECA-ED)+ GKD*(EK-ED)\}/TD$$

where DENDINPUT is obtained by dividing the input current by the total resting conductance of the dendrite and so has units of voltage. GSD is proportional to the input resistance from soma to dendrite, and hence multiplies the difference between ES and ED; GCA is the dendrite's calcium conductance (modelled below), ECA is the calcium battery (assumed constant at 50mv), and GKD is proportional to the dendrite's potassium conductance (modelled below). All potentials are relative to resting potential.

The soma's voltage is raised artificially to 50mv for 1 msec after the soma's voltage exceeds a (fixed) threshold, thus simplifying the action potential.

The potassium conductance in the soma, GKS, is governed by :

$$dGKS/dt=\{-GKS+S*B\}/TGK$$

where S is 1 if an action potential has just fired and 0 otherwise, B is an activation rate constant governing the rate of increase of potassium conductance, and TGK is the time constant of the potassium conductance decay. This rather simplified picture of potassium conductance will be replaced by a more realistic version with a Markov state model of the potassium channel in a subsequent publication in preparation. For the present investigation then we are modelling the voltage dependence of the potassium conductance by the following: potassium conductance builds up by a fixed amount (proportional to B/TGK) during each action potential, and thereafter decays exponentially with time constant TGK.

The dendrite's calcium conductance is governed by:

dGCA/dt={-GCA+D*(ED-CSPIKETHRESH)}/TGCA   ED>CSPIKETHRESH
dGCA/dt={-GCA/TGCA}   ED<CSPIKETHRESH

where CSPIKETHRESH is the minimum dendritic voltage above which calcium conducting channels begin to be opened, D is an activation rate governing the rate of increase in calcium conductance, and TGCA is the time constant assumed to govern conductance decay when voltage is below threshold.

The dendrite's internal calcium concentration [CA] is governed by:

d[CA]/dt={-[CA]+A*GCA}/TCA

where TCA is the time constant for the removal of internal CA, and A is a parameter governing the accumulation rate of increase of internal CA for a given conductance and time constant. A is inversely proportional to the effective relevant volume in which calcium is accumulating. An increase in internal calcium buffer would decrease the parameter A.

Finally, the dendrite's potassium conductance is governed by:

dGKD/dt={-GKD+BD}/TGKD   [CA]>CALCTHRESH
dGKD/dt={-GKD}/TGKD   [CA]<CALCTHRESH

where CALCTHRESH is the internal calcium concentration threshold above which the calcium gated potassium channel begins to open, BD is the parameter governing the rate of increase of dendritic potassium conductance, and TGKD is the time constant governing the exponential decay of potassium conductance.

This entire system of equations is taken from the work of MacGregor (MacGregor, 1987).

The system of coupled first order differential equations is integrated using the exponential method, also discussed in MacGregor. Generally a 1 msec timestep is used, with a smaller timestep of .1 msec used for the relaxation between the dendritic voltage ED and the somatic voltage ES.

2.0 THE EFFECT OF CHANGES IN PARAMETERS (TIME CONSTANTS, CONDUCTANCE RATES, ETC.) ON THE MODEL NEURON'S INPUT-OUTPUT PROPERTIES WILL BE EXPLORED

As is clear from a review of the above set of interrelated equations governing the dynamics of the state variables of the model neuron, there are quite a few externally specified parameters (17) even in such a simple model. Presumably the thresholds are fairly well measureable, and the rate constants and time constants may be specified by measurement of time courses in patch clamp experiments. We are nevertheless dealing with parameters of which some are thought to be variable and which are probably modulated explicitly by normal mechanisms in neurons. Therefor we wish to explore the effect that variation of any of these parameters has on the input-output properties of the model neuron. **In fact, we will find indication that the modulation of these parameters, in particular the rate constants governing the dendritic potassium current and internal calcium accumulation, may be very effective targets of neural plasticity. We find that the neuron's input-output properties are more sensitive to these parameters than to modulation of the efficacy of the synapse strength per se.**

2.1   PROTOCOL FOR SYSTEMATIC EXPLORATION OF THE EFFECT OF VARIATION IN THE MODEL'S PARAMETERS ON THE INPUT-OUTPUT PROPERTIES OF THE MODEL NEURON

We started with the parameters all set to a set of benchmarks and drove the neuron with a constant input to the dendrite. (We could have driven the soma instead, or both soma and dendrite, and we could have chosen more complex input streams. See below for trials where we systematically vary the input but the parameter values are held steady.) The input was a steady command input of 35mv. The values of all the benchmark parameters are given in Table 1.

We then systematically halved and doubled each of the 17 parameters in turn, while leaving all other parameters fixed. Note that in all cases and in fact with any driving input this model neuron fires in bursts. This is due to the long time course of the potassium current in the dendrite, which enforces a long refractory period (about 40-80msec) even during continuous stimulation.

2.2   RESULTS OF SYSTEMATIC VARIATION OF PARAMETERS OF MODEL NEURON

The results are summarized in the notes to Table 1. Following are several observations about the different parameters' varying degree of efficacy in modulation of the input-output function.

1) The most striking finding is that variation of the activation rate of the potassium current, particularly the potassium current in the dendrite, is the most effective means of modulating the input-output properties of the model neuron. The transfer function is 250% more sensitive to an increase in the [CA]-gated dendritic potassium current activation rate than it is to an increase in synaptic efficacy per se.

2) Changing the **time constant** of the [CA]-gated potassium current in the dendrite is the only parameter change which effectively modulates the number of **bursts per second** (see Figure 1). Changing the time constant of the voltage-gated potassium current in the soma, does not have any effect on the number of bursts per second.

3.0   MEASUREMENT OF THE INPUT/OUTPUT RELATION OF THE MODEL NEURON

The input/output relation was determined by the following protocol: The input was supplied in the form of a square wave of current injected into the dendritic compartment, and the frequency of the pulses and their magnitude was systematically varied.

The output of the soma, in the form of action potentials fired per second, was plotted against the input rate, defined as the product of the square wave frequency and the magnitude of the injected current. The duration of pulses was kept fixed at 20 msec (but see below), all internal parameters were fixed at their benchmark levels.

3.1   THE SHAPE OF THE INPUT/OUTPUT RELATION

Figure 2 depicts the above described plot in the case where all the internal parameters were fixed at purported "benchmark" values except for the parameters governing intradendritic calcium accumulation.. It is clearly not strictly monotonic (there are resonance points) though a smoothed version is monotonic, and it does not faithfully render a sigmoid.

3.2   THE INPUT/OUTPUT RELATION IS UNCHANGED IF THE SQUARE SHAPE OF THE EPSP DRIVING THE DENDRITE IS REPLACED BY AN ALPHA FUNCTION

The trials in this study were largely conducted using a square wave as the input driving the dendritic compartment. In order to check whether the unphysical square shape of the envelope of this current injection was coloring the results, the input/output relation was measured in a set of trials wherein the alpha function commonly used to model the time course of EPSP's replaced the square pulse. The total current injected per pulse was kept uniform. **The results, shown in Figure 3, are surprising: The input/output relation was almost completely unaltered by the substitution.   This suggests that the detailed shape and fourier spectrum of the time course of synaptic input has nearly no effect of the neuron's output.** Thus it is suggested that very adequate models can be built without the need for a strict modelling of the synaptic EPSP. I expect this effect is due to the temporal integration ongoing in the summation of input to this system, which blurs the exact shape of any input envelope.

3.3   MODULATION OF THE INPUT/OUTPUT RELATION   BY VARIATION OF INTERNAL MODEL PARAMTERS

Figure 1 portrays the input/output relation measured in three cases in which all internal parameters are identical except the rate of accumulation of intradendric calcium. The lower curve is the case where the calcium accumulation rate is highest. Since [Ca] accumulation drives the dendritic potassium current, the activation of which in turn hyperpolarizes the dendrite and thus indirectly suppresses firing in the soma, we expect output in this case to be lower for a given input as is indeed the result observed. Note that the parameter being varied would be expected to be inversely proportional to the amount of available intradendritic calcium buffer. **Hence the amount of**

intradendritic buffer has a profound ability to modulate the transfer function of the system.

4.0 CONCLUSIONS

As regards the shape of the transfer function itself, we have found it to be non-monotonic (there are resonance points) unless it is smoothed. The shape of the transfer function appears little effected by the envelope of the EPSP (i.e. square pulse input produces nearly the same transfer function as the case where alpha functions are substituted for the square pulses in modelling the EPSP).

A parameter sensitivity analysis of a 2 compartment model neuron with active membranes reveals some unexpected results. For example, the input/output (transfer) function of the neuron is 250% more sensitive to the activation rate of the [CA]-gated dendritic potassium current than it is to synaptic efficacy per se. This in turn suggests that, as has indeed been observed (Alkon et al, 1988; Hawkins, 1989; Olds et al, 1989), nature might employ mechanisms other than simply increasing synaptic conductance during the EPSP to enhance the efficacy of the transfer function.

Alkon, D.L. et al, J. Neurochemistry, Volume 51, 903, (1988).

Hawkins, R. D. in Computational Models of Learning in Simple Neural Systems, Hawkins and Bower, Eds., Academic Press, (1989).

MacGregor, R., Neural and Brain Modelling, Academic Press, (1988).

Olds, J. L. et al, Science, Volume 245, 866, (1989).

TABLE 1

RESULTS OF PARAMETER SENSITIVITY ANALYSIS

PROTOCOL: EACH OF THE 17 INTERNAL PARAMETERS OF THE MODEL NEURON WAS VARIED IN TURN, WHILE ALL THE OTHERS WERE KEPT FIXED AT BENCHMARK VALUES. THE DENDRITE WAS DRIVEN IN EACH CASE WITH A STEADY FIXED INPUT AND THE RESULTING BURSTING RATE AND FIRING RATE WAS COUNTED. IN THE FINAL TRIAL, ALL THE PARAMETERS WERE LEFT FIXED AND THE INPUT MAGNITUDE WAS VARIED, TO SIMULATE FOR COMPARISON THE EFFECT OF MODULATION OF SYNAPTIC EFFICACY.

PARAMETER	SYMBOL		VALUE	BURSTS SEC	SPIKES/ BURST	FIRING FREQ.	FIRING FREQ. AS % OF BENCHMARK
SOMATIC MEMBRANE TIME CONSTANT	TS	BENCHMARK	5.0	13.51	2	27.03	100.0%
		LOW	2.5	13.70	2	27.40	101.4%
		HIGH	10.0	12.82	2	25.64	94.9%
DENDRITIC MEMBRANE TIME CONSTANT	TD	BENCHMARK	5.0	13.51	2	27.03	100.0%
		LOW	2.5	13.51	2	27.03	100.0%
		HIGH	10.0	12.66	2	25.32	93.7%

PARAMETER	SYMBOL		VALUE	BURSTS SEC	SPIKES/ BURST	FIRING FREQ.	FIRING FREQ. AS % OF BENCHMARK
THRESHOLD FOR [CA]-GATED POTASSIUM CURRENT IN DENDRITE (1)	CALCTHRESH	BENCHMARK LOW HIGH	20.0 10.0 40.0	13.51 12.82 13.51	2 1 3	27.03 12.82 40.54	100.0% 47.4% 150.0%
ACTIVATION RATE OF SOMATIC POTASSIUM CURRENT (2)	B	BENCHMARK LOW HIGH	33.0 16.5 66.0	13.51 12.99 13.51	2 3 1	27.03 38.96 13.51	100.0% 144.2% 50.0%
ACTIVATION RATE OF DENDRITIC [CA]-GATED POTASSIUM CURRENT	BD	BENCHMARK LOW HIGH	75.0 37.5 150.0	13.51 12.35 13.16	2 4 2	27.03 49.38 26.32	100.0% 182.7% 97.4%
TIME CONSTANT OF SOMATIC POTASSIUM CURRENT (2)	TGK	BENCHMARK LOW HIGH	3.5 1.8 7.0	13.51 13.51 13.33	2 2 2	27.03 27.03 26.67	100.0% 100.0% 98.7%
TIME CONSTANT OF DENDRITIC POTASSIUM CURRENT (3)	TGKD	BENCHMARK LOW HIGH	10.0 5.0 20.0	13.51 21.74 8.00	2 2 3	27.03 43.48 24.00	100.0% 160.9% 88.8%
ACTIVATION RATE OF CALCIUM CONDUCTANCE	D	BENCHMARK LOW HIGH	2.2 1.1 4.4	13.51 14.71 11.11	2 2 4	27.03 29.41 44.44	100.0% 108.8% 164.4%
TIME CONSTANT OF DENDRITIC CALCIUM CONDUCTANCE	TGC	BENCHMARK LOW HIGH	5.0 2.5 10.0	13.51 14.29 12.82	2 2 2	27.03 28.57 25.64	100.0% 105.7% 94.9%
ACCUMULATION RATE OF CALCIUM FOR A GIVEN CALCIUM CONDUCTANCE (4)	A	BENCHMARK LOW HIGH	2.0 1.0 4.0	13.51 13.51 12.99	2 3 1	27.03 40.54 12.99	100.0% 150.0% 48.1%
TIME CONSTANT FOR CALCIUM ACCUMULATION	TCA	BENCHMARK LOW HIGH	5.0 2.5 10.0	13.51 14.71 11.76	2 1 3	27.03 14.71 35.29	100.0% 54.4% 130.6%
INPUT CONDUCTANCE FROM DENDRITE TO SOMA (5)	GDS	BENCHMARK LOW HIGH	5.0 2.5 10.0	13.51 11.90 14.29	2 1 4	27.03 11.90 57.14	100.0% 44.0% 211.4%
INPUT CONDUCTANCE FROM SOMA TO DENDRITE	GSD	BENCHMARK LOW HIGH	5.0 2.5 10.0	13.51 13.89 10.75	2 2 2	27.03 27.78 21.51	100.0% 102.8% 79.6%
SOMATIC FIRING THRESHOLD	THRESHOLD	BENCHMARK LOW HIGH	12.0 6.0 24.0	13.51 15.38 13.16	2 4 1	27.03 61.54 13.16	100.0% 227.7% 48.7%
CA SPIKE THRESHOLD IN DENDRITE (6)	CSPKTHRESH	BENCHMARK LOW HIGH	12.0 6.0 24.0	13.51 14.08 13.70	2 2 2	27.03 28.17 27.40	100.0% 104.2% 101.4%
SYNAPTIC INPUT TO DENDRITE (8)	INPUT	BENCHMARK LOW (7) HIGH	35.0 27.0 70.0	13.51 11.63 16.95	2 2 2	27.03 23.26 33.90	100.0% 86.0% 125.4%

NOTES TO PARAMETER SENSITIVITY ANALYSIS

(1) The number of spikes per burst is altered by modulating the internal calcium concentration required to trigger the dendritic potassium current. In an observation repeated several times herein, it seems clear that modulating the hyperpolarizing potassium current has a marked effectiveness in modulating the neuron's output.

(2) Modulating the activation rate (B) of the somatic potassium current strongly effects firing, but changing the time constant of this current has almost no effect either on bursts/second or spikes/burst.

(3) However, note that, among all 17 parameters of this model neuron, it is only the time constant of the [CA]-gated dendritic potassium current which is effective in modulating the rate of bursting (whereas the somatic potassium current time constant does not seem to effect the model neuron's output at all).

(4) This quantity, the accumulation rate of calcium in the dendrite per unit calcium conductance, would increase as the effectiveness of calcium buffers within the dendrite decreased.

(5) Despite its efficacy in modulating the neuron's output, this parameter is presumably not a likely candidate for plasticity, because it depends on the axial resistance of the cytoplasm, the cross section of the base of the dendrite, and the volume of the soma, all of which seem unlikely to be the subject to modulation.

(6) Surprisingly, the overall input-output relation for the neuron is not much effected by changing the threshold for the voltage gated calcium spike activity in the dendrite.

(7) The minimum dendritic input required to produce any spike activity (that is, to increase the voltage in the soma above firing threshold) may be calculated to be 26.4 with all the other parameters at benchmark values. Hence 27 is an input level that is only 2% above the minimum level to get any firing at all. Note that it appears a 2 spike burst is always produced (with the internal parameters set at the benchmark levels) if any firing at all is elicited. The number of spikes per burst, then, is modulated by conductance activation rates and calcium accumulation rates but not by input. Tables 2 and 3 demonstrate this over a wide range of inputs.

(8) Note that doubling the synaptic input to the dendrite only increases the model neuron's firing rate by 25.4%, but that, for example, doubling the activiation rate of the dendritic calcium current increases the firing rate by 64.4%. Hence we suggest that modulation of synaptic efficacy is not the only choice or even the most effective choice for the mechanism underlying plasticity. Alkon (1988,1989) and others have in fact recently reported that an increase in protein kinase C, leading to a reduction in calcium-activated potassium current, is observed to be associated with conditioning in Hermissenda and rabbit. Thus, plasticity in the nervous system may indeed operate via a whole set of internal dynamic parameters, of which synapse efficacy is only one.

DENDRITIC K–CURRENT TIME CONST: 5 MSEC

FIRING RATE=43.48   BURST RATE=21.74

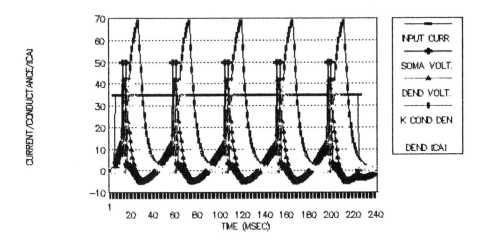

DENDRITIC K–CURRENT TIME CONST: 20 MSEC

FIRING RATE=24.00   BURST RATE=8.00

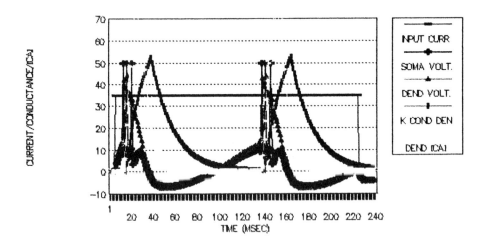

Figure 1

THE INPUT/OUTPUT RELATION
CA ACCUMULATION RATE SET AT 3 LEVELS

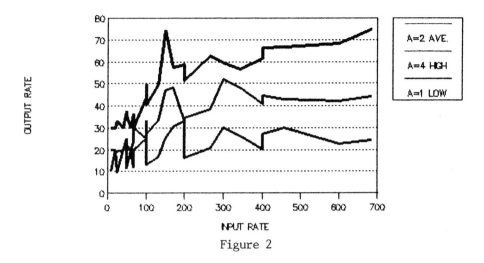

Figure 2

COMPARISON OF INPUT/OUTPUT RELATION
EPSP SQUARE PULSE VS ALPHA FUNCTION

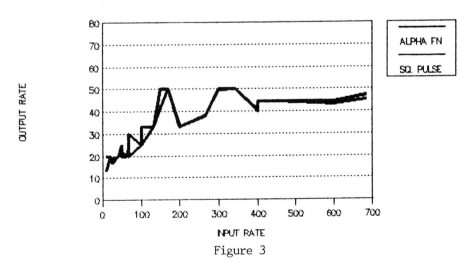

Figure 3

Analytic Solutions to the Formation of Feature-Analysing Cells of a Three-Layer Feedforward Visual Information Processing Neural Net

D.S. Tang
Microelectronics and Computer Technology Corporation
3500 West Balcones Center Drive
Austin, TX 78759-6509
email: tang@mcc.com

ABSTRACT

Analytic solutions to the information-theoretic evolution equation of the connection strength of a three-layer feedforward neural net for visual information processing are presented. The results are (1) the receptive fields of the feature-analysing cells correspond to the eigenvector of the maximum eigenvalue of the Fredholm integral equation of the first kind derived from the evolution equation of the connection strength; (2) a symmetry-breaking mechanism (parity-violation) has been identified to be responsible for the changes of the morphology of the receptive field; (3) the conditions for the formation of different morphologies are explicitly identified.

1 INTRODUCTION

The use of Shannon's information theory (Shannon and Weaver,1949) to the study of neural nets has been shown to be very instructive in explaining the formation of different receptive fields in the early visual information processing, as evident by the works of Linsker (1986,1988). It has been demonstrated that the connection strengths which maximize the information rate from one layer of neurons to the next exhibit center-surround, all-excitatory/all-inhibitory and orientation-selective properties. This could lead to a better understanding on the mechanisms with which the cells are self-organized to achieve adaptive responses to the changing enviroment. However, results from these studies are mainly numerical in nature and therefore do not provide deeper insights as to how and under what conditions the morphologies of the feature-analyzing cells are formed. We present in this paper accurate analytic solutions to the problems posed by Linsker. Namely, we solve analytically the evolution equation of the connection strength, obtain close expressions for the receptive fields and derive the formation conditions for different classes of morphologies. These results are crucial to the understanding of the architecture of neural net as an information processing system. Below, we briefly summarize the analytic techniques involved and the main results we obtained.

2 THREE-LAYER FEEDFORWARD NEURAL NET

The neural net configuration (Fig. 1) is identical to that reported in references 2 and 3 in which a feedforword three-layer neural net is considered. The layers are labelled consecutively as layer-A, layer-B and layer-C.

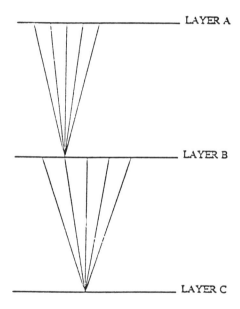

Figure 1: The neural net configuration

The input-output relation for the signals to propagate from one layer to the consecutive layer is assumed to be linear,

$$M_j = \sum_{i=1}^{N_j} C_{ji}(L_i + n_i). \qquad (1)$$

n_i is assumed to be an additive Gaussian white noise with constant standard deviation α and zero mean. L_i and M_j are the ith stochastic input signal and the jth stochastic output signal respectively. C_{ji} is the connection strength which defines the morphology of the receptive field and is to be determined by maximizing the information rate. The spatial summation in equation (1) is to sum over all N_j

inputs located according to a gaussian distributed within the same layer, with the center of the distribution lying directly above the location of the M_j output signal. If the statistical behavior of the input signal is assumed to be Gaussian,

$$P(L) = \frac{e^{-\sum_{ij} L_i Q_{ij}^{-1} L_j}}{(2\pi)^{\frac{N}{2}} \sqrt{Det(Q)}}, \tag{2}$$

then the information rate can be derived and is given by

$$R(M) = \frac{1}{2} ln[1 + \frac{\sum C_i Q_{ij} C_j}{\alpha^2 \sum C_i^2}]. \tag{3}$$

The matrix Q is the correlation of the L's, $Q_{ij} = E[(L_i - \tilde{L})(L_j - \tilde{L})]$ with mean $\tilde{L}$. The set of connection strengths which optimize the information rate subject to a normalization condition, $\sum C_i^2 = A$, and to their overall absolute mean, $(\sum C_i)^2 = B$, constitute physically plausible receptive fields. Below is the solutions to the problem.

3 FREDHOLM INTEGRAL EQUATION

The evolution equation for the connection strength C_n which maximizes the information rate subject to the constraints is

$$\dot{C}_n = \frac{1}{N} \sum_{i=1}^{N} (Q_{ni} + k_2) C_i. \tag{4}$$

k_2 is the Lagrange multiplier. First, we assume that the statistical ensemble of the visual images has the highest information content under the condition of fixed variance. Then, from the maximum entropy principle, it can be shown that the Gaussian distribution with a correlation Q_{ij} being a constant multiple of the kronecker delta function describes the statistics of this ensemble of visual images. It can be shown that the solution to the above equation with Q_{ni} being a kronecker delta function is a constant. Therefore, the connection strengths which defines the linear input-output relation from layer A to layer B is either all-excitatory or all-inhibitory. Hence, without loss of generality, we take the values of the layer A to layer B connection strengths to be all-excitatory. Making use of this result, the correlation function of the output signals at layer B (i.e. the input signals to layer C) is derived

$$Q_{ni} = C_Q exp(-r^2/2r_B^2) \tag{5}$$

where r is the distance between the nth and the ith output signals. $C_Q = \pi N/50$. To study the connection strengths of the input-output relation from layer B to layer C, it is more convenient to work with continuous spatial variables. Then the solutions to the discrete evolution equation which maximizes the information rate are solutions to the following Fredholm integral equation of the first kind with the maximum eigenvalue λ,

$$C(\vec{r}) = \frac{1}{N\lambda} \int_{-\infty}^{+\infty} K(\vec{R}|\vec{r}) C(\vec{R}) d\vec{R} \tag{6}$$

where the kernal is $K(\vec{R}|\vec{r}) = (Q(\vec{R}-\vec{r})+k_2)\rho(\vec{R})$ and the Gaussian input population distribution density is $\rho(\vec{r}) = C_\rho exp(-\frac{r^2}{r_B^2})$ with $C_\rho = \frac{N}{\pi r_B^2}$. In continuous variables, the connection strength is denoted by $C(\vec{r})$. A complete set of solutions to this Fredholm integral equation can be analytically derived. We are interested only in the solutions with the maximum eigenvalues. Below we present the results.

4 ANALYTIC SOLUTIONS

The solution with the maximum eigenvalue has a few number of nodes. This can be constructed as a linear superposition of an infinite number of gaussian functions with different variances and means, which are treated as independent variables to be solved with the Fredholm integral equation. Full details are contained in reference 3.

(a) Symmetric solution $C(-\vec{r}) = C(\vec{r})$:
For $k_2 \neq 0$, the connection strength is

$$C(\vec{r}) = b[1 + Gexp(-\frac{r^2}{2\sigma_0^2}) + \frac{H}{(1-H)}Gexp(-\frac{r^2}{2\sigma_\infty^2})] \tag{7}$$

with $G = \frac{a\pi}{\frac{1}{2r_B^2}+\frac{1}{2a^2}}$ and $H = \frac{a\pi}{\frac{1}{2r_B^2}+\frac{1}{2a^2}+\frac{1}{2\sigma_0^2}}$. Here, $\alpha^2 = .5r_B^2$, $\frac{r_B^2}{\sigma_0^2} = 0.66667$,

$\frac{r_B^2}{\sigma_\infty^2} = 0.73205$ and $a \equiv C_Q C_\rho / N\lambda$.
The eigenvalue is given by

$$\lambda = \frac{k_2 C_\rho \pi}{N}[2\alpha^2 + \frac{G}{\frac{1}{2\sigma_0^2}+\frac{1}{2\alpha^2}} + \frac{H}{(1-H)}G\frac{1}{\frac{1}{2\sigma_\infty^2}+\frac{1}{2\alpha^2}}]. \tag{8}$$

For $k_2 = 0$, the connection strength is

$$C(\vec{r}) = fexp(-\frac{r^2}{2\sigma^2}) \tag{9}$$

and the eigenvalue is

$$\lambda = \frac{C_Q C_\rho \pi}{N[\frac{1}{2r_B^2} + \frac{1}{2\alpha^2} + \frac{1}{2\sigma_\infty^2}]}. \tag{10}$$

These can be shown to be identical to the case of $k_2 \neq 0$ when the limit $k_2 \to 0$ is appropriately taken.
(b) Antisymmetric solution $C(-\vec{r}) = -C(\vec{r})$:
The connection strength is

$$C(\vec{r}) = (fx + gy)exp(-\frac{r^2}{2r_B^2}[1 - \frac{1}{1+\frac{r_B^2}{\alpha^2}+\frac{r_B^2}{\sigma_\infty^2}}]). \tag{11}$$

The eigenvalue is

$$\lambda = \frac{\pi C_Q C_\rho}{N2r_B^2[\frac{1}{2r_B^2} + \frac{1}{2\alpha^2} + \frac{1}{2\sigma_\infty^2}]^2}. \tag{12}$$

In the above equations, b, f and g are normalization constants.

Below are the conditions under which the different morphologies (Fig.2) are formed.

(i)$k_2 > 0$, the symmetric solution has the largest eigenvalue. The receptive field is either all-excitatory or all-inhibitory, Fig.2a.

(ii)$-0.891C_Q < k_2 < 0$, the symmetric solution has the largest eigenvalue. The receptive field has a mexcian-hat appearance, Fig.2b.

(iii)$k_2 < -0.891C_Q$, the anti-symmetric solution has the largest eigenvalue. The receptive field has two regions divided by a straight line of arbitrary direction(degeneracy). The two regions are mirror image of each other. One is totally inhibitory and the other is totally excitatory, Fig.2c.

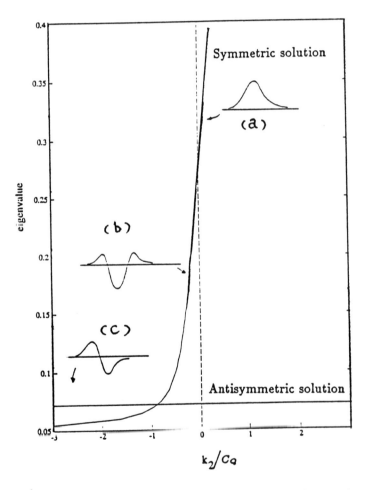

Figure 2: Relations between the receptive field and the maximum eigenvalues. Inserts are examples of the connection strength $C(\vec{r})$ versus the spatial dimension in the x-direction.

Note that the information rate as given by Eq.(3) is invariant under the operation of the spatial reflection, $-\vec{r} \to \vec{r}$. The solutions to the optimaziation problem violates parity-conservation as the overall mean of the connection strength (i.e. equivalently k_2) changes to different values.

Results from numerical simulations agree very well with the analytic results. Numerical simulations are performed from 80 to 600 synapses. The agreement is good even for the case in which the number of synapses are 200.

In summary, we have shown precisely how the mexican-hat morphology emerges as identified by (ii) above. Furthermore, a symmetry-breaking(parity-violation) mechanism has been identified to explain the changes of the morphology from spatially symmetric to anti-symmetric appearance as k_2 passes through $-0.891C_Q$. It is very likely that similar symmetry breaking mechanisms are present in neural nets with lateral connections.

References

1. C.E.Shannon and W. Weaver, The mathematical Theory of Communication (Univ. of Illinois Press,Urbana,1949).
2. R.Linsker, Proc. Natl. Acad. Sci. USA 83,7508(1986); Computer 21 (3), 105(1988).
3. D.S. Tang, Phys.Rev A, 40,6626(1989).

PART II:
SPEECH AND SIGNAL PROCESSING

Practical Characteristics of Neural Network and Conventional Pattern Classifiers on Artificial and Speech Problems*

Yuchun Lee
Digital Equipment Corp.
40 Old Bolton Road,
OGO1-2U11
Stow, MA 01775-1215

Richard P. Lippmann
Lincoln Laboratory, MIT
Room B-349
Lexington, MA 02173-9108

ABSTRACT

Eight neural net and conventional pattern classifiers (Bayesian-unimodal Gaussian, k-nearest neighbor, standard back-propagation, adaptive-stepsize back-propagation, hypersphere, feature-map, learning vector quantizer, and binary decision tree) were implemented on a serial computer and compared using two speech recognition and two artificial tasks. Error rates were statistically equivalent on almost all tasks, but classifiers differed by orders of magnitude in memory requirements, training time, classification time, and ease of adaptivity. Nearest-neighbor classifiers trained rapidly but required the most memory. Tree classifiers provided rapid classification but were complex to adapt. Back-propagation classifiers typically required long training times and had intermediate memory requirements. These results suggest that classifier selection should often depend more heavily on practical considerations concerning memory and computation resources, and restrictions on training and classification times than on error rate.

*This work was sponsored by the Department of the Air Force and the Air Force Office of Scientific Research.

1   Introduction

A shortcoming of much recent neural network pattern classification research has been an overemphasis on back-propagation classifiers and a focus on classification error rate as the main measure of performance. This research often ignores the many alternative classifiers that have been developed (see e.g. [10]) and the practical tradeoffs these classifiers provide in training time, memory requirements, classification time, complexity, and adaptivity. The purpose of this research was to explore these tradeoffs and gain experience with many different classifiers. Eight neural net and conventional pattern classifiers were used. These included Bayesian-unimodal Gaussian, k-nearest neighbor (kNN), standard back-propagation, adaptive-stepsize back-propagation, hypersphere, feature-map (FM), learning vector quantizer (LVQ), and binary decision tree classifiers.

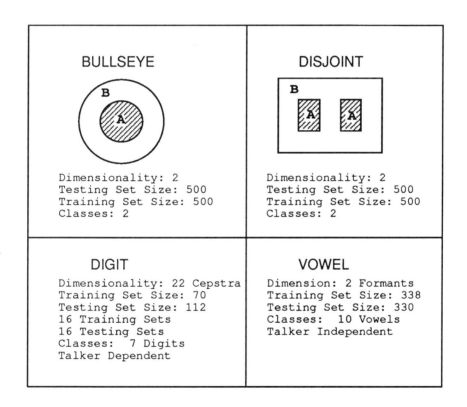

Figure 1: Four problems used to test classifiers.

Classifiers were implemented on a serial computer and tested using the four problems shown in Fig. 1. The upper two artificial problems (Bullseye and Disjoint) require simple two-dimensional convex or disjoint decision regions for minimum error classification. The lower digit recognition task (7 digits, 22 cepstral parameters,

16 talkers, 70 training and 112 testing patterns per talker) and vowel recognition task (10 vowels, 2 formant parameters, 67 talkers, 338 training and 330 testing patterns) use real speech data and require more complex decision regions. These tasks are described in [6, 11] and details of experiments are available in [9].

2   Training and Classification Parameter Selection

Initial experiments were performed to select sizes of classifiers that provided good performance with limited training data and also to select high-performing versions of each type of classifier. Experiments determined the number of nodes and hidden layers in back-propagation classifiers, pruning techniques to use with tree and hypersphere classifiers, and numbers of exemplars or kernel nodes to use with feature-map and LVQ classifiers.

2.1   Back-Propagation Classifiers

In standard back-propagation, weights typically are updated only after each *trial* or *cycle*. A trial is defined as a single training pattern presentation and a cycle is defined as a sequence of trials which sample all patterns in the training set. In group updating, weights are updated every T trials while in trial-by-trial training, weights are updated every trial. Furthermore, in trial-by-trial updating, training patterns can be presented *sequentially* where a pattern is guaranteed to be presented every T trials, or they can be presented *randomly* where patterns are randomly selected from the training set. Initial experiments demonstrated that random trial-by-trial training provided the best convergence rate and error reduction during training. It was thus used whenever possible with all back-propagation classifiers.

All back-propagation classifiers used a single hidden layer and an output layer with as many nodes as classes. The classification decision corresponded to the class of the node in the output layer with the highest output value. During training, the desired output pattern, D, was a vector with all elements set to 0 except for the element corresponding to the correct class of the input pattern. This element of D was set to 1. The mean-square difference between the actual output and this desired output error is minimized when the output of each node is exactly the Bayes *a posteriori* probability for each correct class [1, 10]. Back-propagation with this "1 of m" desired output is thus well justified theoretically because it attempts to estimate minimum-error Bayes probability functions. The number of hidden nodes used in each back-propagation classifier was determined experimentally as described in [6, 7, 9, 11].

Three "improved" back-propagation classifiers with the potential of reduced training times where studied. The first, the *adaptive-stepsize-classifier*, has a global stepsize that is adjusted after every training cycle as described in [4]. The second, the *multiple-adaptive-stepsize classifier*, has multiple stepsizes (one for each weight) which are adjusted after every training cycle as described in [8]. The third classifier uses the conjugate gradient method [9, 12] to minimize the output mean-square error.

The goal of the three "improved" versions of back-propagation was to shorten the often lengthy training time observed with standard back-propagation. These improvements relied on fundamental assumptions about the error surfaces. However, only the multiple-adaptive-stepsize algorithm was used for the final classifier comparison due to the poor performance of the other two algorithms. The adaptive-stepsize classifier often could not achieve adequately low error rates because the global stepsize (η) frequently converged too quickly to zero during training. The multiple-adaptive-stepsize classifier did not train faster than a standard back-propagation classifier with carefully selected stepsize value. Nevertheless, it eliminated the need for pre-selecting the stepsize parameter. The conjugate gradient classifier worked well on simple problems but almost always rapidly converged to a local minimum which provided high error rates on the more complex speech problems.

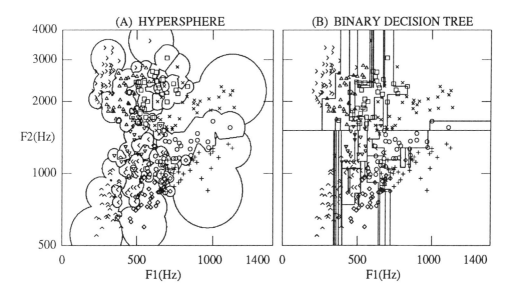

Figure 2: Decision regions formed by the hypersphere classifier (A) and by the binary decision tree classifier (B) on the test set for the vowel problem. Inputs consist of the first two formants for ten vowels in the words $\wedge$ who'd, $\diamond$ hawed, $+$ hod, $\bigcirc$ hud, $\times$ had, $>$ heed, $\triangle$ hid, $\square$ head, $\triangledown$ heard, and $<$ hood as described in [6, 9].

2.2　Hypersphere Classifier

Hypersphere classifiers build decision regions from nodes that form separate hypersphere decision regions. Many different types of hypersphere classifiers have been developed [2, 13]. Experiments discussed in [9], led to the selection of a specific version of hypersphere classifier with "pruning". Each hypersphere can only shrink in size, centers are not repositioned, an ambiguous response (positive outputs from hyperspheres corresponding to different classes) is mediated using a nearest-neighbor rule, and hyperspheres that do not contribute to the classification performance are pruned from the classifier for proper "fitting" of the data and to reduce memory usage. Decision regions formed by a hypersphere classifier for the vowel classification problem are shown in the left side of Fig. 2. Separate regions in this figure correspond to different vowels. Decision region boundaries contain arcs which are segments of hyperspheres (circles in two dimensions) and linear segments caused by the application of the nearest neighbor rule for ambiguous responses.

2.3   Binary Decision Tree Classifier

Binary decision tree classifiers from [3] were used in all experiments. Each node in a tree has only two immediate offspring and the splitting decision is based on only one of the input dimensions. Decision boundaries are thus overlapping *hyper-rectangles* with sides parallel to the axes of the input space and decision regions become more complex as more nodes are added to the tree. Decision trees for each problem were grown until they classified all the training data exactly and then pruned back using the test data to determine when to stop pruning. A complete description of the decision tree classifier used is provided in [9] and decision regions formed by this classifier for the vowel problem are shown in the right side of Fig. 2.

2.4   Other Classifiers

The remaining four classifiers were tuned by selecting coarse sizing parameters to "fit" the problem imposed. Some of these parameters include the number of exemplars in the LVQ and feature map classifiers and k in the k-nearest neighbor classifier. Different types of covariance matrices (full, diagonal, and various types of grand averaging) were also tried for the Bayesian-unimodal Gaussian classifier. Best sizing parameter values for classifiers were almost always not those that that best classified the training set. For the purpose of this study, training data was used to determine internal parameters or weights in classifiers. The size of a classifier and coarse sizing parameters were selected using the test data. In real applications when a test set is not available, alternative methods, such as *cross validation*[3, 14] would be used.

3   Classifier Comparison

All eight classifiers were evaluated on the four problems using simulations programmed in C on a Sun 3/110 workstation with a floating point accelerator. Classifiers were trained until their training error rate converged.

3.1   Error Rates

Error rates for all classifiers on all problems are shown in Fig. 3. The middle solid lines in this figure correspond to the average error rate over all classifiers for each problem. The shaded area is one binomial standard deviation above and below this average. As can be seen, there are only three cases where the error rate of any one classifier is substantially different from the average error. These exceptions are the Bayesian-unimodal Gaussian classifier on the disjoint problem

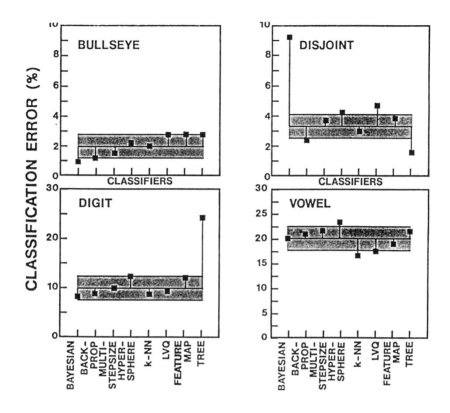

Figure 3: Error rates for all classifiers on all four problems. The middle solid lines correspond to the average error rate over all classifiers for each problem. The shaded area is one binomial standard deviation above and below the average error rate.

and the decision tree classifier on the digit and the disjoint problem. The Bayesian-unimodal Gaussian classifier performed poorly on the disjoint problem because it was unable to form the required bimodal disjoint decision regions. The decision tree classifier performed poorly on the digit problem because the small amount of training data (10 patterns per class) was adequately classified by a minimal 13-node tree which didn't generalize well and didn't even use all 22 input dimensions. The decision tree classifier worked well for the disjoint problem because it forms decision regions parallel to both input axes as required for this problem.

3.2   Practical Characteristics

In contrast to the small differences in error rate, differences between classifiers on practical performance issues such as training and classification time, and memory usage were large. Figure 4 shows that the classifiers differed by orders of magnitude in training time. Shown in log-scale, the k nearest neighbor stands out distinctively

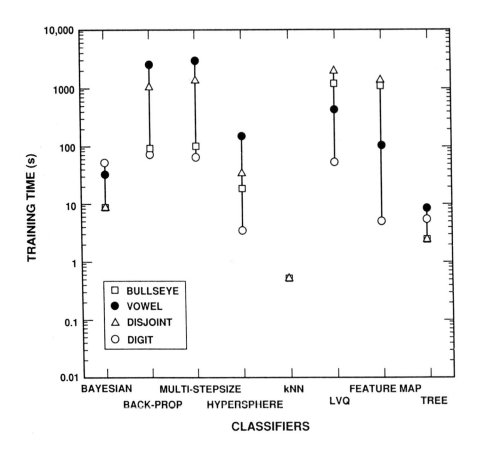

Figure 4: Training time of all classifiers on all four problems.

as the fastest trained classifier by many orders of magnitude. Depending on the problem, Bayesian-unimodal Gaussian, hypersphere, decision tree, and feature map classifiers also have reasonably short training times. LVQ and back-propagation classifiers often required the longest training time. It should be noted that alternative implementations, for example using parallel computers, would lead to different results.

Adaptivity or the ability to adapt using new patterns after complete training also differed across classifiers. The k-nearest neighbor and hypersphere classifiers are able to incorporate new information most readily. Others such as back-propagation and LVQ classifiers are more difficult to adapt and some, such as decision tree classifiers, are not designed to handle further adaptation after training is complete.

The binary decision tree can classify patterns much faster than others. Unlike most classifiers that depend on "distance" calculations between the input pattern and all stored exemplars, the decision tree classifier requires only a few numerical comparisons. Therefore, the decision tree classifier was many orders of magnitude faster

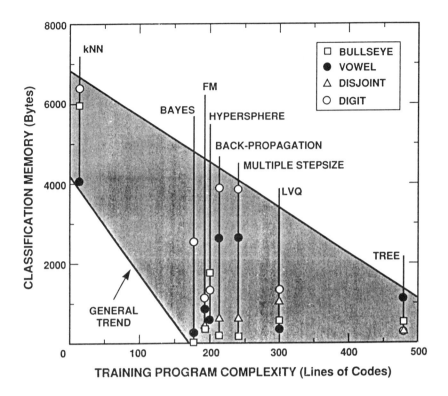

Figure 5: Classification memory usage versus training program complexity for all classifiers on all four problems.

in classification than other classifiers. However, decision tree classifiers require the most complex training algorithm. As a rough measurement of the ease of implementation, subjectively measured by the number of lines in the training program, the decision tree classifier is many times more complex than the simplest training program– that of the k-nearest neighbor classifier. However, the k-nearest neighbor classifier is one of the slowest in classification when implemented serially without complex search techniques such as k-d trees [5]. These techniques greatly reduce classification time but make adaptation to new training data more difficult and increase complexity.

4   Trade-Offs Between Performance Criteria

No one classifier out-performed the rest on all performance criteria. The selection of a "best" classifier depends on practical problem constraints which differ across problems. Without knowing these constraints or associating explicit costs with various performance criteria, a classifier that is "best" can not be meaningfully determined. Instead, there are numerous trade-off relationships between various criteria.

One trade-off shown in Fig. 5 is classification memory usage versus the complexity of the training algorithm. The far upper left corner, where training is very simple and memory is not efficiently utilized, contains the k-nearest neighbor classifier. In contrast, the binary decision tree classifier is in the lower right corner, where the overall memory usage is minimized and the training process is very complex. Other classifiers are intermediate.

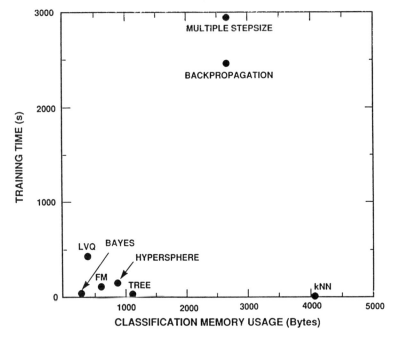

Figure 6: Training time versus classification memory usage of all classifiers on the vowel problem.

Figure 6 shows the relationship between training time and classification memory usage for the vowel problem. The k-nearest neighbor classifier consistently provides the shortest training time but requires the most memory. The hypersphere classifier optimizes these two criteria well across all four problems. Back-propagation classifiers frequently require long training times and require intermediate amounts of memory.

5   Summary

This study explored practical characteristics of neural net and conventional pattern classifiers. Results demonstrate that classification error rates can be equivalent across classifiers when classifiers are powerful enough to form minimum error decision regions, when they are rigorously tuned, and when sufficient training data is provided. Practical characteristics such as training time, memory requirements, and classification time, however, differed by orders of magnitude. In practice, these factors are more likely to affect classifier selection. Selection will often be driven by practical considerations concerning memory and computation resources, restrictions on training, test, and adaptation times, and ease of use and implementation. The many existing neural net and conventional classifiers allow system designers to trade these characteristics off. Tradeoffs will vary with implementation hardware (e.g. serial versus parallel, analog versus digital) and details of the problem (e.g. dimension of the input vector, complexity of decision regions). Our current research efforts are exploring these tradeoffs on more difficult problems and studying additional classifiers including radial-basis-function classifiers, high-order networks, and Gaussian mixture classifiers.

References

[1] A. R. Barron and R. L. Barron. Statistical learning networks: A unifying view. In *1988 Symposium on the Interface: Statistics and Computing Science*, Reston, Virginia, April 21-23 1988.

[2] B. G. Batchelor. Classification and data analysis in vector space. In B. G. Batchelor, editor, *Pattern Recognition*, chapter 4, pages 67–116. Plenum Press, London, 1978.

[3] L. Breiman, J. H. Friedman, R. A. Olshen, and C. J. Stone. *Classification and Regression Trees*. Wadsworth International Group, Belmont, CA, 1984.

[4] L. W. Chan and F. Fallside. An adaptive training algorithm for back propagation networks. *Computer Speech and Language*, 2:205–218, 1987.

[5] J. H. Friedman, J. L. Bentley, and R. A. Finkel. An algorithm for finding best matches in logarithmic expected time. *ACM Transactions on Mathematical Software*, 3(3):209–226, September 1977.

[6] W. M. Huang and R. P. Lippmann. Neural net and traditional classifiers. In D. Anderson, editor, *Neural Information Processing Systems*, pages 387–396, New York, 1988. American Institute of Physics.

[7] William Y. Huang and Richard P. Lippmann. Comparisons between conventional and neural net classifiers. In *1st International Conference on Neural Networks*, pages IV–485. IEEE, June 1987.

[8] R. A. Jacobs. Increased rates of convergence through learning rate adaptation. *Neural Networks*, 1:295–307, 1988.

[9] Yuchun Lee. Classifiers: Adaptive modules in pattern recognition systems. Master's thesis, Massachusetts Institute of Technology, Department of Electrical Engineering and Computer Science, Cambridge, MA, May 1989.

[10] R. P. Lippmann. Pattern classification using neural networks. *IEEE Communications Magazine*, 27(11):47–54, November 1989.

[11] Richard P. Lippmann and Ben Gold. Neural classifiers useful for speech recognition. In *1st International Conference on Neural Networks*, pages IV–417. IEEE, June 1987.

[12] W. H. Press, B. P. Flannery, S. A. Teukolsky, and W. T. Vetterling, editors. *Numerical Recipes*. Cambridge University Press, New York, 1986.

[13] D. L. Reilly, L. N. Cooper, and C. Elbaum. A neural model for category learning. *Biological Cybernetics*, 45:35–41, 1982.

[14] M. Stone. Cross validation choice and assessment of statistical predictions. *Journal of the Royal Statistical Society*, B-36:111–147, 1974.

Dimensionality Reduction and Prior Knowledge in E-set Recognition

Kevin J. Lang[1]
Computer Science Dept.
Carnegie Mellon University
Pittsburgh, PA 15213
USA

Geoffrey E. Hinton
Computer Science Dept.
University of Toronto
Toronto, Ontario M5S 1A4
Canada

ABSTRACT

It is well known that when an automatic learning algorithm is applied to a fixed corpus of data, the size of the corpus places an upper bound on the number of degrees of freedom that the model can contain if it is to generalize well. Because the amount of hardware in a neural network typically increases with the dimensionality of its inputs, it can be challenging to build a high-performance network for classifying large input patterns. In this paper, several techniques for addressing this problem are discussed in the context of an isolated word recognition task.

1 Introduction

The domain for our research was a speech recognition task that requires distinctions to be learned between recordings of four highly confusable words: the names of the letters "B", "D", "E", and "V". The task was created at IBM's T. J. Watson Research Center, and is difficult because many speakers were included and also because the recordings were made under noisy office conditions using a remote microphone. One hundred male speakers said each of the 4 words twice, once for training and again for testing. The words were spoken in isolation, and the recordings averaged 1.1 seconds in length. The signal-to-noise ratio of the data set has been estimated to be about 15 decibels, as compared to

---

[1] Now at NEC Research Institute, 4 Independence Way, Princeton, NJ 08540.

50 decibels for typical lip-mike recordings (Brown, 1987). The key feature of the data set from our point of view is that each utterance contains a tiny information-laden event — the release of the consonant — which can easily be overpowered by meaningless variation in the strong "E" vowel and by background noise.

Our first step in processing these recordings was to convert them into spectrograms using a standard DFT program. The spectrograms encoded the energy in 128 frequency bands (ranging up to 8 kHz) at 3 msec intervals, and so they contained an average of about 45,000 energy values. Thus, a naive back-propagation network which devoted a separate weight to each of these input components would contain far too many weights to be properly constrained by the task's 400 training patterns.

As described in the next section, we drastically reduced the dimensionality of our training patterns by decreasing their resolution in both frequency and time and also by using a segmentation algorithm to extract the most relevant portion of each pattern. However, our network still contained too many weights, and many of them were devoted to detecting spurious features. This situation motivated the experiments with our network's objective function and architecture that will be described in sections 3 and 4.

2   Reducing the Dimensionality of the Input Patterns

Because it would have been futile to feed our gigantic raw spectrograms into a back-propagation network, we first decreased the time resolution of our input format by a factor of 4 and the frequency resolution of the format by a factor 8. While our compression along the time axis preserved the linearity of the scale, we combined different numbers of raw freqencies into the various frequency bands to create a mel scale, which is linear up to 2 kHz and logarithmic above that, and thus provides more resolution in the more informative lower frequency bands.

Next, a segmentation heuristic was used to locate the consonant in each training pattern so that the rest of the pattern could be discarded. On average, all but 1/7 of each recording was thrown away, but we would have liked to have discarded more. The useful information in a word from the E-set is concentrated in a roughly 50 msec region around the consonant release in the word, but current segmentation algorithms aren't good enough to accurately position a 50 msec window on that region. To prevent the loss of potentially useful information, we extracted a 150 msec window from around each consonant release. This safeguard meant that our networks contained about 3 times as many weights as would be required with an ideal segmentation.

We were also concerned that segmentation errors during recognition could lower our final system's performance, so we adopted a simple segmentation-free testing method in which the trained network is scanned over the full-length version of each testing utterance. Figures 3(a) and 3(b) show the activation traces generated by two different networks when scanned over four sample utterances. To the right of each of the capital letters which identifies a particular sample word is a set of 4 wiggly lines that should be viewed as the output of a 4-channel chart recorder which is connected to the network's four output units. Our recognition rule for unsegmented utterances states that the output unit which

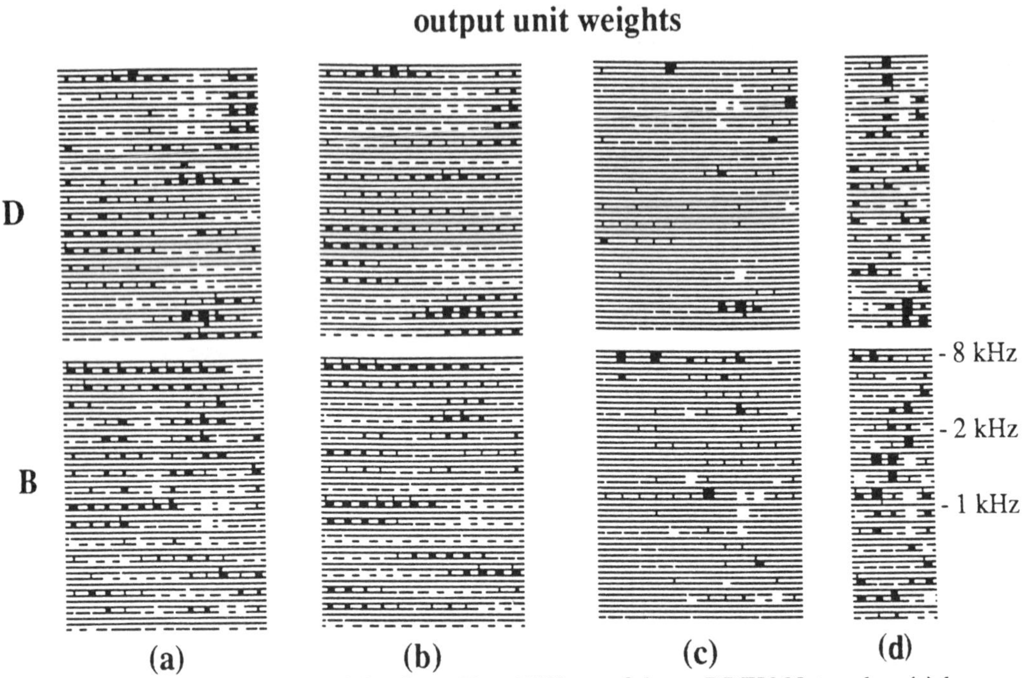

output unit weights

Figure 1: Output Unit Weights from Four Different 2-layer BDEV Networks: (a) baseline, (b) smoothed, (c) decayed, (d) TDNN

generates the largest activation spike (and hence the highest peak in the chart recorder's traces) on a given utterance determines the network's classification of that utterance.[2]

To establish a performance baseline for the experiments that will be described in the next two sections, we trained the simple 2-layer network of figure 2(a) until it had learned to correctly identify 94 percent of our training segments.[3]

This network contains 4 output units (one for each word) but no hidden units.[4] The weights that this network used to recognize the words **B** and **D** are shown in figure 1(a). While these weight patterns are quite noisy, people who know how to read spectrograms can see sensible feature detectors amidst the clutter. For example, both of the units appear to be stimulated by an energy burst near the 9th time frame. However, the units expect to see this energy at different frequencies because the tongue position is different in the consonants that the two units represent.

Unfortunately, our baseline network's weights also contain many details that don't make

---

[2]One can't reasonably expect a network that has been trained on pre-segmented patterns to function well when tested in this way, but our best network (a 3-layer TDNN) actually does perform better in this mode than when trained and tested on segments selected by a Viterbi alignment with an IBM hidden Markov model. Moreover, because the Viterbi alignment procedure is told the identity of the words in advance, it is probably more accurate than any method that could be used in a real recognition system.

[3]This rather arbitrary halting rule for the learning procedure was uniformly employed during the experiments of sections 2, 3 and 4.

[4]Experiments performed with multi-layer networks support the same general conclusions as the results reported here.

any sense to speech recognition experts. These spurious features are artifacts of our small, noisy training set, and are partially to blame for the very poor performance of the network; it achieved only 37 percent recognition accuracy when scanned across the unsegmented testing utterances.

3   Limiting the Complexity of a Network using a Cost Function

Our baseline network performed poorly because it had lots of free parameters with which it could model spurious features of the training set. However, we had already taken our brute force techniques for input dimensionality reduction (pre-segmenting the utterances and reducing the resolution of input format) about as far as possible while still retaining most of the useful information in the patterns. Therefore it was necessary to resort to a more subtle form of dimensionality reduction in which the back-propagation learning algorithm is allowed to create complicated weight patterns only to the extent that they actually reduce the network's error.

This constraint is implemented by including a cost term for the network's complexity in its objective function. The particular cost function that should be used is induced by a particular definition of what constitutes a complicated weight pattern, and this definition should be chosen with care. For example, the rash of tiny details in figure 1(a) originally led us to penalize weights that were different from their neighbors, thus encouraging the network to develop smooth, low-resolution weight patterns whenever possible.

$$C = \frac{1}{2} \sum_i \frac{1}{||\mathcal{N}_i||} \sum_{j \in \mathcal{N}_i} (w_i - w_j)^2 \tag{1}$$

To compute the total tax on non-smoothness, each weight w_i was compared to all of its neighbors (which are indexed by the set $\mathcal{N}_i$). When a weight differed from a neighbor, a penalty was assessed that was proportional to the square of their difference. The term $||\mathcal{N}_i||^{-1}$ normalized for the fact that units at the edge of a receptive field have fewer neighbors than units in the middle.

When a cost function is used, a tradeoff factor λ is typically used to control the relative importance of the error and cost components of the overall objective function $O = E + \lambda C$. The gradient of the overall objective function is then $\nabla O = \nabla E + \lambda \nabla C$. To compute ∇C, we needed the derivative of our cost function with respect to each weight w_i. This derivative is just the difference between the weight and the average of its neighbors: $\frac{\partial C}{\partial w_i} = w_i - \frac{1}{||\mathcal{N}_i||} \sum_{j \in \mathcal{N}_i} w_j$, so minimizing the combined objective function was equivalent to minimizing the network's error while simultaneously smoothing the weight patterns by decaying each weight towards the average of its neighbors.

Figure 1(b) shows the **B** and **D** weight patterns of a 2-layer network that was trained under the influence of this cost function. As we had hoped, sharp transitions between neighboring weights occurred primarily in the maximally informative consonant release of each word, while the spurious details that had plagued our baseline network were smoothed out of existence. However, this network was even worse at the task of generalizing to unsegmented test cases than the baseline network, getting only 35 percent of them correct.

While equation 1 might be a good cost function for some other task, it doesn't capture our prior knowledge that the discrimination cues in E-set recognition are highly localized in time. This cost function tells the network to treat unimportant neighboring input components similarly, but we really want to tell the network to ignore these components altogether. Therefore, a better cost function for this task is the one associated with standard weight decay:

$$C = \frac{1}{2} \sum_i w_i^2 \tag{2}$$

Equation 2 causes weights to remain close to zero unless they are particularly valuable for reducing the network's error on the training set. Unfortunately, the weights that our network learns under the influence of this function merely look like smaller versions of the baseline weights of figure 1(a) and perform just as poorly. No matter what value is used for λ, there is very little size differentiation between the weights that we know to be valuable for this task and the weights that we know to be spurious. Weight decay fails because our training set is so small that spurious weights do not appear to be as irrelevant as they really are for performing the task in general. Fortunately, there is a modified form of weight decay (Scalettar and Zee, 1988) that expresses the idea that the disparity between relevant and irrelevant weights is greater than can be deduced from the training set:

$$C = \frac{1}{2} \sum_i \frac{w_i^2}{2.5 + w_i^2} \tag{3}$$

The weights of figure 1(c) were learned under the influence of equation 3.[5] In these patterns, the feature detectors that make sense to speech recognition experts stand out clearly above a highly suppressed field of less important weights. This network generalizes to 48 percent of the unsegmented test cases, while our earlier networks had managed only 37 percent accuracy.

4   A Time-Delay Neural Network

The preceding experiments with cost functions show that controlling attention (rather than resolution) is the key to good performance on the **BDEV** task. The only way to accurately classify the utterances in this task is to focus on the tiny discrimination cues in the spectrograms while ignoring the remaining material in the patterns.

Because we know that the **BDEV** discrimination cues are highly localized in time, it would make sense to build a network whose architecture reflected that knowledge. One such network (see figure 2(b)) contains many copies of each output unit. These copies apply identical weight patterns to the input in all possible positions. The activation values

---

[5]We trained with $\lambda = 100$ here as opposed to the setting of $\lambda = 10$ that worked best with standard weight decay.

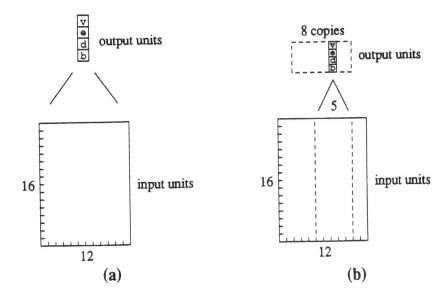

Figure 2: Conventional and Time-Delay 2-layer Networks

from all of the copies of a given output unit are summed to generate the overall output value for that unit.[6]

Now, assuming that the learning algorithm can construct weight patterns which recognize the characteristic features of each word while rejecting the rest of the material in the words, then when an instance of a particular word is shown to the network, the only unit that will be activated is the output unit copy for that word which happens to be aligned with the recognition cues in the pattern. Then, the summation step at the output stage of the network serves as an OR gate which transmits that activation to the outside world.

This network architecture, which has been named the "Time-Delay Neural Network" or "TDNN", has several useful properties for E-set recognition, all of which are consequences of the fact that the network essentially performs its own segmentation by recognizing the most relevant portion of each input and rejecting the rest. One benefit is that sharp weight patterns can be learned even when the training patterns have been sloppily segmented. For example, in the TDNN weight patterns of figure 1(d), the release-burst detectors are localized in a single time frame, while in the earlier weight patterns from conventional networks they were smeared over several time frames.

Also, the network learns to actively discriminate between the relevant and irrelevant portions of its training segments, rather than trying to ignore the latter by using small weights. This turns out to be a big advantage when the network is later scanned across unsegmented utterances, as evidenced by the vastly different appearances of the output

---

[6]We actually designed this network before performing our experiments with cost functions, and were originally attracted by its translation invariance rather than by the advantages mentioned here (Lang, 1987).

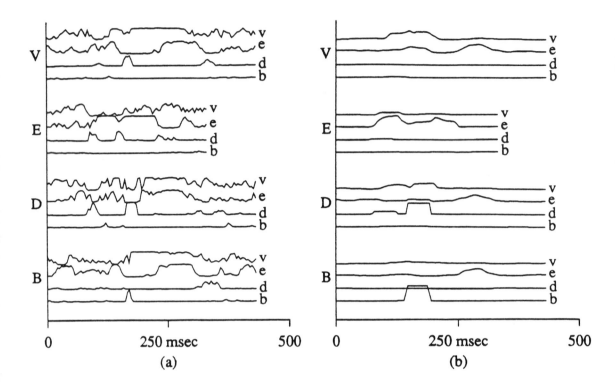

Figure 3: Output Unit Activation Traces of a Conventional Network and a Time-Delay Network, on Four Sample Utterances

activity traces in figures 3(a) and 3(b).[7]

Finally, because the TDNN can locate and attend to the most relevant portion of its input, we are able to make its receptive fields very narrow, thus reducing the number of free parameters in the network and making it highly trainable with the small number of training cases that are available in this task. In fact, the scanning mode generalization rate of our 2-layer TDNN is 65 percent, which is nearly twice the accuracy of our baseline 2-layer network.

5 Comparison with other systems

The 2-layer networks described up to this point were trained and tested under identical conditions so that their performances could be meaningfully compared. No attempt was made to achieve really high performance in these experiments. On the other hand when

---

[7]While the main text of this paper compares the performance of a sequence of 2-layer networks, the plots of figure 3 show the output traces of 3-layer versions of the networks. The correct plots could not be conveniently generated because our CMU Common Lisp program for creating them has died of bit rot.

we trained a 3-layer TDNN using the slightly fancier methodology described in (Lang, Hinton, and Waibel, 1990),[8] we obtained a system that generalized to about 91 percent of the unsegmented test cases. By comparison, the standard, large-vocabulary IBM hidden Markov model accounts for 80 percent of the test cases, and the accuracy of human listeners has been measured at 94 percent. In fact, the TDNN is probably the best automatic recognition system built for this task to date; it even performs slightly better than the continuous acoustic parameter, maximum mutual information hidden Markov model proposed in (Brown, 1987).

6   Conclusion

The performance of a neural network can be improved by building *a priori* knowledge into the network's architecture and objective function. In this paper, we have exhibited two successful examples of this technique in the context of a speech recognition task where the crucial information for making an output decision is highly localized and where the number of training cases is limited. Tony Zee's modified version of weight decay and our time-delay architecture both yielded networks that focused their attention on the short-duration discrimination cues in the utterances. Conversely, our attempts to use weight smoothing and standard weight decay during training got us nowhere because these cost functions didn't accurately express our knowledge about the task.

Acknowledgements

This work was supported by Office of Naval Research contract N00014-86-K-0167, and by a grant from the Ontario Information Techology Research Center. Geoffrey Hinton is a fellow of the Canadian Institute for Advanced Research.

References

P. Brown. (1987) *The Acoustic-Modeling Problem in Automatic Speech Recognition.* Doctoral Dissertation, Carnegie Mellon University.

K. Lang. (1987) *Connectionist Speech Recognition.* PhD Thesis Proposal, Carnegie Mellon University.

K. Lang, G. Hinton, and A. Waibel. (1990) A Time-Delay Neural Network Architecture for Isolated Word Recognition. *Neural Networks* 3(1).

R. Scalettar and A. Zee. (1988) In D. Waltz and J. Feldman (eds.), *Connectionist Models and their Implications*, p. 309. Publisher: A. Blex.

---

[8]Wider but less precisely aligned training segments were employed, as well as randomly selected "counter-example" segments that further improved the network's already good "E" and background noise rejection. Also, a preliminary cross-validation run was performed to locate a nearly optimal stopping point for the learning procedure. When trained using this improved methodology, a conventional 3-layer network achieved a generalization score in the mid 50's.

A Continuous Speech Recognition System Embedding MLP into HMM

Hervé Bourlard
Philips Research Laboratory
Av. van Becelaere 2, Box 8
B-1170 Brussels, Belgium

Nelson Morgan
Intl. Comp. Sc. Institute
1947 Center Street, Suite 600
Berkeley, CA 94704, USA

ABSTRACT

We are developing a phoneme based, speaker-dependent continuous speech recognition system embedding a Multilayer Perceptron (MLP) (i.e., a feedforward Artificial Neural Network), into a Hidden Markov Model (HMM) approach. In [Bourlard & Wellekens], it was shown that MLPs were approximating Maximum a Posteriori (MAP) probabilities and could thus be embedded as an emission probability estimator in HMMs. By using contextual information from a sliding window on the input frames, we have been able to improve frame or phoneme classification performance over the corresponding performance for simple Maximum Likelihood (ML) or even MAP probabilities that are estimated without the benefit of context. However, recognition of words in continuous speech was not so simply improved by the use of an MLP, and several modifications of the original scheme were necessary for getting acceptable performance. It is shown here that word recognition performance for a simple discrete density HMM system appears to be somewhat better when MLP methods are used to estimate the emission probabilities.

1 INTRODUCTION

We have performed a number of experiments with a 1000-word vocabulary continuous speech recognition task. Our frame classification results [Bourlard et al., 1989] are consistent with other research showing the capabilities of MLPs trained with back-propagation-styled learning schemes for the recognition of voiced-unvoiced speech segments [Gevins & Morgan, 1984], isolated phonemes [Watrous & Shastri, 1987; Waibel et al., 1988; Makino et al., 1983], or of isolated words [Peeling & Moore, 1988]. These results indicate that "neural network" approaches can, for some problems, perform pattern classification at least as well as traditional HMM approaches. However, this is not particularly mysterious. When traditional statistical assumptions (distribution, independence of multiple features, etc.) are not valid, systems which do not rely on these assumptions can work better (as discussed in [Niles et al., 1989]). Furthermore, networks provide an easy way to incorporate multiple sources of evidence (multiple features, contextual windows, etc.) without restrictive assumptions.

However, it is not so easy to improve the recognition of words in continuous speech by the use of an MLP. For instance, while it has been shown that the outputs of a feedforward network can be used as emission probabilities in an HMM [Bourlard et al., 1989], the corresponding word recognition performance can be very poor. This is true even when the same network demonstrates extremely good performance at the frame or phoneme levels. We have developed a hybrid MLP-HMM algorithm which (for a preliminary experiment) appears to exceed performance of the same HMM system using standard statistical approaches to estimate the emission probabilities. This was only possible after the original algorithm was modified in ways that did not necessarily maximize the frame recognition performance for the training set. We will describe these modifications below, along with experimental results.

2   METHODS

As shown by both theoretical [Bourlard & Wellekens, 1989] and experimental [Bourlard & Morgan, 1989] results, MLP output values may be considered to be good estimates of MAP probabilities for pattern classification. Either these, or some other related quantity (such as the output normalized by the prior probability of the corresponding class) may be used in a Viterbi search to determine the best time-warped succession of states (speech sounds) to explain the observed speech measurements. This hybrid approach (MLP to estimate probabilities, HMM to incorporate them to recognize continuous speech as a succession of words) has the potential of exploiting the interpolating capabilities of MLPs while using a Dynamic Time Warping (DTW) procedure to capture the dynamics of speech.

However, to achieve good performance at the word level, the following modifications of this basic scheme were necessary:

- MLP training methods - a new cross-validation [Stones, 1977] training algorithm was designed in which the stopping criterion was based on performance for an independent validation set [Morgan & Bourlard, 1990]. In other words, training was stopped when performance on a second set of data began going down, and not when training error leveled off. This greatly improved generalization, which could be further tested on a third independent validation set.

- probability estimation from the MLP outputs - In the original scheme [Bourlard & Wellekens, 1989], MLP outputs were used as MAP probabilities for the HMM directly. While this helped frame performance, it hurt word performance. This may have been due at least partly to a mismatch between the relative frequency of phonemes in the training sets and test (word recognition) sets. Division by the prior class probabilities as estimated from the training set removed this effect of the priors on the DTW. This led to a small decrease in frame classification performance, but a large (sometimes 10 - 20%) improvement in word recognition rates (see Table 1 and accompanying description).

- word transition costs for the underlying HMM - word transition penalties had to be increased for larger contextual windows to avoid a large number of insertions; see Section 4. This is shown to be equivalent to keeping the same word transition cost but scaling the log probabilities down by a number which reflected the dependence of neighboring frames. A reasonable value for this can be determined from recognition on a small number of sentences (e.g., 50), choosing a value which results in insertions at most equal to the number of deletions.

- segmentation of training data - much as with HMM systems, an iterative procedure was required to time align the training labels in a manner that was statistically consistent with the recognition methods used. In our most recent experiments, we segmented the data using an iterative Viterbi alignment starting from a segmentation based on average phoneme durations, and terminated at the segmentation which led to the best performance on an independent test set. For one of our speakers, we had available a more accurate frame labeling (produced by an automatic but more complex procedure [Aubert, 1987]) to use as a start point for the iteration, which led to even better performance.

3   EXPERIMENTAL APPROACH

We have been using a speaker-dependent German database (available from our collaboration with Philips) called SPICOS [Ney & Noll, 1988]. The speech had been sampled at a rate of 16 kHz, and 30 points of smoothed, "mel-scaled" logarithmic spectra (over bands from 200 to 6400 Hz) were calculated every 10-ms from a 512-point FFT over a 25-ms window. For our experiments, the mel spectrum and the energy were vector-quantized to pointers into a single speaker-dependent table of prototypes.

Two independent sets of vocabularies for training and test are used. The training data-set consists of two sessions of 100 German sentences per speaker. These sentences are representative of the phoneme distribution in the German language and include 2430 phonemes in each session. The two sessions of 100 sentences are phonetically segmented on the basis of 50 phonemes, using a fully automated procedure [Aubert, 1987]. The test set consists of one session of 200 sentences per speaker. The recognition vocabulary contains 918 words (including the "silence" word) and the overlap between training and recognition is 51 words. Most of the latter are articles, prepositions and other structural words. Thus, the training and test are essentially vocabulary-independent. Initial tests used sentences from a single male speaker. The final algorithms were tested on an additional male and female speaker.

The acoustic vectors were coded on the basis of 132 prototype vectors by a simple binary representation with only one bit 'on'. Multiple frames were used as input to provide context to the network. In the experiments reported here, the context was 9 frames, while the size of the output layer was kept fixed at 50 units, corresponding to the 50 phonemes to be recognized. The input field contained $9 \times 132 = 1188$ units, and the total number of possible inputs was thus equal to 132^9. There were 26767 training patterns (from the first training session of 100 sentences) and 26702 independent test patterns (from the second training session of 100 sentences). Of course, this represented only a very small fraction of the possible inputs, and generalization was thus potentially difficult. Training was done by the classical "error-back propagation" algorithm, starting by minimizing an entropy criterion, and then the standard least-mean-square error criterion. In each iteration, the complete training set was presented, and the parameters were updated after each training pattern. To avoid overtraining of the MLP, improvement on a cross-validation set was checked after each iteration and if classification was decreasing, the adaptation parameter of the gradient procedure was reduced, otherwise it was kept constant. Later on this approach was systematized by splitting the data in three parts: one for training, one for cross-validation and a third one absolutely independent of the training procedure for the actual validation. No significant difference was observed between classification rates for the last two data sets.

In [Bourlard et al., 1989] this procedure was shown yielding improved frame classification performance over simple ML and MAP estimates. However, acceptable word recognition perfomance was still difficult to reach.

4   WORD RECOGNITION RESULTS

The output values of the MLP were evaluated for each frame, and (after division by the prior probability of each phoneme) were used as emission probabilities in a discrete HMM system. In this system, each phoneme was modeled with a single conditional density, repeated $D/2$ times, where D was a prior estimate of the duration of the phoneme. Only selfloops and sequential transitions were permitted. A Viterbi decoding was then used for recognition of the first hundred sentences of the test session (on which word entrance penalties were optimized), and our best results were validated by a further recognition on the second hundred sentences of the test set. Note that this same simplified HMM was used for both the ML reference system (estimating probabilities directly from relative frequencies) and the MLP system, and that the same input features were used for both.

Table 1 shows the recognition rate (100% - error rate, where errors includes insertions, deletions, and substitutions) for the first 100 sentences of the test session. All runs except the last were done with 20 hidden units in the MLP, as suggested by frame performance. Note the significant positive effect of division of the MLP outputs, which are trained to approximate MAP probabilities, by estimates of the prior probabilities for each class (denoted "MLP/priors" in Table 1).

Table 1: Word Recognition, speaker m003

system method	size of context	% correct	
		test	validation
MLP	1	27.3	
MLP/priors	1	49.7	
MLP	9	40.9	
MLP/priors	9	51.9	52.2
ML	1	52.6	52.5
MLP/priors (0 hidden)	9	53.3	

Table 2: Word Recognition using Viterbi segmentation, speaker m003

method	context	test
MLP/priors (0 hidden)	9	65.3
ML	1	56.9

Word transition probabilities were optimized for both the Maximum Likelihood and MLP style HMMs. This led to a word exit probability of 10^{-8} for the ML and for 1-frame MLP's, and 10^{-14} for an MLP with 9 frames of context. After these adjustments, performance was essentially the same for the two approaches. Performance on the last hundred sentence of the test session (shown in the last column of Table 1) validated that the two systems generalized equivalently despite these tunings.

An initial time alignment of the phonetic transcription with the data (for this speaker) had previously been calculated using a program incorporating speech-specific knowledge [Aubert, 1987]. This labeling had been used for the targets of the frame-based training described above. We then used this alignment as a "bootstrap" segmentation for an iterative Viterbi procedure, much as is done in conventional HMM systems. As with the MLP training, the data was divided into a training and cross-validation set, and the best segmentation (corresponding to the best validation set frame classification rate) was used for later training. For both cross-validation procedures, we switched to a training set of 150 sentences (two repetitions of 75 sentences) and a cross-validation set of 50 sentences (two repetitions of 25 each). Finally, since the best performance in Table 1 was achieved using no hidden layer, we continued our experiments using this simpler network, which also required only a simple training procedure (entropy error criterion only). Table 2 shows this performance for the full 200 recognition sentences (test + validation sets from Table 1).

Two of the more puzzling observations in this work were the need to increase word entrance penalties with the width of the input context and the difficulty to reflect good frame performance at the word level. MLPs can make better frame level discriminations than simple statistical classifiers, because they can easily incorporate multiple sources of evidence (multiple frames, multiple features) without simplifying assumptions. However, when the input features within a contextual window are roughly independent, the Viterbi algorithm will already incorporate all of the context in choosing the best HMM state sequence explaining an utterance. If emission probabilities are estimated from the outputs of an MLP which has a $2c + 1$ frame contextual input, the probability to observe a feature sequence $\{f_1, f_2, \ldots, f_N\}$ (where f_n represents the feature vector at time n) on a particular HMM state q_k is estimated as:

$$\prod_{i=1}^{N} p(f_{i-c}, \ldots, f_i, \ldots, f_{i+c}|q_k),$$

where Bayes' rule has already been used to convert the MLP outputs (which estimate MAP probabilities) into ML probabilities. If independence is assumed, and if boundary effects (context extending before frame 1 or after frame N) are ignored (assume $(2c+1) \ll N$), this becomes:

$$\prod_{i=1}^{N} \prod_{j=-c}^{c} p(f_{i+j}|q_k) = \prod_{i=1}^{N} \left[p(f_i|q_k) \right]^{2c+1},$$

where the latter probability is just the classical Maximum Likelihood solution, raised to the power $2c + 1$. Thus, if the features are independent over time, to keep the effect of transition costs the same as for the simple HMM, the log probabilities must be scaled down by the size of the contextual window. Note that, in the more realistic case where dependencies exist between frames, the optimal scaling factor will be less than $2c + 1$, down to a minimum of 1 for the case in which frames are completely dependent (e.g., same within a constant factor); the scaling factor should thus reflect the time correlation of the input features. Thus, if the features are assumed independent over time, there is no advantage to be gained by using an MLP to extract contextual information for the estimation of emission probabilities for an HMM Viterbi decoding. In general, the relation between the MLP and ML solutions will be more complex, because of interdependence over time of the input features. However, the above relation may give some insight as to the difficulty we have met in improving word recognition performance with a single discrete feature (despite large improvements at the frame level). More positively, our results show that the probabilities estimated by MLPs can be used at least as effectively as conventional estimates and that some advantage can be gained by providing more information for estimating these probabilities.

We have duplicated our recognition tests for two other speakers from the same data base. In this case, we labeled each training set (from the original male plus a male and a female speaker) using a Viterbi iteration initialized from a time-alignment based on a simple estimate of average phoneme duration. This reduced all of the recognition scores, underlining the necessity of a good start point for the Viterbi iteration. However, as can be seen from the Table 3 results (measured over the full 200 recognition sentences), the MLP-based methods appear to consistently offer at least some measurable improvement over the simpler estimation technique. In particular, the performance for the two systems differed significantly ($p < 0.001$) for two out of three speakers, as well as for a multispeaker

Table 3: Word Recognition for 3 speakers, simple initialization

speaker	MLE	MLP
m003	54.4	59.7
m001	47.4	51.9
w010	54.2	54.3

comparison over the three speakers (in each case using a normal approximation to a binomial distribution for the null hypothesis).

5   CONCLUSION

These results show some of the improvement for MLPs over conventional HMMs which one might expect from the frame level results. MLPs can sometimes make better frame level discriminations than simple statistical classifiers, because they can easily incorporate multiple sources of evidence (multiple frames, multiple features), which is difficult to do in HMMs without major simplifying assumptions. In general, the relation between the MLP and ML word recognition is more complex. Part of the difficulty with good recognition may be due to our choice of discrete, vector-quantized features, for which no metric is defined over the prototype space. Despite these limitations, it now appears that the probabilities estimated by MLPs may offer improved word recognition through the incorporation of context in the estimation of emission probabilities. Furthermore, our new result shows the effectiveness of Viterbi segmentation in labeling training data for an MLP. This result appears to remove a major handicap of MLP use, i.e. the requirement for hand-labeled speech, and also offers the possibility to deal with more complex HMMs.

Acknowledgments

Support from the International Computer Science Institute (ICSI) and Philips Research for this work is gratefully acknowledged. Chuck Wooters of ICSI and UCB provided much-needed assistance, and Xavier Aubert of Philips put together our Spicos materials.

References

X. Aubert, (1988), "Supervised Segmentation with Application to Speech Recognition", in *Proc. Eur. Conf. Speech Technology*, Edinburgh, p.161-164.

H. Bourlard, N. Morgan, & C.J. Wellekens, (1989), "Statistical Inference in Multilayer Perceptrons and Hidden Markov Models with Applications in Continuous Speech Recognition", to appear in *Neuro Computing, Algorithms, and Applications*, NATO ASI Series.

H. Bourlard, H. & N. Morgan, (1989), "Merging Multilayer Perceptrons and Hidden Markov Models: Some Experiments in Continuous Speech Recognition" International Computer Science Institute TR-89-033.

H. Bourlard & C.J. Wellekens, (1989), "Links between Markov models and multilayer perceptrons", to be published in *IEEE Trans. on Pattern Analysis and Machine Intelligence*, 1990.

A. Gevins & N. Morgan, (1984), "Ignorance-Based Systems", *Proc. IEEE Intl. Conf. on Acoustics, Speech, & Signal Processing*, Vol. 3, 39A5.1-39A5.4, San Diego.

S. Makino, T. Kawabata, T. & K. Kido, (1983), "Recognition of consonants based on the Perceptron Model", *Proc. IEEE Intl. Conf. on Acoustics, Speech, & Signal Processing*, Vol. 2, pp. 738-741, Boston, Mass.

N. Morgan & H. Bourlard, (1989), "Generalization and Parameter Estimation in Feedforward Nets: Some Experiments", *Advances in Neural Information Processing Systems II*, Morgan Kaufmann.

H. Ney & A. Noll, (1988), "Phoneme Modeling Using Continuous Mixture Densities", *Proc. IEEE Intl. Conf. on Acoustics, Speech, & Signal Processing*, Vol. 1, pp. 437-440, New York.

L. Niles, H. Silverman, G. Tajchman & M. Bush, (1989), "How Limited Training Data Can Allow a Neural Network Classifier to Outperform an 'Optimal' Statistical Classifier", *Proc. IEEE Intl. Conf. on Acoustics, Speech, & Signal Processing*, Vol. 1, pp. 17-20, Glasgow, Scotland.

S.M. Peeling, S.M. & R.K. Moore, (1988), "Experiments in Isolated Digit Recognition Using the Multi-Layer Perceptron", Royal Speech and Radar Establishment, Technical Report 4073, Malvern, Worcester.

M. Stone, (1987), "Cross-validation: a review", *Math. Operationforsch. Statist. Ser. Statist.*, vol.9, pp. 127-139.

A. Waibel, T. Hanazawa, G. Hinton, K. Shikano & K. Lang, (1988), "Phoneme Recognition: Neural Networks vs. Hidden Markov Models", *Proc. IEEE Intl. Conf. on Acoustics, Speech, & Signal Processing*, Vol. 1, pp. 107-110, New York.

R. Watrous & L. Shastri, (1987), Learning phonetic features using connectionist networks: an experiment in speech recognition", *Proceedings of the First Intl. Conference on Neural Networks*, IV-381-388, San Diego, CA.

HMM Speech Recognition
with Neural Net Discrimination*

William Y. Huang and **Richard P. Lippmann**
Lincoln Laboratory, MIT
Room B-349
Lexington, MA 02173-9108

ABSTRACT

Two approaches were explored which integrate neural net classifiers with Hidden Markov Model (HMM) speech recognizers. Both attempt to improve speech pattern discrimination while retaining the temporal processing advantages of HMMs. One approach used neural nets to provide second–stage discrimination following an HMM recognizer. On a small vocabulary task, Radial Basis Function (RBF) and back–propagation neural nets reduced the error rate substantially (from 7.9% to 4.2% for the RBF classifier). In a larger vocabulary task, neural net classifiers did not reduce the error rate. They, however, outperformed Gaussian, Gaussian mixture, and $k-$nearest neighbor (KNN) classifiers. In another approach, neural nets functioned as low–level acoustic–phonetic feature extractors. When classifying phonemes based on single 10 msec. frames, discriminant RBF neural net classifiers outperformed Gaussian mixture classifiers. Performance, however, differed little when classifying phones by accumulating scores across all frames in phonetic segments using a single node HMM recognizer.

*This work was sponsored by the Department of the Air Force and the Air Force Office of Scientific Research.

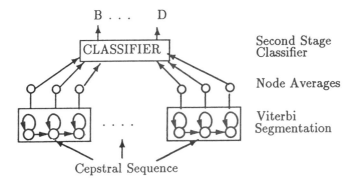

Figure 1: Second stage discrimination system. HMM recognition is based on the accumulated scores from each node. A second stage classifier can adjust the weights from each node to provide improved discrimination.

1 Introduction

This paper describes some of our current efforts to integrate discriminant neural net classifiers into HMM speech recognizers. The goal of this work is to combine the temporal processing capabilities of the HMM approach with the superior recognition rates provided by discriminant classifiers. Although neural nets are well developed for static pattern classification, neural nets for dynamic pattern recognition require further research. Current conventional HMM recognizers rely on likelihood scores provided by non–discriminant classifiers, such as Gaussian mixture [11] and histogram [5] classifiers. Non–discriminant classifiers are sensitive to assumptions concerning the shape of the probability density function and the robustness of the Maximum Likelihood (ML) estimators. Discriminant classifiers have a number of potential advantages over non–discriminant classifiers on real world problems. They make fewer assumptions concerning underlying class distributions, can be robust to outliers, and can lead to efficient parallel analog VLSI implementation [4, 6, 7, 8]. Recent efforts in applying discriminant training to HMM recognizers have led to promising techniques, including Maximum Mutual Information (MMI) training [2] and corrective training [5]. These techniques maintain the same structure as in a conventional HMM recognizer but use a different overall error criteria to estimate parameters. We believe that a significant improvement in recognition rate will result if discriminant classifiers are included directly in the HMM structure.

This paper examines two integration strategies: second stage classification and discriminant pre–processing. In second stage classification, discussed in Sec. 2, classifiers are used to provide post-processing for an HMM isolated word recognizer. In discriminant pre-processing, discussed in Sec. 3, discriminant classifiers replace the maximum likelihood classifiers used in conventional HMM recognizers.

2   Second Stage Classification

HMM isolated–word recognition requires one Markov model per word. Recognition involves accumulating scores for an unknown input across the nodes in each word model, and selecting that word model which provides the maximum accumulated score. In the case of discriminating between minimal pairs, such as those in the E–set vocabulary (the letters {BCDEGPTVZ}), it is desired that recognition be focused on the nodes that correspond to the small portion of the utterance that are different between words. In the second stage classification approach, illustrated in Fig. 1, the HMMs at the first layer are the components of a fully–trained isolated–word HMM recognizer. The second stage classifier is provided with matching scores and duration from each HMM node. A simple second stage classifier which sums the matching scores of the nodes for each word would be equivalent to an HMM recognizer. It is hoped that discriminant classifiers can utilize the additional information provided by the node dependent scores and duration to deliver improved recognition rates.

The second stage system of Fig. 1 was evaluated using the 9 letter E-set vocabulary and the {BDG} vocabulary. Words were taken from the TI–46 Word database, which contains 10 training and 16 testing tokens per word per talker and 16 talkers. Evaluation was performed in the speaker dependent mode; thus, there were a total of 30 training and 48 testing tokens per talker for the {BDG}-set task and 90 training and 144 testing tokens per talker for the E-set task. Spectral pre–processing consisted of extracting the first 12 mel–scaled cepstral coefficients [10], ignoring the 0th cepstral coefficient (energy), for each 10 ms frame. An HMM isolated word recognizer was first trained using the forward–backward algorithm. Each word was modeled using 8 HMM nodes with 2 additional noise nodes at each end. During classification, each test word was segmented using the Viterbi decoding algorithm on all word models. The average matching score and duration of all non–noise nodes were used as a static pattern for the second stage classifier.

2.1   Classifiers

Four second stage classifiers were used: (1) Multi–layer perceptron (MLP) classifiers trained with back–propagation, (2) Gaussian mixture classifiers trained with the Expectation Maximization (EM) algorithm [9], (3) RBF classifiers [8] with weights trained using the pseudoinverse method computed via Singular Value Decomposition (SVD), and (4) KNN classifiers. Covariance matrices in the Gaussian mixture classifiers were constrained to be diagonal and tied to be the same between mixture components in all classes. The RBF classifiers were of the form

$$\text{Decide Class } i = \operatorname*{Argmax}_{i} \sum_{j=1}^{J} w_{ij} \text{EXP} \left(-\frac{\|\vec{x} - \vec{\mu}_j\|^2}{2h\sigma_j^2} \right) \qquad (1)$$

where

$$\begin{aligned}
\vec{x} &= \text{acoustic vector input,} \\
i &= \text{class label,} \\
J &= \text{number of centers,} \\
w_{ij} &= \text{weight from } j^{\text{th}} \text{ center to } i^{\text{th}} \text{ class output,} \\
(\vec{\mu}_j, \sigma_j^2) &= j^{\text{th}} \text{ center and variance, and} \\
h &= \text{spread factor.}
\end{aligned}$$

The center locations ($\vec{\mu}_i$'s) were obtained from either k-means or Gaussian mixture clustering. The variances (σ_j's) were either the variances of the individual k-means clusters or those of the individual Gaussian mixture components, depending on which clustering algorithm was used. Results for $k = 1$ are reported for the KNN classifier because this provided best performance.

The Gaussian mixture classifier was selected as a reference conventional non–discriminant classifier. A Gaussian mixture classifier can provide good models for multi-modal and non–Gaussian distributions by using many mixture components. It can also generalize to the more common, well–known unimodal Gaussian classifier which provides poor performance when the input distribution is not Gaussian. Very few benchmarking studies have been performed to evaluate the relative performance of Gaussian mixture and neural net classifiers, although mixture models have been used successfully in HMM recognizers [11]. RBF classifiers were used because they train rapidly, and recent benchmarking studies show that they perform as well as MLP classifiers on speech problems [8].

			GAUSSIAN		RBF†		RBF‡		
			Mixtures per Class		Centers per Class		Total Number of Centers		KNN
Vocab	HMM	MLP	1	3	1	3	30	70	($k = 1$)
{BDG}	7.9%	5.9%	5.6%	9.1%	11.9%	5.7%	4.2%		6.0%
{E–Set}	11.3%	13.4%	21.2%	20.6%	15.8%	13.7%	15.8%	12.8%	36.0%

†   Centers from Gaussian mixture clustering, h=150.
‡   Centers from k-means clustering. h=150.

Table 1: Percentage errors from the second stage classifier, averaged over all 16 talkers.

2.2   Results of Second Stage Classification

Table 1 shows the error rates for the second stage system of Fig. 1, averaged over all talkers. The second stage system improved performance over the baseline HMM system when the vocabulary was small (B, D and G). Error rates decreased from 7.9% for the baseline HMM recognizer to 4.2% for the RBF second stage classifier. There was no improvement for the E-set vocabulary task. The best RBF second stage classifier degraded the error rate from 11.3% with the baseline HMM to 12.8%. In the E-set results, MLP and RBF classifiers, with error rates of 13.4%

and 12.8%, performed considerably better than the Gaussian (21.2%), Gaussian mixture (20.6%) and KNN classifiers (36.0%).

The second stage approach is effective for a very small vocabulary but not for a larger vocabulary task. This may be due to a combination of limited training data and the increased complexity of decision regions as vocabulary size and dimensionality gets large. When the vocabulary size increased from 3 to 9, the input dimensionality of the classifiers scaled up by a factor of 3 (from 48 to 144) but the number of training tokens increased only by the same factor (from 30 to 90). It is, in general, possible for the amount of training tokens required for good performance to scale up exponentially with the input dimensionality. MLP and RBF classifiers appear to be affected by this problem but not as strongly as Gaussian, Gaussian mixture, and KNN classifiers.

3   Discriminant Pre–Processing

Second stage classifiers will not work well if the nodal matching scores do not lead to good discrimination. Current conventional HMM recognizers use non–discriminant classifiers based on ML estimators to generate these scores. In the discriminant pre–processing approach, the ML classifiers in an HMM recognizer are replaced by discriminant classifiers.

All the experiments in this section are based on the phonemes /b,d,ʤ/ from the speaker dependent TI–46 Word database. Spectral pre–processing consisted of extracting the first 12 mel–scaled cepstral coefficients and ignoring the 0th cepstral coefficient (energy), for each 10 ms frame. For multi–frame inputs, adjacent frames were 20 msec. apart (skipping every other frame). The database was segmented with a conventional high–performance continuous–observation HMM recognizer using forced Viterbi decoding on the correct word. The phonemes /b/, /d/ and /ʤ/ from the letters "B", "D" and "G" (/#_i/ context) were then extracted. This resulted in an average of 95 training and 158 testing frames per talker per word using the 10 training and 16 testing words per talker in the 16 talker database. Talker dependent results, averaged over all 16 talkers, are reported here.

Preliminary experiments using MLP, RBF, KNN, Gaussian, and Gaussian mixture classifiers indicated that RBF classifiers with Gaussian basis functions and a spread factor of 50 consistently yielded close to best performance. RBF classifiers also provided much shorter training times than MLP classifiers. RBF classifiers (as in Eq. 1) with $h = 50$ were thus used in all experiments presented in this section. The parameters of the RBF classifiers were determined as described in Sec. 2.1 above.

Gaussian mixture classifiers were used as reference conventional non–discriminant classifiers. In the preliminary experiments, they also provided close to best performance, and outperformed KNN and unimodal Gaussian classifiers. Covariance matrices were constrained, as described in Sec. 2.1. Although full and independent covariance matrices were advantageous for the unimodal Gaussian classifier and Gaussian mixture classifiers with few mixture components, best performance was provided using many mixture components and constrained covariance matri-

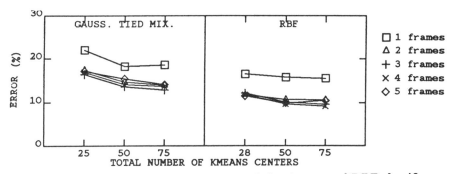

Figure 2: Frame–level error rates for Gaussian tied–mixture and RBF classifiers as a function of the total number of unique centers. Multi–frame results had context frames adjoined together at the input. Centers for both classifiers were determined using k–means clustering.

ces. A Gaussian "tied–mixture" classifier was also used. This is a Gaussian mixture classifier where all classes share the same mixture components but have different mixture weights. It is trained in two stages. In the first stage, class independent mixture centers are computed by k–means clustering, and mixture variances are the variances of the individual k–means clusters. In the second stage, the ML estimates of the class dependent mixture weights are computed while holding mixture components fixed.

3.1   Frame Level Results

Error rates for classifying phonemes based on single frames are shown in Fig. 2 for the Gaussian tied–mixture classifier (left) and RBF classifier (right). These results were obtained using k-means centers. Superior frame–level error rates were consistently provided by the RBF classifier in all experimental variations of this study. This is expected since RBF classifiers use an objective function which is directly related to classification error, whereas the objective of non–discriminant classifiers, modeling the class dependent probability density functions, is only indirectly related to classification error.

3.2   Phone Level Results

In a single node HMM, classifier scores for the frames in a phone segment are accumulated to obtain phone–level results. For conventional HMM recognizers that use non–discriminant classifiers, this score accumulation is done by assuming independent frames, which allows the frame–level scores to be multiplied together:

$$Prob(\text{phone}) = Prob(\vec{x}_1, \vec{x}_2, ... \vec{x}_N)$$
$$= Prob(\vec{x}_1)Prob(\vec{x}_2) \cdots Prob(\vec{x}_N) \tag{2}$$

where $\vec{x} ... \vec{x}_N$ are input frames in an N–frame phone. Eq. 2 does not apply to non–discriminant classifiers. RBF classifier outputs are not constrained to lie between 0 and 1. They do not necessarily behave like probabilities and do not perform

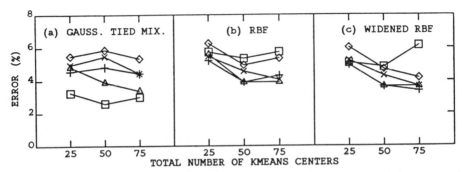

Figure 3: Phone–level error rates using (a) Gaussian tied–mixture, (b) RBF and (c) 5% widened RBF classifiers, as a function of the total number of unique centers. Gaussian classifier phone–level results were obtained by accumulating frame–level scores via multiplication. RBF classifier frame–level scores were accumulated via addition. Symbols are as in Fig. 2.

well when their frame scores are multiplied together. The RBF classifier's frame–level scores were thus accumulated, instead, by addition. Phone–level error rates obtained by accumulating frame–level scores from the Gaussian tied–mixture and RBF classifiers are shown in Fig.'s 3(a) and (b). Best performance was provided by the Gaussian tied–mixture classifier with 50 k–means centers and no context frames (2.6% error rate, versus 3.9% for the RBF classifier with 75 centers and 1 context frame).

The good phone–level performance provided by the Gaussian tied–mixture classifier in Fig. 3(a) is partly due to the near correctness of the Gaussian mixture distribution assumption and the independent frames assumption (Eq. 2). To address the poor phone–level performance of the RBF classifier, we examine solutions that use smoothing to directly extend good frame–level results to acceptable phone–level performance. Smoothing was performed both by passing the classifier outputs through a sigmoid function[1] and by increasing the spread (h in Eq. 1) *after* RBF weights were trained. Increasing h was more effective.

Increasing h has the effect of "widening" the basis functions. This smoothes the discriminant functions produced by the RBF classifier to compensate for limited training data. If basis function widening occurs before weights are trained, then weights training will effectively compensate for the increase. This was verified in preliminary experiments, which showed that if h was increased before weights were trained, little difference in performance was observed as h varies from 50 to 200. Increasing h by 5% after weights were trained resulted in a slightly different frame–level performance (sometimes better, sometimes worse), but a significant improvement in phone–level results for all experimental variations of this study. In Fig. 3(c), a 5% widening of the basis function improved the performance of the baseline

---

[1] The sigmoid function is of the form $y = 1/\left(1 + e^{-(x-.5)^2}\right)$ where x is the input (an output from the RBF classifier) and y is the output used for classification.

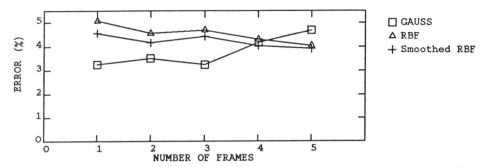

Figure 4: Phone–level error rates, as a function of the number of frames, for Gaussian mixture with 9 mixtures per class, and RBF classifiers with centers from the Gaussian mixture classifier (27 total centers for this 3 class task).

RBF classifier. It did not, however, improve performance over that provided by the Gaussian tied–mixture classifier without context frames at the input. The lowest error rate provided by the smoothed RBF is now 3.4% using 75 k–means centers and 2 context frames (compared with 2.6% for the Gaussian tied–mixture classifier with 50 centers and no context).

Error rates for the Gaussian mixture classifier with 9 mixtures per class is plotted versus the number of frames in Fig. 4, along with the results for RBF classifiers with centers taken from the Gaussian mixture classifier. Similar behavior was observed in all experimental variations of this study. There are three main observations: (1) The Gaussian mixture classifier without context frames provided best performance but degraded as the number of input frames increased, (2) RBF classifiers can out-perform Gaussian mixture classifiers with many input frames, and (3) widening the basis functions after weights were trained improved the RBF classifier's performance.

4   Summary

Two techniques were explored that integrated discriminant classifiers into HMM speech recognizers. In second–stage discrimination, an RBF second–stage classifier halved the error rates in a {BDG} vocabulary task but provided no performance improvement in an E-set vocabulary task. For integrating at the pre–processing level, RBF classifiers provided superior frame–level performance over conventional Gaussian mixture classifiers. At the phone–level, best performance was provided by a Gaussian mixture classifier with a single frame input; however, the RBF classifier outperformed the Gaussian mixture classifier when the input contained multiple context frames. Both sets of experiments indicated an ability for the RBF classifier to integrate the large amount of information provided by inputs with high dimensionality. They suggest that an HMM recognizer integrated with RBF and other discriminant classifiers may provide improved recognition by providing better frame–level discrimination and by utilizing features that are ignored by current "state–of–the–art" HMM speech recognizers. This is consistent with the results of

Franzini [3] and Bourlard [1], who used many context frames in their implementation of discriminant pre–processing which embedded MLPs' into HMM recognizers.

Current efforts focus on studying techniques to improve the performance of discriminant classifier for phones, words, and continuous speech. Approaches include accumulating scores from lower level speech units and using objective functions that depend on higher level speech units, such as phones and words. Work is also being performed to integrate discriminant classification algorithms into HMM recognizers using Viterbi training.

References

[1] H. Bourlard and N. Morgan. Merging multilayer perceptrons in hidden Markov models: Some experiments in continuous speech recognition. Technical Report TR–89–033, International Computer Science Institute, Berkeley, CA., July 1989.

[2] Peter F. Brown. *The Acoustic-Modeling Problem in Automatic Speech Recognition.* PhD thesis, Carnegie Mellon University, May 1987.

[3] Michael A. Franzini, Michael J. Witbrock, and Kai-Fu Lee. A connectionist approach to continuous speech recognition. In *Proceedings of the IEEE ICASSP*, May 1989.

[4] William Y. Huang and Richard P. Lippmann. Comparisons between conventional and neural net classifiers. In *1st International Conference on Neural Network*, pages IV–485. IEEE, June 1987.

[5] Kai-Fu Lee and Sanjoy Mahajan. Corrective and reinforcement leaning for speaker-independent continuous speech recognition. Technical Report CMU-CS-89-100, Computer Science Department, Carnegie–Mellon University, January 1989.

[6] Yuchun Lee and Richard Lippmann. Practical characteristics of neural network and conventional pattern classifiers on artificial and speech problems. In *Advances in Neural Information Processing Systems 2*, Denver, CO., 1989. IEEE, Morgan Kaufmann. In Press.

[7] R. P. Lippmann. Review of neural networks for speech recognition. *Neural Computation*, 1(1):1–38, 1989.

[8] Richard P. Lippmann. Pattern classification using neural networks. *IEEE Communications Magazine*, 27(11):47–63, Nov. 1989.

[9] G. J. McLachlan. *Mixture Models.* Marcel Dekker, New York, N. Y., 1988.

[10] D. B. Paul. A speaker-stress resistant HMM isolated word recognizer. In *Proceedings of the IEEE ICASSP*, pages 713–716, April 1987.

[11] L. R. Rabiner, B.-H. Juang, S. E. Levinson, and M. M. Sondhi. Recognition of isolated digits using hidden Markov models with continuous mixture densities. *AT&T Technical Journal*, 64(6):1211–1233, 1985.

Connectionist Architectures for Multi-Speaker Phoneme Recognition

John B. Hampshire II and **Alex Waibel**
School of Computer Science
Carnegie Mellon University
Pittsburgh, PA 15213-3890

ABSTRACT

We present a number of Time-Delay Neural Network (TDNN) based architectures for multi-speaker phoneme recognition (/b,d,g/ task). We use speech of two females and four males to compare the performance of the various architectures against a baseline recognition rate of 95.9% for a single TDNN on the six-speaker /b,d,g/ task. This series of modular designs leads to a highly modular multi-network architecture capable of performing the six-speaker recognition task at the speaker *de*pendent rate of 98.4%. In addition to its high recognition rate, the so-called "Meta-Pi" architecture learns — without direct supervision — to recognize the speech of one particular male speaker using internal models of *other* male speakers exclusively.

1   INTRODUCTION

References [1,2] have show the Time-Delay Neural Network to be an effective classifier of acoustic phonetic speech from individual speakers. The objective of this research has been to extend the TDNN paradigm to the multi-speaker phoneme recognition task, with the eventual goal of producing connectionist structures capable of speaker *independent* phoneme recognition. In making the transition from single to multi-speaker tasks, we have focused on modular architectures that perform the over-all recognition task by integrating a number of smaller task-specific networks.

Table 1: A synopsis of multi-speaker /b,d,g/ recognition results for six TDNN-based architectures.

Architecture	Type	Features	Size (connections)	Recognition Rate 3-speakers	6-speakers
TDNN	baseline single net		6,233	97.3%	95.9%
FSTDNN	single net	•Frequency shift invariance	(1-ply) 5,357 (2-ply) 6,947	96.8% 97.2%	— —
Multiple TDNNs	multi net	•arbitrated classification	18,700	98.6%	97.1 %
Modular TDNN	multi net	•2-stage training	18,650 37,400	97.3% —	— 96.3%
SID	multi net	•2-stage training •Multiple TDNN modules	144,000	—	98.3%
Meta-Pi	multi net	•2-stage training •Multiple TDNN modules •Bayesian MAP learning •no explicit speaker I.D.	144,000	—	98.4%

1.1 DATA

The experimental conditions for this research are detailed in [1]. Japanese speech data from six professional announcers (2 female, 4 male) was sampled for the /b, d, g/ phonemes (approximately 250 training and 250 testing tokens per phoneme, per speaker). Training for all of the modular architectures followed a general two-stage process: in the first stage, speaker-dependent modules were trained on speech tokens from specific individuals; in the second stage, the over-all modular structure was trained with speech tokens from all speakers.

1.2 RESULTS

Owing to the number of architectures investigated, we present only brief descriptions of each structure. Additional references are provided for readers interested in more detailed descriptions of particular architectures. Table 1 summarizes our recognition results for all of the network architectures described below. We list the type of architecture (single or multi network), the important features of the design, its over-all size (in terms of total connections), and its recognition performance on the specified multi-speaker task. There are two principal multi-speaker tasks: a three male task, and a four male/two female task: the six speaker task is considerably more difficult than its three speaker counterpart, owing to the higher acoustic variance of combined male/female speech.

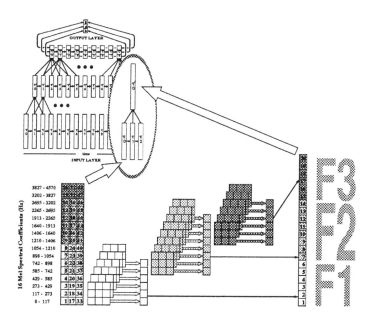

Figure 1: The Frequency Shifting TDNN (FSTDNN) architecture.

2   ARCHITECTURE DESCRIPTIONS

TDNN: The TDNN [1,2] serves as our baseline multi-speaker experiment. Its recognition performance on single speaker speech is typically 98.5% [1,3]. The high acoustic variance of speech drawn from six speakers — two of whom are female — reduces the TDNN's performance significantly (95.9%). This indicates that architectures capable of adjusting to markedly different speakers are necessary for robust multi-speaker and speaker-independent recognition.

FSTDNN: In this design, a frequency shift invariant feature is added to the original TDNN paradigm. The resulting architecture maps input speech into a first hidden layer with three frequency ranges roughly corresponding to the three formants F1 – F3 (see figure 1). Two variations of the basic design have been tested [4]: the first is a "one-ply" architecture (depicted in the figure), while the second is a "two-ply" structure that uses two plies of input to first hidden layer connections. While the frequency shift invariance of this architecture has intuitive appeal, the resulting network has a very small number of unique connections from the input to the first hidden layer ($\sim$ 30, 1-ply). This paucity of connections has two ramifications. First, it creates a crude replica of the input layer state in the first hidden layer; as a result, feature detectors that form in the connections between the input and first hidden layers of the standard TDNN are now formed in the connections between the first and second hidden layers of the FSTDNN. Second, the crude input to first hidden layer replication results in some loss of information; thus, the feature detectors of the FSTDNN operate on what can be viewed as a degraded version of

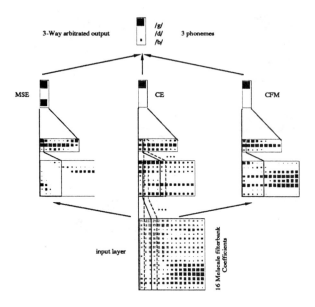

Figure 2: The Multiple TDNN architecture: three identical networks trained with three different objective functions.

the original input. The resulting over-all structure's recognition performance is typically worse ($\sim$ 97%) than the baseline TDNN for the multi-speaker /b,d,g/ task.

Multiple TDNN: This design employs three TDNNs trained with the MSE, Cross Entropy [5], and CFM [3] objective functions (see figure 2). The different objective functions used to train the TDNNs form consistently different internal representations of the speech signal. We exploit these differing representations by using the (potentially) conflicting outputs of the three networks to form a global arbitrated classification decision. Taking the normalized sum of the three networks' outputs constitutes a simple arbitration scheme that typically reduces the single TDNN error rate by 30%.

Modular TDNN: In this design, we use the connection strengths of TDNNs fully trained on individual speakers to form the initial connections of a larger multi-speaker network. This resulting network's higher layer connections are retrained [6] to produce the final multi-speaker network. This technique allows us to integrate speaker-dependent networks into a larger structure, limiting the over-all training time and network complexity of the final multi-speaker architecture. The 3-speaker modular TDNN (shown in figures 3 and 4) shows selective response to different tokens of speech. In figure 3, the network responds to a /d/ phone with only one sub-network (associated with speaker "MNM"). In fact, this /d/ *is* spoken by "MNM". In figure 4, the same network responds to a /b/ phone spoken by "MHT" with all sub-networks. This selective response to utterances indicates that the network is sensitive to utterances that are prototypical for all speakers as well

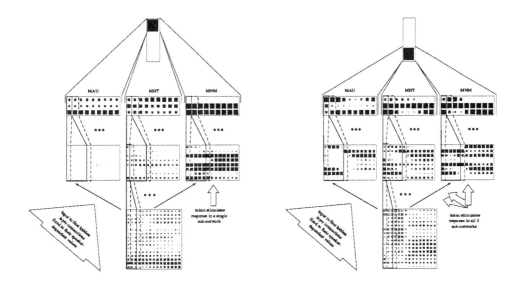

Figure 3: 3-speaker Modular TDNN responding to input with one module.

Figure 4: 3-speaker Modular TDNN responding to input with three modules.

as those that are unique to an individual. The recognition rate for the 3-speaker modular TDNN is comparable to the baseline TDNN rate (97.3%); however, the 6-speaker modular TDNN (not shown) yields a substantially lower recognition rate (96.3%). We attribute this degraded performance to the manner in which this modular structure integrates its sub-networks. In particular, the sub-networks are integrated by the connections from the second hidden to output layers. This scheme uses a very small number of connections to perform the integrating function. As the number of speakers increases and the acoustic variance of their speech becomes significant, the connection topology becomes inadequate for the increasingly complex integration function. Interconnecting the sub-networks between the first and second hidden layers would probably improve performance, but the improvement would be at the expense of modularity. We tried using a "Connectionist Glue" enhancement to the 6-speaker network [4], but found that it did not result in a significant recognition improvement.

Stimulus Identification (SID) network: This network architecture is conceptually very similar to the Integrated Neural Network (INN) [7]. Figure 5 illustrates the network in block diagram form. Stimulus specific networks (in this case, multiple TDNNs) are trained to recognize the speech of an individual. Each of these multiple TDNNs forms a module in the over-all network. The modules are integrated by a superstructure (itself a multiple TDNN) trained to recognize the identity of the input stimulus (speaker). The output activations of the integrating superstructure constitute multiplicative connections that gate the outputs of the modules in order to form a global classification decision.

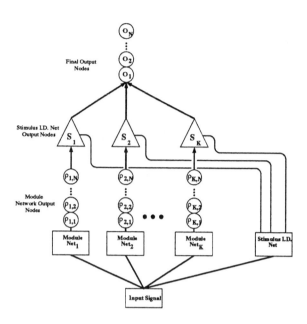

Figure 5: A block diagram of the Stimulus identification (SID) network, which is very similar to the Integrated Neural Network (INN) [7].

Reference [8] details the SID network's performance. The major advantages of this architecture are its high degree of modularity (all modules and the integrating superstructure can be trained independently) and it's high recognition rate (98.3%). It's major disadvantage is that it has no explicit mechanism for handling new speakers (see [8]).

The Meta-Pi Network: This network architecture is very similar to the SID network. Figure 6 illustrates the network in action. Stimulus specific networks (in this case, multiple TDNNs) are trained to recognize the speech of an individual. Each of these multiple TDNNs forms a module in the over-all network. The modules are integrated by a superstructure (itself a multiple TDNN) trained in Bayesian MAP fashion to maximize the phoneme recognition rate of the over-all structure: the equations governing the error back-propagation through the Meta-Pi superstructure link the global objective function with the output states of the network's speaker-dependent modules [8]. As with the the SID network, the output activations of the integrating superstructure constitute multiplicative connections that gate the outputs of the modules in order to form a global classification decision. However, as mentioned above, the integrating superstructure is *not* trained independently from the modules it integrates. While this Bayesian MAP training procedure is not as modularized as the SID network's training procedure, the resulting recognition rate is comparable. Additionally, the Meta-Pi network forms very broad representations of speaker *types* in order to perform its integration task. Reference [8] shows that *the Meta-Pi superstructure learns — without direct supervision — to perform its integra-*

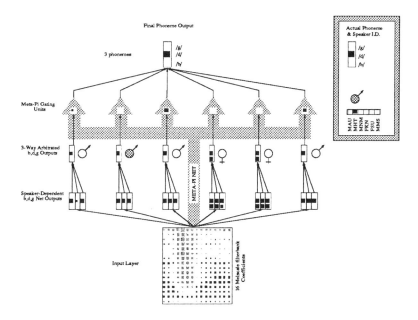

Figure 6: The Meta-Pi network responding to the speech of one male (MHT) using models of *other* males' speech exclusively.

tion function based on gross formant features of the speakers being processed; explicit speaker identity is irrelevant. A by-product of this learning procedure and the general representations that it forms is that the Meta-Pi network *learns to recognize the speech of one male using modules trained for* other *males exclusively* (see figure 6 and [8]).

3   CONCLUSION

We have presented a number of TDNN-based connectionist architectures for multi-speaker phoneme recognition. The Meta-Pi network combines the best features of a number of these designs with a Bayesian MAP learning rule to form a connectionist classifier that performs multi-speaker phoneme recognition at speaker-*de*pendent rates. We believe that the Meta-Pi network's ability to recognize the speech of one male using only models of other male speakers is significant. It suggests speech recognition systems that can maintain their own database of speaker models, adapting to new speakers when possible, spawning new speaker-dependent learning processes when necessary, and eliminating redundant or obsolete speaker-dependent modules when appropriate. The one major disadvantage of the Meta-Pi network is its size. We are presently attempting to reduce the network's size by 67% (target size: 48,000 connections) without a statistically significant loss in recognition performance.

Acknowledgements

We wish to thank Bell Communications Research, ATR Interpreting Telephony Research Laboratories, and the National Science Foundation (EET-8716324) for their support of this research. We thank Bellcore's David Burr, Daniel Kahn, and Candace Kamm and Seimens' Stephen Hanson for their comments and suggestions, all of which served to improve this work. We also thank CMU's Warp/iWarp[1] group for their support of our computational requirements. Finally, we thank Barak Pearlmutter, Dean Pomerleau, and Roni Rosenfeld for their stimulating conversations, insight, and constructive criticism.

References

[1] Waibel, A., Hanazawa, T., Hinton, G., Shikano, K., and Lang, K., "Phoneme Recognition Using Time-Delay Neural Networks," *IEEE Transactions on Acoustics, Speech and Signal Processing*, vol. ASSP-37, March, 1989, pp. 328-339.

[2] Lang, K. "A Time-Delay Neural Network Architecture for Speech Recognition," Ph.D. Dissertation, *Carnegie Mellon University technical report CMU-CS-89-185*, July, 31, 1989.

[3] Hampshire, J., Waibel, A., "A Novel Objective Function for Improved Phoneme Recognition Using Time-Delay Neural Networks," *Carnegie Mellon University Technical Report CMU-CS-89-118*, March, 1989. *A shorter version of this technical report is published in the IEEE Proceedings of the 1989 International Joint Conference on Neural Networks, vol. 1, pp. 235-241.*

[4] Hampshire, J., Waibel, A., "Connectionist Architectures for Multi-Speaker Phoneme Recognition," *Carnegie Mellon University Technical Report CMU-CS-89-167*, August, 1989.

[5] Hinton, G. E., "Connectionist Learning Procedures," *Carnegie Mellon University Technical Report CMU-CS-87-115 (version 2)*, December, 1987, pg. 14.

[6] Waibel, A., Sawai, H., and Shikano, K., "Modularity and Scaling in Large Phonemic Neural Networks", *IEEE Transactions on Acoustics, Speech and Signal Processing*, vol. ASSP-37, December, 1989, pp. 1888-1898.

[7] Matsuoka, T., Hamada, H., and Nakatsu, R., "Syllable Recognition Using Integrated Neural Networks," *IEEE Proceedings of the 1989 International Joint Conference on Neural Networks*, Washington, D.C., June 18-22, 1989, vol. 1, pp. 251-258.

[8] Hampshire, J., Waibel, A., "The Meta-Pi Network: Building Distributed Knowledge Representations for Robust Pattern Recognition," *Carnegie Mellon University Technical Report CMU-CS-89-166*, August, 1989.

---

[1]iWarp is a registered trademark of Intel Corporation.

Training Stochastic Model Recognition Algorithms as Networks can lead to Maximum Mutual Information Estimation of Parameters

John S. Bridle
Royal Signals and Radar Establishment
Great Malvern   Worcs.
UK   WR14 3PS

ABSTRACT

One of the attractions of neural network approaches to pattern recognition is the use of a discrimination-based training method. We show that once we have modified the output layer of a multilayer perceptron to provide mathematically correct probability distributions, and replaced the usual squared error criterion with a probability-based score, the result is equivalent to Maximum Mutual Information training, which has been used successfully to improve the performance of hidden Markov models for speech recognition. If the network is specially constructed to perform the recognition computations of a given kind of stochastic model based classifier then we obtain a method for discrimination-based training of the parameters of the models. Examples include an HMM-based word discriminator, which we call an 'Alphanet'.

1   INTRODUCTION

It has often been suggested that one of the attractions of an adaptive neural network (NN) approach to pattern recognition is the availability of discrimination-based training (*e.g.* in Multilayer Perceptrons (MLPs) using Back-Propagation). Among the disadvantages of NN approaches are the lack of theory about what can be computed with any particular structure, what can be learned, how to choose a network architecture for a given task, and how to deal with data (such as speech) in which an underlying sequential structure is of the essence. There have been attempts to build internal dynamics into neural networks, using recurrent connections, so that they might deal with sequences and temporal patterns [1, 2], but there is a lack of relevant theory to inform the choice of network type.

Hidden Markov models (HMMs) are the basis of virtually all modern automatic speech recognition systems. They can be seen as an extension of the parametric statistical approach to pattern recognition, to deal (in a simple but principled way) with temporal patterning. Like most parametric models, HMMs are usually trained using within-class maximum-likelihood (ML) methods, and an EM algorithm due to Baum and Welch is particularly attractive (see for instance [3]). However, recently some success has been demonstrated using discrimination-based training methods, such as the so-called Maximum Mutual Information criterion [4] and Corrective Training[5].

This paper addresses two important questions:

- How can we design Neural Network architectures with at least the desirable properties of methods based on stochastic models (such as hidden Markov models)?

- What is the relationship between the inherently discriminative neural network training and the analogous MMI training of stochastic models?

We address the first question in two steps. Firstly, to make sure that the outputs of our network have the simple mathematical properties of conditional probability distributions over class labels we recommend a generalisation of the logistic nonlinearity; this enables us (but does not require us) to replace the usual squared error criterion with a more appropriate one, based on relative entropy. Secondly, we also have the option of designing networks which exactly implement the recognition computations of a given stochastic model method. (The resulting 'network' may be rather odd, and not very 'neural', but this is engineering, not biology.) As a contribution to the investigation of the second question, we point out that optimising the relative entropy criterion is exactly equivalent to performing Maximum Mutual Information Estimation.

By way of illustration we describe three 'networks' which implement stochastic model classifiers, and show how discrimination training can help.

2   TRAINABLE NETWORKS AS PARAMETERISED CONDITIONAL DISTRIBUTION FUNCTIONS

We consider a trainable network, when used for pattern classification, as a vector function $Q(x, \theta)$ from an input vector x to a set of indicators of class membership, $\{Q_j\}, \quad j = 1, \ldots N$. The parameters θ modify the transfer function. In a multilayer perceptron, for instance, the parameters would be values of weights. Typically, we have a training set of pairs $(x_t, c_t), \quad t = 1, \ldots T$, of inputs and associated true class labels, and we have to find a value for θ which specialises the function so that it is consistent with the training set. A common procedure is to minimise $E(\theta)$, the sum of the squares of the differences between the network outputs and true class indicators, or targets:

$$E(\theta) = \sum_{t=1}^{T} \sum_{j=1}^{N} (Q_j(x_t, \theta) - \delta_{j,c_t})^2,$$

where $\delta_{j,c} = 1$ if $j = c$, otherwise 0. E and Q will be written without the θ argument where the meaning is clear, and we may drop the t subscript.

It is well known that the value of $F(x)$ which minimises the expected value of $(F(x) - y)^2$ is the expected value of y given x. The expected value of δ_{j,c_t} is $P(C = j \mid X = x_t)$, the probability that the class associated with x_t is the jth class.

From now on we shall assume that the desired output of a classifier network is this conditional probability distribution over classes, given the input.

The outputs must satisfy certain simple constraints if they are to be interpretable as a probability distribution. For any input, the outputs must all be positive and they must sum to unity. The use of logistic nonlinearities at the outputs of the network ensures positivity, and also ensures that each output is less than unity. These constraints are appropriate for outputs that are to be interpreted as probabilities of Boolean events, but are not sufficient for 1-from-N classifiers.

Given a set of unconstrained values, $V_j(x)$, we can ensure both conditions by using a Normalised Exponential transformation:

$$Q_j(\pmb{x}) = \mathrm{e}^{V_j(\pmb{x})} / \sum_k \mathrm{e}^{V_k(\pmb{x})}$$

This transformation can be considered a multi-input generalisation of the logistic, operating on the whole output layer. It preserves the rank order of its input values, and is a differentiable generalisation of the 'winner-take-all' operation of picking the maximum value. For this reason we like to refer to it as **softmax**. Like the logistic, it has a simple implementation in transistor circuits [6].

If the network is such that we can be sure the values we have are all positive, it may be more appropriate just to normalise them. In particular, if we can treat them as likelihoods of the data given the possible classes, $L_j(\pmb{x}) = P(\pmb{X} = \pmb{x} \mid C = j)$, then normalisation produces the required conditional distribution (assuming equal prior probabilities for the classes).

3   RELATIVE ENTROPY SCORING FOR CLASSIFIERS

In this section we introduce an information-theoretic criterion for training 1-from-N classifier networks, to replace the squared error criterion, both for its intrinsic interest and because of the link to discriminative training of stochastic models. the class with highest likelihood. This is justified by

$$P(c \mid \pmb{x}) = P(\pmb{x} \mid c)P(c)/P(\pmb{x}),$$

if we assume equal priors $P(c)$ (this can be generalised) and see that the denominator $P(\pmb{x}) = \sum_c P(\pmb{x} \mid c)P(c)$ is the same for all classes.

It is also usual to train such classifiers by maximising the data likelihood given the correct classes. Maximum Likelihood (ML) training is appropriate if we are choosing from a family of pdfs which includes the correct one. In most real-life applications of pattern classification we do not have knowledge of the form of the data distributions, although we may have some useful ideas. In that case ML may be a rather bad approach to pdf estimation *for the purpose of pattern classification*, because what matters is the *relative* densities.

An alternative is to optimise a measure of success in pattern classification, and this can make a big difference to performance, particularly when the assumptions about the form of the class pdfs is badly wrong.

To make the likelihoods produced by a SM classifier look like NN outputs we can simply normalise them:

$$Q_j(\boldsymbol{x}) = L_j(\boldsymbol{x})/\sum_k L_k(\boldsymbol{x}).$$

Then we can use Neural Network optimisation methods to adjust the parameters.

a sum, weighted by the joint probability, of the MI of the joint events

$$I(X, Y) = \sum_{(x,y)} P(X\!=\!x, Y\!=\!y)\log\frac{P(X\!=\!x, Y\!=\!y)}{P(X\!=\!x)P(Y\!=\!y)}$$

For discrimination training of sets of stochastic models, Bahl et.al. suggest maximising the Mutual Information, I, between the training observations and the choice of the corresponding correct class.

$$I(\boldsymbol{X}, C) = \sum_t \log\frac{P(C\!=\!c_t, \boldsymbol{X}\!=\!\boldsymbol{x}_t)}{P(C\!=\!c_t)P(\boldsymbol{X}\!=\!\boldsymbol{x})} = \sum_t \log\frac{P(C\!=\!c_t\,|\,\boldsymbol{X}\!=\!\boldsymbol{x}_t)P(\boldsymbol{X}\!=\!\boldsymbol{x})}{P(C\!=\!c_t)P(\boldsymbol{X}\!=\!\boldsymbol{x})}.$$

$P(C\!=\!c_t\,|\,\boldsymbol{X} = \boldsymbol{x}_t)$ should be read as the probability that we choose the correct class for the tth training example. If we are choosing classes according to the conditional distribution computed using parameters θ then $P(C = c_t\,|\,\boldsymbol{X} = \boldsymbol{x}_t) = Q_{c_t}(\boldsymbol{x}, \theta)$, and

$$I(\boldsymbol{X}, C) = \sum_t \log\frac{Q_{c_t}(\boldsymbol{x}_t, \vartheta)}{P(C\!=\!c_t)} = \sum_t \log Q_{c_t}(\boldsymbol{x}_t, \theta) - \sum_t \log P(C\!=\!c_t).$$

If the second term involving the priors is fixed, we are left with maximising

$$\sum_t \log Q_{c_t}(\boldsymbol{x}_t, \theta) = -J.$$

The RE-based score we use is $J = -\sum_{t=1}^T \sum_{j=1}^N P_{jt}\log Q_j(\boldsymbol{x}_t)$, where P_{jt} is the probability of class j associated with input $\boldsymbol{x}_t$ in the training set. If as usual the training set specifies only one true class, c_t for each $\boldsymbol{x}_t$ then $P_{j,t} = \delta_{j,c_t}$ and

$$J = -\sum_{t=1}^T \log Q_{c_t}(\boldsymbol{x}_t),$$

the sum of the logs of the outputs for the correct classes.

J can be derived from the Relative Entropy of distribution Q with respect to the true conditional distribution P, averaged over the input distribution:

$$\int d\boldsymbol{x}\, P(\boldsymbol{X} = \boldsymbol{x})G(Q\,|\,P), \quad \text{where} \quad G(Q\,|\,P) = -\sum_c P(c\,|\,\boldsymbol{x})\log\frac{P(c\,|\,\boldsymbol{x})}{Q_c(\boldsymbol{x})}.$$

information, cross entropy, asymmetric divergence, directed divergence, I-divergence, and Kullback-Leibler number. RE scoring is the basis for the Boltzmann Machine learning algorithm [7] and has also been proposed and used for adaptive networks with continuous-valued outputs [8, 9, 10, 11], but usually in the form appropriate to separate logistics and independent Boolean targets. An exception is [12].

There is another way of thinking about this 'log-of correct-output' score. Assume that the way we would use the outputs of the network is that, rather than choosing the class with the largest output, we choose randomly, picking from the distribution specified by the outputs. (Pick class j with probability Q_j.) The probability of choosing the class c_t for training sample $\boldsymbol{x}_t$ is simply $Q_{c_t}(\boldsymbol{x}_t)$. The probability of choosing the correct class labels for *all* the training set is $\prod_{t=1}^{T} Q_{c_t}(\boldsymbol{x}_t)$. We simply seek to maximise this probability, or what is equivalent, to minimise minus its log:

$$J = -\sum_{t=1}^{T} \log Q_{c_t}(\boldsymbol{x}_t).$$

In order to compute the partial derivatives of J wrt to parameters of the network, we first need $\frac{\partial J}{\partial Q_j} = -P_{jt}/Q_j$ The details of the back-propagation depend on the form of the network, but if the final non-linearity is a normalised exponential (softmax),

$$Q_j(x) = \exp(V_j(x)) / \sum_k \exp(V_k(x)), \quad \text{then [6]} \quad \frac{\partial J_t}{\partial V_j} = (Q_j(\boldsymbol{x}_t) - \delta_{j,c_t}).$$

We see that the derivative before the output nonlinearity is the difference between the corresponding output and a one-from-N target. We conclude that softmax output stages and 1-from-N RE scoring are natural partners.

4 DISCRIMINATIVE TRAINING

In stochastic model (probability-density) based pattern classification we usually compute likelihoods of the data given models for each class, $P(\boldsymbol{x} \,|\, c)$, and choose. So minimising our J criterion is also maximising Bahl's mutual information. (Also see [13].)

5 STOCHASTIC MODEL CLASSIFIERS AS NETWORKS
5.1 EXAMPLE ONE: A PAIR OF MULTIVARIATE GAUSSIANS

The conditional distribution for a pair of multivariate Gaussian densities with the same arbitrary covariance matrix is a logistic function of a weighted sum of the input coordinates (plus a constant). Therefore, even if we make such incorrect assumptions as equal priors and spherical unit covariances, it is still possible to find values for the parameters of the model (the positions of the means of the assumed distributions) for which the form of the conditional distribution is correct. (The means may be far from the means of the true distributions and from the data means.) Of course in this case we have the alternative of using a weighted-sum logistic unit to compute the conditional probability: the parameters are then the weights.

5.2 EXAMPLE TWO: A MULTI-CLASS GAUSSIAN CLASSIFIER

Consider a model in which the distributions for each class are multi-variate Gaussian, with equal isotropic unit variances, and different means, $\{\boldsymbol{m}_j\}$. The probability distribution over class labels, given an observation $\boldsymbol{x}$, is $P(c = j \,|\, \boldsymbol{x}) = e^{V_j} / \sum_k e^{V_k}$, where $V_j = -||\boldsymbol{x} - \boldsymbol{m}_j||^2$. This can be interpreted as a one-layer feed-forward non-linear network. The usual weighted sums are replaced by squared Euclidean distances, and the usual logistic output non-linearities are replaced by a normalised exponential.

For a particular two-dimensional 10-class problem, derived from Peterson and Barney's formant data, we have demonstrated [6] that training such a network can cause the ms to move from their "natural" positions at the data means (the in-class maximum likelihood estimates), and this can improve classification performance on unseen data (from 68% correct to 78%).

5.3   EXAMPLE THREE: ALPHANETS

Consider a set of hidden Markov models (HMMs), one for each word, each parameterised by a set of state transition probabilities, $\{a_{ij}^k\}$, and observation likelihood functions $\{b_j^k(\boldsymbol{x})\}$, where a_{ij}^k is the probability that in model k state i will be followed by state j, and $b_j^k(\boldsymbol{x})$ is the likelihood of model k emitting observation $\boldsymbol{x}$ from state j. For simplicity we insist that the end of the word pattern corresponds to state N of a model.

The likelihood, $L_k(\boldsymbol{x}_1^M)$ of model k generating a given sequence $\boldsymbol{x}_1^M \triangleq \boldsymbol{x}_1, \ldots, \boldsymbol{x}_M$ is a sum, over all sequences of states, of the joint likelihood of that state sequence and the data:

$$L_k(\boldsymbol{x}_1^M) = \sum_{s_1 \ldots s_M} \prod_{t=2}^{M} a_{s_{t-1}, s_t}^k \, b_{s_t}^k(\boldsymbol{x}_t) \quad \text{with} \quad s_M = N.$$

This can be computed efficiently via the forward recursion [3]

$$\alpha_{jk}(t) = b_j^k(\boldsymbol{x}_t) \sum_i a_{ij}^k \alpha_{ik}(t-1), \qquad \text{giving} \qquad L_k(\boldsymbol{x}_1^M) = \alpha_{Nk}(M),$$

which we can think of as a recurrent network. (Note that t is used as a time index here.)

If the observation sequence $\boldsymbol{x}_1^M$ could only have come from one of a set of known, equally likely models, then the posterior probability that it was from model k is

$$P(C=k \mid \boldsymbol{x}_1^M) = Q_k(\boldsymbol{x}_1^M) = L_k(\boldsymbol{x}_1^M) \bigg/ \sum_l L_l(\boldsymbol{x}_1^M).$$

These numbers are the output of our special "recurrent neural network" for isolated word discrimination, which we call an "Alphanet" [14]. Backpropagation of partial derivatives of the J score has the form of the **backward** recurrence used in the Baum-Welch algorithm, but they include discriminative terms, and we obtain the gradient of the relative entropy/mutual information.

6   CONCLUSIONS

Discrimination-based training is different from within-class parameter estimation, and it may be useful. (Also see [15].) Discrimination-based training for stochastic models and for networks are not distinct, and in some cases can be mathematically identical.

The notion of specially constructed 'network' architectures which implement stochastic model recognition algorithms provides a way to construct fertile hybrids. For instance, a Gaussian classifier (or a HMM classifier) can be preceeded by a nonlinear transformation (perhaps based on semilinear logistics) and all the parameters of the system adjusted together. This seems a useful approach to automating the discovery of 'feature detectors'.

© British Crown Copyright 1990

References

[1] R P Lippmann. Review of neural networks for speech recognition. *Neural Computation*, 1(1), 1989.

[2] R L Watrous. Connectionist speech recognition using the temporal flow model. In *Proc. IEEE Workshop on Speech Recognition*, June 1988.

[3] A B Poritz. Hidden Markov models: a guided tour. In *Proc. IEEE Int. Conf. Acoustics Speech and Signal Processing*, pages 7–13, 1988.

[4] L R Bahl, P F Brown, P V de Souza, and R L Mercer. Maximum mutual information estimation of hidden Markov model parameters. In *Proc. IEEE Int. Conf. Acoustics Speech and Signal Processing*, pages 49–52, 1986.

[5] L R Bahl, P F Brown, P V de Souza, and R L Mercer. A new algorithm for the estimation of HMM parameters. In *Proc. IEEE Int. Conf. Acoustics Speech and Signal Processing*, pages 493–496, 1988.

[6] J S Bridle. Probabilistic interpretation of feedforward classification network outputs, with relationships to statistical pattern recognition. In F Fougelman-Soulie and J Hérault, editors, *Neuro-computing: algorithms, architectures and applications*, Springer-Verlag, 1989.

[7] D H Ackley, G E Hinton, and T J Sejnowski. A learning algorithm for Boltzmann machines. *Cognitive Science*, 9:147–168, 1985.

[8] L Gillick. Probability scores for backpropagation networks. July 1987. Personal communication.

[9] G E Hinton. *Connectionist Learning Procedures*. Technical Report CMU-CS-87-115, Carnegie Mellon University Computer Science Department, June 1987.

[10] E B Baum and F Wilczek. Supervised learning of probability distributions by neural networks. In D Anderson, editor, *Neural Information Processing Systems*, pages 52–61, Am. Inst. of Physics, 1988.

[11] S Solla, E Levin, and M Fleisher. Accelerated learning in layered neural networks. *Complex Systems*, January 1989.

[12] E Yair and A Gersho. The Boltzmann Perceptron Network: a soft classifier. In D Touretzky, editor, *Advances in Neural Information Processing Systems 1*, San Mateo, CA: Morgan Kaufmann, 1989.

[13] P S Gopalakrishnan, D Kanevsky, A Nadas, D Nahamoo, and M A Picheny. Decoder selection based on cross-entropies. In *Proc. IEEE Int. Conf. Acoustics Speech and Signal Processing*, pages 20–23, 1988.

[14] J S Bridle. Alphanets: a recurrent 'neural' network architecture with a hidden Markov model interpretation. *Speech Communication*, Special Neurospeech issue, February 1990.

[15] L Niles, H Silverman, G Tajchman, and M Bush. How limited training data can allow a neural network to out-perform an 'optimal' classifier. In *Proc. IEEE Int. Conf. Acoustics Speech and Signal Processing*, 1989.

Speaker Independent Speech Recognition with Neural Networks and Speech Knowledge

Yoshua Bengio
Dept Computer Science
McGill University
Montreal, Canada H3A2A7

Renato De Mori
Dept Computer Science
McGill University

Regis Cardin
Dept Computer Science
McGill University

ABSTRACT

We attempt to combine neural networks with knowledge from speech science to build a speaker independent speech recognition system. This knowledge is utilized in designing the preprocessing, input coding, output coding, output supervision and architectural constraints. To handle the temporal aspect of speech we combine delays, copies of activations of hidden and output units at the input level, and Back-Propagation for Sequences (BPS), a learning algorithm for networks with local self-loops. This strategy is demonstrated in several experiments, in particular a nasal discrimination task for which the application of a speech theory hypothesis dramatically improved generalization.

1 INTRODUCTION

The strategy put forward in this research effort is to combine the flexibility and learning abilities of neural networks with as much knowledge from speech science as possible in order to build a speaker independent automatic speech recognition system. This knowledge is utilized in each of the steps in the construction of an automated speech recognition system: preprocessing, input coding, output coding, output supervision, architectural design. In particular for preprocessing we explored the advantages of various possible ways of processing the speech signal, such as comparing an ear model *vs.* Fast Fourier Transform (FFT), or compressing the frame sequence in such a way as to conserve an approximately constant rate of change. To handle the temporal aspect of speech we propose to combine various algorithms depending of the demands of the task, including an algorithm for a type of recurrent network which includes only self-loops and is local in space and time (BPS). This strategy is demonstrated in several experiments, in particular a nasal discrimination task for which the application of a speech theory hypothesis drastically improved generalization.

2 Application of Speech Knowledge

2.1 Preprocessing

Our previous work has shown us that the choice of preprocessing significantly influences the performance of a neural network recognizer. (*e.g.*, Bengio & De Mori 1988) Different types of preprocessing processes and acoustic features can be utilized at the input of a neural network. We used several acoustic features (such as counts of zero crossings), filters derived from the FFT, energy levels (of both the signal and its derivative) and ratios (Gori, Bengio & De Mori 1989), as well as an ear model and synchrony detector.

Ear model *vs.* FFT

We performed experiments in speaker-independent recognition of 10 english vowels on isolated words that compared the use of an ear model with an FFT as preprocessing. The FFT was done using a mel scale and the same number of filters (40) as for the ear model. The ear model was derived from the one proposed by Seneff (1985). Recognition was performed with a neural network with one hidden layer of 20 units. We obtained 87% recognition with the FFT preprocessing *vs.* 96% recognition with the ear model (plus synchrony detector to extract spectral regularity from the instantaneous output of the ear model)(Bengio, Cosi, De Mori 1989). This was an example of the successful application of knowledge about human audition to the automatic recognition of speech with machines.

Compression in time resulting in constant rate of change

The motivation for this processing step is the following. The rate of change of the speech signal, (as well as the output of networks performing acoustic→phonetic mappings) varies a lot. It would be nice to have more temporal precision in parts of the signal where there is a lot of variation (bursts, fast transitions) and less temporal precision in more stable parts of the signal (e.g., vowels, silence).

Given a sequence of vectors (parameters, which can be acoustic parameters, such as spectral coefficients, as well as outputs from neural networks) we transform it by compressing it in time in order to obtain a shorter sequence where frames refer to segments of varying length of the original sequence.

Very simple Algorithm that *maps sequence X(t) → sequence Y(t)* where X and Y are vectors:

```
{ Accumulate and average X(t), X(t+1)...X(t+n) in Y(s) as
long as the sum of the Distance(X(t),X(t+1)) + ... +
Distance(X(t+n-1),X(t+n)) is less than a threshold.
When this threshold is reached,
  t←t+n+1;
  s←s+1; }
```

The advantages of this system are the following: 1) more temporal precision where needed, 2) reduction of the dimensionality of the problem, 3) constant rate of change of the resulting signal so that when using input windows in a neural net, the windows may have less frames, 4) better generalization since several realizations of the same word spoken at different rates of speech tend to be reduced to more similar sequences.

Initial results when this system is used to compress spectral parameters (24 mel-scaled FFT filters + energy) computed every 5 ms were interesting. The task was the classification of phonemes into 14 classes. The size of the database was reduced by 30%. The size of the window was reduced (4 frames instead of 8), hence the network size was reduced as well. Half the size of the window was necessary in order to obtain similar performance on the training set. Generalization on the test set was slightly better (from 38% to 33% classification error by frame). The idea to use a measure of rate of change to process speech is not new (Atal, 1983) but we believe that it might be particularly useful when the recognition device is a neural network with an input of several frames of acoustic parameters.

2.2   Input coding

Our previous work has shown us that information should be as easily accessible as possible to the network. For example, compression of the spectral information into cepstrum coefficients (with first few coefficients having very large variance) resulted in poorer performance with respect to experiments done with the spectrum itself. The recognition was performed with a neural network where units compute the sigmoid of the weighted sum of their inputs. The task was the broad classification of phonemes in 4 classes. The error on the test set increased from 15% to 20% when using cepstral rather than spectral coefficients.

Another example concerns the recognition experiments for which there is a lot of variance in the quantities presented in the input. A grid representation with coarse coding improved learning time as well as generalization (since the problem became more separable and thus the network needed less hidden units). (Bengio, De Mori, 1988).

2.3   Output coding

We have chosen an output coding scheme based on phonetic features defined by the way speech is produced. This is generally more difficult to learn but results in better generalization, especially with respect to new sounds that had not been seen by the network during the training. We have demonstrated this with experiments on vowel recognition in which the networks were trained to recognized the place and the manner of articulation (Bengio, Cosi, De Mori 89). In addition the resulting representation is more compact than when using one output for each phoneme. However, this representation remains meaningful i.e. each output can be attributed a meaning almost independently of the values of the other outputs.

In general, an explicit representation is preferred to an arbitrary and compact one (such as a compact binary coding of the classes). Otherwise, the network must perform an additional step of encoding. This can be costly in terms of the size of the networks, and generally also in terms of generalization (given the need for a larger number of weights).

2.4   Output supervision

When using a network with some recurrences it is not necessary that supervision be provided at every frame for every output (particularly for transition periods which are difficult to label). Instead the supervision should be provided to the network when the speech signal clearly corresponds to the categories one is trying to learn. We have used this approach when performing the discrimination between /b/ and /d/ with the BPS (Back Propagation for Sequences) algorithm (self-loop only, *c.f.* section 3.3).

Giving additional information to the network through more supervision (with extra output units) improved learning time and generalization (*c.f.* section 4).

2.5   Architectural design

Hypothesis about the nature of the processing to be performed by the network based on speech science knowledge enables to put constraints on the architecture. These constraints result in a network that generalizes better than a fully connected network. This strategy is most useful when the speech recognition task has been modularized in the appropriate way so that the same architectural constraints do not have to apply to all of the subtasks. Here are several examples of application of modularization. We initially explored modularization by acoustic context (different networks are triggered when various acoustic contexts are detected)(Bengio, Cardin, De Mori, Merlo 89) We also implemented modularisation by independent articulatory features (vertical and horizontal place of articulation) (in Bengio, Cosi, De Mori, 89). Another type of modularization, by subsets of phonemes, was explored by several researchers, in particular Alex Waibel (Waibel 88).

3   Temporal aspect of the speech recognition task

Both of the algorithms presented in the following subsections assume that one is using the Least Mean Square Error criterion, but both can be easily modified for any type of error criterion. We used and sometimes combined the following techniques:

3.1   Delays

If the speech signal is preprocessed in such a way as to obtain a frame of acoustic parameters for every interval of time, one can use delays from the input units representing these acoustic parameters to implement an input window on the input sequence, as in NETtalk, or using this strategy at every level as in TDNNs (Waibel 88). Even when we use a recurrent network, a small number of delays on the outgoing links of the input units might be useful. It enables the network to make a direct comparison between successive frames.

3.2   BPS (Back Propagation for Sequences)

This is a learning algorithm that we have introduced for networks that have a certain constrained type of recurrence (local self-loops). It permits to compute the gradient of the error with respect to all weights. This algorithm has the same order of space and time requirements as backpropagation for feedforward networks. Experiments with the /b/ vs. /d/ speaker independent discrimination yielded 3.45% error on the test set for the BPS network as opposed to 6.9% error for a feedforward network (Gori, Bengio, De Mori 89).

BPS equations:

feedforward pass:

•dynamic units: these have a local self-loop and their input must directly come from the input layer.

$$X_i(t+1) = W_{ii} X_i(t) + \sum_j W_{ij} f(X_j(t))$$

$$\partial X_i(t+1)/\partial W_{ij} = W_{ii} \partial X_i(t)/\partial W_{ij} + f(X_j(t)) \qquad \text{for } i{!=}j$$

$$\partial X_i(t)/\partial W_{ii} = W_{ii} \partial X_i(t)/\partial W_{ii} + X_i(t) \qquad \text{for } i{==}j$$

•static units, *i.e.*, without feedback, follow usual Back-Propagation (BP) equations (Rumelhart et al. 1986):

$$X_i(t+1) = \sum_j W_{ij} f(X_j(t))$$

$$\partial X_i(t+1)/\partial W_{ij} = f(X_j(t))$$

Backpropagation pass, after every frame: as usual but using above definition of $\partial X_i(t)/\partial W_{ii}$ instead of the usual $f(X_j(t))$.

This algorithm has a time complexity $O(L \cdot N_w)$(as static BP) It needs space $O(N_u)$, where L is the length of a sequence, N_w is the number of weights and N_u is the number of units. Note that it is local in time (it is causal, no backpropagation in time) and in space (only information coming from direct neighbors is needed).

3.3   Discrete Recurrent Net without Constraints

This is how we compute the gradient in an unconstrained discrete recurrent net. The derivation is similar to the one of Pearlmutter (1989). It is another way to view the computation of the gradient for recurrent networks, called time unfolding, which was presented by (Rumelhart et al. 1986). Here the units have a memory of their past activations during the forward pass (from frame 1 to L) and a "memory" of the future $\partial E/\partial Xi$ during the backward pass (from frame L down to frame 1).

Forward phase: consider the possibility of an arbitrary number of connections from unit i to unit j, each having a different delay d.

$$Xi(t) = \sum_{j,d} Wijd\ f(Xi(t\text{-}d)) + I(i,t)$$

Here, the basic idea is to compute $\partial E/\partial Wijd$ by computing $\partial E/\partial Xi(t)$:

$$\partial E/\partial Wijd = \sum_t \partial E/\partial Xi(t)\ \partial Xi(t)/\partial Wijd$$

where $\partial Xi(t)/\partial Wijd = f(Xj(t\text{-}d))$ as usual. In the *backward phase* we backpropagate $\partial E/\partial Xi(t)$ recursively from the last time frame=L down to frame 1:

$$\partial E/\partial Xi(t) = \sum_{k,d} Wkid\ \partial E/\partial Xk(t\text{+}d)\ f'(Xj(t))$$
$$+(\text{if i is an output unit})(f(Xi(t))\text{-}Yi^*(t))\ f'(Xi(t))$$

where $Yi^*(t)$ is the target output for unit i at time t. In this equation the first term represents backpropagation from future times and downstream units, while the second one comes from direct external supervision. This algorithm works for any connectivity of the recurrent network with delays. Its time complexity is $O(L \cdot Nw)$ (as static BP). However the space requirements are $O(L \cdot Nu)$. The algorithm is local in space but not in time; however, we found that restriction not to be very important in speech recognition, where we consider at most a few hundred frames of left context (one sentence).

4 Nasal experiment

As an example of the application of the above described strategy we have performed the following experiment with the discrimination of nasals /m/ and /n/ in a fixed context. The speech material consisted of 294 tokens from 70 training speakers (male and female with various accents) and 38 tokens from 10 test speakers. The speech signal is preprocessed with an ear model followed by a generalized synchrony detector yielding 40 spectral parameters every 10 ms. Early experiments with a simple output coding {vowel, m, n}, a window of two consecutive frames as input, and a two-layer fully connected architecture with 10 hidden units gave poor results: 15% error on the test set. A speech theory hypothesis claiming that the most critical discriminatory information for the nasals is available during the transition between the vowel and the nasal inspired us to try the following output coding: {vowel, transition to m, transition to n, nasal}. Since the transition was more important we chose as input a window of 4 frames at times t, t-10ms, t-30ms and t-70ms. To reduce the connectivity the architecture included a constrained first hidden layer of 40 units where each unit was meant to correspond to one of the 40 spectral frequencies of the preprocessing stage. Each such hidden unit associated with filter bank F was connected (when possible) to input units corresponding to

frequency banks   (F-2,F-1,F,F+1,F+2)

and times   (t,t-10ms,t-30ms,t-70ms).

Experiments with this feedforward delay network (160 inputs--40 hidden--10 hidden--4 outputs) showed that, indeed the strongest clues about the identity of the nasal seemed to be available during the transition and for a very short time, just before the steady part of the nasal started. In order to extract that critical information from the stream of outputs of this network, a second network was trained on the outputs of the first one to provide clearly the discrimination of the nasal during the whole of the nasal. That higher level network used the BPS algorithm to learn about the temporal nature of the task and keep the detected critical information during the length of the nasal. Recognition performance reached a plateau of 1.14% errors on the training set. Generalization was very good with only 2.63% error on the test set.

5 Future experiments

One of the advantages of using phonetic features instead of phonemes to describe the speech is that they could help to learn more robustly about the influence of context. If one uses a phonemic representation and tries to characterize the influence of the past phoneme on the current phoneme, one faces the problem of poor statistical sampling of many of the corresponding diphones (in a realistic database). On the other hand, if speech is characterized by several independent dimensions such as horizontal and vertical place of articulation and voicing, then the number of possible contexts to consider for each value of one of the dimensions is much more limited. Hence the set of examples characterizing those contexts is much richer.

We now present some observations on continuous speech based on our initial work with the TIMIT database in which we try learning articulatory features. Although we have obtained good results for the recognition of articulatory features (horizontal and vertical place of articulation) for isolated words, initial results with continuous speech are less encouraging. Indeed, whereas the measured place of articulation (by the networks) for phonemes in isolated speech corresponds well to expectations (as defined by acousticians who physically measured these features for isolated short words), this is not the case for continuous speech. In the latter case, phonemes have a much shorter duration so that the articulatory features are most of the time in transition, and the place of articulation generally does not reach the expected target values (although it always moves in the right *direction*). This is probably due to the inertia of the production system and to coarticulation effects. In order to attack that problem we intend to perform the following experiments. We could use the subset of the database for which the phoneme duration is sufficiently long to learn an approximation of the articulatory features. We could then improve that approximation in order to be able to learn about the trajectories of these features found in the transitions from one phoneme to the next. This could be done by using a two stage network (similar to the encoder network) with a bottleneck in the middle. The first stage of the network produces phonetic features and receives supervision only on the steady parts of the speech. The second stage of the network (which would be a recurrent network) has as input the trajectory of the approximation of the phonetic features and produces as output the previous, current and next phoneme. As an additional constraint, we propose to use self-loops with various time constants on the units of the bottleneck. Units that represent fast varying descriptors of speech will have a short time constant, while units that we want to have represent information about the past acoustic context will have a slightly longer time constant and units that could represent very long time range information – such as information about the speaker or the recording conditions – will receive a very long time constant.

This paper has proposed a general strategy for setting up a speaker independent speech recognition system with neural networks using as much speech knowledge as possible. We explored several aspects of this problem including preprocessing, input coding, output coding, output supervision, architectural design, algorithms for recurrent networks, and have described several initial experimental results to support these ideas.

References

Atal B.S. (1983), Efficient coding of LPC parameters by temporal decomposition, *Proc. ICASSP 83* , Boston, pp 81-84.

Bengio Y., Cardin R., De Mori R., Merlo E. (1989) Programmable execution of multi-layered networks for automatic speech recognition, *Communications of the Association for Computing Machinery,* 32 (2).

Bengio Y., Cardin R., De Mori R., (1990), Speaker independent speech recognition with neural networks and speech knowledge, in D.S. Touretzky (ed.), *Advances in Neural Networks Information Processing Systems 2,* San Mateo, CA: Morgan Kaufmann.

Bengio Y., De Mori R., (1988), Speaker normalization and automatic speech recognition using spectral lines and neural networks, *Proc. Canadian Conference on Artificial Intelligence (CSCSI-88)* , Edmonton Al., May 88.

Bengio Y., Cosi P., De Mori R., (1989), On the generalization capability of multi-layered networks in the extraction of speech properties, *Proc. Internation Joint Conference of Artificial Intelligence (IJCAI 89)"* , Detroit, August 89, pp. 1531-1536.

Gori M., Bengio Y., De Mori R., (1989), BPS: a learning algorithm for capturing the dynamic nature of speech, *Proc. IEEE International Joint Conference on Neural Networks,* Washington, June 89.

Pearlmutter B.A., Learning state space trajectories in recurrent neural networks, (1989), *Neural Computation, vol. 1, no. 2,* pp. 263-269.

Rumelhart D.E., Hinton G., Williams R.J., (1986), Learning internal representation by error propagation, in *Parallel Distributed Processing, exploration in the microstructure of cognition, vol. 1,* MIT Press 1986.

Seneff S., (1985), Pitch and spectral analysis of speech based on an auditory synchrony model, *RLE Technical report 504, MIT.*

Waibel A., (1988), Modularity in neural networks for speech recognition, *Advances in Neural Networks Information Processing Systems 1.* San Mateo, CA: Morgan Kaufmann.

The Effects of Circuit Integration on a Feature Map Vector Quantizer

Jim Mann
MIT Lincoln Laboratory
244 Wood St.
Lexington, MA 02173
email: mann@vlsi.ll.mit.edu

ABSTRACT

The effects of parameter modifications imposed by hardware constraints on a self-organizing feature map algorithm were examined. Performance was measured by the error rate of a speech recognition system which included this algorithm as part of the front-end processing. System parameters which were varied included weight (connection strength) quantization, adaptation quantization, distance measures and circuit approximations which include device characteristics and process variability. Experiments using the TI isolated word database for 16 speakers demonstrated degradation in performance when weight quantization fell below 8 bits. The competitive nature of the algorithm relaxes constraints on uniformity and linearity which makes it an excellent candidate for a fully analog circuit implementation. Prototype circuits have been fabricated and characterized following the constraints established through the simulation efforts.

1 Introduction

The self-organizing feature map algorithm developed by Kohonen [Kohonen, 1988] readily lends itself to the task of vector quantization for use in such areas as speech recognition. However, in considering practical implementations, it is necessary to

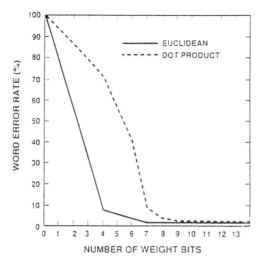

Figure 1: Recognition performance of the Euclidean and dot product activity calculators plotted as a function of weight precision.

understand the limitations imposed by circuitry on algorithm performance. In order to test the effects of these constraints on overall performance a simulation was written which permits ready variation of critical system parameters.

The feature map algorithm was placed in the frontend of a discrete hidden Markov model (HMM) speech recognition program as the vector quantizer (VQ) in order to track the effects of feature map algorithm modifications by monitoring overall word recognition accuracy. The system was tested on TI's 20 isolated word database consisting of 16 speakers. Each speaker had 1 training session consisting of 10 repetitions of each word in the vocabulary and 8 test sessions consisting of 2 repetitions of each word.

The key parameters tested include; quantization of both the weight coefficients and learning rule, and several different activation computations, the dot product and the mean squared error (i.e. squared Euclidean distance), as well as the circuit approximations to these calculators.

2   Results

A unique dependency between weight quantization and distance measure emerged from the simulations and is illustrated in the graph presented in Figure 1. The network equipped with the mean squared error activity calculator shows a "knee" in the word error rate at 6 bits of precision in the weight representation. The overall performance dropped only slightly between the essentially ideal floating point case, at 1.45% error rate, and the 6 bit case, at 2.99% error rate. At 4 bits, the error rate climbs to 7.62%. This still corresponds to a recognition accuracy of better than 92% but does show a marked degradation in performance.

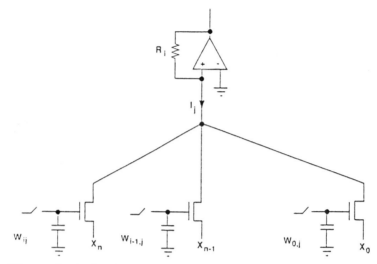

Figure 2: A circuit approximation to the dot product calculator.

The dot product does not degrade as gracefully with reduced precision in the weight representation as the mean squared error activity calculation. This is due to the normalization required on the input, and subsequently the weight vectors, which compresses the space onto the unit hypersphere. This step is necessary because of the inherent sensitivity of this metric to vector magnitude in making decisions of relative distance. Here the "knee" in the error curve occurs at 8 bits. Below 8 bits, performance drops off dramatically, reaching 40.6% error rate at 6 bits. The double precision floating point case starts off at 1.68% and is 3.44% at 8 bits.

Circuit approximations to these activity calculators were also included in the simulations. An approximation to the dot product operation can be implemented with single transistors operating in the ohmic region at each connection as illustrated in Figure 2.

These area related considerations can often overshadow the performance penalties associated with their implementation. The simulation results from this circuit approximation match the performance of the digital calculation of the dot product almost exactly as seen in Figure 3. This indicates that the performance of the system depends more on the monotonicity of the product operation performed at each connection then its linearity.

Effects of process variations on transistor thresholds were also examined. There appears to be a gradual decrease in system performance with increasing variability in transistor thresholds as seen in Figure 4. The cause of this phenomena remains to be investigated.

A weight adjustment rule which simplifies circuitry consists of quantizing the learning rate gain term. An integer step is added to or subtracted from the weight depending on the magnitude of the difference between it and the input. In the

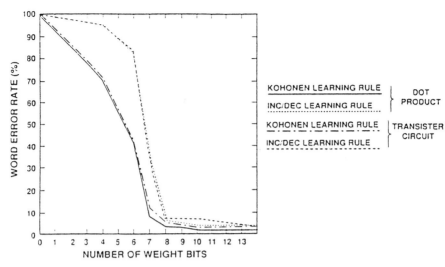

Figure 3: Similarity between the transistor circuit simulation and the digital calculation of the dot product

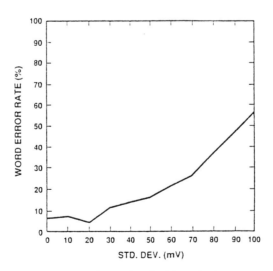

Figure 4: The effects of transistor threshold variation on recognition performance. (8 bit weight; Gaussian distributed, mean(Vth) = 0.75 volts).

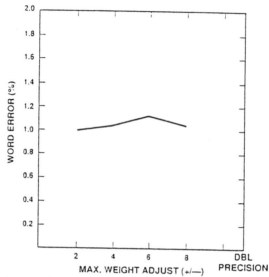

Figure 5: Word recognition error rate as a function of learning rate gain quantization.

simplest case, a fixed increment or decrement operation is performed based only upon the sign of the difference between the two terms. Even in this simplest case no degradation in performance was noted while using an 8 bit weight representation as demonstrated in the graph shown in Figure 5. In fact, performance was often improved over the original learning rule. The error rates using an increment/decrement learning rule with 8 weight bits was 0.97% and 2.0% for the mean squared error and the dot product, respectively.

An additional learning rule is being tested, targeted at a floating gate implementation which uses a "flash" EPROM memory structure at each synapse. Weight changes are restricted to positive adjustments locally while all negative adjustments are made globally to all weights. This corresponds to a forgetting term, or constant weight decay, in the learning rule. This rule was chosen to be compatible with one technique in non-volatile charge storage which allows selective write but only block erase.

3   Hardware

A prototype synaptic array and weight adaptation circuit have been designed and fabricated [Mann, 1989]. A single transistor synapse computes its contribution to the dot product activity calculation. The weight is stored dynamically as charge on the gate of the synapse transistor. The input is represented as a voltage on the drain of the transistor. The current through the transistor is proportional to the product of the gate voltage (i.e. the weight) and the drain voltage (i.e. the input strength) with the source connected to a virtual ground (see Figure 2). The sources of several of these synapse connected together form the accumulation needed to realize the dot product. Circuitry for accessing stored weight information has also been included.

The synapse array works as expected except for circuitry used to read the weight contents. This circuit requires very high on-chip voltages causing other circuits to latch-up when the clocks are turned on.

The weight adaptation circuit performs the simple increment/decrement operation based on the comparison between the input and weight magnitudes. Both quantities are first converted to a digital representation by a flash A/D converter before comparison. This circuit also performs the required refresh operation on weight contents, much like that required for dynamic RAM's but requiring analog charge storage. This insures that weight drift is constrained to lie within boundaries defined by the precision of the weight representation determined by the A/D conversion process. This circuit was functional in the refresh and increment modes, but would not decrement correctly.

Further tests are being conducted to establish the causes of the circuit problems detected thus far. Additional work is proceeding on a non-volatile charge storage version of this device. Some test structures have been fabricated and are currently being characterized for compatibility with this task.

This work was supported by the Department of the Air Force.

References

T. Kohonen. (1988) Self-Organization and Associative Memory, Berlin: Springer-Verlag.

J. Mann & S. Gilbert. (1989) An Analog Self-Organizing Neural Network Chip. In D. S. Touretzky (ed.), *Advances in Neural Information Processing Systems 1*, 739-747. San Mateo, CA: Morgan Kaufmann.

Combining Visual and Acoustic Speech Signals with a Neural Network Improves Intelligibility

T.J. Sejnowski
The Salk Institute
and
Department of Biology
The University of
California at San Diego
San Diego, CA 92037

B.P. Yuhas
M.H. Goldstein, Jr.
Department of Electrical
and Computer
Engineering
The Johns Hopkins
University
Baltimore, MD 21218

R.E. Jenkins
The Applied Physics
Laboratory
The Johns Hopkins
University
Laurel, MD 20707

ABSTRACT

Acoustic speech recognition degrades in the presence of noise. Compensatory information is available from the visual speech signals around the speaker's mouth. Previous attempts at using these visual speech signals to improve automatic speech recognition systems have combined the acoustic and visual speech information at a symbolic level using heuristic rules. In this paper, we demonstrate an alternative approach to fusing the visual and acoustic speech information by training feedforward neural networks to map the visual signal onto the corresponding short-term spectral amplitude envelope (STSAE) of the acoustic signal. This information can be directly combined with the degraded acoustic STSAE. Significant improvements are demonstrated in vowel recognition from noise-degraded acoustic signals. These results are compared to the performance of humans, as well as other pattern matching and estimation algorithms.

1   INTRODUCTION

Current automatic speech recognition systems rely almost exclusively on the acoustic speech signal, and as a consequence, these systems often perform poorly in noisy environments. To compensate for noise-degradation of the acoustic signal, one can either attempt to remove the noise from the acoustic signal or supplement the acoustic signal with other sources of speech information. One such source is the visible movements of the mouth. For humans, visual speech signals can improve speech perception when the acoustic signal is degraded by noise (Sumby and Pollack, 1954) and can serve as a source of speech information when the acoustic signal is completely absent through lipreading. How can these visual speech signals be used to improve the automatic recognition of speech?

One speech recognition system that has extensively used the visual speech signals was developed by Eric Petajan (1987). For a limited vocabulary, Petajan demonstrated that the visual speech signals can be used to significantly improve automatic speech recognition compared to the acoustic recognition alone. The system relied upon a codebook of images that were used to translate incoming images into corresponding symbols. These symbol strings were then compared to stored sequences representing different words in the vocabulary. This categorical treatment of speech signals is required because of the computational limitations of currently available digital serial hardware.

This paper proposes an alternative method for processing visual speech signals based on analog computation in a distributed network architecture. By using many interconnected processors working in parallel large amounts of data can be handled concurrently. In addition to speeding up the computation, this approach does not require segmentation in the early stages of processing; rather, analog signals from the visual and auditory pathways flow through networks in real time and can be combined directly.

Results are presented from a series of experiments that use neural networks to process the visual speech signals of two talkers. In these preliminary experiments, the results are limited to static images of vowels. We demonstrate that these networks are able to extract speech information from the visual images, and that this information can be used to improve automatic vowel recognition.

2   VISUAL AND ACOUSTIC SPEECH SIGNALS

The acoustic speech signal can be modeled as the response of the vocal tract filter to a sound source (Fant, 1960). The resonances of the vocal tract are called *formants*. They often appear as peaks in the short-term power spectrum, and are sufficient to identify the individual vowels (Peterson and Barney, 1953). The overall shape of the short-time spectra is important for general speech perception (Cole, 1980).

The configuration of the articulators define the shape of the vocal tract and the corresponding resonance characteristics of the filter. While some of the articulators are visible on the face of the speaker (e.g., the lips, teeth and sometimes the tip of the tongue), others are not. The contribution of the visible articulators to the acoustic signal results in speech sounds that are much more susceptible to acoustic noise distortion than are the contributions from the hidden articulators (Petajan, 1987), and therefore, the visual speech signal tends to complement the acoustic signal. For example, the visibly distinct speech sounds /b/ and /k/ are among the first pairs to be confused when presented acoustically in the presence of noise. Because of this complementary structure, the perception of speech in noise is greatly improved when both speech signals are present. How and at what level are these two speech signals being combined?

In previous attempts at using the visual speech signals, the information from the visual signal was incorporated into the recognition system after the signals were categorized (Petajan, 1987). In the approach taken here, visual signals will be used to resolve ambiguities in the acoustic signal before either is categorized. By combining these two sources of information at an early stage of processing, it is possible to reduce the number of erroneous decisions made and increase the amount of information passed to later stages of processing (Summerfield, 1987). The additional information provided by the visual signal can serve to constrain the possible interpretations of an ambiguous acoustic signal, or it can serve as an alternative source of speech information when the acoustical signal is heavily noise-corrupted. In either case, a massive amount of computation must be performed on the raw data. New massively-parallel architectures based on neural networks and new training procedures have made this approach feasible.

3   INTERPRETING THE VISUAL SIGNALS

In our approach, the visual signal was mapped directly into an acoustic representation closely related to the vocal tract's transfer function (Summerfield, 1987). This representation allowed the visual signal to be fused with the acoustic signal prior to any symbolic encoding.

The visual signals provide only a partial description of the vocal tract transfer function and that description is usually ambiguous. For a given visual signal there are many possible configurations of the full vocal tract, and consequently many possible corresponding acoustic signals. The goal was to define a *good* estimate of that acoustic signal from the visual signal and then use that estimate in conjunction with any residual acoustic information.

The speech signals used in these experiments were obtained from a male speaker who was video taped while seated facing the camera, under well-lit conditions. The visual and acoustic signals were then transferred and stored on laser disc (Bernstein and Eberhardt, 1986), which allowed the access of individual video frames and the corresponding sound track. The NTSC video standard is based upon 30 frames per second and words are preserved as a series of frames on the laser disc. A data set was constructed of 12 examples of 9 different vowels (Yuhas *et al.*, 1989).

A reduced area-of-interest in the image was automatically defined and centered around the mouth. The resulting sub-image was sampled to produce a topographically accurate image of 20 x 25 pixels that would serve to represent the visual speech signal. While not the most efficient encoding one could use, it is faithful to the parallel approach to computation advocated here and represents what one might observe through an array of sensors.

Along with each video frame on the laser disc there is 33 ms of acoustic speech. The representation chosen for the acoustic output structure was the short-time spectral amplitude envelope (STSAE) of the acoustic signal, because it is essential to speech recognition and also closely related to the vocal tract's transfer function. It can be calculated from the short-term power spectrum of the acoustic signal. The speech signal was sampled and cepstral analysis was used to produced a smooth envelope of the original power spectrum that could be sampled at 32 frequencies.

Figure 1: Typical lip images presented to the network.

Three-layered feedforward networks with non-linear units were used to perform the mapping. A lip image was presented across 500 input units, and an estimated STSAE was produced across 32 output units. Networks with five hidden units were found to provide the necessary bandwidth while minimizing the effects of over-learning. The standard backpropagation technique was used to compute the error gradients for training the network. However, instead of using a fixed-step steepest-descent algorithm for updating the weights, the error gradient was used in a conjugate-gradient algorithm. The weights were changed only after all of the training patterns were presented.

4 INTEGRATING THE VISUAL AND ACOUSTIC SPEECH SIGNALS

To evaluate the spectral estimates, a feedforward network was trained to recognize vowels from their STSAE's. With no noise present, the trained network could correctly categorized 100% of the 54 STSAE's in its training set: thus serving as a *perfect* recognizer for this data. The vowel recognizer was then presented with speech information through two channels, as shown in Fig. 2. The path on the bottom represents the information obtained from the acoustic signal, while the path on the top provides information obtained from the corresponding visual speech signal.

To assess the performance of the recognizer in noise, clean spectral envelopes were systematically degraded by noise and then presented to the recognizer. In this particular condition, no visual input was given to the network. The noise was introduced by adding a normalized random vector to the STSAE. Noise corrupted vectors were produced at 3 dB intervals from -12 dB to 24 dB. At each step 6 different vectors were produced, and the performance reported was the average. Fig. 3 shows the recognition rates as a function of the speech-to- noise ratio. At a speech-to-noise ratio of -12 dB, the recognizer was operating at chance or 11.1%.

Next, a network trained to estimate the spectral envelopes from images was used to provide an independent STSAE input into the recognizer (along the top of Fig. 2). This network was not trained on any of the data that was used in training the vowel recognizer. The task remained to combine these two STSAE's.

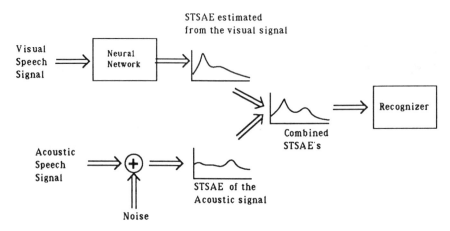

Figure 2: A vowel recognizer that integrates the acoustic and visual speech signals.

We considered three different ways of combining the estimates obtained from visual signals with the noised degraded acoustic envelopes. The first approach was to simply average the two envelopes, which proved to be less than optimal. The recognizer was able to identify 55.6% of the STSAE estimated from the visual signal, but when the visual estimate was combined with the noise degraded acoustic signal the recognizer was only capable of 35% at a S/N of -12 dB. Similarly, at very high signal-to-noise ratios, the combined input produced poorer results than the acoustic signal alone provided. To correct for this, the two inputs needed to be weighted according to the relative amount of information available from each source. A weighting factor was introduced which was a function of speech-to-noise:

$$\alpha \, S_{Visual} \; + \; (1 - \alpha) \, S_{Acoustic} \tag{1}$$

The optimal value for the parameter α was found empirically to vary linearly with the speech-to-noise ratio in dB. The value for α ranged from approximately 0.8 at S/N of -12dB to 0.0 at 24 dB. The results obtained from using the α weighted average are shown in Fig. 3.

The third method used to fuse the two STSAE's was with a second-order neural network (Rumelhart *et al.* 1986). Sigma-pi networks were trained to take in noise-degraded acoustic envelopes and estimated envelopes from the corresponding visual speech signal. The networks were able to recreate the noise-free acoustic envelope with greater accuracy than any of the other methods, as measured by mean squared error. This increased accuracy did not however translate into improved recognition rates.

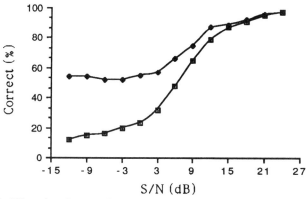

Figure 3: The visual contribution to speech recognition in noise. The lower curve shows the performance of the recognizer under varying signal-to-noise conditions using only the acoustic channel. The top curve shows the final improvement when the two channels were combined using the α weighted average.

5 COMPARING PERFORMANCE

The performance of the network was compared to more traditional signal-processing techniques.

5.1 K-NEAREST NEIGHBORS

In this first comparison, an estimate of the STSAE was obtained using a k-nearest neighbors approach. The images in the training set were stored along with their corresponding STSAE calculated from the acoustic signal. These images served as the data base of stored templates. Individual images from the test set were correlated against all of the stored images and the closest k images were selected. The acoustic STSAE corresponding to the k selected images were then averaged to produce an estimate of the STSAE corresponding to the test image. Using this procedure for various values of k, average MSE was calculated for the test set. This procedure was then repeated with the test and training set reversed.

For values of k between 2 and 6 the k-nearest neighbor estimator was able to produce STSAE estimates with approximately the same accuracy as the neural networks. Those networks evaluated after 500 training epochs produced estimates with 9% more error than the KNN approach, while those weights corresponding to the networks' *best* performance, as defined above, produced estimates with 5% less error.

5.1.1 PRINCIPAL COMPONENT ANALYSIS

A second method of comparison was to obtain an STSAE estimate using a combination of optimal linear techniques. The first step was to encode the images using a Hotelling transform, which produces an optimal encoding of an image with respect to a least-mean-squared error. The encoded image y_i was computed from the normalized image x_i using

$$y_i = A(x_i - m_x) \tag{2}$$

where m_x was the mean image. A was a transformation matrix whose rows were the five largest eigenvectors of the covariance matrix of the images. The vector y_i represents the image as do the hidden units of the neural network.

The second step was to find a mapping from the encoded image vector y_i to the corresponding short-term spectral envelope s_i using a linear least-squares fit. For the y_i's calculated above, a B was found that provided the best estimate of the desired s_i:

$$s_i = By_i \tag{3}$$

If we think of the matrix A as corresponding to the weights from the input layer to the hidden units, then B maps the hidden units to the output units.

The networks trained to produce STSAE estimates were far superior to those obtained using the coefficients of A and B. This was true not only for the training data from which A and B were calculated, but also for the test data set. When compared to networks trained for 500 epochs, the networks produced estimates of the STSAE's that were 46% better on the training set and 12% better on the test set.

6   CONCLUSION

Humans are capable of combining information received through distinct sensory channels with great speed and ease. The combined use of the visual and acoustic speech signals is just one example of integrating information across modalities. Sumby and Pollack (1954) have shown that the relative improvement provided by the visual signal varies with the signal-to-noise ratio of the acoustic signal. By combining the speech information available from the two speech signals before categorizing, we obtained performance that was comparable to that demonstrated by humans.

We have shown that visual and acoustic speech information can be effectively fused without requiring categorical preprocessing. The low-level integration of the two speech signals was particularly useful when the signal-to-noise ratio ranged from 3 dB to 15 dB, where the combined signals were recognized with a greater accuracy than either of the two component signals alone. In contrast, an independent categorical decisions on each channel would have required additional information in the form of *ad hoc* rules to produce the same level of performance.

Lip reading research has traditionally focused on the identification and evaluation of visual features (Montgomery and Jackson, 1983). Reducing the original speech signals to a finite set of predefined parameters or to discrete symbols can waste a tremendous amount of information. For an automatic recognition system this information may prove to be useful at a later stage of processing. In our approach, speech information in the visual signal is accessed without requiring discrete feature analysis or making categorical decisions.

This line of research has consequences for other problems, such as target identification based on multiple sensors. For example, the same problems arise in designing systems that combine radar and infrared data. Mapping into a common representation using neural network models could also be applied to these problem domains. The key insight is to combine this information at a stage prior to categorization. Neural network learning procedures allow systems to be constructed for performing the mappings as long as sufficient data are available to train the network.

Acknowledgements

This research was supported by grant AFOSR-86-0256 from the Air Force Office of Scientific Research and by the Applied Physics Laboratory's IRAD.

References

Bernstein, L.E. and Eberhardt, S.P. (1986). *Johns Hopkins Lipreading Corpus I-II*, Johns Hopkins University, Baltimore, MD

Cole, R.A. (1980). (Ed.) *Perception and Production of Fluent Speech*, Lawrence Erlbaum Assoc, Publishers, Hillsdale, NJ

Fant, G. (1960). *Acoustic Theory of Speech Production.* Mouton & Co., Publishers, The Hague, Netherlands

Montgomery, A. and Jackson, P.L. (1983). Physical Characteristics of the lips underlying vowel lipreading. J. Acoust. Soc. Am. *73*, 2134-2144.

Petajan, E.D. (1987). An improved Automatic Lipreading System To Enhance Speech Recognition. *Bell Laboratories Technical Report No. 11251-871012-111TM.*

Peterson, G.E. and Barney, H.L. (1952). Control Methods Used in a Study of the Vowels. J. Acoust. Soc. Am. *24*, 175-184.

Rumelhart, D.E., Hinton, G.E. and Williams, R.J. (1986). Learning internal representations by error propagation. In: D.E. Rumelhart and J.L. McClelland. (Eds.) *Parallel Distributed Processing in the Microstructure of Cognition: Vol 1. Foundations* MIT Press, Cambridge, MA

Sumby, W.H. and Pollack, I. (1954). Visual Contribution to Speech Intelligibility in Noise. J. Acoust. Soc. Am. *26*, 212-215.

Summerfield, Q.(1987). Some preliminaries to a comprehensive account of audio-visual speech perception. In: B. Dodd and R. Campbell (Eds.) *Hearing by Eye: The Pschology of Lip-Reading*, Lawrence-Erlbaum Assoc, Hillsdale, NJ.

Yuhas, B.P., Goldstein, M.H. Jr. and Sejnowski, T.J. (1989). Integration of Acoustic and Visual Speech Signals Using Neural Networks. IEEE Comm Magazine *27*, November 65-71.

Using A Translation-Invariant Neural Network To Diagnose Heart Arrhythmia

Susan Ciarrocca Lee
The Johns Hopkins University
Applied Physics Laboratory
Laurel, Maryland 20707

ABSTRACT

Distinctive electrocardiogram (ECG) patterns are created when the heart is beating normally and when a dangerous arrhythmia is present. Some devices which monitor the ECG and react to arrhythmias parameterize the ECG signal and make a diagnosis based on the parameters. The author discusses the use of a neural network to classify the ECG signals directly, without parameterization. The input to such a network must be translation-invariant, since the distinctive features of the ECG may appear anywhere in an arbritrarily-chosen ECG segment. The input must also be insensitive to the episode-to-episode and patient-to-patient variability in the rhythm pattern.

1 INTRODUCTION

Figure 1 shows internally-recorded transcardiac ECG signals for one patient. The top trace is an example of normal sinus rhythm (NSR). The others are examples of two arrhythmias: ventricular tachycardia (VT) and ventricular fibrillation (VF). Visually, the patterns are quite distinctive. Two problems make recognition of these patterns with a neural net interesting.

The first problem is illustrated in Figure 2. All traces in Figure 2 are one second samples of NSR, but the location of the QRS complex relative to the start of the sample is shifted. Ideally, one would like a neural network to recognize each of these presentations as NSR, without preprocessing the data to "center" it. The second problem can be discerned by examining the two VT traces in Figure 1. Although quite similar, the two patterns are not exactly the same. Substantial variation in signal shape and repetition rate for NSR and VT (VF is inherently random) can be expected, even among rhythms generated by a single patient. Patient-to-patient variations are even greater. The neural network must ignore variations within rhythm types, while retaining the distinctions between rhythms. This paper discusses a simple transformation of the ECG time series input which is both translation-invariant and fairly insensitive to rate and shape changes within rhythm types.

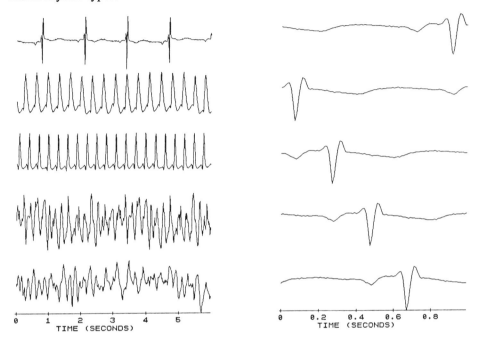

Figure 1: ECG Rhythm Examples   **Figure 2:** Five Examples of NSR

2 DISCUSSION

If test input to a first order neural network is rescaled, rotated, or translated with respect to the training data, it generally will not be recognized. A second or higher order network can be made invariant to these transformations by constraining the weights to meet certain requirements[Giles, 1988]. The input to the jth hidden unit in a second order network with N inputs is:

$$\sum_{i=1}^{N} w_{ij}x_i + \sum_{i=1}^{N-1} \sum_{k=1}^{N-i} w_{(i,i+k)j}x_i x_{i+k} \tag{1}$$

Translation invariance is introduced by constraining the weights on the first order inputs to be independent of input position, and the second order weights to depend only on the difference between indices (k), rather than on the index pairs (i,i+k)[Giles, 1988]. Rewriting equation (1) with these constraints gives:

$$w_j \sum_{i=1}^{N} x_i + \sum_{k=1}^{N-1} w_{kj} \sum_{i=1}^{N-k} x_i x_{i+k} \qquad (2)$$

This is equivalent to a first order neural network where the original inputs, x_i, have been replaced by new inputs, y_i, consisting of the following sums:

$$y_0 = \sum_{i=1}^{N} x_i \ , \qquad y_k = \sum_{i=1}^{N-k} x_i x_{i+k} \ , \quad k=1,2,...,N-1 \qquad (3)$$

While a network with inputs in the form of equation (3) is translation invariant, it is quite sensitive to shape and rate variations in the ECG input data. For ECG recognition, a better function to compute is:

$$y_0 = \sum_{i=1}^{N} ABS(x_i) \ , \quad y_k = \sum_{i=1}^{N-k} ABS(x_i - x_{i+k}) \ , \qquad k=1,2,...,N-1 \quad (4)$$

Both equations (3) and (4) produce translation-invariant outputs, as long as the input time series contains a "shape" which occupies only part of the input window, for example, the single cycle of the sine function in Figure 3a. A periodic time series, like the sine wave in Figure 3b, will not produce a truly translation-invariant output. Fortunately, the translation sensitivity introduced by applying equations (3) or (4) to periodic time series is small for small k, and only becomes important when k becomes large. One can see this by considering the extreme case, when k=N-1, and the final "sum" in equation (4) becomes the absolute value of the difference between the first and the last point in the input time series; clearly, this value will vary as the sine wave in Figure 3b is moved through the input window. If the upper limit on the sum over k gets no larger than N/2,

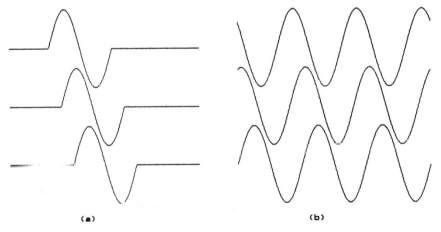

(a)   (b)

Figure 3: Examples of signals which will (a) and will not (b) have invariant transforms

equations (3) and (4) provide a neural network input which is nearly translation-invariant for realistic time series. Additionally, the output of equation (4) can be used to discriminate among NSR, VT, and VF, but is not unduly sensitive to variations within each rhythm type.

The ECG signals used in this experiment were drawn from a data set of internally recorded transcardiac ECG signals digitized at 100 Hz. The data set comprised 203 10-45 second segments obtained from 52 different patients. At least one segment of NSR and one segment of an arrhythmia was available for each patient. In addition, an "exercise" NSR at 150 BPM was artificially constructed by cutting baseline out of the natural resting NSR segment. Arrhythmia detection systems which parameterize the ECG can have difficulty distinguishing high rate NSR's from slow arrhythmias.

To obtain a training data set for the neural network, short pieces were extracted from the original rhythm segments. Since the rhythms are basically periodic, it was possible to chose the endpoints so that the short, extracted piece could be be repeated to produce a facsimile of the original signal. The upper trace in Figure 4 shows an original VT segment. The boxed area is the extracted piece. The lower trace shows the extracted piece chained end-to-end to construct a segment as long as the original. The segments

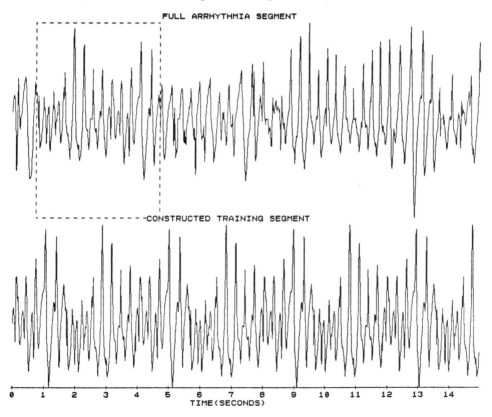

Figure 4: Original and Artificially-Constructed Training Segments

constructed from the short, extracted pieces were used as training input. Typically, the training data segment contained less than 25% of the original data.

The length of the input window was arbitrarily set at 1.35 seconds (135 points); by choosing this window, all NSR inputs were guaranteed to include at least one QRS complex. The upper limit on the sum over k in equation (4) was set to 50. The resulting 51 inputs were presented to a standard back propagation network with seven hidden units and four outputs. Although one output is sufficient to discriminate between NSR and an arrhythmia, the networks were trained to differentiate among two types of VT (generally distinguished by rate), and VF as well.

A separate training set was constructed and a separate network was trained for each patient. The weights thus derived for a given patient were then tested on that patient's original rhythm segments. To test the translation invariance of the network, every possible presentation of an input rhythm segment was tested. To do this, a sliding window of 135 points was moved through the input data stream one point (1/100th of a second) at a time. At each point, the output of equation (4) (appropriately normalized) was presented to the network, and the resulting diagnosis recorded.

3 RESULTS

A percentage of correct diagnoses was calculated for each segment of data. For a segment T seconds long, there are 100x(T-1.35) different presentations of the rhythm. Presentations which included countershock, burst pacing, gain changes on the recording equipment, post-shock rhythms, etc. were excluded, since the network had not been trained to recognize these phenomena. The percentage correct was then calculated for the remaining presentations as:

100x(Number of correct diagnoses)/(Number of presentations)

The percentage of correct diagnoses for each patient was calculated similarly, except that all segments for a particular patient were included in the count. Table 1 presents these results.

Table 1: Results

	Patients	Segments
100% Correct	29	163
99%-90% Correct	19	23
90%-80% Correct	3	6
80%-70% Correct	0	4
<70% Correct	0	1
Could Not Be Trained	1	6
Total	52	203

The network could not be trained for one patient. This patient had two arrhythmia segments, one identified as VT and the other as VF. Visually, the two traces were extremely similiar; after twenty thousand iterations, the network could not distinguish them. The network could certainly have been trained to distinguish between NSR and those two rhythms, but this was not attempted.

The number of segments for which all possible presentations of the rhythm were diagnosed correctly clearly establishes the translation invariance of the input. The network was also quite successful in distinguishing among NSR and various arrhythmias. Unfortunately, for application in inplantable defibrillators or even critical care monitoring, the network must be more nearly perfect.

The errors the network made could be separated into two broad classes. First, short segments of very erratic arrhythmias were misdiagnosed as NSR. Figure 5 illustrates this type of error. The error occurs because NSR is mainly characterized by a lack of correlation. Typically, the misdiagnosed segment is quite short, 1 second or less. This type of error might be avoided by using longer (longer than 1.35 second) input windows which could bridge the erratic segments. Also, a more responsive automatic gain control on the signal might help, since the erratic segments generally had a smaller amplitude

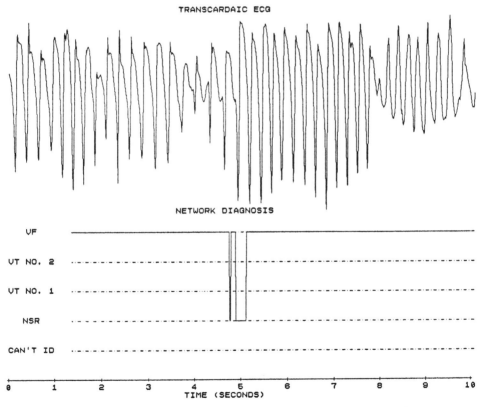

Figure 5: Ventricular Fibrillation Segment Misdiagnosed as NSR

than the surrounding segments. The network response to input windows containing large shifts in the amplitude of the input signal (for example, countershock and gain changes) was usually NSR.

The second class of errors occurred when the network misdiagnosed rhythms which were not included in the training set. For example, one patient had a few beats of a very slow VT in his NSR segment. This slow VT was not extracted for training. Only a fast (200 BPM) VT and VF were presented to this network as possible arrhythmias. Consequently, during testing, the network identified the slow VT as NSR. The network did identify some rhythms it was not trained on, but only if these rhythms did not vary too much from the training rhythms. Generally, the rate of the "unknown" rhythm had to be within 20 BPM of a training rhythm to be recognized. Morphology is also important, in that very regular rhythms, such as the top trace in Figure 6, and noisier rhythms, like the bottom trace, appear quite different to the network.

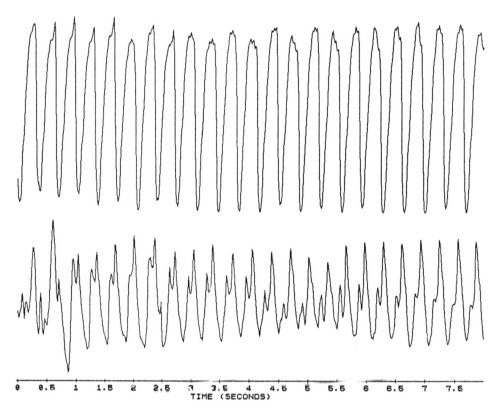

Figure 6: Ventricular Tachycardias with Significant Morphology Differences

The misdiagnosis of rhythms not included in the training set can only be corrected by enlarging the training set. In the future, an attempt will be made to create a "generic" set of typical arrhythmias drawn from the entire data set, rather than taking arrhythmia samples from each patient only. Since the networks can generalize somewhat, it is possible that a network trained on an individual patient's NSR and the "generic" arrhythmia set may be able to recognize all arrhythmias, whether they are included in the training set or not.

References

C. Giles, R. Griffin, T. Maxwell, "Encoding Geometric Invariances in Higher-Order Neural Networks", <u>Neural Information Processing Systems</u>, American Institute of Physics, New York, 1988, pp.301-309

A Neural Network for Real-Time Signal Processing

Donald B. Malkoff
General Electric / Advanced Technology Laboratories
Moorestown Corporate Center
Building 145-2, Route 38
Moorestown, NJ 08057

ABSTRACT

This paper describes a neural network algorithm that (1) performs temporal pattern matching in real-time, (2) is trained on-line, with a single pass, (3) requires only a single template for training of each representative class, (4) is continuously adaptable to changes in background noise, (5) deals with transient signals having low signal-to-noise ratios, (6) works in the presence of non-Gaussian noise, (7) makes use of context dependencies and (8) outputs Bayesian probability estimates. The algorithm has been adapted to the problem of passive sonar signal detection and classification. It runs on a Connection Machine and correctly classifies, within 500 ms of onset, signals embedded in noise and subject to considerable uncertainty.

1 INTRODUCTION

This paper describes a neural network algorithm, STOCHASM, that was developed for the purpose of real-time signal detection and classification. Of prime concern was capability for dealing with transient signals having low signal-to-noise ratios (SNR).

The algorithm was first developed in 1986 for real-time fault detection and diagnosis of malfunctions in ship gas turbine propulsion systems (Malkoff, 1987). It subsequently was adapted for passive sonar signal detection and classification. Recently, versions for information fusion and radar classification have been developed.

Characteristics of the algorithm that are of particular merit include the following:

- It performs well in the presence of either Gaussian or non-Gaussian noise, even where the noise characteristics are changing.

- Improved classifications result from temporal pattern matching in real-time, and by taking advantage of input data context dependencies.

- The network is trained on-line. Single exposures of target data require one pass through the network. Target templates, once formed, can be updated on-line.

- Outputs consist of numerical estimates of closeness for each of the template classes, rather than nearest-neighbor "all-or-none" conclusions.

- The algorithm is implemented in parallel code on a Connection Machine.

Simulated signals, embedded in noise and subject to considerable uncertainty, are classified within 500 ms of onset.

2 GENERAL OVERVIEW OF THE NETWORK

2.1 REPRESENTATION OF THE INPUTS

Sonar signals used for training and testing the neural network consist of pairs of simulated chirp signals that are superimposed and bounded by a Gaussian envelope. The signals are subject to random fluctuations and embedded in white noise. There is considerable overlapping (similarity) of the signal templates. Real data has recently become available for the radar domain.

Once generated, the time series of the sonar signal is subject to special transformations. The outputs of these transformations are the values which are input to the neural network. In addition, several higher-level signal features, for example, zero crossing data, may be simultaneously input to the same network, for purposes of information fusion. The transformations differ from those used in traditional signal processing. They contribute to the real-time performance and temporal pattern matching capabilities of the algorithm by possessing all the following characteristics:

- **Time-Origin Independence:** The sonar input signal is transformed so the resulting time-frequency representation is independent of the starting time of the transient with respect to its position within the observation window (Figure 1). "Observation window" refers to the most recent segment of the sonar time series that is currently under analysis.

- **Translation Independence:** The time-frequency representation obtained by transforming the sonar input transient does not shift from one network input node to another as the transient signal moves across most of the observation window (Figure 1). In other words, not only does the representation remain the same while the transient moves, but its position relative to specific network nodes also does not change. Each given node continues to receive its usual kind of information about the sonar transient, despite the relative position of the transient in the window. For example, where the transform is an FFT, a specific input layer node will always receive the output of one specific frequency bin, and none other.

Where the SNR is high, translation independence could be accomplished by a simple time-transformation of the representation before sending it to the neural network. This is not possible in conditions where the SNR is sufficiently low that segmentation of the transient becomes impossible using traditional methods such as auto-regressive analysis; it cannot be determined at what time the transient signal originated and where it is in the observation window.

- The representation gains time-origin and translation independence without sacrificing knowledge about the signal's temporal characteristics or its complex infrastructure. This is accomplished by using (1) the absolute value of the Fourier transform (with respect to time) of the spectrogram of the sonar input, or (2) the radar Woodward Ambiguity Function. The derivation and characterization of these methods for representing data is discussed in a separate paper (Malkoff, 1990).

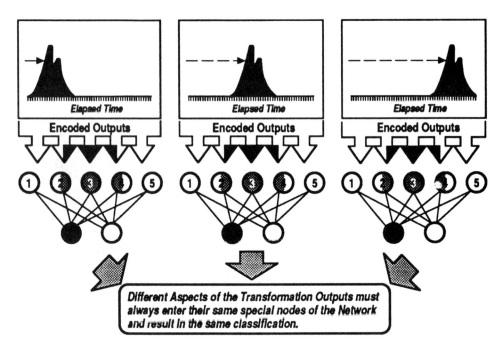

Figure 1: Despite passage of the transient, encoded data enters the same network input nodes (translation independence) and has the same form and output classification (time-origin independence).

2.2   THE NETWORK ARCHITECTURE

Sonar data, suitably transformed, enters the network input layer. The input layer serves as a noise filter, or discriminator. The network has two additional layers, the hidden and output layers (Figure 2). Learning of target templates, as well as classification of unknown targets, takes place in a single "feed-forward" pass through these layers. Additional exposures to the same target lead to further enhancement of the template, if training, or refinement of the classification probabilities, if testing.

The hidden layer deals only with data that passes through the input filter. This data predominantly represents a target. Some degree of context dependency evaluation of the data is achieved. Hidden layer data and its permutations are distributed and maintained intact, separate, and transparent. Because of this, credit (error) assignment is easily performed.

In the output layer, evidence is accumulated, heuristically evaluated, and transformed into figures of merit for each possible template class.

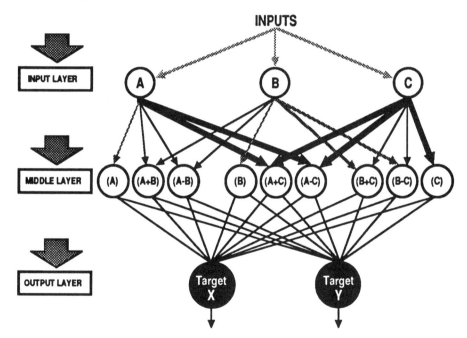

Figure 2: STOCHASM network architecture.

2.2.1   The Input Layer

Each input layer node receives a succession of samples of a unique part of the sonar representation. This series of samples is stored in a first-in, first-out queue.

With the arrival of each new input sample, the mean and standard deviation of the values in the queue are recomputed at every node. These statistical parameters are used to detect and extract a signal from the background noise by computing a threshold for each node. Arriving input values that exceed the threshold are passed to the hidden layer and not entered into the queues. Passed values are expressed in terms of z-values (the number of standard deviations that the input value differs from the mean of the queued values). Hidden layer nodes receive only data exceeding thresholds; they are otherwise inactive.

2.2.2   The Hidden Layer

There are three basic types of hidden layer nodes:

- The first type receive values from only a single input layer node; they reflect absolute changes in an input layer parameter.

- The second type receive values from a pair of inputs where each of those values simultaneously deviates from normal in the same direction.

- The third type receive values from a pair of inputs where each of those values simultaneously deviates from normal in opposite directions.

For N data inputs, there are a total of N^2 hidden layer nodes.

Values are passed to the hidden layer only when they exceed the threshold levels determined by the input node queue. The hidden layer values are stored in first-in, first-out queues, like those of the input layer. If the network is in the testing mode, these values represent signals awaiting classification. The mean and standard deviation are computed for each of these queues, and used for subsequent pattern matching. If, instead, the network is in the training mode, the passed values and their statistical descriptors are stored as templates at their corresponding nodes.

2.2.3   Pattern Matching Output Layer

Pattern matching consists of computing Bayesian likelihoods for the undiagnosed input relative to each template class. The computation assumes a normal distribution of the values contained within the queue of each hidden layer node. The statistical parameters of the queue representing undiagnosed inputs are matched with those of each of the templates. For example, the number of standard deviations distance between the means of the "undiagnosed" queue and a template queue may be used to demarcate an area under a normal probability distribution. This area is then used as a weight, or measure, for their closeness of match. Note that this computation has a non-linear, sigmoid-shaped output.

The weights for each template are summed across all nodes. Likelihood values are computed for each template. *A priori* data is used where available, and the results normalized for final outputs. The number of computations is minimal and done in parallel; they scale linearly with the number of templates per node. If more computer processing hardware were available, separate processors could be assigned for each template of every node, and computational time would be of constant complexity.

3 PERFORMANCE

The sonar version was tested against three sets of totally overlapping double chirp signals, the worst possible case for this algorithm. Where training and testing SNR's differed by a factor of anywhere from 1 to 8, 46 of 48 targets were correctly recognized.

In extensive simulated testing against radar and jet engine modulation data, classifications were better than 95% correct down to -25 dB using the unmodified sonar algorithm.

4 DISCUSSION

Distinguishing features of this algorithm include the following capabilities:

- Information fusion.

- Improved classifications.

- Real-time performance.

- Explanation of outputs.

4.1 INFORMATION FUSION

In STOCHASM, normalization of the input data facilitates the comparison of separate data items that are diverse in type. This is followed by the fusion, or combination, of all possible pairs of the set of inputs. The resulting combinations are transferred to the hidden layer where they are evaluated and matched with templates. This allows the combining of different features derived either from the same sensor suite or from several different sensor suites. The latter is often one of the most challenging tasks in situation assessment.

4.2 IMPROVED CLASSIFICATIONS

4.2.1 Multiple Output Weights per Node

In STOCHASM, each hidden layer node receives a single piece of data representing some key feature extracted from the undiagnosed target signal. In contrast, the node has many separate output weights; one for every target template. Each of those output weights represents an actual correlation between the undiagnosed feature data and one of the individual target templates. STOCHASM optimizes the correlations of an unknown input with each possible class. In so doing, it also generates figures of merit (numerical estimates of closeness of match) for ALL the possible target classes, instead of a single "all-or-none" classification.

In more popularized networks, there is only one output weight for each node. Its effectiveness is diluted by having to contribute to the correlation between one undiagnosed feature data and MANY different templates. In order to achieve reasonable classifications, an extra set of input connection weights is employed. The connection weights provide a somewhat watered-down numerical estimate of the contribution of their particular input data feature to the correct classification, ON THE AVERAGE, of targets representing all possible classes. They employ iterative procedures to compute values for those weights, which prevents real-time training and generates sub-optimal correlations. Moreover, because all of this results in only a single output for each hidden layer node, another set of connection weights between the hidden layer node and each node of the output layer is required to complete the classification process. Since these tend to be fully connected layers, the number of weights and computations is prohibitively large.

4.2.2   Avoidance of Nearest-Neighbor Techniques

Some popular networks are sensitive to initial conditions. The determination of the final values of their weights is influenced by the initial values assigned to them. These networks require that, before the onset of training, the values of weights be randomly assigned. Moreover, the classification outcomes of these networks is often altered by changing the order in which training samples are submitted to the network. Networks of this type may be unable to express their conclusions in figures of merit for all possible classes. When inputs to the network share characteristics of more than one target class, these networks tend to gravitate to the classification that initially most closely resembles the input, for an "all-or-none" classification. STOCHASM has none of these drawbacks

4.2.3   Noisy Data

The algorithm handles SNR's of lower-than-one and situations where training and testing SNR's differ. Segmentation of one dimensional patterns buried in noise is done automatically. Even the noise itself can be classified. The algorithm can adapt on-line to changing background noise patterns.

4.3   REAL-TIME PERFORMANCE

There is no need for back-propagation/gradient-descent methods to set the weights during training. Therefore, no iterations or recursions are required. Only a single feed-forward pass of data through the network is needed for either training or classification. Since the number of nodes, connections, layers, and weights is relatively small, and the algorithm is implemented in parallel, the compute time is fast enough to keep up with real-time in most application domains.

4.4   EXPLANATION OF OUTPUTS

There is strict separation of target classification evidence in the nodes of this network. In addition, the evidence is maintained so that positive and negative correlation data is separate and easily accessible. This enables improved credit (error) assignment that leads to more effective classifications and the potential for making available to the operator real-time explanations of program behavior.

4.5   FUTURE DIRECTIONS

Previous versions of the algorithm dynamically created, destroyed, or re-arranged nodes and their linkages to optimize the network, minimize computations, and eliminate unnecessary inputs. This algorithm also employed a multi-level hierarchical control system. The control system, on-line and in real-time, adjusted sampling rates and queue lengths, governing when the background noise template is permitted to adapt to current noise inputs, and the rate at which it does so. Future versions of the Connection Machine version will be able to effect the same procedures.

Efforts are now underway to:

1. Improve the temporal pattern matching capabilities.

2. Provide better heuristics for the computation of final figures of merit from the massive amount of positive and negative correlation data resident within the hidden layer nodes.

3. Adapt the algorithm to radar domains where time and spatial warping problems are prominent.

4. Simulate more realistic and complex sonar transients, with the expectation the algorithm will perform better on those targets.

5. Apply the algorithm to information fusion tasks.

References

Malkoff, D.B., "The Application of Artificial Intelligence to the Handling of Real-Time Sensor Based Fault Detection and Diagnosis," *Proceedings of the Eighth Ship Control Systems Symposium,* Volume 3, Ministry of Defence, The Hague, pp 264-276. Also presented at the Hague, Netherlands, October 8, 1987.

Malkoff, D.B., "A Framework for Real-Time Fault Detection and Diagnosis Using Temporal Data," *The International Journal for Artificial Intelligence in Engineering,* Volume 2, No. 2, pp 97-111, April 1987.

Malkoff, D.B. and L. Cohen, "A Neural Network Approach to the Detection Problem Using Joint Time-Frequency Distributions," *Proceedings of the IEEE 1990 International Conference on Acoustics, Speech, and Signal Processing,* Albuquerque, New Mexico, April 1990 (to appear).

PART III:
VISION

Learning Aspect Graph Representations from View Sequences

Michael Seibert and Allen M. Waxman
Lincoln Laboratory, Massachusetts Institute of Technology
Lexington, MA 02173-9108

ABSTRACT

In our effort to develop a modular neural system for invariant learning and recognition of 3D objects, we introduce here a new module
architecture called an *aspect network* constructed around adaptive
axo-axo-dendritic synapses. This builds upon our existing system
(Seibert & Waxman, 1989) which processes 2D shapes and classifies
them into view categories (i.e., *aspects*) invariant to illumination,
position, orientation, scale, and projective deformations. From a
sequence of views, the aspect network learns the transitions between these aspects, crystallizing a graph-like structure from an
initially amorphous network. Object recognition emerges by accumulating evidence over multiple views which activate competing
object hypotheses.

1   INTRODUCTION

One can "learn" a three-dimensional object by exploring it and noticing how its
appearance changes. When moving from one view to another, intermediate views
are presented. The imagery is continuous, unless some feature of the object appears
or disappears at the object's "horizon" (called the occluding contour). Such *visual
events* can be used to partition continuously varying input imagery into a discrete
sequence of aspects. The sequence of aspects (and the transitions between them) can
be coded and organized into a representation of the 3D object under consideration.
This is the form of 3D object representation that is learned by our *aspect network*.
We call it an *aspect network* because it was inspired by the aspect graph concept
of Koenderink and van Doorn (1979). This paper introduces this new network

which learns and recognizes sequences of aspects, and leaves most of the discussion of the visual preprocessing to earlier papers (Seibert & Waxman, 1989; Waxman, Seibert, Cunningham, & Wu, 1989). Presented in this way, we hope that our ideas of sequence learning, representation, and recognition are also useful to investigators concerned with speech, finite-state machines, planning, and control.

1.1 2D VISION BEFORE 3D VISION

The aspect network is one module of a more complete vision system (Figure 1) introduced by us (Seibert & Waxman, 1989). The early stages of the complete system learn and recognize 2D views of objects, invariant to the scene illumina-

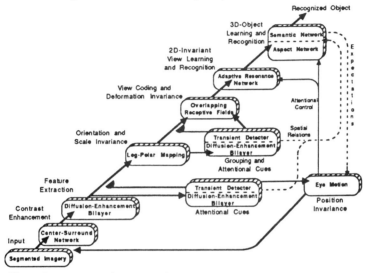

Figure 1: *Neural system architecture for 3D object learning and recognition.* The aspect network is part of the upper-right module.

tion and an object's orientation, size, and position in the visual field. Additionally, projective deformations such as foreshortening and perspective effects are removed from the learned 2D representations. These processing steps make use of Diffusion-Enhancement Bilayers (DEBs)[1] to generate attentional cues and featural groupings. The point of our neural preprocessing is to generate a sequence of views (i.e., aspects) which depends on the object's orientation in 3-space, but which does not depend on how the 2D images happen to fall on the retina. If no preprocessing were done, then the 3D representation would have to account for every possible 2D appearance in addition to the 3D information which relates the views to each other. Compressing the views into aspects avoids such combinatorial problems, but may result in an ambiguous representation, in that some aspects may be common to a number of objects. Such ambiguity is overcome by learning and recognizing a

---

[1]This architecture was previously called the NADEL (Neural Analog Diffusion-Enhancement Layer), but has been renamed to avoid causing any problems or confusion, since there is an active researcher in the field with this name.

sequence of aspects (i.e., a *trajectory* through the aspect graph). The partitioning and sequence recognition is analogous to building a symbol alphabet and learning syntactic structures within the alphabet. Each symbol represents an aspect and is encoded in our system as a separate category by an Adaptive Resonance Network architecture (Carpenter & Grossberg, 1987). This unsupervised learning is competitive and may proceed on-line with recognition; no separate training is required.

1.2 ASPECT GRAPHS AND OBJECT REPRESENTATIONS

Figure 2 shows a simplified aspect graph for a prismatic object.[2] Each node of

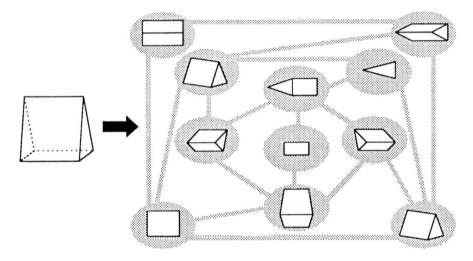

Figure 2: *Aspect Graph.* A 3D object can be represented as a graph of the characteristic view-nodes with adjacent views encoded by arcs between the nodes.

the graph represents a characteristic view, while the allowable transitions among views are represented by the arcs between the nodes. In this depiction, symmetries have been considered to simplify the graph. Although Koenderink and van Doorn suggested assigning aspects based on topological equivalences, we instead allow the ART 2 portion of our 2D system to decide when an invariant 2D view is sufficiently different from previously experienced views to allocate a new view category (aspect).

Transitions between adjacent aspects provide the key to the aspect network representation and recognition processes Storing the transitions in a self-organizing synaptic weight array becomes the learned view-based representation of a 3D object. Transitions are exploited again during recognition to distinguish among objects with similar views. Whereas most investigators are interested in the computational complexity of generating aspect graphs from CAD libraries (Bowyer, Eggert, Stewman,

---

[2] Neither the aspect graph concept nor our aspect network implementation is limited to simple polyhedral objects, nor must the objects even be convex, i.e., they may be self-occluding.

& Stark, 1989), we are interested in designing it as a self-organizing representation, learned from visual experience and useful for object recognition.

2 ASPECT-NETWORK LEARNING

The view-category nodes of ART 2 excite the aspect nodes (which we also call the x-nodes) of the aspect network (Figure 3). The aspect nodes fan-out to the dendritic

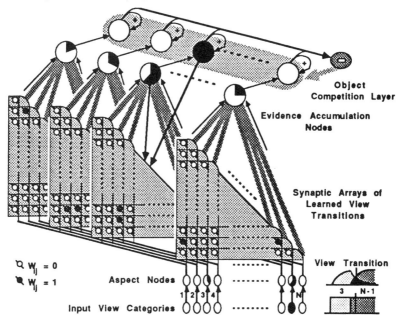

Figure 3: *Aspect Network*. The learned graph representations of 3D objects are realized as weights in the synaptic arrays. Evidence for experienced view-trajectories is simultaneously accumulated for all competing objects.

trees of *object neurons*. An object neuron consists of an adaptive synaptic array and an evidence accumulating y-node. Each object is learned by a single object neuron. A view sequence leads to accumulating activity in the y-nodes, which compete to determine the "recognized object" (i.e., maximally active z-node) in the "object competition layer". Gating signals from these nodes then modulate learning in the corresponding synaptic array, as in competitive learning paradigms. The system is designed so that the learning phase is integral with recognition. Learning (and forgetting) is always possible so that existing representations can always be elaborated with new information as it becomes available.

Differential equations govern the dynamics and architecture of the aspect network. These shunting equations model cell membrane and synapse dynamics as pioneered by Grossberg (1973, 1989). Input activities to the network are given by equation (1), the learned aspect transitions by equation (2), and the objects recognized from the experienced view sequences by equation (3).

2.1   ASPECT NODE DYNAMICS

The aspect node activities are governed by equation (1):

$$\frac{dx_i}{dt} \equiv \dot{x}_i = I_i - \lambda_x x_i, \tag{1}$$

where λ_x is a passive decay rate, and $I_i = 1$ during the presentation of aspect i and zero otherwise as determined by the output of the ART 2 module in the complete system (Figure 1). This equation assures that the activities of the aspect nodes build and decay in nonzero time (see the timetraces for the input I-nodes and aspect x-nodes in Figure 3). Whenever an aspect transition occurs, the activity of the previous aspect decays (with rate λ_x) and the activity of the new aspect builds (again with rate λ_x in this case, which is convenient but not necessary). During the transient time when both activities are nonzero, only the synapses between these nodes have both pre- and post-synaptic activities which are significant (i.e., above the threshold) and Hebbian learning can be supported. The overlap of the pre- and post-synaptic activities is transient, and the extent of the transient is controlled by the selection of λ_x. This is the fundamental parameter for the dynamical behavior of the entire network, since it defines the response time of the aspect nodes to their inputs. As such, nearly every other parameter of the network depends on it.

2.2   VIEW TRANSITION ENCODING BY ADAPTIVE SYNAPSES

The aspect transitions that represent objects are realized by synaptic weights on the dendritc trees of object neurons. Equation (2) defines how the (initially small and random) weight relating aspect i, aspect j, and object k changes:

$$\frac{dw_{ij}^k}{dt} \equiv \dot{w}_{ij}^k = \kappa_w w_{ij}^k \left(1 - w_{ij}^k\right) \left\{\Phi_w \left[(x_i + \epsilon)(x_j + \epsilon)\right] - \lambda_w\right\} \Theta_y(\dot{y}_k)\Theta_z(z_k). \tag{2}$$

Here, κ_w governs the rate of evolution of the weights relative to the x-node dynamics, and λ_w is the decay rate of the weights. Note that a small "background level" of activity ϵ is added to each x-node activity. This will be discussed in connection with (3) below. $\Phi_\phi(\gamma)$ is a threshold-linear function; that is: $\Phi_\phi(\gamma) = \gamma$ if $\gamma > \phi_{th}$ and zero otherwise. $\Theta_\theta(\gamma)$ is a binary-threshold function of the absolute-value of γ, that is: $\Theta_\theta(\gamma) = 1.0$ if $\mid \gamma \mid > \theta_{th}$ and zero otherwise.

Although this equation appears formidable, it can be understood as follows. Whenever simultaneous above-threshold activities arise presynaptically at node x_i and postsynaptically at node x_j, the Hebbian product $(x_i + \epsilon)(x_j + \epsilon)$ causes $\dot{w}_{ij}^k$ to be positive (since above threshold, $(x_i + \epsilon)(x_j + \epsilon) > \lambda_w$) and the weight w_{ij}^k learns the transition between the aspects x_i and x_j. By symmetry, w_{ji}^k would also learn, but all other weights decay ($\dot{w} \propto -\lambda_w$). The product of the shunting terms $w_{ij}^k(1 - w_{ij}^k)$ goes to zero (and thus inhibits further weight changes) only when w_{ij}^k approaches either zero or unity. This shunting mechanism limits the range of weights, but also assures that these fixed points are invariant to input-activity magnitudes, decay-rates, or the initial and final network sizes.

The gating terms $\Theta_y(\dot{y}_k)$ and $\Theta_z(z_k)$ modulate the learning of the synaptic arrays w_{ij}^k. As a result of competition between multiple object hypotheses (see equation (4) below), only one z_k-node is active at a time. This implies recognition (or initial object neuron assignment) of "Object-k," and so only the synaptic array of Object-k adapts. All other synaptic arrays w_{ij}^l ($l \neq k$) remain unchanged. Moreover, learning occurs only during aspect transitions. While $\dot{y}_k \neq 0$ both learning and forgetting proceed; but while $\dot{y}_k \approx 0$ adaptation ceases though recognition continues (e.g. during a long sustained view).

2.3   OBJECT RECOGNITION DYNAMICS

Object nodes y_k accumulate evidence over time. Their dynamics are governed by:

$$\frac{dy_k}{dt} \equiv \dot{y}_k = \kappa_y \left\{ \left[\sum_i \sum_{j>i} \Phi_y \left[(x_i + \epsilon)\, w_{ij}^k\, (x_j + \epsilon) \right] \right] - \lambda_y y_k \right\}. \tag{3}$$

Here, κ_y governs the rate of evolution of the object nodes relative to the x-node dynamics, λ_y is the passive decay rate of the object nodes, $\Phi_y(\cdot)$ is a threshold-linear function, and ϵ is the same small positive constant as in (2). The same Hebbian-like product (i.e., $(x_i + \epsilon)(x_j + \epsilon)$) used to learn transitions in (2) is used to detect aspect transitions during recognition in (3) with the addition of the synaptic term w_{ij}^k, which produces an axo-axo-dendritic synapse (see Section 3). Using this synapse, an aspect transition must not only be detected, but it must also be a permitted one for Object-k (i.e., $w_{ij}^k > 0$) if it is to contribute activity to the y_k-node.

2.4   SELECTING THE MAXIMALLY ACTIVATED OBJECT

A "winner-take-all" competition is used to select the maximally active object node. The activity of each evidence accumulation y-node is periodically sampled by a corresponding object competition z-node (see Figure 3). The sampled activities then compete according to Grossberg's shunted short-term memory model (Grossberg, 1973), leaving only one z-node active at the expense of the activities of the other z-nodes. In addition to signifying the 'recognized' object, outputs of the z-nodes are used to inhibit weight adaptation of those weights which are not associated with the winning object via the $\Theta_z(z_k)$ term in equation (2). The competition is given by a first-order differential equation taken from (Grossberg, 1973):

$$\frac{dz_k}{dt} \equiv \dot{z}_k = \kappa_z \left[f(z_k) - z_k \{ \lambda_z + \sum_l f(z_l) \} \right]. \tag{4}$$

The function $f(z)$ is chosen to be faster-than-linear (e.g. quadratic). The initial conditions are reset periodically to $z_k(0) = y_k(t)$.

3   THE AXO-AXO-DENDRITIC SYNAPSE

Although the learning is very closely Hebbian, the network requires a synapse that is more complex than that typically analyzed in the current modeling literature.

Instead of an axo-dendritic synapse, we utilize an *axo-axo-dendritic* synapse (Shepard, 1979). Figure 4 illustrates the synaptic anatomy and our functional model. We interpret the structure by assuming that it is the conjunction of activities in

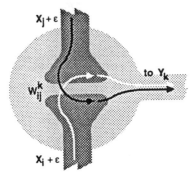

Figure 4: *Axo-axo-dendritic Synapse Model.* The Hebbian-like w_{ij}^k-weight adapts when simultaneous axonal activities x_i and x_j arise. Similarly, a conjunction of both activities is necessary to significantly stimulate the dendrite to node y_k.

both axons (as during an aspect transition) that best stimulates the dendrite. If, however, significant activity is present on only one axon (a sustained static view), it can stimulate the dendrite to a small extent in conjunction with the small base-level activity ϵ present on all axons. This property supports object recognition in static scenes, though object learning requires dynamic scenes.

4   SAMPLE RESULTS

Consider two objects composed of three aspects each with one aspect in common: the first has aspects 0, 2, and 4, while the second has aspects 0, 1, and 3. Figure 5 shows the evolution of the node activities and some of the weights during two aspect sequences. With an initial distribution of small, random weights, we present the repetitive aspect sequence $4 \rightarrow 2 \rightarrow 0 \rightarrow \cdots$, and learning is engaged by Object-1. The attention of the system is then redirected with a saccadic eye motion (the short-term memory node activities are reset to zero) and a new repetitive aspect sequence is presented: $3 \rightarrow 1 \rightarrow 0 \rightarrow \cdots$. Since the weights for these aspect transitions in the Object-1 synaptic array decayed as it learned its sequence, it does not respond strongly to this new sequence and Object-2 wins the competition. Thus, the second sequence is learned (and recognized!) by Object-2's synaptic weight array. In these simulations (1) - (4) were implemented by a Runge-Kutta coupled differential equation integrator. Each aspect was presented for $T = 4$ time-units. The equation parameters were set as follows: $I = 1$, $\lambda_x \approx \ln(0.1)/T$, $\lambda_y \approx 0.3$, $\lambda_w \approx 0.02$, $\kappa_y \approx 0.3$, $\kappa_w \approx 0.6$, $\epsilon \approx 0.03$, and thresholds of $\theta_y \approx 10^{-5}$ for $\Theta_y(\dot{y}_k)$ in equation (2), $\theta_z \approx 10^{-5}$ for $\Theta_z(z_k)$ in equation (2), $\phi_y > \epsilon^2$ for Φ_y in equation (3), $\phi_w > \max[\epsilon I/\lambda_x + \epsilon^2, (I/\lambda_x)^2 \exp(-\lambda_x T)]$ for Φ_w in equation (2). The ϕ_w constraint insures that only transitions are learned, and they are learned only when $t < T$.

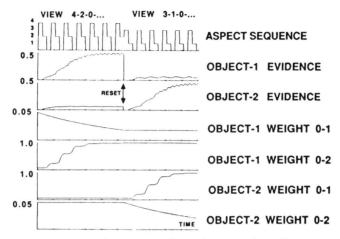

Figure 5: *Node activity and synapse adaptation vs. time.* Two separate representations are learned automatically as aspect sequences of the objects are experienced.

Acknowledgments

This report is based on studies performed at Lincoln Laboratory, a center for research operated by the Massachusetts Institute of Technology. The work was sponsored by the Department of the Air Force under Contract F19628-85-C-0002.

References

Bowyer, K., Eggert, D., Stewman, J., & Stark, L. (1989). Developing the aspect graph representation for use in image understanding. *Proceedings of the 1989 Image Understanding Workshop.* Wash. DC: DARPA. 831-849.

Carpenter, G. A., & Grossberg, S. (1987). ART 2: Self-organization of stable category recognition codes for analog input patterns. *Applied Optics*, **26**(23), 4919-4930.

Grossberg, S. (1973). Contour enhancement, short term memory, and constancies in reverberating neural networks. *Studies in Applied Mathematics*, **52**(3), 217-257.

Koenderink, J. J., & van Doorn, A. J. (1979). The internal representation of solid shape with respect to vision. *Biological Cybernetics*, **32**, 211-216.

Seibert, M., Waxman, A. M. (1989). Spreading Activation Layers, Visual Saccades, and Invariant Representations for Neural Pattern Recognition Systems. *Neural Networks.* 2(1). 9-27.

Shepard, G. M. (1979). **The synaptic organization of the brain.** New York: Oxford University Press.

Waxman, A. M., Seibert, M., Cunningham, R., & Wu, J. (1989). Neural analog diffusion-enhancement layer and spatio-temporal grouping in early vision. In: **Advances in neural information processing systems**, D. S. Touretzky (ed.), San Mateo, CA: Morgan Kaufman. 289-296.

TRAFFIC: Recognizing Objects Using Hierarchical Reference Frame Transformations

Richard S. Zemel
Computer Science Dept.
University of Toronto
Toronto, ONT M5S 1A4

Michael C. Mozer
Computer Science Dept.
University of Colorado
Boulder, CO 80309-0430

Geoffrey E. Hinton
Computer Science Dept.
University of Toronto
Toronto, ONT M5S 1A4

ABSTRACT

We describe a model that can recognize two-dimensional shapes in an unsegmented image, independent of their orientation, position, and scale. The model, called TRAFFIC, efficiently represents the structural relation between an object and each of its component features by encoding the fixed viewpoint invariant transformation from the feature's reference frame to the object's in the weights of a connectionist network. Using a hierarchy of such transformations, with increasing complexity of features at each successive layer, the network can recognize multiple objects in parallel. An implementation of TRAFFIC is described, along with experimental results demonstrating the network's ability to recognize constellations of stars in a viewpoint-invariant manner.

1 INTRODUCTION

A key goal of machine vision is to recognize familiar objects in an unsegmented image, independent of their orientation, position, and scale. Massively parallel models have long been used for lower-level vision tasks, such as primitive feature extraction and stereo depth. Models addressing "higher-level" vision have generally been restricted to pattern matching types of problems, in which much of the inherent complexity of the domain has been eliminated or ignored.

The complexity of object recognition stems primarily from the difficult search required to find the correspondence between features of candidate objects and image features. Images contain spurious features, which do not correspond to any object features; objects in an image may have missing or occluded features; and noisy measurements make it impossible to align object features to image features exactly. These problems are compounded in realistic domains, where images are not segmented and normalized and the number of candidate objects is large.

In this paper, we present a structured, general model of object recognition – called *TRAFFIC* (a loose acronym for "transforming feature instances") – that addresses these difficult problems through a combination of strategies. First, we directly build constraints on the spatial relationships between features of an object directly into the architecture of a connectionist network. We thereby limit the space of possible matches by constructing only plausible assignments of image features to objects. Second, we embed this construction into a hierarchical architecture, which allows the network to handle unsegmented, non-normalized images, and also allows for a wide range of candidate objects. Third, we allow TRAFFIC to discover the critical spatial relationships among features through training on examples of the target objects in various poses.

2   MODEL HIGHLIGHTS

The following sections outline the three fundamental aspects of TRAFFIC. For a more complete discussion of the details of TRAFFIC, see (Zemel, 1989).

2.1   ENCODING STRUCTURAL RELATIONS

The first key aspect of TRAFFIC concerns its encoding and use of the fixed spatial relations between a rigid object and each of its component features. If we assume that each feature has an intrinsic reference frame, then for a rigid object and a particular feature of that object, there is a *fixed* viewpoint-independent transformation from the feature's reference frame to the object's. This transformation can be used to predict the object's reference frame from the feature's. To recognize objects, TRAFFIC takes advantage of the fact that all features of the same object will predict the identical reference frame for that object (the "viewpoint consistency constraint" (Lowe, 1987)).

Each reference frame transformation can be expressed as a matrix multiplication that is efficiently implemented in a connectionist network. Consider a two-layer network, with one layer containing units representing particular features, the other containing units representing objects. For two-dimensional shapes, each feature is described by a set of four *instantiation units*. These real-valued units represent the parameter values associated with the feature: (x,y)-position, orientation, and scale. The objects have a set of instantiation units as well. The units representing particular features are connected to the units representing each object containing that feature, thereby assigning each feature-object pair its own set of weighted connections. The fixed matrix that describes the transformation from the feature's intrinsic reference frame to the object's can be directly implemented in the set of weights connecting the instantiation units of the feature and the object.

We can describe any instantiation, or any transformation between instantiations, as a vector of four parameters. Let $P_{if} = (x_{if}, y_{if}, c_{if}, s_{if})$ specify the reference frame of the feature with respect to the image, where x_{if} and y_{if} represent the coordinates of the feature origin relative to the image frame, c_{if} and s_{if} represent the scale and angle of the feature frame w.r.t. the image frame. Rather than encoding these values directly, c_{if} represents the product of the scale and the cosine of the angle, while s_{if} represesents the product of the scale and the sine of the angle.[1] Let $P_{io} = (x_{io}, y_{io}, c_{io}, s_{io})$, specify the reference frame of the object with respect to the image. Finally, let $P_{fo} = (x_{fo}, y_{fo}, c_{fo}, s_{fo})$ specify the transformation from the reference frame of the object to that of the feature.

Each of these sets of parameters can be placed into a transformation matrix which converts points in one reference frame to points in another. We can express P_{if} as the matrix T_{if}, a transformation from the feature frame to the image frame:

$$T_{if} = \begin{bmatrix} c_{if} & s_{if} & x_{if} \\ -s_{if} & c_{if} & y_{if} \\ 0 & 0 & 1 \end{bmatrix}$$

Likewise, we can express P_{fo} as the matrix T_{fo}, a transformation from the object to feature frame, and P_{io} as T_{io}, a transformation from the object to image frame. Because T_{fo} is fixed for a given feature-object pair and T_{if} is derived from the image, T_{io} can easily be computed by composing these two transforms: $T_{io} = T_{if}T_{fo}$.

The four parameters underlying T_{io} can then be extracted, which results in the following four equations for P_{io}:

$$\begin{aligned} x_{io} &= c_{if}x_{fo} + s_{if}y_{fo} + x_{if} \\ y_{io} &= -s_{if}x_{fo} + c_{if}y_{fo} + y_{if} \\ c_{io} &= c_{if}c_{fo} - s_{if}s_{fo} \\ s_{io} &= c_{if}s_{fo} + s_{if}c_{fo} \end{aligned}$$

This transformation is easily implemented in a network by connecting the units representing P_{if} to the units representing P_{io} with the appropriate weights (Figure 1). In this manner, TRAFFIC directly encodes the reference frame transformation from a feature to an object in the connections from the set of units representing the feature's reference frame to units representing the object's frame. The specification of an object's reference frame can therefore be derived directly from each of its component features on the basis of the structural relationship between the feature and the object. Because each feature of an object should predict the same reference frame parameters for the object, we can determine whether the object is really present in the image by checking to see if the various features make identical

---

[1] We represent angles by their sines and cosines to avoid the discontinuities involved in representing orientation by a single number and to eliminate the non-linear step of computing $\sin \theta_{if}$ from θ_{if}. Note that we represent the four degrees of freedom in the instantiation parameters using four units; a neurally plausible extension to this scheme which does not require single units with arbitrary precision could allocate a *pool* of units to each of these parameters.

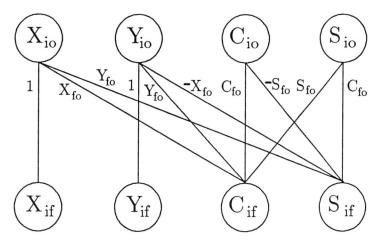

Figure 1: The matrix T_{fo} is a fixed coordinate transformation from the reference frame of feature f to the reference frame of object o. This figure shows how T_{fo} can be built into the weights connecting the object-instantiation units and the feature-instantiation units.

predictions. In Section 2.3 we discuss how the object instantiation is formed in cases where the object parameters predicted by the features do not agree perfectly.

2.2 FEATURE ABSTRACTION HIERARCHY

TRAFFIC recursively extends the notion of reference frame transformations between features and objects in a hierarchical architecture. It is impractical to hope that any network will be able to directly map low-level input features to complex objects. The input features must be simple enough to be easily extracted from images without relying on sophisticated segmentation and interpretation. If they are simple, however, they will be unable to uniquely predict the object's reference frame, since a complex object may contain many copies of a single simple feature.

To address this problem, we adopt a hierarchical approach, introducing several layers of intermediate features between the input and output layers. In each layer, several features are grouped together to form an 'object' in the layer above; this 'object' then serves as a feature for 'objects' in the next layer. The lowest layer contains simple features, such as edges and various corner types. The objects to be recognized appear at the top of the hierarchy – the output layer of the network.

This composition hierarchy builds up a description of objects by selectively grouping sets of features, forming an increasingly abstract set of features. The power of this representation comes in the sharing of a set of features in one layer by objects in the layer above.

To represent multiple features of the same type simultaneously, we carve up the image into spatially-contiguous *regions*, each allowing the representation of one instance of each feature. The network can thus represent several instances of a feature type simultaneously, provided they lie in different regions.

We tailor the regions to the abstraction hierarchy as follows. In the lowest layers, the features are simple and numerous, so we need many regions, but with only a few feature types per region. In upper layers of the hierarchy, the features become increasingly complex and span a larger area of the image; the number of feature types increases and the regions become larger, while the instantiation units retain accurate viewpoint information. In the highest layer, there is a single region, and it spans the entire original image. At this level, the network can recognize and specify parameters for a single instance of each object it has been trained on.

2.3   FORMING OBJECT HYPOTHESES

The third key aspect of TRAFFIC is its method of combining information from features to determine both an object's reference frame and an overall estimate of the likelihood that the object is actually present in the image. This likelihood, called the object's *confidence*, is represented by an additional unit associated with each object.

Each feature individually predicts the object's reference frame, and TRAFFIC forms a single vector of object instantiation-parameters by averaging the predicted instantiations, weighted by the confidence of their corresponding features.[2] Every set of units representing an object is sensitive to feature instances appearing in a fixed area of the image – the *receptive field* of the object. The confidence of the object is then a function of the confidence of the features lying in its receptive field, as well as the variance of their predictions, because low variance indicates a highly self-consistent object instantiation.

Once the network has been defined – the regions, receptive fields, and feature types specified at each level, and the reference frame transformations encoded in the weights – recognition occurs in a single bottom-up pass through the network. TRAFFIC accepts as input a set of simple features and a description of their pose in the image. At each layer in turn, the network forms many candidate object instantiations from the set of feature instantiations in the layer below, and then suppresses the object instantiations that are not consistently predicted by several of their component features. At the output level of the network, the confidence unit of each object describes the likelihood that that object is in the image, and its instantiation units specify its pose.

3   IMPLEMENTING TRAFFIC

The domain we selected for study involves the recognition of constellations of stars. This problem has several interesting properties: the image is by nature unseg-

---

[2] This averaging technique contains an implicit assumption that the maximum expected deviation of a prediction from the actual value is a function of the number of features, and that there will always be enough good values to smooth out any large deviations. We are currently exploring improved methods of forming object hypotheses.

mented; there are many false partial matches; no bottom-up cues suggest a natural frame of reference; and it requires the ability to perform 2-D transformation-invariant recognition.

Each image contains the set of visible stars in a region of the sky. The input to TRAFFIC is a set of features that represent triples of stars in particular configurations. This input is computed by first dividing the image into regions and extracting every combination of three stars within each region. The star triplets (more precisely, the inner angles of the triangles formed by the triplets) are fed into an unsupervised competitive-learning network whose task is to categorize the configuration as one of a small number of types – the primitive feature types for the input layer of TRAFFIC.

The architecture we implemented had an input layer, two intermediate layers, and an output layer.[3] Eight constellations were to be recognized, each represented by a single unit in the output layer. We used a simple unsupervised learning scheme to determine the feature types in the intermediate layers of the hierarchy, working up sequentially from the input layer. During an initial phase of training, the system samples many regions of the sky at random, creating features at one layer corresponding to the frequently occurring combinations of features in the layer below. This scheme forms flexible intermediate representations tailored to the domain, but not hand-coded for the particular object set.

This sampling method determined the connection weights through the intermediate layers of the network. Back propagation was then used to set the weights between the penultimate layer and the output layer.[4] The entire network could have been trained using back propagation, but the combined unsupervised-supervised learning method we used is much simpler and quicker, and worked well for this problem.

4 EXPERIMENTAL RESULTS

We have run several experiments to test the main properties of the network, detailed further in (Zemel, 1989). Each image used in training and testing contained one of the eight target constellations, along with other nearby stars.

The first experiment tested the basic recognition capability of the system, as well as its ability to learn useful connections between objects and features. The training set consisted of a single view of each constellation. The second experiment examined the network's ability to recognize a constellation independent of its position and orientation in the image. We expanded the set of training images to include four different views of each of the eight constellations, in various positions and orientations. The test set contained two novel views of the eight constellations. In both experiments, the network quickly (< 150 epochs) learned to identify the target object. Learning was slower in the second experiment, but the network performance

---

[3] The details of the network, such as the number of regions and feature types per layer, the number of connections, etc., are discussed in (Zemel, 1989).

[4] In this implementation, we used a less efficient method of encoding the transformations than the method discussed in Section 2.1, but both versions perform the same transformations.

was identical for the training and testing images.

The third experiment tested the network's ability not only to recognize an instance of a constellation, but to correctly specify its reference frame. In most simulations, the network produced a correct description of the target object instantiation across the training and testing images.

A final experiment confirmed that the network did *not* recognize an instance of an object when the features of the object were present in the input but were not in the correct relation to one another. The confidence level of the target object decreased proportionately as random noise was added to the instantiation parameters of input features. This shows that the upper layers of the network perform the important function of detecting the spatial relations of features from non-local areas of the image.

5   RELATED WORK

TRAFFIC resembles systems based on the Hough transform (Ballard, 1981; Hinton, 1981) in that evidence from various feature instances is combined using the viewpoint consistency constraint. However, while these Hough transform models need a unit for every possible viewpoint of an object, TRAFFIC reduces hardware requirements by using real-valued units to represent viewpoints.[5] TRAFFIC also resembles the approach of (Mjolsness, Gindi and Anandan, 1989), which relies on a large optimization search to simultaneously find the best set of object instantiations and viewpoint parameters to fit the image data. The TRAFFIC network carries out a similar type of search, but the limited connectivity and hierarchical architecture of the network constrains the search. The feature abstraction hierachy used in TRAFFIC is common to many recognition systems. The pattern recognition technique known as hierarchical synthesis (Barrow, Ambler and Burstall, 1972), employs a similar architecture, as do several connectionist models (Denker et al., 1989; Fukushima, 1980; Mozer, 1988). Each of these systems achieve position- and rotation-invariance by removing position information in the upper layers of the hierarchy. The TRAFFIC hierarchy, on the other hand, maintains and manipulates accurate viewpoint information throughout, allowing it to consider relations between features in non-local areas of the image.

6   CONCLUSIONS AND FUTURE WORK

The experiments demonstrate that TRAFFIC is capable of recognizing a limited set of two-dimensional objects in a viewpoint-independent manner based on the structural relations among components of the objects. We are currently testing the network's ability to perform multiple-object recognition and its robustness with respect to noise and occlusion. We are also currently developing a probabilistic framework for combining the various predictions to form the most likely object

---

[5] Many other recognition systems, such as Lowe's SCERPO system (1985), represent object reference frame information as sets of explicit parameters.

instantiation hypothesis. This probabilistic framework may increase the robustness of the model and allow it to handle deviations from object rigidity.

Another extension to TRAFFIC we are currently exploring concerns the creation of a pre-processing network to specify reference frame information for input features directly from a raw image. We train this network using an unsupervised learning method based on the mutual information between neighboring image patches (Becker and Hinton, 1989). Our aim is to apply this method to learn the mappings from features to objects throughout the network hierarchy.

Acknowledgements

This research was supported by grants from the Ontario Information Technology Research Center, grant 87-2-36 from the Alfred P. Sloan foundation, and a grant from the James S. McDonnell Foundation to Michael Mozer.

References

Ballard, D. H. (1981). Generalizing the Hough transform to detect arbitrary shapes. *Pattern Recognition*, 13(2):111–122.

Barrow, H. G., Ambler, A. P., and Burstall, R. M. (1972). Some techniques for recognising structures in pictures. In *Frontiers of Pattern Recognition*. Academic Press, New York, NY.

Becker, S. and Hinton, G. E. (1989). Spatial coherence as an internal teacher for a neural network. Technical Report Technical Report CRG-TR-89-7, University of Toronto.

Bolles, R. C. and Cain, R. A. (1982). Recognizing and locating partially visible objects: The local-feature-focus method. *International Journal of Robotics Research*, 1(3):57–82.

Denker, J. S., Gardner, W. L., Graf, H. P., Henderson, D., Howard, R. E., Hubbard, W., D., J. L., Baird, H. S., and Guyon, I. (1989). Neural network recognizer for hand-written zip code digits. In Touretzky, D. S., editor, *Advances in neural information processing systems I*, pages 323–331, San Mateo, CA. Morgan Kaufmann Publishers, Inc.

Fukushima, K. (1980). Neocognitron: A self-organizing neural network model for a mechanism of pattern recognition unaffected by shift in position. *Biological Cybernetics*, 36:193–202.

Hinton, G. E. (1981). A parallel computation that assigns canonical object-based frames of reference. In *Proceedings of the 7th International Joint Conference on Artificial Intelligence*, pages 683–685, Vancouver, BC, Canada.

Huttenlocher, D. P. and Ullman, S. (1987). Object recognition using alignment. In *First International Conference on Computer Vision*, pages 102–111, London, England.

Lowe, D. G. (1985). *Perceptual Organization and Visual Recognition*. Kluwer Academic Publishers, Boston.

Lowe, D. G. (1987). The viewpoint consistency constraint. *International Journal of Computer Vision*, 1:57–72.

Mjolsness, E., Gindi, G., and Anandan, P. (1989). Optimization in model matching and perceptual organization. *Neural Computation*, 1:218–299.

Mozer, M. C. (1988). The perception of multiple objects: A parallel, distributed processing approach. Technical Report 8803, University of California, San Diego, Institute for Cognitive Science.

Zemel, R. S. (1989). TRAFFIC: A connectionist model of object recognition. Technical Report Technical Report CRG-TR-89-2, University of Toronto.

A self-organizing multiple-view representation of 3D objects

Daphna Weinshall
Center for Biological
Information Processing
MIT E25-201
Cambridge, MA 02139

Shimon Edelman
Center for Biological
Information Processing
MIT E25-201
Cambridge, MA 02139

Heinrich H. Bülthoff
Dept. of Cognitive and
Linguistic Sciences
Brown University
Providence, RI 02912

ABSTRACT

We demonstrate the ability of a two-layer network of thresholded summation units to support representation of 3D objects in which several distinct 2D views are stored for each object. Using unsupervised Hebbian relaxation, the network learned to recognize ten objects from different viewpoints. The training process led to the emergence of compact representations of the specific input views. When tested on novel views of the same objects, the network exhibited a substantial generalization capability. In simulated psychophysical experiments, the network's behavior was qualitatively similar to that of human subjects.

1   Background

Model-based object recognition involves, by definition, a comparison between the input image and models of different objects that are internal to the recognition system. The form in which these models are best stored depends on the kind of information available in the input, and on the trade-off between the amount of memory allocated for the storage and the degree of sophistication required of the recognition process.

In computer vision, a distinction can be made between representation schemes that use 3D object-centered coordinate systems and schemes that store viewpoint-specific information such as 2D views of objects. In principle, storing enough 2D views would allow the system to use simple recognition techniques such as template matching. If only a few views of each object are remembered, the system must have the capability to normalize the appearance of an input object, by carrying out appropriate geometrical transformations, before it can be directly compared to the stored representations.

What representation strategy is employed by the human visual system? The notion that objects are represented in viewpoint-dependent fashion is supported by the finding that commonplace objects are more readily recognized from certain so-called canonical vantage points than from other, random viewpoints (Palmer et al. 1981). Namely, canonical views are identified more quickly (and more accurately) than others, with response times decreasing monotonically with increasing subjective goodness.[1]

The monotonic increase in the recognition latency with misorientation of the object relative to a canonical view prompts the interpretation of the recognition process in terms of a mechanism related to mental rotation. In the classical mental rotation task (see Shepard & Cooper 1982), the subject is required to decide whether two simultaneously presented images are two views of the same 3D object. The average latency of correct response in this task is linearly dependent on the difference in the 3D attitude of the object in the two images. This dependence is commonly accounted for by postulating a process that attempts to rotate the 3D shapes perceived in the two images into congruence before making the identity decision. The rotation process is sometimes claimed to be analog, in the sense that the representation of the object appears to pass through intermediate orientation stages as the rotation progresses (Shepard & Cooper 1982).

Psychological findings seem to support the involvement of some kind of mental rotation in recognition by demonstrating the dependence of recognition latency for an unfamiliar view of an object on the distance to its closest familiar view. There is, however, an important qualification. Practice with specific objects appears to cause this strategy to be abandoned in favor of a more memory-intensive, less time-consuming direct comparison strategy. Under direct comparison, many views of the objects are stored and recognition proceeds in essentially constant time, provided that the presented views are sufficiently close to one of the stored views (Tarr & Pinker 1989, Edelman et al. 1989).

From the preceding outline, it appears that a faithful model of object representation in the human visual system should provide both for the ability to "rotate" 3D objects and for the fast direct-comparison strategy that supersedes mental rotation for highly familiar objects. Surprisingly, it turns out that mental rotation in recognition can be replicated by a self-organizing memory-intensive model based on direct comparison. The rest of the present paper describes such a model, called CLF (conjunctions of localized features; see Edelman & Weinshall 1989).

---

[1] Canonical views of objects can be reliably identified in subjective judgement as well as in recognition tasks. For example, when asked to form a mental image of an object, people usually imagine it as seen from a canonical perspective.

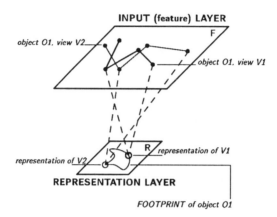

Figure 1: The network consists of two layers, F (input, or feature, layer) and R (representation layer). Only a small part of the projections from F to R are shown. The network encodes input patterns by making units in the R-layer respond selectively to conjunctions of features localized in the F-layer. The curve connecting the representations of the different views of the same object in R-layer symbolizes the association that builds up between these views as a result of practice.

2   The model

The structure of the model appears in Figure 1 (see Edelman & Weinshall 1989 for details). The first (input, or feature) layer of the network is a feature map. In our experiments, vertices of wire-frame objects served as the input features. Every unit in the (feature) F-layer is connected to all units in the second (representation) R-layer. The initial strength of a "vertical" (V) connection between an F-unit and an R-unit decreases monotonically with the "horizontal" distance between the units, according to an inverse square law (which may be considered the first approximation to a Gaussian distribution). In our simulations the size of the F-layer was 64×64 units and the size of the R-layer – 16×16 units. Let (x, y) be the coordinates of an F-unit and (i, j) – the coordinates of an R-unit. The initial weight between these two units is $w_{xyij}|_{t=0} = (\sigma[1 + (x - 4i)^2 + (y - 4j)^2])^{-1}$, where $\sigma = 50$ and $(4i, 4j)$ is the point in the F-layer that is directly "above" the R-unit (i, j).

The R-units in the representation layer are connected among themselves by lateral (L) connections, whose initial strength is zero. Whereas the V-connections form the representations of individual views of an object, the L-connections form associations among different views of the same object.

2.1   Operation

During training, the input to the model is a sequence of appearances of an object, encoded by the 2D locations of concrete sensory features (vertices) rather than a list of abstract features. At the first presentation of a stimulus several representation units are active, all with different strengths (due to the initial distribution of vertical connection strengths).

2.1.1   Winner Take All

We employ a simple winner-take-all (WTA) mechanism to identify for each view of the input object a few most active R-units, which subsequently are recruited to represent that view. The WTA mechanism works as follows. The net activities of the R-units are uniformly thresholded. Initially, the threshold is high enough to ensure that all activity in the R-layer is suppressed. The threshold is then gradually decreased, by a fixed (multiplicative) amount, until some activity appears in the R-layer. If the decrease rate of the threshold is slow enough, only a few units will remain active at the end of the WTA process. In our implementation, the decrease rate was 0.95. In most cases, only one winner emerged.

Note that although the WTA can be obtained by a simple computation, we prefer the stepwise algorithm above because it has a natural interpretation in biological terms. Such an interpretation requires postulating two mechanisms that operate in parallel. The first mechanism, which looks at the activity of the R-layer, may be thought as a high fan-in OR gate. The second mechanism, which performs uniform adjustable thresholding on all the R-units, is similar to a global bias. Together, they resemble feedback-regulated global arousal networks that are thought to be present, e.g., in the medulla and in the limbic system of the brain (Kandel & Schwartz 1985).[2]

2.1.2   Adjustment of weights and thresholds

In the next stage, two changes of weights and thresholds occur that make the currently active R-units (the winners of the WTA stage) selectively responsive to the present view of the input object. First, there is an enhancement of the V-connections from the active (input) F-units to the active R-units (the winners). At the same time, the thresholds of the active R-units are raised, so that at the presentation of a different input these units will be less likely to respond and to be recruited anew. We employ Hebbian relaxation to enhance the V-connections from the input layer to the active R-unit (or units). The connection strength v_{ab} from F-unit a to R-unit $b = (i, j)$ changes by

$$\Delta v_{ab} = \min \left\{ \alpha v_{ab} A_a \cdot A_{ij}, v^{max} - v_{ab} \right\} \cdot \frac{v^{max} - v_{ab}}{v^{max}} \tag{1}$$

where A_{ij} is the activation of the R-unit (i, j) after WTA, v^{max} is an upper bound on a connection strength and α is a parameter controlling the rate of convergence. The threshold of a winner R-unit is increased by

---

[2] The relationship of this approach to other WTA algorithms is discussed in Edelman & Weinshall 1989.

$$\Delta T_b = \delta \sum_a \Delta v_{ab} A_a \qquad (2)$$

where $\delta \leq 1$. This rule keeps the thresholded activity level of the unit growing while the unit becomes more input specific. As a result, the unit encodes the spatial structure of a specific view, responding selectively to that view after only a few (two or three) presentations.

2.1.3   Between-views association

The principle by which specific views of the same object are grouped is that of temporal association. New views of the object appear in a natural order, corresponding to their succession during an arbitrary rotation of the object. The lateral (L) connections in the representation layer are modified by a time-delay Hebbian relaxation. L-connection w_{bc} between R-units $b = (i, j)$ and $c = (l, m)$ that represent successive views is enhanced in proportion to the closeness of their peak activations in time, up to a certain time difference K:

$$\Delta w_{bc} = \sum_{|k| < K} AM(b, c) \cdot \gamma_k A_{ij}^t \cdot A_{lm}^{t+k} \cdot \frac{w^{max} - w_{bc}}{w^{max}} \qquad (3)$$

The strength of the association between two views is made proportional to a coefficient, $AM(b, c)$, that measures the strength of the apparent motion effect that would ensue if the two views were presented in succession to a human subject (see Edelman & Weinshall 1989).

2.1.4   Multiple-view representation

The appearance of a new object is explicitly signalled to the network, so that two different objects do not become associated by this mechanism. The parameter γ_k decreases with $|k|$ so that the association is stronger for units whose activation is closer in time. In this manner, a *footprint* of temporally associated view-specific representations is formed in the second layer for each object. Together, the view-specific representations form a distributed multiple-view representation of the object.

3   Testing the model

We have subjected the CLF network to simulated experiments, modeled after the experiments of (Edelman et al. 1989). Some of the results of the real and simulated experiments appear in Figures 2 and 3. In the experiments, each of ten novel 3D wire-frame objects served in turn as target. The task was to distinguish between the target and the other nine, non-target, objects. The network was first trained on a set of projections of the target's vertices from 16 evenly spaced viewpoints. After learning the target using Hebbian relaxation as described above, the network

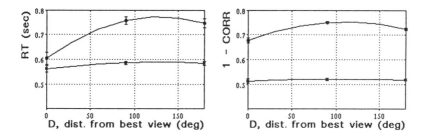

Figure 3: Another comparison of human performance (left panel) with that of the CLF model (right panel). Define the **best view** for each object as the view with the shortest RT (highest CORR). If recognition involves rotation to the best (canonical) view, RT or CORR should depend monotonically on $D = D(target, view)$, the distance between the best view and the actually shown view. (The decrease in RT or CORR at $D = 180°$ is due to the fact that for the wire-frame objects used in the experiments the view diametrically opposite the best one is also easily recognized.) For both human subjects and the model, the dependence is clear for the first session of the experiment (upper curves), but disappears with practice (second session – lower curves).

We note that blurring the input prior to its application to the F-layer can significantly extend the generalization ability of the CLF model. Performing autoassociation on a dot pattern blurred with a Gaussian is computationally equivalent to correlating the input with a set of templates, realized as Gaussian receptive fields. This, in turn, appears to be related to interpolation with Radial Basis Functions (Moody & Darken 1989, Poggio & Girosi 1989, Poggio & Edelman 1989).

4   Summary

We have described a two-layer network of thresholded summation units which is capable of developing multiple-view representations of 3D objects in an unsupervised fashion, using fast Hebbian learning. Using this network to model the performance of human subjects on similar stimuli, we replicated psychophysical experiments that investigated the phenomena of canonical views and mental rotation. The model's performance closely parallels that of the human subjects, even though the network has no a priori mechanism for "rotating" object representations. In the model, a semblance of rotation is created by progressive activation of object footprints (chains of representation units created through association during training). Practice causes the footprints to lose their linear structure through the creation of secondary association links between random representation units, leading to the disappearance of orientation effects. Our results may indicate that a different interpretation of findings that are usually taken to signify mental rotation is possible. The foot-

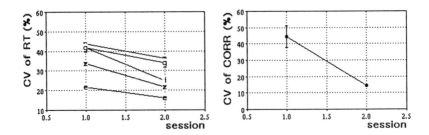

Figure 2: Performance of five human subjects (left panel) and of the CLF model (right panel). The variation of the performance measure (for human subjects, response time RT; for the model, correlation CORR between the input and a stored representation) over different views of an object serves as an estimate of the strength of the canonical views phenomenon. In both human subjects and the model, practice appears to reduce the strength of this phenomenon.

was tested on a sequence of inputs, half of which consisted of familiar views of the target, and half of views of other, not necessarily familiar, objects.

The presentation of an input to the F-layer activated units in the representation layer. The activation then spread to other R-units via the L-connections. After a fixed number of lateral activation cycles, we correlated the resulting pattern of activity with footprints of objects learned so far. The object whose footprint yielded the highest correlation was recognized by definition. In the beginning of the testing stage, this correlation, which served as an analog of response time,[3] exhibited strong dependence on object orientation, replicating the effect of mental rotation in recognition. During testing, successive activation of R-units through association strengthened the L-connection between them, leading to an obliteration of the linear structure of R-unit sequences responsible for mental rotation effects.

3.1   Generalization to novel views

The usefulness of a recognition scheme based on multiple-view representation depends on its ability to classify correctly novel views of familiar objects. To assess the generalization ability of the CLF network, we have tested it on views obtained by rotating the objects away from learned views by as much as 23° (see Figure 4). The classification rate was better than chance for the entire range of rotation. For rotations of up to 1° it was close to perfect, decreasing to 30% at 23° (chance level was 10% because we have used ten objects). One may compare this result with the finding (Rock & DiVita 1987) that people have difficulties in recognizing or imagining wire-frame objects in a novel orientation that differs by more than 30° from a familiar one.

---

[3] The justification for this use of correlation appears in Edelman & Weinshall 1989.

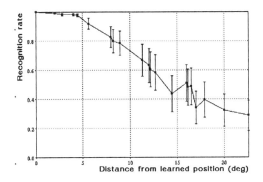

Figure 4: Performance of the network on novel orientations of familiar objects (mean of 10 objects, bars denote the variance).

prints formed in the representation layer in our model provide a hint as to what the substrate upon which the mental rotation phenomena are based may look like.

References

[1] S. Edelman, H. Bülthoff, and D. Weinshall. Stimulus familiarity determines recognition strategy for novel 3D objects. MIT A.I. Memo No. 1138, 1989.

[2] S. Edelman and D. Weinshall. A self-organizing multiple-view representation of 3D objects. MIT A.I. Memo No. 1146, 1989.

[3] E. R. Kandel and J. H. Schwartz. *Principles of neural science.* Elsevier, 1985.

[4] J. Moody and C. Darken. Fast learning in networks of locally tuned processing units. *Neural Computation*, 1:281–289, 1989.

[5] S. Palmer, E. Rosch, and P. Chase. Canonical perspective and the perception of objects. In J. Long and A. Baddeley, eds, *Attn. & Perf. IX*, 135–151. Erlbaum, 1981.

[6] T. Poggio and S. Edelman. A network that learns to recognize 3D objects. *Nature*, 1989, in press.

[7] T. Poggio and F. Girosi. A theory of networks for approximation and learning. MIT A.I. Memo No. 1140, 1989.

[8] I. Rock and J. DiVita. A case of viewer-centered object perception. *Cognitive Psychology*, 19:280–293, 1987.

[9] R. N. Shepard and L. A. Cooper. *Mental images and their transformations.* MIT Press, 1982.

[10] M. Tarr and S. Pinker. Mental rotation and orientation-dependence in shape recognition. *Cognitive Psychology*, 21, 1989.

Contour-Map Encoding of Shape for Early Vision

Pentti Kanerva
Research Institute for Advanced Computer Science
Mail Stop 230-5, NASA Ames Research Center
Moffett Field, California 94035

ABSTRACT

Contour maps provide a general method for
recognizing two-dimensional shapes. All but
blank images give rise to such maps, and people
are good at recognizing objects and shapes
from them. The maps are encoded easily in
long feature vectors that are suitable for
recognition by an associative memory. These
properties of contour maps suggest a role for
them in early visual perception. The prevalence
of direction-sensitive neurons in the visual
cortex of mammals supports this view.

INTRODUCTION

Early vision refers here to the first stages of visual
perception of an experienced (adult human) observer.
Overall, visual perception results in the identification of
what is being viewed: We recognize an image as the letter A
because it looks to us like other As we have seen. Early
vision is the beginning of this process of identification--
the making of the first guess.

Early vision cannot be based on special or salient
features. For example, we normally think of the letter A
as being composed of two slanted strokes, / and \, meeting
at the top and connected in the middle by a horizontal
stroke, -. The strokes and their coincidences define all
the features of A. However, we recognize the As in Figure 1
even though the strokes and the features, if present at all,
do not stand out in the images.

Most telling about human vision is that we can recognize
such As after seeing more or less normal As only. The
challenge of early vision, then, is to find general encoding
mechanisms that turn these quite dissimilar images of the
same object into similar internal representations while
leaving the representations of different objects dissimilar;
and to find basic pattern-recognition mechanisms that work
with these representations. Since our main work is on
associative memories, we have been interested in ways to
encode images into long feature vectors suitable for such
memories. The contour-map method of this paper encodes a
variety of images into vectors for associative memories.

REPRESENTING AN IMAGE AS A CONTOUR MAP

Images take many forms: line drawings, silhouettes,
outlines, dot-matrix pictures, gray-scale pictures, color
pictures, and the like, and pictures that combine all these
elements. Common to all is that they occupy a region of
(two-dimensional) space. An early representation of an
image should therefore be concerned with how the image
controls its space or, in technical terms, how might it be
represented as a field.
    Let us consider first a gray-scale image. It defines
a field by how dark it is in different places (image
intensity--a scalar field--the image itself is the field).
A related field is given by how the darkness changes from
place to place (gradient of intensity--a vector field).
Neither one is quite right for recognizing As because
reversing the field (turning dark to light and light to
dark) leaves us with the "same" A. However, the dark-
and-light reversal leaves the contour lines of the image
unchanged (i.e., lines of uniform intensity--technically
a tangent field perpendicular to the gradient field). My
proposal is to base initial recognition on the contour
lines.
    In line drawings and black-and-white images, which have
only two darkness levels or "colors", the contour lines are
not well defined. This is overcome by propagating the lines
and the edges of the image outward and inward over areas of

FIGURE 1. Various kinds of As.

uniform image intensity, in the manner of contour lines, roughly parallel to the lines and the edges. Figure 2 shows only a few such lines, but, in fact, the image is covered with them, running roughly parallel to each other. As a rule, exactly one contour line runs through any given point. Computing its direction is discussed near the end of the paper.

ENCODING THE CONTOUR MAP

Table 1 shows how the direction of the contour at a point can be encoded in three trits (-1, 0, 1 ternary variables). The code divides 180 degrees into six equal sectors and assigns a codeword to each sector. The distance between two codewords is the number of (Hamming) units by which the words differ (L1 distance). The code is circular, and the distance between codewords is related directly to the difference in direction: Directions 30, 60, and 90 degrees apart are encoded with words that are 2, 4, and 6 units apart, respectively. The code wraps around, as do tangents, so that directions 180 degrees apart are encoded the same. For finer discrimination we would use some finer circular code. The zero-word 000, which is equally far from all other words in the code, is used for points at which the direction of the contour is ill-defined, such as the very centers of circles.

This encoding makes the direction of the contour at any point on a map into a three-component vector. To encode the entire map, the vector field is sampled at a fixed, finite set of points, and the encodings of the sample points are concatenated in fixed order into a long vector. In preliminary studies we have used small sample sizes: 7 x 5 (= 35) sample points, each encoded into three trits, for a total vector of (3 x 35 =) 105 trits, and 8 x 8 sample points by three trits for a total vector of 192 trits.

FIGURE 2.   Propagating the contour.

For an example, Figure 3 shows the digit 4 drawn on a 21-by-15-pixel grid. It also shows a 7 x 5 sampling grid laid over the image and the direction of the contour at the sample points (shown by short line segments). Below the image are the three-trit encodings of the sample points starting at the upper left corner and progressing by rows, concatenated into a 105-trit encoding of the entire image. In this encoding, + means +1 and - means -1.

From Positions of the Code to Directional Sensors

Each position of the three-trit code can be thought of as a directional sensor. For example, the center position senses contours at 90 degrees, plus or minus 45 degrees: It is 1 when the direction of the contour is closer to vertical than to horizontal (see Table 1). Similarly, each position of the long (105-trit) code for the entire map can be thought of as a sensor for a specific direction--plus or minus--at a specific location on the map.

An array of sensors will thus encode an image. The sensors are like the direction-sensitive cells of the visual cortex. Such cells, of course, are not laid down with perfect regularity over the cortex, but that does not mean

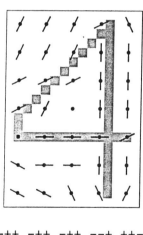

TABLE 1

Coarse Circular Code for
   Direction of Contour
========================

Direction, degrees	Codeword
0 $\pm$ 15	1 -1 1
30 $\pm$ 15	-1 -1 1
60 $\pm$ 15	-1 1 1
90 $\pm$ 15	-1 1 -1
120 $\pm$ 15	1 1 -1
150 $\pm$ 15	1 -1 -1
180 $\pm$ 15	1 -1 1
. . .	. . .
Undefined	0 0 0

========================

```
-++ -++ -++ --+ ++-
-++ -++ -++ -+- -+-
--+ --+ --+ -+- -+-
--+ -++ 000 -+- -+-
000 +-+ +-+ +-+ --+
+-- +-+ +-+ -+- -+-
+-- +-- ++- ++- -++
```

FIGURE 3. Encoding an image.

that they could not perform as encoders. Accordingly, a direction-sensitive cell can be thought of as a feature detector that encodes for a certain direction at a certain location in the visual or attentional field. An irregular array of randomly oriented sensors laid over images would produce perfectly good encodings of their contour maps.

COMPARING TWO CONTOUR MAPS

How closely do two contour maps resemble each other? For simplicity, we will compare maps of equal size (and shape) only. The maps are compared point to point. The difference at a point is the difference in the direction of the contour at that point on the two maps--that is, the magnitude of the lesser of the two angles made by the two contour lines that run through the two points that correspond to each other on the two maps. The maximum difference at a point is therefore 90 degrees. The entire maps are then compared by adding the pointwise differences over all the points (by integrating over the area of the map).

The purpose of the encoding is to make the comparing of maps simple. The code is so constructed that the difference of two maps at a point is roughly proportional to the distance between the two (3-trit) codewords--one from each map--for that point. We need not even concern ourselves with the finding of the lesser of the two angles made by the crossing of the two contours; the distance between codewords accounts for that automatically.

Entire maps are then compared by adding together the distances at the (35) sample points. This is equivalent to computing the distance between the (105-trit) codewords for the two maps. This distance is proportional to the difference between the maps, and it is approximately so because the maps are sampled at a small number of points and because the direction at each point is coded coarsely.

COMPUTING THE DIRECTION OF THE CONTOUR

We have not explored widely how to compute contours from images and merely outline here one method, not exactly biological, that works for line drawings and two-tone images and that can be generalized to gray-scale images and even to many multicolor images. We have also experimented with oriented, difference-of-Gaussian filters of Parent and Zucker (1985) and with cortex transforms of Watson (1987).

The contours are based on a simple model of attraction, akin to gravity, by assuming that the lines and the edges of the image attract according to their distance from the point. The net attraction at any point on the image defines a gradient field, and the contours are perpendicular to it.

In practice we work with pixels and assume, for the sake of the gravity model, that pixels of the same color--same as that of the sample point P for which we are computing the direction--have mass zero and those of the opposite color have mass one. For the direction to be independent of scale, the attractive force must be inversely proportional to some power of the distance. Powers greater than 2 make the computation local. For example, power 7 means that one pixel, twice as far as another, contributes only 1/128 as much as the other to the net force. To make the attraction somewhat insensitive to noise, a small constant, 3, is added to the distance. (The values 7 and 3 were chosed after a small amount of experimentation.) Hence, pixel X (of mass 1) attracts P with a magnitude

$$[d(P,X) + 3]^{-7}$$

force in the direction of X, where d(P,X) is the (Euclidean) distance between P and X. The vector sum of the forces over all pixels X (of mass 1) then is the attractive force at point P, and the direction of the contour at P is perpendicular to it. The magnitude of the vector sum is scaled by dividing it with the sum of the magnitudes of its components. This scaled magnitude indicates how well the direction is defined in the image.

When this computation is made at a point on a (one-pixel wide) line, the result is a zero-vector (the gradient at the top of a ridge is zero). However, we want to use the direction of the line itself as the direction of the contour. To this end, we compute at each sample point P another vector that detects linear features, such as lines. This computation is based on the above attraction model, modified as follows: Pixels of the same color as P's now have mass one and those of the opposite color have mass zero (the pixel at P being always regarded as having mass zero); and the direction of the force, instead of being the angle from P to X, is twice that angle. The doubling of the angle makes attractive forces in opposite directions (along a line) reenforce each other and in perpendicular directions cancel out each other. The angle of the net force is then halved, and the magnitude of the force is scaled as above.

The two computations yield two vectors, both representing the direction of the contour at a point. They can be combined into a single vector by doubling their angles, to eliminate 180-degree ambiguities, by adding together the resulting vectors, and by halving the angle of the sum. The direction of the result gives the direction of the contour, and the magnitude of the result indicates how well

this direction is defined. If the magnitude is below some
threshold, the direction is taken to be undefined and is
encoded with 000.

SOME COMPARISONS

The method is very general, which is at once its virtue and
limitation. The virtue is that it works where more specific
methods fail, the limitation that the specific methods are
needed for specific problems.

   In our preliminary experiments with handwritten Zip-code
digits, low-pass filtering (blurring) an image, as a method
of encoding it, and contour maps resulted in similar rates
of recognition by a sparse distributed memory. Higher rates
on this same task were gotten by Denker et al. (1989) by
encoding the image in terms of features specific to
handwriting.

   To get an idea of the generality of contour maps, Figure
4 shows encoded maps of ten normal digits like that in
Figure 3, and for three unusual digits barely recognizable
by humans. The labels for the unusual ones and for their
maps, 8a, 8b, and 9a, tell what digits they were intented
to be. Table 2 of distances between the encoded maps
shows that 8 gives only the second best match to 8a and 8b,
whereas the digit closest to 9a indeed is 9. This suggest
that a system trained on normal letters and digits would do

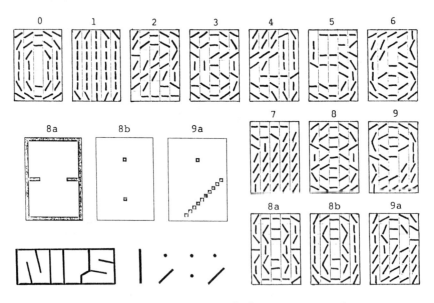

FIGURE 4. Contour maps of digits. Unusual text.

TABLE 2
Distances Between Normal and Unusual Digits of Figure 4

	0	1	2	3	4	5	6	7	8	9
8a	62	95	80	74	91	87	83	86	67	79
8b	38	71	88	64	77	73	65	88	51	73
9a	70	89	66	90	109	99	103	62	83	59

a fair job at recognizing the 'NIPS 1989' at the bottom of
Figure 4. Systems that encode characters as bit maps, or
that take them as composed of strokes, likewise trained,
would not do nearly as well. Going back to the As of Figure
1, they can, with one exception, be recognized based on the
map of a normal A. Logograms are a rich source of images of
this kind. They are excellent for testing a vision system
for generality. Finally, other oriented fields, not just
contour maps, can be encoded with methods similar to this
for recognition by an associative memory.

Acknowledgements

This research was supported by the National Aeronautics and
Space Administration (NASA) with cooperative agreement No.
NCC2-387 with the Universities Space Research Association.
The idea of contour maps was inspired by the gridfonts of
Douglas Hofstadter (1985). The first experiments with the
contour-map method were done by Bruno Olshausen. The
gravity model arose from discussions with Lauri Kanerva.
David Rogers made the computer-drawn illustrations.

References

Denker, J.S., Gardner, W.R., Graf, H.P., Henderson, D.,
    Howard, R.E., Hubbard, W., Jackel, L.D., Baird, H.S., and
    Guyon, I. (1989) Neural Network Recognizer for Hand-
    Written Zip Code Digits. In D.S. Touretzky (ed.),
    Advances in Neural Information Systems, Volume I.
    San Mateo, California: Kaufmann. 323-331.
Hofstadter, D.R. (1985) Metamagical Themas. New Your:
    Basic Books.
Parent, P., and Zucker, S.W. (1985) Trace Inference,
    Curvature Consistency, and Curve Detection. Report CIM-
    86-3, McGill Research Center for Intelligent Machines,
    Montreal, Canada.
Watson, A.W. (1987) The Cortex Transform: Rapid
    Computation of Simulated Neural Images. Computer Vision,
    Graphics, and Image Processing 39(3):311-327.

Neurally Inspired Plasticity in Oculomotor Processes

Paul A. Viola

Artificial Intelligence Laboratory

Massachusetts Institute of Technology

Cambridge, MA 02139

ABSTRACT

We have constructed a two axis camera positioning system which is roughly analogous to a single human eye. This Artificial-Eye (A-eye) combines the signals generated by two rate gyroscopes with motion information extracted from visual analysis to stabilize its camera. This stabilization process is similar to the vestibulo-ocular response (VOR); like the VOR, A-eye learns a system model that can be incrementally modified to adapt to changes in its structure, performance and environment. A-eye is an example of a robust sensory system that performs computations that can be of significant use to the designers of mobile robots.

1   Introduction

We have constructed an "artificial eye" (A-eye), an autonomous robot that incorporates a two axis camera positioning system (figure 1). Like a the human oculomotor system, A-eye can estimate the rotation rate of its body with a gyroscope and estimate the rotation rate of its "eye" by measuring image slip across its "retina". Using the gyroscope to sense rotation, A-eye attempts to stabilize its camera by driving the camera motors to counteract body motion. The conversion of gyro output to motor command is dependent on the characteristics of the gyroscope, the structure of camera lensing system and the response of the motors. A correctly functioning stabilization system must model the characteristics of each of these external variables.

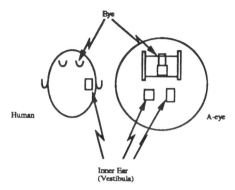

Figure 1: The construction of A-eye can be viewed in rough analogy to the human oculomotor system. In place of an eye, A-eye has a camera on a two axis positioning platform. In place of the circular canals of the inner ear, A-eye has two rate gyroscopes that measure rotation in perpendicular axes.

Since camera motion implies stabilization error, A-eye uses a visual estimate of camera motion to incrementally update its system model. When the camera is correctly stabilized there is no statistically significant slip. Whenever a particular gyro measurement is associated with a result camera motion, A-eye makes an incremental change to its response to that particular measurement to reduce that error in the future.

A-eye was built for two reasons: to facilitate the operation of complex visually guided mobile robots and to explore the applicability of simple learning techniques to the construction of a robust robot.

2 Autonomous Robots

An autonomous robot must function correctly for long periods of time without human intervention. It is certainly difficult to create an autonomous robot or process that will function accurately, both initially and perpetually. To achieve such a goal, autonomous processes must be able to adapt both to unforeseen aspects of the environment and inaccuracies in construction. One approach to attaining successful autonomous performance would entail the full characterization of the robot's structure, its performance requirements, and its relationship with the environment. Since clearly both the robot and its environment are susceptible to change any characterization could not be static. In contrast, our approach only partially categorizes the robot's structure, environment, and task. Without more detailed information initial performance is inaccurate. However, by using a measure of error in performance initially partial categorization can incrementally improved. In addition, a change to system performance can be compensated continually. In this way the extensive analysis and engineering that would be required to characterize, foresee and circumvent variability can be greatly reduced.

3   The VOR

The oculomotor processes found in vertebrates are well studied examples of adaptive, visually guided processing [Gou85]. The three oculomotor processes found almost universally in vertebrates (the vestibulo-ocular response, the optokinetic system, and the saccadic system), accurately perform ocular positioning tasks with little or no conscious direction. The response times of these systems demonstrate that little high level, "conscious", processing could take place. In a limited sense these processes are autonomous, and it should come as no surprise that they are quite plastic. Such plasticity is necessary to counteract the foreseeable changes in the eye due to growth and aging and the unforeseeable changes due to illness and injury.

The VOR works to counteract the motion of a creature in its environment. A correctly functioning VOR ensures that a creature "sees" as little unintended motion as possible. Miles [FAM81] and others have demonstrated that the VOR is an adaptive motor response, capable of significant recalibration in a matter of days. Adaptation can be demonstrated by the use of inverting or magnifying spectacles. While wearing these glasses the correct orbital motion of the eye, given a particular head motion, is significantly different from the normal response. Initially, the response to head motion is an incorrect eye motion. With time eye motion begins to approach the correct counteracting motion. This kind of adaptation allows an animal to continue functioning in spite of injury or illness.

4   The Device

A-eye is a small autonomous robot that incorporates a CCD camera, a three wheel base, a two axis pitch/yaw camera positioning platform, and two rate gyroscopes. On board processing includes a Motorola microcontroller and 68020 based video processing board. Including batteries, A-eye is a foot high cylinder that is 12 inches wide. In its present configuration A-eye can run autonomously for up to three hours (figure 2).

A-eye's goal is to learn how to keep its camera stable as its base trundles down corridors. There are two sources of information regarding the motion of A-eye's base: gyro rotation measurements and optical flow. Rate gyroscopes measure base rotation rate directly. Visual analysis can be used to estimate motion by a number of methods of varying complexity (see [Hil83] for a good overview). By attempting to measure only camera rotation from slip complexity can be avoided. The simple method we have chosen measures the slip of images across the retina.

4.1   Visual Rotation Estimation

Our approach to camera rotation estimation uses a pre-processing subunit commonly known as a "Reichard detector" which for clarity we will call a *shift and correlate unit* [PR73]. A *shift and correlate unit* has as its inputs a set of samples

Figure 2: A photo of the current state of A-eye.

from a blurred area of the retina. It shifts these inputs spatially and correlates them with a previous, unshifted set of inputs. When two succeeding images are identical except for a spatial shift, the units which perform that shift respond strongly. Clearly the activity of a *shift and correlate unit* contains information about retinal motion. Due to the size and direction of shift, some detectors will be sensitive to small motions, others large motions, and each will be sensitive to a particular direction of motion.

The input from the *shift and correlate units* is used to build value-unit encoded retinal velocity map, in which each unit is sensitive to a different direction and range of velocities. The map has 9 units in a 3 by 3 grid (fig 3). To create such a map, each of the *shift and correlate units* is connected to every map unit. By moving the camera, displaced images that are examples of motion, are generated. The motor command that generated this motion example corresponds to a unit in the visual velocity map. Connection weights are updated by a standard least squares learning rule. In operation, the most active unit represents the estimate of visual motion.

4.2   Gyroscope Rotation Estimation

Contrary to first intuition, vertebrates do not rely on visual information to stabilize their eyes. Instead head rotation information measured by the inner ear, or the vestibula, is used keep the eyes stable. Animals do not measure ocular motion directly from visual information for two reasons: a) the response rates of photoreceptors prevent useful visual processing during rapid eye movements [Gou85] b) the

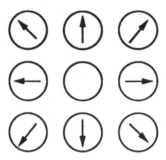

Figure 3: The 9 unit velocity map has 1 unit for each of the 8 "chess moves".

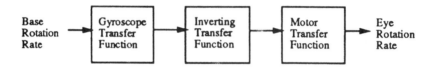

Figure 4: Open-loop control of ocular position based on gyroscope output.

required visual analysis takes approximately 100ms[1]. These difficulties combine to prevent rapid response to unexpected head and body motions. A-eye is beset with similar limitations and we have chosen a similar solution.

The output of the gyroscope is some function of head rotation rate. Stabilization is achieved by driving the ocular motors directly in opposition to the measured velocity (fig 4). This counteract rotation of the base in one direction by moving the camera in the opposite direction. Such an open-loop system is very simple and can perform well; they are unfortunately very reliant on proper calibration and recalibration to maintain performance [Oga70].

A-eye maintains calibration information in the form of a function from gyroscope output to motor velocity command. This function is an 8 unit gaussian radial basis approximation network [TP89]. Basis function approximation has excellent computational properties while representing wide variety of smooth functions. Weights are modified with a simple least squares update rule, based errors in camera motion detected visually.

5   Training A-eye

A-eye learns to perform the VOR in a two phase process. First, the measurement of visual motion is calibrated to the generation of camera motion commands. Second,

---

[1] Ocular following, the tendency to follow the motion of a scene in the absence of head motion, has a typical latency of 100ms [FM87].

the stabilizing motor responses to gyroscope measurements are approximated. This approximation is modified based on a visual estimate of camera motion.

By observing motor commands and comparing them to the resulting visual motion, a map from visual motion to appropriate motor command can be learned. To train the visual motion map, A-eye performs a set of characteristic motions and observes the results. Each motor command is categorized as one of the 9 distinct motions encoded by the visual motion map. With each motion, the connections from *shift and correlate units* to the visual motion map are updated so that issuing a motor command results in activity in the correct visual motion unit. Because no reference is made to external variables, this measure of visual motion is completely relative to the function of the camera motors. The visual motion map plays the role of error signal for later learning.

By observing both the gyroscope output and the visual response from head motion, A-eye learns the appropriate compensating eye motion for all head motions. Eye compensation motions are the result of motor commands generated by the approximation network applied to the gyroscope output. Incorrect responses will cause visual motion. This motion, as measured by the visual motion detector, is the error signal that drives the modification of the approximation network. This is the heart of the adaptation in the VOR.

5.1   Results

While training the motion detector and approximation network there are 5 training events per second (the visual analysis takes about 200 msec). Training the visual motion detector can take up to 10 minutes (in a few environments the weights refuse to settle on the correct values). While it is possible to hand wire a detector that is 95% accurate, most learned detectors worked well, attaining 85% accuracy. In both cases, the detectors have the desirable capability of rejecting object motion whenever there is actual camera motion (this is due to the global nature of the analysis).

The approximation network converges to a function that performs well in minutes (figure 5). Analysis of the images generated by the camera leads us to bound the cumulative error in rotation over a 1 minute trial at 5 degrees (we believe this approaches the accuracy limitations inherent in the gyroscope).

An approach to reducing this gyroscope error involves yet another oculomotor process: optokinetic nystagmus (OKN). This is the tendency for an otherwise undirected eye to follow visual motion in the absence of vestibular cues. A-eye's visual motion map is in motor coordinates. By directing the camera in the opposite direction from observed motion, residual errors in VOR can be reduced.

6   Application

We claim that the stabilization that results from a correctly calibrated VOR is useful both for navigation and scene analysis. A stable inertial reference can act to assist tactical navigation when traversing rough terrain. Large body attitude

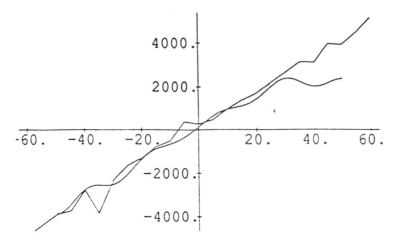

Figure 5: A correct transfer function (rough) and the learned (smoother) approximation.

changes, that can result from such travel, make it difficult to maintain a navigational bearing. However, when there exists a relatively stable inertial reference frame less analysis need be performed to predict or sense changes in bearing by other means.

The VOR is especially applicable to legged vehicles, where the terrain and the form of locomotion can cause constant rapid changes in attitude [Rai89] [Ang89]. The task of adapting conventional vision systems to such vehicles is formidable. As the rate of pitching increases, the quality of video images degrade, while the task of finding a correspondence between successive images will increase in complexity. With the addition of the visual stabilization that A-eye can provide, an otherwise complex visual analysis task can be much simplified.

7   Conclusions

A-eye is in part a response to the observation that static calibration is a disastrous weakness. Static calibration not only forces an engineer to expend additional effort at design time, it requires constant performance monitoring and recalibration. By creating a device that monitors its own performance and adapts to changes, significant work can be saved in design and at numerous times during the lifetime of the device.

A-eye is also in part a confirmation that simple, tractable and reliable learning mechanisms are sufficient to perform useful motor learning.

Finally, A-eye is in part a demonstration that useful visual processing can be performed in real-time with an reasonable amount of computation. This processing yields the additional side-benefit of simplifying the complex task of visual recognition.

Acknowledgements

This report describes research done at the Artificial Intelligence Laboratory of the Massachusetts Institute of Technology. Support for this research was provided by Hughes Artificial Intelligence Center contract #SI-804475-D, the Office of Naval Research contract N00014-86-K-0685, and the Defense Advanced Research Projects Agency under Office of Naval Research contract N00014-85-K-0124.

References

[Ang89]   Colin Angle. Genghis, a six legged autonomous walking robot. Master's thesis, MIT, 1989.

[FAM81]   S. G. Lisberger F. A. Miles. Plasticity in the vestibulo-ocular reflex: A new hypothesis. *Ann. Rev. Neurosci.*, 4:273–299, 1981.

[FM87]   K. Kawano F.A. Miles. Visual stabilization of the eyes. *TINS*, 4(10):153–158, 1987. Reference on Opto-kinetic nystagmus latency.

[Gou85]   Peter Gouras. Oculomotor system. In James Schwartz Eric Kandel, editor, *Principles of Neuroscience*, chapter 34. Elsevier Science Publishing, 1985.

[Hil83]   Ellen C. Hildreth. *The Measurement of Visual Motion.* The MIT Press, 1983. Good book on the extraction of motion from edges.

[Oga70]   Katsuhiko Ogata. *Modern Control Engineering.* Prentice-Hall, Englewood Cliffs, N.J., 1970. Steady State Frequency Response (page 372).

[PR73]   T. Poggio and W. Reichard. Considerations on models of movement detection. *Kybernetic*, 13:223–227, 1973.

[Rai89]   Marc H. Raibert. Trotting, pacing, and bounding by a quadruped robot. *Journal of Biomechanics*, 1989.

[TP89]   Federico Girosi Tomaso Poggio. A theory of networks for approximation and learning. AI Memo 1140, MIT, 1989.

Model Based Image Compression and Adaptive Data Representation by Interacting Filter Banks

Toshiaki Okamoto, Mitsuo Kawato, Toshio Inui
ATR Auditory and
Visual Perception Research Laboratories
Sanpeidani, Inuidani, Seika-cho, Soraku-gun
Kyoto 619-02, Japan

Sei Miyake
NHK Science and
Technical Research Laboratories
1-10-11, Kinuta, Setagaya
Tokyo 157, Japan

Abstract

To achieve high-rate image data compression while maintainig a high quality reconstructed image, a good image model and an efficient way to represent the specific data of each image must be introduced. Based on the physiological knowledge of multi-channel characteristics and inhibitory interactions between them in the human visual system, a mathematically coherent parallel architecture for image data compression which utilizes the Markov random field image model and interactions between a vast number of filter banks, is proposed.

1. Introduction

Data compression has been one of the most important and active areas in information theory and computer science. The goal of image coding is reducing the number of bits in data representation as much as possible, and reconstructing a faithful duplicate of the original image. In order to achieve a high compression ratio while maintaining the high quality of the reconstructed image, a good image model and an efficient way to represent image data must be found. Based on physiological knowledge of the human visual system, we propose a mathematically coherent parallel architecture for the image data compression, which utilizes a stochastic image model and interactions between a vast number of filter banks.

2. Model based image compression and dynamic spatial filtering

The process of reconstructing an original image from compressed data is an ill-posed problem, since an infinite number of original images lead to the same compressed data and solutions to the inverse problem can not uniquely be determined. The coupled Markov random field (MRF) image model proposed by Geman and Geman is introduced to resolve this ill-posedness. The mean field approximation of the MRF is equivalent to a recurrent type neural network with the Ljapunov function (see Koch. Marroquin and Yuille as a special case where the form of the Ljapunov function is predetermined). Correspondingly, a similar deterministic framework of image compression in which the MRF is replaced by the recurrent network, can be developed.

Further, even if a good MRF model is introduced for a family of images, the data for each image must be known in order to reconstruct it. In previous studies of image data compression, representation of image data is fixed in each schema. On the other hand, in this paper, an adaptive data representation is proposed, tuned to each image by competion and cooperation of a vast number of filter banks.

Fig. 1 shows a block diagram of the proposed communication system. Procedures at the encoder side are (1) partial partition and segmentation of the image by the line process of the MRF which represents the image discontinuity, (2) learning of energy parameters which uses the line process to define the MRF model in each segmented area of the image, (3) adaptive data representation of images by cooperation and competition of a vast number of filter banks. (4) Information about energy value parameters, the types of selected filter and their outputs, and the line processes is transmitted, through communication channel. (5) Image reconstruction is carried out at the decorder site by stochastic relaxation based on the aquired MRF model, output from the selected filters, and the line process. These procedures are explained in detail below.

1. The set of line processes represents discontinuities in the 3-dimensional world such as occluding contours or boundaries between different objects. It is not necessarily closed, but it can posess a strong tendency to do so if the MRF model is appropriately chosen. Based on this property, the image can be partially segmented into several regions.

2. If we adopt the MRF image model, the occurrence probability $\Pi(\omega)$ of each configuration ω is Gibbsian :

$$\Pi(\omega)=\frac{\exp\{-U(\omega)/T\}}{Z}$$

Furthermore, the energy $U(\omega)$ can be expressed as a summation of local potential $V_C(\omega)$, which depends on the configuration only in the clique C.

$$U(\omega)=\sum_{C \in S_c} V_C(\omega)$$

Determination of the local energy V_C is equivalent to defining a specific MRF model of the image. Determination of the local energy is equivalent to assigning a real value V_{ℓ_i} to every possible configuration within the clique C. These energy parameters are estimated so that the Kullback divergence G between the real image distribution P and the model image distribution P' is minimized :

$$G(V)=\sum_{\omega}P(\omega)\log\{\frac{P(\omega)}{P'(\omega,V_C)}\}$$

The following learning equation can be derived in approximately the same way as the learning rule of the Boltzmann machine (Ackley, Hinton, Sejnowski, 1985).

$$\Delta V_{\xi_i}=-\varepsilon\frac{\partial G}{\partial V_{\xi_i}}=-\eta\{<\sum_{C\in S_c}I_i(C)>_{real}-<\sum_{C\in S_c}I_i(C)\}>_{desir}$$

Here $I_i(C)$ is the characteristic function of the specific configuration ξ_i of the clique C, that is, $I_i(C)=1$ if $\{y_s; s\in C\}=\xi_i$ otherwise, $I_i(C)=0$. The first term on the right side is the average number of configurations in the real image. The second term on the right side is the average number of each configuration ξ_i generated in the MRF with the energy V_C when part of the image configuration is fixed to the given image.

3. This procedure is based on the multi-channel characteristics of the human visual system, inhibitory interaction between X-cell and Y-cell systems, and interactions between columns with different orientation selectivity, etc. We prepare a vast number of filters centered at each site s in a variety of sizes, shapes and orientations. In particular, we use two-dimensional Gaussian filters $G_s(\omega)$ to represent the DC components (i.e. average luminance) of the gray level, and use the first-order derivative of the Gaussian filters $\nabla G_s(\omega)$ to represent the gradient of the gray levels. The filters whose receptive fields significantly intersect with the line process are inhibited. Inhibitory interactions between filters of similar, shape and orientation at nearby sites are introduced

as well as self excitation to find the N-maximum outputs of ∇G_s, and to find the N-minimum outputs of the Laplacian Gaussian ΔG_s. Of course, 2N must be less than the number of sites to attain data compression.

4. We transmit the local potential energy, the site of the line process, and the outputs from the N − maximum, and the outputs from the N Gaussain filters which correspond to the N − minimum Laplacian Gaussain filters.

5. Image reconstruction is carried out by the usual stochastic relaxation, that is, energy minimization with simulated annealing. However, because we have data constraints as output from the 2N selected filters, we need to minimize the sum of the MRF model energy and the data constraint energy :

$$E_{post}(\omega)=U(\omega)+\lambda\{\sum_{k=1}^{N}(G_{\bar{k}}-G_k(\omega))^2+\sum_{k=1}^{N}(\nabla G_{\bar{k}}-\nabla G_k(\omega))^2\}$$

If we do not further compress the filter outputs, the regularization parameter is increased to infinity during constrained stochastic relaxation.

3. Experimental results

First, we ascertained that the proposed energy learning rule works well for various images. Here, we report only one example from the data compression experiments. We used the shown in Fig. 2a to examine the potential of our scheme. The image data consists of 256 pixels, each of which has 8 bit gray levels. We used the dynamic spatial sampling of filter banks. Fig 2a also shows selected sample points in the image as black dots, as well as a few examples of selected filter shapes. Note that not only the density of the sampling points, but also the selected filter shapes are appropriate local characteristics of the image. Fig. 2b shows the reconstructed image after 20 iterations of the relaxation computation. The signal to noise ratio of the reconstructed images was about 38dB.

References

D. H., Ackley, G. E. Hinton, and T. J. Sejnowski, : "A Learning algorithm for Boltzmann Machines.", Cognitive Science, vol. 9, pp.147 − 169, (1985).

S. Geman and D. Geman, : "Stochastic relaxation, Gibbs distribution, and the Basian restoration of images", IEEE Trans. vol. PAMI − 6, pp.721 − 741, (1984).

S. Hongo, M. Kawato, T. Inui, and S. Miyake, ; "Contour extraction of images on parallel computer", Proc. of 1th IJCNN, (1989).

T. Inui, M. Kawato and R. Suzuki : "The mechanism of mental scanning in foveal vision", Biol. Cybern. vol. 30, pp.147 − 155, (1978).

C. Koch, J. Marroquin, and A. Yuille : "Analog 'neural' networks in early vision", Proc. Natl. Acad. Sci. USA, vol. 83, pp.4263 − 4267, (1986).

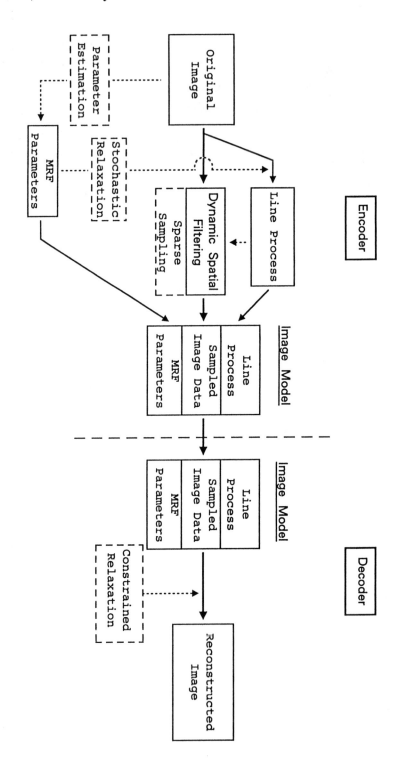

Fig. 1 Model Based Communication System

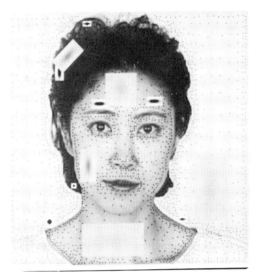

(a) sampled data points
and filters

(b) reconstructed image

Fig. 2 Computer simulation
of image data compression

PART IV:
OPTIMIZATION AND CONTROL

Neuronal Group Selection Theory: A Grounding in Robotics

Jim Donnett and Tim Smithers
Department of Artificial Intelligence
University of Edinburgh
5 Forrest Hill
Edinburgh EH1 2QL
SCOTLAND

ABSTRACT

In this paper, we discuss a current attempt at applying the organizational principle Edelman calls Neuronal Group Selection to the control of a real, two-link robotic manipulator. We begin by motivating the need for an alternative to the position-control paradigm of classical robotics, and suggest that a possible avenue is to look at the primitive animal limb 'neurologically ballistic' control mode. We have been considering a selectionist approach to coordinating a simple perception-action task.

1 MOTIVATION

The majority of industrial robots in the world are mechanical manipulators — often arm-like devices consisting of some number of rigid links with actuators mounted where the links join that move adjacent links relative to each other, rotationally or translationally. At the joints there are typically also sensors measuring the relative *position* of adjacent links, and it is in terms of *position* that manipulators are generally controlled (a desired motion is specified as a desired position of the end effector, from which can be derived the necessary positions of the links comprising the manipulator). Position control dominates largely for historical reasons, rooted in *bang-bang control*: manipulators bumped between mechanical stops placed so as to enforce a desired trajectory for the end effector.

1.1   SERVOMECHANISMS

Mechanical stops have been superceded by position-controlling servomechanisms, negative feedback systems in which, for a typical manipulator with revolute joints, a desired joint angle is compared with a feedback signal from the joint sensor signalling actual measured angle; the difference controls the motive power output of the joint actuator proportionally.

Where a manipulator is constructed of a number of links, there might be a servomechanism for each joint. In combination, it is well known that joint motions can affect each other adversely, requiring careful design and analysis to reduce the possibility of unpleasant dynamical instabilities. This is especially important when the manipulator will be required to execute fast movements involving many or all of the joints. We are interested in such dynamic tasks, and acknowledge some successful servomechanistic solutions (see [Andersson 1988], who describes a ping pong playing robot), but seek an alternative that is not as computationally expensive.

1.2   ESCAPING POSITION CONTROL

In Nature, fast reaching and striking is a primitive and fundamental mode of control. In fast, time-optimal, neurologically ballistic movements (such as horizontal rotations of the head where subjects are instructed to turn it as fast as possible, [Hannaford and Stark 1985]), muscle activity patterns seem to show three phases: a launching phase (a burst of agonist), a braking phase (an antagonist burst), and a locking phase (a second agonist burst). Experiments have shown (see [Wadman *et al.* 1979]) that at least the first 100 mS of activity is the same even if a movement is blocked mechanically (without forewarning the subject), suggesting that the launch is specified from predetermined initial conditions (and is not immediately modified from proprioceptive information). With the braking and locking phases acting as a damping device at the end of the motion, the complete motion of the arm is essentially specified by the initial conditions — a mode radically differing from traditional robot positional control. The overall coordination of movements might even seem naive and simple when compared with the intricacies of servomechanisms (see [Braitenberg 1989, Nahvi and Hashemi 1984] who discuss the crane driver's strategy for shifting loads quickly and time-optimally).

The concept of letting insights (such as these) that can be gained from the biological sciences shape the engineering principles used to create artificial autonomous systems is finding favour with a growing number of researchers in robotics. As it is not generally trivial to see how life's devices can be mapped onto machines, there is a need for some fundamental experimental work to develop and test the basic theoretical and empirical components of this approach, and we have been considering various robotics problems from this perspective.

Here, we discuss an experimental two-link manipulator that performs a simple manipulation task — hitting a simple object perceived to be within its reach. The perception of the object specifies the initial conditions that determine an arm motion that reaches it. In relating initial conditions with motor currents, we have been considering a scheme based on Neuronal Group Selection Theory [Edelman 1987, Reeke and Edelman 1988], a theory of brain organization. We believe this to be the first attempt to apply selectionist ideas in a real machine, rather than just in simulation.

2   NEURONAL GROUP SELECTION THEORY

Edelman proposes Neuronal Group Selection (NGS) [Edelman 1978] as an organizing principle for higher brain function — mainly a biological basis for perception — primarily applicable to the mammalian (and specifically, human) nervous system [Edelman 1981]. The essential idea is that groups of cells, structurally varied as a result of developmental processes, comprise a population from which are selected those groups whose function leads to adaptive behaviour of the system. Similar notions appear in immunology and, of course, evolutionary theory, although the effects of neuronal group selection are manifest in the lifetime of the organism.

There are two premises on which the principle rests. The first is that the unit of selection is a cell group of perhaps 50 to 10,000 neurons. Intra-group connections between cells are assumed to vary (greatly) between groups, but other connections in the brain (particularly inter-group) are quite specific. The second premise is that the kinds of nervous systems whose organization the principle addresses are able to adapt to circumstances not previously encountered by the organism or its species [Edelman 1978].

2.1   THREE CENTRAL TENETS

There are three important ideas in the NGS theory [Edelman 1987].

- A first selective process (cell division, migration, differentiation, or death) results in structural diversity providing a *primary repertoire* of variant cell groups.

- A second selective process occurs as the organism experiences its environment; group activity that correlates with adaptive behaviour leads to differential amplification of intra- and inter-group synaptic strengths (the connectivity pattern remains unchanged). From the primary repertoire are thus selected groups whose adaptive functioning means they are more likely to find future use — these groups form the *secondary repertoire*.

- Secondary repertoires themselves form populations, and the NGS theory additionally requires a notion of *reentry*, or connections between repertoires, usually arranged in maps, of which the well-known retinotopic mapping of the visual system is typical. These connections are critical for they correlate motor and sensory repertoires, and lend the world the kind of spatiotemporal continuity we all experience.

2.2   REQUIREMENTS OF SELECTIVE SYSTEMS

To be selective, a system must satisfy three requirements [Reeke and Edelman 1988]. Given a configuration of input signals (ultimately from the sensory epithelia, but for 'deeper' repertoires mainly coming from other neuronal groups), if a group responds in a specific way it has *matched* the input [Edelman 1978]. The first requirement of a selective system is that it have a sufficiently large repertoire of variant elements to ensure that an adequate match can be found for a wide range of inputs. Secondly, enough of the groups in a repertoire must 'see' the diverse input signals effectively and quickly so that selection can operate on these groups. And finally, there must be a means for 'amplifying' the contribution, to the repertoire, of groups whose operation when matching input signals has led to adaptive behaviour.

In determining the necessary number of groups in a repertoire, one must consider the relationship between repertoire size and the specificity of member groups. On the one hand, if groups are very specific, repertoires will need to be very large in order to recognize a wide range of possible inputs. On the other hand, if groups are not as discriminating, it will be possible to have smaller numbers of them, but in the limit (a single group with virtually no specificity) different signals will no longer be distinguishable. A simple way to quantify this might be to assume that each of N groups has a fixed probability, p, of matching an input configuration; then a typical measure [Edelman 1978] relating the effectiveness of recognition, r, to the number of groups is $r = 1 - (1 - p)^N$ (see Fig. 1).

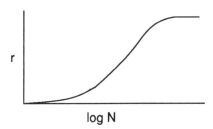

Figure 1: Recognition as a Function of Repertoire Size

From the shape of the curve in Fig. 1, it is clear that, for such a measure, below some lower threshold for N, the efficacy of recognition is equally poor. Similarly, above an upper threshold for N, recognition does not improve substantially as more groups are added.

3   SELECTIONISM IN OUR EXPERIMENT

Our manipulator is required to touch an object perceived to be within reach. This is a well-defined but non-trivial problem in motor-sensory coordination. Churchland proposes a geometrical solution for his two-eyed 'crab' [Churchland 1986], in which eye angles are mapped to those joint angles (the crab has a two-link arm) that would bring the end of the arm to the point currently foveated by the eyes. Such a novel solution, in which computation is implicit and massively parallel, would be welcome; however, the crab is a simulation, and no heed is paid to the question of how the appropriate sensory-motor mapping could be generated for a real arm.

Reeke and Edelman discuss an automaton, Darwin III, similar to the crab, but which by selectional processes develops the ability to manipulate objects presented to it in its environment [Reeke and Edelman 1988]. The Darwin III simulation does not account for arm dynamics; however, Edelman suggests that the training paradigm is able to handle dynamic effects as well as the geometry of the problem [Edelman 1989]. We are attempting to implement a mechanical analogue of Darwin III, somewhat simplified, but which will experience the real dynamics of motion.

3.1   EXPERIMENTAL ARCHITECTURE AND HARDWARE

The mechanical arrangement of our manipulator is shown in Fig. 2. The two links have agonist/antagonist tendon-drive arrangement, with an actuator per tendon. There are strain gauges in-line with the tendons. A manipulator 'reach' is specified by six parameters: burst amplitude and period for each of the three phases, launch, brake, and lock.

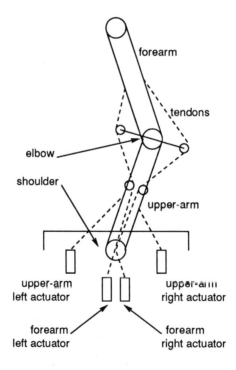

Figure 2: Manipulator Mechanical Configuration

At the end of the manipulator is an array of eleven pyroelectic-effect infrared detectors arranged in a U-shaped pattern. The *relative* location of a warm object presented to the arm is registered by the sensors, and is converted to eleven 8-bit integers. Since the sensor output is proportional to detected infrared energy flux, objects at the same temperature will give a more positive reading if they are close to the sensors than if they are further away. Also, a near object will register on adjacent sensors, not just on the one oriented towards it. Therefore, for a single, small object, a histogram of the eleven values will have a peak, and showing two things (Fig. 3): the sensor 'seeing' the most flux indicates the relative direction of the object, and the sharpness of the peak is proportional to the distance of the object.

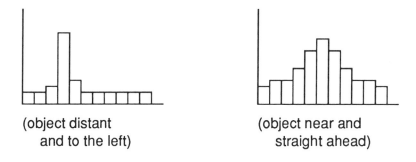

(object distant
and to the left)

(object near and
straight ahead)

Figure 3: Histograms for Distant Versus Near Objects

Modelled on Darwin III [Reeke and Edelman 1988], the architecture of the selectional perception-action coordinator is as in Fig. 4. The boxes represent repertoires of appropriately interconnected groups of 'neurons'.

Darwin III responds mainly to contour in a two-dimensional world, analogous to the recognition of histogram shape in our system. Where Darwin III's 'unique response' network is sensitive to line segment lengths and orientations, ours is sensitive to the length of subsequences in the array of sensor output values in which values increase or decrease by the same amount, and the amounts by which they change; similarly, where Darwin III's 'generic response' network is sensitive to presence of or *changes* in orientation of lines, ours responds to the presence of the subsequences mentioned above, and the positions in the array where two subsequences abut.

The recognition repertoires are reciprocally connected, and both connect to the motor repertoire which consists of ballistic-movement 6-tuples. The system considers 'touching perceived object' to be adaptive, so when recognition activity correlates with a given 6-tuple, amplification ensures that the same response will be favoured in future.

4   WORK TO DATE

As the sensing system is not yet functional, this aspect of the system is currently simulated in an IBM PC/AT. The rest of the electrical and mechanical hardware is in place. The major difficulty currently faced is that the selectional system will become computationally intensive on a serial machine.

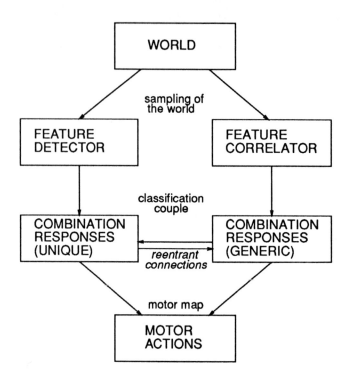

Figure 4: Experimental Architecture

For each possible ballistic 'reach', there must be a representation for the 'reach 6-tuple'. Therefore, the motor repertoire must become large as the dexterity of the manipulator is increased. Similarly, as the array of sensors is extended (resolution increased, or field of view widened), the classification repertoires must also grow. On a serial machine, polling the groups in the repertoires must be done one at a time, introducing a substantial delay between the registration of object and the actual touch, precluding the interception by the manipulator of fast moving objects. We are exploring possibilities for parallelizing the selectional process (and have for this reason constructed a network of processing elements), with the expectation that this will lead us closer to fast, dynamic manipulation, at minimal computational expense.

References

Russell L. Andersson. *A Robot Ping-Pong Player: Experiment in Real-Time Intelligent Control.* MIT Press, Cambridge, MA, 1988.

Valentino Braitenberg. "Some types of movement", in C.G. Langton, ed., *Artificial Life*, pp. 555–565, Addison-Wesley, 1989.

Paul M. Churchland. "Some reductive strategies in cognitive neurobiology". Mind, **95**:279-309, 1986.

Jim Donnett and Tim Smithers. "Behaviour-based control of a two-link ballistic arm". Dept. of Artificial Intelligence, University of Edinburgh, Research Paper *RP 458*, 1990.

Gerald M. Edelman. "Group selection and phasic reentrant signalling: a theory of higher brain function", in G.M. Edelman and V.B. Mountcastle, eds., *The Mindful Brain*, pp. 51–100, MIT Press, Cambridge, MA, 1978.

Gerald M. Edelman. "Group selection as the basis for higher brain function", in F.O. Schmitt et al., eds., *Organization of the Cerebral Cortex*, pp. 535–563, MIT Press, Cambridge, MA, 1981.

Gerald M. Edelman. *Neural Darwinism: The Theory of Neuronal Group Selection.* Basic Books, New York, 1987.

Gerald M. Edelman. Personal correspondence, 1989.

Blake Hannaford and Lawrence Stark. "Roles of the elements of the triphasic control signal". Experimental Neurology, **90**:619–634, 1985.

M.J. Nahvi and M.R. Hashemi. "A synthetic motor control system; possible parallels with transformations in cerebellar cortex", in J.R. Bloedel et al., eds., *Cerebellar Functions*, pp. 67–69, Springer-Verlag, 1984.

George N. Reeke Jr. and Gerald M. Edelman. "Real brains and artificial intelligence", in Stephen R. Graubard, ed., *The Artificial Intelligence Debate*, pp. 143–173, The MIT Press, Cambridge, MA, 1988.

W.J. Wadman, J.J. Denier van der Gon, R.H. Geuse, and C.R. Mol. "Control of fast goal-directed arm movements". Journal of Human Movement Studies, **5**:3–17, 1979.

Using Local Models to Control Movement

Christopher G. Atkeson
Department of Brain and Cognitive Sciences
and the Artificial Intelligence Laboratory
Massachusetts Institute of Technology
NE43-771, 545 Technology Square
Cambridge, MA 02139
cga@ai.mit.edu

ABSTRACT

This paper explores the use of a model neural network for motor learning. Steinbuch and Taylor presented neural network designs to do nearest neighbor lookup in the early 1960s. In this paper their nearest neighbor network is augmented with a local model network, which fits a local model to a set of nearest neighbors. The network design is equivalent to local regression. This network architecture can represent smooth nonlinear functions, yet has simple training rules with a single global optimum. The network has been used for motor learning of a simulated arm and a simulated running machine.

1   INTRODUCTION

A common problem in motor learning is approximating a continuous function from samples of the function's inputs and outputs. This paper explores a neural network architecture that simply remembers experiences (samples) and builds a local model to answer any particular query (an input for which the function's output is desired). This network design can represent smooth nonlinear functions, yet has simple training rules with a single global optimum for building a local model in response to a query. Our approach is to model complex continuous functions using simple local models. This approach avoids the difficult problem of finding an appropriate structure for a global model. A key idea is to form a training set for the local model network after a query to be answered is known. This approach allows us to include in the training set only relevant experiences (nearby samples). The local model network, which may be a simple network architecture such as a perceptron, forms a model of the portion of the function near the query point. This local model is then used to predict the output of the function, given the input. The local model network is retrained with a new training set to answer the next query. This approach minimizes interference between old and new data, and allows the range of generalization to depend on the density of the samples.

Steinbuch (Steinbuch 1961, Steinbuch and Piske 1963) and Taylor (Taylor 1959, Taylor 1960) independently proposed neural network designs that used a local representation to do nearest neighbor lookup and pointed out that this approach could be used for control. They used a layer of hidden units to compute an inner product of each stored vector with the input vector. A winner-take-all circuit then selected the hidden unit with the highest activation. This type of network can find nearest neighbors or best matches using a Euclidean distance metric (Kazmierczak and Steinbuch 1963). In this paper their nearest neighbor lookup network (which I will refer to as the memory network) is augmented with a local model network, which fits a local model to a set of nearest neighbors.

The ideas behind the network design used in this paper have a long history. Approaches which represent previous experiences directly and use a similar experience or similar experiences to form a local model are often referred to as nearest neighbor or k-nearest neighbor approaches. Local models (often polynomials) have been used for many years to smooth time series (Sheppard 1912, Sherriff 1920, Whittaker and Robinson 1924, Macauley 1931) and interpolate and extrapolate from limited data. Lancaster and Šalkauskas (1986) refer to nearest neighbor approaches as "moving least squares" and survey their use in fitting surfaces to arbitrarily spaced points. Eubank (1988) surveys the use of nearest neighbor estimators in nonparametric regression. Farmer and Sidorowich (1988) survey the use of nearest neighbor and local model approaches in modeling chaotic dynamic systems.

Crain and Bhattacharyya (1967), Falconer (1971), and McLain (1974) suggested using a weighted regression to fit a local polynomial model at each point a function evaluation was desired. All of the available data points were used. Each data point was weighted by a function of its distance to the desired point in the regression. McIntyre, Pollard, and Smith (1968), Pelto, Elkins, and Boyd (1968), Legg and Brent (1969), Palmer (1969), Walters (1969), Lodwick and Whittle (1970), Stone (1975) and Franke and Nielson (1980) suggested fitting a polynomial surface to a set of nearest neighbors, also using distance weighted regression. Cleveland (1979) proposed using robust regression procedures to eliminate outlying or erroneous points in the regression process. A program implementing a refined version of this approach (LOESS) is available by sending electronic mail containing the single line, *send dloess from a*, to the address netlib@research.att.com (Grosse 1989). Cleveland, Devlin and Grosse (1988) analyze the statistical properties of the LOESS algorithm and Cleveland and Devlin (1988) show examples of its use. Stone (1977, 1982), Devroye (1981), Cheng (1984), Li (1984), Farwig (1987), and Müller (1987) provide analyses of nearest neighbor approaches. Franke (1982) compares the performance of nearest neighbor approaches with other methods for fitting surfaces to data.

2   THE NETWORK ARCHITECTURE

The memory network of Steinbuch and Taylor is used to find the nearest stored vectors to the current input vector. The memory network computes a measure of the distance between each stored vector and the input vector in parallel, and then a "winner take all" network selects the nearest vector (nearest neighbor). Euclidean distance has been chosen as the distance metric, because the Euclidean distance is invariant under rotation of the coordinates used to represent the input vector.

The memory network consists of three layers of units: input units, hidden or memory units, and output units. The squared Euclidean distance between the input vector ($\mathbf{i}$) and a weight vector ($\mathbf{w}_k$) for the connections of the input units to hidden unit k is given by:

$$d_k^2 = (\mathbf{i} - \mathbf{w}_k)^{\mathrm{T}}(\mathbf{i} - \mathbf{w}_k) = \mathbf{i}^{\mathrm{T}}\mathbf{i} - 2\mathbf{i}^{\mathrm{T}}\mathbf{w}_k + \mathbf{w}_k^{\mathrm{T}}\mathbf{w}_k$$

Since the quantity $\mathbf{i}^{\mathrm{T}}\mathbf{i}$ is the same for all hidden units, minimizing the distance between the input vector and the weight vector for each hidden unit is equivalent to maximizing:

$$\mathbf{i}^{\mathrm{T}}\mathbf{w}_k - 1/2\mathbf{w}_k^{\mathrm{T}}\mathbf{w}_k$$

This quantity is the inner product of the input vector and the weight vector for hidden unit k, biased by half the squared length of the weight vector.

Dynamics of the memory network neurons allow the memory network to output a sequence of nearest neighbors. These nearest neighbors form the selected training sequence for the local model network. Memory unit dynamics can be used to allocate "free" memory units to new experiences, and to forget old training points when the capacity of the memory network is fully utilized.

The local model network consists of only one layer of modifiable weights preceded by any number of layers with fixed connections. There may be arbitrary preprocessing of the inputs of the local model, but the local model is linear in the parameters used to form the fit. The local model network using the LMS training algorithm performs a linear regression of the transformed inputs against the desired outputs. Thus, the local model network can be used to fit a linear regression model to the selected training set. With multiplicative interactions between inputs the local model network can be used to fit a polynomial surface (such as a quadratic) to the selected training set. An alternative implementation of the local model network could use a single layer of "sigma-pi" units.

This network design has simple training rules. In the memory network the weights are simply the values of the components of input and output vectors, and the bias for each memory unit is just half the squared length of the corresponding input weight vector. No search for weights is necessary, since the weights are directly

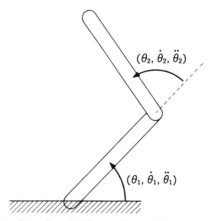

Figure 1: Simulated Planar Two-joint Arm

given by the data to be stored. The local model network is linear in the weights, leading to a single optimum which can be found by linear regression or gradient descent. Thus, convergence to the global optimum is guaranteed when forming a local model to answer a particular query.

This network architecture was simulated using k-d tree data structures (Friedman, Bentley, and Finkel 1977) on a standard serial computer and also using parallel search on a massively parallel computer, the Connection Machine (Hillis 1985). A special purpose computer is being built to implement this network in real time.

3 APPLICATIONS

The network has been used for motor learning of a simulated arm and a simulated running machine. The network performed surprisingly well in these simple evaluations. The simulated arm was able to follow a desired trajectory after only a few practice movements. Performance of the simulated running machine in following a series of desired velocities was also improved. This paper will report only on the arm trajectory learning.

Figure 1 shows the simulated 2-joint planar arm. The problem faced in this simulation is to learn the correct joint torques to drive the arm along the desired trajectory (the inverse dynamics problem). In addition to the feedforward control signal produced by the network described in this paper, a feedback controller was also used.

Figure 2 shows several learning curves for this problem. The first point in each of the curves shows the performance generated by the feedback controller alone. The error measure is the RMS torque error during the movement. The highest curve shows the performance of a nearest neighbor method without a local model. The nearest point was used to generate the torques for the feedforward command, which were then summed with the output from the feedback controller. The second

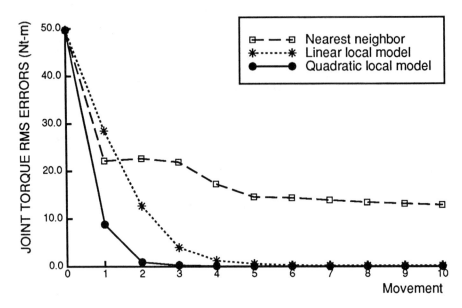

Figure 2: Learning curves from 3 different network designs on the two joint arm trajectory learning problem.

curve shows the performance using a linear local model. The third curve shows the performance using a quadratic local model. Adding the local model network greatly speeds up learning. The network with the quadratic local model learned more quickly than the one with the local linear model.

4   WHY DOES IT WORK?

In this learning paradigm the feedback controller serves as the teacher, or source of new data for the network. If the feedback controller is of poor quality, the nearest neighbor function approximation method tends to get "stuck" with a non-zero error level. The use of a local model seems to eliminate this stuck state, and reduce the dependence on the quality of the feedback controller.

Fast training is achieved by modularizing the network: the memory network does not need to search for weights in order to store the samples, and local models can be linear in the unknown parameters, leading to a single optimum which can be found by linear regression or gradient descent.

The combination of storing all the data and only using a certain number of nearby samples to form a local model minimizes interference between old and new data, and allows the range of generalization to depend on the density of the samples.

There are many issues left to explore. A disadvantage of this approach is the limited capacity of the memory network. In this version of the proposed neural network architecture, every experience is stored. Eventually all the memory units will be used up. To use memory units more sparingly, only the experiences which are sufficiently different from previous experiences could be stored. Memory requirements could also be reduced by "forgetting" certain experiences, perhaps those that have not been referenced for a long time, or a randomly selected experience. It is an empirical question as to how large a memory capacity is necessary for this network design to be useful.

How should the distance metric be chosen? So far distance metrics have been devised by hand. Better distance metrics may be based on the stored data and a particular query. How far will this approach take us? Experiments using more complex systems and actual physical implementations, with the inevitable noise and high order dynamics, need to be done.

Acknowledgments

B. Widrow and J. D. Cowan made the author aware of the work of Steinbuch and Taylor (Steinbuch and Widrow 1965, Cowan and Sharp 1988).

This paper describes research done at the Whitaker College, Department of Brain and Cognitive Sciences, Center for Biological Information Processing and the Artificial Intelligence Laboratory of the Massachusetts Institute of Technology. Support was provided under Office of Naval Research contract N00014-88-K-0321 and under Air Force Office of Scientific Research grant AFOSR-89-0500. Support for CGA was provided by a National Science Foundation Engineering Initiation Award and Presidential Young Investigator Award, an Alfred P. Sloan Research Fellowship, the W. M. Keck Foundation Assistant Professorship in Biomedical Engineering, and a Whitaker Health Sciences Fund MIT Faculty Research Grant.

References

Cheng, P.E. (1984), "Strong Consistency of Nearest Neighbor Regression Function Estimators", *Journal of Multivariate Analysis,* 15:63-72.

Cleveland, W.S. (1979), "Robust Locally Weighted Regression and Smoothing Scatterplots", *Journal of the American Statistical Association,* 74:829-836.

Cleveland, W.S. and S.J. Devlin (1988), "Locally Weighted Regression: An Approach to Regression Analysis by Local Fitting", *Journal of the American Statistical Association,* 83:596-610.

Cleveland, W.S., S.J. Devlin and E. Grosse (1988), "Regression by Local Fitting: Methods, Properties, and Computational Algorithms", *Journal of Econometrics,* 37:87-114.

Cowan, J.D. and D.H. Sharp (1988), "Neural Nets", *Quarterly Reviews of Biophysics,* 21(3):365-427.

Crain, I.K. and B.K. Bhattacharyya (1967), "Treatment of nonequispaced two dimensional data with a digital computer", *Geoexploration,* 5:173-194.

Devroye, L.P. (1981), "On the Almost Everywhere Convergence of Nonparametric Regression Function Estimates", The Annals of Statistics, 9(6):1310-1319.

Eubank, R.L. (1988), *Spline Smoothing and Nonparametric Regression,* Marcel Dekker, New York, pp. 384-387.

Falconer, K.J. (1971), "A general purpose algorithm for contouring over scattered data points", Nat. Phys. Lab. Report NAC 6.

Farmer, J.D., and J.J. Sidorowich (1988), "Predicting Chaotic Dynamics", in *Dynamic Patterns in Complex Systems,* J.A.S. Kelso, A.J. Mandell, and M.F. Shlesinger, (eds.), World Scientific, New Jersey, pp. 265-292.

Farwig, R. (1987), "Multivariate Interpolation of Scattered Data by Moving Least Squares Methods", in J.C. Mason and M.G. Cox (eds), *Algorithms for Approximation,* Clarendon Press, Oxford, pp. 193-211.

Franke, R. (1982), "Scattered Data Interpolation: Tests of Some Methods", *Mathematics of Computation,* 38(157):181-200.

Franke, R. and G. Nielson (1980), "Smooth Interpolation of Large Sets of Scattered Data", *International Journal Numerical Methods Engineering,* 15:1691-1704.

Friedman, J.H., J.L. Bentley, and R.A. Finkel (1977), "An Algorithm for Finding Best Matches in Logarithmic Expected Time", *ACM Trans. on Mathematical Software,* 3(3):209-226.

Grosse, E. (1989), "LOESS: Multivariate Smoothing by Moving Least Squares", in C.K. Chui, L.L. Schumaker, and J.D. Ward (eds.), *Approximation Theory VI,* Academic Press, Boston, pp. 1-4.

Hillis, D. (1985), *The Connection Machine,* MIT Press, Cambridge, Mass.

Kazmierczak, H. and K. Steinbuch (1963), "Adaptive Systems in Pattern Recognition", *IEEE Transactions on Electronic Computers,* EC-12:822-835.

Lancaster, P. and K. Šalkauskas (1986), *Curve And Surface Fitting,* Academic Press, New York.

Legg, M.P.C. and R.P. Brent (1969), "Automatic Contouring", *Proc. 4th Australian Computer Conference,* 467-468.

Li, K.C. (1984), "Consistency for Cross-Validated Nearest Neighbor Estimates in Nonparametric Regression", *The Annals of Statistics,* 12:230-240.

Lodwick, G.D., and J. Whittle (1970), "A technique for automatic contouring field survey data", *Australian Computer Journal,* 2:104-109.

Macauley, F.R. (1931), *The Smoothing of Time Series,* National Bureau of Economic Research, New York.

McIntyre, D.B., D.D. Pollard, and R. Smith (1968), "Computer Programs For Automatic Contouring", *Kansas Geological Survey Computer Contributions 23,*

University of Kansas, Lawrence, Kansas.

McLain, D.H. (1974), "Drawing Contours From Arbitrary Data Points", *The Computer Journal,* 17(4):318-324.

Müller, H.G. (1987), "Weighted Local Regression and Kernel Methods for Nonparametric Curve Fitting", *Journal of the American Statistical Association,* 82:231-238.

Palmer, J.A.B. (1969), "Automated mapping", *Proc. 4th Australian Computer Conference,* 463-466.

Pelto, C.R., T.A. Elkins, and H.A. Boyd (1968), "Automatic contouring of irregularly spaced data", *Geophysics,* 33:424-430.

Sheppard, W.F. (1912), "Reduction of Errors by Means of Negligible Differences", *Proceedings of the Fifth International Congress of Mathematicians,* E. W. Hobson and A. E. H. Love (eds), Cambridge University Press, II:348-384.

Sherriff, C.W.M. (1920), "On a Class of Graduation Formulae", *Proceedings of the Royal Society of Edinburgh,* XL:112-128.

Steinbuch, K. (1961), "Die lernmatrix", *Kybernetik,* 1:36-45.

Steinbuch, K. and U.A.W. Piske (1963), "Learning Matrices and Their Applications", *IEEE Transactions on Electronic Computers,* EC-12:846-862.

Steinbuch, K. and B. Widrow (1965), "A Critical Comparison of Two Kinds of Adaptive Classification Networks", *IEEE Transactions on Electronic Computers,* EC-14:737-740.

Stone, C.J. (1975), "Nearest Neighbor Estimators of a Nonlinear Regression Function", *Proc. of Computer Science and Statistics: 8th Annual Symposium on the Interface,* pp. 413-418.

Stone, C.J. (1977), "Consistent Nonparametric Regression", *The Annals of Statistics,* 5:595-645.

Stone, C.J. (1982), "Optimal Global Rates of Convergence for Nonparametric Regression", *The Annals of Statistics,* 10(4):1040-1053.

Taylor, W.K. (1959), "Pattern Recognition By Means Of Automatic Analogue Apparatus", *Proceedings of The Institution of Electrical Engineers,* 106B:198-209.

Taylor, W.K. (1960), "A parallel analogue reading machine", *Control,* 3:95-99.

Taylor, W.K. (1964), "Cortico-thalamic organization and memory", *Proc. Royal Society B,* 159:466-478.

Walters, R.F. (1969), "Contouring by Machine: A User's Guide", *American Association of Petroleum Geologists Bulletin,* 53(11):2324-2340.

Whittaker, E., and G. Robinson (1924), *The Calculus of Observations,* Blackie & Son, London.

Learning to Control an Unstable System with Forward Modeling

Michael I. Jordan
Brain and Cognitive Sciences
MIT
Cambridge, MA 02139

Robert A. Jacobs
Computer and Information Sciences
University of Massachusetts
Amherst, MA 01003

ABSTRACT

The forward modeling approach is a methodology for learning control when data is available in distal coordinate systems. We extend previous work by considering how this methodology can be applied to the optimization of quantities that are distal not only in space but also in time.

In many learning control problems, the output variables of the controller are not the natural coordinates in which to specify tasks and evaluate performance. Tasks are generally more naturally specified in "distal" coordinate systems (e.g., endpoint coordinates for manipulator motion) than in the "proximal" coordinate system of the controller (e.g., joint angles or torques). Furthermore, the relationship between proximal coordinates and distal coordinates is often not known a priori and, if known, not easily inverted.

The forward modeling approach is a methodology for learning control when training data is available in distal coordinate systems. A *forward model* is a network that learns the transformation from proximal to distal coordinates so that distal specifications can be used in training the controller (Jordan & Rumelhart, 1990). The forward model can often be learned separately from the controller because it depends only on the dynamics of the controlled system and not on the closed-loop dynamics.

In previous work, we studied forward models of kinematic transformations (Jordan, 1988, 1990) and state transitions (Jordan & Rumelhart, 1990). In the current paper, we go beyond the spatial credit assignment problems studied in those papers and broaden the application of forward modeling to include cases of temporal credit assignment (cf. Barto, Sutton, & Anderson, 1983; Werbos, 1987). As discussed below, the function to be modeled in such cases depends on a time integral of the closed-loop dynamics. This fact has two important implications. First, the data needed for learning the forward model can no longer be obtained solely by observing the instantaneous state or output of the plant. Second, the forward model is no longer independent of the controller: If the parameters of the controller are changed by a learning algorithm, then the closed-loop dynamics change and so does the mapping from proximal to distal variables. Thus the learning of the forward model and the learning of the controller can no longer be separated into different phases.

1 FORWARD MODELING

In this section we briefly summarize our previous work on forward modeling (see also Nguyen & Widrow, 1989 and Werbos, 1987).

1.1 LEARNING A FORWARD MODEL

Given a fixed control law, the learning of a forward model is a system identification problem. Let $\mathbf{z} = g(\mathbf{s}, \mathbf{u})$ be a system to be modeled, where $\mathbf{z}$ is the output or the state-derivative, $\mathbf{s}$ is the state, and $\mathbf{u}$ is the control. We require the forward model to minimize the cost functional

$$J_m = \frac{1}{2} \int (\mathbf{z} - \hat{\mathbf{z}})^T (\mathbf{z} - \hat{\mathbf{z}}) dt. \tag{1}$$

where $\hat{\mathbf{z}} = \hat{g}(\mathbf{s}, \mathbf{u}, \mathbf{v})$ is the parameterized function computed by the model. Once the minimum is found, backpropagation through the model provides an estimate $\frac{\partial \hat{\mathbf{z}}}{\partial \mathbf{u}}$ of the system Jacobian matrix $\frac{\partial \mathbf{z}}{\partial \mathbf{u}}$ (cf. Jordan, 1988).

1.2 LEARNING A CONTROLLER

Once the forward model is sufficiently accurate, it can be used in the training of the controller. Backpropagation through the model provides derivatives that indicate how to change the outputs of the controller. These derivatives can be used to change the parameters of the controller by a further application of backpropagation. Figure 1 illustrates the general procedure.

This procedure minimizes the "distal" cost functional

$$J = \frac{1}{2} \int (\mathbf{z}^* - \mathbf{z})^T (\mathbf{z}^* - \mathbf{z}) dt, \tag{2}$$

where $\mathbf{z}^*$ is a reference signal. To see this, let the controller output be given as a function $\mathbf{u} = \mathbf{f}(\mathbf{s}, \mathbf{z}^*, \mathbf{w})$ of the state $\mathbf{s}^*$, the reference signal $\mathbf{z}^*$, and a parameter vector $\mathbf{w}$. Differentiating J with respect to $\mathbf{w}$ yields

$$\nabla_{\mathbf{w}} J = - \int \frac{\partial \mathbf{u}}{\partial \mathbf{w}}^T \frac{\partial \mathbf{z}}{\partial \mathbf{u}}^T (\mathbf{z}^* - \mathbf{z}) dt. \tag{3}$$

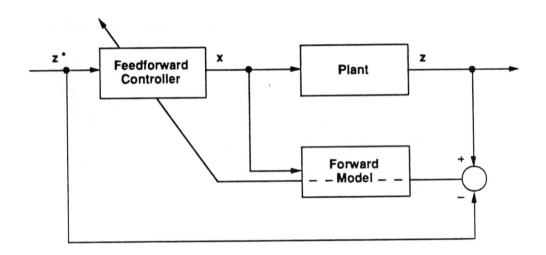

Figure 1: Learning a Controller. The Dashed Line Represents Backpropagation.

The Jacobian matrix $\frac{\partial \mathbf{z}}{\partial \mathbf{u}}$ cannot be assumed to be available a priori, but can be estimated by backpropagation through the forward model. Thus the error signal available for learning the controller is the estimated gradient

$$\hat{\nabla}_{\mathbf{w}} J = - \int \frac{\partial \mathbf{u}}{\partial \mathbf{w}}^T \frac{\hat{\delta} \mathbf{z}}{\partial \mathbf{u}}^T (\mathbf{z}^* - \mathbf{z}) dt. \tag{4}$$

We now consider a task in which the foregoing framework must be broadened to allow a more general form of distal task specification.

2   THE TASK

The task is to learn to regulate an unstable nonminimum-phase plant. We have chosen the oft-studied (e.g., Barto, Sutton, & Anderson, 1983; Widrow & Smith, 1964) problem of learning to balance an inverted pendulum on a moving cart. The plant dynamics are given by:

$$\begin{bmatrix} M + m & mlcos\theta \\ mlcos\theta & I \end{bmatrix} \begin{bmatrix} \ddot{x} \\ \ddot{\theta} \end{bmatrix} + \begin{bmatrix} -mlsin\theta \\ -mglsin\theta \end{bmatrix} \dot{\theta}^2 = \begin{bmatrix} F \\ 0 \end{bmatrix}$$

where m is the mass of the pole, M is the mass of the cart, l is half the pole length, I is the inertia of the pole around its base, and F is the force applied to the cart.

The task we studied is similar to that studied by Barto, Sutton, & Anderson (1983). A state-feedback controller provides forces to the cart, and the system evolves until failure occurs (the cart reaches the end of the track or the pole reaches a critical angle). The system learns from failure; indeed, it is assumed that the *only* teaching information provided by the environment is the signal that failure has occurred.

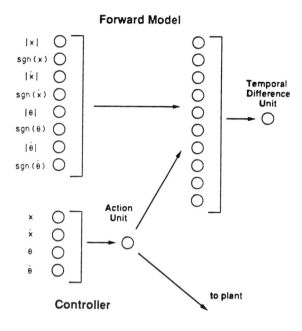

Figure 2: The Network Architecture

There are several differences between our task and that studied by Barto, Sutton, &
Anderson (1983). First, disturbances (white noise) are provided by the environment
rather than by the learning algorithm. This implies that in our experiments the
level of noise seen by the controller does not diminish to zero over the course of
learning. Second, we used real-valued forces rather than binary forces. Finally, we
do not assume the existence of a "reset button" that reinitializes the system to the
origin of state space; upon failure the system is restarted in a random configuration.

3   OUR APPROACH

In our approach, the control system learns a model that relates the current state of
the plant and the current control signal to a prediction of future failure. We make
use of a temporal difference algorithm (Sutton, 1988) to learn the transformation
from (state, action) pairs to an estimate of the inverse of the time until failure.
This mapping is then used as a differentiable forward model in the learning of the
controller—the controller is changed so as to minimize the output of the model and
thereby maximize the time until failure.

The overall system architecture is shown in Figure 2. We describe each component
in detail in the following sections.

An important feature that distinguishes this architecture from previous work (e.g.,

Barto, Sutton, & Anderson, 1983) is the path from the action unit into the forward model. This path is necessary for supervised learning algorithms to be used (see also Werbos, 1987).

3.1   LEARNING THE FORWARD MODEL

Temporal difference algorithms learn to make long term predictions by achieving local consistency between predictions at neighboring time steps, and by grounding the chain of predictions when information from the environment is obtained. In our case, if $z(t)$ is the inverse of the time until failure, then consistency is defined by the requirement that $z^{-1}(t) = z^{-1}(t+1) + 1$. The chain is grounded by defining $z(T) = 1$, where T is the time step on which failure occurs.

To learn to estimate the inverse of the time until failure, the following temporal difference error terms are used. For time steps on which failure does not occur,

$$e(t) = \frac{1}{1 + \hat{z}^{-1}(t+1)} - \hat{z}(t),$$

where $\hat{z}(t)$ denotes the output of the forward model. When failure occurs, the target for the forward model is set to unity:

$$e(t) = 1 - \hat{z}(t)$$

The error signal $e(t)$ is propagated backwards at time $t + 1$ using activations saved from time t. Standard backpropagation is used to compute the changes to the weights.

3.2   LEARNING THE CONTROLLER

If the controller is performing as desired, then the output of the forward model is zero (that is, the predicted time-until-failure is infinity). This suggests that an appropriate distal error signal for the controller is zero minus the output of the forward model.

Given that the forward model has the control action as an input, the distal error can be propagated backward to the hidden units of the forward model, through the action unit, and into the controller where the weights are changed (see Figure 2).

Thus the controller is changed in such a way as to minimize the output of the forward model and thereby maximize the time until failure.

3.3   LEARNING THE FORWARD MODEL AND THE CONTROLLER SIMULTANEOUSLY

As the controller varies, the mapping that the forward model must learn also varies. Thus, if the forward model is to provide reasonable derivatives, it must be continuously updated as the controller changes. We find that it is possible to train the forward model and the controller simultaneously, provided that we use a larger learning rate for the forward model than for the controller.

4   MISCELLANY

4.1   RESET

Although previous studies have assumed the existence of a "reset button" that can restart the system at the origin of state space, we prefer not to make such an assumption. A reset button implies the existence of a controller that can stabilize the system, and the task of learning is to *find* such a controller. In our simulations, we restart the system at random points in state space after failure occurs.

4.2   REDUNDANCY

The mapping learned by the forward model depends on both the state and the action. The action, however, is itself a function of the state, so the action unit provides redundant information. This implies that the forward model could have arbitrary weights in the path from the action unit and yet make reasonable predictions. Such a model, however, would yield meaningless derivatives for learning the controller. Fortunately, backpropagation tends to produce meaningful weights for a path that is correlated with the outcome, even if that path conveys redundant information. To further bias things in our favor, we found it useful to employ a larger learning rate in the path from the action unit to the hidden units of the forward model (0.9) than in the path from the state units (0.3).

4.3   REPRESENTATION

As seen in Figure 2, we chose input representations that take advantage of symmetries in the dynamics of the cart-pole system. The forward model has even symmetry with respect to the state variables, whereas the controller has odd symmetry.

4.4   LONG-TERM BEHAVIOR

There is never a need to "turn off" the learning of the forward model. Once the pole is being successfully balanced in the presence of fluctuations, the average time until failure goes to infinity. The forward model therefore learns to predict zero in the region of state space around the origin, and the error propagated to the controller also goes to zero.

5   RESULTS

We ran twenty simulations starting with random initial weights. The learning rate for the controller was 0.05 and the learning rate for the forward model was 0.3, except for the connection from the action unit where the learning rate was 0.9. Eighteen runs converged to controller configurations that balanced the pole, and two runs converged on local minima. Figure 3 shows representative learning curves for six of the successful runs.

To obtain some idea of the size of the space of correct solutions, we performed an exhaustive search of a lattice in a rectangular region of weight space that contained

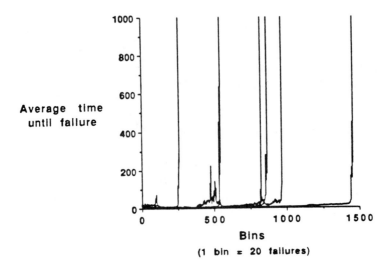

Figure 3: Learning Curves for Six Runs

all of the weight configurations found by our simulations. As shown in Figure 4, only 15 out of 10,000 weight configurations were able to balance the pole.

6   CONCLUSIONS

Previous work within the forward modeling paradigm focused on models of fixed kinematic or dynamic properties of the controlled plant (Jordan, 1988, 1990; Jordan & Rumelhart, 1990). In the current paper, the notion of a forward model is broader. The function that must be modeled depends not only on properties of the controlled plant, but also on properties of the controller. Nonetheless, the mapping is well-defined, and the results demonstrate that it can be used to provide appropriate incremental changes for the controller.

These results provide further demonstration of the applicability of supervised learning algorithms to learning control problems in which explicit target information is not available.

Acknowledgments

The first author was supported by BRSG 2 S07 RR07047-23 awarded by the Biomedical Research Support Grant Program, Division of Research Resources, National Institutes of Health and by a grant from Siemens Corporation. The second author was supported by the Air Force Office of Scientific Research, through grant AFOSR-87-0030.

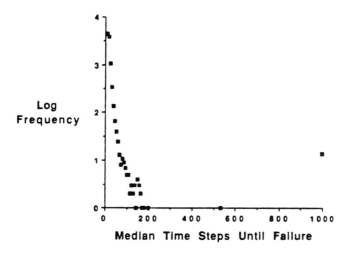

Figure 4: Performance of Population of Controllers

References

Barto, A. G., Sutton, R. S., & Anderson, C. W. (1983). Neuronlike adaptive elements that can solve difficult learning control problems. *IEEE Transactions on Systems, Man, and Cybernetics, SMC-13*, 834-846.

Jordan, M. I. (1988). *Supervised learning and systems with excess degress of freedom.* (COINS Tech. Rep. 88-27). Amherst, MA: University of Massachusetts, Computer and Information Sciences.

Jordan, M. I. (1990). Motor learning and the degrees of freedom problem. In M. Jeannerod, (Ed). *Attention and Performance, XIII.* Hillsdale, NJ: Erlbaum.

Jordan, M. I. & Rumelhart, D. E. (1990). *Supervised learning with a distal teacher.* Paper in preparation.

Nguyen, D. & Widrow, B. (1989). The truck backer-upper: An example of self-learning in neural networks. In: *Proceedings of the International Joint Conference on Neural Networks.* Piscataway, NJ: IEEE Press.

Sutton, R. S. (1987). Learning to predict by the methods of temporal differences. *Machine Learning, 3*, 9-44.

Werbos, P. (1987). Building and understanding adaptive systems: A statistical/numerical approach to factory automation and brain research. *IEEE Transactions on Systems, Man, and Cybernetics, 17*, 7-20.

Widrow, B. & Smith, F. W. (1964). Pattern-recognizing control systems. In: *Computer and Information Sciences Proceedings*, Washington, D.C.: Spartan.

A Self-organizing Associative Memory System for Control Applications

Michael Hormel
Department of Control Theory and Robotics
Technical University of Darmstadt
Schlossgraben 1
6100 Darmstadt/W.-Germany

ABSTRACT

The CMAC storage scheme has been used as a basis for a software implementation of an associative memory system AMS, which itself is a major part of the learning control loop LERNAS. A major disadvantage of this CMAC-concept is that the degree of local generalization (area of interpolation) is fixed. This paper deals with an algorithm for self-organizing variable generalization for the AMS, based on ideas of T. Kohonen.

1 INTRODUCTION

For several years research at the Department of Control Theory and Robotics at the Technical University of Darmstadt has been concerned with the design of a learning real-time control loop with neuron-like associative memories (LERNAS) for the control of unknown, nonlinear processes (Ersue, Tolle, 1988). This control concept uses an associative memory system AMS, based on the cerebellar cortex model CMAC by Albus (Albus, 1972), for the storage of a predictive nonlinear process model and an appropriate nonlinear control strategy (Fig. 1).

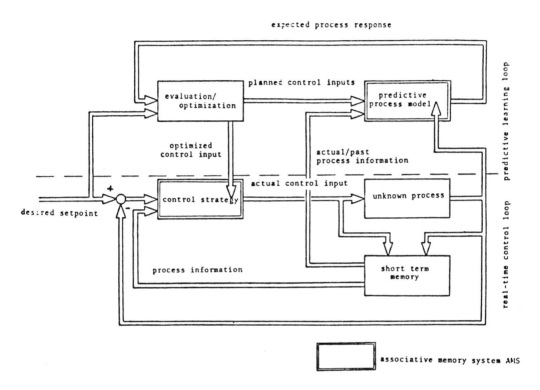

Figure 1: The learning control loop LERNAS

One problem for adjusting the control loop to a process is, however, to find a suitable set of parameters for the associative memory. The parameters in question determine the degree of generalization within the memory and therefore have a direct influence on the number of training steps required to learn the process behaviour. For a good performance of the control loop it is desirable to have a very small generalization around a given setpoint but to have a large generalization elsewhere. Actually, the amount of collected data is small during the transition phase between two setpoints but is large during setpoint control. Therefore a self-organizing variable generalization, adapting itself to the amount of available data would be very advantageous.

Up to now, when working with fixed generalization, finding the right parameters has meant to find the best compromise between performance and learning time required to generate a process model. This paper will show a possibility to introduce a self-organizing variable generalization capability into the existing AMS/CMAC algorithm.

2 THE AMS-CONCEPT

The associative memory system AMS is based on the "Cerebellar Model Articulation Controller CMAC" as presented by J.S. Albus. The information processing structure of AMS can be divided into three stages.

1.) Each component of a n-dimensional input vector (stimulus) activates a fixed number ρ of sensory cells, the receptive fields of which are overlapping. So $n \cdot \rho$ sensory cells become active.

2.) The active sensory cells are grouped to form ρ n-dimensional vectors. These vectors are mapped to ρ association cells. The merged receptive fields of the sensory cells described by one vector can be seen as a hypercube in the n-dimensional input space and therefore as the receptive field of the association cell. In normal applications the total number of available association cells is about $100 \cdot \rho$.

3.) The association cells are connected to the output cells by modifiable synaptic weights. The output cell computes the mean value of all weights that are connected to active association cells (active weights).

Figure 2 shows the basic principle of the associative memory system AMS.

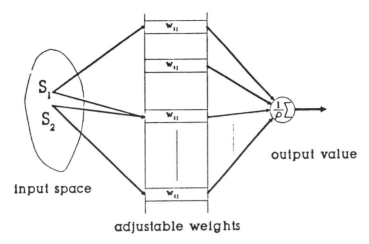

Figure 2: The basic mechanism of AMS

During training the generated output is compared with a desired output, the error is computed and equally distributed
over all active weights. For the mapping of sensory cells to
association cells a hash-coding mechanism is used.

3 THE SELF-ORGANIZING FEATURE MAP

An approach for explaining the self-organizing capabilities
of the nervous system has been presented by T. Kohonen (Kohonen, 1988).

In his "self-organizing feature map" a network of laterally
interconnected neurons can adapt itself according to the
density of trained points in the input space. Presenting a
n-dimensional input vector to the network causes every neuron to produce an output signal which is correlated with the
similarity between the input vector and a "template vector"
which may be stored in the synaptic weights of the neuron.
Due to the "mexican-hat" coupling function between the neurons, the one with the maximum output activity will excite
its nearest neighbours but will inhibit neurons farther a-
way, therefore generating a localized response in the network. The active cells can now adapt their input weights in
order to increase their similarity to the input vector. If
we define the receptive field of a neuron by the number of
input vectors for which the neurons activity is greater than

that of any other neuron in the net, this yields the effect that in areas with a high density of trained points the receptive fields become small whereas in areas with a low density of trained points the size of the receptive fields is large. As mentioned above this is a desired effect when working with a learning control loop.

4 SELF-ORGANIZING VARIABLE GENERALIZATION

Both of the approaches above have several advantages and disadvantages when using them for real-time control applications.

In the AMS algorithm one does not have to care for predefining a network and the coupling functions or coupling matrices among the elements of the network. Association and weight cells are generated when they are needed during training and can be adressed very quickly to produce a memory response. One of the disadvantages is the fixed generalization once the parameters of a memory unit have been chosen.

Unlike AMS, the feature map allows the adaption of the network according to the input data. This advantage has to be payed for by extensive search for the best matching neuron in the network and therefore the response time of the network may be too large for real-time control when working with big networks.

These problems can be overcome when allowing that the mapping of sensory cells to association cells in AMS is no longer fixed but can be changed during training.

To accomplish this a template vector $\underline{t}$ is introduced for every association cell. This vector $\underline{t}$ serves as an indicator for the stimuli by which the association cell has been accessed previously. During an associative recall for a stimulus $\underline{s}_0$ a preliminary set of ρ association cells is activated by the hash coding mechanism. Due to the self-organizing process during training the template vectors do not need to correspond to the input vector $\underline{s}_0$. For the search for the best matching cell the template vector $\underline{t}_0$ of the accessed association cell is compared to the stimulus and a difference vector is calculated.

$$\underline{\delta}_i = \underline{t}_i - \underline{s}_0 \qquad\qquad i = 0,\ldots,n_s \qquad\qquad (1)$$

n_s number of searching steps

This vector can now be used to compute a virtual stimulus which compensates the mapping errors of the hash-coding mechanism.

$$\underline{s}_{i+1} = \underline{s}_i - \underline{\delta}_i \qquad\qquad i = 0,\ldots,n_s \qquad\qquad (2)$$

The best matching cell is found for

$$j = \min_i \| \underline{\delta}_i \| \qquad\qquad i = 0,\ldots,n_s \qquad\qquad (3)$$

and can be adressed by the virtual stimulus $\underline{s}_j$ when using the hash coding mechanism. This search mechanism ensures that the best matching cell is found even if self organization is in effect.

During training the template vectors of the association cells are updated by

$$\underline{t}(k+1) = \alpha(k,d)\cdot(\underline{s}(k) - \underline{t}(k)) + \underline{t}(k) \qquad\qquad (4)$$

d   lateral distance of neurons in the network

where $\underline{t}(k)$ denotes the value of the template vector at time k and $\underline{s}(k)$ denotes the stimulus. $\alpha(k,d)$ is a monotonic decreasing function of time and the lateral distance between neurons in the network.

5 SIMULATION RESULTS

Figure 3 and 4 show some simulation results of the presented algorithm for the dase of a two dimensional stimulus vector.

Figure 3 shows the expected positions in input space of the untrained template vectors (x denotes untrained association cells).

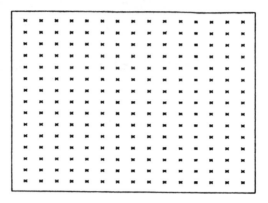

Figure 3: Untrained Network

Figure 4 shows the network after 2000 training steps with stimuli of gaussian distribution in input space. The position of the template vectors of trained cells has shifted into the direction of the better trained areas, so that more association cells are used to represent this area than before. Therefore the stored information will be more exact in this area.

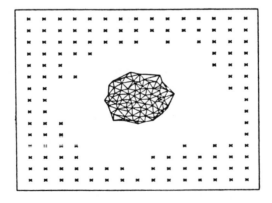

Figure 4: Network after 2000 training steps

6 CONCLUSION

The new algorithm presented above introduces the capability to adapt the storage mechanisms of a CMAC-type associative memory according to the arriving stimuli. This will result in various degrees of generalization depending on the number of trained points in a given area. It therefore will make it unnecessary to choose a generalization factor as a compromise between several constraints when representing nonlinear functions by storing them in this type of associative memory. Some results on tests will be presented together with a comparison on respective results for the original AMS.

Acknowledgements

This work was sponsored by the German Ministry for Research and Technology (BMFT) under grant no. ITR 8800 B/5

References

E. Ersue, H. Tolle. (1988) *Learning Control Structures with Neuron-Like Associative memories*. In: v. Seelen, Shaw, Leinhos (Eds.) Organization of Neural Networks, VCH Verlagsgesellschaft, Weinheim, FRG, 1988

J.S. Albus (1972) *Theoretical and experimental aspects of a cerebellar model*, PhD thesis, University of Maryland, USA

E. Ersue, X. Mao (1983) *Control of pH by Use of a Self-organizing Concept with Associative Memories*. ACI'83, Kopenhagen, Denmark

E. Ersue, J. Militzer (1984) *Real-time Implementation of an Associative Memory-based Learning Control Scheme for Nonlinear Multivariable Systems*. Symposium on "Applications of Multivariable System Techniques", Plymouth, UK

T. Kohonen. (1988) *Self-Organization and Associative Memory*, 2nd Ed., Springer Verlag

Operational Fault Tolerance
of CMAC Networks

Michael J. Carter   Franklin J. Rudolph   Adam J. Nucci
Intelligent Structures Group
Department of Electrical and Computer Engineering
University of New Hampshire
Durham, NH 03824-3591

ABSTRACT

The performance sensitivity of Albus' CMAC network was studied for the scenario in which faults are introduced into the adjustable weights after training has been accomplished. It was found that fault sensitivity was reduced with increased generalization when "loss of weight" faults were considered, but sensitivity was <u>increased</u> for "saturated weight" faults.

1   INTRODUCTION

Fault-tolerance is often cited as an inherent property of neural networks, and is thought by many to be a natural consequence of "massively parallel" computational architectures. Numerous anecdotal reports of fault-tolerance experiments, primarily in pattern classification tasks, abound in the literature. However, there has been surprisingly little rigorous investigation of the fault-tolerance properties of various network architectures in other application areas. In this paper we investigate the fault-tolerance of the CMAC (Cerebellar Model Arithmetic Computer) network [Albus 1975] in a systematic manner. CMAC networks have attracted much recent attention because of their successful application in robotic manipulator control [Ersu 1984, Miller 1986, Lane 1988]. Since fault-tolerance is a key concern in critical control tasks, there is added impetus to study this aspect of CMAC performance. In particular, we examined the effect on network performance of faults introduced into the adjustable weight layer after training has been accomplished in a fault-free environment. The degradation of approximation error due to faults was studied for the task of learning simple real functions of a single variable. The influence of receptive field width and total CMAC memory size on the fault sensitivity of the network was evaluated by means of simulation.

2   THE CMAC NETWORK ARCHITECTURE

The CMAC network shown in Figure 1 implements a form of distributed table lookup. It consists of two parts: 1) an address generator module, and 2) a layer of adjustable weights. The address generator is a fixed algorithmic transformation from the input space to the space of weight addresses. This transformation has two important properties: 1) Only a fixed number C of weights are activated in response to any particular input, and more importantly, only these weights are adjusted during training; 2) It is *locally generalizing,* in the sense that any two input points separated by Euclidean distance less than some threshold produce activated weight subsets that are close in Hamming distance, i.e. the two weight subsets have many weights in common. Input points that are separated by more than the threshold distance produce non-overlapping activated weight subsets. The first property gives rise to the extremely fast training times noted by all CMAC investigators. The number of weights activated by any input is referred to as the "generalization parameter", and is typically a small number ranging from 4 to 128 in practical applications [Miller 1986]. Only the activated weights are summed to form the response to the current input. A simple delta rule adjustment procedure is used to update the activated weights in response to the presentation of an input-desired output exemplar pair. Note that there is no adjustment of the address generator transformation during learning, and indeed, there are no "weights" available for adjustment in the address generator. It should also be noted that the hash-coded mapping is in general necessary because there are many more resolution cells in the input space than there are unique finite combinations of weights in the physical memory. As a result, the local generalization property will be disturbed because some distant inputs share common weight addresses in their activated weight subsets due to hashing collisions.

While the CMAC network readily lends itself to the task of learning and mimicking multidimensional nonlinear transformations, the investigation of network fault-tolerance in this setting is daunting! For reasons discussed in the next section, we opted to study CMAC fault-tolerance for simple one-dimensional input and output spaces without the use of the hash-coded mapping.

3   FAULT-TOLERANCE EXPERIMENTS

We distinguish between two types of fault-tolerance in neural networks [Carter 1988]: operational fault-tolerance and learning fault-tolerance. Operational fault-tolerance deals with the sensitivity of network performance to faults introduced after learning has been accomplished in a fault-free environment. Learning fault-tolerance refers to the sensitivity of network performance to faults (either permanent or transient) which are present during training. It should be noted that the term fault-tolerance as used here applies only to faults that represent perturbations in network parameters or topology, and does **not** refer to noisy or censored input data. Indeed, we believe that the latter usage is both inappropriate and inconsistent with conventional usage in the computer fault-tolerance community.

3.1   EXPERIMENT DESIGN PHILOSOPHY

Since the CMAC network is widely used for learning nonlinear functions (e.g. the motor drive voltage to joint angle transformation for a multiple degree-of-freedom robotic manipulator), the obvious measure of network performance is function approximation error. The sensitivity of approximation error to faults is the subject of this paper. There are several types of faults that are of concern in the CMAC architecture. Faults that occur in the address generator module may ultimately have the most severe impact on approximation error since the selection of incorrect weight addresses will likely produce a bad response. On the other hand, since the address generator is an algorithm rather than a true network of simple computational units, the fault-tolerance of any serial processor implementation of the algorithm will be difficult to study. For this reason we initially elected to study the fault sensitivity of the adjustable weight layer only.

The choice of fault types and fault placement strategies for neural network fault tolerance studies is not at all straightforward. Unlike classical fault-tolerance studies in digital systems which use "stuck-at-zero" and "stuck-at-one" faults, neural networks which use analog or mixed analog/digital implementations may suffer from a host of fault types. In order to make some progress, and to study the fault tolerance of the CMAC network at the <u>architectural</u> level rather than at the device level, we opted for a variation on the "stuck-at" fault model of digital systems. Since this study was concerned only with the adjustable weight layer, and since we assumed that weight storage is most likely to be digital (though this will certainly change as good analog memory technologies are developed), we considered two fault models which are admittedly severe. The first is a "loss of weight" fault which results in the selected weight being set to zero, while the second is a "saturated weight" fault which might correspond to the situation of a stuck-at-one fault in the most significant bit of a single weight register.

The question of fault placement is also problematic. In the absence of a specific circuit level implementation of the network, it is difficult to postulate a model for fault distribution. We adopted a somewhat perverse outlook in the hope of characterizing the network's fault tolerance under a worst-case fault placement strategy. The insight gained will still prove to be valuable in more benign fault placement tests (e.g. random fault placement), and in addition, if one can devise network modifications which yield good fault-tolerance in this extreme case, there is hope of still better performance in more typical instances of circuit failure. When placing "loss of weight" faults, we attacked large magnitude weight locations first, and continued to add more such faults to locations ranked in descending order of weight magnitude. Likewise, when placing saturated weight faults we attacked small magnitude weight locations first, and successive faults were placed in locations ordered by ascending weight magnitude. Since the activated weights are simply summed to form a response in CMAC, faults of both types create an error in the response which is equal to the weight change in the faulted location. Hence, our strategy was designed to produce the maximum output error for a given number of faults. In placing faults of either type, however, we did not place two faults within a single activated weight subset. Our strategy was thus not an absolute worst-case strategy, but was still more stressful than a purely random fault placement strategy. Finally, we did not mix fault types in any single experiment.

The fault tolerance experiments presented in the next section all had the same general structure. The network under study was trained to reproduce (to a specified level of approximation error) a real function of a single variable, $y=f(x)$, based upon presentation of (x,y) exemplar pairs. Faults of the types described previously were then introduced, and the resulting degradation in approximation error was logged versus the number of faults. Many such experiments were conducted with varying CMAC memory size and generalization parameter while learning the same exemplar function. We considered smoothly varying functions (sinusoids of varying spatial frequency) and discontinuous functions (step functions) on a bounded interval.

3.2   EXPERIMENT RESULTS AND DISCUSSION

In this section we present the results of experiments in which the function to be learned is held fixed, while the generalization parameter of the CMAC network to be tested is varied. The total number of weights (also referred to here as memory locations) is the same in each batch of experiments. Memory sizes of 50, 250, and 1000 were investigated, but only the results for the case N=250 are presented here. They exemplify the trends observed for all memory sizes.

Figure 2 shows the dependence of RMS (root mean square) approximation error on the number of loss-of-weight faults injected for generalization parameter values C=4, 8, 16. The task was that of reproducing a single cycle of a sinusoidal function on the input interval. Note that approximation error was diminished with increasing generalization at any fault severity level. For saturated weight faults, however, approximation error increased with increasing generalization! The reason for this contrasting behavior becomes clear upon examination of Figure 3. Observe also in Figure 2 that the increase in RMS error due to the introduction of a single fault can be as much as an order of magnitude. This is somewhat deceptive since the scale of the error is rather small (typically 10^{-3} or so), and so it may not seem of great consequence. However, as one may note in Figure 3, the effect of a single fault is highly localized, so RMS approximation error may be a poor choice of performance measure in selected applications. In particular, saturated weight faults in nominally small weight magnitude locations create a large relative response error, and this may be devastating in real-time control applications. Loss-of-weight faults are more benign, and their impact may be diluted by increasing generalization. The penalty for doing so, however, is increased sensitivity to saturated weight faults because larger regions of the network mapping are affected by a single fault.

Figure 4 displays some of the results of fault-tolerance tests with a discontinuous exemplar function. Note the large variation in stored weight values necessary to reproduce the step function. When a large magnitude weight needed to form the step transition was faulted, the result was a double step (Figure 4(b)) or a shifted transition point (Figure 4(c)). The extent of the fault impact was diminished with <u>decreasing</u> generalization. Since pattern classification tasks are equivalent to learning a discontinuous function over the input feature space, this finding suggests that improved fault-tolerance in such tasks might be obtained by reducing the generalization parameter C. This would limit the shifting of pattern class boundaries in the presence of weight faults. Preliminary experiments, however, also showed that learning of discontinuous exemplar functions proceeded much more slowly with small values of the generalization parameter.

4   CONCLUSIONS AND OPEN QUESTIONS

The CMAC network is well-suited to applications that demand fast learning of unknown multidimensional, static mappings (such as those arising in nonlinear control and signal processing systems). The results of the preliminary investigations reported here suggest that the fault-tolerance of conventional CMAC networks may not be as great as one might hope on the basis of anecdotal evidence in the prior literature with other network architectures. Network fault sensitivity does not seem to be uniform, and the location of particularly sensitive weights is very much dependent on the exemplar function to be learned. Furthermore, the obvious fault-tolerance enhancement technique of increasing generalization (i.e. distributing the response computation over more weight locations) has the undesirable effect of **increasing** sensitivity to saturated weight faults. While the local generalization feature of CMAC has the desirable attribute of limiting the region of fault impact, it suggests that global approximation error measures may be misleading. A low value of RMS error degradation may in fact mask a much more severe response error over a small region of the mapping. Finally, one must be cautious in making assessments of the fault-tolerance of a fixed network on the basis of tests using a single mapping. Discontinuous exemplar functions produce stored weight distributions which are much more fault-sensitive than those associated with smoothly varying functions, and such functions are clearly of interest in pattern classification.

Many important open questions remain concerning the fault-tolerance properties of the CMAC network. The effect of faults on the address generator module has yet to be determined. Collisions in the hash-coded mapping effectively propagate weight faults to remote regions of the input space, and the impact of this phenomenon on overall fault-tolerance has not been assessed. Much more work is needed on the role that exemplar function smoothness plays in determining the fault-tolerance of a fixed topology network.

Acknowledgements

The authors would like to thank Tom Miller, Fil Glanz, Gordon Kraft, and Edgar An for many helpful discussions on the CMAC network architecture. This work was supported in part by an Analog Devices Career Development Professorship and by a General Electric Foundation Young Faculty Grant awarded to M.J. Carter.

References

J.S. Albus. (1975) "A new approach to manipulator control: the Cerebellar Model Articulation Controller (CMAC)," *Trans. ASME- J. Dynamic Syst., Meas., Contr. 97* ; 220-227.

M.J. Carter. (1988) "The illusion of fault-tolerance in neural networks for pattern recognition and signal processing," *Proc. Technical Session on Fault-Tolerant Integrated Systems*, Durham, NH: University of New Hampshire.

E. Ersu and J. Militzer. (1984) "Real-time implementation of an associative memory-based learning control scheme for non-linear multivariable processes," *Proc. 1st Measurement and Control Symposium on Applications of Multivariable Systems Techniques;* 109-119.

S. Lane, D. Handelman, and J. Gelfand. (1988) "A neural network computational map approach to reflexive motor control," *Proc. IEEE Intelligent Control Conf.*, Arlington, VA.

W.T. Miller. (1986) "A nonlinear learning controller for robotic manipulators," *Proc. SPIE: Intelligent Robots and Computer Vision* **726**; 416-423.

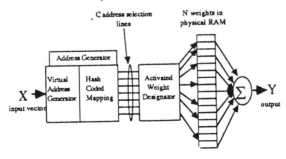

Figure 1: CMAC Network Architecture

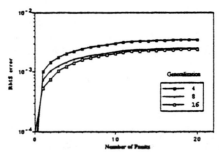

Figure 2: Sinusoid Approximation Error vs. Number of "Loss-of-Weight" Faults

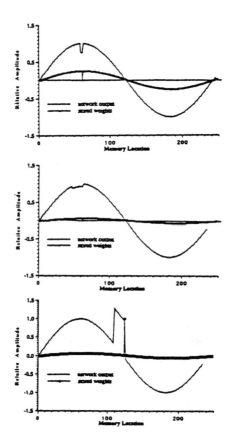

Figure 3: Network Response and Stored Weight Values. a) single lost weight, generalization C=4; b) single lost weight, C=16; c) single saturated weight, C=16.

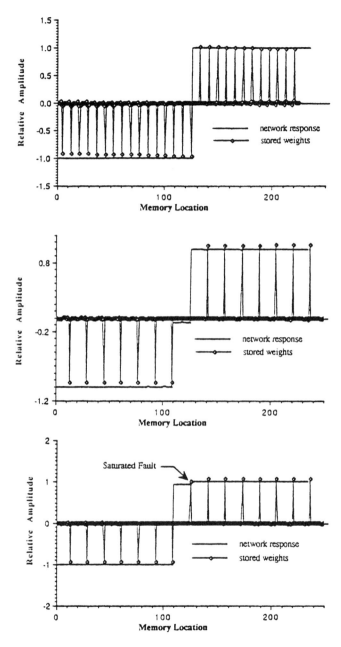

Figure 4: Network Response and Stored Weight Values. a) no faults, transition at location 125, C=8; b) single lost weight, C=16; c) single saturated weight, C=16.

Neural Network Weight Matrix Synthesis Using Optimal Control Techniques

O. Farotimi   A. Dembo   T. Kailath
               Information Systems Lab.
               Electrical Engineering Dept.
               Stanford University,
               Stanford, CA 94305

ABSTRACT

Given a set of input-output training samples, we describe a procedure for determining the time sequence of weights for a dynamic
neural network to model an arbitrary input-output process. We
formulate the input-output mapping problem as an optimal control problem, defining a performance index to be minimized as a
function of time-varying weights. We solve the resulting nonlinear two-point-boundary-value problem, and this yields the training
rule. For the performance index chosen, this rule turns out to be a
continuous time generalization of the outer product rule earlier suggested heuristically by Hopfield for designing associative memories.
Learning curves for the new technique are presented.

1 INTRODUCTION

Suppose that we desire to model as best as possible some unknown map $\phi : \mathcal{U} \to \mathcal{V}$, where $\mathcal{U}, \mathcal{V} \subseteq \mathcal{R}^n$. One way we might go about doing this is to collect as many input-output samples $\{(\theta_{in}, \theta_{out}) : \phi(\theta_{in}) = \theta_{out}\}$ as possible and "find" some function f . $\mathcal{U} \to \mathcal{V}$ such that a suitable distance metric $d(f(x(t)), \phi(x(t)))|_{x \in \{\theta_{in} : \phi(\theta_{in}) = \theta_{out}\}}$ is minimized.

In the foregoing, we assume a system of ordinary differential equations motivated by dynamic neural network structures[1] [2]. In particular we set up an n-dimensional neural network; call it $\mathcal{N}$. Our goal is to synthesize a possibly time varying weight matrix for $\mathcal{N}$ such that for initial conditions $x(t_0)$, the input-output transformation, or flow $f : x(t_0) \rightarrow f(x(t_f))$ associated with $\mathcal{N}$ approximates closely the desired map ϕ.

For the purposes of synthesizing the weight program for $\mathcal{N}$, we consider another system, say $\mathcal{S}$, a formal nL-dimensional system of differential equations comprising L n-dimensional subsystems. With the exception that all L n-dimensional subsystems are *constrained to have the same weight matrix*, they are otherwise identical and decoupled. We shall use this system to determine the optimal weight program given L input-output samples. The resulting time program of weights is then applied to the original n-dimensional system $\mathcal{N}$ during normal operation. We emphasize the difference between this scheme and a simple L-fold replication of $\mathcal{N}$: the latter will yield a practically unwieldy $nL \times nL$ weight matrix sequence, and in fact will generally not discover the underlying map from $\mathcal{U}$ to $\mathcal{V}$, discovering instead *different* maps for each input-output sample pair. By constraining the weight matrix sequence to be an identical $n \times n$ matrix for each subsystem during this synthesis phase, our scheme in essence forces the weight sequence to capture some underlying relationship between *all* the input-output pairs. This is arguably the best estimate of the map given the information we have.

Using formal optimal control techniques[3], we set up a performance index to maximize the correlation between the system $\mathcal{S}$ output and the desired output. This optimization technique leads in general to a nonlinear two-point-boundary-value problem, and is not usually solvable analytically. For this particular performance index we are able to derive an analytical solution to the optimization problem. The optimal interconnection matrix at each time is the sum (over the index of all samples) of the outer products between each desired output n-vector and the corresponding subsystem output. At the end of this synthesis procedure, the weight matrix sequence represents an optimal time-varying program for the weights of the n-dimensional neural network $\mathcal{N}$ that will approximate $\phi : \mathcal{U} \rightarrow \mathcal{V}$.

We remark that in the ideal case, the weight matrix at the final time (i.e *one* element of the time sequence) corresponds to the symmetric matrix suggested empirically by Hopfield for associative memory applications[4]. It becomes clear that the Hopfield matrix is suboptimal for associative memory, being just one point on the optimal weight trajectory; it is optimal only in the special case where the initial conditions coincide exactly with the desired output.

In Section 2 we outline the mathematical formulation and solution of the synthesis technique, and in Section 3 we present the learning curves. The learning curves also by default yield the system performance *over the training samples*, and we compare this performance to that of the outer product rule. In Section 4 we give concluding remarks and give the directions of our future work.

Although the results here are derived for a specific case of the neuron state equation, and a specific choice of performance index, in further work we have extended the results to very general state equations and performance indices.

2   SYNTHESIS OF WEIGHT MATRIX TIME SEQUENCE

Suppose we have a training set consisting of L pairs of n-dimensional vectors $(\tilde{\theta}^{(r)}{}_i, \theta^{(r)}{}_i), r = 1, 2, \ldots, L, i = 1, 2, \ldots, n$. For example, in an autoassociative system in which we desire to store $\theta^{(r)}{}_i, r = 1, 2, \ldots, L, i = 1, 2, \ldots, n$, we can choose the $\tilde{\theta}^{(r)}{}_i, r = 1, 2, \ldots, L, i = 1, 2, \ldots, n$ to be sample points in the neighborhood of $\theta^{(r)}{}_i$ in n-dimensional space. The idea here is that by training the network to map samples in the neighborhood of an exemplar to the exemplar, it will have developed a map that can smoothly interpolate (or *generalize*) to other points around the exemplar that may not be in the training set. In this paper we deal with the issue of finding the weight matrix that transforms the neural network dynamics into such a map. We demonstrate through simulation results that such a map can be achieved. For autoassociation, and using error vectors drawn from the training set, we show that the method here performs better (in an error-correcting sense) than the outer product rule. We are still investigating the performance of the network in generalizing to samples outside the training set.

We construct an n-dimensional *neural network* system $\mathcal{N}$ to model the underlying input-output map according to

$$\mathcal{N} : \quad \dot{\boldsymbol{x}}(t) = -\boldsymbol{x}(t) + \boldsymbol{W}(t)\boldsymbol{g}(\boldsymbol{x}(t)), \tag{1}$$

We interpret $\boldsymbol{x}$ as the neuron activation, $\boldsymbol{g}(\boldsymbol{x}(t))$ is the neuron output, and $\boldsymbol{W}(t)$ is the neural network weight matrix.

To determine the appropriate $\boldsymbol{W}(t)$, we define an nL-dimensional *formal* system of differential equations, $\mathcal{S}$

$$\mathcal{S} : \quad \dot{\boldsymbol{x}}^*(t) = -\boldsymbol{x}_*(t) + \boldsymbol{W}_*(t)\boldsymbol{g}(\boldsymbol{x}_*), \quad \boldsymbol{g}(\boldsymbol{x}_*(t_0)) = \tilde{\boldsymbol{\theta}} \tag{2}$$

formed by concatenating the equations for $\mathcal{N}$ L times. $\boldsymbol{W}_*(t)$ is block-diagonal with *identical* blocks $\boldsymbol{W}(t)$. $\boldsymbol{\theta}$ is the concatenated vector of sample desired outputs, $\tilde{\boldsymbol{\theta}}$ is the concatenated vector of sample inputs.

The performance index for $\mathcal{S}$ is

$$\min_{\boldsymbol{w}_j} J = \min_{\boldsymbol{w}_j} \left\{ -\boldsymbol{x}_*{}^T(t_f)\boldsymbol{\theta} + \frac{1}{2} \int_{t_0}^{t_f} \left(-2\boldsymbol{x}_*{}^T(t)\boldsymbol{\theta} + \beta Q + \beta^{-1} \sum_{j=1}^{n} \boldsymbol{w}_j^T(t)\boldsymbol{w}_j(t) \right) dt \right\} \tag{3}$$

The performance index is chosen to *minimize the negative of the correlation* between the (concatenated) neuron activation and the (concatenated) desired output vectors, or equivalently *maximize the correlation* between the activation and the desired output at the final time t_f, (the term $-\boldsymbol{x}_*{}^T(t_f)\boldsymbol{\theta}$). Along the way from initial time t_0 to final time t_f, the term $-\boldsymbol{x}_*{}^T(t)\boldsymbol{\theta}$ under the integral penalizes decorrelation of the neuron activation and the desired output. $\boldsymbol{w}_j(t), j = 1, 2, \ldots, n$ are the rows of $\boldsymbol{W}(t)$, and β is a positive constant. The term $\beta^{-1}\sum_{j=1}^{n} \boldsymbol{w}_j^T(t)\boldsymbol{w}_j(t)$ effects a bound on the magnitude of the weights. The term

$$Q(g(\boldsymbol{x}(t))) = \sum_{j=1}^{n}\sum_{r=1}^{L}\sum_{u=1}^{n}\sum_{v=1}^{L} \theta_j{}^{(r)}\theta_j{}^{(v)}g(x_u{}^{(v)})g(x_u{}^{(r)}),$$

and its meaning will be clear when we examine the optimal path later. $g(\cdot)$ is assumed C^1 differentiable.

Proceeding formally[3], we define the *Hamiltonian*:

$$
\begin{aligned}
H &= \frac{1}{2}\left(-2\boldsymbol{x}^T(t)\boldsymbol{\theta} + Q + \sum_{j=1}^{n} \boldsymbol{w}_j^T(t)\boldsymbol{B}\boldsymbol{w}_j(t)\right) + \boldsymbol{\lambda}^T(t)\left(-\boldsymbol{x}(t) + \boldsymbol{W}_*(t)g(\boldsymbol{x}(t))\right) \quad (4) \\
&= \frac{1}{2}\left(-2\boldsymbol{x}^T(t)\boldsymbol{\theta} + Q + \sum_{j=1}^{n} \boldsymbol{w}_j^T(t)\boldsymbol{B}\boldsymbol{w}_j(t)\right) - \boldsymbol{\lambda}^T(t)\boldsymbol{x}(t) + \sum_{r=1}^{L}\sum_{j=1}^{n}\lambda^{(r)}{}_j \boldsymbol{w}_j^T(t)g^{(r)}(\boldsymbol{x}(t))
\end{aligned}
$$

where

$$\boldsymbol{\lambda}^T(t) = \begin{bmatrix} \lambda^{(1)}{}_1(t) & \lambda^{(1)}{}_2(t) & \cdots & \lambda^{(L)}{}_n(t) \end{bmatrix}$$

is the vector of Lagrange multipliers, and we have used the fact that $\boldsymbol{W}_*(t)$ is block-diagonal with identical blocks $\boldsymbol{W}(t)$ in writing the summation of the last term in the second line of equation (4). The *Euler-Lagrange equations* are then given by

$$-\dot{\boldsymbol{\lambda}} = \left(\frac{\partial H}{\partial \boldsymbol{x}}\right)^T = \frac{1}{2}\left(\frac{\partial Q}{\partial \boldsymbol{x}}\right)^T - (\boldsymbol{\theta} + \boldsymbol{\lambda}(t)) + \left(\frac{\partial g}{\partial \boldsymbol{x}}\right)^T \boldsymbol{W}_*{}^T(t)\boldsymbol{\lambda}(t) \quad (5)$$

$$\boldsymbol{\lambda}(t_f) = -\boldsymbol{\theta} \quad (6)$$

$$0 = \frac{\partial H}{\partial \boldsymbol{w}_j} = \boldsymbol{w}_j^T\boldsymbol{B} + \sum_{r=1}^{L}\lambda^{(r)}{}_j g^{(r)}{}^T(\boldsymbol{x}(t)) \quad (7)$$

From equation (7) we have

$$w_{ij}(t) = -\beta\sum_{r=1}^{L}\lambda^{(r)}{}_i g(x_j{}^{(r)}(t)) \quad (8)$$

Choosing

$$\boldsymbol{\lambda}(t) = -\boldsymbol{\theta} \quad (9)$$

satisfies the final condition (6), and with some algebra we find that this choice is also consistent with equations (5) and (7). The optimal weight program is therefore

$$w_{ij}(t) = \beta\sum_{r=1}^{L}\theta^{(r)}{}_i g(x_j{}^{(r)}(t)) \quad (10)$$

This describes the weight paradigm to be applied to the n-dimensional neural network system $\mathcal{N}$ in order to model the underlying map described by the sample points. A similar result can be derived for the discrete-time network $x(k + 1) = W(k)g(x(k))$:

$$w_{ij}(k) = \beta \sum_{r=1}^{L} \theta^{(r)}{}_i g(x_j{}^{(r)}(k))$$

2.1   REMARKS

- *Meaning of Q.*
  On the optimal path, using equation (10), it is straightforward to show that

$$\beta Q = \beta^{-1} \sum_{j=1}^{n} w_j^T(t) w_j(t)$$

  Thus Q acts like another integral constraint term on the weights.

- *The Optimal Return Function.*
  The optimal return function[3], which is the value of the performance index on the optimal path can be shown to be

$$J^o(x_*, t) = -x_*{}^T(t)\theta$$

  Thus the optimal weight matrix $W(t)$ seeks at every instant to minimize the negative correlation (or maximize the correlation) on the optimal path in the formal system S (and hence in the neural network $\mathcal{N}$).

- *Comparison with outer product rule.*
  It is worthwhile to compare equation (10) with the outer product rule:

$$w_{ij} = \beta \sum_{r=1}^{L} \theta^{(r)}{}_i \theta^{(r)}{}_j \tag{11}$$

  We see that the outer product rule is just one point on the weight trajectory defined by equation (10) - the point at final time t_f when $g(x_j{}^{(r)}(t_f)) = \theta^{(r)}{}_j$.

3   LEARNING CURVES

In our simulation we considered 14 8-dimensional vectors as the desired outputs. The *weight synthesis* or *learning* phase is as follows: we initialized the 112-dimensional *formal synthesis system* S with a corrupted version of the vector set, and used equation (10) to find the optimal 8×8 weight matrix sequence for an *8-dimensional neural network* $\mathcal{N}$ to correctly classify any of the corrupted 14 vectors. The weight sequence is recorded. This procedure is required *only once* for any given training set. After this learning is completed, the normal operation of the neural network $\mathcal{N}$ consists in running it using the weights obtained from the synthesis phase above. The resulting network describes a continuous input-output map. At points belonging to the training set this map coincides with the underlying map we are trying to model. For points outside the training set, it performs a nonlinear interpolation (generalization) the nature of which is determined by the training set as well as the neuron state equation. Figure 1 shows the learning procedure through time. The curves labeled *"Optimally Trained Network"* shows the behavior of two correlation measures as the training proceeds. One correlation measure used was the cosine of the angle between the desired vector ($\boldsymbol{\theta}$) and the neuron activation ($\boldsymbol{x}$) vector. The other correlation measure was the cosine of the angle between the desired vector ($\boldsymbol{\theta}$) and the neuron output ($g(\boldsymbol{x}(t))$) vector. Given our system initialization in equation (2), the correlation $g(\boldsymbol{x}(t))^T\boldsymbol{\theta}$ more accurately represents our objective, although the performance index (3) reflects the correlation $\boldsymbol{x}^T\boldsymbol{\theta}$. The reason for our performance index choice is that the weight trajectory yielded by $g(\boldsymbol{x}(t))^T\boldsymbol{\theta}$ leads the system to an all-zero, trivial equilibrium for a sigmoid $g(\cdot)$ (we used such a $g(\cdot)$ with saturation values at $+1$ and -1 in our simulations). This is not the case for the weight trajectory yielded by $\boldsymbol{x}^T\boldsymbol{\theta}$. Since $g(\boldsymbol{x}(t))$ is monotonic with $\boldsymbol{x}$, $\boldsymbol{x}^T\boldsymbol{\theta}$ represented an admissible alternative choice for the performance index. The results bear this out. Another possible choice is $(g(\boldsymbol{x}(t)) + \boldsymbol{x})^T\boldsymbol{\theta}$. This gives similar results upon simulation. The correlation measures are plotted on the ordinate. The abscissa is the number of computer iterations. A discrete-time network with real-valued parameters was used. The total number of errors in the 14 8-bit binary $\{1, -1\}$ vectors used to initialize the system was 21. This results in an average of 1.5 errors per 8-bit vector. We note that the learning was completed in two time steps. Therefore, in this case at least, we see that the storage requirement is not intensive - only two weight matrices need to be stored during the synthesis phase.

We note that the learning phase by default also represents the autoassociative system error-correcting performance over input samples *drawn from the training set*. Therefore over the training set we can compare this performance with that of the outer product rule (11). By considering corrupted input vectors from the training set, we compare the error-correcting capabilities of the two methods, *not* their capacities to store uncorrupted vectors. In fact we see that the two weight rules become identical when we initialize with the true vectors (this equivalence is not a peculiarity of the new technique, but merely a consequence of the particular performance index *chosen*). In other words, this comparison is a test of the extent of the basins of attraction around the desired memories for the two techniques. Looking at the curves labeled *"Conventional Outer Product"*, we see that the new technique performs better than the outer product rule.

4   CONCLUSIONS AND FURTHER WORK

We have described a technique for training neural networks based on formal tools from optimal control theory. For a specific example consisting of learning the input-output map in a training set we derived the relevant weight equations and illustrated the learning phase of the method. This example gives a weight rule that turns out to be a continuous-time generalization of the outer-product rule. Using corrupted vectors from the training set, we show that the new rule performs better in error-correction than the outer-product rule. Simulations on the generalization capabilities of the method are ongoing and are not included in the present work.

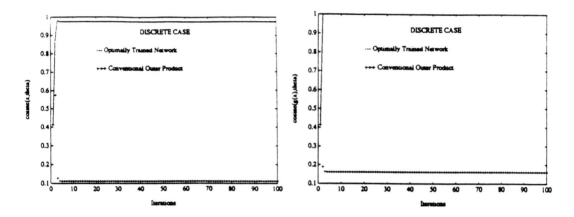

Figure 1: Learning Curves

Although we considered a *training set* consisting of input-output vector pairs as the starting point for the procedure, a closer examination shows that this is not required. More generally, what is required is a performance index that reflects the objective of the training. Also in our ongoing work we have extended the results to more general forms of the state equation and the performance index. Using an appropriate performance index we are investigating a network for the Travelling Salesman Problem and related applications like Tracking and Data Association.

References

[1] Michael A. Cohen & Stephen Grossberg, "Absolute Stability of Global Pattern Formation and Parallel Memory Storage by Competitive Neural Networks," *IEEE Transactions on Systems, Man and Cybernetics* SMC-13 (1983), 815–826.

[2] J. J. Hopfield & D. W. Tank, "Neural Computation of Decisions in Optimization Problems," *Biological Cybernetics* 52 (1985), 141–152.

[3] Arthur E. Bryson & Yu-Chi Ho, *Applied Optimal Control*, Hemisphere, 1975.

[4] J. J. Hopfield, "Neural Networks and Physical Systems with Emergent Collective Computational Abilities," *Proceedings of the National Academy of Sciences* 79 (1982), 2554–2558.

Generalized Hopfield Networks
and
Nonlinear Optimization

Gintaras V. Reklaitis
Dept. of Chemical Eng.
Purdue University
W. Lafayette, IN. 47907

Athanasios G. Tsirukis[1]
Dept. of Chemical Eng.
Purdue University
W. Lafayette, IN. 47907

Manoel F. Tenorio
Dept. of Electrical Eng.
Purdue University
W. Lafayette, IN. 47907

ABSTRACT

A nonlinear neural framework, called the Generalized Hopfield network, is proposed, which is able to solve in a parallel distributed manner systems of nonlinear equations. The method is applied to the general nonlinear optimization problem. We demonstrate GHNs implementing the three most important optimization algorithms, namely the Augmented Lagrangian, Generalized Reduced Gradient and Successive Quadratic Programming methods. The study results in a dynamic view of the optimization problem and offers a straightforward model for the parallelization of the optimization computations, thus significantly extending the practical limits of problems that can be formulated as an optimization problem and which can gain from the introduction of nonlinearities in their structure (eg. pattern recognition, supervised learning, design of content-addressable memories).

---

[1] To whom correspondence should be addressed.

1 RELATED WORK

The ability of networks of highly interconnected simple nonlinear analog processors (neurons) to solve complicated optimization problems was demonstrated in a series of papers by Hopfield and Tank (Hopfield, 1984), (Tank, 1986).

The Hopfield computational model is almost exclusively applied to the solution of combinatorially complex linear decision problems (eg. Traveling Salesman Problem). Unfortunately such problems can not be solved with guaranteed quality, (Bruck, 1987), getting trapped in locally optimal solutions.

Jeffrey and Rossner, (Jeffrey, 1986), extended Hopfield's technique to the nonlinear unconstrained optimization problem, using Cauchy dynamics. Kennedy and Chua, (Kennedy, 1988), presented an analog implementation of a network solving a nonlinear optimization problem. The underlying optimization algorithm is a simple transformation method, (Reklaitis, 1983), which is known to be relatively inefficient for large nonlinear optimization problems.

2 LINEAR HOPFIELD NETWORK (LHN)

The computation in a Hopfield network is done by a collection of highly interconnected simple neurons. Each processing element, i, is characterized by the activation level, u_i, which is a function of the input received from the external environment, I_i, and the state of the other neurons. The activation level of i is transmitted to the other processors, after passing through a filter that converts u_i to a 0-1 binary value, V_i.

The time behavior of the system is described by the following model:

$$C_i(\frac{du_i}{dt}) = \sum_j T_{ij}V_j - \frac{u_i}{R_i} + I_i$$

where T_{ij} are the interconnection strengths. The network is characterized as linear, because the neuron inputs appear linearly in the neuron's constitutive equation. The steady-state of a Hopfield network corresponds to a local minimum of the corresponding quadratic Lyapunov function:

$$E = -\frac{1}{2}\sum_i \sum_j T_{ij}V_1V_j + \sum_i I_iV_i + \sum_i (\frac{1}{R_i}) \int_0^{V_i} s_i^{-1}(V)dV$$

If the matrix $[T_{ij}]$ is symmetric, the steady state values of V_i are binary These observations turn the Hopfield network to a very useful discrete optimization tool. Nonetheless, the linear structure poses two major limitations: The Lyapunov (objective) function can only take a quadratic form, whereas the feasible region can only have a hypercube geometry ($-1 \leq V_i \leq 1$). Therefore, the Linear Hopfield Network is limited to solve optimization problems with quadratic objective function and linear constraints. The general nonlinear optimization problem requires arbitrarily nonlinear neural interactions.

3 THE NONLINEAR OPTIMIZATION PROBLEM

The general nonlinear optimization problem consists of a search for the values of the independent variables x_i, optimizing a multivariable objective function so that some conditions (equality, h_i, and inequality, g_j, constraints) are satisfied at the optimum.

$$optimize\ f(x_1, x_2, ..., x_n)$$

$$subject\ to$$

$$h_i(x_1, x_2, ..., x_n) = 0 \qquad i = 1,2,...,K, \quad K < N$$

$$a_j \leq g_j(x_1, x_2, ..., x_n) \leq b_j \qquad j = 1,2,...,M$$

$$x_k^L \leq x_k \leq x_k^U \qquad k = 1,2,...,N$$

The influence of the constraint geometry on the shape of the objective function is described in a unified manner by the Lagrangian Function:

$$L = f - v^T h$$

The v_i variables, also known as Lagrange multipliers, are unknown weighting parameters to be specified. In the optimum, the following conditions are satisfied:

$$\nabla_x L = 0 \qquad (N\ equations) \tag{1}$$

$$\nabla_v L = 0 \qquad (K\ equations) \tag{2}$$

From (1) and (2) it is clear that the optimization problem is transformed into a nonlinear equation solving problem. In a Generalized Hopfield Network each neuron represents an independent variable. The nonlinear connectivity among them is determined by the specific problem at hand and the implemented optimization algorithm. The network is designed to relax from an initial state to a steady-state that corresponds to a locally optimal solution of the problem.

Therefore, the optimization algorithms must be transformed into a dynamic model - system of differential equations - that will dictate the nonlinear neural interactions.

4 OPTIMIZATION METHODS

Cauchy and Newton dynamics are the two most important unconstrained optimization (equation solving) methods, adopted by the majority of the existing algorithms.

4.1 CAUCHY'S METHOD

This is the famous steepest descent algorithm, which tracks the direction of the largest change in the value of the objective function, f. The "equation of motion" for a Cauchy dynamic system is:

$$\frac{dx}{dt} = -\nabla f \quad ; \quad x(0) = x_o$$

4.2   NEWTON'S METHOD

If second-order information is available, a more rapid convergence is produced using Newton's approximation:

$$\frac{dx}{dt} = \pm (\nabla^2 f)^{-1} \nabla f \quad ; \quad x(0) = x_o$$

The steepest descent dynamics are very efficient initially, producing large objective-value changes, but close to the optimum they become very small, significantly increasing the convergence time. In contrast, Newton's method has a fast convergence close to the optimum, but the optimization direction is uncontrollable. The Levenberg - Marquardt heuristic, (Reklaitis, 1983), solves the problem by adopting Cauchy dynamics initially and switch to Newton dynamics near the optimum. Figure 1 shows the optimization trajectory of a Cauchy network. The algorithm converges to locally optimal solutions.

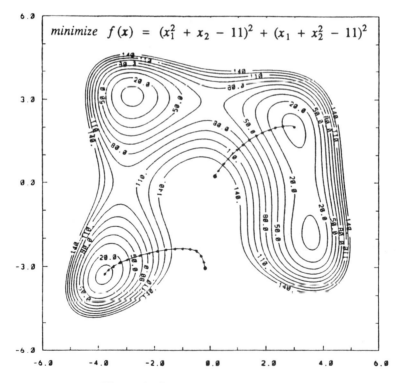

Figure 1: Convergence to Local Optima

5 CONSTRAINED OPTIMIZATION

The constrained optimization algorithms attempt to conveniently manipulate the equality and inequality constraints so that the problem is finally reduced to an unconstrained optimization, which is solved using Cauchy's or Newton's methods. Three are the most important constrained optimization algorithms: The Augmented Lagrangian, the Generalized Reduced Gradient (GRG) and the Successive Quadratic Programming (SQP). Corresponding Generalized Hopfield Networks will be developed for all of them.

5.1   TRANSFORMATION METHODS - AUGMENTED LAGRANGIAN

According to the transformation methods, a measure of the distance from the feasibility region is attached to the objective function and the problem is solved as an unconstrained optimization one. A transformation method was employed by Hopfield. These algorithms are proved inefficient because of numerical difficulties implicitly embedded in their structure, (Reklaitis, 1983). The Augmented Lagrangian is specifically designed to avoid these problems. The transformed unconstrained objective function becomes:

$$P(x,\sigma,\tau) = f(x) + R \sum_{j} \{ <g_j(x) + \sigma_j>^2 - \sigma_j^2 \}$$
$$+ R \sum_{i} \{ [h_i(x) + \tau_i]^2 - \tau_i^2 \}$$

where R is a predetermined weighting factor, and σ_j, τ_i the corresponding inequality - equality Lagrange multipliers. The operator $<a>$ returns a for $a \leq 0$. Otherwise it returns 0.

The design of an Augmented Lagrangian GHN requires $(N+K)$ neurons, where N is the number of variables and K is the number of constraints. The neuron connectivity of a GHN with Cauchy performance is described by the following model:

$$\frac{dx}{dt} = -\nabla_x P = -\nabla f - 2R <g + \sigma>^T \nabla g - 2R [h + \tau]^T \nabla h$$

$$\frac{d\sigma}{dt} = +\nabla_\sigma P = 2R <g + \sigma> - 2R \sigma$$

$$\frac{d\tau}{dt} = +\nabla_\tau P = 2R h$$

where ∇g and ∇h are matrices, eg. $\nabla h = [\nabla h_1, ..., \nabla h_k]$.

5.2   GENERALIZED REDUCED GRADIENT

According to the GRG method, K variables (**basics**, $\hat{x}$) are determined by solving the K nonlinear constraint equations, as functions of the rest $(N-K)$ variables (**non-basics**, $\bar{x}$). Subsequently the problem is solved as a reduced-dimension unconstrained optimization problem. Equations (1) and (2) are transformed to:

$$\nabla \tilde{f} = \nabla \bar{f} - \nabla \hat{f} (\nabla \hat{h})^{-1} \nabla \bar{h} = 0$$

$$h(x) = 0$$

The constraint equations are solved using Newton's method. Note that the Lagrange multipliers are explicitly eliminated. The design of a GRG GHN requires N neurons, each one representing an independent variable. The neuron connectivity using Cauchy dynamics for the unconstrained optimization is given by:

$$\frac{d\bar{x}}{dt} = - \nabla \tilde{f} = - \nabla \bar{f} + \nabla \hat{f} (\nabla \hat{h})^{-1} \nabla \bar{h} \tag{3}$$

$$h(x) = 0 \quad (\rightarrow \frac{d\hat{x}}{dt} = h (\nabla \hat{h})^{-1}) \tag{4}$$

$$x(0) = x_0$$

System (3)-(4) is a differential - algebraic system, with an inherent sequential character: for each small step towards lower objective values, produced by (3), the system of nonlinear constraints should be solved, by relaxing equations (4) to a steady-state. The procedure is repeated until both equations (3) and (4) reach a steady state.

5.3   SUCCESSIVE QUADRATIC PROGRAMMING

In the SQP algorithm equations (1) and (2) are simultaneously solved as a nonlinear system of equations with both the independent variables, x, and the Lagrange multipliers, v, as unknowns. The solution is determined using Newton's method.

The design of an SQP GHN requires $(N+K)$ neurons representing the independent variables and the Lagrange multipliers. The connectivity of the network is determined by the following state equations:

$$\frac{dz}{dt} = \pm [\nabla^2 L]^{-1} (\nabla L)$$

$$z(0) = z_0$$

where z is the augmented set of independent variables:

$$z = [x; v]$$

5.4   COMPARISON OF THE NETWORKS

The Augmented Lagrangian network is very easily programmed. Newton dynamics should be used very carefully because the operator $<a>$ is not smooth at $a = 0$.

The GRG network requires K fewer neurons compared to the other networks. It requires more programming effort because of the inversion of the constraint Jacobian.

The SQP network is algorithmically the most effective, because second order information is used in the determination of both the variables and the multipliers. It is the most tedious to program because of the inversion of the Lagrange Hessian. All the GHNs are proved to be stable, (Tsirukis, 1989). The following example was solved by all three networks.

$$minimize \quad f(\boldsymbol{x}) \; = \; -x_1 \, x_2^2 \, x_3^3 \, / \, 81$$

$$subject \; to$$

$$h_1(\boldsymbol{x}) \; = \; x_1^3 + x_2^2 + x_3 - 13 \; = \; 0$$

$$h_2(\boldsymbol{x}) \; = \; x_2^2 \, x_3^{-1/2} - 1 \; = \; 0$$

Convergence was achieved by all the networks starting from both feasible and infeasible initial points. Figures 2 and 3 depict the algorithmic superiority of the SQP network.

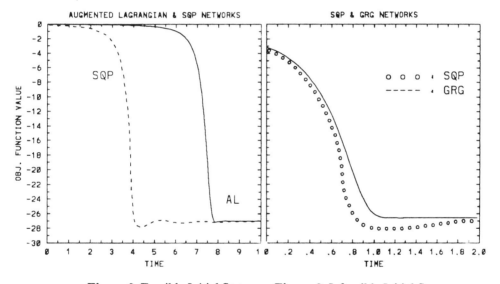

Figure 2. Feasible Initial State.   **Figure 3.** Infeasible Initial State.

6 OPTIMIZATION & PARALLEL COMPUTATION

The presented model can be directly translated into a parallel nonlinear optimizer - nonlinear equation solver - which efficiently distributes the computational burden to a large number of digital processors (at most N+K). Each one of them corresponds to an optimization variable, continuously updated by numerically integrating the state equations:

$$x_j^{(t+1)} \; = \; \phi \, (\, \boldsymbol{x}^{(t)} , \boldsymbol{x}^{(t+1)})$$

where ϕ depends on the optimization algorithm and the integration method. After each update the new value is communicated to the network.

The presented algorithm has some unique features: The state equations are differentials of the same function, the Lagrangian. Therefore, a simple integration method (eg. explicit) can be used for the steady-state computation. Also, the integration in each processor can be done asynchronously, independent of the state of the other processors. Thus, the algorithm is robust to intercommunication and execution delays.

Acknowledgements

An extended version of this work has appeared in (Tsirukis, 1990). The authors wish to thank M.I.T. Press Journals for their permission to publish it in the present form.

References

Bruck, J. and J. Goodman (1988). *On the Power of Neural Networks for Solving Hard Problems*. Neural Information Processing Systems, D.Z. Anderson (ed.), American Institute of Physics, New York, NY, 137-143.

Hopfield J.J. (1984), *Neurons with Graded Response have Collective Computational Properties like those of Two-state Neurons,* Proc. Natl. Acad. Sci. USA, vol. 81, 3088-3092.

Jeffrey, W. and R. Rosner (1986), *Neural Network Processing as a Tool for Function Optimization,* Neural Networks for Computing. J.S. Denker (ed.), American Institute of Physics, New York, NY, 241-246.

Kennedy, M.P. and L.O. Chua (1988), *Neural Networks for Nonlinear Programming,* IEEE Transactions on Circuits and Systems, vol. 35, no. 5, pp. 554-562.

Reklaitis, G.V., A. Ravindran and K.M. Ragsdell (1983), *Engineering Optimization: Methods and Applications,* Wiley - Interscience.

Tank, D.W. and J.J. Hopfield (1986), *Simple "Neural" Optimization Networks: An A/D Converter, Signal Decision Circuit, and a Linear Programming Circuit,* IEEE Transactions on circuits and systems, CAS-33, no. 5.

Tsirukis, A. G., Reklaitis, G.V., and Tenorio, M.F. (1989). *Computational properties of Generalized Hopfield Networks applied to Nonlinear Optimization.* Tech. Rep. TREE 89-69, School of Electrical Engineering, Purdue University.

Tsirukis, A. G., Reklaitis, G.V., and Tenorio, M.F. (1990). *Nonlinear Optimization using Generalized Hopfield Networks,* Neural Computation, vol. 1, no. 4.

PART V:
OTHER APPLICATIONS

Incremental Parsing by Modular Recurrent Connectionist Networks

Ajay N. Jain   Alex H. Waibel
School of Computer Science
Carnegie Mellon University
Pittsburgh, PA 15213

ABSTRACT

We present a novel, modular, recurrent connectionist network architecture which learns to robustly perform incremental parsing of complex sentences. From sequential input, one word at a time, our networks learn to do semantic role assignment, noun phrase attachment, and clause structure recognition for sentences with passive constructions and center embedded clauses. The networks make syntactic and semantic predictions at every point in time, and previous predictions are revised as expectations are affirmed or violated with the arrival of new information. Our networks induce their own "grammar rules" for dynamically transforming an input sequence of words into a syntactic/semantic interpretation. These networks generalize and display tolerance to input which has been corrupted in ways common in spoken language.

1   INTRODUCTION

Previously, we have reported on experiments using connectionist models for a small parsing task using a new network formalism which extends back-propagation to better fit the needs of sequential symbolic domains such as parsing (Jain, 1989). We showed that connectionist networks could learn the complex dynamic behavior needed in parsing. The task included passive sentences which require dynamic incorporation of previously unseen right context information into partially built syntactic/semantic interpretations. The trained parsing network exhibited predictive behavior and was able to modify or confirm

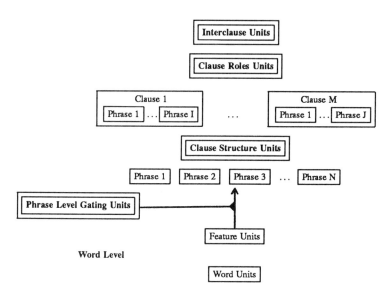

Figure 1: High-level Parsing Architecture.

hypotheses as sentences were sequentially processed. It was also able to generalize well and tolerate ill-formed input.

In this paper, we describe work on extending our parsing architecture to grammatically complex sentences.[1] The paper is organized as follows. First, we briefly outline the network formalism and the general architecture. Second, the parsing task is defined and the procedure for constructing and training the parser is presented. Then the dynamic behavior of the parser is illustrated, and the performance is characterized.

2 NETWORK ARCHITECTURE

We have developed an extension to back-propagation networks which is specifically designed to perform tasks in sequential domains requiring symbol manipulation (Jain, 1989). It is substantially different from other connectionist approaches to sequential problems (e.g. Elman, 1988; Jordan, 1986; Waibel *et al.*, 1989). There are four major features of this formalism. One, units retain partial activation between updates. They can respond to repetitive weak stimuli as well as singular sharp stimuli. Two, units are responsive to both static activation values of other units and their dynamic changes. Three, well-behaved symbol buffers can be constructed using groups of units whose connections are *gated* by other units. Four, the formalism supports recurrent networks. The networks are able to learn complex time-varying behavior using a gradient descent procedure via error back-propagation.

Figure 1 shows a high-level diagram of the general parsing architecture. It is organized into five hierarchical levels: Word, Phrase, Clause Structure, Clause Roles, and Inter-

---

[1] Another presentation of this work appears in Jain and Waibel (1990).

clause. The description will proceed bottom up. A word is presented to the network by stimulating its associated word unit for a short time. This produces a pattern of activation across the feature units which represents the meaning of the word. The connections from the word units to the feature units which encode semantic and syntactic information about words are compiled into the network and are fixed.[2] The Phrase level uses the sequence of word representations from the Word level to build contiguous phrases. Connections from the Word level to the Phrase level are modulated by gating units which learn the required conditional assignment behavior. The Clause Structure level maps phrases into the constituent clauses of the input sentence. The Clause Roles level describes the roles and relationships of the phrases in each clause of the sentence. The final level, Inter-clause, represents the interrelationships among the clauses. The following section defines a parsing task and gives a detailed description of the construction and training of a parsing network which performs the task.

3   INCREMENTAL PARSING

In parsing spoken language, it is desirable to process input one word at a time as words are produced by the speaker and to incrementally build an output representation. This allows tight bi-directional coupling of the parser to the underlying speech recognition system. In such a system, the parser processes information as soon as it is produced and provides predictive information to the recognition system based on a rich representation of the current context. As mentioned earlier, our previous work applying connectionist architectures to a parsing task was promising. The experiment described below extends our previous work to grammatically complex sentences requiring a significant scale increase.

3.1   Parsing Task

The domain for the experiment was sentences with up to three clauses including non-trivial center-embedding and passive constructions.[3] Here are some example sentences:

- Fido dug up a bone near the tree in the garden.
- I know the man who John says Mary gave the book.
- The dog who ate the snake was given a bone.

Given sequential input, one word at a time, the task is to incrementally build a representation of the input sentence which includes the following information: phrase structure, clause structure, semantic role assignment, and interclause relationships. Figure 2 shows a representation of the desired parse of the last sentence in the list above.

---

[2]Connectionist networks have been used for lexical acquisition successfully (Miikkulainen and Dyer, 1989). However, in building large systems, it makes sense from an efficiency perspective to precompile as much lexical information as possible into a network. This is a pragmatic design choice in building large systems.

[3]The training set contained over 200 sentences. These are a subset of the sentences which form the example set of a parser based on a left associative grammar (Hausser, 1988). These sentences are grammatically interesting, but they do not reflect the statistical structure of common speech.

```
[Clause 1:    [The dog RECIP] [was given ACTION] [a bone PATIENT]]
[Clause 2:    [who AGENT] [ate ACTION] [the snake PATIENT]
              (RELATIVE to Clause 1, Phrase 1)]
```

Figure 2: Representation of an Example Sentence.

3.2   Constructing the Parser

The architecture for the network follows that given in Figure 1. The following paragraphs describe the detailed network structure bottom up. The constraints on the numbers of objects and labels are fixed for a particular network, but the architecture itself is scalable. Wherever possible in the network construction, modularity and architectural constraints have been exploited to minimize training time and maximize generalization. A network was constructed from three separate recurrent subnetworks trained to perform a portion of the parsing task on the training sentences. The performance of the full network will be discussed in detail in the next section.

The Phrase level contains three types of units: *phrase block* units, *gating* units, and *hidden* units. There are 10 phrase blocks, each being able to capture up to 4 words forming a phrase. The phrase blocks contain sets of units (called slots) whose target activation patterns correspond to word feature patterns of words in phrases. Each slot has an associated gating unit which learns to conditionally assign an activation pattern from the feature units of the Word level to the slot. The gating units have input connections from the hidden units. The hidden units have input connections from the feature units, gating units, and phrase block units. The direct recurrence between the gating and hidden units allows the gating units to learn to inhibit and compete with one another. The indirect recurrence arising from the connections between the phrase blocks and the hidden units provides the context of the current input word. The target activation values for each gating unit are dynamically calculated during training; each gating unit must learn to become active at the proper time in order to perform the phrasal parsing. Each phrase block with its associated gating and hidden units has its weights slaved to the other phrase blocks in the Phrase level. Thus, if a particular phrase construction is only present in one position in the training set, all of the phrase blocks still learn to parse the construction.

The Clause Roles level also has shared weights among separate clause modules. This level is trained by simulating the sequential building and mapping of clauses to sets of units containing the phrase blocks for each clause (see Figure 1). There are two types of units in this level: *labeling* units and *hidden* units. The labeling units learn to label the phrases of the clauses with semantic roles and attach phrases to other (within-clause) phrases. For each clause, there is a set of units which assigns role labels (agent, patient, recipient, action) to phrases. There is also a set of units indicating phrasal modification. The hidden units are recurrently connected to the labeling units to provide context and competition as with the Phrase level; they also have input connections from the phrase blocks of a single clause. During training, the targets for the labeling units are set at the beginning of the input presentation and remain static. In order to minimize global error across the training set, the units must learn to become active or inactive as soon as possible in the input. This forces the network to learn to be predictive.

The Clause Structure and Interclause levels are trained simultaneously as a single module. There are three types of units at this level: *mapping*, *labeling*, and *hidden* units. The mapping units assign phrase blocks to clauses. The labeling units indicate relative clause and a subordinate clause relationships. The mapping and labeling units are recurrently connected to the hidden units which also have input connections from the phrase blocks of the Phrase level. The behavior of the Phrase level is simulated during training of this module. This module utilizes no weight sharing techniques. As with the Clause Roles level, the targets for the labeling and mapping units are set at the beginning of input presentation, thus inducing the same type of predictive behavior.

4   PARSING PERFORMANCE

The separately trained submodules described above were assembled into a single network which performs the full parsing task. No additional training was needed to fine-tune the full parsing network despite significant differences between actual subnetwork performance and the simulated subnetwork performance used during training. The network successfully modeled the large diverse training set. This section discusses three aspects of the parsing network's performance: dynamic behavior of the integrated network, generalization, and tolerance to noisy input.

4.1   Dynamic Behavior

The dynamic behavior of the network will be illustrated on the example sentence from Figure 2: "The dog who ate the snake was given a bone." This sentence was not in the training set. Due to space limitations, actual plots of network behavior will only be presented for a small portion of the network.

Initially, all of the units in the network are at their resting values. The units of the phrase blocks all have low activation. The word unit corresponding to "the" is stimulated, causing its word feature representation to become active across the feature units of the Word level. The gating unit associated with the slot 1 of phrase block 1 becomes active, and the feature representation of "the" is assigned to the slot; the gate closes as the next word is presented. The remaining words of the sentence are processed similarly, resulting in the final Phrase level representation shown in Figure 2. While this is occurring, the higher levels of the network are processing the evolving Phrase level representation.

The behavior of some of the mapping units of the Clause Structure Level is shown in Figure 3. Early in the presentation of the first word, the Clause Structure level hypothesizes that the first 4 phrase blocks will belong to the first clause—reflecting the dominance of single clause sentences in the training set. After "the" is assigned to the first phrase block, this hypothesis is revised. The network then believes that there is an embedded clause of 3 (possibly 4) phrases following the first phrase. This predictive behavior emerged spontaneously from the training procedure (a large majority of sentences in the training set beginning with a determiner had embedded clauses after the first phrase). The next two words ("dog who") confirm the network's expectation. The word "ate" allows the network to firmly decide on an embedded clause of 3 phrases within

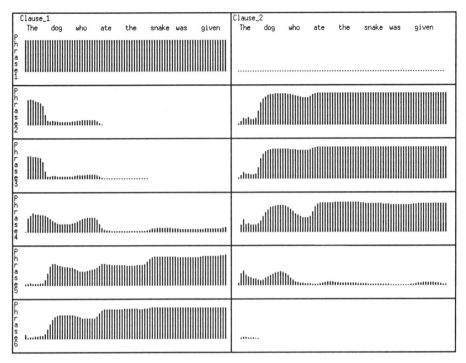

Figure 3: Example of Clause Structure Dynamic Behavior.

the main clause. This is the correct clausal structure of the sentence and is confirmed by the remainder of the input. The Interclause level indicates the appropriate relative clause relationship during the initial hypothesis of the embedded clause.

The Clause Roles level processes the individual clauses as they get mapped through the Clause Structure level. The labeling units for clause 1 initially hypothesize an Agent/Action/Patient role structure with some competition from a Rec/Act/Pat role structure (the Agent and Patient units' activation traces for clause 1, phrase 1 are shown in Figure 4). This prediction occurs because active constructs outnumbered passive ones during training. The final decision about role structure is postponed until just after the embedded clause is presented. The verb phrase "was given" immediately causes the Rec/Act/Pat role structure to dominate. Also, the network indicates that a fourth phrase (e.g. "by Mary") is expected to be the Agent. As with the first clause, an Ag/Act/Pat role structure is predicted for clause 2; this time the prediction is borne out.

4.2 Generalization

One type of generalization is automatic. A detail of the word representation scheme was omitted from the previous discussion. The feature patterns have two parts: a syntactic/semantic part and an identification part. The representations of "John" and "Peter" differ only in their ID parts. Units in the network which learn do not have any input connections from the ID portions of the word units. Thus, when the network learns to

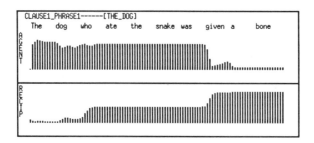

Figure 4: Example of Clause Roles Dynamic Behavior.

parse "John gave the bone to the dog," it will know how to parse "Peter promised the mitt to the boy." This type of generalization is extremely useful, both for addition of new words to the network and for processing many sentences not explicitly trained on.

The network also generalizes to correctly process truly novel sentences—sentences which are distinct (ignoring ID features) from those in the training set. The weight sharing techniques at the Phrase and Clause Structure levels have an impact here. While being difficult to measure generalization quantitatively, some statements can be made about the types of novel sentences which can be correctly processed relative to the training sentences. Substitution of single words resulting in a meaningful sentence is tolerated almost without exception. Substitution of entire phrases by different phrases causes some errors in structural parsing on sentences which have few similar training exemplars. However, the network does quite well on sentences which can be formed from composition between familiar sentences (e.g. interchanging clauses).

4.3   Tolerance to Noise

Several types of noise tolerance are interesting to analyze: ungrammaticality, word deletions (especially poorly articulated short function words), variance in word speed, interword silences, interjections, word/phrase repetitions, etc.   The effects of noise were simulated by testing the parsing network on training sentences which had been corrupted in the ways listed above. Note that the parser was trained only on well-formed sentences.

Sentences in which verbs were made ungrammatical were processed without difficulty (e.g. "We am happy."). Sentences in which verb phrases were badly corrupted produced reasonable interpretations. For example, the sentence "Peter was gave a bone to Fido," received an Ag/Act/Pat/Rec role structure as if "was gave" was supposed to be either "gave" or "has given". Interpretation of corrupted verb phrases was context dependent.

Single clause sentences in which determiners were randomly deleted to simulate speech recognition errors were processed correctly 85 percent of the time.   Multiple clause sentences degraded in a similar manner produced more parsing errors. There were fewer examples of multi-clause sentence types, and this hurt performance. Deletion of function words such as prepositions beginning prepositional phrases produced few errors, but deletions of critical function words such as "to" in infinitive constructions introducing subordinate clauses caused serious problems.

The network was somewhat sensitive to variations in word presentation speed (it was trained on a constant speed), but tolerated inter-word silences. Interjections of "ahh" and partial phrase repetitions were also tested. The network did not perform as well on these sentences as other networks trained for less complex parsing tasks. One possibility is that the weight sharing is preventing the formation of strong attractors for the training sentences. There appears to be a tradeoff between generalization and noise tolerance.

5   CONCLUSION

We have presented a novel connectionist network architecture and its application to a non-trivial parsing task. A hierarchical, modular, recurrent connectionist network was constructed which successfully learned to parse grammatically complex sentences. The parser exhibited predictive behavior and was able to dynamically revise hypotheses. Techniques for maximizing generalization were also discussed. Network performance on novel sentences was impressive. Results of testing the parser's sensitivity to several types of noise were somewhat mixed, but the parser performed well on ungrammatical sentences and sentences with non-critical function word deletions.

Acknowledgments

This research was funded by grants from ATR Interpreting Telephony Research Laboratories and the National Science Foundation under grant number EET-8716324. We thank Dave Touretzky for helpful comments and discussions.

References

J. L. Elman. (1988) *Finding Structure in Time*. Tech. Rep. 8801, Center for Research in Language, University of California, San Diego.

R. Hausser. (1988) *Computation of Language*. Springer-Verlag.

A. N. Jain. (1989) *A Connectionist Architecture for Sequential Symbolic Domains*. Tech. Rep. CMU-CS-89-187, School of Computer Science, Carnegie Mellon University.

A. N. Jain and A. H. Waibel. (1990) Robust connectionist parsing of spoken language. In *Proceedings of the 1990 IEEE International Conference on Acoustics, Speech, and Signal Processing*.

M. I. Jordan. (1986) *Serial Order: A Parallel Distributed Processing Approach*. Tech. Rep. 8604, Institute for Cognitive Science, University of California, San Diego.

R. Miikkulainen and M. G. Dyer. (1989) Encoding input/output representations in connectionist cognitive systems. In D. Touretzky, G. Hinton, and T. Sejnowski (eds.), *Proceedings of the 1988 Connectionist Models Summer School*, pp. 347–356, Morgan Kaufmann Publishers.

A. Waibel, T. Hanazawa, G. Hinton, K. Shikano, and K. Lang. (1989) Phoneme recognition using time-delay neural networks. *IEEE Transactions on Acoustics, Speech, and Signal Processing* 37(3):328–339.

A Computational Basis for Phonology

David S. Touretzky
School of Computer Science
Carnegie Mellon University
Pittsburgh, PA 15213

Deirdre W. Wheeler
Department of Linguistics
University of Pittsburgh
Pittsburgh, PA 15260

ABSTRACT

The phonological structure of human languages is intricate, yet highly constrained. Through a combination of connectionist modeling and linguistic analysis, we are attempting to develop a computational basis for the nature of phonology. We present a connectionist architecture that performs multiple simultaneous insertion, deletion, and mutation operations on sequences of phonemes, and introduce a novel additional primitive, *clustering*. Clustering provides an interesting alternative to both iterative and relaxation accounts of assimilation processes such as vowel harmony. Our resulting model is efficient because it processes utterances entirely in parallel using only feed-forward circuitry.

1   INTRODUCTION

Phonological phenomena can be quite complex, but human phonological behavior is also highly constrained. Many operations that are easily learned by a perceptron-like sequence mapping network are excluded from real languages. For example, as Pinker and Prince (1988) point out in their critique of the Rumelhart and McClelland (1986) verb learning model, human languages never reverse the sequence of segments in a word, but this is an easy mapping for a network to learn. On the other hand, we note that some phonological processes that are relatively common in human languages, such as vowel harmony, appear difficult for a sequence-mapping architecture to learn. Why are only certain types of sequence operations found in human languages, and not others? We suggest that this is a reflection of the limitations of an underlying, genetically-determined, specialized computing architecture. We are searching for this architecture.

Our work was initially inspired by George Lakoff's theory of cognitive phonology (Lakoff, 1988, 1989), which is in turn a development of the ideas of John Goldsmith (to appear). Lakoff proposes a three-level representation scheme. The M (morpho-phonemic) level represents the underlying form of an utterance, the P (phonemic) level is an intermediate form, and the F (phonetic) level is the derived surface form.

Lakoff uses a combination of inter-level mapping rules and intra-level well-formedness conditions to specify the relationships between P- and F-level representations and the M-level input. In a connectionist implementation, the computations performed by the mapping rules are straightforward, but we find the well-formedness conditions troubling. Goldsmith's proposal was that phonology is a goal-directed constraint satisfaction system that operates via parallel relaxation. He cites Smolensky's harmony theory[1] Lakoff has adopted this appeal to harmony theory in his description of how well-formedness conditions could work.

In our model, we further develop the Goldmsith and Lakoff mapping scheme, but we reject harmony-based well-formedness conditions for several reasons. First, harmony theory involves simulated annealing search. The timing constraints of real nervous systems rule out simulated annealing. Second, it is not clear how to construct an energy function for a connectionist network that performs complex discrete phonological operations. Finally there is our desire to explain why certain types of processes occur in human languages and others do not. Harmony theory alone is too unconstrained for this purpose.

We have implemented a model called M^3P (for "Many Maps" Model of Phonology) that allows us to account for virtually all of the phenomena in (Lakoff, 1989) using a tightly-constrained, purely-feedforward computing scheme. In the next section we describe the mapping matrix architecture that is the heart of M^3P. Next we give an example of an iterative process, Yawelmani vowel harmony,[2] which Lakoff models with a P-level well-formedness condition. Such a condition would have to be implemented by relaxation search for a "minimum energy state" in the P-level representation, which we wish to avoid. Finally we present our alternative approach to vowel harmony, using a novel clustering mechanism that eliminates the need for relaxation.

2   THE MAPPING MATRIX ARCHITECTURE

Figure 1 is an overview of our "many maps" model. M-P constructions compute how to go from the M-level representation of an utterance to the P-level representation. The derivation is described as a set of explicit changes to the M-level string. M-P constructions read the segments in the M-level buffer and write the changes, phrased as mutation, deletion, and insertion requests, into slots of a buffer called P-deriv. The M-level and P-deriv buffers are then read by the M-P mapping matrix, which produces the P-level representation as its output. The process is repeated at the next level, with P-F constructions writing changes into an F-deriv buffer, and a P-F map deriving an F-level

---

[1] Smolensky's "harmony theory" should not be confused with the linguistic phenomenon of "vowel harmony."

[2] Yawelmani is a dialect of Yokuts, an American Indian language from California. Our Yawelmani data is drawn from Kenstowicz and Kisseberth (1979), as is Lakoff's.

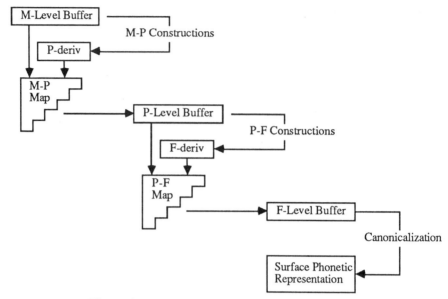

Figure 1: Overview of the "many maps" model.

representation. A final step called "canonicalization" cleans up the representations of the individual segments.

Figure 2 shows the effect of an M-P construction that breaks up CCC consonant clusters by inserting a vowel after the first consonant, producing CiCC. The input in this case is the Yawelmani word /?ugnhin/ "drinks", and the desired insertion is indicated in P-deriv. The mapping matrix derives the P-level representation right-justified in the buffer, with no segment gaps or collisions. It can do this even when mutliple simultaneous insertions and deletions are being performed. But it cannot perform arbitrary sequence manipulations, such as reversing all the segments of an utterance. Further details of the matrix architecture are given in (Touretzky, 1989) and (Wheeler and Touretzky, 1989).

3   ITERATIVE PHENOMENA

Several types of phonological processes operate on groups of adjacent segments, often by making them more similar to an immediately preceding (or following) trigger segment. Vowel harmony and voicing assimilation are two examples. In Yawelmani, vowel harmony takes the following form: an [αhigh] vowel that is preceded by an [αhigh] round vowel becomes round and back. In the form /do:s+al/ "might report", the non-round, back vowel /a/ is [−high], as is the preceding round vowel /o/. Therefore the /a/ becomes round, yielding the surface form [do:sol]. Similarly, in /dub+hin/ "leads by the hand", the [+high] vowel /i/ is preceded by the [+high] round vowel /u/, so the /i/ becomes round and back, giving [dubhun]. In /bok'+hin/ "finds", the /i/ does not undergo harmony because it differs in height from the preceding vowel.

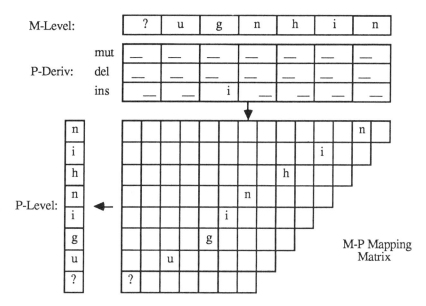

Figure 2: Performing an insertion via the M-P mapping matrix.

Harmony is described as an iterative process because it can apply to entire sequences of vowels, as in the following derivation:

/t'ul+sit+hin/   "burns for"
/t'ul+sut+hin/   *harmony on second vowel*
/t'ul+sut+hun/   *harmony on third vowel*

In Yawelmani we saw an epenthesis process that inserts a high vowel /i/ to break up lengthy consonant clusters. Epenthetic vowels may either undergo or block harmony. With the word /logw+xa/ "let's pulverize", epenthesis inserts an /i/ to break up the /gwx/ cluster, producing /logiw+xa/. Now the /a/ is preceded by a [+high, −round] vowel, so harmony does not apply, whereas in /do:s+al/, which has the same sequence of underlying vowels, it did. This is an instance of epenthesis blocking harmony. In other environments the epenthetic vowel may itself undergo harmony. For example:

/ʔugn+hin/   "drinks"
/ʔuginhin/   *epenthesis*
/ʔugunhin/   *harmony on epenthetic vowel*
/ʔugunhun/   *harmony on third vowel*

The standard generative phonology analysis of harmony utilizes the following rule, applying after epenthesis, that is supposed to iterate through the utterance from left to right, changing one vowel at a time:

$$\left[\begin{array}{c} +\text{syll} \\ \alpha\text{high} \end{array} \right] \rightarrow \left[\begin{array}{c} +\text{round} \\ +\text{back} \end{array} \right] / \left[\begin{array}{c} +\text{syll} \\ +\text{round} \\ \alpha\text{high} \end{array} \right] C_0 \_\_$$

Lakoff offers an alternative account of epenthesis and harmony that eliminates iteration. He states epenthesis as an M-P construction:

M: C   C   {C,#}
      | | |
P: [ ]   i   [ ]

The harmony rule is stated as a P-level well-formedness condition that applies simultaneously throughout the buffer:

P: If [+syll, +round, αhigh] C_0 X,
         then if X = [+syll, αhigh], then X = [+round, +back].

Starting with /ʔugn+hin/ at M-level, Lakoff's model would settle into a representation of /ʔugunhun/ at P-level. We repeat again the crucial point that this representation is not derived by sequential application of rules; it is merely *licensed* by one application of epenthesis and two of harmony. The actual computation of the P-level representation would be performed by a parallel relaxation process, perhaps using simulated annealing, that somehow determines the sequence that best satisfies all applicable constraints at P-level.

4   THE CLUSTERING MECHANISM

Our account of vowel harmony must differ from Lakoff's because we do not wish to rely on relaxation in our model. Instead, we introduce special clustering circuitry to recognize sequences of segments that share certain properties. The clustering idea is meant to be analogous to perceptual grouping in vision. Sequences of adjacent visually-similar objects are naturally perceived as a whole. A similar mechanism operating on phonological sequences, although unprecedented in linguistic theory, does not appear implausible. Crucial to our model is the principle that perceived sequences may be operated on as a unit. This allows us to avoid iteration and give a fully-parallel account of vowel harmony.

The clustering mechanism is controlled by a small number of language-specific parameters. The rule shown below is the P-F clustering rule for Yawelmani. Cluster type [+syllabic] indicates that the rule looks only at vowels. (This is implemented by an additional mapping matrix that extracts the vowel projection of the P-level buffer. The clustering mechanism actually looks at the output of this matrix rather than at the P-level buffer directly.) The trigger of a cluster is a round vowel of a given height, and the elements are the subsequent adjacent vowels of matching height. Application of the rule causes elements (but not triggers) to undergo a change; in this case, they become round and back.

Yawelmani vowel harmony — P-F mapping:

Cluster type:	[+syllabic]
Trigger:	[+round, αhigh]
Element:	[αhigh]
Change:	[+round, +back]

The following hypothetical vowel sequence illustrates the application of this clustering rule. Consonants are omitted for clarity:

	1	2	3	4	5	6	7	8	9
	i	u	i	i	e	o	o	a	i
trigger:		+				+			
element:			+	+			+	+	

The second vowel is round, so it's a trigger. Since the third and fourth vowels match it in height, they become elements. The fifth vowel is [−high], so it is not included in the cluster. The sixth vowel triggers a new cluster because it's round; it is also [−high]. The seventh and eighth vowels are also [−high], so they can be elements, but the ninth vowel is excluded from the cluster because is [+high]. Note that vowel 7 is an element, but it also meets the specification for a trigger. Given a choice, our model prefers to mark segments as elements rather than triggers because only elements undergo the specified change. The distinction is moot in Yawlemani, where triggers are already round and back, but it matters in other languages; see (Wheeler and Touretzky, 1989) for details.

Figures 2 and 3 together show the derivation of the Yawelmani word [ʔugunhun] from the underlying form /ʔugn+hin/. In figure 2 an M-P construction inserted a high vowel. In figure 3 the P-F clustering circuitry has examined the P-level buffer and marked the triggers and elements. Segments that were marked as elements then have the change [+round, +back] written into their corresponding mutation slots in F-deriv. Finally, the P-F mapping matrix produces the sequence /ʔugunhun/ as the F-level representation of the utterance.

5   DISCUSSION

We could not justify the extra circuitry required for clustering if it were suitable only for Yawelmani vowel harmony. The same mechanism handles a variety of other iterative phenomena, including Slovak and Gidabal vowel shortening, Icelandic umlaut, and Russian voicing assimilation. The full mechanism has some additional parameters beyond those covered in the discussion of Yawelmani. For example, clustering may proceed from right-to-left (as is the case in Russian) instead of from left-to-right. Also, clusters may be of either bounded or unbounded length. Bounded clusters are required for alternation processes, such as Gidabal shortening. They cover exactly two segments: a trigger and one element. We are making a deliberate analogy here with metrical phonology (stress systems), where unbounded feet may be of arbitrary length, but bounded feet always contain exactly two syllables. No language has strictly trisyllabic feet. We predict a similar constraint will hold for iterative phenomena when they are reformulated in parallel clustering terms, i.e., no language requires bounded-length clusters with more than one element.

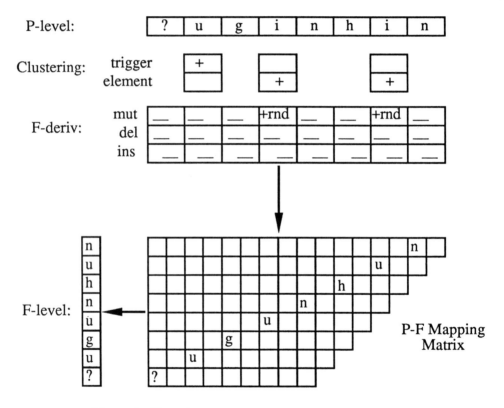

Figure 3: Clustering applied to Yawelmani vowel harmony.

Our model makes many other predictions of constraints on human phonology, based on limitations of the highly-structured "many maps" architecture. We are attempting to verify these predictions, and also to extend the model to additional aspects of phonological behavior, such as syllabification and stress.

Acknowledgements

This research was supported by a contract from Hughes Research Laboratories, by the Office of Naval Research under contract number N00014-86-K-0678, and by National Science Foundation grant EET-8716324. We thank George Lakoff for encouragement and support, John Goldsmith for helpful correspondence, and Gillette Elvgren III for implementing the simulations.

References

Goldsmith, J. (to appear) Phonology as an intelligent system. To appear in a festschrift for Leila Gleitman, edited by D. Napoli and J. Kegl.

Kenstowicz, M., and Kisseberth, C. (1979) *Generative Phonology: Description and Theory*. San Diego, CA: Academic Press.

Lakoff, G. (1988) A suggestion for a linguistics with connectionist foundations. In D. S. Touretzky, G. E. Hinton, and T. J. Sejnowski (eds.), *Proceedings of the 1988 Connectionist Models Summer School*, pp. 301-314. San Mateo, CA: Morgan Kaufmann.

Lakoff, G. (1989) Cognitive phonology. Draft of paper presented at the UC-Berkeley Workshop on Constraints vs Rules, May 1989.

Pinker, S., and Prince, A. (1988) On language and connectionism: analysis of a parallel distributed processing model of language acquisition. In S. Pinker & J. Mehler (eds.), *Connections and Symbols*. Cambridge, Massachusetts: MIT Press.

Rumelhart, D. E., and McClelland, J. L. (1986) On learning the past tenses of English verbs. In J. L. McClelland and D. E. Rumelhart (eds.), *Parallel Distributed Processing: Explorations in the MicroStructure of Cognition*, volume 2. Cambridge, Massachusetts: MIT Press.

Smolensky, P. (1986) Information processing in dynamical systems: foundations of harmony theory. In D. E. Rumelhart and J. L. McClelland (eds.), *Parallel Distributed Processing: Explorations in the MicroStructure of Cognition*, volume 1. Cambridge, Massachusetts: MIT Press.

Touretzky, D. S. (1989) Toward a connectionist phonology: the "many maps" approach to sequence manipulation. *Proceedings of the Eleventh Annual Conference of the Cognitive Science Society*, pp. 188-195. Hillsdale, NJ: Erlbaum.

Wheeler, D. W., and Touretzky, D. S. (1989) A connectionist implementation of cognitive phonology. Technical report CMU-CS-89-144, Carnegie Mellon University, School of Computer Science. To appear in G. Lakoff and L. Hyman (eds.), *Proceedings of the UC-Berkeley Phonology Workshop on Constraints vs, Rules*, University of Chicago Press.

HIGHER ORDER RECURRENT NETWORKS & GRAMMATICAL INFERENCE

C. L. Giles*, G. Z. Sun, H. H. Chen, Y. C. Lee, D. Chen
Department of Physics and Astronomy
and
Institute for Advanced Computer Studies
University of Maryland, College Park, MD 20742
* NEC Research Institute
4 Independence Way, Princeton, N.J. 08540

ABSTRACT

A higher order single layer recursive network easily learns to simulate a deterministic finite state machine and recognize regular grammars. When an enhanced version of this neural net state machine is connected through a common error term to an external analog stack memory, the combination can be interpreted as a neural net pushdown automata. The neural net finite state machine is given the primitives, push and pop, and is able to read the top of the stack. Through a gradient descent learning rule derived from the common error function, the hybrid network learns to effectively use the stack actions to manipulate the stack memory and to learn simple context-free grammars.

INTRODUCTION

Biological networks readily and easily process temporal information; artificial neural networks should do the same. Recurrent neural network models permit the encoding and learning of temporal sequences. There are many recurrent neural net models, for example see [Jordan 1986, Pineda 1987, Williams & Zipser 1988]. Nearly all encode the current state representation of the models in the activity of the neuron and the next state is determined by the current state and input. From an automata perspective, this dynamical structure is a state machine. One formal model of sequences and machines that generate and recognize them are formal grammars and their respective automata. These models formalize some of the foundations of computer science. In the Chomsky hierarchy of formal grammars [Hopcroft & Ullman 1979] the simplest level of complexity is defined by the finite state machine and its regular grammars. {All machines and grammars described here are deterministic.} The next level of complexity is described by pushdown automata and their associated context-free grammars. The pushdown automaton is a finite state machine with the added power to use a stack memory. Neural networks should be able to perform the same type of computation and thus solve such learning problems as grammatical inference [Fu 1982] .

Simple grammatical inference is defined as the problem of finding (learning) a grammar from a finite set of strings, often called the teaching sample. Recall that a grammar {phrase-structured} is defined as a 4-tuple (N, V, P, S) where N and V are a nonterminal and terminal vocabularies, P is a finite set of production rules and S is the start symbol. Here grammatical inference is also defined as the learning of the machine that recognizes the teaching and testing samples. Potential applications of grammatical inference include such various areas as pattern recognition, information retrieval, programming language design, translation and compiling and graphics languages [Fu 1982].

There has been a great deal of interest in teaching neural nets to recognize grammars and simulate automata [Allen 1989, Jordan 1986, Pollack 1989, Servant-Schreiber et. al. 1989,Williams & Zipser 1988]. Some important extensions of that work are discussed here. In particular we construct recurrent higher order neural net state machines which have no hidden layers and seem to be at least as powerful as any neural net multilayer state machine discussed so far. For example, the learning time and training sample size are significantly reduced. In addition, we integrate this neural net finite state machine with an external stack memory and inform the network through a common objective function that it has at its disposal the symbol at the top of the stack and the operation primitives of push and pop. By devising a common error function which integrates the stack and the neural net state machine, this hybrid structure learns to effectively use the stack to recognize context-free grammars. In the interesting work of [Williams & Zipser 1988] a recurrent net learns only the state machine part of a Turing Machine, since the associated move, read, write operations for each input string are known and are given as part of the training set. However, the model we present learns how to manipulate the push, pop, and read primitives of an external stack memory plus learns the additional necessary state operations and structure.

HIGHER ORDER RECURRENT NETWORK

The recurrent neural network utilized can be considered as a higher order modification of the network model developed by [Williams & Zipser 1988]. Recall that in a recurrent net the activation state S of the neurons at time (t+1) is defined as in a state machine automata:

$$S(t+1) = F \{ S(t), I(t); W \} \quad , \tag{1}$$

where F maps the state S and the input I at time t to the next state. The weight matrix W forms the mapping and is usually learned. We use a higher order form for this mapping:

$$S_i(t+1) = g\{ \Sigma W_{ijk} S_j(t) I_k(t) \} \quad , \tag{2}$$

where the range of i, j is the number of state neurons and k the number of input neurons; g is defined as g(x)=1/(1+exp(-x)). In order to use the net for grammatical inference, a learning rule must be devised.   To learn the mapping F and the weight matrix W, given a sample set of P strings of the grammar, we construct the following error function E :

$$E = \Sigma E_r^2 = \Sigma\, (\, T_r - S_o(t_p)\,)^2 \qquad , \qquad (3)$$

where the sum is over P samples . The error function is evaluated at the end of a presented sequence of length t_p and S_o is the activity of the output neuron. For a recurrent net, the output neuron is a designated member of the state neurons. The target value of any pattern is 1 for a legal string and 0 for an illegal one. Using a gradient descent procedure, we minimize the error E function for only the rth pattern. The weight update rule becomes

$$\Delta W_{ijk} = -\eta\, \nabla_W E = \eta\, E_r\, \{\, \partial S_o(t_p)\, /\, \partial W_{ijk}\, \}\, , \qquad (4)$$

where η is the learning rate. Using eq. (2), $\partial S_o(t_p)\, /\, \partial W_{ijk}$ is easily calculated using the recursion relationship and the choice of an initial value for $\partial S_i(t = 0)/\partial W_{ijk}$,

$$\partial S_l(t+1)/\partial W_{ijk} = h_l\, (S_l(t+1))\, \{\, \delta_{li}\, S_j(t)\, I_k(t) + \Sigma\, W_{lmn}\, I_n(t)\, \partial S_m(t)/\partial W_{ijk}\, \}\ (5)$$

where h(x) = dg/dx. Note that this requires $\partial S_i(t)\, /\, \partial W_{ijk}$ be updated as each element of each string is presented and to have a known initial value. Given an adequate network topology, the above neural net state machine should be capable of learning any regular grammar of arbitrary string length or a more complex grammar of finite length.

FINITE STATE MACHINE SIMULATION

In order to see how such a net performs, we trained the net on a regular grammar, the dual parity grammar. An arbitrary length string of 0's and 1's has dual parity if the string contains an even number of 0's and an even number of 1's. The network architecture was 3 input neurons and either 3, 4, or 5 state neurons with fully connected second order interconnection weights. The string vocabulary 0,1,e (end symbol) used a unary representation. The initial training set consisted of 30 positive and negative strings of increasing sting length up to length 4. After including in the training all strings up to length 10 which resulted in misclassification(about 30 strings), the neural net state machine perfectly recognized on all strings up to length 20. Total training time was usually 500 epochs or less.

By looking closely at the dynamics of learning, it was discovered that for different inputs the states of the network tended to cluster around three values plus the initial state. These four states can be considered as possible states of an actual finite state machine and the movement between these states as a function of input can be interpreted as the state transitions of a state machine. Constructing a state machine yields a perfect four state machine which will recognize any dual parity grammar. Using minimization procedures [Fu 1982], the extraneous state transitions can be reduced to the minimal 4-

state machine. The extracted state machine is shown in Fig. 1. However, for more complicated grammars and different initial conditions, it might be difficult to extract the finite state machine. When different initial weights were chosen, different extraneous transition diagrams with more states resulted. What is interesting is that the neural net finite state machine learned this simple grammar perfectly. A first order net can also learn this problem; the higher order net learns it much faster. It is easy to prove that there are finite sate machines that cannot be represented by first order, single layer recurrent nets [Minsky 1967]. For further discussion of higher order state machines, see [Liu, et. al. 1990].

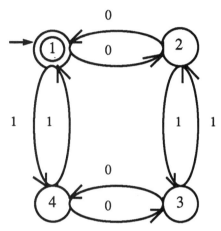

FIGURE 1: A learned four state machine; state 1 is both the start and the final state.

NEURAL NET PUSHDOWN AUTOMATA

In order to easily learn more complex deterministic grammars, the neural net must somehow develop and/or learn to use some type of memory, the simplest being a stack memory. Two approaches easily come to mind. Teach the additional weight structure in a multilayer neural network to serve as memory [Pollack 1989] or teach the neural net to use an external memory source. The latter is appealing because it is well known from formal language theory that a finite stack machine requires significantly fewer resources than a finite state machine for bounded problems such as recognizing a finite length context-free grammar. To teach a neural net to use a stack memory poses at least three problems: 1) how to construct the stack memory, 2) how to couple the stack memory to the neural net state machine, and 3) how to formulate the objective function such that its optimization will yield effective learning rules.

Most straight-forward is formulating the objective function so that the stack is coupled to the neural net state machine. The most stringent condition for a pushdown automata to accept a context-free grammar is that the pushdown automata be in a final state and the stack be empty. Thus, the error function of eq. (3) above is modified to include both final state and stack length terms:

$$E = \Sigma E_r^2 = \Sigma (T_r - S_o(t_p) + L(t_p))^2 , \qquad (6)$$

where $L(t_p)$ is the final stack length at time t_p, i.e. the time at which the last symbol of the string is presented. Therefore, for legal strings $E = 0$, if the pushdown automata is in a final state and the stack is empty.

Now consider how the stack can be connected to the neural net state machine. Recall that for a pushdown automata [Fu 1982], the state transition mapping of eq. (1) includes an additional argument, the symbol R(t) read from the top of the stack and an additional stack action mapping. An obvious approach to connecting the stack to the neural net is to let the activity level of certain neurons represent the symbol at the top of the stack and others represent the action on the stack. The pushdown automata has an additional stack action of reading or writing to the top of the stack based on the current state, input, and top stack symbol. One interpretation of these mappings would be extensions of eq. (2):

$$S_i(t+1) = g\{ \Sigma W^s_{ijk} S_j(t) V_k(t) \} \qquad (7)$$

$$A_i(t+1) = f\{ \Sigma W^a_{ijk} S_j(t) V_k(t) \} \qquad (8)$$

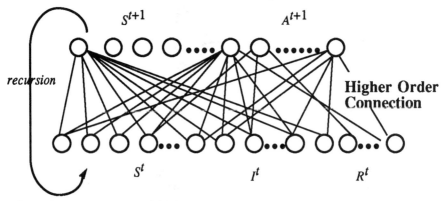

FIGURE 2:. Single layer higher order recursive neural network that is connected to a stack memory. A represents action neurons connected to the stack; R represents memory buffer neurons which read the top of the stack. The activation proceeds upward from states, input, and stack top at time t to states and action at time t+1. The recursion replaces the states in the bottom layer with the states in the top layer.

where $A_j(t)$ are output neurons controlling the action of the stack; $V_k(t)$ is either the input neuron value $I_k(t)$ or the connected stack memory neuron value $R_k(t)$, dependent on the index k; and f=2g-1. The current values $S_j(t)$, $I_k(t)$, and $R_k(t)$ are all fully connected through 2nd order weights with no hidden neurons. The mappings of eqs. (7) and (8) define the recursive network and can be implemented concurrently and in parallel. Let A(t=0) & R(t=0)= 0. The neuron state values range continuously from 0 to 1 while the neuron action values range from -1 to 1. The neural network part of the architecture is depicted in Fig. 2. The number of read neurons is equal to the coding representation of the stack. For most applications, one action neuron suffices.

In order to use the gradient descent learning rule described in eq. (4), the stack length must have continuous values. (Other types of learning algorithms may not require a continuous stack.) We now explain how a continuous stack is used and connected to the action and read neurons. Interpret the stack actions as follows: push (A>0), pop (A<0), no action (A=0). For simplicity, only the current input symbol is pushed ; then the number of input and stack memory neurons are equal. (If the input symbol is a, then only Aa of that value is pushed into the stack) T he stack consists of a summation of analog symbols. By definition, all symbols up in unit depth one are in the read neuron R at time t.. If A<0 (pop), a depth of |A| of all symbols in that depth is removed from the stack. In the next time step what remains in R is a unit length from the current stack top. An attempt to pop an empty stack occurs if not enough remains in the stack to pop depth |A|. Further description of this operation with examples can be found in [Sun, et. al.1990]. Since the action operation A removes or adds to the stack, the stack length at time t+1 is $L(t+1) = L(t) + A(t)$, where L(t=0) = 0.

With the recursion relations, stack construction, and error function defined, the learning algorithms may be derived from eqs. (4) & (6)

$$\Delta W_{ijk} = \eta \ E_r \ \{ \ \partial S_l(t_p)/\partial W_{ijk} - \partial L(t_p)/\partial W_{ij} \ . \tag{9}$$

The derivative terms may be derived from the recurrent relations eqs. (7) & (8) and the stack length equation. They are

$$\partial S_l(t+1)/\partial W_{ijk} = h_l \ S_l(t+1) \ \{ \ \delta_{il} \ S_j(t) \ V_k(t) + \Sigma \ W_{lmn} \ V_n(t) \ \partial S_m(t)/\partial W_{ijk} +$$
$$\Sigma \ W_{lmn} \ S_m(t) \ \partial R_n(t)/\partial W_{ijk} \ \} \tag{10}$$

and

$$\partial L(t+1)/\partial W_{ijk} = \partial L(t)/\partial W_{ijk} + \partial A(t)/\partial W_{ijk} \ . \tag{11}$$

Since the change $\partial R_k(t)/\partial W_{ijk}$ must contain information about past changes in action A, we have

$$\partial R_k(t)/\partial W_{ijk} = \Sigma \ \partial R_k(t)/\partial A(t) \ \partial A(t)/\partial W_{ijk} \cong \Delta_R \ \partial A(t)/\partial W_{ijk} \tag{12}$$

where Δ_R = 0,1, or -1 and depends on the top and bottom symbols read in R(t). This approximation assumes that the read changes are only effected by actions which occurred in the recent past. The change in action with respect to the weights is defined by a recursion derived from eq. (8) and has the same form as eq. (10). For the case of popping an empty stack, the weight change increases the stack length for a legal string; otherwise nothing happens. It appears that all these derivatives are necessary to adequately integrate the neural net to the continuous stack memory.

PUSHDOWN AUTOMATA SIMULATIONS

To test this theoretical development, we trained the neural net pushdown automaton on two context-free grammars, 1^n0^n and the parenthesis grammar (balanced strings of parentheses). For the parenthesis grammar, the net architecture consisted of a 2nd order fully interconnected single layer net with 3 state neurons, 3 input neurons, and 2 action neurons (one for push & one for pop). In 20 epochs with fifty positive and negative training samples of increasing length up to length eight , the network learned how to be a perfect pushdown automaton. We concluded this after testing on all strings up to length 20 and through a similar analysis of emergent state-stack values. Using a similar clustering analysis and heuristic reduction approach, the minimal pushdown automaton emerges. It should be noted that for this pushdown automaton, the state machine does very little and is easily learned Fig. 3 shows the pushdown automaton that emerged; the 3-tuple represents (input symbol, stack symbol, action of push or pop). The 1^n0^n was also successfully trained with a small training set and a few hundred epochs of learning. This should be compared to the more computationally intense learning of layered networks [Allen 1989]. A minimal pushdown automaton was also derived. For further details of the learning and emergent pushdown automata, see [Sun, et.al. 1990].

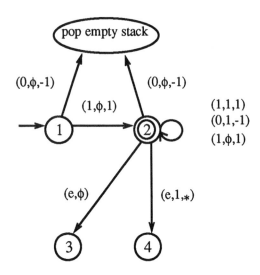

FIGURE 3: Learned neural network pushdown automaton for parenthesis balance checker where the numerical results for states (1), (2), (3), and (4) are (1,0,0), (.9,.2,.2), (.89,.17,.48) and (,79,.25,.70). State (1) is the start state. State (3) is a legal end state. Before feeding the end symbol, a legal string must end at state (2) with empty stack.

CONCLUSIONS

This work presents a different approach to incorporating and using memory in a neural network. A recurrent higher order net learned to effectively employ an external stack memory to learn simple context-free grammars. However, to do so required the creation of a continuous stack structure. Since it was possible to reduce the neural network to the ideal pushdown automaton, the neural network can be said to have "perfectly" learned these simple grammars. Though the simulations appear very promising, many questions remain. Besides extending the simulations to more complex grammars, there are questions of how well such architectures will scale for "real" problems. What became evident was the power of the higher order network; again demonstrating its speed of learning and sparseness of training sets. Will the same be true for more complex problems is a question for further work.

REFERENCES

R.A. Allen, Adaptive Training for Connectionist State Machines, *ACM Computer Conference*, Louisville, p.428, (1989).

D. Angluin & C.H. Smith, Inductive Inference: Theory and Methods, *ACM Computing Surveys*, Vol. 15, No. 3, p. 237, (1983).

K.S. Fu, *Syntactic Pattern Recognition and Applications,* Prentice-Hall, Englewood Cliffs, N.J. (1982).

J.E. Hopcroft & J.D. Ullman, *Introduction to Automata Theory, Languages, and Computation*, Addison Wesley, Reading, Ma. (1979).

M.I. Jordan, Attractor Dynamics and Parallelism in a Connectionist Sequential Machine, *Proceedings of the Eigtht Conference of the Cognitive Science Society*, Amherst, Ma, p. 531 (1986).

Y.D. Liu, G.Z. Sun, H.H. Chen, Y.C. Lee, C.L. Giles, Grammatical Inference and Neural Network State Machines, *Proceedings of the International Joint Conference on Neural Networks*, M. Caudill (ed), Lawerence Erlbaum, Hillsdale, N.J., vol 1. p.285 (1990).

M.L. Minsky, *Computation: Finite and Infinite Machines*, Prentice-Hall, Englewood, N.J., p. 55 (1967).

F.J. Pineda, Generalization of Backpropagation to Recurrent Neural Networks, *Phys. Rev. Lett.*, vol 18, p. 2229 (1987).

J.B. Pollack, Implications of Recursive Distributed Representations, *Advances in Neural Information Systems 1*, D.S. Touretzky (ed), Morgan Kaufmann, San Mateo, Ca, p. 527 (1989).

D. Servan-Schreiber, A. Cleeremans & J.L. McClelland, Encoding Sequential Structure in Simple Recurrent Networks, *Advances in Neural Information Systems 1*, D.S. Touretzky (ed), Morgan Kaufmann, San Mateo, Ca, p. 643 (1989).

G.Z. Sun, H.H. Chen, C.L. Giles, Y.C. Lee, D. Chen, Connectionist Pushdown Automata that Learn Context-free Grammars, *Proceedings of the International Joint Conference on Neural Networks*, M. Caudill (ed), Lawerence Erlbaum, Hillsdale, N.J., vol 1. p.577 (1990).

R. J. Williams & D. Zipser, A Learning Algorithm for Continually Running Fully Recurrent Neural Networks, Institute for Cognitive Science Report 8805, U. of CA, San Diego, La Jolla, Ca 92093, (1988).

Bayesian Inference of Regular Grammar and Markov Source Models

Kurt R. Smith and Michael I. Miller
Biomedical Computer Laboratory
and
Electronic Signals and Systems Research Laboratory
Washington University, St. Louis, MO 63130

ABSTRACT

In this paper we develop a Bayes criterion which includes the Rissanen complexity, for inferring regular grammar models. We develop two methods for regular grammar Bayesian inference. The first method is based on treating the regular grammar as a 1-dimensional Markov source, and the second is based on the combinatoric characteristics of the regular grammar itself. We apply the resulting Bayes criteria to a particular example in order to show the efficiency of each method.

1 MOTIVATION

We are interested in segmenting electron-microscope autoradiography (EMA) images by learning representational models for the textures found in the EMA image. In studying this problem, we have recognized that both structural and statistical features may be useful for characterizing textures. This has motivated us to study the source modeling problem for both structural sources and statistical sources. The statistical sources that we have examined are the class of one and two-dimensional Markov sources (see [Smith 1990] for a Bayesian treatment of Markov random field texture model inference), while the structural sources that we are primarily interested in here are the class of regular grammars, which are important due to the role that grammatical constraints may play in the development of structural features for texture representation.

2 MARKOV SOURCE INFERENCE

Our primary interest here is the development of a complete Bayesian framework for the process of inferring a regular grammar from a training sequence. However, we have shown previously that there exists a 1-D Markov source which generates the regular language defined via some regular grammar [Miller, 1988]. We can therefore develop a generalized Bayesian inference procedure over the class of 1-D Markov sources which enables us to learn the Markov source corresponding to the optimal regular grammar. We begin our analysis by developing the general structure for Bayesian source modeling.

2.1 BAYESIAN APPROACH TO SOURCE MODELING

We state the Bayesian approach to model learning: Given a set of source models $\{\theta_0, \theta_1, \cdots, \theta_{M-1}\}$ and the observation x, choose the source model θ_i which most accurately represents the unknown source that generated x. This decision is made by calculating Bayes risk over the possible models which produces a general decision criterion for the model learning problem:

$$\underset{\{\theta_0, \theta_1, \cdots, \theta_{M-1}\}}{max} log\, P(x|\theta_i) + log\, P_i \, . \tag{2.1}$$

Under the additional assumption that the apriori probabilities over the candidate models are equivalent, the decision criterion becomes

$$\underset{\{\theta_0, \theta_1, \cdots, \theta_{M-1}\}}{max} log\, P(x|\theta_i) \, , \tag{2.2}$$

which is the quantity that we will use in measuring the *accuracy* of a model's representation.

2.2 STOCHASTIC COMPLEXITY AND MODEL LEARNING

It is well known that when given finite data, Bayesian procedures of this kind which do not have any prior on the models suffer from the fundamental limitation that they will predict models of greater and greater complexity. This has led others to introduce priors into the Bayes hypothesis testing procedure based on the complexity of the model being tested [Rissanen, 1986]. In particular, for the Markov case the complexity is directly proportional to the number of transition probabilities of the particular model being tested with the prior exponentially decreasing with the associated complexity. We now describe the inclusion of the complexity measure in greater detail.

Following Rissanen, the basic idea is to uncover the model which assigns maximum probability to the observed data, while also being as simple as possible so as to require a small Kolmogorov description length. The complexity associated with a model having k real parameters and a likelihood with n independent samples, is the now well-known $\frac{k}{2} log\, n$ which allows us to express the generalization of the original Bayes procedure (2.2) as the quantity

$$\max_{\{\theta_0,\theta_1,\ldots,\theta_{M-1}\}} \log P(x_n|\hat{\theta_i}) - \frac{k_{\theta_i}}{2} \log n \; . \tag{2.3}$$

Note well that $\hat{\theta_i}$ is the k_{θ_i}-dimensional parameter parameterizing model θ_i, which must be estimated from the observed data x_n. An alternative view of (2.3) is discovered by viewing the second term as the prior in the Bayes model (2.1) where the prior is defined as

$$P_{\theta_i} = e^{-\frac{k_{\theta_i}}{2} \log n} \; . \tag{2.4}$$

2.3 1-D MARKOV SOURCE MODELING

Consider that x_n is a 1-D n-length string of symbols which is generated by an unknown finite-state Markov source. In examining (2.3), we recognize that for 1-D Markov sources $\log P(x|\hat{\theta_i})$ may be written as $\log \prod_{j=1}^{n-1} P_{\theta_i}(S(x_j)|S(x_{j-1}))$ where $S(x_.)$ is a state function which evaluates to a state in the Markov source state set S_{θ_i}. Using this notation, the Bayes hypothesis test for 1-D Markov sources may be expressed as:

$$\max_{\{\theta_0,\theta_1,\ldots,\theta_{M-1}\}} \sum_{j=1}^{n-1} \log P_{\theta_i}(S(x_j)|S(x_{j-1})) \, , \tag{2.5}$$

For the general Markov source inference problem, we know only that the string x_n was generated by a 1-D Markov source, with the state set S_{θ_i} and the transition probabilities $P_{\theta_i}(S_k|S_l)$, $k,l \in S_{\theta_i}$ unknown. They must therefore be included in the inference procedure. To include the complexity term for this case, we note that the number of parameters to be estimated for model θ_i is simply the number of entries in the state-transition matrix $\hat{P}_{\theta_i}$, i.e. $k_{\theta_i} = |S_{\theta_i}|^2$. Therefore for 1-D Markov sources, the generalized Bayes hypothesis test including complexity may be stated as

$$\max_{\{\theta_0,\theta_1,\ldots,\theta_{M-1}\}} \frac{1}{n} \sum_{j=1}^{n-1} \log \hat{P}_{\theta_i}(S(x_j)|S(x_{j-1})) - \frac{|S_{\theta_i}|^2}{2n} \log n \, , \tag{2.6}$$

where we have divided the entire quantity by n in order to express the criterion in terms of bits per symbol. Note that a candidate Markov source model θ_i is initially specified by its order and corresponding state set S_{θ_i}.

The procedure for inferring 1-D Markov source models can thus be stated as follows. Given a sequence x_n from some unknown source, consider candidate Markov source models by computing the state function $S(x_.)$ (determined by the candidate model order) over the entire string x_n. Enumerating the state transitions which occur in x_n provides an estimate of the state-transition matrix $\hat{P}_{\theta_i}$ which is then used to compute (2.6). Now, the inferred Markov source becomes the one maximizing (2.6).

3 REGULAR GRAMMAR INFERENCE

Although the Bayes criterion developed for 1-D Markov sources (2.6) is a sufficient model learning criterion for the class of regular grammars, we will now show that by taking advantage of the apriori knowledge that the source is a regular grammar, the inference procedure can be made much more efficient. This apriori knowledge brings a special structure to the regular grammar inference problem in that not all allowable sets of Markov probabilities correspond to regular grammars. In fact, as shown in [Miller, 1988], corresponding to each regular grammar is a unique set of candidate probabilities, implying that the Bayesian solution which takes this into account will be far more efficient. We demonstrate that now.

3.1 BAYESIAN CRITERION USING GRAMMAR COMBINATORICS

Our approach is to use the combinatoric properties of the regular grammar in order to develop the optimal Bayes hypothesis test. We begin by defining the regular grammar.

Definition: A regular grammar G is a quadruple (V_N, V_T, S_S, R) where V_N, V_T are finite sets of non-terminal symbols (or states) and terminal symbols respectively, S_S is the sentence start state, and R is a finite set of production rules consisting of the transformation of a non-terminal symbol to either a terminal followed by a non-terminal, or a terminal alone, i.e.,

$$S_i \rightarrow W_j S_k \ or \ S_i \rightarrow W_j, \quad where \ W_j \in V_T, S_i, S_k \in V_N .$$

In the class of regular grammars that we consider, we define the *depth* of the language as the maximum number of terminal symbols which make up a nonterminal symbol. Corresponding to each regular grammar is an associated incidence matrix B with the i,k^{th} entry $B_{i,k}$ equal to the number of times there is a production for some terminal j and non-terminals i,k of the form $S_i \rightarrow W_j S_k \in R$. Also associated with each grammar G_i is the set of all n-length strings produced by the grammar, denoted as the regular language $\mathbf{\mathit{L}}_n(G_i)$.

Now we make the quite reasonable assumption that no string in the language $\mathbf{\mathit{L}}_n(G_i)$ is more or less probable apriori than any other string in that language. This indicates that all n-length strings that can be generated by G_i are equiprobable with a probability dictated by the combinatorics of the language as

$$P(x_n|G_i) = \frac{1}{|\mathbf{\mathit{L}}_n(G_i)|} , \tag{3.1}$$

where $|\mathbf{\mathit{L}}_n(G_i)|$ denotes the number of n-length sequences in the language which can be computed by considering the combinatorics of the language as follows:

$$|\mathbf{\mathit{L}}_n(G_i)| = \lambda_{G_i}{}^n ,$$

with λ_{G_i} corresponding to the largest eigenvalue of the state-transition matrix B_{G_i}. This results from the combinatoric growth rate being determined by the sum of the entries in the nth power state-transition matrix $B_{G_i}^n$, which grows as the largest eigenvalue λ_{G_i} of B_{G_i} [Blahut, 1987]. We can now write (3.1) in these terms as

$$P(x_n|G_i) = \lambda_{G_i}^{-n}, \tag{3.2}$$

which expresses the probability of the sequence x_n in terms of the combinatorics of G_i.

We now use this combinatoric interpretation of the probability to develop Bayes decision criterion over two candidate grammars. Assume that there exists a finite space of sequences X, all of which may be generated by one of the two possible grammars $\{G_0, G_1\}$. Now by dividing this observation space X into two decision regions, X_0 (for G_0) and X_1 (for G_1), we can write Bayes risk R in terms of the observation probabilities $P(x_n|G_0), P(x_n|G_1)$:

$$R = \sum_{x_n \in X_1} P(x_n|G_0) + \sum_{x_n \in X_0} P(x_n|G_1). \tag{3.3}$$

This implementation of Bayes risk assumes that sequences from each grammar occur equiprobably apriori and that the cost of choosing the incorrect grammar is equal to 1. Now incorporating the combinatoric counting probabilities (3.2), we can rewrite (3.3) as

$$R = \sum_{x_n \in X_1} \lambda_{G_0}^{-n} + \sum_{x_n \in X_0} \lambda_{G_1}^{-n}$$

which can be rewritten

$$R = \frac{1}{2} + \sum_{x_n \in X_0} \left\{ \lambda_{G_1}^{-n} - \lambda_{G_0}^{-n} \right\}. \tag{3.4}$$

The risk is therefore minimized by choosing G_0 if $\lambda_{G_1}^{-n} < \lambda_{G_0}^{-n}$ and G_1 if $\lambda_{G_1}^{-n} > \lambda_{G_0}^{-n}$. This establishes the *likelihood ratio* for the grammar inference problem:

$$\frac{\lambda_{G_1}^{-n}}{\lambda_{G_0}^{-n}} \mathrel{\substack{G_1 \\ > \\ < \\ G_0}} 1 \,,$$

which can alternatively be expressed in terms of the *log* as

$$\max_{\{G_0, G_1\}} -n \log \lambda_{G_i}.$$

Recognizing this as the *maximum likelihood* decision, this decision criterion is easily generalized to M hypothesis. Now by ignoring any complexity component, the generalized Bayes test for a regular grammar can be stated as

$$\max_{\{G_0, G_1, \ldots, G_{M-1}\}} - n \log \lambda_{G_i} , \tag{3.5}$$

where λ_{G_i} is the largest eigenvalue of the estimated incidence matrix $\widehat{B}_{G_i}$ corresponding to grammar G_i where $\widehat{B}_{G_i}$ is estimated from x_n.

The complexity factor to be included in this Bayesian criterion differs from the complexity term in (2.3) due to the fact that the parameters to be estimated are now the entries in the $\widehat{B}_{G_i}$ matrix which are strictly binary. From a description length interpretation then, these parameters can be fully described using 1 bit per entry in $\widehat{B}_{G_i}$. The complexity term is thus simply $|S_{G_i}|^2$ which now allows us to write the Bayes inference criterion for regular grammars as

$$\max_{\{G_0, G_1, \ldots, G_{M-1}\}} - \log \lambda_{G_i} - \frac{|S_{G_i}|^2}{n} , \tag{3.6}$$

in terms of bits per symbol. We can now state the algorithm for inferring grammars.

Regular Grammar Inference Algorithm

1. Initialize the grammar depth to $d=1$.

2. Compute $|S_G| = |V_T|^d$.

3. Using the state function $S_d(x_i)$ corresponding to the current depth, compute the state transitions at all sites x_i in the observed sequence x_n in order to estimate the incidence matrix $\widehat{B}_{G_i}$ for the grammar currently being considered.

4. Compute λ_{G_i} from $\widehat{B}_{G_i}$. (recall that this is the largest eigenvalue of $\widehat{B}_{G_i}$).

5. Using λ_{G_i} and $|S_{G_i}|$ compute (3.6) - denote this as $I_{G_i} = - \log \lambda_{G_i} - \frac{|S_{G_i}|^2}{n}$.

6. Increase the grammar depth $d=d+1$ and goto 2 (i.e. test another candidate grammar) until I_{G_i} discontinues to increase.

The regular grammar of minimum depth which maximizes I_{G_i} (i.e. maximizes (3.6)) is then the optimal regular grammar source model for the given sequence x_n.

3.2 REGULAR GRAMMAR INFERENCE RESULTS

To compare the efficiency of the two Bayes criteria (2.6) and (3.6), we will consider a regular grammar inference experiment. The regular grammar that we will attempt to learn, which we refer to as the 4-0,1s regular grammar, is a run-length constrained binary grammar which disallows 4 consecutive occurrences of a 0 or a 1. Referring to the regular grammar definition, we note that this regular grammar can be described by its incidence matrix

$$
B_{4\text{-}0,1} = \begin{bmatrix} 0 & 0 & 0 & 1 & 0 & 0 \\ 1 & 0 & 0 & 1 & 0 & 0 \\ 0 & 1 & 0 & 1 & 0 & 0 \\ 0 & 0 & 1 & 0 & 1 & 0 \\ 0 & 0 & 1 & 0 & 0 & 1 \\ 0 & 0 & 1 & 0 & 0 & 0 \end{bmatrix},
$$

where the states corresponding to row and column indices are

$$
S_1 = 000,\ S_2 = 00,\ S_3 = 0,\ S_4 = 1,\ S_5 = 11,\ S_6 = 111.
$$

Note that this regular grammar has a depth equal to 3 and thus the corresponding Markov source has an order equal to 3.

The inference experiment may be described as follows. Given a training set of length 16 strings from the 4-0,1s language, we apply the Bayes criteria (2.6) and (3.6) in an attempt to infer the regular grammar in each case. We compute the criteria for five candidate models of order/depth 1 through 5 (recall that this defines the size of the state set for the Markov source and the regular grammar, respectively).

Treating the unknown regular grammar as a Markov source, we estimate the corresponding state-transition matrix $\hat{P}$ and then compute the Bayes criterion according to (2.6) for each of the five candidate models. We compute the criterion as a function of the number of training samples for each candidate model and plot the result in Figure 1a.

Similarly, we estimate the incidence matrix $\hat{B}$ and compute the Bayes criterion according to (3.6) for each of the five regular grammar candidate models, and plot the results as a function of the number of training samples in Figure 1b.

We compare the two Bayesian criteria by examining Figures 1a and 1b. Note that criterion (3.6) discovers the correct regular grammar (depth = 3) after only 50 training samples (Figure 1b), while the equivalent Markov source (order = 3) is found only after almost 500 training samples have been used in computing (2.6) (Figure 1a). This points out that a much more efficient inference procedure exists for regular grammars by taking advantage of the apriori grammar information (i.e. only the depth and the binary incidence matrix $\hat{B}$ must be estimated), whereas for 1-D Markov sources, both the order and the real-valued state-transition matrix $\hat{P}$ must be estimated.

4. CONCLUSION

In conclusion, we stress the importance of casting the source modeling problem within a Bayesian framework which incorporates priors based on the model complexity and known model attributes. Using this approach, we have developed an efficient Bayesian

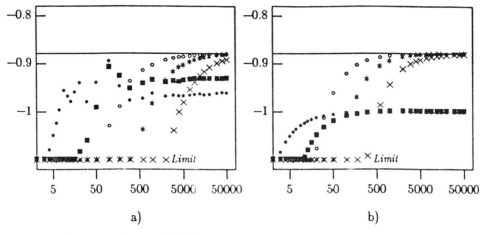

a)   b)

Grammar depth d /Markov order: $\bullet = 1, \blacksquare = 2, \circ = 3, * = 4, \times = 5$.

Figure 1: Results of computing Bayes criterion measures (2.6) and (3.6) vs. the number of training samples - a) Markov source criterion (2.6); b) Regular grammar combinatoric criterion (3.6).

framework for inferring regular grammars. This type of Bayesian model is potentially quite useful for the texture analysis and image segmentation problem where a consistent framework is desired for considering both structural and statistical features in the texture/image representation.

Acknowledgements

This research was supported by the NSF via a Presidential Young Investigator Award ECE-8552518 and by the NIH via a DRR Grant RR-1380.

References

Blahut, R. E. (1987), *Principles and Practice of Information Theory* , Addison-Wesley Publishing Co., Reading, MA.

Miller, M. I., Roysam, B, Smith, K. R., and Udding, J. T (1988), "Mapping Rule-Based Regular Grammars to Gibbs Distributions", *AMS-IMS-SIAM Joint Conference on SPATIAL STATISTICS AND IMAGING,* American Mathematical Society.

Rissanen, J. (1986), "Stochastic Complexity and Modeling", *Annals of Statistics*, 14, no.3, pp. 1080-1100.

Smith, K. R., Miller, M. I. (1990), "A Bayesian Approach Incorporating Rissanen Complexity for Learning Markov Random Field Texture Models", Proceedings of Int. Conference on Acoustics, Speech, and Signal Processing, Albuquerque, NM.

Handwritten Digit Recognition with a Back-Propagation Network

Y. Le Cun, B. Boser, J. S. Denker, D. Henderson,
R. E. Howard, W. Hubbard, and L. D. Jackel
AT&T Bell Laboratories, Holmdel, N. J. 07733

ABSTRACT

We present an application of back-propagation networks to hand-written digit recognition. Minimal preprocessing of the data was required, but architecture of the network was highly constrained and specifically designed for the task. The input of the network consists of normalized images of isolated digits. The method has 1% error rate and about a 9% reject rate on zipcode digits provided by the U.S. Postal Service.

1   INTRODUCTION

The main point of this paper is to show that large back-propagation (BP) networks can be applied to real image-recognition problems without a large, complex preprocessing stage requiring detailed engineering. Unlike most previous work on the subject (Denker et al., 1989), the learning network is directly fed with images, rather than feature vectors, thus demonstrating the ability of BP networks to deal with large amounts of low level information.

Previous work performed on simple digit images (Le Cun, 1989) showed that the architecture of the network strongly influences the network's generalization ability. Good generalization can only be obtained by designing a network architecture that contains a certain amount of *a priori* knowledge about the problem. The basic design principle is to minimize the number of free parameters that must be determined by the learning algorithm, without overly reducing the computational power of the network. This principle increases the probability of correct generalization because

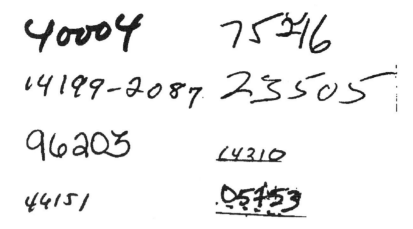

Figure 1: Examples of original zipcodes from the testing set.

it results in a specialized network architecture that has a reduced entropy (Denker et al., 1987; Patarnello and Carnevali, 1987; Tishby, Levin and Solla, 1989; Le Cun, 1989). On the other hand, some effort must be devoted to designing appropriate constraints into the architecture.

2   ZIPCODE RECOGNITION

The handwritten digit-recognition application was chosen because it is a relatively simple machine vision task: the input consists of black or white pixels, the digits are usually well-separated from the background, and there are only ten output categories. Yet the problem deals with objects in a real two-dimensional space and the mapping from image space to category space has both considerable regularity and considerable complexity. The problem has added attraction because it is of great practical value.

The database used to train and test the network is a superset of the one used in the work reported last year (Denker et al., 1989). We emphasize that the method of solution reported here relies more heavily on automatic learning, and much less on hand-designed preprocessing.

The database consists of 9298 segmented numerals digitized from handwritten zipcodes that appeared on real U.S. Mail passing through the Buffalo, N.Y. post office. Examples of such images are shown in figure 1. The digits were written by many different people, using a great variety of sizes, writing styles and instruments, with widely varying levels of care. This was supplemented by a set of 3349 printed digits coming from 35 different fonts. The training set consisted of 7291 handwritten digits plus 2549 printed digits. The remaining 2007 handwritten and 700 printed digits were used as the test set. The printed fonts in the test set were different from the printed fonts in the training set.One important feature of this database, which

Figure 2: Examples of normalized digits from the testing set.

is a common feature to all real-world databases, is that both the training set and the testing set contain numerous examples that are ambiguous, unclassifiable, or even misclassified.

3 PREPROCESSING

Acquisition, binarization, location of the zipcode, and preliminary segmentation were performed by Postal Service contractors (Wang and Srihari, 1988). Some of these steps constitute very hard tasks in themselves. The segmentation (separating each digit from its neighbors) would be a relatively simple task if we could assume that a character is contiguous and is disconnected from its neighbors, but neither of these assumptions holds in practice. Many ambiguous characters in the database are the result of mis-segmentation (especially broken 5's) as can be seen on figure 2.

At this point, the size of a digit varies but is typically around 40 by 60 pixels. Since the input of a back-propagation network is fixed size, it is necessary to normalize the size of the characters. This was performed using a linear transformation to make the characters fit in a 16 by 16 pixel image. This transformation preserves the aspect ratio of the character, and is performed after extraneous marks in the image have been removed. Because of the linear transformation, the resulting image is not binary but has multiple gray levels, since a variable number of pixels in the original image can fall into a given pixel in the target image. The gray levels of each image are scaled and translated to fall within the range −1 to 1.

4 THE NETWORK

The remainder of the recognition is entirely performed by a multi-layer network. All of the connections in the network are adaptive, although heavily constrained, and are trained using back-propagation. This is in contrast with earlier work (Denker et al., 1989) where the first few layers of connections were hand-chosen constants. The input of the network is a 16 by 16 normalized image and the output is composed of 10 units: one per class. When a pattern belonging to class i is presented, the desired output is $+1$ for the ith output unit, and -1 for the other output units.

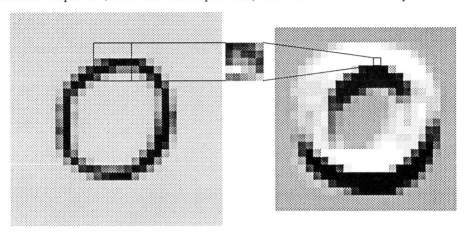

Figure 3: Input image (left), weight vector (center), and resulting feature map (right). The feature map is obtained by scanning the input image with a single neuron that has a local receptive field, as indicated. White represents -1, black represents $+1$.

A fully connected network with enough discriminative power for the task would have far too many parameters to be able to generalize correctly. Therefore a restricted connection-scheme must be devised, guided by our prior knowledge about shape recognition. There are well-known advantages to performing shape recognition by detecting and combining local features. We have required our network to do this by constraining the connections in the first few layers to be local. In addition, if a feature detector is useful on one part of the image, it is likely to be useful on other parts of the image as well. One reason for this is that the salient features of a distorted character might be displaced slightly from their position in a typical character. One solution to this problem is to scan the input image with a single neuron that has a local receptive field, and store the states of this neuron in corresponding locations in a layer called a *feature map* (see figure 3). This operation is equivalent to a convolution with a small size kernel, followed by a squashing function. The process can be performed in parallel by implementing the feature map as a plane of neurons whose weight vectors are constrained to be equal. That is, units in a feature map are constrained to perform the same operation on different parts of the image. An interesting side-effect of this *weight sharing* technique, already described in (Rumelhart, Hinton and Williams, 1986), is to reduce the number of free parameters by a large amount, since a large number of units share the same weights. In addition, a certain level of shift invariance is present in the system: shifting the input will shift the result on the feature map, but will leave it unchanged otherwise. In practice, it will be necessary to have multiple feature maps, extracting different features from the same image.

	1	2	3	4	5	6	7	8	9	10	11	12
1	X	X	X	x	X	X						
2		X	X	X	X	X						
3							X	X	X	x	X	X
4								X	X	X	X	X

Table 1: Connections between H2 and H3.

The idea of local, convolutional feature maps can be applied to subsequent hidden layers as well, to extract features of increasing complexity and abstraction. Interestingly, higher level features require less precise coding of their location. Reduced precision is actually advantageous, since a slight distortion or translation of the input will have reduced effect on the representation. Thus, each feature extraction in our network is followed by an additional layer which performs a local averaging and a subsampling, reducing the resolution of the feature map. This layer introduces a certain level of invariance to distortions and translations. A functional module of our network consists of a layer of shared-weight feature maps followed by an averaging/subsampling layer. This is reminiscent of the Neocognitron architecture (Fukushima and Miyake, 1982), with the notable difference that we use backprop (rather than unsupervised learning) which we feel is more appropriate to this sort of classification problem.

The network architecture, represented in figure 4, is a direct extension of the ones described in (Le Cun, 1989; Le Cun et al., 1990a). The network has four hidden layers respectively named H1, H2, H3, and H4. Layers H1 and H3 are shared-weights feature extractors, while H2 and H4 are averaging/subsampling layers.

Although the size of the active part of the input is 16 by 16, the actual input is a 28 by 28 plane to avoid problems when a kernel overlaps a boundary. H1 is composed of 4 groups of 576 units arranged as 4 independent 24 by 24 feature maps. These four feature maps will be designated by H1.1, H1.2, H1.3 and H1.4. Each unit in a feature map takes its input from a 5 by 5 neighborhood on the input plane. As described above, corresponding connections on each unit in a given feature map are constrained to have the same weight. In other words, all of the 576 units in H1.1 uses the same set of 26 weights (including the bias). Of course, units in another map (say H1.4) share *another* set of 26 weights.

Layer H2 is the averaging/subsampling layer. It is composed of 4 planes of size 12 by 12. Each unit in one of these planes takes inputs on 4 units on the corresponding plane in H1. Receptive fields do not overlap. All the weights are constrained to be equal, even within a single unit. Therefore, H2 performs a local averaging and a 2 to 1 subsampling of H1 in each direction.

Layer H3 is composed of 12 feature maps. Each feature map contains 64 units arranged in a 8 by 8 plane. As before, these feature maps will be designated as H2.1, H2.2 ⋯ H2.12. The connection scheme between H2 and H3 is quite similar to the one between the input and H1, but slightly more complicated because H3 has multiple 2-D maps. Each unit receptive field is composed of one or two 5 by

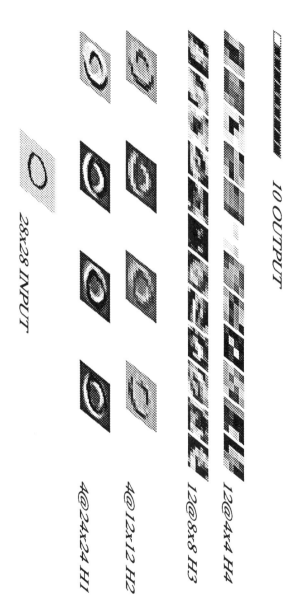

10 OUTPUT

12@4x4 H4

12@8x8 H3

4@12x12 H2

4@24x24 H1

28x28 INPUT

Figure 4: Network Architecture with 5 layers of fully-adaptive connections.

5 neighborhoods centered around units that are at identical positions within each H2 maps. Of course, all units in a given map are constrained to have identical weight vectors. The maps in H2 on which a map in H3 takes its inputs are chosen according to a scheme described on table 1. According to this scheme, the network is composed of two almost independent modules. Layer H4 plays the same role as layer H2, it is composed of 12 groups of 16 units arranged in 4 by 4 planes.

The output layer has 10 units and is fully connected to H4. In summary, the network has 4635 units, 98442 connections, and 2578 independent parameters. This architecture was derived using the Optimal Brain Damage technique (Le Cun et al., 1990b) starting from a previous architecture (Le Cun et al., 1990a) that had 4 times more free parameters.

5   RESULTS

After 30 training passes the error rate on training set (7291 handwritten plus 2549 printed digits) was 1.1% and the MSE was .017. On the whole test set (2007 handwritten plus 700 printed characters) the error rate was 3.4% and the MSE was 0.024. All the classification errors occurred on handwritten characters.

In a realistic application, the user is not so much interested in the raw error rate as in the number of rejections necessary to reach a given level of accuracy. In our case, we measured the percentage of test patterns that must be rejected in order to get 1% error rate. Our rejection criterion was based on three conditions: the activity level of the most-active output unit should by larger than a given threshold t_1, the activity level of the second most-active unit should be smaller than a given threshold t_2, and finally, the difference between the activity levels of these two units should be larger than a given threshold t_d. The best percentage of rejections on the complete test set was 5.7% for 1% error. On the handwritten set only, the result was 9% rejections for 1% error. It should be emphasized that the rejection thresholds were obtained using performance measures on the *test set*. About half the substitution errors in the testing set were due to faulty segmentation, and an additional quarter were due to erroneous assignment of the desired category. Some of the remaining images were ambiguous even to humans, and in a few cases the network misclassified the image for no discernible reason.

Even though a second-order version of back-propagation was used, it is interesting to note that the learning takes only 30 passes through the training set. We think this can be attributed to the large amount of redundancy present in real data. A complete training session (30 passes through the training set plus test) takes about 3 days on a SUN SPARCstation 1 using the SN2 connectionist simulator (Bottou and Le Cun, 1989).

After successful training, the network was implemented on a commercial Digital Signal Processor board containing an AT&T DSP-32C general purpose DSP chip with a peak performance of 12.5 million multiply-add operations per second on 32 bit floating point numbers. The DSP operates as a coprocessor in a PC connected to a video camera. The PC performs the digitization, binarization and segmentation

Figure 5: Atypical data. The network classifies these correctly, even though they are quite unlike anything in the training set.

of the image, while the DSP performs the size-normalization and the classification. The overall throughput of the digit recognizer including image acquisition is 10 to 12 classifications per second and is limited mainly by the normalization step. On normalized digits, the DSP performs more than 30 classifications per second.

6 CONCLUSION

Back-propagation learning was successfully applied to a large, real-world task. Our results appear to be at the state of the art in handwritten digit recognition. The network had many connections but relatively few free parameters. The network architecture and the constraints on the weights were designed to incorporate geometric knowledge about the task into the system. Because of its architecture, the network could be trained on a low-level representation of data that had minimal preprocessing (as opposed to elaborate feature extraction). Because of the redundant nature of the data and because of the constraints imposed on the network, the learning time was relatively short considering the size of the training set. Scaling properties were far better than one would expect just from extrapolating results of back-propagation on smaller, artificial problems. Preliminary results on alphanumeric characters show that the method can be directly extended to larger tasks.

The final network of connections and weights obtained by back-propagation learning was readily implementable on commercial digital signal processing hardware. Throughput rates, from camera to classified image, of more than ten digits per second were obtained.

Acknowledgments

We thank the US Postal Service and its contractors for providing us with the zip-code database. We thank Henry Baird for useful discussions and for providing the printed-font database.

References

Bottou, L.-Y. and Le Cun, Y. (1989). *SN2: A Simulator for Connectionist Models.* Neuristique SA, Paris, France.

Denker, J., Schwartz, D., Wittner, B., Solla, S. A., Howard, R., Jackel, L., and Hopfield, J. (1987). Large Automatic Learning, Rule Extraction and Generalization. *Complex Systems*, 1:877–922.

Denker, J. S., Gardner, W. R., Graf, H. P., Henderson, D., Howard, R. E., Hubbard, W., Jackel, L. D., Baird, H. S., and Guyon, I. (1989). Neural Network Recognizer for Hand-Written Zip Code Digits. In Touretzky, D., editor, *Neural Information Processing Systems*, volume 1, pages 323–331, Denver, 1988. Morgan Kaufmann.

Fukushima, K. and Miyake, S. (1982). Neocognitron: A new algorithm for pattern recognition tolerant of deformations and shifts in position. *Pattern Recognition*, 15:455–469.

Le Cun, Y. (1989). Generalization and Network Design Strategies. In Pfeifer, R., Schreter, Z., Fogelman, F., and Steels, L., editors, *Connectionism in Perspective*, Zurich, Switzerland. Elsevier.

Le Cun, Y., Boser, B., Denker, J. S., Henderson, D., Howard, R. E., Hubbard, W., and Jackel, L. D. (1990a). Back-Propagation Applied to Handwritten Zipcode Recognition. *Neural Computation*, 1(4).

Le Cun, Y., Denker, J. S., Solla, S., Howard, R. E. ., and Jackel, L. D. (1990b). Optimal Brain Damage. In Touretzky, D., editor, *Neural Information Processing Systems*, volume 2, Denver, 1989. Morgan Kaufman.

Patarnello, S. and Carnevali, P. (1987). Learning Networks of Neurons with Boolean Logic. *Europhysics Letters*, 4(4):503–508.

Rumelhart, D. E., Hinton, G. E., and Williams, R. J. (1986). Learning internal representations by error propagation. In *Parallel distributed processing: Explorations in the microstructure of cognition*, volume I, pages 318–362. Bradford Books, Cambridge, MA.

Tishby, N., Levin, E., and Solla, S. A. (1989). Consistent Inference of Probabilities in Layered Networks: Predictions and Generalization. In *Proceedings of the International Joint Conference on Neural Networks*, Washington DC.

Wang, C. H. and Srihari, S. N. (1988). A Framework for Object Recognition in a Visually Complex Environment and its Application to Locating Address Blocks on Mail Pieces. *International Journal of Computer Vision*, 2:125.

Recognizing Hand–Printed Letters and Digits

Gale L. Martin   James A. Pittman
MCC, Austin, Texas 78759

ABSTRACT

We are developing a hand–printed character recognition system using a multi–layered neural net trained through backpropagation. We report on results of training nets with samples of hand–printed digits scanned off of bank checks and hand–printed letters interactively entered into a computer through a stylus digitizer. Given a large training set, and a net with sufficient capacity to achieve high performance on the training set, nets typically achieved error rates of 4–5% at a 0% reject rate and 1–2% at a 10% reject rate. The topology and capacity of the system, as measured by the number of connections in the net, have surprisingly little effect on generalization. For those developing practical pattern recognition systems, these results suggest that a large and representative training sample may be the single, most important factor in achieving high recognition accuracy. From a scientific standpoint, these results raise doubts about the relevance to backpropagation of learning models that estimate the likelihood of high generalization from estimates of capacity. Reducing capacity does have other benefits however, especially when the reduction is accomplished by using local receptive fields with shared weights. In this latter case, we find the net evolves feature detectors resembling those in visual cortex and Linsker's orientation–selective nodes.

Practical interest in hand–printed character recognition is fueled by two current technology trends: one toward systems that interpret hand–printing on hard–copy documents and one toward notebook–like computers that replace the keyboard with a stylus digitizer. The stylus enables users to write and draw directly on a flat panel display. In this paper, we report on results applying multi–layered neural nets trained through backpropagation (Rumelhart, Hinton, & Williams, 1986) to both cases.

Developing pattern recognition systems is typically a two–stage process. First, intuition and experimentation are used to select a set of features to represent the raw input pattern. Then a variety of well–developed techniques are used to optimize the classifier system that assumes this featural representation. Most applications of backpropagation learning to character recognition use the learning capabilities only for this latter stage--developing the classifier system (Burr, 1986; Denker, Gardner, Graf, Henderson, Howard, Hubbard, Jackel, Baird, & Guyon, 1989; Mori & Yokosawa, 1989; Weideman, Manry, & Yau, 1989). However, backpropagation learning affords the opportunity to optimize feature selection and pattern classification simultaneously . We avoid using pre-determined features as input to the net in favor of using a pre-segmented, size-normalized grayscale array for each character. This is a first step toward the goal of approximating the raw input projected onto the human retina, in that no pre-processing of the input is required.

We report on results for both hand-printed digits and letters. The hand-printed digits come from a set of 40,000 hand-printed digits scanned from the numeric amount region of "real-world" bank checks. They were pre-segmented and size-normalized to a 15x24 grayscale array. The test set consists of 4,000 samples and training sets varied from 100 to 35,200 samples. Although it is always difficult to compare recognition rates arising from different pattern sets, some appreciation for the difficulty of categorization can be gained using human performance data as a benchmark. An independent person categorizing the test set of pre-segmented, size-normalized digits achieved an error rate of 3.4%. This figure is considerably below the near-perfect performance of operators keying in numbers directly from bank checks, because the segmentation algorithm is flawed.

Working with letters, as well as digits, enables tests of the generality of results on a different pattern set having more than double the number of output categories. The hand-printed letters come from a set of 8,600 upper-case letters collected from over 110 people writing with a stylus input device on a flat panel display. The stylus collects a sequence of x-y coordinates at 200 points per second at a spatial resolution of 1000 points per inch. The temporal sequence for each character is first converted to a size-normalized bitmap array, keeping aspect ratio constant. We have found that recognition accuracy is significantly improved if these bitmaps are blurred through convolution with a gaussian distribution. Each pattern is represented as a 15x24 grayscale image. A test set of 2,368 samples was extracted by selecting samples from 18 people, so that training sets were generated by people different from those generating the test set. Training set sizes ranged from 500 to roughly 6,300 samples.

1   HIGH RECOGNITION ACCURACY

We find relatively high recognition accuracy for both pattern sets. Table 1[1] reports the minimal error rates achieved on the test samples for both pattern sets, at various reject rates. In the case of the hand-printed digits, the 4% error rate (0% rejects) ap-

---

1.   Effects of the number of training samples and network capacity and topology are reported in the next section. Nets were trained to error rates of 2-3%. Training began with a learning rate of .05 and a momentum value of .9. The learning rate was decreased when training accuracy began to oscillate or had stabilized for a large number of training epochs. We evaluate the output vector on a winner-take-all basis, as this consistently improves accuracy and results in network parameters having a smaller effect on performance.

proaches the 3.4% errors made by the human judge. This suggests that further improvements to generalization will require improving segmentation accuracy. The fact that an error rate of 5% was achieved for letters is promising. Accuracy is fairly high,

Table 1: Error rates of best nets trained on largest sample sets and tested on new samples

REJECT RATE	DIGITS	LETTERS
0%	4%	5%
5%	3%	3%
10%	1%	2%
35%	.001%	.003%

even though there are a large number of categories (26). This error rate may be adequate for applications where contextual constraints can be used to significantly boost accuracy at the word-level.

2 MINIMAL NETWORK CAPACITY AND TOPOLOGY EFFECTS

The effects of network parameters on generalization have both practical and scientific significance. The practical developer of pattern recognition systems is interested in such effects to determine whether limited resources should be spent on trying to optimize network parameters or on collecting a larger, more representative training set. For the scientist, effects of capacity bear on the relevance of learning models to backpropagation.

A central premise of most general models of learning-by-example is that the size of the initial search space--the capacity of the system--determines the number of training samples needed to achieve high generalization performance. Learning is conceptualized as a search for a function that maps all possible inputs to their correct outputs. Learning occurs by comparing successive samples of input-output pairs to functions in a search space. Functions inconsistent with training samples are rejected. Very large training sets narrow the search down to a function that closely approximates the desired function and yields high generalization. The capacity of a learning system--the number of functions it can represent--determines generalization, since a larger initial search space requires more training samples to narrow the search sufficiently . This suggests that to improve generalization, capacity should be minimized. Unfortunately, it is typically unclear how to minimize capacity without eliminating the desired function from the search space. A heuristic, which is often suggested, is that *simple is usually better.* It receives support from experience in curve fitting. Low-order polynomials typically extrapolate and interpolate better than high-order polynomials (Duda & Hart, 1973).

Extensions of the heuristic to neural net learning propose reducing capacity by reducing the number of connections or the number of bits used to represent each connection weight (Baum & Haussler, 1989; Denker, Schwartz, Wittner, Solla, Howard, Jackel, & Hopfield,1987). We manipulated the capacity of nets in a number of ways: 1) varying the number of hidden nodes, 2) limiting connectivity between layers so that nodes received input from only local areas, and 3) sharing connection weights between hidden nodes. We found only negligible effects on generalization.

2.1 NUMBER OF HIDDEN NODES

Figure 1 presents generalization results as a function of training set size for nets having one hidden layer and varying numbers of hidden nodes. The number of free parameters (i.e., number of connections and biases) in each case is presented in parentheses. Despite considerable variation in the number of free parameters, using nets with fewer hidden nodes did not improve generalization.

Baum & Haussler (1989) estimate the number of training samples required to achieve an error rate e (where $0 < e \leq 1/8$) on the generalization test, when an error rate of $e/2$ has been achieved on the training set. They assume a feed–forward net with one hidden layer and W connections. The estimates are distribution–free in the sense that calculations assume an arbitrary to–be–learned function. If the number of training samples is of order $\frac{W}{\epsilon} \log \frac{N}{\epsilon}$, where N refers to the number of nodes, then it is a near certainty that the net will achieve generalization rates of $(1 - e)$. This estimate is the upper–bound on the number of training samples needed. They also provide a lower

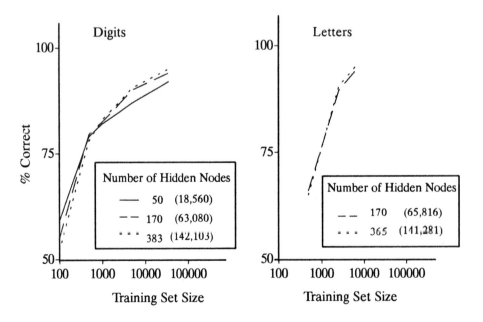

Figure 1. Effect of number of hidden nodes and training set size on generalization.

bound estimate, on the order of W/e. Using fewer than this number of samples will, for some functions, fail to achieve generalization rates of $(1 - e)$. The fact that we find no advantage to reducing the number of connections conflicts with Baum & Haussler's estimates and the underlying assumption that capacity plays a strong role in determining generalization.

Baum & Haussler also suggest using a constant of proportionality of 1 in their estimates. This implies that achieving error rates of 10% or less on new samples requires about 10 times as many training examples as there are connection weights in the net. For our largest nets, this implies a requirement of roughly a million training samples, which most developers would regard as prohibitively large. We found that about 5,000 samples were sufficient. Thus, a *sufficiently large* training sample does not imply a *prohibitively large* sample, at least for character recognition. We find that sample sizes of the order of thousands to tens of thousands yield performance very close to human levels. One reason for the discrepancy is that Baum & Haussler's estimates are distribution-free in the sense that they reflect worst-case scenarios across all possible functions the net might learn. Presumably, the functions underlying most natural pattern recognition tasks are not representative of the set of all possible functions. These results raise doubts about the relevance to natural pattern recognition of learning models based on worst-case analyses, because content may greatly impact generalization.

2.2 LOCAL CONNECTIVITY AND SHARED WEIGHTS

A more biologically plausible way to reduce capacity is to limit connectivity between layers to local areas and to use shared weights. For example, visual cortex contains neurons, each of which is responsive to a feature such as an oriented line appearing in a small, local region on the retina (Hubel & Wiesel, 1979). A given oriented line-detector is essentially replicated across the visual field, so that the same feature can be detected wherever it appears. In this sense, the connections feeding into an oriented-line detector are shared across all similar line-detectors for different areas of the visual field. In an artificial neural net, local structure is achieved by limiting connectivity. A given hidden node receives input from only local areas in the input or hidden layer preceding it. Weight sharing is achieved by linking the incoming weights across a set of hidden nodes. Corresponding weights leading into these nodes are randomly initialized to the same values and forced to have equivalent updates during learning. In this way the net evolves the same local feature set that is invariant across the input array. Several demonstrations exist indicating that local connectivity and shared weights improve generalization performance in tasks where position invariance is required (le Cun, 1989; Rumelhart, Hinton, & Williams, 1986).

We examined the benefits of using local receptive fields with shared weights for hand-printed character recognition, where position invariance was not required. This does not minimize the importance of position invariance. However, it is only one of many necessary invariants underlying reliable pattern recognition. Unfortunately, most of these invariants have not been explicitly specified. So we don't know how to bias a net toward discovering them. Testing the role of local receptive fields with shared weights in situations where position invariance is not required is relevant to discovering whether these constraints have a role other than in promoting position invariance.

As indicated in Figure 2, we find only slightly improved generalization in moving from nets with global connectivity between layers to nets with local receptive fields or to nets with local receptive fields and shared weights. This is true despite the fact that the number of free parameters is substantially reduced. The positive effects that do occur are at relatively small training set sizes. This may explain why others have reported a greater degree of improved generalization by using local receptive fields (Honavar & Uhr, 1988). The data reported are for networks with two hidden layers. *Global* nets had 150 nodes in the first layer and 50 nodes in the second. In the *Local* nets, first hidden layer nodes (540) received input from 5x8 local and overlapping regions (offset by 2 pixels) on the input array. Second hidden layer nodes (100) and output layer nodes had global receptive fields. The *Local, Shared* nets had 540 nodes in the first hidden layer with shared weights and, at the second hidden layer, either 102 (digits) or 180 (letters) nodes with local, overlapping, and shared receptive fields of size 4x6 on the 1st

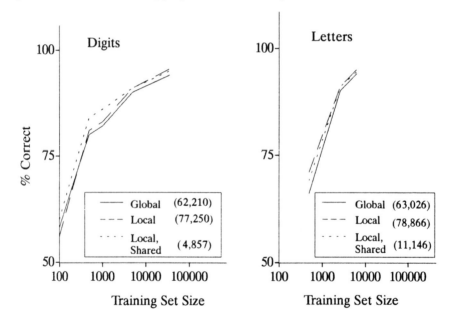

Figure 2.   Effects of net capacity and topology on generalization.

hidden layer. We have experimented with a large variety of different net architectures of this sort, varying the number of hidden nodes, the sizes and overlap of local receptive fields, and the use of local receptive fields with and without shared weights in one or both hidden layers. The fact that we've found little difference in generalization for two different pattern sets across such variations in network architectures argues for the generality of the results.

2.3   DISCUSSION

Given an architecture that enables relatively high training performance, we find only small effects of network capacity and topology on generalization performance. A large training set yields relatively high recognition accuracy in a robust way across most net architectures with which we've worked. These results suggest some practical advice to those developing hand–printed character recognition systems. If optimizing generalization performance is the goal, it is probably better to devote limited resources to collecting a very large, representative training set than to extensive experimentation with different net architectures. The variations in net capacity and topology we've examined do not substantially affect generalization performance for sufficiently large training sets. *Sufficiently large* should be interpreted as on the order of a thousand to tens of thousands of samples for hand–printed character recognition.

From a theoretical standpoint, the negligible effects of network capacity on generalization performance contradicts the central premise of machine learning that the size of the initial hypothesis space determines learning performance. This challenges the relevance, to backpropagation learning, of statistical models that estimate likelihood of high generalization performance from estimates of capacity. Due to the gradient descent nature of backpropagation learning, not all functions that can be represented will be visited during learning. The negligible effects of capacity suggest that the number of functions visited during learning constitutes only a very small percentage of the total possible functions that can be represented.

There are a number of reasons for believing that capacity might impact generalization performance in other circumstances. We regularly train only to 2–3% error rates. This helps to avoid the possibility of overfitting the data, although we have seen no indication of this when we have trained to higher levels, as long as we use large training sets. It is also possible that the number of connections is not a good measure of capacity. For example, the amount of information that can be passed on by a given connection may be a better measure than the number of connections. At this conference, le Cun, Denker, Solla, Howard, & Jackel have also presented evidence that removing unimportant weights from a network may be a better way to reduce capacity. However, the fact that generalization rates come very close to human accuracy levels, even for nets with extremely large numbers of free parameters, suggests that general effects of net capacity and topology are, at best, small in comparison to effects of training set size. We don't deny that there are likely to be net topologies that push performance up to human accuracy levels, presumably by biasing the net toward discovering the range of invariants that underlie human pattern recognition. The problem is that only a few of these invariants have been explicitly specified (e.g., position, size, rotation), and so it is not possible to bias a net toward discovering the full range.

3 ADVANTAGES OF REDUCING CAPACITY

Although reducing gross indicators of capacity may not significantly improve generalization, there are good practical and scientific reasons for doing it. A good reason to
reduce the number of connections is to speed processing. Also, using local receptive
fields with shared weights biases a net toward position invariance, and toward producing a simpler, more modular internal representation which can be replicated across a
large retina. This has important implications for developing nets that combine character segmentation with recognition.

Using local receptive fields with shared weights also offers promise for increasing our
understanding of how the net correctly classifies patterns because the number of distinct receptive fields is greatly reduced. Figure 3 depicts Hinton diagrams of local re-

Digits   Letters

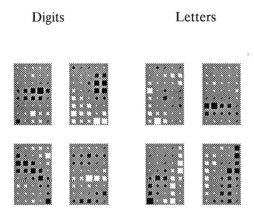

Figure 3. Receptive fields that evolved in 1st hidden layer nodes in nets with
local receptive fields having shared weights.

ceptive fields from 1st hidden layer nodes in nets with shared weights trained on digits
or letters. Each of the eight large, gray rectangles corresponds to the receptive field
for a hidden node. The four on the left came from a net trained on digits; those on
the right from a net trained on letters. Within each of these eight, the black rectangles
correspond to negative weights and the white to positive weights. The size of the black
and white rectangles reflects the magnitude of the weights.

The local feature detectors that develop for both pattern sets appear to be oriented
line and edge detectors. These are similar to oriented line and edge detectors found
in visual cortex (Hubel & Wiesel, 1979) and to Linsker's (1986,1988) orientation–selective nodes, which emerge from a self–adaptive net exposed to random patterns. In
Linsker's case, the feature detectors develop as an emergent property of the principle
that the signal transformation occurring from one layer to the next should maximize
the information that output signals convey about input signals. The fact that similar

feature detectors emerge in backpropagation nets trained on "natural" patterns is interesting because there were no explicit constraints to maximize information flow between layers in the backpropagation nets and because categorization is typically viewed as an abstraction process involving considerable loss of category-irrelevant information.

References

Baum, E. and Haussler, D. (1989) What size net gives valid generalization? in D. S. Touretzky (Ed.) *Advances in neural information processing systems I*, Morgan Kaufman.

Burr, D. J. (1986) A neural network digit recognizer. *Proceedings of the 1986 International conference on systems, man and cybernetics*, Atlanta, Georgia. pp. 1621–1625.

Denker, J. S., Gardner, W. R., Graf, H. P., Henderson, D., Howard, R. E., Hubbard, W., Jackel, L. D., Baird, H. S., and Guyon, I. (1989) Neural network recognizer for hand-written zip code digits in D. S. Touretzky (Ed.) *Advances in neural information processing systems I*, Morgan Kaufman.

Denker, J. S., Schwartz, D., Wittner, B., Solla, S., Howard, R. E., Jackel, L. D., & Hopfield, J. (1987) Large automatic learning, rule extraction and generalization. *Complex Systems, 1*, pp. 877–933.

Duda, R. O., and Hart, P. E. (1973) *Pattern classification and scene analysis.* NY: John Wiley & Sons.

Honavar, V. and Uhr, L. (1988) Experimental results indicate that generation, local receptive fields and global convergence improve perceptual learning in connectionist networks. CS-TR 805. Computer Science Department, University of Wisconsin-Madison.

Hubel, D. H. and Wiesel, T. N. (1979) Brain mechanisms of vision. *Scientific American, 241*, pp. 150–162.

le Cun, Y. (1989) Generalization and network design strategies. Technical Report CRG-TR-89-4, Department of Computer Science, University of Toronto.

Linsker, R. (1986) From basic network principles to neural architecture; Emergence of orientation-selective cells. *Proceedings of the National Academy of Sciences, USA, 83*, pp. 8390–8394.

Linsker, R. (1988) Towards an organizing principle for a layered perceptual network in D. Anderson (Ed.) *Neural information processing systems.* American Institute of Physics.

Mori, Y. and Yokosawa, K. (1989) Neural networks that learn to discriminate similar kanji characters. in . D. S. Touretzky (Ed.) *Advances in neural information processing systems I*, Morgan Kaufman.

Rumelhart, D. E., Hinton, G. E., & Williams, R. J. Learning internal representations by error propagation in D. E. Rumelhart & J. L. McClelland (Editors) *Parallel distributed processing: V. 1.* Cambridge, Mass.: MIT Press, 1986

Weideman, W. E., Manry, M T. & Yau, H. C. (1989) A comparison of a nearest neighbor classifier and a neural network for numeric handprint character recognition. IEEE International Conference on Neural Networks, Washington, D. C., 1989.

Acknowledgements

We would like to thank the NCR corporation for loaning us the set of hand-printed digits and Joyce Conner, Janet Kilgore, and Kay Bauer for their invaluable help in collecting the set of hand-printed letters.

A LARGE-SCALE NEURAL NETWORK WHICH RECOGNIZES HANDWRITTEN KANJI CHARACTERS

Yoshihiro Mori   Kazuki Joe
ATR Auditory and Visual Perception Research Laboratories
Sanpeidani Inuidani Seika-cho Soraku-gun Kyoto 619-02 Japan

ABSTRACT

We propose a new way to construct a large-scale neural network for 3,000 handwritten Kanji characters recognition. This neural network consists of 3 parts: a collection of small-scale networks which are trained individually on a small number of Kanji characters; a network which integrates the output from the small-scale networks, and a process to facilitate the integration of these neworks. The recognition rate of the total system is comparable with those of the small-scale networks. Our results indicate that the proposed method is effective for constructing a large-scale network without loss of recognition performance.

1 INTRODUCTION

Neural networks have been applied to recognition tasks in many fields, with good results [Denker,1988][Mori,1988][Weideman,1989]. They have performed better than conventional methods. However these networks currently operate with only a few categories, about 20 to 30. The Japanese writing system at present is composed of about 3,000 characters. For a network to recognize this many characters, it must be given a large number of categories while maintaining its level of performance.

To train small-scale neural networks is not a difficult task. Therefore, exploring methods for integrating these small-scale neural networks is important to construct a large-scale network. If such methods could integrate small-scale networks without loss of the performance, the scale of neural networks would be extended dramatically. In this paper, we propose such a method for constructing a large-scale network whose object is to recognize 3,000 handwritten Kanji characters, and report the result of a part of this network. This method is not limited to systems for character recognition, and can be applied to any system which recognizes many categories.

2 STRATEGIES FOR A LARGE-SCALE NETWORK

Knowing the current recognition and generalization capacity of a neural network, we realized that constructing a large-scale monolithic network would not be efficient or effective. Instead, from the start we decided on a building blocks approach [Mori,1988][Waibel,1988]. There are two strategies to mix many small-scale networks.

2.1 Selective Neural Network (SNN)

In this strategy, a large-scale neural network is made from many small-scale networks which are trained individually on a small number of categories, and a network (SNN) which selects the appropriate small-scale network (Fig. 1). The advantage of this strategy is that the information passed to a selected small-scale networks is always appropriate for that network. Therefore, training these small-scale networks is very easy. But on the other hand, increasing the number of categories will substantially increase the training time of the SNN, and may make it harder for the SNN to retain high performance. Furthermore, the error rate of the SNN will limit the performance of the whole system.

2.2 Integrative Neural Network (INN)

In this strategy, a large-scale neural network is made from many small-scale networks which are trained individually on a small number of categories, and a network (INN) which integrates the output from these small-scale networks(Fig. 2). The advantage of this strategy is that every small-scale network gets information and contributes to finding the right answer. Therefore, it is possible to use the knowledge distributed among each small-scale network. But in some respects, various devices are needed to make the integration easier.

The common advantage with both strategies just mentioned is that the size of each neural network is relatively small, and it does not take a long time to train these networks. Each small-scale networks is considered an independent part of the whole system. Therefore, retraining these networks (to improve the performance of the whole system) will not take too long.

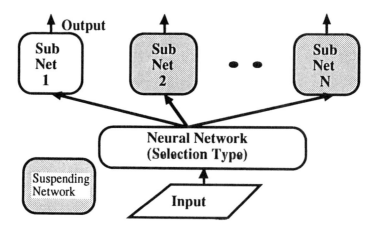

Fig. 1 SNN Strategy

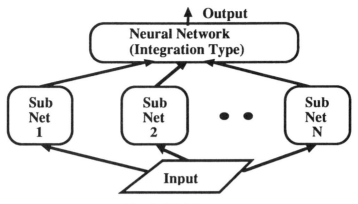

Fig. 2 INN Strategy

3 STRUCTURE OF LARGE-SCALE NETWORK

The whole system is constructed using three kinds of neural networks. The first one, called a SubNet, is an ordinary three layered feed forward type neural network trained using the Back Propagation learning algorithm. The second kind of network is called a SuperNet. This neural network makes its decision by integrating the outputs from all the SubNets. This network is also a 3-layered feed-forward net, but is larger than the Subnets. The last network, which we call an OtherFilter, is devised to improve the integration of the SuperNet. This OtherFilter network was designed using the LVQ algorithm [Khonen,1988]. There are also some changes made in the BP learning algorithm especially for pattern recognition [Joe,1989].

We decided that, based on the time it takes for learning, there should be 9 categories in each small-scale network. The 3,000 characters are separated into these small groups through the K-means clustering method, which allows similar characters to be grouped together. The separation occurs in two stages. First, 11 groups of 270 characters each are formed, then each group is separated into 30 smaller units. In this way, 330 groups of 9 characters each are obtained. We choose the INN strategy to use distributed knowledge to full advantage. The 9-character units are SubNets, which are integrated in 2 stages. First 30 SubNets are integrated by a higher level network SuperNet. Altogether, 11 SuperNets are needed to recognize all 3,000 characters. SuperNets are in turn integrated by a higher level network, the HyperNet. More precisely, the role and structure of these kinds of networks are as follows:

3.1 SubNet

A feature vector extracted from handwritten patterns is used as the input (described in Section 4.1). The number of units in the output layer is the same as the number of categories to be recognized by the SubNet. In short, the role of a SubNet is to output the similarity between the input pattern and the categories allotted to the SubNet. (Fig. 3)

3.2 SuperNet

The outputs from each SubNet filtered by the OtherFilter network are used as the input to the SuperNet. The number of units in an output layer is the same as the number of SubNets belonging to a SuperNet. In short, the role of SuperNet is to select the SubNet which covers the category corresponding to the input patterns. (Fig. 5)

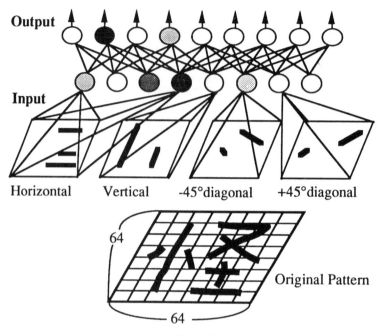

Fig. 3 SubNet

3.3 OtherFIlter

45(9x5) reference vectors are assigned to each SubNet. LVQ is used to adapt these reference vectors, so that each input vector has a reference of the correct SubNet as its closest reference vector. The OtherFilter method is to first measure the distance between all the reference vectors and one input vector. The mean distance and normal deviation of distance are calculated. The distance between a SubNet and an input vector is defined to be the smallest distance of that SubNet's reference vectors to the input vector.

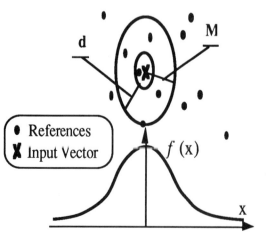

Fig4. Shape of OtherFilter

$$f(x_n) = 1 / (1 + e^{(x_n - M + 2d)/Cd}) \quad (1)$$

x_n : The Distance of Nth SubNet
M : The Mean of x_n
d : The Variance of x_n
C : Constant

This distance modified by equation (1) is multiplied by the outputs of the SubNet, and fed into the SuperNet. The outputs of SubNets whose distance is greater than the mean distance are suppressed, and the outputs of SubNets whose distance is smaller than the mean distance are amplified. In this way, the outputs of SubNets are modified to improve the integration of the higher level SuperNet. (Fig. 5)

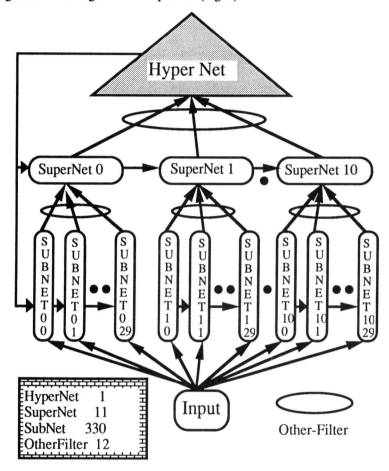

Fig5. Outline of the Whole System

4 RECOGNITION EXPERIMENT

4.1 TRAINING PATTERN

The training samples for this network were chosen from a database of about 3000 Kanji characters [Saito 1985]. For each character, there are 200 handwritten samples from different writers. 100 are used as training samples, and the remaining 100 are used to test recognition accuracy of the trained network. All samples in the database consist of 64 by 63 dots.

Fig. 6 Examples of training pattern

4.2 LDCD FEATURE

If we were to use this pattern as the input to our neural net, the number of units required in the input layer would be too large for the computational abilities of current computers. Therefore, a feature vector extracted from the handwritten patterns is used as the input. In the "LDCD feature" [Hagita 1983], there are 256 dimensions computing a line segment length along four directions: horizontal, vertical, and two diagonals in the 8 by 8 squares into which the handwritten samples are divided.

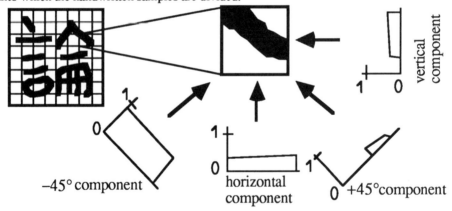

Fig 7. LDCD Feature

4.3 RECOGNITION RESULTS

In the work reported here, one SuperNet, 30 SubNets and one OtherFilter were constructed for recognition experiments. SubNets were trained until the recognition of training samples reaches at least 99%. With these SubNets, the mean recognition rate of test patterns was 92%. This recognition rate is higher than that of conventional methods. A SuperNet which integrates the output modified by OtherFilter from 30 trained SubNets was then constructed. The number of units in the input layer of the SuperNet was 270. This SuperNet was trained until the performance of training samples becomes at least 93%. With this SuperNet, the recognition rate of test patterns was 74%, though that of OtherFilter was 72%. The recognition rate of a system without the OtherFilter of test patterns was 55%.

5 CONCLUSION

We have here proposed a new way of constructing a large-scale neural network for the recognition of 3,000 handwritten Kanji characters. With this method, a system recognizing 270 Kanji characters was constructed. This system will become a part of a system recognizing 3,000 Kanji characters. Only a modest training time was necessary owing to the modular nature of the system. Moreover, this modularity means that only a modest re-training time is necessary for retraining an erroneous neural network in the whole system. The overall system performance can be improved by retraining just that neural network, and there is no need to retrain the whole system. However, the performance of the OtherFilter is not satisfactory. We intend to improve the OtherFilter, and build a large-scale network for the recognition of 3,000 handwritten Kanji characters by the method reported here.

Acknowledgments

We are grateful to Dr. Yodogawa for his support and encouragement. Special thanks to Dr. Sei Miyake for the ideas he provided in our many discussions. The authors would like to acknowledge, with thanks, the help of Erik McDermott for his valuable assistance in writing this paper in English.

References

[Denier,1988]   J.S.Denker, W.R.Gardner, H.P. Graf, D.Henderson, R.E. Howard, W.Hubbard, L.D.Jackel, H.S.Baird, I.Guyon : "Neural Network Recognizer for Hand-Written ZIP Code Digits", NEURAL INFORMATION PROCESSING SYSTEMS 1, pp.323-331, Morgan Kaufmann, 1988

[Mori,1988]   Y.Mori, K.Yokosawa : "Neural Networks that Learn to Discriminate Similar Kanji Characters", NEURAL INFORMATION PROCESSING SYSTEMS 1, pp.332-339, Morgan Kaufmann, 1988

[Weideman,1989]W.E.Weideman, M.T.Manry, H.C.Yau ; "A COMPARISON OF A NEAREST NEIGHBOR CLASSIFIER AND A NEURAL NETWORK FOR NUMERIC HANDPRINT CHARACTER RECOGNITION", IJCNN89(Washington), Vol.I, pp.117-120, June 1989

[Waibel,1988]   Alex Waibel, "Consonant Recognition by Modular Construction of Large Phonemic Time-Delay Neural Networks", NEURAL INFORMATION PROCESSING SYSTEMS 1, pp.215-223, Morgan Kaufmann, 1988

[Joe,1989]   K.Joe, Y.Mori, S.Miyake : "Simulation of a Large-Scale Neural Networks on a Parallel Computer", 4th Hypercube Concurrent Computers,1989

[Khonen,1988]   T.Kohonen, G.Barna, R.Chrisley : "Statistical Pattern Recognition with Neural Networks", IEEE, Proc.of ICNN, Vol.I, pp.61-68, July 1988

[Saito,1985]   T.Saito, H.Yamada, K.Yamamoto : "On the Data Base ETL9 of Handprinted Characters in JIS Chinese Characters and Its Analysis", J68-D, 4, 757-764, 1985

[Hagita,1983]   N.Hagita, S.Naito, I.Masuda : "Recognition of Handprinted Chinese Characters by Global and Local Direction Contributivity Density-Feature", J66-D, 6, 722-729,1983

A Neural Network to Detect Homologies in Proteins

Yoshua Bengio
School of Computer Science
McGill University
Montreal, Canada H3A 2A7

Yannick Pouliot
Department of Biology
McGill University
Montreal Neurological Institute

Samy Bengio
Département d'Informatique
Université de Montreal

Patrick Agin
Département d'Informatique
Université de Montreal

ABSTRACT

In order to detect the presence and location of immunoglobulin (Ig) domains from amino acid sequences we built a system based on a neural network with one hidden layer trained with back propagation. The program was designed to efficiently identify proteins exhibiting such domains, characterized by a few localized conserved regions and a low overall homology. When the National Biomedical Research Foundation (NBRF) NEW protein sequence database was scanned to evaluate the program's performance, we obtained very low rates of false negatives coupled with a moderate rate of false positives.

1 INTRODUCTION

Two amino acid sequences from proteins are homologous if they can be aligned so that many corresponding amino acids are identical or have similar chemical properties. Such subsequences (domains) often exhibit similar three dimensional structure. Furthemore, sequence similarity often results from common ancestors. Immunoglobulin (Ig) domains are sets of β-sheets bound by cysteine bonds and with a characteristic tertiary structure. Such domains are found in many proteins involved in immune, cell adhesion and receptor functions. These proteins collectively form the immunoglobulin superfamily (for review, see Williams and Barclay, 1987). Members of the superfamily often possess several Ig domains. These domains are characterized by well-conserved groups of amino acids localized to specific subregions. Other residues outside of these regions are often poorly conserved, such that there is low overall homology between Ig domains, even though they are clearly members of the same superfamily.

Current search programs incorporating algorithms such as the Wilbur-Lipman algorithm (1983) or the Needleman-Wunsch algorithm (1970) and its modification by Smith and Waterman (1981) are ill-designed for detecting such domains because they implicitly consider each amino acid to be equally important. This is not the case for residues within domains such as the Ig domain, since only some amino acids are well conserved, while most are variable. One solution to this problem are search algorithms based upon the statistical occurrence of a residue at a particular position (Wang et al., 1989; Gribskov et al., 1987). The Profile Analysis set of programs published by the University of Wisconsin Genetics Computer Group (Devereux et al., 1984) rely upon such an algorithm. Although Profile Analysis can be applied to search for domains (c.f. Blaschuk, Pouliot & Holland 1990), the output from these programs often suffers from a high rate of false negatives and positives. Variations in domain length are handled using the traditional method of penalties proportional to the number of gaps introduced, their length and their position. This approach entails a significant amount of spurious recognition if there is considerable variation in domain length to be accounted for.

We have chosen to address these problems by training a neural network to recognize accepted Ig domains. Perceptrons and various types of neural networks have been used previously in biological research with various degrees of success (cf. Stormo et al., 1982; Qian and Sejnowski, 1988). Our results suggest that they are well suited for detecting relatively cryptic sequence patterns such as those which characterize Ig domains. Because the design and training procedure described below is relatively simple, network-based search programs constitute a valid solution to problems such as searching for proteins assembled from the duplication of a domain.

2 ALGORITHM, NETWORK DESIGN AND TRAINING

The network capitalizes upon data concerning the existence and localization of highly conserved groups of amino acids characteristic of the Ig domain. Its design is similar in several respects to neural networks we have used in the study of speech recognition (Bengio et al., 1989). Four conserved subregions (designated P1-P4) of the Ig domain homology were identified. These roughly correspond to β-strands B, C, E and F, respectively, of the Ig domain (see also Williams and Barclay, 1988). Amino acids in these four groups are not necessarily all conserved, but for each subregion they show a distribution very different from the distribution generally observed elsewhere in these proteins. Hence the first and most important stage of the system learns about these joint distributions. The program scans proteins using a window of 5 residues.

The first stage of the system consists of a 2-layer feedforward neural network (5 × 20 inputs - 8 hidden - 4 outputs; see Figure 1) trained with back propagation (Rumelhart *et al.*, 1986). Better results were obtained for the recognition of these conserved regions with this architecture than without hidden layer (similar to a perceptron). The second stage evaluates, based upon the stream of outputs generated by the first stage, whether and where a region similar to the Ig domain has been detected. This stage currently uses a simple dynamic programming algorithm, in which constraints about order of subregions and distance between them are explicitly programmed. We force the recognizer to detect a sequence of high values (above a threshold) for the four conserved regions, in the correct order and such that the sum of the values obtained at the four recognized regions is greater than a certain threshold. Weak penalties are applied for violations of distance constraints between conserved subregions (e.g., distance between P1 and P2, P2 and P3, etc) based upon simple rules derived from our analysis of Ig domains. These rules have little impact if strong homologies are detected, such that the program easily handles the large variation in domain size exhibited by Ig domains. It was necessary to explicitly formulate these constraints given the low number of training examples as well as the assumption that the distance between groups is not a critical discriminating factor. We have assumed that inter-region subsequences probably do not significantly influence discrimination.

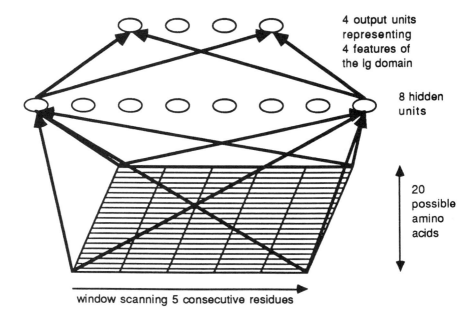

Figure 1: Structure of the neural network

```
filename : A22771.NEW
input sequence name : Ig epsilon chain C region - Human
HOMOLOGY starting at 24
VTLGCLATGYFPEPVMVTWDTGSLNGTTMTLPATTLTLSGHYATISLLTVSGAWAKQMFTC
   P1           P2           P3                            P4
Ending at 84. Score = 3.581
HOMOLOGY starting at 130
IQLLCLVSGYTPGTINITWLEDGQVMDVDLSTASTTQEGELASTQSELTLSQKHWLSDRTYTC
   P1           P2                        P3               P4
Ending at 192. Score = 3.825
HOMOLOGY starting at 234
PTITCLVVDLAPSKGTVNLTWSRASGKPVNHSTRKEEKQRNGTLTVTSTLPVGTRDWIEGETYQC
   P1           P2                            P3           P4
Ending at 298. Score = 3.351
HOMOLOGY starting at 340
RTLACLIQNFMPEDISVQWLHNEVQLPDARHSTTQPRKTKGSGFFVFSRLEVTRAEWEQKDEFIC
   P1           P2                            P3           P4
Ending at 404. Score = 3.402
```

Figure 2: Sample output from a search of NEW. Ig domains
present within the constant region of an epsilon Ig chain
(NBRF file number A22771) are listed with the position of
P1-P4 (see text). The overall score for each domain is also listed.

As a training set we used a group of 30 proteins comprising bona fide Ig
domains (Williams and Barclay, 1987). In order to increase the size of the
training set, additional sequences were stochastically generated by substituting
residues which are not in critical positions of the domain. These substitutions
were designed not to affect the local distribution of residues to minimize
changes in the overall chemical character of the region.

The program was evaluated and optimized by scanning the NBRF protein databases (PROTEIN and NEW) version 19. Results presented below are based
upon searches of the NEW database (except where otherwise noted) and were
generated with a cutoff value of 3.0. Only complete sequences from vertebrates, insects (including *Drosophila melanogaster*) and eukaryotic viruses
were scanned. This corresponds to 2422 sequences out of the 4718 present in
the NEW database. Trial runs with the program indicated that a cutoff threshold of between 2.7 and 3.0 eliminates the vast majority of false positives with
little effect upon the rate of false negatives. A sample output is listed in Figure 2.

3   RESULTS

When the NEW protein sequence database of NBRF was searched as
described above, 191 proteins were identified to possess at least one Ig
domain. A scan of the 4718 proteins comprising the NEW database required
an average of 20 hours of CPU time on a VAX 11/780. This is comparable to
other computationally intensive programs (e.g., Profile Analysis). When run
on a SUN 4 computer, similar searches required 1.3 hours of CPU time. This
is sufficiently fast to allow the user to alter the cutoff threshold repeatedly
when searching for proteins with low homology.

Table 1: Output from a search of the NEW protein sequence database. Domains are sorted according to overall score.

3.0087	Class II histocompatib. antigen, HLA-DR beta-1 chain precursor (REM) - Human
3.0148	Nonspecific cross-reacting antigen precursor - Human
3.0161	Platelet-derived growth factor receptor precursor - Mouse
3.0164	Tla class I histocompatib. antigen, T13-c alpha chain - Mouse
3.0164	Tla class I histocompatib. antigen, T3-b alpha chain - Mouse
3.0223	Vitronectin receptor alpha chain precursor - Human
3.0226	T-cell surface glycoprotein Ly-3 precursor - Mouse
3.0244	Kinase-related transforming protein (src) (EC 2.7.1.-) - Avian sarcoma virus
3.0350	Ig alpha-1 chain C region - Human
3.0350	Ig alpha-1 chain C region - Human
3.0350	Ig alpha-2 chain C region, A2m(1) allotype - Human
3.0409	Granulocyte-macrophage colony-stimulating factor 1 precursor - Mouse
3.0481	HLA class I histocompatib. antigen, alpha chain precursor - Human
3.0492	NADH-ubiquinone oxidoreductase (EC 1.6.5.3), chain 5 - Fruit fly (Drosophila)
3.0508	NADH-ubiquinone oxidoreductase (EC 1.6.5.3), chain 1 - Fruit fly (Drosophila)
3.0518	HLA class II histocompatib. antigen, DP beta chain precursor - clone
3.0518	HLA class II histocompatib. antigen, DP4 beta chain precursor - Human
3.0518	HLA class II histocompatib. antigen, DPw4 beta-1 chain precursor - Human
3.0520	Class II histocompatib. antigen, HLA-DQ beta chain precursor (REM) - Human
3.0561	Protein-tyrosine kinase (EC 2.7.1.112), lymphocyte - Mouse
3.0669	H-2 class II histocompatib. antigen, A-beta-2 chain precursor - Mouse
3.0723	T-cell receptor gamma chain precursor V region (MNG8) - Mouse
3.0723	T-cell receptor gamma chain precursor V region (RAG11) - Mouse
3.0723	T-cell receptor gamma chain precursor V region (RAG4) - Mouse
3.0723	T-cell receptor gamma chain precursor V region (RAG42) - Mouse
3.0723	T-cell receptor gamma chain precursor V region (RAG50) - Mouse
3.0750	T-cell receptor beta chain V region (C.F6) - Mouse
3.0760	Ig heavy chain V region - Mouse 2S1.3
3.0781	T-cell receptor beta chain V region (SUP-T1) - Human
3.0787	H-2 class I histocompatib. antigen, Q7 alpha chain precursor - Mouse
3.0787	H-2 class I histocompatib. antigen, Q8 alpha chain precursor - Mouse
3.0982	Myelin-associated glycoprotein 1B236 long form precursor - Rat
3.0982	Myelin-associated glycoprotein 1B236 short form precursor - Rat
3.0982	Myelin-associated glycoprotein precursor, brain - Rat
3.0982	Myelin-associated large glycoprotein precursor - Rat
3.0998	Class I histocompatib. antigen, BoLA alpha chain precursor (BL3-6) - Bovine
3.0998	Class I histocompatib. antigen, BoLA alpha chain precursor (BL3-7) - Bovine
3.1048	H-2 class I histocompatib. antigen, K-k alpha chain precursor - Mouse
3.1086	Ig heavy chain precursor V region - Mouse VGAM3-2
3.1128	T-cell receptor alpha chain precursor V region (MD13) - Mouse
3.1129	T-cell receptor delta chain V region (DN-4) - Mouse
3.1192	T-cell receptor beta chain precursor V region (VAK) - Mouse
3.1265	T-cell receptor gamma chain precursor V region (K20) - Human
3.1347	T-cell receptor alpha chain precursor V region (HAP05) - Human
3.1623	T-cell surface glycoprotein CD8 precursor - Human
3.1623	T-cell surface glycoprotein CD8 protein precursor - Human
3.1776	Ig gamma-3 chain C region, G3m(b) allotype - Human
3.1931	Hypothetical protein HQLF2 - Cytomegalovirus (strain AD169)
3.2041	Sodium channel protein II - Rat
3.2044	Ig heavy chain V region - African clawed frog
3.2147	SURF-1 protein - Mouse
3.2207	T-cell receptor alpha chain precursor V region (HAP10) - Human
3.2300	Beta-2-microglobulin precursor - Human
3.2300	Beta-2-microglobulin, modified - Human
3.2306	Pregnancy-specific beta-1 glycoprotein E precursor - Human
3.2344	IgE Fc receptor alpha chain precursor - Human
3.2420	T-cell surface glycoprotein CD2 precursor - Rat
3.2422	H-2 class II histocompatib. antigen, I-A (NOD) beta chain precursor - Mouse
3.2552	HLA class II histocompatib. antigen, DPw4 alpha-1 chain precursor - Human
3.2552	HLA class II histocompatib. antigen, SB alpha chain precursor - Human
3.2654	T-cell surface glycoprotein CD8, 37K chain precursor - Rat
3.2726	Myelin P0 protein - Bovine
3.2814	Ig alpha-1 chain C region - Human
3.2814	Ig alpha-1 chain C region - Human
3.2820	Thy-1 membrane glycoprotein precursor - Mouse
3.2840	Smh class II histocompatib. antigen precursor - Ehrenberg's mole-rat
3.3039	X-linked chronic granulomatous disease protein - Human
3.3083	Pregnancy-specific beta-1 glycoprotein C precursor - Human
3.3083	Pregnancy-specific beta-1 glycoprotein D precursor - Human
3.3084	T-cell receptor beta chain precursor V region (16) - Human
3.3251	Ig gamma-1/Ig gamma-2b Fc receptor precursor - Mouse
3.3414	Hypothetical hybrid Ig/T-cell receptor precursor V region (SUP-T1) - Human
3.3414	Ig heavy chain precursor V-II region - Human 71-2
3.3414	Ig heavy chain precursor V-II region - Human 71-4
3.3417	Neural cell adhesion protein precursor - Mouse
3.3511	Ig epsilon chain C region - Human
3.3511	Ig epsilon chain C region - Human
3.3522	T-cell receptor alpha chain V region (BDFL alpha-1) - Mouse
3.3605	Biliary glycoprotein 1 - Human
3.3838	T-cell receptor gamma-1 chain C region (MNG1 and MNG7) - Mouse
3.3838	T-cell receptor gamma-1 chain C region - Mouse
3.3861	T-cell gamma chain precursor V region (V3) - Mouse
3.4024	Ig epsilon chain C region - Human
3.4024	Ig epsilon chain C region - Human
3.4110	Ig heavy chain V region - Mouse H36-2
3.4133	Ig heavy chain V region - Mouse H37-60
3.4152	Ig heavy chain V region - Mouse H18-S415
3.4155	Ig kappa chain V region - Mouse HP9
3.4178	Ig heavy chain V region - Mouse IF6
3.4198	Ig kappa chain V region - Mouse HIC5-4D1
3.4199	Ig heavy chain V region - Mouse 3D10
3.4199	Ig heavy chain V region - Mouse II CR-Id 11
3.4211	Ig heavy chain V region - Mouse HP22 and HP27
3.4213	Pregnancy-specific beta-1 glycoprotein C precursor - Human
3.4213	Pregnancy-specific beta-1 glycoprotein D precursor - Human
3.4218	T-cell receptor beta chain precursor V region (4.C3) - Mouse
3.4218	T-cell receptor beta chain precursor V region (B10) - Mouse
3.4282	Sodium channel protein II - Rat
3.4295	Ig kappa chain V region (H28-A2) - Mouse H28-A2
3.4295	Ig kappa chain V region - Mouse H158-89H4
3.4295	Ig kappa chain V region - Mouse H37-311
3.4295	Ig kappa chain V region - Mouse H37-40
3.4295	Ig kappa chain V region - Mouse H37-43
3.4295	Ig kappa chain V region - Mouse H37-45
3.4295	Ig kappa chain V region - Mouse H37-80
3.4295	Ig kappa chain V region - Mouse H37-84
3.4295	Ig kappa chain V regions - Mouse H35-C6 and H220-25
3.4338	T-cell receptor alpha chain precursor V region (P71) - Mouse
3.4572	T-cell surface glycoprotein CD3 epsilon chain - Human
3.4594	T-cell surface glycoprotein CD8 precursor - Mouse
3.4594	T-cell surface glycoprotein Lyt-2 precursor - Mouse
3.4595	T-cell receptor alpha chain precursor V region (HAP08) - Human
3.4606	T-cell receptor gamma-2 chain C region (MNG8 and MNG9) - Mouse
3.4614	T-cell receptor gamma chain C region (PEER) - Human
3.4614	T-cell receptor gamma-1 chain C region - Human
3.4614	T-cell receptor gamma-2 chain C region - Human
3.4620	Ig heavy chain V region - Mouse H146-24B3
3.4620	Ig heavy chain V region - Mouse H158-89H4
3.4620	Ig heavy chain V region - Mouse H35-C6
3.4620	Ig heavy chain precursor V region - Mouse MAK33
3.4690	T-cell receptor beta-1 chain C region - Human
3.4690	T-cell receptor beta-1 chain C region - Mouse
3.4690	T-cell receptor beta-2 chain C region - Human
3.4690	T-cell receptor beta-2 chain C region - Human
3.4769	Ig gamma-3 chain C region, G3m(b) allotype - Human
3.4798	Ig kappa chain V region - Mouse H146-24B3
3.4798	Ig kappa chain V region - Mouse H36-2
3.4798	Ig kappa chain V region - Mouse H37-62
3.4798	Ig kappa chain V region - Mouse H37-82
3.4810	Ig kappa chain V-I region - Human Wil(1)
3.4840	Peroxidase (EC 1.11.1.7) precursor - Human
3.4888	Platelet-derived growth factor receptor precursor - Mouse
3.4965	Notch protein - Fruit fly
3.4965	Notch protein - Fruit fly
3.4983	T-cell receptor beta chain precursor V region (MT1-1) - Human
3.4983	T-cell receptor beta-2 chain precursor V region MOLT-4 - Human
3.4998	Ig kappa chain precursor V region - Mouse Ser-a
3.5035	Alkaline phosphatase (EC 3.1.3.1) precursor - Human
3.5061	Ig heavy chain V region - Mouse H37-82
3.5082	Class II histocompatib. antigen, HLA-DR beta-2 chain precursor (REM) - Human
3.5082	H-2 class II histocompatib. antigen, E-a/k beta-2 chain precursor - Mouse
3.5082	H-2 class II histocompatib. antigen, E-d beta-2 chain precursor - Mouse
3.5082	HLA class II histocompatib. antigen, DR 1 beta chain (clone 69) - Human
3.5082	HLA class II histocompatib. antigen, DR beta chain precursor
3.5082	HLA class II histocompatib. antigen, DR beta chain precursor A5) - Human
3.5082	HLA class II histocompatib. antigen, DR-1 beta chain precursor - Human
3.5082	HLA class II histocompatib. antigen, DR-4 beta chain - Human
3.5082	HLA class II histocompatib. antigen, DR-5 beta chain precursor - Human
3.5094	Ig lambda-5 chain C region - Mouse
3.5144	Ig alpha-2 chain C region, A2m(1) allotype - Human
3.5150	Ig heavy chain V region - Mouse H28-A2
3.5180	Biliary glycoprotein 1 - Human
3.5193	Ig heavy chain V region - Mouse H37-45
3.5193	Ig heavy chain V regions - Mouse H37-80 and H37-43
3.5211	Ig lambda chain precursor V region - Rat
3.5264	Ig heavy chain V region - Mouse H37-62
3.5316	Ig heavy chain V region - Mouse H37-311
3.5334	Ig heavy chain V region - Mouse H37-40
3.5372	T-cell receptor beta chain precursor V region (ATL12-2) - Human
3.5435	Ig heavy chain V region - Mouse HIC5-401
3.5579	Ig heavy chain V region - Mouse H37-84
3.5603	Ig lambda-2 chain C region - Rat
3.5666	Ig heavy chain V region - Mouse B1-8 (tentative sequence)
3.5709	Biliary glycoprotein 1 - Human
3.5748	Nonspecific cross-reacting antigen precursor - Human
3.5815	Ig epsilon chain C region - Human
3.5815	Ig epsilon chain C region - Human
3.5894	Neural cell adhesion protein precursor - Mouse
3.5912	Ig kappa chain V region - Mouse H37-60
3.5971	Ig kappa chain precursor V region - Rat IR2
3.6020	Ig kappa chain V region - Mouse 1F6
3.6020	Ig kappa chain V region - Mouse 3D10
3.6027	T-cell receptor beta chain V region (KO-ATL) - Human
3.6071	Ig heavy chain V region - Mouse HP20
3.6071	Ig heavy chain V region - Mouse HP25
3.6120	T-cell receptor alpha chain V region (5C.C7) - Mouse
3.6120	T-cell receptor alpha chain V region (C.F6) - Mouse
3.6120	T-cell receptor alpha chain precursor V region (2B4) - Mouse
3.6120	T-cell receptor alpha chain precursor V region (4.C3) - Mouse
3.6120	T-cell receptor alpha chain precursor V region (B10) - Mouse
3.6302	HLA class II histocompatib. antigen DX alpha chain precursor - Human
3.6302	HLA class II histocompatib. antigen, DQ alpha chain precursor - Human
3.6461	T-cell receptor alpha chain precursor V region (HAP58) - Human
3.6465	Ig kappa chain precursor V chain - Mouse Ser-b
3.6539	Neural cell adhesion protein precursor - Mouse
3.6636	Ig heavy chain V region - Mouse B1-8.V1/V2 (tentative sequence)
3.6778	Ig kappa chain precursor V-III region - Human SU-DHL-6
3.6798	Ig kappa chain V region - Mouse H18-S415
3.6803	Myelin-associated glycoprotein 1B236 long form precursor - Rat
3.6803	Myelin-associated glycoprotein 1B236 short form precursor - Rat
3.6803	Myelin-associated glycoprotein precursor, brain - Rat
3.6803	Myelin-associated large glycoprotein precursor - Rat
3.7102	Ig kappa chain V-III region - Human Ger
3.7170	Ig kappa chain V-I region - Human Wil(2)
3.7341	Ig lambda chain C region - Chicken
3.7505	Ig kappa chain precursor V-I region - Human Nalm-6
3.7535	Ig heavy chain precursor V region - Mouse 129
3.7600	Ig lambda-5 chain C region - Mouse
3.7779	Ig heavy chain V region - Mouse HP12
3.7907	Ig kappa chain V region 305 precursor - Human
3.7907	Ig kappa chain precursor V-III - Human Nalm-6
3.7909	Ig heavy chain V region - Mouse HP21
3.8087	Neural cell adhesion protein precursor - Mouse
3.8180	Ig mu chain C region, b allele - Mouse
3.8247	Ig epsilon chain C region - Human
3.8247	Ig epsilon chain C region - Human
3.8440	Ig kappa chain precursor V region - Mouse MAK33
3.8678	Ig kappa chain precursor V region - Rat IR162

Table 2: Efficiency of detection for some Ig superfamily proteins present in NEW. Mean scores of recognized Ig domains for each protein type are listed. Recognition efficiency is calculated by dividing the number of proteins correctly identified (i.e., bearing at least one Ig domain) by the total number of proteins identified by their file description as containing an Ig domain, multiplied by 100. Numbers in parentheses indicate the number of complete protein sequences of each type for each species. All complete sequences for light and heavy immunoglobulin chains of human and mouse origin were scanned. The threshold was set at 3.0. ND: not done.

Protein	Mean score of detected domains (max 4.00)	Recognition efficiency for Ig-bearing proteins (see legend)
Immunoglobulins, mouse, all forms	3.50	98.2 % (55)
Immunoglobulins, human, all forms	3.48	93.8 % (16)
H-2 class II, all forms	3.33	ND
HLA class II, all forms	3.36	ND
T-cell receptor chains, mouse, all forms	3.32	ND
T-cell receptor chains, human, all forms	3.41	ND

The vast majority of proteins which scored above 3.0 were of human, mouse, rat or rabbit origin. A few viral and insect proteins also scored above the threshold. All proteins in the training set and present in either the NEW or PROTEIN databases were detected. Proteins detected in the NEW database arc listed in Table I and sorted according to score. Even though only human MHC class I and II were included in the training set, both mouse H-2 class I and II were detected. Bovine and rat transplantation antigens were also detected. These proteins are homologs of human MHC's. For proteins which include more than one Ig domain contiguously arranged (e.g., carcinoembryonic antigen), all domains were detected if they were sufficiently well conserved. However, domains lacking a feature or possessing a degenerate feature scored much lower (usually below 3.0) such that they are not recognized when using a threshold value of 3. Recognition of human and mouse immunoglobulin sequences was used to measure recognition efficiency. The rate of false negatives for immunoglobulins was very low for both species (Table II). Table III lists the 13 proteins categorized as false positives detected when searching with a threshold of 3.0. Relative to the total number of domains detected, this corresponds to a false positive rate of 6.8%. In the strict sense some of these proteins are not false positives because they do exhibit the expected features of the Ig domain in the correct order. However, inter-feature distances for these pseudo-domains are very different from those observed in bona fide Ig domains. Proteins which are rich in β-sheets, such as rat sodium channel II and fruit-fly NADH-ubiquinone oxidoreductase chain 1 are also abundant among the set of false positives. This is not surprising since the Ig domain is composed of β-strands. One solution to this problem lies in the use of a larger training set as well as the addition of a more intelligent second stage designed to evaluate inter-feature distances so as to increase the specificity of detection.

Table 3: False positives obtained when searching NEW with a threshold of 3.0. Proteins categorized as false positives are listed. See text for details.

3.0244 Kinase-related transforming protein (src) (EC 2.7.1.-)
3.0409 Granulocyte-macrophage colony-stimulating
3.0492 NADH-ubiquinone oxidoreductase (EC 1.6.5.3), chain 5
3.0508 NADH-ubiquinone oxidoreductase (EC 1.6.5.3), chain 1
3.0561 Protein-tyrosine kinase (EC 2.7.1.112), lymphocyte - Mouse
3.1931 Hypothetical protein HQLF2 - Cytomegalovirus (strain AD169)
3.2041 Sodium channel protein II - Rat
3.2147 SURF-1 protein - Mouse
3.3039 X-linked chronic granulomatous disease protein - Human
3.4840 Peroxidase (EC 1.11.1.7) precursor - Human
3.4965 Notch protein - Fruit fly
3.4965 Notch protein - Fruit fly
3.5035 Alkaline phosphatase (EC 3.1.3.1) precursor - Human

5 DISCUSSION

The detection of specific protein domains is becoming increasingly important since many proteins are constituted of a succession of domains. Unfortunately, domains (Ig or otherwise) are often only weakly homologous with each other. We have designed a neural network to detect proteins which comprise Ig domains to evaluate this approach in helping to solve this problem. Alternatives to neural network-based search programs exist. Search programs can be designed to recognize the flanking Cys-termini regions to the exclusion of other domain features since these flanks are the best conserved features of Ig domains (*cf.* Wang *et al.*, 1989). However, even Cys-termini can exhibit poor overall homology and therefore generate statistically insignificant homology scores when analyzed with the ALIGN program (NBRF) (cf. Williams and Barclay, 1987). Other search programs (such as Profile Analysis) cannot efficiently handle the large variations in domain size exhibited by the Ig domain (mostly comprised between 45 and 70 residues). Search results become corrupted by high rates of false positives and negatives. Since the size of the NBRF protein databases increases considerably each year, the problem of false positives promises to become crippling if these rates are not substantially decreased. In view of these problems we have found the application of a neural network to the detection of Ig domains to be an advantageous solution. As the state of biological knowledge advances, new Ig domains can be added to the training set and training resumed. They can learn the statistical features of the conserved subregions that permit detection of an Ig domain and generalize to new examples of this domain that have a similar distribution. Previously unrecognized and possibly degenerate homologous sequences are therefore likely to be detected.

Acknowledgments

This research was supported by a grant from the Canadian Natural Sciences and Engineering Research Council to Y.B. We thank CISTI for graciously allowing us access to their experimental BIOMOLE system.

References

Bengio Y., Cardin R., De Mori R., Merlo E. (1989) Programmable execution of multi-layered networks for automatic speech recognition, *Communications of the Association for Computing Machinery*, 32 (2).

Bengio Y., Cardin R., De Mori R., (1990), Speaker independent speech recognition with neural networks and speech knowledge, in D.S. Touretzky (ed.), *Advances in Neural Networks Information Processing Systems 2*

Blaschuk O.W., Pouliot Y., Holland P.C., (1990). Identification of a conserved region common to cadherins and influenza strain A hemagglutinins. *J. Molec. Biology*, 1990, in press.

Devereux, J., Haeberli, P. and Smithies, O. (1984) A comprehensive set of sequence analysis programs for the VAX. *Nucl. Acids Res.* 12, 387-395.

Gribskov, M., McLachlan, M., and Eisenber, D. (1987) Profile analysis: Detection of distantly related proteins. *Proc. Natl. Acad. Sci.* USA, 84:4355-4358.

Needleman, S. B. and Wunsch, C. D. (1970) A general method applicable to the search for similarities in the amino acid sequence of two proteins. *J. Mol. Biol.* 48, 443-453.

Qian, N. and Sejnowski, T. J. (1988) Predicting the secondary structure of globular proteins using neural network models. *J. Mol. Biol.* 202, 865-884.

Rumelhart D.E., Hinton G.E. & Williams R.J. (1986) Learning internal representation by error propagation. *Parallel Distributed Processing*, Vol. 1, MIT Press, Cambridge, pp. 318-362.

Smith, T. F. and Waterman, W. S. (1981). Identification of common molecular subsequences. *J. Mol. Biol. 147*, 195-197.

Stormo, G. D., Schneider, T. D., Gold, L. and Ehrenfeucht, A. Use of the "perceptron" algorithm to distinguish translational initiation sites in E. coli. *Nucl. Acids Res. 10*, 2997-3010.

Wang, H., Wu, J. and Tang, P. (1989) Superfamily expands. *Nature,* 337, 514.

Wilbur, W. J. and Lipman, D. J. (1983). Rapid similarity searches of nucleic acids and protein data banks. *Proc. Natl. Acad. Sci.* USA 80, 726-730.

Williams, A. F. and Barclay, N. A. (1988) The immunoglobulin superfamily - domains for cell surface recognition. *Ann. Rev. Immunol.*, 6, 381-405.

Rule Representations in a Connectionist Chunker

David S. Touretzky   Gillette Elvgren III
School of Computer Science
Carnegie Mellon University
Pittsburgh, PA 15213

ABSTRACT

We present two connectionist architectures for chunking of symbolic rewrite rules. One uses backpropagation learning, the other competitive learning. Although they were developed for chunking the same sorts of rules, the two differ in their representational abilities and learning behaviors.

1 INTRODUCTION

Chunking is a process for generating, from a sequence of if-then rules, a more complex rule that accomplishes the same task in a single step. It has been used to explain incremental human performance improvement in a wide variety of cognitive, perceptual, and motor tasks (Newell, 1987). The SOAR production system (Laird, Newell, & Rosenbloom, 1987) is a classical AI computer program that implements a "unified theory of cognition" based on chunking.

SOAR's version of chunking is a symbolic process that examines the working memory trace of rules contributing to the chunk. In this paper we present two connectionist rule-following architectures that generate chunks a different way: they use incremental learning procedures to infer the environment in which the chunk should fire. The first connectionist architecture uses backpropagation learning, and has been described previously in (Touretzky, 1989a). The second architecture uses competitive learning. It exhibits more robust behavior than the previous one, at the cost of some limitations on the types of rules it can learn.

The knowledge to be chunked consists of context-sensitive rewrite rules on strings. For example, given the two rules

R1:   D → B / _ E   "change D to B when followed by E"
R2:   A → C / _ B   "change A to C when followed by B"

the model would go through the following derivation: ADE → (Rule R1) ABE → (Rule R2) CBE. Rule R1's firing is what enables rule R2 to fire. The model detects this and formulates a chunked rule (R1-R2) that can accomplish the same task in a single step:

R1-R2:   AD → CB / _ E

Once this chunk becomes active, the derivation will be handled in a single step, this way: ADE → (Chunk R1-R2) CBE. The chunk can also contribute to the formation of larger chunks.

2   CHUNKING VIA BACKPROPAGATION

Our first experiment, a three-layer backpropagation chunker, is shown in Figure 1. The input layer is a string buffer into which symbols are shifted one at a time, from the right. The output layer is a "change buffer" that describes changes to be made to the string. The changes supported are deletion of a segment, mutation of a segment, and insertion of a new segment. Combinations of these changes are also permitted.

Rules are implemented by hidden layer units that read the input buffer and write changes (via their α connections) into the change buffer. Then separate circuitry, not shown in the figure, applies the specified changes to the input string to update the state of the input buffer. The details of this string manipulation circuitry are given in (Touretzky, 1989b; Touretzky & Wheeler, 1990).

We will now go through the ADE derivation in detail. The model starts with an empty input buffer and two rules: R1 and R2.[1] After shifting the symbol A into the input buffer, no rule fires—the change buffer is all zeros. After shifting in the D, the input buffer contains AD, and again no rule fires. After shifting in the E the input buffer contains ADE, and rule R1 fires, writing a request in the change buffer to mutate input segment 2 (counting from the right edge of the buffer) to a B. The input buffer and change buffer states are saved in temporary buffers, and the string manipulation circuitry derives a new input buffer state, ABE. This now causes rule R2 to fire.[2] It writes a request into the change buffer to mutate segment 3 to a C. Since it was R1's firing that triggered R2, the conditions exist for chunk formation. The model combines R1's requested change with that of R2, placing the result in the "chunked change buffer" shown on the right in Figure 1. Backpropagation is used to teach the hidden layer that when it sees the input buffer pattern that triggered R1 (ADE in this case) it should produce via its β connections the combined change pattern shown in the chunked change buffer.

The model's training is "self supervised:" its own behavior (its history of rule firings) is the source of the chunks it acquires. It is therefore important that the chunking

---

[1] The initial rule set is installed by an external teacher using backpropagation.

[2] Note that R1 applies to positions 1 and 2 of the buffer (counting from the right edge), while R2 applies to positions 2 and 3. Rules are represented in a position-independent manner, allowing them to apply anywhere in the buffer that their environment is satisfied. The mechanism for achieving this is explained in (Touretzky, 1989a).

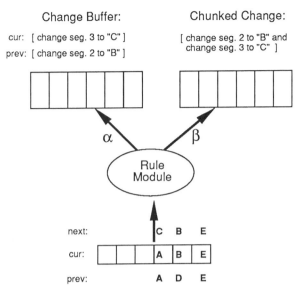

Figure 1: Architecture of the backpropagation chunker.

process not introduce any behavioral errors during the intermediate stages of learning, since no external teacher is present to force the model back on track should its rule representations become corrupted. The original rules are represented in the α connections and the chunked rules are trained using the β connections, but the two rule sets share the same hidden units and input connections, so interference can indeed occur. The model must actively preserve its α rules by continuous rehearsal: after each input presentation, backpropagation learning on a contrast-enhanced version of the α change pattern is used to counteract any interference caused by training on the β patterns. Eventually, when the β weights have been learned correctly, they can replace the α weights.

The parameters of the model were adjusted so that the initial rules had a distributed representation in the hidden layer, i.e., several units were responsible for implementing each rule. Analysis of the hidden layer representations after chunking revealed that the model had split off some of the R1 units to represent the R1-R2 chunk; the remainder were used to maintain the original R1 rule.

The primary flaw of this model is fragility. Constant rehearsal of the original rule set, and low learning rates, are required to prevent the α rules from being corrupted before the β rules have been completely learned. Furthermore, it is difficult to form long rule chains, because each chunk further splits up the hidden unit population. Repeated splitting and retraining of hidden units proved difficult, but the model did manage to learn an R1-R2-R3 chunk that supersedes the R1-R2 chunk, so that ADE mutates directly to CFE. The third rule was:

R3: $B \rightarrow F\ /\ C\ \_\ E$ "change B to F when between C and E"

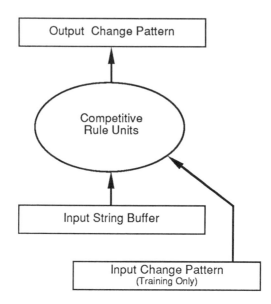

Figure 2: Architecture of the competitive learning chunker.

3   CHUNKING VIA COMPETITIVE LEARNING

Our second chunker, shown in Figure 2, minimizes interference between rules by using competitive learning to assign each rule a dedicated unit. As in the previous case, the model is taught its initial rules by showing it input buffer states and desired change buffer states. Chunks are then formed by running strings through the input buffer and watching for pairs of rules that fire sequentially. The model recruits new units for the chunks and teaches them to produce the new change buffer patterns (formed by composing the changes of the two original rules) in appropriate environments.

A number of technical problems had to be resolved in order to make this scheme work. First, we want to assign a separate unit to each rule, but not to each training example; otherwise the model will use too many units and not generalize well. Second, the encoding for letters we chose (see Table 1) is based on a Cartesian product, and so input patterns are highly overlapping and close together in Hamming space. This makes the job of the competitive learning algorithm more difficult. Third, there must be some way for chunks to take priority over the component rules from which they were formed, so that an input sequence like ADE fires the chunk R1-R2 rather than the original rule R1. As we trace through the operation of the chunker we will describe our solutions to these problems.

Rule units in the competitive layer are in one of three states: *inactive* (waiting to be recruited), *plastic* (currently undergoing learning), and *active* (weights finalized; ready to compete and fire.) They also contain a simple integrator (a counter) that is used to move them from the plastic to the active state. Initially all units are inactive and the counter

Table 1: Input code for both chunking models.

A	1	0	1	0	0
B	1	0	0	1	0
C	1	0	0	0	1
D	0	1	1	0	0
E	0	1	0	1	0
F	0	1	0	0	1

is zero. As in any competitive learning scheme, the rule units' input weights are kept normalized to unit vectors (Rumelhart & Zipser, 1986).

When the teacher presents a novel instance, we must determine if there is already some partially-trained rule unit whose weights should be shaped by this instance. Due to our choice of input code, it is not possible to reliably assign training instances to rule units based solely on the input pattern, because "similar" inputs (close in Hamming space) may invoke entirely different rules. Our solution is to use the desired change pattern as the primary index for selecting a pool of plastic rule units; the input buffer pattern is then used as a secondary cue to select the most strongly activated unit from this pool.

Let's consider what happens with the training example DE $\rightarrow$ BE. The desired change pattern "mutate segment 2 to a B" is fed to the competitive layer, and the network looks for plastic rule units whose change patterns exactly match the desired pattern.[3] If no such unit is found, one is allocated from the inactive pool, its status is changed to "plastic," its input buffer weights are set to match the pattern in the input buffer, and its change pattern input and and change pattern output weights are set according to the desired change pattern.

Otherwise, if a pool of suitable plastic units already exists, the input pattern DE is presented to the competitive layer and the selected plsatic units compete to see which most closely matches the input. The winning unit's input buffer weights are then adjusted by competitive learning to move the weight vector slightly closer to this input buffer vector. The unit's counter is also bumped.

Several presentations are normally required before a rule unit's input weights settle into their correct values, since the unit must determine from experience which input bit values are significant and which should be ignored. For example, rule S1 in Table 2 (the asterisk indicates a wildcard) can be learned from the training instances ACF and ADF, since as Table 1 shows, the letters C and D in the second segment have no bits in common. Therefore the learning algorithm will concentrate virtually all of the weight vector's magnitude in the connections that specify "A" as the first segment and "F" as the third.

Each time a rule unit's weights are adjusted by competitive learning, its counter is in-

---

[3]The units' thresholds are raised so that they can only become active if their weight vectors match the input change buffer vector exactly.

cremented. When the counter reaches a suitable value (currently 25), the unit switches from the plastic to the active state. It is now ready to compete with other units for the right to fire; its weights will not change further.

We now consider the formation of the model's first chunk. Assume that rules R1 and R2 have been acquired successfully. The model is trained by running random strings through the input buffer and looking for sequences of rule firings. Suppose the model is presented with the input string BFDADE. R1 fires, producing BFDABE; this then causes R2 to fire, producing BFDCBE. The model proceeds to form a chunk. The combined change pattern specifies that the penultimate segment should be mutated to "B," and the antepenultimate to "C." Since no plastic rule unit's change pattern weights match this change, a fresh unit is allocated and its change buffer weights are set to reproduce this pattern. The unit's input weights are set to detect the pattern BFDADE.

After several more examples of the R1-R2 firing sequence, the competitive learning algorithm will discover that the first three input buffer positions can hold anything at all, but the last three always hold ADE. Hence the weight vector will be concentrated on the last three positions. When its counter reaches a value of 25, the rule unit will switch to the active state.

Now consider the next time an input ending in ADE is presented. The network is in performance mode now, so there is nothing in the input change buffer; the model is looking only at the input string buffer. The R1 unit will be fully satisfied by the input; its normalized weight vector concentrates on just the last two positions, "DE," which match exactly. The R1-R2 unit will also be fully satisfied; its normalized weight vector looks for the sequence ADE. The latter unit is the one we want to win the competition. We achieve this by scaling the activation function of competitive units by an additional factor: the degree of distributedness of the weight vector. Units that distribute their input weight over a larger number of connections likely represent complex chunks, and should therefore have their activation boosted over rules with narrowly focused input vectors.

Once the unit encoding the R1-R2 chunk enters the active state, its more distributed input weights assure that it will always win over the R1 unit for an input like ADE. The R1 unit may still be useful to keep around, though, to handle a case like FDE → FBE that does not trigger R2.

Sometimes a new chunk is learned that covers the same length input as the old, e.g., chunk R1-R2-R3 that maps ADE → CFE looks at exactly the same input positions as chunk R1-R2. We therefore introduce one additional term into the activation function. As part of the learning process, active units that contribute to the formation of a new chunk are given a permanent, very small inhibitory bias. This ensures that R1-R2 will always lose the competition to R1-R2-R3 once that chunk goes from plastic to active, even though their weights are distributed to an equal degree.

Another special case that needs to be handled is when the competitive algorithm wrongly splits a rule between two plastic units in the same pool, e.g., one unit might be assigned the cases {A,B,C}ADE, and the other the cases {D,E,F}ADE. (In other words, one unit looks for the bit pattern 10xxx in the first position, and the other unit looks for 01xxx.)

This is bad because it allows the weights of each unit to be more distributed than they need to be. To correct the problem, whenever a plastic unit wins a competition our algorithm makes sure that the nearest runner up is considerably less active than the winner. If its activation is too high, the runner up is killed. This causes the survivor to readjust its weights to describe the rule correctly, i.e., it will look for the input pattern ADE. If the runner up was killed incorrectly (meaning it is really needed for some other rule), it will be resurrected in response to future examples.

Finally, active units have a decay mechanism that is kept in check by the unit's firing occasionally. If a unit does not fire for a long time (200 input presentations), its weights decay to zero and it returns to the inactive state. This way, units representing chunks that have been superseded will eventually be recycled.

4   DISCUSSION

Each of the two learning architectures has unique advantages. The backpropagation learner can in principle learn arbitrarily complex rules, such as replacing a letter with its successor, or reversing a subset of the input string. Its use of a distributed rule representation allows knowledge of rule R1 to participate in the forming of the R1-R2 chunk. However, this representation is also subject to interference effects, and as is often the case with backprop, learning is slow.

The competitive architecture learns very quickly. It can form a greater number of chunks, and can handle longer rule chains, since it avoids inteference by assigning a dedicated unit to each new rule it learns.

Both learners are sensitive to changes in the distribution of input strings; new chunks can form any time they are needed. Chunks that are no longer useful in the backprop model will eventually fade away due to non-rehearsal; the hidden units that implement these chunks will be recruited for other tasks. The competitive chunker uses a separate decay mechanism to recycle chunks that have been superseded.

This work shows that connectionist techniques can yield novel and interesting solutions to symbol processing problems. Our models are based on a sequence manipulation architecture that uses a symbolic description of the changes to be made (via the change buffer), but the precise environments in which rules apply are never explicitly represented. Instead they are induced by the learning algorithm from examples of the models' own behavior. Such self-supervised learning may play an important role in cognitive development. Our work shows that it is possible to correctly chunk knowledge even when one cannot predict the precise environment in which the chunks should apply.

Acknowledgements

This research was supported by a contract from Hughes Research Laboratories, by the Office of Naval Research under contract number N00014-86-K-0678, and by National Science Foundation grant EET-8716324. We thank Allen Newell, Deirdre Wheeler, and Akihiro Hirai for helpful discussions.

Table 2: Initial rule set for the competitive learning chunker.

$$
\begin{array}{lll}
\text{S1:} & \text{A*F} & \rightarrow \text{B*F} \\
\text{S2:} & \text{BD} & \rightarrow \text{BF} \\
\text{S3:} & \{\text{D,E,F}\}\text{*E} & \rightarrow \{\text{A,B,C}\}\text{*A} \\
\text{S4:} & \{\text{B,E}\}\text{B} & \rightarrow \text{CB} \\
\text{S5:} & \{\text{A,D}\}\text{C} & \rightarrow \{\text{C,F}\}\text{C}
\end{array}
$$

Table 3: Chunks formed by the competitive learning chunker.

Chunk	(Component Rules)
EA*F → CB*F	(S1,S4)
ABD → CBF	(S1,S2,S4)
AADF → CBFF	(S1,S2,S1,S4)
BE*E → CB*A	(S3,S4)
DEB → FEB	(S4,S5)

References

Laird, J. E., Newell, A., and Rosenbloom, P. S. (1987) Soar: An architecture for general intelligence. *Artificial Intelligence* 33(1):1-64.

Newell, A. (1987) The 1987 William James Lectures: Unified Theories of Cognition. Given at Harvard University.

Rumelhart, D E., and Zipser, D. (1986) Feature discovery by competitive learning. In D. E. Rumelhart and J. L. McClelland (eds.), *Parallel Distributed Processing: Explorations in the Microstructure of Cognition.* Cambridge, MA: MIT Press.

Touretzky, D. S. (1989a) Chunking in a connectionist network. *Proceedings of the Eleventh Annual Conference of the Cognitive Science Society,* pp. 1-8. Hillsdale, NJ: Erlbaum.

Touretzky, D. S. (1989b) Towards a connectionist phonology: the "many maps" approach to sequence manipulation. *Proceedings of the Eleventh Annual Conference of the Cognitive Science Society,* pp. 188-195. Hillsdale, NJ: Erlbaum.

Touretzky, D. S., and Wheeler, D. W. (1990) A computational basis for phonology. In D. S. Touretzky (ed.), *Advances in Neural Information Processing Systems 2.* San Mateo, CA: Morgan Kaufmann.

Discovering the Structure of a Reactive Environment by Exploration

Michael C. Mozer
Department of Computer Science
and Institute of Cognitive Science
University of Colorado
Boulder, CO 80309-0430

Jonathan Bachrach
Department of Computer
and Information Science
University of Massachusetts
Amherst, MA 01003

ABSTRACT

Consider a robot wandering around an unfamiliar environment, performing actions and sensing the resulting environmental states. The robot's task is to construct an internal model of its environment, a model that will allow it to predict the consequences of its actions and to determine what sequences of actions to take to reach particular goal states. Rivest and Schapire (1987a, 1987b; Schapire, 1988) have studied this problem and have designed a symbolic algorithm to strategically explore and infer the structure of "finite state" environments. The heart of this algorithm is a clever representation of the environment called an *update graph*. We have developed a connectionist implementation of the update graph using a highly-specialized network architecture. With back propagation learning and a trivial exploration strategy — choosing random actions — the connectionist network can outperform the Rivest and Schapire algorithm on simple problems. The network has the additional strength that it can accommodate stochastic environments. Perhaps the greatest virtue of the connectionist approach is that it suggests generalizations of the update graph representation that do not arise from a traditional, symbolic perspective.

1 INTRODUCTION

Consider a robot placed in an unfamiliar environment. The robot is allowed to wander around the environment, performing actions and sensing the resulting environmental states. With sufficient exploration, the robot should be able to construct an internal model of the environment, a model that will allow it to predict the consequences of its actions and to determine what sequence of actions must be taken to reach a particular goal state. In this paper, we describe a connectionist network that accomplishes this task, based on a representation of finite-state automata developed by Rivest and Schapire

(1987a, 1987b; Schapire, 1988).

The environments we wish to consider can be modeled by a finite-state automaton (*FSA*). In each environment, the robot has a set of discrete *actions* it can execute to move from one environmental state to another. At each environmental state, a set of binary-valued *sensations* can be detected by the robot. To illustrate the concepts and methods in our work, we use as an extended example a simple environment, the *n*-room world (from Rivest and Schapire). The *n*-room world consists of *n* rooms arranged in a circular chain. Each room is connected to the two adjacent rooms. In each room is a light bulb and light switch. The robot can sense whether the light in the room where it currently stands is on or off. The robot has three possible actions: move to the next room down the chain (D), move to the next room up the chain (U), and toggle the light switch in the current room (T).

2 MODELING THE ENVIRONMENT

If the FSA corresponding to the *n*-room world is known, the sensory consequences of any sequence of actions can be predicted. Further, the FSA can be used to determine a sequence of actions to take to obtain a certain goal state. Although one might try developing an algorithm to learn the FSA directly, there are several arguments against doing so (Schapire, 1988). Most important is that the FSA often does not capture structure inherent in the environment. Rather than trying to learn the FSA, Rivest and Schapire suggest learning another representation of the environment called an *update graph*. The advantage of the update graph is that in environments with regularities, the number of nodes in the update graph can be much smaller than in the FSA (e.g., $2n$ versus 2^n for the *n*-room world). Rivest and Schapire's formal definition of the update graph is based on the notion of *tests* that can be performed on the environment, and the equivalence of different tests. In this section, we present an alternative, more intuitive view of the update graph that facilitates a connectionist interpretation.

Consider a three-room world. To model this environment, the essential knowledge required is the status of the lights in the current room (CUR), the next room up from the current room (UP), and the next room down from the current room (DOWN). Assume the update graph has a node for each of these environmental variables. Further assume that each node has an associated value indicating whether the light in the particular room is on or off.

If we know the values of the variables in the current environmental state, what will their new values be after taking some action, say U? When the robot moves to the next room up, the new value of CUR becomes the previous value of UP; the new value of DOWN becomes the previous value of CUR; and in the three-room world, the new value of UP becomes the previous value of DOWN. As depicted in Figure 1a, this action thus results in shifting values around in the three nodes. This makes sense because moving up does not affect the status of any light, but it does alter the robot's position with respect to the three rooms. Figure 1b shows the analogous flow of information for the action D. Finally, the action T should cause the status of the current room's light to be complemented while the other two rooms remain unaffected (Figure 1c). In Figure 1d, the three sets of links from Figures 1a-c have been superimposed and have been labeled with the appropriate action.

One final detail: The Rivest and Schapire update graph formalism does not make use of the "complementation" link. To avoid it, each node may be split into two values, one representing the status of a room and the other its complement (Figure 1e). Toggling thus involves exchanging the values of CUR and $\overline{\text{CUR}}$. Just as the values of CUR, UP, and DOWN must be shifted for the actions U and D, so must their complements.

Given the update graph in Figure 1e and the value of each node for the current environmental state, the result of any sequence of actions can be predicted simply by shifting values around in the graph. Thus, as far as predicting the input/output behavior of the environment is concerned, the update graph serves the same purpose as the FSA.

A defining and nonobvious (from the current description) property of an update graph is that each node has exactly one incoming link for each action. We call this the *one-input-per-action* constraint. For example, CUR gets input from $\overline{\text{CUR}}$ for the action T, from UP for U, and from DOWN for D.

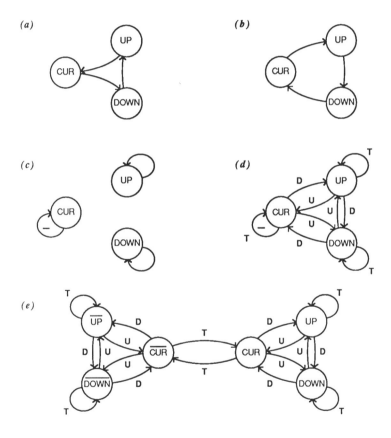

Figure 1: (a) Links between nodes indicating the desired information flow on performing the action U. CUR represents that status of the lights in the current room, UP the status of the lights in the next room up, and DOWN the status of the lights in the next room down. (b) Links between nodes indicating the desired information flow on performing the action D. (c) Links between nodes indicating the desired information flow on performing the action T. The "−" on the link from CUR to itself indicates that the value must be complemented. (d) Links from the three separate actions superimposed and labeled by the action. (e) The complementation link can be avoided by adding a set of nodes that represent the complements of the original set. This is the update graph for a three-room world.

3 THE RIVEST AND SCHAPIRE ALGORITHM

Rivest and Schapire have developed a symbolic algorithm (hereafter, *the RS algorithm*) to strategically explore an environment and learn its update graph representation. The RS algorithm formulates explicit hypotheses about regularities in the environment and tests these hypotheses one or a relatively small number at a time. As a result, the algorithm may not make full use of the environmental feedback obtained. It thus seems worthwhile to consider alternative approaches that could allow more efficient use of the environmental feedback, and hence, more efficient learning of the update graph. We have taken connectionist approach, which has shown quite promising results in preliminary experiments and suggests other significant benefits. We detail these benefits below, but must first describe the basic approach.

4 THE UPDATE GRAPH AS A CONNECTIONIST NETWORK

How might we turn the update graph into a connectionist network? Start by assuming one unit in a network for each node in the update graph. The activity level of the unit represents the truth value associated with the update graph node. Some of these units serve as "outputs" of the network. For example, in the three-room world, the output of the network is the unit that represents the status of the current room. In other environments, there may several sensations in which case there will be several output units.

What is the analog of the labeled links in the update graph? The labels indicate that values are to be sent down a link when a particular action occurs. In connectionist terms, the links should be *gated* by the action. To elaborate, we might include a set of units that represent the possible actions; these units act to multiplicatively gate the flow of activity between units in the update graph. Thus, when a particular action is to be performed, the corresponding action unit is activated, and the connections that are gated by this action become enabled. If the action units form a local representation, i.e., only one is active at a time, exactly one set of connections is enabled at a time. Consequently, the gated connections can be replaced by a set of weight matrices, one per action. To predict the consequences of a particular action, the weight matrix for that action is plugged into the network and activity is allowed to propagate through the connections. Thus, the network is dynamically rewired contingent on the current action.

The effect of activity propagation should be that the new activity of a unit is the previous activity of some other unit. A linear activation function is sufficient to achieve this:

$$X(t) = W_{a(t)}X(t-1) , \tag{1}$$

where $a(t)$ is the action selected at time t, $W_{a(t)}$ is the weight matrix associated with this action, and $X(t)$ is the activity vector that results from taking action $a(t)$. Assuming weight matrices which have zeroes in each row except for one connection of strength 1 (the one-input-per-action constraint), the activation rule will cause activity values to be copied around the network.

5 TRAINING THE NETWORK TO BE AN UPDATE GRAPH

We have described a connectionist network that can behave as an update graph, and now turn to the procedure used to learn the connection strengths in this network. For expository purposes, assume that the number of units in the update graph is known in advance.

(This is not necessary, as we show in Mozer & Bachrach, 1989.) A weight matrix is required for each action, with a potential non-zero connection between every pair of units. As in most connectionist learning procedures, the weight matrices are initialized to random values; the outcome of learning will be a set of matrices that represent the update graph connectivity.

If the network is to behave as an update graph, the one-input-per-action constraint must be satisfied. In terms of the connectivity matrices, this means that each row of each weight matrix should have connection strengths of zero except for one value which is 1. To achieve this property, additional constraints are placed on the weights. We have explored a combination of three constraints:

$$(1) \sum_j w_{aij}^2 = 1, \quad (2) \sum_j w_{aij} = 1, \quad \text{and (3) } w_{aij} \geq 0,$$

where w_{aij} is the connection strength to i from j for action a. Constraint 1 is satisfied by introducing an additional cost term to the error function. Constraints 2 and 3 are rigidly enforced by renormalizing the $\mathbf{W}_{ai}$ following each weight update. The normalization procedure finds the shortest distance projection from the updated weight vector to the hyperplane specified by constraint 2 that also satisfies constraint 3.

At each time step t, the training procedure consists the following sequence of events:

1. An action, $a(t)$, is selected at random.

2. The weight matrix for that action, $\mathbf{W}_{a(t)}$, is used to compute the activities at t, $\mathbf{X}(t)$, from the previous activities $\mathbf{X}(t-1)$.

3. The selected action is performed on the environment and the resulting sensations are observed.

4. The observed sensations are compared with the sensations predicted by the network (i.e., the activities of units chosen to represent the sensations) to compute a measure of error. To this error is added the contribution of constraint 1.

5. The back propagation "unfolding-in-time" procedure (Rumelhart, Hinton, & Williams, 1986) is used to compute the derivative of the error with respect to weights at the current and earlier time steps, $\mathbf{W}_{a(t-i)}$, for $i = 0 \cdots \tau - 1$.

6. The weight matrices for each action are updated using the overall error gradient and then are renormalized to enforce constraints 2 and 3.

7. The temporal record of unit activities, $\mathbf{X}(t-i)$ for $i = 0 \cdots \tau$, which is maintained to permit back propagation in time, is updated to reflect the new weights. (See further explanation below.)

8. The activities of the output units at time t, which represent the predicted sensations, are replaced by the actual observed sensations.

Steps 5-7 require further elaboration. The error measured at time t may be due to incorrect propagation of activities from time $t-1$, which would call for modification of the weight matrix $\mathbf{W}_{a(t)}$. But the error may also be attributed to incorrect propagation of activities at earlier times. Thus, back propagation is used to assign blame to the weights at earlier times. One critical parameter of training is the amount of temporal history, τ, to consider. We have found that, for a particular problem, error propagation beyond a certain critical number of steps does not improve learning performance, although any fewer does indeed harm performance. In the results described below, we set τ for a particular problem to what appeared to be a safe limit: one less than the number of nodes in the update graph solution of the problem.

To back propagate error in time, we maintain a temporal record of unit activities. However, a problem arises with these activities following a weight update: the activities are no longer consistent with the weights — i.e., Equation 1 is violated. Because the error derivatives computed by back propagation are exact only when Equation 1 is satisfied, future weight updates based on the inconsistent activities are not assured of being correct. Empirically, we have found the algorithm extremely unstable if we do not address this problem.

In most situations where back propagation is applied to temporally-extended sequences, the sequences are of finite length. Consequently, it is possible to wait until the end of the sequence to update the weights, at which point consistency between activities and weights no longer matters because the system starts fresh at the beginning of the next sequence. In the present situation, however, the sequence of actions does not terminate. We thus were forced to consider alternative means of ensuring consistency. The most successful approach involved updating the activities after each weight change to force consistency (step 7 of the list above). To do this, we propagated the earliest activities in the temporal record, $X(t-\tau)$, forward again to time t, using the updated weight matrices.

6 RESULTS

Figure 2 shows the weights in the update graph network for the three-room world after the robot has taken 6,000 steps. The Figure depicts a connectivity pattern identical to that of the update graph of Figure 1e. To explain the correspondence, think of the diagram as being in the shape of a person who has a head, left and right arms, left and right legs, and a heart. For the action U, the head — the output unit — receives input from the left leg, the left leg from the heart, and the heart from the head, thereby forming a three-unit loop. The other three units — the left arm, right arm, and right leg — form a

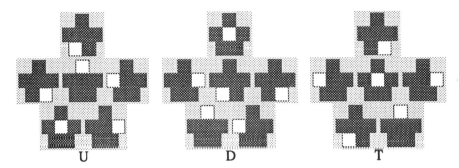

U   D   T

Figure 2: Weights learned after 6,000 exploratory steps in the three-room world. Each large diagram represents the weights corresponding to one of the three actions. Each small diagram contained within a large diagram represents the connection strengths feeding into a particular unit for a particular action. There are six units, hence six small diagrams. The output unit, which indicates the state of the light in the current room, is the protruding "head" of the large diagram. A white square in a particular position of a small diagram represents the strength of connection from the unit in the homologous position in the large diagram to the unit represented by the small diagram. The area of the square is proportional to the connection strength.

similar loop. For the action D, the same two loops are present but in the reverse direction. These two loops also appear in Figure 1e. For the action T, the left and right arms, heart, and left leg each keep their current value, while the head and the right leg exchange values. This corresponds to the exchange of values between the CUR and $\overline{\text{CUR}}$ nodes of the Figure 1e.

In addition to learning the update graph connectivity, the network has simultaneously learned the correct activity values associated with each node for the current state of the environment. Armed with this information, the network can predict the outcome of any sequence of actions. Indeed, the prediction error drops to zero, causing learning to cease and the network to become completely stable.

Now for the bad news: The network does not converge for every set of random initial weights, and when it does, it requires on the order of 6,000 steps. However, when the weight constraints are removed, that the network converges without fail and in about 300 steps. In Mozer and Bachrach (1989), we consider why the weight constraints are harmful and suggest several remedies. Without weight constraints, the resulting weight matrix, which contains a collection of positive and negative weights of varying magnitudes, is not readily interpreted. In the case of the n-room world, one reason why the final weights are difficult to interpret is because the net has discovered a solution that does not satisfy the RS update graph formalism; it has discovered the notion of complementation links of the sort shown in Figure 1d. With the use of complementation links, only three units are required, not six. Consequently, the three unnecessary units are either cut out of the solution or encode information redundantly.

Table 1 compares the performance of the RS algorithm against that of the connectionist network without weight constraints for several environments. Performance is measured in terms of the median number of actions the robot must take before it is able to predict the outcome of subsequent actions. (Further details of the experiments can be found in Mozer and Bachrach, 1989.) In simple environments, the connectionist update graph can outperform the RS algorithm. This result is quite surprising when considering that the action sequence used to train the network is generated at random, in contrast to the RS algorithm, which involves a strategy for exploring the environment. We conjecture that the network does as well as it does because it considers and updates many hypotheses in parallel at each time step. In complex environments, however, the network does poorly. By "complex", we mean that the number of nodes in the update graph is quite large and the number of distinguishing environmental sensations is relatively small. For example, the network failed to learn a 32-room world, whereas the RS algorithm succeeded. An intelligent exploration strategy seems necessary in this case: random actions will take too long to search the state space. This is one direction our future work will take.

Beyond the potential speedups offered by connectionist learning algorithms, the connectionist approach has other benefits.

Table 1: Number of Steps Required to Learn Update Graph

Environment	RS Algorithm	Connectionist Update Graph
Little Prince World	200	91
Car Radio World	27,695	8,167
Four-Room World	1,388	1,308
32-Room World	52,436	fails

- Performance of the network appears insensitive to prior knowledge of the number of nodes in the update graph being learned. In contrast, the RS algorithm requires an upper bound on the update graph complexity, and performance degrades significantly if the upper bound isn't tight.

- The network is able to accommodate "noisy" environments, also in contrast to the RS algorithm.

- During learning, the network continually makes predictions about what sensations will result from a particular action, and these predictions improve with experience. The RS algorithm cannot make predictions until learning is complete; it could perhaps be modified to do so, but there would be an associated cost.

- Treating the update graph as matrices of connection strengths has suggested generalizations of the update graph formalism that don't arise from a more traditional analysis. First, there is the fairly direct extension of allowing complementation links. Second, because the connectionist network is a linear system, any rank-preserving linear transform of the weight matrices will produce an equivalent system, but one that does not have the local connectivity of the update graph (see Mozer & Bachrach, 1989). The linearity of the network also allows us to use tools of linear algebra to analyze the resulting connectivity matrices.

These benefits indicate that the connectionist approach to the environment-modeling problem is worthy of further study. We do not wish to claim that the connectionist approach supercedes the impressive work of Rivest and Schapire. However, it offers complementary strengths and alternative conceptualizations of the learning problem.

Acknowledgements

Our thanks to Rob Schapire, Paul Smolensky, and Rich Sutton for helpful discussions. This work was supported by a grant from the James S. McDonnell Foundation to Michael Mozer, grant 87-2-36 from the Sloan Foundation to Geoffrey Hinton, and grant AFOSR-87-0030 from the Air Force Office of Scientific Research, Bolling AFB, to Andrew Barto.

References

Mozer, M. C., & Bachrach, J. (1989). *Discovering the structure of a reactive environment by exploration* (Technical Report CU-CS-451-89). Boulder, CO: University of Colorado, Department of Computer Science.

Rivest, R. L., & Schapire, R. E. (1987). Diversity-based inference of finite automata. In *Proceedings of the Twenty-Eighth Annual Symposium on Foundations of Computer Science* (pp. 78-87).

Rivest, R. L., & Schapire, R. E. (1987). A new approach to unsupervised learning in deterministic environments. In P. Langley (Ed.), *Proceedings of the Fourth International Workshop on Machine Learning* (pp. 364-375).

Rumelhart, D. E., Hinton, G. E., & Williams, R. J. (1986). Learning internal representations by error propagation. In D. E. Rumelhart & J. L. McClelland (Eds.), *Parallel distributed processing: Explorations in the microstructure of cognition. Volume I: Foundations* (pp. 318-362). Cambridge, MA: MIT Press/Bradford Books.

Schapire, R. E. (1988). *Diversity-based inference of finite automata.* Unpublished master's thesis, Massachusetts Institute of Technology, Cambridge, MA.

Designing Application-Specific Neural Networks Using the Genetic Algorithm

Steven A. Harp, Tariq Samad, Aloke Guha
Honeywell SSDC
1000 Boone Avenue North
Golden Valley, MN 55427

ABSTRACT

We present a general and systematic method for neural network design based on the genetic algorithm. The technique works in conjunction with network learning rules, addressing aspects of the network's gross architecture, connectivity, and learning rule parameters. Networks can be optimized for various application-specific criteria, such as learning speed, generalization, robustness and connectivity. The approach is model-independent. We describe a prototype system, *NeuroGENESYS*, that employs the backpropagation learning rule. Experiments on several small problems have been conducted. In each case, NeuroGENESYS has produced networks that perform significantly better than the randomly generated networks of its initial population. The computational feasibility of our approach is discussed.

1 INTRODUCTION

With the growing interest in the practical use of neural networks, addressing the problem of customizing networks for specific applications is becoming increasingly critical. It has repeatedly been observed that different network structures and learning parameters can substantially affect performance. Such important aspects of neural network applications as generalization, learning speed, connectivity and tolerance to network damage are strongly related to the choice of network architecture. Yet there are few analytic results, and few heuristics, that can help the application developer design an appropriate network.

We have been investigating the use of the genetic algorithm (Goldberg, 1989; Holland, 1975) for designing application-specific neural networks (Harp, Samad and Guha, 1989ab). In our approach, the genetic algorithm is used to evolve appropriate network structures and values of learning parameters. In contrast, other recent applications of the genetic algorithm to neural networks (e.g., Davis [1988], Whitley [1988]) have largely restricted the role of the genetic algorithm to updating weights on a predetermined network structure—another logical approach.

Several first-generation neural network application development tools already exist. However, they are only partly effective: the complexity of the problem, our limited understanding of the interdependencies between various network design choices, and the extensive human effort involved permit only limited exploration of the design space. An objective of our research is the development of a next-generation neural network application development tool that can synthesize optimized custom networks. The genetic algorithm has been distinguished by its relative immunity to high dimensionality, local minima and noise, and it is therefore a logical candidate for solving the network optimization problem.

2 GENETIC SYNTHESIS OF NEURAL NETWORKS

Fig. 1 outlines our approach. A network is represented by a *blueprint*—a bit-string that encodes a number of characteristics of the network, including structural properties and learning parameter values. Each blueprint directs the creation of an actual network with random initial weights. An instantiated network is trained using some predetermined training algorithm and training data, and the trained network can then be tested in various ways—e.g., on non-training inputs, after disabling some units, and after perturbing learned weight values. After testing, a network is evaluated—a *fitness* estimate is computed for it based on appropriate criteria. This process of instantiation, training, testing and evaluation is performed for each of a population of blueprints.

After the entire population is evaluated, the next *generation* of blueprints is produced. A number of *genetic operators* are employed, the most prominent of these being *crossover*, in which two parent blueprints are spliced together to produce a child blueprint (Goldberg, 1989). The higher the fitness of a blueprint, the greater the probability of it being selected as a parent for the subsequent generation. Characteristics that are found useful will thereby tend to be emphasized in the next generation, whereas harmful ones will tend to be suppressed.

The definition of network performance depends on the application. If the application requires good generalization capabilities, the results of testing on (appropriately chosen) non-training data are important. If a network capable of real-time learning is required, the learning rate must be optimized. For fast response, the size of the network must be minimized. If hardware (especially VLSI) implementation is a consideration, low connectivity is essential. In most applications several such criteria must be considered. This important aspect of application-specific network design is covered by the fitness function. In our approach, the fitness of a network can be an arbitrary function of several distinct

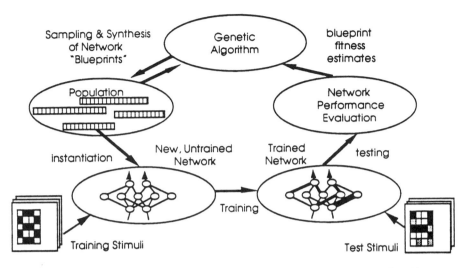

Figure 1: A population of network "blueprints" is cyclically updated by the genetic algorithm based on their fitness.

performance and cost criteria, some or all of which can thereby be simultaneously optimized.

3 NEUROGENESYS

Our approach is model-independent: it can be applied to any existing or future neural network model (including models without a training component). As a first prototype implementation we have developed a working system called *NeuroGENESYS*. The current implementation uses a variant (Samad, 1988) of the backpropagation learning algorithm (Werbos, 1974; Rumelhart, Hinton, and Williams, 1985) as the training component and is restricted to feedforward networks.

Within these constraints, NeuroGENESYS is a reasonably general system. Networks can have arbitrary directed acyclic graph structures, where each vertex of the graph corresponds to an *area* or layer of units and each edge to a *projection* from one area to another. Units in an area have a spatial organization; the current system arrays units in 2 dimensions. Each projection specifies independent radii of connectivity, one for each dimension. The radii of connectivity allow localized receptive field structures. Within the receptive fields connection densities can be specified. Two learning parameters are associated with both projections and areas. Each projection has a learning rate parameter ("η" in backpropagation) and a decay rate for η. Each area has η and η-decay parameters for threshold weights.

These network characteristics are encoded in the genetic blueprint. This bitstring is composed of several segments, one for each area. An area segment consists of an area parameter specification (APS) and a variable number of projection specification fields (PSFs), each of which describes a projection from the area to some other area. Both the APS and the PSF contain values for several parameters for areas and projections respectively. Fig. 2 shows a simple area segment. Note that the target of a projection can be specified through either *Absolute* or *Relative* addressing. More than one projections are possible between two given areas; this allows the generation of receptive field structures at different scales and with different connection densities, and it also allows the system to model the effect of larger initial weights. In our current implementation, all initial weights are randomly generated small values from a fixed uniform distribution. In the near future, we intend to incorporate some aspects of the distribution in the genetic blueprint.

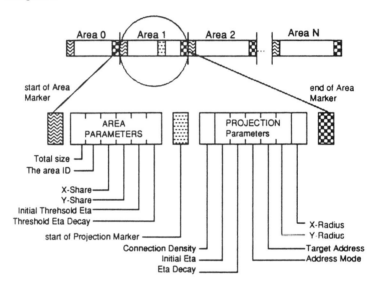

Figure 2: Network Blueprint Representation

In NeuroGENESYS, the score of a blueprint is computed as a linear weighted sum of several performance and cost criteria, including learning speed, the results of testing on a "test set", the numbers of units and weights in the network, the results of testing (on the training set) after disabling some of the units, the results of testing (on the training set) after perturbing the learned weight values, the average fanout of the network, and the maximum fanout for any unit in the network. Other criteria can be incorporated as needed. The user of Neuro-GENESYS supplies the weighting factors at the start of the experiment, thereby controlling which aspects of the network are to be optimized.

4 EXPERIMENTS

NeuroGENESYS can be used for both classification and function approximation problems. We have conducted experiments on three classification problems—digit recognition from 4×8 pixel images, exclusive-OR (XOR), and simple convexity detection; and one function approximation problem—modeling one cycle of a sine function. Various combinations of the above criteria have been used. In most experiments NeuroGENESYS has produced appropriate network designs in a relatively small number of generations (< 50).

Our first experiment was with digit recognition, and NeuroGENESYS produced a solution that surprised us: The optimized networks had no hidden layers yet learned perfectly. It had not been obvious to us that this digit recognition problem is linearly separable. Even in the simple case of no-hidden-layer networks, our earlier remarks on application-specific design can be appreciated. When NeuroGENESYS was asked to optimize for average fanout for the digit recognition task as well as for perfect learning, the best network produced learned perfectly (although comparatively slowly) and had an average fanout of three connections per unit; with learning speed as the sole optimization criterion, the best network produced learned substantially faster (48 iterations) but it had an average fanout of almost an order of magnitude higher.

The XOR problem, of course, is prototypically non-linearly-separable. In this case, NeuroGENESYS produced many fast-learning networks that had a "bypass" connection from the input layer directly to the output layer (in addition to connections to and from hidden layers); it is an as yet unverified hypothesis that these bypass connections accelerate learning.

In one of our experiments on the sine function problem, NeuroGENESYS was asked to design networks for moderate accuracy—the error cutoff during training was relatively high. The networks produced typically had one hidden layer of two units, which is the minimum possible configuration for a sufficiently crude approximation. When the experiment was repeated with a low error cutoff, intricate multilayer structures were produced that were capable of modeling the training data very accurately (Fig. 3). Fig. 4 shows the learning curve for one sine function experiment. The "Average" and "Best" scores are over all individuals in the generation, while "Online" and "Offline" are running averages of Average and Best, respectively. Performance on this problem is quite sensitive to initial weight values, hence the non-monotonicity of the Best curve. Steady progress overall was still being observed when the experiment was terminated.

We have conducted control studies using random search (with best retention) instead of the genetic algorithm. The genetic algorithm has consistently proved superior. Random search is the weakest possible optimization procedure, but on the other hand there are few sophisticated alternatives for this problem—the search space is discontinuous, largely unknown, and highly nonlinear.

5 COMPUTATIONAL EFFICIENCY

Our approach requires the evaluation of a large number of networks. Even on some of our small-scale problems, experiments have taken a week or longer, the bottleneck being the neural network training algorithm. While computational feasibility is a real concern, for several reasons we are optimistic that this approach will be practical for realistic applications:

- The hardware platform for our experiments to date has been a Symbolics computer without any floating-point support. This choice has been ideal

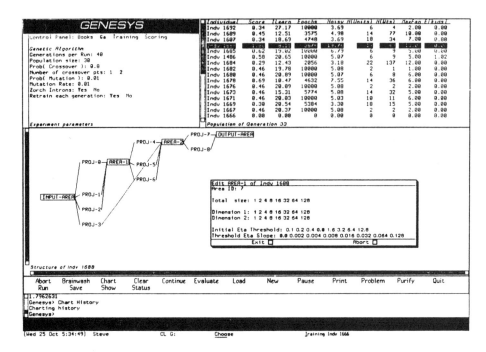

Figure 3: The NeuroGENESYS interface, showing a network structure optimised for the sine function problem

for program development, and NeuroGENESYS' user interface features would not have been possible without it, but the performance penalty has been severe (relative to machines with floating point hardware).

- The genetic algorithm is an inherently parallel optimization procedure, a feature we soon hope to take advantage of. We have recently implemented a networked version of NeuroGENESYS that will allow us to retain the desirable aspects of the Symbolics version and yet achieve substantial speedup in execution (we expect two to three orders of magnitude): up to 30 Apollo workstations, a VAX, and 10 Symbolics computers can now be evaluating different networks in parallel (Harp, Samad and Guha, 1990).

- The current version of NeuroGENESYS employs the backpropagation learning rule, which is notoriously slow for many applications. However, faster-learning extensions of backpropagation are continually being developed. We have incorporated one recent extension (Samad, 1988), but others, especially common ones such as including a "momentum" term in the weight update rule (Rumelhart, Hinton and Williams, 1985), could also be considered. More generally, learning in neural networks is a topic of intensive research and it is likely that more efficient learning algorithms will become popular in the near future.

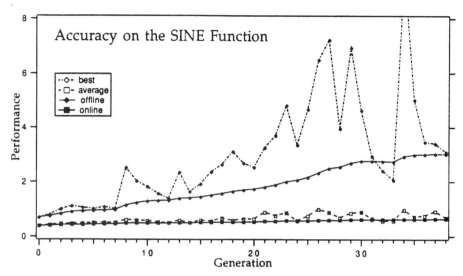

Figure 4: A learning curve for the sine function problem

- The genetic algorithm is an active field of research itself. Improvements, many of which are concerned with convergence properties, are frequently being reported and could reduce the computational requirements for its application significantly.

- The genetic algorithm is an iterative optimization procedure that, on the average, produces better solutions with each passing generation. Unlike some other optimization techniques, useful results can be obtained during a run. The genetic algorithm can thus take advantage of whatever time and computational resources are available for an application.

- Just as there is no strict termination requirement for the genetic algorithm, there is no constraint on its initialization. In our experiments, the zeroth generation consisted of randomly generated networks. Not surprisingly, almost all of these are poor performers. However, better better ways of selecting the initial population are possible. In particular, the initial population can consist of manually optimized networks. Manual optimization of neural networks is currently the norm, but it leaves much of the design space unexplored. Our approach would allow a human application developer to design one or more networks that could be the starting point for further, more systematic optimization by the genetic algorithm. Other initialization approaches are also possible, such as using optimized networks from similar applications, or using heuristic guidelines to generate networks.

It should be emphasized that computational efficiency is not the only factor that must be considered in evaluating this (or any) approach. Others such as the potential for improved performance of neural network applications and the costs and benefits associated with alternative approaches for designing network applications are also critically important.

6 FUTURE RESEARCH

In addition to running further experiments, we hope in the future to develop versions of NeuroGENESYS for other network models, including hybrid models that incorporate supervised and unsupervised learning components.

Space restrictions have precluded a detailed description of NeuroGENESYS and our experiments. The interested reader is referred to (Harp, Samad, and Guha, 1989ab, 1990).

References

Davis, L. (1988). Properties of a hybrid neural network-classifier system. In *Advances in Neural Information Processing Systems 1*, D.S. Touretzky (Ed.). San Mateo: Morgan Kaufmann.

Goldberg, D.E. (1989). *Genetic Algorithms in Search, Optimization and Machine Learning*. Addison-Wesley.

Harp, S.A., T. Samad, and A. Guha (1989a). Towards the genetic synthesis of neural networks. *Proceedings of the Third International Conference on Genetic Algorithms*, J.D. Schaffer (ed.). San Mateo: Morgan Kaufmann.

Harp, S.A., T. Samad, and A. Guha (1989b). *Genetic Synthesis of Neural Networks*. Technical Report I4852-CC-1989-2. Honeywell SSDC, 1000 Boone Avenue North, Golden Valley, MN 55427.

Harp, S.A., T. Samad, and A. Guha (1990). Genetic synthesis of neural network architecture. In *The Genetic Algorithms Handbook*, L.D. Davis (Ed.). New York: Van Nostrand Reinhold. (To appear.)

Holland, J. (1975). *Adaptation in Natural and Artificial Systems*. Ann Arbor: University of Michigan Press.

Rumelhart, D.E., G.E. Hinton, and R.J. Williams (1985). *Learning Internal Representations by Error-Propagation*, ICS Report 8506, Institute for Cognitive Science, UCSD, La Jolla, CA.

Samad, T. (1988). Back-propagation is significantly faster if the expected value of the source unit is used for update. *Neural Networks*, 1, Sup. 1.

Werbos, P. (1974). *Beyond Regression: New Tools for Prediction and Analysis in the Behavioral Sciences*. Ph.D. Thesis, Harvard University Committee on Applied Mathematics, Cambridge, MA.

Whitley, D. (1988). *Applying Genetic Algorithms to Neural Net Learning*. Technical Report CS-88-128, Department of Computer Science, Colorado State University.

Predicting Weather Using a Genetic Memory: a Combination of Kanerva's Sparse Distributed Memory with Holland's Genetic Algorithms

David Rogers
Research Institute for Advanced Computer Science
MS 230-5, NASA Ames Research Center
Moffett Field, CA 94035

ABSTRACT

Kanerva's sparse distributed memory (SDM) is an associative-memory model based on the mathematical properties of high-dimensional binary address spaces. Holland's genetic algorithms are a search technique for high-dimensional spaces inspired by evolutionary processes of DNA. "Genetic Memory" is a hybrid of the above two systems, in which the memory uses a genetic algorithm to dynamically reconfigure its physical storage locations to reflect correlations between the stored addresses and data. For example, when presented with raw weather station data, the Genetic Memory discovers specific features in the weather data which correlate well with upcoming rain, and reconfigures the memory to utilize this information effectively. This architecture is designed to maximize the ability of the system to scale-up to handle real-world problems.

INTRODUCTION

The future success of neural networks depends on an ability to "scale-up" from small networks and low-dimensional toy problems to networks of thousands or millions of nodes and high-dimensional real-world problems. (The *dimensionality* of a problem refers to the number of variables needed to describe the problem domain.) Unless neural networks are shown to be scalable to real-world problems, they will likely remain restricted to a few specialized applications.

Scaling-up adds two types of computational demands to a system. First, there is a linear increase in computational demand proportional to the increased number of variables. Second, there is a greater, nonlinear increase in computational demand due to the number of interactions that can occur between the variables. This latter effect is primarily responsible for the difficulties encountered in scaling-up many systems. In general, it is difficult to scale-up a system unless it is specifically designed to function well in high-dimensional domains.

Two systems designed to function well in high-dimensional domains are Kanerva's sparse distributed memory (Kanerva, 1988) and Holland's genetic algorithms (Holland, 1986). I hypothesized that a hybrid of these two systems would preserve this ability to operate well in high-dimensional environments, and offer grater functionality than either individually. I call this hybrid *Genetic Memory*. To test its capabilities, I applied it to the problem of forecasting rain from local weather data.

Kanerva's sparse distributed memory (SDM) is an associative-memory model based on the mathematical properties of high-dimensional binary address spaces. It can be represented as a three-layer neural-network with an extremely large number of nodes (1,000,000+) in the middle layer. In its standard formulation, the connections between the input layer and the hidden layer (the *input representation* used by the system) are fixed, and learning is done by changing the values of the connections between the hidden layer and the output layer.

Holland's genetic algorithms are a search technique for high-dimensional spaces inspired by evolutionary processes of DNA. Members of a set of binary strings competes for the opportunity to recombine. Recombination is done by selecting two "successful" members of the population to be the parents. A new string is created by splicing together pieces of each parent. Finally, the new string is placed into the set, and some "unsuccessful" older string removed.

"Genetic Memory" is a hybrid of the above two systems. In this hybrid, a genetic algorithm is used to reconfigure the connections between the input layer and the hidden layer. The connections between the hidden layer and the output layer are changed using the standard method for a sparse distributed memory. The "success" of an input representation is determined by how well it reflects correlations between addresses and data, using my previously presented work on statistical prediction (Rogers, 1988). Thus, we have two separate learning algorithms in the two levels. The memory uses the genetic algorithm to dynamically reconfigure its input representation to better reflect correlations between collections of input variables and the stored data.

I applied this Genetic Memory architecture to the problem of predicting rain given only local weather features such as the air pressure, the cloud cover, the month, the temperature, etc. The weather data contained 15 features, sampled every 4-hours over a 20-year period on the Australian coast. I coded each state into a 256-bit address, and stored at that address a single bit which denoted whether it rained in the 4 hours following that weather state. I allowed the genetic algorithm to reconfigure the memory while it scanned the file of weather states.

The success of this procedure was measured in two ways. First, once the training was completed, the Genetic Memory was better at predicting rain than was the standard sparse distributed memory. Second, I had access to the input representations discovered by the Genetic Memory and could view the specific combinations of features that predicted rain. Thus, unlike many neural networks, the Genetic Memory allows the user to inspect the internal representations it discovers during training.

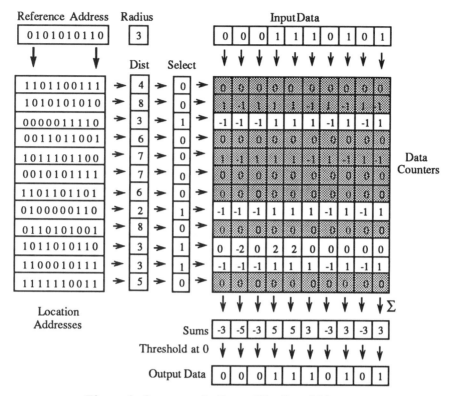

Figure 1: Structure of a Sparse Distributed Memory

SPARSE DISTRIBUTED MEMORY

Sparse distributed memory can be best illustrated as a variant of random-access memory (RAM). The structure of a twelve-location SDM with ten-bit addresses and ten-bit data is shown in figure 1.

A *memory location* is a row in this figure. The *location addresses* are set to random addresses. The *data counters* are initialized to zero. All operations begin with *addressing* the memory; this entails finding the Hamming distance between the *reference address* and each of the location addresses. If this distance is less than or equal to the *Hamming radius*, the select-vector entry is set to 1, and that location is termed *selected*. The ensemble of such selected locations is called the *selected set*. Selection is noted in the figure as non-gray rows. A *radius* is chosen so that only a small percentage of the memory locations are selected for a given reference address.

When *writing* to the memory, all selected counters beneath elements of the *input data* equal to 1 are incremented, and all selected counters beneath elements of the *input data* equal to 0 are decremented. This completes a write operation. When *reading* from the memory, the selected data counters are summed columnwise into the register *sums*. If the value of a sum is greater than or equal to zero, we set the corresponding bit in the *output data* to 1; otherwise, we set the bit in the *output data* to 0. (When reading, the contents of the *input data* are ignored.)

This example makes clear that a datum is *distributed* over the data counters of the selected locations when writing, and that the datum is reconstructed during reading by *averaging* the sums of these counters. However, depending on what additional data were written into some of the selected locations, and depending on how these data correlate with the original data, the reconstruction may contain noise.

The SDM model can also be described as a fully-connected three-layer feed-forward neural network. In this model, the location addresses are the weights between the input layer and the hidden units, and the data counters are the weights between the hidden units and the output layer. Note that the number of hidden-layer nodes (at least 1,000 and possibly up to 1,000,000) is much larger than is commonly used for artificial neural networks. It is unclear how well standard algorithms, such as back-propagation, would perform with such a large number of units in the hidden layer.

HOLLAND'S GENETIC ALGORITHMS

Genetic Algorithms are a search technique for high-dimensional spaces inspired by the evolutionary processes of DNA. The domain of a genetic algorithm is a *population of fixed-length binary strings* and a *fitness function*, which is a method for evaluating the fitness of each of the members. We use this fitness function to select two highly-ranked members for recombination, and one lowly-ranked member for replacement. (The selection may be done either *absolutely*, with the best and worst members always being selected, or *probabilisticly*, with the members being chosen proportional to their fitness scores.)

The member selected as *bad* is removed from the population. The two members selected as *good* are then recombined to create a new member to take its place in the population. In effect, the genetic algorithm is a search over a high-dimensional space for strings which are highly-rated by the fitness function.

The process used to create new members of the population is called *crossover*. In a crossover, we align the two good candidates end-to-end and segment them at one or more crossover-points. We then create a new string by starting the transcription of bits at one of the parent strings, and switching the transcription to the other parent at the crossover-points. This new string is placed into the population, taking the place of the poorly-rated member.

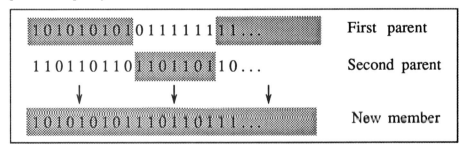

Figure 2: Crossover of two binary strings

By running the genetic algorithm over the population many times, the population "evolves" towards members which are rated more fit by our fitness function.

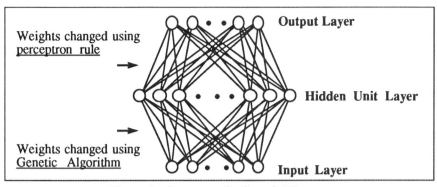

Figure 3: Structure of a Genetic Memory

Holland has a mathematical proof that genetic algorithms based on the crossover procedure are an extremely efficient method for searching a high-dimensional space.

GENETIC MEMORY

Genetic Memory is a hybrid of Kanerva's Sparse Distributed Memory and Holland's Genetic Algorithms. In this hybrid, the location addresses of the SDM are not held constant; rather, a Genetic Algorithm is used to move them to more advantageous positions in the address space. If we view SDM as a neural net, this hybrid uses a genetic algorithm to change the weights in the connections between the input layer and the hidden unit layer, while the connections between the hidden unit layer and the output layer at changed using the standard method for a SDM.

Most other work which combined neural networks and genetic algorithms kept *multiple* networks; the Genetic Algorithm was used to recombine the more successful of these networks to create new entire networks.

In a Genetic Memory there is a *single* network with different algorithms changing the weights in different layers. Thus, a Genetic Memory incorporates the Genetic Algorithm directly into the operation of a single network.

AUSTRALIAN WEATHER DATA

The weather data was collected at a single site on the Australian coast. A sample was taken every 4 hours for 25 years; the file contains over 58,000 weather samples

The file contained 15 distinct features, including year, month, day of the month, time of day, pressure, dry bulb temperature, wet bulb temperature, dew point, wind speed, wind direction, cloud cover, and whether it rained in the past four hours.

For this work, I coded each weather sample into a 256-bit word. Each weather sample was coded into a 256-bit binary address, giving each feature a 16-bit field in that address. The feature values were coarse-coded into a simple thermometer-style code. For example, figure 4 shows the code used for month.

PROCEDURE FOR WEATHER PREDICTION

In the standard SDM model, the locations addresses are held constant. In a Genetic Memory, the location addresses are reconfigured using a Genetic Algorithm.

```
JAN: 1111111100000000      JUL: 1000000001111111
FEB: 0111111111000000      AUG: 1100000000111111
MAR: 0011111111100000      SEP: 1111000000011111
APR: 0000111111110000      OCT: 1111100000001111
MAY: 0000011111111000      NOV: 1111110000000011
JUN: 0000001111111110      DEC: 1111111000000001
```

Figure 4: 16-bit code used for month

The fitness function used is based on my work on statistical prediction and presented at NIPS-88 [Rogers 1988]. This work assigns a number to each physical storage location (a row in the figure) which is a measure of the *predictiveness* of that location. Highly-predictive locations are recombined using crossover; the newly-created location address is given to a location which is relatively unpredictive. *The data counter is a measure of the correlation between the selection of a location and the occurrence of a given bit value.* Thus, we can use the data counters to judge the fitness, i.e., the predictiveness, of each memory location.

To train the memory, we present the memory with each weather state in turn. The memory is *not* shown the data a multiple number of times. For each state, the memory is addressed with the 256-bit address which represents it. **"0"** is written to the memory if it does not rain in the next four hours, and **"1"** if it does. After the memory has seen a given number of weather samples, the Genetic Algorithm is performed to replace a poorly-predictive location with a new address created from two predictive addresses.

The procedure is continued until the memory has seen 50,000 weather samples, and has performed ~5,000 genetic recombinations.

ANALYSIS OF RESULTS

The initial results from the Genetic Memory procedure was conducted on a memory with 1,000 storage locations. The weather sample set consisted of a sequence of weather samples taken every 4 hours over a period of 20 years. In the sample set, it rained in the next 4 hours for ~10% of the samples, and was dry in the next four hours in ~90% of the samples.

The Genetic Memory was testing by storing ~50,000 weather samples. The samples were given to the memory in chronological order. During the course of storage, the memory reconfigured itself with ~5,000 genetic recombinations. A Genetic Memory and a standard Sparse Distributed Memory were tested against 1,000 previously unseen weather samples. In initial experiments, the Genetic Memory had 50% fewer errors than the Sparse Distributed Memory.

However, the Genetic Memory does not only show an improvement in performance, it allows the user to analyze the genetically-determined memory locations to discover how the memory improved its performance.

By studying highly-rated memory locations in the Genetic Memory, we can *open the black box:* that is, access the parameters the memory has decided are the most effective in associating the sample addresses with the sample data. This ability to access the parameters the system found effective has two important implications. First, the parameters may offer insights into the underlying physical processes in the system under study. Second, knowledge of *how* the system predicts may be vital for determining the robustness and the envelope of applicability of the memory prior to embedding into a real-world system.

Simply scoring the performance of a system is not enough. We must be able to "open the black box" to study why the system performs as it does.

OPENING THE BLACK BOX

When the training is completed, we can analyze the structure of memory locations which performed well to discover *which features* they found most discriminatory and *which values* of those features were preferred. For example, here is a memory location which was rated highly-fit for predicting rain after training:

1101001100000011 1111011110101011 <u>0111111100010000</u> 1100000011011010
0100110011111011 1111110000000011 0111111011000000 0011101101100110
0000001011110110 0110000001000010 0001001110110100 0100000111111111
0000000111111110 0000000011111111 0011011111111111 0100110000001000

By measuring the distance between a given 16-bit field and all possible values for that field, we can discover *which values* of the feature are most desired. (Closer in hamming distance is better.) The absolute range of values is the *sensitivity* of the location to changes along that feature dimension. Figure 5 shows an analysis of the 16-bit field for month in the given memory location:

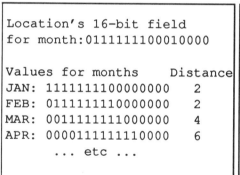
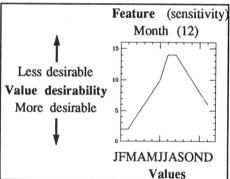

Figure 5: Analyzing a location field

In this case, the location finds January and February the most desirable months for rain, and July and August the least desirable months.

The relative sensitivity towards different features measures which features are most important in making the prediction of rain. In this case, we have a change of distance of 12 bits, which makes this location very sensitive to the value of the month.

We can estimate which features are the most important in predicting rain by looking at the relative sensitivity of the different fields in the location to changes in their feature. The following graphs show the most sensitive features of the previously shown memory location towards predicting rain; that is, the location is very sensitive to the combination of all these fields with the proper values.

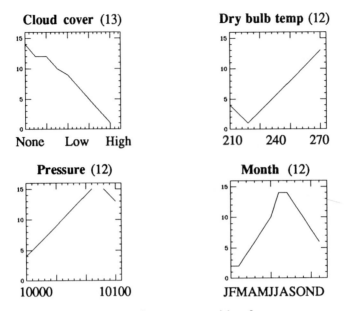

Figure 6: The four most sensitive features

The "most preferred values" of these fields are the *minima* of these graphs. For example, this location greatly prefers January and February over June and July. The preferences of this location are for the month to be January or February, for low pressure, high cloud cover, and low temperature. Surprisingly, whether it rained in the *last* four hours is not one of the most important features for this location.

We can also look some of the least sensitive features. The following graphs show the least sensitive features of the memory location towards predicting rain; that is, the location is relatively insensitive to the values of these features.

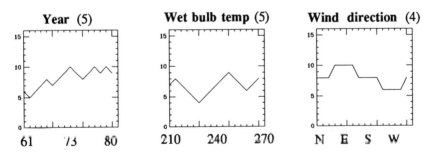

Figure 7: The three least sensitive features

This set contains some fields that one *would* expect to be relatively unimportant, such as year. Fields such as wind direction is unimportant to this location, but interestingly other highly-rated locations find it to be very useful in other regions of the weather space.

COMPARISON WITH DAVIS' METHOD

Davis' Algorithm has been shown to be a powerful new method for augmenting the power of a backpropagation-based system. The following is an attempt to contrast our approaches, without denigrating the importance his groundbreaking work. The reader is referred to his book for detailed information about his approach.

It is difficult to directly compare the performance of these techniques given the preliminary nature of the experiments done with Genetic Memory. However, it is possible to compare architectural features of the systems, and estimate the relative strengths a weaknesses.

• **Backpropagation vs. Associative Memories:** Davis' approach relies on the performance of the backpropagation algorithm for the central learning cycle of the system. Associative memories have a far quicker learning cycle than backpropagation networks, and have been shown to have preferential characteristics after training in some domains. A system based on an associative memory may share these advantages over a system based on backpropagation.

• **Scalability:** Many issues concerning the scalability of backpropagation networks remain unresolved. It is not simple to build backpropagation networks of thousands or hundreds of thousands of units. In contrast, Kanerva's Sparse Distributed Memory is specifically designed for such massive construction; one implementation on the Connection Machine can contain 1,000,000 hidden units. The Genetic Memory shares this property.

• **Unity:** Davis' algorithm has two levels of processing. The first level consists of standard backpropagation networks, and the second is a meta-level which manipulates these networks. The Genetic Memory has incorporated both algorithms into a single network; both algorithms are operating simultaneously.

My intuition is that *different algorithms may be best suited for the different layers of a neural network.* Layers with a large fan-out (such as the input layer to the layer of hidden units) may be best driven by an algorithm suited to high-dimensional searching, such as Genetic Algorithms or a Kohonen-style self-organizing system. Layers with a large fan-in (such as the hidden-unit layer to the output layer) may be best driven by a hill-climbing algorithms such a backpropagation.

CONCLUSIONS

• Real-world problems are often "high-dimensional", that is, are described by large numbers of dependent variables. Algorithms must be specifically designed to function well in such high-dimensional spaces. Genetic Memory is such an algorithm .

• Genetic Memory, while sharing some features with Davis' approach, has fundamental differences that may make it more appropriate to some problems and easier to scale to extremely-large (> 100,000 node) systems.

• The incorporation of the Genetic Algorithm improves the recall performance of a standard associative memory.

• The structure of the Genetic Memory allows the user to access the parameters discovered by the Genetic Algorithm and used to assist in making the associations stored in the memory.

Acknowledgments

This work was supported in part by Cooperative Agreements NCC 2-408 and NCC 2-387 from the National Aeronautics and Space Administration (NASA) to the Universities Space Research Association (USRA). Funding related to the Connection Machine was jointly provided by NASA and the Defense Advanced Research Projects Agency (DARPA). All agencies involved were very helpful in promoting this work, for which I am grateful.

The entire RIACS staff and the SDM group has been supportive of my work. Bruno Olshausen was a vital sounding-board. Pentti Kanerva trusted my intuitions even when the payoff wasn't yet clear. And finally, thanks to Doug Brockman, who decided to wait for me.

References

Davis, L., *Genetic algorithms and simulated annealing,* London, England: Pitman Publishing (1987).

Holland, J. H., *Adaptation in natural and artificial systems,* Ann Arbor: University of Michigan Press (1975).

Holland, J. H., "Escaping brittleness: the possibilities of general-purpose learning algorithms applied to parallel rule-based systems," in *Machine learning, an artificial intelligence approach, Volume II,* R. J. Michalski, J. G. Carbonell, and T. M. Mitchell, eds. Los Altos, California: Morgan Kaufmann (1986).

Kanerva, Pentti., "Self-propagating Search: A Unified Theory of Memory," Center for the Study of Language and Information Report No. CSLI-84-7 (1984).

Kanerva, Pentti., *Sparse distributed memory,* Cambridge, Mass: MIT Press, 1988.

Rogers, David, "Using data-tagging to improve the performance of Kanerva's sparse distributed memory," Research Institute for Advanced Computer Science Technical Report 88.1, NASA Ames Research Center (1988a).

Rogers, David, "Kanerva's Sparse Distributed Memory: an Associative Memory Algorithm Well-Suited to the Connection Machine," *Int. J. High-Speed Comput.,* **2**, pp. 349-365 (1989).

Rogers, David, "Statistical Prediction with Kanerva's Sparse Distributed Memory," *Advances in Neural Information Processing Systems I,* San Mateo: Morgan-Kaufman (1989).

NEURAL NETWORK VISUALIZATION

Jakub Wejchert
Gerald Tesauro
IBM Research
T.J. Watson Research
Center
Yorktown Heights
NY 10598

ABSTRACT

We have developed graphics to visualize static and dynamic information in layered neural network learning systems. Emphasis was placed on creating new visuals that make use of spatial arrangements, size information, animation and color. We applied these tools to the study of back-propagation learning of simple Boolean predicates, and have obtained new insights into the dynamics of the learning process.

1 INTRODUCTION

Although neural network learning systems are being widely investigated by many researchers via computer simulations, the graphical display of information in these simulations has received relatively little attention. In other fields such as fluid dynamics and chaos theory, the development of "scientific visualization" techniques (1,3) have proven to be a tremendously useful aid to research, development, and education. Similar benefits should result from the application of these techniques to neural networks research.

In this article, several visualization methods are introduced to investigate learning in neural networks which use the back-propagation algorithm. A multi-window environment is used that allows different aspects of the simulation to be displayed simultaneously in each window.

As an application, the toolkit is used to study small networks learning Boolean functions. The animations are used to observe the emerging structure of connection strengths, to study the temporal behaviour, and to understand the relationships and effects of parameters. The simulations and graphics can run at real-time speeds.

2   VISUAL REPRESENTATIONS

First, we introduce our techniques for representing both the instantaneous dynamics of the learning process, and the full temporal trajectory of the network during the course of one or more learning runs.

2.1   The Bond Diagram

In the first of these diagrams, the geometrical structure of a connected network is used as a basis for the representation. As it is of interest to try to see how the internal configuration of weights relates to the problem the network is learning, it is clearly worthwhile to have a graphical representation that explicitly includes weight information integrated with network topology. This differs from "Hinton diagrams" (2), in which data may only be indirectly related to the network structure. In our representation nodes are represented by circles, the area of which are proportional to the threshold values. Triangles or lines are used to represent the weights or their rate of change. The triangles or line segments emanate from the nodes and point toward the connecting nodes. Their lengths indicate the magnitude of the weight or weight derivative. We call this the "bond diagram".

In this diagram, one can look at any node and clearly see the magnitude of the weights feeding into and out of it. Also, a sense of direction is built into the picture since the bonds point to the node that they are connected to. Further, the collection of weights form distinct patterns that can be easily perceived, so that one can also infer global information from the overall patterns formed.

2.2   The Trajectory Diagram

A further limitation of Hinton diagrams is that they provide a relatively poor representation of dynamic information. Therefore, to understand more about the dynamics of learning we introduce another visual tool that gives a two-dimensional projection of the weight space of the network. This represents the learning process as a trajectory in a reduced dimensional space. By representing the value of the error function as the color of the point in weight space, one obtains a sense of the contours of the error hypersurface, and the dynamics of the gradient-descent evolution on this hypersurface. We call this the "trajectory diagram".

The scheme is based on the premise that the human user has a good visual notion of vector addition. To represent an n-dimensional point, its axial components are defined as vectors and then are plotted radially in the plane; the vector sum of these is then calculated to yield the point representing the n-dimensional position.

It is obvious that for n > 2 the resultant point is not unique, however, the method does allow one to infer information about families of similar trajectories, make comparisons between trajectories and notice important deviations in behaviour.

2.3 Implementation

The graphics software was written in C using X-Windows v. 11. The C code was interfaced to a FORTRAN neural network simulator. The whole package ran under UNIX, on an RT workstation. Using the portability of X-Windows the graphics could be run remotely on different machines using a local area network. Excecution time was slow for real-time interaction except for very small networks (typically up 30 weights). For larger networks, the Stellar graphics workstation was used, whereby the simulator code could be vectorized and parallelized.

3 APPLICATION EXAMPLES

With the graphics we investigated networks learning Boolean functions: binary input vectors were presented to the network through the input nodes, and the teacher signal was set to either 1 or 0. Here, we show networks learning majority, and symmetry functions. The output of the majority function is 1 only if more than half of the input nodes are on; simple symmetry distiguishes between input vectors that are symmetric or anti-symmetric about a central axis; general symmetry identifies perfectly symmetric patterns out of all other permutations. Using the graphics, one can watch how solutions to a particular problem are obtained, how different parameters affect these solutions, and observe stages at which learning decisions are made.

At the start of the simulations the weights are set to small random values. During learning, many example patterns of vectors are presented to the input of the network and weights are adjusted accordingly. Initially the rate of change of weights is small, later as the simulation gets under way the weights change rapidly, until small changes are made as the system moves toward the final solution. Distinct patterns of triangles show the configuration of weights in their final form.

3.1 The Majority Function

Figure 1 shows a bond diagram for a network that has learnt the majority function. During the run, many input patterns were presented to the network during which time the weights were changed. The weights evolve from small random values through to an almost uniform set corresponding to the solution of the problem. Towards the end, a large output node is displayed and the magnitudes of all the weights are roughly uniform, indicating that a large bias (or threshold) is required to offset the sum of the weights. Majority is quite a simple problem for the network to learn; more complicated functions require hidden units.

3.2 The Simple Symmetry Function

In this case only symmetric or perfectly anti-symmetric patterns are presented and the network is taught to distinguish between these. In solving this problem, the

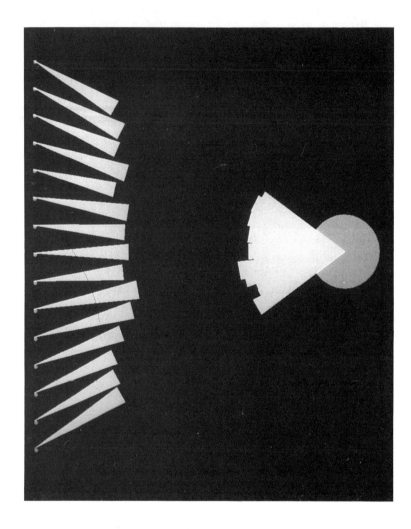

Figure 1: A near-final configuration of weights for the majority function. All the weights are positive. The disc corresponds to the threshold of the output unit.

network chose (correctly) that it needs only two units to make the decision whether the input is totally symmetric or totally anti-symmetric. (In fact, any symmetrically separated input pair will work.) It was found that the simple pattern created by the bond representation carries over into the more general symmetry function, where the network must identify perfectly symmetric inputs from all the other permutations.

3.3 The General Symmetry Function

Here, the network is required to detect symmtery out of all the possible input patterns. As can be seen from the bond diagram (figure 2) the network has chosen a hierarchical structure of weights to solve the problem, using the basic pattern of weights of simple symmtery. The major decision is made on the outer pair and additional decisions are made on the remaining pairs with decreasing strength. As before, the choice of pairs in the hierarchy depends on the initial random weights. By watching the animations, we could make some observations about the stages of learning. We found that the early behavior was the most critical as it was at this stage that the signs of the weights feeding to the hidden units were determined. At the later stages the relative magnitudes of the weights were adapted.

3.4 The Visualization Environment

Figure 3 shows the visualization environment with most of the windows active. The upper window shows the total error, and the lower window the state of the output unit. Typically, the error initially stays high then decreases rapidly and then levels off to zero as final adjustments are made to the weights. Spikes in this curve are due to the method of presenting patterns at random. The state of the output unit initially oscillates and then bifurcates into the two requires output states.

The two extra windows on the right show the trajectory diagrams for the two hidden units. These diagrams are generalizations of phase diagrams: components of a point in a high dimensional space are plotted radially in the plane and treated as vectors whose sum yields a point in the two-dimensional representation. We have found these diagrams useful in observing the trajectories of the two hidden units, in which case they are representations of paths in a six-dimensional weight space. In cases where the network does converge to a correct solution, the paths of the two hidden units either try to match each other (in which case the configurations of the units were identical) or move in opposite directions (in which case the units were opposites).

By contrast, for learning runs which do not converge to global optima we found that usually one of the hidden units followed a normal trajectory whereas the other unit was not able to achieve the appropriate match or anti-match. This is because the signs of the weights to the second hidden unit were not correct and the learning algorithm could not make the necessary adjustments. At a certain point early in learning the unit would travel off on a completely different trajectory. These observations suggest a heuristic that could improve learning by setting initial trajectories in the "correct" directions.

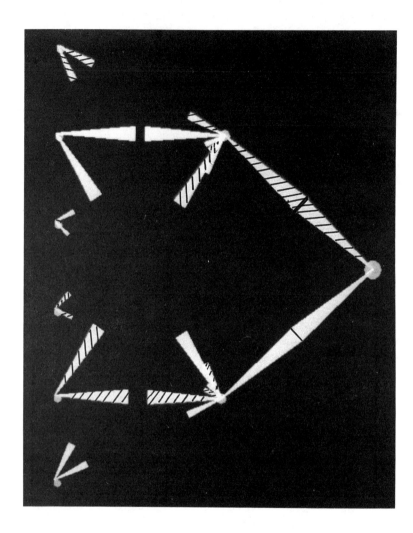

Figure 2: The bond diagram for a network that has learnt the symmetry function. There are six input units, two hidden and one output. Weights are shown by bonds emanating from nodes. In the graphics positive and negative weights are colored red and blue respectively. In this grey-scale photo the negative weights are marked with diagonal lines to distinguish them from positive weights.

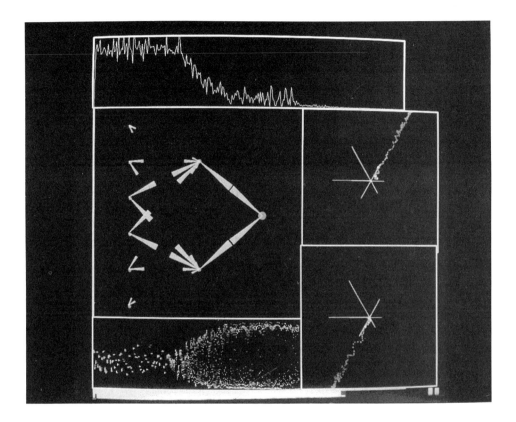

Figure 3: An example of the graphics with most of the windows active; the command line appears on the bottom. The central window shows the bond diagram of the General Symmetry function. The upper left window shows the total error, and the lower left window the state of the output unit. The two windows on the right show the trajectory diagrams for the two hidden units. The "spokes" in this diagram correspond to the magnitude of the weights. The trace of dots are the paths of the two units in weight space.

In general, the trajectory diagram has similar uses to a conventional phase plot: it can distinguish between different regions of configuration space; it can be used to detect critical stages of the dynamics of a system; and it gives a "trace" of its time evolution.

4   CONCLUSION

A set of computer graphics visualization programs have been designed and interfaced to a back-propagation simulator. Some new visualization tools were introduced such as the bond and trajectory diagrams. These and other visual tools were integrated into an interactive multi-window environment.

During the course of the work it was found that the graphics was useful in a number of ways: in giving a clearer picture of the internal representation of weights, the effects of parameters, the detection of errors in the code, and pointing out aspects of the simulation that had not been expected beforehand. Also, insight was gained into principles of designing graphics for scientific processes.

It would be of interest to extend our visualization techniques to include large networks with thousands of nodes and tens of thousands of weights. We are currently examining a number of alternative techniques which are more appropriate for large data-set regimes.

Acknowledgements

We wish to thank Scott Kirkpatrick for help and encouragment during the project. We also thank members of the visualization lab and the animation lab for use of their resources.

References

(1) McCormick B H, DeFanti T A Brown M D (Eds), "Visualization in Scientific Computing" Computer Graphics 21, 6, November (1987). See also "Visualization in Scientific Computing-A Synopsis", IEEE Computer Graphics and Applications, July (1987).

(2) Rumelhart D E, McClelland J L, "Parallel Distributed Processing: Explorations in the Microstructure of Cognition. Volume 1" MIT Press, Cambridge, MA (1986).

(3) Tufte E R, "The Visual Display of Quantitative Information", Graphic Press, Chesire, CT (1983).

PART VI:
NEW LEARNING ALGORITHMS

Sigma-Pi Learning:
On Radial Basis Functions and Cortical
Associative Learning

Bartlett W. Mel   **Christof Koch**
Computation and Neural Systems Program
Caltech, 216-76
Pasadena, CA 91125

ABSTRACT

The goal in this work has been to identify the neuronal elements of the cortical column that are most likely to support the learning of nonlinear associative maps. We show that a particular style of network learning algorithm based on locally-tuned receptive fields maps naturally onto cortical hardware, and gives coherence to a variety of features of cortical anatomy, physiology, and biophysics whose relations to learning remain poorly understood.

1   INTRODUCTION

Synaptic modification is widely believed to be the brain's primary mechanism for long-term information storage. The enormous practical and theoretical importance of biological synaptic plasticity has stimulated interest among both experimental neuroscientists and neural network modelers, and has provided strong incentive for the development of computational models that can both explain and predict.

We present here a model for the synaptic basis of associative learning in cerebral cortex. The main hypothesis of this work is that the principal output neurons of a cortical association area learn functions of their inputs as locally-generalizing lookup tables. As abstractions, locally-generalizing learning methods have a long history in statistics and approximation theory (see Atkeson, 1989; Barron & Barron,

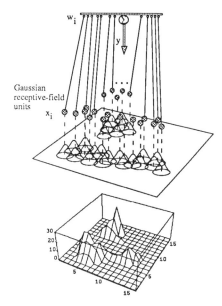

Figure 1: A Neural Lookup Table. A nonlinear function of several variables may be decomposed as a weighted sum over a set of localized "receptive fields" units.

1988). Radial Basis Function (RBF) methods are essentially similar (see Broomhead & Lowe, 1988) and have recently been discussed by Poggio and Girosi (1989) in relation to regularization theory. As is standard for network learning problems, locally-generalizing methods involve the learning of a map $f(\underline{x}) : \underline{x} \mapsto y$ from example $(\underline{x}, y)$ pairs. Rather than operate directly on the input space, however, input vectors are first "decoded" by a population of "receptive field" units with centers ξ_i that each represents a local, often radially-symmetric, region in the input space. Thus, an output unit computes its activation level $y = \sum_i w_i g(x - \xi_i)$, where g defines a "radial basis function", commonly a Gaussian, and w_i is its weight (Fig. 1). The learning problem can then be characterized as one of finding weights $\underline{w}$ that minimize the mean squared error over the N element training set. Learning schemes of this type lend themselves directly to very simple Hebb-type rules for synaptic modification since the initially nonlinear learning problem is transformed into a linear one in the unknown parameters $\underline{w}$ (see Broomhead & Lowe, 1988).

Locally-generalizing learning algorithms as neurobiological models date at least to Albus (1971) and Marr (1969, 1970); they have also been explored more recently by a number of workers with a more pure computational bent (Broomhead & Lowe, 1988; Lapedes & Farber, 1988; Mel, 1988, 1989; Miller, 1988; Moody, 1989; Poggio & Girosi, 1989).

2   SIGMA-PI LEARNING

Unlike the classic thresholded linear unit that is the mainstay of many current connectionist models, the output of a *sigma-pi* unit is computed as a sum of contributions from a set of independent multiplicative clusters of input weights (adapted from Rumelhart & McClelland, 1986): $y = \sigma(\sum_j w_j c_j)$, where $c_j = \prod_i v_i x_i$ is the product of weighted inputs to cluster j, w_j is the weight on cluster j as a whole, and σ is an optional thresholding nonlinearity applied to the sum of total cluster activity. During learning, the output may also by clamped by an unconditioned teacher input, i.e. such that $y = t_i(\underline{x})$. Units of this general type were first proposed by Feldman & Ballard (1982), and have been used occasionally by other connectionist modelers, most commonly to allow certain inputs to gate others or to allow the activation of one unit to control the strength of interconnection between two other units (Rumelhart & McClelland, 1986). The use of *sigma-pi* units as function lookup tables was suggested by Feldman & Ballard (1982), who cited a possible relevance to local dendritic interactions among synaptic inputs (see also Durbin & Rumelhart, 1989).

In the present work, the specific nonlinear interaction among inputs to a *sigma-pi* cluster is not of primary theoretical importance. The crucial property of a cluster is that its output should be AND-like, i.e. selective for the simultaneous activity of *all* of its k input lines[1].

2.1   NETWORK ARCHITECTURE

We assume an underlying d-dimensional input space $\mathcal{X} \in R^d$ over which functions are to be learned. Vectors in $\mathcal{X}$ are represented by a population X of N units whose state is denoted by $\underline{x} \in R^N$. Within X, each of the d dimensions of $\mathcal{X}$ is individually value-coded, i.e. consists of a set of units with gaussian receptive fields distributed in overlapping fashion along the range of allowable parameter values, for example, the angle of a joint, or the orientation of a visual stimulus at a specific retinal location. (A more biologically realistic case would allow for individual units in X to have *multi*-dimensional gaussian receptive fields, for example a 4-d visual receptive field encoding retinal x and y, edge orientation, and binocular disparity.)

We assume a map $t(\underline{x}) : \underline{x} \mapsto \underline{y}$ is to be learned, where the components of $\underline{y} \in R^M$ are represented by an output population Y of M units. According to the familiar single-layer feedforward network learning paradigm, X projects to Y via an "associational" pathway with modifiable synapses. We consider the task of a single output unit y_i (hereafter denoted by y), whose job is to estimate the underlying teacher function $t_i(\underline{x}) : \underline{x} \mapsto y$ from examples. Output unit y is assumed to have access to the entire input vector $\underline{x}$, and a single unconditioned teacher input t_i. We further assume that

---

[1] A local threshold function can act as an AND in place of a multiplication, and for purposes of biological modeling, is a more likely dendritic mechanism than pure multiplication. In continuing work, we are exploring the more detailed interactions between Hebb-type learning rules and various post-synaptic nonlinearities, specifically the NMDA channel, that could underlie a multiplication relation among nearby inputs.

all possible clusters c_j of size 1 through $k = k_{max}$ pre-exist in y's dendritic field, with cluster weights w_j initially set to 0, and input weights v_i within each cluster set equal to 1. Following from our assumption that each of the input lines x_i represents a 1-dimensional gaussian receptive field in $\mathcal{X}$, a multiplicative cluster of k such inputs can yield a k-dimensional receptive field in $\mathcal{X}$ that may then be weighted. In this way, a *sigma-pi* unit can directly implement an RBF decomposition over $\mathcal{X}$. Additionally, since a *sigma-pi* unit is essentially a massively parallel lookup table with clusters as stored table entries, it is significant that the *sigma-pi* function is inherently *modular*, such that groups of *sigma-pi* units that receive the same teacher signal can, by simply adding their outputs, act as a single much larger virtual *sigma-pi* unit with correspondingly increased table capacity[2]. A neural architecture that allows system storage capacity to be multiplied by a factor of k by growing k neurons in the place of one, is one that should be strongly preferred by biological evolution.

2.2   THE LEARNING RULE

The cluster weights w_j are modified during training according to the following self-normalizing Hebb rule:

$$\dot{w}_j = \alpha \ c_{jp} \ t_p - \beta w_j,$$

where α and β are small positive constants, and c_{jp} and t_p are, respectively, the jth cluster response and teacher signal in state p. The steady state of this learning rule occurs when $w_j = \frac{\alpha}{\beta} < c_j t >$, which tries to maximize the correlation[3] of cluster output and teacher signal over the training set, while minimizing total synaptic weight for all clusters. The inputs weights v_i are unmodified during learning, representing the degree of cluster membership for each input line.

We briefly note that because this Hebb-type learning rule is truly local, i.e. depends only upon activity levels available directly at a synapse to be modified, it may be applied transparently to a group of neurons driven by the same global teacher input (see above discussion of *sigma-pi* modularity). Error-correcting rules that modify synapses based on a difference between desired vs. actual neural output do not share this property.

3   TOWARD A BIOLOGICAL MODEL

In the remainder of this paper we examine the hypothesis that *sigma-pi* units underlie associative learning in cerebral cortex. To do so, we identify the six essential elements of the *sigma-pi* learning scheme and discuss the evidence for each: i) a population of output neurons, ii) a focal teacher input, iii), a diffuse association input, iv) Hebb-type synaptic plasticity, v) local dendritic multiplication (or thresholding), and vi) a cluster reservoir.

Following Eccles (1985), we concern ourselves here with the cytoarchitecture of "generic" association cortex, rather than with the more specialized (and more often studied) primary sensory and motor areas. We propose the cortical circuit of fig.

---

[2] This assumes the global thresholding nonlinearity σ is weak, i.e. has an extended linear range.
[3] Strictly speaking, the average product.

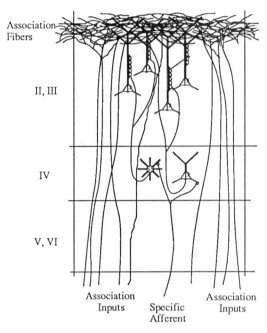

Figure 2: Elements of the cortical column in a generic association cortex.

2 to contain all of the basic elements necessary for associative learning, closely paralleling the accounts of Marr (1970) and Eccles (1985) at this level of description. We limit our focus to the cortically-projecting "output" pyramids of layers II and III, which are posited to be *sigma-pi* units. These cells are a likely locus of associative learning as they are well situated to receive both teacher and associational input pathways. With reference to the modularity property of *sigma-pi* learning (sec. 2.1), we interpret the aggregates of layer II/III pyramidal cells whose apical dendrites rise toward the cortical surface in tight clumps (on the order of 100 cells, Peters, 1989), as a single virtual *sigma-pi* unit.

3.1 THE TEACHER INPUT

We tentatively define the "teacher" input to an association area to be those inputs that terminate primarily in layer IV onto spiny stellate cells or small pyramidal cells. Lund et al. (1985) points out that spiny stellate cells are most numerous in primary sensory areas, but that the morphologically similar class of small pyramidal cells in layer IV seem to mimick the spiny stellates in their local, vertically oriented excitatory axonal distributions. The layer IV spiny stellates are known to project primarily up (but also down) a narrow vertical cylinder in which they sit, probably making powerful "cartridge" synapses onto overlying pyramidal cells. These excitatory interneurons are presumably capable of strongly depolarizing entire output cells (Szentagothai, 1977), thus providing the needed unit-wide teacher signals to the output neurons. We therefore assume this teacher pathway plays a role analagous to the presumed role of cerebellar climbing fibers (Albus, 1971; Marr,

1969) The inputs to layer IV can be of both thalamic and/or cortical origin.

3.2 THE ASSOCIATIONAL INPUT

A second major form of extrinsic excitatory input with access to layer II/III pyramidal cells is the massive system of horizontal fibers in layer I. The primary source of these fibers is currently believed to be long range excitatory association fibers from both other cortical and subcortical areas (Jones, 1981). In accordance with Marr (1970) and Eccles (1985), we interpret this system of horizontal fibers, which virtually permeates the dendritic fields of the layer II/III pyramidal cells, as the primary *conditioned* input pathway at which cortical associative learning takes place. There is evidence that an individual layer I fibers can make excitatory synapses on apical dendrites of pyramidal cells across an area of cortex 5-6mm in diameter (Szentagothai, 1977).

3.3 HEBB RULES, MULTIPLICATION, AND CLUSTERING

The process of cluster formation in *sigma-pi* learning is driven by a local Hebb-type rule. Long term Hebb-type synaptic modification has been demonstrated in several cortical areas, dependent only upon local post-synaptic depolarization (Kelso et al., 1986), and thought to be mediated by the the voltage-dependent NMDA channel (see Brown et al., 1988). In addition to the standard tendency for LTP with pre- and post-synaptic correlation, *sigma-pi* learning implicitly specifies cooperation among pre-synaptic units, in the sense that the largest increase in cluster weight w_j occurs when all inputs x_i to a cluster are simultaneously and strongly active. This type of cooperation among pre-synaptic inputs should follow directly from the assumption that local post-synaptic depolarization is the key ingredient in the induction of LTP. In other words, like-activated synaptic inputs must inevitably contribute to each other's enhancement during learning to the extent they are clustered on a post-synaptic dendrite. This type of cooperativity in learning gives key importance to *dendritic space* in neural learning, and has not until very recently been modelled at a biophysical level (T. Brown, pers. comm; J. Moody, pers. comm.).

In addition to its possible role in enhancing like-activated synaptic clusters however, the NMDA channel may be hypothesized to simultaneously underlie the "multiplicative" interaction among neighboring inputs needed for ensuring cluster-selectivity in *sigma-pi* learning. Thus, if sufficiently endowed with NMDA channels, cortical pyramidal cells could respond highly selectively to associative input "vectors" whose active afferents are spatially clumped, rather than scattered uniformly, across the dendritic arbor. The possibility that dendritic computations could include local multiplicative nonlinearities is widely accepted (e.g. Shepherd et al., 1985; Koch et al., 1983).

3.4 A VIRTUAL CLUSTER RESERVOIR

The abstract definition of *sigma-pi* learning specifies that all possible clusters c_j of size $1 < k < k_{max}$ pre-exist on the "dendrites" of each virtual *sigma-pi* unit (which we have previously proposed to consist of a vertically aggregated clump of 100 pyramidal cells that receive the same teacher input from layer 4). During learning, the weight on each cluster is governed by a simple Hebb rule. Since the number of *possible* clusters of size k overwhelms total available dendritic space for even small k^4, it must be possible to *create* a cluster when it is needed. We propose that the complex 3-d mesh of axonal and dendritic arborizations in layer 1 are ideal for maximizing the probability that arbitrary (small) subsets of association axons cross *near* to each other in space at some point in their collective arborizations. Thus, we propose that the tangle of axons within a dendrite's receptive field gives rise to an enormous set of *almost*-clusters, poised to "latch" onto a post-synaptic dendrite when called for by a Hebb-type learning rule. This geometry of pre- and post-synaptic interface is to be strongly contrasted with the architecture of cerebellum, where the afferent "parallel" fibers have no possibility of clustering on post-synaptic dendrites.

Known biophysical mechamisms for the sprouting and guidance of growth cones during development, in some cases driven by neural activity seem well suited to the task of cluster formation over small distances in the adult brain.

4   CONCLUSIONS

The locally-generalizing, table-based *sigma-pi* learning scheme is a parsimonious mechanisms that can account for the learning of nonlinear associative maps in cerebral cortex. Only a single layer of excitatory synapses is modified, under the control of a Hebb-type learning rule. Numerous open questions remain however, for example the degree to which clusters of active synapses scattered across a pyramidal dendritic tree can function independently, providing the necessary AND-like selectivity.

Acknowledgements

Thanks are due to Ojvind Bernander, Rodney Douglas, Richard Durbin, Kamil Grajski, David Mackay, and John Moody for numerous helpful discussions. We acknowledge support from the Office of Naval Research, the James S. McDonnell Foundation, and the Del Webb Foundation.

References

Albus, J.S. A theory of cerebellar function. *Math. Biosci.*, 1971, *10*, 25-61.

Atkeson, C.G. Using associative content-addressable memories to control robots, MIT A.I. Memo 1124, September 1989.

Barron, A.R. & Barron, R.L. Statistical learning networks: a unifying view. Presented at the *1988 Symposium on the Interface: Statistics and Computing Science*, Reston, Virginia.

Bliss, T.V.P. & Lømo, T. Long-lasting potentiation of synaptic transmission in the dentate area of the anaesthetized rabbit following stimulation of the perforant path. *J. Physiol.*, 1973, *232*, 331-356.

---

[4] For example, assume a 3-d learning problem and clusters of size $k = 3$; with 100 afferents per input dimension, there are $100^3 = 10^6$ possible clusters. If we assume 5,000 available association synapses per pyramidal cell, there is dendritic space for at most 166,000 clusters of size 3.

Broomhead, D.S. & Lowe, D. Multivariable functional interpolation and adaptive networks. *Complex Systems*, 1988, *2*, 321-355.

Brown, T.H., Chapman, P.F., Kairiss, E.W., & Keenan, C.L. Long-term synaptic potentiation. *Science*, 1988, *242*, 724-728.

Durbin, R. & Rumelhart, D.E. Product units: a computationally powerful and biologically plausible extension to backpropagation networks. *Complex Systems*, 1989, *1*, 133.

Eccles, J.C. The cerebral neocortex: a theory of its operation. In *Cerebral Cortex, vol. 2*, A. Peters & E.G. Jones, (Eds.), Plenum: New York, 1985.

Feldman, J.A. & Ballard, D.H. Connectionist models and their properties. *Cognitive Science*, 1982, *6*, 205-254.

Giles, C.L. & Maxwell, T. Learning, invariance, and generalization in high-order neural networks. *Applied Optics*, 1987, *26(23)*, 4972-4978.

Hebb, D.O. *The organization of behavior.* New York: Wiley, 1949.

Jones, E.G. Anatomy of cerebral cortex: columnar input-ouput relations. In *The organization of cerebral cortex*, F.O. Schmitt, F.G. Worden, G. Adelman, & S.G. Dennis, (Eds.), MIT Press: Cambridge, MA, 1981.

Kelso, S.R., Ganong, A.H., & Brown, T.H. Hebbian synapses in hippocampus. *PNAS* USA, 1986, *83*, 5326-5330.

Koch, C., Poggio, T., & Torre, V. Nonlinear interactions in a dendritic tree: localization, timing, and role in information processing. *PNAS*, 1983, *80*, 2799-2802.

Lapedes, A. & Farber, R. How neural nets work. In *Neural Information Processing Systems*, D.Z. Anderson, (Ed.), American Institute of Physics: New York, 1988.

Lund, J.S. Spiny stellate neurons. In *Cerebral Cortex, vol. 1*, A. Peters & E.G. Jones, (Eds.), Plenum: New York, 1985.

Marr, D. A theory for cerebral neocortex. *Proc. Roy. Soc. Lond. B*, 1970, *176*, 161-234.

Marr, D. A theory of cerebellar cortex. *J. Physiol.*, 1969, *202*, 437-470.

Mel, B.W. MURPHY: A robot that learns by doing. In *Neural Information Processing Systems*, D.Z. Anderson, (Ed.), American Institute of Physics: New York, 1988.

Mel, B.W. MURPHY: A neurally inspired connectionist approach to learning and performance in vision-based robot motion planning. Ph.D. thesis, University of Illinois, 1989.

Miller W.T., Hewes, R.P., Glanz, F.H., & Kraft, L.G. Real time dynamic control of an industrial manipulator using a neural network based learning controller. Technical Report, Dept. of Electrical and Computer Engineering, University of New Hampshire, 1988.

Moody, J. & Darken, C. Learning with localized receptive fields. In *Proc. 1988 Connectionist Models Summer School*, Morgan-Kaufmann, 1988.

Peters, A. Plenary address, 1989 Soc. Neurosc. Meeting, Phoenix, AZ.

Poggio, T. & Girosi, F. Learning, networks and approximation theory. *Science*, In press.

Rumelhart, D.E., Hinton, G.E., & McClelland, J.L. A general framework for parallel distributed processing. In *Parallel distributed processing: explorations in the microstructure of cognition, vol. 1*, D.E. Rumelhart, J.L. McClelland, (Eds.), Cambridge, MA: Bradford, 1986.

Shepherd, G.M., Brayton, R.K., Miller, J.P., Segev, I., Rinzel, J., & Rall, W. Signal enhancement in distal cortical dendrites by means of interactions between active dendritic spines. *PNAS*, 1985, *82*, 2192-2195.

Szentagothai, J. The neuron network of the cerebral cortex: a functional interpretation. (1977) *Proc. R. Soc. Lond. B.*, 201:219-248.

Algorithms for Better Representation and Faster Learning in Radial Basis Function Networks

Avijit   Saha[1]
James D. Keeler

Microelectronics and Computer Technology corporation
3500 West Balcones Center Drive
Austin, Tx 78759

ABSTRACT

In this paper we present upper bounds for the learning rates for hybrid models that employ a combination of both self-organized and supervised learning, using radial basis functions to build receptive field representations in the hidden units. The learning performance in such networks with nearest neighbor heuristic can be improved upon by multiplying the individual receptive field widths by a suitable overlap factor. We present results indicating optimal values for such overlap factors. We also present a new algorithm for determining receptive field centers. This method negotiates more hidden units in the regions of the input space as a function of the output and is conducive to better learning when the number of patterns (hidden units) is small.

1 INTRODUCTION

Functional approximation of experimental data originating from a continuous dynamical process is an important problem. Data is usually available in the form of a set S consisting of $\{x,y\}$ pairs, where x is a input vector and y is the corresponding output vector. In particular, we consider networks with a single layer of hidden units and the jth output unit computes $y_j = \Sigma f_\alpha R_\alpha\{ x_j, x_\alpha, \sigma_\alpha\}$, where, y_j is the

---

[1] University of Texas at Austin, Dept. of ECE, Austin TX 78712

network output due to input x_j, f_α is the synaptic weight associated with the αth hidden neuron and the jth output unit; $R_\alpha\{ x(t_j), x_\alpha, \sigma\}$ is the Radial Basis Function (RBF) response of the αth hidden neuron. This technique of using a superposition of RBF for the purposes of approximation has been considered before by [Medgassy '58] and more recently by [Moody '88], [Casdagli '89] and [Poggio '89]. RBF networks are particularly attractive since such networks are potentially 1000 times faster than the ubiquitous backpropagation network for comparable error rates [Moody '88].

The essence of the network model we consider is described in [Moody '88]. A typical network that implements a receptive field response consists of a layer of linear input units, a layer of linear output units and an intermediate (hidden) layer of non-linear response units. Weights are associated with only the links connecting the hidden layer to the output layer. For the single output case the real valued functional mapping $f : R^n \rightarrow R$ is characterized by the following equations:

$$O(x_i) = \Sigma f_\alpha R_\alpha (x_i) \qquad (1)$$

$$O(x_i) = \Sigma f_\alpha R_\alpha (x_i) / \Sigma R_\alpha (x_i) \qquad (2)$$

$$R_\alpha(x_i) = e^{- (|x_\alpha - x_i| / \sigma_\alpha)^2} \qquad (3)$$

where x_α is a real valued vector associated with the αth receptive field (hidden) unit and is of the same dimension as the input. The output can be normalized by the sum of the responses of the hidden units due to any input, and the expression for the output using normalized response function is presented in Equation 2. The x_α values the centers of the receptive field units and σ_α are their widths. Training in such networks can be performed in a two stage hybrid combination of independent processes. In the first stage, a clustering of the input data is performed. The objective of this clustering algorithm is to establish appropriate x_α values for each of the receptive field units such that the cluster points represent the input distribution in the best possible manner. We use competetive learning with the nearest neighbor heuristic as our clustering algorithm (Equation 5). The degree or quality of clustering achieved is quantified by the sum-square measure in Equation 4, which is the objective function we are trying to minimize in the clustering phase.

$$TSS\text{-}KMEANS = \Sigma (x_{\alpha-closest} - x_i)^2 \qquad (4)$$

$$x_{\alpha-closest} = x_{\alpha-closest} + \lambda (x_i - x_{\alpha-closest}) \qquad (5)$$

After suitable cluster points (x_α values) are determined the next step is to determine the σ_α or widths for each of the receptive fields. Once again we use the nearest neighbor heuristic where σ_α (the width of the αth neuron) is set equal to the euclidian distance between x_α and its nearest neighbor. Once the receptive field centers x_α and the widths (σ_α) are found, the receptive field responses can be calculated for any input using Equation 3. Finally, the f_α values or weights on links connecting the hidden layer units to the output are determined using the well-known gradient descent learning rule. Pseudo inverse methods are usually impractical in these problems. The rules for the objective function and weight update are given by equations 6 and 7.

$$E \;\; = \;\; \Sigma_i \, (\, O(x_i) \, - \, t_i \,)^2 \tag{6}$$

$$f_\alpha \;\; = \;\; f_\alpha \, + \, \eta \, \{ (\, O(x_i) \, - \, t_i \,) \, \} \, R_\alpha \, (x_i) \tag{7}$$

where, i is the number of input patterns, x_i is the input vector and t_i is the target output for the ith pattern.

2   LEARNING RATES

In this section we present an adaptive formulation for the network learning rate η (Equation 7). Learning rates (η) in such networks that use gradient descent are usually chosen in an adhoc fashion. A conservative value for η is usually sufficient. However, there are two problems with such an approach. If the learning rate is not small enough the TSS (Total Sums of Squares) measure can diverge to high values instead of decreasing. A very conservative estimate on the other hand will work with almost all sets of data but will unnecessarily slow down the learning process. The choice of learning rate is crucial, since for real-time or hardware implementations of such systems there is very little scope for interactive monitoring.

This problem is addressed by the Theorem 1. We present the proof for this theorem for the special case of a single output. In the gradient descent algorithm, weight updates can be performed after each presentation of the entire set of patterns (per epoch basis or after each pattern (per pattern basis); both cases are considered. Equation p.3 gives the upper bound for η when updates are done on a per epoch basis. Only positive values of η should be considered. Equations p.4 and p.5 gives the bounds for η when updates are done on a per pattern basis without and with normalized response function respectively. We present some simulation results for the logistic map { x(t+1) = r x(t) [1 - x(t)] } data in Figure 1. The plots are shown only for the normalized response case, and the learning rate was set to η = $\mu\{ \, (\, \Sigma \, R_\alpha)^2 \, / \, \Sigma \, (R_\alpha)^2 \}$. We used a fixed number of 20 hidden units, and r was set to 4.0. The network TSS did not diverge until μ was set arbitrarily close to 1.

This is shown in Figure 1 which indicates that, with the normalized response function, if the sum of squares of the hidden unit responses is nearly equal to the square of the sum of the responses, then a high effective learning rate (η) can be used.

Theorem 1 : The TSS measure of a network will be decreasing in time, provided the learning rate η does not exceed $\Sigma_i \, e_i \, \Sigma_\alpha \, E_\alpha R_{\alpha i} / \{ \, \Sigma_i \, (\Sigma_\alpha \, E_\alpha R_{\alpha i} \,)^2 \}$ if the network is trained on a per epoch basis, and $1 / \Sigma_\alpha (R_{\alpha i} \,)^2$ when updates are done on a per pattern basis. With normalized response function, the upper bound for the learning rate is $(\Sigma_\alpha R_{\alpha i} \,)^2 / \Sigma_\alpha (R_{\alpha i} \,)^2$. Note similar result of [Widrow 1985].

Proof :
$$\text{TSS}(t) \;=\; \Sigma_i (\, t_i - \Sigma_\alpha f_\alpha R_{\alpha i})^2 \qquad (p.1)$$
where N is the number of exemplars, and K is the number of receptive fields and t_i is the ith target output.

$$\text{TSS}\,(t+1) \;=\; \Sigma_i \, (\, t_i - \Sigma_\alpha (\, f_\alpha + \Delta f_\alpha) R_{\alpha i})^2 \qquad (p.2)$$

$$\text{where,} \; \Delta f_\alpha \;=\; - \, \eta \, \frac{\delta(\text{TSS}(t)}{\delta f_\alpha}$$

$$= \; 2 \, \eta \, \Sigma_i \, e_i \, R_{\alpha i}$$

$$= \; 2 \, \eta \, E_\alpha \qquad \text{where,} \, E_\alpha \; = \; \Sigma_i \, e_i \, R_{\alpha i}$$

For stability, we impose the condition $\text{TSS}(t) - \text{TSS}\,(t+1) \geq 0$. From Eqns (p.1) and (p.2) above and substituting $\eta \, 2 E_\alpha$ for Δf_α, we have :

$$\text{TSS}(t) - \text{TSS}\,(t+1) \geq \Sigma_i \, e_i^2 - \Sigma_i (\, t_i - \Sigma_\alpha f_\alpha R_{\alpha i} - \Sigma_\alpha \, 2 \, \eta \, E_\alpha \, R_{\alpha i})^2$$

Expanding the RHS of the above expression and substituting e_i appropriately :

$$\text{TSS}(t) - \text{TSS}\,(t+1) \geq -4 \, \eta \, \Sigma_i \, e_i \, \Sigma_\alpha E_\alpha \, R_{\alpha i} + 4 \, \eta^2 \, \Sigma_i \, (\Sigma_\alpha E_\alpha \, R_{\alpha i})^2$$

$\therefore$ From the above inequality it follows that for stability in per epoch basis training, the upper bound for learning rate η is given by :

$$\eta \; \leq \; \Sigma_i \, e_i \, \Sigma_\alpha E_\alpha \, R_{\alpha i} / \Sigma_i \, (\Sigma_\alpha E_\alpha R_{\alpha i})^2 \qquad (p.3)$$

If updates are done on a per pattern basis, then N = 1 and we drop the summation over N and the index i and we obtain the following bound :

$$\eta \; \leq \; 1 / \Sigma_\alpha (R_{\alpha i} \,)^2. \qquad (p.4)$$

With normalized response function the upper bound for the learning rate is :

$$\eta \; \leq \; (\Sigma_\alpha R_{\alpha i} \,)^2 / \Sigma_\alpha (R_{\alpha i} \,)^2. \qquad ((p.5)$$

$$\text{Q.E.D.}$$

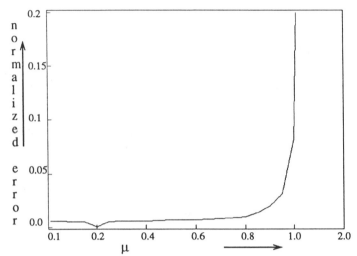

Figure 1: Normalized error vs. fraction (μ)
of maximum allowable learning rate

3 EFFECT OF WIDTH (σ) ON APPROXIMATION ERROR

In the nearest-neighbor heuristic σ values of the hidden units are set equal to the euclidian distance between its center and the center of its nearest neighbor. This method is preferred mainly because it is computationally inexpensive. However, the performance can be improved by increasing the overlap between nearby hidden unit responses. This is done by multiplying the widths obtained with the nearest neighbor heuristic by an overlap factor m as shown in Equation 3.1.

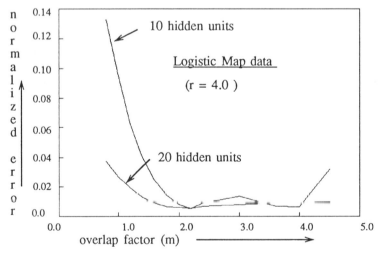

Figure 2: Normalized errors vs. overlap factor for the
logistic map.

$$\sigma_\alpha = m \cdot \| x_\alpha - x_{\alpha\text{-nearest}} \| \qquad (3.1)$$

and $\| \cdot \|$ is the euclidian distance norm.

In Figures 2 and 3 we show the network performance (normalized error) as a function of m. In the logistic map case a value of r = 4.0 was used, predicting 1 timestep into the future; training set size was 10 times the number of hidden units and test set size was 70 patterns. The results for the Mackey-Glass data are with parameter values a = 0.1, b = 0.2, Δ = 6, D = 4. The number of training patterns was 10 times the number of hidden units and the normalized error was evaluated based on the presentation of 900 unseen patterns. For the Mackey-Glass data the optimal values were rather well-defined; whereas for the logistic map case we found that the optimal values were spread out over a range.

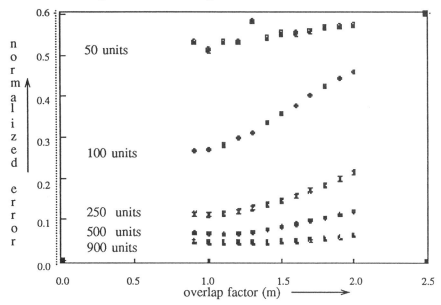

Figure 2: Normalized errors vs. overlap factor for varying number of hidden units, Mackey-Glass data.

4 EXTENDED METRIC CLUSTERING

In this method clustering is done in higher dimensions. In our experiments we set the initial K hidden unit center values based on the first K exemplars. The receptive fields are assigned vector values of dimensions determined by the size of the input and the output vectors. Each center value was set equal to the vector obtained by concatenating the input and the corresponding output. During the clustering phase the output y_i is concatenated with the input x_i and presented to the hidden layer.

This method finds cluster points in the (I+O)-dimensional space of the input-output map as defined by Equations 4.1, 4.2 and 4.3.

$$X_\alpha = <x_\alpha, y_\alpha> \qquad (4.1)$$

$$X_i = <x_i, y_i> \qquad (4.2)$$

$$X_{\alpha\text{-new}} = X_{\alpha\text{-old}} + \lambda(X_\alpha - X_i) \qquad (4.3)$$

Once the cluster points or the centers are determined we disable the output field, and only the input field is used for computing the widths and receptive field responses. In Figure 3 we present a comparison of the performances of such a network with and without the enhanced metric clustering. Variable size networks of only Gaussian RBF units were used. The plots presented are for the Mackey-Glass data with the same parameter values used in [Farmer 88]. This method works significantly better when the number of hidden units is low.

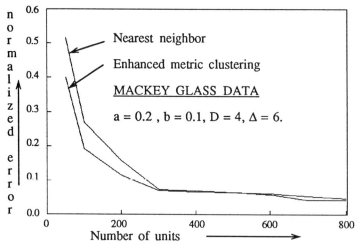

Figure 3 : Performance of enhanced metric clustering algorithmm.

5 CONCLUSIONS

One of the emerging application areas for neural network models is real time signal processing. For such applications and hardware implementations, adaptive methods for determining network parameters are essential. Our derivations for learning rates are important in such situations. We have presented results indicating that in RBF networks, performance can be improved by tuning the receptive field widths by some suitable overlap factor. We have presented an extended metric algorithm that negotiates hidden units based on added output information. We have observed more than 20% improvement in the normalized error measure when the number of training patterns, and therefore the number of hidden units, used is reasonably small.

References

M. Casdagli. (1989) "Nonlinear Prediction of Chaotic Time Series" <u>Physica 35D</u>, 335 -356.

D. J. Farmer and J. J. Sidorowich. (1988). "Exploiting Chaos to Predict the Future and Reduce Noise". Tech. Report No. LA-UR-88-901, Los Alamos National Laboratory.

John Moody and Christen Darken (1989)."Learning with Localised Receptive Fields". <u>In: Eds: D. Touretzky, Hinton and Sejnowski: Proceedings of the 1988 Connectionist Models Summer School</u>. Morgan Kaufmann Publishing, San Mateo, CA.

P. Medgassy. (1961) <u>Decomposition of Superposition of Distribution Functions,</u> Publishing house of the Hungarian Academy of Sciences, Budapest, 1961.

T. Poggio and F. Girosi. (1989). "A Theory of Networks for Approximation and Learning", A.I. Memo No. 1140, Massachusetts Institute of Technology.

B. Widrow and S. Stearns (1985). <u>Adaptive Signal Processing.</u> Prentice-Hall Inc., Englewood Cliffs, NJ, pp 49,102.

Learning in higher-order 'artificial dendritic trees'

Tony Bell
Artificial Intelligence Laboratory
Vrije Universiteit Brussel
Pleinlaan 2, B-1050 Brussels, BELGIUM
(tony@arti.vub.ac.be)

ABSTRACT

If neurons sum up their inputs in a non-linear way, as some simulations suggest, how is this distributed fine-grained non-linearity exploited during learning? How are all the small sigmoids in synapse, spine and dendritic tree lined up in the right areas of their respective input spaces? In this report, I show how an abstract atemporal highly nested tree structure with a quadratic transfer function associated with each branchpoint, can self organise using only a single global reinforcement scalar, to perform binary classification tasks. The procedure works well, solving the 6-multiplexer and a difficult phoneme classification task as well as back-propagation does, and faster. Furthermore, it does not calculate an error gradient, but uses a statistical scheme to build moving models of the reinforcement signal.

1. INTRODUCTION

The computational territory between the linearly summing McCulloch-Pitts neuron and the non-linear differential equations of Hodgkin & Huxley is relatively sparsely populated. Connectionists use variants of the former and computational neuroscientists struggle with the exploding parameter spaces provided by the latter. However, evidence from biophysical simulations suggests that the voltage transfer properties of synapses, spines and dendritic membranes involve many detailed non-linear interactions, not just a squashing function at the cell body. Real neurons may indeed be higher-order nets.

For the computationally-minded, higher order interactions means, first of all, quadratic terms. This contribution presents a simple learning principle for a binary tree with a logistic/quadratic transfer function at each node. These functions, though highly nested, are shown to be capable of changing their shape in concert. The resulting tree structure receives inputs at its leaves, and outputs an estimate of the probability that the input pattern is a member of one of two classes at the top.

A number of other schemes exist for learning in higher-order neural nets. Sigma-Pi units, higher-order threshold logic units (Giles & Maxwell, 87) and product units (Durbin & Rumelhart, 89) are all examples of units which learn coefficients of non-linear functions. Product unit networks, like Radial Basis Function nets, consist of a layer of non-linear transformations, followed by a normal Perceptron-style layer. The scheme presented here has more in common with the work reviewed in Barron (88) (see also Tenorio 90) on polynomial networks in that it uses low order polynomials in a tree of low degree. The differences lie in a global rather than layer-by-layer learning scheme, and a transfer function derived from a gaussian discriminant function.

2. THE ARTIFICIAL DENDRITIC TREE (ADT)

The network architecture in Figure 1(a) is that of a binary tree which propagates real number values from its leaf nodes (or inputs) to its root node which is the output. In this simple formulation, the tree is construed as a binary classifier. The output node signals a number between 1 and 0 which represents the probability that the pattern presented to the tree was a member of the positive class of patterns or the negative class. Because the input patterns may have extremely high dimension and the tree is, at least initially, constrained to be binary, the depth of the tree may be significant, at least more than one might like to back-propagate through. A transfer function is associated with each 'hidden' node of the tree and the output node. This will hereafter be referred to as a *Z-function*, for the simple reason that it takes in two variables X and Y, and outputs Z. A cascade of Z-functions performs the computation of the tree and the learning procedure consists of changing these functions. The tree is referred to as an *Artificial Dendritic Tree* or ADT with the same degree of licence that one may talk of Artificial Neural Networks, or ANNs.

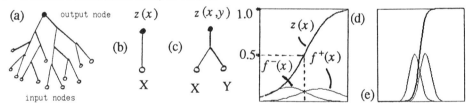

Figure 1: (a) an Artificial Dendritic Tree, (b) a 1D Z-node (c) a 2D Z-node (d) A 1D Z-function constructed from2 gaussians (e) approximating a step function

2.1. THE TRANSFER FUNCTION

The idea behind the Z-function is to allow the two variables arriving at a node to interact locally in a non-linear way which contributes to the global computation of the tree. The transfer function is derived from statistical considerations. To simplify, consider the one-dimensional case of a variable X travelling on a wire as in Figure 1(b). A statistical estimation procedure could observe the distribution of values of X when the global pattern was positive or negative and derive a decision rule from these. In Figure 1(d), the two density functions $f^+(x)$ and $f^-(x)$ are plotted. Where they meet, the local computation must answer that, based on its information, the global pattern is positively classified with probability 0.5. Assuming that there are equal numbers of positive and negative patterns (ie: that the *a priori* probability of positive is 0.5), it is easy to see that the *conditional probability* of being in the positive class given our value for X, is given by equation (1).

$$z(x) = P[class=+ve \mid x] = \frac{f^+(x)}{f^+(x)+f^-(x)} \qquad (1)$$

This can be also derived from Bayesian reasoning (Therrien, 89). The form of $z(x)$ is shown with the thick line in Figure 1(d) for the given $f^+(x)$ and $f^-(x)$. If $f^+(x)$ and $f^-(x)$ can be usefully approximated by normal (gaussian) curves as plotted above, then (1) translates into (2):

$$z(x) = \frac{1}{1+e^{-input}} \quad , \quad input = \beta^-(x) - \beta^+(x) + \ln\left[\frac{\alpha^-}{\alpha^+}\right] \qquad (2)$$

This can be obtained by substituting equation (4) overleaf into (1) using the definitions of α and β given. The exact form α and β take depends on the number of variables input. The first striking thing is that the form of (2) is exactly that of the back-propagation logistic function. The second is that *input* is a polynomial quadratic expression. For Z-functions with 2 inputs (x,y) using formulas (4.2) it takes the form:

$$w_1x^2+w_2y^2+w_3xy+w_4x+w_5y+w_6 \qquad (3)$$

The w's can be thought of as weights just as in backprop, defining a 6D space of transfer functions. However optimising the w's directly through gradient descent may not be the best idea (though this is what Tenorio does), since for any error function E, $\partial E/\partial w_4 = x\partial E/\partial w_1 = y\partial E/\partial w_3$. That is, the axes of the optimisation are not indepen-dent of each other. There are, however, two sets of 5 independent parameters which the w's in (3) are actually composed from if we calculate *input* from (4.2). These are μ_x^+, σ_x^+, μ_y^+, σ_y^+ and r^+, denoting the means, standard deviations and correlation coefficient defining the two-dimensional distribution of (x,y) values which should be positively classified. The other 5 variables define the negative distribution.

Thus 2 Gaussians (hereafter referred to as the *positive* and *negative models*) define a quadratic transfer function (called the *Z-function*) which can be interpreted as express-ing conditional probability of positive class membership. The shape of these functions can be altered by changing the statistical parameters defining the distributions which underly them. In Figure 1(d), a 1-dimensional Z-function is seen to be sigmoidal though it need not be monotonic at all. Figure 2(b)-(h) shows a selection of 2D Z-functions. In general the Z-function divides its N-dimensional input space with a N-1 dimensional hypersurface. In 2D, this will be an ellipse, a parabola, a hyperbola or some combination of the three. Although the dividing surface is quadratic, the Z-function is still a logistic or squashing function. The exponent *input* is actually equivalent to the *log likelihood ratio* or $\ln(f^+(x)/f^-(x))$, commonly used in statistics.

In this work, 2-dimensional gaussians are used to generate Z-functions. There are compelling reasons for this. One dimensional Z-functions are of little use since they do not reduce information. Z-functions of dimension higher than 1 perform optimal class-based information reduction by propagating conditional probabilities of class membership. But 2D Z-functions using 2D gaussians are of particular interest because they include in their function space all boolean functions of two variables (or at least analogue versions of these functions). For example the gaussians which would come to represent the positive and negative exemplar patterns for XOR are drawn as ellipses in Figure 2(a). They have equal means and variances but the negative exemplar patterns are correlated while the positive ones are anti-correlated. These models automatically give rise to the XOR surface in Figure 2(b) if put through equation (2). An interesting observation is that a problem of Nth order (XOR is 2nd order, 3-parity is 3rd order etc) can be solved by a polynomial of degree N (Figure 2d). Since 2nd degree polynomials like (3) are used in our system, there is one step up in power from 1st degree systems like the Perceptron. Thus 3-parity is to the Z-function unit what XOR is to the Perceptron (in this case not *quadratically separable*).

A GAUSSIAN IS: $f(x)=\dfrac{1}{\alpha}e^{-\beta(x)}$ $\qquad\qquad\qquad\qquad\qquad$ (4)

in one dimension: $\alpha=(2\pi)^{1/2}\sigma_x$ $\qquad\qquad\qquad\qquad\qquad$ (4.1.1)

$\qquad\qquad\qquad\quad \beta(x)=\dfrac{(x-\mu_x)^2}{2\sigma_x{}^2}$ $\qquad\qquad\qquad\qquad$ (4.1.2)

in two dimensions: $\alpha=2\pi\sigma_x\sigma_y(1-r^2)^{1/2}$ $\qquad\qquad\qquad$ (4.2.1)

$\qquad\qquad\quad \beta(x,y)=\dfrac{1}{2(1-r^2)}\left[\dfrac{(x-\mu_x)^2}{\sigma_x{}^2}+\dfrac{(y-\mu_y)^2}{\sigma_y{}^2}-2r\dfrac{(x-\mu_x)(y-\mu_y)}{\sigma_x\sigma_y}\right]$ (4.2.2)

in n dimensions: $\alpha=(2\pi)^{n/2}|K|^{1/2}$ $\qquad\qquad\qquad\qquad$ (4.n.1)

$\qquad\qquad\quad \beta(\underline{x})=\dfrac{1}{2}(\underline{x}-\underline{m})^T K^{-1}(\underline{x}-\underline{m})$ $\qquad\qquad\quad$ (4.n.2)

$\mu_x=E[x]$ $\qquad\qquad\quad$ *is the expected value or mean of* x

$\sigma_x^2=E[x^2]-\mu_x{}^2$ $\qquad$ *is the variance of* x

$r=\dfrac{E[xy]-\mu_x\mu_y}{\sigma_x\sigma_y}$ $\qquad$ *is the correlation coefficient of a bivariate gaussian*

$\underline{m}=E[\underline{x}]$ $\qquad\qquad\quad$ *is the mean vector of a multivariate gaussian*

$K=E[(\underline{x}-\underline{m})(\underline{x}-\underline{m})^T]$ *is the covariance matrix of a multivariate gaussian with* $|K|$ *its determinant*

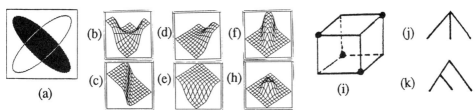

Figure 2: (a) two anti-correlated gaussians seen from above (b) the resulting Z-function (c)-(h) Some other 2D Z-functions. (i) 3-parity in a cube cannot be solved by a 3D Z-function (j) but yields to a cascade of 2D ones (k).

2.2. THE LEARNING PROCEDURE

If gaussians are used to model the distribution of inputs x which give positive and negative classification *errors*, rather than just the distribution of positively and negatively classified x, then it is possible to formulate an incremental learning procedure for training Z-functions. This procedure enables the system to deal with data which is not gaussianly distributed.

2.2.1. Without hidden units: learning a step function.

A simple example illustrates this principle. Consider a network consisting entirely of a 1-dimensional Z-function, as in Figure 1(b). The input is a real number from 0 to 1 and the output is to be a step function, such that 0.5-1.0 is classed positively (output 1.0) and 0.0-0.5 should output 0.0. The 4 parameters of the Z-function (μ^+,μ^-,σ^+,σ^-) are initialised randomly and example patterns are presented to the 'tree'. On each presentation t, the error δ in the response is calculated by $\delta_t \leftarrow d_t - o_t$, the desired minus the actual output at time t, and 2 of the parameters are altered. If the error is positive, the positive model is altered, otherwise the negative model is altered. Changing a model consists of 'sliding' the estimates of the appropriate first and second moments ($E[x]$ and $E[x^2]$) according to a 'moving-average' scheme:

$$E[x]_t \leftarrow \varepsilon\delta_t x_t + (1-\varepsilon\delta_t)E[x]_{t-1} \tag{5.1}$$

$$E[x^2]_t \leftarrow \varepsilon\delta_t x_t^2 + (1-\varepsilon\delta_t)E[x^2]_{t-1} \tag{5.2}$$

where ε is a plasticity or learning rate, x_t is the value input and $E[x]_{t-1}$ was the previous estimate of the mean value of x for the appropriate gaussian. This rule means that at any moment, the parameters determining the positive and negative models are weighted averages of recent inputs which have generated errors. The influence which a particular input has had decays over time. This algorithm was run with ε=0.1. After 100 random numbers had been presented, with error signals from the step-function changing the models, the models come to well represent the distribution of positive and negative inputs. At this stage the models and their associated Z-function are those shown in Figure 1(d). But now, most of the error reinforcement will be coming from a small region around 0.5, which means that since the gaussians are modelling the errors, they will be drawn towards the centre and become narrower. This has the effect, Figure 1(e), of increasing the gain of the sigmoidal Z-function. In the limit, it will converge to a perfect step function as the gaussians become infinitesimally separated delta functions. This initial demonstration shows the *automatic gain adjustment* property of the Z-function.

2.2.2. With hidden units: the 6-multiplexer.

The first example showed how a 1D Z-function can minimise error by modelling it. This example shows how a cascade of 2-dimensional Z-functions can co-operate to solve a 3rd order problem. A 6-multiplexer circuit receives as input 6 bits, 4 of which are data bits and 2 are address bits. If the address bits are 00, it must output the contents of the first data bit, if 01, the second, 10 the third and 11 the fourth. There are 64 different input patterns. Choosing an tree architecture is a difficult problem in general, but the first step is to choose one which we know can solve the problem. This is illustrated in Figure 3(a). This is an architecture for which there exists a solution using binary Boolean functions.

The tree's solution was arrived at as follows: each node was initialised with 10 random values: $E[x]$, $E[y]$, $E[x^2]$, $E[y^2]$ and $E[xy]$ for each of its positive and negative models. The learning rate ε was set to 0.02 and input patterns were generated and propagated up to the top node, where an error measurement was made. The error was then broadcast *globally to all nodes*, each one, in effect, being told to respond more positively (or negatively) should the same circumstances arise again, and adjusting their Z-functions in the same way as equations (5). This time, however, 5 parameters were adjusted per node per presentation, instead of 2. Again, which model (positive or negative) is adjusted depends on the sign of the error at the top of the tree.

The tree learns after about 200 random bit patterns are presented (7 seconds on a Symbolics). After 300 presentations (the state depicted in Figure 3a), the mean squared error is falling steadily to zero. An adequate back-propagation network takes 6000 presentations to converge on a solution. The solution achieved is a rather messy combination of half-hearted XORs and NXORs, and ambiguous AND/ORs. The problem was tried with different trees. In general any tree of sufficient richness can solve the problem though larger trees take longer. Trees for which no nice solutions exist, ie: those with fewer than 6 well-chosen inputs from the address bits can sometimes still perform rather well. A tree with straight convergence, only one contact per address bit, can still quickly approach 80% performance, but further training is destructive. Figure 3(b) shows a tree trained to output 1 if half or more of its 8 inputs were on.

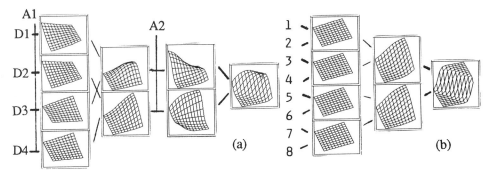

Figure 3: Solving the 6-multiplexer (a) and the 8-majority predicate (b)

2.2.3. Phoneme classification.

A good question was if such a tree could perform well on a large problem, so a typical back-propagation application was attempted. Space does not permit a full account here, but the details appear in Bell (89). The data came from 100 speakers speaking the confusable E-set phonemes (B, D, E and V). This was the same data as that used by Lang & Hinton (88). Four trees were built out of 192 input units and the trees trained using a learning schedule of ϵ falling from 0.01 to 0.001 over the course of 30 presentations of each of 668 training patterns. Generalisation to a test set was 88.5%, 0.5% worse than an equivalently simple backprop net. A more sophisticated backprop net, using time-delays and multiresolution training could reach 93% generalisation. Thirty epochs with the trees took some 16 hours on a Sun 3-260 whereas the backprop experiments were performed on a Convex supercomputer. The conclusion from these experiments is that trees some 8 levels deep are capable of almost matching normal back-propagation on a large classification task in a fraction of the training time. Attempts to build time-symmetry into the trees have not so far been successful.

3. DISCUSSION

Even within the context of other connectionist learning procedures, there is something of an air of mystery about this one. The apparatus of gradient descent, either for individual units or for the whole tree is absent or at least hidden.

3.1. HOW DOES IT WORK?

It is necessary to reflect on the effect of modelling errors. Models of errors are an attempt to push a node's outputs towards the edge of its parent's input square. Where the model is perfect, it is simple for the node above to model the model by applying a sigmoid, and so on to the top of the tree, where the error disappears. But the modelling is actually done in a totally distributed and collaborative way. The identification of 1.0 with positive error (top output too small) means that Z-functions are more likely to be monotonic towards (1,1) the further they are from the inputs.

Two standard problems are overcome in unusual ways. The first, *credit assignment*, is solved because different Z-functions are able to model different errors, giving them different roles. Although all nodes receive the same feedback, some changes to a node's model will be swiftly undone when the new errors that result from them begin to be broadcast. Other nodes can change freely either because they are not yet essential to the computation or because there exist alterations of their models tolerable to the nodes above. The second problem is *stability*. In backprop, the way the error diffuses through the net ensures that the upper weights are slaved to the lower ones because the lower are changing more slowly. In this system, the upper nodes are slaved to the lower ones because they are explicitly modelling their activities. Conversely, the lower nodes will never be allowed to change too quickly since the errors generated by sluggish top nodes will throw them back into the behaviour the top nodes expect. For a low enough learning rate ε, the solutions are stable.

Amongst the real problems with this system are the following. First, the credit assignment is not solved for units receiving the same input variables, making many normal connectionist architectures impossible. Second, the system can only deal with 2 classes. Third, as with other algorithms, choice of architecture is a 'black art'.

3.2. BIOPHYSICS & REAL NEURONS

The name 'Artificial Dendritic Tree' is perhaps overdoing it. The tree has no dynamic properties, activation flows in only one direction, the branchpoints of the tree routinely implement XOR and the 'cell' as a whole implements phoneme recognition (only a small step from grandmothers). The title was kept because what drove the work was a search for a computational explanation of how fine-grained local non-linearities of low degree could combine in a learning process. Work in computational neuroscience, in particular with compartmental models (Koch & Poggio 87; Rall & Segev 88; Segev et al 89, Shepherd & Brayton 87) have shown that it is likely that many non-linear effects take place between synapse and soma. Synaptic transfer functions can be sigmoidal, spines with active channels may mutually excite each other (even implement boolean computations) and inhibitory inputs can 'veto' firing in a highly non-linear fashion (silent inhibition). The dendritic membrane itself is filled with active ion channels, whose boosting or quenching properties depend in a complex way on the intracellular voltage levels or Ca^{2+} concentration (itself dependent on voltage). Thus we may be able to consider the membrane itself as a distributed processing system, meaning that the synapses are no longer the privileged sites of learning which they have tended to be since Hebb. Active channels can serve to implement threshold functions just as well at the dendritic branchpoints as at the soma, where they generate spikes. There are many different kinds of ion channel (Yamada et al, 89) with inhomogenous distributions over the dendritic tree. A neuron's DNA may generate a certain 'base set' of channel proteins that span a non-linear function space just as our parameters span the Z-function space. The properties of a part of dendritic membrane could be seen as a point in *channel space*. Viewed this way, the neuron becomes one large computer. When one considers the Purkinje cell of the cerebellum with 100,000 inputs, as many spines, a massive arborisation full of active channels, many of them Ca-permeable or Ca-dependent, with spiking and plateau potentials occurring in the dendritic tree, the notion that the cell may be implementing a 99,999 dimensional hyperplane starts to recede. here is an extra motivation for considering the cell as a complex computer. Algorithms such as back-propagation would require feedback circuits to send error. If the cell is the feedback unit, then reinforcement can occur as a spike at the soma reinvades the dendritic tree. Thus nerves may not spike just for axonal purposes, but also to penetrate the electrotonic length of the dendrites. This was thought to be a component of Hebbian learning at the synapses, but it could be the basis of more if the dendritic membrane computes.

4. Acknowledgements

To Kevin Lang for the speech data and to Rolf Pfeifer and Luc Steels for support. Further credits in Bell (90). The author is funded by ESPRIT B.R.A. 3234.

5. References

Barron A & Barron R (88) Statistical Learning Networks: a unifying view, in Wegman E (ed) *Proc. 20th Symp. on Comp. Science & Statistics* [see also this volume]

Bell T (89) Artificial Dendritic Learning, in Almeida L. (ed) *Proc. EURASIP Workshop on Neural Networks*, Lecture notes in Computer Science, Springer-Verlag. [also VUB AI-lab Memo 89-20].

Durbin R & Rumelhart D (89) Product Units: A Computationally Powerful and Biologically Plausible Extension to Backpropagation Nets, *Neural Computation 1*

Giles C.L. & Maxwell T (87) Learning, invariance and generalisation in high-order neural networks, *Applied Optics* vol 26, no. 23

Koch C & Poggio T (87) Biophysics of Computational Systems: Neurons, synapses and membranes, in G. Edelman et al (eds), *Synaptic Function*, John Wiley.

Lang K & Hinton G (88) The Development of the Time-Delay Neural Network Architecture for Speech Recognition, *Tech Report CMU-CS-88-152*

Rall W & Segev I (88) Excitable Dendritic Spine Clusters: non-linear synaptic processing, in R.Cotterill (ed) *Computer Simulation in Brain Science*, Camb.U.P.

Segev I, Fleshman J & Burke R. (89) Compartmental Models of Complex Neurons, in *Methods in Neuronal Modelling*

Shepherd G & Brayton R (87) Logic operations are properties of computer simulated interactions between excitable dendritic spines, *Neuroscience*, vol 21, no. 1 1987 Koch C & Segev I (eds) MIT press 1989

Tenorio M & Lee W (90) Self-Organizing Network for Optimal Supervised Learning, *IEEE Transactions in Neural Networks*, 1990 [see also this volume]

Therrien C (89) *Decision Estimation and Classification.*

Yamada W, Koch C & Adams P (89) Multiple Channels and Calcium Dynamics, in *Methods in Neuronal Modelling* Koch C & Segev I (eds) MIT press 1989.

Adjoint Operator Algorithms for Faster Learning in Dynamical Neural Networks

Jacob Barhen   Nikzad Toomarian   Sandeep Gulati

Center for Space Microelectronics Technology
Jet Propulsion Laboratory
California Institute of Technology
Pasadena, CA 91109

ABSTRACT

A methodology for faster supervised learning in dynamical nonlinear neural networks is presented. It exploits the concept of *adjoint operators* to enable computation of changes in the network's response due to perturbations in all system parameters, using the solution of a single set of appropriately constructed linear equations. The lower bound on speedup per learning iteration over conventional methods for calculating the neuromorphic energy gradient is $O(N^2)$, where N is the number of neurons in the network.

1   INTRODUCTION

The biggest promise of artifcial neural networks as computational tools lies in the hope that they will enable fast processing and synthesis of complex information patterns. In particular, considerable efforts have recently been devoted to the formulation of efficent methodologies for learning (e.g., Rumelhart et al., 1986; Pineda, 1988; Pearlmutter, 1989; Williams and Zipser, 1989; Barhen, Gulati and Zak, 1989). The development of learning algorithms is generally based upon the minimization of a neuromorphic energy function. The fundamental requirement of such an approach is the computation of the gradient of this objective function with respect to the various parameters of the neural architecture, e.g., synaptic weights, neural gains, etc. The paramount contribution to the often excessive cost of learning using dynamical neural networks arises from the necessity to solve, at each learning iteration, one set of equations for each parameter of the neural system, since those parameters affect both directly and indirectly the network's energy.

In this paper we show that the concept of adjoint operators, when applied to dynamical neural networks, not only yields a considerable algorithmic speedup, but also puts on a firm mathematical basis prior results for "recurrent" networks, the derivations of which sometimes involved much heuristic reasoning. We have already used adjoint operators in some of our earlier work in the fields of energy-economy modeling (Alsmiller and Barhen, 1984) and nuclear reactor thermal hydraulics (Barhen et al., 1982; Toomarian et al., 1987) at the Oak Ridge National Laboratory, where the concept flourished during the past decade (Oblow, 1977; Cacuci et al., 1980).

In the sequel we first motivate and construct, in the most elementary fashion, a computational framework based on adjoint operators. We then apply our results to the Cohen-Grossberg-Hopfield (CGH) additive model, enhanced with terminal attractor (Barhen, Gulati and Zak, 1989) capabilities. We conclude by presenting the results of a few typical simulations.

2   ADJOINT OPERATORS

Consider, for the sake of simplicity, that a problem of interest is represented by the following system of N coupled nonlinear equations

$$\bar{\varphi}(\bar{u}, \bar{p}) = 0 \qquad (2.1)$$

where $\bar{\varphi}$ denotes a nonlinear operator[1] . Let $\bar{u}$ and $\bar{p}$ represent the N-vector of dependent state variables and the M-vector of system parameters, respectively. We will assume that generally $M >> N$ and that elements of $\bar{p}$ are, in principle, independent. Furthermore, we will also assume that, for a specific choice of parameters, a unique solution of Eq. (2.1) exists. Hence, $\bar{u}$ is an implicit function of $\bar{p}$. A system "response", R, represents any result of the calculations that is of interest. Specifically

$$R = R(\bar{u}, \bar{p}) \qquad (2.2)$$

i.e., R is a known nonlinear function of $\bar{p}$ and $\bar{u}$ and may be calculated from Eq. (2.2) when the solution $\bar{u}$ in Eq. (2.1) has been obtained for a given $\bar{p}$. The problem of interest is to compute the "sensitivities" of R, i.e., the derivatives of R with respect to parameters p_μ, $\mu = 1, \cdots, M$. By definition

$$\frac{dR}{dp_\mu} = \frac{\partial R}{\partial p_\mu} + \frac{\partial R}{\partial \bar{u}} \cdot \frac{\partial \bar{u}}{\partial p_\mu} \qquad (2.3)$$

---

[1] If differential operators appear in Eq. (2.1), then a corresponding set of boundary and/or initial conditions to specify the domain of φ must also be provided. In general an inhomogeneous "source" term can also be present. The learning model discussed in this paper focuses on the adiabatic approximation only. Nonadiabatic learning algorithms, wherein the response is defined as a functional, will be discussed in a forthcoming article.

Since the response R is known analytically, the computation of $\partial R/\partial p_\mu$ and $\partial R/\partial \bar{u}$ is straightforward. The quantity that needs to be determined is the vector $\partial \bar{u}/\partial p_\mu$. Differentiating the state equations (2.1), we obtain a set of equations to be referred to as "forward" sensitivity equations

$$\frac{\partial \bar{\varphi}}{\partial \bar{u}} \cdot \frac{\partial \bar{u}}{\partial p_\mu} = -\frac{\partial \bar{\varphi}}{\partial p_\mu} \tag{2.4}$$

To simplify the notations, we are omitting the "transposed" sign and denoting the N by N forward sensitivity matrix $\partial \bar{\varphi}/\partial \bar{u}$ by A, the N-vector $\partial \bar{u}/\partial p_\mu$ by ${}^\mu \bar{q}$ and the "source" N-vector $-\partial \bar{\varphi}/\partial p_\mu$ by ${}^\mu \bar{s}$. Thus

$$A \, {}^\mu \bar{q} = {}^\mu \bar{s} \tag{2.5}$$

Since the source term in Eq. (2.5) explicitly depends on μ, computing dR/dp_μ, requires solving the above system of N algebraic equations for each parameter p_μ. This difficulty is circumvented by introducing adjoint operators. Let A^* denote the formal adjoint[2] of the operator A. The adjoint sensitivity equations can then be expressed as

$$A^* \, {}^\mu \bar{q}^* = {}^\mu \bar{s}^*. \tag{2.6}$$

By definition, for algebraic operators

$${}^\mu \bar{q}^* \cdot (A \, {}^\mu \bar{q}) = {}^\mu \bar{q}^* \cdot {}^\mu \bar{s} = {}^\mu \bar{q} \cdot (A^* \, {}^\mu \bar{q}^*) = {}^\mu \bar{q} \cdot {}^\mu \bar{s}^* \tag{2.7}$$

Since Eq. (2.3), can be rewritten as

$$\frac{dR}{dp_\mu} = \frac{\partial R}{\partial p_\mu} + \frac{\partial R}{\partial \bar{u}} \, {}^\mu \bar{q} , \tag{2.8}$$

if we identify

$$\frac{\partial R}{\partial \bar{u}} \equiv {}^\mu \bar{s}^* \equiv \bar{s}^* \tag{2.9}$$

we observe that the source term for the adjoint equations is independent of the specific parameter p_μ. Hence, the *solution of a single set of adjoint equations will provide all the information required to compute the gradient of R with respect to all parameters*. To underscore that fact we shall denote ${}^\mu \bar{q}^*$ as $\bar{v}$. Thus

$$\frac{dR}{dp_\mu} = \frac{\partial R}{\partial p_\mu} - \bar{v} \cdot \frac{\partial \bar{\varphi}}{\partial p_\mu} \tag{2.10}$$

We will now apply this computational framework to a CGH network enhanced with terminal attractor dynamics. The model developed in the sequel differs from our

---

[2] Adjoint operators can only be considered for densely defined linear operators on Banach spaces (see e.g., Cacuci, 1980). For the neural application under consideration we will limit ourselves to real Hilbert spaces. Such spaces are self-dual. Furthermore, the domain of an adjoint operator is determined by selecting appropriate adjoint boundary conditions[1]. The associated bilinear form evaluated on the domain boundary must thus be also generally included.

earlier formulations (Barhen, Gulati and Zak, 1989; Barhen, Zak and Gulati, 1989) in avoiding the use of constraints in the neuromorphic energy function, thereby eliminating the need for differential equations to evolve the concomitant Lagrange multipliers. Also, the usual activation dynamics is transformed into a set of equivalent equations which exhibit more "congenial" numerical properties, such as "contraction".

3   APPLICATIONS TO NEURAL LEARNING

We formalize a neural network as an adaptive dynamical system whose temporal evolution is governed by the following set of coupled nonlinear differential equations

$$\dot{z}_n \; + \; \kappa_n \, z_n \;\; = \;\; \sum_m \omega_{nm} \, T_{nm} \, g_\gamma(z_m) \; + \; {}^k I_n \qquad (3.1)$$

where z_n represents the mean soma potential of the nth neuron and T_{nm} denotes the synaptic coupling from the $m-$th to the $n-$th neuron. The weighting factor ω_{nm} enforces topological considerations. The constant κ_n characterizes the decay of neuron activity. The sigmoidal function $g_\gamma(\cdot)$ modulates the neural response, with gain given by γ_m; typically, $g_\gamma(z) = \tanh(\gamma z)$. The "source" term $^k I_n$, which includes dimensional considerations, encodes contribution in terms of attractor coordinates of the k-th training sample via the following expression

$$^k I_n \;\; = \;\; \begin{cases} [{}^k a_n]^{1-\beta} \, [{}^k a_n \; - \; g_\gamma(z_n)\,]^\beta & \textbf{if } n \in S_X \\ 0 & \textbf{if } n \in S_H \cup S_Y \end{cases} . \qquad (3.2)$$

The topographic input, output and hidden network partitions S_X, S_Y and S_H are architectural requirements related to the encoding of mapping-type problems for which a number of possibilities exist (Barhen, Gulati and Zak, 1989; Barhen, Zak and Gulati, 1989). In previous articles (ibid; Zak, 1989) we have demonstrated that in general, for $\beta = (2i+1)^{-1}$ and i a strictly positive integer, such attractors have infinite local stability and provide opportunity for learning in real-time. Typically, β can be set to 1/3. Assuming an adiabatic framework, the fixed point equations at equilibrium, i.e., as $\dot{z}_n \rightarrow 0$, yield

$$\frac{\kappa_n}{\gamma_n} \, g^{-1}({}^k \tilde{u}_n) \;\; = \;\; \sum_m \omega_{nm} \, T_{nm} \, {}^k \tilde{u}_m \; + \; {}^k \tilde{I}_n \qquad (3.3)$$

where $u_n = g_\gamma(z_n)$ represents the neural response. The superscript $\sim$ denotes quantities evaluated at steady state. Operational network dynamics is then given by

$$\dot{u}_n \; + \; u_n \;\; = \;\; g_\gamma \left[\frac{\gamma_n}{\kappa_n} \sum_m \omega_{nm} \, T_{nm} \, u_m \; + \; \frac{\gamma_n}{\kappa_n} \, {}^k I_n \right] \qquad (3.4)$$

To proceed formally with the development of a supervised learning algorithm, we consider an approach based upon the minimization of a constrained "neuromorphic" energy function E given by the following expression

$$E(\bar{u}, \bar{p}) \;\; = \;\; \frac{1}{2} \sum_k \sum_n [\, {}^k \tilde{u}_n \; - \; {}^k a_n \,]^2 \qquad \forall \, n \in S_X \cup S_Y \qquad (3.5)$$

We relate adjoint theory to neural learning by identifying the neuromorphic energy function, E in Eq. (3.5), with the system response R. Also, let $\bar{p}$ denote the following system parameters:

$$\bar{p} = \{ T_{11}, \cdots T_{NN} \mid \kappa_1, \cdots \kappa_N \mid \gamma_1, \cdots \gamma_N \mid \cdots \}$$

The proposed objective function enforces convergence of every neuron in S_X and S_Y to attractor coordinates corresponding to the components in the input-output training patterns, thereby prompting the network to learn the embedded invariances. Lyapunov stability requires an energy-like function to be monotonically decreasing in time. Since in our model the internal dynamical parameters of interest are the synaptic strengths T_{nm} of the interconnection topology, the characteristic decay constants κ_n and the gain parameters γ_n this implies that

$$\dot{E} = \sum_n \sum_m \frac{dE}{dT_{nm}} \dot{T}_{nm} + \sum_n \frac{dE}{d\kappa_n} \dot{\kappa}_n + \sum_n \frac{dE}{d\gamma_n} \dot{\gamma}_n < 0 \qquad (3.6)$$

For each adaptive system parameter, p_μ, Lyapunov stability will be satisfied by the following choice of equations of motion

$$\dot{p}_\mu = -\tau_p \frac{dE}{dp_\mu} \qquad (3.7)$$

Examples include

$$\dot{T}_{nm} = -\tau_T \frac{dE}{dT_{nm}} \quad ; \quad \dot{\gamma}_n = -\tau_\gamma \frac{dE}{d\gamma_n} \quad ; \quad \dot{\kappa}_n = -\tau_\kappa \frac{dE}{d\kappa_n}$$

where the time-scale parameters τ_T, τ_κ and $\tau_\gamma > 0$. Since E depends on p_μ both directly and indirectly, previous methods required solution of a system of N equations for each parameter p_μ to obtain dE/dp_μ from $d\tilde{u}/dp_\mu$. Our methodology (based on **adjoint operators**), yields all derivatives $dE/dp_\mu, \forall \mu$, by solving a single set of N linear equations.

The nonlinear neural operator for each training pattern k, $k = 1, \cdots K$, at equilibrium is given by

$$^k\varphi_n \left(^k\tilde{u}, \bar{p} \right) = g \left[\frac{1}{\kappa_n} \sum_{m'} \omega_{nm'} T_{nm'} \, ^k\tilde{u}_{m'} + \frac{1}{\kappa_n} \, ^k\tilde{I}_n \right] - \, ^k\tilde{u}_n = 0 \qquad (3.8)$$

where, without loss of generality we have set γ_n to unity. So, in principle $^k\tilde{u}_n = {}^k\tilde{u}_n [T, \bar{\kappa}, \bar{\gamma}, {}^ka_n, \cdots]$. Using Eqs. (3.8), the forward sensitivity matrix can be computed and compactly expressed as

$$^kA_{nm} = \frac{\partial \, ^k\varphi_n}{\partial \, ^k\tilde{u}_m} = \, ^k\hat{g}_n \frac{1}{\kappa_n} \left[\omega_{nm} T_{nm} + \frac{\partial \, ^k\tilde{I}_n}{\partial \, ^k\tilde{u}_m} \right] - \delta_{nm}$$

$$= \frac{1}{\kappa_n} \, ^k\hat{g}_n \, \omega_{nm} T_{nm} - \, ^k\eta_n \, \delta_{nm}. \qquad (3.9)$$

where

$$^k\eta_n = \begin{cases} 1 + \frac{[^k a_n]^{2/3}}{3\kappa_n} {}^k\hat{g}_n \, [^k a_n - {}^k\tilde{u}_n \,]^{-2/3} & \text{if } n \in S_X \\ 1 & \text{if } n \in S_H \cup S_Y \end{cases}. \quad (3.10)$$

Above, $^k\hat{g}_n$ represents the derivative of g with respect to $^k\tilde{u}_n$, i.e., if $g \equiv tanh$, then

$$^k\hat{g}_n = 1 - [^k g_n]^2 \quad \text{where} \quad ^k g_n = g\left[\frac{1}{\kappa_n} \left(\sum_m \omega_{nm} \, T_{nm} \, {}^k\tilde{u}_m + {}^k\tilde{I}_n \right) \right] \quad (3.11)$$

Recall that the formal adjoint equation is given as $A^*\bar{v} = \bar{s}^*$; here

$$^k A^*_{nm} = \frac{1}{\kappa_m} {}^k\hat{g}_m \, \omega_{mn} \, T_{mn} - {}^k\eta_m \, \delta_{mn} \quad (3.12)$$

Using Eqs. (2.9) and (3.5), we can compute the formal **adjoint source**

$$^k s^*_n \equiv \frac{\partial E}{\partial {}^k\tilde{u}_n} = \begin{cases} ^k\tilde{u}_n - {}^k a_n & \text{if } n \in S_X \cup S_Y \\ 0 & \text{if } n \in S_H \end{cases} \quad (3.13)$$

The system of adjoint fixed-point equations can then be constructed using Eqs. (3.12) and (3.13), to yield :

$$\sum_m \frac{1}{\kappa_m} {}^k\hat{g}_m \, \omega_{mn} \, T_{mn} \, {}^k\tilde{v}_m - \sum_m {}^k\eta_m \, \delta_{mn} \, {}^k\tilde{v}_m = {}^k s^*_n \quad (3.14)$$

Notice that the above coupled system, (3.14), is linear in $^k\tilde{v}$. Furthermore, it has the same mathematical characteristics as the operational dynamics (3.4). Its components can be obtained as the equilibrium points, (i.e., $\dot{v}_i \to 0$) of the **adjoint neural dynamics**

$$\dot{v}_n + {}^k\eta_n \, v_n = \sum_m \frac{1}{\kappa_m} {}^k\hat{g}_m \, \omega_{mn} \, T_{mn} \, v_m - {}^k s^*_n \quad (3.15)$$

As an implementation example, let us conclude by deriving the learning equations for the synaptic strengths, T_μ. Recall that

$$\frac{dE}{dT_\mu} = \frac{\partial E}{\partial T_\mu} + \sum_k {}^k\tilde{v} \cdot {}^{\mu k}\bar{s} \qquad \mu = (i, j) \quad (3.16)$$

We differentiate the steady state equations (3.8) with respect to T_{ij}, to obtain the forward source term,

$$^{\mu k} s_n = -\frac{\partial {}^k\varphi_n}{\partial T_{ij}} = -{}^k\hat{g}_n \left[\frac{1}{\kappa_n} \sum_l \omega_{nl} \, \delta_{in} \, \delta_{jl} \, {}^k\tilde{u}_l + 0 \right]$$

$$= -\frac{1}{\kappa_n} {}^k\hat{g}_n \, \delta_{in} \, \omega_{nj} \, {}^k\tilde{u}_j \quad (3.17)$$

Since by definition, $\partial E/\partial T_{nm} = 0$, the explicit energy gradient contribution is obtained as

$$\dot{T}_{nm} = -\tau_T \left[-\frac{\omega_{nm}}{\kappa_n} \sum_k {}^k\tilde{v}_n \, {}^k\hat{g}_n \, {}^k\tilde{u}_m \right] \tag{3.18}$$

It is straightforward to obtain learning equations for γ_n and κ_n in a similar fashion.

4 ADAPTIVE TIME-SCALES

So far the adaptive learning rates, i.e., τ_p in Eq.(3.7), have not been specified. Now we will show that, by an appropriate selection of these parameters the convergence of the corresponding dynamical systems can be considerably improved. Without loss of generality, we shall assume $\tau_T = \tau_\kappa = \tau_\gamma = \tau$, and we shall seek τ in the form (Barhen et al, 1989; Zak 1989)

$$\tau \propto |\nabla E|^{-\beta} \tag{4.1}$$

where ∇E denotes the vector with components $\nabla_T E$, $\nabla_\gamma E$ and $\nabla_\kappa E$. It is straightforward to show that

$$\frac{d}{dt} |\nabla E| = -\chi |\nabla E|^{1-\beta} \tag{4.2}$$

as ∇E tends to zero, where χ is an arbitrary positive constant. If we evaluate the relaxation time of the energy gradient, we find that

$$t_E = \int_{|\nabla E|_0}^{|\nabla E| \to 0} \frac{d|\nabla E|}{|\nabla E|^{1-\beta}} = \begin{cases} \infty & \text{if } \beta \le 0 \\ \frac{1}{\beta} |\nabla E|_0^\beta < \infty & \text{if } \beta > 0 \end{cases} \tag{4.3}$$

Thus, for $\beta \le 0$ the relaxation time is infinite, while for $\beta > 0$ it is finite. The dynamical system (3.19) suffers a qualitative change for $\beta > 0$: it loses uniqueness of solution. The equilibrium point $|\nabla E| = 0$ becomes a singular solution being intersected by all the transients, and the Lipschitz condition is violated, as one can see from

$$\frac{d}{d|\nabla E|} \left(\frac{d|\nabla E|}{dt} \right) = -\chi |\nabla E|^{-\beta} \longrightarrow -\infty \tag{4.4}$$

where $|\nabla E|$ tends to zero, while β is strictly positive. Such infinitely stable points are "terminal attractors". By analogy with our previous results we choose $\beta = 2/3$, which yields

$$\tau = \left(\sum_n \sum_m [\nabla_T E]_{nm}^2 + \sum_n [\nabla_\gamma E]_n^2 + \sum_n [\nabla_\kappa E]_n^2 \right)^{-1/0} \tag{4.5}$$

The introduction of these adaptive time-scales dramatically improves the convergence of the corresponding learning dynamical systems.

5 SIMULATIONS

The computational framework developed in the preceding section has been applied to a number of problems that involve learning nonlinear mappings, including Exclusive-OR, the hyperbolic tangent and trignometric functions, e.g., sin. Some of these mappings (e.g., XOR) have been extensively benchmarked in the literature, and provide an adequate basis for illustrating the computational efficacy of our proposed formulation. Figures 1(a)-1(d) demonstrate the temporal profile of various network elements during learning of the XOR function. A six neuron feedforward network was used, that included self-feedback on the output unit and bias. Fig. 1(a) shows the LMS error during the training phase. The worst-case convergence of the output state neuron to the presented attractor is displayed in Fig. 1(b). Notice the rapid convergence of the input state due to the terminal attractor effect. The behavior of the adaptive time-scale parameter τ is depicted in Fig. 1(c). Finally, Fig. 1(d) shows the evolution of the energy gradient components.

The test setup for signal processing applications, i.e., learning the sin function and the tanh sigmoidal nonlinearlity, included a 8-neuron fully connected network with no bias. In each case the network was trained using as little as 4 randomly sampled training points. Efficacy of recall was determined by presenting 100 random samples. Fig. (2) and (3b) illustrate that we were able to approximate the sin and the hyperbolic tangent functions using 16 and 4 pairs respectively. Fig. 3(a) demonstrates the network performance when 4 pairs were used to learn the hyperbolic tangent.

We would like to mention that since our learning methodology involves terminal attractors, extreme caution must be exercised when simulating the algorithms in a digital computing environment. Our discussion on sensitivity of results to the integration schemes (Barhen, Zak and Gulati, 1989) emphasizes that explicit methods such as Euler or Runge-Kutta shall not be used, since the presence of terminal attractors induces extreme stiffness. Practically, this would require an integration time-step of infinitesimal size, resulting in numerical round-off errors of unacceptable magnitude. Implicit integration techniques such as the Kaps-Rentrop scheme should therefore be used.

6 CONCLUSIONS

In this paper we have presented a theoretical framework for faster learning in dynamical neural networks. Central to our approach is the concept of *adjoint operators* which enables computation of network neuromorphic energy gradients with respect to all system parameters using the solution of a single set of linear equations. If C_F and C_A denote the computational costs associated with solving the forward and adjoint sensitivity equations (Eqs. 2.5 and 2.6), and if M denotes the number of parameters of interest in the network, the speedup achieved is

$$S^{F \to A} = \frac{M \; C_F}{C_A}$$

If we assume that $C_F \simeq C_A$ and that $M = N^2 + 2N + \cdots$, we see that the lower bound on speedup per learning iteration is $O(N^2)$. Finally, particular care must be execrcised when integrating the dynamical systems of interest, due to the extreme stiffness introduced by the terminal attractor constructs.

Acknowledgements

The research described in this paper was performed by the Center for Space Microelectronics Technology, Jet Propulsion Laboratory, California Institute of Technology, and was sponsored by agencies of the U.S. Department of Defense, and by the Office of Basic Energy Sciences of the U.S. Department of Energy, through interagency agreements with NASA.

References

R.G. Alsmiller, J. Barhen and J. Horwedel. (1984) "The Application of Adjoint Sensitivity Theory to a Liquid Fuels Supply Model", *Energy*, 9(3), 239-253.

J. Barhen, D.G. Cacuci and J.J. Wagschal. (1982) "Uncertainty Analysis of Time-Dependent Nonlinear Systems", *Nucl. Sci. Eng.*, 81, 23-44.

J. Barhen, S. Gulati and M. Zak. (1989) "Neural Learning of Constrained Nonlinear Transformations", *IEEE Computer*, 22(6), 67-76.

J. Barhen, M. Zak and S. Gulati. (1989) " Fast Neural Learning Algorithms Using Networks with Non-Lipschitzian Dynamics", in *Proc. Neuro-Nimes '89*, 55-68, EC2, Nanterre, France.

D.G. Cacuci, C.F. Weber, E.M. Oblow and J.H. Marable. (1980) "Sensitivity Theory for General Systems of Nonlinear Equations", *Nucl. Sci. Eng.*, 75, 88-110.

E.M. Oblow. (1977) "Sensitivity Theory for General Non-Linear Algebraic Equations with Constraints", ORNL/TM-5815, Oak Ridge National Laboratory.

B.A. Pearlmutter. (1989) "Learning State Space Trajectories in Recurrent Neural Networks", *Neural Computation*, 1(3), 263-269.

F.J. Pineda. (1988) "Dynamics and Architecture in Neural Computation", *Journal of Complexity*, 4, 216-245.

D.E. Rumelhart and J.L. Mclelland. (1986) *Parallel and Distributed Procesing*, MIT Press, Cambridge, MA.

N. Toomarian, E. Wacholder and S. Kaizerman. (1987) "Sensitivity Analysis of Two-Phase Flow Problems", *Nucl. Sci. Eng.*, 99(1), 53-81.

R.J. Williams and D. Zipser. (1989) "A Learning Algorithm for Continually Running Fully Recurrent Neural Networks", *Neural Computation*, 1(3), 270-280.

M. Zak. (1989) "Terminal Attractors", *Neural Networks*, 2(4), 259-274.

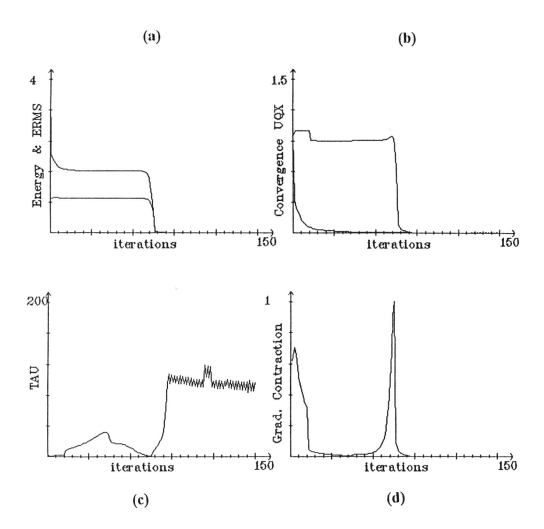

Figure 1(a)-(d).   **Learning the Exclusive-OR function using a 6-neuron (including bias) feedforward dynamical network with self-feedback on the output unit.**

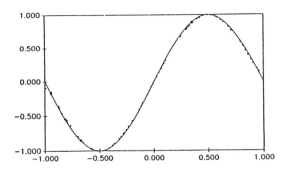

Figure 2.   Learning the Sin function using a fully connected, 8-neuron
network with no bias. The training set comprised of
4 points that were randomly selected.

3(a)

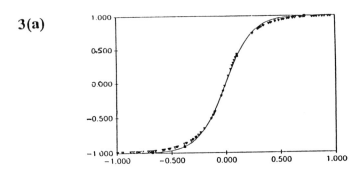

3(b)

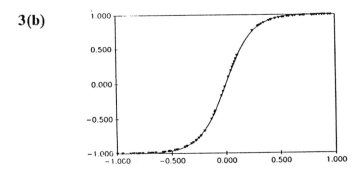

Figure 3.   Learning the Hyperbolic Tangent function using a fully connected,
8-neuron network with no bias. (a) using 4 randomly selected
training samples; (b) using 16 randomly selected training samples.

Discovering high order features with mean field modules

Conrad C. Galland and Geoffrey E. Hinton
Physics Dept. and Computer Science Dept.
University of Toronto
Toronto, Canada
M5S 1A4

ABSTRACT

A new form of the deterministic Boltzmann machine (DBM) learning procedure is presented which can efficiently train network modules to discriminate between input vectors according to some criterion. The new technique directly utilizes the free energy of these "mean field modules" to represent the probability that the criterion is met, the free energy being readily manipulated by the learning procedure. Although conventional deterministic Boltzmann learning fails to extract the higher order feature of shift at a network bottleneck, combining the new mean field modules with the mutual information objective function rapidly produces modules that perfectly extract this important higher order feature without direct external supervision.

1 INTRODUCTION

The Boltzmann machine learning procedure (Hinton and Sejnowski, 1986) can be made much more efficient by using a mean field approximation in which stochastic binary units are replaced by deterministic real-valued units (Peterson and Anderson, 1987). Deterministic Boltzmann learning can be used for "multicompletion" tasks in which the subsets of the units that are treated as input or output are varied from trial to trial (Peterson and Hartman, 1988). In this respect it resembles other learning procedures that also involve settling to a stable state (Pineda, 1987). Using the multicompletion paradigm, it should be possible to force a network to explicitly extract important higher order features of an ensemble of training vectors by forcing the network to pass the information required for correct completions through a narrow bottleneck. In back-propagation networks with two or three hidden layers, the use of bottlenecks sometimes allows the learning to explictly discover important underlying features (Hinton, 1986) and our original aim was to demonstrate that the same idea could be used effectively in a DBM with three hidden layers. The initial simulations using conventional techniques were not successful, but when we combined a new type of DBM learning with a new objective function, the resulting network extracted the crucial higher order features rapidly and perfectly.

2   THE MULTI-COMPLETION TASK

Figure 1 shows a network in which the input vector is divided into 4 parts. A1 is a random binary vector. A2 is generated by shifting A1 either to the right or to the left by one "pixel", using wraparound. B1 is also a random binary vector, and B2 is generated from B1 by using the same shift as was used to generate A2 from A1. This means that any three of A1, A2, B1, B2 uniquely specify the fourth (we filter out the ambiguous cases where this is not true). To perform correct completion, the network must explicitly represent the shift in the single unit that connects its two halves. Shift is a second order property that cannot be extracted without hidden units.

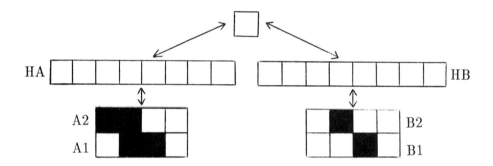

Figure 1.

3   SIMULATIONS USING STANDARD DETERMINISTIC BOLTZMANN LEARNING

The following discussion assumes familiarity with the deterministic Boltzmann learning procedure, details of which can be obtained from Hinton (1989). During the positive phase of learning, each of the 288 possible sets of shift matched four-bit vectors were clamped onto inputs A1, A2 and B1, B2, while in the negative phase, one of the four was allowed to settle unclamped. The weights were changed after each training case using the on-line version of the DBM learning procedure. The choice of which input not to clamp changed systematically throughout the learning process so that each was left unclamped equally often. This technique, although successful in problems with only one hidden layer, could not train the network to correctly perform the multicompletion task where any of the four input layers would settle to the correct state when the other three were clamped. As a result, the single central unit failed to extract shift. In general, the DBM learning procedure, like its stochastic predecessor, seems to have difficulty learning tasks in multi-hidden layer nets. This failure led to the development of the new procedure which, in one form, manages to correctly extract shift without the need for many hidden layers or direct external supervision.

4   A NEW LEARNING PROCEDURE FOR MEAN FIELD MODULES

A DBM with unit states in the range $[-1, 1]$ has free energy

$$F = -\sum_{i<j} y_i y_j w_{ij} + T \sum_i \left[\frac{(1+y_i)}{2} \log \frac{(1+y_i)}{2} + \frac{(1-y_i)}{2} \log \frac{(1-y_i)}{2} \right] \qquad (1)$$

The DBM settles to a free energy minimum, F^*, at a non-zero temperature, where the states of the units are given by

$$y_i = \tanh(\frac{1}{T} \sum_j y_j w_{ij}) \qquad (2)$$

At the minimum, the derivative of F^* with respect to a particular weight (assuming $T = 1$) is given by (Hinton, 1989)

$$\frac{\cdot \partial F^*}{\partial w_{ij}} = -y_i y_j \qquad (3)$$

Suppose that we want a network module to discriminate between input vectors that "fit" some criterion and input vectors that don't. Instead of using a net with an output unit that indicates the degree of fit, we could view the negative of the mean field free energy of the whole module as a measure of how happy it is with the clamped input vector. From this standpoint, we can define the probability that input vector α fits the criterion as

$$p_\alpha = \frac{1}{(1 + e^{F_\alpha^*})} \qquad (4)$$

where F_α^* is the equilibrium free energy of the module with vector α clamped on the inputs.

Supervised training can be performed by using the cross-entropy error function (Hinton, 1987):

$$C = -\sum_{i=\alpha}^{N_+} \log(p_\alpha) - \sum_{j=\beta}^{N_-} \log(1 - p_\beta) \qquad (5)$$

where the first sum is over the N_+ input cases that fit the criterion, and the second is over the N_- cases that don't. The cross-entropy expression is used to specify error derivatives for p_α and hence for F_α^*. Error derivatives for each weight can then be obtained by using equation (3), and the module is trained by gradient descent to have high free energy for the "negative" training cases and low free energy for the "positive" cases.

Thus, for each positive case

$$
\begin{aligned}
-\frac{\partial \log(p_\alpha)}{\partial w_{ij}} &= \frac{1}{1 + e^{F_\alpha^*}} e^{F_\alpha^*} \frac{\partial F_\alpha^*}{\partial w_{ij}} \\
&= \frac{1}{1 + e^{-F_\alpha^*}} (-y_i y_j)
\end{aligned}
$$

For each negative case,

$$
\begin{aligned}
-\frac{\partial \log(1 - p_\beta)}{\partial w_{ij}} &= -\frac{1}{1 + e^{-F_\beta^*}} e^{-F_\beta^*} \frac{\partial F_\beta^*}{\partial w_{ij}} \\
&= \frac{1}{1 + e^{F_\beta^*}} (y_i y_j)
\end{aligned}
$$

To test the new procedure, we trained a shift detecting module, composed of the the input units A1 and A2 and the hidden units HA from figure 1, to have low free energy for all and only the right shifts. Each weight was changed in an on-line fashion according to

$$
\Delta w_{ij} = \epsilon \, \frac{1}{1 + e^{-F_\alpha^*}} \, y_i y_j
$$

for each right shifted case, and

$$
\Delta w_{ij} = -\epsilon \, \frac{1}{1 + e^{F_\beta^*}} \, y_i y_j
$$

for each left shifted case. Only 10 sweeps through the 24 possible training cases were required to successfully train the module to detect shift. The training was particularly easy because the hidden units only receive connections from the input units which are always clamped, so the network settles to a free energy minimum in one iteration. Details of the simulations are given in Galland and Hinton (1990).

5   MAXIMIZING MUTUAL INFORMATION BETWEEN MEAN FIELD MODULES

At first sight, the new learning procedure is inherently supervised, so how can it be used to *discover* that shift is an important underlying feature? One method is to use two modules that each supervise the other. The most obvious way of implementing this idea quickly creates modules that always agree because they are always "on". If, however, we try to maximize the mutual information between the stochastic binary variables represented by the free energies of the modules, there is a strong pressure for each binary variable to have high entropy across cases because the mutual information between binary variables A and B is:

$$I(A; B) = H_A + H_B - H_{AB} \tag{6}$$

where H_{AB} is the entropy of the joint distribution of A and B over the training cases, and H_A and H_B are the entropies of the individual distributions.

Consider two mean field modules with associated stochastic binary variables $A, B \in \{0, 1\}$. For a given case α,

$$p(A^\alpha = 1) = \frac{1}{1 + e^{F^*_{A,\alpha}}} \tag{7}$$

where $F^*_{A,\alpha}$ is the free energy of the A module with the training case α clamped on the input.

We can compute the probability that the A module is on or off by averaging over the input sample distribution, with P^α being the prior probability of an input case α:

$$p(A = 1) = \sum_\alpha P^\alpha p(A^\alpha = 1)$$

$$p(A = 0) = 1 - p(A = 1)$$

Similarly, we can compute the four possible values in the joint probability distribution of A and B:

$$p(A = 1, B = 1) = \sum_\alpha P^\alpha p(A^\alpha = 1) p(B^\alpha = 1)$$

$$p(A = 0, B = 1) = p(B = 1) - p(A = 1, B = 1)$$

$$p(A = 1, B = 0) = p(A = 1) - p(A = 1, B = 1)$$

$$p(A = 0, B = 0) = 1 - p(B = 1) - p(A = 1) + p(A = 1, B = 1)$$

Using equation (3), the partial derivatives of the various individual and joint probability functions with respect to a weight w_{ik} in the A module are readily calculated.

$$\frac{\partial p(A = 1)}{\partial w_{ik}} = \sum_\alpha P^\alpha \frac{\partial p(A^\alpha = 1)}{\partial w_{ik}}$$

$$= \sum_\alpha P^\alpha \left(p(A^\alpha = 1) - 1 \right) p(A^\alpha = 1)(y_i y_k) \tag{8}$$

$$\frac{\partial p(A=1, B=1)}{\partial w_{ik}} = \sum_{\alpha} P^{\alpha} \frac{\partial p(A^{\alpha}=1)}{\partial w_{ik}} p(B^{\alpha}=1) \tag{9}$$

The entropy of the stochastic binary variable A is

$$H_A = - <\log p(A)> = - \sum_{a=0,1} p(A=a) \log p(A=a)$$

The entropy of the joint distribution is given by

$$\begin{aligned} H_{AB} &= - <\log p(A,B)> \\ &= - \sum_{a,b} p(A=a, B=b) \log p(A=a, B=b) \end{aligned}$$

The partial derivative of $I(A; B)$ with respect to a single weight w_{ik} in the A module can now be computed; since H_B does not depend on w_{ik}, we need only differentiate H_A and H_{AB}. As shown in Galland and Hinton (1990), the derivative is given by

$$\begin{aligned} \frac{\partial I(A; B)}{\partial w_{ik}} &= \frac{\partial H_A}{\partial w_{ik}} - \frac{\partial H_{AB}}{\partial w_{ik}} \\ &= \sum_{\alpha} P^{\alpha} \left(p(A^{\alpha}=1)-1\right) p(A^{\alpha}=1)(y_i y_k) \left[\log \frac{p(A=1)}{p(A=0)}\right. \\ &\left. - p(B^{\alpha}=1) \log \frac{p(A=1, B=1)}{p(A=0, B=1)} - p(B^{\alpha}=0) \log \frac{p(A=1, B=0)}{p(A=0, B=0)}\right] \end{aligned}$$

The above derivation is drawn from Becker and Hinton (1989) who show that mutual information can be used as a learning signal in back-propagation nets. We can now perform gradient ascent in $I(A; B)$ for each weight in both modules using a two-pass procedure, the probabilities across cases being accumulated in the first pass.

This approach was applied to a system of two mean field modules (the left and right halves of figure 1 without the connecting central unit) to detect shift. As in the multi-completion task, random binary vectors were clamped onto inputs A1, A2 and B1, B2 related only by shift. Hence, the only way the two modules can provide mutual information to each other is by representing the shift. Maximizing the mutual information between them created perfect shift detecting modules in only 10 two-pass sweeps through the 288 training cases. That is, after training, each module was found to have low free energy for either left or right shifts, and high free energy for the other. Details of the simulations are again given in Galland and Hinton (1990).

6   SUMMARY

Standard deterministic Boltzmann learning failed to extract high order features in a network bottleneck. We then explored a variant of DBM learning in which the free energy of a module represents a stochastic binary variable. This variant can efficiently discover that shift is an important feature without using external supervision, provided we use an architecture and an objective function that are designed to extract higher order features which are invariant across space.

Acknowledgements

We would like to thank Sue Becker for many helpful comments. This research was supported by grants from the Ontario Information Technology Research Center and the National Science and Engineering Research Council of Canada. Geoffrey Hinton is a fellow of the Canadian Institute for Advanced Research.

References

Becker, S. and Hinton, G. E. (1989). Spatial coherence as an internal teacher for a neural network. Technical Report CRG-TR-89-7, University of Toronto.

Galland, C. C. and Hinton, G. E. (1990). Experiments on discovering high order features with mean field modules. University of Toronto Connectionist Research Group Technical Report, forthcoming.

Hinton, G. E. (1986) Learning distributed representations of concepts. *Proceedings of the Eighth Annual Conference of the Cognitive Science Society*, Amherst, Mass.

Hinton, G. E. (1987) Connectionist learning procedures. Technical Report CMU-CS-87-115, Carnegie Mellon University.

Hinton, G. E. (1989) Deterministic Boltzmann learning performs steepest descent in weight-space. *Neural Computation*, **1**.

Hinton, G. E. and Sejnowski, T. J. (1986) Learning and relearning in Boltzmann machines. In Rumelhart, D. E., McClelland, J. L., and the PDP group, *Parallel Distributed Processing: Explorations in the Microstructure of Cognition. Volume 1: Foundations*, MIT Press, Cambridge, MA.

Hopfield, J. J. (1984) Neurons with graded response have collective computational properties like those of two-state neurons. *Proceedings of the National Academy of Sciences U.S.A.*, **81**, 3088–3092.

Peterson, C. and Anderson, J. R. (1987) A mean field theory learning algorithm for neural networks. *Complex Systems*, **1**, 995–1019.

Peterson, C. and Hartman, E. (1988) Explorations of the mean field theory learning algorithm. Technical Report ACA-ST/HI-065-88, Microelectronics and Computer Technology Corporation, Austin, TX.

Pineda, F. J. (1987) Generalization of backpropagation to recurrent neural networks. *Phys. Rev. Lett.*, **18**, 2229–2232.

The CHIR Algorithm for Feed Forward

Networks with Binary Weights

Tal Grossman
Department of Electronics
Weizmann Institute of Science
Rehovot 76100 Israel

ABSTRACT

A new learning algorithm, Learning by Choice of Internal Represetations (CHIR), was recently introduced. Whereas many algorithms reduce the learning process to minimizing a cost function over the *weights*, our method treats the *internal representations* as the fundamental entities to be determined. The algorithm applies a search procedure in the space of internal representations, and a cooperative adaptation of the weights (e.g. by using the perceptron learning rule). Since the introduction of its basic, single output version, the CHIR algorithm was generalized to train any feed forward network of binary neurons. Here we present the generalised version of the CHIR algorithm, and further demonstrate its versatility by describing how it can be modified in order to train networks with binary (± 1) weights. Preliminary tests of this binary version on the random teacher problem are also reported.

I. INTRODUCTION

Learning by Choice of Internal Representations (CHIR) was recently introduced [1,11] as a training method for feed forward networks of binary units.

Internal Representations are defined as the states taken by the hidden units of a network when patterns (e.g. from the training set) are presented to the input layer of the network. The CHIR algorithm views the internal representations associated with various inputs as the basic independent variables of the learning process. Once such representations are formed, the weights can be found by simple and local learning procedures such as the Perceptron Learning Rule (PLR) [2]. Hence the problem of learning becomes one of *searching for proper internal representations*, rather than of minimizing a cost function by varying the values of weights, which is the approach used by back propagation (see, however [3],[4] where "back propagation of desired states" is described). This basic idea, of viewing the internal representations as the fundamental entities, has been used since by other groups [5-7]. Some of these works, and the main differences between them and our approach, are briefly disscussed in [11]. One important difference is that the CHIR algorithm, as well as another similar algorithm, the MRII [8], try to solve the learning problem for a fixed architecture, and are not guaranteed to converge. Two other algorithms [5,6] always find a solution, but at the price of increasing the network size during learning in a manner that resembles similar algorithms developed earlier [9,10]. Another approach [7] is to use an error minimizing algorithm which treats the internal representations as well as the weights as the relevant variables of the search space.

To be more specific, consider first the single layer perceptron with its Perceptron Learning Rule (PLR) [2]. This simple network consists of N input (source) units j, and a single target unit i. This unit is a binary linear threshold unit, i.e. when the source units are set in any one of $\mu = 1, ..M$ patterns, i.e. $S_j = \xi_j^\mu$, the state of unit i, $S_i = \pm 1$ is determined according to the rule

$$S_i = sign(\sum_j W_{ij} S_j + \theta_i) \ . \tag{1}$$

Here W_{ij} is the (unidirectional) weight assigned to the connection from unit j to i; θ_i is a local bias. For each of the M input patterns, we require that the target unit (determined using (1)) will take a preassigned value ξ_i^μ. Learning takes place in the course of a training session. Starting from any arbitrary initial guess for the weights, an input ν is presented, resulting in the output taking some value S_i^ν. Now modify every weight according to the rule

$$W_{ij} \rightarrow W_{ij} + \eta(1 - S_i^\nu \xi_i^\nu)\xi_i^\nu \xi_j^\nu \ , \tag{2}$$

where $\eta > 0$ is a step size parameter ($\xi_j^\nu = 1$ is used to modify the bias θ). Another input pattern is presented, and so on, until all inputs draw the correct output. The Perceptron convergence theorem states [2] that the PLR will find a solution (if one exists), in a finite number of steps. Nevertheless, one needs, for each unit, both the desired input and output states in order to apply the PLR.

Consider now a two layer perceptron, with N input, H hidden and K output units (see Fig.1). The elements of the network are binary linear threshold units i, whose states $S_i = \pm 1$ are determined according to (1). In a typical task for such a network, M specified output patterns, $S_i^{out,\mu} = \xi_i^{out,\mu}$, are required in response to $\mu = 1, ..., M$ input patterns. If a solution is found, it first maps each input onto an internal representation generated on the hidden layer, which, in turn, produces the correct output. Now imagine that we are *not* supplied with the weights that solve the problem; however the correct internal representations *are* revealed. That is, we are given a *table* with M rows, one for each input. Every row has H bits $\xi_i^{h,\mu}$, for $i = 1..H$, specifying the state of the hidden layer obtained in response to input pattern μ. One can now view each hidden-layer cell i as the target of the PLR, with the N inputs viewed as source. Given sufficient time, the PLR will converge to a set of weights W_{ij}, connecting input unit j to hidden unit i, so that indeed the input-hidden association that appears in column i of our table will be realized. In order to obtain the correct output, we apply the PLR in a learning process that uses the hidden layer as source and each output unit as a target, so as to realize the correct output. In general, however, one is not supplied with a correct table of internal representations. Finding such a table is the goal of our approach.

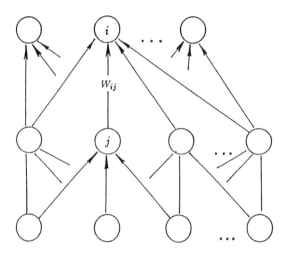

Figure 1. A typical three layered feed forward network (two layered perceptron) with N input, H hidden and K output units. The unidirectional weight W_{ij} connects unit j to unit i. A layer index is implicitly included in each unit's index.

During learning, the CHIR algorithm alternates between two phases : in one it generates the internal representations, and in the other it uses the updated representations in order to search for weights, using some single layer learning rule. This general scheme describes a large family of possible algorithms, that use different ways to change the internal representations, and update the weights.

A simple algorithm based on this general scheme was introduced recently [1,11]. In section II we describe the multiple output version of CHIR [11]. In section III we present a way to modify the algorithm so it can train networks with binary weights, and the preliminary results of a few tests done on this new version. In the last section we shortly discuss our results and describe some future directions.

II. THE CHIR ALGORITHM

The CHIR algorithm that we describe here implements the basic idea of learning by choice of internal representations by breaking the learning process into four distinct procedures that are repeated in a cyclic order :

1. SETINREP: Generate a table of internal representations $\{\xi_i^{h,\nu}\}$ by presenting each input pattern from the training set and recording the states of the hidden units, using Eq.(1), with the existing couplings W_{ij} and θ_i.

2. LEARN23: The current table of internal representations is used as the training set, the hidden layer cells are used as source, and each output as the target unit of the PLR. If weights W_{ij} and θ_i that produce the desired outputs are found, the problem has been solved. Otherwise stop after I_{23} learning sweeps, and keep the current weights, to use in CHANGE INREP.

3. CHANGE INREP: Generate a new table of internal representations, which reduces the error in the output : We present the table sequentially, row by row (pattern by pattern), to the hidden layer. If for pattern ν the wrong output is obtained, the internal representation $\xi^{h,\nu}$ is changed.

This is done simply by choosing (at random) a hidden unit i, and checking the effect of flipping the sign of $\xi_i^{h,\nu}$ on the total output error, i.e. the number of wrong bits. If the output error is not increased, the flip is accepted and the table of internal representations is changed accordingly. Otherwise the flip is rejected and we try another unit. When we have more than one output unit, it might happen that an error in one output unit can not be corrected without introducing an error in another unit. Therefore we allow only for a pre-specified number of attempted flips, I_{in}, and go on to the next pattern even if the output error was not eliminated completely. This procedure ends with a modified, "improved" table which is our next guess of internal representations. Note that this new table does not necessarily yield a totally correct output for all the patterns. In such a case, the learning process will go on even if this new table is perfectly realized by the next stage - LEARN12.

4. LEARN12: Present an input pattern; if the output is wrong, apply the PLR with the first layer serving as source, treating every hidden layer site separately as target. If input ν does yield the correct output, we insert the current state of the hidden layer as the internal representation associated with pattern ν, and no learning steps are taken. We sweep in this manner the training set, modifying weights W_{ij}, (between input and hidden layer), hidden-layer thresholds θ_i, and, as explained above, internal representations. If the network has achieved error-free performance for the entire training set, learning is completed. Otherwise, after I_{12} training sweeps (or if the current internal representation is perfectly realized), abort the PLR stage, keeping the present values of W_{ij}, θ_i, and start SETINREP again.

The idea in trying to learn the current internal representation even if it does not yield the perfect output is that it can serve as a better input for the next LEARN23 stage. That way, in each learning cycle the algorithm tries to improve the overall performance of the network.

This algorithm can be further generalized for multi-layered feed forward networks by applying the CHANGE INREP and LEARN12 procedures to each of the hidden layers, one by one, from the last to the first hidden layer.

There are a few details that need to be added.

a) The "impatience" parameters: I_{12} and I_{23}, which are rather arbitrary, are introduced to guarantee that the PLR stage is aborted if no solution is found, but they have to be large enough to allow the PLR to find a solution (if one exists) with sufficiently high probability. Similar considerations are valid for the I_{in} parameter, the number of flip attempts allowed in the CHANGE INREP procedure. If this number is too small, the updated internal representations may not improve. If it is too large, the new internal representations might be too different from the previous ones, and therefore hard to learn.

The optimal values depend, in general, on the problem and the network size. Our experience indicates, however, that once a "reasonable" range of values is found, performance is fairly insensitive to the precise choice. In addition, a simple rule of thumb can always be applied : "Whenever learning is getting hard, increase the parameters". A detailed study of this issue is reported in [11].

b) The Internal representations updating scheme: The CHANGE INREP procedure that is presented here (and studied in [11]) is probably the simplest and "most primitive" way to update the InRep table. The choice of the hidden units to be flipped is completely blind and relies only on the single bit of information about the improvement of the total output error. It may even happen that no change in the internal representaion is made, although such a change is needed. This procedure can certainly be made more efficient, e.g. by probing the fields induced on all the hidden units to be flipped and then choosing one (or more) of them by applying a "minimal disturbance" principle as in [8]. Nevertheless it was shown [11] that even this simple algorithm works quite well.

c) The weights updating schemes: In our experiments we have used the simple PLR with a fixed increment ($\eta = 1/2$, $\Delta W_{ij} = \pm 1$) for weight learning. It has the advantage of allowing the use of discrete (or integer) weights. Nevertheless, it is just a component that can be replaced by other, perhaps more sophisticated methods, in order to achieve, for example, better stability [12], or to take into account various constraints on the weights, e.g. binary weights [13]. In the following section we demonstrate how this can be done.

III. THE CHIR ALGORITHM FOR BINARY WEIGHTS

In this section we describe how the CHIR algorithm can be used in order to train feed forward networks with binary weights. According to this strong constraint, all the weights in the system (including the thresholds) can be either +1 or -1. The way to do it within the CHIR framework is simple: instead of applying the PLR (or any other single layer, real weights algorithm) for the updating of the weights, we can use a binary perceptron learning rule. Several ways to solve the learning problem in the binary weight perceptron were suggested recently [13]. The one that we used in the experiments reported here is a modified version of the directed drift algorithm introduced by Venkatesh [13]. Like the standard PLR, the directed drift algorithm works on-line, namely, the patterns are presented one by one, the state of a unit i is calculated according to (1), and whenever an error occurs the incoming weights are updated. When there is an error it means that

$$\xi_i^\nu h_i^\nu < 0$$

Namely, the field $h_i^\nu = \sum_j W_{ij}\xi_j^\nu$, (induced by the current pattern ξ_j^ν) is "wrong". If so, there must be some weights that pull it to the wrong direction. These are the weights for which

$$\xi_i^\nu W_{ij}\xi_j^\nu < 0.$$

Here ξ_i^ν is the desired output of unit i for pattern ν. The updating of the weights is done simply by flipping (i.e. $W_{ij} \to -W_{ij}$) at random k of these weights.

The number of weights to be changed in each learning step, k, can be a pre-fixed parameter of the algorithm, or, as suggested by Venkatesh, can be decreased gradually during the learning process in a way similar to a cooling schedule (as in simulated annealing). What we do is to take $k = |h|/2 + 1$, making sure, like in relaxation algorithms, that just enough weights are flipped in order to obtain the desired target for the current pattern. This simple and local rule is now "plugged" into the Learn12 and Learn23 procedures instead of (2), and the initial weights are chosen to be +1 or -1 at random.

We tested the binary version of CHIR on the "random teacher" problem. In this problem a "teacher network" is created by choosing a random set of +1/-1 weights for the given architecture. The training set is then created by presenting M input patterns to the network and recording the resulting output as the desired output patterns. In what follows we took $M = 2^N$ (exhaustive learning), and an N:N:1 architecture.

The "time" parameter that we use for measuring performance is the number of sweeps through the training set of M patterns ("epochs") needed in order to find the solution. Namely, how many times each pattern was presented to the network. In the experiments presented here, all possible input patterns were presented sequentially in a fixed order (within the perceptron learning sweeps). Therefore in each cycle of the algorithm there are $I_{12} + I_{23} + 1$ such sweeps. Note that according to our definition, a single sweep involves the updating of only one layer of weights or internal representations. for each network size, N, we created an ensemble of 50 independent runs, with different ranodom teachers and starting with a different random choice of initial weights.

We calculate, as a performance measure, the following quantities:

a. The median number of sweeps, t_m.

b. The "inverse average rate", τ, as defined by Tesauro and Janssen in [14].

c. The success rate, S, i.e. the fraction of runs in which the algorithm finds a solution in less than the maximal number of training cycles I_{max} specified.

The results,with the typical parameters, for N=3,4,5,6, are given in Table 1.

Table 1. The Random Teacher problem with N:N:1 architecture.

N	I_{12}	I_{23}	I_{in}	I_{max}	t_m	τ	S
3	20	10	5	20	14	9	1.00
4	25	10	7	60	87	37	1.00
5	40	15	9	300	430	60	1.00
6	70	40	11	900	15000	1100	0.71

As mentioned before, these are only preliminary results. No attempt was made to to optimize the learning parameters.

IV. DISCUSSION

We presented a generalized version of the CHIR algorithm that is capable of training networks with multiple outputs and hidden layers. A way to modify the basic algortihm so it can be applied to networks with binary weights was also explained and tested. The potential importance of such networks, e.g. in hardware implementation, makes this modified version particularly interesting.

An appealing feature of the CHIR algorithm is the fact that it does not use any kind of "global control", that manipulates the internal representations (as is used for example in [5,6]). The mechanism by which the internal representations are changed is local in the sense that the change is done for each unit and each pattern without conveying any information from other units or patterns (representations). Moreover, the feedback from the "teacher" to the system is only a single bit quantity, namely, whether the output is getting worse or not (in contrast to BP, for example, where one informs each and every output unit about its individual error).

Other advantages of our algorithm are the simplicity of the calculations, the need for only integer, or even binary weights and binary units, and the good performance. It should be mentioned again that the CHIR training sweep involves much less computations than that of back-propagation. The price is the extra memory of MH bits that is needed during the learning process in order to store the internal representations of all M training patterns. This feature is biologically implausible and may be practically limiting. We are developing a method that does not require such memory. The learning method that is currently studied for that purpose [15], is related to the MRII rule, that was recently presented by Widrow and Winter in [8]. It seems that further research will be needed in order to study the practical differences and the relative advantages of the CHIR and the MRII algorithms.

Acknowledgements : I am gratefull to Prof. Eytan Domany for many useful suggestions and comments. This research was partially supported by a grant from Minerva.

References

[1] Grossman T., Meir R. and Domany E., *Complex Systems* **2**, 555 (1989). See also in D. Touretzky (ed.), *Advances in Neural Information Processing Systems 1*, (Morgan Kaufmann, San Mateo 1989).

[2] Minsky M. and Papert S. 1988, *Perceptrons* (MIT, Cambridge);

Rosenblatt F. *Principles of neurodynamics* (Spartan, New York, 1962).

[3] Plaut D.C., Nowlan S.J., and Hinton G.E., Tech.Report CMU-CS-86-126,

Carnegie-Mellon University (1986).

[4] Le Cun Y., *Proc. Cognitiva* **85**, 593 (1985).

[5] Rujan P. and Marchand M., in the *Proc. of the First International Joint Conference Neural Networks - Washington D.C. 1989*, Vol.II, pp. 105. and to appear in *Complex Systems*.

[6] Mezard M. and Nadal J.P., J.Phys.A. **22**, 2191 (1989).

[7] Krogh A., Thorbergsson G.I. and Hertz J.A., in these Proceedings.

R. Rohwer, to apear in the *Proc. of DANIP, GMD Bonn*, April 1989, J. Kinderman and A. Linden eds ;

Saad D. and Merom E., preprint (1989).

[8] Widrow B. and Winter R., *Computer* **21**, No.3, 25 (1988).

[9] See e.g. Cameron S.H., IEEE TEC **EC-13**,299 (1964) ; Hopcroft J.E. and Mattson R.L., IEEE TEC **EC-14**, 552 (1965).

[10] Honavar V. and Uhr L. in the *Proc. of the 1988 Connectionist Models Summer School*, Touretzky D., Hinton G. and Sejnowski T. eds. (Morgan Kaufmann, San Mateo, 1988).

[11] Grossman T., to be published in *Complex Systems* (1990).

[12] Krauth W. and Mezard M., J.Phys.A, **20**, L745 (1988).

[13] Venkatesh S., preprint (1989) ;

Amaldi E. and Nicolis S., J.Phys.France **50**, 2333 (1989).

Kohler H., Diederich S., Kinzel W. and Opper M., preprint (1989).

[14] Tesauro G. and Janssen H., *Complex Systems* **2**, 39 (1988).

[15] Nabutovski D., unpublished.

The Cascade-Correlation Learning Architecture

Scott E. Fahlman and **Christian Lebiere**
School of Computer Science
Carnegie-Mellon University
Pittsburgh, PA 15213

ABSTRACT

Cascade-Correlation is a new architecture and supervised learning algorithm for artificial neural networks. Instead of just adjusting the weights
in a network of fixed topology, Cascade-Correlation begins with a minimal network, then automatically trains and adds new hidden units one
by one, creating a multi-layer structure. Once a new hidden unit has
been added to the network, its input-side weights are frozen. This unit
then becomes a permanent feature-detector in the network, available for
producing outputs or for creating other, more complex feature detectors. The Cascade-Correlation architecture has several advantages over
existing algorithms: it learns very quickly, the network determines its
own size and topology, it retains the structures it has built even if the
training set changes, and it requires no back-propagation of error signals
through the connections of the network.

1   DESCRIPTION OF CASCADE-CORRELATION

The most important problem preventing the widespread application of artificial neural
networks to real-world problems is the slowness of existing learning algorithms such as
back-propagation (or "backprop"). One factor contributing to that slowness is what we
call the *moving target problem*: because all of the weights in the network are changing
at once, each hidden units sees a constantly changing environment. Instead of moving
quickly to assume useful roles in the overall problem solution, the hidden units engage in
a complex dance with much wasted motion. The Cascade-Correlation learning algorithm
was developed in an attempt to solve that problem. In the problems we have examined,
it learns much faster than back-propagation and solves some other problems as well.

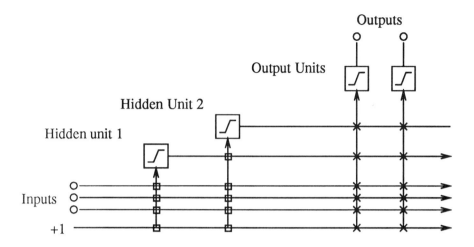

Figure 1: The Cascade architecture, after two hidden units have been added. The vertical lines sum all incoming activation. Boxed connections are frozen, X connections are trained repeatedly.

Cascade-Correlation combines two key ideas: The first is the *cascade architecture*, in which hidden units are added to the network one at a time and do not change after they have been added. The second is the learning algorithm, which creates and installs the new hidden units. For each new hidden unit, we attempt to maximize the magnitude of the *correlation* between the new unit's output and the residual error signal we are trying to eliminate.

The cascade architecture is illustrated in Figure 1. It begins with some inputs and one or more output units, but with no hidden units. The number of inputs and outputs is dictated by the problem and by the I/O representation the experimenter has chosen. Every input is connected to every output unit by a connection with an adjustable weight. There is also a *bias* input, permanently set to +1.

The output units may just produce a linear sum of their weighted inputs, or they may employ some non-linear activation function. In the experiments we have run so far, we use a symmetric sigmoidal activation function (hyperbolic tangent) whose output range is -1.0 to +1.0. For problems in which a precise analog output is desired, instead of a binary classification, linear output units might be the best choice, but we have not yet studied any problems of this kind.

We add hidden units to the network one by one. Each new hidden unit receives a connection from each of the network's original inputs and also from every pre-existing hidden unit. The hidden unit's input weights are frozen at the time the unit is added to the net; only the output connections are trained repeatedly. Each new unit therefore adds a new one-unit "layer" to the network, unless some of its incoming weights happen to be zero. This leads to the creation of very powerful high-order feature detectors; it also may lead to very deep networks and high fan-in to the hidden units. There are a number of possible strategies for minimizing the network depth and fan-in as new units are added, but we have not yet explored these strategies.

The learning algorithm begins with no hidden units. The direct input-output connections are trained as well as possible over the entire training set. With no need to back-propagate through hidden units, we can use the Widrow-Hoff or "delta" rule, the Perceptron learning algorithm, or any of the other well-known learning algorithms for single-layer networks. In our simulations, we use Fahlman's "quickprop" algorithm [Fahlman, 1988] to train the output weights. With no hidden units, this acts essentially like the delta rule, except that it converges much faster.

At some point, this training will approach an asymptote. When no significant error reduction has occurred after a certain number of training cycles (controlled by a "patience" parameter set by the operator), we run the network one last time over the entire training set to measure the error. If we are satisfied with the network's performance, we stop; if not, we attempt to reduce the residual errors further by adding a new hidden unit to the network. The unit-creation algorithm is described below. The new unit is added to the net, its input weights are frozen, and all the output weights are once again trained using quickprop. This cycle repeats until the error is acceptably small (or until we give up).

To create a new hidden unit, we begin with a *candidate unit* that receives trainable input connections from all of the network's external inputs and from all pre-existing hidden units. The output of this candidate unit is not yet connected to the active network. We run a number of passes over the examples of the training set, adjusting the candidate unit's input weights after each pass. The goal of this adjustment is to maximize S, the sum over all output units o of the magnitude of the correlation (or, more precisely, the covariance) between V, the candidate unit's value, and E_o, the residual output error observed at unit o. We define S as

$$S = \sum_o \left| \sum_p (V_p - \overline{V})(E_{p,o} - \overline{E_o}) \right|$$

where o is the network output at which the error is measured and p is the training pattern. The quantities $\overline{V}$ and $\overline{E_o}$ are the values of V and E_o averaged over all patterns.

In order to maximize S, we must compute $\partial S/\partial w_i$, the partial derivative of S with respect to each of the candidate unit's incoming weights, w_i. In a manner very similar to the derivation of the back-propagation rule in [Rumelhart, 1986], we can expand and differentiate the formula for S to get

$$\partial S/\partial w_i = \sum_{p,o} \sigma_o (E_{p,o} - \overline{E_o}) f'_p I_{i,p}$$

where σ_o is the sign of the correlation between the candidate's value and output o, f'_p is the derivative for pattern p of the candidate unit's activation function with respect to the sum of its inputs, and $I_{i,p}$ is the input the candidate unit receives from unit i for pattern p.

After computing $\partial S/\partial w_i$ for each incoming connection, we can perform a gradient ascent to maximize S. Once again we are training only a single layer of weights. Once again we use the quickprop update rule for faster convergence. When S stops improving, we install the new candidate as a unit in the active network, freeze its input weights, and continue the cycle as described above.

Because of the absolute value in the formula for S, a candidate unit cares only about the *magnitude* of its correlation with the error at a given output, and not about the sign of the correlation. As a rule, if a hidden unit correlates positively with the error at a given unit, it will develop a negative connection weight to that unit, attempting to cancel some of the error; if the correlation is negative, the output weight will be positive. Since a unit's weights to different outputs may be of mixed sign, a unit can sometimes serve two purposes by developing a positive correlation with the error at one output and a negative correlation with the error at another.

Instead of a single candidate unit, it is possible to use a *pool* of candidate units, each with a different set of random initial weights. All receive the same input signals and see the same residual error for each pattern and each output. Because they do not interact with one another or affect the active network during training, all of these candidate units can be trained in parallel; whenever we decide that no further progress is being made, we install the candidate whose correlation score is the best. The use of this pool of candidates is beneficial in two ways: it greatly reduces the chance that a useless unit will be permanently installed because an individual candidate got stuck during training, and (on a parallel machine) it can speed up the training because many parts of weight-space can be explored simultaneously.

The hidden and candidate units may all be of the same type, for example with a sigmoid activation function. Alternatively, we might create a pool of candidate units with a mixture of nonlinear activation functions—some sigmoid, some Gaussian, some with radial activation functions, and so on—and let them compete to be chosen for addition to the active network. To date, we have explored the all-sigmoid and all-Gaussian cases, but we do not yet have extensive simulation data on networks with mixed unit-types.

One final note on the implementation of this algorithm: While the weights in the output layer are being trained, the other weights in the active network are frozen. While the candidate weights are being trained, none of the weights in the active network are changed. In a machine with plenty of memory, it is possible to record the unit-values and the output errors for an entire epoch, and then to use these cached values repeatedly during training, rather than recomputing them repeatedly for each training case. This can result in a tremendous speedup as the active network grows large.

Figure 2: Training points for the two-spirals problem, and output pattern for one network trained with Cascade-Correlation.

2   BENCHMARK RESULTS

2.1   THE TWO-SPIRALS PROBLEM

The "two-spirals" benchmark was chosen as the primary benchmark for this study because it is an extremely hard problem for algorithms of the back-propagation family to solve. It was first proposed by Alexis Wieland of MITRE Corp. The net has two continuous-valued inputs and a single output. The training set consists of 194 X-Y values, half of which are to produce a +1 output and half a -1 output. These training points are arranged in two interlocking spirals that go around the origin three times, as shown in Figure 2a. The goal is to develop a feed-forward network with sigmoid units that properly classifies all 194 training cases. Some hidden units are obviously needed, since a single linear separator cannot divide two sets twisted together in this way.

Wieland (unpublished) reported that a modified version of backprop in use at MITRE required 150,000 to 200,000 epochs to solve this problem, and that they had never obtained a solution using standard backprop. Lang and Witbrock [Lang, 1988] tried the problem using a 2-5-5-5-1 network (three hidden layers of five units each). Their network was unusual in that it provided "shortcut" connections: each unit received incoming connections from every unit in *every* earlier layer, not just from the immediately preceding layer. With this architecture, standard backprop was able to solve the problem in 20,000 epochs, backprop with a modified error function required 12,000 epochs, and quickprop required 8000. This was the best two-spirals performance reported to date. Lang and Witbrock also report obtaining a solution with a 2-5-5-1 net (only ten hidden units in all), but the solution required 60,000 quickprop epochs.

We ran the problem 100 times with the Cascade-Correlation algorithm using a sigmoidal activation function for both the output and hidden units and a pool of 8 candidate units. All trials were successful, requiring 1700 epochs on the average. (This number counts both the epochs used to train output weights and the epochs used to train candidate units.) The number of hidden units built into the net varied from 12 to 19, with an average of 15.2 and a median of 15. Here is a histogram of the number of hidden units created:

Hidden Units	Number of Trials	
12	4	####
13	9	#########
14	24	########################
15	19	###################
16	24	########################
17	13	#############
18	5	#####
19	2	##

In terms of training epochs, Cascade-Correlation beats quickprop by a factor of 5 and standard backprop by a factor of 10, while building a network of about the same complexity (15 hidden units). In terms of actual computation on a serial machine, however, the speedup is much greater than these numbers suggest. In backprop and quickprop, each training case requires a forward and a backward pass through all the connections in the network; Cascade-Correlation requires only a forward pass. In addition, many of the Cascade-Correlation epochs are run while the network is much smaller than its final size. Finally, the cacheing strategy described above makes it possible to avoid re-computing the unit values for parts of the network that are not changing.

Suppose that instead of epochs, we measure learning time in *connection crossings*, defined as the number of multiply-accumulate steps necessary to propagate activation values forward through the network and error values backward. This measure leaves out some computational steps, but it is a more accurate measure of computational complexity than comparing epochs of different sizes or comparing runtimes on different machines. The Lang and Witbrock result of 20,000 backprop epochs requires about 1.1 billion connection crossings. Their solution using 8000 quickprop epochs on the same network requires about 438 million crossings. An average Cascade-Correlation run with a pool of 8 candidate units requires about 19 million crossings—a 23-fold speedup over quickprop and a 50-fold speedup over standard backprop. With a smaller pool of candidate units the speedup (on a serial machine) would be even greater, but the resulting networks might be somewhat larger.

Figure 2b shows the output of a 12-hidden-unit network built by Cascade-Correlation as the input is scanned over the X-Y field. This network properly classifies all 194 training points. We can see that it interpolates smoothly for about the first 1.5 turns of the spiral, but becomes a bit lumpy farther out, where the training points are farther apart. This "receptive field" diagram is similar to that obtained by Lang and Witbrock using backprop, but is somewhat smoother.

2.2 N-INPUT PARITY

Since parity has been a popular benchmark among other researchers, we ran Cascade-Correlation on N-input parity problems with N ranging from 2 to 8. The best results were obtained with a sigmoid output unit and hidden units whose output is a Gaussian function of the sum of weighted inputs. Based on five trials for each value of N, our results were as follows:

N	Cases	Hidden Units	Average Epochs
2	4	1	24
3	8	1	32
4	16	2	66
5	32	2–3	142
6	64	3	161
7	128	4–5	292
8	256	4–5	357

For a rough comparison, Tesauro and Janssens [Tesauro, 1988] report that standard back-prop takes about 2000 epochs for 8-input parity. In their study, they used $2N$ hidden units. Cascade-Correlation can solve the problem with fewer than N hidden units because it uses short-cut connections.

As a test of generalization, we ran a few trials of Cascade-Correlation on the 10-input parity problem, training on either 50% or 25% of the 1024 patterns and testing on the rest. The number of hidden units built varied from 4 to 7 and training time varied from 276 epochs to 551. When trained on half of the patterns, performance on the test set averaged 96% correct; when trained on one quarter of the patterns, test-set performance averaged 90% correct. Note that the nearest neighbor algorithm would get almost all of the test-set cases wrong.

3 DISCUSSION

We believe that that Cascade-Correlation algorithm offers the following advantages over network learning algorithms currently in use:

- There is no need to guess the size, depth, and connectivity pattern of the network in advance. A reasonably small (though not optimal) net is built automatically, perhaps with a mixture of unit-types.

- Cascade-Correlation learns fast. In backprop, the hidden units engage in a complex dance before they settle into distinct useful roles; in Cascade-Correlation, each unit sees a fixed problem and can move decisively to solve that problem. For the problems we have investigated to date, the learning time in epochs grows roughly as $N \log N$, where N is the number of hidden units ultimately needed to solve the problem.

- Cascade-Correlation can build deep nets (high-order feature detectors) without the dramatic slowdown we see in deep back-propagation networks.

- Cascade-Correlation is useful for *incremental learning*, in which new information is added to an already-trained net. Once built, a feature detector is never cannibalized. It is available from that time on for producing outputs or more complex features.

- At any given time, we train only one layer of weights in the network. The rest of the network is constant, so results can be cached.

- There is never any need to propagate error signals backwards through network connections. A single residual error signal can be broadcast to all candidates. The weighted connections transmit signals in only one direction, eliminating one difference between these networks and biological synapses.

- The candidate units do not interact, except to pick a winner. Each candidate sees the same inputs and error signals. This limited communication makes the architecture attractive for parallel implementation.

4 RELATION TO OTHER WORK

The principal differences between Cascade-Correlation and older learning architectures are the dynamic creation of hidden units, the way we stack the new units in multiple layers (with a fixed output layer), the freezing of units as we add them to the net, and the way we train new units by hill-climbing to maximize the unit's correlation with the residual error. The most interesting discovery is that by training one unit at a time instead of training the whole network at once, we can speed up the learning process considerably, while still creating a reasonably small net that generalizes well.

A number of researchers [Ash, 1989,Moody, 1989] have investigated networks that add new units or receptive fields within a single layer in the course of learning. While single-layer systems are well-suited for some problems, these systems are incapable of creating higher-order feature detectors that combine the outputs of existing units. The idea of building feature detectors and then freezing them was inspired in part by the work of Waibel on modular networks [Waibel, 1989], but in his model the structure of the sub-networks must be fixed before learning begins.

We know of only a few attempts to build up multi-layer networks as the learning progresses. Our decision to look at models in which each unit can see all pre-existing units was inspired to some extent by work on progressively deepening threshold-logic models by Merrick Furst and Jeff Jackson at Carnegie Mellon. (They are not actively pursuing this line at present.) Gallant [Gallant, 1986] briefly mentions a progressively deepening perceptron model (his "inverted pyramid" model) in which units are frozen after being installed. However, he has concentrated most of his research effort on models in which new hidden units are generated at random rather than by a deliberate training process. The SONN model of Tenorio and Lee [Tenorio, 1989] builds a multiple-layer topology to suit the problem at hand. Their algorithm places new two-input units at randomly selected locations, using a simulated annealing search to keep only the most useful ones—a very different approach from ours.

Acknowledgments

We would like to thank Merrick Furst, Paul Gleichauf, and David Touretzky for asking good questions that helped to shape this work. This research was sponsored in part by the National Science Foundation (Contract EET-8716324) and in part by the Defense Advanced Research Projects Agency (Contract F33615-87-C-1499).

References

[Ash, 1989]   Ash, T. (1989) "Dynamic Node Creation in Back-Propagation Networks", Technical Report 8901, Institute for Cognitive Science, University of California, San Diego.

[Fahlman, 1988]   Fahlman, S. E. (1988) "Faster-Learning Variations on Back-Propagation: An Empirical Study" in *Proceedings of the 1988 Connectionist Models Summer School*, Morgan Kaufmann.

[Gallant, 1986]   Gallant, S. I. (1986) "Three Constructive Algorithms for Network Learning" in *Proceedings, 8th Annual Conference of the Cognitive Science Society*.

[Lang, 1988]   Lang, K. J. and Witbrock, M. J. (1988) "Learning to Tell Two Spirals Apart" in *Proceedings of the 1988 Connectionist Models Summer School*, Morgan Kaufmann.

[Moody, 1989]   Moody, J. (1989) "Fast Learning in Multi-Resolution Hierarchies" in D. S. Touretzky (ed.), *Advances in Neural Information Processing Systems 1*, Morgan Kaufmann.

[Rumelhart, 1986]   Rumelhart, D. E., Hinton, G. E., and Williams, R. J. (1986) "Learning Internal Representations by Error Propagation" in Rumelhart, D. E. and McClelland, J. L.,*Parallel Distributed Processing: Explorations in the Microstructure of Cognition*, MIT Press.

[Tenorio, 1989]   Tenorio, M. F., and Lee, W. T. (1989) "Self-Organizing Neural Nets for the Identification Problem" in D. S. Touretzky (ed.), *Advances in Neural Information Processing Systems 1*, Morgan Kaufmann.

[Tesauro, 1988]   Tesauro, G. and Janssens, B. (1988) "Scaling Relations in Back-Propagation Learning" in *Complex Systems 2* 39-44.

[Waibel, 1989]   Waibel, A. (1989) "Consonant Recognition by Modular Construction of Large Phonemic Time-Delay Neural Networks" in D. S. Touretzky (ed.), *Advances in Neural Information Processing Systems 1*, Morgan Kaufmann.

Meiosis Networks

Stephen José Hanson [1]
Learning and Knowledge Acquisition Group
Siemens Research Center
Princeton, NJ 08540

ABSTRACT

A central problem in connectionist modelling is the control of network and architectural resources during learning. In the present approach, weights reflect a coarse prediction history as coded by a distribution of values and parameterized in the mean and standard deviation of these weight distributions. Weight updates are a function of both the mean and standard deviation of each connection in the network and vary as a function of the error signal ("stochastic delta rule"; Hanson, 1990). Consequently, the weights maintain information on their central tendency and their "uncertainty" in prediction. Such information is useful in establishing a policy concerning the size of the nodal complexity of the network and growth of new nodes. For example, during problem solving the present network can undergo "meiosis", producing two nodes where there was one "overtaxed" node as measured by its coefficient of variation. It is shown in a number of benchmark problems that meiosis networks can find minimal architectures, reduce computational complexity, and overall increase the efficiency of the representation learning interaction.

---

[1] Also a member of the Cognitive Science Laboratory, Princeton University, Princeton, NJ 08542

1 INTRODUCTION

Search problems which involve high dimensionality, a-priori constraints and nonlinearities are hard. Unfortunately, learning problems in biological systems involve just these sorts of properties. Worse, one can characterize the sort of problem that organisms probably encounter in the real world as those that do not easily admit solutions that involve, simple averaging, optimality, linear approximation or complete knowledge of data or nature of the problem being solved. We would contend there are three basic properties of real learning result in an ill-defined set problems and heterogeneous set of solutions:

- Data are continuously available but incomplete; the learner must constantly update parameter estimates with stingy bits of data which may represent a very small sample from the possible population

- Conditional distributions of response categories with respect to given features are unknown and must be estimated from possibly unrepresentative samples.

- Local (in time) information may be misleading, wrong, or nonstationary, consequently there is a poor tradeoff between the present use of data and waiting for more and possibly flawed data-- consequently updates must be small and revocable.

These sorts of properties represent only one aspect of the learning problem faced by real organisms in real environments. Nonetheless, they underscore why "weak" methods--methods that assume little about the environment in which they are operating --are so critical.

1.1 LEARNING AND SEARCH

It is possible to precisely characterize the search problem in terms of the resources or degress of freedom in the learning model. If the task the learning system is to perform is classification then the system can be analyzed in terms of its ability to dichotomize stimulus points in feature space.

Dichotomization Capability: Network Capacity Using a linear *fan-in* or hyperplane type neuron we can characterize the degrees of freedom inherent in a network of units with thresholded output. For example, with linear boundaries, consider 4 points, well distributed in a 2-dimensional feature space. There are exactly 14 linearly separable dichotomies that can be formed with the 4 target points. However, there are actually 16 (2^4) possible dichotomies of 4 points in 2 dimensions consequently, the number of possible dichotomies or arbitrary categories that are linearly implementable can be thought of as a capacity of the linear network in k dimensions with n examples. The general category capacity measure (Cover, 1965) can be written as:

$$C(n,k)=2 \sum_{j=0}^{k} \frac{(n-1)!}{(n-1-j)!\,j!}, \quad n > k+1 \qquad (1)$$

Note the dramatic growth in C as a function of k, the number of feature dimensions, for example, for 25 stimuli in a 5 dimensional feature space there are 100,670 linear dichotomies. Undertermination in these sorts of linear networks is the rule not the exception. This makes the search process and the nature of constraints on the search process critical in finding solutions that may be useful in the given problem domain.

1.2   THE STOCHASTIC DELTA RULE

Actual mammalian neural systems involve noise. Responses from the same individual unit in isolated cortex due to cyclically repeated identical stimuli will never result in identical bursts Transmission of excitation through neural networks in living systems is essentially stochastic in nature. The typical activation function used in connectionist models must be assumed to be an average over many intervals, since any particular neuronal pulse train appears quite random [in fact, Poisson; for example see Burns,1968; Tomko & Crapper, 1974].

This suggests that a particular neural signal in time may be modeled by a *distribution* of synaptic values rather then a single value. Further this sort of representation provides a natural way to affect the synaptic efficacy in time. In order to introduce noise adaptively, we require that the synaptic modification be a function of a random increment or decrement proportional in size to the present error signal. Consequently, the weight delta or gradient itself becomes a random variable based on prediction performance. Thus, the noise that seems ubiquitous and apparently useless throughout the nervous system can be turned to at least three advantages in that it provides the system with mechanisms for (1) entertaining multiple response hypotheses given a single input (2) maintaining a coarse prediction history that is local, recent, and cheap, thus providing punctate credit assignment opportunities and finally, (3) revoking parameterizations that are easy to reach, locally stable, but distant from a solution.

Although it is possible to implement the present principle a number of different ways we chose to consider a connection strength to be represented as a distribution of weights with a finite mean and variance (see Figure 1).

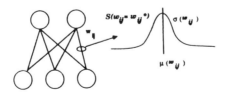

Figure 1: Weights as Sampling Distributions

A forward activation or recognition pass consists of randomly sampling a weight from the existing distribution calculating the dot product and producing an output for that pass.

$$x_i = \sum_j w^*_{ij} y_j \qquad (2)$$

where the sample is found from,

$$S(w_{ij}=w^*_{ij}) = \mu_{w_{ij}} + \sigma_{w_{ij}} \phi(w_{ij};0,1) \qquad (3)$$

Consequently $S(w_{ij}=w^*_{ij})$ is a random variable constructed from a finite mean $\mu_{w_{ij}}$ and standard deviation $\sigma_{w_{ij}}$ based on a normal random variate (ϕ) with mean zero and standard deviation one. Forward recognition passes are therefore one to many mappings, each sampling producing a different weight depending on the mean and standard deviation of the particular connection while the system remains stochastic.

In the present implementation there are actually three separate equations for learning. The mean of the weight distribution is modified as a function of the usual gradient based upon the error, however, note that the random sample point is retained for this gradient calculation and is used to update the mean of the distribution for that synapse.

$$\mu_{w_{ij}}(n+1) = \alpha \left(-\frac{\partial E}{\partial w^*_{ij}}\right) + \mu_{w_{ij}}(n) \qquad (4)$$

Similarly the standard deviation of the weight distribution is modified as a function of the gradient, however, the sign of the gradient is ignored and the update can only increase the variance if an error results. Thus errors immediately increase the variance of the synapse to which they may be attributed.

$$\sigma_{w_{ij}}(n+1) = \beta \left| -\frac{\partial E}{\partial w^*_{ij}} \right| + \sigma_{w_{ij}}(n) \qquad (5)$$

A third and final learning rule determines the decay of the variance of synapses in the network,

$$\sigma_{w_{ij}}(n+1) = \varsigma \sigma_{w_{ij}}(n), \quad \varsigma < 1. \qquad (6)$$

As the system evolves for ς less than one, the last equation of this set guarantees that the variances of all synapses approach zero and that the system itself becomes deterministic prior to solution. For small ς the system evolves very rapidly to deterministic, while larger ςs allow the system to revisit chaotic states as needed during convergence. A simpler implementation of this algorithm involves just the gradient itself as a random variable (hence, the name "stochastic delta rule"), however this approach confounds the growth in variance of the weight distribution with the decay and makes parametric studies more complicated to implement.

The stochastic delta rule implements a local, adaptive simulated annealing (cf. Kirkpatrick, S., Gelatt, C. D. & Veechi, M., 1983) process occuring at different rates in the network dependent on prediction history. Various benchmark tests of this basic algorithm are discussed in Hanson (1990).

1.3   MEIOSIS

In the SDR rule disscussed above, the standard deviation of the weight distributions might be seen as uncertainty measure concerning the weight value and strength. Consequently, changes in the standard deviation can be taken as a measure of the "prediction value" of the connection. Hidden units with significant uncertainty have low prediction value and are performing poorly in reducing errors. If hidden unit uncertainty increases beyond the cumulative weight value or "signal" to that unit then the complexity of the architecture can be traded off with the uncertainty per unit. Consequently, the unit "splits" into two units each copying half the architecture information to each of the new two units.

Networks are initialized with a random mean and variance values (where the variance is started in the interval (10,-10)). Number of hidden units in all problems was initialized at one. The splitting policy is fixed for all problems to occur when both the C.V. (standard deviation relative to the mean) for the input and output to the hidden unit exceeds 100%, that is, when the composite variance of the connection strengths is 100% of the composite mean value of the connection strengths:

$$\frac{\sum\limits_{i}\sigma_{ij}}{\sum\limits_{i}\mu_{ij}}>1.0 \text{ and } \frac{\sum\limits_{k}\sigma_{jk}}{\sum\limits_{k}\mu_{jk}}>1.0$$

Meiosis then proceeds as follows (see Figure 2)

- A forward stochastic pass is made producing an output
- Output is compared to target producing errors which are then used to update the mean and variance of weight.
- The composite input and output variance and means are computed for each hidden units
- For those hidden units whose composite C.V.s are > 1.0 node splitting occurs; half the variance is assigned to each new node with a jittered mean centered at the old mean

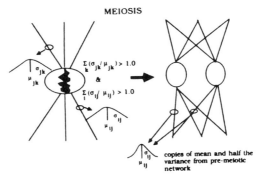

Figure 2: Meiosis

There is no stopping criteria. The network stops creating nodes based on the prediction error and noise level (β,ς) .

1.4   EXAMPLES

1.4.1   Parity Benchmark: Finding the Right number of units

Small parity problems (Exclusive-or and 3BIT parity) were used to explore sensitivity of the noise parameters on node splitting and to benchmark the method. All runs were with fixed learning rate ($\eta = .5$) and momentum ($\alpha = .75$). Low values of zeta ($<.7$) produce minimal or no node splitting, while higher values ($>.99$) seem to produce continuous node spliting without regard to the problem type. Zeta was fixed (.98) and beta, the noise per step parameter was varied between values .1 and .5. The following runs were unaffected by varying beta between these two values.

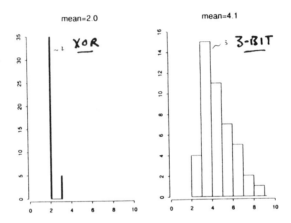

Figure 3: Number of Hidden Units at Convergence

Shown in Figure 3 are 50 runs of Exclusive-or and 50 runs of 3 BIT PARITY. Histograms show for exclusive-or that almost all runs ($>95\%$) ended up with 2 hidden units while for the 3BIT PARITY case most runs produce 3 hidden units, however with considerably more variance, some ending with 2 while a few runs ended with as many 9 hidden units. The next figure (Figure 4) shows histograms for

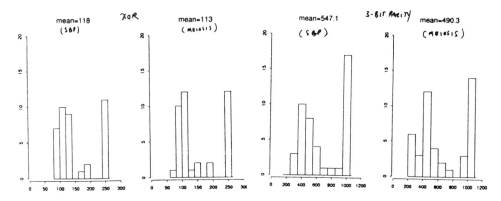

Figure 4: Convergence Times

the convergence time showing a slight advantage in terms of convergence for the meiosis networks for both exclusive-or and 3 BIT PARITY.

1.4.2 Blood NMR Data: Nonlinear Separability

In the Figure 5 data were taken from 10 different continuous kinds of blood measurements, including, total lipid content, cholesterol (mg/dl), High density lipids, low-density lipids, triglyceride, etc as well as some NMR measures. Subjects were previously diagnosed for presence (C) or absence (N) of a blood disease.

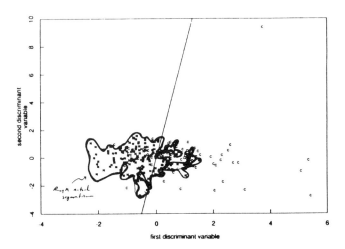

Figure 5: Blood NMR Separability

The data consisted of 238 samples, 146 Ns and 92 Cs. Shown in the adjoining figure is a Perceptron (linear discriminant analysis) response to the data. Each original data point is projected into the first two discriminant variables showing about 75% of the data to be linearly separable (k-k/2 jackknife tests indicate about 52% transfer rates). However, also shown is a rough non-linear envelope around one class of subjects(N) showing the potentially complex decision region for this data.

1.4.3   Meiosis Learning curves

Data was split into two groups (118,120) for learning and transfer tests. Learning curves for both the meiosis network and standard back-propagation are shown in the Figure 6. Also shown in this display is the splitting rate for the meiosis network showing it grow to 7 hidden units and freezing during the first 20 sweeps.

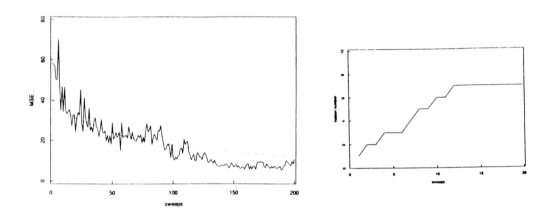

Figure 6: Learning Curves and Splitting Rate

1.4.4   Transfer Rate

Backpropagation was run on the blood data with 0 (perceptron), 2, 3, 4, 5, 6, 7, and 20 hidden units. Shown is the median transfer rate of 3 runs for each hidden unit network size. Transfer rate seemed to hover near 65% as the number of hidden units approached 20. A meiosis network was also run 3 times on the data (using β .40 and ς .98). Transfer Rate shown in Figure 7 was always above 70% at the 7 hidden unit number.

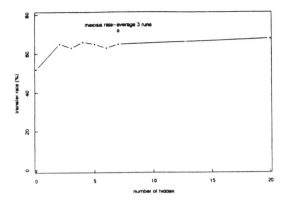

Figure 7: Transfer Rate as a Function of Hidden Unit Number

1.5   Conclusions

The key property of the present scheme is the integration of representational aspects that are sensitive to network prediction and at the same time control the architectural resources of the network. Consequently, with Meiosis networks it is possible to dynamically and opportunistically control network complexity and therefore indirectly its learning efficiency and generalization capacity. Meiosis Networks were defined upon earlier work using local noise injections and noise related learning rules. As learning proceeds the meiosis network can measure the prediction history of particular nodes and if found to be poor, can split the node and opportunistically to increase the resources of the network. Further experiments are required in order to understand different advantages of splitting policies and their affects on generalization and speed of learning.

References

Burns, B. D. The uncertain nervous system, London: Edward Arnold Ltd., 1968.

Cover, T. M. Geometrical and statistical properties of systems of linear inequalities with applications to pattern recognition. IEEE Trans. Elec. Computers, Vol EC-14,3, pp 236-334, 1965.

Hanson, S. J. A stochastic version of the delta rule. Physica D, 1990.

Hanson, S. J. & Burr D. J. Minkowski Back-propagation: learning in connectionist models with non-euclidean error signals, Neural Information Processing Systems, American Institute of Physics 1988.

Hanson, S. J. & Pratt, L. A comparison of different biases for minimal network construction with back-propagation, Advances in Neural Information Processing, D. Touretzsky, Morgan-Kaufmann, 1989.

Kirkpatrick, S., Gelatt, C. D. & Veechi, M. Optimization by simulated annealing, Science, 220, 671-680, 1983.

Tomko, G. J. & Crapper, D. R. Neural variability: Non-stationary response to identical visual stimuli, Brain Research, 79, p 405-418, 1974

The Cocktail Party Problem: Speech/Data Signal Separation Comparison between Backpropagation and SONN

John Kassebaum   Manoel Fernando Tenorio   Christoph Schaefers
jak@ec.ecn.purdue.edu   tenorio@ee.ecn.purdue.edu

Parallel Distributed Structures Laboratory
School of Electrical Engineering
Purdue University
W. Lafayette, IN. 47907

ABSTRACT

This work introduces a new method called Self Organizing Neural Network (SONN) algorithm and compares its performance with Back Propagation in a signal separation application. The problem is to separate two signals; a modem data signal and a male speech signal, added and transmitted through a 4 khz channel. The signals are sampled at 8 khz, and using supervised learning, an attempt is made to reconstruct them. The SONN is an algorithm that constructs its own network topology during training, which is shown to be much smaller than the BP network, faster to trained, and free from the trial-and-error network design that characterize BP.

1. INTRODUCTION

The research in Neural Networks has witnessed major changes in algorithm design focus, motivated by the limitations perceived in the algorithms available at the time. With the extensive work performed in that last few years using multilayered networks, it was soon discovered that these networks present limitations in tasks that: (a) are difficult to determine problem complexity a priori, and thus design network of the correct size, (b) training not only takes prohibitively long times, but requires a large number of samples as well as fine parameter adjustment, without guarantee of convergence, (c) such networks do not handle the system identification task efficiently for systems whose time varying structure changes radically, and, (d) the trained network is little more than a black box of weights and connections, revealing little about the problem structure; being hard to find the justification for the algorithm weight choice, or an explanation for the output decisions based on an input vector. We believe that this need is sparking the emergence of a third generation of algorithms to address such questions.

2. THE SELF ORGANIZING NEURAL NETWORK ALGORITHM

2.1 SELF ORGANIZING NETWORK FAMILY

A family of Self Organizing Structure (SOS) Algorithms can be readily designed with our present knowledge, and can be used as a tool to research the motivating questions. Each individual algorithm in this family might have different characteristics, which are summarized in the following list:

- A search strategy for the structure of the final model

- A rule of connectivity

- A performance criteria

- A transfer function set with appropriate training rule

As we will show here, by varying each one of these components, a different behavior of the algorithm can be imposed.

Self organizing structure algorithms are not new. These algorithms have been present in the statistical literature since the mid 70's in a very different context. As far as we know, the first one to propose such an algorithm was Ivahnenko [1971] which was followed by a host of variations on that original proposal [Duffy&Franklin, 1975; Ikeda, et al., 1976; Tomura&Kondo, 1980; Farlow,1989]. Ivahnenko's subfamily of algorithms (GMDH - Group Method of Data Handling) can be characterized in our classification by the same four-tuple criterion: (1) gradient descent local search, (2) creation of regular feedforward layers with elements pairwisely connected, (3) least-mean-squares estimation, and (4) a single element set comprised of a 2 order bivariate function.

Here we want to present our subfamily (SON - Self Organizing Networks) of the SOS algorithm family, characterized differently by: (1) global optimization search, (2) arbitrary connectivity based on an arbitrary number of neuron inputs, (3) Structure Estimation Criteria (SEC) (a variation of Rissanen's [1983]. Minimum Description Length Criteria, extended to the hierarchical case), and, (4) for training speed, activation functions are restricted to be linear on the parameters and the output functions need to be invertible, no other restriction is imposed in kind or number. The particular algorithm presented here is called the Self Organizing

Neural Network (SONN) [Tenorio&Lee, 1988,1989; Tenorio 1990 a,b]. It was composed of: (1) a graph synthesis procedure based on Simulated Annealing [Kirkpatrick et al., 1983]; (2) two input neurons that are arbitrarily connected; (3) the Structure Estimation Criteria; and, (4) a set of all polynomials that are special cases of 2nd order bivariates and inclusive, followed or not by sigmoid functions. The SONN algorithm performs a search in the model space by the construction of hypersurfaces. A network of nodes, each node representing a hypersurface, is organized to be an approximate model of the real system. Below, the components of SONN are discussed.

2.2 THE ALGORITHM STRUCTURE

The mechanisms behind the algorithm works as follows. First, create a set of terminals which are the output of the nodes available for connection to other nodes. This set is initialized with the output of the input nodes; in other words, the input variables themselves. From this set, with uniform probability, select a subset (2 in our case) of terminals, and used them as inputs to the new node. To construct the new node, select all the function of the set of prototype functions (activation followed by output function), and evaluate the SEC using the terminals as inputs. Selecting the best function, test for the acceptance of that node according to the Simulated Annealing move acceptance criterion. If the new node is accepted, place its output in the set of terminals and iterate until the optimum model is found. The details of the algorithm can be found in [Tenorio&Lee, 1989].

2.2.1 The Prototype Functions

Consider the Mahalanobis distance:

$$y_j = \text{sig}\{(\mathbf{x} - \mu)\mathcal{X}^{-1} \,(\mathbf{x} - \mu)^t\} \tag{1}$$

This distance can be rewritten as a second order function, whose parameters are the indirect representation of the covariance matrix $\mathcal{X}$ and the mean vector μ. This function is linear in the parameters, which makes it easy to perform training, and it is the function with the smallest degree of non linearity; only simpler is the linear case. Interestingly enough, this is the same prototype function used in the GMDH algorithm to form the Ivahnenko polynomial for apparently completely different reasons. In the SONN, this function is taken to be 2-input and all its possible variations (32) by setting parameters to zero are included in the set of activation functions. This set combined with the output function (the identify or sigmoid), for the set of prototype functions, used by the algorithm in the node construction.

2.2.2 Evaluation of the Model Based on the MDL Criterion

The selection rule of the neuron transfer function was based on a modification of the Minimal Description Length (MDL) information criterion. In [Rissanen, 1978], the principle of minimal description for statistical estimation was developed. The reason for the choice of such a criterion is that, in general the accuracy of the model can increase at the expense of simplicity in the number of parameters. The increase of complexity might also be accompanied by the overfitting of the model. To overcome this problem, the MDL provides a trade-off between the accuracy and the complexity of the model by including the structure estimation term of the final model. The final model (with the minimal MDL) is optimum in the sense of being a consistent estimate of the number of parameters while achieving the minimum error [Rissanen, 1980]. Given a sequence of observations $X_1, X_2, ..., X_N$ from the random variable X, the dominant term of the MDL in [Rissanen, 1978] is:

$$MDL = -\log f(x \,|\, \theta) + 0.5 \ k \log N \qquad (2)$$

where $f(x \,|\, \theta)$ is the estimated probability density function of the model, k is the number of parameters, and N is the number of observations. The first term is actually the negative of the maximum likelihood (ML) with respect to the estimated parameter. The second term describes the structure of the models and it is used as a penalty for the complexity of the model.

3. EXAMPLE - THE COCKTAIL PARTY PROBLEM

The Cocktail Party Problem is the name given to the phenomenon that people can understand and track speech in a noisy environment, even when the noise is being made by other speakers. A simpler version of this problem is presented here: a 4 khz channel is excited with male speech and modem data additively at the same time. The task presented to the network is to separate both signals.

To compare the accuracy of the signal separation between the SONN and the Back Propagation algorithms a normalized RMSE is used as a performance index:

$$\text{normalized RMSE} = \frac{\text{RMSE}}{\text{StandardDevision}} \qquad (3)$$

3.1. EXPERIMENTS WITH BACK PROPAGATION

In order to design a filter using Back Propagation for this task, several architectures were considered. Since the input and output to the problem are time series, and such architectures are static, modifications to the original paradigm is required to deal with the time dimension. Several proposals have been made in this respect: tapped delay filters, recurrent architectures, low pass filter transfer functions, modified discriminant functions, and self excitatory connections (see [Wah, Tenorio, Merha, and Fortes, 90]). The best result for this task was achieved by two tapped delay lines in the input layer, one for the input signal, the other for the output signal. The network was trained to recognize the speech signal from the mixed signal. The mixed signal had a speech to modem data energy ratio of 4:1, or 2.5 dB.

The network was designed to be a feedforward with 42 inputs (21 delayed versions of the input signal, and similarly for the output signal), 15 hidden units, and a single output unit. The network was trained with a single phoneme, taking about

10 cpu-hours on a Sequent machine. The network when presented with the trained phoneme added to the modem data, produced a speech reconstructability error equal to a nRMSE of 0.910. Previously several different configurations of the network were tried as well as different network parameters, and signal ratios of 1:1; all with poor results. Few networks actually converged to a final solution. A major problem with the BP architecture is that it can perfectly filter the signal in the first few samples, just to later demonstrate increasing amounts of cumulative errors; this instability may be fruit of the recurring nature of the architecture, and suboptimal weight training (Figure 2). The difficulty in finding and fine tuning the architecture, the training convergence, and time requirements led us to later stop pursuing the design of these filters with Back Propagation strategies.

3.2. EXPERIMENTS WITH SONN

At that time, the SONN algorithm had been successfully used for identification and prediction tasks [Tenorio&Lee; 88,89,90]. To make the task more realistic with possible practical utilization of this filter (Data-Over-Voice Circuits), the energy ratio between the voice and the modem data was reduced to 1:1, or 0 dB. A tapped delay line containing 21 delayed versions of the mixed signal was presented to the algorithm. Two sets of prototype functions were used, and both contained the full set of 32 variations of 2nd order bivariates. The first set had the identity (SONN-I experiments) and the second had a sigmoid (SONN-SIG experiments) as the output function for each node.

SONN-I created 370 nodes, designing a final model with 5 nodes. The final symbolic transfer function which represents the closed form function of the network was extracted. Using a Gould Powernode 9080, this search took 98.6 sec, with an average of 3.75 nodes/sec. The final model had an nRMSE of 0.762 (Figure 3) for reconstructed speech with the same BP data; with 19 weights. Training with the modem signal led to nRMSE of 0.762 (Figure 4) for the BP data. A search using the SONN-SIG model was allowed to generate 1000 nodes, designing a final model with 5 nodes. With the same computer, the second search took 283.42 sec, with an average 3.5 nodes/sec. The final model had an nRMSE comparable to the SONN-I (better by 5-10%); with 20 weights. The main characteristics of both signals were captured, specially if one looks at the plots and notices the same order of nonlinearity between the real and estimated signals (no over or under estimation). Because of the forgiving nature of the human speech perception, the voice after reconstruction, although sightly muffled, remains of good quality; and the reconstructed modem signal can be used to reconstruct the original digital message, without much further post processing. The SONN does not present cumulative errors during the reconstruction, and when test with different (unseen, from the same speaker) speech data, performed as well as with the test data. We have yet to fully explore the implication of that to different speakers and with speaker of different gender or language. These results will be reported elsewhere.

4. COMPARISON BETWEEN THE TWO ALGORITHMS

Below we outline the comparison between the two algorithms drawn from our experience with this signal separation problem.

4.1. ADVANTAGES

The following were advantages of the SONN approach over the BP paradigm. The most striking difference was found in the training times, and in the amount of data required for training. The BP required 42 inputs (memories), where as the SONN functioned with 21 inputs, actually using as few as 4 in the final model (input variable selection). The SONN removed the problem of model estimation and architecture design. The number of connections with the SONN models is as low as 8 for 20 weights (relevant connections), as compared with 645 connections and weights for the BP model. The accuracy and complexity of the model can be trade for learning time as in BP, but the models that were more accurate also required less parameters than BP. The networks are not required to be homogeneous, thus contributing to smaller models as well. Above all, the SONN can produce both the C code for the network as well as the sequence of individual node symbolic functions; the SONN-I can also produce the symbolic representation of the closed form function of the entire network.

4.2. DISADVANTAGES

Certain disadvantages of using self-organizing topology networks with stochastic optimization algorithms were also apparent. The learning time of the SONN is non deterministic, and depends on the model complexity and starting point. Those are characteristic of the Simulated Annealing (SA) algorithm. These disadvantages are also present in the BP approach for different reasons. The connectivity of the model is not known a priori, which does not permit hardware implementation algorithms with direct connectivity emulation. Because the SONN selects nodes from a growing set with uniform probability, the probability of choosing a pair of nodes decreases with the inverse of the square of the number of nodes. Thus algorithm effectiveness decreases with processing time. Careful plotting of the SEC, nRMSE, and complexity trajectories during training reveal that the first 10% of the processing time achieves 90% of the final steady state values. Biasing the node selection procedure might be an alternative to modify this behavior. Simulated Annealing also required parametric tuning of the algorithm by setting" the initial and final temperature, the duration of the search at each temperature and the temperature decay. Alternative algorithms such as A* might produce a better alternative to stochastic search algorithms.

5. CONCLUSION AND FUTURE WORK

In this study, we proposed a new approach for the signal separation filter design based on a flexible, self-organizi   neural network (SONN) algorithm. The variable structure provides the oppo: nity to search and construct the optimal model based on input-output observations. The hierarchical v   ion of the MDL, ' 'led the Structure Estimation Criteria, was used to guide   trade-off betwee   the model complexity and the accuracy of the estimation. The SONN approach demonstrates potential usefulness as a tool for non linear signal processing function design.

We would like to explore the use of high level knowledge for function selection and connectivity. Also, the issues involving estimator and deterministic searches are still open. Currently we are exploring the use of SONN for digital circuit synthesis, and studying how close the architecture generated here can approach the design of natural structures when performing similar functions. More classification problems, and problems involving dynamical systems (adaptive control and signal processing) need to be explored to give us the experience needed to tackle the problems for which it was designed.

6. NOTE

The results reported here were originally intended for two papers accepted for presentation at the NIPS'89. The organizing committee asked us to fuse the into a single presentation for organizational purposes. In the limited time and the small space allocated for the presentation of these results, we sought a compromise between the reporting of the results and the description and comments on our experience with the algorithm. The interested reader should look at the other references about the SONN listed here and forthcoming papers.

REFERENCE

A. G. Ivakhnenko, (1971) "Polynomial Theory of Complex Systems," IEEE Trans. S.M.C, Vol. SMC-1, no.4, pp. 364-378, Oct.

J. J. Duffy and M. A. Franklin, (1975) "A Learning Identification Algorithm and its Application to an Environmental System," IEEE Trans. S. M. C., Vol. SMC-5, no. 2, pp. 226-240.

S. Ikeda, M. Ochiai and Y. Sawarogi, (1976) "Sequential GMDH Algorithm and its Application to River Flow Prediction," IEEE Trans S.M.C., Vol. SMC-6, no.7, pp. 473-479, July.

H. Tamura, T. Kondo, (1980) "Heuristics Free Group Method of Data Handling Algorithm of Generating Optimal Partial Polynomials with Application to Air Pollution Predication," Int. J. Systems Sci., 11,no.9, pp. 1095-1111.

J. Rissanen (1978) "Modeling by Shortest Data Description," Automatica, Vol.14, pp. 465-471.

J. Rissanen, (1980) "Consistent Order Estimation of Autoregression Processes by Shortest Description of Data," Analysis and Optimation of Stochastic System, Jacobs et al eds. NY Academic.

J. Rissanen, (1983) "A Universal Prior for Integers and Estimation by Minimum Description Length," Annuals of Statistics, Vol.11, no. 2, pp. 416-431.

S.Kirkpatrick, C.D. Gelatt, M.P. Vecchi, (1983) "Optimization by Simulated Annealing," Science, vol.220, pp. 671-680, May.

M. F. M. Tenorio and W.-T. Lee, (1988) "Self-Organizing Neural Network for the Identification Problem," *Advances in Neural Information Processing Systems I,* David S. Touretzky ed., pp. 57-64.

M. F. M. Tenorio and W.-T. Lee, (1989) "Self-Organizing Neural Network for the

Identification Problem," School of Electrical Engineering, Purdue University, Tech Report TR-EE 89-20, June.

M. F. M. Tenorio and W. -T. Lee, (1990) "Self-Organizing Network for the Identification Problem," (expanded) IEEE Trans. on the Neural Networks, to appear.

M. F. M. Tenorio, (1990) "The Self-Organizing Neural Network Algorithm: Adapting Topology for Optimum Supervised Learning," IEEE Hawaii Conference in Systems Science, 22, January.

M. F. Tenorio, (1990) "Self-Organizing Neural Network for the Signal Separation Problem," to be submitted.

B. Wah, M. Tenorio, P. Mehra, J. Fortes, (1990) *Artificial Neural Networks: Theory, Algorithms, Application and Implementations,*" IEEE press.

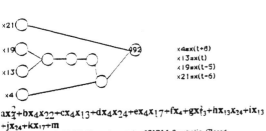

$$x_4 = x(t+8)$$
$$x_{13} = x(t)$$
$$x_{19} = x(t-5)$$
$$x_{21} = x(t-6)$$

$$ax_7^2 + bx_4x_{22} + cx_4x_{13} + dx_4x_{24} + ex_4x_{17} + fx_4 + gx_{13}^2 + hx_{13}x_{24} + ix_{13} + jx_{24} + kx_{17} + m$$

Figure 1: The SONN-SIG Network and the SONN-I Symbolic Closed Form

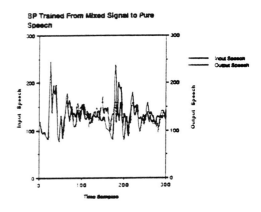

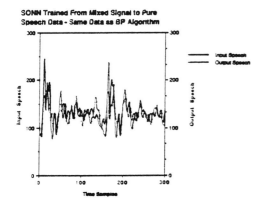

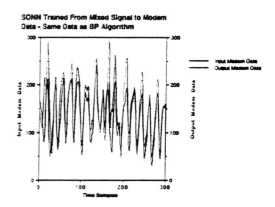

Generalization and scaling in reinforcement learning

David H. Ackley
Michael L. Littman
Cognitive Science Research Group
Bellcore
Morristown, NJ 07960

ABSTRACT

In *associative reinforcement learning*, an environment generates input vectors, a learning system generates possible output vectors, and a reinforcement function computes feedback signals from the input-output pairs. The task is to discover and remember input-output pairs that generate rewards. Especially difficult cases occur when rewards are rare, since the expected time for any algorithm can grow exponentially with the size of the problem. Nonetheless, if a reinforcement function possesses regularities, and a learning algorithm exploits them, learning time can be reduced below that of non-generalizing algorithms. This paper describes a neural network algorithm called *complementary reinforcement back-propagation* (*CRBP*), and reports simulation results on problems designed to offer differing opportunities for generalization.

1   REINFORCEMENT LEARNING REQUIRES SEARCH

Reinforcement learning (Sutton, 1984; Barto & Anandan, 1985; Ackley, 1988; Allen, 1989) requires more from a learner than does the more familiar supervised learning paradigm. Supervised learning supplies the correct answers to the learner, whereas reinforcement learning requires the learner to *discover* the correct outputs before they can be stored. The reinforcement paradigm divides neatly into search and learning aspects: When rewarded the system makes internal adjustments to learn the discovered input-output pair; when punished the system makes internal adjustments to search elsewhere.

1.1   MAKING REINFORCEMENT INTO ERROR

Following work by Anderson (1986) and Williams (1988), we extend the backprop-agation algorithm to associative reinforcement learning. Start with a "garden variety" backpropagation network: A vector i of n binary input units propagates through zero or more layers of hidden units, ultimately reaching a vector s of m sigmoid units, each taking continuous values in the range (0,1). Interpret each s_j as the *probability* that an associated random bit o_j takes on value 1. Let us call the continuous, deterministic vector s the *search vector* to distinguish it from the stochastic binary output vector o.

Given an input vector, we forward propagate to produce a search vector s, and then perform m independent Bernoulli trials to produce an output vector o. The $i - o$ pair is evaluated by the reinforcement function and reward or punishment ensues. Suppose reward occurs. We therefore want to make o more likely given i. Backpropagation will do just that if we take o as the desired target to produce an error vector $(o - s)$ and adjust weights normally.

Now suppose punishment occurs, indicating o does not correspond with i. By choice of error vector, backpropagation allows us to push the search vector in any direction; which way should we go? In absence of problem-specific information, we cannot pick an appropriate direction with certainty. Any decision will involve assumptions. A very minimal "don't be like o" assumption—employed in Anderson (1986), Williams (1988), and Ackley (1989)—pushes s directly *away from* o by taking $(s - o)$ as the error vector. A slightly stronger "be like not-o" assumption—employed in Barto & Anandan (1985) and Ackley (1987)—pushes s directly *toward the complement of* o by taking $((1 - o) - s)$ as the error vector. Although the two approaches always agree on the signs of the error terms, they differ in magnitudes. In this work, we explore the second possibility, embodied in an algorithm called *complementary reinforcement back-propagation* (*CRBP*).

Figure 1 summarizes the *CRBP* algorithm. The algorithm in the figure reflects three modifications to the basic approach just sketched. First, in step 2, instead of using the s_j's directly as probabilities, we found it advantageous to "stretch" the values using a parameter ν. When $\nu < 1$, it is not necessary for the s_j's to reach zero or one to produce a deterministic output. Second, in step 6, we found it important to use a smaller learning rate for punishment compared to reward. Third, consider step 7: Another forward propagation is performed, another stochastic binary output vector o^* is generated (using the procedure from step 2), and o^* is compared to o. If they are identical and punishment occurred, or if they are different and reward occurred, then another error vector is generated and another weight update is performed. This loop continues until a different output is generated (in the case of failure) or until the original output is regenerated (in the case of success). This modification improved performance significantly, and added only a small percentage to the total number of weight updates performed.

0. Build a back propagation network with input dimensionality n and output dimensionality m. Let $t = 0$ and $t_e = 0$.
1. Pick random $i \in 2^n$ and forward propagate to produce s_j's.
2. Generate a binary output vector o. Given a uniform random variable $\xi \in [0, 1]$ and parameter $0 < \nu \le 1$,

$$o_j = \begin{cases} 1, & \text{if } \left(s_j - \frac{1}{2}\right)/\nu + \frac{1}{2} \ge \xi; \\ 0, & \text{otherwise.} \end{cases}$$

3. Compute reinforcement $r = f(i, o)$. Increment t. If $r < 0$, let $t_e = t$.
4. Generate output errors e_j. If $r > 0$, let $t_j = o_j$, otherwise let $t_j = 1 - o_j$. Let $e_j = (t_j - s_j)s_j(1 - s_j)$.
5. Backpropagate errors.
6. Update weights. $\Delta w_{jk} = \eta e_k s_j$, using $\eta = \eta_+$ if $r \ge 0$, and $\eta = \eta_-$ otherwise, with parameters $\eta_+, \eta_- > 0$.
7. Forward propagate again to produce new s_j's. Generate temporary output vector o^*. If $(r > 0$ and $o^* \ne o)$ or $(r < 0$ and $o^* = o)$, go to 4.
8. If $t_e \ll t$, exit returning t_e, else go to 1.

Figure 1: Complementary Reinforcement Back Propagation—CRBP

2   ON-LINE GENERALIZATION

When there are many possible outputs and correct pairings are rare, the computational cost associated with the search for the correct answers can be profound. The search for correct pairings will be accelerated if the search strategy can effectively *generalize* the reinforcement received on one input to others. The speed of an algorithm on a given problem relative to non-generalizing algorithms provides a measure of generalization that we call *on-line generalization*.

0. Let x be an array of length 2^n. Set the $x[i]$ to random numbers from 0 to $2^m - 1$. Let $t = t_e = 0$.
1. Pick a random input $i \in 2^n$.
2. Compute reinforcement $r = f(i, x[i])$. Increment t.
3. If $r < 0$ let $x[i] = (x[i] + 1) \bmod 2^m$, and let $t_e = t$.
4. If $t_e \ll t$ exit returning t_e, else go to 1.

Figure 2: The Table Lookup Reference Algorithm $T_{\text{ref}}(f, n, m)$

Consider the table-lookup algorithm $T_{\text{ref}}(f, n, m)$ summarized in Figure 2. In this algorithm, a separate storage location is used for each possible input. This prevents the memorization of one $i - o$ pair from interfering with any other. Similarly, the selection of a candidate output vector depends only on the slot of the table corresponding to the given input. The learning speed of T_{ref} depends only on the input and output dimensionalities and the number of correct outputs associated with each input. When a problem possesses n input bits and n output bits, and there is only one correct output vector for each input vector, T_{ref} runs in about 4^n time (counting each input-output judgment as one.) In such cases one expects to take at least 2^{n-1} just to find *one* correct $i-o$ pair, so exponential time cannot be avoided without *a priori* information. How does a generalizing algorithm such as $CRBP$ compare to T_{ref}?

3   SIMULATIONS ON SCALABLE PROBLEMS

We have tested $CRBP$ on several simple problems designed to offer varying degrees and types of generalization. In all of the simulations in this section, the following details apply: Input and output bit counts are equal (n). Parameters are dependent on n but independent of the reinforcement function f. η_+ is hand-picked for each n,[1] $\eta_- = \eta_+/10$ and $\nu = 0.5$. All data points are medians of five runs. The stopping criterion $t_e \ll t$ is interpreted as $t_e + \max(2000, 2^{n+1}) < t$. The fit lines in the figures are least squares solutions to $a \times b^n$, to two significant digits.

As a notational convenience, let $c = \frac{1}{n} \sum_{j=1}^{n} i_j$ — the fraction of ones in the input.

3.1 n-MAJORITY

Consider this "majority rules" problem: [if $c > \frac{1}{2}$ then $o = 1^n$ else $o = 0^n$]. The $i-o$ mapping is many-to-1. This problem provides an opportunity for what Anderson (1986) called "output generalization": since there are only two correct output states, every pair of output bits are completely correlated in the cases when reward occurs.

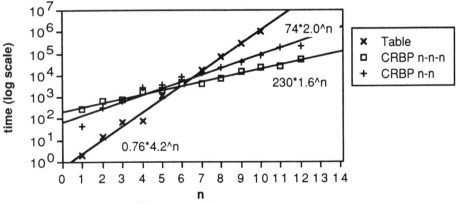

Figure 3: The n-majority problem

Figure 3 displays the simulation results. Note that although T_{ref} is faster than $CRBP$ at small values of n, $CRBP$'s slower growth rate $(1.6^n$ vs $4.2^n)$ allows it to cross over and begin outperforming T_{ref} at about 6 bits. Note also—in violation of

---

[1]For $n = 1$ to 12, we used $\eta_+ = \{2.000, 1.550, 1.130, 0.979, 0.783, 0.709, 0.623, 0.525, 0.280, 0.219, 0.170, 0.121\}$.

some conventional wisdom—that although n-majority is a linearly separable problem, the performance of *CRBP* with hidden units is better than without. Hidden units can be helpful—even on linearly separable problems—when there are opportunities for output generalization.

3.2 n-COPY AND THE 2^k-ATTRACTORS FAMILY

As a second example, consider the n-copy problem: $[o = i]$. The $i-o$ mapping is now 1-1, and the values of output bits in rewarding states are completely uncorrelated, but the value of each output bit is completely correlated with the value of the corresponding input bit. Figure 4 displays the simulation results. Once again, at

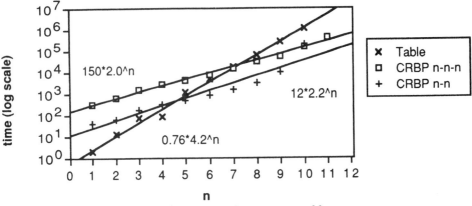

Figure 4: The n-copy problem

low values of n, T_{ref} is faster, but *CRBP* rapidly overtakes T_{ref} as n increases. In n-copy, unlike n-majority, *CRBP* performs better without hidden units.

The n-majority and n-copy problems are extreme cases of a spectrum. n-majority can be viewed as a "2-attractors" problem in that there are only two correct outputs—all zeros and all ones—and the correct output is the one that i is closer to in hamming distance. By dividing the input and output bits into two groups and performing the majority function independently on each group, one generates a "4-attractors" problem. In general, by dividing the input and output bits into $1 \leq k \leq n$ groups, one generates a "2^k-attractors" problem. When $k = 1$, n-majority results, and when $k = n$, n-copy results.

Figure 5 displays simulation results on the $n = 8$-bit problems generated when k is varied from 1 to n. The advantage of hidden units for low values of k is evident, as is the advantage of "shortcut connections" (direct input-to-output weights) for larger values of k. Note also that combination of both hidden units and shortcut connections performs better than either alone.

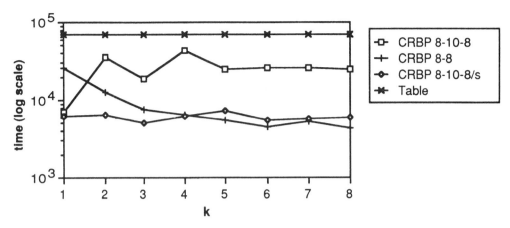

Figure 5: The 2^k-attractors family at $n = 8$

3.3 n-EXCLUDED MIDDLE

All of the functions considered so far have been linearly separable. Consider this "folded majority" function: [if $\frac{1}{3} < c \leq \frac{2}{3}$ then $o = 0^n$ else $o = 1^n$]. Now, like n-majority, there are only two rewarding output states, but the determination of which output state is correct is not linearly separable in the input space. When $n = 2$, the n-excluded middle problem yields the EQV (i.e., the complement of XOR) function, but whereas functions such as n-parity [if nc is even then $o = 0^n$ else $o = 1^n$] get more non-linear with increasing n, n-excluded middle does not.

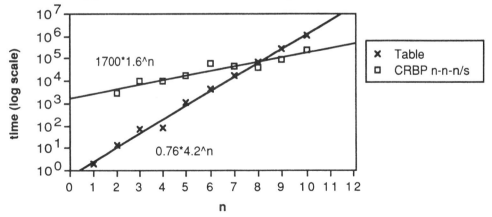

Figure 6: The n-excluded middle problem

Figure 6 displays the simulation results. *CRBP* is slowed somewhat compared to the linearly separable problems, yielding a higher "cross over point" of about 8 bits.

4   STRUCTURING DEGENERATE OUTPUT SPACES

All of the scaling problems in the previous section are designed so that there is a single correct output for each possible input. This allows for difficult problems even at small sizes, but it rules out an important aspect of generalizing algorithms for associative reinforcement learning: If there are multiple satisfactory outputs for given inputs, a generalizing algorithm may *impose structure* on the mapping it produces.

We have two demonstrations of this effect, "Bit Count" and "Inverse Arithmetic." The Bit Count problem simply states that the number of 1-bits in the output should equal the number of 1-bits in the input. When $n = 9$, T_{ref} rapidly finds solutions involving hundreds of different output patterns. $CRBP$ is slower—especially with relatively few hidden units—but it regularly finds solutions involving just 10 output patterns that form a sequence from 0^9 to 1^9 with one bit changing per step.

$$
\begin{array}{llll}
0 + 0 \times 4 = 0 & 0 + 2 \times 4 = 8 & 0 + 4 \times 4 = 16 & 0 + 6 \times 4 = 24 \\
1 + 0 \times 4 = 1 & 1 + 2 \times 4 = 9 & 1 + 4 \times 4 = 17 & 1 + 6 \times 4 = 25 \\
2 + 0 \times 4 = 2 & 2 + 2 \times 4 = 10 & 2 + 4 \times 4 = 18 & 2 + 6 \times 4 = 26 \\
3 + 0 \times 4 = 3 & 3 + 2 \times 4 = 11 & 3 + 4 \times 4 = 19 & 3 + 6 \times 4 = 27 \\
\\
4 + 0 \times 4 = 4 & 4 + 2 \times 4 = 12 & 4 + 4 \times 4 = 20 & 4 + 6 \times 4 = 28 \\
5 + 0 \times 4 = 5 & 5 + 2 \times 4 = 13 & 5 + 4 \times 4 = 21 & 5 + 6 \times 4 = 29 \\
6 + 0 \times 4 = 6 & 6 + 2 \times 4 = 14 & 6 + 4 \times 4 = 22 & 6 + 6 \times 4 = 30 \\
7 + 0 \times 4 = 7 & 7 + 2 \times 4 = 15 & 7 + 4 \times 4 = 23 & 7 + 6 \times 4 = 31 \\
\\
2 + 2 - 4 = 0 & 2 + 2 + 4 = 8 & 6 + 6 + 4 = 16 & 0 + 6 \times 4 = 24 \\
3 + 2 - 4 = 1 & 3 + 2 + 4 = 9 & 7 + 6 + 4 = 17 & 1 + 6 \times 4 = 25 \\
2 + 2 \div 4 = 2 & 2 + 2 \times 4 = 10 & 2 + 4 \times 4 = 18 & 2 + 6 \times 4 = 26 \\
3 + 2 \div 4 = 3 & 3 + 2 \times 4 = 11 & 3 + 4 \times 4 = 19 & 3 + 6 \times 4 = 27 \\
\\
6 + 2 - 4 = 4 & 6 + 2 + 4 = 12 & 4 \times 4 + 4 = 20 & 4 + 6 \times 4 = 28 \\
7 + 2 - 4 = 5 & 7 + 2 + 4 = 13 & 5 + 4 \times 4 = 21 & 5 + 6 \times 4 = 29 \\
6 + 2 \div 4 = 6 & 6 + 2 \times 4 = 14 & 6 + 4 \times 4 = 22 & 6 + 6 \times 4 = 30 \\
7 + 2 \div 4 = 7 & 7 + 2 \times 4 = 15 & 7 + 4 \times 4 = 23 & 7 + 6 \times 4 = 31 \\
\end{array}
$$

Figure 7: Sample $CRBP$ solutions to Inverse Arithmetic

The Inverse Arithmetic problem can be summarized as follows: Given $i \in 2^5$, find $x, y, z \in 2^3$ and $\circ, \diamond \in \{+_{(00)}, -_{(01)}, \times_{(10)}, \div_{(11)}\}$ such that $x \circ y \diamond z = i$. In all there are 13 bits of output, interpreted as three 3-bit binary numbers and two 2-bit operators, and the task is to pick an output that evaluates to the given 5-bit binary input under the usual rules: operator precedence, left-right evaluation, integer division, and division by zero fails.

As shown in Figure 7, $CRBP$ sometimes solves this problem essentially by discovering positional notation, and sometimes produces less-globally structured solutions, particularly as outputs for lower-valued i's, which have a wider range of solutions.

5   CONCLUSIONS

Some basic concepts of supervised learning appear in different guises when the paradigm of reinforcement learning is applied to large output spaces. Rather than a "learning phase" followed by a "generalization test," in reinforcement learning the *search problem is a generalization test*, performed simultaneously with learning. Information is put to work as soon as it is acquired.

The problem of of "overfitting" or "learning the noise" seems to be less of an issue, since learning stops automatically when consistent success is reached. In experiments not reported here we gradually increased the number of hidden units on the 8-bit copy problem from 8 to 25 without observing the performance decline associated with "too many free parameters."

The 2^k-attractors (and 2^k-folds—generalizing Excluded Middle) families provide a starter set of sample problems with easily understood and distinctly different extreme cases.

In degenerate output spaces, generalization decisions can be seen directly in the discovered mapping. Network analysis is not required to "see how the net does it."

The possibility of ultimately generating useful new knowledge via reinforcement learning algorithms cannot be ruled out.

References

Ackley, D.H. (1987) *A connectionist machine for genetic hillclimbing.* Boston, MA: Kluwer Academic Press.

Ackley, D.H. (1989) Associative learning via inhibitory search. In D.S. Touretzky (ed.), *Advances in Neural Information Processing Systems 1*, 20–28. San Mateo, CA: Morgan Kaufmann.

Allen, R.B. (1989) Developing agent models with a neural reinforcement technique. *IEEE Systems, Man, and Cybernetics Conference.* Cambridge, MA.

Anderson, C.W. (1986) Learning and problem solving with multilayer connectionist systems. University of Mass. Ph.D. dissertation. COINS TR 86–50. Amherst, MA.

Barto, A.G. (1985) Learning by statistical cooperation of self-interested neuron-like computing elements. *Human Neurobiology*, 4:229–256.

Barto, A.G., & Anandan, P. (1985) Pattern recognizing stochastic learning automata. *IEEE Transactions on Systems, Man, and Cybernetics, 15*, 360–374.

Rumelhart, D.E., Hinton, G.E., & Williams, R.J. (1986) Learning representations by back-propagating errors. *Nature, 323*, 533–536.

Sutton, R.S. (1984) Temporal credit assignment in reinforcement learning. University of Mass. Ph.D. dissertation. COINS TR 84–2. Amherst, MA.

Williams, R.J. (1988) Toward a theory of reinforcement–learning connectionist systems. College of Computer Science of Northeastern University Technical Report NU–CCS–88–3. Boston, MA.

The 'Moving Targets' Training Algorithm

Richard Rohwer
Centre for Speech Technology Research
Edinburgh University
80, South Bridge
Edinburgh EH1 1HN SCOTLAND

ABSTRACT

A simple method for training the dynamical behavior of a neural network is derived. It is applicable to any training problem in discrete-time networks with arbitrary feedback. The algorithm resembles back-propagation in that an error function is minimized using a gradient-based method, but the optimization is carried out in the hidden part of state space either instead of, or in addition to weight space. Computational results are presented for some simple dynamical training problems, one of which requires response to a signal 100 time steps in the past.

1 INTRODUCTION

This paper presents a minimization-based algorithm for training the dynamical behavior of a discrete-time neural network model. The central idea is to treat hidden nodes as target nodes with variable training data. These "moving targets" are varied during the minimization process. Werbos (Werbos, 1983) used the term "moving targets" to describe the qualitative idea that a network should set itself intermediate objectives, and vary these objectives as information is accumulated on their attainability and their usefulness for achieving overall objectives. The (coincidentally) like-named algorithm presented here can be regarded as a quantitative realization of this qualitative idea.

The literature contains several temporal training algorithms based on minimization of an error measure with respect to the weights. This type of method includes the straightforward extension of the back-propagation method to back-propagation through time (Rumelhart, 1986), the methods of Rohwer and Forrest (Rohwer, 1987), Pearlmutter (Pearlmutter, 1989), and the forward propagation of derivatives (Robinson, 1988, Williams 1989a, Williams 1989b, Kuhn, 1990). A careful comparison of moving targets with back-propagation in time and teacher forcing appears in (Rohwer, 1989b). Although applicable only to fixed-point training, the algorithms of Almeida (Almeida, 1989) and Pineda (Pineda, 1988) have much in common with these dynamical training algorithms. The formal relationship between these and the method of Rohwer and Forrest is spelled out in (Rohwer 1989a).

2 NOTATION AND STATEMENT OF THE TRAINING PROBLEM

Consider a neural network model with arbitrary feedback as a dynamical system in which the dynamical variables x_{it} change with time according to a dynamical law given by the mapping

$$\left. \begin{array}{rcl} x_{it} & = & \sum_j w_{ij} f(x_{j,t-1}) \quad i > 0 \\ x_{0t} & = & \text{bias constant} \end{array} \right\} \tag{1}$$

unless specified otherwise. The *weights* w_{ij} are arbitrary parameters representing the connection strength from node j to node i. f is an arbitrary differentiable function. Let us call any given variable x_{it} the *"activation"* on node i at time t. It represents the total input into node i at time t. Let the *"output"* of each node be denoted by $y_{it} = f(x_{it})$. Let node 0 be a *"bias node"*, assigned a positive constant activation so that the weights w_{i0} can be interpreted as activation thresholds.

In normal back-propagation, a network architecture is defined which divides the network into input, hidden, and target nodes. The moving targets algorithm makes itself applicable to arbitrary training problems by defining analogous concepts in a manner dependent upon the training data, but independent of the network architecture. Let us call a node-time pair an *"event"*. To define a training problem, the set of all events must be divided into three disjoint sets, the *input* events I, *target* events T, and *hidden* events H. A node may participate in different types of event at different times. For every input event $(it) \in I$, we require *training data* X_{it} with which to overrule the dynamical law (1) using

$$x_{it} = X_{it} \quad (it) \in I. \tag{2}$$

(The bias events $(0t)$ can be regarded as a special case of input events.) For each target event $(it) \in T$, we require training data X_{it} to specify a desired activation value for event $(0t)$. No notational ambiguity arises from referring to input and target data with the same symbol X because I and T are required to be disjoint sets. The training data says nothing about the hidden events in H. There is no restriction on how the initial events $(i0)$ are classified.

3   THE "MOVING TARGETS" METHOD

Like back-propagation, the moving targets training method uses (arbitrary) gradient-based minimization techniques to minimize an *"error"* function such as the *"output deficit"*

$$E_{\text{od}} = \tfrac{1}{2} \sum_{(it)\in T} \{y_{it} - Y_{it}\}^2, \tag{3}$$

where $y_{it} = f(x_{it})$ and $Y_{it} = f(X_{it})$. A modification of the output deficit error gave the best results in numerical experiments. However, the most elegant formalism follows from an *"activation deficit"* error function:

$$E_{\text{ad}} = \tfrac{1}{2} \sum_{(it)\in T} \{x_{it} - X_{it}\}^2, \tag{4}$$

so this is what we shall use to present the formalism.

The basic idea is to treat the hidden node activations as variable target activations. Therefore let us denote these variables as X_{it}, just as the (fixed) targets and inputs are denoted. Let us write the computed activation values x_{it} of the hidden and target events in terms of the inputs and (fixed and moving) targets of the previous time step. Then let us extend the sum in (4) to include the hidden events, so the error becomes

$$E = \tfrac{1}{2} \sum_{(it)\in T\cup H} \left\{ \sum_j w_{ij} f(X_{j,t-1}) - X_{it} \right\}^2. \tag{5}$$

This is a function of the weights w_{ij}, and because there are no x's present, the full dependence on w_{ij} is explicitly displayed. We do not actually have desired values for the X_{it} with $(it) \in H$. But any values for which weights can be found which make (5) vanish would be suitable, because this would imply not only that the desired targets are attained, but also that the dynamical law is followed on both the hidden and target nodes. Therefore let us regard E as a function of both the weights and the "moving targets" $X_{it}, (it) \in H$. This is the essence of the method. The derivatives with respect to all of the independent variables can be computed and plugged into a standard minimization algorithm.

The reason for preferring the activation deficit form of the error (4) to the output deficit form (3) is that the activation deficit form makes (5) purely quadratic in the weights. Therefore the equations for the minimum,

$$dE/dw_{ij} = \partial E/\partial w_{ij} = 0, \tag{6}$$

form a linear system, the solution of which provides the optimal weights for any given set of moving targets. Therefore these equations might as well be used to define the weights as functions of the moving targets, thereby making the error (5) a *function of the moving targets alone.*

The derivation of the derivatives with respect to the moving targets is spelled out in (Rohwer, 1989b). The result is:

$$\frac{dE}{dX_{as}} = \sum_i \chi_{i,s+1} e_{i,s+1} w_{ia} f'_{as} - \chi_{as} e_{as}, \tag{7}$$

where

$$\chi_{it} = \begin{cases} 1 & (it) \in T \cup H \\ 0 & (it) \notin T \cup H \end{cases} \tag{8}$$

$$e_{it} = \sum_j w_{ij} f(X_{j,t-1}) - X_{it}, \tag{9}$$

$$f'_{it} = \left. \frac{df(x)}{dx} \right|_{x=X_{it}}, \tag{10}$$

and

$$w_{ij} = \sum_k \left(\sum_t \chi_{it} X_{it} Y_{k,t-1} \right) M_{kj}^{(i)-1}, \tag{11}$$

where $M^{(a)-1}$ is the inverse of $M^{(a)}$, the correlation matrix of the node outputs defined by

$$M_{ij}^{(a)} = \sum_t \chi_{at} Y_{i,t-1} Y_{j,t-1}. \tag{12}$$

In the event that any of the matrices M are singular, a pseudo-inversion method such as singular value decomposition (Press, 1988) can be used to define a unique solution among the infinite number available.

Note also that (11) calls for a separate matrix inversion for each node. However if the set of input nodes remains fixed for all time, then all these matrices are equal.

3.1 FEEDFORWARD VERSION

The basic ideas used in the moving targets algorithm can be applied to feedforward networks to provide an alternative method to back-propagation. The hidden node activations for each training example become the moving target variables. Further details appear in (Rohwer, 1989b). The moving targets method for feedforward nets is analogous to the method of Grossman, Meir, and Domany (Grossman, 1990a, 1990b) for networks with discrete node values. Birmiwal, Sarwal, and Sinha (Birmiwal, 1989) have developed an algorithm for feedforward networks which incorporates the use of hidden node values as fundamental variables and a linear system of equations for obtaining the weight matrix. Their algorithm differs from the feedforward version of moving targets mainly in the (inessential) use of a specific minimization algorithm which discards most of the gradient information except for the signs of the various derivatives. Heileman, Georgiopoulos, and Brown (Heileman, 1989) also have an algorithm which bears some resemblance to the feedforward version of moving targets. Another similar algorithm has been developed by Krogh, Hertz, and Thorbergasson (Krogh, 1989, 1990).

4   COMPUTATIONAL RESULTS

A set of numerical experiments performed with the activation deficit form of the algorithm (4) is reported in (Rohwer, 1989b). Some success was attained, but greater progress was made after changing to a quartic output deficit error function with temporal weighting of errors:

$$E_{\text{quartic}} = \tfrac{1}{4} \sum_{(it) \in T} (1.0 + at)\{y_{it} - Y_{it}\}^4. \tag{13}$$

Here a is a small positive constant. The quartic function is dominated by the terms with the greatest error. This combats a tendency to fail on a few infrequently seen state transitions in order to gain unneeded accuracy on a large number of similar, low-error state transitions. The temporal weighting encourages the algorithm to focus first on late-time errors, and then work back in time. In some cases this helped with local minimum difficulties. A difficulty with convergence to chaotic attractors reported in (Rohwer, 1989b) appears to have mysteriously disappeared with the adoption of this error measure.

4.1   MINIMIZATION ALGORITHM

Further progress was made by altering the minimization algorithm. Originally the conjugate gradient algorithm (Press, 1988) was used, with a linesearch algorithm from Fletcher (Fletcher, 1980). The new algorithm might be called "curvature avoidance". The change in the gradient with each linesearch is used to update a moving average estimate of the absolute value of the diagonal components of the Hessian. The linesearch direction is taken to be the component-by-component quotient of the gradient with these curvature averages. Were it not for the absolute values, this would be an unusual way of estimating the conjugate gradient. The absolute values are used to discourage exploration of directions which show any hint of being highly curved. The philosophy is that by exploring low-curvature directions first, narrow canyons are entered only when necessary.

4.2   SIMULATIONS

Several simulations have been done using fully connected networks. Figure 1 plots the node outputs of a network trained to switch between different limit cycles under input control. There are two input nodes, one target node, and 2 hidden nodes, as indicated in the left margin. Time proceeds from left to right. The oscillation period of the target node increases with the binary number represented by the two input nodes. The network was trained on one period of each of the four frequencies.

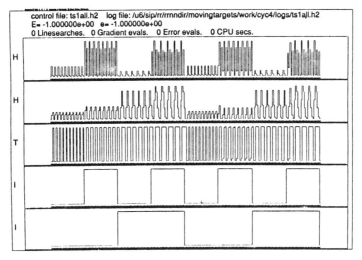

Figure 1: Controlled switching between limit cycles

Figure 2 shows the operation of a network trained to detect whether an even or odd number of pulses have been presented to the input; a temporal version of parity detection. The network was trained on the data preceding the third input pulse.

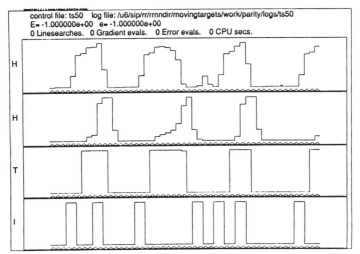

Figure 2: Parity detection

Figure 3 shows the behavior of a network trained to respond to the second of two input pulses separated by 100 time steps. This demonstrates a unique (in the author's knowledge) capability of this method, an ability to utilize very distant temporal correlations when there is no other way to solve the problem. This network was trained and tested on the same data, the point being merely to show that training is possible in this type of problem. More complex problems of this type frequently get stuck in local minima.

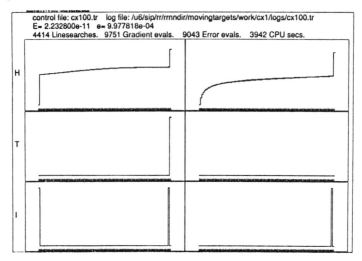

control file: cx100.tr   log file: /u6/sip/rr/rrnndir/movingtargets/work/cx1/logs/cx100.tr
E= 2.232800e-11 e= 9.977818e-04
4414 Linesearches. 9751 Gradient evals.   9043 Error evals.   3942 CPU secs.

Figure 3: Responding to temporally distant input

5   CONCLUDING REMARKS

The simulations show that this method works, and show in particular that distant temporal correlations can be discovered. Some practical difficulties have emerged, however, which are currently limiting the application of this technique to 'toy' problems. The most serious are local minima and long training times. Problems involving large amounts of training data may present the minimization problem with an impractically large number of variables. Variations of the algorithm are being studied in hopes of overcomming these difficulties.

Acknowledgements

This work was supported by ESPRIT Basic Research Action 3207 ACTS.

References

L. Almeida, (1989), "Backpropagation in Non-Feedforward Networks", in *Neural Computing Architectures*, I. Aleksander, ed., North Oxford Academic.

K. Birmiwal, P. Sarwal, and S. Sinha, (1989), "A new Gradient-Free Learning Algorithm", Tech. report, Dept. of EE, Southern Illinois U., Carbondale.

R. Fletcher, (1980), *Practical Methods of Optimization*, v1, Wiley.

T. Grossman, (1990a), "The CHIR Algorithm: A Generalization for Multiple Output and Multilayered Networks", to appear in *Complex Systems*.

T. Grossman, (1990b), this volume.

G. L. Heileman, M. Georgiopoulos, and A. K. Brown, (1989), "The Minimal Disturbance Back Propagation Algorithm", Tech. report, Dept. of EE, U. of Central Florida, Orlando.

A. Krogh, J. A. Hertz, and G. I. Thorbergsson, (1989), "A Cost Function for Internal Representations", NORDITA preprint 89/37 S.

A. Krogh, J. A. Hertz, and G. I. Thorbergsson, (1990), this volume.

G. Kuhn, (1990) "Connected Recognition with a Recurrent Network", to appear in Proc. NEUROSPEECH, 18 May 1989, as special issue of *Speech Communication*, **9**, no. 2.

B. Pearlmutter, (1989), "Learning State Space Trajectories in Recurrent Neural Networks", *Proc. IEEE IJCNN 89*, Washington D. C., II-365.

F. Pineda, (1988), "Dynamics and Architecture for Neural Computation", *J. Complexity* **4**, 216.

W. H. Press, B. P. Flannery, S. A. Teukolsky, and W. T. Vetterling, (1988), *Numerical Recipes in C, The Art of Scientific Computing*, Cambridge.

A. J. Robinson and F. Fallside, (1988), "Static and Dynamic Error Propagation Networks with Applications to Speech Coding", *Neural Information Processing Systems*, D. Z. Anderson, Ed., AIP, New York.

R. Rohwer and B. Forrest, (1987), "Training Time Dependence in Neural Networks" *Proc. IEEE ICNN*, San Diego, II-701.

R. Rohwer and S. Renals, (1989a), "Training Recurrent Networks", in *Neural Networks from Models to Applications*, L. Personnaz and G. Dreyfus, eds., I.D.S.E.T., Paris, 207.

R. Rohwer, (1989b), "The 'Moving Targets' Training Algorithm", to appear in *Proc. DANIP*, GMD Bonn, J. Kinderman and A. Linden, Eds.

D. Rumelhart, G. Hinton and R. Williams, (1986), "Learning Internal Representations by Error Propagation" in *Parallel Distributed Processing*, v. 1, MIT.

P. Werbos, (1983) *Energy Models and Studies*, B. Lev, Ed., North Holland.

R. Williams and D. Zipser, (1989a), "A Learning Algorithm for Continually Running Fully Recurrent Neural Networks", *Neural Computation* **1**, 270.

R. Williams and D. Zipser, (1989b), "Experimental Analysis of the Real-time Recurrent Learning Algorithm", *Connection Science* **1**, 87.

Training Connectionist Networks with Queries and Selective Sampling

Les Atlas
Dept. of E.E.

David Cohn
Dept. of C.S. & E.

Richard Ladner
Dept. of C.S. & E.

M.A. El-Sharkawi, R.J. Marks II, M.E. Aggoune, and D.C. Park
Dept. of E.E.
University of Washington, Seattle, WA 98195

ABSTRACT

"Selective sampling" is a form of directed search that can greatly increase the ability of a connectionist network to generalize accurately. Based on information from previous batches of samples, a network may be trained on data selectively sampled from regions in the domain that are unknown. This is realizable in cases when the distribution is known, or when the cost of drawing points from the target distribution is negligible compared to the cost of labeling them with the proper classification. The approach is justified by its applicability to the problem of training a network for power system security analysis. The benefits of selective sampling are studied analytically, and the results are confirmed experimentally.

1 Introduction: Random Sampling vs. Directed Search

A great deal of attention has been applied to the problem of generalization based on random samples drawn from a distribution, frequently referred to as "learning from examples." Many natural learning learning systems however, do not simply rely on this passive learning technique, but instead make use of at least some form of directed search to actively examine the problem domain. In many problems, directed search is provably more powerful than passively learning from randomly given examples.

Typically, directed search consists of membership queries, where the learner asks for the classification of specific points in the domain. Directed search via membership queries may proceed simply by examining the information already given and determining a *region of uncertainty*, the area in the domain where the learner believes mis-classification is still possible. The learner then asks for examples exclusively from that region.

This paper discusses one form of directed search: *selective sampling*. In Section 2, we describe theoretical foundations of directed search and give a formal definition of selective sampling. In Section 3 we describe a neural network implementation of this technique, and we discuss the resulting improvements in generalization on a number of tasks in Section 4.

2   Learning and Selective Sampling

For some arbitrary domain learning theory defines a *concept* as being some subset of points in the domain. For example, if our domain is $\Re^2$, we might define a concept as being all points inside a region bounded by some particular rectangle.

A *concept class* is simply the set of concepts in some description language.

A concept class of particular interest for this paper is that defined by neural network architectures with a single output node. *Architecture* refers to the number and types of units in a network and their connectivity. The *configuration* of a network specifies the weights on the connections and the thresholds of the units [1].

A single-output architecture plus configuration can be seen as a specification of a concept classifier in that it classifies the set of all points producing a network output above some threshold value. Similarly, an architecture may be seen as a specification of a concept class. It consists of all concepts classified by configurations of the network that the learning rule can produce (figure 1).

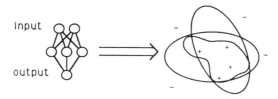

input

output

Figure 1: A network architecture as a concept class specification

2.1   Generalization and formal learning theory

An *instance*, or training example, is a pair $(x, f(x))$ consisting of a point x in the domain, usually drawn from some distribution $\mathcal{P}$, along with its classification

---

[1] For the purposes of this discussion, a neural network will be considered to be a feedforward network of neuron-like components that compute a weighted sum of their inputs and modify that sum with a sigmoidal transfer function. The methods described, however should be equally applicable to other, more general classifiers as well.

according to some target concept f. A concept c is *consistent* with an instance $(x, f(x))$ if $c(x) = f(x)$, that is, if the concept produces the same classification of point x as the target. The $error(c, f, \mathcal{P})$ of a concept c, with respect to a target concept f and a distribution $\mathcal{P}$, is the probability that c and f will disagree on a random sample drawn from $\mathcal{P}$.

The generalization problem, is posed by formal learning theory as: for a given concept class C, an unknown target f, and an arbitrary error rate ϵ, how many samples do we have to draw from an arbitrary distribution $\mathcal{P}$ in order to find a concept $c \in C$ such that $error(c, f, \mathcal{P}) \leq \epsilon$ with high confidence? This problem has been studied for neural networks in (Baum and Haussler, 1989) and (Haussler, 1989).

2.2 $\mathcal{R}(S^m)$, the region of uncertainty

If we consider a concept class C and a set S^m of m instances, the classification of some regions of the domain may be implicitly determined; all concepts in C that are consistent with all of the instances may agree in these parts. What we are interested in here is what we define to be the *region of uncertainty*:

$$\mathcal{R}(S^m) = \{x : \exists c_1, c_2 \in C, \; c_1, c_2 \text{ are consistent with all } s \in S^m, \text{ and } c_1(x) \neq c_2(x)\}.$$

For an arbitrary distribution $\mathcal{P}$, we can define a measure on the size of this region as $\alpha = \Pr[x \in \mathcal{R}(S^m)]$. In an incremental learning procedure, as we classify and train on more points, α will be monotonically non-increasing. A point that falls outside $\mathcal{R}(S^m)$ will leave it unchanged; a point inside will further restrict the region. Thus, α is the probability that a new, random point from $\mathcal{P}$ will reduce our uncertainty.

A key point is that since $\mathcal{R}(S^m)$ serves as an envelope for consistent concepts, it also bounds the potential error of any consistent hypothesis we choose. If the error of our current hypothesis is ϵ, then $\epsilon \leq \alpha$. Since we have no basis for changing our current hypothesis without a contradicting point, ϵ is also the probability of an additional point reducing our error.

2.3 Selective sampling is a directed search

Consider the case when the cost of drawing a point from our distribution is small compared to the cost of finding the point's proper classification. Then, after training on n instances, if we have some inexpensive method of testing for membership in $\mathcal{R}(S^n)$, we can "filter" points drawn from our distribution, selecting, classifying and training on only those that show promise of improving our representation.

Mathematically, we can approximate this filtering by defining a new distribution $\mathcal{P}'$ that is zero outside $\mathcal{R}(S^n)$, but maintains the relative distribution of $\mathcal{P}$. Since the next sample from $\mathcal{P}'$ would be guaranteed to land inside the region, it would have, with high confidence, the effect of at least $1/\alpha$ samples drawn from $\mathcal{P}$.

The filtering process can be applied iteratively. Start out with the distribution $\mathcal{P}_{0,n} = \mathcal{P}$. Inductively, train on n samples chosen from $\mathcal{P}_{i,n}$ to obtain a new region of uncertainty, $\mathcal{R}(S^{i,n})$, and define from it $\mathcal{P}_{i+1,n} = \mathcal{P}'_{i,n}$. The total number of training points to calculate $\mathcal{P}'_{i,n}$ is $m = in$.

Selective sampling can be contrasted with random sampling in terms of efficiency. In random sampling, we can view training as a single, non-selective pass where $n = m$. As the region of uncertainty shrinks, so does the probability that any given additional sample will help. The efficiency of the samples decreases with the error.

By filtering out useless samples before committing resources to them, as we can do in selective sampling, the efficiency of the samples we *do* classify remains high. In the limit where $n = 1$, this regimen has the effect of querying: each sample is taken from a region based on the cumulative information from all previous samples, and each one will reduce the size of $\mathcal{R}(S^m)$.

3   Training Networks with Selective Sampling

A leading concern in connectionist research is how to achieve good generalization with a limited number of samples. This suggests that selective sampling, properly implemented, should be a useful tool for training neural networks.

3.1   A naïve neural network querying algorithm

Since neural networks with real-valued outputs are generally trained to within some tolerance (say, less than 0.1 for a zero and greater than 0.9 for a one), one is tempted to use the part of the domain between these limits as $\mathcal{R}(S^m)$ (figure 2).

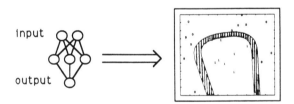

Figure 2: The region of uncertainty captured by a naïve neural network

The problem with applying this naïve approach to neural networks is that when training, a network tends to become "overly confident" in regions that are still unknown. The $\mathcal{R}(S^m)$ chosen by this method will in general be a very small subset of the true region of uncertainty.

3.2   Version-space search and neural networks

Mitchell (1978) describes a learning procedure based on the partial-ordering in generality of the concepts being learned. One maintains two sets of plausible hypotheses: S and G. S contains all "most specific" concepts consistent with present information, and G contains all consistent "most general" concepts. The "version space," which is the set of *all* plausible concepts in the class being considered, lies between these two bounding sets. Directed search proceeds by examining instances that fall in the difference of S and G. Specifically, the search region for a version-space search is equal to $\{\bigcup s\Delta g : s \in S, g \in G\}$. If an instance in this region proves positive, then some s in S will have to generalize to accommodate the new information; if it proves negative, some g in G will have to be modified to exclude it. In either case, the version space, the space of plausible hypotheses, is reduced with every query.

This search region is exactly the $\mathcal{R}(S^m)$ that we are attempting to capture. Since s and g consist of most specific/general concepts *in the class we are considering*, their analogues are the most specific and most general networks consistent with the known data.

This search may be roughly implemented by training two networks in parallel. One network, which we will label N_S, is trained on the known examples as well as given a large number of random "background" patterns, which it is trained to classify with as negative. The global minimum error for N_S is achieved when it classifies all positive training examples as positive and as much else as possible as negative. The result is a "most specific" configuration consistent with the training examples.

Similarly, N_G is trained on the known examples and a large number of random background examples which it is to classify as positive. Its global minimum error is achieved when it classifies all negative training examples as negative and as much else possible as positive.

Assuming our networks N_S and N_G converge to near-global minima, we can now define a region $\mathcal{R}_{s\Delta g}$, the symmetric difference of the outputs of N_S and N_G. Because N_S and N_G lie near opposite extremes of $\mathcal{R}(S^m)$, we have captured a well-defined region of uncertainty to search (figure 3).

3.3   Limitations of the technique

The neural network version-space technique is not without problems in general application to directed search. One limitation of this implementation of version

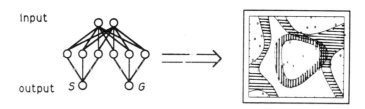

Figure 3: $\mathcal{R}_{s\Delta g}$ contains the difference between decision regions of N_S and N_G as well as their own regions of uncertainty.

space search is that a version space is bounded by a *set* of most general and most specific concepts, while an *S-G* network maintains only one most general and most specific network. As a result, $\mathcal{R}_{s\Delta g}$ will contain only a subset of the true $\mathcal{R}(S^m)$.

This limitation is softened by the global minimizing tendency of the networks. As new examples are added and the current N_S (or N_G) is forced to a more general (or specific) configuration, the network will relax to another, now more specific (or general) configuration. The effect is that of a traversal of concepts in S and G. If the number of samples in each pass is kept sufficiently small, all "most general" and most specific" concepts in $\mathcal{R}(S^m)$ may be examined without excessive sampling on one particular configuration.

There is a remaining difficulty inherent in version-space search itself: Haussler (1987) points out that even in some very simple cases, the size of S and G may grow exponentially in the number of examples.

A limitation inherent to neural networks is the necessary assumption that the networks N_S and N_G will in fact converge to global minima, and that they will do so in a reasonable amount of time. This is not always a valid assumption; it has been shown that in (Blum and Rivest, 1989) and (Judd, 1988) that the network loading problem is NP-complete, and that finding a global minimum may therefore take an exponential amount of time.

This concern is ameliorated by the fact that if the number of samples in each pass is kept small, the failure of one network to converge will only result in a small number of samples being drawn from a less useful area, but will not cause a large-scale failure of the technique.

4   Experimental Results

Experiments were run on three types of problems: learning a simple square-shaped region in $\Re^2$, learning a 25-bit majority function, and recognizing the secure region of a small power system.

4.1   The square learner

A two-input network with one hidden layer of 8 units was trained on a distribution of samples that were positive inside a square-shaped region at the center of the domain and negative elsewhere. This task was chosen because of its intuitive visual appeal (figure 4).

The results of training an S-G network provide support for the method. As can be seen in the accompanying plots, the N_S plots a tight contour around the positive instances, while N_G stretches widely around the negative ones.

4.2   Majority function

Simulations training on a 25-bit majority function were run using selective sampling in 2, 3, 4 and 20 passes, as well as baseline simulations using random sampling for error comparison.

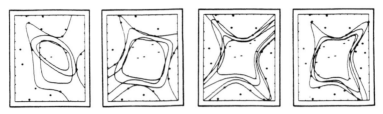

Figure 4: Learning a square by selective sampling

In all cases, there was a significant improvement of the selective sampling passes over the random sampling ones (figure 5). The randomly sampled passes exhibited a roughly logarithmic generalization curve, as expected following Blumer et al (1988).

The selectively sampled passes, however, exhibited a steeper, more exponential drop in the generalization error, as would be expected from a directed search method. Furthermore, the error seemed to decrease as the sampling process was broken up into smaller, more frequent passes, pointing at an increased efficiency of sampling as new information was incorporated earlier into the sampling process.

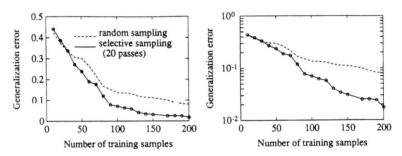

Figure 5: Error rates for random vs. selective sampling

4.3   Power system security analysis

If various load parameters of a power system are within a certain range, the system is secure. Otherwise it risks thermal overload and brown-out. Previous research (Aggoune et al, 1989) determined that this problem was amenable to neural network learning, but that random sampling of the problem domain was inefficient in terms of samples needed. The fact that arbitrary points in the domain may be analyzed for stability makes the problem well-suited to learning by means of selective sampling.

A baseline case was tested using 3000 data points representing power system configurations and compared with a two-pass, selectively-sampled data set. The latter was trained on an initial 1500 points, then on a second 1500 derived from a S-G network as described in the previous section. The error for the baseline case was 0.86% while that of the selectively sampled case was 0.56%.

5   Discussion

In this paper we have presented a theory of selective sampling, described a connectionist implementation of the theory, and examined the performance of the resulting system in several domains.

The implementation presented, the S-G network, is notable in that, even though it is an imperfect implementation of the theory, it marks a sharp departure from the standard method of training neural networks. Here, the network itself decides what samples are worth considering and training on. The results appear to give near-exponential improvements over standard techniques.

The task of active learning is an important one; in the natural world much learning is directed at least somewhat by the learner. We feel that this theory and these experiments are just initial forays into the promising area of self-training networks.

Acknowledgements

This work was supported by the National Science Foundation, the Washington Technology Center, and the IBM Corporation. Part of this work was done while D. Cohn was at IBM T.J. Watson Research Center, Yorktown Heights, NY 10598.

References

M. Aggoune, L. Atlas, D. Cohn, M. Damborg, M. El-Sharkawi, and R. Marks II. Artificial neural networks for power system static security assessment. In *Proceedings, International Symposium on Circuits and Systems*, 1989.

Eric Baum and David Haussler. What size net gives valid generalization? In *Neural Information Processing Systems*, Morgan Kaufmann 1989.

Anselm Blumer, Andrej Ehrenfeucht, David Haussler, and Manfred Warmuth. Learnability and the Vapnik-Chervonenkis dimension. *UCSC Tech Report UCSC-CRL-87-20*, October 1988.

Avrim Blum and Ronald Rivest. Training a 3-node neural network is NP-complete. In *Neural Information Processing Systems*, Morgan Kaufmann 1989.

David Haussler. Learning conjunctive concepts in structural domains. In *Proceedings, AAAI '87*, pages 466-470. 1987.

David Haussler. Generalizing the pac model for neural nets and other learning applications. *UCSC Tech Report UCSC-CRL-89-30*, September 1989.

Stephen Judd. On the complexity of loading shallow neural networks. *Journal of Complexity*, 4:177-192, 1988.

Tom Mitchell. Version spaces: an approach to concept learning. *Tech Report CS-78-711*, Dept. of Computer Science, Stanford Univ., 1978.

Leslie Valiant. A theory of the learnable. *Communications of the ACM*, 27:1134-1142, 1984.

Maximum Likelihood Competitive Learning

Steven J. Nowlan[1]
Department of Computer Science
University of Toronto
Toronto, Canada
M5S 1A4

ABSTRACT

One popular class of unsupervised algorithms are competitive algorithms. In the traditional view of competition, only one competitor, the winner, adapts for any given case. I propose to view competitive adaptation as attempting to fit a blend of simple probability generators (such as gaussians) to a set of data-points. The maximum likelihood fit of a model of this type suggests a "softer" form of competition, in which all competitors adapt in proportion to the relative probability that the input came from each competitor. I investigate one application of the soft competitive model, placement of radial basis function centers for function interpolation, and show that the soft model can give better performance with little additional computational cost.

1   INTRODUCTION

Interest in unsupervised learning has increased recently due to the application of more sophisticated mathematical tools (Linsker, 1988; Plumbley and Fallside, 1988; Sanger, 1989) and the success of several elegant simulations of large scale self-organization (Linsker, 1986; Kohonen, 1982). One popular class of unsupervised algorithms are competitive algorithms, which have appeared as components in a variety of systems (Von der Malsburg, 1973; Fukushima, 1975; Grossberg, 1978).

Generalizing the definition of Rumelhart and Zipser (1986), a competitive adaptive system consists of a collection of modules which are structurally identical except, possibly, for random initial parameter variation. A set of rules is defined which allow the modules to compete in some way for the right to respond to some subset

---

[1]The author is visiting the University of Toronto while completing a PhD at Carnegie Mellon University.

of the inputs. Typically a module is a single unit, but this need not be the case. Often, parameter restrictions are used to prevent "uninteresting" representations in which the entire set of input patterns are represented by one module.

Most of the work on competitive systems, especially within the neural network literature, has focused on a fairly extreme form of competition in which only the winner of the competition for a particular case is updated. Variants on this theme are the schemes in which, in addition to the winner, all of the losers are updated in some uniform fashion[2]. Within the statistical pattern recognition literature (Duda and Hart, 1973; McLachlan and Basford, 1988) a rather different form of competition is frequently encountered. In this form, which will be referred to as "soft" competition, all competitors are updated but the amount of update is proportional to how well each competitor did in the competition for the current case. Under a statistical model, this "soft" form of competition performs exact gradient descent in likelihood, while the more traditional winner-take-all, or "hard" competition, is an approximation to gradient descent in likelihood.

In this paper I demonstrate the superiority of "soft" competitive learning by comparing "hard" and "soft" algorithms in a classification application. The classification network consists of a layer of Radial Basis Functions (RBF's) followed by a layer of linear units which attempt to find a least mean square (LMS) fit to the desired output function (Broomhead and Lowe, 1988; Lee and Kill, 1988; Niranjan and Fallside, 1988). A network of this type can form a smooth approximation to an arbitrary function, with the RBF centers serving as control points for fitting the function (Keeler and Kowalski, 1989; Poggio and Girosi, 1989). A competitive learning component adjusts the centers of the RBF's in an unsupervised fashion, before the weights to the output units are adapted. Comparisons of hard and soft algorithms for placing the RBF's on a hand-drawn digit recognition problem and a subset of a speaker independant vowel recognition problem suggest that the soft algorithm is superior. Comparisons are also made with more traditional classifiers on the same problems.

2   COMPETITIVE PLACEMENT OF RBF'S

Radial Basis Function networks have been shown to be quite effective for some tasks, however a major limitation is that a very large number of RBF's may be required in high dimensional spaces. One method for using RBF's places the centers of the RBF's at the interstices of some coarse lattice defined over the input space (Broomhead and Lowe, 1988). If we assume the lattice is uniform with k divisions along each dimension, and the dimensionality of the input space is d, a uniform lattice would require k^d RBF's. This exponential growth makes the use of such a uniform lattice impractical for any high dimensional space. Another choice is to center the RBF's on the first n training samples, but this method is subject to sampling error,

---

[2]The feature maps of Kohonen (1982) are actually a special case in which a few units are adapted at once, however the units which are adapted in addition to the winner are selected by a neighbourhood function rather than by how well they represent the current data.

and a very large number of samples can be required to adequately represent the distribution of inputs. This is particularly true in high dimensional spaces where it is extremely difficult to visualize the input distribution and determine whether the training examples adequately represent this distribution.

Moody and Darken (1988) have suggested a method in which a much smaller number of RBF's are used, however the centers of these RBF's are allowed to adapt to the input samples, so they learn to represent only the part of the input space actually represented by the data. The adaptive strategy also allows the center of each RBF to be determined by a large number of training samples, greatly reducing sampling error. In their method, an unsupervised algorithm (a version of k-means) is used to select the centers of the RBF's and some *ad hoc* heuristics are suggested for adjusting the size of the RBF's to get a smooth interpolator. The weights from the hidden to the output layer are adapted to minimize a Least Mean Square (LMS) criterion. Moody and Darken were able to attain performance levels equivalent to a multi-layer Back Propagation network on a chaotic time series prediction task and a vowel discrimination task. Significant savings in training time were also reported.

The k-means algorithm used by Moody and Darken can be easily reformulated as a form of competitive adaptation. In the basic k-means algorithm (Duda and Hart, 1973) the training samples are first assigned to the class of the closest mean. The means are then recomputed as the average of the samples in their class. This two step process is repeated until the means stop changing. This is simply the "batch" version of a competitive learning scheme in which the activity of each competing unit is proportional to the distance between its weight vector and the current input vector, and the winning unit on each case adapts by adding a portion of the current input to its weight vector (with appropriate normalization).

We will now consider a statistical formalization of a competitive process for placing the centers of RBF's. Let each competing unit represent a radially symmetric (spherical) gaussian probability distribution, with the weight vector of the unit $\vec{\mu}_j$ representing the center or mean of the gaussian. The probability that the gaussian associated with unit j generated an input vector $\vec{x}_k$ is

$$p(\vec{x}_k) = \frac{1}{K\sigma_j} e^{-\frac{(x_k - \mu_j)^2}{2\sigma_j^2}} \tag{1}$$

where K is a normalization constant, and the covariance matrix is $\sigma_j^2 I$.

A collection of M such units is a model of the input distribution. The parameters of these M gaussians can be adjusted so that the overall average likelihood of generating the training examples is maximized. The likelihood of generating a set of observations $\{\vec{x}_1, \vec{x}_2, \ldots, \vec{x}_n\}$ from the current model is

$$L = \prod_k P(\vec{x}_k) \tag{2}$$

where $P(\vec{x}_k)$ is the probability of generating observation $\vec{x}_k$ under the current model. (For mathematical convenience we usually work with $\log L$.) If gaussian i is selected with probability π_i and a sample is drawn from the selected gaussian, the probability of observing $\vec{x}_k$ is

$$P(\vec{x}_k) = \sum_{i=1}^{N} \pi_i \, p_i(\vec{x}_k) \tag{3}$$

where $p_i(\vec{x}_k)$ is the probability of observing $\vec{x}_k$ under gaussian distribution i. The summation in (3) is awkward to work with, and frequently one of the $p_i(\vec{x}_k)$ is much larger than any of the others. Therefore, a convenient approximation for (3) is

$$P(\vec{x}_k) = \mathrm{MAX}_{i=1}^{N} \pi_i \, p_i(\vec{x}_k) \tag{4}$$

This is equivalent to assigning all of the responsibility for an observation to the gaussian with the highest probability of generating that observation. This approximation is frequently referred to as the "winner-take-all" assumption. It may also be regarded as a "hard" competitive decision among the gaussians. When we use (3) directly, all of the gaussians share responsibility for each observation in proportion to their probability of generating the observation. This sharing of responsibility can be regarded as a "soft" competitive decision among the gaussians.

The maximum likelihood estimate for the mean of each gaussian in our model can be found by evaluating $\partial \log L / \partial \vec{\mu}_j = 0$. We will consider a simple model in which we assume that π_j and σ_j are the same for all of the gaussians, and compare the hard and soft estimates for $\vec{\mu}_j$.

With the hard approximation, substituting (4) in (2), the maximum likelihood estimate of $\vec{\mu}_j$ has the simple form

$$\hat{\vec{\mu}}_j = \frac{\sum_{k \in C_j} \vec{x}_k}{N_j} \tag{5}$$

where C_j is the set of cases closest to gaussian j, and N_j is the size of this set. This is identical to the expression for $\vec{\mu}_j$ in the k-means algorithm.

Rather than using the approximation in (4) we can find the exact maximum likelihood estimates for $\vec{\mu}_j$ by substituting (3) in (2). The estimate for the mean is now

$$\hat{\vec{\mu}}_j = \frac{\sum_k p(j|\vec{x}_k)\vec{x}_k}{\sum_k p(j|\vec{x}_k)} \tag{6}$$

where $p(j|\vec{x}_k)$ is the probability, given that we have observed $\vec{x}_k$, of gaussian j having generated $\vec{x}_k$. For the simple model used here

$$p(j|\vec{x}_k) = \frac{p_j(\vec{x}_k)}{\sum_{i=1}^{M} p_i(\vec{x}_k)}$$

Comparing (6) and (5), the hard competitive model uses the average of the cases unit j is closest to in recomputing its mean, while the soft competitive model uses the average of all the cases weighted by $p(j|\vec{x}_k)$.

We can use either the approximate or exact likelihood algorithm to position the RBF's in an interpolation network. If $\vec{x}_k$ is the current input, each RBF unit computes $p_j(\vec{x}_k)$ as its output activation a_j. For the hard competitive model, a winner-take-all operation then sets $a_j = 1$ for the most active unit and $a_i = 0$ for all other units. Only the winning unit will update its mean vector, and for this update we use the iterative version of (5). In the soft competitive model we normalize each a_j by dividing it by the sum of a_j over all RBF's. In this case the mean vectors of all of the hidden units are updated according to the iterative version of (6). The computational cost difference between the winner-take-all operation in the hard model and the normalization in the soft model is negligible; however, if the algorithms are implemented sequentially, the soft model requires more computation because all of the means, rather than just the mean of the winner, are updated for each case.

The two models described in this section are easily extended to allow each spherical gaussian to have a different variance σ_j^2. The activation of each RBF unit is now a function of $(\vec{x}_k - \vec{\mu}_j)/\sigma_j$, but the expressions for the maximum likelihood estimates of $\vec{\mu}_j$ are the same. Expressions for updating σ_j^2 can be found by solving $\partial \log L/\partial \sigma_j^2 = 0$. Some simulations have also been performed with a network in which each RBF had a diagonal covariance matrix, and each of the d variance components was estimated separately (Nowlan, 1990).

3   APPLICATION TO TWO CLASSIFICATION TASKS

The architecture described above was used for a digit classification and a vowel discrimination task. The networks were trained by first using the soft or hard competitive algorithm to determine the means and variances of the RBF's, and, once these were learned, then training the output layer of weights. The weights from the RBF's to the output layer were trained using a recursive least squares algorithm, allowing an exact LMS solution to be found with one pass through the training set. (A target of $+1$ was used for the correct output category and -1 for all of the other categories.) For the hard competitive model the unnormalized probabilities $p_j(\vec{x})$ were used as the RBF unit outputs, while the soft competitive model used the normalized probabilities $p(j|\vec{x})$.

The first task required the classification of a set of hand drawn digits from 12 subjects. There were 480 input patterns, divided into 320 training patterns and 160 testing patterns, with examples from all subjects in both groups. Each pattern was digitized on a 16 by 16 grid. These 256 dimensional binary vectors were used as input to the classification network, and there were 10 output units.

Networks with 40 and 150 spherical gaussians were simulated. Both hard and soft algorithms were used with all configurations. The performance of these networks on the testing set is summarized in Table 1. This table also contains performance results for a multi-layer back propagation network, a two layer linear network, and a nearest neighbour classifier on the same task. The nearest neighbour classifier used all 320 labeled training samples and based its decision on the class of the

Type of Classifier	% Correct on Test Set
40 Sph. Gauss. – Hard	87.6%
40 Sph. Gauss. – Soft	91.8%
150 Sph. Gauss. – Hard	90.1%
150 Sph. Gauss. – Soft	94.0%
Layered BP Net	94.5%
Linear Net	60.0%
Nearest Neighbour	83.1%

Table 1: Summary of Performance for Digit Classification

nearest neighbour only[3]. The relatively poor performance of the nearest neighbour classifier is one indication of the difficulty of this task. The two layer linear network was trained with a recursive least squares algorithm[4]. The back propagation network was developed specifically for this task (le Cun, 1987), and used a specialized architecture with three layers of hidden units, localized receptive fields, and weight sharing to reduce the number of free parameters in the system.

Table 1 reveals that the networks were trained using the soft competitive algorithm to determine means and variances of the RBF's were superior in performance to identical networks trained with the hard competitive algorithm. The RBF network using 150 spherical gaussians was able to equal the performance level of the sophisticated back propagation network, and a network with 40 spherical RBF's performed considerably better than the nearest neighbour classifier.

The second task was a speaker independent vowel recognition task. The data consisted of a digitized version of the first and second formant frequencies of 10 vowels for multiple male and female speakers (Peterson and Barney, 1952). Moody and Darken (1988) have previously applied to this data an architecture which is very similar to the one suggested here, and Huang and Lippmann (1988) have compared the performance of a number of different classifiers on this same data. More recently, Bridle (1989) has applied a supervised algorithm which uses a "softmax" output function to this data. This softmax function is very similar to the equation for $p(j|\vec{x}_k)$ used in the soft competitive model. The results from these studies are included in Table 2 along with the results for RBF networks using both hard and soft competition to determine the RBF parameters. All of the classifiers were trained on a set of 338 examples and tested on a separate set of 333 examples.

As with the digit classification task, the RBF networks trained using the soft adaptive procedure show uniformly better performance than equivalent networks trained using the hard adaptive procedure. The results obtained for the hard adaptive pro-

---

[3] Two, three, and five nearest neighbour classifiers were also tried, but they all performed worse than nearest neighbour.

[4] This network was included to show that the linear layer is not doing all of the work in the hybrid RBF networks.

Type of Classifier	% Correct on Test Set
20 Sph. Gauss. – Hard	75.1%
20 Sph. Gauss. – Soft	82.6%
100 Sph. Gauss. – Hard	82.6%
100 Sph. Gauss. – Soft	87.1%
20 RBF's (Moody *et al*)	73.3%
100 RBF's (Moody *et al*)	82.0%
K Nearest Neighbours (Lippmann *et al*)	82.0%
Gaussian Classifier (Lippmann *et al*)	79.7%
2 Layer BP Net (Lippmann *et al*)	80.2%
Feature Map (Lippmann *et al*)	77.2%
2 Layer Softmax (Bridle)	78.0%

Table 2: Summary of Performance for Vowel Classification

cedure with 20 and 100 spherical gaussians are very close to Moody and Darken's results, which is expected since the procedures are identical except for the manner in which the variances are obtained. Table 2 also reveals that the RBF network with 100 spherical gaussians, trained with the soft adaptive procedure, performed better than any of the other classifiers that have been applied to this data.

4 DISCUSSION

The simulations reported in the previous section provide strong evidence that the exact maximum likelihood (or soft) approach to determining the centers and sizes of RBF's leads to better classification performance than the winner-take-all approximation. In both tasks, for a variety of numbers of RBF's, the exact maximum likelihood approach outperformed the approximate method. Comparing (5) and (6) reveals that this improved performance can be obtained with little additional computational burden.

The performance of the RBF networks on these two classification tasks also shows that hybrid approaches which combine unsupervised and supervised procedures are capable of competent levels of performance on difficult problems. In the digit classification task the hybrid RBF network was able to equal the performance level of a sophisticated multi-layer supervised network, while in the vowel recognition task the hybrid network obtained the best performance level of any of the classification networks. One reason why the hybrid model is interesting is that since the hidden unit representation is independent of the classification task, it may be used for many different tasks without interference between the tasks. (This is actually demonstrated in the simulations described, since each category in the two tasks can be regarded as a separate classification problem.) Even if we are only interested in using the network for one task, there are still advantages to the hybrid approach. In many domains, such as speech, unlabeled samples can be obtained much more cheaply than labeled samples. To avoid over-fitting, the amount of training data must generally be considerably greater than the number of free parameters in the model. In the hybrid models, especially in high dimensional input spaces, most of the parameters are in the unsupervised part of the model[5]. The unsupervised stage may be trained with a large body of unlabeled samples, and a much smaller body of labeled samples can be used to train the output layer.

The performance on the digit classification task also shows that RBF networks can deal effectively with tasks with high (256) dimensional input spaces and highly non-gaussian input distributions. The competitive network was able to succeed on this task with a relatively small number of RBF's because the data was actually distributed over a much lower dimensional subspace of the input space. The soft competitive network automatically concentrates its representation on this subspace, and in this fashion performs a type of implicit dimensionality reduction. Moody (1989) has also mentioned this type of dimensionality reduction as a factor in the success of some of the models he has worked with.

The success of the soft adaptive strategy in these interpolation networks encourages one to extend the soft interpretation in other directions. The feature maps of Kohonen (1982) incorporate a hard competitive process, and a soft version of the feature map algorithm could be developed. In addition, there is a class of decision-directed, or "bootstrap", learning algorithms which use their own outputs to provide a training signal. These algorithms can be regarded as hard competitive processes, and new algorithms which use the soft assumption may be developed from the bootstrap procedure (Nowlan and Hinton, 1989). Bridle (1989) has suggested a different type of output unit for supervised networks, which incorporates the idea of a "softmax" type of competition. Finally, the maximum likelihood approach is easily extended to non-gaussian models, and one model of particular interest would be the Boltzmann machine.

Acknowledgements

I would like to thank Richard Lippmann of Lincoln Laboratories and John Moody of Yale University for making the vowel formant data available to me. I would also like to thank Geoff Hinton, and the members of the Connectionist Research Group of the University of Toronto, for many helpful comments and suggestions while conducting this research and preparing this paper.

References

Bridle, J. (1989). Probabilistic interpretation of feedforward classification network outputs, with relationships to statistical pattern recognition. In Fougelman-Soulie, F. and Herault, J., editors, *Neuro-computing: algorithms, architectures and applications*. Springer-Verlag.

Broomhead, D. and Lowe, D. (1988). Multivariable functional interpolation and adaptive networks. *Complex Systems*, 2:321–355.

Duda, R. and Hart, P. (1973). *Pattern Classification And Scene Analysis*. Wiley and Son.

Fukushima, K. (1975). Cognitron: A self-organizing multilayered neural network. *Biological Cybernetics*, 20:121–136.

---

[5] In the digit task, there are over 25 times as many parameters in the unsupervised part of the network as there are in the supervised part.

Grossberg, S. (1978). A theory of visual coding, memory, and development. In *Formal theories of visual perception*. John Wiley and Sons, New York.

Huang, W. and Lippmann, R. (1988). Neural net and traditional classifiers. In Anderson, D., editor, *Neural Information Processing Systems*. American Institute of Physics.

Keeler, E. H. J. and Kowalski, J. (1989). Layered neural networks with gaussian hidden units as universal approximators. MCC Technical Report ACT-ST-272-89, MCC.

Kohonen, T. (1982). Self-organized formation of topologically correct feature maps. *Biological Cybernetics*, 43:59–69.

le Cun, Y. (1987). *Modèles Connexionnistes de l'Apprentissage*. PhD thesis, Université Pierre et Marie Curie, Paris, France.

Lee, S. and Kill, R. (1988). Multilayer feedforward potential function networks. In *Proceedings IEEE Second International Conference on Neural Networks*, page I:161, San Diego, California.

Linsker, R. (1986). From basic network principles to neural architecture: Emergence of spatial opponent cells. *Proceedings of the National Academy of Sciences USA*, 83:7508–7512.

Linsker, R. (1988). Self-organization in a perceptual network. *IEEE Computer Society*, pages 105–117.

McLachlan, G. and Basford, K. (1988). *Mixture Models: Inference and Applications to Clustering*. Marcel Dekker, New York.

Moody, J. (1989). Fast learning in multi-resolution hierarchies. Technical Report YALEU/DCS/RR-681, Yale University.

Moody, J. and Darken, C. (1988). Learning with localized receptive fields. In D. Touretzky, G. Hinton, T. S., editor, *Proceedings of the 1988 Connectionist Models Summer School*, pages 133–143. Morgan Kauffman.

Niranjan, M. and Fallside, F. (1988). Neural networks and radial basis functions in classifying static speech patterns. Technical Report CUEDIF-INFENG17R22, Engineering Dept., Cambridge University. to appear in Computers Speech and Language.

Nowlan, S. (1990). Maximum likelihood competition in RBF networks. Technical Report CRG-TR-90-2, University of Toronto Connectionist Research Group.

Nowlan, S. and Hinton, G. (1989). Maximum likelihood decision-directed adaptive equalization. Technical Report CRG-TR-89-8, University of Toronto Connectionist Research Group.

Peterson, G. and Barney, H. (1952). Control methods used in a study of vowels. *The Journal of the Acoustical Society of America*, 24:175–184.

Plumbley, M. and Fallside, F. (1988). An information theoretic approach to unsupervised connectionist models. In D. Touretzky, G Hinton, T. S., editor, *Proceedings of the 1988 Connectionist Models Summer School*, pages 239–245. Morgan Kauffmann.

Poggio, G. and Girosi, F. (1989). A theory of networks for approximation and learning. A.I. Memo 1140, MIT.

Rumelhart, D. E. and Zipser, D. (1986). Feature discovery by competitive learning. In *Parallel distributed processing: Explorations in the microstructure of cognition*, volume I. Bradford Books, Cambridge, MA.

Sanger, T. (1989). An optimality principle for unsupervised learning. In Touretzky, D., editor, *Advances in Neural Information Processing Systems 1*, pages 11–19. Morgan Kauffman.

Von der Malsburg, C. (1973). Self-organization of orientation sensitive cells in striate cortex. *Kybernetik*, 14:85–100.

Unsupervised Learning in Neurodynamics Using the Phase Velocity Field Approach

Michail Zak   Nikzad Toomarian

Center for Space Microelectronics Technology
Jet Propulsion Laboratory
California Institute of Technology
Pasadena, CA 91109

ABSTRACT

A new concept for unsupervised learning based upon examples introduced to the neural network is proposed. Each example is considered as an interpolation node of the velocity field in the phase space. The velocities at these nodes are selected such that all the streamlines converge to an attracting set imbedded in the subspace occupied by the cluster of examples. The synaptic interconnections are found from learning procedure providing selected field. The theory is illustrated by examples.

This paper is devoted to development of a new concept for unsupervised learning based upon examples introduced to an artificial neural network. The neural network is considered as an adaptive nonlinear dissipative dynamical system described by the following coupled differential equations:

$$\dot{u}_i + \kappa u_i = \sum_{j=1}^{N} T_{ij} g(u_j) + I_i \qquad i = 1, 2, \ldots, N \tag{1}$$

in which u is an N-dimensional vector, function of time, representing the neuron activity, T is a constant matrix whose elements represent synaptic interconnections between the neurons, g is a monotonic nonlinear function, I_i is the constant exterior input to each neuron, and κ is a positive constant.

Let us consider a pattern vector $\tilde{u}$ represented by its end point in an n-dimensional phase space, and suppose that this pattern is introduced to the neural net in the form of a set of vectors - examples $u^{(k)}, k = 1, 2 \ldots K$ (Fig. 1). The difference between these examples which represent the same pattern can be caused not only by noisy measurements, but also by the invariance of the pattern to some changes in the vector coordinates (for instance, to translations, rotations etc.). If the set of the points $u^{(k)}$ is sufficiently dense, it can be considered as a finite-dimensional approximation of some subspace $\theta^{(\ell)}$.

Now the goal of this study is formulated as following: find the synaptic interconnections T_{ij} and the input to the network I_i such that any trajectory which is originated inside of $\theta^{(\ell)}$ will be entrapped there. In such a performance the subspace $\theta^{(\ell)}$ practically plays the role of the basin of attraction to the original pattern $\tilde{u}$. However, the position of the attractor itself is not known in advance: the neural net has to create it based upon the introduced representative examples. Moreover, in general the attractor is not necessarily static: it can be periodic, or even chaotic.

The achievement of the goal formulated above would allow one to incorporate into a neural net a set of attractors representing the corresponding clusters of patterns, where each cluster is imbedded into the basin of its attractor. Any new pattern introduced to such a neural net will be attracted to the "closest" attractor. Hence, the neural net would learn by examples to perform content-addressable memory and pattern recognition.

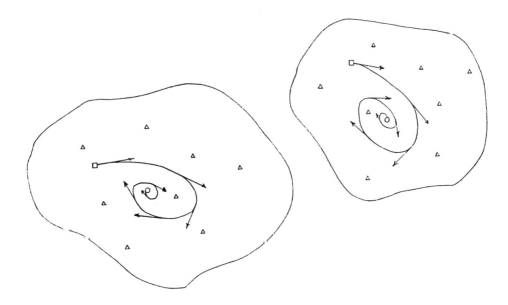

Fig. 1: Two-Dimensional Vectors as Examples, u^k, and Formation of Clusters θ.

Our approach is based upon the utilization of the original clusters of the example points $u^{(k)}$ as interpolation nodes of the velocity field in the phase space. The assignment of a certain velocity to an example point imposes a corresponding constraint upon the synaptic interconnections T_{ij} and the input I_i via Eq. (1). After these unknowns are found, the velocity field in the phase space is determined by Eq. (1). Hence, the main problem is to assign velocities at the point examples such that the required dynamical behavior of the trajectories formulated above is provided.

One possibility for the velocity selection based upon the geometrical center approach was analyzed by M. Zak, (1989). In this paper a "gravitational attraction" approach to the same problem will be introduced and discussed.

Suppose that each example-point $u^{(k)}$ is attracted to all the other points $u^{(k')}(k' \neq k)$ such that its velocity is found by the same rule as a gravitational force:

$$v_i^{(k)} = v_o \sum_{\substack{k'=1 \\ k' \neq k}}^{K} \frac{u_i^{(k')} - u_i^{(k)}}{\left[\sum_{j=1}^{n} (u_j^{(k')} - u_j^{(k)})^2 \right]^{3/2}} \tag{2}$$

in which v_o is a constant scale coefficient.

Actual velocities at the same points are defined by Eq. (1) rearranged as:

$$\dot{u}_i^{(k)} = \sum_{j=1}^{N} T_{ij} g(u_j^{(\kappa)} - u_{oi}) - \kappa(u_i^{(k)} - u_{oi}) \qquad \begin{array}{l} i = 1, 2, \ldots, N \\ k = 1, 2, \ldots, K \end{array} \tag{3}$$

The objective is to find synaptic interconnections T_{ij} and center of gravity u_{oi} such that they minimize the distance between the assigned velocity (Eq. 2) and actual calculated velocities (Eq. 3).

Introducing the energy:

$$E = \frac{1}{2} \sum_{k=1}^{K} \sum_{i=1}^{N} (v_i^{(k)} - \dot{u}_i^{(k)})^2 \tag{4}$$

one can find T_{ij} and u_{oi} from the condition:

$$E \to \min$$

i.e., as the static attractor of the dynamical system:

$$\dot{u}_{oi} = -\alpha^2 \frac{\partial E}{\partial u_{oi}} \tag{5a}$$

$$\dot{T}_{ij} = -\alpha^2 \frac{\partial E}{\partial T_{ij}} \tag{5b}$$

in which α is a time scale parameter for learning. By appropriate selection of this parameter the convergence of the dynamical system can be considerably improved (J. Barhen, S. Gulati, and M. Zak, 1989).

Obviously, the static attractor of Eqs. (5) is unique. As follows from Eq. (3)

$$\frac{\partial \dot{u}_i^{(k)}}{\partial u_j^{(k)}} = T_{ij} \frac{dg_j^{(k)}}{du_j^{(k)}}. \qquad (i \neq j) \qquad (6)$$

Since $g(u)$ is a monotonic function, $\operatorname{sgn} \frac{dg_j^{(k)}}{du_j^{(k)}}$ is constant which in turn implies that

$$\operatorname{sgn} \frac{\partial \dot{u}_i^{(k)}}{\partial u_j^{(k)}} = \text{const} \quad (i \neq j) \qquad (7)$$

Applying this result to the boundary of the cluster one concludes that the velocity at the boundary is directed inside of the cluster (Fig. 2).

For numerical illustration of the new learning concept developed above, we select 6 points in the two dimensional space, (i.e., two neurons) which constructs two separated clusters (Fig. 3, points 1-3 and 16-18 (three points are the minimum to form a cluster in two dimensional space)). Coordinates of the points in Fig. 3 are given in Table 1. The assigned velocity v_i^k calculated based on Eq. 2 and $v_o = 0.04$ are shown in dotted line. For a random initialization of T_{ij} and u_{oi}, the energy decreases sharply from an initial value of 10.608 to less than 0.04 in about 400 iterations and at about 2000 iterations the final value of 0.0328 has been achieved, (Fig. 4). To carry out numerical integration of the differential equations, first order Euler numerical scheme with time step of 0.01 has been used. In this simulation the scale parameter α^2 was kept constant and set to one. By substituting the calculated T_{ij} and u_{oi} into Eq. (3) for point u^k, $(k = 1, 2, 3, 16, 17, 18)$, one will obtain the calculated velocities at these points (shown as dashed lines in Fig. 3). As one may notice, the assigned and calculated velocities are not exactly the same. However, this small difference between the velocities are of no importance as long as the calculated velocities are directed toward the interior of the cluster. This directional difference of the velocities is one of the reasons that the energy did not vanish. The other reason is the difference in the value of these velocities, which is of no importance either, based on the concept developed.

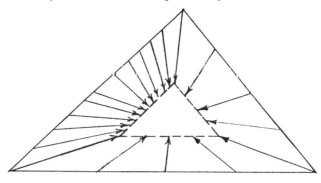

Fig. 2: Velocities at Boundaries are directed Toward Inside of the Cluster.

In order to show that for different initial conditions, Eq. 3 will converge to an attractor which is inside one of the two clusters, this equation was started from different points (4-15, 19-29). In all points, the equation converges to either (0.709,0.0) or (-0.709,0.0). However, the line $x = 0$ in this case is the dividing line, and all the points on this line will converge to u_o.

The decay coefficient κ and the gain of the hyperbolic tangent were chosen to be 1. However, during the course of this simulation it was observed that the system is very sensitive to these parameters as well as v_o, which calls for further study in this area.

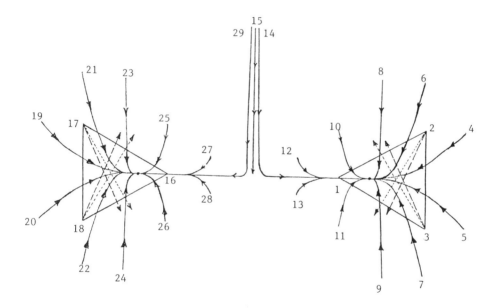

Fig. 3: •   Cluster 1 (1-3) and Cluster 2 (16-19).

•   Assigned Velocity (· ·)   Calculated Velocity (- -)

•   Activation Dynamics initiated at different points.

Table 1. - Coordinate of Points in Figure 4.

point	X	Y	point	X	Y
1	0.50	0.00	16	-0.50	0.00
2	1.00	0.25	17	-1.00	0.25
3	1.00	-0.25	18	-1.00	0.25
4	1.25	0.25	19	-1.25	0.25
5	1.25	-0.25	20	-1.25	-0.25
6	1.00	0.50	21	-1.00	0.50
7	1.00	-0.50	22	-1.00	-0.50
8	0.75	0.50	23	-0.75	0.50
9	0.75	-0.50	24	-0.75	-0.50
10	0.50	0.25	25	-0.50	-0.25
11	0.50	-0.25	26	-0.50	-0.25
12	0.25	0.10	27	-0.25	0.10
13	0.25	-0.10	28	-0.25	-0.10
14	0.02	1.00	29	-0.02	1.00
15	0.00	1.00			

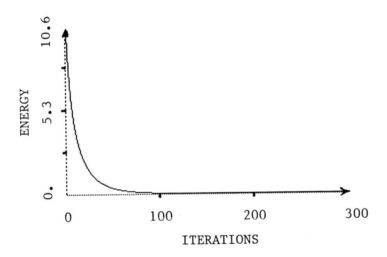

Fig 4: Profile of Neuromorphic Energy over Time Iterations

Acknowledgement

This research was carried out at the Center for Space Microelectronic Technology, Jet Propulsion Laboratory, California Institute of Technology. Support for the work came from Agencies of the U.S. Department of Defense, including the Innovative Science and Technology Office of the Strategic Defense Initiative Organization and the Office of the Basic Energy Sciences of the US Dept. of Energy, through an agreement with the National Aeronautics and Space Administration.

References

M. Zak (1989), "Unsupervised Learning in Neurondynamics Using Example Interaction Approach", Appl. Math. Letters, Vol. 2, No. 3, pp. 381- 286.

J. Barhen, S. Gulati, M. Zak (1989), "Neural Learning of Constrained nonlinear Transformations", IEEE Computer, Vol. 22(6), pp. 67-76.

A Method for the Associative Storage
of Analog Vectors

Amir Atiya (*) and Yaser Abu-Mostafa (**)
(*) Department of Electrical Engineering
(**) Departments of Electrical Engineering and Computer Science
California Institute Technology
Pasadena, Ca 91125

ABSTRACT

A method for storing analog vectors in Hopfield's continuous feedback model is proposed. By analog vectors we mean vectors whose components are real-valued. The vectors to be stored are set as equilibria of the network. The network model consists of one layer of visible neurons and one layer of hidden neurons. We propose a learning algorithm, which results in adjusting the positions of the equilibria, as well as guaranteeing their stability. Simulation results confirm the effectiveness of the method.

1 INTRODUCTION

The associative storage of binary vectors using discrete feedback neural nets has been demonstrated by Hopfield (1982). This has attracted a lot of attention, and a number of alternative techniques using also the discrete feedback model have appeared. However, the problem of the distributed associative storage of analog vectors has received little attention in literature. By analog vectors we mean vectors whose components are real-valued. This problem is important because in a variety of applications of associative memories like pattern recognition and vector quantization the patterns are originally in analog form and therefore one can save having the costly quantization step and therefore also save increasing the dimension of the vectors. In dealing with analog vectors, we consider feedback networks of the continuous-time graded-output variety, e.g. Hopfield's model (1984):

$$\frac{d\mathbf{u}}{dt} = -\mathbf{u} + \mathbf{W}\mathbf{f}(\mathbf{u}) + \mathbf{a}, \qquad \mathbf{x} = \mathbf{f}(\mathbf{u}), \qquad (1)$$

where $\mathbf{u} = (u_1, ..., u_N)^T$ is the vector of neuron potentials, $\mathbf{x} = (x_1, ..., x_N)^T$ is the vector of firing rates, $\mathbf{W}$ is the weight matrix, $\mathbf{a}$ is the threshold vector, and $\mathbf{f}(\mathbf{u})$ means the vector $(f(u_1), ..., f(u_N))^T$, where f is a sigmoid-shaped function.

The vectors to be stored are set as equilibria of the network. Given a noisy version of any of the stored vectors as the initial state of the network, the network state has to reach eventually the equilibrium state corresponding to the correct vector. An important requirement is that these equilibria be asymtotically stable, otherwise the attraction to the equilibria will not be guaranteed. Indeed, without enforcing this requirement, our numerical simulations show mostly unstable equilibria.

2 THE MODEL

It can be shown that there are strong limitations on the set of memory vectors which can be stored using Hopfield's continuous model (Atiya and Abu-Mostafa 1990). To relieve these limitations, we use an architecture consisting of both visible and hidden units. The outputs of the visible units correspond to the components of the stored vector. Our proposed architecture will be close to the continuous version of the BAM (Kosko 1988). The model consists of one layer of visible units and another layer of hidden units (see Figure 1). The output of each layer is fed as an input to the other layer. No connections exist within each of the layers. Let $\mathbf{y}$ and $\mathbf{x}$ be the output vectors of the hidden layer and the visible layer respectively. Then, in our model,

$$\frac{d\mathbf{u}}{dt} = -\mathbf{u} + \mathbf{W}\mathbf{f}(\mathbf{z}) + \mathbf{a} \equiv \mathbf{e}, \qquad \mathbf{y} = \mathbf{f}(\mathbf{u}) \qquad (2a)$$

$$\frac{d\mathbf{z}}{dt} = -\mathbf{z} + \mathbf{V}\mathbf{f}(\mathbf{u}) + \mathbf{b} \equiv \mathbf{h}, \qquad \mathbf{x} = \mathbf{f}(\mathbf{z}) \qquad (2b)$$

where $\mathbf{W} = [w_{ij}]$ and $\mathbf{V} = [v_{ij}]$ are the weight matrices, $\mathbf{a}$ and $\mathbf{b}$ are the threshold vectors, and f is a sigmoid function (monotonically increasing) in the range from -1 to 1, for example

$$f(u) = \tanh(u).$$

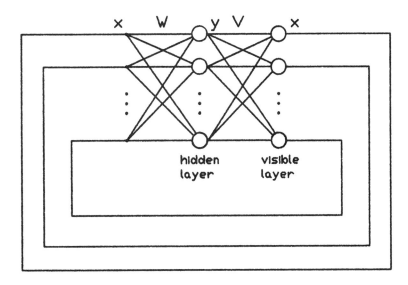

Figure 1: The model

As we mentioned before, for a basin of attraction to exist around a given memory vector, the corresponding equilibrium has to be asymtotically stable. For the proposed architecture a condition for stability is given by the following theorem.

Theorem: An equilibrium point $(\mathbf{u}^*, \mathbf{z}^*)$ satisfying

$$f'^{1/2}(u_i^*)\sum_j |w_{ij}| f'^{1/2}(z_j^*) < 1 \qquad (3a)$$

$$f'^{1/2}(z_i^*)\sum_j |v_{ij}| f'^{1/2}(u_j^*) < 1 \qquad (3b)$$

for all i is asymptotically stable.

Proof: We linearize (2a), (2b) around the equilibrium. We get

$$\frac{d\mathbf{q}}{du} = \mathbf{J}\mathbf{q},$$

where

$$q_i = \begin{cases} u_i - u_i^*, & \text{if } i = 1, ..., N_1 \\ z_{i-N_1} - z_{i-N_1}^*, & \text{if } i = N_1 + 1, ..., N_1 + N_2, \end{cases}$$

N_1 and N_2 are the number of units in the hidden layer and the visible layer respectively, and $\mathbf{J}$ is the Jacobian matrix, given by

$$\mathbf{J} = \begin{pmatrix} \frac{\partial e_1}{\partial u_1} & \cdots & \frac{\partial e_1}{\partial u_{N_1}} & \frac{\partial e_1}{\partial z_1} & \cdots & \frac{\partial e_1}{\partial z_{N_2}} \\ \vdots & & \vdots & \vdots & & \vdots \\ \frac{\partial e_{N_1}}{\partial u_1} & \cdots & \frac{\partial e_{N_1}}{\partial u_{N_1}} & \frac{\partial e_{N_1}}{\partial z_1} & \cdots & \frac{\partial e_{N_1}}{\partial z_{N_2}} \\ \frac{\partial h_1}{\partial u_1} & \cdots & \frac{\partial h_1}{\partial u_{N_1}} & \frac{\partial h_1}{\partial z_1} & \cdots & \frac{\partial h_1}{\partial z_{N_2}} \\ \vdots & & \vdots & \vdots & & \vdots \\ \frac{\partial h_{N_2}}{\partial u_1} & \cdots & \frac{\partial h_{N_2}}{\partial u_{N_1}} & \frac{\partial h_{N_2}}{\partial z_1} & \cdots & \frac{\partial h_{N_2}}{\partial z_{N_2}} \end{pmatrix},$$

the partial derivatives evaluated at the equilibrium point. Let Λ_1 and Λ_2 be respectively the $N_1 \times N_1$ and $N_2 \times N_2$ diagonal matrices with the ith diagonal element being respectively $f'(u_i^*)$ and $f'(z_i^*)$. Furthermore, let

$$\Lambda = \begin{pmatrix} \Lambda_1 & 0 \\ 0 & \Lambda_2 \end{pmatrix}.$$

The Jacobian is evaluated as

$$\mathbf{J} = \begin{pmatrix} -\mathbf{I}_{N_1} & \mathbf{W}\Lambda_2 \\ \mathbf{V}\Lambda_1 & -\mathbf{I}_{N_2} \end{pmatrix}$$

where $\mathbf{I}_L$ means the $L \times L$ identity matrix. Let

$$\mathbf{A} = \begin{pmatrix} -\Lambda_1^{-1} & \mathbf{W} \\ \mathbf{V} & -\Lambda_2^{-1} \end{pmatrix}.$$

Then,

$$\mathbf{J} = \mathbf{A}\mathbf{\Lambda}.$$

Eigenvalues of $\mathbf{A}\mathbf{\Lambda}$ are identical to the eigenvalues of $\mathbf{\Lambda}^{1/2}\mathbf{A}\mathbf{\Lambda}^{1/2}$ because if λ is an eigenvalue of $\mathbf{A}\mathbf{\Lambda}$ corresponding to eigenvector $\mathbf{v}$, then

$$\mathbf{A}\mathbf{\Lambda}\mathbf{v} = \lambda\mathbf{v},$$

and hence

$$(\mathbf{\Lambda}^{1/2}\mathbf{A}\mathbf{\Lambda}^{1/2})(\mathbf{\Lambda}^{1/2}\mathbf{v}) = \lambda(\mathbf{\Lambda}^{1/2}\mathbf{v}).$$

Now, we have

$$\mathbf{\Lambda}^{1/2}\mathbf{A}\mathbf{\Lambda}^{1/2} = \begin{pmatrix} -\mathbf{I}_{N_1} & \mathbf{\Lambda}_1^{1/2}\mathbf{W}\mathbf{\Lambda}_2^{1/2} \\ \mathbf{\Lambda}_2^{1/2}\mathbf{V}\mathbf{\Lambda}_1^{1/2} & -\mathbf{I}_{N_2} \end{pmatrix}.$$

By Gershgorin's Theorem (Franklin 1968), an eigenvalue of $\mathbf{J}$ has to satisfy at least one of the inequalities:

$$|\lambda + 1| \le f'^{1/2}(u_i^*)\sum_j |w_{ij}|f'^{1/2}(z_j^*) \qquad i = 1, ..., N_1$$

$$|\lambda + 1| \le f'^{1/2}(z_i^*)\sum_j |v_{ij}|f'^{1/2}(u_j^*) \qquad i = 1, ..., N_2.$$

It follows that under conditions (3a), (3b) that the eigenvalues of $\mathbf{J}$ will have negative real parts, and hence the equilibrium of the original system (2a), (2b) will be asymptotically stable.

Thus, if the hidden unit values are driven far enough into the saturation region (i.e. with values close to 1 or -1), then the corresponding equilibrium will be stable because then, $f'(u_i^*)$ will be very small, causing Inequalities (3) to be satisfied. Although there is nothing to rule out the existence of spurious equilibria and limit cycles, if they occur then they would be far away from the memory vectors because each memory vector has a basin of attraction around it. In our simulations we have never encountered limit cycles.

3 TRAINING ALGORITHM

Let $\mathbf{x}^m, m = 1, ..., M$ be the vectors to be stored. Each $\mathbf{x}^m$ should correspond to the visible layer component of one of the asymptotically stable equilibria. We design the network such that the hidden layer component of the equilibrium corresponding to $\mathbf{x}^m$ is far into the saturation region. The target hidden layer component $\mathbf{y}^m$ can be taken as a vector of 1's and -1's, chosen arbitrarily for example by generating the components randomly. Then, the weights have to satisfy

$$y_j^m = f(\sum_l w_{jl}x_l^m + a_j),$$

$$x_i^m = f[\sum_j v_{ij}f(\sum_l w_{jl}x_l^m + a_j) + b_i].$$

Training is performed in two steps. In the first step we train the weights of the hidden layer. We use steepest descent on the error function

$$E_1 = \sum_{m,j} \|y_j^m - f(\sum_l w_{jl} x_l^m + a_j)\|^2.$$

In the second step we train the weights of the visible layer, using steepest descent on the error function

$$E_2 = \sum_{m,i} \|x_i^m - f[\sum_j v_{ij} f(\sum_l w_{jl} x_l^m + a_j) + b_i]\|^2.$$

We remark that in the first step convergence might be slow since the targets are 1 or -1. A way to have fast convergence is to stop if the outputs are within some constant (say 0.2) from the targets. Then we multiply the weights and the thresholds of the hidden layer by a big positive constant, so as to force the outputs of the hidden layer to be close to 1 or -1.

4 IMPLEMENTATION

We consider a network with 10 visible and 10 hidden units. The memory vectors are randomly generated (the components are from -0.8 to 0.8 rather than the full range to have a faster convergence). Five memory vectors are considered. After learning, the memory is tested by giving memory vectors plus noise (100 vectors for a given variance). Figure 2 shows the percentage correct recall in terms of the signal to noise ratio. Although we found that we could store up to 10 vectors, working close to the full capacity is not recommended, as the recall accuracy deteriorates.

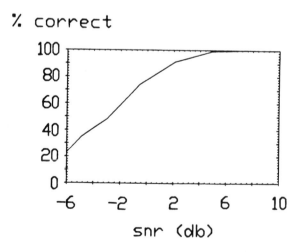

Figure 2: Recall accuracy versus signal to noise ratio

Acknowledgement

This work is supported by the Air Force Office of Scientific Research under grant AFOSR-88-0231.

References

J. Hopfield (1982), "Neural networks and physical systems with emergent collective computational abilities", *Proc. Nat. Acad. Sci. USA*, vol. 79, pp. 2554-2558.

J. Hopfield (1984), "Neurons with graded response have collective computational properties like those of two state neurons", *Proc. Nat. Acad. Sci. USA*, vol. 81, p. 3088-3092.

A. Atiya and Y. Abu-Mostafa (1990), "An analog feedback associative memory", to be submitted.

B. Kosko (1988), "Bidirectional associative memories", *IEEE Trans. Syst. Man Cybern.*, vol. SMC-18, no. 1, pp. 49-60.

J. Franklin (1968) *Matrix Theory*, Prentice-Hall, Englewood Cliffs, New Jersey.

PART VII:
EMPIRICAL ANALYSES

Optimal Brain Damage

Yann Le Cun, John S. Denker and Sara A. Solla
AT&T Bell Laboratories, Holmdel, N. J. 07733

ABSTRACT

We have used information-theoretic ideas to derive a class of practical and nearly optimal schemes for adapting the size of a neural network. By removing unimportant weights from a network, several improvements can be expected: better generalization, fewer training examples required, and improved speed of learning and/or classification. The basic idea is to use second-derivative information to make a tradeoff between network complexity and training set error. Experiments confirm the usefulness of the methods on a real-world application.

1 INTRODUCTION

Most successful applications of neural network learning to real-world problems have been achieved using highly structured networks of rather large size [for example (Waibel, 1989; Le Cun et al., 1990a)]. As applications become more complex, the networks will presumably become even larger and more structured. Design tools and techniques for comparing different architectures and minimizing the network size will be needed. More importantly, as the number of parameters in the systems increases, overfitting problems may arise, with devastating effects on the generalization performance. We introduce a new technique called Optimal Brain Damage (OBD) for reducing the size of a learning network by selectively deleting weights. We show that OBD can be used both as an automatic network minimization procedure and as an interactive tool to suggest better architectures.

The basic idea of OBD is that it is possible to take a perfectly reasonable network, delete half (or more) of the weights and wind up with a network that works just as well, or better. It can be applied in situations where a complicated problem must be solved, and the system must make optimal use of a limited amount of training data. It is known from theory (Denker et al., 1987; Baum and Haussler, 1989; Solla et al., 1990) and experience (Le Cun, 1989) that, for a fixed amount of training data, networks with too many weights do not generalize well. On the other hand, networks with too few weights will not have enough power to represent the data accurately. The best generalization is obtained by trading off the training error and the network complexity.

One technique to reach this tradeoff is to minimize a cost function composed of two terms: the ordinary training error, plus some measure of the network complexity. Several such schemes have been proposed in the statistical inference literature [see (Akaike, 1986; Rissanen, 1989; Vapnik, 1989) and references therein] as well as in the NN literature (Rumelhart, 1988; Chauvin, 1989; Hanson and Pratt, 1989; Mozer and Smolensky, 1989).

Various complexity measures have been proposed, including Vapnik-Chervonenkis dimensionality (Vapnik and Chervonenkis, 1971) and description length (Rissanen, 1989). A time-honored (albeit inexact) measure of complexity is simply the number of non-zero free parameters, which is the measure we choose to use in this paper [but see (Denker, Le Cun and Solla, 1990)]. Free parameters are used rather than connections, since in constrained networks, several connections can be controlled by a single parameter.

In most cases in the statistical inference literature, there is some *a priori* or heuristic information that dictates the order in which parameters should be deleted; for example, in a family of polynomials, a smoothness heuristic may require high-order terms to be deleted first. In a neural network, however, it is not at all obvious in which order the parameters should be deleted.

A simple strategy consists in deleting parameters with small "saliency", i.e. those whose deletion will have the least effect on the training error. Other things being equal, small-magnitude parameters will have the least saliency, so a reasonable initial strategy is to train the network and delete small-magnitude parameters in order. After deletion, the network should be retrained. Of course this procedure can be iterated; in the limit it reduces to continuous weight-decay during training (using disproportionately rapid decay of small-magnitude parameters). In fact, several network minimization schemes have been implemented using non-proportional weight decay (Rumelhart, 1988; Chauvin, 1989; Hanson and Pratt, 1989), or "gating coefficients" (Mozer and Smolensky, 1989). Generalization performance has been reported to increase significantly on the somewhat small problems examined. Two drawbacks of these techniques are that they require fine-tuning of the "pruning" coefficients to avoid catastrophic effects, and also that the learning process is significantly slowed down. Such methods include the implicit hypothesis that the appropriate measure of network complexity is the number of parameters (or sometimes the number of units) in the network.

One of the main points of this paper is to move beyond the approximation that "magnitude equals saliency", and propose a theoretically justified saliency measure.

Our technique uses the second derivative of the objective function with respect to the parameters to compute the saliencies. The method was validated using our handwritten digit recognition network trained with backpropagation (Le Cun et al., 1990b).

2   OPTIMAL BRAIN DAMAGE

Objective functions play a central role in this field; therefore it is more than reasonable to define the saliency of a parameter to be the change in the objective function caused by deleting that parameter. It would be prohibitively laborious to evaluate the saliency directly from this definition, i.e. by temporarily deleting each parameter and reevaluating the objective function.

Fortunately, it is possible to construct a local model of the error function and *analytically predict* the effect of perturbing the parameter vector. We approximate the objective function E by a Taylor series. A perturbation δU of the parameter vector will change the objective function by

$$\delta E = \sum_i g_i \delta u_i + \frac{1}{2} \sum_i h_{ii} \delta u_i^2 + \frac{1}{2} \sum_{i \neq j} h_{ij} \delta u_i \delta u_j + O(\|\delta U\|^3) \qquad (1)$$

Here, the δu_i's are the components of δU, the g_i's are the components of the gradient G of E with respect to U, and the h_{ij}'s are the elements of the Hessian matrix H of E with respect to U:

$$g_i = \frac{\partial E}{\partial u_i} \qquad \text{and} \qquad h_{ij} = \frac{\partial^2 E}{\partial u_i \partial u_j} \qquad (2)$$

The goal is to find a set of parameters whose deletion will cause the least increase of E. This problem is practically insoluble in the general case. One reason is that the matrix H is enormous (6.5 x 10^6 terms for our 2600 parameter network), and is very difficult to compute. Therefore we must introduce some simplifying approximations. The "diagonal" approximation assumes that the δE caused by deleting several parameters is the sum of the δE's caused by deleting each parameter individually; cross terms are neglected, so third term of the right hand side of equation 1 is discarded. The "extremal" approximation assumes that parameter deletion will be performed after training has converged. The parameter vector is then at a (local) minimum of E and the first term of the right hand side of equation 1 can be neglected. Furthermore, at a local minimum, all the h_{ii}'s are non-negative, so any perturbation of the parameters will cause E to increase or stay the same. Thirdly, the "quadratic" approximation assumes that the cost function is nearly quadratic so that the last term in the equation can be neglected. Equation 1 then reduces to

$$\delta E = \frac{1}{2} \sum_i h_{ii} \delta u_i^2 \qquad (3)$$

2.1 COMPUTING THE SECOND DERIVATIVES

Now we need an efficient way of computing the diagonal second derivatives h_{ii}. Such a procedure was derived in (Le Cun, 1987), and was the basis of a fast back-propagation method used extensively in various applications (Becker and Le Cun, 1989; Le Cun, 1989; Le Cun et al., 1990a). The procedure is very similar to the back-propagation algorithm used for computing the first derivatives. We will only outline the procedure; details can be found in the references.

We assume the objective function is the usual mean-squared error (MSE); generalization to other additive error measures is straightforward. The following expressions apply to a single input pattern; afterward E and H must be averaged over the training set. The network state is computed using the standard formulae

$$x_i = f(a_i) \quad \text{and} \quad a_i = \sum_j w_{ij} x_j \tag{4}$$

where x_i is the state of unit i, a_i its total input (weighted sum), f the squashing function and w_{ij} is the connection going from unit j to unit i. In a shared-weight network like ours, a single parameter u_k can control one or more connections: $w_{ij} = u_k$ for all $(i, j) \in V_k$, where V_k is a set of index pairs. By the chain rule, the diagonal terms of H are given by

$$h_{kk} = \sum_{(i,j) \in V_k} \frac{\partial^2 E}{\partial w_{ij}^2} \tag{5}$$

The summand can be expanded (using the basic network equations 4) as:

$$\frac{\partial^2 E}{\partial w_{ij}^2} = \frac{\partial^2 E}{\partial a_i^2} x_j^2 \tag{6}$$

The second derivatives are back-propagated from layer to layer:

$$\frac{\partial^2 E}{\partial a_i^2} = f'(a_i)^2 \sum_l w_{li}^2 \frac{\partial^2 E}{\partial a_l^2} - f''(a_i) \frac{\partial E}{\partial x_i} \tag{7}$$

We also need the boundary condition at the output layer, specifying the second derivative of E with respect to the last-layer weighted sums:

$$\frac{\partial^2 E}{\partial a_i^2} = 2f'(a_i)^2 - 2(d_i - x_i)f''(a_i) \tag{8}$$

for all units i in the output layer.

As can be seen, computing the diagonal Hessian is of the same order of complexity as computing the gradient. In some cases, the second term of the right hand side of the last two equations (involving the second derivative of f) can be neglected. This corresponds to the well-known Levenberg-Marquardt approximation, and has the interesting property of giving guaranteed positive estimates of the second derivative.

2.2 THE RECIPE

The OBD procedure can be carried out as follows:

1. Choose a reasonable network architecture
2. Train the network until a reasonable solution is obtained
3. Compute the second derivatives h_{kk} for each parameter
4. Compute the saliencies for each parameter: $s_k = h_{kk}u_k^2/2$
5. Sort the parameters by saliency and delete some low-saliency parameters
6. Iterate to step 2

Deleting a parameter is defined as setting it to 0 and freezing it there. Several variants of the procedure can be devised, such as decreasing the values of the low-saliency parameters instead of simply setting them to 0, or allowing the deleted parameters to adapt again after they have been set to 0.

2.3 EXPERIMENTS

The simulation results given in this section were obtained using back-propagation applied to handwritten digit recognition. The initial network was highly constrained and sparsely connected, having 10^5 connections controlled by 2578 free parameters. It was trained on a database of segmented handwritten zipcode digits and printed digits containing approximately 9300 training examples and 3350 test examples. More details can be obtained from the companion paper (Le Cun et al., 1990b).

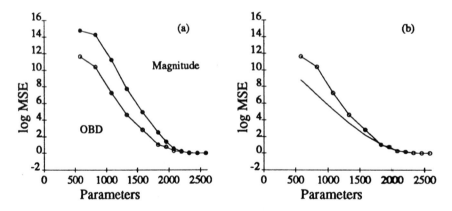

Figure 1: (a) Objective function (in dB) versus number of parameters for OBD (lower curve) and magnitude-based parameter deletion (upper curve). (b) Predicted and actual objective function versus number of parameters. The predicted value (lower curve) is the sum of the saliencies of the deleted parameters.

Figure 1a shows how the objective function increases (from right to left) as the number of remaining parameters decreases. It is clear that deleting parameters by order of saliency causes a significantly smaller increase of the objective function than deleting them according to their magnitude. Random deletions were also tested for the sake of comparison, but the performance was so bad that the curves cannot be shown on the same scale.

Figure 1b shows how the objective function increases (from right to left) as the number of remaining parameters decreases, compared to the increase predicted by the Quadratic-Extremum-Diagonal approximation. Good agrement is obtained for up to approximately 800 deleted parameters (approximately 30% of the parameters). Beyond that point, the curves begin to split, for several reasons: the off-diagonal terms in equation 1 become disproportionately more important as the *number* of deleted parameters increases, and higher-than-quadratic terms become more important when *larger-valued* parameters are deleted.

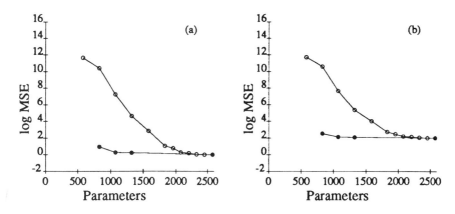

Figure 2: Objective function (in dB) versus number of parameters, without retraining (upper curve), and after retraining (lower curve). Curves are given for the training set (a) and the test set (b).

Figure 2 shows the log-MSE on the training set and the on the test set before and after retraining. The performance on the training set and on the test set (after retraining) stays almost the same when up to 1500 parameters (60% of the total) are deleted.

We have also used OBD as an interactive tool for network design and analysis. This contrasts with the usual view of weight deletion as a more-or-less automatic procedure. Specifically, we prepared charts depicting the saliency of the 10,000 parameters in the digit recognition network reported last year (Le Cun et al., 1990b). To our surprise, several large groups of parameters were expendable. We were able to excise the second-to-last layer, thereby reducing the number of parameters by a factor of two. The training set MSE increased by a factor of 10, and the generalization MSE increased by only 50%. The 10-category classification error on the test set actually decreased (which indicates that MSE is not the optimal objective function for this task). OBD motivated other architectural changes, as can be seen by comparing the 2600-parameter network in (Le Cun et al., 1990a) to the 10,000-parameter network in (Le Cun et al., 1990b).

3 CONCLUSIONS AND OUTLOOK

We have used Optimal Brain Damage interactively to reduce the number of parameters in a practical neural network by a factor of four. We obtained an additional factor of more than two by using OBD to delete parameters automatically. The network's speed improved significantly, and its recognition accuracy increased slightly. We emphasize that the starting point was a state-of-the-art network. It would be too easy to start with a foolish network and make large improvements; a technique that can help improve an already-good network is particularly valuable.

We believe that the techniques presented here only scratch the surface of the applications where second-derivative information can and should be used. In particular, we have also been able to move beyond the approximation that "complexity equals number of free parameters" by using second-derivative information. In (Denker, Le Cun and Solla, 1990), we use it to to derive an improved measure of the network's *information content*, or complexity. This allows us to compare network architectures on a given task, and makes contact with the notion of Minimum Description Length (MDL) (Rissanen, 1989). The main idea is that a "simple" network whose description needs a small number of bits is more likely to generalize correctly than a more complex network, because it presumably has extracted the essence of the data and removed the redundancy from it.

Acknowledgments

We thank the US Postal Service and its contractors for providing us with the database. We also thank Rich Howard and Larry Jackel for their helpful comments and encouragements. We especially thank David Rumelhart for sharing unpublished ideas.

References

Akaike, H. (1986). Use of Statistical Models for Time Series Analysis. In *Proceedings ICASSP 86*, pages 3147–3155, Tokyo. IEEE.

Baum, E. B. and Haussler, D. (1989). What Size Net Gives Valid Generaliztion? *Neural Computation*, 1:151–160.

Becker, S. and Le Cun, Y. (1989). Improving the Convergence of Back-Propagation Learning with Second-Order Methods. In Touretzky, D., Hinton, G., and Sejnowski, T., editors, *Proc. of the 1988 Connectionist Models Summer School*, pages 29–37, San Mateo. Morgan Kaufman.

Chauvin, Y. (1989). A Back-Propagation Algorithm with Optimal Use of Hidden Units. In Touretzky, D., editor, *Neural Information Processing Systems*, volume 1, Denver, 1988. Morgan Kaufmann.

Denker, J., Schwartz, D., Wittner, B., Solla, S. A., Howard, R., Jackel, L., and Hopfield, J. (1987). Large Automatic Learning, Rule Extraction and Generalization. *Complex Systems*, 1:877–922.

Denker, J. S., Le Cun, Y., and Solla, S. A. (1990). Optimal Brain Damage. To appear in Computer and System Sciences.

Hanson, S. J. and Pratt, L. Y. (1989). Some Comparisons of Constraints for Minimal Network Construction with Back-Propagation. In Touretzky, D., editor, *Neural Information Processing Systems*, volume 1, Denver, 1988. Morgan Kaufmann.

Le Cun, Y. (1987). *Modèles Connexionnistes de l'Apprentissage*. PhD thesis, Université Pierre et Marie Curie, Paris, France.

Le Cun, Y. (1989). Generalization and Network Design Strategies. In Pfeifer, R., Schreter, Z., Fogelman, F., and Steels, L., editors, *Connectionism in Perspective*, Zurich, Switzerland. Elsevier.

Le Cun, Y., Boser, B., Denker, J. S., Henderson, D., Howard, R. E., Hubbard, W., and Jackel, L. D. (1990a). Handwritten Digit Recognition with a Back-Propagation Network. In Touretzky, D., editor, *Neural Information Processing Systems*, volume 2, Denver, 1989. Morgan Kaufman.

Le Cun, Y., Boser, B., Denker, J. S., Henderson, D., Howard, R. E., Hubbard, W., and Jackel, L. D. (1990b). Back-Propagation Applied to Handwritten Zipcode Recognition. *Neural Computation*, 1(4).

Mozer, M. C. and Smolensky, P. (1989). Skeletonization: A Technique for Trimming the Fat from a Network via Relevance Assessment. In Touretzky, D., editor, *Neural Information Processing Systems*, volume 1, Denver, 1988. Morgan Kaufmann.

Rissanen, J. (1989). *Stochastic Complexity in Statistical Inquiry*. World Scientific, Singapore.

Rumelhart, D. E. (1988). personal communication.

Solla, S. A., Schwartz, D. B., Tishby, N., and Levin, E. (1990). Supervised Learning: a Theoretical Framework. In Touretzky, D., editor, *Neural Information Processing Systems*, volume 2, Denver, 1989. Morgan Kaufman.

Vapnik, V. N. (1989). Inductive Principles of the Search for Empirical Dependences. In *Proceedings of the second annual Workshop on Computational Learning Theory*, pages 3–21. Morgan Kaufmann.

Vapnik, V. N. and Chervonenkis, A. Y. (1971). On the Uniform Convergence of Relative Frequencies of Events to Their Probabilities. *Th. Prob. and its Applications*, 17(2):264–280.

Waibel, A. (1989). Consonant Recognition by Modular Construction of Large Phonemic Time-Delay Neural Networks. In Touretzky, D., editor, *Neural Information Processing Systems*, volume 1, pages 215–223, Denver, 1988. Morgan Kaufmann.

Asymptotic Convergence of Backpropagation: Numerical Experiments

Subutai Ahmad
ICSI
1947 Center St.
Berkeley, CA 94704

Gerald Tesauro
IBM Watson Labs.
P. O. Box 704
Yorktown Heights, NY
10598

Yu He
Dept. of Physics
Ohio State Univ.
Columbus, OH 43212

ABSTRACT

We have calculated, both analytically and in simulations, the rate of convergence at long times in the backpropagation learning algorithm for networks with and without hidden units. Our basic finding for units using the standard sigmoid transfer function is $1/t$ convergence of the error for large t, with at most logarithmic corrections for networks with hidden units. Other transfer functions may lead to a slower polynomial rate of convergence. Our analytic calculations were presented in (Tesauro, He & Ahamd, 1989). Here we focus in more detail on our empirical measurements of the convergence rate in numerical simulations, which confirm our analytic results.

1   INTRODUCTION

Backpropagation is a popular learning algorithm for multilayer neural networks which minimizes a global error function by gradient descent (Werbos, 1974: Parker, 1985; LeCun, 1985; Rumelhart, Hinton & Williams, 1986). In this paper, we examine the rate of convergence of backpropagation late in learning when all of the errors are small. In this limit, the learning equations become more amenable to analytic study. By expanding in the small differences between the desired and actual output states, and retaining only the dominant terms, one can explicitly solve for the leading-order behavior of the weights as a function of time. This is true both for single-layer networks, and for multilayer networks containing hidden units. We confirm our analysis by empirical measurements of the convergence rate in numerical simulations.

In gradient-descent learning, one minimizes an error function E according to:

$$\Delta \vec{w} = -\epsilon \frac{\partial E}{\partial \vec{w}} \qquad (1)$$

where $\Delta \vec{w}$ is the change in the weight vector at each time step, and the learning rate ϵ is a small numerical constant. The convergence of equation 1 for single-layer networks with general error functions and transfer functions is studied in section 2. In section 3, we examine two standard modifications of gradient-descent: the use of a "margin" variable for turning off the error backpropagation, and the inclusion of a "momentum" term in the learning equation. In section 4 we consider networks with hidden units, and in the final section we summarize our results and discuss possible extensions in future work.

2   CONVERGENCE IN SINGLE-LAYER NETWORKS

The input-output relationship for single-layer networks takes the form:

$$y_p = g(\vec{w} \cdot \vec{x}_p) \qquad (2)$$

where $\vec{x}_p$ represents the state of the input units for pattern p, $\vec{w}$ is the real-valued weight vector of the network, g is the input-output transfer function (for the moment unspecified), and y_p is the output state for pattern p. We assume that the transfer function approaches 0 for large negative inputs and 1 for large positive inputs.

For convenience of analysis, we rewrite equation 1 for continuous time as:

$$\dot{\vec{w}} = -\epsilon \sum_p \frac{\partial E_p}{\partial \vec{w}} = -\epsilon \sum_p \frac{\partial E_p}{\partial y_p} \frac{\partial y_p}{\partial \vec{w}} = -\epsilon \sum_p \frac{\partial E_p}{\partial y_p} g'(h_p) \vec{x}_p \qquad (3)$$

where E_p is the individual error for pattern p, $h_p = \vec{w} \cdot \vec{x}_p$ is the total input activation of the output unit for pattern p, and the summation over p is for an arbitrary subset of the possible training patterns. E_p is a function of the difference between the actual output y_p and the desired output d_p for pattern p. Examples of common error functions are the quadratic error $E_p = (y_p - d_p)^2$ and the "cross-entropy" error (Hinton, 1987) $E_p = d_p \log y_p + (1 - d_p) \log(1 - y_p)$.

Instead of solving equation 3 for the weights directly, it is more convenient to work with the outputs y_p. The outputs evolve according to:

$$\dot{y}_p = -\epsilon g'(h_p) \sum_q \frac{\partial E_q}{\partial y_q} g'(h_q) \vec{x}_q \cdot \vec{x}_p \qquad (4)$$

Let us now consider the situation late in learning when the output states are approaching the desired values. We define new variables $\eta_p = y_p - d_p$, and assume

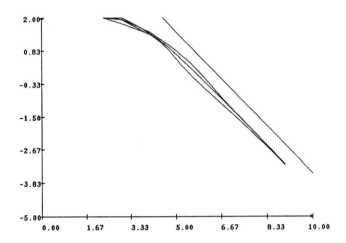

Figure 1: Plots of ln(error) vs. ln(epochs) for single-layer networks learning the majority function using standard backpropagation without momentum. Four different learning runs starting from different random initial weights are shown. In each case, the asymptotic behavior is approximately $E \sim 1/t$, as seen by comparison with a reference line of slope -1.

that η_p is small for all p. For reasonable error functions, the individual errors E_p will go to zero as some power of η_p, i.e., $E_p \sim \eta_p^{\gamma}$. (For the quadratic error, $\gamma = 2$, and for the cross-entropy error, $\gamma = 1$.) Similarly, the slope of the transfer function should approach zero as the output state approaches 1 or 0, and for reasonable transfer functions, this will again follow a power law, i.e., $g'(h_p) \sim \eta_p^{\beta}$. Using the definitions of η, γ and β, equation 4 becomes:

$$\dot{\eta}_p \sim |\eta_p|^{\beta} \sum_q \eta_q^{\gamma-1} |\eta_q|^{\beta} \, \vec{x}_q \cdot \vec{x}_p + \text{higher order} \tag{5}$$

The absolute value appears because g is a non-decreasing function. Let η_r be the slowest to approach zero among all the η_p's. We then have for η_r:

$$\dot{\eta}_r \sim \eta_r^{2\beta+\gamma-1} \tag{6}$$

Upon integrating we obtain

$$\eta_r \sim t^{-1/(2\beta+\gamma-2)} \; ; \; E \sim \eta_r^{\gamma} \sim t^{-\gamma/(2\beta+\gamma-2)} \tag{7}$$

When $\beta = 1$, i.e., $g' \sim \eta$, the error function approaches zero like $1/t$, independent of γ. Since $\beta = 1$ for the standard sigmoid function $g(x) = (1+e^{-x})^{-1}$, one expects to see $1/t$ behavior in the error function in this case. This behavior was in fact first seen in the numerical experiments of (Ahmad, 1988; Ahmad & Tesauro, 1988). The behavior was obtained at relatively small t, about 20 cycles through the training set. Figure 1 illustrates this behavior for single-layer networks learning a data set containing 200 randomly chosen instances of the majority function. In each case, the behavior at long times in this plot is approximately a straight line, indicating power-law decrease of the error. The slopes are in each case within a few percent of the theoretically predicted value of -1.

It turns out that $\beta = 1$ gives the fastest possible convergence of the error function. This is because $\beta < 1$ yields transfer functions which do not saturate at finite values, and thus are not allowed, while $\beta > 1$ yields slower convergence. For example, if we take the transfer function to be $g(x) = 0.5[1 + (2/\pi)\tan^{-1} x]$, then $\beta = 2$. In this case, the error function will go to zero as $E \sim t^{-\gamma/(\gamma+2)}$. In particular, when $\gamma = 2$, $E \sim 1/\sqrt{t}$.

3   MODIFICATIONS OF GRADIENT DESCENT

One common modification to strict gradient-descent is the use of a "margin" variable μ such that, if the difference between network output and teacher signal is smaller than μ, no error is backpropagated. This is meant to prevent the network from devoting resources to making its output arbitrarily close to the teacher signal, which is usually unnecessary. It is clear from the structure of equations 5, 6 that the margin will not affect the basic $1/t$ error convergence, except in a rather trivial way. When a margin is employed, certain driving terms on the right-hand side of equation 5 will be set to zero as soon as they become small enough. However, as long as *some* non-zero driving terms are present, the basic polynomial solution of equation 7 will be unaltered. Of course, when *all* the driving terms disappear because they are all smaller than the margin, the network will stop learning, and the error will remain constant at some positive value. Thus the prediced behavior is $1/t$ decrease in the error followed eventually by a rapid transition to constant non-zero error. This agrees with what is seen numerically in Figure 2.

Another popular generalization of equation 1 includes a "momentum" term:

$$\Delta \vec{w}(t) = -\epsilon \frac{\partial E}{\partial \vec{w}}(t) + \alpha \Delta \vec{w}(t-1) \tag{8}$$

In continuous time, this takes the form:

$$\alpha \ddot{\vec{w}} + (1 - \alpha)\dot{\vec{w}} = -\epsilon \frac{\partial E}{\partial \vec{w}} \tag{9}$$

Turning this into an equation for the evolution of outputs gives:

$$\alpha \ddot{y}_p - \alpha g''(h_p)[\frac{\dot{y}_p}{g'(h_p)}]^2 + (1 - \alpha)\dot{y}_p = -\epsilon g'(h_p)\sum_q \frac{\partial E_q}{\partial y_q} g'(h_q)\vec{x}_q \cdot \vec{x}_p \tag{10}$$

Once again, exapanding y_p, E_p and g' in small η_p yields a second-order differential equation for η_p in terms of a sum over other η_q. As in equation 6, the sum will be

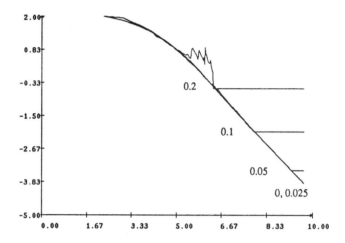

Figure 2: Plot of ln(error) vs. ln(epochs) for various values of margin variable μ as indicated. In each case there is a $1/t$ decrease in the error followed by a sudden transition to constant error. This transition occurs earlier for larger values of μ.

controlled by some dominant term r, and the equation for this term is:

$$C_1 \ddot{\eta}_r \ + \ C_2 \eta_r^{-1} \dot{\eta}_r^2 \ + \ C_3 \dot{\eta}_r \ \sim \ \eta_r^{2\beta + \gamma - 1} \tag{11}$$

where C_1, C_2 and C_3 are numerical constants. For polynomial solutions $\eta_r \sim t^z$, the first two terms are of order t^{z-2}, and can be neglected relative to the third term which is of order t^{z-1}. The resulting equation thus has exactly the same form as in the zero momentum case of section 2, and therefore the rate of convergence is the same as in equation 7. This is demonstrated numerically in Figure 3. We can see that the error behaves as $1/t$ for large t regardless of the value of momentum constant α. Furthermore, although it is not required by the analytic theory, the numerical prefactor appears to be the same in each case.

Finally, we have also considered the effect on convergence of schemes for adaptively altering the learning rate constant ϵ. It was shown analytically in (Tesauro, He & Ahmad, 1989) that for the scheme proposed by Jacobs (1988), in which the learning rate could in principle increase linearly with time, the error would decrease as $1/t^2$ for sigmoid units, instead of the $1/t$ result for fixed ϵ.

4   CONVERGENCE IN NETWORKS WITH HIDDEN UNITS

We now consider networks with a single hidden layer. In (Tesauro, He & Ahmad, 1989), it was shown that if the hidden units saturate late in learning, then the convergence rate is no different from the single-layer rate. This should be typical

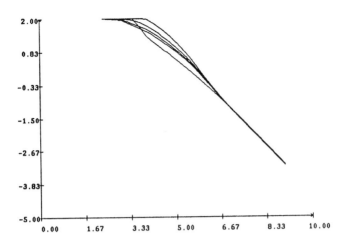

Figure 3: Plot of ln(error) vs. ln(epochs) for single-layer networks learning the majority function, with momentum constant $\alpha = 0, 0.25, 0.5, 0.75, 0.99$. Each run starts from the same random initial weights. Asymptotic $1/t$ behavior is obtained in each case, with the same numerical prefactor.

of what usually happens. However, assuming for purposes of argument that the hidden units do not saturate, when one goes through a small η expansion of the learning equation, one obtains a coupled system of equations of the following form:

$$\dot{\eta} \sim \eta^{2\beta+\gamma-1}[1 + \Omega^2] \tag{12}$$

$$\dot{\Omega} \sim \eta^{\gamma+\beta-1} \tag{13}$$

where Ω represents the magnitude of the second layer weights, and for convenience all indices have been suppressed and all terms of order 1 have been written simply as 1.

For $\beta > 1$, this system has polynomial solutions of the form $\eta \sim t^z$, $\Omega \sim t^\lambda$, with $z = -3/(3\gamma + 4\beta - 4)$ and $\lambda = z(\gamma + \beta - 1) - 1$. It is interesting to note that these solutions converge slightly faster than in the single-layer case. For example, with $\gamma = 2$ and $\beta = 2$, $\eta \sim t^{-3/10}$ in the multilayer case, but as shown previously, η goes to zero only as $t^{-1/4}$ in the single-layer case. We emphasize that this slight speed-up will only be obtained when the hidden unit states do not saturate. To the extent that the hidden units saturate and their slopes become small, the convergence rate will return to the single-layer rate.

When $\beta = 1$ the above polynomial solution is not possible. Instead, one can verify that the following is a self-consistent leading order solution to equations 12, 13:

$$\eta \sim t^{-1/\gamma}ln^{-2/3\gamma}t \tag{14}$$

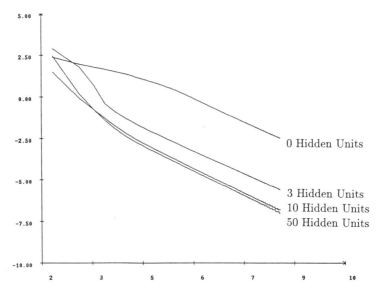

Figure 4: Plot of ln(error) vs. ln(epochs) for networks with varying numbers of hidden units (as indicated) learning majority function data set. Approximate $1/t$ behavior is obtained in each case.

$$\Omega \sim ln^{1/3}t \tag{15}$$

Recall that in the single-layer case, $\eta \sim t^{-1/\gamma}$. Therefore, the effect of multiple layers could provide at most only a logarithmic speed-up of convergence when the hidden units do not saturate. For practical purposes, then, we expect the convergence of networks with hidden units to be no different empirically from networks without hidden units. This is in fact what our simulations find, as illustrated in Figure 4.

5   DISCUSSION

We have obtained results for the asymptotic convergence of gradient-descent learning which are valid for a wide variety of error functions and transfer functions. We typically expect the same rate of convergence to be obtained regardless of whether or not the network has hidden units. However, it may be possible to obtain a slight polynomial speed-up when $\beta > 1$ or a logarithmic speed-up when $\beta = 1$. We point out that in all cases, the sigmoid provides the maximum possible convergence rate, and is therefore a "good" transfer function to use in that sense.

We have not attempted analysis of networks with multiple layers of hidden units; however, the analysis of (Tesauro, He & Ahmad, 1989) suggests that, to the extent that the hidden unit states saturate and the g' factors vanish, the rate of convergence would be no different even in networks with arbitrary numbers of hidden layers.

Another important finding is that the expected rate of convergence does not depend on the use of all 2^n input patterns in the training set. The same behavior should be seen for general subsets of training data. This is also in agreement with our numerical results, and with the results of (Ahamd, 1988; Ahmand & Tesauro, 1988).

In conclusion, a combination of analysis and numerical simulations has led to insight into the late stages of gradient-descent learning. It might also be possible to extend our approach to times earlier in the learning process, when not all of the errors are small. One might also be able to analyze the numbers, sizes and shapes of the basins of attraction for gradient-descent learning in feed-forward networks. Another important issue is the behavior of the generalization performance, i.e., the error on a set of test patterns not used in training, which was not addressed in this paper. Finally, our analysis might provide insight into the development of new algorithms which might scale more favorably than backpropagation.

References

S. Ahmad. (1988) A study of scaling and generalization in neural networks. Master's Thesis, Univ. of Illinois at Urbana-Champaign, Dept. of Computer Science.

S. Ahmad & G. Tesauro. (1988) Scaling and generalization in neural networks: a case study. In D. S. Touretzky et al. (eds.), *Proceedings of the 1988 Connectionist Models Summer School*, 3-10. San Mateo, CA: Morgan Kaufmann.

G. E. Hinton. (1987) Connectionist learning procedures. Technical Report No. CMU-CS-87-115, Dept. of Computer Science, Carnegie-Mellon University.

R. A. Jacobs. (1988) Increased rates of convergence through learning rate adaptation. *Neural Networks* 1:295-307.

Y. Le Cun. (1985) A learning procedure for asymmetric network. *Proceedings of Cognitiva (Paris)* 85:599-604.

D. B. Parker. (1985) Learning-logic. Technical Report No. TR-47, MIT Center for Computational Research in Economics and Management Science.

D. E. Rumelhart, G. E. Hinton, & R. J. Williams. (1986) Learning representations by back-propagating errors. *Nature* **323**:533-536.

G. Tesauro, Y. He & S. Ahmad. (1989) Asymptotic convergence of backpropagation. *Neural Computation* 1:382-391.

P. Werbos. (1974) Ph. D. Thesis, Harvard University.

Comparing the Performance of Connectionist and Statistical Classifiers on an Image Segmentation Problem

Sheri L. Gish   W. E. Blanz
IBM Almaden Research Center
650 Harry Road
San Jose, CA 95120

ABSTRACT

In the development of an image segmentation system for real time image processing applications, we apply the classical decision analysis paradigm by viewing image segmentation as a pixel classification task. We use supervised training to derive a classifier for our system from a set of examples of a particular pixel classification problem. In this study, we test the suitability of a connectionist method against two statistical methods, Gaussian maximum likelihood classifier and first, second, and third degree polynomial classifiers, for the solution of a "real world" image segmentation problem taken from combustion research. Classifiers are derived using all three methods, and the performance of all of the classifiers on the training data set as well as on 3 separate entire test images is measured.

1   Introduction

We are applying the trainable machine paradigm in our development of an image segmentation system to be used in real time image processing applications. We view image segmentation as a classical decision analysis task; each pixel in a scene is described by a set of measurements, and we use that set of measurements with a classifier of our choice to determine the region or object within a scene to which that pixel belongs. Performing image segmentation as a decision analysis task provides several advantages. We can exploit the inherent trainability found in decision analysis systems [1] and use supervised training to derive a classifier from a set of examples of a particular pixel classification problem. Classifiers derived using the trainable machine paradigm will exhibit the property of generalization, and thus can be applied to data representing a set of problems similar to the example problem. In our pixel classification scheme, the classifier can be derived solely from the quantitative characteristics of the problem data. Our approach eliminates the dependency on qualitative characteristics of the problem data which often is characteristic of explicitly derived classification algorithms [2,3].

Classical decision analysis methods employ statistical techniques. We have compared a connectionist system to a set of alternative statistical methods on classification problems in which the classifier is derived using supervised training, and have found that the connectionist alternative is comparable, and in some cases preferable, to the statistical alternatives in terms of performance on problems of varying complexity [4]. That comparison study also analyzed the alternative methods in terms of cost of implementation of the solution architecture in digital LSI. In terms of our cost analysis, the connectionist architectures were much simpler to implement than the statistical architectures for the more complex classification problems; this property of the connectionist methods makes them very attractive implementation choices for systems requiring hardware implementations for difficult applications.

In this study, we evaluate the performance of a connectionist method and several statistical methods as the classifier component of our real time image segmentation system. The classification problem we use is a "real world" pixel classification task using images of the size (200 pixels by 200 pixels) and variable data quality typical of the problems a production system would be used to solve. We thus test the suitability of the connectionist method for incorporation in a system with the performance requirements of our system, as well as the feasibility of our exploiting the advantages the simple connectionist architectures provide for systems implemented in hardware.

2   Methods

2.1   The Image Segmentation System

The image segmentation system we use is described in [5], and summarized in Figure 1. The system is designed to perform low level image segmentation in real time; for production, the feature extraction and classifier system components are implemented in hardware. The classifier parameters are derived during the Training Phase. A user at a workstation outlines the regions or objects of interest in a training image. The system performs low level feature extraction on the training image, and the results of the feature extraction plus the input from the user are combined automatically by the system to form a training data set. The system then applies a supervised training method making use of the training data set in order to derive the coefficients for the classifier which can perform the pixel classification task. The feature extraction process is capable of computing 14 classes of features for each pixel; up to 10 features with the highest discriminatory power are used to describe all of the pixels in the image. This selection of features is based only on an analysis of the results of the feature extraction process and is independent of the supervised learning paradigm being used to derive the classifier [6]. The identical feature extraction process is applied in both the Training and Running Phases for a particular image segmentation problem.

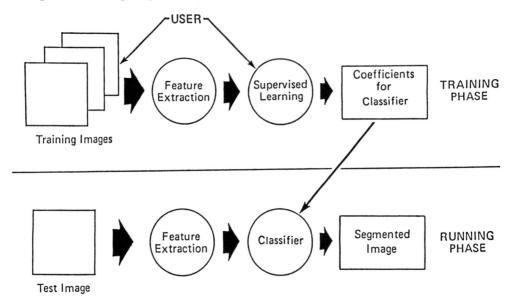

Figure 1: Diagram of the real time image segmentation system.

2.2   The Image Segmentation Problem

The image segmentation problem used in this study is from combustion research and is described in [3]. The images are from a series of images of a combustion chamber taken by a high speed camera during the inflammation process of a gas/air mixture. The segmentation task is to determine the area of inflamed gas in the image; therefore, the pixels in the image are classified into 3 different classes: cylinder, uninflamed gas, and flamed gas (See Figure 2). Exact determination of the area of flamed gas is not possible using pixel classification alone, but the greater the success of the pixel classification step, the greater the likelihood that a real time image segmentation system could be used successfully on this problem.

2.3   The Classifiers

The set of classifiers used in this study is composed of a connectionist classifier based on the Parallel Distributed Processing (PDP) model described in [7] and two statistical methods: a Gaussian maximum likelihood classifier (a Bayes classifier), and a polynomial classifier based on first, second, and third degree polynomials. This set of classifiers was used in a general study comparing the performance of

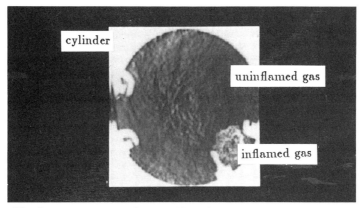

Figure 2: The image segmentation problem is to classify each image pixel into 1 of 3 regions.

the alternatives on a set of classification problems; all of the classifiers as well as adaptation procedures are described in detail in that study [4]. Implementation and adaptation of all classifiers in this study was performed as software simulation. The connectionist classifier was implemented in CMU Common Lisp running on an IBM RT workstation.

The connectionist classifier architecture is a multi-layer feedforward network with one hidden layer. The network is fully connected, but there are only connections between adjacent layers. The number of units in the input and output layers are determined by the number of features in the feature vector describing each pixel and a binary encoding scheme for the class to which the pixel belongs, respectively. The number of units in the hidden layer is an architectural "free parameter." The network used in this study has 10 units in the input layer, 12 units in the hidden layer, and 3 units in the output layer.

Network activation is achieved by using the continuous, nonlinear *logistic* function defined in [8]. The connectionist adaptation procedure is the application of the backpropagation learning rule also defined in [8]. For this problem, the learning rate $\eta = 0.01$ and the momentum $\alpha = 0.9$; both terms were held constant throughout adaptation. The presentation of all of the patterns in the training data set is termed a *trial*; network weights and unit biases were updated after the presentation of each pattern during a trial.

The training data set for this problem was generated automatically by the image segmentation system. This training data set consists of approximately 4,000 ten element (feature) vectors (each vector describes one pixel); each vector is labeled as belonging to one of the 3 regions of interest in the image. The training data set was constructed from one entire training image, and is composed of vectors statistically representative of the pixels in each of the 3 regions of interest in that image.

All of the classifiers tested in this study were adapted from the same training data set. The connectionist classifier was defined to be converged for this problem before it was tested. Network convergence is determined from the results of two separate tests. In the first test, the difference between the network output and the target output averaged over the entire training data set has to reach a minimum. In the second test, the performance of the network in classifying the training data set is measured, and the number of misclassifications made by the network has to reach a minimum. Actual network performance in classifying a pattern is measured after post-processing of the output vector. The real outputs of each unit in the output layer are assigned the values of 0 or 1 by application of a 0.5 decision threshold. In our binary encoding scheme, the output vector should have only one element with the value 1; that element corresponds to one of the 3 classes. If the network produces an output vector with either more than one element with the value 1 or all elements with the value 0, the pattern generating that output is considered rejected. For the test problem in this study, all of the classifiers were set to reject patterns in the test data samples. All of the statistical classifiers had a rejection threshold set to 0.03.

3 Results

The performance of each of the classifiers (connectionist, Gaussian maximum likelihood, and linear, quadratic, and cubic polynomial) was measured on the training data set and test data representing 3 entire images taken from the series of combustion chamber images. One of those images, labeled Image 1, is the image from which the training data set was constructed. The performance of all of the classifiers is summarized in Table 1.

Although all of the classifiers were able to classify the training data set with comparably few misclassifications, the Gaussian maximum likelihood classifier and the quadratic polynomial classifier were unable to perform on any of the 3 entire test images. The connectionist classifier was the only alternative tested in this study to deliver acceptable performance on all 3 test images; the connectionist classifier had lower error rates on the test images than it delivered on the training data sample. Both the linear polynomial and cubic polynomial classifiers performed acceptably on the test Image 2, but then both exhibited high error rates on the other two test images. For this image segmentation problem, only the connectionist method generalized from the training data set to a solution with acceptable performance.

In Figure 3, the results from pixel classification performed by the connectionist and polynomial classifiers on all 3 test images are portrayed as segmented images. The actual test images are included at the left of the figure.

4 Conclusions

Our results demonstrate the feasibility of the application of a connectionist decision analysis method to the solution of a "real world" image segmentation problem. The

Data Set	Connectionist Classifier		Polynomial Classifier			Gaussian Classifier	
	Error[a]	Reject[b]	Degree	Error	Reject	Error	Reject
Training Data	10.40%	1.64%	1	11.25%	1.62%	12.84%	0.12%
			2	9.61%	1.41%		
			3	8.13%	1.05%		
Image 1[c]	8.84%	1.72%	1	41.70%	4.63%	94.27%	0.00%
			2	57.55%	3.66%		
			3	25.86%	0.28%		
Image 2	5.82%	1.53%	1	12.01%	2.00%	69.09%	0.01%
			2	68.01%	0.58%		
			3	4.68%	0.26%		
Image 3	6.31%	1.63%	1	19.68%	5.43%	88.35%	0.00%
			2	45.89%	1.41%		
			3	25.75%	0.28%		

[a]Percent misclassifications for all patterns.

[b]Percent of all patterns rejected.

[c]Image from which training data set was taken.

Table 1: A summary of the performance of the classifiers.

inclusion of a connectionist classifier in our supervised segmentation system will allow us to meet our performance requirements under real world problem constraints.

Although the application of connectionism to the solution of real time machine vision problems represents a new processing method, our solution strategy has remained consistent with the decision analysis paradigm. Our connectionist classifiers are derived solely from the quantitative characteristics of the problem data; our connectionist architecture thus remains simple and need not be re-designed according to qualitative characteristics of each specific problem to which it will be applied. Our connectionist architecture is independent of the image size; we have applied the identical architecture successfully to images which range in size from 200 pixels by 200 pixels to 512 pixels by 512 pixels [9]. In most research to date in which neural networks are applied to machine vision, entire images explicitly are mapped to networks by making each pixel in an image correspond to a different unit in a network layer (see [10,11] for examples). This "pixel map" representation makes scaling up to larger image sizes from the idealized "toy" research images a significant problem.

Most statistical pattern classification methods require that problem data satisfy the assumptions of statistical models; unfortunately, real world problem data are complex and of variable quality and thus rarely can be used to guide the choice of an appropriate method for the solution of a particular problem *a priori*. For the image segmentation problem reported in this study, our classifier performance results show that the problem data actually did not satisfy the assumptions behind the statistical models underlying the Gaussian maximum likelihood classifier or the polynomial

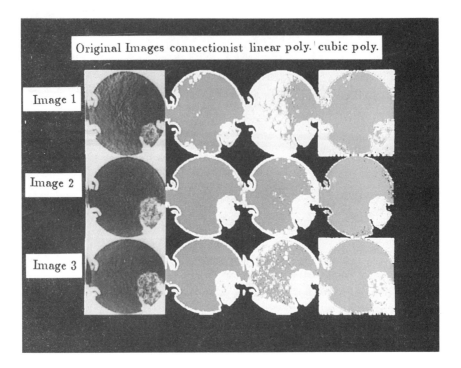

Figure 3: The grey levels assigned to each region are: Black — cylinder, Light Grey — uninflamed gas, Grey — flamed gas. Original images are at the left of the figure.

classifiers. It appears that the Gaussian model least fits our problem data, the polynomial classifiers provide a slightly better fit, and the connectionist method provides the fit required for the solution of the problem. It is also notable that all the alternative methods in this study could be adapted to perform acceptably on the training data set, but extensive testing on several different entire images was required in order to demonstrate the true performance of the alternative methods on the actual problem, rather than just on the training data set.

These results show that a connectionist method is a viable choice for a system such as ours which requires a simple architecture readily implemented in hardware, the flexibility to handle complex problems described by large amounts of data, and the robustness to not require problem data to meet many model assumptions *a priori*.

References

[1] R. O. Duda and P. E. Hart. *Pattern Classification and Scene Analysis*. Wiley, New York, 1973.

[2] W. E. Blanz, J. L. C. Sanz, and D. Petkovic. Control-free low-level image segmentation: Theory, architecture,and experimentation. In J. L. C. Sanz, editor, *Advances of Machine Vision, Applications and Architectures*, Springer-Verlag, 1988.

[3] B. Straub and W. E. Blanz. Combined decision theoretic and syntactic approach to image segmentation. *Machine Vision and Applications*, 2(1):17–30, 1989.

[4] Sheri L. Gish and W. E. Blanz. *Comparing a Connectionist Trainable Classifier with Classical Statistical Decision Analysis Methods*. Research Report RJ 6891 (65717), IBM, June 1989.

[5] W. E. Blanz, B. Shung, C. Cox, W. Greiner, B. Dom, and D. Petkovic. *Design and implementation of a low level image segmentation architecture – LISA*. Research Report RJ 7194 (67673), IBM, December 1989.

[6] W. E. Blanz. Non-parametric feature selection for multiple class processes. In *Proc. 9th Int. Conf. Pattern Recognition*, Rome, Italy, Nov. 14–17 1988.

[7] David E. Rumelhart, James L. McClelland, et al. *Parallel Distributed Processing*. MIT Press, Cambridge, Massachusetts, 1986.

[8] David E. Rumelhart, Geoffrey E. Hinton, and Ronald J. Williams. Learning internal representations by error propagation. In David E. Rumelhart, James L. McClelland, et al., editors, *Parallel Distributed Processing*, chapter 8, MIT Press, Cambridge, Massachusetts, 1986.

[9] W. E. Blanz and Sheri L. Gish. *A Connectionist Classifier Architecture Applied To Image Segmentation*. Research Report RJ 7193 (67672), IBM, December 1989.

[10] K. Fukushima, S. Miyake, and T. Ito. Neocognitron: a neural network model for a mechanism of visual pattern recognition. *IEEE Transactions on Systems, Man, and Cybernetics*, SMC-13(5):826–834, 1983.

[11] Y. Hirai. A model of human associative processor. *IEEE Transactions on Systems, Man, and Cybernetics*, SMC–13(5):851–857, 1983.

Performance Comparisons Between Backpropagation Networks and Classification Trees on Three Real-World Applications

Les Atlas
Dept. of EE, FT-10
University of Washington
Seattle, Washington 98195

Ronald Cole
Dept. of CS&E
Oregon Graduate Institute
Beaverton, Oregon 97006

Jerome Connor, Mohamed El-Sharkawi, and Robert J. Marks II
University of Washington

Yeshwant Muthusamy
Oregon Graduate Institute

Etienne Barnard
Carnegie-Mellon University

ABSTRACT

Multi-layer perceptrons and trained classification trees are two very different techniques which have recently become popular. Given enough data and time, both methods are capable of performing arbitrary non-linear classification. We first consider the important differences between multi-layer perceptrons and classification trees and conclude that there is not enough theoretical basis for the clear-cut superiority of one technique over the other. For this reason, we performed a number of empirical tests on three real-world problems in power system load forecasting, power system security prediction, and speaker-independent vowel identification. In all cases, even for piecewise-linear trees, the multi-layer perceptron performed as well as or better than the trained classification trees.

1 INTRODUCTION

In this paper we compare regression and classification systems. A regression system can generate an output Y for an input X, where both X and Y are continuous and, perhaps, multi-dimensional. A classification system can generate an output class, C, for an input X, where X is continuous and multi-dimensional and C is a member of a finite alphabet.

The statistical technique of Classification And Regression Trees (CART) was developed during the years 1973 (Meisel and Michalpoulos) through 1984 (Breiman *et al*). As we show in the next section, CART, like the multi-layer perceptron (MLP), can be trained to solve the exclusive-OR problem. Furthermore, the solution it provides is extremely easy to interpret. Moreover, both CART and MLPs are able to provide arbitrary piecewise linear decision boundaries. Although there have been no links made between CART and biological neural networks, the possible applications and paradigms used for MLP and CART are very similar.

The authors of this paper represent diverse interests in problems which have the commonality of being both important and potentially well-suited for trainable classifiers. The **load forecasting** problem, which is partially a regression problem, uses past load trends to predict the critical needs of future power generation. The **power security** problem uses the classifier as an interpolator of previously known states of the system. The **vowel recognition** problem is representative of the difficulties in automatic speech recognition due to variability across speakers and phonetic context.

In each problem area, large amounts of real data were used for training and disjoint data sets were used for testing. We were careful to ensure that the experimental conditions were identical for the MLP and CART. We concentrated only on performance as measured in error on the test set and did not do any formal studies of training or testing time. (CART was, in general, quite a bit faster.)

In all cases, even with various sizes of training sets, the multi-layer perceptron performed as well as or better than the trained classification trees. We also believe that integration of many of CART's well-designed attributes into MLP architectures could only improve the already promising performance of MLP's.

2 BACKGROUND

2.1 Multi-Layer Perceptrons

The name "artificial neural networks" has in some communities become almost synonymous with MLP's trained by back-propagation. Our power studies made use of this standard algorithm (Rumelhart *et al*, 1986) and our vowel studies made use of a conjugate gradient version (Barnard and Casasent, 1989) of back-propagation. In all cases the training data consisted of ordered pairs $\{(X,Y)\}$ for regression, or $\{(X,C)\}$ for classification. The input to the network is X and the output is, after training, hopefully very close to Y or C.

When MLP's are used for regression, the output, Y, can take on real values between 0 and 1. This normalized scale was used as the prediction value in the power forecasting problem. For MLP classifiers the output is formed by taking the (0,1) range of the output neurons and either thresholding or finding a peak. For example, in the vowel study we chose the maximum of the 12 output neurons to indicate the vowel class.

2.2   Classification and Regression Trees (CART)

CART has already proven to be useful in diverse applications such as radar signal classification, medical diagnosis, and mass spectra classification (Breiman *et al*, 1984). Given a set of training examples $\{(X,C)\}$, a binary tree is constructed by sequentially partitioning the p-dimensional input space, which may consist of quantitative and/or qualitative data, into p-dimensional polygons. The trained classification tree divides the domain of the data into non-overlapping regions, each of which is assigned a class label C. For regression, the estimated function is piecewise constant over these regions.

The first split of the data space is made to obtain the best global separation of the classes. The next step in CART is to consider the partitioned training examples as two completely unrelated sets—those examples on the left of the selected hyper-plane, and those on the right. CART then proceeds as in the first step, treating each subset of the training examples independently. A question which had long plagued the use of such sequential schemes was: when should the splitting stop? CART implements a novel, and very clever approach; splits continue until every training example is separated from every other, then a pruning criterion is used to sequentially remove less important splits.

2.3   Relative Expectations of MLP and CART

The non-linearly separable exclusive-OR problem is an example of a problem which both MLP and CART can solve with zero error. The left side of Figure 1 shows a trained MLP solution to this problem and the right side shows the very simple trained CART solution. For the MLP the values along the arrows represent trained multiplicative weights and the values in the circles represent trained scalar offset values. For the CART figure, y and n represent yes or no answers to the trained thresholds and the values in the circles represent the output Y. It is interesting that CART did not train correctly for equal numbers of the four different input cases and that one extra example of one of the input cases was sufficient to break the symmetry and allow CART to train correctly. (Note the similarity to the well-known requirement of random and different initial weights for training the MLP).

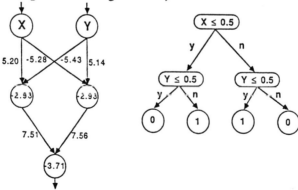

Figure 1:   The MLP and CART solutions to the exclusive-OR problem.

CART trains on the exclusive-OR very easily since a piecewise-linear partition in the input space is a perfect solution. In general, the MLP will construct classification regions with smooth boundaries, whereas CART will construct regions with ''sharp'' corners (each region being, as described previously, an intersection of half planes). We would thus expect MLP to have an advantage when classification boundaries tend to be smooth and CART to have an advantage when they are sharper.

Other important differences between MLP and CART include:

For an MLP the number of hidden units can be selected to avoid overfitting or underfitting the data. CART fits the complexity by using an automatic pruning technique to adjust the size of the tree. The selection of the number of hidden units or the tree size was implemented in our experiments by using data from a second training set (independent of the first).

An MLP becomes a classifier through an ad hoc application of thresholds or peak-picking to the output value(s). Great care has gone into the CART splitting rules while the usual MLP approach is rather arbitrary.

A trained MLP represents an approximate solution to an optimization problem. The solution may depend on initial choice of weights and on the optimization technique used. For complex MLP's many of the units are independently and simultaneously adjusting their weights to best minimize output error.

MLP is a distributed topology where a single point in the input space can have an effect across all units or analogously, one weight, acting alone, will have minimal affect on the outputs. CART is very different in that each split value can be mapped onto one segment in the input space. The behavior of CART makes it much more useful for data interpretation. A trained tree may be useful for understanding the structure of the data. The usefulness of MLP's for data interpretation is much less clear.

The above points, when taken in combination, do not make a clear case for either MLP or CART to be superior for the best performance as a trained classifier. We thus believe that the empirical studies of the next sections, with their consistent performance trends, will indicate which of the comparative aspects are the most significant.

3 LOAD FORECASTING

3.1   The Problem

The ability to predict electric power system loads from an hour to several days in the future can help a utility operator to efficiently schedule and utilize power generation. This ability to forecast loads can also provide information which can be used to strategically trade energy with other generating systems. In order for these forecasts to be useful to an operator, they must be accurate and computationally efficient.

3.2   Methods

Hourly temperature and load data for the Seattle/Tacoma area were provided for us by the Puget Sound Power and Light Company. Since weekday forecasting is a more critical problem for the power industry than weekends, we selected the hourly data for all Tuesdays through Fridays in the interval of November 1, 1988 through January 31, 1989. These data consisted of 1368 hourly measurements that consisted of the 57 days of data collected.

These data were presented to both the MLP and the CART classifier as a 6-dimensional input with a single, real-valued output. The MLP required that all values be normalized to the range (0,1). These same normalized values were used with the CART technique. Our training and testing process consisted of training the classifiers on 53 days of the data and testing on the 4 days left over at the end of January 1989. Our training set consisted of 1272 hourly measurements and our test set contained 96 hourly readings.

The MLP we used in these experiments had 6 inputs (plus the trained constant bias term) 10 units in one hidden layer and one output. This topology was chosen by making use of data outside the training and test sets.

3.3   Results

We used an l_1 norm for the calculation of error rates and found that both techniques worked quite well. The average error rate for the MLP was 1.39% and CART gave 2.86% error. While this difference (given the number of testing points) is not statistically significant, it is worth noting that the trained MLP offers performance which is at least as good as the current techniques used by the Puget Sound Power and Light Company and is currently being verified for application to future load prediction.

4   POWER SYSTEM SECURITY

The assessment of security in a power system is an ongoing problem for the efficient and reliable generation of electric power. Static security addresses whether, after a disturbance, such as a line break or other rapid load change, the system will reach a steady state operating condition that does not violate any operating constraint and cause a "brown-out" or "black-out."

The most efficient generation of power is achieved when the power system is operating near its insecurity boundary. In fact, the ideal case for efficiency would be full knowledge of the absolute boundaries of the secure regions. Due to the complexity of the power systems, this full knowledge is impossible. Load flow algorithms, which are based on iterative solutions of nonlinearly constrained equations, are conventionally used to slowly and accurately determine points of security or insecurity. In real systems the trajectories through the regions are not predictable in fine detail. Also these changes can happen too fast to compute new results from the accurate load flow equations.

We thus propose to use the sparsely known solutions of the load flow equations as a training set. The test set consists of points of unknown security. The error of the test set can then be computed by comparing the result of the trained classifier to load flow equation solutions.

Our technique for converting this problem to a problem for a trainable classifier involves defining a training set $\{(X,C)\}$ where X is composed of real power, reactive power, and apparent power at another bus. This 3-dimensional input vector is paired with the corresponding security status (C=1 for secure and C=0 for insecure). Since the system was small, we were able to generate a large number of data points for training and testing. In fact, well over 20,000 total data points were available for the (disjoint) training and test sets.

4.1 Results

We observed that for any choice of training data set size, the error rate for the MLP was always lower than the rate for the CART classifier. At 10,000 points of training data, the MLP had an error rate of 0.78% and CART has an error rate of 1.46%. While both of these results are impressive, the difference was statistically significant ($p > .99$).

In order to gain insight into the reasons for differences in importance, we looked at classifier decisions for 2-dimensional slices of the input space. While the CART boundary sometimes was a better match, certain pathological difficulties made CART more error-prone than the MLP. Our other studies also showed that there were worse interpolation characteristics for CART, especially for sparse data. Apparently, starting with nonlinear combinations of inputs, which is what the MLP does, is better for the accurate fit than the stair-steps of CART.

5 SPEAKER-INDEPENDENT VOWEL CLASSIFICATION

Speaker-independent classification of vowels excised from continuous speech is a most difficult task because of the many sources of variability that influence the physical realization of a given vowel. These sources of variability include the length of the speaker's vocal tract, phonetic context in which the vowel occurs, speech rate and syllable stress.

To make the task even more difficult the classifiers were presented only with information from a single spectral slice. The spectral slice, represented by 64 DFT coefficients (0-4 kHz), was taken from the center of the vowel, where the effects of coarticulation with surrounding phonemes are least apparent.

The training and test sets for the experiments consisted of featural descriptions, X, paired with an associated class, C, for each vowel sample. The 12 monophthongal vowels of English were used for the classes, as heard in the following words: b*eat*, b*i*t, b*e*t, b*a*t, r*o*ses, th*e*, b*u*t, b*oo*t, b*oo*k, b*ough*t, c*o*t, b*ir*d. The vowels were excised from the wide variety of phonetic contexts in utterances of the TIMIT database, a standard acoustic phonetic corpus of continuous speech, displaying a wide range of American dialectical variation (Fisher *et al*, 1986) (Lamel *et al*, 1986). The training set consisted of 4104 vowels from 320 speakers. The test set consisted of 1644 vowels (137 occurrences of each vowel) from a different set of 100 speakers.

The MLP consisted of 64 inputs (the DFT coefficients, each normalized between zero and one), a single hidden layer of 40 units, and 12 output units; one for each vowel category. The networks were trained using backpropagation with conjugate gradient optimization (Barnard and Casasent, 1989). The procedure for training and testing a network proceeded as follows: The network was trained on 100 iterations through the 4104 training vectors. The trained network was then evaluated on the training set and a different set of 1644 test vectors (the test set). The network was then trained for an additional 100 iterations and again evaluated on the training and test sets. This process was continued until the network had converged; convergence was observed as a consistent decrease or leveling off of the classification percentage on the test data over successive sets of 100 iterations.

The CART system was trained using two separate computer routines. One was the CART program from California Statistical Software; the other was a routine we designed ourselves. We produced our own routine to ensure a careful and independent test of the CART concepts described in (Breiman *et al*, 1984).

5.1   Results

In order to better understand the results, we performed listening experiments on a sub-set of the vowels used in these experiments. The vowels were excised from their sentence context and presented in isolation. Five listeners first received training in the task by classifying 900 vowel tokens and receiving feedback about the correct answer on each trial. During testing, each listener classified 600 vowels from the test set (50 from each category) without feedback. The average classification performance on the test set was 51%, compared to chance performance of 8.3%. Details of this experiment are presented in (Muthusamy *et al*, 1990). When using the scaled spectral coefficients to train both techniques, the MLP correctly classified 47.4% of the test set while CART employing uni-variate splits performed at only 38.2%.

One reason for the poor performance of CART with uni-variate splits may be that each coefficient (corresponding to energy in a narrow frequency band) contains little information when considered independently of the other coefficients. For example, reduced energy in the 1 kHz band may be difficult to detect if the energy in the 1.06 kHz band was increased by an appropriate amount. The CART classifier described above operates by making a series of inquiries about one frequency band at a time, an intuitively inappropriate approach.

We achieved our best CART results, 46.4%, on the test set by making use of arbitrary hyper-planes (linear combinations) instead of univariate splits. This search-based approach gave results which were within 1% of the MLP results.

6   CONCLUSIONS

In all cases the performance of the MLP was, in terms of percent error, better than CART. However, the difference in performance between the two classifiers was only significant (at the $p > .99$ level) for the power security problem.

There are several possible reasons for the sometimes superior performance of the MLP technique, all of which we are currently investigating. One advantage may stem from the ability of MLP to easily find correlations between large numbers of variables. Although it is possible for CART to form arbitrary nonlinear decision boundaries, the efficiency of the recursive splitting process may be inferior to MLP's nonlinear fit. Another relative disadvantage of CART may be due to the successive nature of node growth. For example, if the first split that is made for a problem turns out, given the successive splits, to be suboptimal, it becomes very inefficient to change the first split to be more suitable.

We feel that the careful statistics used in CART could also be advantageously applied to MLP. The superior performance of MLP is not yet indicative of best performance and it may turn out that careful application of statistics may allow further advancements in the MLP technique. It also may be possible that there would be input representations that would cause better performance for CART than for MLP.

There have been new developments in trained statistical classifiers since the development of CART. More recent techniques, such as projection pursuit (Friedman and Stuetzle, 1984), may prove as good as or superior to MLP. This continued interplay between MLP techniques and advanced statistics is a key part of our ongoing research.

Acknowledgements

The authors wish to thank Professor R.D. Martin and Dr. Alan Lippman of the University of Washington Department of Statistics and Professors Aggoune, Damborg, and Hwang of the University of Washington Department of Electrical Engineering for their helpful discussions. David Cohn and Carlos Rivera assisted with many of the experiments.

We also would like to thank Milan Casey Brace of Puget Power and Light for providing the load forecasting data.

This work was supported by a National Science Foundation Presidential Young Investigator Award for L. Atlas and also by separate grants from the National Science Foundation and Washington Technology Center.

References

P. E. Barnard and D. Casasent, "Image Processing for Image Understanding with Neural Nets," *Proc. Int. Joint Conf. on Neural Nets*, Washington, DC, June 18-22, 1989.

L. Breiman, J.H. Friedman, R.A. Olshen, and C.J. Stone, **Classification and Regression Trees,** Wadsworth International, Belmont, CA, 1984.

W. Fisher, G. Doddington, and K. Goudie-Marshall, "The DARPA Speech Recognition Research Database: Specification and Status," *Proc. of the DARPA Speech Recognition Workshop,* pp. 93-100, February 1986.

J.H. Friedman and W. Stuetzle, "Projection Pursuit Regression," *J. Amer. Stat. Assoc.* **79**, pp. 599-608, 1984.

L. Lamel, R. Kassel, and S. Seneff, "Speech Database Development: Design and Analysis of the Acoustic-Phonetic Corpus," *Proc. of the DARPA Speech Recognition Workshop*, pp. 100-110, February 1986.

W.S. Meisel and D.A. Michalpoulos, "A Partitioning Algorithm with Application in Pattern Classification and the Optimization of Decision Trees," *IEEE Trans. Computers* **C-22**, pp. 93-103, 1973.

Y. Muthusamy, R. Cole, and M. Slaney, "Vowel Information in a Single Spectral Slice: Cochleagrams Versus Spectrograms," *Proc. ICASSP '90*, April 3-6, 1990. (to appear)

D.E. Rumelhart, G.E. Hinton, and R.J. Williams, "Learning Internal Representations by Error Propagation," Ch. 2 in **Parallel Distributed Processing**, D.E. Rumelhart, J.L. McClelland, and the PDP Research Group, MIT Press, Cambridge, MA, 1986.

Generalization and Parameter Estimation in Feedforward Nets: Some Experiments

N. Morgan[†]
[†]International Computer Science Institute
Berkeley, CA 94704, USA

H. Bourlard[†‡]
[‡]Philips Research Laboratory Brussels
B-1170 Brussels, Belgium

ABSTRACT

We have done an empirical study of the relation of the number of parameters (weights) in a feedforward net to generalization performance. Two experiments are reported. In one, we use simulated data sets with well-controlled parameters, such as the signal-to-noise ratio of continuous-valued data. In the second, we train the network on vector-quantized mel cepstra from real speech samples. In each case, we use back-propagation to train the feedforward net to discriminate in a multiple class pattern classification problem. We report the results of these studies, and show the application of cross-validation techniques to prevent overfitting.

1 INTRODUCTION

It is well known that system models which have too many parameters (with respect to the number of measurements) do not generalize well to new measurements. For instance, an autoregressive (AR) model can be derived which will represent the training data with no error by using as many parameters as there are data points. This would generally be of no value, as it would only represent the training data. Criteria such as the Akaike Information Criterion (AIC) [Akaike, 1974, 1986] can be used to penalize both the complexity of AR models and their training error variance. In feedforward nets, we do not currently have such a measure. In fact, given the aim of building systems which are biologically plausible, there is a temptation to assume the usefulness of indefinitely large adaptive networks. In contrast to our best guess at Nature's tricks, man-made systems for pattern recognition seem to require nasty amounts of data for training. In short, the design of massively parallel systems is limited by the number of parameters that can be learned with available training data. It is likely that the only way truly massive systems can be built is with the help of prior information, e.g., connection topology and weights that need not be learned [Feldman et al, 1988].

Learning theory [Valiant, V.N., 1984; Pearl, J., 1978] has begun to establish what is possible for trained systems. Order-of-magnitude lower bounds have been established for the number of required measurements to train a desired size feedforward net [Baum&Haussler, 1988]. Rules of thumb suggesting the number of samples required for specific distributions could be useful for practical problems. Widrow has suggested having a training sample size that is 10 times the number of weights in a network ("Uncle Bernie's Rule")[Widrow, 1987]. We have begun an empirical study of the relation of the number of parameters in a feedforward net (e.g. hidden units, connections, feature dimension) to generalization performance for data sets with known discrimination complexity and signal-to-noise ratio. In the experiment reported here, we are using simulated data sets with controlled parameters, such as the number of clusters of continuous-valued data. In a related practical example, we have trained a feedforward network on vector-quantized mel cepstra from real speech samples. In each case, we are using the back-propagation algorithm [Rumelhart et al, 1986] to train the feedforward net to discriminate in a multiple class pattern classification problem. Our results confirm that estimating more parameters than there are training samples can degrade generalization. However, the peak in generalization performance (for the difficult pattern recognition problems tested here) can be quite broad if the networks are not trained too long, suggesting that previous guidelines for network size may have been conservative. Furthermore, cross-validation techniques, which have also proved quite useful for autoregressive model order determination, appear to improve generalization when used as a stopping criterion for iteration, and thus preventing overtraining.

2 RANDOM VECTOR PROBLEM

2.1 METHODS

Studies based on synthesized data sets will generally show behavior that is different from that seen with a real data set. Nonetheless, such studies are useful because of the ease with which variables of interest may be altered. In this case, the object was to manufacture a difficult pattern recognition problem with statistically regular variability between the training and test sets. This is actually no easy trick; if the problem is too easy, then even very small nets will be sufficient, and we would not be modeling the problem of doing hard pattern classification with small amounts of training data. If the problem is too hard, then variations in performance will be lost in the statistical variations inherent to methods like back-propagation, which use random initial weight values.

Random points in a 4-dimensional hyperrectangle (drawn from a uniform probability distribution) are classified arbitrarily into one of 16 classes. This group of points will be referred to as a cluster. This process is repeated for 1-4 nonoverlapping hyperrectangles. A total of 64 points are chosen, 4 for each class. All points are then randomly perturbed with noise of uniform density and range specified by a desired signal-to-noise ratio (SNR). The noise is added twice to create 2 data sets, one to be used for training, and the other for test. Intuitively, one might expect that 16-64 hidden units would be required to transform the training space for classification by the output layer. However, the variation between training and test and the relatively small amount of data (256 numbers) suggest that for large numbers of parameters (over 256) there should be a significant degrading of generalization. Another issue was how performance in such a situation would vary over large numbers of iterations.

Simulations were run on this data using multi-layer perceptrons(MLP) (i.e., layered feedforward networks) with 4 continuous-valued inputs, 16 outputs, and a hidden layer of sizes ranging from 4 to 128. Nets were run for signal-to-noise ratios of 1.0 and 2.0, where the SNR is defined as the ratio of the range of the original cluster points to the range of the added random values. Error back-propagation without momentum was used, with an adaptation constant of .25 . For each case, the 64 training patterns were used 10,000 times, and the resulting network was tested on the second data set every 100 iterations so that generalization could be observed during the learning. Blocks of ten scores were averaged to stabilize the generalization estimate. After this smoothing, the standard deviation of error (using the normal approximation to the binomial distribution) was roughly 1%. Therefore, differences of 3% in generalization performance are significant at a level of .001 . All computation was performed on Sun4-110's using code written in C at ICSI. Roughly a trillion floating point operations were required for the study.

2.2   RESULTS

Table I shows the test performance for a single cluster and a signal-to-noise ratio of 1.0 . The chart shows the variation over a range of iterations and network size (specified both as #hidden units, and as ratio of #weights to #measurements, or "weight ratio"). Note that the percentages can have finer gradation than 1/64, due to the averaging, and that the performance on the training set is given in parentheses. Test performance is best for this case for 8 hidden units (24.7%), or a weight ratio of .62 (after 2000 iterations), and for 16 units (21.9%), or a weight ratio of 1.25 (after 10000 iterations). For larger networks, the performance degrades, presumably because of the added noise. At 2000 iterations, the degradation is statistically significant, even in going from 8 to 16 hidden units. There is further degradation out to the 128-unit case. The surprising thing is that, while this degradation is quite noticeable, it is quite graceful considering the order-of-magnitude range in net sizes. An even stronger effect is the loss of generalization power when the larger nets are more fully trained. All of the nets generalized better when they were trained to a relatively poor degree, especially the larger ones.

Table I — Test (and training) scores: 1 cluster, SNR = 1.0

#hidden units	#weights / #inputs	%Test (Train) Correct after N Iterations			
		1000	2000	5000	10000
4	.31	9.2(4.4)	21.7(15.6)	12.0(25.9)	15.6(34.4)
8	.62	11.4(5.2)	24.7(17.0)	20.6(29.8)	21.4(63.9)
16	1.25	13.6(6.9)	21.1(18.4)	18.3(37.2)	21.9(73.4)
32	2.50	12.8(6.4)	18.4(18.3)	17.8(41.7)	13.0(80.8)
64	5.0	13.6(7.7)	18.3(20.8)	19.7(34.4)	18.0(79.2)
128	10.0	11.6(6.7)	17.7(19.1)	12.2(34.7)	15.6(75.6)

Table II shows the results for the same 1-cluster problem, but with higher SNR data (2.0). In this case, a higher level of test performance was reached, and it was reached for a larger net with more iterations (40.8% for 64 hidden units after 5000 iterations). At this point in the iterations, no real degradation was seen for up to 10 times the number of weights as data samples. However, some signs of performance loss for the largest nets was evident after 10000 iterations. Note that after 5000 iterations, the networks were only half-trained (roughly 50% error on the training set). When they were 80-90% trained, the larger nets lost considerable ground. For instance, the 10 x net (128 hidden units) lost performance from 40.5% to 28.1% during these iterations. It appears that the higher signal-to-noise of this example permitted performance gains for even higher overparametrization factors, but that the result was even more sensitive to training for too many iterations.

Table II — Test (and training) scores: 1 cluster, SNR = 2.0

#hidden units	#weights / #inputs	%Test (Train) Correct after N Iterations			
		1000	2000	5000	10000
4	.31	18.1(8.4)	25.6(29.1)	32.2(29.8)	26.9(29.2)
8	.62	22.5(12.8)	31.1(34.7)	34.5(44.5)	33.3(62.2)
16	1.25	22.0(11.6)	33.4(32.8)	33.6(57.2)	29.4(78.3)
32	2.50	25.6(13.3)	33.4(35.2)	39.4(51.1)	34.2(87.0)
64	5.0	26.4(13.9)	36.1(35.0)	40.8(45.2)	33.6(86.9)
128	10.0	26.9(12.0)	34.5(34.5)	40.5(47.2)	28.1(91.1)

Table III shows the performance for a 4-cluster case, with SNR = 1.0 . Small nets are omitted here, because earlier experiments showed this problem to be too hard. The best performance (21.1%) is for one of the larger nets at 2000 iterations, so that the degradation effect is not clearly visible for the undertrained case. At 10000 iterations, however, the larger nets do poorly.

Table III — Test (and training) scores: 4 cluster, SNR = 1.0

#hidden units	#weights / #inputs	%Test (Train) Correct after N Iterations			
		1000	2000	5000	10000
32	2.50	13.8(12.7)	18.3(23.6)	15.8(38.8)	9.4(71.4)
64	5.0	13.6(12.7)	18.4(23.6)	14.7(42.7)	18.8(71.6)
96	7.5	15.3(13.0)	21.1(24.7)	15.9(45.5)	16.3(78.1)
128	10.	15.2(13.1)	19.1(23.8)	17.5(40.5)	10.5(70.9)

Figure 1 illustrates this graphically. The "undertrained" case is relatively insensitive to the network size, as well as having the highest raw score.

3   SPEECH RECOGNITION

3.1   METHODS

In an ongoing project at ICSI and Philips, a German language data base consisting of 100 training and 100 test sentences (both from the same speaker) were used for training of a multi-layer-perceptron (MLP) for recognition of phones at the frame level, as well as to estimate probabilities for use in the dynamic programming algorithm for a discrete Hidden Markov Model (HMM) [Bourlard & Wellekens, 1988; Bourlard et al, 1989]. Vector-quantized mel cepstra were used as binary input to a hidden layer. Multiple frames were used as input to provide context to the network. While the size of the output layer was kept fixed at 50 units, corresponding to the 50 phonemes to be recognized, the hidden layer was varied from 20 to 200 units, and the input context was kept fixed at 9 frames of speech. As the acoustic vectors were coded on the basis of 132 prototype vectors by a simple binary vector with only one bit 'on', the input field contained $9 \times 132 = 1188$ units, and the total number of possible inputs was thus equal to 132^9. There were 26767 training patterns and 26702 independent test patterns. Of course, this represented only a very small fraction of the possible inputs, and generalization was thus potentially difficult. Training was done by the classical "error-back propagation" algorithm, starting by minimizing an entropy criterion [Solla et al, 1988] and then the standard least-mean-square error (LMSE) criterion. In each iteration, the complete training set was presented, and the parameters were updated after each training pattern.

To avoid overtraining of the MLP, (as was later demonstrated by the random vector experiment described above), improvement on the test set was checked after each iteration. If the classification rate on the test set was decreasing, the adaptation parameter of the gradient procedure was decreased, otherwise it was kept constant. In another experiment this approach was systematized by splitting the data in three parts: one for the training, one for the test and a third one absolutely independent of the training procedure for validation. No significant difference was observed between classification rates for the test and validation data.

Other than the obvious difference with the previous study (this used real data), it is important to note another significant point: in this case, we stopped iterating (by any one particular criterion) when that criterion was leading to no new test set performance improvement. While we had not yet done the simulations described above, we had observed the necessity for such an approach over the course of our speech research. We expected this to ameliorate the effects of overparameterization.

3.2   RESULTS

Table IV shows the variation in performance for 5, 20, 50, and 200 hidden units. The peak at 20 hidden units for test set performance, in contrast to the continued improvement in training set performance, can be clearly seen. However, the effect is certainly a mild one given the wide range in network size; using 10 times the number of weights as in the "peak" case only causes a degradation of 3.1%. Note, however, that for this experiment, the more sophisticated training procedure was used which halted training when generalization started to degrade.

For comparison with classical approaches, results obtained with Maximum Likelihood (ML) and Bayes estimates are also given. In those cases, it is not possible to use contextual information, because the number of parameters to be learned would be $50 * 132^9$ for the 9 frames of context. Therefore, the input field was restricted to a single frame. The number of parameters for these two last classifiers was then $50 * 132 = 6600$, or a parameter/measurement ratio of .25 . This restriction explains why the Bayes classifier, which is inherently optimal for a given pattern classification problem, is shown here as yielding a lower performance than the potentially suboptimal MLP.

Table IV — Test Run: Phoneme Recognition on German data base

hidden units	#parameters/#training_numbers	training	test
5	.23	62.8	54.2
20	.93	75.7	62.7
50	2.31	73.7	60.6
200	9.3	86.7	59.6
ML	.25	45.9	44.8
Bayes	.25	53.8	53.0

4 CONCLUSIONS

While both studies show the expected effects of overparameterization, (poor generalization, sensitivity to overtraining in the presence of noise), perhaps the most significant result is that it was possible to greatly reduce the sensitivity to the choice of network size by directly observing the network performance on an independent test set during the course of learning (cross-validation). If iterations are not continued past this point, fewer measurements are required. This only makes sense because of the interdependence of the learned parameters, particularly for the undertrained case. In any event, though, it is clear that adding parameters over the number required for discrimination is wasteful of resources. Networks which require many more parameters than there are measurements will certainly reach lower levels of peak performance than simpler systems. For at least the examples described here, it is clear that both the size of the MLP and the degree to which it should be trained are parameters which must be learned from experimentation with the data set. Further study might, perhaps, yield enough results to permit some rule of thumb dependent on properties of the data, but our current thinking is that these parameters should be determined dynamically by testing on an independent test set.

References

Akaike, H. (1974), "A new look at the statistical model identification." *IEEE Trans. autom. Control*, AC-10, 667-674

Akaike, H. (1986), "Use of Statistical Models for Time Series Analysis", Vol. 4, Proc. IEEE Intl. Conference on Acoustics, Speech, and Signal Processing, Tokyo, 1986, pp.3147-3155

Baum, E.B., & Haussler, D., (1988), "What Size Net Gives Valid Generalization?", Neural Computation, In Press

Bourlard, H., Morgan, N., & Wellekens, C.J., (1989), "Statistical Inference in Multilayer Perceptrons and Hidden Markov Models, with Applications in Continuous Speech Recognition", NATO Advanced Research Workshop, Les Arcs, France

Feldman, J.A., Fanty, M.A., and Goddard, N., (1988) "Computing with Structured Neural Networks", Computer, vol. 21, No.3, pp 91-104

Pearl,J., (1978), "On the Connection Between the Complexity and Credibility of Inferred Models", Int. J. General Systems, Vol.4, pp. 155-164

Rumelhart, D.E., Hinton, G.E., & Williams, R.J., (1986), "Learning internal representations by error propagation" in *Parallel Distributed Processing* (D.E. Rumelhart & J.L. McClelland, Eds.), ch. 15, Cambridge, MA: MIT Press

Valiant, L.G., (1984), "A theory of the learnable", Comm. ACM V27, N11 pp1134-1142

Widrow, B, (1987) "ADALINE and MADALINE" , Plenary Speech, Vol. I, Proc. IEEE 1st Intl. Conf. on Neural Networks, San Diego, CA, 143-158

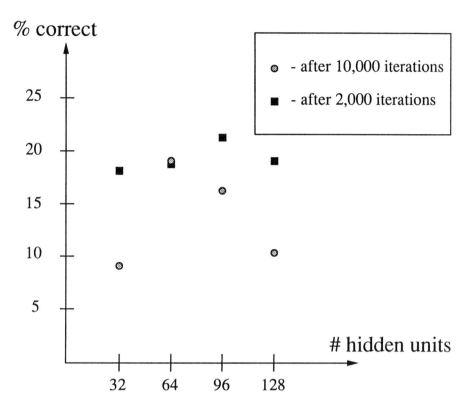

Figure 1: Sensitivity to net size

Subgrouping Reduces Complexity and Speeds Up Learning in Recurrent Networks

David Zipser
Department of Cognitive Science
University of California, San Diego
La Jolla, CA 92093

1 INTRODUCTION

Recurrent nets are more powerful than feedforward nets because they allow simulation of dynamical systems. Everything from sine wave generators through computers to the brain are potential candidates, but to use recurrent nets to emulate dynamical systems we need learning algorithms to program them. Here I describe a new twist on an old algorithm for recurrent nets and compare it to its predecessors.

2 BPTT

In the beginning there was BACKPROPAGATION THROUGH TIME (BPTT) which was described by Rumelhart, Williams, and Hinton (1986). The idea is to add a copy of the whole recurrent net to the top of a growing feedforward network on each update cycle. Backpropagating through this stack corrects for past mistakes by adding up all the weight changes from past times. A difficulty with this method is that the feedforward net gets very big. The obvious solution is to truncate it at a fixed number of copies by killing an old copy every time a new copy is added. The truncated-BPTT algorithm is illustrated in Figure 1. It works well, more about this later.

3 RTRL

It turns out that it is not necessary to keep an ever growing stack of copies of the recurrent net as BPTT does. A fixed number of parameters can record all of past time. This is done in the REAL TIME RECURRENT LEARNING (RTRL) algorithm of Williams and Zipser (1989). The derivation is given elsewhere (Rumelhart, Hinton, & Williams, 1986), but a

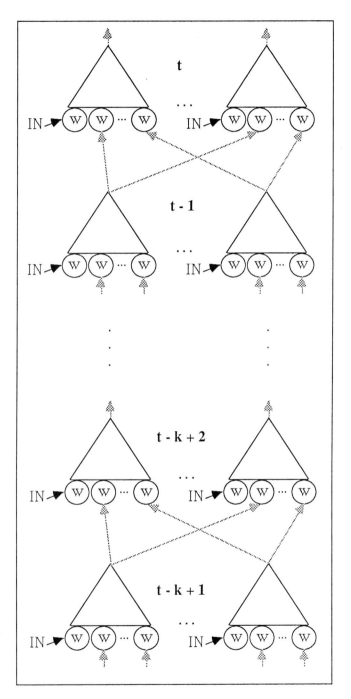

Figure 1: BPTT.

simple rational comes from the fact that error backpropagation is linear, which makes it possible to collapse the whole feedforward stack of BPTT into a few fixed size data structures. The biggest and most time consuming to update of these is the matrix of p values whose update rule is

$$p_{ij}^k (t+1) = f'(s_k(t)) \left[\sum_{l \in U} w_{kl} \, p_{ij}^l(t) + \delta_{ik} z_j(t) \right]$$

$$i \in U, \; j \in U \cup I, \; k \in U$$

where $z_k(t)$ represents the value of a signal, either an input or recurrent; the sets of subscriptss are defined so that if z_k is an input then $k \in I$ and if z_k is a signal from a recurrently connected unit then $k \in U$, s_k are *net* values; d_{ik} is the Kronecker delta; and w_{kl} is the recurrent weight matrix. For a network with n units and w weights there are nw of these p values, and it takes $O(wn^2)$ operations to update them. As n gets big this gets very big and is computationally unpleasant. This unpleasantness is cured to some degree by the new variant of RTRL described below.

4 SUBGROUPED RTRL

The value of n in the factor wn^2, which causes all the trouble for RTRL, can be reduced by viewing a recurrent network as consisting of a set of subnetworks all connected together. A fully recurrent network with n units and m inputs can be divided into g fully recurrent subnets, each with n/g units (assuming g is a factor of n). Each unit in a subnet will receive as input the original m inputs and the activities of the $n - n/g$ units in the other subnets. The effect of subgrouping is to reduce the number of p values per weight to n/g and the number of operations to update the p to $O(wn^2/g^2)$. If g is increased in proportion to n, which keeps the size of the sub-nets constant, n^2/g^2 is a constant and the complexity is reduced to $O(w)$. If all this is confusing try Figure 2.

5 TESTING THESE ALGORITHMS

To see if the subgrouped algorithm works, I compared its performance to RTRL and BPTT on the problem of training a Turing machine to balance parentheses. The network "sees" the same tape as the Turing machine, and is trained to produce the same outputs. A fully recurrent network with 12 units was the smallest that learned this task. All three algorithms learned the task in about the same number of learning cycles. RTRL and subgrouped RTRL succeeded 50%, and BPTT succeeded 80% of the time. Subgrouped RTRL was 10 times faster than RTRL, whereas BPTT was 28 times faster.

References

Rumelhart, D. E., Hinton, G. E., & Williams, R. J. (1986). Learning internal representations by error propagation. In D. E. Rumelhart, J. L. McClelland, & the PDP Research Group (Eds.), *Parallel distributed processing: Explorations in the microstructure of cognition. Vol. 1. Foundationa.* Cambridge, MA: MIT Press.

Williams, R. J., & Zipser, D. (1989). A learning algorithm for continually running fully recurrent neural networks. *Neural Computation, 1,* 270-280.

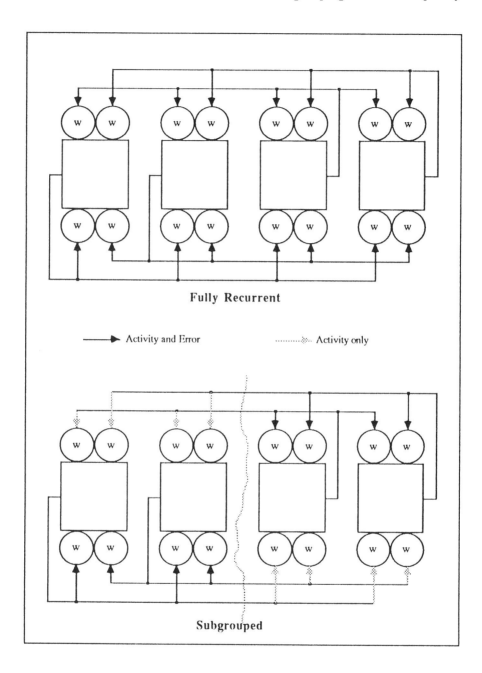

Figure 2: Subgrouped-RTRL

Dynamic Behavior of Constrained Back-Propagation Networks

Yves   Chauvin[1]
Thomson–CSF, Inc.
630 Hansen Way, Suite 250
Palo Alto, CA. 94304

ABSTRACT

The learning dynamics of the back–propagation algorithm are investigated when complexity constraints are added to the standard Least Mean Square (LMS) cost function. It is shown that loss of generalization performance due to overtraining can be avoided when using such complexity constraints. Furthermore, "energy," hidden representations and weight distributions are observed and compared during learning. An attempt is made at explaining the results in terms of linear and non–linear effects in relation to the gradient descent learning algorithm.

1 INTRODUCTION

It is generally admitted that generalization performance of back–propagation networks (Rumelhart, Hinton & Williams, 1986) will depend on the relative size of the training data and of the trained network. By analogy to curve–fitting and for theoretical considerations, the generalization performance of the network should decrease as the size of the network and the associated number of degrees of freedom increase (Rumelhart, 1987; Denker et al., 1987; Hanson & Pratt, 1989).

This paper examines the dynamics of the standard back–propagation algorithm (BP) and of a constrained back–propagation variation (CBP), designed to adapt the size of the network to the training data base. The performance, learning dynamics and the representations resulting from the two algorithms are compared.

---

1.   Also in the Psychology Department, Stanford University, Stanford, CA. 94305

2 GENERALIZATION PERFORMANCE

2.1 STANDARD BACK-PROPAGATION

In Chauvin (In Press), the generalization performance of a back–propagation network was observed for a classification task from spectrograms into phonemic categories (single speaker, 9 phonemes, 10msx16frequencies spectrograms, 63 training patterns, 27 test patterns). This performance was examined as a function of the number of training cycles and of the number of (logistic) hidden units (see also, Morgan & Bourlard, 1989). During early learning, the performance of the network appeared to be basically independent of the number of hidden units (provided a minimal size). However, after prolonged training, performance started to decrease with training at a rate that was a function of the size of the hidden layer. More precisely, from 500 to 10,000 cycles, the generalization performance (in terms of percentage of correctly classified spectrograms) decreased from about 93% to 74% for a 5 hidden unit network and from about 95% to 62% for a 10 hidden unit network. These results confirmed the basic hypothesis proposed in the Introduction but only with a sufficient number of training cycles (overtraining).

2.2 CONSTRAINED BACK-PROPAGATION

Several constraints have been proposed to "adapt" the size of the trained network to the training data. These constraints can act directly on the weights, or on the net input or activation of the hidden units (Rumelhart, 1987; Chauvin, 1987, 1989, In Press; Hanson & Pratt, 1989; Ji, Snapp & Psaltis, 1989; Ishikawa, 1989; Golden and Rumelhart, 1989). The complete cost function adopted in Chauvin (In Press) for the speech labeling task was the following:

$$C = aE_r + \beta E_n + \gamma W = a \sum_{ip}^{OP} (t_{ip} - o_{ip})^2 + \beta \sum_{ip}^{HP} \frac{o_{ip}^2}{1 + o_{ip}^2} + \gamma \sum_{ij}^{W} \frac{w_{ij}^2}{1 + w_{ij}^2} \qquad [\,1\,]$$

E_r is the usual LMS error computed at the output layer, E_n is a function of the squared activations of the hidden units and W is a function of the squared weights throughout the network. This constrained back–propagation (CBP) algorithm basically eliminated the overtraining effect: the resulting generalization performance remained constant (about 95%) throughout the complete training period, independently of the original network size.

3 ERROR AND ENERGY DYNAMICS

Using the same speech labeling task as in Chauvin (In Press), the dynamics of the global variables of the network defined in Equation 1 (E_r , E_n , and W) were observed during training of a network with 5 hidden units. Figure 1 represents the error and energy dynamics for the standard (BP) and the constrained back–propagation algorithm (CBP). For BP and CBP, the error on the training patterns kept

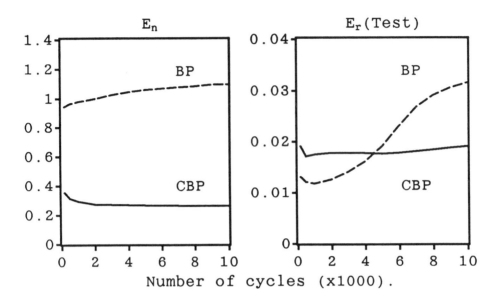

Figure 1. "Energy" (left) and generalization error – LMS averaged over the test patterns and output units – (right) when using the standard (BP) or the constrainted (CBP) back–propagation algorithm during a typical run.

decreasing during the entire training period (more slowly for CBP). The W dynamics over the entire network were similar for BP and CBP (but the distributions were different, see below).

3.1 STANDARD BACK-PROPAGATION

As shown in Figure 1, the "energy" E_n (Equation 1) of the hidden layer slightly increases during the entire learning period, long after the minimum was reached for the test error (around 200 cycles). This "energy" reaches a plateau after long overtraining, around 10,000 cycles. The generalization error reaches a minimum and later increases as training continues, also slowly reaching a plateau around 10,000 cycles.

3.2 CONSTRAINED BACK-PROPAGATION

With CBP, the "energy" decreases to a much lower level during early learning and remains about constant throughout the complete training period. The error quickly decreases during early learning and remains about constant during the rest of the training period, apparently stabilized by the energy and weight constraints given in Equation 1.

4   REPRESENTATION

The hidden unit activations and weights of the networks were examined after learning, using BP or CBP. A hidden unit was considered "dead" when its contribution to any output unit (computed as the product of its activation times the corresponding outgoing weight) was at least 50 times smaller than the total contribution from all hidden units, over the entire set of input patterns.

4.1   STANDARD BACK–PROPAGATION

As also observed by Hanson et al. (1989), standard back–propagation usually makes use of most or all hidden units: the representation of the input patterns is well distributed over the entire set of hidden units, even if the network is oversized for the task.   The exact representation depends on the initial weights.

4.2   CONSTRAINED BACK–PROPAGATION

Using the constraints described in Equation 1, the hidden layer was reduced to 2 or 3 hidden units for all the observed runs (2 hidden units corresponds to the minimal size network necessary to solve the task). All the other units were actually "killed" during learning, independently of the size of the original network (from 4 to 11 units in the simulations). Both the constraints on the hidden unit activations (E_n) and on the weights (W) contribute to this reduction.

Figure 2 represents an example of the resulting weights from the input layer to a remaining hidden unit. As we can see, a few weights ended up dominating the entire set: they actually "picked up" a characteristic of the input spectrograms that allow the disctinction between two phoneme categories (this phenomenon was also predicted and observed by Rumelhart, 1989). In this case, the weights "picked up" the 10th and 14th frequency components of the spectrograms, both present during the 5th time interval. The characteristics of the spectrum make the corresponding hidden unit especially responsive to the [G] phoneme. The specific non-linear W constraint on the input–to–hidden weights used by CBP forced that hidden unit to acquire a very local receptor field. Note that this was not always observed in the simulations. Some hidden units acquired broad receptor fields with weights distributed over the entire spectrogram (as it is always the case with standard BP). No statistical comparison was made to compute the relative ratio of local to distributed units, which probably depends on the exact form of the reduction constraint used in CBP.

5   INTERPRETATION OF RESULTS

We observed that the occurrence of overfitting effects depends both on the size of the network *and* on the number of training cycles. At this point, a better theoretical understanding of the back–propagation learning dynamics would be useful to explain this dependency (Chauvin, In Preparation). This section presents an informal interpretation of the results in terms of linear and non–linear phenomena.

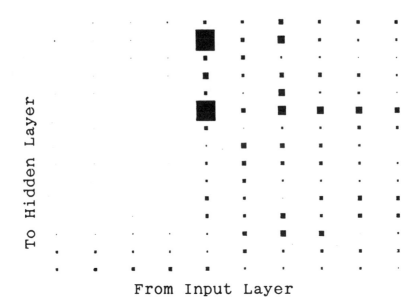

Figure 2. Typical fan-in weights after learning from the input layer to a hidden unit using the constrained back-propagation algorithm.

5.1 LINEAR PHENOMENA

These linear phenomena might be due to probable correlations between sample plus observation noise at the input level and the desired classification at the output level. The gradient descent learning rule should eventually make use of these correlations to decrease the LMS error. However, these correlations are specific to the used training data set and should have a negative impact on the performance of the network on a testing data set. Figure 3 represents the generalization performance of linear networks with 1 and 7 hidden units (averaged over 5 runs) for the speech labeling task described above. As predicted, we can see that overtraining effects are actually generated by linear networks (as they would with a one-step algorithm; e.g., Vallet et al., 1989). Interestingly, they occur even when the size of the network is minimum. These effects should obviously decrease by increasing the size of the training data set (therefore reducing the effect of sample and observation noise).

5.2 NON-LINEAR PHENOMENA

The second type of effect is non-linear. This is illustrated in Chauvin (In Press) with a curve-fitting problem. In the first problem, a non-linear back-propagation network (1 input unit, 1 output unit, 2 layers of 20 hidden units) is trained to fit a function composed of two linear segments separated by a discontinuity. The mapping realized by the network over the entire interval is observed as a function of the number of training cycles. It appears that the interpolated fit reaches a minimum

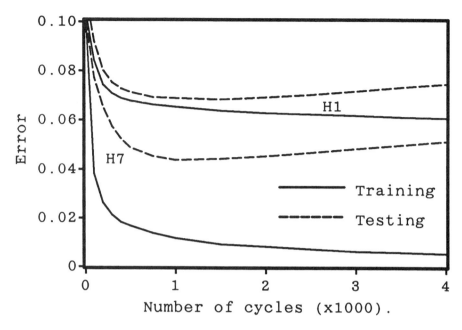

Figure 3. LMS error for the training and test data sets of a speech labeling task as a function of the number of training cycles. A one hidden and a 7 hidden unit linear network are considered.

and gets worse with the number of training cycles *and* with the size of the sample training set around the discontinuity.

This phenomenon is evocative of an effect in interpolation theory known as the Runge effect (Steffenssen, 1950). In this case, a "well–behaved" bell–like function, $f(x) = 1/(1 + x^2)$, uniformly sampled $n+1$ times over a $[-D, +D]$ interval, is fitted with a polynomial of degree n. Runge showed that over the considered interval, the maximum distance between the fitted function and the fitting polynomial goes to infinity as n increases. Note that in theory, there is no overfitting since the number of degree of freedoms associated with the polynomial matches the number of data points. However, the interpolation "overfitting effect" actually increases with the sampling data set, that is with the increased accuracy in the description of the fitted function. (Runge also showed that the effect may disappear by changing the size of the sampled interval or the distribution of the sampling data points.)

We can notice that in the piecewise linear example, a linear network would have computed a linear mapping using only two degrees of freedom (the problem is then equivalent to one–dimensional linear regression). With a non–linear network, simulations show that the network actually computes the desired mapping by slowly fitting higher and higher "frequency components" present in the desired mapping (reminiscent of the Gibb's phenomenon observed with successive Fourier series approximations of a square wave; e.g., Sommerfeld, 1949). The discontinuity, considered as a singular point with high frequency components, is fitted during later stages of learning. Increasing the number of sampling points around the discontinuilty generates an effect similar to the Runge effect with overtraining. In this sense, the notion of degrees of freedom in non–linear neural networks is not only a function of the network architecture – the "capacity" of the network – and of the non–linearities of the fitted function but also of the learning algorithm (gradient descent), which *gradually* "adjusts" the "capacity" of the network to fit the nonlinearities required by the desired function.

A practical classification task might generate not only linear overtraining effects due to sample and observation noise but also non–linear effects if a continuous input variable (such as a frequency component in the speech example) has to be classified in two different bins. It is also easy to imagine that noise may generate non–linear effects. At this stage, the non–linear effects involved in back–propagation networks composed of logistic hidden units are poorly understood. In general, both effects will probably occur in non–linear networks and might be difficult to assess. However, because of the gradient descent procedure, both effects seem to depend on the amount of training relative to the capacity of the network. The use of complexity constraints acting on the complexity of the network seems to constitute a promising solution to the overtraining problem in both the linear and non–linear cases.

Acknowledgements

I am greatful to Pierre Baldi, Fred Fisher, Matt Franklin, Richard Golden, Julie Holmes, Erik Marcade, Yoshiro Miyata, David Rumelhart and Charlie Schley for helpful comments.

References

Chauvin, Y. (1987). Generalization as a function of the number of hidden units in back–propagation networks. *Unpublished Manuscript*. University of California, San Diego, CA.

Chauvin, Y. (1989). A back–propagation algorithm with optimal use of the hidden units. In D. Touretzky (Ed.), *Advances in Neural Information Processing Systems 1*. Palo Alto, CA: Morgan Kaufman.

Chauvin, Y. (In Press). Generalization performance of back–propagation networks. *Proceedings of the 1990 European conference on Signal Processing (Eurasip)*. Springer–Verlag.

Chauvin, Y. (In Preparation). Generalization performance of LMS trained linear networks.

Chauvin, Y. (1989). A back–propagation algorithm with optimal use of the hidden units. In D. Touretzky (Ed.), *Advances in Neural Information Processing Systems 1*. Palo Alto, CA: Morgan Kaufman.

Chauvin, Y. (1989). A back–propagation algorithm with optimal use of the hidden units. In D. Touretzky (Ed.), *Advances in Neural Information Processing Systems 1*. Palo Alto, CA: Morgan Kaufman.

Denker, J. S., Schwartz, D. B., Wittner, B. S., Solla, S. A., Howard, R. E., Jackel, L. D., & Hopfield, J. J. (1987). Automatic learning, rule extraction, and generalization. *Complex systems, 1*, 877–922.

Golden, R.M., & Rumelhart, D.E. (1989). *Improving generalization in multi–layer networks through weight decay and derivative minimization.* Unpublished Manuscript. Stanford University, Palo Alto, CA.

Hanson, S. J. & Pratt, L. P. (1989). Comparing biases for minimal network construction with back–propagation. In D. Touretzky (Ed.), *Advances in Neural Information Processing Systems 1*. Palo Alto, CA: Morgan Kaufman.

Ishikawa M. (1989). A structural learning algorithm with forgetting of weight link weights. *Proceedings of the IJCNN International Joint Conference on Neural Networks, II,* 626. Washington D.C., June 18–22, 1989.

Ji, C., Snapp R. & Psaltis D. (1989). Generalizing smoothness constraints from discrete samples. *Unpublished Manuscript.* Department of Electrical Engineering. California Institute of Technology, CA.

Morgan, N. & Bourlard, H. (1989). *Generalization and parameter estimation in feedforward nets: some experiments.* Paper presented at the Snowbird Conference on Neural Networks, Utah.

Rumelhart, D. E., Hinton G. E., Williams R. J. (1986). Learning internal representations by error propagation. In D. E. Rumelhart & J. L. McClelland (Eds.) *Parallel Distributed Processing: Explorations in the Microstructures of Cognition (Vol. I).* Cambridge, MA: MIT Press.

Rumelhart, D. E. (1987). Talk given at Stanford University, CA.

Rumelhart, D. E. (1989). Personal Communication.

Sommerfeld, A. (1949). *Partial differential equations in physics.* (Vol. VI). Academic Press: New York, NY.

Steffenssen, J. F. (1950). *Interpolation.* Chelsea: New York, NY.

Vallet, F., Cailton, J.–G. & Refregier P. (1989). Solving the problem of overfitting of the pseudo–inverse solution for classification learning. *Proceedings of the IJCNN Conference, II,* 443–450. Washington D.C., June 18–22, 1989.

Synergy Of Clustering Multiple Back Propagation Networks

William P. Lincoln* and Josef Skrzypek†
UCLA Machine Perception Laboratory
Computer Science Department
Los Angeles, CA 90024

ABSTRACT

The properties of a cluster of multiple back-propagation (BP) networks are examined and compared to the performance of a single BP network. The underlying idea is that a synergistic effect within the cluster improves the performance and fault tolerance. Five networks were initially trained to perform the same input-output mapping. Following training, a cluster was created by computing an average of the outputs generated by the individual networks. The output of the cluster can be used as the desired output during training by feeding it back to the individual networks. In comparison to a single BP network, a cluster of multiple BP's generalization and significant fault tolerance. It appear that cluster advantage follows from simple maxim "you can fool some of the single BP's in a cluster all of the time but you cannot fool all of them all of the time" {Lincoln}

1 INTRODUCTION

Shortcomings of back-propagation (BP) in supervised learning has been well documented in the past {Soulie, 1987; Bernasconi, 1987}. Often, a network of a finite size does not learn a particular mapping completely or it generalizes poorly. Increasing the size and number of hidden layers most often does not lead to any improvements {Soulie,

---

* also with Hughes Aircraft Company
† to whom the correspondence should be addressed

1987}. The central question that this paper addresses is whether a "synergy" of clustering multiple back-prop nets improves the properties of the clustered system over a comparably complex non-clustered system. We use the formulation of back-prop given in {Rumelhart, 1986}. A cluster is shown in figure 1. We start with five, three-layered, back propagation networks that "learn" to perform the same input-output mapping. Initially the nets are given different starting weights. Thus after learning, the individual nets are expected to have different internal representations. An input to the cluster is routed to each of the nets. Each net computes its output and the judge uses these outputs, $\hat{y}_k$ to form the cluster output, $\hat{y}$. There are many ways of forming $\hat{y}$ but for the sake of simplicity, in this paper we consider the following two rules:

$$simple \ \ average : \hat{y} \ = \ \sum_{K=1}^{N} \frac{1}{N} \hat{y}_k \tag{1.1}$$

$$convex \ \ combination : \hat{y} \ = \ \sum_{K=1}^{N} W_k y_k \tag{1.2}$$

Cluster function 1.2 adds an extra level of fault tolerance by giving the judge the ability to bias the outputs based on the past reliability of the nets. The W_k are adjusted to take into account the recent reliability of the net. One weight adjustment rule is $W_k = W_k \cdot G \cdot \dfrac{e}{e_k}$ where $e = \dfrac{1}{N} \sum_{k=1}^{N} e_k$, G is the gain of adjustment and $e_k = ||\hat{y} - \hat{y}_k||$ is the network deviation from the cluster output. Also, in the absence of an initial training period with a perfect teacher the cluster can collectively self-organize. The cluster in this case is performing an "averaging" of the mappings that the individual networks perform based on their initial distribution of weights. Simulations have been done to verify that self organization does in fact occur. In all the simulations, convergence occurred before 1000 passes.

Besides improved learning and generalization our clustered network displays other desirable characteristics such as fault tolerance and self-organization. Feeding back the cluster's output to the N individual networks as the desired output in training endows the cluster with fault tolerance in the absence of a teacher. Feeding back also makes the cluster continuously adaptable to changing conditions. This aspects of clustering is similar to the tracking capabilities of adaptive equalizers. After the initial training period it is usually assumed that no teacher is present, or that a teacher is present only at relatively infrequent intervals. However, if the failure rate is large enough, the performance of a single, non-clustered net will degrade during the periods when no teacher is present.

2 CLUSTERING WITH FEEDBACK TO INCREASE FAULT TOLERANCE IN THE ABSENCE OF A PERFECT TEACHER.

When a teacher is not present, $\hat{y}$ can be used as the desired output and used to continuously train the individual nets. In general, the correct error that should be back-propagated, $d_k = y - \hat{y}_k$, will differ from the actual error, $\hat{d}_k = \hat{y} - \hat{y}_k$ If d_k and $\hat{d}_k$ differ significantly, the error of the individual nets (and thus the cluster as a whole) can increase over time. This phenomenon is called drift. Because of drift, retraining using $\hat{y}$ as the desired output may seem disadvantageous when no faults exist within the nets. The possibility of drift is decreased by training the nets to a sufficiently small error. In fact under these circumstance with sufficiently small error, it is possible to see the error to decrease even further.

It is when we assume that faults exist that retraining becomes more advantageous. If the failure rate of a network node is sufficiently low, the injured net can be retrained using the judge's output. By having many nets in the cluster the effect of the injured net's output on the cluster output can be minimized. Retraining using $\hat{y}$ adds fault tolerance but causes drift if the nets did not complete learning when the teacher was removed.

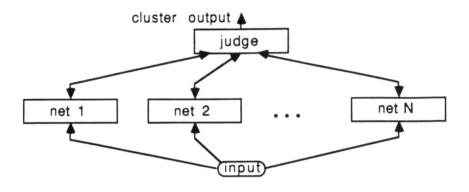

Figure 1: A cluster of N back-prop nets.

3   EXPERIMENTAL METHODS.

To test the ideas outlined in this paper an abstract learning problem was chosen. This abstract problem was used because many neural network problems require similar separation and classification of a group of topologically equivalent sets in the process of learning {Lippman, 1987}. For instance, images categorized according to their characteristics. The input is a 3-dimensional point, $P = (x,y,z)$. The problem is to categorize the point P into one of eight sets. The 8 sets are the 8 spheres of radius 1 centered at $x = (\pm 1)$, $y = (\pm 1)$, $z = (\pm 1)$ The input layer consists of three continuous nodes. The size of the output layer was 8, with each node trained to be an indicator function for its associated sphere. One hidden layer was used with full connectivity between layers. Five nets with the above specifications were used to form a cluster. Generalization was tested using points outside the spheres.

4   CLUSTER ADVANTAGE.

The performance of a single net is compared to performance of a five net cluster when the nets are not retrained using $\hat{y}$. The networks in the cluster have the same structure and size as the single network. Average errors of the two systems are compared. A useful measure of the cluster advantage is obtained by taking the ratio of an individual net's error to the cluster error. This ratio will be smaller or larger than 1 depending on the relative magnitudes of the cluster and individual net's errors. Figures 2a and 2b show the cluster advantage plotted versus individual net error for 256 and 1024 training passes respectively. It is seen that when the individual nets either learn the task completely or don't learn at all there is not a cluster advantage. However, when the task is learned even marginally, there is a cluster advantage.

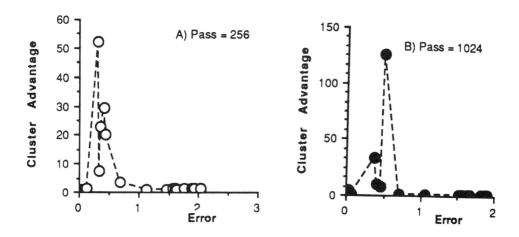

Figure 2: Cluster Advantage versus Error.
Data points from more than one learning task are shown.
A) After 256 training passes. B) After 1024 training passes.

The cluster's increased learning is based on the synergy between the individual networks and not on larger size of a cluster compared to an individual network. An individual net's error is dependent on the size of the hidden layer and the length of the training period. However, in general the error is not a decreasing function of the size of the hidden layer throughout its domain, i.e. increasing the size of the hidden layer does not always result in a decrease in the error. This may be due to the more direct credit assignment with the smaller number of nodes. Figures 4a and 4b show an individual net's error versus hidden layer size for different training passes. The point to this pedagogics is to counter the anticipated argument: "a cluster should have a lower error based on the fact that it has more nodes".

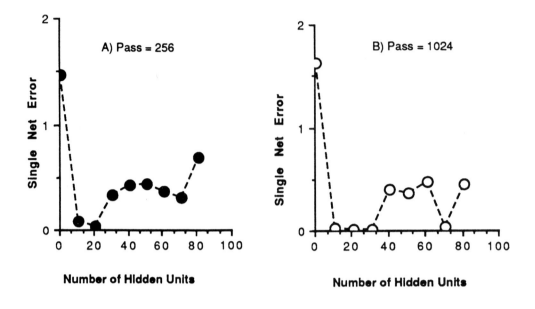

Figure 3: Error of a single BP network is a nonlinear funtion
of the number of hidden nodes.
A) After 256 training passes B) After 1024 training passes

5 FAULT TOLERANCE.

the judge's output as the desired output and retraining the individual networks, fault tolerance is added. The fault tolerant capabilities of a cluster of 5 were studied. The size of the hidden layer is 15. After the nets were trained, a failure rate of 1 link in the cluster per 350 inputs was introduced. This failure rate in terms of a single unclustered net is 1 link per 1750 (=5.350) inputs. The link that is chosen to fail in the cluster was randomly selected from the links of all the networks in the cluster. When a link failed its weight was set to 0. The links from the nets to the judge are considered immune from faults in this comparison. A pass consisted of 1 presentation of a random point from each of the 8 spheres. Figure 4 shows the fault tolerant capabilities of a cluster. By knowing the behavior of the single net in the presence of faults, the fault tolerant behavior of any conventional configuration (i.e. comparison and spares) of single nets can be determined, so that this form of fault tolerance can be compared with conventional fault tolerant schemes.

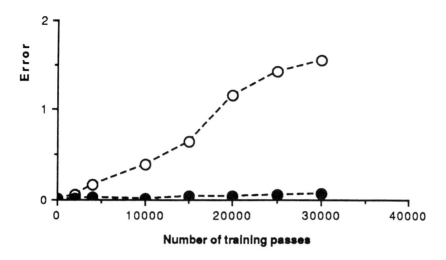

Figure 4: Fault tolerance of a cluster using feedback
from the "judge" as a desired training output.
Error as a function of time (# of training passes) without link
failures (solid circles) and with link failures (open cirles).
Link failure rate = 1 cluster link per 350 inputs
or 1 single net link per 1750 (=5 nets*350) inputs

6 CONCLUSIONS.

Clustering multiple back-prop nets has been shown to increase the performance and fault tolerance over a single network. Clustering has exhibited very interesting self organization. Preliminary investigations are restricted to a few simple examples. Nevertheless, there are some interesting results that appear to be rather general and which can thus be expected to remain valid for much larger and complex systems. The clustering ideas presented in this paper are not specific to back-prop but can apply to any nets trained with a supervised learning rule. The results of this paper can be viewed in an enlightening way. Given a set of weights, the cluster performs a mapping. There is empirical evidence of local minimum in this "mapping space". The initial point in the mapping space is taken to be when the cluster output begins to be fed back. Each time a new cluster output is fed back the point in the mapping space moves. The step size is related to the step size of the back prop algorithm. Each task is conjectured to have a local minimum in the mapping space. If the point moves away from the desired local minimum, drift occurs. A fault moves the point away from the local minimum. Feedback moves the point closer to the local minimum. Self organization can be viewed as finding the local minimum of the valley that the point is initially placed based on the initial distribution of weights.

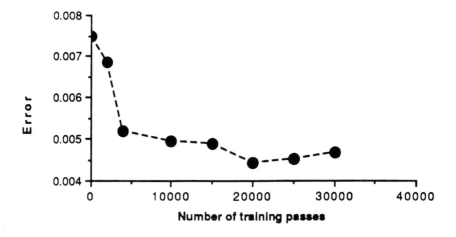

Figure 5: Cluster can continue to learn in the absence of a
teacher if the feedback from the judge is used as a
desired training output. No link failures.

6.1 INTERPRETATION OF RESULTS.

The results of the previous section can be interpreted from the viewpoint of the model
described in this section. This model attempts to describe how the state of the nets change
due to possibly incorrect error terms being back-propagated, and how in turn the state of
the net determines its performance. The state of a net could be defined by its weight
string. Given its weight string, there is a duality between the mapping that the net is performing and its error. When a net is being trained towards a particular mapping, its
current weight string determines the error of the net. The back-propagation algorithm is
used to change the weight string so that the error decreases. The duality is that at any
time a net is performing some mapping (it may not be the desired mapping) it is performing that mapping with no error. This duality has significance in connection with self-
organization which can be viewed as taking an "average" of the N mappings.

While the state of a net could be defined by its weight string, a state transition due to a backward error propagation is not obvious. A more useful definition of the state of a net is its error. (The error can be estimated by taking a representative sample of input vectors and propagating them through the net and computing the average error of the outputs.) Having defined the state, a description of the state transition rules can now be given.

output of net (i) = f (state of net (i) , input)

state of net (i) = g (state of net (i) , output of net (1) ,...,output of net(N))

delta error (i) = error (i) at t+1 - error (i) at t

cluster mistake = | correct output - cluster output |

This model says that for positive constants A and B:

delta error = A * (cluster mistake - B)

This equation has the property that the error increase or decrease is proportional to the size of the cluster mistake. The equilibrium is when the mistake equals B. An assumption is made that an individual net's mistake is a guassian random variable z_i with mean and variance equal to its error. For the purposes of this analysis, the judge uses a convex combination of the net outputs to form the cluster output. Using the assumptions of this model, it can be shown that a strategy of increasing the relative weight in the convex combination of a net that has a relatively small error and conversely decreasing the relative weight for poorly performing nets. (1,2) is an example weight adjustment rule. This rule has the effect of increasing the weight of a network that produced a network deviation that was smaller than average. The opposite effect is seen for a network that produced a network deviation that was larger than average.

6.1.1   References.

D.E. Rumelhart, J.L. McClelland, and the PDP Research Group. Parallel Distributed Processing (PDP): Exploration in the Microstructure of Cognition (Vol. 1). MIT Press, Cambridge, Massachusetts, 1986.

R.P. Lippman. An Introduction to Computing with Neural Nets. IEEE ASSP magazine, Vol. 4, pp. 4-22, April, 1987.

F.F. Soulie, P. Gallinari, Y. Le Cun, and S. Thiria. Evaluation of network architectures on test learning tasks. IEEE First International Conference on Neural Networks, San Diego, pp. II653-II660, June 1987.

J. Bernasconi. Analysis and Comparison of Different Learning Algorithms for Pattern Association Problems. Neural Information Processing Systems, Denver, Co, pp. 72-81, 1987.

Abraham Lincoln. Personal communication.

PART VIII:
THEORETICAL ANALYSES

Coupled Markov Random Fields and Mean Field Theory

Davi Geiger[1]
Artificial Intelligence
Laboratory, MIT
545 Tech. Sq. # 792
Cambridge, MA 02139

and

Federico Girosi
Artificial Intelligence
Laboratory, MIT
545 Tech. Sq. # 788
Cambridge, MA 02139

ABSTRACT

In recent years many researchers have investigated the use of Markov Random Fields (MRFs) for computer vision. They can be applied for example to reconstruct surfaces from sparse and noisy depth data coming from the output of a visual process, or to integrate early vision processes to label physical discontinuities. In this paper we show that by applying mean field theory to those MRFs models a class of neural networks is obtained. Those networks can speed up the solution for the MRFs models. The method is not restricted to computer vision.

1   Introduction

In recent years many researchers (Geman and Geman, 1984) (Marroquin et. al. 1987) (Gamble et. al. 1989) have investigated the use of Markov Random Fields (MRFs) for early vision. Coupled MRFs models can be used for the reconstruction of a function starting from a set of noisy sparse data, such as intensity, stereo, or motion data. They have also been used to integrate early vision processes to label physical discontinuities. Two fields are usually required in the MRFs formulation of a problem: one represents the function that has to be reconstructed, and the other is associated to its discontinuities. The reconstructed function, say f, has

---

[1] New address is Siemens Corporate Research, 755 College Road East, Princeton NJ 08540

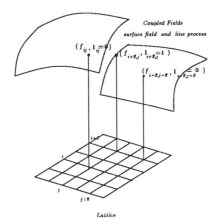

Figure 1: *The square lattice with the line process l and the field f defined at some pixels.*

a continuous range and the discontinuity field, say l, is a binary field (1 if there is a discontinuity and 0 otherwise, see figure 1). The essence of the MRFs model is that the probability distribution of the configuration of the fields, for a given a set of data, has a Gibbs distribution for some cost functional dependent upon a small neighborhood. Since the fields have a discrete range, to find the solution becomes a combinatorial optimization problem, that can be solved by means of methods like the Monte Carlo one (simulated annealing (Kirkpatrick and all, 1983), for example). However it has a main drawback: the amount of computer time needed for the implementation.

We propose to approximate the solution of the problem formulated in the MRFs frame with its "average solution." The mean field theory (MFT) allows us to find deterministic equations for MRFs whose solution approximates the solution of the statistical problem. A class of neural networks can naturally solve these equations (Hopfield, 1984) (Koch et. al., 1985) (Geiger and Yuille, 1989). An advantage of such an approach is that the solution of the networks is faster than the Monte Carlo techniques, commonly used to deal with MRFs.

A main novelty in this work, and a quite general one, is to show that the binary field representing the discontinuities can be averaged out to yield an effective theory independent of the binary field. The possibility of writing a set of equations describing the network is also useful for a better understanding of the nature of the solution and of the parameters of the model. We show the network performance in an example of image reconstruction from sparse data.

2   MRFs and Bayes approach

One of the main attractions of MRFs models in vision is that they can deal directly with discontinuities. We consider coupled MRFs depending upon two fields, f and l. For the problem of image reconstruction the field f represents the field to be smoothed and l represents the discontinuities. In this case l is a binary field, assuming the values 1 if there is a discontinuity and 0 otherwise. The Markov property asserts that the probability of a certain value of the field at any given site in the lattice depends only upon neighboring sites. According to the Clifford-Hammersley theorem, the prior probability of a state of the fields f and l has the Gibbs form:

$$P(f, l) = \frac{1}{Z} e^{-\beta U(f,l)} \tag{2.1}$$

where f and l are the fields, e.g. the surface-field and its discontinuities, Z is the normalization constant also known as the partition function, $U(f, l) = \sum_i U_i(f, l)$ is an energy function that can be computed as the sum of local contributions from each lattice site i, and β is a parameter that is called the inverse of the natural temperature of the field. If a sparse observation g for any given surface-field f is given and a model of the noise is available then one knows the conditional probability $P(g|f, l)$. Bayes theorem then allows us to write the posterior distribution:

$$P(f, l|g) = \frac{P(g|f, l) P(f, l)}{P(g)} \equiv \frac{1}{Z} e^{-\beta V(f|g)} . \tag{2.2}$$

For the case of a sparse image corrupted by white gaussian noise

$$V(f, l|g) = \sum_i \lambda_i (f_i - g_i)^2 + U_i(f, l) \tag{2.3}$$

where $\lambda_{ij} = 1$ or 0 depending on whether data are available or not. $V(f, l|g)$ is sometimes called the visual cost function. The solution for the problem is the given by some estimate of the fields. The maximum of the posterior distribution or other related estimates of the "true" data-field value can not be computed analytically, but sample distributions of the field with the probability distribution of (2.2) can be obtained using Monte Carlo techniques such as the Metropolis algorithm. These algorithms sample the space of possible values of the fields according to the probability distribution $P(f, l|g)$.

A drawback of coupled MRFs has been the amount of computer time used in the Metropolis algorithm or in simulated annealing (Kirkpatrick et. al., 1983).

A justification for using the mean field (MF) as a measure of the fields, f for example, resides in the fact that it represents the minimum variance Bayes estimator. More precisely, the average variance of the field f is given by

$$Var_f = \sum_{f,l}(f - \bar{f})^2 P(f,l|g)$$

where $\bar{f}$ is a given estimate of the field, the $\sum_{f,l}$ represents the sum over all the possible configurations of f and l, and Var_f is the variance. Minimizing Var_f with respect to all possible values of $\bar{f}$ we obtain

$$\frac{\partial}{\partial \bar{f}} Var_f = 0 \Rightarrow \bar{f} = \sum_{f,l} f P(f,l|g)$$

This equation for $\bar{f}$ defines the deterministic MF equations.

2.1   MFT and Neural Networks

To connect MRFs to neural networks, we use Mean field theory (MFT) to obtain deterministic equations from MRFs that represent a class of neural networks.

The mean field for the values f and l at site i are given by

$$\bar{f}_i = \sum_{f,l} f_i P(f,l|g) \quad \text{and} \quad \bar{l}_i = \sum_{f,l} l_i P(f,l|g) \tag{2.4}$$

The sum over the binary process, $l_i = 0,1$ gives for (2.3), using the mean field approximation,

$$\bar{f}_i = \sum_f f_i \frac{e^{-\beta\lambda_i(f_i-g_i)^2}}{Z_i}\left(e^{-\beta U_i(f,l_{j\neq i},l_i=0)} + e^{-\beta U_i(f,l_{j\neq i},l_i=1)}\right)$$

$$\bar{l}_i = \sum_f \frac{e^{-\beta[\lambda_i(f_i-g_i)^2+U_i(f,l_{j\neq i},l_i=1)]}}{Z_i} \tag{2.5}$$

where the partition function Z where factorized as $\prod_i Z_i$. In this case

$$Z_i = \sum_f e^{-\beta\lambda_i(f_i-g_i)^2}\left(e^{-\beta U_i(f,l_{j\neq i},l_i=0)} + e^{-\beta U_i(f,l_{j\neq i},l_i=1)}\right).$$

Another way to write the equation for f is

$$\bar{f}_i = \sum_f f_i \frac{e^{-\beta V_i^{effective}}}{Z_i} \tag{2.6}$$

where

$$V_i^{effective}(f) = \lambda_i(f_i - g_i)^2 - \frac{1}{\beta}ln(e^{-\beta U_i(f, l_{j\neq i}, l_i=0)} + e^{-\beta U_i(f, l_{j\neq i}, l_i=1)}) \quad (2.7)$$

The important result obtained here is that the effective potential does not dependend on the binary field l_i. The line process field has been eliminated to yield a temperature dependent effective potential (also called visual cost function). The interaction of the field f with itself has changed after the line process has been averaged out. We interpret this result as the effect of the interaction of the line processes with the field f to yield a new temperature dependent potential.

The computation of the sum over all the configurations of the field f is hard and we use the saddle point approximation. In this case is equivalent to minimize $V^{effective}(f)$. A dynamical equation to find the minimum of $V^{effective}$ is given by introducing a damping force $\frac{\partial f}{\partial t}$ that brings the system to equilibrium. Therefore the mean field equation under the mean field and saddle point approximation becomes

$$\frac{\partial}{\partial f_i}V_i^{effective}(f, \bar{l}) = \frac{\partial f_i}{\partial t} \quad (2.8)$$

Equation (2.8) represents a class of unsupervised neural networks coupled to (2.5). The mean field solution is given by the fixed point of (2.8) and (2.5) it is attained after running (2.8) and (2.5) as $t \mapsto \infty$. This network is better understood with an example of image reconstruction.

3   Example: Image reconstruction

To reconstruct images from sparse data and to detect discontinuities we use the weak membrane model where $U_i(f, l)$ in two dimensions is given by

$$U_{i,j}(f, h, v) = \alpha \sum_{i,j}[(f_{i,j} - f_{i,j-1})^2(1-h_{i,j}) + (f_{i,j} - f_{i-1,j})^2(1-v_{i,j})] + \gamma(h_{i,j} + v_{i,j})$$

$$(3.1)$$

and α and γ are positive parameters.

The first term, contains the interaction between the field and the line processes: if the horizontal or vertical gradient is very high at site (i, j) the corresponding line process will be very likely to be active ($h_{i,j} = 1$ or $v_{i,j} = 1$), to make the visual cost function decrease and signal a discontinuity. The second term takes into account the price we pay each time we create a discontinuity and is necessary to prevent the creation of discontinuities everywhere. The effective cost function (2.7) then becomes

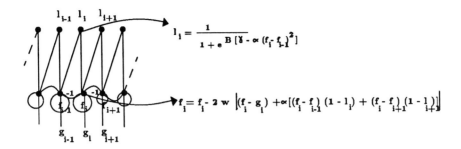

Figure 2: *The network is represented for the one dimensional case. The lines are the connections*

$$V_{ij}^{eff} = \sum_{i,j}\left[\lambda_{ij}(f_{i,j}-g_{i,j})^2+\alpha(\Delta_{i,j}^h)^2+(\Delta_{i,j}^v)^2-\frac{1}{\beta}ln[(1+e^{-\beta(\gamma-\alpha\Delta_{i,j}^h{}^2)})(1+e^{-\beta(\gamma-\alpha\Delta_{i,j}^v{}^2)})]\right]$$

$$(3.2)$$

where $\Delta_{i,j}^h = f_{i,j} - f_{i-1,j}$, $\Delta_{i,j}^v = f_{i,j} - f_{i,j-1}$ and (2.5) is then given by

$$\bar{h}_{i,j} = \frac{1}{1+e^{\beta(\gamma-\alpha(\bar{f}_{i,j}-\bar{f}_{i-1,j})^2)}} \quad and \quad \bar{v}_{i,j} = \frac{1}{1+e^{\beta(\gamma-\alpha(\bar{f}_{i,j}-\bar{f}_{i,j-1})^2)}} \qquad (3.3).$$

we point out here that while the line process field is a binary field, its mean value is a continuous (analog) function in the range between 0 and 1.

Discretizing (2.8) in time and applying for (3.2), we obtain

$$\bar{f}_{ij}^{n+1} = \bar{f}_{ij}^n - \omega\left[\lambda_{ij}(\bar{f}_{i,j}^n - g_{i,j}) - \alpha(\bar{f}_{i,j}^n - \bar{f}_{i,j-1}^n)(1-\bar{v}_{i,j}^n) + \alpha(\bar{f}_{i,j+1}^n - \bar{f}_{i,j}^n)(1-\bar{v}_{i,j+1}^n)\right.$$
$$\left. -\alpha(\bar{f}_{i,j}^n - \bar{f}_{i-1,j}^n)(1-\bar{h}_{i,j}^n) + \alpha(\bar{f}_{i+1,j}^n - \bar{f}_{i,j}^n)(1-\bar{h}_{i+1,j}^n)\right] \qquad (3.4)$$

where $\bar{h}_{i,j}$ and $\bar{v}_{i,j}$ are given by the network (3.3) and n is the time step on the algorithm. We notice that (3.4) is coupled with (3.3) such that the field f is updated by (3.4) at step n and then (3.3) updates the field h and v before (3.4) updates field f again at step $n+1$.

This is a simple unsupervised neural network where the imput are the fields f and the output is the line process field h or v. This network is coupled to the network (2.8) to solve for the field f and then constitute the global network for this problem (see figure 2). It has been shown by many authors and (Geiger and Yuille, 1989) that these class of networks is equivalent to Hopfield networks (Hopfield, 1984) (Koch et. al., 1985).

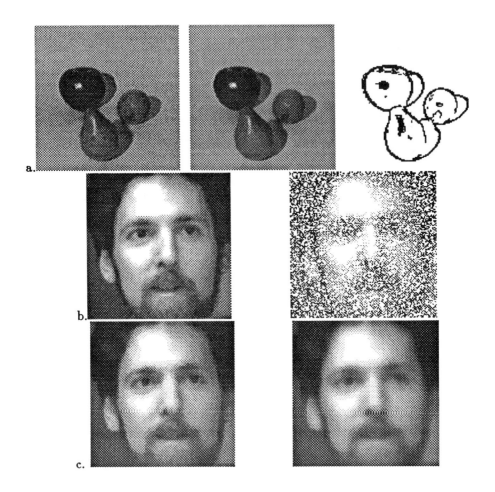

Figure 3: *a. The still life image 128 × 128 pixels. The image smoothed with*
γ = 1400 and α = 4 for 9 iterations. The line process field (needs thinning). b. A
face image of 128 × 128 pixels. Randomly chosen 50 % of the original image (for
display the other 50% are filled with white dots). c. The network described above is
applied to smooth and fill in using the same parameters and for 10 iterations. For
comparison we show the results of simply bluring the sparse data (no line process
field).

An important connection we make is to show (Geiger and Girosi, 1989) (Geiger,
1989) that the work of Blake and Zisserman (Blake and Zisserman, 1987) can be
seen as an approximation of these results.

In the zero temperature limit ($\beta \to \infty$) (3.3) becomes the Heaviside function (1 or 0) and the interpretation is simple: when the horizontal or vertical gradient are larger than a threshold ($\sqrt{\frac{\gamma}{\alpha}}$) a vertical or horizontal discontinuity is created.

4   Results

We applied the network to a real still life image and the result was an enhancement of specular edges, shadow edges and some other contours while smoothing out the noise (see Figure 3a). This result is consistent with all the images we have used. From one face image we produced sparse data by randomly suppressing 50% of the data. (see Figure 3b). We then applied the neural network to reconstruct the image.

Acknowledgements

We are grateful to Tomaso Poggio for his guidance and support.

References

A. Blake and A. Zisserman. (1987) *Visual Reconstruction*. Cambridge, Mass: MIT Press.

E. Gamble and D. Geiger and T. Poggio and D. Weinshall. (1989) *Integration of vision modules and labeling of surface discontinuities*. Invited paper to IEEE Trans. Sustems, Man & Cybernetics, December.

D. Geiger and F. Girosi. (1989) *Parallel and deterministic algorithms for MRFs: surface reconstruction and integration*. A.I. Memo No.1114. Artificial Intelligence Laboratory of MIT.

D. Geiger. (1989) *Visual models with statistical field theory*. Ph.D. thesis. MIT, Physics department and Artificial Intelligence Laboratory.

D. Geiger and A. Yuille. (1989) *A common framework for image segmentation and surface reconstruction*. Harvard Robotics Laboratory Technical Report, 89-7, Harvard, August.

S. Geman and D. Geman. (1984) *Stochastic Relaxation, Gibbs Distributions, and the Bayesian Restoration of Images*. Pattern Analysis and Machine Intelligence, PAMI-6:721–741.

J. J. Hopfield. (1984) *Neurons with graded response have collective computational properties like those of two-state neurons*. Proc. Natl. Acad. Sci., 81:3088-3092,

S. Kirkpatrick and C. D. Gelatt and M. P. Vecchi. (1983) *Optimization by Simulated Annealing*. Science, 220:219–227.

C. Koch and J. Marroquin and A. Yuille. (1985) *Analog 'Neuronal' Networks in Early Vision*. Proc. Natl. Acad. Sci., 83:4263-4267.

J. L. Marroquin and S. Mitter and T. Poggio. (1987) *Probabilistic Solution of Ill-Posed Problems in Computational Vision*. J. Amer. Stat. Assoc., 82:76-89.

Complexity of Finite Precision Neural Network Classifier

Amir Dembo[1]
Inform. Systems Lab.
Stanford University
Stanford, Calif. 94305

Kai-Yeung Siu
Inform. Systems Lab.
Stanford University
Stanford, Calif. 94305

Thomas Kailath
Inform. Systems Lab.
Stanford University
Stanford, Calif. 94305

ABSTRACT

A rigorous analysis on the finite precision computational aspects of neural network as a pattern classifier via a probabilistic approach is presented. Even though there exist negative results on the capability of perceptron, we show the following positive results: Given n pattern vectors each represented by cn bits where $c > 1$, that are uniformly distributed, with high probability the perceptron can perform all possible binary classifications of the patterns. Moreover, the resulting neural network requires a vanishingly small proportion $O(\log n/n)$ of the memory that would be required for complete storage of the patterns. Further, the perceptron algorithm takes $O(n^2)$ arithmetic operations with high probability, whereas other methods such as linear programming takes $O(n^{3.5})$ in the worst case. We also indicate some mathematical connections with VLSI circuit testing and the theory of random matrices.

1   Introduction

It is well known that the perceptron algorithm can be used to find the appropriate parameters in a linear threshold device for pattern classification, provided the pattern vectors are linearly separable. Since the number of parameters in a perceptron is significantly fewer than that needed to store the whole data set, it is tempting to

---

[1] The coauthor is now with the Mathematics and Statistics Department of Stanford University.

conclude that when the patterns are linearly separable, the perceptron can achieve a reduction in storage complexity. However, Minsky and Papert [1] have shown an example in which both the learning time and the parameters increase exponentially, when the perceptron would need much more storage than does the whole list of patterns.

Ways around such examples can be explored by noting that analysis that assumes real arithmetic and disregards finite precision aspects might yield misleading results. For example, we present below a simple network with one real valued weight that can simulate all possible classifications of n real valued patterns into k classes, when unlimited accuracy and continuous distribution of the patterns are assumed. For simplicity, let us assume the patterns are real numbers in $[0, 1]$. Consider the following sequence $\{x_{i,j}\}$ generated by each pattern x_i for $i = 1, \ldots, n$:

$$x_{i,1} = k \cdot x_i \mod k$$
$$x_{i,j} = k \cdot x_{i,j-1} \mod k \ \ for \, j > 1$$
$$\sigma(x_i, j) = [x_{i,j}]$$

where $[\,]$ denotes the integer part.

Let $f : \{x_1, \ldots, x_n\} \to \{0, \ldots, k-1\}$ denote the desired classification of the patterns. It is easy to see that for any continuous distribution on $[0, 1]$, there exists a j such that $\sigma(x_i, j) = f(x_i)$, with probability one. So, the network $y = \sigma(x, w)$ may simulate any classification with $w = j$ determined from the desired classification as shown above.

So in this paper, we emphasize the finite precision computational aspects of pattern classification problems and provide partial answers to the following questions:

- *Can the perceptron be used as an efficient form of memory?*

- *Does the 'learning' time of perceptron become too long to be practical most of the time even when the patterns are assumed to be linearly separable?*

- *How do the convergence results compare to those obtained by solving system of linear inequalities?*

We attempt to answer the above questions by using a probabilistic approach. The theorems will be presented without proofs; details of the proof will appear in a complete paper. In the following analysis, the phrase 'with high probability' means the probability of the underlying event goes to 1 as the number of patterns goes to infinity. First, we shall introduce the classical model of a perceptron in more details and give some known results on its limitation as a pattern classifier.

2   The Perceptron

A perceptron is a linear threshold device which computes a linear combination of the coordinates of the pattern vector, compares the value with a threshold and outputs $+1$ or -1 if the value is larger or smaller than the threshold respectively. More formally, we have

Output:

$$\text{sign}\{< \vec{w}, \vec{x} > -\theta\} = \text{sign}\{\sum_{i=1}^{d} x_i \cdot w_i - \theta\}$$

Input:

$$\vec{x} = (x_1, \ldots, x_d) \in R^d$$

Parameters:

weights $\vec{w} = (w_1, \ldots, w_d) \in R^d$

threshold $\theta \in R$

$$\text{sign}\{y\} = \left\{ \begin{array}{ll} +1 & \text{if } y \geq 0 \\ -1 & \text{otherwise} \end{array} \right.$$

Given m patterns $\vec{x_1}, \ldots, \vec{x_m}$ in R^d, there are 2^m possible ways of classifying each of the patterns to ± 1. When a desired classification of the patterns is achieveable by a perceptron, the patterns are said to be linearly separable. Rosenblatt(1962) [2] showed that if the patterns are linearly separable, then there is a 'learning' algorithm which he called *perceptron learning algorithm* to find the appropriate parameters $\vec{w}$ and θ. Let $\sigma_i = \pm 1$ be the desired classification of the pattern $\vec{x_i}$. Also, let $\vec{y_i} = \sigma_i \cdot \vec{x_i}$. The perceptron learning algorithm runs as follows:

1. Set $k = 1$, choose an initial value of $\vec{w}(k) \neq 0$.
2. Select an $i \in \{1, \ldots, n\}$, set $\vec{y}(k) = \vec{y_i}$.
3. If $\vec{w}(k) \cdot \vec{y}(k) \geq 0$, goto 2. Else
4. Set $\vec{w}(k + 1) = \vec{w}(k) + \vec{y}(k)$, $k = k + 1$, goto 2.

The algorithm terminates when step 3 is true for all $\vec{y_i}$. If the patterns are linearly separable, then the above perceptron algorithm is guaranteed to converge in finitely many iterations, i.e. Step 4 would be reached only finitely often.

The existence of such simple and elegant 'learning' algorithm had brought a great deal of interests during the 60's. However, the capability of the perceptron is very limited since only a small portion of the 2^m possible binary classifications can be achieved. In fact, Cover(1965) [3] has shown that a perceptron can at most classify the patterns into

$$2 \sum_{i=0}^{d-1} \binom{m-1}{i} = O(m^{d-1})$$

different ways out of the 2^m possibilities.

The above upper bound $O(m^{d-1})$ is achieved when the pattern vectors are *in general position* i.e. every subset of d vectors in $\{\vec{x_1}, \ldots, \vec{x_m}\}$ are linearly independent. An immediate generalization of this result is the following:

Theorem 1 *For any function $f(\vec{w}, \vec{x})$ which lies in a function space of dimension r, i.e. if we can write*

$$f(\vec{w}, \vec{x}) = \alpha_1(\vec{w}) f_1(\vec{x}) + \ldots + \alpha_r(\vec{w}) f_r(\vec{x})$$

then the number of possible classifications of m patterns by $sign\{f(\vec{w}, \vec{x})\}$ is bounded by $O(m^{r-1})$

3   A New Look at the Perceptron

The reason why perceptron is so limited in its capability as a pattern classifier is that the dimension of the pattern vector space is kept fixed while the number of patterns is increased. We consider the binary expansion of each coordinate and view the real pattern vector as a binary vector, but in a much higher dimensional space. The intuition behind this is that we are now making use of every bit of information in the pattern. Let us assume that each pattern vector has dimension d and that each coordinate is given with m bits of accuracy, which grows with the number of patterns n in such a way that $d \cdot m = c \cdot n$ for some $c > 1$. By considering the binary expansion, we can treat the patterns as binary vectors, i.e. each vector belongs to $\{+1, -1\}^{cn}$. If we want to classify the patterns into k classes, we can use $\log k$ number of binary classifiers, each classifying the patterns into the corresponding bit of the binary encoding of the k classes. So without loss of generality, we assume that the number of classes equals 2. Now the classification problem can be viewed as an implementation of a partial Boolean function whose value is only specified on

n inputs out of the 2^{cn} possible ones. For arbitrary input patterns, there does not seem to exist an efficient way other than complete storage of the patterns and the use of a look-up table for classification, which will require $O(n^2)$ bits. It is natural to ask if this is the best we can do. Surprisingly, using probabilistic method in combinatorics [4] (counting arguments), we can show the following:

Theorem 2 *For n sufficiently large, there exists a system that can simulate all possible binary classifications with parameter storage of $n + 2\log n$ bits.*

Moreover, a recent result from the theory of VLSI testing [5], implies that at least $n + \log n$ bits are needed. As the proof of theorem 1 is non-constructive, both the learning of the parameters and the retrieval of the desired classification in the 'optimal' system may be too complex for any practical purpose. Besides, since there is almost no redundancy in the storage of parameters in such an 'optimal' system, there will be no 'generalization' properties. i.e. It is difficult to predict what the output of the system would be on patterns that are not trained. However, a perceptron classifier, while sub-optimal in terms of Theorem 3 below, requires only $O(n \log n)$ bits for parameter storage, compared with $O(n^2)$ bits for a table look up classifier. In addition, it will exhibit 'generalization' properties in the sense that new patterns that are close in Hamming distance to those trained patterns are likely to be classified into the same class. So, if we allow some vanishingly small probability of error, we can give an affirmative answer to the first question raised at the beginning:

Theorem 3 *Assume the n pattern vectors are uniformly distributed over $\{+1, -1\}^{cn}$, then with high probability, the patterns can be classified into all 2^n possible ways using perceptron algorithm. Further, the storage of parameters requires only $O(n \log n)$ bits.*

In other words, when the input patterns are given with high precision, perceptron can be used as an efficient form of memory.

The known upper bound on the learning time of perceptron depends on the maximum length of the input pattern vectors, and the minimum distance δ of the pattern vectors to a separating hyperplane. In the following analysis, our probabilistic assumption guarantees the pattern vectors to be linearly independent with high probability and thus linearly separable. In order to give an probabilistic upper bound on the learning time of the perceptron, we first give a lower bound on the minimum distance δ with high probability:

Lemma 1 *Let n be the number of pattern vectors each in R^m, where $m = (1 + \epsilon)n$ and ϵ is any constant > 0. Assume the entries of each vector v are iid random variables with zero mean and bounded second moment. Then with probability $\to 1$*

as $n \to \infty$, there exists a separating hyperplane and a $\delta^* > 0$ such that each vector is at a distance of at least δ^* from it.

In our case, each coordinate of the patterns is assumed to be equally likely ± 1 and clearly the conditions in the above lemma are satisfied. In general, when the dimension of the pattern vectors is larger than and increases linearly with the number of patterns, the above theorem applies provided the patterns are given with high enough precision that a continuous distribution is a sufficiently good model for analysis.

The above lemma makes use of a famous conjecture from the theory of random matrices [6] which gives a lower bound on the minimum singular value of a random matrix. We actually proved the conjecture during our course of study, which states which states that the minimum singular value of a cn by n random matrix with $c > 1$, grows as $\sqrt{n}$ almost surely.

Theorem 4 *Let A_n be a $cn \times n$ random matrix with $c > 1$, whose entries are i.i.d. entries with zero mean and bounded second moment, $\sigma(\cdot)$ denote the minimum singular value of a matrix. Then there exists $\beta > 0$ such that*

$$\liminf_{n \to \infty} \sigma(\frac{A_n}{\sqrt{n}}) > \beta$$

with probability 1.

Note that our probabilistic assumption on the patterns includes a wide class of distributions, in particular the zero mean normal and symmetric uniform distribution on a bounded interval. In addition, they satisfy the following condition:

(∗) There exists a $\alpha > 0$ such that $P\{|v| > \alpha \sqrt{n}\} \to 0$ as $n \to \infty$.

Before we answer the last two questions raised at the beginning, we state the following known result on the perceptron algorithm as a second lemma:

Lemma 2 *Suppose there exists a unit vector w^* such that $w^* \cdot v > \delta$ for some $\delta > 0$ and for all pattern vectors v. Then the perceptron algorithm will converge to a solution vector in $\leq N^2/\delta^2$ number of iterations, where N is the maximum length of the pattern vectors.*

Now we are ready to state the following

Theorem 5 *Suppose the patterns satisfy the probabilistic assumptions stated in*

Lemma 1 and the condition (*), then with high probability, the perceptron takes $O(n^2)$ *arithmetic operations to terminate.*

As mentioned earlier, another way of finding a separating hyperplane is to solve a system of linear inequalities using linear programming, which requires $O(n^{3.5})$ arithmetic operations [7]. Under our probabilistic assumptions, the patterns are linearly independent with high probability, so that we can actually solve a system of linear equations. However, this still requires $O(n^3)$ arithmetic operations. Further, these methods require batch processing in the sense that all patterns have to be stored in advance in order to find the desired parameters, in constrast to the sequential 'learning' nature of the perceptron algorithm. So for training this neural network classifier, perceptron algorithm seems more preferable.

When the number of patterns is polynomial in the total number of bits representing each pattern, we may first extend each vector to a dimension at least as large as the number of patterns, and then apply the perceptron to compress the storage of parameters. One way of adding these extra bits is to form products of the coordinates within each pattern. Note that by doing so, the coordinates of each pattern are pairwise independent. We conjecture that theorem 3 still applies, implying even more reduction in storage requirements. Simulation results strongly support our conjecture.

4   Conclusion

In this paper, the finite precision computational aspects of pattern classification problems are emphasized. We show that the perceptron, in contrast to common belief, can be quite efficient as a pattern classifier, provided the patterns are given with high enough precision. Using a probabilistic approach, we show that the perceptron algorithm can even outperform linear programming under certain conditions. During the course of this work, we also discovered some mathematical connections with VLSI circuit testing and the theory of random matrices. In particular, we have proved an open conjecture regarding the minimum singular value of a random matrix.

Acknowledgements

This work was supported in part by the Joint Services Program at Stanford University (US Army, US Navy, US Air Force) under Contract DAAL03-88-C-0011, and NASA Headquarters, Center for Aeronautics and Space Information Sciences (CASIS) under Grant NAGW-419-S5.

References

[1] M. Minsky and S. Papert, *Perceptrons*, The MIT Press, expanded edition, 1988.

[2] F. Rosenblatt, *Principles of Neurodynamics*, Spartan Books, New York, 1962.

[3] T. M. Cover, "Geometrical and Statistical Properties of Systems of Linear Inequalities with Applications in Pattern Recognition", *IEEE Trans. on Electronic Computers*, **EC-14**:326–34, 1965.

[4] P. Erdös and J. Spencer, *Probabilistic Methods in Combinatorics*, Academic Press/Akademiai Kiado, New York-Budapest, 1974.

[5] G. Seroussi and N. Bshouty, "Vector Sets for Exhaustive Testing of Logic Circuits", *IEEE Trans. Inform. Theory*, **IT-34**:513–522, 1988.

[6] J. Cohen, H. Kesten and C. Newman, editor, *Random Matrices and Their Applications*, volume 50 of *Contemporary Mathematics*, American Mathematical Society, 1986.

[7] N. Karmarkar, "A New Polynomial-Time Algorithm for Linear Programming", *Combinatorica 1*, pages 373–395, 1984.

The Perceptron Algorithm Is Fast for Non-Malicious Distributions

Erice B. Baum
NEC Research Institute
4 Independence Way
Princeton, NJ 08540

Abstract: Within the context of Valiant's protocol for learning, the Perceptron algorithm is shown to learn an arbitrary half-space in time $O(\frac{n^2}{\epsilon^3})$ if D, the probability distribution of examples, is taken uniform over the unit sphere S^n. Here ϵ is the accuracy parameter. This is surprisingly fast, as "standard" approaches involve solution of a linear programming problem involving $\Omega(\frac{n}{\epsilon})$ constraints in n dimensions. A modification of Valiant's distribution independent protocol for learning is proposed in which the distribution and the function to be learned may be chosen by adversaries, however these adversaries may not communicate. It is argued that this definition is more reasonable and applicable to real world learning than Valiant's. Under this definition, the Perceptron algorithm is shown to be a distribution independent learning algorithm. In an appendix we show that, for uniform distributions, some classes of infinite V-C dimension including convex sets and a class of nested differences of convex sets are learnable.

§1: Introduction

The Perceptron algorithm was proved in the early 1960s[Rosenblatt,1962] to converge and yield a half space separating any set of linearly separable classified examples. Interest in this algorithm waned in the 1970's after it was emphasized[Minsky and Papert, 1969] (1) that the class of problems solvable by a single half space was limited, and (2) that the Perceptron algorithm, although converging in finite time, did not converge in polynomial time. In the 1980's, however, it has become evident that there is no hope of providing a learning algorithm which can learn arbitrary functions in polynomial time and much research has thus been restricted to algorithms which learn a function drawn from a particular class of functions. Moreover, learning theory has focused on protocols like that of [Valiant, 1984] where we seek to classify, not a fixed set of examples, but examples drawn from a probability distribution. This allows a natural notion of "generalization". There are very few classes which have yet been proven learnable in polynomial time, and one of these is the class of half spaces. Thus there is considerable theoretical interest now in studying the problem of learning a single half space, and so it is natural to reexamine the Perceptron algorithm within the formalism of Valiant.

In Valiant's protocol, a class of functions is called learnable if there is a learning algorithm which works in polynomial time independent of the distribution D generating the examples. Under this definition the Perceptron learning algorithm is not a polynomial time learning algorithm. However we will argue in section 2 that this definition is too restrictive. We will consider in section 3 the behavior of the Perceptron algorithm if D is taken to be the uniform distribution on the unit sphere S^n. In this case, we will see that the Perceptron algorithm converges remarkably rapidly. Indeed we will give a time bound which is faster than any bound known to us for any algorithm solving this problem. Then, in section 4, we will present what we believe to be a more natural definition of distribution independent learning in this context, which we will call Nonmalicious distribution independent learning. We will see that the Perceptron algorithm is indeed a polynomial time nonmalicious distribution independent learning algorithm. In Appendix A, we sketch proofs that, if one restricts attention to the uniform distribution, some classes with infinite Vapnik-Chervonenkis dimension such as the class of convex sets and the class of nested differences of convex sets (which we define) are learnable. These results support our assertion that distribution independence is too much to ask for, and may also be of independent interest.

§2: Distribution Independent Learning

In Valiant's protocol[Valiant, 1984], a class F of Boolean functions on $\Re^n$ is called learnable if a learning algorithm A exists which satisfies the following conditions. Pick some probability distribution D on $\Re^n$. A is allowed to call examples, which are pairs $(x, f(x))$, where x is drawn according to the distribution D. A is a valid learning algorithm for F if for any probability distribution D on $\Re^n$, for any $0 < \delta, \epsilon < 1$, for any $f \in F$, A calls examples and, with probability at least $1 - \delta$ outputs in time bounded by a polynomial in n, δ^{-1}, and ϵ^{-1} a hypothesis g such that the probability that $f(x) \neq g(x)$ is less than ϵ for x drawn according to D.

This protocol includes a natural formalization of 'generalization' as prediction.For more discussion see [Valiant, 1984]. The definition is restrictive in demanding that A work for an arbitrary probability distribution D. This demand is suggested by results on uniform convergence of the empirical distribution to the actual distribution. In particular, if F has Vapnik-Chervonenkis (V-C) dimension[1] d, then it has been proved[Blumer et al, 1987] that all A needs to do to be a valid learning algorithm is to call $M_0(\epsilon, \delta, d) = max(\frac{4}{\epsilon} log \frac{2}{\delta}, \frac{8d}{\epsilon} log \frac{13}{\epsilon})$ examples and to find in polynomial time a function $g \in F$ which correctly classifies these.

Thus, for example, it is simple to show that the class H of half spaces is Valiant learnable[Blumer et al, 1987]. The V-C dimension of H is $n + 1$. All we need to do to learn H is to call $M_0(\epsilon, \delta, n + 1)$ examples and find a separating half space using Karmarkar's algorithm [Karmarkar, 1984]. Note that the Perceptron algorithm would not work here, since one can readily find distributions for which the Perceptron algorithm would be expected to take arbitrarily long times to find a separating half space.

---

[1] We say a set $S \subset R^n$ is shattered by a class F of Boolean functions if F induces all Boolean functions on S. The V-C dimension of F is the cardinality of the largest set S which F shatters.

Now, however, it seems from three points of view that the distribution independent definition is too strong. First, although the results of [Blumer et al., 1987] tell us we can gather enough information for learning in polynomial time, they say nothing about when we can actually find an algorithm A which learns in polynomial time. So far, such algorithms have only been found in a few cases, and (see, e.g. [Baum, 1989a]) these cases may be argued to be trivial.

Second, a few classes of functions have been proved (modulo strong but plausible complexity theoretic hypotheses) unlearnable by construction of cryptographically secure subclasses. Thus for example [Kearns and Valiant, 1988] show that the class of feedforward networks of threshold gates of some constant depth, or of Boolean gates of logarithmic depth, is not learnable by construction of a cryptographically secure subclass. The relevance of such results to learning in the natural world is unclear to us. For example, these results do not rule out a learning algorithm that would learn almost any log depth net. We would thus prefer a less restrictive definition of learnability, so that if a class were proved unlearnable, it would provide a meaningful limit on pragmatic learning.

Third, the results of [Blumer et al, 1987] imply that we can only expect to learn a class of functions F if F has finite V-C dimension. Thus we are in the position of assuming an enormous amount of information about the class of functions to be learned- namely that it be some specific class of finite V-C dimension, but nothing whatever about the distribution of examples. In the real world, by contrast, we are likely to know at least as much about the distribution D as we know about the class of functions F. If we relax the distribution independence criterion, then it can be shown that classes of infinite Vapnik-Chervonenkis dimension are learnable. For example, for the uniform distribution, the class of convex sets and a class of nested differences of convex sets (both of which trivially have infinite V-C dimension) are shown to be learnable in Appendix A.

§3: The Perceptron Algorithm and Uniform Distributions

The Perceptron algorithm yields, in finite time, a half-space (w_H, θ_H) which correctly classifies any given set of linearly separable examples [Rosenblatt, 1962]. That is, given a set of classified examples $\{x_\pm^\mu\}$ such that, for some (w_t, θ_t), $w_t \cdot x_+^\mu > \theta_t$ and $w_t \cdot x_-^\mu < \theta_t$ for all μ, the algorithm converges in finite time to output a (w_H, θ_H) such that $w_H \cdot x_+^\mu \geq \theta_H$ and $w_H \cdot x_-^\mu < \theta_H$. We will normalize so that $\vec{w}_t \cdot \vec{w}_t = 1$. Note that $|w_t \cdot x - \theta_t|$ is the Euclidean distance from x to the separating hyperplane $\{y : w_t \cdot y = \theta_t\}$.

The algorithm is the following. Start with some initial candidate (w_0, θ_0), which we will take to be $(\vec{0}, 0)$. Cycle through the examples. For each example, test whether that example is correctly classified. If so, proceed to the next example. If not, modify the candidate by

$$(w_{k+1} = w_k \pm x_\pm^\mu, \theta_{k+1} = \theta_k \mp 1) \tag{1}$$

where the sign of the modification is determined by the classification of the missclassified example.

In this section we will apply the Perceptron algorithm to the problem of learning in the probabilistic context described in section 2, where however the distribution D generating examples is uniform on the unit sphere S^n. Rather than have a fixed set of examples, we apply the algorithm in a slightly novel way: we call an example, perform a Perceptron update step, discard the example, and iterate until we converge to accuracy ϵ.[f2] If we applied the Perceptron algorithm in the standard way, it seemingly would not converge as rapidly. We will return to this point at the end of this section.

Now the number of updates the Perceptron algorithm must make to learn a given set of examples is well known to be $O(\frac{1}{l^2})$, where l is the minimum distance from an example to the classifying hyperplane (see eg. [Minsky and Papert, 1969]). In order to learn to ϵ accuracy in the sense of Valiant, we will observe that for the uniform distribution we do not need to correctly classify examples closer to the target separating hyperplane than $\Omega(\frac{\epsilon}{\sqrt{n}})$. Thus we will prove that the Perceptron algorithm will converge (with probability $1 - \delta$) after $O(\frac{n}{\epsilon^2})$ updates, which will occur after $O(\frac{n}{\epsilon^3})$ presentations of examples.

Indeed take $\theta_t = 0$ so the target hyperplane passes through the origin. Parallel hyperplanes a distance $\kappa/2$ above and below the target hyperplane bound a band B of probability measure

$$P(\kappa) = \int_{-\kappa/2}^{\kappa/2} (\sqrt{1 - z^2})^{n-2} dz \, \frac{A_{n-1}}{A_n} \qquad (2)$$

(for $n \geq 2$), where $A_n = \frac{2\pi^{(n+1)/2}}{\Gamma((n+1)/2)}$ is the area of S^n. See figure 1. Using the readily

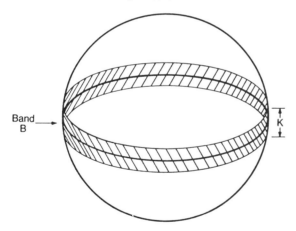

Figure 1: The target hyperplane intersects the sphere S^n along its equator (if $\theta_t = 0$) shown as the central line. Points in (say) the upper hemisphere are classified as positive examples and those in the lower as negative examples. The band B is formed by intersecting the sphere with two planes parallel to the target hyperplane and a distance $\kappa/2$ above and below it.

[f2] We say that our candidate half space has accuracy ϵ when the probability that it missclassifies an example drawn from D is no greater than ϵ.

obtainable (e.g. by Stirling's formula) bound that $\frac{A_{n-1}}{A_n} < \sqrt{n}$, and the fact that the integrand is nowhere greater than 1, we find that for $\kappa = \epsilon/2\sqrt{n}$, the band has measure less than $\epsilon/2$. If $\theta_t \neq 0$, a band of width κ will have less measure than it would for $\theta_t = 0$. We will thus continue to argue (without loss of generality) by assuming the worst case condition that $\theta_t = 0$.

Since B has measure less than $\epsilon/2$, if we have not yet converged to accuracy ϵ, there is no more than probability $1/2$ that the next example on which we update will be in B. We will show that once we have made $m_0 = max(144ln\frac{\delta}{2}, \frac{48}{\kappa^2})$ updates, we have converged unless more than $7/12$ of the updates are in B. The probability of making this fraction of the updates in B, however, is less than $\delta/2$ if the probability of each update lying in B is not more than $1/2$. We conclude with confidence $1-\delta/2$ that the probability our next update will be in B is greater than $1/2$ and thus that we have converged to ϵ-accuracy.

Indeed, consider the change in the quantity

$$N(\alpha) = \| \alpha w_t - w_k \|^2 + \| \alpha \theta_t - \theta_k \|^2 \tag{3}$$

when we update.

$$\Delta N \equiv \| \alpha w_t - w_{k+1} \|^2 + \| \alpha \theta_t - \theta_{k+1} \|^2 - \| \alpha w_t - w_k \|^2 - \| \alpha \theta_t - \theta_k \|^2 =$$

$$\mp 2\alpha w_t \cdot x_\pm \pm 2\alpha\theta_t \pm 2w_k \cdot x_\pm \mp 2\theta_k + \| x \|^2 + 1. \tag{4}$$

Now note that $\pm(w_k \cdot x_\pm - \theta_k) < 0$ since x was missclassified by (w_k, θ_k) (else we would not update). Let $A = (\mp(w_t \cdot x_\pm - \theta_t))$. If $x \in B$, then $A \leq 0$. If $x \notin B$, then $A \leq -\kappa/2$. Recalling $x^2 = 1$, we see that $\Delta N < 2$ for $x \in B$ and $\Delta N < -\alpha\kappa + 2$ for $x \notin B$. If we choose $\alpha = 8/\kappa$, we find that $\Delta N \leq -6$ for $x \notin B$. Recall that, for $k = 0$, with $(w_0, \theta_0) = (0, 0)$, we have $N = \alpha^2 = 64/\kappa^2$. Thus we see that if we have made O updates on points outside B, and I updates on points in B, $N < 0$ if $6O - 2I > 64/\kappa^2$. But N is positive semidefinite. Once we have made $48/\kappa^2$ total updates, at least $7/12$ of the updates must thus have been on examples in B.

If you assume that the probability of updates falling in B is less than $1/2$ (and thus that our hypothesis half space is not yet at ϵ - accuracy), then the probability that more than $7/12$ of $m_0 = max(144ln\frac{\delta}{2}, \frac{48}{\kappa^2})$ updates fall in B is less than $\delta/2$. To see this define $LE(p, m, r)$ as the probability of having at most r successes in m independent Bernoulli trials with probability of success p and recall, [Angluin and Valiant,1070], for $0 \leq \beta \leq 1$ that

$$LE(p, m, (1 - \beta)mp) \leq e^{-\beta^2 mp/2}. \tag{5}$$

Applying this formula with $m = m_0, p = 1/2, \beta = 1/6$ shows the desired result. We conclude that the probability of making m_0 updates without converging to ϵ accuracy is less than $\delta/2$.

However, as it approaches $1 - \epsilon$ accuracy, the algorithm will only update on a fraction ϵ of the examples. To get, with confidence $1 - \delta/2$, m_0 *updates*, it suffices to call $M = 2m_o/\epsilon$ examples. Thus we see that the Perceptron algorithm converges, with confidence $1 - \delta$, after we have called

$$M = \frac{2}{\epsilon} max(144 ln\frac{\delta}{2}, \frac{48n}{\epsilon^2}) \tag{6}$$

examples.

Each example could be processed in time of order 1 on a "neuron" which computes $w_k \cdot x$ in time 1 and updates each of its "synaptic weights" in parallel. On a serial computer, however, processing each example will take time of order n, so that we have a time of order $O(n^2/\epsilon^3)$ for convergence on a serial computer.

This is remarkably fast. The general learning procedure, described in section 2, is to call $M_0(\epsilon, \delta, n+1)$ examples and find a separating halfspace, by some polynomial time algorithm for linear programming such as Karmarkar's algorithm. This linear programming problem thus contains $\Omega(\frac{n}{\epsilon})$ constraints in n dimensions. Even to write down the problem thus takes time $\Omega(\frac{n^2}{\epsilon})$. The upper time bound to solve this given by [Karmarkar, 1984] is $O(n^{5.5}\epsilon^{-2})$. For large n the Perceptron algorithm is faster by a factor of $n^{3.5}$. Of course it is likely that Karmarkar's algorithm could be proved to work faster than $\Omega(n^{5.5})$ for the particular distribution of examples of interest. If, however, Karmarkar's algorithm requires a number of iterations depending even logarithmically on n, it will scale worse (for large n) than the Perceptron algorithm.[3]

Notice also that if we simply called $M_0(\epsilon, \delta, n + 1)$ examples and used the Perceptron algorithm, in the traditional way, to find a linear separator for this set of examples, our time performance would not be nearly as good. In fact, equation 2 tells us that we would expect one of these examples to be a distance $O(\frac{\epsilon}{n^{1.5}})$ from the target hyperplane, since we are calling $\Omega(\frac{n}{\epsilon})$ examples and a band of width $O(\frac{\epsilon}{n^{1.5}})$ has measure $\Omega(\frac{\epsilon}{n})$. Thus this approach would take time $\Omega(\frac{n^4}{\epsilon^3})$, or a factor of n^2 worse than the one we have proposed.

An alternative approach to learning using only $O(\frac{n}{\epsilon})$ examples, would be to call $M_0(\frac{\epsilon}{4}, \delta, n + 1)$ examples and apply the Perceptron algorithm to these until a fraction $1 - \epsilon/2$ had been correctly classified. This would suffice to assure that the hypothesis half space so generated would (with confidence $1 - \delta$) have error less than ϵ, as is seen from [Blumer et al, 1987, Theorem A3.3]. It is unclear to us what time performance this procedure would yield.

§4: Non-Malicious Distribution Independent Learning

Next we propose modification of the distribution independence assumption, which we have argued is too strong to apply to real world learning. We begin with an informal description. We allow an adversary (adversary 1) to choose the

---

[3] We thank P. Vaidya for a discussion on this point.

function f in the class F to present to the learning algorithm A. We allow a second adversary (adversary 2) to choose the distribution D arbitrarily. We demand that (with probability $1 - \delta$) A converge to produce an ϵ-accurate hypothesis g. Thus far we have not changed Valiant's definition. Our restriction is simply that before their choice of distribution and function, adversaries 1 and 2 are not allowed to exchange information. Thus they must work independently. This seems to us an entirely natural and reasonable restriction in the real world.

Now if we pick any distribution and any hyperplane *independently*, it is highly unlikely that the probability measure will be concentrated close to the hyperplane. Thus we expect to see that under our restriction, the Perceptron algorithm is a distribution independent learning algorithm for H and converges in time $O(\frac{n^2}{\epsilon^3 \delta^2})$ on a serial computer.

If adversary 1 and adversary 2 do not exchange information, the least we can expect is that they have no notion of a preferred direction on the sphere. Thus our informal demand that these two adversaries do not exchange information should imply, at least, that adversary 1 is equally likely to choose any w_t (relative e.g. to whatever direction adversary 2 takes as his z axis). This formalizes, sufficiently for our current purposes, the notion of Nonmalicious Distribution Independence.

Theorem 1: Let U be the uniform probability measure on S^n and D any other probability distribution on S^n. Let R be any region on S^n of U-measure $\epsilon\delta$ and let x label some point in R. Choose a point y on S^n randomly according to U. Consider the region R' formed by translating R rigidly so that x is mapped to y. Then the probability that the measure $D(R') > \epsilon$ is less than δ.

Proof: Fix any point $z \in S^n$. Now choose y and thus R'. The probability $z \in R'$ is $\epsilon\delta$. Thus in particular, if we choose a point p according to D and then choose R', the probability that $p \in R'$ is $\epsilon\delta$.

Now assume that there is probability greater than δ that $D(R') > \epsilon$. Then we arrive immediately at a contradiction, since we discover that the probability that $p \in R'$ is greater than $\epsilon\delta$. **Q.E.D.**

Corollary 2: The Perceptron algorithm is a Non-malicious distribution independent learning algorithm for half spaces on the unit sphere which converges, with confidence $1 - \delta$ to accuracy $1 - \epsilon$ in time of order $O(\frac{n^2}{\epsilon^3 \delta^2})$ on a serial computer.

Proof sketch: Let $\kappa' = \epsilon\delta/2\sqrt{n}$. Apply Theorem 1 to show that a band formed by hyperplanes a distance $\kappa'/2$ on either side of the target hyperplane has probability less than δ of having measure for examples greater than $\epsilon/2$. Then apply the arguments of the last section, with κ' in place of κ. **Q.E.D.**

Appendix A: Convex Sets Are Learnable for Uniform Distribution

In this appendix we sketch proofs that two classes of functions with infinite V-C dimension are learnable. These classes are the class of convex sets and a class of nested differences of convex sets which we define. These results support our conjecture that full distribution independence is too restrictive a criterion to ask for if we want our results to have interesting applications. We believe these results are also of independent interest.

Theorem 3: The class C of convex sets is learnable in time polynomial in ϵ^{-1} and δ^{-1} if the distribution of examples is uniform on the unit square in d dimensions.

Remarks: (1) C is well known to have infinite V-C dimension. (2) So far as we know, C is not learnable in time polynomial in d as well.

Proof Sketch:[14] We work, for simplicity, in 2 dimensions. Our arguments can readily be extended to d dimensions.

The learning algorithm is to call M examples (where M will be specified). The positive examples are by definition within the convex set to be learned. Let M_+ be the set of positive examples. We classify examples as negative if they are linearly separable from M_+, i.e. outside of c_+, the convex hull of M_+.

Clearly this approach will never missclassify a negative example, but may miss-classify positive examples which are outside c_+ and inside c_t. To show ϵ- accuracy,

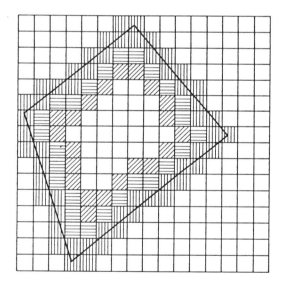

Figure 2: The boundary of the target concept c_t is shown. The set I_1 of little squares intersecting the boundary of c_t are hatched vertically. The set I_2 of squares just inside I_1 are hatched horizontally. The set I_3 of squares just inside I_2 are hatched diagonally. If we have an example in each square in I_2, the convex hull of these examples contains all points inside c_t except possibly those in $I_1, I_2,$ or I_3.

---

[14] This proof is inspired by arguments presented in [Pollard, 1984], pp22-24. After this proof was completed, the author heard D. Haussler present related, unpublished results at the 1989 Snowbird meeting on Neural Computation.

we must choose M large enough so that, with confidence $1 - \delta$, the symmetric difference of the target set c_t and c_+ has area less than ϵ.

Divide the unit square into k^2 equal subsquares. (See figure 2.) Call the set of subsquares which the boundary of c_t intersects I_1. It is easy to see that the cardinality of I_1 is no greater than $4k$. The set I_2 of subsquares just inside I_1 also has cardinality no greater than $4k$, and likewise for the set I_3 of subsquares just inside I_2. If we have an example in each of the squares in I_2, then c_t and c_+ clearly have symmetric difference at most equal the area of $I_1 \cup I_2 \cup I_3 \leq 12k \times k^{-2} = 12/k$. Thus take $k = 12/\epsilon$. Now choose M sufficiently large so that after M trials there is less than δ probability we have not got an example in each of the $4k$ squares in I_2. Thus we need $LE(k^{-2}, M, 4k) < \delta$. Using equation 5, we see that $M = \frac{500}{\epsilon^2} ln \delta$ will suffice. **Q.E.D.**

Actually, one can learn (for uniform distributions) a more complex class of functions formed out of nested convex regions. For any set $\{c_1, c_2, ..., c_l\}$ of l convex regions in $\Re^d$, let $R_1 = c_1$ and for $j = 2, ..., l$ let $R_j = R_{j-1} \cap c_j$. Then define a concept $f = R_1 - R_2 + R_3 - ... R_l$. The class C of concepts so formed we call nested convex sets. See figure 3.

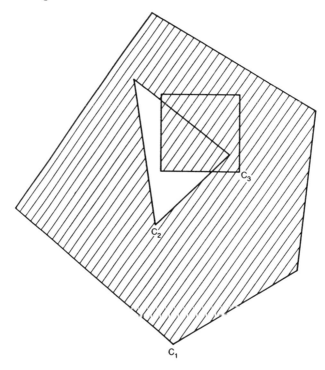

Figure 3: c_1 is the five sided region, c_2 is the triangular region, and c_3 is the square. The positive region $c_1 - c_2 \cup c_1 + c_3 \cup c_2 \cup c_1$ is shaded.

This class can be learned by an iterative procedure which peels the onion. Call a sufficient number of examples. (One can easily see that a number polynomial in l, ϵ, and δ but of course exponential in d will suffice.) Let the set of examples so obtained be called S. Those negative examples which are linearly separable from all positive examples are in the outermost layer. Class these in set S_1. Those positive examples which are linearly separable from all negative examples in $S - S_1$ lie in the next layer- call this set of positive examples S_2. Those negative examples in $S - S_1$ linearly separable from all positive examples in $S - S_2$ lie in the next layer, S_3. In this way one builds up $l + 1$ sets of examples. (Some of these sets may be empty.) One can then apply the methods of Theorem 3 to build a classifying function from the outside in. If the innermost layer S_{l+1} is (say) negative examples, then any future example is called negative if it is not linearly separable from S_{l+1}, or is linearly separable from S_l and not linearly separable from S_{l-1}, or is linearly separable from S_{l-2} but not linearly separable from S_{l-3}, etc.

Acknowledgement: I would like to thank L.E. Baum for conversations and L. G. Valiant for comments on a draft. Portions of the work reported here were performed while the author was an employee of Princeton University and of the Jet Propulsion Laboratory, California Institute of Technology, and were supported by NSF grant DMR-8518163 and agencies of the US Department of Defence including the Innovative Science and Technology Office of the Strategic Defence Initiative Organization.

References

ANGLUIN, D., VALIANT, L.G. (1979), Fast probabilistic algorithms for Hamiltonian circuits and matchings, J. of Computer and Systems Sciences, 18, pp 155-193.

BAUM, E.B., (1989), On learning a union of half spaces, Journal of Complexity V5, N4.

BLUMER, A., EHRENFEUCHT,A., HAUSSLER,D., and WARMUTH,M. (1987), Learnability and the Vapnik-Chervonenkis Dimension, U.C.S.C. tech. rep. UCSC-CRL-87-20, and J. ACM, to appear.

KARMARKAR, N., (1984), A new polynomial time algorithm for linear programming, Combinatorica 4, pp373-395

KEARNS, M, and VALIANT, L., (1989), Cryptographic limitations on learning Boolean formulae and finite automata, Proc. 21st ACM Symp. on Theory of Computing, pp433-444.

MINSKY, M, and PAPERT,S., (1969), *Perceptrons, and Introduction to Computational Geometry*, MIT Press, Cambridge MA.

POLLARD, D. (1984), *Convergence of stochastic processes*, New York: Springer-Verlag.

ROSENBLATT, F. (1962), *Principles of Neurodynamics*, Spartan Books, N.Y.

VALIANT, L.G., (1984), A theory of the learnable, Comm. of ACM V27, N11, pp1134-1142.

Sequential Decision Problems
and Neural Networks

A. G. Barto
Dept. of Computer and
Information Science
Univ. of Massachusetts
Amherst, MA 01003

R. S. Sutton
GTE Laboratories Inc.
Waltham, MA 02254

C. J. C. H. Watkins
25B Framfield
Highbury, London
N5 1UU

ABSTRACT

Decision making tasks that involve delayed consequences are very common yet difficult to address with supervised learning methods. If there is an accurate model of the underlying dynamical system, then these tasks can be formulated as sequential decision problems and solved by Dynamic Programming. This paper discusses reinforcement learning in terms of the sequential decision framework and shows how a learning algorithm similar to the one implemented by the Adaptive Critic Element used in the pole-balancer of Barto, Sutton, and Anderson (1983), and further developed by Sutton (1984), fits into this framework. Adaptive neural networks can play significant roles as modules for approximating the functions required for solving sequential decision problems.

1   INTRODUCTION

Most neural network research on learning assumes the existence of a supervisor or teacher knowledgeable enough to supply desired, or target, network outputs during training. These network learning algorithms are function approximation methods having various useful properties. Other neural network research addresses the question of where the training information might come from. Typical of this research is that into *reinforcement learning* systems; these systems learn without detailed instruction about how to interact successfully with reactive environments. Learning tasks involving delays between actions and their consequences are particularly difficult to address with supervised learning methods, and special reinforcement learning algorithms have been developed to handle them. In this paper, reinforcement learning is related to the theory of sequential decision problems and to the computational methods known as Dynamic Programming (DP). DP methods are not learning methods because they rely on complete prior knowledge of the task, but their theory is nevertheless relevant for understanding and developing learning methods.

An example of a sequential decision problem invloving delayed consequences is the version of the pole-balancing problem studied by Barto, Sutton, and Anderson (1983). In this problem the consequences of control decisions are not immediately available because training information comes only in the form of a "failure signal" occurring when the pole falls past a critical angle or when the cart hits an end of the track. The learning system used by Barto et al. (1983), and subsequently systematically explored by Sutton (1984), consists of two different neuron-like adaptive elements: an Associative Search Element (ASE), which implemented and adjusted the control rule, or decision policy, and an Adaptive Critic Element (ACE), which used the failure signal to learn how to provide useful moment-to-moment evaluation of control decisions. The focus of this paper is the algorithm implemented by the ACE: What computational task does this algorithm solve, and how does it solve it?

Sutton (1988) analyzed a class of learning rules which includes the algorithm used by the ACE, calling them Temporal Difference, or TD, algorithms. Although Sutton briefly discussed the relationship between TD algorithms and DP, he did not develop this perspective. Here, we discuss an algorithm slightly different from the one implemented by the ACE and call it simply the "TD algorithm" (although the class of TD algorithms includes others as well). The earliest use of a TD algorithm that we know of was by Samuel (1959) in his checkers player. Werbos (1977) was the first we know of to suggest such algorithms in the context of DP, calling them "heuristic dynamic programming" methods. The connection to dynamic programming has recently been extensively explored by Watkins (1989), who uses the term "incremental dynamic programming." Also related is the "bucket brigade" used in classifier systems (see Liepins et al., 1989), the adaptive controller developed by Witten (1977), and certain animal learning models (see Sutton and Barto, to appear). Barto, Sutton, and Watkins (to appear) discuss the relationship between TD algorithms and DP more extensively than is possible here and provide references to other related research.

2   OPTIMIZING DELAYED CONSEQUENCES

Many problems require making decisions whose consequences emerge over time periods of variable and uncertain duration. Decision-making strategies must be formed that take into account expectations of both the short-term and long-term consequences of decisions. The theory of sequential decision problems is highly developed and includes formulations of both deterministic and stochastic problems (the books by Bertsekas, 1976, and Ross, 1983, are two of the many relevant texts). This theory concerns problems such as the following special case of a stochastic problem. A decision maker (DM) interacts with a discrete-time stochastic dynamical system in such a way that, at each time step, the DM observes the system's current state and selects an action. After the action is performed, the DM receives (at the next time step) a certain amount of *payoff* that depends on the action and the current state, and the system makes a transition to a new state determined by the current state, the action, and random disturbances. Upon observing the new state, the DM chooses another action and continues in this manner for a sequence of time steps. The objective of the task is to form a rule for the DM to use in selecting actions, called a *policy*, that maximizes a measure of the total amount of payoff accumulated over time. The amount of time over which this measure is computed is the *horizon* of the problem, and a maximizing policy is an *optimal policy*. One commonly studied measure of cumulative payoff is the *expected infinite-horizon discounted return*, defined below. Because the objective is to maximize a measure of cumulative payoff, both short- and long-term consequences of decisions are important. Decisions that produce high immediate payoff may prevent high payoff from being received later on, and hence such decisions should not necessarily be included in optimal policies.

More formally (following the presentation of Ross, 1983), a policy is a mapping, denoted π, that assigns an action to each state of the underlying system (for simplicity, here we consider only the special case of deterministic policies). Let x_t denote the system state at time step t, and if the DM uses policy π, the action it takes at step t is $a_t = \pi(x_t)$. After the action is taken, the system makes a transition from state $x = x_t$ to state $y = x_{t+1}$ with a probability $P_{xy}(a_t)$. At time step $t+1$, the DM receives a payoff, r_{t+1}, with expected value $R(x_t, a_t)$. For any policy π and state x, one can define the expected infinite-horizon discounted return (which we simply call the *expected return*) under the condition that the system begins in state x, the DM continues to use policy π throughout the future, and γ, $0 \leq \gamma < 1$, is the discount factor:

$$E_\pi \left[\sum_{t=0}^{\infty} \gamma^t r_{t+1} | x_0 = x \right], \tag{1}$$

where x_0 is the initial system state, and E_π is the expectation assuming the DM uses policy π. The objective of the decision problem is to form a policy that maximizes the expected return defined by Equation 1 for each state x.

3   DYNAMIC PROGRAMMING

Dynamic Programming (DP) is a collection of computational methods for solving stochastic sequential decision problems. These methods require a model of the dynamical system underlying the decision problem in the form of the state transition probabilities, $P_{xy}(a)$, for all states x and y and actions a, as well as knowledge of the function, $R(x, a)$, giving the payoff expectations for all states x and actions a. There are several different DP methods, all of which are iterative methods for computing optimal policies, and all of which compute sequences of different types of *evaluation functions*. Most relevant to the TD algorithm is the evaluation function for a given policy. This function assigns to each state the expected value of the return assuming the problem starts in that state and the given policy is used. Specifically, for policy π and discount factor γ, the evaluation function, V_γ^π, assigns to each state, x, the expected return given the initial state x:

$$V_\gamma^\pi(x) = E_\pi[\textstyle\sum_{t=0}^\infty \gamma^t r_{t+1} | x_0 = x].$$

For each state, the evaluation function provides a prediction of the return that will accrue throughout the future whenever this state is encountered if the given policy is followed. If one can compute the evaluation function for a state merely from observing that state, this prediction is effectively available *immediately* upon the system entering that state. Evaluation functions provide the means for assessing the temporally extended consequences of decisions in a temporally local manner.

It can be shown (e.g., Ross, 1983) that the evaluation function V_γ^π is the unique function satisfying the following condition for each state x:

$$V_\gamma^\pi(x) = R(x, \pi(x)) + \gamma \textstyle\sum_y P_{xy}(\pi(x)) V_\gamma^\pi(y). \tag{2}$$

DP methods for solving this system of equations (i.e., for determining V_γ^π) typically proceed through successive approximations. For dynamical systems with large state sets the solution requires considerable computation. For systems with continuous state spaces, DP methods require approximations of evaluation functions (and also of policies). In their simplest form, DP methods rely on lookup-table representations of these functions, based on discretizations of the state space in continuous cases, and are therefore exponential in the state space dimension. In fact, Richard Bellman, who introduced the term Dynamic Programming (Bellman, 1957), also coined the phrase "curse of dimensionality" to describe the difficulty of representing these functions for use in DP. Consequently, any advance in function approximation methods, whether due to theoretical insights or to the development of hardware having high speed and high capacity, can be used to great advantage in DP. Artificial neural networks therefore have natural applications in DP.

Because DP methods rely on complete prior knowledge of the decision problem, they are not learning methods. However, DP methods and reinforcement learning methods are closely related, and many concepts from DP are relevant to the case of incomplete prior knowledge. Payoff values correspond to the available evaluation signals (the "primary reinforcers"), and the values of an evaluation function correspond to improved evaluation signals (the "secondary reinforcers") such a those produced by the ACE. In the simplest reinforcement learning systems, the role of the dynamical system model required by DP is played by the real system itself. A reinforcement learning system improves performance by interacting directly with the real system. A system model is not required.[1]

---

[1] Although reinforcement learning methods can greatly benefit from such models (Sutton, to appear).

4   THE TD ALGORITHM

The TD algorithm approximates V_γ^π for a given policy π in the absence of knowledge of the transition probabilities and the function determining expected payoff values. Assume that each system state is represented by a feature vector, and that V_γ^π can be approximated adequately as a function in a class of parameterized functions of the feature vectors, such as a class of functions parameterized by the connection weights of a neural network. Letting $\phi(x_t)$ denote the feature vector representing state x_t, let the estimated evaluation of x_t be

$$V_t(x_t) = f(v_t, \phi(x_t)),$$

where v_t is the weight vector at step t and f depends on the class of models assumed. In terms of a neural network, $\phi(x_t)$ is the input vector at time t, and $V_t(x_t)$ is the output at time t, assuming no delay across the network.

If we knew the true evaluations of the states, then we could define as an error the difference between the true evaluations and the estimated evaluations and adjust the weight vector v_t according to this error using supervised-learning methods. However, it is unrealistic to assume such knowledge in sequential decision tasks. Instead the TD algorithm uses the following update rule to adjust the weight vector:

$$v_{t+1} = v_t + \alpha \left[r_{t+1} + \gamma V_t(x_{t+1}) - V_t(x_t) \right] \frac{\partial f}{\partial v_t}(\phi(x_t)). \tag{3}$$

In this equation, α is a positive step-size parameter, r_{t+1} is the payoff received at time step $t+1$, $V_t(x_{t+1})$ is the estimated evaluation of the state at $t+1$ using the weight vector v_t (i.e., $V_t(x_{t+1}) = f(v_t, \phi(x_{t+1}))$,[2] and $\frac{\partial f}{\partial v_t}(\phi(x_t))$ is the gradient of f with respect to v_t evaluated at $\phi(x_t)$. If f is the inner product of v_t and $\phi(x_t)$, this gradient is just $\phi(x_t)$, as it is for a single linear ACE element. In the case of an appropriate feedforward network, this gradient can be computed by the error backpropagation method as illustrated by Anderson (1986). One can think of Equation 3 as the usual supervised-learning rule using $r_{t+1} + \gamma V_t(x_{t+1})$ as the "target" output in the error term.

To understand why the TD algorithm uses this target, assume that the DM is using a fixed policy for selecting actions. The output of the critic at time step t, $V_t(x_t)$, is intended to be a prediction of the return that will accrue after time step t. Specifically, $V_t(x_t)$ should be an estimate for the expected value of

$$r_{t+1} + \gamma r_{t+2} + \gamma^2 r_{t+3} + \dots,$$

where r_{t+k} is the payoff received at time step $t+k$. One way to adjust the weights would be to *wait forever* and use the actual return as a target. More practically,

---

[2] Instead of using v_t to evaluate the state at $t+1$, the learning rule used by the ACE by Barto et al. (1983) uses v_{t+1}. This closely approximates the algorithm described here if the weights change slowly.

one could wait n time steps and use what Watkins (1989) calls the n-*step truncated return* as a target:

$$r_{t+1} + \gamma r_{t+2} + \gamma^2 r_{t+3} + \ldots + \gamma^{n-1} r_{t+n}.$$

However, it is possible to do better than this. One can use what Watkins calls the *corrected n-step truncated return* as a target:

$$r_{t+1} + \gamma r_{t+2} + \gamma^2 r_{t+3} + \ldots + \gamma^{n-1} r_{t+n} + \gamma^n V_t(x_{t+n}),$$

where $V_t(x_{t+n})$ is the estimated evaluation of state x_{t+n} using the weight values at time t. Because $V_t(x_{t+n})$ is an estimate of the expected return from step $t + n + 1$ onwards, $\gamma^n V_t(x_{t+n})$ is an estimate for the missing terms in the n-step truncated return from state x_t. To see this, note that $\gamma^n V_t(x_{t+n})$ approximates

$$\gamma^n [r_{t+n+1} + \gamma r_{t+n+2} + \gamma^2 r_{t+n+3} + \ldots].$$

Multiplying through by γ^n, this equals

$$\gamma^n r_{t+n+1} + \gamma^{n+1} r_{t+n+2} + \ldots,$$

which is the part of the series missing from the n-step truncated return. The weight update rule for the TD algorithm (Equation 3) uses the corrected 1-step truncated return as a target, and using the n-step truncated return for $n > 1$ produces obvious generalizations of this learning rule at the cost of requiring longer delay lines for implementation.

The above justification of the TD algorithm is based on the assumption that the critic's output $V_t(x)$ is in fact a useful estimate of the expected return starting from any state x. Whether this estimate is good or bad, however, the expected value of the n-step corrected truncated return is always better (Watkins, 1989). Intuitively, this is true because the n-step corrected truncated return includes more data, namely the payoffs r_{t+k}, $k = 1, \ldots, n$. Surprisingly, as Sutton (1988) shows, the corrected truncated return is often a better estimate of the actual expected return than is the actual return itself.

Another way to explain the TD algorithm is to refer to the system of equations from DP (Equation 2), which the evaluation function for a given policy must satisfy. One can obtain an error based on how much the current estimated evaluation function, V_t, departs from the desired condition given by Equation 2 for the current state, x_t:

$$R(x_t, a_t) + \gamma \sum_y P_{x_t,y}(a_t) V_t(y) - V_t(x_t).$$

But the function R and the transition probabilities, $P_{x_t,y}(a_t)$, are not known. Consequently, one substitutes r_{t+1}, the payoff actually received at step $t + 1$, for the expected value of this payoff, $R(x_t, a_t)$, and substitutes the current estimated evaluation of the state actually *reached* in one step for the expectation of the estimated evaluations of states *reachable* in one step. That is, one uses $V_t(x_{t+1})$ in place of $\sum_y P_{x_t,y}(a_t) V_t(y)$. Using the resulting error in the usual supervised-learning rule yields the TD algorithm (Equation 3).

5   USING THE TD ALGORITHM

We have described the TD algorithm above as a method for approximating the evaluation function associated with a fixed policy. However, if the fixed policy and the underlying dynamical system are viewed together as an autonomous dynamical system, i.e, a system without input, then the TD algorithm can be regarded purely as a prediction method, a view taken by Sutton (1988). The predicted quantity can be a discounted sum of any observable signal, not just payoff. For example, in speech recognition, the signal might give the identity of a word at the word's end, and the prediction would provide an anticipatory indication of the word's identity. Unlike other adaptive prediction methods, the TD algorithm does not require fixing a prediction time interval.

More relevant to the topic of this paper, the TD algorithm can be used as a component in methods for improving policies. The pole-balancing system of Barto et al. (1983; see also Sutton, 1984) provides one example in which the policy changes while the TD algorithm operates. The ASE of that system changes the policy by attempting to improve it according to the current estimated evaluation function. This approach is most closely related to the policy improvement algorithm of DP (e.g., see Bertsekas, 1976; Ross, 1983) and is one of several ways to use TD-like methods for improving policies; others are described by Watkins (1989) and Werbos (1987).

6   CONCLUSION

Decision making problems involving delayed consequences can be formulated as stochastic sequential decision problems and solved by DP if there is a complete and accurate model of the underlying dynamical system. Due to the computational cost of exact DP methods and their reliance on complete and exact models, there is a need for methods that can provide approximate solutions and that do not require this amount of prior knowledge. The TD algorithm is an incremental, on-line method for approximating the evaluation function associated with a given policy that does not require a system model. The TD algorithm directly adjusts a parameterized model of the evaluation function—a model that can take the form of an artificial neural network. The TD learning process is a Monte-Carlo approximation to a successive approximation method of DP. This perspective provides the necessary framework for extending the theory of TD algorithms as well as that of other algorithms used in reinforcement learning. Adaptive neural networks can play significant roles as modules for approximating the required functions.

Acknowledgements

A. G. Barto's contribution was supported by the Air Force Office of Scientific Research, Bolling AFB, through grants AFOSR-87-0030 and AFOSR-89-0526.

References

C. W. Anderson. (1986) *Learning and Problem Solving with Multilayer Connectionist Systems.* PhD thesis, University of Massachusetts, Amherst, MA.

A. G. Barto, R. S. Sutton, and C. W. Anderson. (1983) Neuronlike elements that can solve difficult learning control problems. *IEEE Transactions on Systems, Man, and Cybernetics*, 13:835–846.

A. G. Barto, R. S. Sutton, and C. Watkins. (to appear) Learning and sequential decision making. In M. Gabriel and J. W. Moore, editors, *Learning and Computational Neuroscience*. The MIT Press, Cambridge, MA.

R. E. Bellman. (1957) *Dynamic Programming*. Princeton University Press, Princeton, NJ.

D. I. Bertsekas. (1976) *Dynamic Programming and Stochastic Control*. Academic Press, New York.

Liepins, G. E., Hilliard, M.R., Palmer, M., and Rangarajan, G. (1989) Alternatives for classifier system credit assignment. *Proceedings of the Eleventh International Joint Conference on Artificial Intelligence*, 756–761.

S. Ross. (1983) *Introduction to Stochastic Dynamic Programming*. Academic Press, New York.

A. L. Samuel. (1959) Some studies in machine learning using the game of checkers. *IBM Journal on Research and Development*, 210–229.

R. S. Sutton. (1984) *Temporal Credit Assignment in Reinforcement Learning*. PhD thesis, University of Massachusetts, Amherst, MA.

R. S. Sutton. (1988) Learning to predict by the methods of temporal differences. *Machine Learning*, 3:9–44.

R. S. Sutton (to appear) First results with Dyna, an integrated architecture for learning planning and reacting. *Proceedings of the 1990 AAAI Symposium on Planning in Uncertain, Unpredictable, or Changing Environments.*

R. S. Sutton and A. G. Barto. (to appear) Time-derivative models of Pavlovian reinforcement. In M. Gabriel and J. W. Moore, editors, *Learning and Computational Neuroscience*. The MIT Press, Cambridge, MA.

C. J. C. H. Watkins. (1989) *Learning from Delayed Rewards*. PhD thesis, Cambridge University, Cambridge, England.

P. J. Werbos. (1977) Advanced forecasting methods for global crisis warning and models of intelligence. *General Systems Yearbook*, 22:25–38.

P. J. Werbos. (1987) Building and understanding adaptive systems: A statistical/numerical approach to factory automation and brain research. *IEEE Transactions on Systems, Man, and Cybernetics*, 17:7–20.

I. H. Witten. (1977). An adaptive optimal controller for discrete-time markov environments. *Information and Control*, 34:286–295.

Analysis of Linsker's Simulations
of Hebbian rules

David J. C. MacKay
Computation and Neural Systems
Caltech 164–30 CNS
Pasadena, CA 91125
mackay@aurel.cns.caltech.edu

Kenneth D. Miller
Department of Physiology
University of California
San Francisco, CA 94143 - 0444
ken@phyb.ucsf.edu

ABSTRACT

Linsker has reported the development of centre–surround receptive fields and oriented receptive fields in simulations of a Hebb–type equation in a linear network. The dynamics of the learning rule are analysed in terms of the eigenvectors of the covariance matrix of cell activities. Analytic and computational results for Linsker's covariance matrices, and some general theorems, lead to an explanation of the emergence of centre–surround and certain oriented structures.

Linsker [Linsker, 1986, Linsker, 1988] has studied by simulation the evolution of weight vectors under a Hebb–type teacherless learning rule in a feed–forward linear network. The equation for the evolution of the weight vector **w** of a single neuron, derived by ensemble averaging the Hebbian rule over the statistics of the input patterns, is:[1]

$$\frac{\partial}{\partial t} w_i = k_1 + \sum_j (Q_{ij} + k_2) w_j \quad \text{subject to} \quad -w_{\max} \le w_i \le w_{\max} \tag{1}$$

---

[1]Our definition of equation 1 differs from Linsker's by the omission of a factor of $1/N$ before the sum term, where N is the number of synapses.

where $\mathbf{Q}$ is the covariance matrix of activities of the inputs to the neuron. The covariance matrix depends on the covariance function, which describes the dependence of the covariance of two input cells' activities on their separation in the input field, and on the location of the synapses, which is determined by a synaptic density function. Linsker used a gaussian synaptic density function.

Depending on the covariance function and the two parameters k_1 and k_2, different weight structures emerge. Using a gaussian covariance function (his layer $\mathcal{B} \to \mathcal{C}$), Linsker reported the emergence of non–trivial weight structures, ranging from saturated structures through centre–surround structures to bi–lobed oriented structures.

The analysis in this paper examines the properties of equation (1). We concentrate on the gaussian covariances in Linsker's layer $\mathcal{B} \to \mathcal{C}$, and give an explanation of the structures reported by Linsker. Several of the results are more general, applying to any covariance matrix $\mathbf{Q}$. Space constrains us to postpone general discussion, and criteria for the emergence of centre–surround weight structures, technical details, and discussion of other model networks, to future publications [MacKay, Miller, 1990].

1   ANALYSIS IN TERMS OF EIGENVECTORS

We write equation (1) as a first order differential equation for the weight vector $\mathbf{w}$:

$$\dot{\mathbf{w}} = (\mathbf{Q} + k_2 \mathbf{J})\mathbf{w} + k_1 \mathbf{n} \quad \text{subject to} \quad -w_{\max} \le w_i \le w_{\max} \tag{2}$$

where $\mathbf{J}$ is the matrix $J_{ij} = 1 \, \forall i, j$, and $\mathbf{n}$ is the DC vector $n_i = 1 \, \forall i$. This equation is linear, up to the hard limits on w_i. These hard limits define a hypercube in weight space within which the dynamics are confined. We make the following assumption:

Assumption 1 *The principal features of the dynamics are established before the hard limits are reached. When the hypercube is reached, it captures and preserves the existing weight structure with little subsequent change.*

The matrix $\mathbf{Q} + k_2 \mathbf{J}$ is symmetric, so it has a complete orthonormal set of eigenvectors[2] $\mathbf{e}^{(a)}$ with real eigenvalues λ_a. The linear dynamics within the hypercube can be characterised in terms of these eigenvectors, each of which represents an independently evolving weight configuration. First, equation (2) has a fixed point at

$$\mathbf{w}^{\mathrm{FP}} = -k_1 (\mathbf{Q} + k_2 \mathbf{J})^{-1} \mathbf{n} = -k_1 \sum_a \frac{\mathbf{e}^{(a)} \cdot \mathbf{n}}{\lambda_a} \mathbf{e}^{(a)} \tag{3}$$

Second, relative to the fixed point, the component of $\mathbf{w}$ in the direction of an eigenvector grows or decays exponentially at a rate proportional to the corresponding eigenvalue. Writing $\mathbf{w}(t) = \sum_a w_a(t) \mathbf{e}^{(a)}$, equation (2) yields

$$w_a(t) - w_a^{\mathrm{FP}} = (w_a(0) - w_a^{\mathrm{FP}}) e^{\lambda_a t} \tag{4}$$

---

[2] The indices a and b will be used to denote the eigenvector basis for $\mathbf{w}$, while the indices i and j will be used for the synaptic basis.

Thus, the principal emergent features of the dynamics are determined by the following three factors:

1. The principal eigenvectors of $\mathbf{Q} + k_2\mathbf{J}$, that is, the eigenvectors with largest positive eigenvalues. These are the fastest growing weight configurations.

2. Eigenvectors of $\mathbf{Q} + k_2\mathbf{J}$ with negative eigenvalue. Each is associated with an attracting constraint surface, the hyperplane defined by $w_a = w_a^{\mathrm{FP}}$.

3. The location of the fixed point of equation (1). This is important for two reasons: a) it determines the location of the constraint surfaces; b) the fixed point gives a "head start" to the growth rate of eigenvectors $\mathbf{e}^{(a)}$ for which $|w_a^{\mathrm{FP}}|$ is large compared to $|w_a(0)|$.

2   EIGENVECTORS OF Q

We first examine the eigenvectors and eigenvalues of $\mathbf{Q}$. The principal eigenvector of $\mathbf{Q}$ dominates the dynamics of equation (2) for $k_1 = 0$, $k_2 = 0$. The subsequent eigenvectors of $\mathbf{Q}$ become important as k_1 and k_2 are varied.

2.1   PROPERTIES OF CIRCULARLY SYMMETRIC SYSTEMS

If an operator commutes with the rotation operator, its eigenfunctions can be written as eigenfunctions of the rotation operator. For Linsker's system, in the continuum limit, the operator $\mathbf{Q} + k_2\mathbf{J}$ is unchanged under rotation of the system. So the eigenfunctions of $\mathbf{Q} + k_2\mathbf{J}$ can be written as the product of a radial function and one of the angular functions $\cos l\theta$, $\sin l\theta$, $l = 0, 1, 2...$ To describe these eigenfunctions we borrow from quantum mechanics the notation $n = 1, 2, 3...$ and $l = $ s, p, d... to denote the total number of number of nodes in the function $= 0, 1, 2...$ and the number of angular nodes $= 0, 1, 2...$ respectively. For example, "2s" denotes a centre–surround function with one radial node and no angular nodes (see figure 1).

For monotonic and non-negative covariance functions, we conjecture that the eigenfunctions of $\mathbf{Q}$ are ordered in eigenvalue by their numbers of nodes such that the eigenfunction $[nl]$ has larger eigenvalue than either $[(n + 1)l]$ or $[n(l + 1)]$. This conjecture is obeyed in all analytical and numerical results we have obtained.

2.2   ANALYTIC CALCULATIONS FOR $k_2 = 0$

We have solved analytically for the first three eigenfunctions and eigenvalues of the covariance matrix for layer $\mathcal{B} \to \mathcal{C}$ of Linsker's network, in the continuum limit (Table 1). 1s, the function with no changes of sign, is the principal eigenfunction of $\mathbf{Q}$; 2p, the bilobed oriented function, is the second eigenfunction; and 2s, the centre–surround eigenfunction, is third.[3]

Figure 1(a) shows the first six eigenfunctions for layer $\mathcal{B} \to \mathcal{C}$ of [Linsker, 1986].

---

[3]2s is degenerate with 3d at $k_2 = 0$.

Table 1: The first three eigenfunctions of the operator $Q(\mathbf{r}, \mathbf{r}')$
$Q(\mathbf{r}, \mathbf{r}') = e^{-(\mathbf{r}-\mathbf{r}')^2/2C}e^{-r'^2/2A}$, where C and A denote the characteristic sizes of the covariance function and synaptic density function. $\mathbf{r}$ denotes two-dimensional spatial position relative to the centre of the synaptic arbor, and $r = |\mathbf{r}|$. The eigenvalues λ are all normalised by the effective number of synapses.

Name	Eigenfunction	λ/N
1s	$e^{-r^2/2R}$	lC/A
2p	$r\cos\theta e^{-r^2/2R}$	l^2C/A
2s	$(1 - r^2/r_0^2)e^{-r^2/2R}$	l^3C/A

$$R = \frac{C}{2}\left(1 + \sqrt{1 + 4A/C}\right)$$
$$l = \frac{R-C}{R} \quad (0 < l < 1)$$
$$r_0^2 = \frac{2A}{\sqrt{1+4A/C}}$$

Figure 1: Eigenfunctions of the operator $Q + k_2 J$.
Largest eigenvalue is in the top row. Eigenvalues (in arbitrary units): (a) $k_2 = 0$: 1s, 2.26; 2p, 1.0; 2s & 3d (only one 3d is shown), 0.41. (b) $k_2 = -3$: 2p, 1.0; 2s, 0.66; 1s, -17.8. The greyscale indicates the range from maximum negative to maximum positive synaptic weight within each eigenfunction. Eigenfunctions of the operator $(e^{-(\mathbf{r}-\mathbf{r}')^2/2C} + k_2)e^{-r'^2/2A}$ were computed for $C/A = 2/3$ (as used by Linsker for most layer $\mathcal{B} \to \mathcal{C}$ simulations) on a circle of radius 12.5 grid intervals, with $\sqrt{A} = 6.15$ grid intervals.

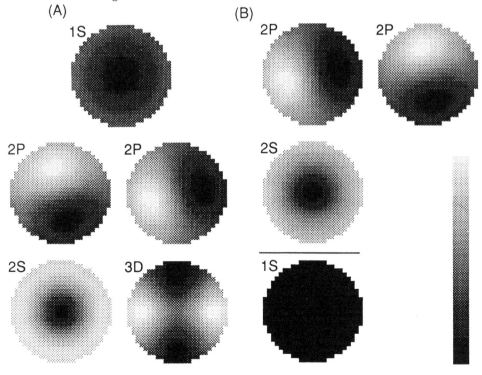

3   THE EFFECTS OF THE PARAMETERS k_1 AND k_2

Varying k_2 changes the eigenvectors and eigenvalues of the matrix $\mathbf{Q}+k_2\mathbf{J}$. Varying k_1 moves the fixed point of the dynamics with respect to the origin. We now analyse these two changes, and their effects on the dynamics.

Definition: Let $\hat{\mathbf{n}}$ be the unit vector in the direction of the DC vector $\mathbf{n}$. We refer to $(\mathbf{w} \cdot \hat{\mathbf{n}})$ as the *DC component* of $\mathbf{w}$. The DC component is proportional to the sum of the synaptic strengths in a weight vector. For example, 2p and all the other eigenfunctions with angular nodes have zero DC component. Only the s–modes have a non–zero DC component.

3.1   GENERAL THEOREM: THE EFFECT OF k_2

We now characterise the effect of adding $k_2\mathbf{J}$ to *any* covariance matrix $\mathbf{Q}$.

Theorem 1 *For any covariance matrix $\mathbf{Q}$, the spectrum of eigenvectors and eigenvalues of $\mathbf{Q} + k_2\mathbf{J}$ obeys the following:*
1. Eigenvectors of $\mathbf{Q}$ with no DC component, and their eigenvalues, are unaffected by k_2.
2. The other eigenvectors, with non–zero DC component, vary with k_2. Their eigenvalues increase continuously and monotonically with k_2 between asymptotic limits such that the upper limit of one eigenvalue is the lower limit of the eigenvalue above.
3. There is at most one negative eigenvalue.
4. All but one of the eigenvalues remain finite. In the limits $k_2 \to \pm\infty$ there is a DC eigenvector $\hat{\mathbf{n}}$ with eigenvalue $\to k_2 N$, where N is the dimensionality of $\mathbf{Q}$, i.e. the number of synapses.

The properties stated in this theorem, whose proof is in [MacKay, Miller, 1990], are summarised pictorially by the spectral structure shown in figure 2.

3.2   IMPLICATIONS FOR LINSKER'S SYSTEM

For Linsker's circularly symmetric systems, all the eigenfunctions with angular nodes have zero DC component and are thus independent of k_2. The eigenvalues that vary with k_2 are those of the s–modes. The leading s–modes at $k_2 = 0$ are 1s, 2s; as k_2 is decreased to $-\infty$, these modes transform continuously into 2s, 3s respectively (figure 2).[4] 1s becomes an eigenvector with negative eigenvalue, and it approaches the DC vector $\hat{\mathbf{n}}$. This eigenvector enforces a constraint $\mathbf{w} \cdot \hat{\mathbf{n}} = \mathbf{w}^{FP} \cdot \hat{\mathbf{n}}$, and thus determines that the final average synaptic strength is equal to $\mathbf{w}^{FP} \cdot \mathbf{n}/N$.

Linsker used $k_2 = -3$ in [Linsker, 1986]. This value of k_2 is sufficiently large that the properties of the $k_2 \to -\infty$ limit hold [MacKay, Miller, 1990], and in the following we concentrate interchangeably on $k_2 = -3$ and $k_2 \to -\infty$. The computed eigenfunctions for Linsker's system at layer $\mathcal{B} \to \mathcal{C}$ are shown in figure 1(b) for

---

[4] The 2s eigenfunctions at $k_2 = 0$ and $k_2 = -\infty$ both have one radial node, but are not identical functions.

Figure 2: General spectrum of eigenvalues of $Q + k_2 J$ as a function of k_2.
A: Eigenvectors with DC component. B: Eigenvectors with zero DC component.
C: Adjacent DC eigenvalues share a common asymptote. D: There is only one
negative eigenvalue.
The annotations in brackets refer to the eigenvectors of Linsker's system.

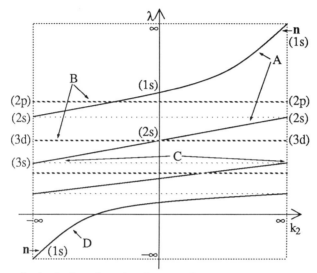

$k_2 = -3$. The principal eigenfunction is 2p. The centre–surround eigenfunction 2s
is the principal *symmetric* eigenfunction, but it still has smaller eigenvalue than 2p.

3.3   EFFECT OF k_1

Varying k_1 changes the location of the fixed point of equation (2). From equation
(3), the fixed point is displaced from the origin only in the direction of eigenvectors
that have non–zero DC component, that is, only in the direction of the s–modes.
This has two important effects, as discussed in section 1: a) The s–modes are given
a head start in growth rate that increases as k_1 is increased. In particular, the
principal s–mode, the centre–surround eigenvector 2s, may outgrow the principal
eigenvector 2p. b) The constraint surface is moved when k_1 is changed. For large
negative k_2, the constraint surface fixes the average synaptic strength in the final
weight vector. To leading order in $1/k_2$, Linsker showed that the constraint is:
$\sum w_j = k_1/|k_2|$.[5]

3.4   SUMMARY OF THE EFFECTS OF k_1 AND k_2

We can now anticipate the explanation for the emergence of centre–surround cells:
For $k_1 = 0$, $k_2 = 0$, the dynamics are dominated by 1s. The centre–surround

---

[5] To second order, this expression becomes $\sum w_j = k_1/|k_2 + \bar{q}|$, where $\bar{q} = \langle Q_{ij} \rangle$, the average
covariance (averaged over i and j). The additional term largely resolves the discrepancy between
Linsker's g and $k_1/|k_2|$ in [Linsker, 1986].

eigenfunction 2s is third in line behind 2p, the bi–lobed function. Making k_2 large and negative removes 1s from the lead. 2p becomes the principal eigenfunction and dominates the dynamics for $k_1 \simeq 0$, so that the circular symmetry is broken. Finally, increasing $k_1/|k_2|$ gives a head start to the centre–surround function 2s. Increasing $k_1/|k_2|$ also increases the final average synaptic strength, so large $k_1/|k_2|$ also produces a large DC bias. The centre–surround regime therefore lies sandwiched between a 2p–dominated regime and an all–excitatory regime. $k_1/|k_2|$ has to be large enough that 2s dominates over 2p, and small enough that the DC bias does not obscure the centre–surround structure. We estimate this parameter regime in [MacKay, Miller, 1990], and show that the boundary between the 2s– and 2p–dominated regimes found by simulated annealing on the energy function may be different from the boundary found by simulating the time–development of equation (1), which depends on the initial conditions.

4   CONCLUSIONS AND DISCUSSION

For Linsker's $\mathcal{B} \rightarrow \mathcal{C}$ connections, we predict four main parameter regimes for varying k_1 and k_2.[6] These regimes, shown in figure 3, are dominated by the following weight structures:

$k_2 = 0$, $k_1 = 0$:	The principal eigenvector of $\mathbf{Q}$, 1s.
$k_2 =$ large positive and/or $k_1 =$ large	The flat DC weight vector, which leads to the same saturated structures as 1s.
$k_2 =$ large negative, $k_1 \simeq 0$	The principal eigenvector of $\mathbf{Q} + k_2\mathbf{J}$ for $k_2 \rightarrow -\infty$, 2p.
$k_2 =$ large negative, $k_1 =$ intermediate	The principal circularly symmetric function which is given a head start, 2s.

Higher layers of Linsker's network can be analysed in terms of the same four regimes; the principal eigenvectors are altered, so that different structures can emerge. The development of the interesting cells in Linsker's system depends on the use of negative synapses and on the use of the terms k_1 and k_2 to enforce a constraint on the final percentages of positive and negative synapses. Both of these may be biologically problematic [Miller, 1990]. Linsker suggested that the emergence of centre–surround structures may depend on the peaked synaptic density function that he used [Linsker, 1986, page 7512]. However, with a flat density function, the eigenfunctions are qualitatively unchanged, and centre–surround structures can emerge by the same mechanism.

Acknowledgements

D.J.C.M. is supported by a Caltech Fellowship and a Studentship from SERC, UK.

K.D.M. thanks M. P. Stryker for encouragement and financial support while this work was undertaken. K.D.M. was supported by an N.E.I. Fellowship and the In-

---

[6]not counting the symmetric regimes $(k_1, k_2) \leftrightarrow (-k_1, k_2)$ in which all the weight structures are inverted in sign.

Figure 3: Parameter regimes for Linsker's system. The DC bias is approximately constant along the radial lines, so each of the regimes with large negative k_2 is wedge-shaped.

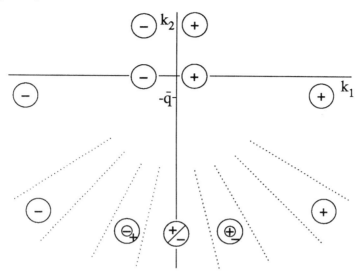

ternational Joint Research Project Bioscience Grant to M. P. Stryker (T. Tsumoto, Coordinator) from the N.E.D.O., Japan.

This collaboration would have been impossible without the internet/NSFnet, long may their daemons flourish.

References

[Linsker, 1986] R. Linsker. From Basic Network Principles to Neural Architecture (series), *PNAS USA*, **83**, Oct.-Nov. 1986, pp. 7508-7512, 8390-8394, 8779-8783.

[Linsker, 1988] R. Linsker. Self-Organization in a Perceptual Network, *Computer*, March 1988.

[Miller, 1990] K.D. Miller. "Correlation-based mechanisms of neural development," in *Neuroscience and Connectionist Theory*, M.A. Gluck and D.E. Rumelhart, Eds. (Lawrence Erlbaum Associates, Hillsboro NJ) (in press).

[MacKay, Miller, 1990] D.J.C. MacKay and K.D. Miller. "Analysis of Linsker's Simulations of Hebbian rules" (submitted to *Neural Computation*); and "Analysis of Linsker's application of Hebbian rules to linear networks" (submitted to *Network*).

Analog Neural Networks of Limited Precision I: Computing with Multilinear Threshold Functions (Preliminary Version)

Zoran Obradovic and Ian Parberry
Department of Computer Science,
Penn State University,
University Park, Pa. 16802.

ABSTRACT

Experimental evidence has shown analog neural networks to be extremely fault-tolerant; in particular, their performance does not appear to be significantly impaired when precision is limited. Analog neurons with limited precision essentially compute k-ary weighted multilinear threshold functions, which divide R^n into k regions with $k-1$ hyperplanes. The behaviour of *k-ary neural networks* is investigated. There is no canonical set of threshold values for $k>3$, although they exist for binary and ternary neural networks. The weights can be made integers of only $O((z+k)\log(z+k))$ bits, where z is the number of processors, without increasing hardware or running time. The weights can be made ± 1 while increasing running time by a constant multiple and hardware by a small polynomial in z and k. Binary neurons can be used if the running time is allowed to increase by a larger constant multiple and the hardware is allowed to increase by a slightly larger polynomial in z and k. Any symmetric k-ary function can be computed in constant depth and size $O(n^{k-1}/(k-2)!)$, and any k-ary function can be computed in constant depth and size $O(nk^n)$. The *alternating neural networks* of Olafsson and Abu-Mostafa, and the *quantized neural networks* of Fleisher are closely related to this model.

1 INTRODUCTION

Neural networks are typically circuits constructed from processing units which compute simple functions of the form $f(w_1,...,w_n):\mathbf{R}^n \to S$ where $S \subseteq \mathbf{R}$, $w_i \in \mathbf{R}$ for $1 \le i \le n$, and

$$f(w_1,...,w_n)(x_1, \ldots, x_n) = g\left(\sum_{i=1}^{n} w_i x_i\right)$$

for some *output function* $g:\mathbf{R} \to S$. There are two choices for the set S which are currently popular in the literature. The first is the *discrete model*, with $S = \mathbf{B}$ (where $\mathbf{B}$ denotes the Boolean set $\{0,1\}$). In this case, g is typically a *linear threshold function* $g(x) = 1$ iff $x \ge 0$, and f is called a *weighted linear threshold function*. The second is the *analog model*, with $S = [0,1]$ (where $[0,1]$ denotes $\{r \in \mathbf{R} | 0 \le r \le 1\}$). In this case, g is typically a monotone increasing function, such as the *sigmoid function* $g(x) = (1 + c^{-x})^{-1}$ for some constant $c \in \mathbf{R}$. The analog neural network model is popular because it is easy to construct processors with the required characteristics using a few transistors. The digital model is popular because its behaviour is easy to analyze.

Experimental evidence indicates that analog neural networks can produce accurate computations when the precision of their components is limited. Consider what actually happens to the analog model when the precision is limited. Suppose the neurons can take on k distinct excitation values (for example, by restricting the number of digits in their binary or decimal expansions). Then S is isomorphic to $\mathbf{Z}_k = \{0,...,k-1\}$. We will show that g is essentially the *multilinear threshold function* $g(h_1, h_2,...,h_{k-1}):\mathbf{R} \to \mathbf{Z}_k$ defined by

$$g(x) = i \ \ iff \ \ h_i \le x < h_{i+1}.$$

Here and throughout this paper, we will assume that $h_1 \le h_2 \le ... \le h_{k-1}$, and for convenience define $h_0 = -\infty$ and $h_k = \infty$. We will call f a *k-ary weighted multilinear threshold function* when g is a multilinear threshold function.

We will study neural networks constructed from k-ary multilinear threshold functions. We will call these *k-ary neural networks*, in order to distinguish them from the standard 2-ary or *binary neural network*. We are particularly concerned with the resources of *time*, *size* (number of processors), and *weight* (sum of all the weights) of k-ary neural networks when used in accordance with the classical computational paradigm. The reader is referred to (Parberry, 1990) for similar results on binary neural networks. A companion paper (Obradovic & Parberry, 1989b) deals with learning on k-ary neural networks. A more detailed version of this paper appears in (Obradovic & Parberry, 1989a).

2 A K-ARY NEURAL NETWORK MODEL

A *k-ary neural network* is a weighted graph $M = (V, E, w, h)$, where V is a set of processors and $E \subseteq V \times V$ is a set of connections between processors. Function $w:V \times V \to \mathbf{R}$ assign weights to interconnections and $h:V \to \mathbf{R}^{k-1}$ assign a set of $k-1$ thresholds to each of the processors. We assume that if $(u,v) \notin E$, $w(u,v) = 0$. The *size* of M is defined to be the number of processors, and the *weight* of M is

$$\sum_{u,v \in V} |w(u,v)|.$$

The processors of a k-ary neural network are relatively limited in computing power. A *k-ary function* is a function $f:\mathbf{Z}_k^n \to \mathbf{Z}_k$. Let F_k^n denote the set of all n-input k-ary functions. Define $\Theta_k^n:\mathbf{R}^{n+k-1} \to F_k^n$ by $\Theta_k^n(w_1,...,w_n,h_1,...,h_{k-1}):\mathbf{R}_k^n \to \mathbf{Z}_k$, where

$$\Theta_k^n(w_1,...,w_n,h_1,...,h_{k-1})(x_1,...x_n) = i \ \ iff \ h_i \le \sum_{i=1}^n w_i x_i < h_{i+1}.$$

The set of *k-ary weighted multilinear threshold functions* is the union, over all $n \in \mathbf{N}$, of the range of Θ_k^n. Each processor of a k-ary neural network can compute a k-ary weighted multilinear threshold function of its inputs.

Each processor can be in one of k states, 0 through $k-1$. Initially, the input processors of M are placed into states which encode the input. If processor v was updated during interval t, its state at time $t-1$ was i and output was j, then at time t its state will be j. A k-ary neural network *computes* by having the processors change state until a stable configuration is reached. The *output* of M are the states of the output processors after a stable state has been reached. A neural network M_2 is said to be $f(t)$-*equivalent* to M_1 iff for all inputs x, for every computation of M_1 on input x which terminates in time t there is a computation of M_2 on input x which terminates in time $f(t)$ with the same output. A neural network M_2 is said to be *equivalent* to M_1 iff it is t-equivalent to it.

3 ANALOG NEURAL NETWORKS

Let f be a function with range [0,1]. Any limited-precision device which purports to compute f must actually compute some function with range the k rational values $\mathbf{R}_k = \{i/k-1 | i \in \mathbf{Z}_k, 0 \le i < k\}$ (for some $k \in \mathbf{N}$). This is sufficient for all practical purposes provided k is large enough. Since $\mathbf{R}_k$ is isomorphic to $\mathbf{Z}_k$, we will formally define the limited precision variant of f to be the function $f_k:X \to \mathbf{Z}_k$ defined by $f_k(x) = round(f(x).(k-1))$, where $round:\mathbf{R} \to \mathbf{N}$ is the natural rounding function defined by $round(x) = n$ iff $n-0.5 \le x < n+0.5$.

Theorem 3.1 : Let $f(w_1,...,w_n):\mathbf{R}^n \to [0,1]$ where $w_i \in \mathbf{R}$ for $1 \le i \le n$, be defined by

$$f(w_1,...,w_n)(x_1, \ldots ,x_n) = g(\sum_{i=1}^n w_i x_i)$$

where $g:\mathbf{R} \to [0,1]$ is monotone increasing and invertible. Then $f(w_1,...,w_n)_k:\mathbf{R}^n \to \mathbf{Z}_k$ is a k-ary weighted multilinear threshold function.

Proof: It is easy to verify that $f(w_1,...,w_n)_k = \Theta_k^n(w_1,...,w_n,h_1,...,h_{k-1})$, where $h_i = g^{-1}((2i-1)/2(k-1))$. $\square$

Thus we see that analog neural networks with limited precision are essentially k-ary neural networks.

4 CANONICAL THRESHOLDS

Binary neural networks have the advantage that all thresholds can be taken equal to zero (see, for example, Theorem 4.3.1 of Parberry, 1990). A similar result holds for ternary neural networks.

Theorem 4.1 : For every n-input ternary weighted multilinear threshold function there is an equivalent $(n+1)$-input ternary weighted multilinear threshold function with threshold values equal to zero and one.

Proof: Suppose $w=(w_1,...,w_n)\in \mathbf{R}^n$, $h_1,h_2\in \mathbf{R}$. Without loss of generality assume $h_1<h_2$. Define $\hat{w}=(\hat{w}_1,...,\hat{w}_{n+1})\in \mathbf{R}^{n+1}$ by $\hat{w}_i=w_i/(h_2-h_1)$ for $1\le i\le n$, and $\hat{w}_{n+1}=-h_1/(h_2-h_1)$. It can be demonstrated by a simple case analysis that for all $x=(x_1,...,x_n)\in \mathbf{Z}_k^n$,

$$\Theta_3^n(w,h_1,h_2)(x)=\Theta_3^{n+1}(\hat{w},0,1)(x_1,...,x_n,1).$$

□

The choice of threshold values in Theorem 4.1 was arbitrary. Unfortunately there is no canonical set of thresholds for $k>3$.

Theorem 4.2 : For every $k>3$, $n\ge 2$, $m\ge 0$, $h_1,...,h_{k-1}\in \mathbf{R}$, there exists an n-input k-ary weighted multilinear threshold function

$$\Theta_k^n(w_1,...,w_n,t_1,...,t_{k-1}):\mathbf{Z}_k^n\rightarrow \mathbf{Z}_k,$$

such that for all $(n+m)$-input k-ary weighted multilinear threshold functions

$$\Theta_k^{n+m}(\hat{w}_1,\ .\ .\ .\ ,\hat{w}_{n+m},h_1,...,h_{k-1}):\mathbf{Z}_k^{m+n}\rightarrow \mathbf{Z}_k$$

and $y_1,...,y_m\in \mathbf{R}$, there exists $x=(x_1,...,x_n)\in \mathbf{Z}_k^n$ such that

$$\Theta_k^n(w_1,...,w_n,t_1,...,t_{k-1})(x)\ne\Theta_k^{n+m}(\hat{w}_1,\ .\ .\ .\ ,\hat{w}_{n+m},h_1,...,h_{k-1})(x_1,...,x_n,y_1,...,y_m).$$

Proof (Sketch): Suppose that $t_1,...,t_{k-1}\in \mathbf{R}$ is a canonical set of thresholds, and w.l.o.g. assume $n=2$. Let $h=(h_1,...,h_{k-1})$, where $h_1=h_2=2$, $h_3=4$, $h_i=5$ for $4\le i<k$, and $f=\Theta_k^2(1,1,h)$.

By hypothesis there exist $w_1,...,w_{m+2}$ and $y=(y_1,...,y_m)\in \mathbf{R}^m$ such that for all $x\in \mathbf{Z}_k^2$,

$$f(x)=\Theta_k^{m+2}(w_1,...,w_{m+2},t_1,...,t_{k-1})(x,y).$$

Let $S=\sum_{i=1}^m w_{i+2}y_i$. Since $f(1,0)=0$, $f(0,1)=0$, $f(2,1)=2$, $f(1,2)=2$, it follows that

$$2(w_1+w_2+S)<t_1+t_3. \tag{1}$$

Since $f(2,0)=2$, $f(1,1)=2$, and $f(0,2)=2$, it follows that

$$w_1 + w_2 + S \geq t_2. \tag{2}$$

Inequalities (1) and (2) imply that

$$2t_2 < t_1 + t_3. \tag{3}$$

By similar arguments from $g = \Theta_k^2(1,1,1,3,3,4,...,4)$ we can conclude that

$$2t_2 > t_1 + t_3. \tag{4}$$

But (4) contradicts (3). $\square$

5   NETWORKS OF BOUNDED WEIGHT

Although our model allows each weight to take on an infinite number of possible values, there are only a finite number of threshold functions (since there are only a finite number of k-ary functions) with a fixed number of inputs. Thus the number of n-input threshold functions is bounded above by some function in n and k. In fact, something stronger can be shown. All weights can be made integral, and $O((n+k)\log(n+k))$ bits are sufficient to describe each one.

Theorem 5.1 : For every k-ary neural network M_1 of size z there exists an equivalent k-ary neural network M_2 of size z and weight $((k-1)/2)^z (z+1)^{(z+k)/2+ O(1)}$ with integer weights.

Proof (Sketch): It is sufficient to prove that for every weighted threshold function $f_k^n(w_1,...,w_n,h_1,...,h_{k-1}):\mathbf{Z}_k^n \to \mathbf{Z}_k$ for some $n \in \mathbf{N}$, there is an equivalent weighted threshold function $g_k^n(w_1^*,...,w_n^*,h_1^*,...,h_{k-1}^*)$ such that $|w_i^*| \leq ((k-1)/2)^n (n+1)^{(n+k)/2+ O(1)}$ for $1 \leq i \leq n$. By extending the techniques used by Muroga, Toda and Takasu (1961) in the binary case, we see that the weights are bounded above by the maximum determinant of a matrix of dimension $n+k-1$ over $\mathbf{Z}_k$. $\square$

Thus if k is bounded above by a polynomial in n, we are guaranteed of being able to describe the weights using a polynomial number of bits.

6   THRESHOLD CIRCUITS

A k-ary neural network with weights drawn from $\{\pm 1\}$ is said to have *unit weights*. A unit-weight directed acyclic k-ary neural network is called a *k-ary threshold circuit*. A k-ary threshold circuit can be divided into layers, with each layer receiving inputs only from the layers above it. The *depth* of a k-ary threshold circuit is defined to be the number of layers. The weight is equal to the number of edges, which is bounded above by the square of the size. Despite the apparent handicap of limited weights, k-ary threshold circuits are surprisingly powerful.

Much interest has focussed on the computation of symmetric functions by neural networks, motivated by the fact that the visual system appears to be able to recognize objects regardless of their position on the retina. A function $f: \mathbf{Z}_k^n \to \mathbf{Z}_k$ is called *symmetric* if its output remains the same no matter how the input is permuted.

Theorem 6.1 : Any symmetric k-ary function on n inputs can be computed by a k-ary threshold circuit of depth 6 and size $(n+1)^{k-1}/(k-2)!+ O(kn)$.

Proof: Omitted. ☐

It has been noted many times that neural networks can compute any Boolean function in constant depth. The same is true of k-ary neural networks, although both results appear to require exponential size for many interesting functions.

Theorem 6.2 : Any k-ary function of n inputs can be computed by a k-ary threshold circuit with size $(2n+1)k^n+k+1$ and depth 4.

Proof: Similar to that for $k=2$ (see Chandra et. al., 1984; Parberry, 1990). ☐

The interesting problem remaining is to determine which functions require exponential size to achieve constant depth, and which can be computed in polynomial size and constant depth. We will now consider the problem of adding integers represented in k-ary notation.

Theorem 6.3 : The sum of two k-ary integers of size n can be computed by a k-ary threshold circuit with size $O(n^2)$ and depth 5.

Proof: First compute the carry of x and y in quadratic size and depth 3 using the standard elementary school algorithm. Then the ith position of the result can be computed from the ith position of the operands and a carry propagated in that position in constant size and depth 2. ☐

Theorem 6.4 : The sum of n k-ary integers of size n can be computed by a k-ary threshold circuit with size $O(n^3+kn^2)$ and constant depth.

Proof: Similar to the proof for $k=2$ using Theorem 6.3 (see Chandra et. al., 1984; Parberry, 1990). ☐

Theorem 6.5 : For every k-ary neural network M_1 of size z there exists an $O(t)$-equivalent unit-weight k-ary neural network M_2 of size $O((z+k)^4\log^3(z+k))$.

Proof: By Theorem 5.1 we can bound all weights to have size $O((z+k)\log(z+k))$ in binary notation. By Theorem 6.4 we can replace every processor with non-unit weights by a threshold circuit of size $O((z+k)^3\log^3(z+k))$ and constant depth. ☐

Theorem 6.5 implies that we can assume unit weights by increasing the size by a polynomial and the running time by only a constant multiple provided the number of logic levels is bounded above by a polynomial in the size of the network. The number of thresholds can also be reduced to one if the size is increased by a larger polynomial:

Theorem 6.6 : For every k-ary neural network M_1 of size z there exists an $O(t)$-equivalent unit-weight binary neural network M_2 of size $O(z^4k^4)(\log z + \log k)^3$ which outputs the binary encoding of the required result.

Proof: Similar to the proof of Theorem 6.5. ☐

This result is primarily of theoretical interest. Binary neural networks appear simpler, and hence more desirable than analog neural networks. However, analog neural networks are actually more desirable since they are easier to build. With this in mind, Theorem 6.6 simply serves as a limit to the functions that an analog neural network can be expected to compute efficiently. We are more concerned with constructing a model of the computational abilities of neural networks, rather than a model of their implementation details.

7 NONMONOTONE MULTILINEAR NEURAL NETWORKS

Olafsson and Abu-Mostafa (1988) study information capacity of functions $f(w_1,...,w_n):\mathbf{R}^n \to \mathbf{B}$ for $w_i \in \mathbf{R}$, $1 \le i \le n$, where

$$f(w_1,...,w_n)(x_1, \ldots, x_n) = g(\sum_{i=1}^{n} w_i x_i)$$

and g is the *alternating threshold function* $g(h_1,h_2,...,h_{k-1}):\mathbf{R}\to\mathbf{B}$ for some monotone increasing $h_i \in \mathbf{R}$, $1 \le i < k$, defined by $g(x)=0$ if $h_{2i} \le x < h_{2i+1}$ for some $0 \le i \le n/2$. We will call f an *alternating weighted multilinear threshold function*, and a neural network constructed from functions of this form *alternating multilinear neural networks*. Alternating multilinear neural networks are closely related to k-ary neural networks:

Theorem 7.1 : For every k-ary neural network of size z and weight w there is an equivalent alternating multilinear neural network of size $z \log k$ and weight $(k-1)w \log (k-1)$ which produces the output of the former in binary notation.

Proof (Sketch): Each k-ary gate is replaced by $\log k$ gates which together essentially perform a "binary search" to determine each bit of the k-ary gate. Weights which increase exponentially are used to provide the correct output value. □

Theorem 7.2 : For every alternating multilinear neural network of size z and weight w there is a 3t-equivalent k-ary neural network of size $4z$ and weight $w+4z$.

Proof (Sketch): Without loss of generality, assume k is odd. Each alternating gate is replaced by a k-ary gate with identical weights and thresholds. The output of this gate goes with weight one to a k-ary gate with thresholds $1,3,5,...,k-1$ and with weight minus one to a k-ary gate with thresholds $-(k-1),...,-3,-1$. The output of these gates goes to a binary gate with threshold k. □

Both k-ary and alternating multilinear neural networks are a special case of *nonmonotone multilinear neural networks*, where $g:\mathbf{R}\to\mathbf{R}$ is the defined by $g(x)=c_i$ iff $h_i \le x < h_{i+1}$, for some monotone increasing $h_i \in \mathbf{R}$, $1 \le i < k$, and $c_0,...,c_{k-1} \in \mathbf{Z}_k$. Nonmonotone neural networks correspond to analog neural networks whose output function is not necessarily monotone nondecreasing. Many of the result of this paper, including Theorems 5.1, 6.5, and 6.6, also apply to nonmonotone neural networks. The size, weight and running time of many of the upper-bounds can also be improved by a small amount by using nonmonotone neural networks instead of k-ary ones. The details are left to the interested reader.

8 MULTILINEAR HOPFIELD NETWORKS

A multilinear version of the Hopfield network called the *quantized neural network* has been studied by Fleisher (1987). Using the terminology of (Parberry, 1990), a quantized neural network is a simple symmetric k-ary neural network (that is, its interconnection pattern is an undirected graph without self-loops) with the additional property that all processors have an identical set of thresholds. Although the latter assumption is reasonable for binary neural networks (see, for example, Theorem 4.3.1 of Parberry, 1990), and ternary neural networks (Theorem 4.1), it is not necessarily so for k-ary neural networks with $k > 3$ (Theorem 4.2). However, it is easy to extend Fleisher's main result to give the following:

Theorem 8.1 : Any productive sequential computation of a simple symmetric k-ary neural network will converge.

9 CONCLUSION

It has been shown that analog neural networks with limited precision are essentially k-ary neural networks. If k is limited to a polynomial, then polynomial size, constant depth k-ary neural networks are equivalent to polynomial size, constant depth binary neural networks. Nonetheless, the savings in time (at most a constant multiple) and hardware (at most a polynomial) arising from using k-ary neural networks rather than binary ones can be quite significant. We do not suggest that one should actually construct binary or k-ary neural networks. Analog neural networks can be constructed by exploiting the analog behaviour of transistors, rather than using extra hardware to inhibit it. Rather, we suggest that k-ary neural networks are a tool for reasoning about the behaviour of analog neural networks.

Acknowledgements

The financial support of the Air Force Office of Scientific Research, Air Force Systems Command, USAF, under grant numbers AFOSR 87-0400 and AFOSR 89-0168 and NSF grant CCR-8801659 to Ian Parberry is gratefully acknowledged.

References

Chandra A. K., Stockmeyer L. J. and Vishkin U., (1984) "Constant depth reducibility," *SIAM J. Comput.,* vol. 13, no. 2, pp. 423-439.

Fleisher M., (1987) "The Hopfield model with multi-level neurons," *Proc. IEEE Conference on Neural Information Processing Systems,* pp. 278-289, Denver, CO.

Muroga S., Toda I. and Takasu S., (1961) "Theory of majority decision elements," *J. Franklin Inst.,* vol. 271., pp. 376-418.

Obradovic Z. and Parberry I., (1989a) "Analog neural networks of limited precision I: Computing with multilinear threshold functions (preliminary version)," Technical Report CS-89-14, Dept. of Computer Science, Penn. State Univ.

Obradovic Z. and Parberry I., (1989b) "Analog neural networks of limited precision II: Learning with multilinear threshold functions (preliminary version)," Technical Report CS-89-15, Dept. of Computer Science, Penn. State Univ.

Olafsson S. and Abu-Mostafa Y. S., (1988) "The capacity of multilevel threshold functions," *IEEE Trans. Pattern Analysis and Machine Intelligence,* vol. 10, no. 2, pp. 277-281.

Parberry I., (To Appear in 1990) "A Primer on the Complexity Theory of Neural Networks," in *A Sourcebook of Formal Methods in Artificial Intelligence,* ed. R. Banerji, North-Holland.

Time Dependent Adaptive Neural Networks

Fernando J. Pineda

Center for Microelectronics Technology
Jet Propulsion Laboratory
California Institute of Technology
Pasadena, CA 91109

ABSTRACT

A comparison of algorithms that minimize error functions to train the trajectories of recurrent networks, reveals how complexity is traded off for causality. These algorithms are also related to time-independent formalisms. It is suggested that causal and scalable algorithms are possible when the activation dynamics of adaptive neurons is fast compared to the behavior to be learned. Standard continuous-time recurrent backpropagation is used in an example.

1 INTRODUCTION

Training the time dependent behavior of a neural network model involves the minimization of a function that measures the difference between an actual trajectory and a desired trajectory. The standard method of accomplishing this minimization is to calculate the gradient of an error function with respect to the weights of the system and then to use the gradient in a minimization algorithm (e.g. gradient descent or conjugate gradient).

Techniques for evaluating gradients and performing minimizations are well developed in the field of optimal control and system identification, but are only now being introduced to the neural network community. Not all algorithms that are useful or efficient in control problems are realizable as physical neural networks. In particular, physical neural network algorithms must satisfy locality, scaling and causality constraints. Locality simply is the constraint that one should be able to update each connection using only presynaptic and postsynaptic information. There should be no need to use information from neurons or connections that are not in physical contact with a given connection. Scaling, for this paper, refers to the scaling law that governs the amount of computation or hardware that is required to perform the weight updates. For neural networks, where the number of weights can become very large, the amount of hardware or computation required to calculate the gradient must scale linearly with the number of weights. Otherwise, large networks are not possible. Finally, learning algorithms must be causal since physical neural networks must evolve forwards in time. Many algorithms for learning time-dependent behavior, although they are seductively elegant and computationally efficient, cannot be implemented as physical systems because the gradient evaluation requires time evolution in two directions. In this paper networks that violate the causality constraint will be referred to as unphysical.

It is useful to understand how scalability and causality trade off in various gradient evaluation algorithms. In the next section three related gradient evaluation algorithms are derived and their scaling and causality properties are compared. The three algorithms demonstrate a natural progression from a causal algorithm that scales poorly to an a causal algorithm that scales linearly.

The difficulties that these exact algorithms exhibit appear to be inescapable. This suggests that approximation schemes that do not calculate exact gradients or that exploit special properties of the tasks to-be-learned may lead to physically realizable neural networks. The final section of this paper suggests an approach that could be exploited in systems where the time scale of the to-be-learned task is much slower than the relaxation time scale of the adaptive neurons.

2 ANALYSIS OF ALGORITHMS

We will begin by reviewing the learning algorithms that apply to time-dependent recurrent networks. The control literature generally derives these algorithms by taking a variational approach (e.g. Bryson and Ho, 1975). Here we will take a somewhat unconventional approach and restrict ourselves to the domain of differential equations and their solutions. To begin with, let us take a concrete example. Consider the neural system given by the equation

$$\frac{dx_i}{dt} = x_i + \sum_{i=1}^{n} w_{ij} f(x_j) + I_i \tag{1}$$

Where f(.) is a sigmoid shaped function (e.g. tanh(.)) and I_i is an external input This system is a well studied neural model (e.g. Aplevich, 1968; Cowan, 1967; Hopfield, 1984; Malsburg, 1973; Sejnowski, 1977). The goal is to find the weight matrix $\mathbf{w}$ that causes the states $\mathbf{x}(t)$ of the output units to follow a specified trajectory x(t). The actually trajectory depends not only on the weight matrix but also on the external input vector $\mathbf{I}$. To find the weights one minimizes a measure of the difference between the actual trajectory $\mathbf{x}(t)$ and the desired trajectory $\xi(t)$. This measure is a functional of the trajectories and a function of the weights. It is given by

$$E(\mathbf{w}, t_f, t_o) = \frac{1}{2} \sum_{i \in O} \int_{t_o}^{t_f} dt \left(x_i(t) - \xi_i(t) \right)^2 \tag{2}$$

where O is the set of output units. We shall, only for the purpose of algorithm comparison, make the following assumptions: (1) That the networks are fully connected (2) That all the interval $[t_o,t_f]$ is divided into q segments with numerical integrations performed using the Euler method and (3) That all the operations are performed with the same precision. This will allow us to easily estimate the amount of computation and memory required for each algorithm relative to the others.

2.1 ALGORITHM A

If the objective function E is differentiated with respect to w_{rs} one obtains

$$\frac{\partial E}{\partial w_{rs}} = - \sum_{i=1}^{n} \int_{t_o}^{t_f} dt \, J_i(t) \, p_{irs}(t) \tag{3a}$$

where

$$J_i = \begin{cases} \xi_i(t) - x_i(t) & if \ i \in O \\ 0 & if \ i \notin O \end{cases} \tag{3b}$$

and where

$$p_{irs} = \frac{\partial x_i}{\partial w_{rs}} \tag{3c}$$

To evaluate p_{irs}, differentiate equation (1) with respect to w_{rs} and observe that the time derivative and the partial derivative with respect to w_{rs} commute. The resulting equation is

$$\frac{dp_{irs}}{dt} = \sum_{j=1}^{n} L_{ij}(x_j) \, p_{jrs} + s_{ir} \tag{4a}$$

where

$$L_{ij}(x_j) = -\delta_{ij} + w_{ij} f'(x_j) \tag{4b}$$

and where

$$s_{irs} = \delta_{ir} f(x_s) \tag{4c}$$

The initial condition for eqn. (4a) is $p(t_o) = 0$. Equations (1), (3) and (4) can be used to calculate the gradient for a learning rule. This is the approach taken by Williams and Zipser (1989) and also discussed by Pearlmutter(1988). Williams and Zipser further observe that one can use the instantaneous value of $p(t)$ and $J(t)$ to update the weights continually provided the weights change slowly. The computationally intensive part of this algorithm occurs in the integration of equation (4a). There are n^3 components to p hence there are n^3 equations. Accordingly the amount of hardware or memory required to perform the calculation will scale like n^3. Each of these equations requires a summation over all the neurons, hence the amount of computation (measured in multiply-accumulates) goes like n^4 per time step, and there are q time steps, hence the total number of multiply-accumulates scales like n^4q Clearly, the scaling properties of this approach are very poor and it cannot be practically applied to very large networks.

2.2 ALGORITHM B

Rather than numerically integrate the system of equations (4a) to obtain $p(t)$, suppose we write down the formal solution. This solution is

$$p_{irs}(t) = \sum_{j=1}^{n} K_{ij}(t,t_o)\, p_{jrs}(t_o) + \sum_{j=1}^{n} \int_{t_o}^{t} dt K_{ij}(t,\tau)\, s_{jrs}(\tau) \tag{5a}$$

The matrix K is defined by the expression

$$K(t_2 t_1) = exp\left(\int_{t_1}^{t_2} d\tau\, L(x(\tau))\right) \tag{5b}$$

This matrix is known as the propagator or transition matrix. The expression for p_{irs} consists of a homogeneous solution and a particular solution. The choice of initial condition $p_{irs}(t_o)$ = 0 leaves only the particular solution. If the particular solution is substituted back into eqn. (3a), one eventually obtains the following expression for the gradient

$$\frac{\partial E}{\partial w_{rs}} = -\sum_{i=1}^{n} \int_{t_o}^{t_f} dt \int_{t_o}^{t} d\tau\, J_i(t) K_{ir}(t,\tau) f(x_s(\tau)) \tag{6}$$

To obtain this expression one must observe that s_{jrs} can be expressed in terms of x_s, i.e. use eqn. (4c). This allows the summation over j to be performed trivially, thus resulting in eqn.(6). The familiar outer product form of backpropagation is not yet manifest in this expression. To uncover it, change the order of the integrations. This requires some care because the limits of the integration are not the same. The result is

$$\frac{\partial E}{\partial w_{rs}} = -\sum_{i=1}^{n} \int_{t_o}^{t_f} d\tau \int_{\tau}^{t_f} dt\, J_i(t) K_{ir}(t,\tau) f(x_s(\tau)) \tag{7}$$

Inspection of this expression reveals that neither the summation over i nor the integration over τ includes $x_s(t)$, thus it is useful to factor it out. Consequently equation (7) takes on the familiar outer product form of backpropagation

$$\frac{\partial E}{\partial w_{rs}} = -\int_{\tau}^{t_f} dt\, y_r(t) f(x_s(t)) \tag{8}$$

Where $y_r(t)$ is defined to be

$$y_r(\tau) = -\sum_{i=1}^{n} \int_{\tau}^{t_f} dt\, J_i(t) K_{ir}(t,\tau) \tag{9}$$

Equation (8), defines an expression for the gradient, provided we can calculate $y_r(t)$ from eqn. (9). In principle, this can be done since the propagator K and the vector J are both completely determined by $x(t)$. The computationally intensive part of this algorithm is the calculation of $K(t,\tau)$ for all values of t and τ. The calculation requires the integration of equations of the form

$$\frac{dK(t,\tau)}{dt} = L(x(t)) K(t,\tau) \tag{10}$$

for q different values of τ. There are n^2 different equations to integrate for each value of τ Consequently there are $n^2 q$ integrations to be performed where the interval from t_o to t_f is divided into q intervals. The calculation of all the components of $K(t,\tau)$, from t_f to t_o, scales like $n^3 q^2$, since each integration requires n multiply-accumulates per time step and there are q time steps. Similarly, the memory requirements scale like $n^2 q^2$. This is because K has n^2 components for each (t,τ) pair and there are q^2 such pairs.

Equation (10) must be integrated forwards in time from $t = \tau$ to $t = t_f$ *and backwards in time* from $t = \tau$ to $t = t_o$. This is because $\mathbf{K}$ must satisfy $\mathbf{K}(\tau, \tau) = 1$ (the identity matrix) for all τ. This condition follows from the definition of $\mathbf{K}$ eqn. (5b). Finally, we observe that expression (9) is the time-dependent analog of the expression used by Rohwer and Forrest (1987) to calculate the gradient in recurrent networks. The analogy can be made somewhat more explicit by writing $\mathbf{K}(t, \tau)$ as the inverse $\mathbf{K}^{-1}(\tau, t)$. Thus we see that $y(t)$ can be expressed in terms of a matrix inverse just as in the Rohwer and Forrest algorithm.

2.3   ALGORITHM C

The final algorithm is familiar from continuous time optimal control and identification. The algorithm is usually derived by performing a variation on the functional given by eqn. (2). This results in a two-point boundary value problem. On the other hand, we know that y is given by eqn. (9). So we simply observe that this is the particular solution of the differential equation

$$-\frac{dy}{dt} = L^{T}(x(t))y + J \tag{11}$$

Where L^T is the transpose of the matrix defined in eqn. (4b). To see this simply substitute the form for y into eqn. (11) and verify that it is indeed the solution to the equation.

The particular solution to eqn. (11) vanishes only if $y(t_f) = 0$. In other words: to obtain $y(t)$ we need only integrate eqn. (11) *backwards* from the final condition $y(t_f) = 0$. This is just the algorithm introduced to the neural network community by Pearlmutter (1988). This also corresponds to the unfolding in time approach discussed by Rumelhart et al. (1986), provided that all the equations are discretized and one takes $\Delta t - 1$.

The two point boundary value problem is rather straight forward to solve because the equation for $x(t)$ is independent of $y(t)$. Both $x(t)$ and $y(t)$ can be obtained with n multiply-accumulates per time step. There are q time steps from t_o to t_f and both $x(t)$ and $y(t)$ have n components, hence the calculation of $x(t)$ and $y(t)$ scales like n^2q. The weight update equation also requires n^2q multiply- accumulates. Thus the computational requirements of the algorithm as a whole scale like n^2q The memory required also scales like n^2q, since it is necessary to save each value of $x(t)$ along the trajectory to compute $y(t)$.

2.4   SCALING VS CAUSALITY

The results of the previous sections are summarized in table 1 below. We see that we have a progression of tradeoffs between scaling and causality. That is, we must choose between a causal algorithm with exploding computational and storage requirements and an a causal algorithm with modest storage requirements. There is no q dependence in the memory requirments because the integral given in eqn. (3a) can be accumulated at each time step. Algorithm B has some of the worst features of both algorithms.

Table 1: Comparison of three algorithms

Algorithm	Memory	Multiply -accumulates	diirection of integations
A	n^3	n^4q	$\mathbf{x}$ and $\mathbf{p}$ are both forward in time
B	n^2q^2	n^3q^2	$\mathbf{x}$ is forward, $\mathbf{K}$ is forward *and* backward
C	n^2q	n^2q	$\mathbf{x}$ is forward, $\mathbf{y}$ is backward in time.

Digital hardware has no difficulties (at least over finite time intervals) with a causal algorithms provided a stack is available to act as a memory that can recall states in reverse order. To the extent that the gradient calculations are carried out on digital machines, it makes sense to use algorithm C because it is the most efficient. In analog VLSI however, it is difficult to imagine how to build a continually running network that uses an a causal algorithm. Algorithm A is attractive for physical implementation because it could be run continually and in real time (Williams and Zipser, 1989). However, its scaling properties preclude the possibility of building very large networks based on the algorithm. Recently, Zipser (1990) has suggested that a divide and conquer approach may reduce the computational and spatial complexity of the algorithm. This approach, although promising, does not always work and there is as yet no convergence proof. How then, is it possible to learn trajectories using local, scalable and causal algorithms? In the next section a possible avenue of attack is suggested.

3 EXPLOITING DISPARATE TIME SCALES

I assert that for some classes of problems there are scalable and causal algorithms that approximate the gradient and that these algorithms can be found by exploiting the disparity in time scales found in these classes of problems. In particular, I assert that when the time scale of the adaptive units is fast compared to the time scale of the behavior to be learned, it is possible to find scalable and causal adaptive algorithms. A general formalism for doing this will not be presented here, instead a simple, perhaps artificial, example will be presented. This example minimizes an error function for a time dependent problem.

It is likely that trajectory generation in motor control problems are of this type. The characteristic time scales of the trajectories that need to be generated are determined by inertia and friction. These mechanical time scales are considerably longer than the electronic time scales that occur in VLSI. Thus it seems that for robotic problems, there may be no need to use the completely general algorithms discussed in section 2. Instead, algorithms that take advantage of the disparity between the mechanical and the electronic time scales are likely to be more useful for learning to generate trajectories.

he task is to map from a periodic input $\mathbf{I}(t)$ to a periodic output $\xi(t)$. The basic idea is to use the continuous-time recurrent-backpropagation approach with slowly varying time-dependent inputs rather than with static inputs. The learning is done in real-time and in a continuous fashion. Consider a set of n "fast" neurons (i=1,..,n) each of which satisfies the additive activation dynamics determined by eqn (1). Assume that the initial weights are sufficiently small that the dynamics of the network would be convergent *if the inputs* **I** *were constant.* The external input vector ξ is applied to the network through the vector **I**. It has been previously shown (Pineda, 1988) that the ij-th component of the gradient of E is equal to $y_i^f f(x_j^f)$ where x_j^f is the steady state solution of eqn. (1) and where y_i^f is a component of the steady state solution of

$$\frac{dy}{dt} = L^T(x^f)y + J \tag{12}$$

where the components of L^T are given by eqn. (4.b). Note that the relative sign between equations (11) and (12) is what enables this algorithm to be causal. Now suppose that instead of a fixed input vector **I**, we use a slowly varying input $I(t/\tau_p)$ where τ_a is the characteristic time scale over which the input changes significantly. If we take as the gradient descent algorithm, the dynamics defined by

$$\tau_w \frac{dw_{rs}}{dt} = y_i(t)x_j(t) \tag{13}$$

where τ_w is the time constant that defines the (slow) time scale over which **w** changes and where x_j is the *instantaneous* solution of eqn. (1) and y_i is the *instantaneous* solution of eqn.(12) . Then in the adiabatic limit the Cartesian product $y_i f(x_j)$ in eqn. (13) approximates the negative gradient of the objective function E, that is

$$y_r^f f(x_s^f(t)) \cong y_r(t)f(x_s(t)) \tag{14}$$

This approach can map one continuous trajectory into another continuous trajectory, provided the trajectories change slowly enough. Furthermore, learning occurs causally and scalably. There is no memory in the model, i.e. the output of the adaptive neurons depends only on their input and not on their internal state. Thus, this network can never learn to perform tasks that require memory unless the learning algorithm is modified to learn the appropriate transitions. This is the major drawback of the adiabatic approach. Some state information can be incorporated into this model by using recurrent connections — in which case the network can have multiple basins and the final state will depend on the initial state of the net as well as on the inputs, but this will not be pursued here.

Simple simulations were performed to verify that the approach did indeed perform gradient descent. One simulation is presented here for the benefit of investigators who may wish to verify the results. A feedforward network topology consisting of two input units, five hidden units and two output units was used for the adaptive network. Units were numbered sequentially, 1 through 9, beginning with the input layer and ending in the output layer. Time dependent external inputs for the two input neurons were generated with time dependence $I_1 = \sin(2\pi t)$ and $I_2 = \cos(2\pi t)$. The targets for the output neurons were $\xi_8 = R \sin(2\pi t)$ and $\xi_9 = R \cos(2\pi t)$ where $R = 1.0 + 0.1\sin(6\pi t)$. All the equations were simultaneously integrated using 4th order Runge-Kutta with a time step of 0.1. A relaxation time scale was introduced into the forward and backward propagation equations by multiplying the time derivatives in eqns. (1) and (12) by τ_x and τ_y respectively. These time scales were set to $\tau_x = \tau_y = 0.5$. The adaptive time scale of the weights was $\tau_w = 1.0$. The error in the network was initially, E =

10 and the integration was cut off when the error reached a plateau at $E = 0.12$. The learning curve is shown in Fig. 1. The trained trajectory did not exactly reach the desired solution. In particular the network did not learn the odd order harmonic that modulates R. By way of comparison, a conventional backpropagation approach that calculated a cumulative gradient over the trajectory and used conjugate gradient for the descent, was able to converge to the global minimum.

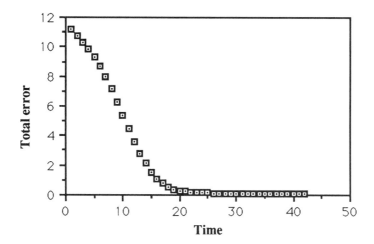

Figure 1: Learning curve. One time unit corresponds to a single oscillation

4 SUMMARY

The key points of this paper are: 1) Exact minimization algorithms for learning time-dependent behavior either scale poorly or else violate causality and 2) Approximate gradient calculations will likely lead to causal and scalable learning algorithms. The adiabatic approach should be useful for learning to generate trajectories of the kind encountered when learning motor skills.

References herein to any specific commercial product, process, or service by trade name, trademark, manufacturer, or otherwise, does not constitute or imply any endorsement by the United States Government or the Jet Propulsion Laboratory, California Institute of Technology. The work described in this paper was carried out at the Center for Space Microelectonrics Technology, Jet Propulsion Laboratory, California Institute of Technology. Support for the work came from the Air Force Office of Scientific Research through an agreement with the National Aeronautics and Space Administration (AFOSR-ISSA-90-0027).

REFERENCES

Aplevich, J. D. (1968). Models of certain nonlinear systems. In E. R. Caianiello (Ed.), *Neural Networks*, (pp. 110-115). Berlin: Springer Verlag.

Bryson, A. E. and Ho, Y. (1975). *Applied Optimal Control: Optimization, Estimation, and*

Control. New York: Hemisphere Publishing Co.

Cowan, J. D. (1967). A mathematical theory of central nervous activity. Unpublished dissertation, Imperial College, University of London.

Hopfield, J. J. (1984). Neurons with graded response have collective computational properties like those of two-state neurons. *Proc. Nat. Acad. Sci. USA, Bio.*, 81, 3088-3092.

Malsburg, C. van der (1973). Self-organization of orientation sensitive cells in striate cortex, *Kybernetic*, 14, 85-100.

Pearlmutter, B. A. (1988), Learning state space trajectories in recurrent neural networks: A preliminary report, *(Tech. Rep. AIP-54)*, Department of Computer Science, Carnegie Mellon University, Pittsburgh, PA

Pineda, F. J. (1988). Dynamics and Architecture for Neural Computation. *Journal of Complexity*, 4, (pp.216-245)

Rowher R, R. and Forrest, B. (1987). Training time dependence in neural networks, In M. Caudil and C. Butler, (Eds.), *Proceedings of the IEEE First Annual International Conference on Neural Networks*, 3, (pp. 701-708). San Diego, California: IEEE.

Rumelhart, D. E., Hinton, G. E., and Willaims, R.J. (1986).   Learning Internal Representations by Error Propagation. In D. E. Rumelhart and J. L. McClelland, (Eds.), *Parallel Distributed Processing*, (pp. 318-362). Cambridge: M.I.T. Press.

Sejnowski, T. J. (1977). Storing covariance with nonlinearly interacting neurons. *Journal of Mathematical Biology*, 4, 303-321.

Williams, R.J. and Zipser, D. (1989). A learning algorithm for continually running fully recurrent neural networks. *Neural Computation*, 1, (pp. 270-280).

Zipser, D. (1990). Subgrouping reduces complexity and speeds up learning in recurrent networks, (this volume).

A Neural Network for Feature Extraction

Nathan Intrator
Div. of Applied Mathematics, and
Center for Neural Science
Brown University
Providence, RI 02912

ABSTRACT

The paper suggests a statistical framework for the parameter estimation problem associated with unsupervised learning in a neural network, leading to an exploratory projection pursuit network that performs feature extraction, or dimensionality reduction.

1 INTRODUCTION

The search for a possible presence of some unspecified structure in a high dimensional space can be difficult due to the *curse of dimensionality* problem, namely the inherent sparsity of high dimensional spaces. Due to this problem, uniformly accurate estimations for all smooth functions are not possible in high dimensions with practical sample sizes (Cox, 1984, Barron, 1988).

Recently, exploratory projection pursuit (PP) has been considered (Jones, 1983) as a potential method for overcoming the curse of dimensionality problem (Huber, 1985), and new algorithms were suggested by Friedman (1987), and by Hall (1988, 1989). The idea is to find low dimensional projections that provide the most revealing views of the full-dimensional data emphasizing the discovery of nonlinear effects such as clustering.

Many of the methods of classical multivariate analysis turn out to be special cases of PP methods. Examples are principal component analysis, factor analysis, and discriminant analysis. The various PP methods differ by the projection index optimized.

Neural networks seem promising for feature extraction, or dimensionality reduction, mainly because of their powerful parallel computation. Feature detecting functions of neurons have been studied in the past two decades (von der Malsburg, 1973, Nass et al., 1973, Cooper et al., 1979, Takeuchi and Amari, 1979). It has also been shown that a simplified neuron model can serve as a principal component analyzer (Oja, 1982).

This paper suggests a statistical framework for the parameter estimation problem associated with unsupervised learning in a neural network, leading to an exploratory PP network that performs feature extraction, or dimensionality reduction, of the training data set. The formulation, which is similar in nature to PP, is based on a minimization of a cost function over a set of parameters, yielding an optimal decision rule under some norm. First, the formulation of a single and a multiple feature extraction are presented. Then a new projection index (cost function) that favors directions possessing multimodality, where the multimodality is measured in terms of the separability property of the data, is presented. This leads to the synaptic modification equations governing learning in Bienenstock, Cooper, and Munro (BCM) neurons (1982). A network is presented based on the multiple feature extraction formulation, and both, the linear and nonlinear neurons are analysed.

2   SINGLE FEATURE EXTRACTION

We associate a feature with each projection direction. With the addition of a threshold function we can say that an input posses a feature associated with that direction if its projection onto that direction is larger than the threshold. In these terms, a one dimensional projection would be a single feature extraction.

The approach proceeds as follows: Given a compact set of parameters, define a family of loss functions, where the loss function corresponds to a decision made by the neuron whether to fire or not for a given input. Let the risk be the averaged loss over all inputs. Minimize the risk over all possible decision rules, and then minimize the risk over the parameter set. In case the risk does not yield a meaningful minimization problem, or when the parameter set over which the minimization takes place can be restricted by some a-priori knowledge, a penalty, i.e. a measure on the parameter set, may be added to the risk.

Define the decision problem $(\Omega, \mathcal{F}_\Omega, P, L, \mathcal{A})$, where $\Omega = (x^{(1)}, \ldots, x^{(n)})$, $x^{(i)} \in R^N$, is a fixed set of input vectors, $(\Omega, \mathcal{F}_\Omega, P)$ the corresponding probability space, $\mathcal{A} = \{0, 1\}$ the decision space, and $\{L_\theta\}_{\theta \in B^M}$, $L_\theta : \Omega \times \mathcal{A} \mapsto R$ is the family of loss functions. B^M is a compact set in R^M. Let $\mathcal{D}$ be the space of all decision rules. The risk $R_\theta : \mathcal{D} \mapsto R$, is given by:

$$R_\theta(\delta) = \sum_{i=1}^{n} P(x^{(i)}) L_\theta(x^{(i)}, \delta(x^{(i)})). \qquad (2.1)$$

For a fixed θ, the optimal decision δ_θ is chosen so that:

$$R_\theta(\delta_\theta) = \min_{\delta \in \mathcal{D}} \{R_\theta(\delta)\} \qquad (2.2)$$

Since the minimization takes place over a finite set, the minimizer exists. In particular, for a given $x^{(i)}$ the decision $\delta_\theta(x^{(i)})$ is chosen so that $L_\theta(x^{(i)}, \delta_\theta(x^{(i)})) \leq L_\theta(x^{(i)}, 1 - \delta_\theta(x^{(i)}))$.

Now we find an optimal $\tilde{\theta}$ that minimizes the risk, namely, $\tilde{\theta}$ will be such that:

$$R_{\tilde{\theta}}(\delta_{\tilde{\theta}}) = \min_{\theta \in B^M} \{R_\theta(\delta_\theta)\}. \tag{2.3}$$

The minimum with respect to θ exits since B^M is compact.

$R_\theta(\delta_\theta)$ becomes a function that depends only on θ, and when θ represents a vector in R^N, R_θ can be viewed as a projection index.

3   MULTI-DIMENSIONAL FEATURE EXTRACTION

In this case we have a single layer network of interconnected units, each performing a single feature extraction. All units receive the same input and the interaction between the units is via lateral inhibition. The formulation is similar to single feature extraction, with the addition of interaction between the single feature extractors. Let Q be the number of features to be extracted from the data. The multiple decision rule $\delta_\theta = (\delta_\theta^{(1)}, \ldots, \delta_\theta^{(Q)})$ takes values in $\mathcal{A} = \{0, 1\}^Q$. The risk of node k is given by: $R_\theta^{(k)}(\delta) = \sum_{i=1}^n P(x^{(i)}) L_\theta^{(k)}(x^{(i)}, \delta^{(k)}(x^{(i)}))$, and the total risk of the network is $R_\theta(\delta) = \sum_{k=1}^Q R_\theta^{(k)}(\delta)$. Proceeding as before, we can minimize over the decision rules δ to get δ_θ, and then minimize over θ to get $\tilde{\theta}$, as in equation (2.3).

The coupling of the equations via the inhibition, and the relation between the different features extracted is exhibited in the loss function for each node and will become clear through the next example.

4   FINDING THE OPTIMAL θ FOR A SPECIFIC LOSS FUNCTION

4.1   A SINGLE BCM NEURON - ONE FEATURE EXTRACTION

In this section, we present an exploratory PP method with a specific loss function. The differential equations performing the optimization turn out to be a good approximation of the low governing synaptic weight modification in the BCM theory for learning and memory in neurons. The formal presentation of the theory, and some theoretical analysis is given in (Bienenstock, 1980, Bienenstock et al., 1982), mean field theory for a network based on these neurons is presented in (Scofield and Cooper, 1985, Cooper and Scofield, 1988), more recent analysis based on the statistical viewpoint is in (Intrator 1990), computer simulations and the biological relevance are discussed in (Saul et al., 1986, Bear et al., 1987, Cooper et al., 1988).

We start with a short review of the notations and definitions of BCM theory. Consider a neuron with input vector $x = (x_1, \ldots, x_N)$, synaptic weights vector $m = (m_1, \ldots, m_N)$, both in R^N, and activity (in the linear region) $c = x \cdot m$.

Define $\Theta_m = E[(x \cdot m)^2]$, $\hat{\phi}(c, \Theta_m) = c^2 - \frac{2}{3}c\Theta_m$, $\phi(c, \Theta_m) = c^2 - \frac{4}{3}c\Theta_m$. The input x, which is a stochastic process, is assumed to be of Type II φ mixing, bounded, and piecewise constant. The φ mixing property specifies the dependency of the future of the process on its past. These assumptions are needed for the approximation of the resulting deterministic equation by a stochastic one and are discussed in detail in (Intrator, 1990). Note that c represents the linear projection of x onto m, and we seek an optimal projection in some sense.

The BCM synaptic modification equations are given by: $\dot{m} = \mu(t)\phi(x \cdot m, \Theta_m)x$, $m(0) = m_0$, where $\mu(t)$ is a global modulator which is assumed to take into account all the global factors affecting the cell, e.g., the beginning or end of the critical period, state of arousal, etc.

Rewriting the modification equation as $\dot{m} = \mu(t)(x \cdot m)(x \cdot m - \frac{4}{3}\theta_m)x$, we see that unlike a classical Hebb-Stent rule, the threshold θ_m is dynamic. This gives the modification equation the desired stability, with no extra conditions such as saturation of the activity, or normalization of $\| m \|$, and also yields a statistically meaningful optimization.

Returning to the statistical formulation, we let $\theta = m$ be the parameter to be estimated according to the above formulation and define an appropriate loss function depending on the cell's decision whether to fire or not. The loss function represents the intuitive idea that the neuron will fire when its activity is greater than some threshold, and will not otherwise. We denote the firing of the neuron by $a = 1$. Define $K = -\mu \int_{\Theta_m}^{\frac{2}{3}\Theta_m} \hat{\phi}(s, \Theta_m)ds$. Consider the following loss function:

$$L_\theta(x, a) = L_m(x, a) = \begin{cases} -\mu \int_{\Theta_m}^{(x \cdot m)} \hat{\phi}(s, \Theta_m)ds, & (x \cdot m) \geq \Theta_m, \ a = 1 \\ K - \mu \int_{\Theta_m}^{(x \cdot m)} \hat{\phi}(s, \Theta_m)ds, & (x \cdot m) < \Theta_m, \ a = 1 \\ -\mu \int_{\Theta_m}^{(x \cdot m)} \hat{\phi}(s, \Theta_m)ds, & (x \cdot m) \leq \Theta_m, \ a = 0 \\ K - \mu \int_{\Theta_m}^{(x \cdot m)} \hat{\phi}(s, \Theta_m)ds, & (x \cdot m) > \Theta_m, \ a = 0 \end{cases} \quad (4.1)$$

It follows from the definition of L_θ and from the definition of δ_θ in (2.2) that

$$L_m(x, \delta_m) = -\mu \int_{\Theta_m}^{(x \cdot m)} \hat{\phi}(s, \Theta_m)ds = -\frac{\mu}{3}\{(x \cdot m)^3 - E[(x \cdot m)^2](x \cdot m)^2\} \quad (4.2)$$

The above definition of the loss function suggests that the decision of a neuron whether to fire or not is based on a dynamic threshold $(x \cdot m) > \Theta_m$. It turns out that the synaptic modification equations remain the same if the decision is based on a fixed threshold. This is demonstrated by the following loss function, which leads to the same risk as in equation (4.3): $K = -\mu \int_0^{\frac{2}{3}\Theta_m} \hat{\phi}(s, \Theta_m)ds$,

$$L_\theta(x, a) = L_m(x, a) = \begin{cases} -\mu \int_0^{(x \cdot m)} \hat{\phi}(s, \Theta_m)ds, & (x \cdot m) \geq 0, \ a = 1 \\ K - \mu \int_0^{(x \cdot m)} \hat{\phi}(s, \Theta_m)ds, & (x \cdot m) < 0, \ a = 1 \\ -\mu \int_0^{(x \cdot m)} \hat{\phi}(s, \Theta_m)ds, & (x \cdot m) \leq 0, \ a = 0 \\ K - \mu \int_0^{(x \cdot m)} \hat{\phi}(s, \Theta_m)ds, & (x \cdot m) > 0, \ a = 0 \end{cases} \quad (4.1')$$

The risk is given by:

$$R_\theta(\delta_\theta) = -\frac{\mu}{3}\{E[(x \cdot m)^3] - E^2[(x \cdot m)^2]\}.\tag{4.3}$$

The following graph represents the ϕ function and the associated loss function $L_m(x, \delta_m)$ of the activity c.

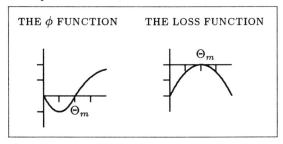

Fig. 1: The Function ϕ and the Loss Functions for a Fixed m and Θ_m.

From the graph of the loss function it follows that for any fixed m and Θ_m, the loss is small for a given input x, when either $x \cdot m$ is close to zero or negative, or when $x \cdot m$ is larger than Θ_m. This suggests, that the preferred directions for a fixed θ_m will be such that the projected single dimensional distribution differs from normal in the center of the distribution, in the sense that it has a multi-modal distribution with a distance between the two peaks larger than θ_m. Rewriting (4.3) we get

$$\frac{R_\theta(\delta_\theta)}{E^2[(x \cdot m)^2]} = -\frac{\mu}{3}\{\frac{E[(x \cdot m)^3]}{E^2[(x \cdot m)^2]} - 1\}.\tag{4.4}$$

The term $E[(x \cdot m)^3]/E^2[(x \cdot m)^2]$ can be viewed as some measure of the skewness of the distribution, which is a measure of deviation from normality and therefore an interesting direction (Diaconis and Friedman, 1984), in accordance with Friedman (1987) and Hall's (1988, 1989) argument that it is best to seek projections that differ from the normal in the center of the distribution rather than in the tails.

Since the risk is continuously differentiable, its minimization can be done via the gradient descent method with respect to m, namely:

$$\frac{\partial m_i}{\partial t} = -\frac{\partial}{\partial m_i} R_\theta(\delta_\theta) = \mu E[\phi(x \cdot m, \Theta_m)x_i].\tag{4.5}$$

Notice that the resulting equation represents an averaged deterministic equation of the stochastic BCM modification equations. It turns out that under suitable conditions on the mixing of the input x and the global function μ, equation (4.5) is a good approximation of its stochastic version.

When the nonlinearity of the neuron is emphasized, the neuron's activity is then defined as $c = \sigma(x \cdot m)$, where σ usually represents a smooth sigmoidal function. Θ_m is then defined as $E[\sigma^2(x \cdot m)]$, and the loss function is similar to the one given by equation (4.1) except that $(x \cdot m)$ is replaced by $\sigma(x \cdot m)$. The gradient of the risk is given by: $-\nabla_m R_m(\delta_m) = \mu E[\phi\big(\sigma(x \cdot m), \Theta_m\big)\sigma'x]$, where σ' represents the derivative of σ at the point $(x \cdot m)$. Note that σ may represent any nonlinear function, e.g. radial symmetric kernels.

4.2   THE NETWORK - MULTIPLE FEATURE EXTRACTION

In this case we have Q identical nodes, which receive the same input and inhibit each other. Let the neuronal activity be denoted by $c_k = x \cdot m_k$. We define the *inhibited* activity $\tilde{c}_k = c_k - \eta \sum_{j \neq k} c_j$, and the threshold $\tilde{\Theta}_m^k = E[\tilde{c}_k^2]$. In a more general case, the inhibition may be defined to take into account the spatial location of adjacent neurons, namely, $\tilde{c}_k = \sum_j \lambda_{jk} c_j$, where λ_{jk} represents different types of inhibitions, e.g. Mexican hat. Since the following calculations are valid for both kinds of inhibition we shall introduce only the simpler one.

The loss function is similar to the one defined in a single feature extraction with the exception that the activity $c = x \cdot m$ is replaced by $\tilde{c}$. Therefore the risk for node k is given by: $R_k = -\frac{\mu}{3}\{E[\tilde{c}_k^3] - (E[\tilde{c}_k^2])^2\}$, and the total risk is given by $R = \sum_{k=1}^{Q} R_k$. The gradient of R is given by:

$$\frac{\partial R}{\partial m_k} = -\mu[1 - \eta(Q - 1)]E[\phi(\tilde{c}_k, \tilde{\Theta}_m^k)x]. \tag{4.6}$$

Equation (4.6) demonstrates the ability of the network to perform exploratory projection pursuit in parallel, since the minimization of the risk involves minimization of nodes $1, \ldots, Q$, which are loosely coupled.

The parameter η represents the amount of lateral inhibition in the network, and is related to the amount of correlation between the different features sought by the network. Experience shows that when $\eta \simeq 0$, the different units may all become selective to the simplest feature that can be extracted from the data. When $\eta(Q - 1) \simeq 1$, the network becomes selective to those inputs that are very far apart (under the l^2 norm), yielding a classification of a small portion of the data, and mostly unresponsiveness to the rest of the data. When $0 < \eta(Q - 1) < 1$, the network becomes responsive to substructures that may be common to several different inputs, namely extract invariant features in the data. The optimal value of η has been estimated by data driven techniques.

When the non linearity of the neuron is emphasized the activity is defined (as in the single neuron case) as $c_k = \sigma(x \cdot m_k)$. $\tilde{c}_k$, $\tilde{\Theta}_m^k$, and R_k are defined as before. In this case $\frac{\partial \tilde{c}_k}{\partial m_j} = -\eta\sigma'(x \cdot m_j)x$, $\frac{\partial \tilde{c}_k}{\partial m_k} = \sigma'(x \cdot m_k)x$, and equation (4.6) becomes:

$$\frac{\partial R}{\partial m_k} = -\mu E\Big[\phi(\tilde{c}_k, \tilde{\Theta}_m^k)\big(\sigma'(x \cdot m_k) - \eta \sum_{j \neq k} \sigma'(x \cdot m_j)\big)x\Big] \tag{4.7}$$

4.3   OPTIMAL NETWORK SIZE

A major problem in network solutions to real world problems is optimal network size. In our case, it is desirable to try and extract as many features as possible on one hand, but it is clear that too many neurons in the network will simply inhibit each other, yielding sub-optimal results. The following solution was adopted: We replace each neuron in the network with a group of neurons which all receive the same input, and the same inhibition from adjacent groups. These neurons differ from one another only in their initial synaptic weights. The output of each neuron is replaced by the average group activity. Experiments show that the resulting network is more robust to noise and outliers in the data. Furthermore, it is observed that groups that become selective to a *true* feature in the data, posses a much smaller inter-group variance of their synaptic weight vector than those which do not become responsive to a coherent feature. We found that eliminating neurons with large inter-group variance and retraining the network, may yield improved feature extraction properties.

The network has been applied to speech segments, in an attempt to extract some features from CV pairs of isolated phonemes (Seebach and Intrator, 1988).

5   DISCUSSION

The PP method based on the BCM modification function, has been found capable of effectively discovering non linear data structures in high dimensional spaces. Using a parallel processor and the presented network topology, the pursuit can be done faster than in the traditional serial methods.

The projection index is based on polynomial moments, and is therefore computationally attractive. When only the nonlinear structure in the data is of interest, a sphering transformation (Huber, 1981, Friedman, 1987), can be applied first to the data for removal of all the location, scale, and correlational structure from the data.

When compared with other PP methods, the highlights of the presented method are *i*) the projection index concentrates on directions where the separability property as well as the non-normality of the data is large, thus giving rise to better classification properties; *ii*) the degree of correlation between the directions, or features extracted by the network can be regulated via the global inhibition, allowing some tuning of the network to different types of data for optimal results; *iii*) the pursuit is done on all the directions at once thus leading to the capability of finding more interesting structures than methods that find only one projection direction at a time. *iv*) the network's structure suggests a simple method for size-optimization.

Acknowledgements

I would like to thank Professor Basilis Gidas for many fruitful discussions.

Supported by the National Science Foundation, the Office of Naval Research, and the Army Research Office.

References

Barron A. R. (1988) Approximation of densities by sequences of exponential families. Submitted to *Ann. Statist.*

Bienenstock E. L. (1980) A theory of the development of neuronal selectivity. Doctoral dissertation, Brown University, Providence, RI

Bienenstock E. L., L. N Cooper, and P. W. Munro (1982) Theory for the development of neuron selectivity: orientation specificity and binocular interaction in visual cortex. *J.Neurosci.* 2:32-48

Bear M. F., L. N Cooper, and F. F. Ebner (1987) A Physiological Basis for a Theory of Synapse Modification. *Science* 237:42-48

Cooper L. N, and F. Liberman, and E. Oja (1979) A theory for the acquisition and loss of neurons specificity in visual cortex. *Biol. Cyb.* 33:9-28

Cooper L. N, and C. L. Scofield (1988) Mean-field theory of a neural network. *Proc. Natl. Acad. Sci. USA* 85:1973-1977

Cox D. D. (1984) Multivariate smoothing spline functions. *SIAM J. Numer. Anal.* 21 789-813

Diaconis P., and D. Freedman (1984) Asymptotics of Graphical Projection Pursuit. *The Annals of Statistics*, 12 793-815.

Friedman J. H. (1987) Exploratory Projection Pursuit. *Journal of the American Statistical Association* 82-397:249-266

Hall P. (1988) Estimating the Direction in which Data set is Most Interesting. *Probab. Theory Rel. Fields* 80, 51-78

Hall P. (1989) On Polynomial-Based Projection Indices for Exploratory Projection Pursuit. *The Annals of Statistics*, 17, 589-605.

Huber P. J. (1981) Projection Pursuit. Research Report PJH-6, Harvard University, Dept. of Statistics.

Huber P. J. (1985) Projection Pursuit. *The Annal. of Stat.* 13:435-475

Intrator N. (1990) An Averaging Result for Random Differential Equations. In Press.

Jones M. C. (1983) The Projection Pursuit Algorithm for Exploratory Data Analysis. Unpublished Ph.D. dissertation, University of Bath, School of Mathematics.

von der Malsburg, C. (1973) Self-organization of orientation sensitivity cells in the striate cortex. *Kybernetik* 14:85-100

Nass M. M., and L. N Cooper (1975) A theory for the development of feature detecting cells in visual cortex. *Biol. Cybernetics* 19:1-18

Oja E. (1982) A Simplified Neuron Model as a Principal Component Analyzer. *J. Math. Biology,* 15:267-273

Saul A., and E. E. Clothiaux, 1986) Modeling and Simulation III: Simulation of a Model for Development of Visual Cortical specificity. *J. of Electrophysiological Techniques,* 13:279-306

Scofield C. L., and L. N Cooper (1985) Development and properties of neural networks. *Contemp. Phys.* 26:125-145

Seebach B. S., and N. Intrator (1988) A learning Mechanism for the Identification of Acoustic Features. (Society for Neuroscience).

Takeuchi A., and S. Amari (1979) Formation of topographic maps and columnar microstructures in nerve fields. *Biol. Cyb.* 35:63-72

On the Distribution of the Number of Local Minima of a Random Function on a Graph

Pierre Baldi
JPL, Caltech
Pasadena, CA 91109

Yosef Rinott
UCSD
La Jolla, CA 92093

Charles Stein
Stanford University
Stanford, CA 94305

1   INTRODUCTION

Minimization of energy or error functions has proved to be a useful principle in the design and analysis of neural networks and neural algorithms. A brief list of examples include: the back- propagation algorithm, the use of optimization methods in computational vision, the application of analog networks to the approximate solution of NP complete problems and the Hopfield model of associative memory.

In the Hopfield model associative memory, for instance, a quadratic Hamiltonian of the form

$$F(x) = \frac{1}{2} \sum_{i,j=1}^{n} w_{ij} x_i x_j \qquad x_i = \pm 1 \qquad (1)$$

is constructed to tailor a particular "landscape" on the n- dimensional hypercube $H^n = \{-1, 1\}^n$ and store memories at a particular subset of the local minima of F on H^n. The synaptic weights w_{ij} are usually constructed incrementally, using a form of Hebb's rule applied to the patterns to be stored. These patterns are often chosen at random. As the number of stored memories grows to and beyond saturation, the energy function F becomes essentially random. In addition, in a general context of combinatorial optimization, every problem in NP can be (polynomially) reduced to the problem of minimizing a certain quadratic form over H^n.

These two types of considerations, associative memory and combinatorial optimization, motivate the study of the number and distribution of local minima of a random function F defined over the hypercube, or more generally, any graph G. Of course, different notions of randomness can be introduced. In the case where F is a quadratic form as in (1), we could take the coefficients w_{ij} to be independent identically distributed gaussian random variables, which yields, in fact, the Sherrington-Kirkpatrick long-range spin glass model of statistical physics. For this model, the expectation of the number of local minima is well known but no rigorous results have been obtained for its distribution (even the variance is not known precisely). A simpler model of randomness can then be introduced, where the values $F(x)$ of the random function at each vertex are assigned randomly and independently from a common distribution: This is in fact the random energy model of Derrida (1981).

2   THE MAIN RESULT

In Baldi, Rinott and Stein (1989) the following general result on random energy models is proven.

Let $G = (V, E)$ be a regular d-graph, i.e., a graph where every vertex has the same number d of neighbors. Let F be a random function on V whose values are independently distributed with a common continuous distribution. Let W be the number of local minima of F, i.e., the number of vertices x satisfying $F(x) > F(y)$ for any neighbor y of x (i.e., $(x, y)\epsilon E$). Let $EW = \lambda$ and Var $W = \sigma^2$. Then

$$EW = \frac{|V|}{d+1} \tag{2}$$

and for any positive real w:

$$\left| P(W \le w) - \Phi\left(\frac{w - \lambda}{\sigma}\right) \right| \le \frac{C}{\sqrt{\sigma}} \tag{3}$$

where Φ is the standard normal distribution and C is an absolute constant.

Remarks:

(a) The proof of (3) ((2) is obvious) is based on a method developed in Stein (1986).

(b) The bound given in the theorem is not asymptotic but holds also for small graphs.

(c) If $|V| \to \infty$ the theorem states that if $\sigma \to \infty$ then the distribution of the number of local minima approaches a normal distribution and (3) gives also a bound of $O(\sigma^{-1/2})$ on the rate of convergence.

(d) The function F simply induces a ranking (or a random permutation) of the vertices of G.

(e) The bound in (3) may not be optimal. We suspect that the optimal rate should scale like σ^{-1} rather than $\sigma^{-1/2}$.

3   EXAMPLES OF APPLICATIONS

(1) Consider a $n \times n$ square lattice (see fig.1) with periodic boundary conditions. Here, $|V_n| = n^2$ and $d = 4$. The expected number of local minima is

$$EW_n = \frac{n^2}{5} \tag{4}$$

and a simple calculations shows that

$$\text{Var } W_n = \frac{13n^2}{225}. \tag{5}$$

Therefore W_n is asymptotically normal and the rate of convergence is bounded by $O(n^{-1/2})$.

(2) Consider a $n \times n$ square lattice, where this time the neighbors of a vertex v are all the points in same row or column as v (see fig.2). This example arises in game theory, where the rows (resp. columns) correspond to different possible strategies of one of two players. The energy value can be interpreted as the cost of the combined choice of two strategies. Here $|V_n| = n^2$ and $d = 2n - 2$. The expected number of local minima (the Nash equilibrium points of game theory) W_n is

$$EW_n = \frac{n^2}{2n - 1} \approx \frac{n}{2} \tag{6}$$

and

$$\text{Var } W_n = \frac{n^2(n - 1)}{2(2n - 1)^2} \approx \frac{n}{8}. \tag{7}$$

Therefore W_n is asymptotically normal and the rate of convergence is bounded by $O(n^{-1/4})$.

(3) Consider the n-dimensional hypercube $H^n = (V_n, E_n)$ (see fig.3). Then $| V_n |= 2^n$ and $d = n$. The expected number of local minima W_n is:

$$EW_n = \frac{2^n}{n + 1} = \lambda_n \tag{8}$$

and

$$\text{Var } W_n = \frac{2^{n-1}(n - 1)}{(n + 1)^2} = \sigma_n^2. \tag{9}$$

Therefore W_n is asymptotically normal and in fact:

$$\left| P(w_n \leq w) - \Phi\left(\frac{w - \lambda_n}{\sigma_n}\right) \right| \leq \frac{C\sqrt{n + 1}}{(n - 1)^{1/4} 2^{(n-1)/4}} = O(\sqrt[4]{n/2^n}). \tag{10}$$

In contrast, if the edges of H^n are randomly and independently oriented with probability .5, then the distribution of the number of vertices having all their adjacent edges oriented inward is asymptotically Poisson with mean 1.

References

P. Baldi, Y. Rinott (1989), "Asymptotic Normality of Some Graph-Related Statistics," Journal of Applied Probability, 26, 171-175.

P. Baldi and Y. Rinott (1989), "On Normal Approximation of Distribution in Terms of Dependency Graphs," Annals of Probability, in press.

P. Baldi, Y. Rinott and C. Stein (1989), "A Normal Approximation for the Number of Local Maxima of a Random Function on a Graph," In: Probability, Statistics and Mathematics: Papers in Honor of Samuel Karlin. T.W. Anderson, K.B. Athreya and D.L. Iglehard, Editors, Academic Press.

B. Derrida (1981), "Random Energy Model: An Exactly Solvable Model of Disordered Systems," Physics Review, B24, 2613- 2626.

C. M. Macken and A. S. Perelson (1989), "Protein Evolution on Rugged Landscapes", PNAS, 86, 6191-6195.

C. Stein (1986), "Approximate Computation of Expectations," Institute of Mathematical Statistics Lecture Notes, S.S. Gupta Series Editor, Volume 7.

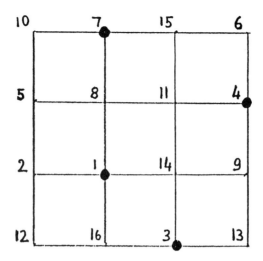

Figure 1:   A ranking of a 4×4 square lattice with periodic boundary conditions and four local minima ($d = 4$).

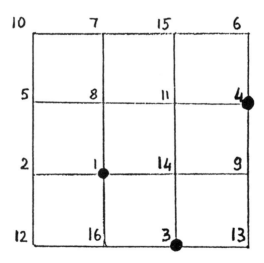

Figure 2:   A ranking of a 4×4 square lattice. The neighbors of a vertex are all the points on the same row and column. There are three local minima ($d = 6$).

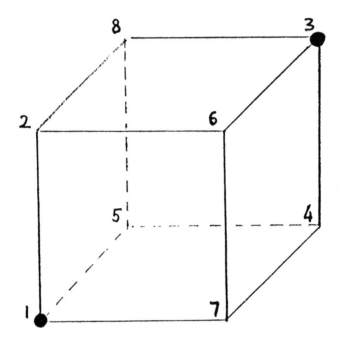

Figure 3:   A ranking of H^3 with two local minima ($d = 3$).

A Cost Function for Internal Representations

Anders Krogh
The Niels Bohr Institute
Blegdamsvej 17
2100 Copenhagen
Denmark

G. I. Thorbergsson
Nordita
Blegdamsvej 17
2100 Copenhagen
Denmark

John A. Hertz
Nordita
Blegdamsvej 17
2100 Copenhagen
Denmark

ABSTRACT

We introduce a cost function for learning in feed–forward neural networks which is an explicit function of the internal representation in addition to the weights. The learning problem can then be formulated as two simple perceptrons and a search for internal representations. Back–propagation is recovered as a limit. The frequency of successful solutions is better for this algorithm than for back–propagation when weights and hidden units are updated on the same timescale i.e. once every learning step.

1   INTRODUCTION

In their review of back–propagation in layered networks, Rumelhart et al. (1986) describe the learning process in terms of finding good "internal representations" of the input patterns on the hidden units. However, the search for these representations is an indirect one, since the variables which are adjusted in its course are the connection weights, not the activations of the hidden units themselves when specific input patterns are fed into the input layer. Rather, the internal representations are represented implicitly in the connection weight values.

More recently, Grossman et al. (1988 and 1989)[1] suggested a way in which the search for internal representations could be made much more explicit. They proposed to make the activations of the hidden units for each of the input patterns

---

[1] See also the paper by Grossman in this volume.

explicit variables to be adjusted iteratively (together with the weights) in the learning process. However, although they found that the algorithm they gave for making these adjustments could be effective in some test problems, it is rather *ad hoc* and it is difficult to see whether the algorithm will converge to a good solution.

If an optimization task is posed in terms of a cost function which is systematically reduced as the algorithm runs, one is in a much better position to answer questions like these. This is the motivation for this work, where we construct a cost function which is an explicit function of the internal representations as well as the connection weights. Learning is then a descent on the cost function surface, and variations in the algorithm, corresponding to variations in the parameters of the cost function, can be studied systematically. Both the conventional back–propagation algorithm and that of Grossman et al. can be recovered in special limits of ours. It is easy to change the algorithm to include constraints on the learning.

A method somewhat similar to ours has been proposed by Rohwer (1989)[2]. He considers networks with feedback but in this paper we study feed–forward networks. Le Cun has also been working along the same lines, but in a quite different formulation (Le Cun, 1987).

The learning problem for a two–layer perceptron is reduced to learning in two simple perceptrons and the search for internal representations. This search can be carried out by gradient descent of the cost function or by an iterative method.

2   THE COST FUNCTION

We work within the standard architecture, with three layers of units and two of connections. Input pattern number μ is denoted ξ_k^μ, the corresponding target pattern ζ_i^μ, and its internal representation σ_i^μ. We use a convention in which i always labels output units, j labels hidden units, and k labels input units. Thus w_{ij} is always a hidden–to–output weight and w_{jk} an input–to–hidden connection weight. Then the actual activations of the hidden units when pattern μ is the input are

$$S_j^\mu = g(h_j^\mu) \equiv g(\sum_k w_{jk}\xi_k^\mu) \tag{1}$$

and those of the output units, when given the internal representations σ_j^μ as inputs, are

$$S_i^\mu = g(h_i^\mu) \equiv g(\sum_j w_{ij}\sigma_j^\mu) \tag{2}$$

where $g(h)$ is the activation function, which we take to be $\tanh h$.

The cost function has two terms, one of which describes simple delta–rule learning (Rumelhart et al., 1986) of the internal representations from the inputs by the first layer of connections, and the other of which describes the same kind of learning of the

---

[2]See also the paper by Rohwer in this volume.

target patterns from the internal representations in the second layer of connections. We use the "entropic" form for these terms:

$$E = \sum_{i\mu\pm} \tfrac{1}{2}(1 \pm \zeta_i^\mu)\ln\left(\frac{1 \pm \zeta_i^\mu}{1 \pm S_i^\mu}\right) + T\sum_{j\mu\pm} \tfrac{1}{2}(1 \pm \sigma_j^\mu)\ln\left(\frac{1 \pm \sigma_j^\mu}{1 \pm S_j^\mu}\right) \tag{3}$$

This form of the cost function has been shown to reduce the learning time (Solla et al., 1988). We allow different relative weights for the two terms through the parameter T. This cost function should now be minimized with respect to the two sets of connection weights w_{ij} and w_{jk} and the internal representations σ_j^μ.

The resulting gradient descent learning equations for the connection weights are simply those of simple one–layer perceptrons:

$$\frac{\partial w_{ij}}{\partial t} \propto -\frac{\partial E}{\partial w_{ij}} = \sum_\mu (\zeta_i^\mu - S_i^\mu)\sigma_j^\mu \equiv \sum_\mu \delta_i^\mu \sigma_j^\mu \tag{4}$$

$$\frac{\partial w_{jk}}{\partial t} \propto -\frac{\partial E}{\partial w_{jk}} = T\sum_\mu (\sigma_j^\mu - S_j^\mu)\xi_k^\mu \equiv T\sum_\mu \delta_j^\mu \xi_k^\mu \tag{5}$$

The new element is the corresponding equation for the adjustment of the internal representations:

$$\frac{\partial \sigma_j^\mu}{\partial t} \propto -\frac{\partial E}{\partial \sigma_j^\mu} = \sum_i \delta_i^\mu w_{ij} + Th_j^\mu - T\tanh^{-1}\sigma_j^\mu \tag{6}$$

The stationary values of the internal representations thus solve

$$\sigma_j^\mu = \tanh(h_j^\mu + T^{-1}\sum_i \delta_i^\mu w_{ij}) \tag{7}$$

which has a simple interpretation: The internal representation variables σ_j^μ are like conventional units except that in addition to the field fed forward into them from the input layer they also feel the back–propagated error field $b_j^\mu \equiv \sum_i \delta_i^\mu w_{ij}$. The parameter T regulates the relative weights of these terms.

Instead of doing gradient descent we have iterated equation (7) to find the internal representations.

One of the advantages of formulating the learning problem in terms of a cost function is that it is easy to implement constraints on the learning. Suppose we want to prevent the network from forming the same internal representations for different output patterns. We can then add the term

$$E = \frac{\gamma}{2}\sum_{ij\mu\nu} \zeta_i^\mu \zeta_i^\nu \sigma_j^\mu \sigma_j^\nu \tag{8}$$

to the energy. We may also want to suppress internal representations where the units have identical values. This may be seen as an attempt to produce efficient representations. The term

$$E = \frac{\gamma'}{2} \sum_\mu \left(\sum_j \sigma_j^\mu \right)^2 \tag{9}$$

is then added to the energy. The parameters γ and γ' can be tuned to get the best performance. With these new terms equation (7) for the internal representations becomes

$$\sigma_j^\mu = \tanh(h_j^\mu + T^{-1} \sum_i \delta_i^\mu w_{ij} + \gamma T^{-1} \sum_{i\nu} \zeta_i^\mu \zeta_i^\nu \sigma_j^\nu + \gamma' T^{-1} \sum_{j'} \sigma_{j'}^\mu). \tag{10}$$

The only change in the algorithm is that this equation is iterated rather than (7). These terms lead to better performance in some problems. The benefit of including such terms is very problem–dependent. We include in our results an example where these terms are useful.

3   SIMPLE LIMITS

It is simple to recover ordinary back–propagation in this model. It is the limit where $T \gg 1$: Expanding (7) we obtain

$$\sigma_j^\mu = S_j^\mu + T^{-1} \sum_i \delta_i^\mu w_{ij} (1 - \tanh^2 h_j^\mu) \tag{11}$$

Keeping only the lowest–order surviving terms, the learning equations for the connection weights then reduce to

$$\frac{\partial w_{ij}}{\partial t} = \sum_\mu [\zeta_i^\mu - \tanh(\sum_{j'} w_{ij'} S_{j'}^\mu)] S_j^\mu \tag{12}$$

and

$$\frac{\partial w_{jk}}{\partial t} = \sum_{i\mu} \delta_i^\mu w_{ij} (1 - \tanh^2 h_j^\mu) \xi_k^\mu \tag{13}$$

which are just the standard back–propagation equations (with an entropic cost function).

Now consider the opposite limit, $T \ll 1$. Then the second term dominates in (7):

$$\sigma_j^\mu \to \text{sgn} \left(\sum_i \delta_i^\mu w_{ij} \right) \tag{14}$$

A similar algorithm to the one of Grossman et al. is then to train the input–to–hidden connection weights with these σ_j^μ as targets while training the hidden–to–output weights with the σ_j^μ obtained in the other limit (7) as inputs. That is, one alternates between high and low T according to which layer of weights one is adjusting.

4 RESULTS

There are many ways to do the optimization in practice. To be able to make a comparison with back–propagation, we have made simulations that, at high T, are essentially the same as back–propagation (in terms of weight adjustment).

In one set of simulations we have kept the internal representations, σ_j^μ, optimal with the given set of connections. This means that after one step of weight changes we have relaxed the σ's. One can think of the σ's as fast–varying and the weights as slowly–varying. In the $T \gg 1$ limit we can use these simulations to get a comparison with back–propagation as described in the previous section.

In our second set of simulations we iterate the equation for the σ's only once after one step of weight updating. All variables are then updated on the same timescale. This turns out to increase the success rate for learning considerably compared to the back–propagation limit. The σ's are updated in random order such that each one is updated once on the average.

The learning rate, momentum, etc. have been chosen optimally for the back–propagation limit (large T) and kept fixed at these values for other values of T (though no systematic optimization of parameters has been done).

We have tested the algorithm on the parity and encoding problems for $T = 1$ and $T = 10$ (the back–propagation limit). Each problem was run 100 times and the average error and success rate were measured and plotted as functions of learning steps (time). One learning step corresponds to one updating of the weights.

For the parity problem (and other similar tasks) the learning did not converge for T lower than about 3. When the weights are small we can expand the tanh on the output in equation (7),

$$\sigma_j^\mu \simeq \tanh(h_j^\mu + T^{-1} \sum_i w_{ij} [\zeta_i^\mu - \sum_{j'} w_{ij'} \sigma_{j'}^\mu]), \tag{15}$$

so the σ_j^μ sits in a spin-glass-like "local field" except for the connection to itself. When the algorithm is started with small random weights this self–coupling $(\sum_i (w_{ij})^2)$ is dominant. Forcing the self–coupling to be small at low w's and gradually increasing it to full strength when the units saturate improves the performance a lot.

For larger networks the self–coupling does not seem to be a problem.

The specific test problems were:

Parity with 4 input units and 4 hidden units and all the 16 patterns in the training set. We stop the runs after 300 sweeps of the training set. For $T = 1$ the self coupling is suppressed.

Encoding with 8 input, 3 hidden and 8 output units and 8 patterns to learn (same input as output). The 8 patterns have -1 at all units but one. We stop the runs after 500 sweeps of the training set.

Both problems were run with fast–varying σ's and with all variables updated on the same timescale. We determined the average learning time of the *successful* runs and the percentage of the 100 trials that were successful. The success criterion was that the sign of the output was correct. The learning times and success rates are shown in table 1.

Table 1: Learning Times and Succes Rates

		Learning times		Success rate	
		T=1	T=10	T=1	T=10
Fast-vary-	Parity	130±10	97±6	30%	48%
ing σ's	Encoding	167±10	88±4	95%	98%
Slow-vary-	Parity	146±10	121±6	36%	57%
ing σ's	Encoding	145±8	64±2	99%	100%

In figure 1 we plot the average error as a function of learning steps and the success rate for each set of runs.

It can seem a disadvantage of this method that it is necessary to store the values of the σ's between learning sweeps. We have therefore tried to start the iteration of equation (7) with the value $\sigma_j^\mu = \tanh(\sum_k w_{jk}\xi_k^\mu)$ on the right hand side. This does not affect the performance much.

We have investigated the effect of including the terms (8) and (9) in the energy. For the same parity problem as above we get an improved success rate in the high T limit.

5   CONCLUSION

The most striking result is the improvement in the success rate when all variables, weights and hidden units, are updated once every learning step. This is in contrast to back–propagation, where the values of the hidden units are completely determined by the weights and inputs. In our formulation this corresponds to relaxing the hidden units fully in every learning cycle and having the parameter $T \gg 1$. There is then an advantage in considering the hidden units as additional variables during the learning phase whose values are not completely determined by the field fed forward to them from the inputs.

The results indicate that the performance of the algorithm is best in the high T limit.

For the parity problem the performance of the algorithm presented here is similar to that of the back–propagation algorithm measured in learning time. The real advantage is the higher frequency of successful solutions. For the encoding problem the algorithm is faster than back–propagation but the success rate is similar ($\simeq$ 100%). The algorithm should also be comparable to back–propagation in cpu time

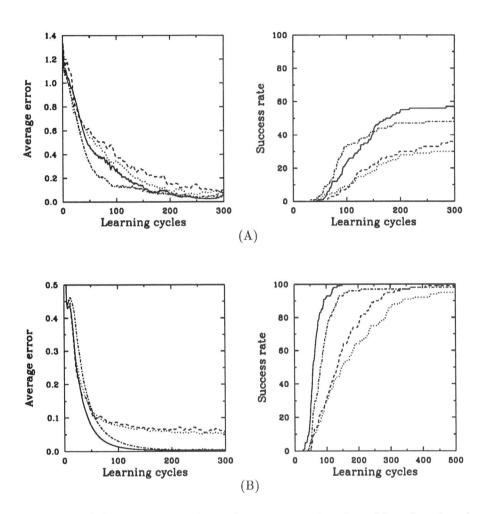

Figure 1: (A) The left plot shows the error as a function of learning time for the 4–parity problem for those runs that converged within 300 learning steps. The curves are: $T = 10$ and slow sigmas (———), $T = 10$ and fast sigmas (·—·—·), $T = 1$ and slow sigmas (------), and $T = 1$ and fast sigmas (········). The right plot is the percentage of converged runs as a function of learning time.
(B) The same as above but for the encoding problem.

in the limit where all variables are updated on the same timescale (once every learning sweep).

Because the computational complexity is shifted from the calculation of new weights to the determination of internal representations, it might be easier to implement this method in hardware than back–propagation is. It is possible to use the method *without* saving the array of internal representations by using the field fed forward from the inputs to generate an internal representation that then becomes a starting point for iterating the equation for σ.

The method can easily be generalized to networks with feedback (as in [Rohwer, 1989]) and it would be interesting to see how it compares to other algorithms for recurrent networks. There are many other directions in which one can continue this work. One is to try another cost function. Another is to use binary units and perceptron learning.

References

Le Cun, Y (1987). Modeles Connexionistes de l'Apprentissage. Thesis, Paris.

Grossman, T, R Meir and E Domany (1988). Learning by Choice of Internal Representations. *Complex Systems* **2**, 555.

Grossman, T (1989). The CHIR Algorithm: A Generalization for Multiple Output and Multilayered Networks. Preprint, submitted to *Complex Systems*.

Rohwer, R (1989). The "Moving Targets" Training Method. Preprint, Edinburgh.

Rumelhart, D E, G E Hinton and R J Williams (1986). Chapter 8 in *Parallel Distributed Processing*, vol 1 (D E Rumelhart and J L McClelland, eds), MIT Press.

Solla, S A, E Levin, M Fleisher (1988). Accelerated Learning in Layered Neural Networks. *Complex Systems* **2**, 625.

PART IX:
HARDWARE IMPLEMENTATION

An Analog VLSI Model of Adaptation in the Vestibulo-Ocular Reflex

Stephen P. DeWeerth and Carver A. Mead
California Institute of Technology
Pasadena, CA 91125

ABSTRACT

The vestibulo-ocular reflex (VOR) is the primary mechanism that controls the compensatory eye movements that stabilize retinal images during rapid head motion. The primary pathways of this system are feed-forward, with inputs from the semicircular canals and outputs to the oculomotor system. Since visual feedback is not used directly in the VOR computation, the system must exploit motor learning to perform correctly. Lisberger(1988) has proposed a model for adapting the VOR gain using image-slip information from the retina. We have designed and tested analog very large-scale integrated (VLSI) circuitry that implements a simplified version of Lisberger's adaptive VOR model.

1   INTRODUCTION

A characteristic commonly found in biological systems is their ability to adapt their function based on their inputs. The combination of the need for precision and the variability inherent in the environment necessitates such learning in organisms. Sensorimotor systems present obvious examples of behaviors that require learning to function correctly. Simple actions such as walking, jumping, or throwing a ball are not performed correctly the first time they are attempted; rather, they require motor learning throughout many iterations of the action.

When creating artificial systems that must execute tasks accurately in uncontrolled environments, designers can exploit adaptive techniques to improve system performance. With this in mind, it is possible for the system designer to take inspiration from systems already present in biology. In particular, sensorimotor systems, due to their direct interfaces with the environment, can gather an immediate indication of the correctness of an action, and hence can learn without supervision. The salient characteristics of the environment are extracted by the adapting system and do not need to be specified in a user-defined training set.

2   THE VESTIBULO-OCULAR REFLEX

The vestibulo-ocular reflex (VOR) is an example of a sensorimotor system that requires adaptation to function correctly. The desired response of this system is a gain of -1.0 from head movements to eye movements (relative to the head), so that, as the head moves, the eyes remain fixed relative to the surroundings. Due to the feed-forward nature of the primary VOR pathways, some form of adaptation must be present to calibrate the gain of the response in infants and to maintain this calibration during growth, disease, and aging (Robinson, 1976).

Lisberger (1988) demonstrated variable gain of the VOR by fitting magnifying spectacles onto a monkey. The monkey moved about freely, allowing the VOR to learn the new relationship between head and eye movements. The monkey was then placed on a turntable, and its eye velocity was measured while head motion was generated. The eye-velocity response to head motion for three different lens magnifications is shown in Figure 1.

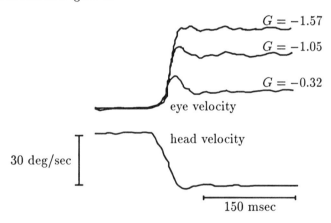

Figure 1: VOR data from Lisberger (1988). A monkey was fitted with magnifying spectacles and allowed to learn the gain needed for an accurate VOR. The monkey's head was then moved at a controlled velocity, and the eye velocity was measured. Three experiments were performed with spectacle magnifications of 0.25, 1.0, and 2.0. The corresponding eye velocities showed VOR gains G of -0.32, -1.05, and -1.57.

Lisberger has proposed a simple model for this adaptation that uses retinal-slip information from the visual system, along with the head-motion information from the vestibular system, to adapt the gain of the forward pathways in the VOR.

Figure 2 is a schematic diagram of the pathways subserving the VOR. There are two parallel VOR pathways from the vestibular system to the motor neurons that control eye movements (Snyder, 1988). One pathway consists of vestibular inputs, VOR interneurons, and motor neurons. This pathway has been shown to exhibit an unmodified gain of approximately -0.3. The second pathway consists of vestibular inputs, floccular target neurons (FTN), and motor neurons. This pathway is the site of the proposed gain adaptation.

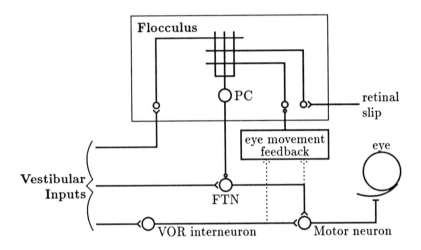

Figure 2: A schematic diagram of the VOR (Lisberger, 1988). Two pathways exist connecting the vestibular neurons to the motor neurons driving the eye muscles. The unmodified pathway connects via the VOR interneurons. The modified pathway (the proposed site of gain adaptation) connects via the floccular target neurons (FTN). Outputs from the Purkinje cells (PC) in the flocculus mediate gain adaptation at the FTNs.

Lisberger's hypothesis is that feedback from the visual system through the flocculus is used to facilitate the adaptation of the gain of the FTNs. Image slip on the retina indicates that the total VOR gain is not adjusted correctly. The relationship between the head motion and the image slip on the retina determines the direction in which the gain must be changed. For example, if the head is turning to the right and the retinal image slip is to the right, the eyes are turning too slowly and the gain should be increased. The direction of the gain change can be considered to be the sign of the product of head motion and retinal image slip.

3   THE ANALOG VLSI IMPLEMENTATION

We implemented a simplified version of Lisberger's VOR model using primarily subthreshold analog very large-scale integrated (VLSI) circuitry (Mead, 1989). We interpreted the Lisberger data to suggest that the gain of the modified pathway varies from zero to some fixed upper limit. This assumption gives a minimum VOR gain equal to the gain of the unmodified pathway, and a maximum VOR gain equal to the sum of the unmodified pathway gain and the maximum modified pathway gain. We designed circuitry for the unmodified pathway to give an overshoot response to a step function similar to that seen in Figure 1.

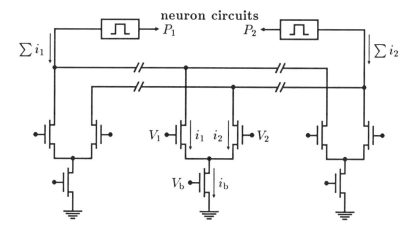

Figure 3: An analog VLSI sensorimotor framework. Each input circuit consists of a bias transistor and a differential pair. The voltage V_b sets a fixed current i_b through the bias transistor. This current is partitioned into currents i_1 and i_2 according to the differential voltage $V_1 - V_2$, and these currents are summed onto a pair of global wires. The global currents are used as inputs to two neuron circuits that convert the currents into pulse trains P_1 and P_2.

The VOR model was designed within the sensorimotor framework shown in Figure 3 (DeWeerth, 1987). The framework consists of a number of input circuits and two output circuits. Each input circuit consists of a bias transistor and a differential pair. The gain of the circuit is set by a fixed current through the bias transistor. This current is partitioned according to the differential input voltage into two currents that pass through the differential-pair transistors. The equations for these currents are

$$i_1 = i_b \frac{1}{1 + e^{V_2 - V_1}} \qquad i_2 = i_b \frac{1}{1 + e^{V_1 - V_2}}$$

The two currents are summed onto a pair of global wires. Each of these global currents is input to a neuron circuit (Mead, 1989) that converts the current linearly into the duty cycle of a pulse train. The pulse trains can be used to drive a pair of antagonistic actuators that can bidirectionally control the motion of a physical plant. We implement a system (such as the VOR) within this framework by augmenting the differential pairs with circuitry that computes the function needed for the particular application.

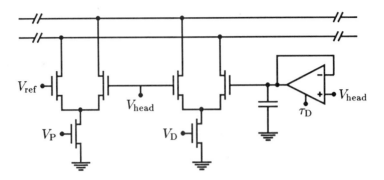

Figure 4: The VLSI implementation of the unmodified pathway. The left differential pair is used to convert proportionally the differential voltage representing head velocity ($V_{\text{head}} - V_{\text{ref}}$) into output currents. The right differential pair is used in conjunction with a first-order section to give output currents related to the derivative of the head velocity. The gains of the two differential pairs are set by the voltages V_{P} and V_{D}.

The unmodified pathway is implemented in the framework using two differential pairs (Figure 4). One of these circuits proportionally converts the head motion into output currents. This circuit generates a step in eye velocity when presented with a step in head velocity. The other differential pair is combined with a first-order section to generate output currents related to the derivative of the head motion. This circuit generates a broad impulse in eye velocity when presented with a step in head velocity. By setting the gains of the proportional and derivative circuits correctly, we can make the overall response of this pathway similar to that of the unmodified pathway seen when Lisberger's monkey was presented with a step in head velocity.

We implement the modified pathway within the framework using a single differential-pair circuit that generates output currents proportional to the head velocity (Figure 5). The system adapts the gain of this pathway by integrating an error signal with respect to time. The error signal is a current, which the circuitry computes by multiplying the retinal image slip and the head velocity. This error current is integrated onto a capacitor, and the voltage on the capacitor is then converted to a current that sets the gain of the modified pathway

4   EXPERIMENTAL METHOD AND RESULTS

To test our VOR circuitry, we designed a simple electrical model of the head and eye (Figure 6). The head motion is represented by a voltage that is supplied by a function generator. The oculomotor plant (the eye and corresponding muscles) is modeled by an RC circuit that integrates output pulses from the VOR circuitry into a voltage that represents eye velocity in head coordinates. We model the magnifying

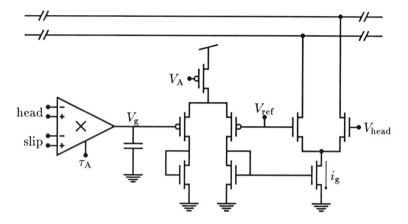

Figure 5: The VLSI implementation of the modified pathway. A differential pair is used to convert proportionally the differential voltage representing head velocity ($V_{\text{head}} - V_{\text{ref}}$) into output currents. Adaptive circuitry capacitively integrates the product of head velocity and retinal image slip as a voltage V_{g}. This voltage is converted to a current i_{g} that sets the gain of the differential pair. The voltage V_{A} sets the maximum gain of this pathway.

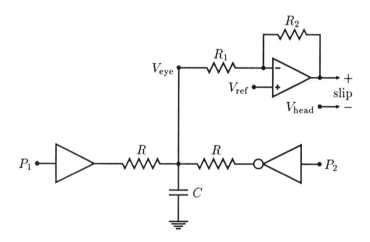

Figure 6: A simple model of the oculomotor plant. An RC circuit (bottom) integrates pulse trains P_1 and P_2 into a voltage V_{eye} that encodes eye velocity. The magnifying spectacles are modeled by an operational amplifier circuit (top), which has a magnification $m = R_2/R_1$. The retinal image slip is encoded by the difference between the output voltage of this circuit and the voltage V_{head} that encodes the head velocity.

spectacles using an operational amplifier circuit that multiplies the eye velocity by a gain before the velocity is used to compute the slip information. We compute the image slip by subtracting the head velocity from the magnified eye velocity.

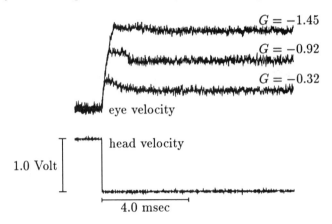

Figure 7: Experimental data from the VOR circuitry. The system was allowed to adapt to spectacle magnifications of 0.25, 1.0, and 2.0. After adaptation, the eye velocities showed corresponding VOR gains of −0.32, −0.92, and −1.45.

We performed an experiment to generate data to compare to the data measured by Lisberger (Figure 1). A head-velocity step was supplied by a function generator and was used as input to the VOR circuitry. The VOR outputs were then converted to an eye velocity by the model of the oculomotor plant. The proportional, derivative, and maximum adaptive gains were set to give a system response similar to that observed in the monkey. The system was allowed to adapt over a number of presentations of the input for each spectacle magnification. The resulting eye velocity data are displayed in Figure 7.

5   CONCLUSIONS AND FUTURE WORK

In this paper, we have presented an analog VLSI implementation of a model of a biological sensorimotor system. The system performs unsupervised learning using signals generated as the system interacts with its environment. This model can be compared to traditional adaptive control schemes (Åström, 1987) for performing similar tasks. In the future, we hope to extend the model presented here to incorporate more of the information known about the VOR.

We are currently designing and testing chips that use ultraviolet storage techniques for gain adaptation. These chips will allow us to achieve adaptive time constants of the same order as those found in biological systems (minutes to hours).

We are also combining our chips with a mechanical model of the head and eyes to give more accurate environmental feedback. We can acquire true image-slip data using a vision chip (Tanner, 1986) that computes global field motion.

Acknowledgments

We thank Steven Lisberger for his suggestions for improving our implementation of the VOR model. We would also like to thank Massimo Sivilotti, Michelle Mahowald, Michael Emerling, Nanette Boden, Richard Lyon, and Tobias Delbrück for their help during the writing of this paper.

References

K.J. Åström, Adaptive feedback control. *Proceedings of the IEEE*, 75:2:185–217, 1987.

S.P. DeWeerth, *An Analog VLSI Framework for Motor Control.* M.S. Thesis, Department of Computer Science, California Institute of Technology, Pasadena, CA, 1987.

S.G. Lisberger, The neural basis for learning simple motor skills. *Science*, 242:728–735, 1988.

C.A. Mead, **Analog VLSI and Neural Systems.** Addison-Wesley, Reading, MA, 1989.

D.A. Robinson, Adaptive gain control of vestibulo-ocular reflex by the cerebellum. *J. Neurophysiology*, 39:954–969, 1976.

L.H. Snyder and W.M. King, Vertical vestibuloocular reflex in cat: asymmetry and adaptation. *J. Neurophysiology*, 59:279–298, 1988.

J.E. Tanner. *Integrated Optical Motion Detection.* Ph.D. Thesis, Department of Computer Science, California Institute of Technology, S223:TR:86, Pasadena, CA, 1986.

Real-Time Computer Vision and Robotics Using Analog VLSI Circuits

Christof Koch   Wyeth Bair   John G. Harris   Timothy Horiuchi
Andrew Hsu   Jin Luo
Computation and Neural Systems Program
Caltech 216-76
Pasadena, CA 91125

ABSTRACT

The long-term goal of our laboratory is the development of analog resistive network-based VLSI implementations of early and intermediate vision algorithms. We demonstrate an experimental circuit for smoothing and segmenting noisy and sparse depth data using the resistive fuse and a 1-D edge-detection circuit for computing zero-crossings using two resistive grids with different space-constants. To demonstrate the robustness of our algorithms and of the fabricated analog CMOS VLSI chips, we are mounting these circuits onto small mobile vehicles operating in a real-time, laboratory environment.

1 INTRODUCTION

A large number of computer vision algorithms for finding intensity edges, computing motion, depth, and color, and recovering the 3-D shapes of objects have been developed within the framework of minimizing an associated "energy" functional. Such a variational formalism is attractive because it allows *a priori* constraints to be explicitly stated. The single most important constraint is that the physical processes underlying image formation, such as depth, orientation and surface reflectance, change slowly in space. For instance, the depths of neighboring points on a surface are usually very similar. Standard regularization algorithms embody this smoothness constraint and lead to quadratic variational functionals with a unique global minimum (Poggio, Torre, and Koch, 1985). These quadratic functionals

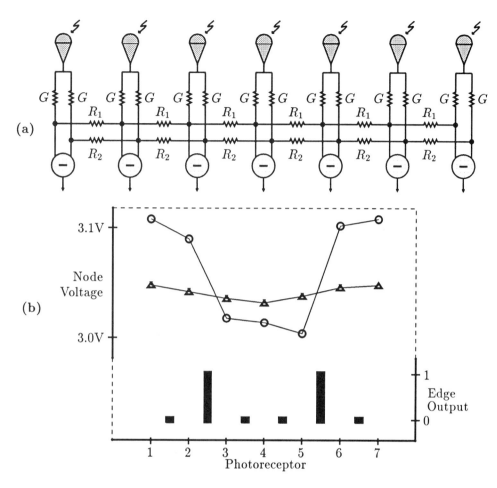

Figure 1: (a) shows the schematic of the zero-crossing chip. The phototransistors logarithmically map light intensity to voltages that are applied via a conductance G onto the nodes of two linear resistive networks. The network resistances R_1 and R_2 can be arbitrarily adjusted to achieve different space-constants. Transconductance amplifiers compute the difference of the smoothed network node voltages and report a current proportional to that difference. The sign of current then drives exclusive-or circuitry (not shown) between each pair of neighboring pixels. The final output is a binary signal indicating the positions of the zero-crossings. The linear network resistances have been implemented using Mead's saturating resistor circuit (Mead, 1989), and the vertical resistors are implemented with transconductance followers. (b) shows the measured response of a seven-pixel version of the chip to a bright background with a shadow cast across the middle three photoreceptors. The circles and triangles show the node voltages on the resistive networks with the smaller and larger space-constants, respectively. Edges are indicated by the binary output (bar chart at bottom) corresponding to the locations of zero-crossings.

can be mapped onto linear resistive networks, such that the stationary voltage distribution, corresponding to the state of least power dissipation, is equivalent to the solution of the variational functional (Horn, 1974; Poggio and Koch, 1985). Smoothness breaks down, however, at discontinuities caused by occlusions or differences in the physical processes underlying image formation (e.g., different surface reflectance properties). Detecting these discontinuities becomes crucial, not only because otherwise smoothness is incorrectly applied but also because the locations of discontinuities are often required for further image analysis and understanding. We describe two different approaches for finding discontinuities in early vision: (1) a 1-D edge-detection circuit for computing zero-crossings using two resistive grids with different space-constants, and (2) a 20 by 20 pixel circuit for smoothing and segmenting noisy and sparse depth data using the resistive fuse.

Finally, while successfully demonstrating a highly integrated circuit on a stationary laboratory bench under controlled conditions is already a tremendous success, this is not the environment in which we ultimately intend them to be used. The jump from a sterile, well-controlled, and predictable environment such as that of the laboratory bench to a noisy and physically demanding environment of a mobile robot can often spell out the true limits of a circuit's robustness. In order to demonstrate the robustness and real-time performance of these circuits, we have mounted two such chips onto small toy vehicles.

2   AN EDGE DETECTION CIRCUIT

The zero-crossings of the Laplacian of the Gaussian, $\nabla^2 G$, are often used for detecting edges. Marr and Hildreth (1980) discovered that the Mexican-hat shape of the $\nabla^2 G$ operator can be approximated by the difference of two Gaussians (DOG). In this spirit, we have built a chip that takes the difference of two resistive-network smoothings of photoreceptor input and finds the resulting zero-crossings. The Green's function of the resistive network, a decaying exponential, differs from the Gaussian, but simulations with digitized camera images have shown that the difference of exponentials (DOE) gives results nearly as good as the DOG. Furthermore, resistive nets have a natural implementation in silicon, while implementing the Gaussian is cumbersome.

The circuit, Figure 1a, uses two independent resistive networks to smooth the voltages supplied by logarithmic photoreceptors. The voltages on the two networks are subtracted and exclusive-or circuitry (not shown) is used to detect zero-crossings. In order to facilitate thresholding of edges, an additional current is computed at each node indicating the strength of the zero-crossing. This is particularly important for robust real-world performance where there will be many small (in magnitude of slope) zero-crossings due to noise. Figure 1b shows the measured response of a seven-pixel version of the chip to a bright background with a shadow cast across the middle three photoreceptors. Subtracting the two network voltage traces shown at the top, we find two zero-crossings, which the chip correctly identifies in the binary output shown at the bottom.

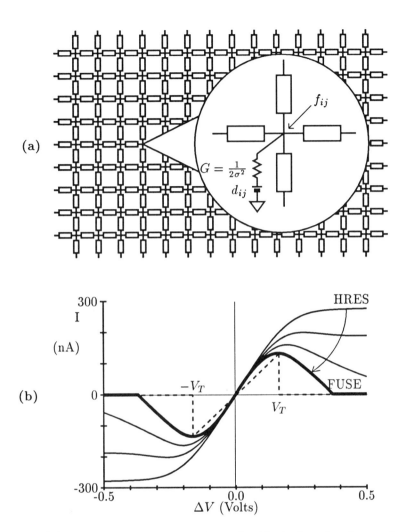

Figure 2: **(a)** Schematic diagram for the 20 by 20 pixel surface interpolation and smoothing chip. A rectangular mesh of resistive fuse elements (shown as rectangles) provide the smoothing and segmentation ability of the network. The data are given as battery values d_{ij} with the conductance G connecting the battery to the grid set to $G = 1/2\sigma^2$, where σ^2 is the variance of the additive Gaussian noise assumed to corrupt the data. **(b)** Measured current-voltage relationship for different settings of the resistive fuse. For a voltage of less than V_T across this two-terminal device, the circuit acts as a resistor with conductance λ. Above V_T, the current is either abruptly set to zero (binary fuse) or smoothly goes to zero (analog fuse). We can continuously vary the I-V curve from the hyperbolic tangent of Mead's saturating resistor (HRES) to that of an analog fuse (Fig. 2b), effectively implementing a continuation method for minimizing the non-convex functional. The I-V curve of a binary fuse is also illustrated.

3   A CIRCUIT FOR SMOOTHING AND SEGMENTING

Many researchers have extended regularization theory to include discontinuities. Let us consider the problem of interpolating noisy and sparse 1-D data (the 2-D generalization is straightforward), where the depth data d_i is given on a discrete grid. Associated with each lattice point is the value of the recovered surface f_i and a binary line discontinuity ℓ_i. When the surface is expected to be smooth (with a first-order, membrane-type stabilizer) except at isolated discontinuities, the functional to be minimized is given by:

$$J(f,\ell) = \lambda \sum_i (f_{i+1} - f_i)^2 (1 - \ell_i) + \frac{1}{2\sigma^2} \sum_i (d_i - f_i)^2 + \alpha \sum_i \ell_i \qquad (1)$$

where σ^2 is the variance of the additive Gaussian noise process assumed to corrupt the data d_i, and λ and α are free parameters. The first term implements the piecewise smooth constraint: if all variables, with the exception of f_i, f_{i+1}, and ℓ_i, are held fixed and $\lambda(f_{i+1} - f_i)^2 < \alpha$, it is "cheaper" to pay the price $\lambda(f_{i+1} - f_i)^2$ and set $\ell_i = 0$ than to pay the larger price α; if the gradient becomes too steep, $\ell_i = 1$, and the surface is segmented at that location. The second term, with the sum only including those locations i where data exist, forces the surface f to be close to the measured data d. How close depends on the estimated magnitude of the noise, in this case on σ^2. The final surface f is the one that best satisfies the conflicting demands of piecewise smoothness and fidelity on the measured data.

To minimize the 2-D generalization of eq. (1), we map the functional J onto the circuit shown in Fig. 2a such that the stationary voltage at every gridpoint then corresponds to f_{ij}. The cost functional J is interpreted as electrical co-content, the generalization of power for nonlinear networks. We designed a two-terminal nonlinear device, which we call a resistive fuse, to implement piecewise smoothness (Fig. 2b). If the magnitude of the voltage drop across the device is less than $V_T = (\alpha/\lambda)^{1/2}$, the fuse acts as a linear resistor with conductance λ. If V_T is exceeded, however, the fuse breaks and the current goes to zero. The operation of the fuse is fully reversible. We built a 20 by 20 pixel fuse network chip and show its segmentation and smoothing performance in Figure 3.

4   AUTONOMOUS VEHICLES

Our goal—beyond the design and fabrication of analog resistive-network chips—is to build mobile testbeds for the evaluation of chips as well as to provide a systems perspective on the usefulness of certain vision algorithms. Due to the small size and power requirements of these chips, it is possible to utilize the vast resource of commercially available toy vehicles. The advantages of toy cars over robotic vehicles built for research are their low cost, ease of modification, high power-to-weight ratio, availability, and inherent robustness to the real-world. Accordingly, we integrated two analog resistive-network chips designed and built in Mead's laboratory onto small toy cars controlled by a digital microprocessor (see Figure 4).

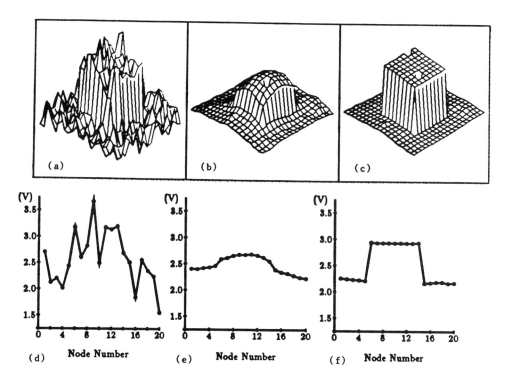

Figure 3: Experimental data from the fuse network chip. We use as input data a tower (corresponding to $d_{ij} = 3.0\ V$) rising from a plane (corresponding to 2.0 V) with superimposed Gaussian noise. (a) shows the input with the variance of the noise set to 0.2 V, (b) the voltage output using the fuse configured as a saturating resistance, and (c) the output when the fuse elements are activated. (d), (e), and (f) illustrate the same behavior along a horizontal slice across the chip for $\sigma^2 = 0.4\ V$. We used a hardware deterministic algorithm of varying the fuse I-V curve of the saturating resistor to that of the analog fuse (following the arrow in Fig. 2b) as well as increasing the conductance λ. This algorithm is closely related to other deterministic approximations based on continuation methods or a Mean Field Theory approach (Koch, Marroquin, and Yuille, 1986; Blake and Zisserman, 1987; Geiger and Girosi, 1989). Notice that the amplitude of the noise in the last case (40% of the amplitude of the voltage step) is so large that a single filtering step on the input (d) will fail to detect the tower. Cooperativity and hysteresis are required for optimal performance. Notice the "bad" pixel in the middle of the tower (in c). Its effect is localized, however, to a single element.

Figure 4: The vehicle in the foreground, facing right, utilizes the center-of-intensity chip for tracking light sources. The vehicle is being controlled by a MC68HC805B6, a micro-controller with on-board RAM, EEPROM, A/D converters, PWM (pulse width modulation) generators, and serial ports. The vehicle in the background utilizes the Silicon Retina for line/movement tracking. This vehicle has two retinas mounted (one facing forwards and one facing backwards) for the investigation of different steering options. The vehicle is controlled by a MC6802 microprocessor.

The first vehicle uses a center-of-intensity chip (DeWeerth, 1988) to follow bright spots of light. The chip uses a 200 x 200 pixel array of photoreceptors with circuitry along the edges to compute the mean, or median, of light intensity. The car can successfully track a flashlight mounted on a human-driven radio-controlled car at approximately 1.5 m/sec. The second vehicle utilizes the Silicon Retina (Mahowald and Mead, 1989) to track edges and movement. The first of two behaviors tracks a black line of tape laid down on the floor of the laboratory at a maximum speed of approximately 1 m/sec. The retina is operated in the "edge-enhancement" mode (i.e., computing a difference-of-Gaussians-like transform) to find any high-contrast edges in a one-dimensional scan across the field of view. The second behavior tracks movement (temporal derivative of the intensity) in two dimensions while "looking" down in front of the vehicle, thus acquiring crude, close-range, distance information. By dangling a small "bug-like" object in its field of view, the car maintains a constant distance from the movement, a behavior reminiscent of a curious puppy playing with an insect.

5   CONCLUSION

By studying analog VLSI circuits, we are finding methodologies for building fast, cheap, low-power vision hardware that detects and utilizes discontinuities. Using sensing strategies that simultaneously take advantage of a robot's mobility and our real-time vision processing will allow the system to perform actions that assist in the acquisition of information, thereby transgressing some of the limitations of the simple sensors. As argued convincingly by Brooks (1987), we believe we can build mobile machines able to explore their environments relying on a small number of special-purpose analog circuits and avoid large, general-purpose and power-hungry digital processors.

Acknowledgements

We thank Misha Mahowald and Steve DeWeerth for making their chips available to us for mounting on our vehicles. Without Carver Mead, none of this research would be possible. Our laboratory is supported by the Office of Naval Research, as well as by Rockwell International and Hughes Aircraft Corporation.

References

Blake, A. and Zisserman, A. (1987) *Visual Reconstruction*. MIT Press: Cambridge, MA.

Brooks, R. A. (1987) *Proc. Workshop in Foundations of AI*. Endicott House: Dedham, MA.

DeWeerth, S. and Mead, C.A. (1988) A two-dimensional visual tracking array. In: *Advanced Research in VLSI: Proceedings of the Fifth MIT Conference*, pp. 259–275. MIT Press: Cambridge, MA.

Geiger, D. and Girosi, F. (1989) Parallel and deterministic algorithms for MRFs: surface reconstruction and integration. AI Memo No. 1114, MIT, Cambridge, MA.

Geman, S. and Geman, D. (1984) Stochastic relaxation, Gibbs distribution and the Bayesian restoration of images. *IEEE Trans. Pattern Anal. Mach. Intell.* 6:721–741.

Harris, J. G., Koch, C., Luo, J. and Wyatt, J. (1989) Resistive fuses: analog hardware for detecting discontinuities in early vision. In: *Analog VLSI Implementations of Neural Systems*, Mead, C. and Ismail, M. (eds.), pp. 27–55. Kluwer: Norwell, MA.

Horn, B. K. P. (1974) Determining lightness from an image. *Computer Graphics and Image Processing* 3:277–299.

Koch, C., Marroquin, J., and Yuille, A. (1986) Analog "neuronal" networks in early vision. *Proc. Natl. Acad. Sci. USA* **83**:4263–4267.

Marr, D. and Hildreth, E.C. (1980) Theory of edge detection. *Proc. Roy. Soc. Lond. B* **207**:187–217.

Mead, C. and Mahowald, M.A., (1988) A silicon model of early visual processing. *Neural Networks* 1:91–97.

Mead, C. A. (1989) *Analog VLSI and Neural Systems*. Addison-Wesley: Reading, MA.

Poggio, T. and Koch, C. (1985) Ill-posed problems in early vision: from computational theory to analogue networks. *Proc. R. Soc. Lond. B* **226**:303–323.

Poggio, T., Torre, V., and Koch, C. (1985) Computational vision and regularization theory. *Nature* **317**:314–319.

A Reconfigurable Analog VLSI Neural Network Chip

Srinagesh Satyanarayana and Yannis Tsividis
Department of Electrical Engineering
and
Center for Telecommunications Research
Columbia University, New York, NY 10027, USA

Hans Peter Graf
AT&T
Bell Laboratories
Holmdel, NJ 07733
USA

ABSTRACT

1024 distributed-neuron synapses have been integrated in an active area of 6.1mm × 3.3mm using a 0.9μm, double-metal, single-poly, n-well CMOS technology. The distributed-neuron synapses are arranged in blocks of 16, which we call '4 × 4 tiles '. Switch matrices are interleaved between each of these tiles to provide programmability of interconnections. With a small area overhead (15 %), the 1024 units of the network can be rearranged in various configurations. Some of the possible configurations are, a 12-32-12 network, a 16-12-12-16 network, two 12-32 networks etc. (the numbers separated by dashes indicate the number of units per layer, including the input layer). Weights are stored in analog form on MOS capacitors. The synaptic weights are usable to a resolution of 1% of their full scale value. The limitation arises due to charge injection from the access switch and charge leakage. Other parameters like gain and shape of nonlinearity are also programmable.

Introduction

A wide variety of problems can be solved by using the neural network framework [1]. However each of these problems requires a different topology and weight set. At a much lower system level, the performance of the network can be improved by selecting suitable neuron gains and saturation levels. Hardware realizations of

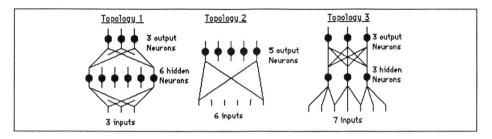

Figure 1: Reconfigurability

neural networks provide a fast means of solving the problem. We have chosen analog circuits to implement neural networks because they provide high synapse density and high computational speed. In order to provide a general purpose hardware for solving a wide variety of problems that can be mapped into the neural network framework, it is necessary to make the topology, weights and other neurosynaptic parameters programmable. Weight programmability has been extensively dealt in several implementations [2 - 9]. However features like programmable topology, neuron gains and saturation levels have not been addressed extensively. We have designed, fabricated and tested an analog VLSI neural network in which the topology, weights and neuron gains and saturations levels are all programmable.

Since the process of design, fabrication and testing is time-consuming and expensive, redesigning the hardware for each application is inefficient. Since the field of neural networks is still in its infancy, new solutions to problems are being searched for everyday. These involve modifying the topology [10] and finding the best weight set. In such an environment, a computational tool that is fully programmable is very desirable.

The Concept of Reconfigurability

We define *reconfigurability* as the ability to alter the topology (the number of layers, number of neurons per layer , interconnections from layer to layer and interconnections within a layer) of the network. The topology of a network does not describe the value of each synaptic weight. It only specifies the presence or absence of a synapse between two neurons (However in the special case of binary weight (0,1), defining the topology specifies the weight). The ability to alter the synaptic weight can be defined as weight programmability. Figure 1 illustrates reconfigurability, whereas Figure 2 shows how the weight value is realized in our implementation. The Voltage V_w across the capacitor represents the synaptic weight. Altering this voltage makes weight programmability possible.

Why is On-Chip Reconfigurability Important ?

Synapses, neurons and interconnections occupy real estate on a chip. Chip sizes are limited due to various factors like yield and cost. Hence only a limited number

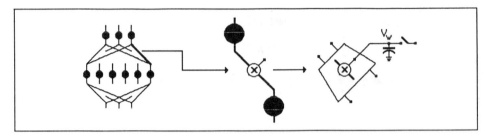

Figure 2: Weight programmability

of synapses can be integrated in a given chip area. Currently the most compact realizations (considering more than 6 bits of synaptic accuracy) permit us to integrate only a few thousand synapses per cm^2. In such a situation every zero-valued (inactive) synapse represents wasted area, and decreases the computational ability per unit area of the chip. If a fixed topology network is used for different problems, it will be underutilized as long as some synapses are set to zero value. On the other hand, if the network is reconfigurable, the limited resources on-chip can be reallocated to build networks with different topologies more efficiently. For example the network with topology-2 of Figure 1 requires 30 synapses. If the network was reconfigurable, we could utilize these synapses to build a two-layer network with 15 synapses in the first layer and 15 in the second layer. In a similar fashion we could also build the network with topology-3 which is a network with localized receptive fields.

The Distributed-Neuron Concept

In order to provide reconfigurability on-chip, we have developed a new cell called the distributed-neuron synapse [11]. In addition to making reconfiguration easy, it has other advantages like being modular hence making design easy, provides automatic gain scaling , avoids large current build-up at any point and makes possible a fault tolerant system.

Figure 3 shows a lumped neuron with N synaptic inputs. We call it 'lumped' because, the circuit that provides the nonlinear function is lumped into one block.

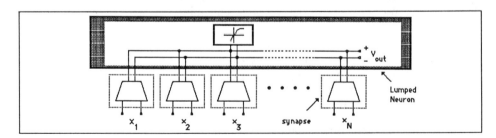

Figure 3: A lumped neuron with N synaptic inputs

The synapses are assumed to be voltage-to-current (transconductor) cells, and the neuron is assumed to be a current-to-voltage cell. Summation is achieved through addition of the synapse output currents in the parallel connection.

Figure 4 shows the equivalent distributed-neuron with N synaptic inputs. It is called 'distributed' because the circuit that functions as the neuron, is split into 'N' parts. One of these parts is integrated with each synapse. This new block (that contains a a synapse and a fraction of the neuron) is called the 'distributed-neuron synapse'. Details of the distributed-neuron concept are described in [11]. It has to be noted that the splitting of the neuron to form the distributed-neuron synapse is done at the summation point where the computation is linear. Hence the two realizations of the neuron are computationally equivalent. However, the distributed-neuron implementation offers a number of advantages, as is now explained.

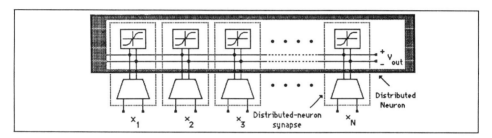

Figure 4: A distributed-neuron with N synaptic inputs

Modularity of the design

As is obvious from Figure 4, the task of building a complete network involves designing one single distributed-neuron synapse module and interconnecting several of them to form the whole system. Though at a circuit level, a fraction of the neuron has to be integrated with each synapse, the system level design is simplified due to the modularity.

Automatic gain normalization

In the distributed-neuron, each unit of the neuron serves as a load to the output of a synapse. As the number of synapses at the input of a neuron increases, the number of neuron elements also increases by the same number. The neuron output is given by:

$$y_j = f\{\frac{1}{N}\sum_{i=1}^{N} w_{ij}x_i - \Theta j\} \qquad (1)$$

Where y_j is the output of the jth neuron, w_{ij} is the weight from the ith synaptic input x_i and Θ_j is the threshold, implemented by connecting in parallel an appropriate number of distributed-neuron synapses with fixed inputs. Assume for the

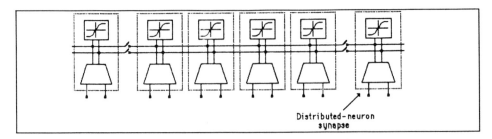

Distributed-neuron
synapse

Figure 5: Switches used for reconfiguration in the distributed-neuron implementation.

moment that all the inputs x_i are at a maximum possible value. Then it is easily seen that y_j is independent of N. This is the manifestation of the automatic gain normalization that is inherent to the idea of distributed-neuron synapses.

Ease of reconfiguration

In a distributed-neuron implementation, reconfiguration involves interconnecting a set of distributed-neuron synapse modules (Figure 5). A neuron of the right size gets formed when the outputs of the required number of synapses are connected. In a lumped neuron implementation, reconfiguration involves interconnecting a set of synapses with a set of neurons. This involves more wiring, switches and logic control blocks.

Avoiding large current build-up in the neuron

In our implementation the synaptic outputs are currents. These currents are summed by Kirchoffs current law and sent to the neuron. Since the neuron is distributed, the total current is divided into N equal parts, where N is the number of distributed-neuron synapses. One of these part flows through each unit of the distributed neuron as illustrated in Figure 4. This obviates the need for large current summation wires and avoids other problems associated with large currents at any single point.

Fault tolerance

On a VLSI chip defects are commonly seen. Some of these defects can short wires, hence corrupting the signals that are carried on them. Defects can also render some synapses and neurons defective. In our implementation, we have integrated switches in-between groups of distributed-neuron synapses (which we call 'tiles') to make the chip reconfigurable (Figure 6). This makes each tile of the chip externally testable. The defective sections of the chip can be isolated and the remaining synapses can thus be reconfigured into another topology as shown in Figure 6.

Circuit Description of the Distributed-Neuron Synapse

Figure 7 shows a distributed-neuron synapse constructed around a differential-input, differential-output transconductance multiplier. A weight converter is used to con-

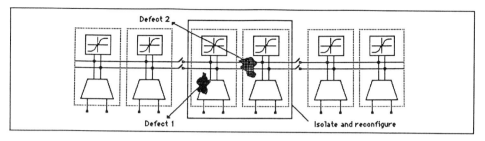

Figure 6: Improved fault tolerance in the distributed-neuron system

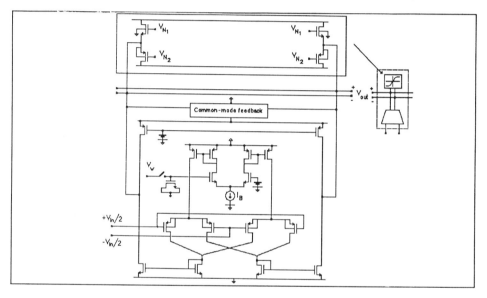

Figure 7: The distributed-neuron synapse circuit

vert the single-ended weight controlling voltage V_w into a set of differential currents that serve as the bias currents of the multiplier. The weight is stored on a MOS capacitor.

The differential nature of the circuit offers several advantages like improved rejection of power supply noise and linearity of multiplication. Common-mode feedback is provided at the output of the synapse. An amplitude limiter that is operational only when the weighted sum exceeds a certain range serves as the distributed-neuron part. The saturation levels of the neuron can be programmed by adjusting V_{N_1} and V_{N_2}. Gains can be set by adjusting the bias current I_B and/or a load (not shown). The measured synapse characteristics are shown in Figure 8 .

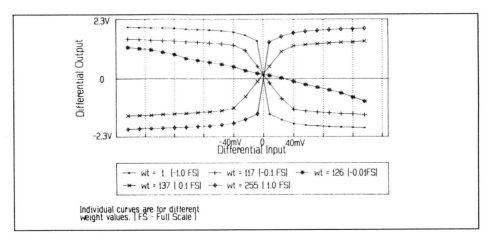

Figure 8: Measured characteristics of the distributed-neuron synapse

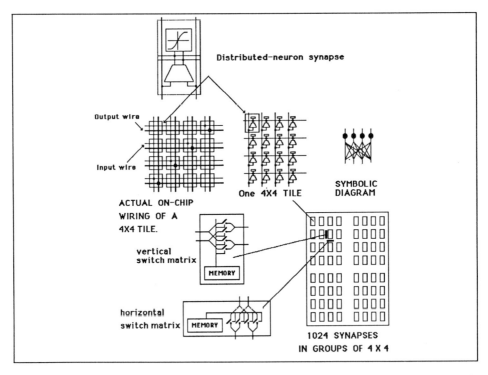

Figure 9: Organization of the distributed-neurons and switches on chip

Organization of the Chip

Figure 9 shows how the distributed-neuron synapses are arranged on-chip. 16 distributed-neuron synapses have been arranged in a 4 × 4 crossbar fashion to form a 4-input–4-output network. We call this a '4 × 4 tile'. Input and output wires are available on all four sides of the tile. This makes interconnections to adjacent blocks easy. Vertical and horizontal switch matrices are interleaved in-between the tiles to select one of the various possible modes of interconnections. These modes can be configured by setting the 4 bits of memory in each switch matrix. 1024 distributed-neuron synapses have been integrated in an active area of 6.1mm × 3.3mm using a 0.9μm, double-metal, single-poly, n-well CMOS technology.

The Weight Update/Refresh Scheme

Weights are stored in analog form on a MOS capacitor. A semi-serial-parallel weight update scheme has been built. 8 pins of the chip are used to distribute the weights to the 1024 capacitors on the chip. Each pin can refresh 128 capacitors contained in a row of tiles. The capacitors in each tile-row are selected one at a time by a decoder. The maximum refresh speed depends on the time needed to charge up the weight storage capacitor and the parasitic capacitances. One complete refresh of all weights on the chip is possible in about 130 μ seconds. However one could refresh at a much slower rate, the lower limit of which is decided by the charge leakage. For a 7-bit precision in the weight at room temperature, a refresh rate in the order of milliseconds should be adequate. Charge injection due to the parasitic capacitances has been kept low by using very small switches. In the first version of the chip, only the distributed-neuron synapses, the switches used for reconfiguration, and the topology memory have been integrated. Weights are stored outside the chip in digital form in a 1K × 8 RAM. The contents of the RAM are continuously read and converted into analog form using a bank of off-chip D/A converters. An advantage of our scheme is that the forward-pass operation is not interrupted by the weight refresh mechanism. A fast weight update scheme of the type used here is very desirable while executing learning algorithms at a high speed. The complete block diagram of the weight refresh/update and testing scheme is shown in Figure 10.

Configuration Examples

In Figure 11 we show some of the network topologies that can be configured with the resources available on the chip. The left-hand side of the figure shows the actual wiring on the chip and the right-hand side shows the symbolic diagram of the network configuration. The darkened tiles have been used for implementing the thresholds. Several other topologies like feedback networks and networks with localized receptive fields can be configured with this chip.

The complete system

Figure 10 shows how the neural network chip fits into a complete system that is necessary for its use and testing. The 'Config-EPROM' stores the bit pattern corre-

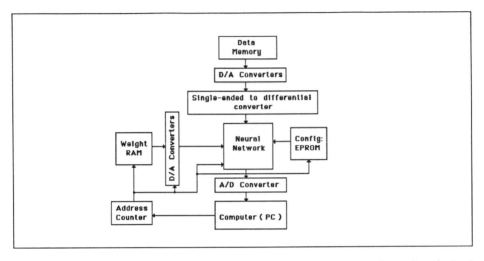

Figure 10: Block diagram of the system for reconfiguration, weight update/refresh and testing.

sponding to the desired topology. This bit pattern is down-loaded into the memory cells of the switch matrices before the start of computation. Input vectors are read out from the 'Data memory' and converted into analog form by D/A converters. The outputs of the D/A converters are further transformed into differential signals and then fed into the chip. The chip delivers differential outputs which are converted into digital form using an A/D converter and stored in a computer for further analysis.

The delay in processing one layer with N inputs driving another layer with an equal number of inputs is typically 1μsec. Hence a 12-32-12 network should take about 6μsecs for one forward-pass operation. However external loads can slow down the computation considerably. This problem can be solved by increasing the bias currents or/and using pad buffers. Each block on the chip has been tested and has been found to function as expected. Tests of the complete chip in a variety of neural network configurations are being planned.

Conclusions

We have designed a reconfigurable array of 1024 distributed-neuron synapses that can be configured into several different types of neural networks. The distributed-neuron concept that is integral to this chip offers advantages in terms of modularity and automatic gain normalization . The chip can be cascaded with several other chips of the same type to build larger systems.

References

[1] Richard Lippmann. Pattern classification using neural networks. *IEEE Communications Magazine*, 27(11):47–64, November 1989.

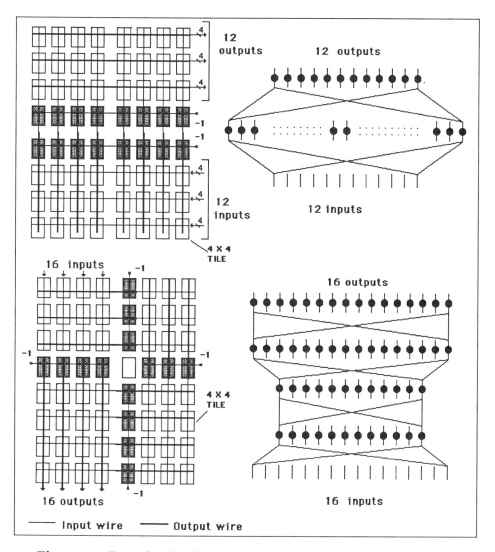

Figure 11: Reconfiguring the network to produce two different topologies

[2] Y. Tsividis and S. Satyanarayana. Analogue circuits for variable-synapse electronic neural networks. *Electronics Letters*, 23(24):1313–1314, November 1987.

[3] Y. Tsividis and D. Anastassiou. Switched-capacitor neural networks. *Electronics Letters*, 23(18):958–959, August 1987.

[4] Paul Mueller et al. *A Programmable Analog Neural Computer and Simulator*, volume 1 of *Advances in Neural Information Processing systems*, pages 712–719. Morgan Kaufmann Publishers, 1989.

[5] D. B. Schwartz, R. E. Howard, and W. E. Hubbard. *Adaptive Neural Networks Using MOS Charge Storage*, volume 1 of *Advances in Neural Information Processing systems*, pages 761–768. Morgan Kaufmann Publishers, 1989.

[6] J. R. Mann and S. Gilbert. *An Analog Self-Organizing Neural Network Chip*, volume 1 of *Advances in Neural Information Processing systems*, pages 739–747. Morgan Kaufmann Publishers, 1989.

[7] Mark Holler, Simon Tam, Hernan Castro, and Ronald Benson. An electrically trainable artificial neural network etann with 10240 'floating gate' synapses. In *IJCNN International Joint Conference on Neural Networks*, volume 2, pages 191–196. International Neural Network Society (INNS) and Institue of Electrical and Electronic Engineers (IEEE), 1989.

[8] S. Eberhardt, T. Duong, and A. Thakoor. Design of parallel hardware neural network systems from custom analog vlsi 'building block' chips. In *IJCNN International Joint Conference on Neural Networks*, volume 2, pages 191–196. International Neural Network Society (INNS) and Institue of Electrical and Electronic Engineers (IEEE), 1989.

[9] F. J. Kub, I. A. Mack, K. K. Moon, C. Yao, and J. Modola. Programmable analog synapses for microelectronic neural networks using a hybrid digital-analog approach. In *IEEE International Conference on Neural Networks, San Diego*, 1988.

[10] Y. Le Cun et al. Handwritten digit recognition: Application of neural network chips and automatic learning. *IEEE Communications Magazine*, 27(11):41–46, November 1989.

[11] S. Satyanarayana, Y. Tsividis, and H. P. Graf. Analogue neural networks with distributed neurons. *Electronics Letters*, 25(5):302–304, March 1989.

Digital-Analog Hybrid Synapse Chips for Electronic Neural Networks

A. Moopenn, T. Duong, and A.P. Thakoor
Center for Space Microelectronics Technology
Jet Propulsion Laboratory/California Institute of Technology
Pasadena, CA 91109

ABSTRACT

Cascadable, CMOS synapse chips containing a cross-bar array of 32x32 (1024) programmable synapses have been fabricated as "building blocks" for fully parallel implementation of neural networks. The synapses are based on a hybrid digital-analog design which utilizes on-chip 7-bit data latches to store quantized weights and two-quadrant multiplying DAC's to compute weighted outputs. The synapses exhibit 6-bit resolution and excellent monotonicity and consistency in their transfer characteristics. A 64-neuron hardware incorporating four synapse chips has been fabricated to investigate the performance of feedback networks in optimization problem solving. In this study, a 7x7, one-to-one assignment net and the Hopfield-Tank 8-city traveling salesman problem net have been implemented in the hardware. The network's ability to obtain optimum or near optimum solutions in real time has been demonstrated.

1 INTRODUCTION

A large number of electrically modifiable synapses is often required for fully parallel analog neural network hardware. Electronic synapses based on CMOS, EEPROM, as well as thin film technologies are actively being developed [1-5]. One preferred approach is based on a hybrid digital-analog design which can easily be implemented in CMOS with simple interface and analog circuitry. The hybrid design utilizes digital memories to store the synaptic weights and digital-to-analog converters to perform analog multiplication. A variety of synaptic chips based on such hybrid designs have been developed and used as "building blocks" in larger neural network hardware systems fabricated at JPL.

In this paper, the design and operational characteristics of the hybrid synapse chips are described. The development of a 64-neuron hardware incorporating several of the synapse chips is also discussed. Finally, a hardware implementation of two global optimization nets, namely, the one-to-one assignment optimization net and the Hopfield-Tank traveling salesman net [6], and their performance based on our 64-neuron hardware are discussed.

2 CHIP DESIGN AND ELECTRICAL CHARACTERISTICS

The basic design and operational characteristics of the hybrid digital analog synapse chips are described in this section. A simplified block diagram of the chips is shown in Fig. 1. The chips consist of an address/data de-multiplexer, row and column address decoders, 64 analog input/output lines, and 1024 synapse cells arranged in the form of a 32x32 cross-bar matrix. The synapse cells along the i-th row have a common output, x_i, and similarly, synapses along the j-th column have a common input, y_j. The synapse input/output lines are brought off-chip for multi-chip expansion to a larger synaptic matrix. The synapse cell, based on a hybrid digital analog design, essentially consists of a 7-bit static latch and a 7-bit, two-quadrant multiplying DAC.

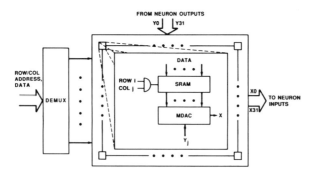

Figure 1: Simplified block diagram of hybrid 32x32x7-bit synapse chip.

A circuit diagram of the 7-bit DAC is shown in Fig. 2. The DAC consists of a current input circuit, a set of binary weighted current sources, and a current steering circuit. The current in the input circuit is mirrored by the binary-weighted current sources for all synapses along a column. In one version of the chips, a single long-channel FET is used to convert the synapse input voltage to a current. In addition, the gate of the transistor is connected internally to the gates of other long channel transistors. This common gate is accessible off-chip and provides a means for controlling the overall "gain" of the synapses in the chip. In a second chip version, an external resistor is employed to perform input voltage to current conversion when a high linearity in the synapse transfer characteristics is desired.

Hybrid 32x32x7-bit synapse chips with and without long channel transistors were fabricated through MOSIS using a 2-micron, n-well CMOS process. Typical measured synapse response (I-V) curves from these chips are shown in Figs. 3a and 3b for weight values of 0, +/- 1, 3, 7, 15, 31, and 63. The curves in Fig. 3a were obtained for a synapse incorporating an on-chip long-channel FET with a gate bias of 5 volts. The non-linear synapse response is evident and can be seen to be similar to that of a "threshold" current source. The non-linear behavior is mainly attributed to the nonlinear drain characteristics of the long channel transistor. It should be pointed out that synapses with such characteristics are especially suited for neural networks with neurons operating in the high gain limit, in which case, the nonlinearity may even be desirable. The set of curves in Fig. 3b were obtained using an external 10-megaohm resistor for the V-I conversion. For input voltages greater than about twice the transistor's threshold voltage (~ 0.8 v), the synapse's current output is a highly linear function of the input voltage. The linear characteristics achieved with the use of external resistors would be applicable in feedforward nets with learning capabilities.

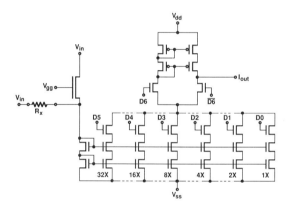

Figure 2: Circuit diagram of 7-bit multiplying DAC.

Figure 4 shows the measured output of the synapse as the weight is incremented from -60 to +60. The synapse exhibits excellent monotonicity and step size consistency. Based on a random sampling of synapses from several chips, the step size standard deviation due to mismatched transistor characteristics is typically less than 25 percent.

3   64-NEURON HARDWARE

The hybrid synapse chips are ideally suited for hardware implementation of feedback neural networks for combinatorial global optimization problem solving or associative recall where the synaptic weights are known a priori. For example, in a Hopfield-type feedback net [7], the weights can be calculated directly from a set of cost parameters or a set of stored vectors. The desired weights are quantized and downloaded into the memories of the synapse chips. On the other hand, in supervised learning applications, learning can be performed off-line, taking into consideration the operating characteristics of the synapses, and the new updated weights are simply reprogrammed into the synaptic hardware during each training cycle.

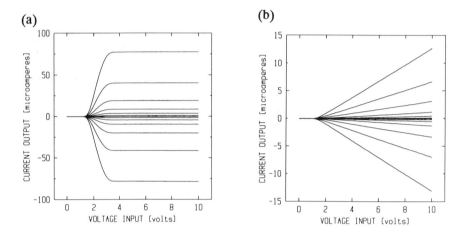

Figure 3: Transfer characteristics of a 7-bit synapse for weight values of 0, +/- 1, 3, 7, 15, 31, 63, (a) with long channel transistors for voltage to current conversion (V_{gg}= 5.0 volts) and (b) with external 10 mega-ohm resistor.

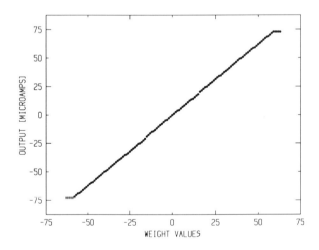

Figure 4: Synapse output as weight value is incremented from -60 to +60. (V_{gg}=V_{in}= 5.0 volts)

A 64-neuron breadboard system incorporating several of the hybrid synapse chips has been fabricated to demonstrate the utility of these building block chips, and to investigate the dynamical properties, global optimization problem solving abilities, and application potential of neural networks. The system consists of an array of 64 discrete neurons and four hybrid synapse chips connected to form a 64x64 crossbar synapse matrix. Each neuron is an operational-amplifier operating as a current summing amplifier. A circuit model of a neuron with some synapses is shown in Fig. 5. The system dynamical equations are given by:

$$\tau_f \, dV_i/dt \; = \; \Sigma \, T_{ij} \, V_j \, - \, V_i \, + \, R_f \, I_i,$$

where V_i is the output of the neuron i, T_{ij} is the synaptic weight from neuron j to neuron i, R_f and C_f are the feedback resistance and capacitance of the neuron, $\tau_f = R_f \, C_f$, and I_i is the external input current. For our system, R_f was about 50 kilo-ohms, and C_f was about 10 pF, a value large enough to ensure stability against oscillations. The system was interfaced to a microcomputer which allows downloading of the synaptic weight data and analog readout of the neuron states.

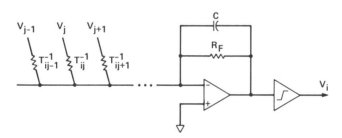

Figure 5: Electronic circuit model of neuron and synapses.

4 GLOBAL OPTIMIZATION NEURAL NETS

Two combinatorial global optimization problems, namely, the one-to-one assignment problem and the traveling salesman problem, were selected for our neural net hardware implementation study. Of particular interest is the performance of the optimization network in terms of the quality and speed of solutions in light of hardware limitations.

In the one-to-one assignment problem, given two sets of N elements and a cost assignment matrix, the objective is to assign each element in one set to an element in the second set so as to minimize the total assignment cost. In our neural net implementation, the network is a Hopfield-type feedback net consisting of an NxN array of assignment neurons. In this representation, a permissible set of one-to-one assignments corresponds to a permutation matrix. Thus, lateral inhibition between assignment neurons is employed to ensure that there is only one active neuron in each row and in each column of the neuron array. To force the network to favor assignment sets with low total assignment cost, each assignment neuron is also given an analog prompt, that is, a fixed analog excitation proportional to a positive constant minus its assignment cost.

An 8-city Hopfield-Tank TSP net was implemented in the 64-neuron hardware. Convergence statistics were similarly obtained from 100 randomly generated 8-city positions. The network was observed to give good solutions using a large synapse gain (common gate bias= 7 volts) and an annealing time of about one neuron time constant (~ 50 usec). As shown in Fig. 6b, the TSP net found tours which were in the best 6%. It gave the best tours in 11% of the cases and the first to third best tours in 31% of the cases. Although these results are quite good, the performance of the TSP net compares less favorably with the assignment net. This can be expected due to the increased complexity of the TSP net. Furthermore, since the initial state is arbitrary, the TSP net is more likely to settle into a local minimum before reaching the global minimum. On the other hand, in the assignment net, the analog prompt helps to establish an initial state which is close to the global minimum, thereby increasing its likelihood of converging to the optimum solution.

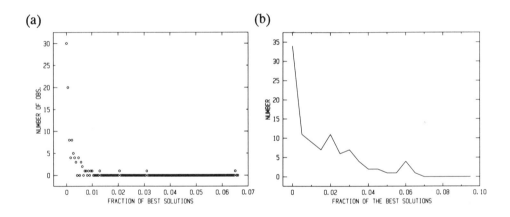

Figure 6: Performance statistics for (a) 7x7 assignment problem and (b) 8-city traveling salesman problem.

5 CONCLUSIONS

CMOS synapse chips based on a hybrid analog-digital design are ideally suited as building blocks for the development of fully parallel and analog neural net hardware. The chips described in this paper feature 1024 synapses arranged in a 32x32 cross-bar matrix with 120 programmable weight levels for each synapse. Although limited by the process variation in the chip fabrication, a 6-bit weight resolution is achieved with our design. A 64-neuron hardware incorporating several of the synapse chips is fabricated to investigate the performance of feedback networks in optimization problem solving. The ability of such networks to provide optimum or near optimum solutions to the one-to-one assignment problem and the traveling salesman problem is demonstrated in hardware. The neural hardware is capable of providing real time solutions with settling times in the 50-500 usec In an energy function description, all valid assignment sets correspond to energy minima of equal depth located at corners of the NxN dimensional hypercube (in the large neuron gain limit). The analog prompt term in the energy function has the effect of "tilting" the energy surface toward the hypercube corners with low total assignment cost. Thus, the assignment net may be described as a first-order global optimization net because the analog cost parameters appear only in the linear term of the energy function, i.e., the analog information simply appears as fixed biases and the interaction between neurons is of a binary nature. Since the energy surface contains a large number of local energy minima ($\sim$ N!) there is the strong possibility that the network will get trapped in a local minimum, depending on its initial state. Simulated annealing can be used to reduce this likelihood. One approach is to start with very low neuron gain, and increasing it slowly as the network evolves to a stable state. An alternative but similar approach which can easily be implemented with the current hybrid synapse chips is to gradually increase the synapse gain.

A 7x7 one-to-one assignment problem was implemented in the 64-neuron hardware to investigate the performance of the assignment optimization net. An additional neuron was used to provide the analog biases (quantized to 6 bits) to the assignment neurons. Convergence statistics were obtained from 100 randomly generated cost assignment matrices. For each cost matrix, the synapse gain and annealing time were optimized and the solution obtained by the hardware was recorded. The network generally performed well with a large synapse gain (common gate bias of 7 volts) and an annealing time of about 10 neuron time constants ($\sim$ 500 usec). The unusually large anneal time observed emphasizes the importance of suppressing the quadratic energy term while maintaining the analog prompt in the initial course of the network's state trajectory. Solution distributions for each cost matrix were also obtained from a computer search for the purpose of rating the hardware solutions. The performance of the assignment net is summarized in Fig. 6. In all cases, the network obtained solutions which were in the best 1%. Moreover, the best solutions were obtained in 40% of the cases, and the first, second, third best in 75% of the cases. These results are very encouraging in spite of the limited resolution of the analog biases and the fact that the analog biases also vary in time with the synapse gain.

The Hopfield-Tank's traveling salesman problem (TSP) network [6] was also investigated in the 64-neuron hardware. In this implementation, the analog cost information (i.e., the inter-city distances) is encoded in the connection strength of the synapses. Lateral inhibition is provided via binary synapses to ensure a valid city tour. However, the intercity distance provides additional interaction between

neurons via excitatory synapses with strength proportional to a positive constant minus the distance. Thus the TSP net, considerably more complex than the assignment net, may be described as a second order global optimization net.
range, which can be further reduced to 1-10 usec with the incorporation of on-chip neurons.

Acknowledgements

The work described in this paper was performed by the Center for Space Microelectronics Technology, Jet Propulsion Laboratory, California Institute of Technology, and was sponsored in part by the Joint Tactical Fusion Program Office and the Defense Advanced Research Projects Agency, through an agreement with the National Aeronautics and Space Administration. The authors thank John Lambe and Assad Abidi for many useful discussions, and Tim Shaw for his valuable assistance in the chip-layout design.

References

1.   S. Eberhardt, T. Duong, and A. Thakoor, "A VLSI Analog Synapse 'Building Block' Chip for Hardware Neural Network Implementations," Proc. IEEE 3rd Annual Parallel Processing Symp., Fullerton, ed. L.H. Canter, vol. 1, pp. 257-267, Mar. 29-31, 1989.

2.   A. Moopenn, A.P. Moopenn, and T. Duong, "Digital-Analog-Hybrid Neural Simulator: A Design Aid for Custom VLSI Neurochips," Proc. SPIE Conf. High Speed Computing, Los Angeles, ed. Keith Bromley, vol. 1058, pp. 147-157, Jan. 17-18, 1989.

3.   M. Holler, S. Tam, H. Castro, R. Benson, "An Electrically Trainable Artificial Neural Network (ETANN) with 10240 'Floating Gate' Synapses," Proc. IJCNN, Wash. D.C., vol. 2, pp. 191-196, June 18-22, 1989.

4.   A.P. Thakoor, A. Moopenn, J. Lambe, and S.K. Khanna, "Electronic Hardware Implementations of Neural Networks," Appl. Optics, vol. 26, no. 23, 1987, pp. 5085-5092.

5.   S. Thakoor, A. Moopenn, T. Daud, and A.P. Thakoor, "Solid State Thin Film Memistor for Electronic Neural Networks," J. Appl. Phys. 1990 (in press).

6.   J.J. Hopfield and D.W. Tank, "Neural Computation of Decisions in Optimization Problems," Biol. Cybern., vol. 52, pp. 141-152, 1985.

7.   J.J. Hopfield, "Neurons with Graded Response Have Collective Computational Properties Like Those of Two-State Neurons," Proc. Nat'l Acad. Sci., vol. 81, 1984, pp. 3088-3092.

Analog Circuits for Constrained Optimization

John C. Platt [1]
Computer Science Department, 256-80
California Institute of Technology
Pasadena, CA 91125

ABSTRACT

This paper explores whether analog circuitry can adequately perform constrained optimization. Constrained optimization circuits are designed using the differential multiplier method. These circuits fulfill time-varying constraints correctly. Example circuits include a quadratic programming circuit and a constrained flip-flop.

1   INTRODUCTION

Converting perceptual and cognitive tasks into constrained optimization problems is a useful way of generating neural networks to solve those tasks. Researchers have used constrained optimization networks to solve the traveling salesman problem [Durbin, 1987] [Hopfield, 1985], to perform object recognition [Gindi, 1988], and to decode error-correcting codes [Platt, 1986].

Implementing constrained optimization in analog VLSI is advantageous, because an analog VLSI chip can solve a large number of differential equations in parallel [Mead, 1989]. However, analog circuits only approximate the desired differential equations. Therefore, we have built test circuits to determine whether analog circuits can fulfill user-specified constraints.

2   THE DIFFERENTIAL MULTIPLIER METHOD

The differential multiplier method (DMM) is a method for creating differential equations that perform constrained optimization. The DMM was originally proposed by [Arrow, 1958] as an economic model. It was used as a neural network by [Platt, 1987].

---

[1]   Current address: Synaptics, 2860 Zanker Road, Suite 105, San Jose, CA 95134

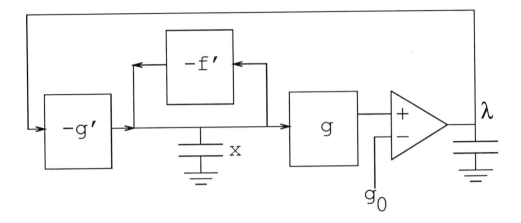

Figure 1. The architecture of the DMM. The x capacitor in the figure represents the x_i neurons in the network. The $-f'$ box computes the current needed for the neurons to minimize f. The rest of the circuitry causes the network to fulfill the constraint $g(\vec{x}) = 0$.

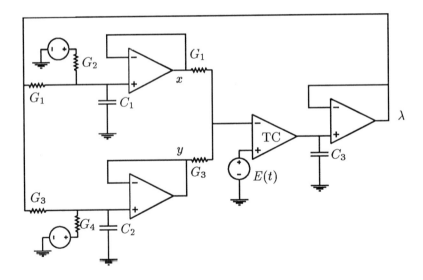

Figure 2. A circuit that implements quadratic programming. x, y, and λ are voltages. "TC" refers to a transconductance amplifier.

A constrained optimization problem is find a $\vec{x}$ such that $f(\vec{x})$ is minimized subject to a constraint $g(\vec{x}) = 0$. In order to find a constrained minimum, the DMM finds the critical points $(\vec{x}, \lambda)$ of the Lagrangian

$$\mathcal{E} = f(\vec{x}) + \lambda g(\vec{x}), \tag{1}$$

by performing gradient *descent* on the variables $\vec{x}$ and gradient *ascent* on the Lagrange multiplier λ:

$$\begin{aligned}
\frac{dx_i}{dt} &= -\frac{\partial \mathcal{E}}{\partial x_i} = -\frac{\partial f}{\partial x_i} - \lambda \frac{\partial g}{\partial x_i}, \\
\frac{d\lambda}{dt} &= +\frac{\partial \mathcal{E}}{\partial \lambda} = g(\vec{x}).
\end{aligned} \tag{2}$$

The DMM can be thought of as a neural network which performs gradient descent on a function $f(\vec{x})$, plus feedback circuitry to find the λ that causes the neural network output to fulfill the constraint $g(\vec{x}) = 0$ (see figure 1).

The gradient ascent on the λ is necessary for stability. The stability can be examined by combining the two equations (2) to yield a set of second-order differential equations

$$\frac{d^2 x_i}{dt^2} + \sum_j \left(\frac{\partial^2 f}{\partial x_i \partial x_j} + \lambda \frac{\partial^2 g}{\partial x_i \partial x_j} \right) \frac{dx_j}{dt} + g \frac{\partial g}{\partial x_i} = 0, \tag{3}$$

which is analogous to the equations that govern a spring-mass-damping system. The differential equations (3) converge to the constrained minima if the damping matrix

$$M = \frac{\partial^2 f}{\partial x_i \partial x_j} + \lambda \frac{\partial^2 g}{\partial x_i \partial x_j} \tag{4}$$

is positive definite.

The DMM can be extended to satisfy multiple simultaneous constraints. The stability of the DMM can also be improved. See [Platt, 1987] for more details.

3   QUADRATIC PROGRAMMING CIRCUIT

This section describes a circuit that solves a specific quadratic programming problem for two variables. A quadratic programming circuit is interesting, because the basic differential multiplier method is guaranteed to find the constrained minimum. Also, quadratic programming is useful: it is frequently a sub-problem in a more complex task. A method of solving general nonlinear constrained optimization is sequential quadratic programming [Gill, 1981].

We build a circuit to solve a time-dependent quadratic programming problem for two variables:

$$\min A(x - x_0)^2 + B(y - y_0)^2, \tag{5}$$

subject to the constraint

$$Cx + Dy + E(t) = 0. \tag{6}$$

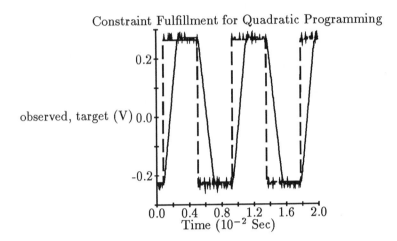

Constraint Fulfillment for Quadratic Programming

Figure 3. Plot of two input voltages of transconductance amplifier. The dashed line is the externally applied voltage $E(t)$. The solid line is the circuit's solution of $-Cx - Dy$. The constraint depends on time: the voltage $E(t)$ is a square wave. The linear constraint is fulfilled when the two voltages are the same. When $E(t)$ changes suddenly, the circuit changes $-Cx - Dy$ to compensate. The unusually shaped noise is caused by digitization by the oscilloscope.

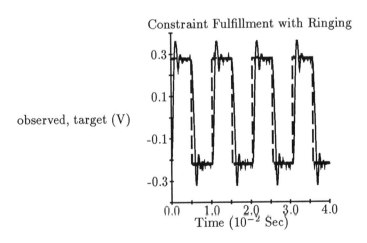

Constraint Fulfillment with Ringing

Figure 4. Plot of two input voltages of transconductance amplifier: the constraint forces are increased, which causes the system to undergo damped oscillations around the constraint manifold.

The basic differential multiplier method converts the quadratic programming problem into a system of differential equations:

$$k_1 \frac{dx}{dt} = -2Ax + 2Ax_0 - C\lambda,$$

$$k_2 \frac{dy}{dt} = -2By + 2By_0 - D\lambda, \tag{7}$$

$$k_3 \frac{d\lambda}{dt} = Cx + Dy + E(t).$$

The first two equations are implemented with a resistor and capacitor (with a follower for zero output impedance). The third is implemented with resistor summing into the negative input of a transconductance amplifier. The positive input of the amplifier is connected to $E(t)$.

The circuit in figure 2 implements the system of differential equations

$$C_1 \frac{dx}{dt} = G_1(\lambda - x) + G_2(V_x - x),$$

$$C_2 \frac{dy}{dt} = G_3(\lambda - y) + G_4(V_y - y), \tag{8}$$

$$C_3 \frac{d\lambda}{dt} = K \left(E(t) - \frac{G_1 x + G_3 y}{G_1 + G_3} \right),$$

where K is the transconductance of the transconductance amplifier. The two systems of differential equations (7) and (8) can match with suitably chosen constants.

The circuit in figure 2 actually performs quadratic programming. The constraint is fulfilled when the voltages on the inputs of the transconductance amplifier are the same. The g function is a difference between these voltages. Figure 3 is a plot of $-Cx - Dy$ and $E(t)$ as a function of time: they match reasonably well. The circuit in figure 2 therefore successfully fulfills the specified constraint.

Decreasing the capacitance C_3 changes the spring constant of the second-order differential equation. The forces that push the system towards the constraint manifold are increased without changing the damping. Therefore, the system becomes underdamped and the constraint is fulfilled with ringing (see figure 4).

The circuit in figure 2 can be easily expanded to solve general quadratic programming for N variables: simply add more x_i neurons, and interconnect them with resistors.

4   CONSTRAINED FLIP-FLOP

A flip-flop is two inverters hooked together in a ring. It is a bistable circuit: one inverter is on while the other inverter is off. A flip-flop can also be considered the simplest neural network: two neurons which inhibit each other.

If the inverters have infinite gain, then the flip-flop in figure 5 minimizes the function

$$\mathcal{E}_{flip-flop} - G_4 V_1 U_2 + G_2 V_2 U_1 - G_1 I_1 U_1 - G_3 I_2 U_2 + \frac{G_1 + G_2}{2} U_1^2 + \frac{G_3 + G_4}{2} U_2^2. \tag{9}$$

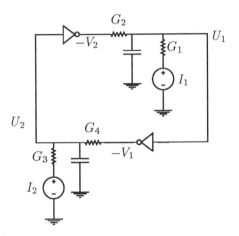

Figure 5. A flip-flop. U_1 and U_2 are voltages.

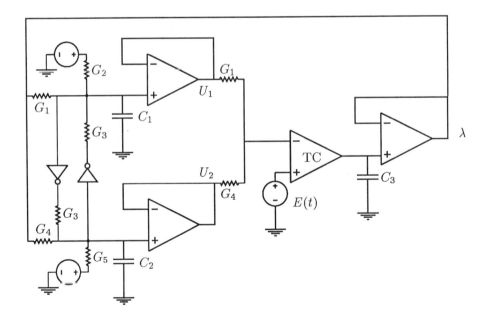

Figure 6. A circuit for constraining a flip-flop. U_1, U_2, and λ are voltages.

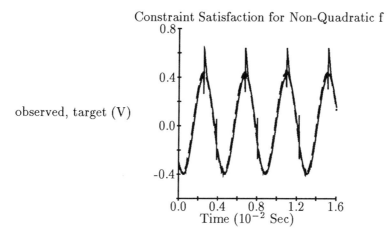

Figure 7. Constraint fulfillment for a non-quadratic optimization function. The plot consists of the two input voltages of the transconductance amplifier. Again, $E(t)$ is the dashed line and $-Cx - Dy$ is the solid line. The constraint is fulfilled when the two voltages are the same. As the constraint changes with time, the flip-flop changes state and the location of the constrained minimum changes abruptly. After the abrupt change, the constraint is temporarily not fulfilled. However, the circuit quickly fulfills the constraint. The temporary violation of the constraint causes the transient spikes in the $-Cx - Dy$ voltage.

Now, we can construct a circuit that minimizes the function in equation (9), subject to some linear constraint $Cx + Dy + E(t) = 0$, where x and y are the inputs to the inverters. The circuit diagram is shown in figure 6. Notice that this circuit is very similar to the quadratic programming circuit. Now, the x and y circuits are linked with a flip-flop, which adds non-quadratic terms to the optimization function.

The voltages $-Cx - Dy$ and $E(t)$ for this circuit are plotted in figure 7. For most of the time, $-Cx - Dy$ is close to the externally applied voltage $E(t)$. However, because $G_1 \neq G_4$ and $G_2 \neq G_5$, the flip-flop moves from one minima to the other and the constraint is temporarily violated. But, the circuitry gradually enforces the constraint again. The temporary constraint violation can be seen in figure 7.

5   CONCLUSIONS

This paper examines real circuits that have been constrained with the differential multiplier method. The differential multiplier method seems to work, even when the underlying circuit is non-linear, as in the case of the constrained flip-flop. Other papers examine applications of the differential multiplier method [Platt, 1987] [Gindi, 1988]. These applications could be built with the same parallel analog hardware discussed in this paper.

Acknowledgement

This paper was made possible by funding from AT&T Bell Labs. Hardware was provided by Carver Mead, and Synaptics, Inc.

References

Arrow, K., Hurwicz, L., Uzawa, H., [1958], *Studies in Linear Nonlinear Programming*, Stanford University Press, Stanford, CA.

Durbin, R., Willshaw, D., [1987], "An Analogue Approach to the Travelling Salesman Problem," *Nature*, **326**, 689–691.

Gill, P. E., Murray, W., Wright, M. H., [1981], *Practical Optimization*, Academic Press, London.

Gindi, G, Mjolsness, E., Anandan, P., [1988], "Neural Networks for Model Matching and Perceptual Organization," *Advances in Neural Information Processing Systems I*, 618–625.

Hopfield, J. J., Tank, D. W., [1985], "'Neural' Computation of Decisions in Optimization Problems," *Biol. Cyber.*, **52**, 141–152.

Mead, C. A., [1989], *Analog VLSI and Neural Systems*, Addison-Wesley, Reading, MA.

Platt, J. C., Hopfield, J. J., [1986], "Analog Decoding with Neural Networks," *Neural Networks for Computing*, Snowbird, UT, 364–369.

Platt, J. C., Barr, A., [1987], "Constrained Differential Optimization," *Neural Information and Processing Systems*, 612–621.

PULSE-FIRING NEURAL CHIPS FOR HUNDREDS OF NEURONS

Michael Brownlow
Lionel Tarassenko
Dept. Eng. Science
Univ. of Oxford
Oxford OX1 3PJ

Alan F. Murray
Dept. Electrical Eng.
Univ. of Edinburgh
Mayfield Road
Edinburgh EH9 3JL

Alister Hamilton
Il Song Han(1)
H. Martin Reekie
Dept. Electrical Eng.
Univ. of Edinburgh

ABSTRACT

We announce new CMOS synapse circuits using only three and four MOSFETs/synapse. Neural states are asynchronous pulse streams, upon which arithmetic is performed directly. Chips implementing over 100 fully programmable synapses are described and projections to networks of hundreds of neurons are made.

1 OVERVIEW OF PULSE FIRING NEURAL VLSI

The inspiration for the use of pulse firing in silicon neural networks is clearly the electrical/chemical pulse mechanism in "real" biological neurons. Asynchronous, digital voltage pulses are used to signal *states* $\{ S_i \}$ through *synapse weights* $\{ T_{ij} \}$ to emulate neural dynamics. Neurons fire voltage pulses of a *frequency* determined by their level of activity but of a constant magnitude (usually 5 Volts) [Murray,1989a]. As indicated in Fig. 1, synapses perform arithmetic directly on these asynchronous pulses, to increment or decrement the receiving neuron's activity. The activity of a receiving neuron i, x_i is altered at a frequency controlled by the sending neuron j, with state S_j by an amount determined by the synapse weight (here, T_{ij}).

---

[1] On secondment from the Korean Telecommunications Authority

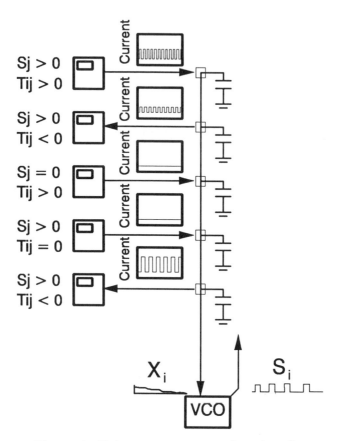

Figure 1 : Pulse stream synapse functionality

A silicon neural network based on this technique is therefore an asynchronous, analog computational structure. It is a hybrid between analog and digital techniques in that the individual neural pulses are digital voltage spikes, with all the robustness to noise and ease of regeneration that this implies. These and other characteristics of pulse stream networks will be discussed in detail later in this paper. Pulse stream methods, developed in Edinburgh, have since been investigated by other groups - see for instance [El-Leithy,1988, Daniell,1989].

1.1. WHY PULSE STREAMS?

There are some advantages in the use of pulse streams, and pulse rate encoding, in implementing neural networks. It should be admitted here that the initial move towards pulse streams was motivated by the desire to implement pseudo-analog circuits on an essentially digital CMOS process. It was a decision based at the time on expediency rather than on great vision on our part, as we did not initially appreciate the full benefits of this form of pulse stream arithmetic [Murray,1987].

For example, the voltages on the terminals of a MOSFET, V_{GS} and V_{DS} could clearly be used to code a neural synapse weight and state respectively, doing away with the need for pulses. In the pulse stream form, however, we can arrange that only V_{GS} is an "unknown". The device equations are therefore easily simplified, and furthermore the body effect is more predictable. In an equivalent continuous - time circuit, V_{DS} will also be a variable, which codes information. Predicting the transistor's operating regime becomes more difficult, and the equation cannot be simplified. Aside of the transistor - level advantages, giving rise to extremely compact synapse circuits, there may be architectural advantages. There are certainly architectural **consequences**. Digital pulses are easier to regenerate, easier to pass between chips, and generally far more noise - insensitive than analog voltages, all of which are significant advantages in the VLSI context. Furthermore, the relationship to the biological exemplar should not be ignored. It is at least interesting - whether it is significant remains to be seen.

2 FULLY ANALOG PULSE STREAM SYNAPSES

Our early pulse stream chips proved the viability of the pulse stream technique [Murray,1988a]. However, the area occupied by the digital weight storage memory was unacceptably large. Furthermore, the use of pseudo-clocks in an analog circuit was both aesthetically unsatisfactory and detrimental to smooth dynamical behaviour, and using separate signal paths for excitation and inhibition was both clumsy and inefficient. Accordingly, we have developed a family of fully programmable, fully analog synapses using dynamic weight storage, and operating on individual pulses to perform arithmetic. We have already reported time-modulation synapses based on this technique, and a later section of this paper will present the associated chips [Murray,1988b, Murray,1989b].

2.1. TRANSCONDUCTANCE MULTIPLIER SYNAPSES

The equation of interest is that for the drain-source current, I_{DS}, for a MOSFET in the *linear* or *triode* region:-

$$I_{DS} = \frac{\mu C_{ox} W}{L} \left[(V_{GS} - V_T) V_{DS} - \frac{V_{DS}^2}{2} \right] \tag{1}$$

Here, C_{ox} is the oxide capacitance/area, μ the carrier mobility, W the transistor gate width, L the transistor gate length, and V_{GS}, V_T, V_{DS} the transistor gate-source, threshold and drain-source voltages respectively.

This expression for I_{DS} contains a useful product term:- $\frac{\mu C_{ox} W}{L} \times V_{GS} \times V_{DS}$. However, it also contains two other terms in $V_{DS} \times V_T$ and V_{DS}^2.

One approach might be to ignore this imperfection in the multiplication, in the hope that the neural parallelism renders it irrelevant. We have chosen, rather, to **remove** the unwanted terms via a second MOSFET, as shown in Fig. 2.

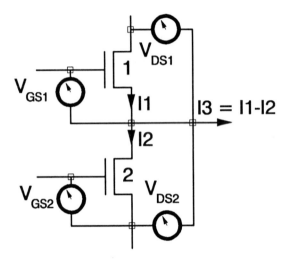

Figure 2 : Use of a second MOSFET to remove nonlinearities
(a transconductance multiplier).

The output current I_3 is now given by:-

$$I_3 = \mu C_{ox} \left[\frac{W_1}{L_1} (V_{GS1} - V_T) V_{DS1} - \frac{W_1}{L_1} \frac{V_{DS1}^2}{2} \right.$$
$$\left. - \frac{W_2}{L_2} (V_{GS2} - V_T) V_{DS2} + \frac{W_2}{L_2} \frac{V_{DS2}^2}{2} \right] \qquad (2)$$

The secret now is to select W_1, L_1, W_2, L_2, V_{GS1}, V_{GS2}, V_{DS1} and V_{DS2} to cancel all terms except

$$\mu C_{ox} \frac{W_1}{L_1} V_{GS1} \times V_{DS1} \qquad (3)$$

This is a fairly well-known circuit, and constitutes a **Transconductance Multiplier**. It was reported initially for use in signal processing chips such as filters [Denyer,1981, Han,1984]. It would be feasible to use it directly in a continuous time network, with analog voltages representing the $\{ S_i \}$. We choose to use it within a pulse-stream environment, to minimise the uncertainty in determining the operating regime, and terminal voltages, of the MOSFETs, as described above.

Fig. 3 shows two related pulse stream synapse based on this technique. The presynaptic neural state S_j is represented by a stream of 0-5V digital, asynchronous voltage pulses V_j. These are used to switch a current sink and source in and out of the synapse, either pouring current to a fixed voltage node (excitation of the postsynaptic neuron), or removing it (inhibition). The magnitude and direction of the resultant current pulses are determined by the synapse weight, currently stored as a dynamic, analog voltage T_{ij}.

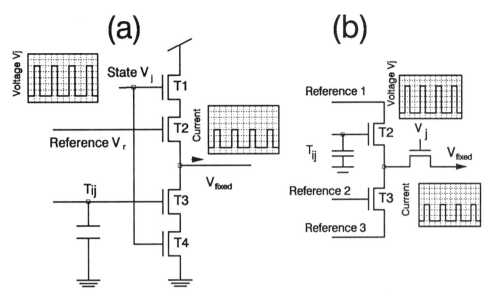

Figure 3 : Use of a transconductance multiplier to
form fully programmable pulse-stream synapses.

The fixed voltage V_{fixed} and the summation of the current pulses to give an
activity $x_i = \sum T_{ij} S_j$ are both provided by an Operational Amplifier
integrator circuit, whose saturation characteristics incidentally apply a
sigmoid nonlinearity. The transistors T1 and T4 act as power supply
"on/off" switches in Fig. 3a, and in Fig 3b are replaced by a single
transistor, in the output "leg" of the synapse, Transistors T2 and T3 form the
transconductance multiplier. One of the transistors has the synapse voltage
T_{ij} on its gate, the other a reference voltage, whose value determines the
crossover point between excitation and inhibition. The gate-source voltages
on T2 and T3 need to be substantially greater than the drain-source
voltages, to maintain linear operation. This is not a difficult constraint to
satisfy.

The attractions of these cells are that all the transistors are n-type, removing
the need for area-hungry isolation well structures, and In Fig. 3a, the
vertical line of drain-source connections is topologically attractive,
producing very compact layout, while Fig. 3b has fewer devices. It is not
yet clear which will prove optimal.

2.2. ASYNCHRONOUS "SWITCHED CAPACITOR" SYNAPSE

Fig. 4 shows a further variant, in the form of a "switched capacitor" pulse
stream synapse. Here the synapse voltage T_{ij} is electrically buffered to
switched capacitor structure, clocked *by the presynaptic neural pulse
waveforms*. Packets of charge are therefore "metered out" to the current
integrator whose magnitude is controlled by T_{ij} (positive or negative), and

whose frequency by the presynaptic pulse rate. The overall principle is therefore the same as that described for the transconductance multiplier synapses, although the circuit level details are different.

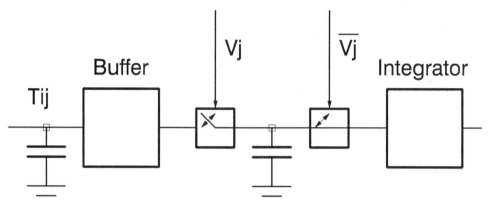

Figure 4 : Asynchronous, "switched capacitor" pulse stream synapse.

Conventional synchronous switched capacitor techniques have been used in neural integration [Tsividis,1987], but nowhere as directly as in this example.

2.3. CHIP DETAILS AND RESULTS

Both the time-modulation and switched capacitor synapses have been tested fully in silicon, and Fig. 5 shows a section of the time-modulation test chip. This synapse currently occupies $174 \times 73 \mu m$.

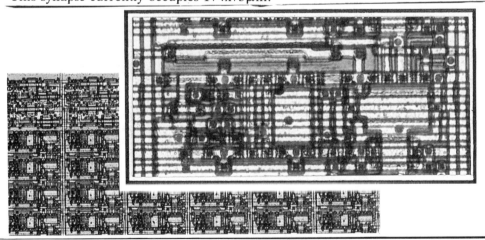

Figure 5 : Section, and single synapse, from time-modulation chip.

Three distinct pulse-stream synapse types have been presented, with different operating schemes and characteristics. None has yet been used to configure a large network, but this is now being done. Current estimates for the number of synapses implementable using the two techniques described above are as shown in Table 1, using an 8mmx8mm die as an example.

The lack of direct scaling between transistor count and synapse count (e.g. why does the factor 4/11 not manifest itself as a much larger increase in synapse count) can be explained. The raw number of transistors is not the only factor in determining circuit area. Routing of power supplies, synapse weight address lines, as well as storage capacitor size all take their toll, and are common to both of the above synapse circuits. Furthermore, in analog circuitry, transistors are almost certainly larger than minimum geometry, and generally significantly larger, to minimise noise problems. This all gives rise to a larger area than might be expected from simple arguments. Clearly, however, we are in position to implement serious sized networks, firstly with the time-modulation synapse, which is fully tested in silicon, and later with the transconductance type, which is still under detailed design and layout.

Table 1 : Estimated synapse count on 8mm die

SYNAPSE	NO. OF TRANSISTORS	ESTIMATED NETWORK SIZE
Time modulation	11	$\simeq 6400$ synapses
Transconductance	4	$\simeq 15000$ synapses
Switched Capacitor	4	$\simeq 14000$ synapses

In addition, we are developing new oscillator forms, techniques to counteract leakage from dynamic nodes, novel inter-chip signalling strategies specifically for pulse-stream systems, and non-volatile (α-Si) pulse stream synapses. These are to be used for applications in text-speech synthesis, pattern analysis and robotics. Details will be published as the work progresses.

Acknowledgements

The authors are grateful to the UK Science and Engineering Research Council, and the European Community (ESPRIT BRA) for its support of this work. Dr. Han is grateful to the Korean Telecommunications Authority, from whence he is on secondment in Edinburgh, and KOSEF(Korea) for partial financial support.

References

Daniell,1989.
P. M. Daniell, W. A. J. Waller, and D. A. Bisset, "An Implementation of Fully Analogue Sum-of-Product Neural Models," *Proc. IEE Conf. on Artificial Neural Networks*, pp. 52-56, ,1989.

Denyer,1981.
P. B. Denyer and J. Mavor, "MOST Transconductance Multipliers for Array Applications," *IEE Proc. Pt. 1*, vol. 128, no. 3, pp. 81-86, June ,1981.

El-Leithy,1988.
N. El-Leithy, M. Zaghloul, and R. W. Newcomb, "Implementation of Pulse-Coded Neural Networks," *Proc. 27th Conf. on Decision and Control*, pp. 334-336, ,1988.

Han,1984.
Il S. Han and Song B. Park, "Voltage-Controlled Linear Resistors by MOS Transistors and their Application to Active RC Filter MOS Integration," *Proc. IEEE*, pp. 1655-1657, Nov., ,1984.

Murray,1987.
A. F. Murray and A. V. W. Smith, "Asynchronous Arithmetic for VLSI Neural Systems," *Electronics Letters*, vol. 23, no. 12, pp. 642-3, June, ,1987.

Murray,1988a.
A. F. Murray and A. V. W. Smith, "Asynchronous VLSI Neural Networks using Pulse Stream Arithmetic," *IEEE Journal of Solid-State Circuits and Systems*, vol. 23, no. 3, pp. 688-697, June, ,1988.

Murray,1988b.
A. F. Murray, L. Tarassenko, and A. Hamilton, "Programmable Analogue Pulse-Firing Neural Networks," *Neural Information Processing Systems Conference*, pp. 671-677, Morgan Kaufmann, ,1988.

Murray,1989a.
A. F. Murray, "Pulse Arithmetic in VLSI Neural Networks," *IEEE MICRO*, vol. 9, no. 6, pp. 64-74, ,1989.

Murray,1989b.
A. F. Murray, A. Hamilton, H. M. Reekie, and L. Tarassenko, "Pulse - Stream Arithmetic in Programmable Neural Networks," *Int. Symposium on Circuits and Systems, Portland, Oregon*, pp. 1210-1212, IEEE, ,1989.

Tsividis,1987.
Y. P. Tsividis and D. Anastassiou, "Switched - Capacitor Neural Networks," *Electronics Letters*, vol. 23, no. 18, pp. 958 - 959, August, ,1987.

VLSI Implementation of a High-Capacity Neural Network Associative Memory

Tzi-Dar Chiueh [1] and Rodney M. Goodman
Department of Electrical Engineering (116-81)
California Institute of Technology
Pasadena, CA 91125, USA

ABSTRACT

In this paper we describe the VLSI design and testing of a high capacity associative memory which we call the exponential correlation associative memory (ECAM). The prototype 3μ-CMOS programmable chip is capable of storing 32 memory patterns of 24 bits each. The high capacity of the ECAM is partly due to the use of special exponentiation neurons, which are implemented via sub-threshold MOS transistors in this design. The prototype chip is capable of performing one associative recall in 3 μs.

1   ARCHITECTURE

Previously (Chiueh, 1989), we have proposed a general model for correlation-based associative memories, which includes a variant of the Hopfield memory and high-order correlation memories as special cases. This new exponential correlation associative memory (ECAM) possesses a very large storage capacity, which scales *exponentially* with the length of memory patterns (Chiueh, 1988). Furthermore, it has been shown that the ECAM is asymptotically stable in both synchronous and

---

[1]Tzi-Dar Chiueh is now with the Department of Electrical Engineering, National Taiwan University, Taipei, Taiwan 10764.

asynchronous updating modes (Chiueh, 1989). The model is based on an architecture consisting of binary connection weights, simple hard-limiter neurons, and specialized nonlinear circuits as shown in Figure 1. The evolution equation of this general model is

$$\mathbf{x}' = sgn\left\{ \sum_{k=1}^{M} f(<\mathbf{u}^{(k)}, \mathbf{x}>) \, \mathbf{u}^{(k)} \right\}, \tag{1}$$

where $\mathbf{u}^{(1)}, \mathbf{u}^{(2)}, \cdots, \mathbf{u}^{(M)}$ are the M memory patterns. $\mathbf{x}$ and $\mathbf{x}'$ are the current and the next state patterns of the system respectively, and sgn is the threshold function, which takes on the value $+1$ if its argument is nonnegative, and -1 otherwise.

We addressed, in particular, the case where $f(\cdot)$ is in the form of an exponentiation, namely, when the evolution equation is given by

$$\mathbf{x}' = sgn\left\{ \sum_{k=1}^{M} a^{<\mathbf{u}^{(k)}, \mathbf{x}>} \, \mathbf{u}^{(k)} \right\}, \tag{2}$$

and a is a constant greater than unity.

The ECAM chip we have designed is *programmable*; that is, one can change the stored memory patterns at will. To perform an associative recall, one first loads a set of memory patterns into the chip. The chip is then switched to the associative recall mode, an input pattern is presented to the ECAM chip, and the ECAM chip then computes the next state pattern according to Equation (2). The components of the next state pattern appear at the output in parallel after the internal circuits have settled. Feedback is easily incorporated by connecting the output port to the input port, in which case the chip will cycle until a fixed point is reached.

2   DESIGN OF THE ECAM CIRCUITS

From the evolution equation of the ECAM, we notice that there are essentially three circuits that need to be designed in order to build an ECAM chip. They are:

- $<\mathbf{u}^{(k)}, \mathbf{x}>$, the correlation computation circuit;

- $\sum_{k=1}^{M} a^{<\mathbf{u}^{(k)}, \mathbf{x}>} \, \mathbf{u}^{(k)}$, the exponentiation, multiplication and summing circuit;

- $sgn(\cdot)$, the threshold circuit.

We now describe each circuit, present its design, and finally integrate all these circuits to get the complete design of the ECAM chip.

2.1   CORRELATION COMPUTATION

In Figure 2, we illustrate a voltage-divider type circuit consisting of NMOS transistors working as controlled resistors (linear resistors or open circuits). This circuit computes the correlation between the input pattern $\mathbf{x}$ and a memory pattern $\mathbf{u}^{(k)}$. If the ith components of these two patterns are the same, the corresponding XOR gate outputs a "0" and there is a connection from the node $V_{ux}^{(k)}$ to VBB; otherwise, there is a connection from $V_{ux}^{(k)}$ to GND. Hence the output voltage will be proportional to the number of positions at which $\mathbf{x}$ and $\mathbf{u}^{(k)}$ match. The maximum output voltage is controlled by an externally supplied bias voltage VBB. Normally, VBB is set to a voltage lower than the threshold voltage of NMOS transistors (VTH) for a reason that will be explained later. Note that the conductance of an NMOS transistor in the ON mode is not fixed, but rather depends on its gate-to-source voltage and its drain-to-source voltage. Thus, some nonlinearity is bound to occur in the correlation computation circuit, however, simulation shows that this effect is small.

2.2   EXPONENTIATION, MULTIPLICATION, AND SUMMATION

Figure 4 shows a circuit that computes the exponentiation of $V_{ux}^{(k)}$, the product of the $u_i^{(k)}$ and the exponential, and the sum of all M products.

The exponentiation function is implemented by an NMOS transistor whose gate voltage is $V_{ux}^{(k)}$. Since VBB, the maximum value that $V_{ux}^{(k)}$ can assume, is set to be lower than the threshold voltage (VTH); the NMOS transistor is in the subthreshold region, where its drain current depends exponentially on its gate-to-source voltage (Mead, 1989). If we temporarily ignore the transistors controlled by $u_i^{(k)}$ or the complement of $u_i^{(k)}$, the current flowing through the exponentiation transistor associated with $V_{ux}^{(k)}$ will scale exponentially with $V_{ux}^{(k)}$. Therefore, the exponentiation function is properly computed.

Since the multiplier $u_i^{(k)}$ assumes either $+1$ or -1, the multiplication can be easily done by forming two branches, each made up of a transmission gate in series with an exponentiation transistor whose gate voltage is $V_{ux}^{(k)}$. One of the two transmission gates is controlled by $u_i^{(k)}$, and the other by the complement of $u_i^{(k)}$. Consequently, when $u_i^{(k)} = 1$, the positive branch will carry a current that scales exponentially with the correlation of the input $\mathbf{x}$ and the kth memory pattern $\mathbf{u}^{(k)}$, while the negative branch is essentially an open circuit, and vice versa.

Summation of the M terms in the evolution equation is done by current summing. The final results are two currents I_i^+ and I_i^-, which need to be compared by a threshold circuit to determine the sign of the ith bit of the next state pattern x_i'. In the ECAM a simple differential amplifier (Figure 3) performs the comparison.

2.3   THE BASIC ECAM CELL

The above computational circuits are then combined with a simple static RAM cell, to make up a basic ECAM cell as illustrated in Figure 5. The final design of an ECAM that stores M N-bit memory patterns can be obtained by replicating the basic ECAM cell M times in the horizontal direction and N times in the vertical direction, together with read/write circuits, sense amplifiers, address decoders, and I/O multiplexers. The prototype ECAM chip is made up of 32×24 ECAM cells, and stores 32 memory patterns each 24 bits wide.

3   ECAM CHIP TEST RESULTS

The test procedure for the ECAM is to first generate 32 memory patterns at random and then program the ECAM chip with these 32 patterns. We then pick a memory pattern at random, flip a specified number of bits randomly, and feed the resulting pattern to the ECAM as an input pattern ($\mathbf{x}$). The output pattern ($\mathbf{x}'$) can then be fed back to the inputs of the ECAM chip. This iteration continues until the pattern at the input is the same as that at the the output, at which time the ECAM chip is said to have reached a stable state. We select 10 sets of 32 memory patterns and for each set we run the ECAM chip on 100 trial input patterns with a fixed number of errors. Altogether, the test consists of 1000 trials.

In Figure 6, we illustrate the ECAM chip test results. The number of successes is plotted against the number of errors in the input patterns for the following four cases: 1) The ECAM chip with $V_{BB} = 5V$; 2) $V_{BB} = 2V$; 3) $V_{BB} = 1V$; and 4) a simulated ECAM in which the exponentiation constant a, equals 2. It is apparent from Figure 6 that as the number of errors increases, the number of successes decreases, which is expected. Also, one notices that the simulated ECAM is by far the best one, which is again not unforeseen because the ECAM chip is, after all, only an approximation of the ideal ECAM model.

What is really unexpected is that the best performance occurs for $V_{BB} = 2V$ rather than $V_{BB} = 1V$ (V_{TH} in this CMOS process). This phenomenon arises because of two contradictory effects brought about by increasing V_{BB}. On the one hand, increasing V_{BB} increases the dynamic range of the exponentiation transistors in the ECAM chip. Suppose that the correlations of two memory patterns $\mathbf{u}^{(l)}$ and $\mathbf{u}^{(k)}$ with the input pattern $\mathbf{x}$ are t_l and t_k, respectively, where $t_l > t_k$; then

$$V_{ux}^{(l)} = \frac{(t_l + N)\,V_{BB}}{2N}, \quad V_{ux}^{(k)} = \frac{(t_k + N)\,V_{BB}}{2N}.$$

Therefore, as V_{BB} increases, so does the difference between $V_{ux}^{(l)}$ and $V_{ux}^{(k)}$, and $\mathbf{u}^{(l)}$ becomes more dominant than $\mathbf{u}^{(k)}$ in the weighted sum of the evolution equation.

Hence, as VBB increases, the error correcting ability of the ECAM chip should improve. On the other hand, as VBB increases beyond the threshold voltage, the exponentiation transistors leave the subthreshold region and may enter saturation, where the drain current is approximately proportional to the *square* of the gate-to-source voltage. Since a second-order correlation associative memory in general possesses a smaller storage capacity than an ECAM, one would expect that with a fixed number of loaded memory patterns, the ECAM should do better than the second-order correlation associative memory. Thus one effect tends to enhance the performance of the ECAM chip, while the other tends to degrade it. A compromise between these two effects is reached, and the best performance is achieved when VBB = 2V.

For the case when VBB = 2V, the drain current versus gate-to-source voltage characteristic of the exponentiation transistors is actually a hybrid of a square function and an exponentiation function. At the bottom it is of an exponential form, and it gradually flattens out to a square function, once the gate-to-source voltage becomes larger than the threshold voltage. Therefore, the ECAM chip with VBB = 2V is a mixture of the second-order correlation associative memory and the pure ECAM. According to the convergence theorem for correlation associative memories (Chiueh, 1989) and the fact that $f(\cdot)$ in the ECAM chip with VBB = 2V is still monotonically nondecreasing, the ECAM chip is still asymptotically stable when VBB = 2V.

We have tested the speed of the ECAM chip using binary image vector quantization as an example problem. The speed at which the ECAM chip can vector-quantize binary images is of interest. We find experimentally that the ECAM chip is capable of doing one associative recall operation, in less than 3 μs, ˥n 4 × 4 blocks. This projects to approximately 49 ms for a 512 × 512 binary image, or more than 20 images per second.

4 CONCLUSIONS

In this paper, we have presented a VLSI circuit design for implementing a high capacity correlation associative memory. The performance of the ECAM chip is shown to be almost as good as a computer-simulated ECAM. Furthermore, we believe that the ECAM chip is more robust than an associative memory using a winner-take-all function, because it obtains its result via iteration, as opposed to one shot. In conclusion, we believe that the ECAM chip provides a fast and efficient way for solving many associative recall problems, such as vector quantization and optical character recognition.

Acknowledgement

This work was supported in part by NSF grant No. MIP – 8711568.

References

T. D. Chiueh and R. M. Goodman. (1988) "High Capacity Exponential Associative Memory," in *Proc. of IEEE ICNN*, Vol. I, pp. 153–160.

T. D. Chiueh. (1989) "Pattern Classification and Associative Recall by Neural Networks," Ph. D. dissertation, California Institute of Technology.

C. A. Mead. (1989) *Analog VLSI and Neural Systems.* Reading, MA : Addison-Wesley.

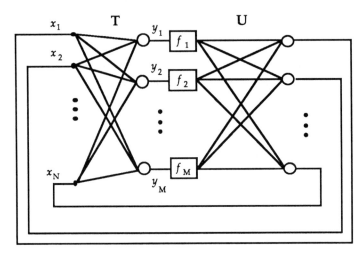

Figure 1: Architecture of the General Correlation-Based Associative Memory

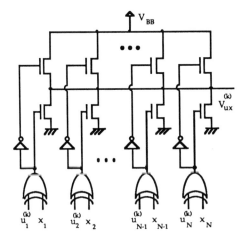

Figure 2: The Correlation Computation Circuit

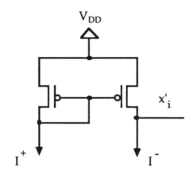

Figure 3: The Threshold Circuit

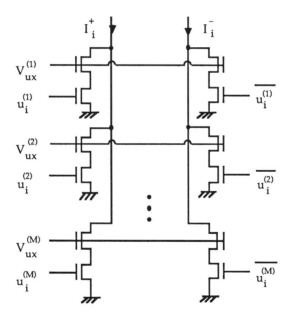

Figure 4: The Exponentiation, Multiplication, and Summation Circuit

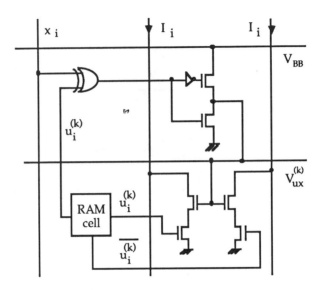

Figure 5: Circuit Diagram of the Basic ECAM Cell

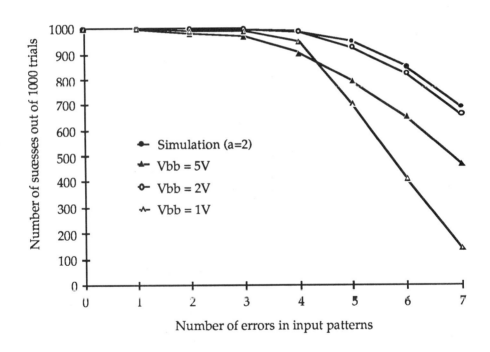

Figure 6: Error Correcting Ability of the ECAM Chip with Different V_{BB} compared with a Simulated ECAM with $a = 2$

An Efficient Implementation of the Back-propagation Algorithm on the Connection Machine CM-2

Xiru Zhang[1]   Michael Mckenna   Jill P. Mesirov   David L. Waltz

Thinking Machines Corporation
245 First Street, Cambridge, MA 02142-1214

ABSTRACT

In this paper, we present a novel implementation of the widely used Back-propagation neural net learning algorithm on the Connection Machine CM-2 – a general purpose, massively parallel computer with a hypercube topology. This implementation runs at about 180 million interconnections per second (IPS) on a 64K processor CM-2. The main interprocessor communication operation used is 2D nearest neighbor communication. The techniques developed here can be easily extended to implement other algorithms for layered neural nets on the CM-2, or on other massively parallel computers which have 2D or higher degree connections among their processors.

1 Introduction

High-speed simulation of large artificial neural nets has become an important tool for solving real world problems and for studying the dynamic behavior of large populations of interconnected processing elements [3, 2]. This work is intended to provide such a simulation tool for a widely used neural net learning algorithm – the Back-propagation (BP) algorithm.[7]

The hardware we have used is the Connection Machine® CM-2.[2] On a 64K processor CM-2 our implementation runs at 40 million *Weight Update Per Second*

---

[1] This author is also a graduate student at Computer Science Department, Brandeis University, Waltham, MA 02254-9110.

[2] Connection Machine is a registered trademark of Thinking Machines Corporation.

(WUPS)[3] for training, or 180 million *Interconnection Per Second* (IPS) for forward-pass, where IPS is defined in the DARPA NEURAL NETWORK STUDY [2] as *"the number of multiply-and-add operations that can be performed in a second" [on a Back-propagation network].* We believe that the techniques developed here can be easily extended to implement other algorithms for layered neural nets on the CM-2, or other massively parallel machines which have 2D or higher degree connections among their processors.

2   The Connection Machine

The Connection Machine CM-2 is a massively parallel computer with up to $65,536$ processors. Each processor has a single-bit processing unit and 64K or 256K bits of local RAM. The processors run in SIMD mode. They are connected in an n-cube topology, which permits highly efficient n dimensional grid communications. The system software also provides *scan* and *spread* operations – e.g., when $n \cdot m$ processors are connected as an $n \times m$ 2D grid, the summation (product, max, *etc.*) of a "parallel variable" value in all the processors on a row of the grid[4] takes only $O(\log m)$ time. It is possible to turn off any subset of the processors so that instructions will only be performed by those processors that are currently active. On the CM-2, every 32 processors share a floating point processing unit; and a 32 bit number can be stored across 32 processors (i.e., one bit per processor). These 32 processors can each access this 32-bit number as if it were stored in its own memory. This is a way of sharing data among processors locally. The CM-2 uses a conventional computer such as a SUN-4, VAX or Symbolics Lisp Machine as a front-end machine. Parallel extensions to the familiar programming languages LISP, C, and FORTRAN, via the front-end, allow the user to program the Connection Machine and the front-end system.

3   The Back-propagation Algorithm

The Back-propagation [7] algorithm works on layered, feed-forward networks (*BP net* for short in the following discussion), where the processing units are arranged in layers – there are an input layer, an output layer, and one or more "hidden layers" (layers between the input and output layers). A BP net computes its output in the following fashion: first an input pattern is set as the output of the units at the input layer; then one layer at a time, from the input to hidden to output layer, the units compute their outputs by applying an activation function to the weighted sum of their inputs (which are the outputs of the unit at the lower layer(s) that are connected to them). The weights come from the links between the units.

The Back-propagation algorithm "trains" a BP net by adjusting the link weights of the net using a set of "training examples." Each training example consists of

---

[3]   This includes the time required to read in the input pattern, propagate activation forward through the network, read in the ideal output pattern, propagate the error signal backward through the network, compute the weight changes, and change the weights.

[4]   That is, to add together one value from each processor on a row of the grid and distribute the sum into all the processors on the same row.

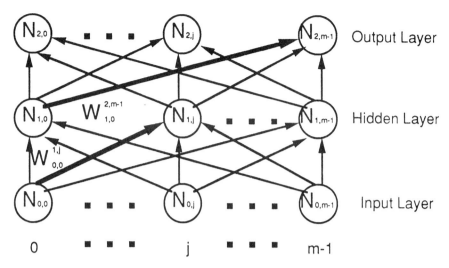

Figure 1: A 3-layer, fully-connected Back-propagation network that has the same number (m) of nodes at each layer.

an input pattern and an ideal output pattern that the user wants the network to produce for that input. The weights are adjusted based on the difference between the ideal output and the actual output of the net. This can be seen as a gradient descent process in the weight space.

After the training is done, the BP net can be applied to inputs that are not in the set of training examples. For a new input pattern IP, the network tends to produce an output similar to the training example whose input is similar to IP. This can be used for interpolation, approximation, or generalization from examples depending on the goal of the user [4].

4   The Implementation

In this section, we explain our implementation by presenting a simple example – a three-layer fully-connected BP network that has the same number of nodes at each layer. It is straightforward to extend it to general cases. For a more detailed discussion, see reference [8].

4.1   A Simple Case

Figure 1 shows a fully-connected 3-layer BP network with m nodes on each layer. In the following discussion, we will use $N_{i,j}$ to denote the jth node (from the left) on layer i, $i \in \{0, 1, 2\}, j \in \{0, 1, \ldots, m - 1\}$; $W_{k,h}^{i,j}$ is the weight of the link from node $N_{k,h}$ to node $N_{i,j}$, and $\delta_{i,j}$ is the error at node $N_{i,j}$.

First, assume we have exactly m processors. We store a "column" of the network in each processor. That is, processor j contains nodes $N_{0,j}$, $N_{1,j}$ and $N_{2,j}$. It also contains the weights of the links going into $N_{1,j}$ and $N_{2,j}$ (i.e., $W_{0,k}^{1,j}$ and $W_{1,k}^{2,j}$ for

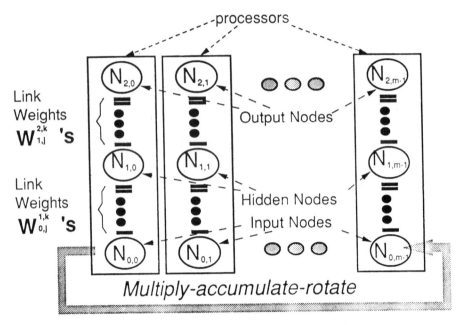

Figure 2: The layout of the example network.

$k \in \{0, 1, \ldots, m-1\}$). See Figure 2. The Back-propagation algorithm consists of three steps: (1) *forward pass* to compute the network output; (2) *backward propagation* to compute the errors at each node; and (3) *weight update* to adjust the weights based on the errors. These steps are implemented as follows:

4.1.1   Forward Pass: $Output(N_{i,j}) = F(\sum_{k=0}^{m-1} W_{i-1,k}^{ij} \cdot Output(N_{i-1,k}))$

We implement *forward pass* as follows:

1. Set the input node values; there is one input node per processor.

2. In each processor, multiply the input node value by the link weight between the input node and the hidden node that is in the same processor; then accumulate the product in the hidden node.

3. Rotate the input node values – each processor sends its input node value to its nearest left neighbor processor, the leftmost processor sends its value to the rightmost processor; i.e., do a left-circular-shift.

4. Repeat the *multiply-accumulate-rotate* cycles in the above two steps (2–3) m times; every hidden node $N_{1,j}$ will then contain $\sum_{k=0}^{m-1} W_{0,k}^{1j} \cdot Output(N_{0,k})$. Now apply the activation function F to that sum. (See Figure 2.)

5. Repeat steps 2–4 for the output layer, using the hidden layer as the input.

4.1.2 Backward Propagation

For the output layer, $\delta_{2,k}$, the error at each node $N_{2,k}$, is computed by

$$\delta_{2,k} = Output(N_{2,k}) \cdot (1 - Output(N_{2,k})) \cdot (Target(N_{2,k}) - Output(N_{2,k})),$$

where $Target(N_{2,k})$ is the ideal output for node $N_{2,k}$. This error can be computed in place, i.e., no inter-processor communication is needed. For the hidden layer,

$$\delta_{1,j} = Output(N_{1,j}) \cdot (1 - Output(N_{1,j})) \cdot \sum_{k=0}^{m-1} W_{1,j}^{2,k} \cdot \delta_{2,k}$$

To compute $\sum_{k=0}^{m-1} W_{1,j}^{2,k} \cdot \delta_{2,k}$ for the hidden nodes, we perform a *multiply-accumulate-rotate* operation similar to the *forward pass*, but from the top down. Notice that the weights between a hidden node and the output nodes are in different processors. So, instead of rotating $\delta_{2,k}$'s at the output layer, we rotate the partial sum of products for the hidden nodes: at the beginning every hidden node $N_{1,j}$ has an accumulator A_j with initial value $= 0$ in processor j. We do a left-circular-shift on the A_j's. When A_j moves to processor k, we set $A_j \leftarrow A_j + W_{1,j}^{2,k} \cdot \delta_{2,k}$. After m rotations, A_j will return to processor j and its value will be $\sum_{k=0}^{m-1} W_{1,j}^{2,k} \cdot \delta_{2,k}$.

4.1.3 Weight Update: $\Delta W_{k,h}^{i,j} = \eta \cdot \delta_{i,j} \cdot Output(N_{k,h})$

$\Delta W_{k,h}^{i,j}$ is the weight increment for $W_{k,h}^{i,j}$, η is the "learning rate" and $\delta_{i,j}$ is the error for node $N_{i,j}$, which is computed in the *backward propagation* step and is stored in processor j. The *weight update* step is done as follows:

1. In each processor j, for the weights between the input layer and hidden layer, compute weight update $\Delta W_{0,k}^{1,j} = \eta \cdot \delta_{1,j} \cdot Output(N_{0,k})$,[5] and add $\Delta W_{0,k}^{1,j}$ to $W_{0,k}^{1,j}$;[6]

2. Rotate the input node values as in step 3 of the *forward pass*.

3. Repeat the above two steps m times, until all the weights between the input layer and the hidden layer are updated.

4. Do the above for weights between the hidden layer and the output layer also.

We can see that the basic operation is the same for all three steps of the Back-propagation algorithm, i.e., *multiply-accumulate-rotate*. On the CM-2, *multiply*, *add* (for accumulate) and *circular-shift* (for rotate) take roughly the same amount of time, independent of the size of the machine. So the CM-2 spends only about 1/3 of its total time doing communication in our implementation.

---

[5] Initially $k = j$, but the input node values will be rotated around in later steps, so $k \neq j$ in general.

[6] $W_{0,k}^{1,j}$ is in the same processor as $\Delta W_{0,k}^{1,j}$ – all the weights going into node $N_{1,j}$ are in processor j. Also we can accumulate $\Delta W_{0,k}^{1,j}$ for several training patterns instead of updating $W_{0,k}^{1,j}$ every time. We can also keep the previous weight change and add a "momentum" term here. (Our implementation actually does all these. They are omitted here to simplify the explanation of the basic ideas.)

4.2   Replication of Networks

Usually, there are more processors on the CM-2 than the width of a BP network. Suppose the network width is m and there are $n \cdot m$ processors; then we make n copies of the network on the CM-2, and do the *forward pass* and *backward propagation* for *different* training patterns on each copy of the network. For the *weight update* step, we can sum up the weight changes from different copies of the network (i.e. from different training patterns), then update the weights in all the copies by this sum. This is equivalent to updating the weights after n training patterns on a single copy of the BP network.

On the CM-2, every 32 processors can share the same set of data (see section 2). We make use of this feature and store the BP network weights across sets of 32 processors. Thus each processor only needs to allocate one bit for each weight. Also, since the weight changes from different training patterns are additive, there is no need to add them up in advance – each copy of the network can update (add to) the weights separately, as long as no two or more copies of the network update the same weight at the same time. (Our implementation guarantees that no such weight update conflict can occur.) See **Figure 3**.

We call the 32 copies of the network that share the same set of weights a *block*. When the number of copies $n > 32$, say $n = 32 \cdot q$, then there will be q blocks on the CM-2. We need to sum up the weight changes from different blocks before updating the weights in each block. This summation takes a very small portion of the total running time (much less than 1%). So the time increase can usually be ignored when there is more than one block.[7] Thus, the implementation speeds up essentially linearly as the number of processors increases.

5   An Example: Character Image Recovery

In this example, a character, such as A, is encoded as a 16×16 pixel array. A 3-layer fully-connected network with 256 input nodes, 128 hidden nodes and 256 output nodes is trained with 64 character pixel arrays, each of which is used both as the input pattern and the ideal output pattern. After the training is done ($maximum\_error < 0.15$),[8] some noisy character images are fed into the network. The network is then used to remove the noise (to recover the images). We can also use the network recursively – to feed the network output back as the input.

Figure 4a shows the ideal outputs (odd columns) and the actual outputs (even columns) of the network after the training. **Figure 4b** shows corrupted character image inputs (odd columns) and the recovered images (even columns). The corrupted inputs have 30% noise, i.e., 30% of the pixels take random values in each image. We can see that most of the characters are recovered.

---

[7] The summation is done using the *scan* and *spread* operations (see section 2), so its time increases only logarithmically in proportion to the number of blocks. Usually there are only a few blocks, thus we could use the nearest neighbor communication here instead without much loss of performance.

[8]   This training took about 400 cycles.

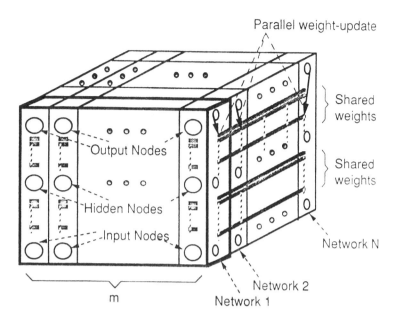

Figure 3: Replication of a BP network and parallel update of network weights. In the *weight update* step, the nodes in each copy of the BP network loop through the weights going into them in the following fashion: in the first loop, Network 1 updates the first weight, Network 2 updates the second weight ... Network N updates the Nth weight; in general, in the Jth loop, Network I updates $[Mod(I + J, N)]th$ weight. In this way, it is guaranteed that no two networks update the same weight at the same time. When the total number of weights going into each node is greater than N, we repeat the above loop.

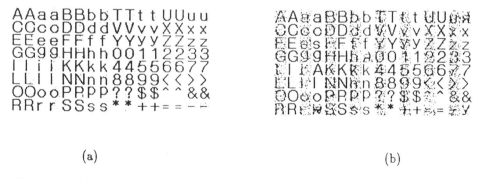

(a)   (b)

Figure 4: (a) Ideal outputs (in odd columns) and the actual after-training outputs (in even columns) of a network with 256 input nodes, 128 hidden nodes and 256 output nodes trained with character images. (b) Noisy inputs (in odd columns) and the corresponding outputs ("cleaned-up" images) produced by the network.

Computer	BP performance (IPS)
CM-2	180 M
Cray X-MP	50 M
WARP (10)	17 M (WUPS)
ANZA plus	10 M
TRW MK V (16)	10 M
Butterfly (64)	8 M
SAIC SIGMA-1	5-8 M
TI Odyessy	5 M
Convex C-1	3.6 M
VAX 8600	2 M
SUN 3	250 K
Symbolics 3600	35 K

Table 1: Comparison of BP implementations on different computers.

In this example, we used a 4K processor CM-2. The BP network had $256 \times 128 + 128 \times 256 = 65,536$ weights. We made 64 copies of the network on the CM-2, so there were 2 blocks. One weight update cycle[9] took 1.66 seconds. Thus the performance is: $(65,536 \times 64) \div 1.66 \approx 2,526,689$ weight update per second (WUPS). Within the 1.66 seconds, the communication between the two blocks took 0.0023 seconds. If we run a network of the same size on a 64K processor CM-2,[10] there will be 32 blocks, and the inter-block communication will take $0.0023 \times \frac{\log 32}{\log 2} = 0.0115$ second.[11] And the overall performance will be:

$$(16 \times 65,536 \times 64) \div (1.66 + 0.0115) = 40,148,888 \text{ WUPS}$$

Forward-pass took 22% of the total time. Thus if we ran the forward pass alone, the speed would be $40,148,888 \div 0.22 \approx 182,494,940$ IPS.

6   Comparison With Other Implementations

This implementation of the Back-propagation algorithm on the CM-2 runs much more efficiently than previous CM implementations (e.g., see [1], [6]). Table 1 lists the speeds of Back-propagation on different machines (obtained from reference [2] and [5]).

---

[9] See footnote 3 for definition.

[10] Assume we have enough training patterns to fill up the CM-2.

[11] We use *scan* and *spread* operations here, so the time used increases logrithmatically.

7   Summary

In this paper, we have shown an example of efficient implementation of neural net algorithms on the Connection Machine CM-2. We used Back-propagation because it is the most widely implemented, and many researchers have used it as a benchmark. The techniques developed here can be easily adapted to implement other algorithms on layered neural nets.

The main communication operation used in this work is the 2D grid nearest neighbor communication. The facility for a group of processors on the CM-2 to share data is important in reducing the amount of space required to store network weights and the communication between different copies of the network. These points should be kept in mind when one tries to use the techniques described here on other machines.

The main lesson we learned from this work is that to implement an algorithm efficiently on a massively parallel machine often requires re-thinking of the algorithm to explore the parallel nature of the algorithm, rather than just a straightforward translation of serial implementations.

Acknowledgement

Many thanks to Alex Singer, who read several drafts of this paper and helped improve it. Lennart Johnsson helped us solve a critical problem. Discussions with other members of the Mathematical and Computational Sciences Group at Thinking Machines Corporation also helped in many ways.

References

[1] Louis G. Ceci, Patrick Lynn, and Phillip E. Gardner. Efficient Distribution of Back-Propagation Models on Parallel Architectures. Tech. Report CU-CS-409-88, Dept. of Computer Science, University of Colorado, September 1988.

[2] MIT Lincoln Laboratory. Darpa Neural Network Study. Final Report, July 1988.

[3] Special Issue on Artificial Neural Systems. IEEE Computer, March 1988.

[4] Tomaso Poggio and Federico Girosi. A Theory of Networks for Approximation and Learning. A.I.Memo 1140, MIT AI Lab, July 1989.

[5] Dean A. Pomerleau, George L. Gusciora David S. Touretzky, and H. T. Kung. Neural Network Simulation at Warp Speed: How We Got 17 Million Connections Per Second. In *IEEE Int. Conf. on Neural Networks*, July 1988. San Diego, CA.

[6] Charles R. Rosenberg and Guy Blelloch. An Implementation of Network Learning on the Connection Machine. In *Proceedings of the Tenth International Joint Conference on Artificial Intelligence*, Milan, Italy, 1987.

[7] D. E. Rumelhart, G. E. Hinton, and R. J. Williams. Learning internal representations by error propagation. In *Parallel Distributed Processing*, chapter 8. MIT Press, 1986.

[8] Xiru Zhang, Michael Mckenna, Jill P. Mesirov, and David L. Waltz. An Efficient Implementation of The Back-Propagation Algorithm On the Connection Machine CM-2. Technical Report RL-89-1, Thinking Machines Corp., 245 First St. Cambridge, MA 02114, 1989.

Performance of Connectionist Learning Algorithms on 2-D SIMD Processor Arrays

Fernando J. Núñez* and Jose A.B. Fortes
School of Electrical Engineering
Purdue University
West Lafayette, IN 47907

ABSTRACT

The mapping of the back-propagation and mean field theory learning algorithms onto a generic 2-D SIMD computer is described. This architecture proves to be very adequate for these applications since efficiencies close to the optimum can be attained. Expressions to find the learning rates are given and then particularized to the DAP array procesor.

1 INTRODUCTION

The digital simulation of connectionist learning algorithms is flexible and accurate. However, with the exception of very small networks, conventional computer architectures spend a lot of time in the execution of simulation software. Parallel computers can be used to reduce the execution time. Vector-pipelined, multiprocessors, and array processors are some of the most important classes of parallel computers[3]. Connectionist or neural net (NN) learning algorithms have been mapped onto all of them.

The focus of this contribution is on the mapping of the back-propagation (BP) and mean field theory (MFT) learning algorithms onto the subclass of SIMD computers with the processors arranged in a square two-dimensional mesh and interconnected by nearest-neighbor links.

The material is organized as follows. In section 2, the execution cost of BP and MFT on sequential computers is found. Two-dimensional SIMD processor arrays are described in section 3, and the costs of the two dominanting operations in the simulations are derived. In section 4 the mapping of BP and MFT is commented

---

* Current address: Motorola Inc., 1301 E Algonquin Rd., Schaumburg, IL 60196

and expressions for the learning rates are obtained. These expressions are particularized to the DAP computer in section 5. Section 6 concludes this work.

2 BACK-PROPAGATION AND MEAN FIELD THEORY

In this paper, two learning algorithms: BP[7] and MFT[4]; and 3-layer nets are considered. The number of neurons in the input, hidden, and output layer is I, H, and O respectively. BP has been used in many applications. Probably, NETtalk[8] is the best known. MFT can also be used to learn arbitrary mappings between two sets, and remarkably, to find approximate solutions to hard optimization problems much more efficiently than a Boltzmann Machine does[4,5].

The output of a neuron i will be denoted as v_i and called *value:* $v_i = f\left(\sum_{j \neq i} a_{ij} v_j - \theta_i\right)$. The summation represents the net input received and will be called *activation*. The neuron thresold is θ_i. A sigmoid-like function f is applied to find the value. The weight of the link from neuron j to neuron i is a_{ij}. Since input patterns are the values of the I layer, only neuron values and activations of the H and O layers must be computed. In BP, the activation error and the value error of the H and O layers are calculated and used to change the weights.

In a conventional computer, the execution time of BP is approximately the time spent in finding the activations, back-propagating the activation error of the O layer, and modifying the I-H and H-O weights. The result is: $(2I + 3O)Ht_m$, where t_m is the time required to perform a multiply/accumulate operation. Since the net has $(I + O)H$ connections, the learning rate in connections per second is:

$$\mathcal{L}_{BP} = \frac{I + O}{(2I + 3O)t_m} \quad CPS$$

In the MFT algorithm, only from the neuron values in equilibrium at the end of the clamped and free annealing phases we can compute the weight increments. It is assumed that in both phases there are A annealing temperatures and that E iterations are enough to reach equilibrium at each temperature[4,5]. With these changes, MFT is now a deterministic algorithm where the annealing phases are composed of AE sweeps. The MFT execution time can be approximated by the time spent in computing activations in the annealing loops. Taking into account that in the clamped phase only the H layer is updated, and that in the free phase both, the H and O layers change their values, the MFT learning performance is found to be:

$$\mathcal{L}_{MFT} = \frac{\mathcal{L}_{BP}}{AE} \quad CPS$$

MFT is AE times more expensive than BP. However, the learning qualities of both algorithms are different and such a direct comparison is simplistic.

3 2-D SIMD PROCESSOR ARRAYS

Two-dimensional single instruction multiple data stream (2-D SIMD) computers are very efficient in the simulation of NN learning algorithms. They can provide massive parallelism at low cost. An SIMD computer is an array of processing elements (PEs) that execute the same instruction in each cycle. There is a single control unit that broadcasts instructions to all the PEs. SIMD architectures operate in a synchronous, lock-step fashion[3]. They are also called *array procesors* because their *raison d'être* is to operate on vectors and matrices.

Example SIMD computers are the Illiac-IV, the Massively Parallel Processor (MPP), the Connection Machine (CM), and the Distributed Array Processor (DAP). With the exception of the CM, whose PE interconnection topology is a hypercube, the other three machines are 2-D SIMD arrays because their PEs are interconnected by a 2-D mesh with wrap-around links (figure 1).

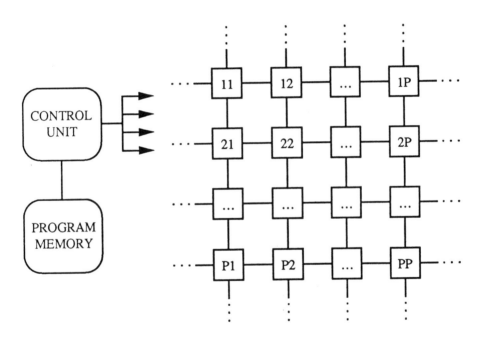

Figure 1: A 2-D SIMD Processor Array

Each PE has its own local memory. The instruction has an address field to access it. The array memory space can be seen as a 3-D volume. This volume is generated by the PE plane, and the depth is the number of memory words that each PE can address. When the control unit issues an address, a plane of the memory volume is being referenced. Then, square blocks of $P{\times}P$ elements are the natural addressing unit of 2-D SIMD processor arrays. There is an activity bit register in each PE to disable the execution of instructions. This is useful to perform operations with a subset of the PEs. It is assumed that there is no overlapping between data processing an data moving operations. In other words, PEs can be either performing some operation on data (this includes accessing the local memory) or exchanging data with other processors.

3.1   MAPPING THE TWO BASIC OPERATIONS

It is characteristic of array processors that the way data is allocated into the PEs memories has a very important effect on performance. For our purposes, two data structures must be considered: vectors and matrices. The storage of vectors is illustrated in figure 2-a. There are two modes: row and column. A vector is split into P-element subvectors stored in the same memory plane. Very large vectors will require two or more planes. The storage of matrices is also very simple. They must be divided into square $P{\times}P$ blocks (figure 2-b). The shading in figure 2 indicates that, in general, the sizes of vectors and matrices do not fit the array dimensions perfectly.

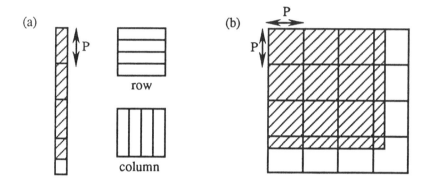

Figure 2: (a) Vector and (b) Matrix Storage

The execution time of BP and MFT in a 2-D SIMD computer is spent, almost completely, in matrix-vector multiply (MVM) and vector outer multiply/accumulate (VOM) operations. They can be decomposed in the following simpler operations involving $P{\times}P$ blocks.

a) Addition $(+)$: $C = A + B$ such that $c_{ij} = a_{ij} + b_{ij}$.
b) Point multiply/accumulate $(\cdot)$: $C' = C + A{\cdot}B$ such that $c'_{ij} = c_{ij} + a_{ij}b_{ij}$.
c) Unit rotation: The result block has the same elements than the original, but rotated one place in one of the four possible directions (N, E, W, and S).
d) Row (column) broadcast: The result of the row (column) broadcast of a vector x stored in row (column) mode is a block X such that $x_{ij} = x_j\ (= x_i)$.

The time required to execute a, b, c, and d will be denoted as t_a, t_m, t_r, and t_b respectively. Next, let us see how the operation $y = Ax$ (MVM) is decomposed in simpler steps using the operations above. Assume that x and y are P-element vectors, and A is a $P{\times}P$ block.

1) Row-broadcast vector x.

2) Point multiply $Y = A \cdot X$.

3) Row addition of block Y, $y_i = \sum_{j=1}^{P} y_{ij} = \sum_{j=1}^{P} a_{ij} x_j$. This requires $\left\lceil \log_2 P \right\rceil$ steps. In each step multiple rotations and one addition are performed. Figure 3 shows how eight values in the same row are added using the recursive doubling technique. Note that the number of rotations doubles in each step. The cost is: $Pt_r + \log_2 Pt_a$. Row addition is an inefficient operation because of the large cost due to communication. Fortunately, for larger data its importance can be diminished by using the scheduling described nextly.

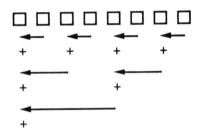

Figure 3: Recursive Doubling

Suppose that x, y, and A have dimensions $m = MP$, $n = NP$, and $n \times m$ respectively. Then, $y = Ax$ must be partitioned into a sequence of non-partitioned block operations as the one explained above. We can write:

$$y^i = \sum_{j=1}^{M} A^{ij} x^j = \sum_{j=1}^{M} (A^{ij} \cdot X^j) u = \left(\sum_{j=1}^{M} A^{ij} \cdot X^j \right) u$$

In this expression, y^i and x^j represent the i-th and j-th P-element subvector of y and x respectively, and A^{ij} is the $P \times P$ block of A with indices i and j. Block X^j is the result of row-broadcasting x^j (x is stored in row mode.) Finally, u is a vector with all its P-elements equal to 1. Note that in the second term M column additions are implicit, while only one is required in the third term because blocks instead of vectors are accumulated. Since y has N subvectors, and the M subvectors of x are broadcast only once, the total cost of the MVM operation is:

$$NMt_m + N(Pt_r + \log_2 Pt_a) + Mt_b$$

After a similar development, the cost of the VOM ($A' = A + yx^T$) operation is:

$$NMt_m + (N + M)t_b$$

If the number of neurons in each layer is not an integer multiple of P, the storage and execution efficiencies decrease. This effect is less important in large networks.

4 LEARNING RATES ON 2-D SIMD COMPUTERS

4.1 BACK-PROPAGATION

The neuron values, activations, value errors, activation errors, and thresolds of the H and O layers are organized as vectors. The weights are grouped into two matrices: I-H and H-O. Then, the scalar operations of the original algorithm are transformed into matrix-vector operations.

From now on, the size of the input, hidden, and output layers will be IP, HP, and OP. As commented before, the execution time is mostly spent in computing activations, values, their errors, and in changing the weights. To compute activations, and to back-propagate the activation error of the O layer MVM operations are performed. The change of weights requires VOM operations. After substituting the expressions of the previous section, the time required to learn a pattern simulating BP on a 2-D SIMD computer is:

$$(2I + 3O)Ht_m + (2I + 3H + 2O)t_b + (2H + O)(Pt_r + \log_2 Pt_a)$$

The time spent in data communication is given by the factors in t_r and t_b. The larger they are, the smaller is the efficiency. For array processors with fast broadcast facilities, and for nets large enough in terms of the array dimensions, the efficiency grows since a smaller fraction of the total execution time is dedicated to moving data. Since the net has $(I + O)HP^2$ connections, the learning rate is P^2 times greater than using a single PE:

$$\mathcal{L}_{SIMD-BP} = \frac{(I + O)P^2}{(2I + 3O)t_m} \quad CPS$$

4.2 MEAN FIELD THEORY

The operations outside the annealing loops can be neglected with small error. In consequence, only the computation of activations in the clamped and free annealing phases is accounted for:

$$AE((2I + 3O)Ht_m + (2I + H + 2O)t_b + (2H + O)(Pt_r + \log_2 Pt_a))$$

Under the same favorable conditions above mentioned, the learning rate is:

$$\mathcal{L}_{SIMD-MFT} = \frac{(I + O)P^2}{AE(2I + 3O)t_m} \quad CPS$$

5 LEARNING PERFORMANCE ON THE DAP

The DAP is a commercial 2-D SIMD processor array developed by ICL. It is a massively parallel computer with bit-level PEs built around a single-bit full adder. In addition to the 2-D PE interconnection mesh, there are row and column broadcast buses that allow the direct transfer of data from any processor row or column to an edge register. Many instructions require a single clock cycle leading to very efficient codings of loop bodies. The DAP-510 computer features $2^5 \times 2^5$ PEs with a maximum local memory of 1Mbit per PE. The DAP-610 has $2^6 \times 2^6$ PEs, and the maximum local memory is 64Kbit. The clock cycle in both machines is 100 ns[1].

With bit-level processors it is possible to tailor the precision of fixed-point computations to the minimum required by the application. The costs in cycles required by several basic operations are given below. These expressions are function of the number of bits of the operands, that has been assumed to be the same for all of them: b bits.

The time required by the DAP to perform a block addition, point multiplication/accumulation, and broadcast is $t_a = 2b$, $t_m = 2b^2$, and $t_b = 8b$ clock cycles respectively. On the other hand, $P + 2b \log_2 P$ cycles is the duration of a row addition. Let us take $b = 8$ bits, and $AE = 24$. This values have been found adequate in many applications. Then, the maximum learning rates of the DAP-610 $(P = 64)$ are:

$$\text{BP: } 100\text{-}160 \; MCPS \qquad \text{MFT: } 4.5\text{-}6.6 \; MCPS$$

where MCPS $\equiv 10^6$ CPS. These figures are 4 times smaller for the DAP-510. It is worth to mention that the performance decreases quadratically with b. The two learning rates of each algorithm correspond to the worst and best case topology.

5.1 EXAMPLES

Let us consider a one-thousand neuron net with 640, 128, and 256 neurons in the input, hidden, and output layer. For the DAP-610 we have $I = 10$, $H = 2$, and $O = 4$. The other parameters are the same than used above. After substituting, we see that the communication costs are less than 10% of the total, demonstrating the efficiency of the DAP in this type of applications. The learning rates are:

$$\text{BP: } 140 \; MCPS \qquad \text{MFT: } 5.8 \; MCPS$$

NETtalk[10] is frequently used as a benchmark in order to compare the performance achieved on different computers. Here, a network with similar dimensions is considered: 224 input, 64 hidden, and 32 output neurons. These dimensions fit perfectly into the DAP-510 since $P = 32$. As before, a data precision of 8 bits has been taken. However, the fact than the input patterns are binary has been exploited to obtain some savings.

The performance reached in this case is 50 $MCPS$. Even though NETtalk is a relatively small network, only 30% of the total execution time is spent in data communication. If the DAP-610 were used, somewhat less than 200 $MCPS$ would be learnt since the output layer is smaller than P what causes some inefficiency.

Finally, BP learning rates of the DAP-610 with 8- and 16-bit operands are compared to those obtained by other machines below[2,6]:

COMPUTER	MCPS
VAX 780	0.027
CRAY-2	7
CM (65K PEs)	13
DAP-610 (8 bits)	100-160
DAP-610 (16 bits)	25-40

6 CONCLUSIONS

Two-dimensional SIMD array processors are very adequate for the simulation of connectionist learning algorithms like BP and MFT. These architectures can execute them at nearly optimum speed if the network is large enough, and there is full connectivity between layers. Other much more costly parallel architectures are outperformed.

The mapping approach described in this paper can be easily extended to any network topology with dense blocks in its global interconnection matrix. However, it is obvious that 2-D SIMD arrays are not a good option to simulate networks with random sparse connectivity.

Acknowledgements

This work has been supported by the Ministry of Education and Science of Spain.

References

[1] (1988) AMT DAP Series, Technical Overview. *Active Memory Technology*.

[2] G. Blelloch & C. Rosenberg. (1987) Network Learning on the Connection Machine. *Proc. 10th Joint Conf. on Artificial Intelligence*, IJCA Inc.

[3] K. Hwang & F. Briggs. (1984) *Computer Architecture and Parallel Processing*, McGraw-Hill.

[4] C. Peterson & J. Anderson. (1987) A Mean Field Theory Learning Algorithm for Neural Networks. *Complex Systems*, 1:995-1019.

[5] C. Peterson & B. Soderberg. (1989) A New Method For Mapping Optimization Problems onto Neural Networks. *Int'l J. of Neural Systems*, 1(1):3-22.

[6] D. Pomerleau, G. Gusciora, D. Touretzky & H.T. Kung. (1988) Neural Network Simulation at Warp Speed: How We Got 17 Million Connections per Second. *Proc. IEEE Int'l Conf. on Neural Networks*, II:143-150.

[7] D. Rumelhart, G. Hinton & R. Williams. (1986) Learning Representations by Back-Propagating Errors. *Nature*, (323):533-536.

[8] T. Sejnowski & C. Rosenberg. (1987) Parallel Networks that Learn to Pronounce English Text. *Complex Systems*, 1:145-168.

Dataflow Architectures:
Flexible Platforms for
Neural Network Simulation

Ira G. Smotroff
MITRE-Bedford Neural Network Group
The MITRE Corporation
Bedford, MA 01730

ABSTRACT

Dataflow architectures are general computation engines optimized for the execution of fine-grain parallel algorithms. Neural networks can be simulated on these systems with certain advantages. In this paper, we review dataflow architectures, examine neural network simulation performance on a new generation dataflow machine, compare that performance to other simulation alternatives, and discuss the benefits and drawbacks of the dataflow approach.

1 DATAFLOW ARCHITECTURES

Dataflow research has been conducted at MIT (Arvind & Culler, 1986) and elsewhere (Hiraki, et. al., 1987) for a number of years. Dataflow architectures are general computation engines that treat each instruction of a program as a separate task which is scheduled in an asynchronous, data-driven fashion. Dataflow programs are compiled into graphs which explicitly describe the data dependencies of the computation. These graphs are directly executed by the machine. Computations which are not linked by a path in the graphs can be executed in parallel. Each machine has a large number of processing elements with hardware that is optimized to reduce task switching overhead to a minimum. As each computation executes and produces a result, it causes all of the following computations that require the result to be scheduled. In this manner, fine grain parallel computation is achieved, with the limit on the amount of possible parallelism determined by the problem and the number of processing elements in the machine.

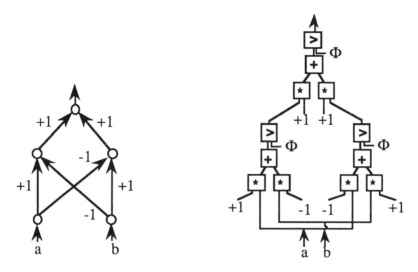

Figure 1: XOR network and its dataflow graph.

1.1 NEURAL NETWORKS & DATAFLOW

The most powerful hardware platforms for neural network simulation were enumerated in the DARPA Neural Network Study (Lincoln Laboratory, 1988): *Supercomputers* offer programming in sequential languages at great cost. *Systolic Arrays* such as the CMU WARP (Pomerleau, 1988) and *"Massively" Parallel* machines such as the Connection Machine (Hillis, 1987), offer power at increasingly reasonable costs, but require specialized low-level programming to map the algorithm to the hardware. *Specialized VLSI* and *Optical devices* (Alspector, 1989) (Farhat, 1987) (Rudnick & Hammerstrom, 1989) offer fast implementations of fixed algorithms[1].

Although dataflow architectures were not included on the DARPA list, there are good reasons for using them for neural network simulation. First, there is a natural mapping between neural networks and the dataflow graphs used to encode dataflow programs (see Figure 1). By expressing a neural network simulation as a dataflow program, one gains the data synchronization and the parallel execution efficiencies that the dataflow architecture provides at an appropriate fine grain of abstraction. The close mapping may allow simple compilation of neural network specifications into executable programs. Second, this ease of programming makes the approach extremely *flexible*, so one can get good performance on a new algorithm the first time it is run, without having to spend additional time determining the best way to map it onto the hardware. Thus dataflow simulations may be particularly appropriate for those who develop new learning algorithms or architectures. Third, high level languages are being developed for dataflow machines, providing environments in which neural nets can be combined with standard calculations; this can't be done with much of the specialized neural network hardware. Last, there may be ways to optimize dataflow architectures for neural network simulation.

---

[1] Hammerstrom's device (Rudnick & Hammerstrom, 1989) may be micro-programmable.

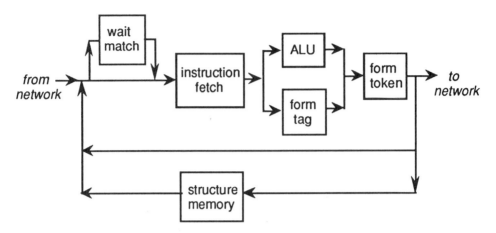

Figure 2: Schematic of a tagged-token dataflow processor.

2 TAGGED-TOKEN DATAFLOW

The *Tagged-token* dataflow approach represents each computation product as a token which is passed to following computations. A schematic view of a tagged-token processor is shown in Figure 2. Execution proceeds in a *Wait-Match-Store* cycle which achieves data synchronization. An instruction to be executed *waits* in the wait-match queue for a token with its operand. If a *match* occurs, the incoming token contains its operand and one of two things happens: for a monadic operation, the instruction is executed and the result is passed on; for a dyadic operation, a check is made to see if the operand is the first or the second one to arrive. If it's the first, the location representing the instruction is *tagged*, the operand is *stored*, and the instruction continues to wait. If it's the second (i.e. the instruction is tagged already) the instruction is executed and a token containing the result is sent to all computations requiring the result. A schematic view of the execution of the XOR network of Figure 1 on a tagged-token dataflow machine is illustrated in Figure 3.

2.1 SPLIT-PHASE TRANSACTIONS

In fine-grain parallel computations distributed over a number of physical devices, the large number of network transactions represent a potential bottleneck. The tagged-token dataflow architecture mitigates this problem in a way that *enhances* the overall parallel execution time. Each network transaction is split into two phases. A process requests an external data value and then goes to sleep. When the token bearing the requested value returns, the process is awakened and the computation proceeds. In standard approaches, a processor must idle while it waits for a result. This non-blocking approach allows other computations to proceed while the value is in transit, *thus masking memory and network latencies.* Independent threads of computation may be interwoven at each cycle, thus allowing the maximum amount of parallel execution at each cycle. As long as the amount of parallelism in the task (i.e. the length of each processor's task queue) is larger than the network latency, the processors never idle. Consequently, massively parallel applications such as neural simulations benefit most from the split-phase transaction approach.

3 NEURAL NETWORK DATAFLOW SIMULATION

To illustrate neural network execution on a dataflow processor, the XOR network in Figure 1 was coded in the dataflow language ID (Nikhil, 1988) and run on the MIT GITA (Graph Interpreter for Tagged-token Architecture) simulator (Nikhil, 1988). Figures 4-6 are ALU operations profiles with the vertical axis representing the number of processors that could be simultaneously kept busy (i.e. the amount of parallelism in the task at a particular instance) and the horizontal axis representing elapsed computation cycles. In addition, Figures 4 & 5 are *ideal* simulations with communication latency of zero time and an infinite number of processors available at all times. The ideal profile width represents the absolute minimum time in which the dataflow calculation could possibly be performed, and is termed the *critical path*. Figure 4 shows the execution profile for a single linear threshold neuron processing its two inputs. The initial peak activity of eleven corresponds to initialization activities, with later peaks corresponding to actual computation steps. The complexity of the profile may be attributed to various dataflow synchronization mechanisms. In figure 5, the ideal execution profile for the XOR net, note the initialization peak similar to the one appearing in the single neuron profile; the peak parallelism of fifty-five corresponds to all five neuron initializations occuring simultaneously. This illustrates the ability of the dataflow approach to automatically expose the inherent parallelism in the overall computation. Note also that the critical path of one hundred fifty one is substantially less than five times the single neuron critical path of eighty-five. Wherever possible, the dataflow approach has performed computation in parallel, and the lengthening of the critical path can be attributed to those computations which had to be delayed until prior computations became available.

Figure 6 represents the execution of the same XOR net under more realistic conditions in which each token operation is subject to a finite network delay. The regular spacing of the profile corresponds to the effect of the network delays. The interesting thing to observe is that the overall critical path length has only increased slightly to one hundred seventy because the average amount of parallelism available as tokens come in from the net is higher. Dataflow's ability to interleave computations thus compensates for much of the network latency effects.

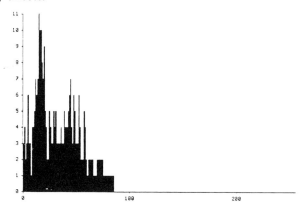

Figure 4: Ideal parallelism profile for dataflow execution – single threshold neuron unit.

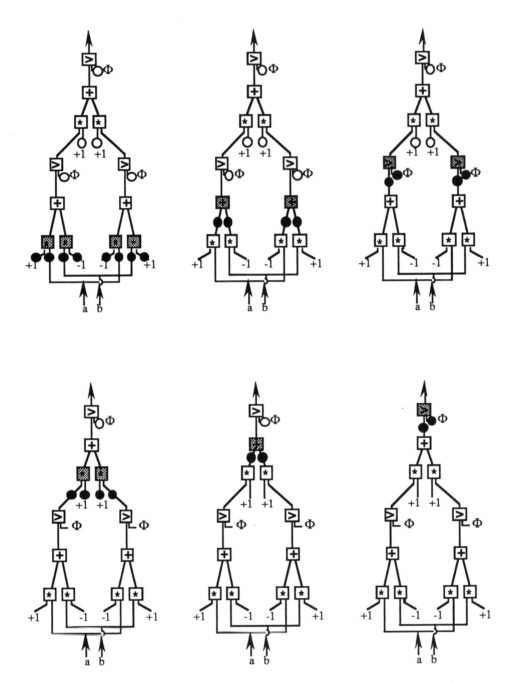

Figure 3: Execution of the XOR network of Figure 1 on a tagged-token dataflow processor. The black dots represent active tokens, the white dots represent waiting tokens, and the shaded boxes represent enabled operations executing.

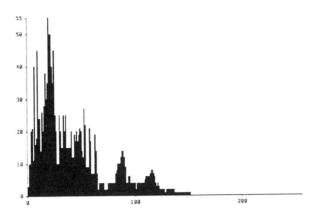

Figure 5: Ideal parallelism profile for dataflow execution of XOR network.

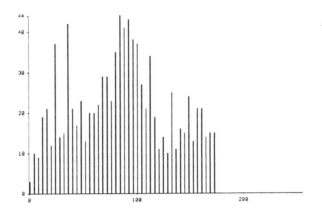

Figure 6: Parallelism profile for dataflow execution of XOR with constant communication latency.

3.1 COST OF THE DATAFLOW APPROACH

The Tagged-Token Dataflow machine executing an ID program performs two to three times as many instructions as an IBM 370 executing an equivalent FORTRAN program. The overhead in dataflow programs is attributable to mechanisms which manage the asynchronous parallel execution. Similar overhead would probably exist in specialized neural network simulators written for dataflow machines. However, this overhead can be justified because the maximum amount of parallelism in the computation is exposed in a straightforward manner, which requires no additional programming effort. On conventional multiprocessors, parallelism must be selectively tailored for each problem. As the amount of parallelism increases, the associated costs increase as well; often they will eventually surpass the cost of dataflow (Arvind ,Culler & Ekanadham, 1988). Thus the parallel performance on the dataflow machine will often surpass that of alternative platforms despite the overhead.

4 THE MONSOON ARCHITECTURE

Early dataflow implementations using a Tagged Token approach had a number of practical barriers (Papadoupoulos, 1988). While useful results were achieved, the cost and expansion limits of the associative memory used for token matching made them impractical. However, the systems did prove the utility of the Tagged Token approach..

Recently, the MONSOON architecture (Papadoupoulos, 1988) was developed to remedy the problems encountered with Tagged Token architectures. The token-matching problem has been solved by treating each token descriptor as an address in a global memory space which is partitioned among the processors in the system; matching becomes a simple RAM operation.

An initial MONSOON prototype has been constructed and a 8 processor machine is scheduled to be built in 1990. Processor elements for that machine are CMOS gate-array implementations being fabricated by Motorola. Each processor board will have a 100 ns cycle time and process at a rate of 7-8 MIPS/2-4 MFLOPS. Total memory for the 8 processor machine is 256 MBytes. Interconnect is provided by a 100 MByte/s packet switch network. The throughput of the 8 processor machine is estimated at 56-64 MIPS/16-32 MFLOPs. This translates to 2-3 million connections per second per processor and 16-24 million connections per second for the machine. Monsoon performance is in the supercomputer class while the projected Monsoon cost is significantly less due to the use of standard process technologies.

A 256 processor machine with CMOS VLSI processors is envisioned. Estimated performance is 40 MIPS per processor and 10,240 MIPS for the machine. Aggregate neural simulation performance is estimated at 2.5-3.8 billion connections per second, assuming an interconnect network of suitable performance.

5 CONCLUSIONS

    i) Dataflow architectures should be cost effective and flexible platforms for neural network simulation if they become widely available.

    ii) As general architectures, their performance will not exceed that of specialized neural network architectures.

    iii) Maximum parallelism is attained simply by using the dataflow approach: no machine or problem-specific tuning is needed. Thus dataflow is seen as an excellent tool for empirical simulation. Excellent performance may be obtained on cost effective hardware, with no special effort required for performance improvement.

    iv) Dataflow architectures optimized for neural network simulation performance may be possible.

References

Alspector, J., Gupta, B. and Allen, R. B. (1989) Performance of a Stochastic Learning Microchip. In D. S. Touretzky (ed.), *Advances in Neural Information Processing Systems 1*, 748-760, San Mateo, CA: Morgan Kaufmann.

Arvind and Culler, D. E..(1986) *Dataflow Architectures,* MIT Technical Report MIT/LCS/TM-294, Cambridge, MA.

Arvind, Culler, D. E., Ekanadham, K. (1988) *The Price of Asynchronous Parallelism: An Analysis of Dataflow Architectures,* MIT Laboratory for Computer Science, Computation Structures Group Memo 278.

DARPA Neural Network Study (1988) Lincoln Laboratory, MIT, Lexington, MA.

Farhat, N.H., and Shai, Z. Y.(1987) Architectures and Methodologies for Self-Organization and Stochastic Learning in Opto-Electronic Analogs of Neural Nets. In *Proceedings of IEEE First International Conference on Neural Networks,* **III**:565-576.

Hillis, W. D.(1986) *The Connection Machine,* Cambridge, MA: The MIT Press.

Hiraki, K., Sekiguchi, S. and Shimada, T. (1987) *System Architecture of a Dataflow Supercomputer.* Technical Report, Computer Systems Division, Electrotechnical Laboratory, 1-1-4 Umezono, Sakura-mura, Niihari-gun, Ibaraki, 305, Japan.

Nikhil, R. S. (1988) *Id World Reference Manual,* Computational Structures Group, MIT Laboratory for Computer Science, Cambridge, MA.

Pomerleau, D. A., Gusciora, G. L., Touretsky and D. S., Kung, H. T.(1988) Neural Simulation at Warp Speed: How we got 17 Million Connections per Second. In *Proceedings of the IEEE International Conference on Neural Networks,* **II**:143-150, San Diego.

Papadoupoulos, G. M. (1988) *Implementation of a General Purpose Dataflow Multiprocessor*, Phd. Thesis, MIT Department of Electrical Engineering and Computer Science, Cambridge, MA.

Rudnick, M. and Hammerstrom, D.(1989) An Interconnection Structure for Wafer Scale Neurocomputers. In *Proceedings of the 1988 Connectionist Models Summer School.* San Mateo, CA: Morgan Kaufmann.

PART X:
HISTORY OF NEURAL NETWORKS

Neural networks: the early days

J.D. Cowan
Department of Mathematics, Committee on
Neurobiology, and Brain Research Institute,
The University of Chicago, 5734 S. Univ. Ave.,
Chicago, Illinois 60637

ABSTRACT

A short account is given of various investigations of neural network properties, beginning with the classic work of McCulloch & Pitts. Early work on neurodynamics and statistical mechanics, analogies with magnetic materials, fault tolerance via parallel distributed processing, memory, learning, and pattern recognition, is described.

1 INTRODUCTION

In this brief account of the early days in neural network research, it is not possible to be comprehensive. This article then is a somewhat subjective survey of some, but not all, of the developments in the theory of neural networks in the twent-five year period, from 1943 to 1968, when many of the ideas and concepts were formulated, which define the field of neural network research. This comprises work on connections with automata theory and computability; neurodynamics, both deterministic and statistical; analogies with magnetic materials and spin systems; reliability via parallel and parallel distributed processing; modifiable synapses and conditioning; associative memory; and supervised and unsupervised learning.

2 McCULLOCH-PITTS NETWORKS

The modern era may be said to have begun with the work of McCulloch and Pitts (1943). This is too well-known to need commenting on. Let me just make some historical remarks. McCulloch, who was by training a psychiatrist and neuroanatomist, spent some twenty years thinking about the representation of event in the nervous system. From 1941 to 1951 he worked in Chicago. Chicago at that time was one of the centers of neural of

Figure1: Warren McCulloch *circa* 1962

network research, mainly through the work of the Rashevsky group in the Committee on Mathematical Biology at the University of Chicago. Rashevsky, Landahl, Rapaport and Shimbel, among others, carried out many early investigations of the dynamics of neural networks, using a mixture of calculus and algebra. In 1942 McCulloch was introduced to Walter Pitts, then a 17 year old student of Rashevsky's. Pitts was a mathematical prodigy who had joined the Committee sometime in 1941. There is an (apocryphal) story that Pitts was led to the Rashevsky group after a chance meeting with the philosopher Bertrand Russell, at that time a visitor to the University of Chicago. In any event Pitts was already working on algebraic aspects of neural networks, and it did not take him long to see the point behind McCulloch's quest for the embodiment of mind. In one of McCulloch later essays (McCulloch 1961) he describes the history of his efforts thus:

> My object, as a psychologist, was to invent a least psychic event, or "psychon", that would have the following properties: First, it was to be so simple an event that it either happened or else it did not happen. Second, it was to happen only if its bound cause had happened-shades of Duns Scotus!-that is, it was to imply its temporal antecedent. Third it was to propose this to subsequent psychons. Fourth, these were to be compounded to produce the equivalents of more complicated propositions concerning their antecedents...In 1921 it dawned on me that these events might be regarded as the all-or-nothing impulses of neurons, combined by convergence upon the next neuron to yield complexes of propositional events.

Their subsequent 1943 paper was remarkable in many respects. It is best appreciated within the *zeitgeist* of the era when it was written. As Papert has documented in his introduction to a collection of McCulloch's papers (McCulloch 1967), 1943 was a seminal year for the development of the science of the mind. Craik's monograph *The Nature of Explanation* and the paper "Behavior, Purpose and Teleology, by Rosenbleuth, Wiener and Bigelow, were also published in 1943. As Papert noted, "The common feature [of these publications] is their recognition that the laws governing the embodiment of mind should be sought among the laws governing information rather than energy or matter". The paper by McCulloch and Pitts certainly lies within this framework.

Figure 2: Walter Pitts *circa* 1952

McCulloch-Pitts networks (hence-forth referred to as MP networks), are finite state automata embodying the logic of propositions, with quantifiers, as McCulloch wished; and permit the framing of sharp hypotheses about the nature of brain mechanisms, in a form equivalent to computer programs. This was a remarkable achievement. It established once and for all, the validity of making formal models of brain mechanisms, if not their veridicality. It also established the possibility of a rigorous theory of mind, in that neural networks with feedback loops can exhibit purposive behavior, or as McCulloch and Pitts put it:

> both the formal and the final aspects of that activity which we are wont to call *mental* are rigorously deducible from present neurophysiology...[and] that in [imaginable networks]..."Mind" no longer "goes more ghostly than a ghost".

2.1 FAULT TOLERANCE

MP networks were the first designed to perform specific logical tasks; and of course logic can be mapped into arithmetic. Landahl, McCulloch and Pitts (1943), for example, noted that the arithmetical operations +, 1-, and x can be obtained in MP networks via the logical operations OR, NOT, and AND. Thus the arithmetical expression a-a.b = a.(1-b) corresponds to the logical expression a AND NOT b, and more generally, all (finite) arithmetical calculations can be implemented in an MP network. But what happens if such a network malfunctions from time to time, or is damaged? It was this problem that attracted von Neumann. In 1951-2, following conversations with McCulloch, and with Bruckner and Gell-Mann, von Neumann took up the problem of designing MP networks to function reliably despite malfunctions and failures of their component neurons, or misconnected wires, or damage to a portion of the network (von Neumann 1956).

Von Neumann solved the reliability problem in two differing ways. His first solution was to make use of the error correcting properties of *majority logic* elements. Such an element executes the logical function $m(a,b,c) = (a$ AND $b)$ OR $(b$ AND $c)$ OR $(c$ AND $a)$. The proceedure is to *triplicate* each logical function to be executed, i.e.; execute each logical function three times in *parallel,* and then feed the outputs through majority logic elements. Let ε be the probability of a majority element malfunctioning, and let η be the probability of error on any of its input lines. The general result is that provided $\varepsilon < 0.007$, an output error η^* equal to about 4ε can be achieved. However the redundancy is high. Let μ be the *logical depth* of the function to be computed, i.e.; the longest serial chain of MP units in the original network. Then about 3^μ MP neurons are required to achieve outputs whose probability of error is about four times the probability of error of the MP units. If $\mu = 3$ the requisite redundancy is 9:1, but if $\mu = 6$ it is about 700:1, and if $\mu = 10$ it is about 60, 000:1. Von Neumann's second solution to the reliability problem was to *multiplex*, i.e.; use N MP circuits to do the job of one. In such networks one bit of information (the choice between "1" and "0") is signaled not by the activation of one MP neuron, but instead by the synchronous activation of many MP neurons. Let Δ be a number between 0 and 1. Then "1" is signaled if ξ, the fraction of activated MP neurons involved in any job, exceeds Δ; otherwise "0" is signalled. Evidently a multiplexed MP network will function reliably only if ξ is close to either 0 or 1. Von Neumann achieved this with networks made up entirely of NAND logic elements. Let ε now be the probability of such an element malfunctioning. Von Neumann then proved that with $\Delta = 0.07$ and $\varepsilon < 0.0107$, η^* can be made to decrease with increasing N. With $\varepsilon = 0.005$, von Neumann showed that $\eta^* \sim aN^{-1/2}10^{-bN}$, where $a = 6.4$ and $b = 8.6 \cdot 10^{-4}$. It follows that η^* can be made less than ε provided $N \geq 2, 000$. This is achieved with a redundancy of 3N:1 that is independent of the logical depth μ; thus for logical computations of large depth the method of multiplexing is superior to majority logic decoding.

2.2 PARALLEL DISTRIBUTED PROCESSING

This solution to the problem of reliable computing with unreliable elements is general since the NAND logic element is universal. Is it biologically plausible? The answer seems to be negative since real neurons have *thousands* of synaptic contacts, so that it is not necessary to concatenate many NAND elements in circuits of large logical depth to implement logical functions of many variables. This suggests that real neurons can implement logical functions of many variables with a probability of error ϵ not much greater than that of the NAND element. This observation motivated Winograd and I (1963) to study the limiting case in which ϵ is independent of the logical complexity of the function to be implemented. In such a case it is possible to use *error-correcting codes* just as is done in noisy communication channels (Shannon 1948, Hamming 1950) in which a message comprising K symbols is transmitted via a signal comprising N signals, N - K of which are used by the receiver for error detection and correction. In the computing case this implies that K *computations* be implemented by an MP-network comprising N/K times as many elements as would be required in the error-free case.

The overall effect of such an encoding scheme is to *distribute* the logical functions to be implemented, over the entire MP network. Such a scheme works most efficiently with large K and N; in effect in a parallel distributed architecture. Thus the Winograd-Cowan scheme is an early example of *Parallel Distributed Processing* or *PDP*. Of course it can be argued that the scheme is not realistic, in that all the extra coding machinery is assumed to be error free. As we have noted this may not be true for simple logical elements, but it may be more plausible for real neurons. In unpublished work Winograd and Cowan studied this issue in more detail and found a realistic optimal scheme involving both multiplexing and PDP (Cowan and Winograd, In preparation).

These solutions to the fault tolerance problem provided an insight into the way neural networks in the brain might function reliably despite damage. Ever since Hughlings Jackson's neurological studies of brain-damaged patients (Taylor, 1932), and Lashley's demonstration of the spared cognitive abilities of brain-damaged rats (Lashley, 1942), it has become apparent that, although different regions of the brain are specialized for differing functions, the scale of such a *localization* of function need not extend down to single neurons. In terms of the von Neumann-Winograd-Cowan analysis, the representation of a bit of information need not be *unary*, but may be redundant or even distributed. There has been much debate on this point. Lashley, for example, proposed that different brain regions are *equipotent* with respect to function (Lashley, 1950)--any region can implement a given task--the very antithesis of regional localization. More recently, Barlow (1972) asserted that the level of redundancy in brain functioning is reduced, the further one moves from peripheral to central regions of the brain, culminating in a unary representation of information deep in the brain. In current terminology, we speak of "grandmother" neurons, supposedly activated only when grandmother is perceived.

2.3 CELL ASSEMBLIES AND NEURODYNAMICS

Lashley's notion of the equipotentiality of brain regions is reflected in the work of Hebb (1949). In his book *The Organization of Behavior*, Hebb proposed that the connectivity of the brain is continually changing as an organism learns differing functional tasks, and that *cell assemblies* are created by such changes. Hebb followed up an early suggestion of Cajal and introduced his now famous postulate: *repeated activation of one neuron by another, across a particular synapse, increases its conductance.* It follows that groups of weakly connected cells, if synchronously activated, will tend to organize into more strongly connected assemblies. Here again, the representation of a bit of information is distributed. Hebb's book has proved to be very influential. The cell assembly theory has triggered many investigations of *learning* in neural networks and of the way in which synchronized neural activity is generated and propagated. Studies of this topic, now known as *neurodynamics*, began with Rashevsky (1938). Rashevsky and his co-workers represented activation and propagation in neural networks in terms of differential equations and tried to make contact with related applications to physical problems. A more elaborate mathematical approach to neurodynamics was introduced by Wiener (1949) in his influential book, *Cybernetics, or Control and Communication in the Animal and the Machine*, and continued with Rosenbleuth, Pitts, and Garcia-Ramos (1952) in a series of investigations of reverberations in excitable networks.

2.4 CONTINUUM NEURODYNAMICS

It was Beurle (1956) however, who first provided a detailed analysis of the triggering and propagation of large-scale brain activity. However Beurle focussed, not on the activation of individual neurons, but on the proportion of neurons becoming activated per unit time in a given volume element of a slab of model brain tissue consisting of randomly connected neurons (see Fig. 3). In modern terms, this is the *continuum approximation* of neural activity. Beurle's work triggered many computer simulations of randomly connected neural networks. Farley and Clark (1961), for example, simulated the action of 1024 randomly connected model neurons, somewhat more complicated and realistic than McCulloch-Pitts neurons. They confirmed the Wiener-Beurle deduction of the existence of traveling and rotating waves in nerve tissue.

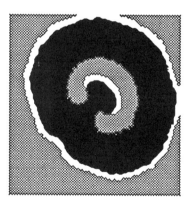

Figure 3. Computer simulation of activity in a sheet of neural tissue. White denotes regions of activated neurons; black, regions of neurons which have just been activated and are therefore insensitive, and gray, regions in which neurons have recovered and are again sensitive to incoming excitation (Reproduced from Beurle 1962).

3 MEMORY & LEARNING

3.1 ANALOGIES WITH LATTICE SPIN SYSTEMS

Following Hebbs work, perhaps the most stimulating suggestion concerning the
properties of cell assemblies was that of Cragg and Temperley (1954), who noted that,
just as neurons can be either *activated* (emitting action potentials), or *quiescent* (at rest),
so can atoms in an assembly or lattice be in one of two energetic states, e.g., with spins
pointing "up" or "down". Furthermore, just as neurons either excite or inhibit one
another, so do spinning atoms exert magnetic forces on their neighbors tending to set
their spins in either the same or opposite direction. Therefore the properties of neurons in
a densely connected network should be analogous to those of spinning atoms (or binary
alloys) in a lattice. Systems of spins showing various kinds of order provide good
models of the properties of magnetic materials. For example, a *ferromagnet*, which
consists of atoms tending to force each other to spin in the same direction, has long-range
order; an *antiferromagnet*, which consists of atoms tending to force each other to spin in
the opposite direction, also has long-range order, whereas a *paramagnet* is disordered. It
is plausible that neural networks should exhibit analogous properties. Cragg and
Temperley therefore suggested (a) that the domain patterns which are a ubiquitous
feature of ferromagnets, comprising patches of "up" or "down" spins, should show up in
neural networks as patches of excited or quiescent neurons, and (b) that neural networks
should show effects similar to ferromagnetic hysteresis in transitions between disordered
and ordered states. This implied that neural domain patterns, once triggered by external
stimuli, should be stable against spontaneous random activity, and could therefore constitute a *memory* of the stimulus (Cragg & Temperley, 1955). It is interesting to note that
20 years later Little (1974) arrived at virtually the same conclusions as Cragg and
Temperley concerning the existence of persistent neural states, via the mathematical
analysis of a lattice spin system.

3.2 MODIFIABLE SYNAPSES

It was Hebb's proposal of synaptic modification during learning, however, that triggered
even more work on neural networks; specifically on *adaptive* networks which could learn
to perform specified tasks. Early work toward this goal was carried out by Uttley (1956),
who demonstrated that neural networks with modifiable connections could indeed learn
to classify simple sets of binary patterns into equivalence classes. Uttley's first suggestion
was that synaptic weights represent *conditional probabilities*. Let $u_i(t)$ be the binary
variable representing the state of the ith neuron at time t, and $\Theta[v]$ the Heaviside step
function Let time be measured in quantal units Δt, $t = n\Delta t$. As is well-known, the acti-
vation of an MP neuron can be expressed by the equation: $u_i(n + 1) = \Theta[\Sigma_j w_{ij} u_j(n) - v_{TH}]$, where w_{ij} is the "weight" of the (j --> i) th connection, and where v_{TH} is the voltage threshold. Suppose instead that $u_i(t+\Delta t) = \Theta[\Sigma_j w_{ij} e_j(t) - v_{TH}]$ where $e_j(t) = \Sigma_k u_i(t-t_k)\tau^{-1}e^{-(t-t_k)/\tau}$, τ is the neural membrane time-constant and t_k denotes the time of

of arrival of an incoming current impulse. This is the so-called "leaky integrate and fire" or LIF neuron, later formally analyzed by Caianiello (1961). By Uttley's hypothesis w_{ij} = - k $\log_2$ [$e_{ij}(t)/e_j(t)$], a time-averaged representation of - $\log_2$ Pr[$u_i(t)/u_j(t)$]. Uttley built a hydraulic computer to calculate such probabilities (see fig. 5 for details), and demonstrated that such machinary could perform simple pattern classification after a period of conditioning. In later work Uttley (1966) introduced the hypothesis that w_{ij} = - k$\log_2$ [$g_{ij}(t)/g_i(t)g_j(t)$], where $g_i(t)$ is a further weighted time average of e $_i(t)$: thus w_{ij} is proportional to the *mutual information* provided by the ith and jth firing patterns.

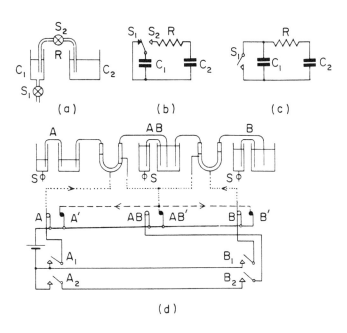

Figure 4: A hydraulic computer of conditional probability. (a) A counter [of Pr{A}] using an exponential scale. A siphon R connects two containers C_1 and C_2; normally tap S_1 is off and S_2 is on. To effect a count S_1 is turned on and S_2 off. C_1 then empties. The two taps are returned to their original positions and a fixed fraction of the liquid in C_2 is siphoned into C_1. The height of the liquid in C_2 is the measure of the total count. (b) An equivalent electrical counter. (c) A simplified electrical counter. (d) A conditional certainty computer which indicates when the conditional probability Pr{AB/A} exceeds a critical value. (Reproduced from Uttley 1959).

3.3 ASSOCIATIVE MEMORY

Another topic which was investigated in the 1950s is *associative memory*, beginning with the work of W.K. Taylor (1956). Fig. 5 shows Taylor's original network. Note it's structural similarity to an elementary Perceptron with no hidden units, except that the units are not M-P neurons, but *analog* devices operating in the fashion shown in Fig. 6.

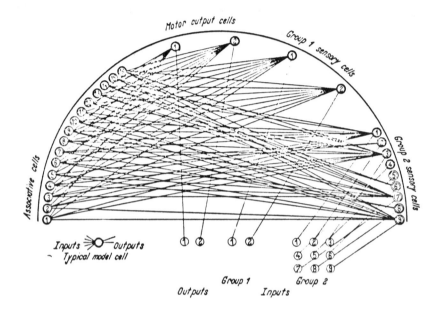

Figure 5: Taylor network. This network uses analog neurons with modifiable weights, and can be trained to associate differing sets of stimulus patterns, see text for details (Reproduced from Taylor 1956).

The training procedure also differs from that in Perceptrons and Adalines: it is simply Hebb's rule. The network learns to associate differing sensory patterns through repeated presentation of pairs of patterns, one of which initially elicits a motor response. Eventually the other pattern triggers the response. Thus Taylor networks exhibit simplePavlovian conditioning, and the associated memory is stored in a distributed fashion in the pattern of weights. In later work (Taylor, 1964) Taylor constructed a more elaborate network in which motor output units inhibit each other, in modern parlance, a "winner-take-all circuit". Such a network is capable of forming associations with paired stimuli in a more reliable and controllable way than the earlier network, and also of pattern discrimination in the style of Perceptrons and Adalines. Taylor suggested that the association areas of cerebral cortex and thalamus contained such networks.

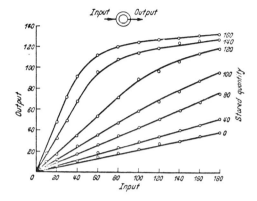

Figure 6: Analog neurons used by Taylor. The output firing rate increases smoothly with increasing input current. There is also a stored quantity which increases with the firing rate, equivalent to a lowering of the threshold. (Reproduced from Taylor 1956).

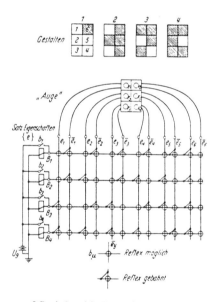

Figure 7: Structure of Steinbuch's Learning Matrix. It consists of a planar array of switches, each of which can be either open or closed. Each switch is connected to a receptor. However there are switches for both receptor ON and receptor OFF configurations. The switches control a set of relays, connected together in a winner-take-all circuit as in a Taylor network. The correspondence between the elements of a Learning matrix--receptors, switches and relays, and those of Perceptrons and Taylor networks is evident (Reproduced from Steinbuch 1961).

Shortly before this a very similar network was introduced by K. Steinbuch (1961), the *"Learning Matrix"* (see Fig. 7). It consists of a planar network of switches interposed between arrays of "sensory" receptors and "motor" effectors. As in Taylor's scheme, the network learns to associate sensory with motor patterns. The associated memory is again stored in the pattern of opened switches.

3.4 PERCEPTRONS AND ADALINES

Some fifteen years after the publication of McCulloch and Pitts' paper, a major approach to the pattern recognition problem was introduced by Rosenblatt (1958) in his work on the *Perceptron*. Shortly thereafter Widrow and Hoff (1960) introduced the Adaline. As is well-known, the only difference between Perceptrons and Adalines lies in the training procedure. What is not appreciated is the confusion which such results generated in the late 1950s and early 1960s. It was not at all clear what had been accomplished. I remember vividly Rosenblatt's first lecture on the Perceptron at MIT, in the fall of 1958. To put it mildly, the lecture was not well-received. However Novikoff's proof of the Perceptron convergence theorem (Novikoff 1963) clarified things somewhat, although the initial claims of the agency sponsoring Rosenblatt's work (ONR), left a residue of disbelief, particularly at MIT. This led to the demonstration by Minsky and Papert (1969) that there are limits to the performance of elementary Perceptrons and Adalines. They proved that such devices are not computationally universal, even with modifiable connections. In addition, they conjectured that hidden units in multilayer Perceptrons cannot be trained, or in other words, that the problem of *assigning credit* to hidden units is unsolvable. Rosenblatt (1961) had almost solved the problem with his *backpropagation* scheme, but as we all know, he had the wrong neurons.

Interestingly, Adalines had been anticpated somewhat in the work of Gabor (1954), one of the early pioneers of communication theory and cybernetics, and the inventor of *holography*, who also invented the *"Learning filter"*. This operates in the following fashion. Let $s(t)$ be a signal of bandwidth F, and let $s_0, s_1, s_2, ..., s_N$ be past samples of $s(t)$. Then the output of a learning filter can be written in the form:

$$O(s) = \sum_0^N w_i s_i + \sum_0^N \sum_0^N w_{ij} s_i s_j + \cdots ,$$

where the coefficients w_{ij} are adjusted via gradient descent to minimize $<(O(s) - s_d)^2>$, where s_d is the desired output. If $s(t)$ is a noisy message, then s_d can be the pure message, and $O(s)$ will be a filtered version of $s(t)$, or s_d can be retarded, in which case $O(s)$ will predict s_d. The learning filter is clearly analogous to a network of input, output, and hidden units, and it seems that Gabor had, in effect, solved the credit assignment problem!

4 ANALOG NEURAL NETWORKS

The MP neuron is of course a very simplified representation of real neural properties. Since 1943 it has been extended and elaborated in a number of ways. Perhaps the first significant extension was the LIF neuron. Neither neural model generates network equations which are mathematically tractable. It was for this reason that I introduced the *sigmoid* firing characteristic (Cowan, 1967) and the smooth firing condition $e_i(t+\Delta t) = \Phi[\tau\sum_j w_{ij}e_j(t) + h_i]$ where $e_i(t)$ is the firing rate of the ith element (a time-averaged version of $u_i(t)$), t is measured in units of τ, $h_i(t)$ is an additional external stimulus, and $\Phi[x]$ is the logistic function. The differential equation version of this condition is of course the equation $\tau de_i/dt = -e_i + \Phi[\tau\sum_{jk}w_{ij}e_j(t) + h_i]$. One of my colleagues at Imperial College, J.J. Sparkes, then devised the transistor circuit shown in fig. 8 to implement the function Φ.

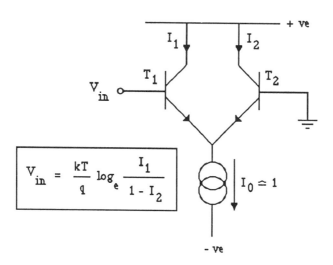

Figure 8: A transistor circuit which implements the logistic function Φ, using the (approximately) exponential collector current- base emitter voltage characteristic of a transistor (Sparkes, personal communication *circa* 1965).

4.1 STATISTICAL NEUROMECHANICS

I made the further observation (Cowan 1968) that if $w_{ij} = -w_{ji}$, $w_{ij} = 0$, and if τ is large, then this equation can be rewritten in the form:

$$\frac{dv_i}{dT} = \sum_j w_{ij}\frac{\partial G}{\partial v_j}$$

where $v_i = \Phi[\tau\sum_{jk}w_{ij}e_j(t) + h_i]$ and $G = \sum_i \{log[1+ q_i exp(v_i)] - q_i v_i\}$, $h_i + \sum_j w_{ij}q_j = 0$, is a "constant of motion" of the network. Since the matrix iW, $W = \{w_{ij}\}$, is Hermitian, we can form the block diagonal matrix W', made out of blocks of the form:

$$\begin{pmatrix} 0 & 1 \\ -1 & 0 \end{pmatrix}$$

by way of the congruence transformation $W' = \Lambda W \tilde{\Lambda}$, where Λ is built up from the eigenvectors of W. Then if $y_i = \Lambda v_i$, we have the Hamiltonian equations $\frac{dy_i}{dT} = \frac{\partial G}{\partial y_j}$.

The physical content of this result is that a network of neural-like elements with *skew-symmetric* coupling constants can generate neutrally stable oscillations in x_i in the range between 0 and 1. Moreover, because G is a constant of the motion, one can introduce a form of equilibrium statistical mechanics, in which the probability of being in the state

$\{y_1, y_2, ..., y_N\}$ takes the form $Z^{-1}\exp[-\alpha G]$, where $Z = \sum_{\{y\}} \exp[-\beta G]$. One can then compute various statistical averages of the behavior of such networks. Of course the skew-symmetry of the coupling coefficients w_{ij} is rather artificial, as is the effective neglect of the damping produced by the term $-e_i$ in the original differential equation. For similar reasons I did not pursue the study of the *symmetric* case!

5 CONCLUSIONS

It is evident that by the late 1960s most of the ideas and concepts necessary to solve the Perceptron credit assignment problem were already formulated, as were many of the ideas underlying Hopfield networks. Why did it take so long? I believe that there are two or three reasons for the lag. One was technological. There weren't personal computers and work stations to try things out on. For example, when Gabor developed the learning filter, it took he and his students a further seven years to implement the filter with analog devices. Similar delays obtained for others. The other reason was in part psychological, in part financial. Minsky and Papert's monograph certainly did not encourage anyone to work on Perceptrons, nor agencies to support them. A third reason was that the analogy between neural networks and lattice spins was premature. The Sherrington-Kirkpatrick *spin-glass* was not invented until 1975.

Acknowledgements

We thank The University of Chicago Brain Research Foundation and the US Department of the Navy, Office of Naval Research, (Grant # N00014-89-J-1099) for partial support of this work.

References:

Barlow, H.B. (1972) Single units and sensation: a neuron doctrine for perceptual psychology? Perception **1**, 371-394.
Beurle, R.L. (1956) Properties of a mass of cells capable of regenerating pulses, Phil. Trans. Roy. Soc.Lond. B, **240**, *669*, 55-94; (1962) Functional organization in random

networks, *Principles of Self-Organization* (Eds.), Von Foerster, H & Zopf, G.W. Jr., Pergamon Press.

Caianiello, E.R. (1961) Outline of a theory of thought processes and thinking machines, J. Theor. Biol., **1**, 204-235.

Cowan, J.D. (1967) A mathematical theory of central nervous activity, *Thesis*, University of London; (1968) Statistical mechanics of nervous nets, *Neural Networks*, (Ed.), E.R. Caianiello, 181-188, Springer-verlag, Berlin;

Cragg, B.G. & Temperley, H.N.V. (1954) The organisation of neurones: a cooperative analogy, EEG Clin.Neurophysiol., **6**, 85-92; (1955) Memory: the analogy with ferromagnetic hysteresis, Brain, **78**, II, 304-316.

Craik, K.J.W. (1943) *The nature of explanation*, Cambridge Univ. Press, Cambridge.

Farley, B.G. & Clark, W. A. (1961) Activity in networks of neuron-like elements, Information Theory, **4**, (Ed.) Cherry, E.C., 242-251, Butterworths, London.

Gabor, D. (1954) Communication theory and cybernetics, IRE Trans., **CT-1**, *4*, 19-31

Hamming, R.W. (1950) Error detecting and error correcting codes, Bell Syst. Tech. J., **29**, 147-160.

Hebb, D.O. (1949) *The Organization of Behavior*, Wiley, New York.

Landahl, H.D., McCulloch, W.S. & Pitts, W. (1943) A statistical consequence of the logical calculus of nervous nets, Bull. Math.Biophys. **5**, 135-137.

Lashley, K.S. (1942) Persistent problems in the evolution of mind, Quart. Rev. Biol., **24**, *1*, 28-42; (1950) In search of the engram, Symp. Soc. Expt. Biol., **4**, 454-482.

Little, W.A. (1974) The existence of persistent states in the brain, Math. Biosci., **19**, 101-120.

McCulloch, W.S. (1961) What Is a Number, that a Man May Know It, and a Man, that He May Know a Number?, General Semantics Bull., 26 - 27, 7-18; (1967) *Embodiments of Mind*, MIT Press, Cambridge Mass.

McCulloch, W.S.& Pitts, W. (1943) A logical calculus of the ideas immanent in nervous activity, Bull. Math. Biophys. **5**, 115-133.

Minsky, M. & Papert, S. (1969) *Perceptrons: an introduction to computational geometry*, MIT Press.

Neumann, J. von (1956) Probabilistic logics and the synthesis of reliable organisms from unreliable components, *Automata Studies*, (Eds.) Shannon, C.E. & McCarthy, J. Princeton University Press, Princeton, New Jersey, 43-98.

Novikoff, A. (1963) On convergence proofs for Perceptrons, *Symp. on Mathematical Theory of Automata*, (Ed.) Fox, J., Polytechnic Press New York (1963), 615-622.

Rashevsky, N. (1938) *Mathematical Biophysics*, Univ. of Chicago Press, Chicago.

Rosenblatt, F. (1958) The Perceptron, a probabilistic model for information storage and organization in the brain, Psych. Rev., **62**, 386-408; (1961) *Principles of Neurodynamics: Perceptrons and the Theory of Brain Mechanisms*, Spartan Books, Washington DC.

Rosenbleuth, A., Wiener, N. & Bigelow, J. (1943) Behavior, Purpose and Teleology, Philosophy of Science, **10**, 18-24.

Rosenbleuth, A., Wiener, N., Pitts, W., & Garcia Ramos, J. (1949) A statistical analysis of synaptic excitation, J. Cell. Comp. Physiol., **34**, 173-205.

Shannon, C.E, (1948) A mathematical theory of communication, Bell Syst. Tech. J., **27**, 379-423; 623-656.

Steinbuch, K. (1961) Die Lernmatrix, Kybernetik, **1**, 1, 36-45.

Taylor, J. (1932) *Selected writings of John Hughlings Jackson*, Hodder & Stoughton, London, reprinted (1958) New York.

Taylor, W.K. (1956) Electrical simulation of some nervous system functional activities, *Information Theory*, **3**, (Ed.) Cherry, E.C., Butterworths, London, 314-328; (1964) Cortico-thalamic organization and memory, Proc. Roy. Soc. Lond. B, **159**, 466-478.

Uttley, A.M. (1956) A theory of the mechanism of learning based on the computation of conditional probabilities, Proc. 1st Int. Conf. on Cybernetics, Namur, Gauthier-Villars, Paris; (1959) The design of conditional probability computers, Information & Control **2**, 1-24; (1966) The transmission of information and the effect of local feedback in theoretical and neural networks, Brain Research **2**, 21-50.

Widrow, B. & Hoff, M.E. (1960) Adaptive switching circuits, WESCON convention record, **IV**, 96-104.

Wiener, N. (1948) *Cybernetics, or Control and Communication in the Animal and the Machine*, Wiley, New York.

Winograd, S. & Cowan, J.D. (1963) *Reliable Computation in the Presence of Noise*, MIT Press, Cambridge, Mass.

SUBJECT INDEX

AUTHOR INDEX